David
Skelton

MONOGRAPHS OF THE HEBREW UNION COLLEGE 36

Yannai on Genesis: An Invitation to Piyyut

Yannai on Genesis
An Invitation to Piyyut

Laura S. Lieber

Hebrew Union College Press
Cincinnati

© 2010 by the Hebrew Union College Press
Hebrew Union College–Jewish Institute of Religion

Library of Congress Cataloging in Publication Data

Lieber, Laura Suzanne.
Yannai on Genesis: an invitation to piyyut / Laura Lieber.
p.cm – (Monographs of the Hebrew Union College; no. 36)
Includes bibliographical references and index.
ISBN 978–0–87820–464–9 (alk. paper)
1, Yannai—Criticism and interpretation, 2. Piyyutim—Criticism, Textual.
3. Bible. O.T. Genesis—Commentaries. 4. Sabbath—Liturgy—Texts.
5. Judaism—Liturgy—Texts. I. Title.
BM760.P5L485 2010
296.4'52—dc22 2010032068

Printed on acid-free paper in the United States of America
Typeset by Posner and Sons Ltd., Jerusalem, Israel
Distributed by Wayne State University Press
4809 Woodward Avenue, Detroit, MI 48201
Toll-free 1-800-978-7323

Contents

Acknowledgments

"Rabbah b. Ḥanah said: Why are the words of the Torah compared to fire?
This is to teach you that just as fire does not ignite of itself,
so, too, the words of the Torah do not endure with one who studies alone."
b. Taʿanit 7a

This book has been many years in the making, and would not now be seeing the light of day without the help and encouragement of many people and institutions. My first debts of gratitude are owed to Michael Meyer, who as the chair of the Hebrew Union College Press Publications Committee has graciously overseen the publication of this work; and to Barbara Selya, the managing editor at the press. Thanks to Barbara's brilliant editorial acumen and tremendous patience, a very complicated manuscript became a book. I am also deeply grateful to Dr. Raphael Posner, who not only typeset the entire volume but accepted the task of taking the material generously given to us by the Academy of the Hebrew Language's Historical Hebrew Dictionary Project (*Maʾagarim*) and transforming it into the beautiful text presented here. I would in particular like to extend my thanks to Dr. Binyamin Elizur of the Academy for his assistance. Finally, I would also like to express my heartfelt gratitude to the Publications Committee at HUC Press for giving me the opportunity to publish this volume, and for the care and attention that was shown to the project at every stage along the way.

Between the covers of this volume can be found the results of many years of working on piyyutim, and thinking about them; none of it would have come to be without the care and encouragement of the many teachers with whom I have been privileged to study over the years, both at Hebrew Union College in Cincinnati and at the University of Chicago. The project would never have been conceived, let alone completed, without the enduring support of two mentors in particular: Richard Sarason, professor of rabbinics and liturgy at HUC; and Michael Fishbane, my doctoral advisor at the University of Chicago. Professor Sarason gave me my first piyyut to read in "Liturgy 1" and encouraged me to pursue my interests at the doctoral level. Professor Fishbane, whose student I will always be, enthusiastically supported my study of piyyut as my interests came into focus, and helped me sharpen my inquiry when my instincts dulled. Both Professors Sarason and Fishbane read full drafts of the manuscript, and their diligent, thoughtful comments helped me not only to refine the points I hoped to make, but to see the coherence and significance of a project that I, lost within the work, had been unable to see. The enthusiasm of these two teachers sustained me through the rough patches, and kept me challenged during the smooth, and will always be gratifying. It is a debt I can repay only by striving to do a fraction as well by my own students. If this work possesses scholarly merit, it is only because I have been blessed with such wonderful teachers.

Many others also helped shape this work into the form it now holds. Marc Bregman, in particular, has patiently read much of the material that now lies between these covers. His insightful and encouraging comments pushed me to think about the material in new ways. He has nurtured in me a love not only of rabbinic texts, but of the rabbinic mind. Likewise, I am grateful to Ruth Langer, whose work on the history and reception of liturgy are my gold standard. Always at the precisely necessary moment, Professor Langer has tried her best to prod me away from complacency and fuzzy assumptions. This work is sharper and more precise as a result of her keen and attentive readings. Other readers and advisors, including Susan Einbinder, Ezra Spicehandler, and Wout van Bekkum (who introduced me to the Historical Dictionary of the Hebrew Language), offered just the right advice at just the right times; their counsel was my good fortune. And I would like to thank Peter Cole and Adina Hoffman for their support and encouragement at many stages of the project, and for their knack of being wherever I happen to be at precisely the right time to nudge me on.

This volume is not a revised dissertation, but a new work, conceived and largely written during five deeply transformative years at Middlebury College. I am grateful to the administration at Middlebury for their support of my research on this project, particularly Carol Rifelj and Sunder Ramaswamy, who, as Deans of Faculty, provided generous financial assistance, including a junior research leave and funds for travel. Beyond administrative support, I could not have written this book without the support and friendship of my colleagues in Religion and Classics, who will be my colleagues and friends forever: Larry Yarbrough, Robert Schine,

James Davis, Elizabeth Morrison, Justin Stearns, Bill Waldron, Marc Witkin, Pavlos Sfyroeras, Maria Hatjigeorgiou, Randy Ganiban, Chris Star, Charlene Barrett, and Diane Tomkinson; and I owe a special debt of thanks and love to Jane Chaplin. I also am grateful to my students at Middlebury who taught me that writing a book—even one on something as seemingly arcane as Byzantine piyyut—is an act of pedagogy. Writing became easier when it became teaching, and teaching became richer when it nourished my writing. Thank you.

Likewise, the final stages of this project have been made possible through the generous support of my new home, Duke University, particularly the generous granting of research leave in the Fall of 2008. I am also grateful for the support and encouragement of my new colleagues, mentors, and friends: Eric Meyers, Carol Meyers, Kalman Bland, Liz Clark, Lucas van Rompay, Malachi Hacohen, Ellen Davis, Joel Marcus, and Steven Sager. These are scholars I hope to emulate as a researcher, writer, and teacher. Likewise, I have benefited from the cheerful and prompt assistance of our department staff: Nancy Hurtgen, Sandra Woods, Jenny Hirtz, and Marissa Lane. My students, undergraduate and graduate, have been willing audiences for reading and critiquing a number of the texts presented here. And I am particularly indebted to Yael Wilfand, my research assistant, for her diligent and comprehensive work on the manuscript at multiple stages, and her insight into the texts themselves.

In addition to the support of my home institutions, this project was made possibly by two external grants. The Lucius N. Littauer Foundation provided a three-summer travel grant, which enabled me to travel to Cambridge, Jerusalem, and New York in order to consult manuscripts and volumes not available to me in Vermont; additionally, the Littauer Foundation has generously provided a publication subvention, significantly defraying the cost of a costly volume. Conversations with the Littauer Foundation's William Frost have always been particularly rewarding. I also am grateful to the Memorial Foundation for Jewish Culture, which provided me with a fellowship that enabled me to take full advantage of a research leave during the year when I was finishing the first full draft of the manuscript. I am gratefuld too for Professor Eric Friedland's special gift towards the book's publication.

Selections of the material presented in this volume benefited from public scrutiny before they were committed to print. Congregation Ohavi Zedek in Burlington, Vermont, and particularly Rabbi Joshua Chasen, welcomed my presentations as scholar-in-residence on a topic that, at first, may have seemed alarmingly obscure. The richness of give-and-take in that forum strengthened my conviction that this material will thrive well beyond academe's walls. Even more so, my time as the scholar-in-residence for the Chicago Association of Reform Rabbis in October 2007 proved tremendously fruitful, and the impact of those days can be detected in the awareness of orality and audience reception that are found here and will no doubt be further developed in future works. I would like to particularly thank Karyn Kedar, Ellen Dreyfuss, and Steven (Simcha) Bob, as well as Andrea Cosnowsky and John Linder, for inviting me.

Finally, no work such as this can be created in isolation. Ellen Haskell has been a friend and sounding board since my first days as a student at the University of Chicago, and to my delight, she is now a colleague down the road at the University of North Carolina–Greensboro; and Deborah Green continues to be, simply, my best friend. My closeness to her is rivaled only by my love for my parents, Michael and Eileen Lieber, my sister Debbie and brother Ken, my remarkably indulgent and enduring husband, Norman Weiner, and the one project I love more than this book: my son, Julian Micah Weiner. Milk and honey are under his tongue, and his voice is sweet to me. I dedicate this book to him, and to beginnings.

An Introduction to the Poet and his Works and this Project

"This is the splendor of Yannai:
–he is extremely old yet entirely new."
Shalom Spiegel, *Fathers of Piyyut*, 386

Saadia Gaon, the leader of Babylonian Jewry in the tenth century, listed him among "the ancient poets."[1] The Karaite scholar Abu Yusuf al-Qirqisani, a contemporary of Saadia's, asserts that Anan ben David, the founder of the Karaite sect of Judaism, derived laws from his poetry.[2] And Gershom Me'or HaGolah, the great Ashkenazic rabbi of the eleventh century, reckoned him among "the early Sages," saying that "he wrote *qerovot*[3] for every single Torah portion (*seder*) of the year."[4] And yet, for all his reputation and productivity, this poet's works were lost to the world for almost a millennium. Only with the discovery of the treasures in the Cairo Genizah at the end of the nineteenth century did this once major Hebrew author emerge from the mists of legend into the world of Jewish literary history.

His name was Yannai, and if his poetry represents a remarkable development in the history of Hebrew letters, its rediscovery has the potential to transform and tremendously enrich our understanding of the history of Hebrew literature and Jewish culture during a formative period. Menachem Schmelzer suggests that the recovery of Yannai's works from the Genizah was a "most revolutionary discovery," noting that they constitute a

1 *Sefer ha-Egron*, ed. N. Allony (Jerusalem: Ha-Akademyah La-Lashon Ha-ʿIvrit, 1969), 154.

2 See Israel Davidson, *Machzor Yannai: A Liturgical Work of the VIIth Century* (New York: Jewish Theological Seminary of America, 1919), xi–xlvi.

3 Liturgical poems embellishing the Amidah, the central prayer of the Jewish liturgy, are called, as a class, *qerovot.*

4 *Teshuvot rabbenu Gershom Me-or ha-Golah*, ed. S. Eidelberg (New York: Yeshiva University, 1955), vol. 1, 55–56.

key piece of evidence for recognizing the central importance of poetry in Byzantine and medieval Judaism.[5] In the early twentieth century, it seemed that the study of Yannai's poetry would transform our understandings of Jewish society in Late Antiquity, and even revolutionize the study of rabbinic literature.[6]

Yet, for all this testimony to his significance, Yannai's particular body of poetry—and even more surprisingly, the entire genre of his work (called "*piyyut*," the Hebrew term for Jewish liturgical poetry), has received relatively little attention from scholars outside of first German and then Israeli academia.[7] That neglect is surprising, given the prominence of Jewish poetry, sacred and secular, in the earliest period of Jewish Studies. Leopold Zunz, a founder of *Wissenschaft des Judentums* (the scientific study of Judaism), wrote multiple landmark volumes devoted to liturgical poetry;[8] Paul Kahle, the famed linguist, found piyyutim a rich resource for understanding the development of Masoretic Hebrew grammar;[9] Franz Delitzsch, a Protestant scholar, featured them prominently in his landmark literary study of Hebrew poetry.[10] Many other major *Wissenschaft* writers, including S. J. Rappoport and S. D. Luzzato, likewise emphasized Hebrew sacred poetry in their writings.

The students and heirs of these groundbreaking scholars, many of whom

5 M. Schmelzer, "The Contribution of the Genizah to the Study of Liturgy and Poetry," *Proceedings of the American Academy for Jewish Research* 63 (1997–2001): 169.

6 See S. Lieberman, "Ḥazzanut Yannai," *Sinai* 4 (1938): 221–50 [Hebrew]. In this essay, Lieberman expressed a hope that someday Yannai's poetry would stand on the shelf next to the volumes of Talmud and midrash because "that is its proper place [כי שם הוא מקומו]" (250).

7 For a survey of the state of Piyyut Studies at present, see Wout Jac. van Bekkum, "The Hebrew Liturgical Poetry of Byzantine Palestine: Recent Research and New Perspectives," *Prooftexts* 28.2 (2008): 232–46. He notes at the very end of this article: "One of my conclusions is that since the days of Leopold Zunz the poetics of piyyut has not attracted sufficient attention in modern academic scholarship, although it may be noted that the situation has clearly improved in recent years" (246).

8 Including: *Literaturgeschichte der synagogalen Poesie* (Berlin: L. Gerschel Verlagsbuchhandlung, 1865); *Der Ritus des synagogalen Gottesdienstes* (Berlin: J. Springer, 1859); and *Die synagogale Poesie des Mittelalters* (1 ed.; Frankfurt am Main: J. Kaufmann, 1920).

9 See P. E. Kahle, *The Cairo Genizah*, 2nd ed. (Oxford: Blackwell, 1959) and "Kerobas aus dem Maḥzor des Jannai," in *Masoreten des Westens* (Hildesheim: Georg Olms Verlagsbuchhandlung, 1967), 1:87–89; see also A. Murtonen (with G. J. Ormann), *Materials for a Non-Masoretic Hebrew Grammar*, 2 vols (Helsinki, 1958).

10 Franz Delitzsch, *Zur Geschichte der jüdischen Poesie seit dem Abschluss der Schriften des Alten Bundes* (Leipzig: Karl Tauchnitz, 1836).

were affiliated with the Schocken Research Institute for the study of Hebrew Poetry—including Jefim (Hayyim) Schirmann, Hayyim Brody, A. M. Habermann, Menachem Zulay, Avraham Mirsky, and others—continued the efforts of their teachers. They devoted tremendous energy to cataloguing, publishing, and analyzing the literatures of the ancient and medieval synagogue, whether found in printed prayerbooks or discovered in manuscripts.[11] When, in the 1930s, many of the great scholars of piyyut fled Europe (the Schocken Institute relocated to Jerusalem in 1934), Piyyut Studies was transformed from a Germanic scholarly field to a largely Israeli—and therefore Hebraic—one. Even piyyut scholars residing in the U.S., such as Shalom Spiegel, published their scholarly articles and monographs primarily in Hebrew, as that was the language of their readership.[12]

The fact that Yannai's poems were composed in a difficult Hebrew idiom, combined with the tendency of the scholarship itself to be in languages other than English, has resulted in an American audience largely unaware of the richness, vastness, and importance of this literature or unable to access it in a substantial way. Furthermore, these poems were handicapped by a reputation for being inferior literature; the study of Andalusian Hebrew poetry—with a reputation as "good" literature—successfully became a field of study in the U.S., despite similar obstacles. For all the inherent relevance of piyyut to the study of more popular fields, particularly midrash (rabbinic interpretation of Scripture) and targum (Aramaic versions of the Bible), this tremendous body of literature has been undervalued in the English-speaking world, even after the Cairo Genizah was recognized as housing a vast quantity of liturgical poetry, works spanning centuries and continents, among its diverse treasures.[13]

---

11 In the introduction to his *Jewish Hymnography: A Literary History* (London; Portland, OR: Littman Library, 1998), Leon Weinberger concisely summarizes the nineteenth and twentieth-century history of Piyyut Studies.

12 For example, Spiegel's brief but influential article, "On the Language of the Payyetanim" was published only in the Hebrew language periodical *HaDoar* 43 (23), 1962–63: 397–400. Similarly, Saul Lieberman's essay, *Ḥazzanut yannai*, was published only in Hebrew.

13 T. Carmi offers a dramatic description of the unlikely discovery of the Genizah and its significance: "The enormous jigsaw puzzle of the *piyut* began to reveal its contours only with the discovery of the Cairo Genizah ('hiding place'). This momentous event—momentous for almost every branch of Hebrew scholarship—has been aptly described as a cluster of miracles. It is a miracle that the community in Fostat (Old Cairo), which is known to have bought its synagogue in the ninth century, perpetuated the customs and liturgy of the Palestinian rite. It was a miracle that they, and subsequent generations,

This is not to say that all scholars in the U.S. have failed to consider these important works. Researchers in related fields—principally Liturgy, Semitics, and Rabbinics—have often noted their importance and included them in their studies. The field of Jewish Liturgy, in particular, has consistently acknowledged the centrality of liturgical poetry; the most important work in English remains Ismar Elbogen's classic study *Jewish Liturgy: A Comprehensive History*, which includes a full chapter on "The Period of the Piyyut" as well as sections on major poets and notes concerning poetic additions to the prayers.[14] As the field of Liturgical Studies developed, so did this element of Piyyut Studies, and in recent years, more and more attention has been paid to piyyutim in the context of understanding liturgical development.[15] Indeed, as Stefan Reif comments in his major work *Judaism and Hebrew Prayer*, "Liturgical poetry will hardly feature [in this study] at all for the simple reason that it has had more than its fair share of scholarly attention for a century and a half."[16] What Reif does not mention—it is not pertinent to his study—is *how* piyyut has been studied in the works he has in mind. Piyyutim have proven a useful tool for liturgical historians in reconstructing the development of liturgies, rites, and rituals, but rarely have scholars

held the written word in such esteem that any piece of writing in Hebrew could not simply be thrown away, but had to be stored in a special lumber-room. It was a miracle that hundreds of thousands of fragments were deposited in this windowless room in the synagogue's attic from the eleventh to nineteenth century. And it was nothing less than a miracle that they were preserved from decay and were not discovered prematurely" ("Introduction," *The Penguin Book of Hebrew Verse* [New York: Penguin Books, 1981], 22).

14 I. Elbogen, *Jewish Liturgy: a Comprehensive History*, trans. R. Scheindlin (Philadelphia: JPS; New York: JTSA, 1993). Originally published in German as *Der jüdische Gottesdienst in seiner geschichtlichen Entwicklung* (1913), updated in 1972 by Joseph Heinemann and published as *Ha-Tefillah be-yisrael be-hitpatḥutah ha-historit* (Hebrew), and finally revised and translated into English by Raymond Scheindlin (1993). Scheindlin is, himself, a noted scholar of Hebrew poetry. Another important work in English that should be mentioned is A. Z. Idelsohn's *Jewish Liturgy and Its Development* (New York: Henry Holt & Co., 1932). This work, while less exhaustive and systematic than Elbogen's study, catalogues an impressive number of piyyutim from various medieval rites.

15 See J. Heinemann's landmark volume *Prayer in the Talmud: Forms and Patterns*, trans. R. Sarason (Berlin/New York: DeGruyter, 1977); and more recently, see especially Ruth Langer, *To Worship God Properly: Tensions Between Liturgical Custom and Halakhah in Judaism* (Cincinnati: Hebrew Union College Press, 1998), which considers extensively the development of piyyutim, Gaonic opposition to the genre, and its eventual normalization. Finally, the works of R. Sarason have been of tremendous value; see especially his entry "Midrash in Liturgy," in *Encyclopedia of Midrash* 1:463–92.

16 S. Reif, *Judaism and Hebrew Prayer: New Perspectives on Jewish Liturgical History* (Cambridge; New York: Cambridge University Press, 1993), 15–16.

addressed these texts seriously as *prayers*. Indeed, the field of Liturgical Studies itself has changed in recent decades, moving in more phenomenological directions; in the context of such research, piyyutim—with their experiential, even theatrical elements, as well as their implicit form of constructive theology—promise to play a prominent role once again.

A growing number of researchers in other fields have also come to recognize the importance of piyyutim. In recent decades, more and more scholarly works have taken these poems into account, understanding them to be important cultural artifacts of the Byzantine era and Middle Ages. Eric Werner's comparative study of early Jewish and Christian liturgical practices (particularly music) made extensive use of piyyutim.[17] Similarly, in recent years, historians attempting to understand the development of Jewish culture have begun to recognize the importance of liturgical poetry as a way of gaining access to the interior life and ritual practices of the Byzantine and medieval synagogue.[18] In the field of Hebrew linguistics, Michael Rand has argued convincingly that the idiosyncratic grammar of the early liturgical poets possesses integrity and merits study in its own right.[19] Scholars of rabbinic literature have begun to treat liturgical poetry as part of the history of Jewish biblical interpretation, on par with midrash and targum.[20] Finally, a few English language monographs have put piyyutim at center stage: Jakob Petuchowski's *Theology and Poetry* and, more recently, Leon Weinberger's *Jewish Hymnography* offer English-language readers general introductions to Piyyut Studies, while Joseph Yahalom and Michael Swartz's volume of Yom Kippur piyyutim, *Avodah: An Anthology of Ancient Poems for Yom Kippur*, is the first major collection of complete

17 Eric Werner, *The Sacred Bridge: The Interdependence of Liturgy and Music in Synagogue and Church during the First Millenium*, vol 1. (New York: Columbia University Press, 1959); vol. 2 (New York: Ktav, 1984).

18 For example: Seth Schwartz, *Imperialism and Jewish Society, 200* B.C.E. *to 640* C.E. (Princeton: Princeton University Press, 2001); Lee Levine, *The Ancient Synagogue: The First Thousand Years* (2d ed.; New Haven: Yale University Press, 2000); and Steven Fine, *Art and Judaism in the Greco-Roman World: Towards a New Jewish Archaeology* (Cambridge/New York: Cambridge University Press, 2005).

19 Michael Rand, *Introduction to the Grammar of Hebrew Poetry in Byzantine Palestine* (Piscataway, NJ: Gorgias Press, 2006). Despite its broad title, this work focuses on the grammar of Qillir.

20 See, for example, Michael Fishbane, *Biblical Myth and Rabbinic Mythmaking* (Oxford and New York: Oxford University Press, 2003).

piyyutim to be translated into English.[21] Hebrew liturgical poems are beginning to get their due.

Whereas Yahalom and Swartz's *Avodah* introduces readers to a specific genre of piyyut, the present work presents a specific poet and his innovative style of poetry, indicating along the way the range of new fields and questions where piyyut may be of particular interest as well as new ways of studying piyyut in its own right. Piyyutim are poised to become an important and fruitful resource for scholars working in the history of Western religions and comparative literature, as well as more commonly studied disciplines within Jewish studies; at the same time, scholars primarily interested in this body of poetry are drawing on the tools of these related disciplines in order to understand their own texts more fully.

This volume highlights new ways of looking at piyyutim in order to bring them to the attention of an audience able to appreciate these rich texts from a diversity of heretofore overlooked vantage points. It explores these works not just from the various perspectives of rabbinics, biblical interpretation, and liturgy, but as texts to be read in the context of Byzantine art, synagogue archaeology, and early Christian hymnography; not only as evidence of rites and rituals, but as poetry to be studied in the context of comparative literature and from the perspectives of aesthetics and phenomenology. In particular, it seeks to understand the piyyutim as rich and beautiful poetic texts that were not only heard but also experienced—not just listened to, but prayed. As such, these poems must be approached "thickly," as literature, theology, and art in their own right. To achieve this goal, this volume includes introductory material useful for the novice as well as analysis and explication of the piyyutim for those who choose to delve more deeply into a broad range of related topics—literary technique, poetics, theology, comparative ancient poetry—and realize the substantial intellectual potential of this field. Annotated translations, meanwhile, add depth and substance to the more overarching observations in the essays. The task of rescuing and resurrecting these poems began a century ago with the discoveries of the Cairo Genizah, but the study of these works is, in many ways, only now beginning.

21 J. Petuchowski, *Theology and Poetry: Studies in the Medieval Piyyut* (London; Boston: Routledge and Kegan Paul, 1978); Weinberger, *Jewish Hymnography*; M. Swartz and J. Yahalom, *Avodah: An Anthology of Ancient Poetry for Yom Kippur* (University Park: Penn State University Press, 2005).

Poetry Lost and Found

What is piyyut? Why does this literature matter and for whom was it written? Who was Yannai, and why does he merit his own monograph? The name "piyyut" derives from the Greek ποιητής ("something made or created"), the same word that gives English the word "poetry"; from this root, the composers of piyyutim are called in Hebrew *payyetanim*, or "poets." This new vocabulary, which first appears in rabbinic writings, immediately distinguishes this genre of late ancient poetry from biblical forms of composition (*shir*, *tehillah*, *mizmor*, etc.) and biblicizing works (such as the Qumranic *Hodayot*) that imitate the biblical style of composition. Even more significantly, this terminology indicates that the rabbinic sources recognized piyyut as something new. As the Greek etymology implies, it arose in the context of Hellenism, although its precise origins are unknown.[22] Indeed, these are the great mysteries of the field: Did piyyut arise as a kind of borrowing from early Christian hymnography? Or are its roots deep within Judaism and its ingrained ("native"?) methods of biblical interpretation, now distilled to its barest poetic essence? This style of writing appears on the scene fully developed and already complex in roughly the fourth or fifth century—a tumultuous period in Near Eastern history—but any clear understanding of its relationship to earlier forms of poetry from the Second Temple period, from the Jewish mystical traditions, from Qumran, and from outside Judaism remains shrouded in mystery. Odds are that the answer is far from simple.

Regardless of their origin, piyyutim are, in essence, poems composed for use in the Jewish liturgical context, either in place of or as adornments to the statutory prayers. The term "piyyut" generally applies to Hebrew compositions, although liturgical poems in other languages (especially Aramaic) may also be called "piyyutim." The earliest examples (works from the so-called "pre-Classical" or "Anonymous" period) are generally dated to the fourth or fifth century in the Land of Israel, and they are typified by the works of Yose ben Yose. The "Classical period," which began with Yannai and was dominated by Qillir, lasted from the fifth to eighth

22 See my entry, "Piyyut" in *The Encyclopedia of Judaism* 3: 2000–2019, for a discussion of the possible origins of this form of poetry.

centuries—overlapping with the Muslim conquest of the Land of Israel, and established the aesthetic trends for centuries after.[23]

Piyyut soon diffused throughout the Jewish world. The inclusion of piyyutim typified the early Palestinian-Jewish rite, and the abundance of liturgical poetry from this early period indicates the same diversity of liturgical practice that the *targumim* (Aramaic renderings of the biblical text) of the Land of Israel also suggest.[24] Babylonian Jewish authorities—favoring uniformity (in the content of prayers as well as in Aramaic translation)—initially resisted the inclusion of piyyutim in the worship service, but as these poems became increasingly popular throughout the Jewish world, the Babylonian leadership eventually discovered ways of accommodating popular tastes. Although the Geonim initially rejected piyyut quite vigorously, by the eighth and ninth centuries they grudgingly permitted their recitation, and by the tenth century, Saadia Gaon—the head of Babylonian Jewry—himself composed numerous piyyutim.[25] The poetic trends first manifested in the Land of Israel prior to the Muslim conquest were preserved, transmitted, and developed during the Middle Ages, first in Italy and then in Ashkenaz (Western, Central, and ultimately Eastern Europe), where the distinctive payyetanic style of poetry flourished well into the medieval period. In the Sephardic world, however, shortly after Saadia's lifetime, the history of Hebrew poetry took a different turn, overtly rejecting many of the stylistic features of classical piyyut in favor of a shorter, more lyrical, more biblicizing style of composition, influenced by the aesthetics and ideals of Arabic poetry.

As the above sketch suggests, the history of piyyut is one of literary and liturgical transformation; in many ways, piyyutim embody and enact Rabbi Eliezer's dictum "Whoever makes his prayer a fixed thing (*qeva*), his prayer is not a true supplication" (*m. Berakhot* 4:4). Piyyutim, which diversified and enlivened the services in the ancient and medieval world (and, to a

---

23 This periodization, now standard, derives from the magisterial volume by E. Fleischer, *Hebrew Liturgical Poetry in the Middle Ages* (Jerusalem: Keter, 1975).

24 For the Eastern-Western divide in terms of regulation of *targumim*, see W. F. Smelik, "Orality, the Targums, and Manuscript Reproduction," in *Paratext and Megatext in Jewish and Christian* Traditions*: The Textual Markers of Contextualization* (ed. A. den Hollander, U. Schmidt and W.F. Smelik; Leiden; Boston, MA: Brill, 2003), 49–81.

25 The most nuanced and comprehensive study of the Geonic opposition to and then accommodation of the Palestinian-Jewish poetic embellishment of the liturgy can be found in Langer, *To Worship God Properly*, especially her chapter "The Language of Prayer: The Challenge of Piyyut," 110–87.

lesser extent, in modern prayerbooks), engaged in a dynamic tension with liturgical fixity. Whether they supplemented or replaced the statutory liturgy, piyyutim built upon a set framework (exactly how "set" varied over time) while simultaneously personalizing and customizing the service to the content and language of the Torah portion and themes of the Sabbath or festival.

Piyyutim also reflected the aesthetic tastes of the community. Despite the ambivalence of the Geonic authorities, the piyyutim were tremendously popular, both in the West and, later, in the East. By the Middle Ages, most of the major liturgical opportunities—particularly the Shema and its blessings, the Amidah, and the various penitential rites, but also the Grace after Meals, the Sanctification of the New Moon, the *nishmat kol ḥai*, and others—were embellished with piyyutim, to the extent that those they chose often serve as the primary distinction of one regional rite from another. The evidence of the Cairo Genizah confirms the tremendous desire for new piyyutim throughout the Jewish world, a hunger that began in the Byzantine world and was sustained throughout the Middle Ages. One Genizah letter published by S. D. Goitein describes the efforts of one Jewish community to obtain new poems from as far away as Marseilles.[26] Even more than this letter, however, the sheer quantity of poetic texts recovered from the Genizah attests to the tremendous popularity of these works.

The Andalusian poetic revolution, reflected in the writings of Solomon ibn Gabirol, Abraham ibn Ezra, Judah Halevi, and others, was, in part, a rebellion against the poetic aesthetics of the earlier Palestinian- Ashkenazic style of piyyutim.[27] For all their protests, however, many famous poems by Iberian Jews are, themselves, technically piyyutim, written in a neo-Classical (i.e., biblicizing) style.[28] No matter their specific place of or-

26 S. D. Goitein, *Jewish Education in Muslim Countries Based on Records from the Cairo Genizah* (Jerusalem: Yad Yitzchak Ben-Ẓvi, 1962), 97–103 [Hebrew].

27 Abraham ibn Ezra famously derided the "Qilliran" style of piyyut. His commentary to Eccl 5:1 is a veritable manifesto for Andalusian neo-Classicism. In this comment, ibn Ezra accuses *payyetanim* of filling their works with riddles and parables; of mixing biblical idiom with that of rabbinic literature (including non-Hebrew loan words); of violating the rules of Hebrew grammar (for example, making a feminine word masculine); and finally, of filling their poems with aggadic allusions. For the Hebrew of this text, see J. Yahalom, "Appendix I," *Sefat ha-shir shel ha-piyyut ha-erets-yisraeli ha-kadum* (Jerusalem: Magnes, 1985), 185–96.

28 The poetry of medieval Spain has received substantially more attention than the piyyut of the pre-Classical and Classical period. For accessible studies that include ample translations of poetry, see Raymond Scheindlin, *The Gazelle: Medieval Hebrew Poems on God, Israel*

igin, piyyut offered each generation's best sacred poets an opportunity to add their voices to the synagogue service, and these poems, while often difficult for modern readers to appreciate, were very much the *kavvanah* ("intentionality")—the responsive, flexible fluidity of meaningful prayer—of their day. As communities became more remote from both the distinctive Hebraic idiom and the Byzantine thematic concerns of these venerable poems, however, these texts became obscure and ossified remnants of the past—the worst examples of rigid *qeva*. Indeed, as Jakob Petuchowski noted, piyyutim were the "*bête noire*" (dark beast) of the early Reform movement and were among the first texts purged from the early Reform prayerbooks.[29]

Nevertheless, the inclusion of contemporary poetry and readings in many modern synagogue services reflects the same impulse that popularized the early piyyutim, often without the congregational liturgists realizing that they are participating in an ancient Jewish tradition. Additionally, in an intriguing "neo-Classical" twist, some modern prayerbooks, particularly those used on the High Holidays (*maḥzorim*), have reintroduced works by the classical poets of Byzantine Palestine, including Yannai.[30]

---

and the Soul (Philadelphia: Jewish Publication Society, 1991) and Peter Cole, *The Dream of the Poem: Hebrew Poetry from Muslim and Christian Spain*, 950–1492 (Princeton: Princeton University Press, 2007).

29 Jakob J. Petuchowski, *Prayerbook Reform in Europe: The Liturgy of European Liberal and Reform Judaism* (New York: World Union for Progressive Judaism, 1968), 30. For an example of the low regard in which *piyyutim* were held by the early Reformers, due to the fact that piyyut language had become completely incomprehensible and its aesthetic alien to the Jews of nineteenth-century Germany, see Gunther Plaut, ed., *The Rise of Reform Judaism* (New York: World Union for Progressive Judaism, 1963), 152–58. Note, in particular, the assertion of Joseph Maier, chair of the First Rabbinical Conference in Brunswick (1844), who considered "the lack of the truly poetic element as a technical defect in our prayer book" (154). Note also, however, the impassioned plea of Gustav Gottheil on behalf of retaining the piyyutim because he believed they elevated the decorum of Shabbat and holiday observance: "I fully recognize the rights of the present to change the prayer [service], but I believe that the religious consciousness of other times also has the right to find expression in our prayers. … I would rather go back to the warmer religious sentiment of antiquity. Therefore I must speak out against the generally condemnatory judgment against piyyutim" (184).

30 Prayerbooks associated with the Conservative movement in the mid-twentieth century in the U.S. have been particularly likely to reintroduce classical piyyut; see, for example, the Silverman *maḥzor* (M. Silverman, ed., *High Holiday Prayerbook: Rosh Hashanah–New Year's Day, Yom Kippur–Day of Atonement* [Hartford: Prayer Book Press, 1951]) and the Harlow *maḥzor* (J. Harlow and the Rabbinical Assembly of America, *Machzor for Rosh Hashanah and Yom Kippur: A Prayer Book for the Days of Awe* [New York: Rabbinical Assembly, 1972]). These prayerbooks reflect the important role that scholars at the Jewish

In sum, piyyutim exist at the intersection of multiple discrete fields of study: as liturgical works, they shed light on the development of the Jewish liturgy; as Hebrew texts from a period when Hebrew was supposedly "dead," they reveal much about the status of the language; as poetry, they reveal transformations in Hebrew literature and aesthetics; as prayer, they offer insight into the concerns and experiences of Jews at various moments in their history; and as a forum for the public interpretation of Scripture, they must be contextualized as part of the same dynamic tradition that produced midrash and targum. Furthermore, because these works were composed for recitation in the synagogue, they often shed an incidental light on the complex reality of that world—issues of topical concern to the congregants, events of contemporary importance, popular theological trends, exegetical motifs, and even the language and intellectual background of the audience.

Though not readily apparent, insights into the cultural history of a fascinating but murky period of Jewish and Western history may also be found within these works. Was Jewish life in this period a story of external coercion and oppression, rebellious messianic foment, or creative independence and interdependence? Scholars have posited variant readings of Jewish history at this moment, and the piyyutim are a major (but overlooked and oversimplified) Jewish voice in the discussion. Likewise, the early piyyutim of the Byzantine period have also proven to be literary complements to the visual art and architecture of the early synagogue, helping scholars place the startlingly rich mosaics discovered during the last century in the Byzantine synagogues within a larger cultural context.

Piyyutim also have much to offer scholars in fields outside of Jewish Studies entirely. In particular, research in Byzantine Christianity—especially Christian hymnography and liturgy—reveals suggestive confluences and parallels with Jewish sources from the same period. Shared traditions of interpretation (convivial and polemical) are readily apparent, as are common rhetorical techniques, although the details of the relationship remain thorny and have defied easy interpretation. In short, scholars from an array of fields, disciplines, and approaches—Jewish and Christian, his-

Theological Seminary (Solomon Schechter and Shalom Spiegel, especially) have played in Genizah and Piyyut Studies as well as the ideological preference in Conservative Judaism to innovate by means of reviving traditional texts.

torical and literary, phenomenological and New Critical—can all find a treasure trove of new material in the piyyutim.

A Poet Lost and Found

A thorough and comprehensive introduction to piyyutim at all these different levels and across the many centuries in which the genre flourished exceeds the scope of a single book (and possibly the abilities of a single author).[31] Instead, in hopes of complementing works already in existence, the present study focuses on a single poet, Yannai, whose historical context and creative output best intersect with the host of interests delineated above.

Yannai lived before the Muslim conquest of the Land of Israel, probably in the sixth century, during the tumultuous reign of the Byzantine emperor Justinian.[32] Yannai's time and place situate him at a critical moment in Jewish cultural history: important rabbinic sources were crystallizing; the synagogue was thriving; the liturgy was taking definitive shape. Looking at Yannai's period more broadly, he probably lived at a time when the Byzantine Empire was undergoing a military resurgence, witnessing a tremendous Christian building program (including Hagia Sophia and the splendid edifices of Ravenna), and experiencing the cultural flowering that created works such as the monumental oeuvre of the Greek hymnist Romanos. It was a period when, under strong imperial leadership, Byzantium truly became a Christian empire.[33] Yannai's works, with their dynamic mixture of messianism, defiance, and restraint, reflect and engage this society in flux and show him to be a poet of transformative importance at a period when Jewish (and Western) culture itself was both coalescing and becoming something new.

---

31 Readers seeking a concise general introduction to "Piyyut" should consult the entries in the *Encyclopaedia Judaica* (s.v., "Piyyut") and the *Encyclopaedia of Judaism* (s.v., "Piyyut"), or, for a more extensive treatment in English, Weinberger's *Jewish Hymnography.*

32 For a discussion of the problems in assigning Yannai a more specific date, see my article "'You Have Skirted This Hill Long Enough': The Tension Between Rhetoric and History in a Byzantine Piyyut" (forthcoming in the *Hebrew Union College Annual* 80 (2010).

33 Averil Cameron articulates with particular eloquence the emergence of Christian Byzantium as an imperial force. Especially worth noting in this context are her two monographs, *Christianity and the Rhetoric of Empire: The Development of Christian Discourse* (Berkeley: University of California Press, 1995); and *The Mediterranean World in Late Antiquity,* A.D. 395–600 (London: Routledge, 1993).

Furthermore, Yannai—"a father of piyyut"[34]—influenced Hebrew sacred poetry for centuries beyond his lifespan. He was the first non-anonymous Hebrew poet, signing his name into his works by means of an acrostic; he was the first to consistently use true end-rhyme; and he was among the first to have written for the weekly service and festivals rather than just particular holidays such as Tisha b'Av, Rosh Hashanah, and Yom Kippur.[35] Many important Classical *payyetanim*, including Judah, Shimon bar Megas, and most famously Qillir, composed works modeled on Yannai's compositions. His poems stand out both for their complex form and their complicated content. As a poet, Yannai drew more intensely and allusively on rabbinic traditions than the poetry of previous generations did. At the same time, however, he was highly original not only in form but in content. Indeed, while much work remains to be done before definitive conclusions can be offered, it is possible that Yannai's exegesis, rather than merely echoing more widespread traditions and methods of aggadah, may well have influenced later prose exegetes; some of Yannai's original interpretations (or, at least, interpretations attested only in Yannai's works) appear in prose *midrashim* from much later dates. The precise mechanism by which this happened remains subject to diverse interpretations, but the commonalities tantalize. Yannai was, in short, a trendsetter in terms of form, style, and content.

The poetic form most associated with Yannai—the *qedushta* (plural, *qedushta'ot*), which embellishes the first three benedictions of the Amidah, "the prayer" *par excellence* of Judaism—became one of the most important genres in the following centuries. The origin of this type of poem is unknown. We do not know whether Yannai invented the *qedushta*, con-

---

34 See S. Spiegel, *Fathers of Piyyut: Texts and Studies toward a History of the Piyyut in Eretz Yisrael*, ed. M. Schmelzer (Jerusalem and New York: Jewish Theological Seminary of America, 1996) [Hebrew]. For a presentation of a variety of texts that attest to Yannai's importance, from the Karaite Abu Yusuf al-Qirqisani to Ephraim of Bonn, see Israel Davidson, *Maḥzor Yannai*, xliii–xlix.

35 Yannai's formal innovations and their consequences for Hebrew poetics are explored in Chapter One.

36 For an intriguing hypothesis on the origin of the *qerova*—the larger genre to which Yannai's *qedushta'ot* belong—see Aharon Mirsky, "The Origins of the Qerova," in *The Piyyut* (Magnes: Jerusalem, 1991), 86–92 [Hebrew]. See, too, E. Fleischer, "Towards a Solution of Some Fundamental Problems in the Structure of the Classical 'Qedushta,'" in *Henoch Yalon Memorial Volume*, ed. E.Y. Kutscher, S. Lieberman, and M.Z. Kaddari (Jerusalem: Kiryat Sefer, 1974), 444–70.

structed it out of diverse but existing styles of poetry which he combined into a single new form, or whether he followed an established poetic structure of which earlier exemplars simply didn't survive.[36] The essential structure of the *qedushta* was adapted to later styles of poetry, notably the genre called the *yotzer* (a poetic cycle adorning the blessings before the Shema), which became popular in Ashkenaz in the Middle Ages. Individual poems within the *qedushta* (which consists of nine or more individual poems, ranging from highly stylized "pattern poems" to unrhymed rhythmic prose) show signs of continuity with the simpler Hebrew poetry of the previous generations, such as that of Yose ben Yose, but also anticipates the intricate developments of medieval Ashkenazic Hebrew poetry.[37]

So influential was Yannai that Jewish tradition considered the most prolific, famous, and enduring Byzantine *payyetan*, Qillir, to be his student; a poet as great as Qillir could only have studied with the greatest poet of the previous generation. At the same time, tradition was also aware of Yannai's strange disappearance from the prayerbook. One legend, cited by Ephraim of Bonn (twelfth century C.E.), goes so far as to assert that Yannai's obscurity was intentionally enacted as punishment for his murder of Qillir in a fit of jealous rage.[38] More likely, Yannai's works simply became obsolete when the so-called "triennial" Torah cycle, for which his works were composed, was eventually replaced by the Babylonian annual cycle of Torah reading, which is still in place today.[39] Later poets and editors did not adapt

---

37 For examples of Yose ben Yose's work, with English translation, see Swartz and Yahalom, *Avodah*.

38 The legend is cited in Eliezer Landshuth, *Amudei ha-avodah: Reshimat rashe ha-paytanim u-meʿat mi-toldotehem al sedar alfabeta im mispar piyutehem ha-nimtsaʾim be-sifre tefilot* (Berlin: Bernstein, 1857–1862), 1:103. Israel Davidson also cites this tradition in his *Maḥzor Yannai*, xlix, as the next-to-last of the medieval sources on this poet. In Davidson's text, Ephraim of Bonn states: "[As for the hymn] 'The firstborn who opened each womb (*onei pitrei raḥmatayim*),' the world states that its source is Rabbi Yannai, the teacher of Rabbi Eleazar berabbi Qillir, but throughout the region of Lombardy it is not said, because it is said about him that he was jealous of Rabbi Eleazar, his student, so he cast a scorpion into his shoe and killed him. May the Lord forgive all who say this about him if it is not true." This passage, in addition to preserving a colorful legend about Yannai, indicates an awareness of Yannai's authorship of the *qedushta* for Exod 12:29 ("And it came to pass at midnight") in at least some circles in the pre-modern period.

39 See Elbogen, *Jewish Liturgy*, 132–34; he notes that the Palestinian synagogue in twelfth-century Cairo still retained the triennial cycle (133). The "triennial" cycle used in many Conservative congregations is a variant of the Babylonian annual cycle, not a recreation of the old Palestinian-Jewish lectionary. Yannai's poems presume that the Torah is read over the course of three and a half to four years, in linear order; modern triennial cycles divide the Babylonian annual Torah portion into thirds, resulting in a non-linear reading of the

his works to a new context, and vigorous younger poets arose to fill the lacunae. Indeed, prior to the rediscovery of Yannai among the texts of the Cairo Genizah, the only extant work by this important poet was his *qedushta* for Exod 12:29 ("And it came to pass at midnight..." [ויהי בחצי הלילה]).[40] Otherwise, despite his importance and the vastness of his creative output (poems for every *sidra*—every Torah portion—of the triennial cycle and the festivals and holidays), Yannai was essentially lost.[41] Fashions changed and the piyyutim of Yannai—once the most influential trendsetter in the world of Hebrew poetry—had become passé.

Being "lost," however, may have served Yannai well in the end; the works of other poets, which remained parts of living liturgical traditions in various Jewish communities, were often edited over time—abbreviated, adapted, and reused to suit local liturgical norms and aesthetic ideals. Particularly as Hebrew receded in popularity and became a more remote "sacred language," opportunities for misunderstanding and mis-transmitting the piyyutim increased. Yannai's works, precisely because they became outmoded early on, were spared this fate. Furthermore, while Yannai's body of work is impressively complete, it is not overwhelming. In contrast, Qillir—one of the most prolific poets in the history of Hebrew—wrote a tremendous number of piyyutim, leaving behind such a vast body of work that scholars have yet to assemble a complete collection, let alone produce a critical edition of his *oeuvre*. Because Yannai's works were so well preserved and are so manageable in size, and because his historical and cultural context is so significant, he provides a unique yet representative point of entry into the field of Piyyut Studies.

Torah. For the text and calendar of the modern Conservative triennial lectionary, see http://www.rabbinicalassembly.org/teshuvot/docs/19861990/eisenberg_triennial.pdf. In this work, I use the term *sidra* to distinguish the triennial Torah portion from the Babylonian *parashah*.

40 The first seven units of this poem were preserved in the Ashkenazi liturgy for Shabbat HaGadol, and in the seventh unit by itself. The hymn "And it came to pass at midnight" is included in the Passover Haggadah; the final two units of the piyyut appear only in Genizah manuscripts, and the final unit is fragmentary. The complete text of this *qedushta* can be found in Z. M. Rabinovitz, *The Liturgical Poems of Rabbi Yannai according to the Triennial Cycle of the Pentateuch and the Holidays*, 2 vols (Jerusalem: Bialik, 1985–1987), I:296–304. A translation of the piyyut can be found in Sarason, "Midrash in the Liturgy," 485–90.

41 Davidson was the first to recognize and publish Yannai texts. See his *Maḥzor Yannai.* The first major edition of Yannai's corpus was published several decades later by Menachem Zulay as *The Liturgical Poems of Yannai: Collected from Geniza-Manuscripts and Other Sources* (Berlin: Shocken, 1938) [Hebrew]. Zulay also published important studies of Yannai's language and forms, as will be noted throughout this study.

The modern history of Yannai studies is intimately connected to the recovery of material from the Cairo Genizah. As noted above, Yannai is one of the great treasures to emerge from that vast and amazing storeroom. In 1919, Israel Davidson published *Maḥzor Yannai*—a slender volume containing eight Genizah fragments and supplemental poems.[42] It caused a stir in part because it indicated that piyyutim were composed at this early period for the weekly Sabbath service as well as the holidays, and thus, by extension, it revealed an appreciation for poetry among the Jews of Byzantine Palestine beyond what had previously been imagined. Almost exactly two decades later, the Schocken Institute for the Study of Medieval Hebrew poetry brought out Menachem Zulay's magnificent *Liturgical Poems of Yannai*, an almost complete edition of Yannai's works. It contained 138 piyyutim, albeit most of them fragmentary, and was one of the last Hebrew books published in Nazi Germany.[43] However, while Zulay provided a body of texts, he did not include commentaries, and it was Saul Lieberman, in *Ḥazzanut Yannai*, who provided a scholarly analysis of Yannai's resonances with rabbinic writings and determined the direction of scholarly study of Yannai in future decades. In the 1960s, Z. M. Rabinovitz followed Lieberman's lead and published *Halakhah and Aggadah in the Liturgical Poetry of Yannai*, a book-length study of Yannai's relationship with classical midrashic and halakhic sources. At last, in the 1980s, Rabinovitz published his critical edition of Yannai's poetry—providing the current generation of scholars with the resources necessary to undertake a variety of in-depth studies. Thus the second century of Yannai scholarship begins.[44]

The Present Work

Our study of Yannai moves from the "small scale" of examining his poetry's language and forms to the "large scale" of its cultural and societal importance. It concludes with an examination of selected intriguing and important motifs. Along the way, important works of scholarship (in Hebrew as

42 Davidson, *Maḥzor Yannai.*

43 Zulay, *The Liturgical Poems of Yannai.*

44 Z. M. Rabinovitz, *Halakhah and Aggadah in the Liturgical Poetry of Yannai* (Tel Aviv: Alexander Kohut, 1965) [Hebrew]; and *The Liturgical Poems of Rabbi Yannai according to the Triennial Cycle of the Pentanteuch and the Holidays*, 2 vols. (Jerusalem: Mosad Bialik, 1985–87) [Hebrew]. For a discussion of Rabinovitz's edition of the Yannai corpus, see the "Issues of Text and Translation," below.

well as English) will be noted. Each chapter builds upon the previous, expanding and deepening the scope and range of analyses presented.

The first chapter approaches Yannai's *qedsuhta'ot* as poetry, a medium in which form is primary. While it may seem obvious to study poetry *as poetry*, scholars have, by and large, neglected the artistic and aesthetic aspects of piyyutim. There was, in the scholarship, something of a sense that these poems were interesting for many reasons, but as poetry they were mediocre or worse—certainly not as lovely as the lyrics of the Hebrew poetry of Andalusia. Indeed, compared to the poetry of Shmuel HaNagid, Judah HaLevi, and Moses ibn Ezra, the classical piyyutim can appear clumsy, long, and willfully obscure. If, however, piyyutim like Yannai's are taken at face value—accepted in principle as meaningful performative pieces reflecting an aesthetic different from our own—then significant artistic merit becomes manifest.

An understanding of a *qedushta*'s intricate structure and its rhetorical effects is vital for a full appreciation of Yannai's artistry. Like a symphony, a *qedushta*'s artistic power and emotional effects emerge cumulatively from the totality of the complicated whole, although each of the component parts of the lengthy poem possesses its own integrity. Indeed, it may be that some units possess a distinctive history; the unit called a *rahit*, in particular, often stands out for both its formal artistry and its resonance with midrashic techniques of exegesis. Furthermore, because *qedushta'ot* were composed for a liturgical setting, these poems by definition engaged an audience, and that aspect of their composition must also be considered—the ways the poems drew the community into the story, into the performance, into the experience. Piyyutim were, after all, not abstract works to be studied, but intense textual phenomena that were to be lived; their artistry is theatrical as well as literary. The poet mediated his listeners' experience at the same time that he constructed it. Precisely because the poetry operates at so many levels, the poet's role must be understood as similarly complex. In many ways, the poet fills the role once held by prophets and priests, but he does so from what seems to be a rabbinic vantage point.

The topic of the second chapter—payyetanic language—is already a very well researched area. Peculiarities in grammar, syntax, and rhetoric were among the first topics to attract attention to these works and to invite scholarly argument, even as the poetics of the piyyutim generated only peripheral interest. The purpose of the essay in this volume is not to replicate or translate the important work done by German and Israeli scholars but to complement their studies by examining Yannai's Genesis *qedushtaʾot* from a more idiosyncratic perspective, in which the performative effects of his use of biblical language are placed in the foreground.

This approach will hopefully open the texts up in a new way to readers perhaps not expert in the field of Hebrew language but interested in questions of why grammatical irregularities and allusions may be important and how vocabulary can be particularly charged. Intertextuality is particularly important at this level; quotation, allusion, and pun were all essential tools in constructing piyyutim, but are often among the most difficult for readers to appreciate. The present treatment attempts to convey a sense of the strange richness and evocative depth of Yannai's language, which works at many levels simultaneously and over time. In truth, with the piyyutim, there will always be new notes to hear, new resonances to catch; the footnotes in the translations provide only tinny echoes of this aural richness, but they are important for conveying to less sensitive modern ears the richness inherent in these works.

Of course, the experiential element and allusive language of the piyyutim lead to questions of context, the focus of the third chapter. The material at the heart of this chapter—the rise of a rich rabbinic culture in the context of Christian Byzantine society—could fill volumes. Yannai's *qedushtaʾot* offer a lens through which this complex period can be examined. They provide a glimpse of an important aspect of Jewish life from literary, artistic, and societal perspectives. His poems are important cultural artifacts, and their richness emerges with even greater clarity when they are regarded as part not only of the ancient synagogue, but also of a wider poetic and artistic revolution in the Byzantine world—one that was played out on the stage of religious ritual and belief as much as in the political sphere.

Just as Yannai mediated the experience of the divine and the sense of the text for his community, he interpreted their experience of the larger world on both a small and larger scale, both as a participant in and a shaper of the culture and society of Late Antiquity. His works, Janus-faced, looked inward to the Jewish prayer experience and outward to the world in which the Jewish community lived—in this case, a Christian world experiencing its own transformative epoch. The relationship between piyyut and early Christian hymnography—and traditions of poetic exegesis—has the potential to be a particularly rich field of study. The poetry of these two communities hints not only at the internal experience of each group but the tense and complicated interactions between them.

The final chapter presents six mini-essays that highlight the significance of these poems as literary works, liturgical texts, and cultural artifacts by considering very specific facets of their content. The first piece explores the relationship of Yannai's works to *Hekhalot* mystical traditions and considers the prominence of angelic figures in his works; the second considers the concept of "holiness" that permeates his works and nuances its liturgical function; the third examines the poet's theology and how he depicts God; the fourth delineates the omnipresent theme of exile and restoration that runs throughout Yannai's poetry; the next examines the depictions of non-Jews in these poems, both negative and positive; and the final essay studies the ways in which he crafts female and feminine characters.

The selected topics are not exhaustive; other threads could be traced just as well, and the ones presented here developed much further. Ideally, these miniature essays will whet appetites to read and study more. Their very incompleteness suggests the wealth of research yet to be done. Indeed, the creation of such an awareness is one goal of this project.

A comprehensive study of Yannai's entire corpus exceeds the confines of a single volume, so I have chosen to concentrate specifically on his piyyutim for Genesis. The Genesis *qedushtaʾot*—there are thirty-one in total, many complete but others fragmentary—display a representative range of techniques, styles, themes, and motifs while highlighting the poet's presentation of some of the most familiar biblical narratives. The limited size of the corpus also makes it possible to include translations. Given this study's interest in understanding Jewish perception of Christianity and the Byzantine Empire, the Genesis material is particularly fruitful because of the prominence of Esau (understood allegorically as Rome and identified, by Yannai's day, with Byzantine Christendom) in the biblical base text. A study of Yannai's piyyutim for the High Holidays and festivals also has great appeal—these works are lengthier than routine Shabbat *qedushtaʾot* and, as a result, contain a rich repository of exposition and exegesis. Their irregularity, however, conflicts with the introductory nature of this work. The routine must be explored before the exceptions can be appreciated.[45]

45 The volume planned to follow this will focus on the place of the Song of Songs–a text that rivals Genesis in terms of its rich history of interpretation–in the context of the Byzantine synagogue.

In sum, Genesis is an important text with a unique (and frequently extensive) history of interpretation in both Judaism and Christianity. When introducing the rich world of piyyut to a diverse audience, it makes sense to begin with a familiar text and well-known stories—to begin "at the beginning."

Issues of Text and Translation

R. Judah said: If one translates a verse literally, he is a liar;
if he adds thereto, he is a blasphemer and a libeler.
b. Kid. 49a

Translation is the art of failure.
Umberto Eco

The translations that constitute the second part of this book work in concert with the first; where the chapters lay out broad points and concepts, the translations provide lengthy, concrete examples of specific compositions. Translating Yannai's *qedushtaʾot* represented a profound challenge, one that this author undertook with no small amount of trepidation. Poetry is best translated by poets—a profession to which the present writer has no pretense. Furthermore, the very features that make Yannai's poetry so impressive—his delightful word play, deft puns, learned allusions, and clever wit—defy attempts to render them in another language; key elements of the works can survive translation but the whole cannot be truly communicated. Readers adept at Hebrew may well argue with specific choices made in these translations, but such is the nature of the endeavor—indeed, the original Hebrew of the poems is presented here in order to facilitate the study of these works by those with the language skills to read them in their original language. Ultimately, the translations should be understood as a bridge into the world of the Hebrew piyyutim; it is my hope that even readers with relatively rudimentary Hebrew skills—in particular, familiarity with biblical Hebrew—will, with practice and a biblical concordance, be able to grasp the brilliance of these works with a minimum of mediation.

The translations presented here balance a variety of competing demands: first, they strive to convey faithfully the *content* of the originals, replicating insofar as possible the vocabulary, puns, allusions, and quotations that texture the Hebrew; second, they attempt to convey the *sound* and *sense* of the original by drawing on the rich vocabulary of the English language; finally, they are intended to be readable as free-standing works of literature, although in no way can the English versions replace the works of Hebrew art they endeavor to convey.

In order to give a sense of the complexity and richness of these compositions, the translations are accompanied by annotations, often benefiting from the work of earlier scholars of Yannai as discussed below, plus my own brief commentaries, which highlight some important or intriguing elements of that particular work. In some cases, these annotations and commentaries link the individual texts to the book's introductory essays or to other translated poems. In other cases, they stand alone. This structure recognizes that some readers will begin with the major essays, turning to the translations for additional depth and specificity. Others will begin with the translations, looking secondarily to the essays or to other poems for a sense of context, and still others will dip into each section without any particular system, moving back and forth between the two halves of the book.

Sources and Editions

The Hebrew text presented here is based on the version provided by the Historical Hebrew Dictionary project (*Maʾagarim*). The Maʾagarim database offers the best, most accurate, most complete, and most current readings of the extant manuscripts.[1] In order to make the text as approachable as possible, the Hebrew text presented here begins with and adapts from that in the electronic database. In particular, technical sigla used to indicate lacunae, corrections, uncertain readings, and copyists' additions have been dispensed with; manuscript abbreviations have, for the most part, been completed; extremely damaged passages have been omitted; and textual variants are noted only when they are highly significant. In addition, while the Maʾagarim text is unvocalized (although the database itself reflects vocalization extant in the manuscripts) due to the technical challenges of creating the electronic database, the present edition has been vocalized except in cases where the reading is dubious. Those wishing to

1 The Historical Hebrew Dictionary Project, accessible (subscription required) via: http://hebrew-treasures.huji.ac.il. I am extremely grateful to the Project staff, in particular Dr. Benjamin Elizur, for permission to use their texts in this volume and for their assistance in working with the material.

understand the full complexity of manuscript work beneath the surface of this edition are encouraged to make use of the apparatus of the Maʾagarim database, which contains a wealth of information about the manuscripts used as well as indicating the textual difficulties smoothed over in the present edition.[2]

The Maʾagarim database text represents a significant advance from the text available in the standard, and more accessible, critical edition of Yannai's work published in the 1980s by Zvi Meir Rabinovitz.[3] In particular, many lacunae and uncertain readings in Rabinovitz's edition have been completed on the basis of manuscripts unavailable to Rabinovitz, at times to the extent of entire units (for example, Poem Six and a *rahit* for the Gen 1:1 *qedushta*). Rabinovitz's volume is itself an updated version of the groundbreaking volume by Menachem Zulay published in 1938.[4] Due to the proliferation of discoveries from the Cairo Genizah, Rabinovitz was able to consult more (and more complete) manuscripts than Zulay had at his disposal. Furthermore, Rabinovitz—whose previous major work examined the relationship of Yannai's compositions to rabbinic and biblical writings[5]—supplied each poem with substantial annotations, paying particular attention to the parallels between the piyyutim and other sources. While his interpretations are not always persuasive, all scholars of Yannai owe Rabinovitz a debt for his efforts. References to Rabinovitz's edition of Yannai appear as "**R**" in the present text's annotations, and while this present volume does not include even a fraction of his ample annotations and

---

2 See also Joseph Yahalom, *Palestinian Vocalised Piyyut Manuscripts in the Cambridge Genizah Collections* (Cambridge: Cambridge University Press, 1997). This volume focuses on those piyyut manuscripts which employed the superlinear vocalization system, and includes many plates with photographs of manuscripts.

3 Z. M. Rabinovitz, *The Liturgical Poems of Rabbi Yannai*, 2 vols. (Jerusalem: Mosad Bialik, 1985–87).

4 M. Zulay, *The Liturgical Poems of Yannai*. This work built on the pioneering work of I. Davidson, who published nine of Yannai's *qedushtaʾot* from the Cairo Genizah twenty years earlier (*Maḥzor Yannai*). Zulay's volume is a remarkable scholarly accomplishment; he assembled 138 poems (many fragmentary) from the vast quantity of Genizah fragments. Saul Lieberman's *Ḥazzanut Yannai*, published a few years after Zulay's volume appeared, delineates the relationship between Yannai's poetry and rabbinic writings, and it serves as the first "commentary" on Zulay's edition of Yannai. All later commentators on Yannai, including Rabinovitz and Nachum M. Bronznick, *The Liturgical Poetry of Yannai*, 2 vols. (Rubin Mass: Jerusalem, 2000, Supp. 2005), cite Zulay and Lieberman frequently.

5 Rabinovitz, *Halakhah and Aggadah*.

commentary, the existence of his critical edition made undertaking the translation element of this project, particularly in the early stages, feasible.

Texts as complicated as these poems lend themselves to ever more detailed annotation, and readers of Yannai can now benefit as well from Nahum Bronznick's two Hebrew volumes of annotations. I have cited his works as "**B1**" and "**B2**," respectively.[6] Bronznick took the Rabinovitz edition as his starting point, noting that while Rabinovitz's volumes were "unquestionably of great value," they nonetheless left some unclear passages unexplained, some biblical allusions unreferenced, and some midrashic sources unidentified.[7] With these shortcomings in mind, Bronznick undertook a massive project: the completion of a commentary on Rabinovitz's volumes—poem by poem, not once, but twice. Bronznick's first volume represents his initial review of the poems, in which he supplies notes on sources, allusions, and interpretations as well as, based on both manuscript readings and learned conjecture, emendations and completions for lacunae. Five years after his initial commentary was published, Bronznick deemed his own work in need of supplementation and revision, resulting in the publication of his second volume, in which he revisited his initial commentary and added even more notes, clarifications, and readings. While Bronzick's commentaries assume a different edition of Yannai than that employed here, they remain eminently useful and his interpretations, annotations, and restorations are frequently noted in the annotations of the present edition. In many places, the Maʾagarim database concurs with or even confirms Bronzick's proposed readings.

In addition to the substantial resources provided by the Maʾagarim database, Rabinovitz's critical edition, and Bronznick's commentary on Rabinovitz, Shalom Spiegel's *Fathers of Poetry*, edited by Menachem Schmelzer, contains annotations of a number of Yannai fragments (the texts themselves are, with one exception, included in the Maʾagarim database), and his contributions have been noted wherever possible.[8] My

---

6 Bronznick, *The Liturgical Poetry of Yannai.* While in the preface to **B2**, Bronzick states, "[T]his volume, coupled with the previous one and taken together with most of the comments by Zvi M. Rabinovitz… make for a comprehensive commentary that will enable even the non-expert to gain an enlightened insight and delightful appreciation of Yannai's multifaceted liturgical poetry," obviously this only holds true if the "non-expert" reader has access to scholarly modern Hebrew.

7 English preface to **B1**.

8 Spiegel, *Fathers of Piyyut.* The piyyutim of Yannai included in this volume are: Gen 17:1, 38:1, and 44:18. Spiegel also includes a very brief fragment of the *qedushah* (Poem Nine)

work benefited also from the opportunities I had to read many of the *qedushta'ot* in their original manuscripts, particularly those housed at Cambridge University. While the various tools now available make Yannai one of the easiest poets to study if one can work in modern Hebrew, inspecting the originals was invaluable for conveying the reality beneath the tidy surface of the various printed editions.

Rabinovitz and Bronznick both offer extensive annotation and discussion of Yannai's poetry—between the two authors, almost every line receives attention—with Bronznick often nuancing Rabinovitz or, in **B2**, his own earlier reading. While I have drawn on the works of both scholars, I have not limited myself to their annotations, but freely added notes and interpretations of my own as I saw necessary or useful—always with an eye towards those insights that will be most engaging to this volume's intended audience and relevant to the discussions in the introductory essays.

It is important to note that the present Hebrew edition is eclectic. Upon rare occasion it differs from the Ma'agarim version, favoring a reading suggested by other scholars or reflecting my own inspection of the manuscripts; such alterations to the Ma'agarim text are indicated in the notes. Likewise, when I accept a line-completion supplied by **R**, **B1**, or **B2**, I use square brackets to indicate the lacuna and reflect the source of the additional text in the notes; nevertheless, it must be borne in mind that these often reflect "educated guesses" rather than actual readings of the manuscripts. In cases where the Ma'agarim text itself contains variants, requiring that one wording be chosen over another based on variations preserved in manuscripts, the present edition represents a judgment as to the "best" reading. Likewise, when manuscripts differ in their lists of quoted intertexts, I have included *all* the potential verses. In places where there are multiple viable but distinctive readings, I have left the Ma'agarim text intact and noted alternative readings (and their translations) in the footnotes. In two cases—the *silluq* for Gen 1:1 and the second *rahit* for Gen 48:1—I have included passages whose attribution to Yannai has been cast into doubt. I do this out of deference to earlier published editions (which remain in many ways more accessible than the Ma'agarim database) and because of the poetic merits of those two units, but with due caution.[9]

---

for a *qedushta* for Gen 27:1 (p. 59), but as that passage does not appear in Rabinovitz's edition or in the Ma'agarim database, I elected not to include that fragment in this edition.

9 This edition also does not include the *qedushta* for Gen 42:1 which is included in Zulay's edition (pp. 59–62) but is absent from Rabinovitz's edition and considered anonymous by

Method of Translation

Abundant in deft allusions and fleeting puns, Yannai's piyyutim are written in an idiosyncratic variation of post-biblical Hebrew that possesses a distinctive cadence and grammar. English simply cannot replicate the consonance, assonance, rhythm, and rhyme of these works, let alone characteristic formal elements such as acrostics or rhyme. Yet, to publish the essays without the accompanying texts and translations would deny readers a sense of the sheer scale of Yannai's output, let alone the texture and variety of his piyyutim.

My approach in translating these poems is, thus, as eclectic as the poems themselves. In some cases, the essential element of a stich, line, or stanza derives from intertextuality and allusion; in others, the primary features are repeated words, refrains, or rhetorical flourishes that embellish lines focused primarily on narrative content. In each case, the translation emphasizes what I believe to be the poem's dominant element. While some formal features, notably acrostics and rhyme, simply cannot be reproduced in English, other elements (consonance, alliteration, repetition, parallelism) can survive translation in some fashion.

Examples:

In some places, the poet emphasizes content over form; that is, while there are formal features within a stanza (acrostics, rhyme, etc.), Yannai's main objective seems to be narration—moving the action of the story forward or giving readers clear, substantial information. These passages are often the easiest to translate because they are the most like prose. The final lines of Poem Six of Yannai's *qedushta* to Gen 38:1 illustrate this tension between form and content and its resolution. The original can be transliterated as:

> **Q**idshah shem tamar haqedoshah // asher kamhah lezeraʿ qedushah
> **R**imat ve-ʿastah qedeshah // ve-hitsliaḥ darkaḥ qedoshah
> **Sh**imrah almenutah penei Adonai // [ve-reyqam] lo hashivah Adonai
> **T**aʾavah lehagziaʿ be-ʿam Adonai // ki hem zeraʿ beyraḥ Adonai
>
> (Poem Six, lines 41–44)

---

the Maʾagarim database. Two badly damaged texts that do appear to be by Yannai—part of the *qedushta* for Gen 24:1 (beyond the *qedushah* which is included here) and various passages from the *qedushta* for Gen 46:28—were, reluctantly, not included in the present edition due to their fragmentary states.

which we have translated as:

> Tamar hallowed the Holy Name // for she hoped for holy seed
> She harlequinned and played the "holy" harlot // and her holy path He prospered
> She preserved her widowhood before the Lord // the Lord did not return her empty
> She longed to grow the garden of the Lord // for they are the seed the Lord has blessed

These two stanzas are typical of the style of Yannai's Poem Six.[10] In terms of form, each line is relatively lengthy (6–8 words per line), embeds the letter of the alphabetical acrostic (here, *qof, resh, shin,* and *tav,* respectively), includes internal and end-rhyme, and employs repeated words/roots. At the same time, in term of content, the poet here uses his format for exposition; he is retelling and interpreting the biblical story.

The English version of this passage does not attempt to replicate two of the most basic formal features of the stanzas: acrostic or rhyme. To do so would result in stilted English and awkward idiom—the opposite of Yannai's clear narrative exposition of the lines. Although at times I have resorted to including the transliteration of key words in the body of the poem (see, for example, the end of Poem One in the *qedushta* for Gen 9:18), English is, quite often, sufficiently flexible to permit the repetition of key words/roots. We see this here in the translation of the two stanzas quoted above: "holy/hallow" (*q-d-sh*) in the first and God's name in the second. The translation does not attempt to replicate the placement of the theme words within the line, but the simple repetition of the words conveys at least some of the sound-play of the original. Furthermore, in the first of the quoted stanzas, every effort was made to include words that begin with the letter "h"—not because the Hebrew original used a single letter so consistently but because this consonance suggests the rich and resonant sound of the original. Thus, the word *rimat,* literally "deceived," is translated as "harlequinned"—a neologism coined both for its sound-play and because the image of the harlequin conveys the element of costume involved in Tamar's seductive deceit. In some cases, two words—e.g., the phrase "holy harlot"—are necessary to capture the nuance of the Hebrew *qedeshah* (lit. a "holy woman" but with connotations of

10 See discussion in Chapter One.

sacred prostitution). In short, the English does not replicate the poetry of the original, but it attempts to create a kind of poetic idiom of its own, while faithfully rendering the sense of the Hebrew.

Translating passages where both form and content are important proved the most challenging, particularly when both elements rely heavily on the resonant language of biblical allusion or when the words themselves convey multiple resonances simultaneously. The following example indicates the challenge of translating passages where allusions and sound-play are almost as important as narrative content. The stanza appears in the first unit (the *magen*) of Yannai's *qedushta* for Gen 16:1, and it represents a relatively typical line where biblical allusions must be preserved and elements of the sound-play retained or recreated. The lines are transliterated as:

> **H**aytah kemo gan naʿul // **v**e-ḥatumah kemo gal naʿul
> **Z**aʿaqah ve-dafqah kapot ha-manʿul // **ḥ**anun leḥonenah mibaʿalah ʿul
>
> (Poem One, lines 5–6)

which we have translated as:

> She was like a garden locked // and she was sealed like fountain locked
> She cried out and knocked upon the latches of the lock // O Gracious One to grant her from her husband, a child.

Although the original Hebrew is deceptively simple, much is lost in translation. For example, the English version sacrifices the acrostic (the embedded letters *heh*, *vav*, *zayin*, and *ḥet*), the rhyme (*ʿul*), the rhythm of the four-word stichs, and the richly resonant sound of the alternating "ah" and "oo" vowels. It also fails to replicate the thick sound of the *ʿayin*, which subtly emphasizes the sound *naʿul* ("locked") that concludes the first three stichs, and the unexpected final word, *ʿul* ("child")—the potent semantic antithesis of Sarai's "locked" (infertile) status.

All elements of form are not lost in translation, however. The English rendering does convey the presence of "lock/locked" in each stich of the first three stichs (if not the pun on "child," which concludes the stanza), and this lends the English a cadence that is faithful at least to the outlines of the Hebrew original. Similarly, the phrase translated here as “latches of the lock” creates alliteration not found in the Hebrew (*kapot ha-manʿul*), but this sound helps suggest the general sense of alliteration present in the original. Similarly, we are fortunate that in English "knock" and "lock" rhyme, as this also creates a resonance with Yannai's Hebrew version. Even if *naʿul* ("lock") and *dafqah* ("knock") do not actually rhyme, other words in the lines *do* rhyme. In sum, the English does not try to replicate the actual *form* of the Hebrew—as if that were possible—but rather to create an English work faithful to the *sense* and the *ambiance* of the Hebrew.

The translation also anticipates several of the key *intertexts* and *subtexts* that undergird the language of the stanza. In places where the biblical verse is quoted in the body of the poem as an intertext[11] or by the present author in the footnotes, the translation of the biblical verse harmonizes with the language of the poem, so as to obscure the relationship as little as possible. Here the key verse, cited as an intertext following the unit, is Song 4:12: "A garden locked is my sister, my bride, a fountain locked, a spring sealed." This biblical language is readily apparent in the language of the poetic stanza: the "garden," "fountain," "locked" and "sealed" are all present, albeit reorganized to create the end-rhyme and acrostic that the poet needs. More subtly, however, this stanza relies on the language of two verses not cited as intertexts but included among the footnotes: Song 5:2 ("Hark, my beloved knocks!"), only with the poet reversing the genders and Sarai knocking at God's door rather than the male lover knocking at his lover's gates; and Song 5:5 ("I arose to open to my beloved, and my hands dripped with myrrh, my fingers with liquid myrrh, upon the latches of the lock"), where the lock is opened, but too late. When God opens the lock, however, it is not—even for the ninety-year-old Sarai—too late.

Additional brief examples illustrate our efforts to preserve the poet's allusiveness while also conveying the sense of his lines. In the second unit of his *qedushta* for Gen 31:3, we have translated Yannai as:

> Pure women, and wise, free of disdain // the pure one, in his wisdom, called them to council
>
> (Poem Two, lines 11–12)

This language emphasizes the tact and subtlety necessary for Jacob and his wives to successfully deceive the vengeful Laban. It praises Rachel, Leah, and Jacob in terms of "wisdom" (literally, "discretion" or "modesty," from the root *ts-n-ʿ*). This line difficult to translate because it relies on a verse

11 The first three units of a *qedushta* are followed by lists of biblical verses quoted in full, which I have called "intertexts." See the discussion in Chapter One.

quoted subsequently as an intertext: Mic 6:8, which is usually translated as "He has told you, O mortal, what is good, and what the Lord seeks from you: nothing except doing justice, keeping loyalty, and walking humbly (*ve-hatsneʿa lekhet*) with your God." In this case, in order to convey the resonance between the poetic line and its biblical subtext, I resorted to altering the translation of the biblical verse (a change significant enough to be mentioned in the notes) in order to highlight the intertextuality. This translation of Micah, while unusual, reflects the way that the biblical language would have been "heard" in the context of the poetic stichs that preceded it. Among all the other things this line does, it offers an interpretation of Micah in which "humility" is transformed into wisdom—not only articulating but enacting the deftness and discretion needed to complete successfully a boldly necessary scheme. The awkward translation highlights Yannai's exegetical move.

In some cases, English barely manages to convey the richness of Yannai's language. He alludes to biblical texts, but they are read through the lens of rabbinic interpretation—either exclusively or in a way that creates meaningful ambiguity. We see this in the *qedushta* to Gen 27:28, where we find a line that I have rendered as:

> In cunning he came / yet he did not—such a sin!—con him;
> but as for the con-man, who came with his "game":
> "The con-man shall not enjoy his game."
>
> (Poem Five, lines 3–5).

These lines are, *in situ*, amply footnoted. As I note in the commentary to this passage, the translation "cunning" (*mirmah*) attempts to capture the ambiguity of the Hebrew: "deceitfulness" (as in the biblical text itself) and "wisdom" (as in, for example, the targumic rendering of the verse). Similarly, the Hebrew underlying the word "game" could also have been translated as "prey"—but that translation would have sacrificed the grimly serious "playful" nuance of the original. It is a happy coincidence that, in so many places, English is able to supply words that capture at least some of the same complicated nuances as Yannai's deft and clever Hebrew.

And yet, it is impossible to render in English the ambiguity of the verb in the first stich: הובא (pronounced "*huva*'"). On the one hand, this verb seems obviously passive (a *hofal*), meaning "he was brought" and suggesting that Rebecca brought Jacob in (and that she is therefore the agent of guilt). At the same time, in rabbinic and payyetanic idiom, the *hofal* can have an active connotation, which would implicate Jacob directly. Furthermore, it is possible that in an oral context, sixth-century listeners may have heard the active phrase הוא בא (*hu ba'*). We chose to translate the ambiguous term simply "he came." In the end, the translation reflects the overall sense of the passage, and notes must convey some of the knottier nuances.

Finally, there are numerous passages where Yannai truly exploits the formal possibilities of Hebrew to their richest potential. In these places (particularly the units called "*r'hitim,*" which are often intricately patterned[12]), where form is so much a part of the unit's structure, English cannot adequately render even a fraction of the Hebrew's complexity. Nonetheless, I have attempted, as much as English would allow, to write lines that convey some of the sensation of the original, even if ultimately footnotes are necessary to understand the true complexity of a passage. Indeed, while English does not lend itself as easily to the rhymes and resonances of Hebrew, it is capable of its own rich and playful sound. A few examples will suffice to demonstrate both the challenge of Yannai's Hebrew in such passages and the techniques used to retain some elements of the original in translation.

The first *rahit* for Yannai's *qedushta* for Gen 11:1 employs a structural device in which he repeats the final word of one line as the first word of the next, within the context of a densely alliterative acrostic. A transliteration of the first three lines (reflecting the letters *alef, bet,* and *gimmel*) reads as follows:

> (alef) *aḥadim aḥudim imrah aḥat avilei adamah* ***bizu***
> (bet) ***bizu*** bevitaḥon bituyam beʾomram benot birah ***gevohah***
> (gimmel) ***gevohah*** gibru garei gayʾ gidufei gaʾavah ***dibru***
> (dalet) **dibru**...

(Poem Seven[1], lines 1–3)

We have translated this as:

> Unified, united, one of speech, fools of the earth, **they disparaged**
> **They disparaged** Him who tested their speech when they said, "Let us build a castle **lofty**"
> **Loftily**, haughtily—they thought heroically—those valley-dwellers, arrogant blasphemers, **they spoke**
> **They spoke**...

12 See the discussion of the form of the *rahit* in Chapter One.

Obviously, English cannot replicate Yannai's intricate acrostic, in which each line contains six words beginning with the same letter and a seventh word that begins with the next letter (i.e., AAAAAAB – BBBBBBC – CCCCCCD, and so forth). With some effort, however, I was able to recreate the "daisy-chain" effect (the technical term is "anadiplosis") of linking the final word of each line with the first word of the next. My efforts were not perfect. "Lofty" is not identical to "loftily," but close enough to suggest the nature of the original.

Translating the *rehitim*, in particular, led me to push English to its limits, and at times I was willing to present somewhat stilted English in order to convey, however roughly, the dramatic intensity of the original language. Thus, the English grammar of the second *rahit* (unit 7^2) for Gen 44:18 is somewhat stilted because the form of the unit—with its reuse of the biblical verse's language "please… do not…"—is the most important single element to preserve. To an extent, the awkwardness of the English mirrors a certain awkwardness in the Hebrew. For example, the eighth line in Hebrew states:

> *Bi adoni sinʾah / al tisnʾa // Bi adoni ʿalilah / al taʿas*
>
> (Poem Seven², lines 15–16)

This is translated as:

> *Please*, my lord, hatred *do not* feel;
> *Please*, my lord, a wicked deed *do not* do!

Of course, it would be more straightforward simply to say, "Please, my lord, do not feel hatred; please, my lord, do not do this wicked deed," but such a translation would obscure the pattern in Yannai's language integral to his rhetoric.

Even more difficult were those units where a single word forms the keystone of a composition, such as in the first *rahit* of the *qedushta* for Gen 32:4. There, the theme word "Edom" (from the root *ʾ-d-m*, "red") becomes the basis for a complicated meditation on Edom (i.e., Rome), its actions, and its fate. In some cases, it proved simply impossible to translate the nuances, such as the line giving voice to messianic yearnings that alludes to Song 5:10 ("my beloved is radiant and ruddy"—*dodi tsaḥ va-ʾadom*). The poetic line is translated in the present volume as: "We yearn for You, O Beloved, radiant and red (*ʾadom*)" (Poem Seven¹, line 11); while in the biblical context, "ruddy" is the more pleasing translation, in the context of this poetic unit, repetition of the word "red," despite some awkwardness, conveys clearly the repetition of the theme-word. In some cases, I had to resort to parentheses to convey the sound-play of Edom – *ʾadom*/red in the body of the piyyut; it was impossible to translate both the sound and the sense—both the form and the content—without recourse to somewhat awkward mechanisms.

In other places, English can more successfully recreate some elements of the form of the underlying Hebrew. For example, in the first line of Poem Four for the *qedushta* to Gen 49:1, the Hebrew is a string of passive participles, all of which convey the idea of concealment and hiddenness; transliterated, it would read:

> *kamus ve-satum / ganuz ve-ḥatum // tamun ve-safun / ʿamus ve-tsafun*
> (Poem Four, lines 1–2)

In English, this appears as:

> Suppressed and sealed / hidden and concealed // secreted and covered / closeted and veiled

To be sure, the passive participles in English lack the strong, regular pattern of the Hebrew form, but English morphology is sufficiently patterned on its own that it lends the translation an organic rhythm of its own. Furthermore, English contains a sufficiently rich vocabulary to supply the needed synonyms for the concept of concealment, thereby permitting relatively "literal" rendering of the line's content (unlike, for example, the lack of synonyms for "lion" in English, which hampered translation of the *qedushta* to Gen 44:18, where many different terms for the king of beasts are employed). The English line ("Suppressed and sealed…" etc.) has its own cleverness and sound-play—a richness of language in English that echoes the Hebrew text it strives to render.

As these brief examples demonstrate, translators of Yannai must balance a variety of delicate demands. They should create, above all, clear and idiomatic English texts that can be comprehended on their own terms. At the same time, translations must provide a sense of the original—for example, introducing alliteration even where it is not present in the Hebrew because this feature is so important generally in Yannai's works. Likewise, occasionally awkward translations may be allowed in order to capture biblical allusions or intricate forms. And, at times, of course, only the generous addition of footnotes and the occasional parentheses enable the reader to appreciate the full complexity of Yannai's verse—but this is true for readers of the Hebrew editions of his texts, as well.

Yannai's poetry is as lovely and lyrical as it is complex. Yannai's voice can conjure sensations of majestic grandeur and delicate grief, thunderous apocalypse and fragile hope. The rich sound and texture of these works ultimately defy translation. Yet, it is my hope that through these texts and translations—as imperfect as they are—the beauty of Yannai's words will be perceived.

Chapter One

"Anatomy of a Qedushta:" How Form Shapes Meaning and Meaning Shapes Form

"My verses are a prophecy, and what's more, they are written in meter."
Judah Halevi

At first glance, the *qedushta*—the genre of piyyut most closely associated with Yannai—looks like a complex and perplexing form. A complete *qedushta* presents its audience with an elliptical, elaborate poetic cycle: it is not one poem but a composition of nine or more interrelated but distinctive units which occur in a fixed order. These poems are called: (1) the *magen*, (2) the *meḥayyeh*, (3) the *meshallesh*, (4) "Poem Four," (5) the *asiriyyah*, (6) "Poem Six," (7) the *rahit* or *r'hitim*, (8) the *silluq*, and (9) the *qedushah*. Written not in a single style but in multiple modes, diverse structures, and shifting voices, these nine units blend biblical allusions with rabbinic exegesis and contemporary commentary, all in a liturgical context; somehow the anthology of texts constitutes a singular whole. Allusive rhymed benedictions anticipate the content of longer, more expansive recapitulations and extensions; terse, formally intricate pattern poems abut rhythmic but unrhymed prose narrations.

The complicated *qedushta* structure, with its dynamic repetitions and creative juxtapositions, can be analyzed from a variety of perspectives: formal and functional, most obviously, but liturgical and theological as well. Through the combination of poetic diversity and synagogue setting, the poems that constitute a complete *qedushta* create additional layers of meaning beyond the words themselves. Poetic structures can generate effects with theological implications as well as aesthetic effects; traditions that are received one way in a prose midrash may be deeply transformed by "translation" into a performed poetic piece. In Yannai's piyyutim, form, content, and context are fully intertwined. As much as theology informs the poetry, poetry shapes the theology, all in the realm of public worship.

Form is, by definition, essential to meaning in any kind of poetry; form is what ultimately distinguishes poetry from prose. In a genre as complex as the *qedushta*, questions concerning the relationship between form and meaning simply become more urgent. What are the effects of the *qedushta*'s many repetitions and changes in pace? Are formal features such as patterned repetitions and amplifications primarily aesthetic or do they offer clues about synagogue performance? How does liturgical poetry differ from prose examples of exegesis and prayer? How do we locate the *qedushta* in the context of Hebrew poetry in general? And above all, what are the distinguishing characteristics of the nine units that make up a single *qedushta*? While many important themes and motifs emerge when we analyze discrete facets of these poems closely, only a holistic exploration of the complete *qedushta* cycle as liturgical poetry reveals the true complexity of these compositions. *Qedushta*ʾ*ot* must be studied much like symphonies, where attention to the parts is balanced by attention to the whole.

Anatomy of a *Qedushta*: A General Overview

The *qedushta* (pl. *qedushta*ʾ*ot*) is a subset of the poetic genre of the *qerova*.[1] The term "*qerova*" encompasses a variety of early poetic forms embellishing the central prayer of Judaism, the Amidah. On the Sabbath and Festi-

1 The term *qerova* probably relates the idea that the prayer leader draws close to (דקרב, in Aramaic) the ark or lectern; see *Mid. Ps* 19:2, which refers to the prayer-leader as חזנא דקרב, "the cantor who approaches." It also recalls the biblical term *qorban*, which suggests that the poem could be perceived as a kind of offering like the Amidah, with the poet a kind of priest. *Qedushta* is a name that comes from the specific focus of the poem on the third benediction of the Amidah. The formal development of piyyut has received significant scholarly attention over the years, although not precisely from the literary-thematic perspective presented here. The definitive classic in the field remains E. Fleischer, *Hebrew Liturgical Poetry in the Middle Ages* (Jerusalem: Keter, 1975) [Hebrew]. On *the qedushta* form in specific, see also Fleischer's essays, "On the Antiquity of the Qedushta," *Ha-Sifrut* 2 (1971): 390–414 [Hebrew] and "Inquiries in the Structure of the Classical *Qedushta*," in *Proceedings of the* 5th *World Congress of Jewish Studies*, vol. 3 (Jerusalem: World Union of Jewish Studies, 1969), 291–95 [Hebrew]. Also important are A. Mirsky's monograph *Formal Foundations of Piyyut* (Jerusalem: Magnes, 1985) [Hebrew] and, more briefly, his essay "Foundation of the Qerova," in *The Piyyut* (Jerusalem: Magnes, 1991), 86–92 [Hebrew]; other essays in this volume are also valuable. Likewise, the anthology of M. Zulay's writings, *Eretz Yisrael and Its Poetry*, ed. E. Hazan (Jerusalem: Magnes, 1995) [Hebrew], contains classic essays that delineate the formal structures of piyyut, notably "The Genealogy of Piyyut in the Land of Israel" (95–125). More recently, the work of Michael Rand stands out, although his focus is on Qillir rather than Yannai; see in particular: M. Rand, "The *Seder Beriyot* in Byzantine-Era Piyyut," *JQR* 95 (2005): 667–83.

vals, the Amidah consists of seven blessings.[2] The term "*qedushta,*" meanwhile, describes a poem embellishing only the Amidah's first three benedictions: the *avot* (God of the ancestors) prayer, the *gevurot* (God's might) prayer, and, in particular, the *qedushat ha-shem* (God's holiness) prayer.[3] As poetry, *qedushta᾽ot* display a variety of distinctive rhythms, but compared to the later Jewish poets of Andalusia or the early hymns of the Christian tradition, such as those of Ephrem the Syrian and Romanos the Melodist, Yannai's works are not truly metrical.[4] Like the Christian hymns, however, it seems quite likely that Yannai's *qedushta᾽ot* were, in some fashion, set to music—a hypothesis supported by the system of vocalization apparent in many manuscripts.[5] While many details of the actual recitation or performance of these works remain unknown (and perhaps unknowable), Yannai's poetry—particularly when read in light of other textual and material sources—offers tantalizing clues to those attempting to reconstruct the rituals of the Byzantine synagogue.

An examination of the structure of a *qedushta*—those details that enable us to identify its component parts even when only fragments are preserved—is the most important place to begin a larger study of the form.

---

2 The Amidah (i.e., "standing prayer") is also called *ha-Tefillah* ("the prayer"—that is, the prayer *par excellence*) in rabbinic sources. For the history of the Amidah, I. Elbogen, *Jewish Liturgy,* 24–62, is the classic source; also important is J. Heinemann, *Prayer in the Talmud.* More recently, see Stefan Reif, *Judaism and Hebrew Prayer.* L. Hoffman, *The Canonization of the Synagogue Service* (Notre Dame: University of Notre Dame Press, 1979) offers perspective that contrasts the cultural contexts of the Land of Israel and Babylonian Jewry. And, for a summary of recent discussions in the context of the early synagogue, see Lee Levine, *The Ancient Synagogue,* especially 162–63.

For the text of the first three blessings of the Amidah—those embellished in the *qedushta*—please see Appendix I.

3 The *Qedushat ha-shem* is also called simply the Qedushah (after the extended insertion added during the reader's repetition); it is so-called in distinction to the *qedushat ha-yom* ("the holiness of the day"), the single blessing that replaces the intermediate blessings of the Amidah on the Sabbath and holidays.

4 See Chapter Three for more on the relationship of Yannai's piyyutim to Byzantine Christian hymnography. Meter does not enter Hebrew poetry until the tenth century, under the influence of Arabic poetics. For a concise discussion of the history of Hebrew metrics and verse, see B. Hrushovski, "Note on the Systems of Hebrew Versification," in *The Penguin Book of Hebrew Verse,* ed. and trans. T. Carmi (New York: Penguin Books, 1981), 57–72. The topic is also discussed in L. Weinberger, *Jewish Hymnography.*

5 The use of superlinear vocalization in many of the surviving manuscripts supports the hypothesis that these piyyutim were musically performed. For an extended (not uncontroversial) discussion of music's role in the synagogue service, see E. Werner, *The Sacred Bridge,* vol. 2. Peter Jeffrey's review essay of *The Sacred Bridge* in *JQR* 77 (1987): 283–98, nuances, emends, and supplements Werner's work.

The nine units follow a specific, almost "scripted," pattern. Overall, the initial poems of each complete piyyut are the most tightly controlled and allusive, while the later poems display freer, somewhat more varied structures and present more opportunity for narrative expansion. The *magen*, the *meḥayyeh*, and the *meshallesh* are the most strictly conventional, in formal terms, incorporating rhyme, acrostics, and intertexts (biblical and liturgical) in predictable ways. The unnamed fourth poem lacks a fixed form (e.g., an acrostic) but has regular rhythm and rhyme. The *asiriyyah* is a ten-line alphabetical acrostic. The unnamed sixth poem, a complete alphabetic acrostic, is the longest single poem and presents the freest narration. The *rahit* contains one or two highly-complex, densely formal "pattern poems." The *silluq*, which is in rhymed prose and can vary in length, serves as a transition to the final poem and builds up communal anticipation for it. The ninth and final poem, also called the *qedushah*, itself segues into the third prayer of the Amidah and integrates its language (particularly the quotations from Isa 6:3 and Ezek 3:12) with the *qedushta*.

In form, the *qedushta* can be seen as symmetrical and hewing to a chiastic structure, with Poem Six acting as the center of the work: the fifth and seventh poems (the *asiriyyah* and *rahit*, respectively) are rapid, intricately structured poems. Poems Four and Eight (the *silluq*) are relatively unfixed in form and serve as transitional poems. Poems One through Three and Poem Nine blend liturgical verses and biblical texts.[6] Complicating this balanced, symmetrical form there are, at the same time, cyclical patterns (the *magen* and *meḥayyeh*, like Poem Six, tend to hew most closely to the content of the *sidra*, the week's Torah portion) and even linear elements (the clear trajectory towards the recitation of "Holy, holy, holy," which undergirds the entire structure). Within a single piyyut, then, we confront a diversity of styles and structures that range from the simple to the ornate; and the juxtaposition of such diverse poems can both dazzle and overwhelm the modern reader. While the poems constituting a *qedushta* can be easily delineated, it remains more difficult to tease out elements of their formal unity beyond the overt thematics that knit them into a single work of art.

---

6 It may be that the structure of the *qedushta* is, in some way, indebted to, grounded in, or influenced by the poetic technique of chiasmus (i.e., the A-B-C-C'-B'-A' structure) familiar from the biblical Psalms but also common in Latin literature. In shorter works, chiasmus is very visible, operating at the level of clause or line; in the *qedushta*, it manifests less obviously, because it operates at the level of the poetic unit.

To further clarify the complex structure of the *qedushta*, it will be useful to survey and analyze samples of each unit of the composition in turn, drawing from the poetic texts presented in the second half of this volume.

Poems One and Two: Magen (shield of Abraham) and meḥayyeh (the one who resurrects)

The initial two units of a *qedushta* are named for the benedictions (*ḥatimot*) that conclude the first two blessings in the Amidah. The *magen* and *meḥayyeh* embellish the *avot* and *gevurot* blessings, respectively and take their names from the language of the benedictions. That is, while the benedictions appear in the text, the standard wordings of the blessings are absent, and the poems take their place.[7] Although each of these two units is a distinct work, they share a common form and function together essentially as a single poem. An example, taken from the *qedushta* for Gen 31:3, will make these formal features more apparent:

אוֹמָנָךְ מְקָרֵב רְחוֹקִים
בְּדוּדֵי נְדוּדֵי מֶרְחַקִים
גּוֹלִים וּמִמֶּרְחֲקוֹתֶיךָ רוֹחֲקִים
דַּרְכָּם מֵעֲלֵיהֶם מַרְחִיקִים

הֵן כְּאִישׁ תָּם הַקָּרוֹב אֲשֶׁר רָחַק
וּבָרַח מֵאִישׁ הַמְּרֻוחָק
זֹאת הָאָרֶץ אֲשֶׁר לוֹ הוּחַק
חֲזוֹר לָהּ דִּיבֵּר אֵלָיו דָּחַק

טַעֲמָךְ אֲשֶׁר רֵיק לֹא יָשׁוּב
יִידַּעְתָּה אֶת שְׁאָר יָשׁוּב
כְּבָה סַעַר שָׂעִיר כְּעַכְשׁוּב
לְחָלָק נַמְתָּה לְחֶלְקָךְ **שׁוּב**

ככתוב ויאמר יי אל יעקב שוב אל ארץ אבותיך ולמולדתך ואהיה עמך
ונאמר שאר ישוב שאר יעקב אל אל גבור
ונאמר זעקתי אליך יי אמרתי אתה מחסי חלקי בארץ החיים

---

7 In the Middle Ages, piyyutim adorned the statutory prayers rather than appearing in their place. The question of whether earlier piyyutim (such as Yannai's) arose during a period of rebellion against the fixed wording of the Amidah or whether they reflect a time before standardized wording had crystallized will be addressed in Chapter Three. The only element of the modern Amidah found in these two poetic units is the concluding benediction.

ונאמר לאמר לך אתן את ארץ כנען חבל נחלתכם
ונאמר ויעמידה ליעקב לחק לישראל ברית **עולם**

עוֹלָם יְסוֹדָךְ
בָּנִיתָהּ בְחַסְדָּךְ
מְמַגֵּן בְּנֵי חֲסִידָךְ
ברוך... מגן...

(magen)
Your ways bring near those who are far
Those driven to wander so far a-field
Exiles, far flung among those who reject You
Their path keeps them far from evil

Indeed, just like the man of purity, who had been near but had gone afar
Fleeing the man of rejection
This is the land bequeathed to him
"Return to it"—with a word, He spoke and compelled him

Your decree: he would not return empty
You declared: a remnant would return
Though the storm of the hairy one, like a dragon, approached
To the smooth one You said, "Return to your portion!"

As it is written: "Then the Eternal said to Jacob: `Return to the land of your ancestors and to your birthplace, and I will be with you'" (Gen 31:3).
And it is said: "A remnant shall return, a remnant of Jacob, to a mighty God" (Isa 10:21)
And it is said: "I cry out to You, O Eternal; (I say), `You are my refuge my portion in the (living) land'" (Ps 142:6)
And it is said: "Say, `To you will I give the land of Canaan, your allotted portion'" (Ps 105:11)
And it is said: "And He confirmed as a decree for Jacob, for Israel as an **eternal** covenant" (Ps 105:10)

The **world** You founded
You built it with Your steadfast love
O Shield of the children of Your faithful one

Blessed... Shield...

מְלָכוֹת בִּיקְרוֹתָיו
נְשׂוּאוֹת תָּם יְקָרוֹתָיו
סוֹכְנוֹתָיו צֵל קוֹרוֹתָיו
עוֹמְדוֹת תַּבְנִית קוֹרוֹתָיו

פִּקּוּד אֲשֶׁר אֵלָיו נִגְלָה
צִימְּדָם וְלָהֶם גִּילָּה
קֵץ גָּע לָשׁוּב מִגּוֹלָה
רְצוּיָה תּוֹכַחַת מְגֻולָּה

שָׂר הַדָּבָר כִּי נָחוּץ
שִׁילַּח אַחֲרֵיהֶם וְהוּא בַּחוּץ
תְּמִימוֹת וּצְנוּעוֹת מִנִּיאוּץ
תָּם בְּהַצְנֵיעַ קְרָאָם לְיִעוּץ

ככתוב וישלח יעקב ויקרא לרחל וללאה השדה אל צאנו
ונאמר בנות מלכים ביקרותיך נצבה שגל לימינך בכתם אופיר
ונאמר הגיד לך אדם מה טוב ומה יי דורש ממך כי אם עשות משפט ואהבת חסד והצנע לכת עם אלהיך
ונאמר ה׳ לי לא אירא מה יעשה לי **אדם**

אָדָם וּבְהֵמָה תּוֹשִׁיעַ
אֵל הַמּוֹשִׁיעַ
תְּחִיַּית טַל לָנוּ תַּשְׁפִּיעַ
ברוך... מחיה...

(meḥayyeh)
The queens among his treasures
The wives of the pure one, his favorites
His stalwarts, sturdy sheltering walls:
The very structure of his dwelling, they stand by

Mindful of what had been revealed
He joined them, and to them he revealed:
“The end arrives, the return from exile”
Desiring that rebuke be revealed

He perceived that the matter was urgent;
He sent for them while he waited outside
Pure women, and wise, free of disdain
The pure one in his wisdom called them to council

As it is written: "Then Jacob sent and called Rachel and Leah to the field, to his flock" (Gen 31:4)
And it is said: "Daughters of queens are among your treasures; your consort stands at your right hand, decked in the fine gold of Ophir" (Ps 45:10)
And it is said: "He has told you, O mortal, what is good, and what the Eternal seeks from you: nothing except doing justice, keeping loyalty, and walking in wisdom with yo(ur God)" (Mic 6:8)
And it is said: "The Eternal is for me, I fear nothing; what can a **man** do to me?" (Ps 118:6)

Man and beast You save
O God who saves
Life-giving dew You pour over us!

Blessed… Who resurrects…

Each poem contains three stanzas of four rhyming stichs (resulting in twelve stichs for each poem), followed by a series of verses and then the appropriate benediction. Embedded in each poem is half of an alphabetic acrostic (indicated in boldface). The *magen* begins each of its twelve stichs with the first twelve letters of the alphabet (*alef* through *lamed*). The *meḥayyeh* completes the acrostic (*mem* through *tav*) in its twelve stichs, reaching the necessary count of twelve letters by doubling each of the last two letters (*shin* and *tav*).

Rhetorically, the use of short, rhyming stichs creates a strong rhythm, reinforced by internal rhyme, assonance, and consonance—all the raw material for Yannai's extensive puns and word-plays. The narration of the poem includes direct address to the deity, which creates a powerful effect as a performance piece: it immediately creates a divine as well as human audience while also reflecting the liturgical setting of the work. No character is named; instead, metonymy (the use of epithets) hints at character identification. The content of each poem is somewhat cryptic. With the help of prefaces, commentary, and annotations, a reader may understand most of what is going on, albeit much also remains obscure. Finally, each unit includes a series of biblical texts,[8] which are simply listed, without explica-

---

8 The significance of these verse lists will be considered in depth in Chapter Three. Daniel Boyarin's understanding of midrash as, in essence, the juxtaposition of two verses with the result of yielding new meaning, is important here. See his *Intertextuality and the Reading of*

tion, before a transition to the benediction. The poet, however, knits the verses to his texts by means of careful verbal transitions, indicated here by boldface.

The quoted biblical verses constitute a crucial element in these first two poems, as they serve both intellectual and liturgical functions. Literarily, the citations provide the vocabulary or imagery of the poetic units that preceded them, hinting at the meaning of some of the cryptic or allusive language in the poems while simultaneously imbuing the poet's words with resonant depth. Exegetically, these texts must have engaged the sixth-century congregation in an act akin to generating midrash—of interpreting diverse verses in the familiar context of the weekly Torah portion and the innovative poetic context created by the *payyetan*. Liturgically, the Torah portion plays an important role as well: the series of verses following the *magen* poem always begins with the first verse of the Torah portion, while the second verse of the week's reading introduces the verse grouping that follows the *meḥayyeh* poem. The specific number of intertexts following the quotation from the *sidra* in these series varies; we find as few verses as four and as many as ten. Nor do the collocations come from any specific books or in any order. Generally, the verses are from the Prophets and the Writings, but quotations from the Pentateuch also occur with some regularity. Resonances between the simple (or at least familiar) language of the biblical verses and their implicit interpretation link these quotations to the bodies of the poems, while word-play, repetition, and enjambment often signal and create the transition—from the verse group to the benediction—that concludes each section.[9]

Formally, Yannai's *magen* and *meḥayyeh* poems display regular and fixed patterns in stichometry, rhyme schemes, and acrostic. The only significant variation from one *qedushta* to the next lies in the number of verses cited after each unit. Noticing these highly formalized patterns does not diminish our appreciation of the poet's creativity (particularly since Yannai appears to have, if not actually created the *qedushta*, at least developed the

---

Midrash (Bloomington: University of Indiana Press, 1990), which provides the terminology of "intertext" employed in this work.

9 The use of transitional phrases between the verse series and the benediction is in keeping with the halakhic obligation to "say something resembling the blessing before the blessing" (see *b. Pesah.* 104a). As Ruth Langer notes, "Although only Babylonian traditions preserve this principle, the Palestinian *payyetanim*, at least in their more elaborate creations, followed strictly the ruling of Shmuel" (*To Worship God Properly*, 27).

artistic potential of the form); their presence actually raises more questions. How does the almost rigid fixity of these first poems' structures contribute to—or constrict—the poet's ability to create meaning? What do these poems achieve through their intricate use of rhyme and acrostic that the longer, more narrative poems, such as the Sixth Poem, do not? Why begin so cryptically, rather than simply summarizing the Torah portion or its explication for the congregation?

The formal constraints that govern these poems provide a key to understanding their playful, even riddle-like content.[10] Conventionality sets up expectations in the reader (or, more accurately, the listener); predictability serves to engage the audience in the act of decipherment. It is easy to visualize Yannai's congregation anticipating the challenges the composer set up for himself and eagerly waiting to see how he would meet them from week to week, perhaps testing themselves against his cleverness. For example, most of the *qedushtaʾot* immediately introduce a main character in the biblical narrative. They do so indirectly, however, by means of an epithet or opaque allusion in the opening lines. For example, "Prisoners of Your hope" (Gen 8:15, Poem One, line 1) refers to the family of Noah in the Ark. "A lover" (Gen 12:1, Poem One, line 1) highlights a specific quality of Abraham to be tested in the lectionary. And "the paths of the pure one" (Gen 33:18, Poem One, line 1) describes Jacob on his journey home. Even more enigmatically and expansively, the *qedushta* for Gen 29:31 opens with an evocative invocation of the deity:

> Your might, O awesome one, is in the heavens
> but You watch over all who stride upon the streets
> Obvious to You is the love of the lovable
> but the hated, the oppressed, You seek out (Poem One, lines 1–4)

With these first words, the audience (including the deity, who is addressed directly) is drawn personally into the drama. The language, while cryptic and vague, suggests a sense of intimacy that resonates with the poem's liturgical setting. In the poem, as in prayer, awe and reverence intersect

---

10 The riddle is a complex literary form in its own right; see Galit Hasan-Rokem and David Shulman, eds., *Untying the Knot: Riddles and Other Enigmatic Modes* (New York: Oxford University Press, 1996).

11 The notation used here indicates the Poem by biblical chapter and verse being embellished and then indicates unit: line. Thus "Gen 12:1, Poem One, line 1" refers to the first line of the *magen* of the *qedushta* for Gen 12:1.

with familiarity and approachability. As a public poet, Yannai worked to engage his audience at once; as a prayer-leader, he directly addressed the deity as "You." Following this engaging opening, strong and suggestive themes of love and hate, oppression and redemption are introduced but not yet developed. The overall narrative content of the *qedushta* is suggested, but the terse nature of the rhetoric works to create and heighten emotional connotations rather than narrative content. These words are the "hook" that draws the audience in as it anticipates and enjoys the way the poet shapes the fixed elements (poetic and liturgical) of the poem.

These opening lines, rich in allusions to key biblical texts and intertexts, serve narrative and exegetical purposes as well as performative functions. Each weekly portion (i.e., the *sidra*), especially in Genesis, contains many story lines—too many to all be included in a single *qedushta*. These opening lines hint at which story and characters will be the focus within the *qedushta* but they do not resolve all ambiguities—indeed, they often challenge the hearers to decipher the poet's intent and direction. Furthermore, much like in the classical midrashic form called a *petiḥta*—a rhetorical structure in which the exegete links "a verse from afar" to the first verse of the Torah portion—the poem's construction engages the community in trying to solve the more general riddle of what theme the poet will develop and how he will move from these opening stichs to the first line of the biblical *sidra*.[12] Similar intellectual engagement arises from the intertexts that follow the poem: How will the poet segue from the biblical story to the blessing required by context? The elliptical, evocative rhetoric of the *magen's* form serves to draw the audience into the world of the *qedushta*.

The *meḥayyeh*, formally very similar to the *magen*, continues and develops the terse, almost cryptic, introduction of the *qedushta*'s major themes and figures. In terms of content, the *magen* and *meḥayyeh* together typically sketch the broad outlines of the poet's interpretation of the passage, delineating key character traits and major narrative arcs by means of epithets and allusions often not explicated until later in the piyyut. For example, the idolatrous rebellion of those who built the Tower of Babel in Gen 11 is indicated in the *meḥayyeh* but not immediately explored: "From the ancients, they never learned... along the paths of ancient error, they strayed" (Gen 11:1; Poem Two, lines 1 and 12). Only later does the poet narrate the details of the tower builders' various sins.

---

12 The relationship between piyyut and *petiḥta* is developed further in Chapter Three.

Likewise, Yannai's initial description of Joseph's descent to Egypt suggests the interpretation he will not develop until later: "Drawn down and bound by human cords // You led (him) as a man leads a lamb" (Gen 39:1, Poem Two, lines 1–2). The lines are clearly theologically fraught, but what exactly do they mean? Members of the community who possessed a background in rabbinic traditions of interpretation could presumably assemble the clues and hear allusions to aggadic traditions preserved in other (prose) sources, particularly with the help of the concatenation of verses after each unit, which supply many of the allusions. Others in the audience, however, would have had to remember the hints, waiting to see if they had correctly assembled and interpreted the clues. Or else they simply relied on the gestalt impression created by the overall content of the poem, which revisits and revises key themes over the course of the complete *qedushta.*

The formal patterning of these two opening units offers intellectual gratification by means of aesthetic, rhetorical, and exegetical conventions. The blessings, verses, and poem are woven together into self-sufficient wholes, but they also build anticipation for the units to come. In the end, the formal structure of the opening units of the *qedushta* results in immediate religious engagement.

Poem Three: meshallesh (the third)

The *meshallesh* (so-called because of its placement in the *qedushta*), strongly resembles the *magen* and *meḥayyeh* but also differs in subtle, significant ways. The *meshallesh* from the *qedushta* for Gen 11:1 illustrates the standard form:

יָשַׁבְתָּה בַּסֵּתֶר שׁוֹחֵק עַל כָּל גָּלוּי
כִּי כָל שְׂחוֹק סֵיתֶר לְפָנֶיךָ גָּלוּי
נְתוֹשׁ נָא מֵאֲדָמָה מַלְכוּת דּוּמָה
וְתַפִּיל אֵימָה עַל כָּל אֻומָּה

יִקְרְאוּ בְשִׁמְךָ כֹּל לֹא קָרְאוּ בְשִׁמְךָ
יִיקָּרֵא שִׁמְךָ עַל קוֹרְאֵי שְׁמָךְ
יָהּ כְּמוֹ בְעַמָּךְ הוּא יִיחוּדָךְ
הֲפוֹךְ עַל כָּל **עַמִּים שָׂפָה בְרוּרָה** לְיַחֲדָךְ

ככתוב כי אז **אהפוך** אל **עמים שפה ברורה** לקרא כלם בשם יי לעבדו שכם אחד
ונאמר יי שפתי תפתח ופי יגיד תהלתך
ואתה קדוש יושב תהילות ישראל אל נא

You dwell in secret, laughing as all is revealed
for all secret laughter is revealed before You
Now pluck up from the earth the kingdom of deathly silence,
and cast down fear upon every Nation

Yea, let them invoke Your name, all who have not invoked Your name
Let Your name be invoked upon all who invoke Your name
Yah, just as Your unity is in Your people
restore to all the nations a pure language to unify You

As it is written: "For then I will restore nations to a pure language, so that they all invoke the Eternal by name and serve Him with one accord." (Zeph 3:9)
And as it is said: "May the Eternal open my lips and my mouth proclaim Your praise." (Ps 51:18)
And You are holy, enthroned on the praises of Israel (Ps 22:4)

Please, God…

Like the *magen* and *meḥayyeh*, the *meshallesh* is composed of rhymed bicola, contains an acrostic (indicated in boldface) and is followed by a series of verses (a lemma and intertexts). Psalm 22:4 concludes the lists of verses, and the phrase "Please, God…" is probably a cue for a fixed liturgical phrase, functioning somewhat like the benedictions in the *magen* and *meḥayyeh*. Also like the first two units, the *meshallesh* embeds an acrostic, but not an alphabetic acrostic; instead, its four lines spell out the poet's name, ינ״י, making Yannai the earliest known Hebrew artist to "sign" his creations.[13] Its length determined by the signature acrostic, the

13 Several centuries prior to Yannai, in the fourth century C.E, the Syriac poet Ephrem of Edessa (also known as "Ephrem the Syrian"), living in the Eastern region of the Roman Empire, was signing his poems by means of an embedded acrostic; the gap of as many as two hundred years between the work of Ephrem and Yannai suggests that the Syriac poet's technique did not influence Hebrew poetry directly but the techniques may nonetheless be related in some more complicated, indirect way. That noted, the Greek Christian hymnographer Romanos the Melodist (possibly a convert from Judaism) employed extensive and intricate acrostics in his works, signing in some fashion all of his *kontakia*; e.g., "By the humble Romanos," "On the Palms, by Romanos," and so forth. Unnamed Byzantine Christian poets also "signed" works (e.g., "A poem by a sinner"). These texts and others are discussed in: D. Krueger, *Writing and Holiness: The Practice of Authorship in the Early Christian East* (Philadelphia: University of Pennsylvania Press, 2004), 159–88. Krueger notes that for Romanos, embedding his signature in poetry was ultimately an act of humility, because it was "invisible" to the ear (172). Yannai's signatures, however, precisely because they were both short and always in the same location, may have been detectable by his listeners.

meshallesh consists of only four lines, each with its own internal rhyme. Additionally, the rhythm of the *meshallesh* is markedly more rapid than that of the *magen* and *meḥayyeh*; the individual stichs are often broken into shorter cola, intensifying the pace of the poem and increasing the sense of tension. The anthology of verses that follows the *meshallesh* begins with the first verse of the haftarah rather than a verse from the Torah portion, and its list of intertexts is noticeably shorter than those that follow the first two poems.

Unlike the *magen* and *meḥayyeh* poems, no benediction follows the *meshallesh*; from this point forward, all poems in the *qedushta* move towards the third blessing of the Amidah, the Qedushah.[14] The quotation from Ps 22:4, which includes the word "holy," may function as a foreshadowing of that blessing—the first hint of a central theme.[15] Finally, in terms of content, the *meshallesh* is most likely to focus on contemporary themes—read through the lens of the Torah portion and haftarah—or future hopes rather than on more straightforward, narrative exegesis of the biblical texts. While Yannai often encoded discussions of his day throughout his *qedushtaʾot*, in the *meshallesh* he was often most direct in addressing his contemporary situation and ambitions, whether a diatribe against Esau- Rome/Christianity, a comparison of Sarah and Zion, or an articulation of messianic expectations.

As significant as these differences are between the first two poems and the third, the change in the lemma (from Torah to haftarah) and intertexts signals the most intriguing shift in orientation in this unit. While the focus of the *magen* and *meḥayyeh* poems was the biblical narrative, albeit cryptically at times, in the *meshallesh*, the poet anticipated and eventually quoted the prophetic voice of the haftarah. With the prophetic texts already in mind, Yannai addressed his congregation's concerns and situation, translating the themes of the lectionary into contemporary terms. The prophetic text was not his starting point, but it became inevitable and fraught with significance by the time he quoted it. Through

14 In order to distinguish the liturgical blessing called "Qedushah" from the poetic unit of the same name, which embellishes that blessing, the poetic unit will be italicized and spelled consistently with a lower-case "q"—as are the other poetic unit names—while the liturgical blessing will be capitalized and Roman.

15 For an interesting hypothesis concerning the role of the transitional biblical texts in the *magen*, *meḥayyeh*, and *meshullash* poems, as well as the standardized quotations from Ps 146:10 and Ps 22:4 at the end of the third section of the *qedushta*, see Fleischer, "Inquiries in the Structure of the Classical *Qedushta*."

the power of simple juxtaposition, the *meshallesh* creates the sense that just as the Prophets spoke to generations past, the poet speaks to his people. The *meshallesh* for Gen 11:1, cited above, provides a clear example of this contemporizing and dynamic application of biblical ideas. It states, in part:

> Pluck now from the earth / the kingdom of deathly silence // cast down fear / upon every Nation...
> Yah, with your people is Your unity // restore to all nations a pure language to unify You (3:2, 4).

In these lines, a pun on *dumah* ("deathly silence") evokes the poet's contemporary antagonist (Rome—i.e., the Byzantine Roman Empire), while the motif of linguistic unity and divine unity anticipates the quotation of Zeph 3:9 that begins the haftarah and is quoted immediately after the allusion. Transformed by Yannai's poetic mediation and empowered by its liturgical context, Zephaniah speaks to a new community—Yannai's congregation—with his words revived by being set in a new context.

Indeed, because of the contemporary orientation of the *meshallesh* and its incorporation of the often dramatic visions articulated by the ancient Prophets, these poems tend to be thematically dense and emotionally intense, despite their brevity. For example, when the character of Esau—understood as the ancestor of both pagan and Christian Rome, oppressor of the Jews and tyrannical ruler of the Holy Land for centuries—enters the biblical narrative in Gen 25, the sense of yearning for redemption becomes particularly keen, at times apocalyptic.[16] We see this trend in Yannai's *qedushta* for Gen 32:4. In the *meshallesh*, the poet shifts his focus from the story of Genesis to his hopes for the future, as seen through the lens of prophetic apocalypse: "Famine shall be their fate / fire fills their future / but You will hear our outcry / as You showed Obadiah the seer!" (Poem Three, lines 7–8). The first and last verses of the brief book of Obadiah, a prophecy describing the cataclysmic fate of Edom and Esau—understood by Yannai and his community as code-words for the Byzantine Empire—follow these fervent stichs. In a piyyut for another week—the *qedushta* for Gen 29:31, with Isa 60:15 as a haftarah—the poet used the contemporary focus of the *meshallesh* to console his community, implicitly identified with the long- suffering, misunderstood matriarch Leah. This contemporary focus of the *meshallesh* is not, however, rigid; in some in-

16 See Chapter Four for more on the topics of Esau and apocalypse.

stances, largely determined by the nature of the haftarah, the poet keeps his focus on the biblical narrative. In the *qedushta* for Gen 12:1, where the haftarah comes from the book of Joshua and reiterates God's promise of the land to Abraham, Yannai does not address the contemporary situation until much later in the poem. And yet, for a community dwelling in the Land of Israel but enduring the experience of foreign rule, God's promises to Abraham and Joshua could have felt not archaic but merely latent and awaiting fulfillment.

Rhetorical embellishments (puns, word-play, and allusions) generate the wit so typical of Yannai's best writing, and the translation of ancient words and ideas into a contemporary setting augment the relevance of these compositions to Yannai's community.[17] Less explicitly, however, form itself contributes immeasurably to poetic meaning. The *meshallesh* is briefer than the *magen* and *meḥayyeh*, and perhaps as a result, its language tends to be thicker and even more reliant on the power of puns and patterns. The resulting dense language demands interpretation, and thus engagement. For example, "O Yah, love those who love You / And hate those who hate You // Watch over Your lovers / Watch out for Your haters" is the translation of the staccato opening Hebrew line of the *meshallesh* for Gen 29:31: *Yah* **ehov ohavekha** / *u*-**sena**ʾ **sonekha** // *netzor* **lemaʾahavekha** / *netor* **le-mesanekha**. The thematic roots employed here—the binary pair "love" and "hate" especially—appear throughout the *magen* and *meḥayyeh* of this *qedushta* as well, but they occur with particular frequency and intensity here in the *meshallesh*. Only one consonant distinguishes Yannai's hope for Israel—that they will be protected (נצר)—and his hope for Christian Rome—that they will get their due (נטר).

Poem Four (unnamed)

Poem Four is quite different from the three poems that precede it. The *meshallesh*, while it differs from the *magen* and *meḥayyeh* in important respects, largely resembles them. All three are brief poems, structured by acrostics and followed by a series of biblical verses. Poem Four interrupts the pattern completely. A less fixed form of poetry, this unnamed unit serves a number of diverse functions, depending on the poet's needs and interests in a given week. The irregularity of this piece makes selecting a

17 Yannai's use of language will be more specifically studied in Chapter Three of this volume.

representative example difficult, but the fourth poem from the *qedushta* for Gen 12:1 provides a good illustration of the *meshallesh's* characteristics:

בְּשַׁעֲרֵי מִזְרָח
הֵיצִיץ אֶזְרָח
וּמֵאוֹפֶל וּמֵחוֹשֶׁךְ צָבָא וְזָרַח
כִּי בְּתוֹעֲבוֹת תֶּרַח
מָאַס וְטָרַח
וּכְעַיִט פָּרַח
וְעָדֶיךָ בָּרַח
צַלְמֵי אָבִיו כִּתֵּת וְשִׁיבֵּר
וְהַרְבֵּה תוֹעִים אֵלֶיךָ חִיבֵּר
נַעַר הָיָה וּכְגָבֵר עַצְמוֹ לָךְ גִּיבֵּר
בְּבִיטָּחוֹן אֲשֶׁר פִּיךָ לוֹ דִּיבֵּר
....
יְדָעֲךָ מְעַט נוֹדַעְתָּה לוֹ הַרְבֵּה
הוּא פָּתַח ...
... קָרוֹב וְקָדוֹשׁ
נוֹרָא מָרוֹם וְקָדוֹשׁ

Within the eastern gates
arose one radiantly pure
within the midst of darkness and gloom, he shone with a radiant light
Indeed, the abominations of Terah he rejected and cast aside
like a falcon, he burst forth and unto You he flew
His father's images he hammered to bits
and many lost souls he brought close to You
Though just a youth, he readied himself to fight for You
Trusting in the promises Your mouth uttered
...
He knew You a little, You made Yourself known to him well
He opened ...
... close and holy
O Awesome, Exalted, and Holy One

As evident from this example (despite the text's fragmentary nature), Poem Four lacks any acrostic. Furthermore, it varies unpredictably in length, typically ranging from five to nine lines. Poem Four may employ thought-rhyme (e.g, juxtaposing "inside" [מבית] and "outside" [בחוץ] in the *qedush-*

ta to Gen 29:31, Poem Four, lines 3–4 and 7–8) in place of the internal- and end-rhyme found in the earlier units. Content, likewise, varies in this unit: Poem Four of the *qedushta* to Gen 11:1 waxes philosophical on the power of language: "Who gives man mouth and lips?" (Poem Four, line 1). Poem Four for Gen 29:31 depicts the poet speaking in his own voice: "Our eyes are weak from our longing love of You, O You whom we love" (Poem Four, line 1). And Poem Four for Gen 33:18 exploits the ambiguous identity of Israel (referring both to Jacob and to his descendents) to craft a poem that serves as a prayer for both: "He dealt blamelessly with him / for he walked in purity" (Poem Four, lines 7–8) In Poem Four of Gen 12:1, however, cited above, the poet explicitly focuses on the biblical narrative, describing the brilliant appearance of Abraham on the stage of history: "Within the eastern gates / arose one radiantly pure" (Poem Four, lines 1–2). Thus of all the styles of poetry appearing in the *qedushta* thus far, Poem Four has the fewest constraints upon it, giving the poet the greatest freedom to construe it as he will.

What specific functions are served by the sudden formal freedom in the fourth unit—especially in the wake of the relative predictability and stability of the first three? These fourth-unit poems obey no rules of structure beyond a sense of rhythm (though not a fixed one), and they follow no standard pattern aside from general conciseness in language. They include neither a list of verses nor any liturgical formulae beyond, irregularly, inclusion of the word "holy" (*qadosh*) in anticipation of the Qedushah.[18] The poem's thematic orientation—whether it is concerned with the past, present, or future—is likewise unpredictable. This very quality seems, perhaps counter-intuitively, to define the poem's formal-aesthetic function. Much like a transition in a symphony—and in anticipation of the eighth poem of the *qedushta*—Poem Four's interruption of the well-established patterns of the first three poems awakens the audience by unsettling expectations. It engages the audience through its very unpredictability: What direction will the poet take? What aspect of the biblical text (its plot, its interpretations, its contemporary resonance) will he highlight? Brief and varied, this poem serves as a palate cleanser, preparing the way for Poem Five, the *asiriyyah*.

18 The idea of God's holiness is first introduced, typically, through the quotation of Ps 22:4 in the *meshullash*.

Poem Five: asiriyyah (ten)

As its name indicates, the *asiriyyah* is a poem of ten lines. In form and content, it is less dense and compact than the *magen*, *meḥayyeh*, and *meshallesh*, but it represents some return to patterning, after the looser structure of Poem Four. Yannai's *qedushta* for Gen 8:15 provides a representative example:

אָז רָז נִרְמַז לוֹ וְדָבָר דִּבּוּר נִדְבַּר לוֹ / בְּבוֹאוֹ לַתֵּיבָה וּבְצֵאתוֹ מִתֵּיבָה
בְּבוֹאוֹ נֶאֱמַר לוֹ בּוֹא אַתָּה וּבָנֶיךָ / וּבְצֵאתוֹ נֶאֱמַר לוֹ צֵא אַתָּה וְאִשְׁתֶּךָ
גַּם בְּבוֹאוֹ לְהֵיאָסֵר נֶאֶסְרָה לוֹ / וּבְצֵאתוֹ לְהִיוָּתֵר הוּתְּרָה לוֹ
דוֹרוֹת לְהַשְׂכִּיל וּלְהַסְכִּית וּלְהַסְכִּים / מִלְהַרְבּוֹת בְּעֵת מִיעוּט וּמִלְּמַלְּאוֹת בְּעֵת חִיסּוּר
הַאִם בָּאַת צָרָה לָעוֹלָם לְהָצֵר בָּהּ / וְאִם בָּאַת שִׂמְחָה לָעוֹלָם לִשְׂמוֹחַ בָּהּ
וְאָמְנָם זֶה כְּלָל בְּחֻוקֵּי לִימּוּד / לִנְהוֹג בְּחֶסֶר וּבְכָפָן גַּלְמוּד
זְכוּת אֲשֶׁר הֶאֱמִין וְהִזְמִין וְהֵימִין / אֲשֶׁר עָשׂ שָׁם עִם כָּל מִין אֲשֶׁר אִיתּוֹ הִטְמִין
חֻודַּשׁ לוֹ מִצְוָוה בְּצֵאתוֹ מִתֵּיבָה / כְּכִי שְׂכַר מִצְוָוה מִצְוָוה וּשְׂכַר נְפָשׁוֹת נְפָשׁוֹת
טַעַם לוֹ הִתְכִּין וְהֵיבִין וְהֶחְכִּים / בְּעֵת כִּי רִיבָּה לוֹ בַּטְּהוֹרִים וּמִיעֵט לוֹ בַּטְּמֵאִים
יָצָא וַיִּמְצָא מִמֶּנָּה לְהַקְרִיב קָרְבָּן / לִמְחַדֵּשׁ לוֹ עוֹלָם מֵחׇורְבָּן אל נא

Then the hint was dropped / and a word discretely spoken,
upon his entry to the ark / and upon his exit
Upon his entry, he was told, “Enter, you and your *sons*;” / But upon his exit, he was told, “Go forth, you and your *wife*”
Indeed, upon his entry into captivity, she was forbidden to him / but upon his going forth to freedom, she was again permitted to him
Later generations would realize, deem wise, and affirm this: / do not increase at a time of decrease; do not be fruitful in a time of want
When trouble comes into the world, all suffer / but when joy comes to the world, all rejoice
And truly, a general rule can be learned from these laws: / how to act when wasted by want and hunger
His merit: he believed so he summoned and sustained; / And [thus] did he do well by every beast concealed in there with him
A new mitzvah was made for him when he went forth from the ark / for the reward of a mitzvah is a mitzvah: the reward of a life is a life
God granted him good sense gave him insight and made him wise / when He multiplied pure creatures but made the impure creatures few
He went out among the pure and found an offering to offer / to the One who would renew a world out of the ruins *Please God…*

As this passage shows, the *asiriyyah* employs an acrostic from *alef* through *yod* (in boldface) as a structuring device. Each line of this poem consists of two to four stichs unified by internal rhyme and augmented by dense internal sound-play: consonance, assonance, and repeated roots. In its rhetorical complexity, the poem resembles or even anticipates the *rahit* (Poem Seven). The *asiriyyah* is simple and spare compared to the *rahit*, but it foreshadows the formal and rhetorical motifs upon which the *rahit* will build, and the two poems share an element of auditory complexity.

Thematically, the wordplay of the *asiriyyah* often highlights or even creates the "measure for measure" theology that emerges with particular clarity in the *rahit*.[19] The binary structure of the *asiriyyah* lends itself to stark contrasts, similar to those seen in the *meshallesh:* loved-unloved, pure-impure, king-slave, smooth-hairy, Jacob-Esau, Joseph-Judah. Indeed, these elements of contrast—repeated, refined, and nuanced, drawn out by pithy juxtaposition and pun—provide the raw materials for Yannai's creativity. At the same time, the liturgical cue indicated in the manuscript, beginning אל נא ("please, God") probably alludes to the prayer language from the Palestinian Amidah, which begins: אל נא לעולם תוערץ, "*O God, may You be revered forever...*"—directly reminding the listeners of the poem's liturgical setting.[20]

In terms of station and content, the *asiriyyah* acts as a transition to (the unnamed) Poem Six of the *qedushta*, which is a lengthy, explicit, and clear explication of the Torah portion. The rapid-paced, rhythmic *asiriyyah*—its form and content predictable only in the most limited ways—serves as an energetic preface to the more leisurely presentation of Poem Six. Its terseness, dictated by the fixed ten-line form, gives the poet a canvas upon which to sketch the outlines of the poem to follow.

Several examples may help display the rhetorical force of this poem. In the *asiriyyah* for the *qedushta* embellishing Gen 31:3, the poet deftly compares the patriarch Jacob, characterized throughout the *qedushta* as pure and pious (if not perfect), with his conniving father-in-law Laban, who is described with a litany of synonyms for "crooked" (Poem Four, lines 1–2). This interpersonal contrast anticipates the unit's larger-scale thematic comparison between exile and restoration. Weak and vulnerable outside

19 See Chapter Four

20 Manuscripts indicate this cue by means of various abbreviations; see Rabinovitz, *The Poetry of Rabbi Yannai*, I:10; see also the discussion by R. Sarason, "Midrash in Liturgy," 485.

the Promised Land, Jacob is first shown living as a slave to Laban and nearly dead from his various trials. The poet assures us, however, that because of human repentance and in fulfillment of the divine promise, Jacob (i.e., Israel) will soon be restored, physically, spiritually, and existentially. The ancestor's biography becomes prophecy, and one good "turn"—that is, *teshuvah* ("repentance")—will lead to another—*shuvah* ("restoration"). The contrasts in this brief poem fall along the axes of exile-restoration, anxiety- security, sin-repentance, and suffering-reward. In the final lines of the *asiriyyah*, the poet applies the exegesis to his own community: "Yah, again return us / and turn us unto You! // Let us live securely / and settle us in stillness!" (Poem Five, lines 19–20). Not every *asiriyyah* concludes with such a direct, contemporary peroration; such thematic consistency would be inconsistent for the *asiriyyah*. Instead, inspired by the themes of this Torah portion—and anticipating the content of the piyyut yet to come—Yannai has used stark poetic rhetoric to craft a powerful frame for his prayer. In the *asiriyyah*, the poet has the formal and rhetorical freedom to begin to articulate his unique understanding of his text.

Poem Six (unnamed)

The punning, rhetorically-powerful ten lines of the *asiriyyah* act as an energizing springboard into the lengthy, subtle, and complex Poem Six, which forms a kind of fulcrum at the center of the *qedushta*. Compared to the previous poems, this unnamed unit is leisurely, expansive, and clear; just a few lines from the opening of Poem Six for Gen 16:1 will demonstrate the similarities and differences between them:

ושרי
אֲשֶׁר נִימְשְׁלָה בַּעֲרֵימַת בֶּטֶן / וְיָבְשָׁה בְּבֶטֶן וְצָמְקָה בְעֶטֶן
בְּעֵת טָהֳרָה מִילַּצְבּוֹת בֶּטֶן / נֶחְנְנָה שָׂכָר פְּרִי הַבָּטֶן
גּוֹרָל עָלְתָה לְאַבְרָם חֶבֶל / עוֹדָם בִּימְעֵי אִימָּם הֶבֶל
דֵּי יְגִיעָם לֹא הָיָה לְהֶיבֶל / כִּי הַיַּלְדוּת וְהַשַּׁחְרוּת הָבֶל
הָיְתָה נַחֲלַת אָבוֹת בְּהוֹן וָבַיִת / וּשְׁתוּלָה בְיַרְכְּתֵי הַבָּיִת
וְהִיא הָיְתָה עִיקָּר הַבָּיִת / וְיוֹשֶׁבֶת עֲקֶרֶת הַבָּיִת

And Sarai...(Gen 16:1)
Whose womb has been compared to a heap of wheat: / her womb was dry and her breasts were withered
While she was pure, her womb unswollen / she was granted a reward: fruit of the womb

The lot was cast: she was meant for Abram / while they were yet in their mothers' wombs
Their quantity of sighs was not for naught / though "youth and black hair are fleeting"
She was the patriarch's portion, along with wealth and home; / with a fair sapling, a wife, taking root within the home
And she was the essence of the home / she who dwelled childless in the home (Poem Six, lines 1–12)

Formally, Poem Six is predictably simple and straightforward. It is a poem of twenty-two lines—a full alphabetic acrostic (as indicated in boldface). It contains eleven stanzas of two lines each (four rhyming bicola per stanza). It is introduced by an incipit from the first or second verse of the Torah portion (in this example, the first word), which may have functioned as a preface or even a kind of refrain for each two-lined stanza. Of all the poems in a full *qedushta*, the sixth unit is usually the most "prosaic"—the least allusive and most explicitly narrative.[21] It is an adagio amidst the more frenetic livelier movements of the symphony. The generous canvas of this particular piece—longer than the first three poems combined, excluding the lists of biblical verses—offers the poet a substantial space in which to develop and present ideas. The sixth poem does not, however, simply recap in a straightforward, narrative style the ideas and motifs from the previous five. Nor is Poem Six exclusively aimed at the less educated levels of society, those unable to grasp the content and subtleties of the earlier units—its simplicity does not make it simplistic. Instead, Yannai here expanded upon themes, motifs, and images from the units that preceded it while also using its open, unhurried space as an opportunity for careful, clear exposition and innovation.

Poem Six is a large, empty stage upon which the poet can create and develop elaborate scenes and conceits. Rarely does it function as a simple expansion of already-introduced motifs. Instead, the loose, open structure—

21 See Shulamit Elizur, "The Congregation at Prayer," in *Knesset Ezra*. Elizur's idea that the *magen* and *meḥayyeh* poems (units 1and 2) function as proems introducing Poem Six and thereby engage the intellectual elites is intriguing, and this hypothesis was fundamental for inspiring the analysis of this chapter. Her thesis appears to be partially correct, but the form and content of the poems in the end serve multiple functions and operate on numerous levels simultaneously. At the same time, the analogy between the opening units of the poem (*magen*, *meḥayyeh*, and *meshullash*) and the *petiḥta* form has been developed further in this study than in her essay.

reminiscent of the first three poems, but with less rigid acrostic demands and many more lines—offers the poet the opportunity to compose complex dialogues between characters, to develop aggadic expansions of narratives, to explore complicated theological conceits, to delve into specific topics, and to teach important theological lessons. Of all the poems in the *qedushta*, this unit presents the blankest slate, providing an unhurried, yet not unlimited, space for exploring whatever seems most compelling to the poet. The most interesting aspects of this unit will tend to be in the area of content; it is not a work of dazzling form, energetic rhythm, or deliciously complex allusions and puns. But it is a poem of substance and creativity nonetheless. Modest as it is in terms of form and artifice, it is the poem easiest to imagine transmitting a teaching, as it is never encumbered by excessive aesthetic demands.

Poem Seven: rahit (the runner)

The *rahit* provides stark formal contrast to the straightforward and leisurely Poem Six. In form, the *rahit* most closely resembles an intensified version of the *asiriyyah* (Poem Five). In effect, then, the slowest poem of the *qedushta* (Poem Six) is bracketed by the two liveliest (Poems Five and Seven, the *asiriyyah* and *rahit*, respectively). And whereas Poem Six emphasizes content, the *rahit* is a study in formal complexity. At the same time, as the next section of this chapter will show, complex rhetoric and form do not necessarily diminish the *rahit's* meaningfulness, particularly in the synagogal context. The first five lines of the *rahit* for Gen 11:1 provide an impressive example of the verbal artistry associated with this unit:

ובכן ודברים אחדים
אֲחָדִים אֲחוּדִים אִימְרָה אַחַת אֱוִילֵי אֲדָמָה בִּיזּוּ
בִּיזּוּ בְּבוֹחֵן בִּיטּוּיָם בְּאָומְרָם בְּנוֹת בִּירָה גְּבוֹהָה
גְּבוֹהָה גִּיבְּרוּ גָּרֵי גַּיְא גִּידּוּפֵי גַּאֲוָה דִּבֵּרוּ
דִּבֵּרוּ דָּהֲרוּ דָּאוּ דְּרוֹךְ דְּרוֹס דְּרִיסַת הַשָּׁמַיִם
הַשָּׁמַיִם הֵמָּה הִשְׁמִימוּם הוּתַל הִיטָּם הֲפַכְפַּךְ וְנוֹאָלוּ

And thus, "Unified of speech" (Gen 11:1b)
Unified, united, one of speech, fools of the earth, they disparaged
They disparaged Him who tested their speech when they said, "Let us
build a castle lofty"
Loftily, haughtily—they thought heroically—those valley-dwellers,
arrogant blasphemers, they spoke

They spoke, they galloped, they soared, stomping, trampling,
 the trampling of Heaven
Heaven wrought their ruin; they were hung; He bent them, they
 were overturned and made fools… (Poem Seven, lines 1-5)

This example, with its six-fold acrostic and enjambment, is particularly complex and should not be taken as typical. In fact, there is no typical *rahit*. It is a tightly patterned poem of varying formal structure, usually of twenty-two lines or stichs and employing dense acrostics and terse, rapid phrasing. Yannai generally builds the *rahit* around a theme word, pair of words, or phrase from the Torah portion—whatever style he deemed best for the particular *qedushta*—and that theme word or phrase is often quoted at the beginning of the unit. While many *r'hitim* utilize end-rhyme and all employ alphabetical acrostics, some rely on assonance and consonance to create a kind of internal rhyme while others favor intense parallelism to create a kind of thought-rhyme, a device reminiscent of biblical poetry but significantly more extreme.[22] The *rahit* dazzles and even overwhelms with artistry, often approaching tongue-twister complexity. Even today, *r'hitim* are pleasurable to read aloud, if at times a challenge to comprehend. Evidence suggests that these individual poems were especially popular: in fact many of Yannai's *qedushta'ot* feature doubled *r'hitim*—two poems in different *rahit*-patterns following one after the other.[23]

But were these poems popular merely because of their aesthetics—the auditory pleasure they provided through their soundplay—or were their narrative and exegetical content and experiential effect also important? How does a style of poetry so vested in verbal complexity still convey meaning? And what is the function of the *rahit* in the context of the *qedushta* as a whole?

While at first the *rahit* may seem to be as close to "art for art's sake" as

22 The classic analysis of parallelism in biblical poetry remains J. Kugel, *The Idea of Biblical Poetry: Parallelism and Its History* (New Haven: Yale University Press, 1981). Yannai's amplification of biblical parallelism is discussed briefly below and at length in Chapter Three.

23 It is possible that the doubled *r'hitim* were alternates—one or the other was intended to be performed rather than both on a single Sabbath. However, the narrative interplay between the two *r'hitim* in many instances strongly suggests that both were meant to be performed together. Shulamit Elizur has considered the received-performed nature of the *qedushta* in her article, "The Congregation at Prayer and the Early *Qedushta*," in *Knesset Ezra: Literature and Life in the Synagogue, Studies presented to Ezra Fleischer*, eds. E. Fleischer and Shulamit Elizur (Jerusalem: Yad Yitsḥak Ben-Tsvi, 1994), 171–90 [Hebrew].

one finds in the *qedushta*, closer inspection reveals that it is a rich and potent vehicle for conveying strong messages to the congregation, quite possibly involving them in the recitation of the *qedushta* as well. The terse, punchy language, far from impeding theology or prayer, may in fact have intensified them. The experience of the *rahit* may well have been as important as its content; after the leisurely exposition of Poem Six, the *rahit* awakens and energizes its listeners. It marks the transition to piyyut as a participatory genre, and as a result it shapes meaning in different ways than the earlier units do.

Poem Six uses its broad, open structure for lengthy narrative exposition; the *rahit*, following immediately on its heels, exploits its tight, rhythmic structure to create dramatic emphasis.[24] For example, the *rahit* for Gen 17:1 begins every stich with the word *berit* ("covenant," from Gen 17:2), emphasizing with refrain-like potency the durability and centrality of that motif from the Torah portion. Similarly, the *rahit* for Gen 9:18 takes the opening word of the *sidra*'s second verse, *me-eleh* ("from these") to expand the biblical story of post-diluvian settlement into a promise of restoration from exile. The brothers Ephraim and Manasseh blur into messianic figures in the *rahit* for Gen 48:1, while the juxtaposition of Jacob and Esau in the *rahit* for Gen 25:19 anticipates the final confrontation between God and the powers of (Byzantine) Rome. The refrain-like repetition of the word *milḥamah* ("war") in the *rahit* for Gen 14:1, meanwhile, creates an almost apocalyptic urgency.

In some instances, such as the first *rahit* for Gen 11:1 and both *r'hitim* for Gen 44:18, the poet uses the complexity of the poem's form to augment the drama of the Torah portion. Patterns can become extremely intricate. The patter-song rhythm and consonance of the first *rahit* for Gen 11:1, shown above, follows an AAAAAAB-BBBBBBC (sixfold) acrostic form, in which the final word of one line is repeated, exactly, at the beginning of the next—a structure technically called "anadiplosis." This highly patterned repetition/interruption formally underscores the theme of disrupted language in the *sidra*. On other occasions, the poet uses the terseness of the form, its definitive compactness, to move quickly from the biblical topic to contemporary hopes and aspirations—using the "runner" (*rahit*) to run, as it were, from past to future, exploiting the brevity of the poem in order to juxtapose concepts and exploit parallels. Messianism, apocalypti-

24 This idea is developed further in the following section.

cism, and prophecy, perhaps hinted at earlier in the *qedushta*, appear boldly (even aggressively) in the *rahit*. For a poem that never ceases to move, the *rahit* is often the most arresting in ultimate content. Its rapid, terse language amplifies the energy of the *qedushta* as a whole, enabling the poet to starkly distill a single theme or articulate a tight cluster of themes.

Poem Eight: silluq (removal or elevation)

The *silluq* functions as a transition to the conclusion. It is characterized by the increasingly ecstatic nature of prayer as the mystically-charged *Qedushah* approaches. The rapid pace and frequently future-looking, if not outright messianic focus of the *rahit* prepare the listener for the *silluq*. For all their synergy in purpose, however, great formal differences distinguish these two units. Rather than being jarring, however, the *silluq* appears to be almost an organic outgrowth of the *rahit*. The *silluq* is so unpredictable in form but so dense in its language that it is as if a *rahit* has simply gone off the rails. The *silluq* for Gen 44:18 provides a fair example:

וְלֹא נִבְהַל שׁוֹר וְלֹא נֶחְפַּז אֲרִי / זֶה מְדַבֵּר וְזֶה מֵשִׁיב / זֶה אוֹמֵר וְזֶה מְקַבֵּל / מוֹכֵר וּמָכוּר /
וּבַת קוֹל מִמָּרוֹם עוֹנָה / הִנֵּה הָעֵת וְהָעוֹנָה / הִנֵּה קְרָב וְהִנֵּה מִלְחָמָה / וְיְיָ אִישׁ מִלְחָמָה /
אוֹמֵר עֵת שָׁלוֹם הִיא / וְהַשַּׁלִּיט מֵעָיו הוֹמִים לְהִתְוַדַּע אֶל אֶחָיו / וְעֵת אֲשֶׁר נִגְלָה לָהֶם /
וּפָנָיו גִּילָּה לָהֶם / נָפְלוּ עַל פְּנֵיהֶם / וּרְעָדָה אֲחָזָתָם / חִיל כַּיּוֹלֵדָה אֲפָפָם / וַיִּתֵּר קִיר לִבָּם /
וַתִּתְעַלֵּף רוּחָם וַתִּתְעַטֵּף נַפְשָׁם / וּמַלְאָכִים אֲשֶׁר לִיווּהוּ / וּבַת קוֹל מִמָּרוֹם קָרְאוּ לָהֶם /
הִנֵּה קָמָה אֲלֻומָּתוֹ / וְנִצְּבוּ חֲלוֹמוֹתָיו / וּפָתְחוּ פִּיהֶם / וְנָתְנוּ שֶׁבַח / לִמְקַיֵּים דְּבָרוֹ וּמַעֲמִיד
עֲצָתוֹ / כִּי בְכֵן יוּקְדַּשׁ
וקרא זה

The ox was not terrified nor did the lion flee / this one speaks and the other responds / this one says and the other replies, / The seller and the sold; / and a heavenly voice from above answers: / "This is the time and the moment! / Here is battle / And here is war! / Though the Lord is a man of war / He says: "A time of peace is this!" / As for the vizier, his stomach / is in knots: / should he reveal himself to his brothers? / And when it was that he was revealed to them / his most private parts he uncovered to them / They fell on their faces / and trembling seized them / throes like a birthing woman enveloped them / and the walls of their hearts trembled / Their spirits grew faint / and their souls grew weak / but angels accompanied him / and a heavenly voice called out to them from on high / Behold his sheaf stood / and his dreams came true / and

they opened their mouths /and gave praise to the One who fulfills His word and who sustains His counsel / for with this He is sanctified
"And the one called

The *silluq* is not, strictly speaking, poetry at all: it does not rhyme, have regular rhythm, or employ acrostics—in short, it is more akin to prose (albeit peculiar prose) than poetry.[25] Its length can vary from as few as two to more than ten lines, and its rhythm may shift in the middle of the passage. And yet, because the *silluq* typically uses short phrases, often linked to each other through densely interlocking repeated words, grammatical structures, or images, it echoes the rhythmical style of the *rahit.* The short, enmeshed phrases, freed of the formal constraints of the *rahit,* extends the *rahit's* breathless pace but without the *rahit's* formal scaffolding. This potential formlessness increases uncertainty and demands concentration. The genre provides no guidance to the audience. That said, in the *silluq* certain features are predictable, especially the use of the root *q-d-sh* ("to be holy, to hallow, to sanctify") and a shift in focus from the biblical story and the human sphere upwards, towards the realm of God and the angels. Direct address of God intensifies and replaces simple narration, while the poet also draws in his own community, both by speaking to both his audiences directly and through numerous rhetorical questions addressed to them. The *silluq*—truly a bridge—forges the strongest connection yet between the poet's two audiences, earthly and heavenly.

The prominence of the poet's own voice in the *silluq* reveals how self-conscious he has become at this point about the liturgical setting of his composition, even beyond the playful interweaving of benedictions that opened the *qedushta.* Knitting together imagery, language, and motifs from the preceding poems with new features such as overt angelology and increasingly persistent direct address of God, the *silluq* functions as a "warm up" for the ecstatic, heaven-meets-earth experience the *qedushta* has anticipated since the *meshallesh,* with its quotation from Ps 22:4: the moment Israel and the angels together praise God with the recitation of "Holy, holy, holy..." It is as if, by his rhetoric, the poet seeks to open a window or line of vision from the synagogue to the realm of the divine.

---

25 It is possible to find the occasional *silluq* that does, in fact, display definitive poetic features; see, for example, the *silluq* for Gen 33:18, which has a very intense rhythm and begins with a reverse-acrostic (תשר"ק) pattern. This formally-complex *silluq* may have been influenced by the unusually intricate *rahit* that precedes it.

The energy of the immanent Qedushah cascades through the poem, and it is hard to imagine a congregation resisting the enthusiasm and liveliness of both the sound and visuals of the *silluq*.

Form and function are essentially inseparable in the *silluq*. Its reliance on the root *q-d-sh* anticipates explicitly the impending recitation of the Qedushah; its frequent use of rhetorical questions and direct address reflects overtly the dialogical-liturgical setting of the piyyut as a whole; and the rhythmic prose, becoming increasingly ecstatic, reflects the rapturous mood of the prayer it introduces. Of all the units of the *qedushta*, the *silluq* most closely resembles the ecstatic-mystical hymns of the *hekhalot* texts and the Qumranic angelic liturgies.[26] By intensifying the pace of the previous poem and anticipating the poem to come, the *silluq* moves the audience smoothly and energetically from the realms of story, theology, and exegesis into the experience of prayer.

Poem Nine: qedushah (sanctification)

The final poem, called a *qedushah* like the prayer it introduces and includes (the third benediction in the Amidah), resolves the building tension created by the *rahit* and *silluq* and satisfies the expectations created by these proximate units by interweaving the central verses of the liturgical Qedushah (Isa 6:3 and Ezek 3:12) into its creative text. And like the *rahit*, Yannai's *qedushah* invites the congregation to participate in the performance. This integrating structure of the *qedushah* is best demonstrated by an example, here taken from the *qedushta* for Gen 9:18:

יוֹצְאֵי מִמַּסְגֵּר אֲשֶׁר הוֹצֵאתָה לִרְוָוחָה יְצוּאֵיהֶם יֹאמְרוּ
קדוש קדוש קדוש יי צבאות מלא כל הארץ כבודו
קָדוֹשׁ מִבַּעֲלֵי שֵׁם וּמַעֲשֶׂה
קָדוֹשׁ מִבַּעֲלֵי לָשׁוֹן מֵובְחָר
קָדוֹשׁ מִבַּעֲלֵי שָׂכָר טוֹב
קדוש קדוש קדוש יי צבאות מלא כל הארץ כבודו
קָדוֹשׁ מִשֵּׁם הֶעֱמִיד עוֹטֶה צִיצִית בְּשֵׁם וּמַעֲשֶׂה
קָדוֹשׁ מִיֶּפֶת הֶעֱמִיד מַמְלִיצֵי דָת בְּלָשׁוֹן מֵובְחָר
קָדוֹשׁ מֵחָם הֶעֱמִיד מַשְׂכִּילִים דְּבֵיק בִּבְרוּכִים

לעומתם כל

מִמְּקוֹמוֹ בָּחַר בְּשֵׁם כְּכִי דָרַשׁ אֵשׁ דָּת

26 See Chapter Four

מִמְּקוֹמוֹ בָּחַר בְּיֶפֶת הוֹגֵי נוֹפֶת צוּפִים
מִמְּקוֹמוֹ קֵירַב מֵחָם גֵּירִים וְחוֹשְׁבֵי שְׁמוֹ

פעמים

מִמְּקוֹמוֹ הוֹצִיא מִתֵּיבָה יַלְדֵי ...
מִמְּקוֹמוֹ בָּנָה עוֹלָמוֹ מִגֶּיזַע תָּמִים
מִמְּקוֹמוֹ הוֹרִישׁ לָהֶם עוֹלָם לַחֲלָקִים

פעמים

The descendants of those who went forth from enclosure,
those You brought out to space to breath,
let (them) say of the One who took them out:
Holy, holy, holy is the Lord of Hosts! The whole earth is filled with His glory!
"*Holy*"—from the masters of great name and deed
"*Holy*"—from the masters of a choice tongue
"*Holy*"—from the masters of a good reward
Holy, holy, holy is the Lord of Hosts! The whole earth is filled with His glory!
"*Holy*"—from Shem, He established those who wrap themselves in *tsitstit*,
(distinguished) in name and (great) in deed
"*Holy*"—from Yafet, He established translations of the Torah
into a chosen tongue
"*Holy*"—from Ham, He established enlightened ones
who cling to the blessed
The one towards the other…

"*From His place*"—He chose Shem: that he would expound the fiery
Torah
"*From His place*"—He chose Yafet: those who would utter honeyed words
"*From His place*"—He brought near from Ham: righteous converts
meditating on His name
Twice…
"*From His place*"—He brought out from the ark the children of [the
righteous one]
"*From His place*"—He built His world from the stock of the pure one
"*From His place*"—He bequeathed to them a world in fair parts divided
Twice…

In form, like the *silluq* that preceded it, the *qedushah* falls somewhere between poetry and prose. But unlike the *silluq*, the *qedushah* follows a basically predictable format. In all cases, Yannai prefaces the first quotation of Isa 6:3 with an introductory line, usually containing three discrete elements from the *qedushta*'s narrative, by means of epithets: in this case, the lineages of Ham, Shem, and Yafet, the sons of Noah. In other poems, the three figures may be Abraham, Isaac, and Jacob; or Abraham as a youth, adult, and elder; or three qualities of the patriarch Jacob. After the first recitation of "Holy, holy, holy..." (which we can assume the congregation participated in reciting), the poem expands on each member of the introductory triad, in lines beginning with the word "holy." These lead into a repetition of Isa 6:3, which again the congregation probably joined or echoed. The final stanza of the poem—rarely extant and possibly not routinely included—treats Ezek 3:12 in a similar manner. Poetry and prayer, poet and community, become thoroughly entwined in the rapturous crescendo.

The juxtaposition of scriptural quotation and poetry, along with the reliance on epithets, immediately recalls the formal structure of the first two poems, the *magen* and *meḥayyeh*. These similarities serve to bring the *qedushta* thematically and aesthetically full circle. The final poem, like the first two, is woven around predictable texts in a stable and conventional context. The passages framing the *qedushah* verses, much like in the first two poems, draw on the biblical Torah portion, weaving allusions to the Torah's content into the fixed language of the prayer. As in the *magen* and *meḥayyeh*, the specific referents of the thematic triad highlighted by the poet in his *qedushah* are often cryptic at first—introduced indirectly, by means of metonymy. The implicit identities are clarified and developed after the first recitation of Isa 6:3. This pattern of clarifying initially obscure references likewise recalls the way opaque language of the early poetic units subsequently becomes clearer (albeit more complicated) in the later poetic units. Meanwhile, the mystical, rapturous elements of Yannai's *qedushah*, as well as its prose-like language, echoes the *silluq*. In terms of context, however, this ninth poem signals a final shift to the audience: the language of prayer becomes primary, while the poetry fades into the background. This ninth poem, then, uses form to unify the *qedushta* as a whole. It is the final link in a series of interlocking pieces, and then—absorbed in the ecstasy of the Qedushah—the piyyut softly dissolves into the liturgy, like a magnificent wave that swelled, reaching up to the heavens, crested, and then faded back to the sea.

"Themes and Variations": Repetition and Refrain

As mentioned in the Introduction, Yannai was a tremendous innovator of Hebrew poetics. He was, so far as we know today, the first to use end-rhyme, the first to use an acrostic signature, the first (in short) to compose complicated, multi-poem poetry such as the *qedushta;* and he did so on a weekly basis. His significance is obvious on the large scale. Many details and features of Yannai's poetry—various patterns and refrains, for example—display the poet's originality and craftsmanship at the most subtle levels, as well. While formal innovations and variations can be found in every poem of the *qedushta*, the seventh poem—the *rahit*—offers the greatest density of such subtle features and deserves special attention.

One of those features is repetition, which may involve a single letter, word, or phrase—with words and phrases possibly functioning in the communal, liturgical context as participatory refrains.[27] Even in those poems where formal elements do not lend themselves to a communal refrain, however (such as dense alliteration), the methodical reiteration of singular elements affects how a poem conveys and shapes meaning. Hearing a word

27 Yannai was not the first poet to employ extensive repetition, nor are the origins of something as complicated as rhyme clear and settled. According to Aharon Mirsky, the intense repetition in the *Shofarot*-poems by Yose ben Yose, the major poet of the pre-Classical period, may well have been a forerunner to rhyme, a formal feature first displayed in Yannai's work. Mirsky also regards rhyme as an organic development from rabbinic literature, notably the rhetorical trope of "measure for measure," which piyyut distills to a kind of essence. See A. Mirsky, "The Origins of the Refrain," in *The Piyyut* (Magnes: Jerusalem, 1991), 302–14 [Hebrew] as well as his introduction to *Piyyutei Yose ben Yose*, (2nd ed.; Jerusalem: Mosad Bialik, 1991), 11–90 [Hebrew]. J. Yahalom, however, has suggested that rhyme such as that used by Yannai developed not out of rabbinic prose, but out of increased intensification of biblical-style poetic parallelism; see his discussion, which includes a summary of previous theories on the origins of rhyme, in *Poetry and Society in Jewish Galilee of Late Antiquity* (Tel-Aviv: Hakibbutz Hameuchad; Jerusalem: Yad Yitshak Ben-Zvi, 1999), 137–62 [Hebrew], which develops the ideas presented in his article, "Rhyme in the Early Piyyut," in *HaSifrut* 2,4 (1971): 762–66 [Hebrew]. Yahalom's English language article "Piyyut as Poetry" offers a succinct synopsis of the history of rhyme in Hebrew poetry, and in this location he suggests a way of harmonizing his understanding of rhyme's origin with a more Mirskian approach. He writes: "One of the most famous rhetorical devices found in midrash is the `*middah keneged middah*,' measure for measure. It relies on different kinds of repetition between two unrelated topics, with regard either to sound and wording or to meaning. In the long run, this kind of repetition furthered the development of the couplet into a rhyming unit. Synonyms and homonyms, paronomasia and alliteration all seem suitable to this end. Ultimately this led to the emergence of end-rhyme based on sound parallelism, but it must have taken a long time for this to evolve" (118–19).

multiple times is different from hearing it once; and words actively spoken together acquire greater power than words passively heard.

Repetition

Throughout his *qedushtaʾot* for Genesis, Yannai employs a variety of rhetorical structures in his *r'hitim*, to both aural-aesthetic and meaningful ends. In some cases, the rhetorical devices are very simple, involving repetitions of single sounds, words, or grammatical patterns, while in others they are exceedingly complex. An example of the simpler varieties can be found in the two *r'hitim* for Gen 30:22. In the first *rahit*, every three or four-word line begins with a narrative preterit (*vav*-consecutive) form in which the initial verb and final word of each line create an alphabetic acrostic. Thus, the line embedding the seventh letter of the alef-bet, the letter *zayin* (in boldface), states: *va-yizkor shetiqat zekhutah* (Poem Seven¹, line 7, translated as "Then He remembered her silence, to her merit"). This embedded acrostic, nestled within a repetitive grammatical scaffolding, provides the major structuring pattern within the unit; the overall result is a pleasing and intricate but very subtle consonance. The use of the narrative preterit creates a neo-biblical sound effect (this construction is not regularly used in rabbinic Hebrew), giving an overall impression of "quotation" (although not directly quoting Scripture). These "pseudo quotations" lend the lines a kind of authority and gravity that is subtly reinforced by the pleasant alliterative sounds.

The second *rahit* for this *qedushta*, a listing of divine attributes, employs a very different formal structure: a reverse acrostic that runs from *tav* to *alef* (a formal device called a "*tashraq*," תשר״ק); each stich consists of a *qal* active participle ("one who...") followed by a noun. The first two lines of this *rahit* exemplify its relatively unsophisticated form (acrostic letters are in boldface): ***t**omekh toledot* / ***sh**omeʿa tefillah* // ***r**oʾeh noladot* / ***q**oreʾ dorot* (Poem Seven², lines 1–2, translated: "[For You are] sustaining offspring / hearkening to prayers // beholding births[28] / summoning generations"). The formal patterning in this *rahit* is easy to detect—it lies close to the surface of the poem rather than deeply embedded and the ear can quickly

28 As noted in the commentary to this piyyut, the idiom *roʾeh noladot* could also be translated as "discerning outcomes"; the more literal translation given here highlights the resonance of this mishnaic idiom with the themes of the *sidra*, in which childbirth and desired outcomes are one and the same. The listener in antiquity may well have heard *both* nuances of the idiom.

pick up its presence. This kind of patterning does not necessarily lend itself to congregational recitation, but an audience would quickly grasp the basic pattern and be able to enjoy the strong and regular rhythm, if not anticipate the precise words. The simple, accessible language of the second *rahit* would also be engaging for the audience, focusing its attention on the variety of God's ways of involving Himself beneficently with the human world.

Refrain

Neither of the *r'hitim* from Gen 30:22 (examined above) includes anything that seems immediately like a refrain, although a refrain can be regarded as simply an essentialized form of repetition—the repetition not of a letter or syntactic pattern but of a discrete word or phrase. It is likely that the invocation of the second *rahit* for Gen 30:22, "For You are…" (כי אתה...), indicated as a heading in the manuscript, could have functioned as a refrain—the congregation may have recited it as a preface to each stanza—but this detail about performance remains hypothetical, even if it seems likely.[29] Other examples

29 Refrain-like phrases do, in fact, occur outside the context of the *rahit*. Poem Six of the *qedushta* for Gen 31:3 works best if one begins every stanza with the opening phrase of the *sidra*: "Return to the land of your ancestors…" The manuscript presents this quotation as an incipit for the poem, but the placement may also indicate that it is a cue for its use as a refrain. The repetition of this phrase would add a level of pathos and intensity to an already moving poem; we can imagine that the experience of a community joining the cantor in reciting such an invocation would be extremely powerful. Biblical incipits in other units may likewise indicate the presence of communal or choral refrains, either original to the poem or added at a later date to suit congregational desire to participate. On the custom of adding refrains to earlier works, see E. Fleischer, *The Refrains of Anonymous* (Jerusalem: Akademon, 1974).

It is unknown how refrains might have been performed in Yannai's day—were they congregational, as hypothesized here, or were they choral responses, as we see in some of Qillir's poetry and in some Christian settings? Yannai's refrains, if such the repeated words in the *r'hitim* are, are notably brief and their precise performance is conjecture. By the time of Qillir, however, we find the use of the *qiqlar*—a short, free-standing refrain (the name is from the Greek "*kuklos*" cycle)—which was possibly performed as a choral response by a professional choir. The Greek name for the form is, itself, suggestive, but as with piyyut in general, we should be cautious about assuming simple and direct importation of Christian practices into the Jewish or vice-versa. The choral response was, after all, employed in biblical times (2 Chron 5:12–14; 7:6) and it is noted as part of the Temple ritual in *m. Tamid*. 7:3–4. Christian ritual may have continued or reinstituted this feature of liturgy without borrowing from contemporary Jewish practice. At the same time, the prohibition on vocal music recorded in *b. Git.* 7a may reflect Babylonian rather than Palestinian sentiment (and custom). Even if that is the case, note that Nathan ha-Kohen ha-Bavli, a tenth century chronicler, mentions that a professional chorus ("a choir of young men with pleasant

of repetition, however, are more clearly suggestive of at least the potential for congregational participation. The reiteration of a specific word or phrase in a fixed pattern certainly seems to be an invitation to what we might call a refrain.[30]

The *rahit* for Gen 17:1 offers an example of this simple kind of repetition, and its form is very typical of Yannai's *r'hitim.* In this example, every six-word line begins with the word *berit* ("covenant") taken from the second verse of the Torah portion; the remainder of the line is governed by an embedded alphabetic acrostic. The results cannot be fully reproduced in English, but the sound of the first three lines (where *alef, bet,* and *gimmel* are the theme letters) are as follows:

> ***berit*** *'ito ʾimanta / ʾizarta ʾoto ʾilaphta*
> *berit* ***b****ivsaro* ***b****eirarta /* ***b****ah* ***b****o* ***b****ararta*
> berit ***g****ivyo* ***g****azarta /* ***g****aʾon* ***g****ezarim* ***g****izarta*

> *A covenant:* with him You confirmed / You bound him, You taught (him)
> *A covenant:* by it You made him pure / through it You made him strong
> *A covenant:* You circumcised his member / cuttings of proud waters (in return) You decreed[31]

Each subsequent line likewise begins with the word "*berit*" and then continues the acrostic and, thus, the dense alliteration and consonance.

---

voices") performed at the installation of the Babylonian exilarch during a Sabbath service (the full text can be found in English translation in N. Stillman, *The Jews of Arab Lands: a History and Sourcebook* [Philadelphia: Jewish Publication Society, 1979], 171–75). It may be, in short, that some form of participatory refrain or chorus was a common and increasingly popular element of payyetanic performance in Late Antiquity.

For a discussion of Qillir's possible use of choirs, see E. Fleischer, *Hebrew Liturgical Poetry,* 132, 148. Weinberger regards the refrains as congregational rather than choral (*Jewish Hymnography,* 47). Pinhas ha-Kohen, roughly contemporary with Qillir, introduced refrains into the *Zulat* unit of his *Yotzerot*; see E. Fleischer, *The Yotzer,* 281–96. The picture of performance offered here is, ultimately, conjecture, but one based on the knowledge that, within half a century or so of Yannai's lifetime, formal refrains (either congregational or choral) were in use within at least some synagogues. On the use of choral refrains in Christian hymnography, see Chapter Three.

30 The custom of reciting the repeated phrases in Ps 118 (to cite one example) as a refrain reflects this same performative impulse, regardless of how the Psalms may have been used pre-70 C.E.

31 For exegetical notes and glosses see the text of this *qedushta* in the second half of the book.

While we do not know how this piyyut was actually performed, it is possible that each line's opening word (reflecting a major motif from the *sidra*), functioned as a kind of refrain or invitation to communal participation: the congregation could have joined the cantor in reciting this word at the beginning of each line. This congregational recitation would have the effect of conveying the centrality of the idea of covenant and encouraging the internalization—the embodying, really—of this idea. *Hearing* the key word twenty-two times would be forceful but passive; *reciting* it the same number of times, as an active participant, would be a profound experience. While this kind of reiteration resembles the technique of subjecting a specific word, phrase, or verse to multiple interpretations in a single unit of midrash (the word "*berit*" is nuanced twenty-two different ways), this form of repetition does not evoke the atmosphere of schoolhouse debate or resemble a work where discrete opinions are only subsequently redacted into a single work. Instead, these manifold interpretations of a key idea receive their potency from their performance, and are strongly the work of a single mind and hand.

Yannai's favored style of *rahit* seems to be, in general, the combination of a refrain-like repetition of a word or phrase in every stanza, combined with an embedded acrostic. The "refrain" can occur at the beginning of the line, as in the Gen 17:1 example above, or at the end of the stich or line. For example, the *rahit* for Gen 35:9 concludes every line with the name "Israel"; that of Gen 38:1 ends each line with "Judah"; and that of Gen 32:4 finishes every line with "Edom." The *rahit* for Gen 48:1 offers a slightly more complex variant on this model, alternating the names "Manasseh" and "Ephraim" in every stich.[32] In each of these cases, the possibility of congregational participation in recitation of the key word suggests a profound psychological-experiential effect, in which a singular, key idea, image, belief, or value is inculcated into the members of the community. At the very least, the element of participation would indicate a liveliness and engagement far beyond passive auditory reception.

In some *qedushta'ot*, Yannai takes this basic form of *rahit* and intensifies it in some way, thereby multiplying the imagined possibilities of communal participation. The *rahit* for Gen 33:18, which contains a triple-repetition/refrain, shows the poet in such an extravagant mood. Each line of this *rahit*

32 Yannai's amplification of biblical parallelism, a midrashic exegetical technique, is treated in Chapter Three.

is comprised of three stichs, each beginning with a variant of the root *sh-l-m*: the first stich opens with "perfect" (*shalem*, the *qal* stative) and contains a second word, describing the patriarch himself; the second begins with "perfected" (*meshullam*, the *puʿal* participle), also containing a second word, this time referring to Jacob's descendants; and the third starts with "to fulfill" (*leshallem*, the *pi'el* infinitive), followed by three words, which elaborate upon the purpose of his return—to fulfill the oath he had made at Bethel in Gen 28. The words that complete each stanza share a common letter, and together the poem contains a complete alphabetic acrostic. Thus, for example, the fourth and fifth stanzas of this poem (embedding the letters *dalet* and *heh*) state:

> *shalem bi-**d**erakhav / meshullam be-**d**ebharav / leshallem **d**ebhebh **d**igul **d**ebharo*
> *shalem be**h**ono / meshullah ba**h**amono / leshallem **h**iddur **h**odayyat **h**egyono*

> Perfect in his ways / perfected in his words / to fulfill his speech's exalted reward
> Perfect in his form / perfected in his following / to fulfill the beauty of his meditative knowledge

Yannai uses poetic form to maximize the potential of grammar, exploring the full range of meanings of the root *sh-l-m*: the *stative* in which wholeness is its own end; the *passive*, in which Jacob/Israel is acted upon; and the *infinitive*, which reveals the purpose behind the first two clauses. The repetition of the root *sh-l-m* in so many forms, with so many nuances, for a total of sixty-six times in twenty-two lines, drives home the message of completeness: a wholeness which typified not only the patriarch Jacob but, like a ripple effect, also his descendents. The variations on the root generate within the poem a sense of totality; hearing—let alone repeating—these words (rather than reading them) has the effect of internalizing the message. The poetic pattern employed by Yannai in this *rahit* expands, distills, and clarifies the semantic possibilities of a familiar word and, by extension, creates a comprehensive world-view (past, present, and future) within the composition. From the perspective of performance and liturgy, structural complexity and repetition do not obscure the message but make it insistent and unmistakable.

The *r'hitim* for Gen 44:18 also dazzle with their complexity of form and depth of meaning. The first *rahit,* while not preserved completely, appears to be a slightly more complicated variant of the standard Yannai *rahit* described above. Each line begins with the opening word of the Torah portion: "*Vayiggash*" ("then he approached"). After this opening phrase follow four words, each beginning with the same letter, creating a four-fold alphabetic acrostic; the final word of each stanza continues the alphabetic acrostic and has the third masculine singular suffix, "his."

For example, the line embedding *tet* as its acrostic reads: *vayiggash **t**oref **t**evaḥ **t**ored be-**t**uv **t**aʿan **t**ohoro* (Poem Seven, lines 3–4, translated as: "Then he approached: he who tears prey, casting off the good sense of his purity"). In this embellishment of Judah's confrontation with the Egyptian vizier, Yannai in many ways is rewriting Scripture: he opens with the words of the Torah portion itself, and then dramatizes the biblical scene with quick, compact rhetoric that emphasizes Judah's brash character, military prowess, and complex motives. Quick words imply a quick person, and Yannai creates a Judah who is fast and touchy. A community that participated in this poem by joining the cantor in the recitation of *vayiggash* ("then [Judah] approached") would be almost participating in the dramatic action of the reimagined biblical scene.

The second *rahit* for this *qedushta* is even more intricate, parsing out the opening words of Judah's address from the first verse of the Torah portion in every bipartite line.[33] The first phrase of each line begins with "*bi adoni*" ("please, my lord"); the second with *ʾal* ("do not"). Each line also constitutes one part of an alphabetic acrostic, resulting in a 22-line work. For example, the first two lines, which include the acrostics for *alef, bet, gimmel,* and *dalet,* read:

> <u>*bi ʾadoni*</u> *ʾav* <u>*ʾal*</u> *teʾabed* // <u>*bi ʾadoni*</u> ***b**en* <u>*ʾal*</u> *te**b**aqqesh*
> <u>*bi ʾadoni*</u> ***g**edi* <u>*ʾal*</u> *ti**g**zol* // <u>*bi ʾadoni*</u> ***d**in* <u>*al*</u> *ti**d**ḥof*

> Please, my lord, a father do not cast away // Please, my lord, a son, do not seek!
> Please, my lord, a kid do not steal // Please, my lord, justice do not thrust aside!

Through sheer force of form, this poem transforms Judah from a vigorous figure of action, as he was in the first *rahit,* into a speech-maker, slowing

---

33 The rhetorical effects of parsing out and rewriting biblical speeches (a technique reminiscent of midrash) will be discussed below in the "Creative Voice" section of this chapter.

down his rhetoric and changing him from a one-man militia into a powerful and imploring man of words. In the narrative *rahit*, Judah is the focus; in the dialogical *rahit*, the vizier Joseph—representing the foreign oppressor—is. Yannai's playful, quicksilver rhetorical style does not obscure his interpretation of the *sidra* but rather embodies it and brings it to life. Congregational participation in this poem would unify the community sympathetically not with Judah's agitated actions but with his desperate, dramatic petition.

Of course, there are any number of subtle variations on these typical forms, and a number of reasons can be put forth to explain their unique diversity within the *rahit*: the poet's impulse to be creative, the community's desire for novelty, the contextually-driven rhetorical function of the unit, and the appealing challenge of integrating the Torah portion's language, among others. Acrostics—particularly the intricate, densely repetitive structures—can probably be attributed to auditory pleasure and, at some level, poetic bravado—unlike later extended "signatures," these acrostics can be heard.[34] The emphases created by the formal patterns, however, are not purely decorative; they generate meaning, both inherently and even more so in the congregational setting. Repetitions of ancestral names—Jacob, Judah, even Edom—exploit the eponymous resonances of these figures. Jacob blurs into Israel, Judah into the Jews, Esau into Rome and, by extension, Byzantium. Biblical characters become timeless figures acting in eternal stories, and promises made to them become eternal. Particularly in the liturgical setting, the stories take place in "mythic" rather than "historical" time.[35] The drama of the Torah portion, then, becomes a

34 Later poets, particularly those of medieval Ashkenaz, embedded tremendous acrostic signatures into their works, undetectable at the auditory level and suggesting playfulness and pride combined with piety and humility, evident only to a reader, not a listener. Lengthy acrostics appear much earlier in Christian hymnography. See D. Kreuger, *Writing and Holiness*, esp. 172–73, where he discusses the ambiguity of Romanos the Melodist signing his works "By the humble Romanos." He notes that lengthy signature acrostics, which cannot be heard, can be understood as an act of piety, and that complicate acrostic compositions are "ascetic… for like the poem's complex metrics, they supply rules that must be followed… creating a rubric of discipline to which the poet submits" (172). In Yannai's compositions, where the acrostics are often densely repetitive, the act of submission to formal constraints is balanced by an apparent delight in showing off.

35 On the issue of time/timelessness in liturgy and the potency of reenacting and reliving historical events (technically called anamnesis), see Ruth Langer, "From Study of Scripture to a Reenactment of Sinai," *Worship* 72 (1998): 43–67; reprinted in the *Journal of Synagogue Music* 31 (2006): 104–25.

lens through which the poet views his own period, and formal features are important in teaching the lesson on a visceral, more than intellectual, level. The repetition of a single word lends a specific, auditory intensity to the narrative content. Over and over again, the word "*berit*" in the *rahit* for Gen 15:1 affirms the unbroken bond between God and Israel; repeating "Jacob" time after time in the *rahit* for Gen 28:10 underscores the connection between the beloved patriarch and his descendents; the hammer-like conclusion "Edom" at the end of every stich of the *rahit* for Gen 32:4 creates a cumulative effect of nearly apocalyptic fury and excitement. More intricate structures, such as the morphological variation on *sh-l-m* in the *rahit* for Gen 33:18, serve to augment even further the impact of the poem; cumulatively, the poem teaches that Jacob—and by extension, Israel—will be restored completely in every way possible. The single concept of wholeness is refracted through a variety of lenses, grammatical and existential: stative, passive, and active; physical, ethical, and national.

The elements of form presented here will, in subsequent chapters, become tools for exploring Yannai's theology and understanding of prayer. The rhetorical tropes and features of his poetry can only be understood when seen as part of the synagogue experience. The prospect of audience participation—active rather than passive reception—in these works enriches the possibilities for the experiential component of the *rahit.*

In sum, repetition and refrain indicate how meaning can emerge out of subtle manipulation of poetic form.[36] Yannai exploits the unique power of poetic language to generate content through simple juxtaposition and sound play, all of which in turn demands that the audience engage in acts of interpretation and decipherment if the content of the words is to be unlocked. Poetry also, however, creates possibilities for ambiguity, double meanings, and even paradox, in ways that are distinctive from prose—even the prose *midrashim* (rabbinic explications of Scripture) and *targumim* (Aramaic versions of the Torah) that are so often the closest parallels to the content of these poems.[37] The next section of this chapter considers the important role that specifically poetic rhetoric plays in the creation of meaning in Yannai's Genesis *qedushtaʾot.*

---

36 Other poetic features, especially rhyme, word-play, and intertextuality, contribute to the creation of meaning in these poems. See Chapter Two, which addresses the role of punning, quotation, and allusion in these *qedushtaʾot.*

37 The relationships among midrash, targum, and piyyut will be explored more fully in Chapter Three.

Paradox and Ambiguity

In the world of rabbinic literature, writing—no matter how opaque it may seem to the modern reader in its edited form—functions primarily to teach and explain, and most sources take the form of prose.[38] The translators of the Aramaic *targumim* used their medium to clarify and elucidate the biblical text for the assembled public. The authors of *midrashim*, for their part, were at pains to clarify the puns and wordplays undergirding and inspiring their exegesis. However cryptic the end result may be, the Sages quoted in the Mishnah attempted to distill and transmit centuries of traditional thought and practice into concise, organized forms. Later generations of scholars continued in this discursive, pedagogical mode; the two Talmuds represent the culmination of the formative phase of this tradition.

To be sure, these classical rabbinic writings were not purely educational. Many are lengthy, convoluted anthologies that must be read with trained eyes and the help of teachers if the lessons contained within them are to emerge with any clarity. Moreover, embedded within these texts are many legends and traditions that exist for reasons other than edification. Furthermore, in terms of content, rabbinic writings often dazzle a reader with linguistic virtuosity and theological daring, creating a sense that the Rabbis themselves were startled by what they found when reading Scripture. In the end, however, these prose works do not seek to obscure or create paradoxes; ambiguities may be introduced, but on a case-by-case basis the Rabbis attempted to explain, contextualize, tame, or resolve them. Rab-

---

38 To be sure, the "texts" that we have now are, themselves, later artifacts that reflect a more fluid, lived, and oral original. Many passages of rabbinic literature—particularly the Mishnah—show evidence of orality and oral transmission that renders their literary quality something between poetry and prose—akin, in many ways, to the rhetoric of the *silluq* in a *qedushta*. Furthermore, many of the "prose" rabbinic sources have poetic passages, particularly the Talmud, which includes poetry that has been incorporated into the liturgy (e.g., *b. Ber.* 60b), laments (e.g., *b. Mo*ʿ*ed Qat.* 25b), and the mystically-charged "Song of the Kine" (*b.* ʿ*Abod. Zar* 24b). Of particular interest here, written *targumim* from fourth- to seventh-century Palestine (particularly the fragmentary *targumim*) have poems embedded in them at certain locations (e.g., the parting of the Sea, the death of Moses, etc.), but these works appear to be later additions to manuscripts, not part of the targumic translation-performance. That is, the *sitz im leben* of these works remains unclear, although the texts are tantalizing. See M. Sokoloff and J. Yahalom, *Jewish Palestinian Aramaic Poetry from Late Antiquity* (Jerusalem: Akademon, 1999). Nevertheless, the complicated poetic-liturgical nature of piyyut sets it apart from these other genres of writing.

binic prose rarely seeks to *create* a lack of clarity, despite the multiple interpretations and often difficult exegesis that often typify the genres. Ideally, the rabbinically-explicated text gains layers and levels of meaning, growing richer and deeper, not murkier. When a passage of midrash or gemara cannot be understood, we assume that fault lies with the reader or that there has been a problem in the transmission of the text—incomplete information, lost cultural assumptions, censorship, and so forth—not that the author of the passage is indulging a willful desire to be ambiguous.[39]

Poetry, however, is not prose, and for all that the *qedushta* may at first suggest a linear explication of the biblical text—superficially more akin to targum than midrash, being the work of a single author for a congregational setting—Yannai seems to delight in using his chosen medium as much to create ambiguity as to resolve it. In the end, the uncertainties in the biblical text that Yannai exploits are similar, even identical, to those familiar from prose sources, particularly midrash, and the daring of his teaching at times matches that of the Rabbis. Poetry, however, demands that the audience do much of the interpretive work—work done by the Sages in the prose texts. The overtones, resonances, and multiple possible meanings are left open, potentially unresolved or subject to manifold, undetermined resolutions (individual conclusions reached by individual listeners). This ability to conflate, confuse, and blur, far from weakening poetic rhetoric, is a source of its power and a major reason liturgical poetry is so compelling. By requiring the audience to participate in making sense of its language and meaning, piyyut weaves the community into the poetry. Piyyutim are active, not passive, texts.

Most likely, most if not all genres of rabbinic writing (including the *targumim*, the Aramaic versions of Scripture) were originally in some fashion oral literature. Even if the material was written down very early in its transmission (for example, if the translator employed a written crib-sheet, the liturgical poet a score, and so forth), in practice these traditions were

---

39 At times, of course, the Rabbis wished to conceal knowledge from non-initiates, and the written texts do preserve that element of intellectual hierarchy; see *b. Sanh.* 68a for an example: "For it once happened that [Rabbi Akiva] and I [Rabbi Eliezer] were walking together on a road, when he said to me, 'My master, teach me about the planting of cucumbers.' I made one statement, and the whole field was filled with cucumbers. Then he said, 'Master, you have taught me how to plant them, now teach me how to pluck them up.' I said something and all the cucumbers gathered in one place." We are not told the magical agricultural phrase, and that is intentional; it is not, however, ambiguous.

primarily heard.[40] The element of audience reception renders the topic of ambiguity particularly pressing, as it is entirely possible for two people hearing the same passage to understand very different things—or even to grasp multiple meanings simultaneously. While this is true of any text, it is particularly true of poetry. Rather than creating "either/or" dichotomies, Yannai crafts "both/and" dualities, exploiting the fact that the liturgical setting can tolerate and even thrive on the ambiguous rhetoric particularly available through poetry.

The most persistent ambiguities in Yannai's *qedushtaʾot* arise from the poet's blurring of boundaries. Individual characters become emblems of nations; singular events transmute into routine occurrences; a line of dialogue thought to be addressed to one character morphs into a prayer addressed to God.[41] In some cases, the poet teaches through the ambiguity and clarifies it, much like we would find in midrash; in other cases, the multiple meanings emerge subtly and remain unresolved. Often blurriness early in a *qedushta* anticipates a thematic shift developed later in one of the

---

40 The topic of orality in early Judaism has received much attention in recent years. A partial bibliography would include: M. Jaffee, *Torah in the Mouth: Writing and Oral Tradition in Palestinian Judaism,* 200 B.C.E.–400 C.E. (Oxford; New York: Oxford University Press, 2001); D. Nelson, "Orality and Mnemonics in Aggadic Literature," in *Midrash and Context: Proceedings of the SBL Consultation on Midrash,* 2004–2005 (Piscataway, NJ: Gorgias Press, 2007), 123–38; and the two classic studies by B. Gerhadsson, now printed together as *Memory and Manuscript: Oral Tradition and Written Transmission in Rabbinic Judaism and Early Christianity; with Tradition and Transmission in Early Christianity* (Grand Rapids: Eerdmans, 1998). It is worth noting that many features of Yannai's piyyutim suggest that these compositions were written very early on—their intense complexity, length, diversity of forms, and so forth—but only the poet possessed a copy of the text. Their reception remained oral for centuries. The cantor's reliance on written texts is exploited by the ninth-century Italian poet Silanus (or Silano) of Venosa in the famous episode in the Chronicle of Ahimaatz (*Megillat aḥimaatz*), where Silanus tricks the visiting emissary from Jerusalem into reading an inappropriate text at the Saturday morning service, thereby starting a riot. See B. Klar, *The Chronicle of Aḥimaatz* (Jerusalem: Tarshish, 1974), 18–19 [Hebrew]; and J. Marcus, "Studies in the Chronicle of Aḥimaaz," *Proceedings of the American Academy for Jewish Research* 5 (1933–34): 85–93.

41 This type of interpretation is hardly unique to Yannai; it appears even within the biblical corpus, where the Prophets retell the stories of the ancestors to illuminate points about the present community (e.g., Hos 12) or texts exploit the eponymous names of founders/ancestors (e.g., Gen 49). This exegetical technique is developed into the typological method of reading in Christianity. For a discussion of this topic, see Isaac Kalimi and Peter J. Haas, eds., *Biblical Interpretation in Judaism and Christianity* (New York: T&T Clark, 2006). The issue here is not the identification of ancestors with their descendents, or the way of reading the past as a lens into the present and future, but the ambiguity poetic rhetoric detects, amplifies, and exploits as a result of these interpretive assumptions.

units. For instance, the poet may make use of the fact that the story of Jacob-Israel foreshadows the story of his eponymous descendents: the early units of the poem will focus on Jacob, while the national allegory becomes more prominent in the *meshallesh* (which, as noted above, tends to focus on contemporary issues). A few examples will highlight these variously interrelated, distinctly poetic phenomena.

Another technique Yannai frequently uses is collapsing biblical time into the present and making the ancient story merge into that of his contemporary community.[42] In the second *rahit* for Gen 25:19, for example, attributes of Jacob and Esau blur into attributes of Jews and Christians-Romans:

> Descendents loved and loathed / loved, and finding compassion, and loathed, receiving rejection…
> Descendents of the soft-spoken and the brusque / the soft-spoken to bring together and the brusque to break apart
> (Poem Seven[2], lines 1–2 and 39–40).

At the level of biblical interpretation, Yannai here simply juxtaposes the gentle Jacob with his harsh twin, contrasting the meekness of the people of Israel with the coarseness of Christian Rome and delineating their resultant, appropriate fates. This structure amplifies a contrast rooted in the biblical narrative and well developed in rabbinic midrash, but the rhetoric of the *rahit* is indeterminate, compelling the readers to consider the biblical story and their own day simultaneously. The poet does not specify a context or interpretation. A person hearing the poem may wonder which interpretation the poet intends as his focus—then or now? To an extent, both should be held in mind together, in synergistic resonance, while the openness of the language invites the listeners to consider the implications separately, comparing both readings of the antithetical pairs in every line and perhaps favoring whichever emphasis speaks most to them. Yannai develops and extends the tension of the biblical narrative; it is as if the twins of the Genesis story, entangled from birth, become mirror images of each other, eternally bound together. From Yannai's perspective, there is ultimately little point in distinguishing

---

42 This phenomenon of collapsing time-frames appears in midrash, as well, although it manifests itself somewhat differently; Marc Bregman refers to this literary technique as writing in "the narrative present." See his article "Past and Present in Midrashic Literature," *Hebrew Annual Review* 2 (1978): 45–59.

the ancestor from his heirs, because in an existential way, they are the same character. The dramatic clash of these two personalities merely anticipates and foreshadows the drama of Yannai's own period—themes he develops more and more explicitly throughout the course of the *qedushta*.[43]

In the *meshallesh* of the *qedushta* for Gen 16:1, Yannai creates an intentional parity—this time a positive one—between the matriarch Sarah and Zion.[44] The opening lines of the unit assert: "O Yah! You compared Zion to the wife of the brave one // similar tests and trials upon them both You set" (Poem Three, lines 1–3). Drawing on images going back to the biblical Prophets, the character Sarah becomes the paradigm for the future of the city of God: just as Sarah was barren but became a mother, so, too, will Zion—currently bereft— become a joyful home, populated with new generations. The first three lines of the poem make the comparison explicit: the first half of each line describes Sarah while the second describes Zion. For example, third and fourth lines state clearly:

> It is said about Sarah, the princess, that she could not bear
> And it was said about Zion, My principality, that she would never bear again.

The final lines of the poem, however, deviate from this pattern, or so it seems:

> Fair-crested, the precious one / by Your own mouth called "mother"—
> Rejoice, O barren one / unto your children He will call!.

On the one hand, these final lines make sense, grammatically and exegetically, as an address to the matriarch alone—as if they were a long "A" part of the line. If so, then the first verse of the haftarah (Isa 54:1, "Rejoice, O barren one"), quoted immediately after the last poetic line, functions like an extended "B" part of the final stanza and serves to describe Sarah's joyful fate. However, it could just as easily be that the complete fourth line of the poem refers to Zion alone (as Isa 54:1 does in context), a shift emphasizing the allegorical element of the poem.

43 For more on this specific theme—Yannai's depictions of Edom/Rome—see Chapter Four.

44 This analogy can be found in *GenR*. 38:14, which links the barrenness of Sarah, Hannah, and Zion directly. See also the discussion of female characters in Chapter Four. The key element to consider here is rhetoric, not content.

This instance of productive ambiguity cannot be decisively resolved, and furthermore, it colors the remainder of the *qedushta*. The surviving final units of the poem (the *asiriyyah*, Poem Six, and half of a *rahit*) focus on Sarah, but all the descriptions of her—her trials, perseverance, and redemption—take on new, nationalistic resonances for the congregation in light of the *meshallesh*. The matriarch's individual story foreshadows the fate of Israel's beloved city, and Sarah's happy ending will become their own.

The *meshallesh* for Gen 29:31 challenges its audience with even bolder ambiguities. Yannai does not identify any of the figures in the poem explicitly. The second line, for example, states:

> Glorify, she who was hated for her voice
> Call to her, because of her voice / and love her, she who is pleasant of voice (Poem Three, lines 5–7)

To whom does this line refer—Leah or Israel? And in the next line, who is "the mother of children"—Leah, mother of six of the twelve tribes, or Zion, the metaphorical mother of Israel? The poet plays with the ambiguity, creating a parallel between the lonely, lovelorn matriarch and the second-class, dispirited community of his own day. Again, because this is a *meshallesh*, the haftarah suggests that the poet is speaking of his own congregation at least as much as he is of the biblical figures; the ambiguity cannot be dismissed.

In short, through this technique, Yannai conflates past, present, and future. God did not listen simply to the prayers of the ancestors once upon a time; poetry transforms history into prophecy as the story of Israel and Israel's God continues to unfold and biblical words speak directly to the new congregation. Strikingly similar interpretations, exegetical theologies, and philosophical messages can be found in midrash (explicitly and implicitly), but the medium of liturgical poetry transforms these ideas into something experienced and prayed. Piyyutim are not texts that invite criticism or debate; the setting does not deny the intellectual (these poems are, as we will see, profoundly learned) but their functional orientation is prayer, not study. Through their performance, the ideas embedded in and conveyed by these poems are implicitly affirmed and internalized.

As these examples suggest, the *meshallesh*, where Yannai typically turns to contemporary issues and introduces the haftarah, provides an easy and appropriate location for blurring past and present. Not surprisingly, the *rahit*—a poem that often employs a dense rhetoric of juxtaposition and unexplicated phrases—presents another ripe location for playful, meaningful ambiguity. Examples can also be found elsewhere. The *magen* poem, where the poet strives to engage and intrigue his audience—it is his opening shot and as an artist he must gain his listeners' attention—also offers opportunities for blurring past and present. For example, in the *magen* for Gen 31:3, the line "Your decree he would not return empty // You declared a remnant would return" (Poem One, lines 9–10) seems to speak in national terms, reminding God of promises to the Israelites. The language draws on Isa 55:11, 10:21, and 7:3, all prophecies addressed to the nation, not an individual, past or present. But *context* suggests that Jacob the patriarch, not Israel the nation, is the focus. The audience is drawn in and implicitly invited to ponder how the fate of the children of Israel closely resembles the fate of their eponymous ancestor. The audience may find itself wondering, "Which Israel does the poet mean?" The poet's reply may well be "Both." The distinction between past and present, between ancestor and descendent, is a false one, and the ambiguity is, itself, perhaps one of the poem's messages.

In the *silluq* for the *qedushta* embellishing Gen 28:10, Yannai playfully but seriously conflates his own congregation with the angelic hosts. Expanding on the legend that the face of Jacob is engraved upon God's throne on high, which results in a kind of "doubling" of the patriarch, Yannai creates a triple identity in which the angelic hosts rename themselves: "One proclaims the name `Jacob' / and another proclaims the name `Israel'" (Poem Eight, lines 7–8, picking up on Isa 44:5). It seems that camps of angels in heaven divide themselves into cohorts named "Jacob" and "Israel." While this tradition concerning the names of the angelic hosts is a tradition Yannai shares with midrash, the aggadah does not develop the potential of this tradition in the way Yannai does.[45]

As the *silluq* progresses, Yannai makes it increasingly unclear whether the angels call out to each other or to the community below—whether the two groups exist in parallel or intersect. Where the midrashic parallel seeks to elucidate, Yannai seeks to confuse. The lack of clarity he creates draws the congregation into the piece at the level of interpretation but also in concrete terms of participation, profoundly deepening their experience

---

45 See *Mek. Mishpatim* 18, which describes the angelic hosts as being named "Jacob" and "Israel," citing as a prooftext Isa 44:5 ("One shall say, `I am the Lord's'; another shall use the name of `Jacob'; another shall mark his arm `of the Lord' and adopt the name of `Israel'").

and understanding of their own acts of prayer. The community doesn't merely act in concert with the angels; it becomes intimately and deeply identified with them. Midrash lacks this liturgical agenda, which stands at the center of piyyut.

At times, the blurriness seems to be complete and irresolvable. In both *r'hitim* for Gen 15:1, it is unclear whether the poet is addressing Abraham in the context of the Torah portion, or the Jewish population of Byzantine Palestine. The first *rahit*, which parses out God's words to Abraham in Gen 15:1, "Do not fear, I am...," creates an alphabetic litany of reassurances: "Do not fear! I am your Hope // Do not cower! I am your Guardian" (Poem Seven, lines 1–2). It is easy to see these lines simply as midrashic expansions of God's words to Abraham—an example of the poet expanding a biblical dialogue.[46] But it is also possible to understand them as consolation of Yannai's own community, and this potential grows more likely as the poem progresses, until the final stich, "Do not dwell in darkness! I am your light!" (Poem Seven[1], line 22) acquires strong overtones of an anticipated national redemption, with the language of Isaiah coloring the poet's images of the future.[47]

Similarly, the second *rahit* for this *qedushta*, which parses out the rest of God's words from Gen 15:1, "Your reward shall be very great," seems to address both Abraham and Israel simultaneously. For example, the opening stanza, "*Your reward* / for the fire into which you went // *Shall be very great* / for the converts you drew close" (Poem Seven[2], lines:1-2) overtly alludes to the legends about Abraham in the ovens of Ur and Abraham the father of converts. But it could easily apply, metaphorically and literally, to Jewish martyrs and Sages in Yannai's period, as well.[48] This *rahit* concludes just as ambiguously: "*Your reward* / for the oath that you heard // *Shall be very great* / for the promises you claimed" (Poem Seven[2], lines 11-12). Is this praise of Abraham's faithfulness and trust, or Israel's? Does "the oath" refer to God's promises to Abram in the land or Israel or to the children of Israel at Sinai? Is "the promise" one of offspring for the patriarch or redemption for the nation? Yannai doesn't explicitly tell us what he means. To specify—to limit—these identities would diminish the poem's power.

46 See next section, "The Creative Voice."

47 The resonances with Isa 9:1 ("The people who have walked in darkness have seen a great light") and Isa 60, a passage dominated by images of divine light and redemption in contrast to the darkness of exile, are particularly strong.

48 See Chapter Four.

Through ambiguity, the *rahit* engages, even demands, attention from the congregation. The reader, or hearer, must decide what this poem is really about, and he may well decide: it is about Abraham, it is about me, it is about *us*. There is no "past" or "present" but only a liturgical-exegetical "now."

Other examples could easily be summoned, even from within the limited corpus of Yannai's *qedushtaʾot* for Genesis. In the poem for "Day Seven" from the unusual *qedushta* for Gen 1:1, the first Sabbath blurs into the contemporary Sabbath observed by Yannai's own community. In the *rahit* for Gen 44:18, Judah's address to the disguised Joseph ("please, my lord") shifts into the poet's personal address to God ("please, my Lord"). In some cases, such as the Gen 15 examples above, the ambiguity is complete; in others, one tone clearly dominates while the second meaning lurks just beneath the surface. There is no single location, inspiration, or paradigm favored by the poet. One recurring feature is suggestive, however: as just seen, Yannai often creates ambiguity by adapting or expanding the reported speech in biblical passages. By doing so, the poet often adopts the voice of biblical characters, male and female, mortal and divine. Yannai's imaginative use of "voice" hints at another level of theological and liturgical significance in his creative constructions and provides the final topic of this chapter.

The Creative Voice

Even a casual skimming of midrashic works reveals the comfort with which the Rabbis put words in biblical characters' mouths—even, quite commonly, writing in the divine voice. In the aggadah, the Sages unselfconsciously expanded upon biblical discourse and invented whole conversations, freely imagining dialogue between the deity and biblical characters or even more contemporary figures. In doing this, the Rabbis reflect, in a distinctive way, the developmental trajectory of the earlier traditions of "rewritten Torah" that were popular in Hellenistic and Greco-Roman Judaism.[49] Yannai does not depart from this midrashic

49 The topic of "rewritten Torah" has generated significant scholarship. While rabbinic sources often engage episodically with this tradition, rewriting specific biblical scenes and episodes, in the Hellenistic and Greco-Roman period, lengthy new versions of biblical works (or works attributed to biblical characters) were composed. One could even categorize Deuteronomy as the forerunner of this genre. J. Charlesworth, ed., *The Old Testament*

habit but rather participates enthusiastically in it; invented dialogue and conversation can be found commonly throughout his *qedushta'ot.* The unique aspects of Yannai's compositions, compared to their prose aggadic relatives, lie not in their existence but in his technique and form.

To an extent, every *qedushta*—indeed, every liturgical text—should be understood as dialogue, in that the poet frequently speaks not *about* God, but *to* Him, directly, in his own voice, and God often responds. The poet creates dialogue because his compositions are, by definition, prayer and he is the prayer-leader. Yannai spoke not only on his own behalf but for his community, and to them, as well. His use of the second-person address ("You" as well as "you") merely amplified and developed the mode of address used in the liturgy. Beyond this inherent liturgical give- and-take, Yannai often seized upon key conversational elements in the Torah portion—dramatic confrontations, vivid debates, memorable speeches—and used these as the basis for reimagining, even rewriting, the scene. He did not simply comment upon the story, explaining the events; he retold them in vibrant and engaging detail, using the rhetoric and aesthetics of poetry and exegesis to draw his audience in. Indeed, the combination of petition, speech, chastisement, and consolation suggests that the piyyut functions in many ways not like the aggadic literature its content frequently evokes, but rather like a *targum* (the Aramaic translations and expansions of the Torah, but with the poetry freed from the constraints of linearity) or, even more provocatively, like piyyut's biblical predecessors, the Psalms and the poetry of the Prophets. Like the psalmists and the Prophets, Yannai stood in the breach, negotiating the space between God and Israel, speaking not only *to* his people and his God, but *for* each party.[50] Even in terms of form, let alone content, the poet staked out a bold position. In periods of Jewish history when there might have been pressure or

---

Pseudepigraph, 2 vols. (Garden City, NY: Doubleday, 1983–1985) remains the most accessible compilation of many "rewritten" biblical texts from antiquity. For secondary sources, see the essays collected in C. Bakhos, ed., *Current Trends in the Study of Midrash* (Leiden: Brill, 2006), especially the chapter by S. Fraade, "Rewritten Bible and Rabbinic Commentary" (59–78); G. Nickelsburg, *Ancient Judaism and Christian Origins: Diversity, Continuity, and Transformation* (Minneapolis: Fortress, 2003); H. Naiman, *Seconding Sinai: The Development of Mosaic Discourse in Second Temple Judaism* (Leiden: Brill, 2003); and J. Kugel, *In Potiphar's House: The Interpretive Life of Biblical Texts* (San Francisco: Harper and Row, 1990).

50 The image of "one who stands in the breach" can be found both in the Psalms (Ps 106:23, describing Moses) and the Prophets (Ezek 22:30). The poet, mediating both prayer and scriptural interpretation, functions as the heir of Moses, the Prophets, and the scribes.

temptation to succumb to Christian supersessionist propaganda—the idea that God no longer favored Israel but had, rather, rejected them in favor of the Church—the poet forcefully kept the conversation between God and Israel going.[51]

But dialogue in general plays an important role in Yannai's poetry. How, and to what effect, does Yannai invent direct speech?

Most often, the inspiration for inventing direct speech lies within the biblical lemma Yannai embellishes, typically the first or second verse of the Torah portion.[52] As a result of this convention, dialogue within a *piyyut* is often an expansion of discourse already present in Scripture, with the specific speakers depending on the voices of the inspirational text. For example, in Poem Six of the *qedushta* for Gen 48:1 ("And it came to pass after these things, that Joseph was told, `Lo, your father is ill'; and he took with him his two sons, Manasseh and Ephraim"), Yannai expands on the content of the message given to Joseph. The anonymous messenger— implied by the biblical text's use of an impersonal grammatical construction rendered in most biblical translations as a passive voice—becomes a true, if anonymous, *character* whose words convey pathos and conjure (in the listener and in Joseph) feelings of filial piety:

---

51 The topic of Christian supersessionism, a belief that established the tenor of much Christian-Jewish interaction (theoretically if not practically) and shaped the anxiety each party felt about the other, is touched on in almost every work on Byzantine Judaism. It is treated here in Chapter Three, but not exhaustively. For a broad discussion of Christian anti-Jewish polemic (and vice-versa), among the many works on this topic, see Ora Limor and Guy G. Stroumsa, eds., *Contra Iudaeos: Ancient and Medieval Polemics between Christians and Jews* (Tübingen: Mohr [Siebeck], 1996). Readers wishing a brief, accessible introduction to the cultural context in which Yannai composed are encouraged to consult O. Irshai, "Confronting a Christian Empire: Jewish Culture in the World of Byzantium," in *Cultures of the Jews: a New History* (ed. D. Biale; New York: Schocken, 2002), 180–221. W. van Bekkum's essay "Anti-Christian Polemics in Hebrew Liturgical Poetry (*Piyyut*) in the Sixth and Seventh Centuries," in *Early Christian Poetry* (eds. J. den Boeft and A. Hilhorst; Leiden: Brill, 1993), 297–308, makes valuable points concerning the difficulty of assuming that what seems polemical in a piyyut really is, although he overestimates the oppression to which Jews were subjected in Byzantine Galilee. On the historical situation, which was defined in many ways by the Jews of the Galilee ignoring (unenforceable) imperial anti-Jewish legislation, see P. T. R. Gray, "Palestine and Justinian's Legislation on Non-Christian Religions," in *Law, Politics and Society in the Ancient Mediterranean World,* eds. Baruch Halpern and Deborah W. Hobson (Sheffield: Sheffield Academic Press, 1993), 241–70, as well as the works noted in Chapter Four.

52 Often, though not always, these dialogues recall similar discursive expansions of ideas found in aggadic midrash; rarely do the prose texts develop the dialogue so extensively, however.

> The one who bore you yearns to behold you // his soul is faint and weak…
> He who loved you most among all his sons // he is sick and calls to you, of all his sons" (Poem Six, lines 21–22 and 25–26).

Yannai transforms the brief informational exchange in the biblical passage into a vivid, extended emotional plea. The still-nameless speaker of the poem now speaks with forceful rhetoric, using parallelism to create dramatic effect and depth of meaning. Jacob didn't just father Joseph, he *loved* him. He didn't just *love* him, he loved him *more* than all his other sons. He doesn't summon all his sons, *just* Joseph. The varying phrases in the repetitions create a sense of resistance, as if the servant were pulling on Joseph's sleeve to urge him—faster, faster!—down the hallway.

A more complex example can be found in the *qedushta* for the Torah portion beginning with Gen 44:18, which states: "Then Judah approached him [Joseph, as Pharaoh's vizier], saying, `Please, my lord, let your servant speak a word in the ear of my lord, and let not your face grow hot against your servant, for you are just like Pharaoh.'" This dramatic scene proves fertile ground for Yannai's conversational imagination, just as it did for the rabbinic aggadists. Although the *sidra* itself contains the longest passage of dialogue in Genesis, Yannai does not paraphrase the original passage but creates his own scene. In the *meḥayyeh* poem, all the brothers speak, although Judah is clearly the leader. The unit opens:

> Deep coursed the devisings of that one's heart[53] // but when the wise one[54] saw him, he saw his brokenness of heart
> The brothers spoke to him with all their heart // on behalf of a brother they poured out heart and soul[55]

Speaking as one, the brothers then assert their piety—both religious and filial—stating, "The children of one man are we all // and One Rock is our King" (Poem Two, lines 5–6) but they do not shy away from confessing their crime against Joseph ("Once, against one brother, we sinned… Once we were whole, but now we are lacking" [Poem Two, lines 7 and 9]) and

53 That is, Joseph.

54 That is, Judah. The language of this stich derives from Prov 20:5, cited among the intertexts that follow this unit.

55 Although in the Torah portion only Judah speaks, here the poet employs the plural and depicts all the brothers as speaking.

pleading for mercy. Yannai's depiction of this scene differs from the biblical passages upon which it is based. In Gen 42, the brothers acknowledge their guilt among themselves (but not to the vizier), while in Gen 44, Judah alone speaks to the vizier, sticking to the story that Joseph was torn by beasts. Beyond these changes of framing and content, however, Yannai's use of dialogue possesses its own intrinsic importance. The repetition of "one" in each stich underscores the unity the brothers now possess, in contrast to the discord they used to display. Yet, paradoxically, their unity is not complete because one brother is missing. "One"—and its variant "once"—become thematic ideas for the brothers: assertions of completeness conceal implicit deep deficiencies.

The drama of this *qedushta* increases in the a*sirayyah*, again through the skillful creation of new speech. At this point in the piyyut, as in Gen 44, Judah alone speaks, venting his frustration and anger:

> If I but say the word / all Zoan [Egypt] will be done for!
> (Poem Five, line 6).

Judah's rhetoric in the poem is brilliant: powerful in its parallelism as he puts forth an argument that blends piety with raw emotional appeal. Threats of violence are tinged with pathos and appeals to justice, reflecting Judah's desperate bafflement at the vizier's eccentric behavior:

> If a slave you need to serve you, here I am! I am your slave!…
> Take for yourself our great wealth / but to this lad [Benjamin] show mercy!" (Poem Five, lines 11and 18)

Judah's desperate entreaty soon gives way to wild threats, and the poem as a whole juxtaposes essential ideas as stark dichotomies: violence-restraint, me-him, wealth-mercy. These are not precisely antithetical pairs. Instead, Yannai creates a kind of slant-thought-rhyme, crafting a slightly unpredictable, off-balance drama in these terse couplets as if they are verbal embodiments of an unpredictable, unbalanced Judah—a patriarch struggling against his own nature, wrestling with his own history and inclinations—as he negotiates an off-kilter, volatile, and perilous situation. The rapid pacing and binary pairs heighten the atmosphere of confrontation, underscoring the content of the lines. This verbal confrontation is developed further in Poem Six:

> Our hand held still until the time you fell upon us // Now indeed, in my bloody garment I will fall upon you!

> Why against us did you plot such a secret? // And why did you not keep for us the promise you swore?" (Poem Six, lines 19–20 and 31–32).

This sense of increasing urgency transfers seamlessly to the *silluq*, when God becomes a speaker, borrowing Judah's aggressive tone: "Though the Lord is a man of war / He says: A time of peace is this!" (Poem Eight, lines 8–9). The vivid, expressive language engages the audience and suggests a theatrical element of performance. The visceral, aural intensity of emotion gives the poem an immediacy, and no doubt the rhetoric contributed substantially to the aesthetic pleasure of hearing (practically participating) in the work, given that the content of the dialogue is interesting in its own right.

As the previous example shows, the poet freely fashioned dialogue between biblical characters, mortal and divine, as is often found in midrash. The *qedushtaʾot* for Gen 8:15 and 12:1 in particular illustrate the poet's willingness to write in the divine voice. In both, Poem Six is written from God's perspective. In the Gen 8:15 cycle, God directly reassures Noah—and his descendents, including the contemporary congregation—that never again will a flood destroy the world. Blurring the biblical story into the future tense, God states: "All of My works I shall not again undo // The Curtain I shall not tatter nor the land again make melt" (Poem Six, lines 21–22). The merism of "heaven and earth" underscores the scope of God's oath: it is all-inclusive, even cosmic, in scale, and it applies to all. In the midst of the (literally) universal speech, however, the poet—in God's voice—hints at particularism:

> Never again shall there be waters to flood // but a downpour of My words instead...
> Before your birth, I selected you for this covenant..."
> (Poem Six, lines 25–26 and 33)

The poet dramatizes the divine oath of Gen 9:11 by juxtaposing the death-dealing effects of rain with the life-giving power of God's word, the metaphoric "waters of life."

But to whom are these remarks addressed? Are the "words" in the line simply the content of the Noahide covenant, or something more? Although at first this line seems to present God speaking to Noah, the poet (through both language and context) implicitly widens the address to include his congregation. The language of "words" (i.e., Torah) and "covenant" cannot be decoupled, especially in the liturgical context, from their living Jewish overtones. The embedded message, then, inoculates the audience against physical fear and existential despair: not only is the natural world stable and secure as the *sidra* promises, but the Jews—through the Torah—have direct access to the secrets of life.

This rhetorical doubling—drawing the audience into history through implicit extension of "then" into "now"—is even more overt in Poem Six for Gen 12:1. This *qedushta* describes and embellishes Abraham's journey from Ur to the land of Israel, and in Poem Six, God's speech to the patriarch becomes an elaborate courtship song sung by God to Abraham and all his heirs. The poem opens with a bold assertion of divine yearning (in God's voice), including a paraphrase from the Song of Songs: "You, for whom I waited from the first, // watching for you for ten generations!...This is the decree which I spoke to you: // `My lover, arise, come away with Me!'" (Poem Six, lines 1–2 and 17–18). The poet undermines the audience's expectations of what a divine decree should state. Where one expects law, God speaks of love; and where one anticipates command or authority, He urges running away together. The romance is not limited to God and Abraham, however. Abraham's descendents play a vital role in the relationship from the beginning. The poet depicts God as again invoking the language of the Song of Songs while He anticipates the creation of Israel, a people who, as the word-play indicates, are fitting heirs to Abraham:

> Let there come forth from you a nation, and let it hearken as you have done // My friend, My sister, arise, come away!...
> Therefore from you I will raise up a great nation // who bless themselves by your name...
> I strengthened you with My arm, so holy // to thereby sanctify, through you, My people, so holy!"
>
> (Poem Six, lines 19–20, 23–24, and 43–44).

By using God's words in Gen 12:1 as a pretext and foundation for an extended divine speech, Yannai expands the biblical dialogue from its original setting into the present day. He writes from a perspective in which his community eavesdrops (as it were) on the intimate conversation of their parents (so to speak), overhearing the story of their love affair. In turn, the community learns about the depth of God's attachment to them, as the poet re-imagines and emphasizes the status of the chosen people. God has loved them all, every generation since the first. The poem and its exegetical basis possess even more power than a mortal love-letter; parallelism and common words yoke Abraham and his children together with God. Thousands of years, and the gulf between the mortal and divine realms, dissolve as the poet speaks in God's voice.

Poems written in biblical voices do not always depend on an explicit anchor in a biblical quotation, however. For example, the *asiriyyah* from the *qedushta* for Gen 15:1 expands the dialogue between God and Abraham that appears in the Torah portion, but it does so without directly quoting the original verse. The poet narrates the action, recreating a "he said-He said" banter, with a rhythm that makes the exchange vigorous and brusque. The opening line of the poem generates a sensation of immediacy, with the poet directly addressing God as if he were narrating the biblical scene: "O Lord God, Your brave one [Abraham] entreats you…" (Poem Five, line 1). The next lines contain the substance of Abraham's complaint—his ongoing childlessness in the face of God's promise of offspring—culminating in an quotation adapted from Eccl 1:3, "What profit have I // for all my labor?" (line 13). God then reassures: "Fear not—neither the one [Lot] nor the other [Eliezer the Damascene]— // Neither one nor the other shall inherit" (lines 16–17). Abraham remains troubled, worrying about the sin he may have committed in killing the Canaanite kings. This anxiety prompts a final divine response, as the poet—interjecting himself into the scene—reminds the deity:

> "You gave him sound advice: `Don't overdo righteousness!' // You wiped out wicked ones; your reward shall be very great!" (lines 22–23).

In tone, this is quite different from the rhapsodic, erotically-charged love song of the *qedushta* for Gen 12:1—all parties sound a little short-tempered, even cranky. Its conclusion, however, is just as reassuring. The patriarch speaks to God and God responds, and neither has a monologue. Abraham's vigor in holding up his end of the argument both entertains and encourages Yannai's audience—complaint and fretting are not out of bounds. Conversely, God's replies—reassuring and mild in their chiding—console the congregation as well as the patriarch and, with their tone of indulgent and even amused rebuke, comfort rather than antagonize. Earlier, in Gen 12, God and Abraham resembled a young couple in love; by Gen 15, they are an old married pair negotiating new developments in their relationship. Undercutting any real tension in the poem, the audience—heirs as they are to Abraham's covenant—knows the outcome (that Abraham will have children). Yet Yannai's words, through their playful rhetoric, draw the community into the scene. Piyyut, blending the intellectual engagement of exegesis with the personal and communal demands of prayer, is a fundamentally active and interactive genre of writing.

Indeed, Yannai often mediates between God and the community. As the prayer leader, he is heir, as it were, to the prophetic role of "standing in the breach"—navigating the space between God and His people. In the end, for all of their artistry and complexity, these works are prayers. Only the Passover Haggadah seeks so strongly to connect the historical past with the present day. Just as at Passover, Jews are commanded to say, "I, myself, went forth from Egypt," in the course of these *piyyutim*, the community itself experiences and relives key moments from the biblical past.[56] In doing so, the powerful connection between God and His people becomes manifest and is reaffirmed. These poems address God on behalf of the people while simultaneously reassuring the people of a positive response.

As many of the examples given above reveal, Yannai keeps his attention fixed both on his text and his context. Often he addresses God directly, affirming positive divine attributes in keeping with the Torah portion's theme and his community's concern:

> "Your might, O Awesome One, is in the heavens // but You watch over all who set feet upon the streets"

begins the *qedushta* for Gen 29:31 (Poem One, lines 1–2). Exploiting a dramatic and visual juxtaposition, Yannai moves, sweepingly, from God's lofty abode to the humble pathways of His people. Reading these lines, the reader or hearer can follow the poet's gaze as he forcibly yokes high and low

---

56 This specific feature of piyyut merits further inquiry; in provocative ways, it resembles the "lived experience" of the Christian Eucharist, in which the Last Supper is recreated and experienced in a controlled liturgical setting. This reanimation of past events into the present and, by extension, the self-conscious use of memory to shape self-understanding, is called, technically, *anamnesis*. While midrash may make parallels between biblical stories and the present day, such "relived Scripture" is unusual in rabbinic Judaism outside of the Passover haggadah and, less overtly, in piyyut. R. Langer has written with particular insightfulness on anamnesis and related phenomena in Judaism, notably in her essay "Liturgy and Sensory Experience," in *Christianity in Jewish Terms* (eds. Tikva Frymer-Kensky et al.; Boulder, Colo.: Westview Press, 2000), 189–95, 386–87; and in "From Study of Scripture to a Reenactment of Sinai." As Langer notes, the Torah service itself offers a version of the anamnetic experience.

together. Addressing God in the second *rahit* for Gen 43:14, the poet waxes rapturous while he pleads for his people to experience God's beneficient presence:[57]

> Singing sweetly of Your holiness / is a multitude that is sweet to You / tribes of the pure one [Jacob] from the people who are consumed / May you sooth their suffering / Let us always know Your strength / Let us sing your praises / Let us rejoice in Your joy-giving / Let us proclaim Your holiness / Let us make a diadem of Your righteousness / Let us show wonder at Your wonders / and let us grow strong in Your strength… (Poem Eight, lines 1-9)

The formal similarities of these stichs—especially the ringing cohortatives "let us…let us…let us"—include the audience in the plea, which borders on the imperative. There is no anger at God in these declarations, but there is an urgency. The poet affirms those qualities—mercy, forgiveness, love, fidelity, justice, covenant, immediacy, presence, protection—that may seem to be most precarious in the minds of a community living in Galilean exile, a short physical journey but an impossible political distance from where, centuries before, the Temple stood.

In the end, while Yannai speaks to God, his real audience is the people, whom he incessantly if obliquely reminds of their own role in this cosmic, national drama: "The fate of Your faithful ones You guard / as for Your enemies, their pride You shatter… Your allies You lead in straight ways / the twisted threads of dreams You explain" (*qedushta* for Gen 41:1, Poem Seven[1], lines 17–18 and 21–22). In the most positive terms possible, through the power of distinctly, uniquely poetic rhetoric, Yannai challenges both his constituencies: each side owes it to the other to be faithful. Without that foundation of mutual obligation (i.e., the covenant) everything else—implicitly, never explicitly, a possibility conjured by extrapolation rather than assertion—loses meaning. Like the Prophets of old, the poet chastises both God and Israel, but writing in the wake of the long catastrophe of exile and political subjugation, Yannai is a gentle scold when he lectures, working to seduce and inspire both his mortal and his divine constituencies,

57 As discussed in Chapter Three, the Jews of Yannai's period were probably not actively, severely persecuted. Even according to the most optimistic reading of the evidence, however, it is clear from Yannai's piyyutim that the Jews in the sixth century experienced existential oppression, living as second-class citizens in the shadow of a triumphant, if fragile, Church. See Gray, "Palestine and Justinian's Legislation on Non-Christian Religions."

drawing his community towards their God gently and drawing God back to His people, through the power of words and word-play.

Many key rhetorical features—sound-play, puns, intertextuality, and insinuation—have so far been mentioned but not directly explored. In the following chapter, Yannai's language, particularly his use of biblical quotation and allusion, will be considered more closely. We now have some idea of *why* Yannai used poetry as his creative medium; next let us consider *how* he knit his works together at the most basic level: words.

Chapter Two

"Inscribed by a Learned Tongue": The Language of Aesthetics and Biblical Intertextuality

"The more expert one were at nuances,
the more poetic one should be."
Horace Walpole

Just as poetry cannot be separated from its most obvious component, structure, it also cannot be isolated from its most basic building block, language. Responding to the constraints of form and demands of aesthetics, every word in poetry serves multiple functions and contributes to both the sound and experience of the poem and its meaningfulness. To add to this complexity, the language of piyyut, Hebrew, is profoundly enriched (even overdetermined) by a long and ongoing tradition of self-reference and allusion. Writers in this tradition mine the themes and phrases of the biblical text and use them as raw material for the creation of allusive and witty works.

Yannai, whose poems embed biblical verses and motifs within the fixed structure of the weekly liturgy, was a master of both quotation and allusion, and he established poetic trends in poetic rhetoric for generations to come. Earlier poets might have quoted a biblical text and alluded to its phrasing, but none did so to the extent or with the depth, intricacy, and concentration that we first see in Yannai's works. To fully appreciate the deftness of Yannai's writing, we must understand his creative and multifaceted mastery of the canonical text. He was an exegetical poet writing for an exegetical community, and the biblical text and its interpretations permeate and flavor every line of his poetry. The array of allusions and quotations—simple and intricate, obvious and subtle—lends his works an extraordinary density, and a sharply attuned ear can detect manifold resonances in a single phrase. The Bible, as read and preached, provided Yannai with a vocabulary of both wit and meaning. In his piyyutim, texts create texture and tradition becomes the language of innovation.

At the same time, Yannai's Hebrew is not simply a pastiche of biblical phrases and images. His innovative use of language raises questions about the status of Hebrew itself in Byzantine Palestine and its influence on Yannai. Was it a living language or a relic? Was it comprehensible only because of its biblical resonances, or does it reflect a more common idiom of Late Antiquity? What external factors shaped Yannai's distinctive style of expression? This chapter will consider the types and functions of language in Yannai's poems, ranging from the role of morphology to the use of biblical quotations and allusions.

The Importance of Words

The intricate and varied formal constraints of the poems that constitute a *qedushta*—the diverse patterns of end-rhyme, rhythm, assonance, and consonance that differ in density and specifics from unit to unit—demand that the (successful) poet be a linguistic virtuoso. Simply put, a poem's most visceral impact derives from its sounds. Through the formal devices of rhyme and cadence, Yannai used Hebrew in ways that surely delighted his audiences in antiquity—and influenced those who came after him. Most famously, Qillir and poets of the Qillir school employed similar forms taken to new extremes, to the point that Yannai's medieval heirs composed works that are amazing to listen to—and often impossible to comprehend. Yannai, in contrast, rarely sacrificed clarity on the altar of art. His diction balances brilliant word-play with aural effects that create aesthetic delight. But his word-plays and puns do not obscure meaning. They create it. Sometimes—like a barely-audible overtone—meaning emerges subtly from the cumulative effects of repetition and the sly, unarticulated implications of puns.

Two rituals appear to have shared primacy in the ancient synagogue of Yannai's day and each contributed to Yannai's poetic lexicon: the statutory prayers, which took the place of the sacrifices in the Temple; and the Torah service, in which the weekly portion from the Torah scroll was read. Yannai's *qedushta'ot* merge the two, synthesizing liturgy and lectionary. Yannai achieves this effect through his overt use of biblical intertexts, from single, highly evocative phrases and allusions to entire narratives to direct quotations, all in the context of a fixed liturgical scaffolding. Fleeting hints and partial quotations are hallmarks of classical payyetanic style, and Yannai mastered and developed this technique, using it to create complex layers of meaning. He evokes complete biblical stories along with their aggadic interpretations by means of a single well-turned phrase while simultaneously anticipating fixed liturgical phrases. In its entirety, each *qedushta* embellishes a specific Torah portion, the lectionary (*sidra*) and haftarah for that week, along with the prayer text of the Amidah. By its very form, then, the *qedushta* is an intertextual literary work.

Yannai's use of the biblical text is most obvious in his quotations from the weekly Torah portion and haftarah, in stations which are fixed by his poetic structures, but closer examination reveals that he integrated verbal motifs from the entire Bible consistently, in what amounts to a dazzling display of biblical holism.[1] The initial three poems (*magen*, *meḥayyeh*, and *meshallesh*) foreshadow the language of the collections of verses that follow each unit. In these poems, allusions invite the audience to guess what the quotations are before the answers are given away. Later poetic units—notably the *rahit*—lack the extensive anthologies of intertexts of the opening poems but nonetheless often build upon explicit quotations from either the first verses of the *sidra* or, less commonly, other key texts (often ones which were cited earlier in the piyyut). In the end, almost every line in one of Yannai's works draws words, phrases, or distinctive images from Scripture. Thus a concordance is often more useful in translating a *qedushta* than a lexicon.

It is important to realize that Yannai both *quotes* and *alludes*. As noted in the Introduction, his poetry—as is true of piyyut in general—does not attempt to biblicize or otherwise imitate biblical forms of poetry.[2] Instead, it draws upon the familiar, canonical literary source as a kind of shorthand, employing a single, meaning-laden word or phrase in order to evoke a world of implicit meaning, both biblical-contextual and exegetical. Yannai freely manipulates quotations as necessary to suit his dramatic conceits and narrative constructs and to fit complicated formal structures, but he also lifts verses and phrases intact, weaving them into complex and innovative *new* compositions.

---

1 For an outline of the units constituting a typical *qedushta*, see Appendix I.

2 This sets piyyut apart from the *hodayot* of Qumran, for example, which largely mimic biblical styles of poetry; see the essays collected in E. Chazon, Ruth Clements and Avital Pinnick, eds., *Liturgical Perspectives: Prayer and Poetry in Light of the Dead Sea Scrolls* (Leiden: Brill, 2003). As we will see in Chapter Three, where biblical poetry emphasizes parallelism and the use of word-pairs, Yannai often delights in breaking word-pairs apart and explicating them separately—reflecting a midrashic more than a neo-biblical sensibility.

For all its richness, Yannai's language is functional as well as ornamental, possibly even didactic.[3] His poems are neither "art for art's sake" nor pedantic. The specific audience for which Yannai composed cannot be settled, although it seems likely that he wrote for a distinctly rabbinic and generally learned community in the Galilee, the hub of rabbinic Judaism in his period.[4] Nevertheless, growing evidence from Late Antiquity suggests that his works were, at the very least, also comprehensible to a more general audience at the time they were composed, however that audience might have been constituted.[5] The status of Hebrew in the sixth century remains an open question, and one complicated by the preference for Hebrew in the context of statutory prayer: Was the liturgy composed in Hebrew precisely because of its archaicness and exoticism, because of its historical (and nostalgic) associations with the Temple and the Bible, because that was the "traditional" Hebrew that the wider community of Aramaic speakers knew and comprehended, or because it remained an elevated register of a true living language? Yannai's poetry does not resolve these

3 Comparison could perhaps be made to Shakespeare's famously innovative use of English. For a consideration of the aural nature of piyyut, see Wout J. van Bekkum, "Hearing and Understanding Piyyut in the Liturgy of the Synagogue," *Zutot* 1 (2001): 58–63. On the topic of payyetanic idiom in the early period, see Shalom Spiegel, "On the Language of the Payyetanim," *Ha-Doar* 43:23 (1962–63): 397–400 [Hebrew]; and specifically on Yannai, M. Zulay, "Matters of Language in the Poetry of Yannai," in *Studies of the Research Institute for Hebrew Poetry in Jerusalem*, vol. 6 (Schocken: Jerusalem, 1945), 165–247 [Hebrew], as well as the articles contained in the anthology of Zulay's articles, *The Land of Israel and Its Poetry.* On the issue of "competency"—the conventions of reading and understanding a text, particularly poetry—see J. Culler, *Structuralist Poetics: Structuralism, Linguistics, and the Study of Literature* (Ithaca: Cornell University Press, 1975).

4 Levine, in *The Ancient Synagogue*, 585–86, argues that congregations in which piyyutim were recited must have been unusually learned. However, the arguments of Mirsky, Zulay, and Spiegel about the living nature of Hebrew in this period, and the comprehensibility of biblical idiom in particular, remain compelling. Of particular interest here is the essay by Steven Fraade, "Rabbinic Views on the Practice of Targum, and Multilingualism in the Jewish Galilee of the Third–Sixth Centuries," in Lee Levine, ed., *The Galilee in Late Antiquity* (New York: JTSA / Cambridge, MA : Harvard University Press, 1992), 253–87; Fraade emphasizes the contextual use of specific languages for specific purposes—a possible explanation for the use of Hebrew in synagogue-based poetry and Aramaic ("vernacular") poetry in non-synagogue contexts, possibly appealing to the same constituency. On this topic, see also Rachel Sroumsa, "People and Identities in Nessana," (Ph.D. diss., Duke University, 2008).

5 The most thorough study of Jewish literacy in antiquity is Catherine Heszer, *Jewish Literacy in Roman Palestine* (Tübingen: Mohr Siebeck, 2001); this volume, however, addresses a period prior to Yannai, and does not take the evidence of piyyut into consideration.

issues—indeed, it can be used to support diverse hypotheses. If anything, Yannai's use of Hebrew (like that of the other early *payyetanim*) complicates the reaching of any simple conclusions.

The very fact that the majority of piyyutim, both before and after Yannai's period, were composed in Hebrew at all—Jewish Palestinian Aramaic was presumably the vernacular in his cultural context—remains something of a puzzle. Although Aramaic poetry is well attested, it seems to have filled a different, less "official" niche in the synagogue world than the Hebrew works. The bilingual nature of Jewish poetry in Late Antiquity may reflect differences in terms of audience or perhaps in the context in which poetry was performed—Hebrew for the synagogue service, Aramaic for other settings.[6] Explaining the presence of these two "registers" of poetry simply in terms of the level of education of audience neglects subtler indications arising from the context, function, and subject matter of the poetry, among other elements.

In some instances, Yannai seems to employ a variety of Hebrew that would fall out of usage by the time of the Islamic conquest.[7] And although it was not the primary language of everyday discourse in sixth-century Galilee, it oversimplifies matters to restrict its classification at the time to a binary choice of "alive" or "dead." The fluid and creative variations of Hebrew grammar, morphology, and lexicon found in Yannai's specific idiom likewise complicate attempts to classify Hebrew as simply "the holy language," whether in the sense of "sacred" or "the language of the sanctuary"—that is, the Temple—or even "the language of the Holy One."[8]

---

6 On the issue of language coding as a form of linguistic register, see Fraade, "Rabbinic Views on the Practice of Targum, and Multilingualism in the Jewish Galilee of the Third-Sixth Centuries." A fine, critical anthology of the Aramaic piyyutim was published by Sokoloff and Yahalom, *Jewish Palestinian Aramaic Poetry.* English translations of some of these poems can be found in M. Klein, *The Fragment Targums of the Pentateuch According to their Extant Sources*, 2 vols. (Rome: Pontifical Institute, 1980). van Bekkum, although he discusses the Aramaic poems only briefly, sees the Aramaic poems as "common" and the Hebrew poems as "elite" but also regards the Hebrew poems as "official" and the Aramaic works as "popular"—a complex matter of register, audience and function. See his essay, "Anti-Christian Polemics in Hebrew Liturgical Poetry (*piyyut*) of the Sixth and Seventh Centuries." On the relationship between Jewish Palestinian Aramaic poetry and Hebrew piyyutim, see Michael Rand, "Observations on the Relationship Between JPA Poetry and the Hebrew Piyyut Tradition—The Case of the *Kinot*," in *Jewish and Christian Liturgy and Worship: New Insights into its History and Interaction* (Jewish and Christian Perspectives Series 15; eds. Albert Gerhards and Clemens Leonhard; Leiden, Boston: Brill, 2007), 127–44.

7 See Spiegel, "On the Language of the Payyetanim."

8 For a very succinct summary of the history of Hebrew and its various practical and

Hebrew may well have served to evoke the authority of tradition. On the other hand, Yannai did not hew rigidly to a strictly "classical" kind of Hebrew, either in diction or grammar. The fact that he composed in Hebrew—as did later poets—may reflect not only its centrality in the early synagogue and evidence of its functionality, but an important stage in the language's ongoing development.

For all that Hebrew may have been a flourishing and vibrant language in the Byzantine period, Yannai's reliance on biblical vocabulary remains telling: the written Torah was the single Hebrew work most likely to be familiar to any Jewish population, particularly one that probably spoke Aramaic as a daily vernacular.[9] Furthermore, the fact that Yannai often viewed his biblical citations through the lens of rabbinic interpretation implies that he wrote for an audience possessing or aspiring to a specific kind of learning—able to comprehend the words and sensitive to their resonances. The patterns of repetition and reiteration that are the hallmarks of his *qedushtaʾot* may be the key to the issues of reception and appreciation of Yannai's poems: the more learned the hearer, the deeper the meaningfulness of the poem and the greater the appreciation. Nevertheless, in the end, there was probably something for everyone to enjoy.

With that in mind, a more systematic exploration of Yannai's use of sound-play, quotation, and allusion offers the best way to understand the complex language of the classical payyetanic tradition, and that is the topic to which we now turn.

Sound Effects

Yannai's poetry, when read aloud, dazzles. End-rhyme, internal rhyme, deft puns, witty sound-play, assonance, consonance, and dramatic pacing texture and unify the poetic units of the *qedushta* like threads of a tapestry.[10] In some instances, the author's displays of playfulness and virtuosity or

ritual uses over time, see David Aaron, "The Doctrine of Hebrew Language Usage," in *The Blackwell Companion to Judaism* (eds. Jacob Neusner and Alan J. Avery-Peck; Blackwell: Oxford, UK/Malden, MA, 2003), 268–87.

9 See, Aharon Mirsky, "Roots of Payyetanic Language," in *The Piyyut* (Magnes: Jerusalem, 1999), 209–18 [Hebrew]. Also note Gerhardsson, *Memory and Manuscript*, especially 56–67 on education.

10 In *Poetry and Society in Jewish Galilee of Late Antiquity* (Tel Aviv: Ha-Kibbutz HaMeuchad, 1999), 14–20 [Hebrew], Joseph Yahalom uses the term "jeweled style" to describe the use of scripture to embellish the poems—a term borrowed from the work of

simple adherence to a chosen pattern simply sound pleasing. In other places, the sounds themselves may acquire significance, or the poet may use aural effects to conjure an *implicit* word by creating a readiness to hear it.[11] Because all of this linguistic play occurs in the context of public performance (they were heard and prayed and not silently considered), these auditory features merit particular consideration. The sound of his poems—generated most basically by his flexible understanding of Hebrew morphology—influences their meaning. Indeed, in some poems (particularly the *r'hitim*), the overall aural impact may well have exceeded any intellectual comprehension of the words. Hebrew is a rich and resonant language, and Yannai mastered its possibilities.

Hebrew—based, like all Semitic languages, on a system of consonantal roots inflected according to specific patterns to create meaning—lends itself to word play and sound-play.[12] It appears that Yannai, like later medieval Hebrew grammarians, understood it to employ a system of either two or three, rather than strictly three, consonantal roots. As a result, the poet's forms are often a challenge for modern Hebraists to decipher because they appear strangely truncated or apocopated. This morphology likely reflects Hebrew grammar as it was understood, composed, and possibly even spoken in Yannai's day—even his most unusual coinages have parallels in biblical or rabbinic prose.[13] At the same time, it enabled the poet to create the sound-play essential to the aesthetics in these *qedushta'ot*. Thus seemingly unusual words and coinages serve both functional and formal ends: they create and convey comprehensible *meaning* while simultaneously reflecting Yannai's distinctive aesthetic.[14]

Although many of these elements of Yannai's creative language defy translation, a few representative constructions can illustrate some of the

---

Michael Roberts, a scholar of late antique Latin literature. The image of "jewelling" aptly describes the intricate and artistic aural embellishments of Yannai's poems as well.

11 Because sound-play, especially unusual coinages, are so difficult to translate, they are treated only briefly here, in order to give some of the flavor of Yannai's verbal style. Interested readers are urged to consult Yahalom's *Sefat ha-shir* for a thorough treatment of the subject of payyetanic diction. More generally, see A. Murtonen, *Materials for a Non-Masoretic Hebrew Grammar.*

12 While not explicitly examining Yannai's language, Rand's *Introduction to the Grammar of Hebrew Poetry*, which focuses on the language of Qillir, is a model study of payyetanic grammar.

13 See Spiegel and Zulay, cited above; Yahalom, in *Sefat ha-shir*, takes a more skeptical view.

14 On the topic of the Bible in the liturgy in the period before Yannai, see Judith New-

issues at stake here and help clarify his idiom which, while unusual, fits patterns of Hebrew usage in his era and in his works. In the *magen* for Gen 11:1 (Poem One, line 8), for example, Yannai employs a *qal* perfect from the root נ-ב-ט, which is attested in biblical Hebrew only in the *hiphil* stem.[15] The forms of the root that appear in Yannai's *qedushta'ot* suggest that he understood the verbal root to be simply ב-ט (as, indeed, those are the only two visible root letters in most forms). For instance, he employs the *qal* coinage בטו (*batu*, "they saw") in place of the standard *hiphil* form הביטו (*hibbitu*); the two forms are semantically equivalent but in Yannai's coinage the letter *nun*, necessary to find the word in a modern lexicon, is left out.[16] Yannai's use of this short form, which looks very strange to those familiar with biblical or modern Hebrew (it is neither the expected *hiphil* nor a normal *qal*), is not random; the bi-syllabic בטו is consistent with the end-rhyme and rhythm required by this poem, and it reflects a logical, albeit "non- standard" understanding of Hebrew grammar. At the same time, this apocopated form is primarily associated with poetry, indicating that it may have sounded unusual—elevated or artificial—even to Yannai's audience. Indeed, Yannai does know and use the standard forms of words, as will be discussed below.[17] But the apocopated coinages so pervade his work (and follow such a clear logic) that we cannot dismiss them as incomprehensible neologisms. Yannai's use of the short forms, such as בטו, must be understood as significant in their own right for specifically poetic reasons but also recognized as suggesting a more-than-idiosyncratic grasp of Hebrew grammar.

Many additional examples of this kind of rhythmic apocopation can be found throughout Yannai's corpus. For example, in the *qedushta* for Gen 15:1, Yannai writes: *ki damam tarti* (תרתי) *lakh le-hattirah* (להתירה) ("indeed, their blood—you were told to let it flow," Poem One, line 11).[18]

---

man, *Praying by the Book: Scripturalization of Prayer in Second Temple Judaism* (Atlanta: Scholars Press, 1999).

15 Modern grammarians will explain that the initial *nun* disappears in most cases where the *nun* would otherwise close a syllable. This phonological phenomenon means that the *nun* is generally elided in speech when in the syllable-closing position. Because the elision of the *nun* happens so frequently in initial-*nun* roots, pre-modern grammarians did not consider it part of the root.

16 Similarly, we find Yannai using גע (*gaᶜ*) as a qal perfect in place of הגיע (*higgiaᶜ* – the hiphil of נ-ג-ע) in his *qedushta* for Gen 31:1 (Poem Two, line 7).

17 E.g., Yannai uses הביט (*hibbît*), the standard (*hiphil*) third masculine singular perfect in his poem for the third Sabbath of Rebuke in Rabinovitz II: 313 (lines 14, 16).

18 In order to convey the sound-play, most examples here are presented in

The word *tarti* is from the root נ-ת-ר ("permit"), which—like the similar root נ-ב-ט—occurs only as a *hiphil* in the Bible. Yannai regards it as if it were from the root ת-ר, however, and coins a *qal* form of that new root in order to highlight the sound-play of the line, a sound-play that picks up on the standard *hiphil* infinitive (להתירה) several words later. Yannai demonstrates amply that he has both standard and innovative morphologies in his repertoire. His choice of form—particularly in those cases where he is not apparently trying to connote any difference in meaning—must, therefore, be determined not simply by grammar or knowledge but rather by form and aesthetics.

In the grammar of Yannai's Hebrew, weak roots—particularly those that are weak either at the beginning or end of the root—are especially malleable and useful for poetic coinages. For example, the root נ-ת-ן ("give") will appear both in standard, expected forms and in unusual variants such as *tattah* (תתה, "you gave") instead of *natatta*. In this case, the shortened form serves the purpose of continuing an acrostic while also maintaining rhythm.[19] The coinage does not reflect a limited or wholly irregular understanding of grammar, however, because in other piyyutim the standard forms are used without differences in meaning. The poet's familiarity with both standard and short forms is readily apparent in a line such as the following, from the *qedushta* to Gen 15:1: *tatti lakh ve-natatta li / mah eitten lakh u-mah titten li* ("[In the past] I gave to You as You gave to me / What can I give you and what will you give me?" Poem Two, lines 11–12). The first form, necessary for the acrostic, is apocopated, while the others are all standard. Similarly, ע-ש-ה ("do, make") and ח-י-ה ("live") appear in "short" forms (clipped forms that look much like the jussive in standard biblical Hebrew) as well as longer, standard forms. Final-weak roots, such as ח-ז-ה ("see") and פ-צ-ה ("open"), and initial-weak roots, such as י-צ-ר ("create") and י-ד-ע ("know"), sometimes appear in standard, "correct" forms but at other times are used in apocopated forms, such as *ḥaz* instead of *ḥazah*, *tsarta* instead of *yatsarta*, and *daʿta* instead of *yadaʿta*.[20] Yannai's use of both short and regular coinages with the same meaning suggest that it was often

transliteration, with the Hebrew supplied when necessary. Readers wishing to examine the Hebrew text should consult the cited texts in the second half of this volume.

19 See *qedushta* for Gen 16:1, Poem Six, line 21. This is not to say that Yannai did not know or use the standard word forms; for example, in the *qedushta* for Gen 12:1, we see the expected *natatta* (Poem Three, line 1).

form, not meaning, that determined his usages.[21] Indeed, the poet displays a clear preference for mono- and bi-syllabic words, including the use of what appear to be jussives used with imperfective meanings (e.g., *ʿaś* in place of *ʿaśeh* in the *qedushta* for Gen 27:28, Poem Five, line 6), again reflecting a bi-consonantal understanding of weak Hebrew roots. These deviations from standard grammar create a distinctively springy pacing. The powerful nature of Yannai's rhythm becomes evident if one replaces his short words with longer, more typical forms.[22]

Yannai's short, pithy formulations are not generally unique coinages, however. In some cases, he employs grammatical forms that also appear in rabbinic prose or even the Bible, while other unusual usages reflect common changes attested in other sources, likely the vernacular vocabulary and inflection of his period and area.[23] In other cases, Yannai favors forms that are unusual but attested in the Bible—coinages well- rooted in Scripture, albeit peculiar-sounding to modern ears. For example, in the *meḥayyeh* for Gen 16:1, the poet writes: *saḥah yiskah le-av be-maʿaneh* ("So mused `she who discerned' to the father aloud"—meaning Sarah answered Abraham; Poem Two, line 3). The word *ʾamrah* would have the same meaning and syllable count as *saḥah* (from the biblically-attested root ש-י-ח , "to speak," but spelled by Yannai with a *samekh*), but it would neither resonate with the appellation *yiskah* (from the root ס-כ-ה, "to see, anticipate, hope") nor would it continue the acrostic. The root ש-י-ח is unusual in the biblical

20 For example, in the *qedushta* for Gen 15:1, we find *ḥaz* instead of *ḥazah* (Poem Six, line 15), where the shortened form contributes to the rhythm of the stich; similarly, Yannai uses *naḥaz* in the *qedushta* for Gen 33:18 (Poen Three, line 3) instead of *naḥazeh*. For *pats* instead of *patsah*, see Gen 15:1 (Poem Five, line 2); for *tsarta* instead of *yatsarta*, see Gen 17:1 (Poem Seven, line 35); for *daʿta* instead of *yadaʿta*, see Gen 12:1 (Poem Two, line 1). It is important to note that these changes in form are often not driven by the demands of the acrostic but instead reveal a preference for the terse, punchy rhythm of short words or, perhaps, norms of Hebrew usage in Yannai's period.

21 In *Sefat ha-shir*, Yahalom notes that in some cases, poets seem to use these bi-forms with different connotations, such as active or passive, while other forms that might seem to be candidates for shortening never appear that way. The precise nuances, mechanisms, and rules governing such forms are still being determined. In the present instance, only examples with interchangeable meanings are being addressed, in recognition that in other instances differences between forms may be meaningful.

22 For example, in the *qedushta* for Gen 31:3, poem 5, the poet uses *ʿaś* for *ʿaśah* (line 3, meaning "he did"); *patstah* for *patsitah* in the first *rahit* for Gen 12:1 (line 17); *naḥaz* for *naḥazeh* in the *meshallesh* for Gen 33:18 (line 3); innumerable other examples could be provided, but these help suggest the nature of the phenomenon.

23 See discussion below on the weakening of gutturals.

text but, as employed by Yannai, absolutely regular in both form and meaning. Yannai also frequently favors the archaic or poetic biblical prepositional form *lamo* (למו, "to him," "to them," or, in some instances, as a long form of the preposition -ל) over the standard *lahem*, which is otherwise more common.[24] Likewise Yannai shows a clear and strong preference for short forms of "from"(מן), rather than the normal, reduplicated forms: *menno* instead of *mimmenno; menni* instead of *mimmenni*.[25] Language that was poetic in the Bible remains poetic in these Byzantine works.

Perhaps because speech—reported and expository—is so common in Yannai's poems, creative synonyms for "to say" are especially common.[26] Much in the way he favors the less-common lexeme ש-י-ח, Yannai frequently—over 100 times[27]—uses forms of the root נ-ו-ם (which may ultimately be a form of the biblically-attested roots נ-א-ם and/or נ-ה-ם in which the middle guttural has disappeared) as a synonym for א-מ-ר and ד-ב-ר. The preference for נ-ו-ם may arise because the initial *nun* suits the acrostic of the stich (see the *qedushta* for Gen 12:1, Poem Three, line 4, where the *nun* supplies the acrostic letter needed to spell ינאי, the poet's name), but in many places, rhythm, sound, or simple authorial preference appears to be the determining factor.

Preference for certain roots and forms sometimes derive from the need to complete an acrostic, or it may be independent of such formal demands and reflect a subtler kind of aesthetic. They may also preserve echoes of a living Hebrew of Yannai's day. In the *magen* (Poem One) for Gen 12:1 (line 12), *namta* ("you said") occurs in the middle of a stich and meets no overt formal need. The poet's general preference for the short, punchy root can be found in the *rahit* for the very same *qedushta*, where Yannai prefaces *namta* with the prefix *ke-* (meaning "when you said"). The *kaf*—not the *nun*—is required by the acrostic. The root נ-ו-ם, while one of Yannai's fa-

---

24 See *Gesenius' Hebrew Grammar* (Oxford: Clarendon Press, 1910), Wilhelm Gesenius, Emil Kautzsch, George Wolseley Collins, and Arthur Ernest Cowley, eds., 2nd English ed. [commonly referred to as "GKC"], §103f for *lamo* specifically and §103k for a discussion of the longer prepositional forms in biblical Hebrew; as the entry in GKC notes, "Poetry is distinguished from prose by the use of longer forms." Yannai continues this biblical tradition of using the lengthier biform in poetry.

25 The best precedent in biblical Hebrew for *menno* (which is not attested in biblical Hebrew at all) would be the first-person singular *menni* (in place of the longer *mimmenni*), which occurs six times in the Bible. See GKC §103i.

26 See Chapter Three for a discussion of reported speech in Yannai's *qedushta'ot*.

27 According to the data entered in *The Historical Hebrew Dictionary Project (ma'agarim)*.

vorites, is neither uniquely his nor particularly poetic. It appears in early rabbinic texts (including the Mekhilta, Sifre, and the Tosefta) as a standard word, despite its absence from biblical Hebrew with this meaning (outside the ossified cognate *ne'um*, "utterance," so common among the biblical Prophets). It does, however, fall out of favor in later rabbinic texts, supplanted by the familiar root א-מ-ר. Yannai's preference for the less-common root suggests not only that it was a useful word at a formal register, but a familiar one as well.[28]

In all these cases, audience comprehension does not seem to have been an issue. Yannai apparently assumed that listeners understood these words, some of which may represent the living Hebrew of his own era, while others would probably have had a "classical" sound even 1,500 years ago. His idiom is at once alive and hoary with age, likely clear but possibly obscure. The demands of aesthetics and form (rhyme, rhythm, and acrostics), as much as meaning, seem to have shaped Yannai's preferences when he was selecting among many options available in the flexible, literate, and apparently vibrant (even if only in rarefied circles) Hebrew of his period.

Rhyme and Reason[29]

As important as these discrete coinages are for understanding the history of the Hebrew language and the register of his speech, Yannai's use of language is most appealing, accessible, and intriguing when considered on a larger scale—phrases, lines, and even whole poems. Almost every unit of a *qedushta* contains aural effects that are both pleasing to the ear and engaging to the mind. At times, these poems provide simple yet illuminating evidence of how Hebrew sounded (or was heard) in Yannai's day. For example, seeming slippages in Yannai's rhymes reveal that *ʿayin* and *ḥet* rhymed to his ear, either naturally or perhaps with effort. Thus we find הצניע rhyming with הצניח in the *qedushta* for Gen 39:1 (Poem Two, lines 5–6) and סלע (*selaʿ*, "stone") and סלח (*selaḥ*, "supplication") in the *magen* for Gen 16:1 (Poem One, lines 1–4). In particular, we can hear in the rhym-

28 See Spiegel, "On the Language of the Payyetanim." The frequency with which Yannai uses forms of נ-ו-ם suggest that Spiegel's hypothesis—that this was a common word in the Hebrew of Yannai's day—is correct. As Spiegel notes, later tradents when copying prose texts that also used the root נ-ו-ם often "corrected" this less familiar word to forms of the much more common א-מ-ר.

29 See Chapter One, n. 26, for a discussion of the origin of rhyme.

ing of Yannai evidence that the guttural letters (*ʾalef*, *heh*, *ḥet*, and *ʿayin*, especially) continued to weaken—a trend that supports phenomena to which other texts written in Jewish Palestinian Aramaic, Samaritan Aramaic, and rabbinic Hebrew bear witness.[30] Yannai's works, functionally lost at a relatively early date, are particularly valuable for the study of this element of language, having been spared the process of "updating" to which texts preserved in ongoing liturgies and academic texts—that is, those that continued to be living texts—were often subjected.

As the following examples will show, Yannai's signature poetic techniques can be found in any poetic unit of a *qedushta*. To begin with a simple illustration, the fifth poem of his *qedushta* for Gen 31:3 concludes:

> Yah, again return to us / and turn us unto You // Let us live securely / and settle us in serenity! (Poem Five, lines 19–20)

Transliterated, this line sounds as follows:

> *Yah ʿod shuveinu / ve-eilekha hashiveinu // betaḥ hoshiveinu / ve-sheqet yashveinu*

Together, the repeated sound-play on a cluster of roots—ש-ו-ב, י-ש-ב, and נ-ש-ב—knit the words into a harmonious whole. The resonance of the consonants *shin* and *bet*, the repeated first-common-plural suffix *-nu*, and the assonance of the vowel patterns create an aesthetically pleasing cumulative aural effect. Meaning also emerges through these sound-clusters: themes of restoration, repentance, and peaceful lives are linked tightly together not just by proximity but by their common sounds. The petitionary nature of the line, picking up on Lam 5:21, follows immediately after a plaintive lament about exile and dispersion. The vocalic harmony among the words in the concluding line suggests, however, that restoration is practically part of the fabric of nature. Language embeds the message so deeply that it is as if the poet is uncovering rather than crafting the message. Due to the resonances,

---

30 See Spiegel, "On the Language of the Payyetanim;" and Edward Y. Kutscher, *Studies in Galilean Aramaic*, trans. Michael Sokoloff (Ramat Gan, Israel: Bar Ilan University Press, 1976). Common interchanges include: *ayin-alef*; *ayin-ḥet*; *ayin-heh*; *heh-ḥet*; *samekh-sin*; *mem-nun*; and *alef-heh*. These changes—essentially the weakening of the gutturals—appear in texts written in Jewish Palestinian Aramaic, Samaritan Aramaic, and rabbinic Hebrew, as well as in Yannai and other piyyutim, and may represent changes in orthography as much as pronunciation. See *b.* ˋ*Erub.* 53b, the *locus classicus* for the Babylonian critique of Galilean ways of speaking.

restoration appears inherent, destined, and inevitable, woven into the very sound of language. The sound inspires and consoles. The poem that follows these lines—a paean to the beauty of the land—picks up on the optimism of the sound-play in the quoted line by opening with the imperative from the Torah portion itself, which may even have functioned as a refrain: "Return to the land of your ancestors"—*shuv el eretz avotekha* (Gen 31:3). The restoration depicted in the final line of the *asiriyyah* transforms the root's next appearance, in the opening of Poem Six, from a simple historical remembrance of Jacob's restoration to a prophecy of his children's return. Past becomes promise through the resonant repetitions of the root, "return." The imperatives of the biblical verses are no longer spoken in the past tense, but have become, instead, imminent—very much in the present tense.

An additional illustration of how the same techniques of root repetition, assonance, consonance, and rhyme amplify both the aesthetic experience of a poem and its meaningfulness can be found in Poem Four of the *qedushta* for Gen 12:1, where the poet rhymes the roots ז-ר-ח, ת-ר-ח, ט-ר-ח, פ-ר-ח, and ב-ר-ח. The resulting stanza states:

> Within the eastern (*mizraḥ*) gates / arose one radiantly pure (*ezraḥ*)[31] // Within the midst of darkness and gloom, he shone (*zaraḥ*) with radiant light
> Indeed, the abominations of Teraḥ (*teraḥ*) / he rejected and cast aside (*taraḥ*) // Like a falcon he burst forth (*peraḥ*) and unto You he flew (*baraḥ*). (Poem Four, lines 1–5)

The combination of vivid images—the dawn in the east (associated with new beginnings, but here also with Ur and the legend that Abram was cast into Nimrod's furnace), Abraham's purity, his rejection of his father's idolatry, his emergence as a radiant savior on the horizon, his vigorous (even uncontainable) piety and virtue, and especially a sense of his magnificent and vital action—all of this emerges from the close concatenation of sounds, from aural resonances that bind together roots of diverse or even opposite meanings in close proximity.[32] The sounds burst

31 Heb. "*ezraḥ*," usually translated as "citizen" (an anachronistic rendering here) or "one born of the land"—an irony in this context, given that Abraham was born outside of the Promised Land. It probably means something like "one of pure descent." I have incorporated the nuances of radiance and purity in my admittedly innovative translation.

32 This line also draws on numerous aggadic interpretations of Scripture; for example,

forth with as much vigor as their images, with all the elements of the poem—auditory, visual, and thematic—working together to create a single effect. Abraham appears on the scene in a nimbus of radiance, as unstoppable, inevitable, and welcome as a hero from the world of myths. This is not the aged, tested patriarch of the biblical narratives but someone altogether different. And, while some of these images come from verses also associated with Abraham in midrashic literature, in Yannai's poetry, the words themselves appear with unmediated directness and force.[33]

The two examples above show how Yannai could create substantial poetic texture out of a variety of resonant words. In many cases, the words chosen—epithets, turns of phrase, whole stichs—are, in truth, biblical allusions (and they often connote broad aggadic traditions associated with the verses or figures). Yannai frequently derives his sound-play from puns latent in the Torah portion itself. For example, the epithet for Abraham, "radiantly pure" (*ezraḥ*) comes from an aggadic reading of Ps 89:1, which happens to rhyme with the name of Abraham's idolatrous father, *Teraḥ*, while the city of Ur lies, geographically, to the East (*mizraḥ*). Yannai complemented these resonant words with vigorous verbs of action (*zaraḥ, taraḥ, peraḥ, baraḥ*) that likewise rhyme.[34]

Similarly, the dense repetition of roots and sounds textures the conclusion of Poem Six for Gen 38:1, which describes Tamar's quest for justice through her seduction of Judah. The second to last stanza puns on the root ק-ד-ש ("holy"), while the final stanza repeats the tetragram ("the Lord") at the conclusion of each stich (an effect that cannot be replicated in English):

> Tamar *hallowed* the *Holy* Name // for she hoped for *holy* seed
> She harlequinned and played the `*holy*' harlot // and her *holy* path He prospered

Abraham is called "*ezraḥ*" (translated as "radiantly pure") in *LevR* 9:1, *PRK* 4, and elsewhere, based on Ps 89:1. This single stich, then, is densely intertextual, using biblical language from the Psalms to evoke a particular midrashic reading. Yannai's use of biblical quotation will be discussed in the following section, allusions to rabbinic tradition in Chapter Four.

33 See the notes to this particular poem for midrashic and biblical sources, as well as the more general discussion in the following chapter.

34 Levels of meaning continue to appear as one scrutinizes Yannai's language; for instance, the poet's use of the verb *baraḥ* ("to flee") echoes Song 8:14, and his phrasing subtly amplifies the verse-source and resonates with the Song of Songs language earlier in the piyyut building on Abraham's image as God's beloved.

She preserved her widowhood before the *Lord* // … the *Lord* did not return her [empty]
She longed to grow the garden of the *Lord* // for they are the seed the *Lord* has blessed (Poem Six, lines 37–44)

The juxtaposition of "holy" and God's name is hardly original, but Yannai exploits the double meanings of *q-d-sh* in order to amplify the irony and drama latent in the biblical story.[35] To reach her hallowed ends, Tamar had to play a "holy woman'"(*qedeshah;* Gen 38:21)—meaning, in biblical idiom, a pagan cult prostitute. God does not reject her for this, but is, instead, completely in league with her. Yannai's word-play amplifies the ironic reversal of the biblical story: to produce holy offspring (she is, after all, the mother of the messianic line of David), Tamar must disguise herself as a whore. The final stanza underscores God's approval of the seemingly questionable course of action depicted in the previous stanza—highlighting the inherent irony of her situation, at once sacred and profane. The verbal repetition, which lends the entire passage pleasing sound and semantic unity, also emphasizes the boldness and correctness of Tamar's actions. The "holy woman" (i.e., prostitute) was, in fact, doing holy work.

Not all payyetanic word-play is as overt as rhyme and repetition. In some cases, Yannai produces effects through the creation of a kind of semantic rhyme—effects that depend on meaning rather than aural affinity. The *asiriyyah* (Poem Five) from the *qedushta* for Gen 17:1 demonstrates this variation on word play by punning, in sequence, on words highlighting the similarity between circumcision and the pruning of trees, both of which were understood to increase fertility: *ʿorlah* ("foreskin"); *milah* ("circumcision"); *gazar* ("to cut/prune"); *etz ha-sadeh* ("the tree of the field"); and *perotav* ("his fruit"). Line-by-line, this language and these images create a kind of "thought rhyme" from which the poet's point emerges: foreskin pairs with tree, circumcision with pruning, and children with fruit. When read together, the lines replicate the process of Abraham contemplating the logic of the implied analogy—with, perhaps, a touch of humor as the patriarch works out the implications of the comparison of his masculine "limb" with the anatomy of a tree. The imagery itself, more than the sound, gives this passage its power.[36]

35 This particular poem is discussed again in Chapter Four.
36 Yannai's interpretation shares much with aggadic embellishments of this story (e.g.,

At his most impressive, Yannai merges semantic and aural resonance. We see this in the opening line of Poem Four for Gen 49:1, which catalogues synonyms for the idea of "hidden." The original "sounds" as follows: *kamus ve-satum / ganuz ve-ḥatum // tamun ve-safun / ʿamus ve-tsafun* ("suppressed and sealed / hidden and concealed // secreted and covered / closeted and veiled;" Poem Four, lines 1–2). The inflection of the *qal* passive participle combined with a series of similar sounding—even, in some cases, etymologically related—roots results in an almost incantational quality to this line, a sense well-suited to the aura of mysterious foreboding at Jacob's deathbed scene. The effect is also pleasing to the ear—form and function are in perfect synch. Similarly, in the *rahit* for Gen 11:1, Yannai aims to impress, creating a visceral sense of language tumbling over itself, much as the bricks of the Tower of Babel fell upon each other. The opening two lines, structured on the letters *aleph* and *bet* respectively, sound as follows:

> *ʾaḥadim ʾaḥudim ʾiimra ʾaḥat ʾevilei ʾadamah* ***bizu***
> ***bizu be****-vo*<u>*h*</u>*en* ***b****ittuyam* ***be****-ʾomram* ***b****enot* ***b****iyrah* ***g****evohah*
>
> Unified, united, one of speech, fools of the earth, they disparaged
> They disparaged Him who tested their speech when they said, "Let us build a castle lofty"(Poem Seven[1], lines 1-2)

The first six words of each line begin with the acrostic letter (*alef* and *bet*, respectively); the seventh word introduces the next letter of the acrostic. Amplifying the formal complexity of this *rahit*, the last word of the first line is repeated as the opening word of the following line, creating a daisy-chain effect (a technique called "anadiplosis"). This pattern holds for all twenty-two lines of the unit. To be sure, this line is clever—the poem as a whole, and particularly this *rahit*, delights in wickedly witty juxtapositions, reversals, and ironies—but just as important to a poem like this is the

---

Gen. Rab 46:4, where it states: "R. Huna said in Bar Kappara's name: Abraham pondered [God's command] and drew an inference: *ʿorlah* (foreskin) is said here (Gen 17:11), and *ʿorlah* occurs in reference to a tree (Lev 19:23): just as *ʿorlah* in the case of trees refers to the place where it yields fruit, so *ʿorlah* employed in reference to man means the member which produces offspring [fruit]"). Poetic rhetoric, however, conveys the common idea with distinctive forcefulness, amplifying in this case the parallelism of the analogy and recreating a sense of Abraham's amazement with immediacy, distilling the midrash down to a kind of essence, although at the cost of explication and precision. Poetic rhetoric is not "better than" prose *midrashim* but a different manifestation of the same tradition and impulse, a lesson shaped in each case by genre and context. See below and Chapter Three.

sound-play of the poem itself. The poet challenges his audience with his verbal virtuosity and dexterity: Can he really keep this up for twenty-two lines? Can we keep up with him? At some point, in a poem this complex, comprehension falls by the wayside and the sound of the line just washes over the audience. The pace is frenetic, and no line really ends, because each connects relentlessly to the following. This *rahit*—i.e., the "runner"—really runs; it races breathlessly ahead on the power of words.

Two final examples will illustrate Yannai's powerful use of language to serve both aesthetic and meaningful ends. The first is the *rahit* (Poem Seven) for Gen 33:18, a very complicated unit that is structured on repetitions of the root ש-ל-ם; in the context of the Torah portion, the root refers to a place name, Shalem, in the territory of Shechem. In this unit, Yannai explores multiple nuances of this lexical root, rendered in translation as: "perfect," "perfected," and "fulfilled." Building on the associations of Jacob with Israel and Shalem with Jerusalem, Yannai crafts a poem in which Jacob's return takes on national-redemptive overtones. He achieves this effect in part by taking advantage of the nuances of related words: he highlights distinctive facets of meaning ("perfect" versus "fulfilled") and blurs boundaries (Israel-the-patriarch becomes Israel-the-nation).[37] Furthermore, Jacob's perfection is not merely praised; it serves a purpose: he is perfect (*shalem*) and perfected (*meshullam*) in order to fulfill (*leshallem*) divine command and covenant. The dexterity with which Yannai handles the twenty-two lines, each of which repeats this root three times, reflects the poet's artistry and creativity. The choice of root and his manipulation of it, however, go beyond poetic whimsy or artistic virtuosity. Through the sheer force of repetition and reinforcement he creates a meaningfulness that both instructs and reassures.

Finally, the first *rahit* (Poem Seven[1]) for Gen 32:4 shows how Yannai could exploit the root א-ד-ם ("red," "ruddy," "Edom"), taking full advantage of its latent apocalyptic and messianic potential. Each stich of the acrostic poem ends with the word *edom/adom*. At times, this word refers to the territory of Edom or, by extension, the Roman Empire. In others, it refers to Esau, the progenitor of the Edomite nation and thereby the oppressor of Yannai's own day, or to the red of Jewish blood on Edom's hands. But in other instances, it refers to God, who is "radiant and ruddy" (צח ואדום) in Song 5:10 and who, according to Isa 63:1-2, will appear at the time

37 See discussion of this *rahit* in Chapter One.

of judgment red with the blood of Edom. The constant repetition of the same word over and over—a pattern interrupted only once, in order to make mention of the doomed town of Sodom (סדום), whose fate anticipates that of Edom as much as its sound does—lends an inexorable, drum-like quality to the messianic, apocalyptic vision of the poet.

This technique differs from punning or rhyming because it is almost exclusively the repetition of a single word. It is not, in and of itself, a clever or sophisticated poetic technique.[38] Aesthetically, however, it has force and appeal precisely because it is simple repetition: it builds upon itself with every stich, becoming in effect an anti-Edom (and thereby anti-Byzantine Roman) cheer, which quite likely involved audience participation—an inviting, intoxicating refrain anticipating eventual revenge. The word *edom* becomes, in the poet's conception, emblematic of a bloody past, an oppressed present, and a violent but triumphant future.

Old Wine in New Bottles: Quotation and Allusion

Yannai may be best understood as a "poet of the book." By Late Antiquity, Judaism was a scriptural religion, a tradition steeped in the study and explication of a single, compact, but remarkably diverse and complex literary work: the Bible. Indeed, Scripture provides the pretext, context, and vocabulary for his creativity. To a certain extent, overt references to Scripture in Yannai's *qedushta'ot* should be expected: these poems embellish the weekly Torah and Haftarah portions, so it only makes sense that they would resonate with and even quote from these subtexts. But quotations, marked and unmarked, appear *throughout* Yannai's *qedushta'ot*, drawing on numerous textual sources that become the raw material for the poet's innovative creativity. In many cases, poetic allusions carry with them latent aggadic ideas—resonances of both *peshat* (contextual meaning) and *drash* (aggadic interpretation). By Yannai's time, biblical words were no longer simple narrative or prose; rather, they conveyed layers of accrued interpretation and implied meaning. At the same time, the biblical words were powerful in their own right; in many places, Yannai uses them to evoke biblical worlds and resonances and to create theological impressions independent of ex-

38 Indeed, this kind of intensive repetition recalls the proto-rhyme of pre-classical piyyut, such as the Shofar service of Yose ben Yose. See Aharon Mirsky, *Yose ben Yose: Poems*, 2nd ed. (Jerusalem: Mosad Bialik 1991), 93–117 [Hebrew], for the text of the poems; and his essay, "The Origins of Rhyme," in *The Piyyut* (Magnes: Jerusalem, 1990), 302–14 [Hebrew].

plicitly midrashic ideas. In short, the language of the Bible provided Yannai with themes, stories, characters, and even words, but it simultaneously became the actual raw material for his creative expression.[39]

Intertexts and Allusion: Hidden in Plain Sight?

The collections of verses—the verses from the lectionary and intertexts—that follow each of the first three poems in a *qedushta* are the most obvious place to find direct quotations from Scripture in Yannai.[40] The appended verse lists, introducing the first two verses of the Torah portion and the first verse of the haftarah, suggest prose origins of piyyut in midrash, but they also provide a textual key for unlocking allusions in the poems themselves.[41] At the same time, the narrative and interpretive content of the poems help shape how the verse anthologies should be read.

A lengthy quotation will help display the complex interrelation between Scripture and piyyut—the interdependence created by Yannai's use of intertextuality. Let us, then, consider the opening poem of Yannai's *qedushta* for *Lekh lekha* (Gen 12:1); although a few lines are fragmentary, the vivid imagery and memorable allusions make this a good place to begin. The complete *magen* (Poem One) is presented below:

A lover amidst Your enemies, You acquired // A creature You endowed, allowed to create

---

39 See William Scott Green and Jacob Neusner, *Writing with Scripture: The Authority and Uses of the Hebrew Bible in the Torah of Formative Judaism* (Minneapolis: Fortress Press, 1989). Also see Boyarin, *Intertextuality and the Reading of Midrash.* The terminology of "intertext" employed here derives from Boyarin's analysis of midrash as an act of "co-citation"—that is, a new understanding that emerges from the juxtaposition of biblical quotations.

The treatment of intertextuality in the present chapter is rudimentary and should be taken as indicating how important this aspect of payyetanic creativity is; piyyut has not yet received as much serious treatment as biblical intertextuality has (in the works of Michael Fishbane, Ben Sommer, Bernard Levinson, and Richard Hayes, among others) or as much as medieval and modern Hebrew literature have (as in the writings of Dan Pagis, Chana Kronfeld, and Ziva Ben-Porat). But, as the following analyses will indicate, classical piyyut provides a rich repository of textual tradition for scholars of Jewish intertextuality; this is an area of Piyyut Studies that merits substantial attention.

40 See Chapter One for a delineation of the formal aspects discussed here, and Appendix I for an outline of the standard *qedushta.*

41 Mirsky, in particular, has argued persuasively for the origins of piyyut in midrash; see his monograph *Formal Foundations of Piyyut,* as well as his essay "Open with that which Concludes," *The Piyyut* (Magnes: Jerusalem, 1990), 181–201 [Hebrew]. See Chapter Three of this volume for a discussion of the relationships among piyyut and other forms of aggadic writing, including midrash.

Radiant among those dwelling in darkness You perceived // The ways of his heart You fathomed

Thus like an only daughter You led him // and like a little sister You drew him near
Clear amidst the clouded when You saw him // like sweet-talking a lass, You enticed him

They burdened ... without ... // You imbued him with a portion of Your power
Because You were so close... // Therefore, with a promise, You said to him, "Go forth!"

As it is written, "The Lord said to Abram, Go forth from your land and from your kindred and from your father's house to the land that I will show you" (Gen 12:1)
And it is said: "Pay heed, O daughter, and see; incline your ear, and forget your father's house" (Ps 45:11)
And it is said: "And let the king be aroused by your charms, for he is your lord; bow down to him" (Ps 45:12)
And it is said: "Draw me after you and let us run! The king has brought me to his chambers; let us exult and rejoice in you! Let us extol your lovemaking beyond wine! Rightly do they love you" (Song 1:4)
...
And it is said: "In all your ways acknowledge Him and He will make your pathways straight" (Prov 3:6)

Our pathways may You set firm / and our hearts may You discern / and... may You shield!
Blessed are You, O Shield of Abraham!

The verse quotations included within this unit are clearly labeled; the poet intended them to be recognized as explicit citations of Scripture. Each is prefaced by a prosaic introductory phrase: "as it is written" (*ka-katuv*) introduces the lemma (in this poem, the first verse of the Torah portion), while "as it is said" (*ve-ne'emar*) precedes each of the subsequent supporting intertexts. Strictly speaking, these verses interrupt the poetry. Viewed in isolation, anthologies of verses such as those listed after the *magen* poem strongly resemble the intertexts that we find in *midrashim*, particularly the form called a *petiḥta*—indeed, Ps 45:11-12 are *petiḥta* verses in *GenR* 39:1

and exegetical verses in *Tanḥumah* and *Tanḥumah Buber Lekh lekha* 3—which suggests that in this case, the poet was drawing on an established exegetical tradition. In its most basic form, midrash arises from the juxtaposition of two verses to be read simultaneously; each verse reveals new insight about the other, which the exegete then articulates. The anthologies of verses embedded in the poem above display this process in its most basic state: the sources are juxtaposed but the exegesis only implied. As in midrash, the lemma and intertexts are meant to be read together; the intertexts interpret the lemma and, in a manner of speaking, while the verses are from disparate locations in Scripture, they exist simultaneously for the later exegetes. This form of intertextuality strongly connects piyyut to midrash; the difference, as noted in Chapter One, lies in the fact that in midrash, the connections between lemma and intertext are generally elucidated, while in piyyut, the same interpretation and effects are achieved by juxtaposition.

The anthologies of verses that appear in the *qedushta* also strongly resemble the litanies of verses in the High Holy Day liturgy, particularly the *selihot* compositions.[42] The *seliḥot* occupy a middle space between poetry and prose, resembling in particular the works of the pre-classical *payyetanim* like Yose ben Yose. The earliest piyyutim (such as the writings of Yose ben Yose and the *aleinu* prayer—all works composed for the High Holidays) include concatenation of verses at significant junctures. Each genre uses biblical texts in different ways, however. In the *seliḥot*, the verses are of central importance—they possess the almost theurgic power to remind the deity of His promises to forgive—while in the piyyutim, whether pre-Classical or Classical, the poetry dominates while the verses appear to

---

42 See Laura Lieber, "Confessing from A–Z: Penitential Themes in Early Synagogue Poetry," in *Penitential Prayer: Origins, Development, and Impact*, vol. 3 (eds., Mark J. Boda, Daniel K. Falk, and Rodney Werline; Society of Biblical Literature: Atlanta, 2008), 99–125; and, on the topic of prayers that are actually composed of biblical verses (*florilegia*), see Ruth Langer, "Biblical Texts in Jewish Prayers: Their History and Function," in *Jewish and Christian Liturgy and Worship: New Insights into its History and Interaction*, Jewish and Christian Perspectives Series 15; eds. Albert Gerhards and Clemens Leonhard; Leiden, Boston: Brill, 2007), 63–90. More generally, see James Kugel, ed., *Prayers that Cite Scripture* (Cambridge, Mass.: Harvard University Center for Jewish Studies: Harvard University Press, 2006) and Newman, *Praying by the Book*, especially the article by Shulamit Elizur, "The Use of Biblical Verses in Hebrew Liturgical Poetry," 83–100. Intertexts are common in the work of pre-classical poets, such as Yose ben Yose, whose Shofar-cycle embellishes the verses that form the core of the Shofar service, while his Avodah poems incorporate key passages from the Mishnah. Yannai's works allude to rabbinic sources but only quote biblical verses in full.

embellish and enrich the poet's words. Nevertheless, for each kind of composition, the quotation of verses remains significant, an essential part of the form. As such, the role of quotations in Yannai's *qedushtaʾot* must not be taken for granted or written off as simple generic convention.

Anthologies of verses are not, in and of themselves, poetry, even when the poet has taken many of the verses from biblical poetry such as the Psalms. In their new context, they remain quotations, not compositions. Nor are such groupings midrash *per se*: text and explication are present, but in a sort of raw state and not in the clear, linear fashion of a prose text. Nor are they exactly prayers—they precede the benediction but are buffered on either side by poetic lines and suggest interpretation more than petition.[43] The function of these lines in the poetry, then, is open to interpretation. Are they trace reminders of a prose (midrashic) origin of parts of the *qedushta*? Or are they hints dropped to reward or challenge the learned? Perhaps elements of both ideas can be affirmed. On the one hand, the presence of lists of verses in the middle of a poetic unit makes sense because of the profoundly midrashic nature of the poems. Yannai displays a deep familiarity with aggadic traditions, both in content and in methods of reading, which were still fluid and crystallizing in his era. At the same time, because these verses demand active engagement from the audience in order to make sense, they represent something of an intellectual challenge or game. Finally, however, these verses, stated in isolation, have a peculiar power of their own, which in turn enriches and deepens poetic lines that precede, follow, or allude to them. The content of the poem strongly suggests, implies, or assumes an interpretation of the lemma and intertexts, but the poet leaves it to his audience to take the final step of piecing all the parts together and hearing their echo in surrounding lines. In this sense, piyyutim demand intellectual engagement—a complement to the likely participatory engagement found in the later poems.

In the example from the *qedushta* for Gen 12:1 given above, Yannai uses biblical language to retell the story of Abraham's call. The poet presents a bold and dramatic scenario, creating and exploiting a variety of tensions in his build-up to the quotation of the biblical summons itself. In the first

43 If we were to understand the congregation to actually be "praying" these verses, we would perhaps understand them to be in violation of *y. Ber.* 1:8, 3d, which asserts, "One may not recite a biblical verse as a blessing." I would assert, however, that these verses were not "prayed" but rather functioned rhetorically and exegetically in the narrative context of the piyyut—closer akin to midrash than a liturgical litany.

stanza, the poet describes Abraham as a bright light piercing through the darkness of his era. He is no mere mortal but a partner with God in creation. The second stanza eroticizes the relationship. Abraham's charms—his purity in a polluted world—lead to his seduction; knowledge leads to intimacy. Sealing the union with the gift of power, in the third stanza God finally speaks to Abraham the opening words of the *sidra*—"Go forth!"—Yannai's elegant (despite being expected) transition to the quotation from Gen 12:1. The verbs in the stanzas describe a clear progression: acquisition, reflection, proximity, union, adornment, speech. Most of these words have overtones of both marriage and covenant. The language itself, however, teases the reader, naggingly familiar yet not from the Torah portion itself. Some of the allusions are clarified, solidified, by the quotations that follow these bold stanzas. The imagery of the "daughter" and the vocabulary of beauty come from Ps 45:11-12. The language of "drawing" Abraham into Canaan echoes Song 1:4. These verses are not organized around an explicit or obvious theme-word but around the opening of the Torah portion. The collection of verses from Ps 45, the Song of Songs, and Proverbs, must all be read in light of Gen 12:1 and the poem in which the quotations are embedded. These are thus not simple, loose collections of verses—some formal obligation to be met or anthology organized purely by internal logic—but are, instead, essential components of the poem and integral to assembling meaning from its words. They deepen the texture of the language and draw the audience in, engaging it in active participation. And they imbue Yannai's allusive vocabulary with depth. The audience does not hear midrash; it generates and understands it from the materials and context the poet has provided. The verses make sense only when the person hearing them connects all the dots.

Allusions to verses *not* in the cluster of intertexts also pepper Yannai's poems, and these also work to draw the audience into the experience of the composition. Indeed, as the following analysis of the *magen* for Gen 12:1 will show, Yannai so saturates his poetry with allusions—or, perhaps, readers become so attuned to allusions that they hear them everywhere—that every glance at his poetry reveals layer upon layer of new meaning generated by fleeting resonances.

At their most obvious, and accessible, these allusions resonate in subtle ways with texts that the poet explicitly quotes elsewhere, adding a depth of texture to the lines—a sensation of richness and resonance at a less overtly intellectualized level. For example, in Isa 41:8, God refers to Abraham as

His lover, a resonance which, if heard, deepens the nuances of the language of the quotation from Ps 45, which appears as an actual intertext—a level of implicit midrash. Song 8:8 (to which Yannai alludes) refers to a "little sister," highlighting the role of Abraham as a "young woman" about to be wed and resonating with the quotation from Song 1:4 that appears as an intertext. And Prov 22:6 describes leading or training a child, implying that God—as the male lover in Song 1:4—will lead Abraham as a teacher as well as a lover.[44] These allusions are not superficial embellishments, however. For instance, Yannai alters the verse from Prov 22 to say "lead a *lass* (*naʿarah)* in the way *she* ought to go"—a subtle but significant change from Prov 22:6, which uses the word *naʿar* ("lad"). In order to maintain the feminized imagery of Abraham rooted in the use of Ps 45, the poet adapts the secondary text as necessary. The allusions are active, not passive; the words are not simply lifted, but shaped. We cannot know how audible these allusions would be in a performed context; it is possible that some deeply learned members of the community would not only hear but appreciate the fleeting references, while to others it might have simply sounded "elevated," "right," or merely pleasant.

As short as the *magen* poem quoted above is, we can still mine from within it further allusions. For example, the idea of "following the way of one's heart" occurs in Isa 57:17 and Prov 7:25, where it is negative, and in Prov 23:19, where it describes the possibility of doing good. If these allusions are heard, the drama of the poem intensifies: Abraham, standing at a critical juncture in his personal (and national) history, must act decisively, and his choice will have significant positive or negative consequences. Which path will he follow? Of course, the soundness and goodness of Abraham's heart aligns him with the wise youth of Prov 23, but the ambiguity of the phrase creates a dramatic tension nonetheless. This network of unquoted allusions add much depth to the poem beyond the "prooftexting" quotation from Prov 3:6 that Yannai actually cites. The quoted text is the obvious source for the imagery of Abraham's "straight pathways" and one that speaks bluntly to the entire audience. But the unquoted texts—the allusions—add a knowing resonance to the line for the satisfaction of those with the knowledge to hear it. In Yannai's poetry, there

---

44 It is possible, of course, that one of these verses is missing from the damaged section of the ms., indicated above by ellipses. Nevertheless, the phenomenon described here holds true of Yannai's *qedushtaʾot* in general.

is always a deeper level of meaning. His works appeal to ears both dulled and profoundly attuned.

Indeed, closer examination of the language of the *magen* quoted above suggests the presence of even more deeply embedded allusions, echoes buried much deeper than the anthologies of intertexts and their charged vocabulary and overtones. Often these reverberations rely on the richness of a single word or phrase and exist as much in the mind of the hearer as that of the poet. For example, the language of acquisition and creation in the first line of the poem (both from the root ק-נ-ה) hints at Gen 14:19, which describes God as "creator (*qoneh*) of heaven and earth"—language found in the Palestinian Jewish version of the Amidah (and preserved in its shortened form, the *magen avot*, still present in modern rites). God created the world; now He is creating His special people. Even more obliquely, this language hints at rabbinic traditions that depict Abraham as a co-creator with God (based on the enigmatic language of Gen 12:5, in which Abram brings with him on his journey "the soul(s) they had made in Haran").[45] Finally, *qinyan* ("acquisition") is a rabbinic term for marriage—a nuance the *eros* of the subsequent stanzas amplifies.

The imagery of "radiance," in turn, anticipates Abraham's epithet "the Ezrahite" (from the root ז-ר-ח), which itself depends on rabbinic interpretations of Ps 89:1, "A *maskil* of Eitan the Ezrahite" (Eitan, lit. "the brave one," is a rabbinic epithet for Abraham). The phrase "with the might of Your power" (*be-koaḥ ḥelakh*) echoes the phrase "power to make might" (*koaḥ laʿasot ḥayl*) in Deut 8:18, which states: "Then you shall remember the Lord, your God, because it is He who gives you the power to make might."[46] Deuteronomy speaks generally; Abraham offers a specific example of one whose power comes directly from the divine source. Even more strikingly, this same phrase recalls the "mighty power"(*koaḥ ḥayl*) mentioned in 2 Chron 26:13, a much more obscure allusion, stating: "And at their command was an army of three hundred and seven thousand five hundred, who made war with mighty power, to help the king against the enemy." If this specific allusion was caught by a particularly astute member of Yannai's audience, in the context of this poem, the Chronicles verse would take on an allegorical air: Abraham, who loves God amidst God's

45 See notes to translation of the *qedushta* for Gen 12:1.

46 In the context of Deut 8:18, *ḥayl* probably means "wealth" or "substance" rather than "power," but in the *qedushta*, the complete range of nuance is invoked.

enemies, is adorned with mighty power by God in order to help God—the King—achieve victory over His enemies.

These poems not only borrow language but use it to generate unfolding levels of significance—resulting in both new richness within the poem, and new levels of meaning when the biblical verse is again encountered. The deeply embedded presence of allusion and interpretation transform both the poetry and the biblical lemma—the poet creates layers upon layers of references, hints, and interpretations, and in a dynamic rather than passive framework. The poems become almost inexhaustible: the closer one studies them, the more nuance, depth, and texture one perceives.

Text cannot be separated from interpretation—certainly not in the rabbinic context—and this poem provides a vivid example of this truism. In general, the imagery in this poem is both bold and engaging, as the poet re-imagines God's summons to the patriarch in unexpectedly romantic and triumphant language. In terms of content, Yannai's conceit closely resembles traditions scattered throughout prose aggadic collections, including works such as *Genesis Rabbah, Midrash ha-Gadol*, and *Tanḥumah*, which interpret Ps 45 in light of the Abraham tradition, just as Yannai does.[47] Yannai's *language*, however, is extensively biblical—a carefully crafted patchwork of phrases that make sense on their own but can be traced back to other contexts (not just the psalm and Genesis), thereby deepening the poem's meaning. At the same time, the poem itself generates understandings of the biblical phrases that differ from the biblical *peshat*; using biblical words, the poet coaxes the audience to generate interpretations that resemble commonplace aggadic understandings. For example, "the king" in Ps 45, Song 1:4 and 2 Chron. 26:13 becomes *the* King, God. The female lover in Song 1:4 now speaks with the voice of Abraham, giving the affirmative response absent in the biblical text. The lovely, worthy princess of Ps 45 who leaves her father's house to wed the king becomes an emblem of Abraham, who leaves his father's house to follow the King. The poem alludes to the language of some of these verses but creates the interpretation of others. The two pieces—poem and verse anthology—com-

47 See Chapter Three for a discussion of the relationship between Yannai and the prose rabbinic corpus; for the sake of continuity, this poem provides an example in that chapter, as well. It is important to note that while Yannai may predate some of the written midrashic collections, the shared traditions may well predate both kinds of sources. *Midrash ha-gadol*, for example, is dated to twelfth-century Yemen but contains traditions that probably predate or are contemporary with Yannai.

plement each other, with Scripture enriching the language of the poem, and the poem deepening the meaning of the texts. The motifs may be familiar, but the fact that the poems are created out of Scripture itself lends them a unique potency.

This single example, examined at length, suggests the complex relationship between Yannai and Scripture. The language of the poem is biblical but does not biblicize; that is, Yannai makes use of biblical words, phrases, and verses, but he does not try to write in their style, or even hew to their grammar. In creating his poetry, he borrows freely from biblical prose, wisdom literature, and prophecy, as well as the Psalms and other poetic works. Indeed, his rhetoric is profoundly indebted to midrash for form and content.[48] His poetry interprets the biblical texts more than it imitates earlier poetic styles. Yannai's aesthetic is payyetanic and rabbinic, both in terms of structure and dense allusiveness; neither in form, sound, or style does it resemble the Psalms or other biblical period poems.[49] Nevertheless, while much of the content and many of the techniques of these poems are "rabbinic," the rhetoric differs from midrash: rather than developing his interpretation through linear exegesis—carefully delineating the connections between lemma and intertexts—the poet first anticipates interpretations through allusions and then elucidates by simple quotation. As a result, while the poetic units can be comprehended in isolation (in terms of language), they are confusing and lacking depth if one cannot decode the allusions.

Quotations and overt allusions are the most obvious use of Scripture in the *qedushta*. Yannai invoked the biblical text in many other ways, as well—shorter, more fleeting references that nonetheless create much of the rich texture of Yannai's work. The various uses of such brief allusions—biblical words, phrases, and images—also need to be teased out, classified, and scrutinized for significance, however, and that is what we will now endeavor to do, in brief.

Hearing the Echoes: The Fleeting Quotation

The groupings of verses that follow the first three poems are the most obvious place to look for direct quotations from Scripture in Yannai's piyyutim, but their function, particularly when understood as part of a

48 See Mirsky, *Formal Foundations of Piyyut*; and Chapter Three.

49 Contrast, for example, the Dead Sea Scrolls *hodayot*, which do biblicize. See n. 2, above.

performed piece, is hardly simple. The Torah portion and haftarah provide not only the themes and concerns but the very language around which these opening units of the poem are structured. Each poem works its way inexorably towards the opening words of the appropriate verse, as well as the theme of the blessing. The destinations, both lectionary and liturgical, are known in advance but the question of how the poet will find his way there remains. In this creation of intellectual tension, the opening poems closely resemble the midrashic *petiḥta*, a stylized form of discourse that begins with an unlikely "verse from afar" (usually from the Writings section of the Hebrew Bible) and works its way, with much cleverness and often false starts, towards the exegetical verse.[50] The opening poems of a *qedushta*, like the *petiḥta*, engage the audience in the intellectual game of, "We know where he is going—but how will he get there?" Unlike the composer of a *petiḥta*, however, the payyetan has *two* goals: he must reach both the appropriate verse from the lectionary *and* the theme of the blessing. In some cases, the transition from poem to quotation is very brief; the *magen* (Poem One) for Gen 11:1 ends with the word "lips" (Poem One, line12), which anticipates the same word in Gen 11:1 itself. In the *magen* for Gen 15:1, however, the entire final stich—"I am a shield to you; fear not!"—alludes both to the verse the poet is about to quote and also to the *ḥatimah* of the benediction (which derives from this verse!).

There are, of course, exceptions to this pattern; the *meḥayyeh* (Poem Two) for Gen 44:18, for instance, ends with a quotation that itself seems rooted in Gen 44:18—not vs. 19, as we would expect. This unusual backtracking serves a rhetorical function, however. The quotation from Gen 44:19 that follows the body of the poem blends seamlessly into the poem's narration. The lemma is not simply supporting the poem but has been integrated into the poet's retelling of the story. Yannai apparently felt free to violate convention in subtle ways in order to dramatize his own poetic narrative. As much as his piyyutim resemble midrash in terms of technique, and the Bible in terms of lexicon and language, Yannai has created something wholly unique with his *qedushta'ot*. The poet uses borrowed tools but the creations are his own.

Indeed, while quotations are most obvious and expected in the first

50 The similarities between the opening poetic units and the midrashic *petiḥta* are further developed in Chapter Three. The overlap between Yannai's intertexts and the opening verses of midrashic *petiḥtot* merits further study.

three units of a *qedushta*, Yannai uses Scripture in a variety of ways, and references permeate his poems. Quotations can be as fleeting as an epithet—"lover" for Abraham (from Isa 41:8), "the pure one" for Jacob (based on Gen 25:27), "the comely one" for Joseph (derived from Gen 39:6), and so forth—or as extensive as whole verses, such as, "There is a time for peace and a time for war" (Eccl 3:8), which opens the fragmentary *rahit* (Poem Seven) for Gen 14:1. In Poem Six for Gen 32:4, Yannai describes the confrontation between Jacob and Esau by weaving together a patchwork of quotations from Genesis, Leviticus, Proverbs and Psalms. In the *rahit* for Gen 28:10, each stanza begins with a quotation from a different source (ranging from Genesis to Micah to Psalms), selected for and unified by their repetition of the name Jacob.[51] The consistent repetition of that single word suggests that "Jacob" functioned as a kind of refrain, possibly inviting audience response.

A very different use of quotation occurs in the dramatic retelling of Dan 7:7-8 found in the second and third *r'hitim* (Poems Seven^2 and 7^3) for Gen 32:4. In part, these units dramatize the biblical story of Daniel's night vision, not only quoting from the biblical text but using biblical Aramaic throughout the poem to create a sensation of "new" Scripture being written. Allusion, quotation, and originality blend so thoroughly that they can become difficult to distinguish from one another.

Beyond Quotation: Lemma-as-Scaffold

In the previous example, quotations and allusions were often marked by their brevity. While certain epithets may repeat within a *qedushta*, and while many allusions are later fleshed out by fuller quotations of whole verses, in general, the references pass quickly by and only the astute listener will perceive many of them. Such is not always the case, however. Yannai often uses certain words or phrases repeatedly in his poems, either in a single unit or throughout a *qedushta*. By and large, those thematic tropes are quotations from the first or second verse of the Torah portion—the lemmas of the first two units.

The piyyut for Gen 31:3 provides a particularly clear illustration of this *sidra*-based theme-word device. The *qedushta* revolves around the lan-

---

51 This *qedushta* is fragmentary, with only the final stanzas of the unusual *rahit*, the *silluq*, and the *qedushah* preserved. As a result, we can't know if the earlier units of the poem were as unusual as the *rahit*, or if they anticipated it in some specific way.

guage of "Return to the land of your ancestors"—God's words to Jacob in the opening verse of the Torah portion. Yannai weaves the language of that verse—"Return (*shuv*) to the land of your ancestors!" (Gen 31:3)—throughout the piyyut. The *magen* (Poem One) concludes with the word, "Return!" transitioning to the series of texts that interweave images of restoration and the eternal gift of the land. The *meḥayyeh* (Poem Two) continues the theme of restoration, as the patriarch spreads the good news to his wives. The *meshallesh* (Poem Three), which focuses on the theme of trusting in God, concludes with a series of puns on the root ש-ו-ב, as do the two verses—Jer 30:10 (the haftarah) and 31:21 (possibly an alternative haftarah[52])—that follow it. The motif of return reappears strongly in the *asiriyyah* (Poem Five), where Yannai increases the drama of the divine-human dialogue by incorporating quotations from Gen 28:15 and 28:21 to underscore the long-standing promises each has made to come back from exile. The final line of the fifth poem, discussed above, creates a tremendously dense sound-play on a variety of roots, including a twofold repetition of ש-ו-ב. Poem Six, a lovely and remarkable ode to Zion, probably had the quotation from Gen 31:3 as a repeated incipit, with the phrase, "Return to the land of your ancestors," prefacing each stanza—which then describes the virtues of the Land. The first *rahit* (Poem Seven[1], which opens with the phrase "And I will be with you," also from Gen 31:3) concludes with the words, "You will return (*tashuv*) to your birthplace in peace" while the second *rahit* (Poem Seven[2]) opens with "You will bring us back (*teshiveinu*) from foreign gates." The *silluq* (Poem Eight) uses the root ש-ו-ב three times in four lines. And the final poem, the *qedushah* (Poem Nine), concludes with a three-fold litany on the images of physical and spiritual return.

The motif of return—Jacob's return from Aram, Israel's return from Exile, the penitent's return in repentance—so permeates this poem that it is difficult to determine whether the biblical verse came first or whether it was simply a pretext for the extended meditation. Yannai adduces numerous verses that incorporate the language of return or intensify the themes of restoration along the way, but Gen 31:3 provides a consistent subtext and structure. The language of the opening verse of the *sidra* permeates the piyyut like a theme-word.

---

52 See Natan Fried, "Alternative Haftarot in the Piyyutim of Yannai and the other early Payyetanim," *Sinai* 61 (1966–67): 268–90 [Hebrew].

In this example, a single root (ש-ו-ב), taken from the first verse of the *sidra*, unifies the poem as a whole. Through this rhetorical technique, Yannai implicitly weaves the opening words of the Torah portion, with their optimistic command of restoration, into the fabric of his *qedushta*. Is every use of the root ש-ו-ב some kind of allusion? Not really—that root is too commonplace to restrict in such a way. And yet its repetition lends it a force that its connection to the Torah portion only strengthens. In Yannai's poetry, a word as simple as "return" takes on complicated, nuanced, intertextual resonances. Words are never *just* words in his poetry.

Speaking Scripturally: Creation of Dialogue

The previous example shows how Yannai would select a single theme, encapsulate it in a single word, and integrate it into his poem, unifying and grounding the *qedushta* in the language of the Torah portion. The example also indicates another clever way Yannai incorporates direct quotations into his poems: the quotation—and occasional invention—of dialogue. In the case of the *qedushta* for Gen 31:3, the phrase "Return to the land of your ancestors" appears multiple times, functionally introducing the divine voice back into the poem at key moments. In other examples, Yannai uses such quotations in a more fleeting manner, such as when God says, "Let us go down" in Poem Five of the *qedushta* for Gen 11:1 (line 12)—a statement framed by Yannai as God's response to a fictional quotation from the tower-builders, "Let us go up." When Yannai blends the quotation from Gen 11:7 with the creative pseudo-quotation, he creates a symmetry between human action and heavenly reaction, all of which amplifies the theology of measure-for-measure that recurs throughout the *qedushta*. Scripture provides part of his language; the wit of the line lies in his response to the biblical quotation.

Yannai does not always invent dialogue, however. Sometimes he weaves it out of disparate biblical verses. For instance, the series of statements in the *asiriyyah* (Poem Five) for Gen 16:1 consists of a pastiche of quotations. To create the dialogue, Yannai juxtaposes the divine promises given to Abraham in Gen 16:5 ("Thus shall it be!"—a reference to Abraham's future progeny) and Gen 18:18 ("Indeed, it shall surely be"—a reference to the great nation that will arise from Abraham) with Sarah's plea of "He has closed me up" (rendered me barren) from Gen 16:2, the second verse of the Torah portion. The result is an artificially created, biblical-but-not-biblical conversation among God, Abraham, and Sarah—"biblical" because each statement is taken directly from Scripture, but "not biblical" because Yannai has lifted them from their original contexts and juxtaposed them in ways not found anywhere else. Indeed, part of the intellectual challenge and playfulness in deciphering Yannai at the level of his use of language derives from hearing *allusions* embedded within *quotations.* We see this, for example, when Sarah refers to herself as "a bundle of myrrh" in Poem Six (line 18) of the *qedushta* for Gen 16:1—an allusion to Song 1:13—and when, in the *qedushta* to Gen 44:18, Yannai seamlessly blends actual quotations with invented dialogue. Within a single poetic unit, Yannai's characters may speak the language of the lemma, quote other parts of Scripture, allude to a text, or utter words invented by the poet's pen. Through this technique, Yannai's *qedushtaʾot* bring the stories of the Torah portions—and often their very language—vividly to life.

Repetitions of Scripture

The term "quotation" in many places actually misrepresents the specific use Yannai makes of the biblical subtext of his poems. In a number of instances, Yannai selects specific key biblical words and phrases—again, usually from the first verse of the Torah portion—and uses them as essential structural elements in specific poems. We see this particularly with the *rahit* poems because they are generally the most intricately-patterned units of a *qedushta* and therefore the most likely to possess such a structuring device.[53] The two *r'hitim* (Poems 7^1 and 7^2) for Gen 44:18 exemplify this technique. In the first *rahit*, each line begins with, "Then he approached"—the opening word (*va-yiggash*) of the *sidra*:

Then he approached:
the one who plows, the hot wrath of … sharp his sword
Then he approached:
he who tears prey[54], casting off the good sense of his purity[55]
Then he approached:
Judah descended ... fear of his pride[56]

(Poem Seven[1], lines 1–3)

53 See Chapter One for a discussion of the form of the *rahit.*

54 That is, the lion (Ps 7:3, 22:4, etc.)—Judah.

55 "Purity" in the sense of mercy, kindness, humility—the attributes of the meek.

56 This line and the following recall the themes of the *qedushta* to Gen 38, in which Judah's new-found humility (there when he admitted to his guilt in the affair with Tamar, here when he expresses remorse for the fate of Joseph) results in an increase in his honor.

Through this repetition of the first word of the Torah portion, the initial, singular action becomes an extended narration of the dramatic scenario. For the second *rahit*, Yannai takes two phrases from within that opening verse—"He said, `Please, my lord… do not'"—and using these quotations as a framework, he creates a new poem of entreaty:

Please, my lord, a father *do not* cast away;
Please, my lord, a son *do not* seek!
Please, my lord, a kid *do not* steal;
Please, my lord, justice *do not* thrust aside![57] (7^2:1-4)

Judah's action—petitionary approach—structures the first *rahit*, while his words—"Please, my lord, do not…"—are reinvented and recreated, expanded and made even more dramatic in the second. Yannai's creative reuse of specific phrases is even more striking in the double *rahit* for Gen 15:1, where the phrase, "Fear not, I am" from Gen 15:1, broken into two halves—"*Fear not…*" and "*I am…*"—structures the first *rahit*, while the phrase "Your reward shall be very great," also from Gen 15:1 and also broken into two pieces—"*Your reward…*" and "*Shall be very great…*"—structures the second *rahit*.[58] The biblical quotations introduce new poems built on their language. Far from being fleeting allusions audible only to the most learned listeners, these quotations become integral to the very structure of the poetic units. Yannai uses the biblical language not as an end in and of itself, but as a starting point for original composition.

The repetitions of the key phrases from the Torah portion within the complex formal structure of the *rahit* (each example noted above contains

---

Judah's maturation is one reason the most important messianic figure—that of the Davidic line—will spring from Judah's lineage rather than from that of another brother (e.g., Joseph) who might seem, superficially, more worthy.

57 Rabinovitz reads the verb here as תעוות ("pervert"), but this violates the pattern of the poem and is not clear in the MS. The verb present here in the MS תחדוף both interrupts the pattern of the poem and is an otherwise unknown root. Most probably the verb should be corrected to the familiar תדחוף ("to push off, drive, hasten").

58 Separating two words joined in biblical rhetoric and then interpreting them similarly yet separately in proximity is a standard midrashic rhetorical device also found in the liturgy. The density and intensity of the use of this rhetorical device, not the device itself, distinguish piyyut, liturgy, and midrash from one another. The similarities among these three forms of writing suggests just how blurred the distinctions can be. See R. Sarason, "Midrash in Liturgy"; and Mirsky, *Formal Foundations of Piyyut.*

a complete alphabetic acrostic) transform the original biblical messages by intensifying them eleven-fold, or even twenty-two-fold. Both the examples given above—and these examples are typical of the *rahit*—reflect a variant on Yannai's tendency to break apart biblical word pairs, separating two words joined in biblical rhetoric (e.g., Ephraim and Manasseh, Justice and Mercy, etc.) and interpreting them separately yet in proximity.[59] In some ways, Yannai's aesthetic, in which word pairs are broken apart, is the antithesis of biblical poetry, which is structured on parallelism. Viewed from another angle, however, it is a classic midrashic-rabbinic amplification of scriptural poetics. Yannai takes this established midrashic trope and amplifies it formally by adding elements such as acrostic and fixed rhythmic patterns. Taking symmetrical or antithetical pairs from the biblical text and then breaking them apart and reading them according to the norms of rabbinic exegesis, Yannai adds an element of performance and artistry that extends the biblical language out of the biblical period and into his own. If we go one step further and imagine these repetitions as having an element of audience participation, then this technique draws the congregation into the act of exegesis at the end of the poem, just as the juxtaposition of lemma and intertexts did at the beginning. Through this technique, biblical words breathe with new life.

Epithets and Metonymy

Epithets (כינויים) are a final, specific kind of quotation that deserves mention. The use of epithets and cognomina—allusive shorthand references to biblical characters (including the deity) that highlight specific aspects of their personality, history, or fate—typify payyetanic style. Indeed, these epithets are a distinctly payyetanic form of poetic metonymy, and critical editions of piyyutim will often include a special index of these terms.[60] It is far more common, and elegant, for a *payyetan* to refer to characters obliquely by epithets than explicitly by name. In some cases, the poet specifies

59 See Yahalom, *Poetry and Society*, 154–60. Yahalom, who regards this kind of device as one of the origins of rhyme, cites as an example the way Yannai breaks up the phrase "iron against iron" from Prov 27:17 in the fifth poem of the Gen 44:18 *qedushta*. Mirsky's essay, "Open with that which Concludes," delineates the relationship between the *rahit*'s formal structure and midrashic tropes. See also the discussion in Chapter Three.

60 For example, Ezra Fleischer, *The Poems of Shelomo Ha-Bavli: Critical Edition with Introduction and Commentary* (Jerusalem: Academy of Sciences and Humanities, 1973); Wout J. van Bekkum, *Hebrew Poetry from Late Antiquity: Liturgical Poems of Yehudah* (Leiden: Brill, 1998).

and clarifies an epithet; for example, "'Sister'—what Rachel was called" (*qedushta* to Gen 30:22, Poem Six, line 1). In this instance perhaps Yannai is implicitly emphasizing that the barren matriarch was not, as yet, called "mother." In other cases, the epithet is delineated in an almost midrashic way, such as in the *qedushta* for Gen 32:4, when the poet describes Joseph as "a man compared (*nimshal*) to a flickering flame" (Poem Five, line 1), drawing on imagery from Obad 18 in the haftarah. Joseph is the logical referent for "the man," but Yannai does not go so far as to spell it out for his audience. Building on this same set of analogies, Yannai later describes Esau simply as "one compared (*medummeh*) to straw"—clearly anticipating the conflagration to follow the brothers' meeting. More often, the epithets are simply used without explanation: "Zoan" and "No-Ammon" refer to Egypt (based on Num 13:11 and Nah 3:8, respectively); "the lion" to Judah (drawing on Gen 49:24); "the ox" is Joseph (based on Deut 33:17); "the barren one" is an epithet for Zion (taken from Isa 54:1); and so forth. Often these epithets can be found in targumic and midrashic literature as well (where, generally, the referent is explicated), but in Yannai's poems the identities are assumed rather than explicated.[61]

These nicknames, while presuming a significant and specific kind of literary competence on the part of the audience, add variety to the poems and enable the poet to introduce both vivid imagery and a tremendous amount of background with a single word or phrase. To describe Zion as "the barren one" is to evoke the whole tragic history of the city and her people (particularly the imagery from Lamentations and the Prophets), creating through sheer force of imagery and connotation a link between the bereft matriarch Sarah and her children, archetypal events of Jewish history, and the Jews of Yannai's day. By depicting Joseph as an ox and Judah as a lion, the confrontation in Genesis 44 takes on a vigor and intensity that simultaneously recalls the apocalyptic battle between Leviathan and Behemoth in Job as well as the Roman circus. Epithets are vivid and efficient, adding nuance and depth as well as drama to Yannai's poems.[62]

The use of metonymy—and the impression of palpable delight in new

---

61 See Laura Lieber, "O My Dove, Let Me See Your Face: Targum, Piyyut, and the Literary Life of the Ancient Synagogue," in *Paratext and Megatext as Channels of Jewish and Christian Traditions*, ed. August den Hollander, Ulrich Schmid, and Willem Smelik (Leiden: Brill, 2003), 109–35.

62 For a discussion of the concept of literary competence, see Culler, *Structuralist Poetics*, especially chap. 6.

coinages—so pervades Yannai (as well as his successors' works) that it is impossible to catalogue them all. Indeed, the anthologies of verses in the first *rahit* for Gen 15:1 and the second *rahit* for Gen 30:22 suggest how extensive the library of epithets could become, particularly when God is the subject: each of these units presents the reader with a complete alphabetic acrostic (both are תשר"ק, or reverse, acrostics) listing of divine epithets. The *rahit* for Gen 15:1 is written in the first person; God identifies Himself to Abraham as "your Hope," "your Guardian," "your Creator," and so forth. The second *rahit* for Gen 30:22, by way of comparison, was composed in the second person, as an address to God, who "hearkens to prayer," "remembers the barren," and "loves the pure." These veritable anthologies of metonyms, which resemble similar lists from piyyutim (or proto-piyyutim) of the anonymous period in the statutory liturgy, often draw upon biblical language. For example, in these two examples, Yannai strongly recalls the list of epithets in Ps 145 (familiarly named after its first word, "the *ashrei*") and Ps 146:6-10—both of which appear in the Morning Blessings in the daily liturgy. Indeed, the Morning Blessings (specifically, the *pesuqei d'zimra*) may be a secondary source for Yannai's language and rhetorical style—an extra layer of reference and resonance, even when the specific attributes he includes are original or drawn from diverse biblical sources. In such instances, Yannai alludes to two essential texts simultaneously: to Scripture itself, and Scripture that is already being prayed as part of the liturgy. Some epithets are verbatim quotations; some are adapted to suit specific constraints of form; and others are Yannai's own coinages, written in a style that mimics the biblical models. The distinctions can be so fine that scholars, in annotating the poems, search desperately at times for the poet's sources only to find that the source must be the poet himself. Tradition and innovation blend; the one passes for the other until, with time, the one *becomes* the other.

Conclusions

Yannai's importance and success as a poet emerge in part from his ability to mine the variety of Hebrew (biblical and otherwise) and shape it in a way that gave access to listeners at a range of levels. It is not possible to annotate his every scriptural reference. Such references—overt and oblique—so saturate Yannai's work that footnotes would quickly overwhelm our text itself. Instead, in the translations that accompany this volume, we have sought to convey a flavor of the allusiveness of the *qedushta.* And much like with audiences in antiquity, some readers will hear overtones that others will miss, although the basic meaning will (ideally) come through.

The above analysis has focused on select idiosyncrasies in Yannai's language and use of scriptural quotations. Despite this narrow concern, and the difficulty of conveying certain nuances in translation, it should be evident to the reader that Yannai, for all his citation from Scripture, viewed these texts through a rabbinic lens and participated in the emergent tradition of rabbinic exegesis. Frequently his quotations and allusions carry with them not merely the biblical context to which the quotations refer, but that biblical context as understood in accord with aggadic interpretations. The verses Yannai quotes or infers in a given *qedushta* often appear in midrashic treatments of the same material. In many cases, familiarity with rabbinic treatments of a topic is the easiest way for modern readers to contextualize and comprehend Yannai's elliptical interpretations. These *qedushtaʾot* could, indeed, be regarded as a re-biblicizing of rabbinic interpretations of Scripture. The interpretation is implicit more often than explicit, and the combination of poetic form and biblical idiom sets these works apart from other works of aggadah.[63] Although midrash is often overtly didactic in style (if not content)—teaching students how to read the text, in light of other texts—liturgical poetry serves many functions, as we have repeatedly noted. In many cases, the use of biblical texts may have functioned to draw the listeners in, requiring them to participate in the art of exegesis in the opening three poems or, more viscerally, in the verbal repetition of key biblical words in the *rahit.* While poems may explicate, they also require explication. The poet, when he does teach, instructs us subtly, working as much by juxtaposition and allusion as by direct articulation. Piyyut is a medium that both caters to and makes demands on its audience.

In the next chapter, the complex connection between Yannai's *qedushtaʾot* and classical rabbinic literature (both aggadic and liturgical) will be further explored. The broad and complicated interrelationships among these genres—all of which are ultimately in some kind of tension with the

63 The impulse to "re-biblicize" rabbinic interpretation has parallels in the *targumim* which, while not written in Hebrew, integrate aggadah into the biblical narrative as a kind of retold Scripture. It is worth noting that both *targum* and piyyut are performative texts composed for use in the synagogue context.

biblical text—will serve as the basis for a more sweeping contextualization of piyyutim in the framework of the ancient synagogue. Indeed, Yannai's creative contribution to Hebrew literature and Jewish biblical interpretation exemplifies the tremendous creativity of Judaism in Late Antiquity, intersecting with midrash, *targum*, liturgy, and art, all forms in critical periods of genesis and synthesis. Exploring Yannai's work in this multifaceted way will enable us to understand his writings as part of a significant Jewish cultural renaissance that was lived at the levels of literature, interpretation, and prayer.

Chapter Three
"New Wine—In New Bottles?": Yannai in the Byzantine World

"The synagogue poets took the gems for their pearl necklace from the midrash, and the string from the Bible"
Zunz, *Poesie*

"Liturgy, art, and preaching worked together to mediate an experience of worship. Biblical motifs, if not always particular biblical narratives, richly inform all three."
Wayne A. Meeks and Martha F. Meeks, *Reading in Christian Communities*

A Complicated Culture

As discussed above, Yannai's poems are built with and upon biblical language. Scripture gave Yannai his plots, his characters, and in many cases his specific words and phrases. But well before the Byzantine period, scriptural words had ceased to be simply a vocabulary in Judaism; then, as now, biblical language evoked layer upon layer of resonant meaning. Thus the *qedushta'ot* studied here reflect more than just an important stage in the development of Hebrew literature, although Yannai is one of the most significant early Jewish writers. These poems must also be understood as an element of the history of biblical interpretation and artifacts of the early synagogue, important both within the Jewish cultural context and as part of the larger societal matrix. Yannai was shaped by and was a shaper of the culture of exegesis in which he lived and for which he wrote. The great scholar Saul Lieberman wrote that Yannai's poems should "stand on the shelf next to the great volumes of *midrashim* and the Talmud (because that is where he belongs [כי שם הוא מקומו])."[1] Note that Lieberman does not say

1 Lieberman, "*Ḥazzanut Yannai*," 250.

piyyut—the genre as a whole—belongs alongside midrash and Talmud (although such is certainly the case), but *Yannai*, the individual *payyetan*. This hyperbole suggests how integral Yannai's poetry is in shaping our understanding of Judaism in Late Antiquity.

Our knowledge about how important aspects of this text-saturated Jewish culture developed in Byzantine society remains uncertain. The abundant but at times conflicting material and literary evidence can challenge and confound contemporary researchers, as can the impulse to draw linear connections between artifacts or the temptation to reach simple conclusions about them. Archaeologists have uncovered over a hundred synagogues in the Land of Israel and in the Diaspora from the early centuries of the Common Era, some displaying strikingly "pagan" iconography—imagery that provides a jarring contrast to stereotypes of "iconoclastic" rabbinic Judaism. Furthermore, these structures date from centuries when literary sources (Jewish and Christian) depict a Judaism that was under attack and in retreat—not undergoing a building boom or cultural renaissance. Liturgists, in turn, have reconstructed multiple Jewish rites, customs, and lectionaries, far more varied than the practices, texts, and traditions of today. Historians of Jewish art and culture, meanwhile, have worked to delineate nuances of acculturation, accommodation, and resistance on the part of a minority community that was simultaneously attracted to, repelled by, and in conflict with a majority Christian society that was, itself, ambivalent towards Judaism.[2] And literary scholars, particularly those who work in rabbinics and Christian hymnography, have spent the last century cataloguing and analyzing vast quantities of newly discovered writings, particularly liturgical poetry—including the works of Yannai—appreciating them for the light they shed on this complicated culture and period. One constant unifies all the disparate sources of evidence and scholarly approaches: the increasingly inarguable recognition that Palestinian Judaism in the Byzantine period, perhaps in response to increasing external pressure if not active oppression, experienced a tremendous

2 Population estimates for the Land of Israel in the sixth century vary, but a rough estimate sets the total population at 1,000,000 to 1,300,000. In rural areas, the population was largely Jewish or Samaritan, with Jews (centered in the Galilee) totaling around 150,000–200,000. These figures are from M. Avi-Yonah, *The Jews of Palestine* (New York: Schocken Books, 1976), 240. Note also the discussion in A. S. Jacobs, "Visible Ghosts and Invisible Demons: The Place of Jews in Early Christian Terra Sancta," in Eric Meyers, ed., *The Galilee Through the Centuries: A Confluence of Cultures* (Winona Lake: Eisenbrauns, 1999), 361.

creative upswell, a dynamic diversification often rooted in bold and innovative interpretations of Scripture. Far from being a *dark* age in which Judaism was defined by persecution and conflict, Late Antiquity is now seen as more of a *lost* age. This was a period of cultural inventiveness and synthesis, of creatively generative tensions and deeply complicated societal impulses. But it is an era waiting to be recovered by modern scholars.

Late Antiquity and the Byzantine period in Palestine (the period from roughly the late third through seventh centuries) were once regarded simply as a time when the Christian church expanded while the synagogue stagnated, a period when monolithic Rabbis (or, in some depictions, a corrupt rabbinic Patriarch) imposed their authority on a weak and dispirited community in the Galilee, while Jewish intellectual energy shifted east to the Babylonian academies.[3] Now, however, we know that these centuries witnessed the building and rebuilding of numerous synagogues, both in Palestine and in the western Diaspora, a small but significant number of them containing literary inscriptions as well as mosaics and frescoes of startling beauty and enigmatic boldness.[4] This same period, particularly in the Galilee, witnessed a flourishing of Aramaic translations (*targumim*), enriched with creative narrative embellishments and existing in tandem

---

3 The traditional association between the rise of piyyutim and external oppressive forces was long accepted as a truism. As early as the 8th century, Pirqoi ben Baboi wrote in the name of his teacher, Yehudai Gaon, that the authorities of Byzantium prohibited the statutory prayers; the piyyutim were a means for subverting this prohibition. See Louis Ginsberg, ed., *Ginzei Schechter* (New York: Jewish Theological Seminary of America, 1928–1929), 2:504–73 and 63–39 [Hebrew]. Israel Davidson and others have suggested that this is an allusion to Justinian's novella of 529 prohibiting "*deuterosis*." In the 12th century, Samau'al ibn Yahya of Fez (a Jewish convert to Islam) echoed the tradition recounted by Judah ben Barzillai of Barcelona (11th century), who located the origin of piyyutim in the oppression of the Jews. More contemporary scholarship, however, has cast doubt on the completeness of such an explanation. Piyyutim predate Justinian by several centuries, and while external pressures may have encouraged the spread of these poems, their origins are not in response to negative cultural pressures. For a presentation of the "traditional" view, with a reproduction of the Justinian novella, see Paul Kahle, *The Cairo Geniza* (London: The British Academy, 1947), 19–35. For a rebuttal of this view, see Fleischer, *Hebrew Liturgical Poetry in the Middle Ages*, 53–54. Joseph Heinemann, who sees the origin of certain piyyutim in Temple times, implicitly disagrees with the "traditional" view. More recently, see G. Stemberger, *Jews and Christians in the Holy Land: Palestine in the Fourth Century*, trans. R. Tushling (Edinburgh: T&T Clark, 2000). For a nuanced discussion of Jewish society in this period more generally, see Stuart Miller, *Sages and Commoners in Late Antique 'Erez Israel* (Tübingen: JCB Mohr [Paul Siebeck], 2006).

4 The major volume on the inscriptions, which are discussed in numerous other sources, remains J. Naveh, *On Stone and Mosaic: The Aramaic and Hebrew Inscriptions from Ancient Synagogues* (Jerusalem: Maariv, 1978) [Hebrew].

with Aramaic piyyutim—a diversity of literary evidence that suggests how Jewish culture developing in the Land of Israel was complexly multilingual and valued dynamism and diversity over conformity.[5] In Hebrew, vast, fluid traditions of rabbinic interpretation began to crystallize into written anthologies, which were eventually edited into the now-familiar volumes of aggadic midrash. During this same period, perhaps out of the same circles that produced the aggadah, the enigmatic *hekhalot* traditions of rabbinic mysticism seem to have appeared and spread. The liturgy, we now know, remained fluid, although it was slowly growing steadily more fixed. And tremendous quantities of highly inventive Hebrew poetry were composed, a literary innovation that would shape Hebrew literature for centuries as the genre known as *piyyut*.

In recent years, some scholars have hesitated to assume that all of these diverse institutions and innovations—social, liturgical, literary— were exclusively "rabbinic" in terms of orientation or leadership. While rabbinic sources display a great deal of interest in the synagogue, the constituency of the early synagogue remains uncertain. It is possible, as some writers have suggested, that groups such as the ancient priestly aristocracy vied with the emergent rabbinic movement for leadership within the Jewish community.[6] Arguing against this "revisionist" view, we should note that the rabbinic sources themselves reflect such a tremendous variety of opinions and interests that even texts and traditions that seem marginal may

5 Willem Smelik, "Orality, Manuscript Reproductions, and the Targums," in *Paratext and Megatext as Channels of Jewish and Christian Traditions*, ed. A.A. den Hollander, U. B. Schmid, and W.F. Smelik (Leiden: Brill, 2003), 49–81. Concerning the Aramaic poems, it is important to note that while these works were often included in written Targum manuscripts, they probably originated outside of the targumic performance. See Rand, "Observations on the Relationship Between JPA [Jewish-Palestinian Aramaic] and the Hebrew Piyyut Tradition—The Case of the *Kinot* [Laments]," 127–34.

6 Questions of Jewish leadership, both in society and within the synagogue communities—including the relative roles and prominence of rabbinic, priestly, and patriarchal factions, have been much refined and nuanced over recent years. Of particular value in many recent studies is the recognition of the importance of priests and priestly concerns in Byzantine Judaism, although the tendency to separate "priestly" Judaism from "rabbinic" Judaism may be overstated in some cases, as a necessary corrective to earlier pictures of Jewish society. For a selection of the most recent understandings, see Seth Schwartz, *Imperialism and Jewish Society*; also Lee Levine, *The Ancient Synagogue*, 381–498; Steven Fine, *Art and Judaism in the Greco-Roman World*, 184–205; Catherine Hezser, *The Social Structure of the Rabbinic Movement in Roman Palestine* (Tübingen: Mohr-Siebeck, 1997), 119–23, 214–25; and Stuart Miller, *Sages and Commoners in Late Antique Erez Israel*. A general overview of the societal situation can be found in the brief and accessible article by Irshai, "Confronting a Christian Empire," 180–221.

well be within the fold; textual evidence (particularly from the Land of Israel) indicates a dynamic rather than a rigid "rabbinic" Judaism—a variety of rabbinic cultures rather than a monolith.[7] It might be most accurate to say that this period witnessed the consolidation and growing prominence of what would come to be called *rabbinic tradition*—a tradition deeply engaged in priestly themes and profoundly invested in the structure and teleology of the Temple cult as well as the intellectual concerns and exegetical methods most commonly associated with the Rabbis. The existence of multiple perspectives does not require the existence of multiple, exclusive groups. Furthermore, many traditions and ideas should be understood as common and shared rather than proprietary and restricted, particularly when effective religiosity and meaningful interpretation are at stake. Highly specified assertions about such a complicated period may be misleading. In the end, diversity at the local-communal level may be the only stereotype we can offer.

When viewed within the framework of the larger societal context of the Byzantine empire in Palestine and its exertion of pressures on Jewish culture, the picture becomes even more complicated. Jews, to be sure, lived under the increasing oppression of a consolidating and increasingly empowered Christian empire, but the tremendous diversity of physical and literary evidence suggests that the Jewish communities responded to this tension by channeling it into confident and unique expression. They found, and did not lose, their voices despite often presenting themselves as (and perhaps at times really being) under attack.[8] Jewish memory certainly recalls this period as one of oppression and suppression; medieval Jewish sources (intriguingly and erroneously) suggest that the origins of piyyut lie in anti-Jewish imperial laws. The reality appears to have been much more complex, even messy, with scholarly evidence providing tantalizingly complicated, sometimes conflicting, clues. Laws enshrined in the

7 The phrasing of this observation derives from Gershon Cohen, *Studies in the Variety of Rabbinic Cultures* (Philadelphia: JPS, 1991).

8 The reality is that despite many laws being enacted that inconvenienced, denigrated, interfered with, or otherwise abused non-Christians, Jews living in Byzantine Palestine apparently ignored the laws in ways that Jews living in Constantinople could not. A convenient discussion of the complexity of Jewish-Christian relations, viewed through the lens of the tension between legal theory and social-political reality in the Galilee during the 6th century C.E. can be found in Gray, "Palestine and Justinian's Legislation on Non-Christian Religions." The fact that Yannai's community was probably spared severe physical oppression does not negate the fact that they seem to have experienced "existential" oppression.

Byzantine legal codes paint one picture; historical accounts (often by Christian authorities forwarding their own agendas) suggest another; and archaeology, a third.[9] Christians, like Jews, were living in a dynamic, contentious, textually focused society, confronting their own crises of identity as they sought to understand their relationship not only to Judaism but to the former enemy, Rome.[10] Nothing in this period appears to be as simple as was once thought. Particularly as the boundaries between research fields blur, scholars have available an array of both new methods and sources; the resulting scholarly energy has reinvigorated the study of antiquity from

---

9 A full treatment of Byzantine Jewish society exceeds the scope of the present volume, but a selected list of sources may be useful. For background in the important and relatively new role of archaeology in the area of Jewish cultural history, see Levine, *The Ancient Synagogue*, the most important and comprehensive presentation of the topic at hand here; and Fine, *Art and Judaism in the Greco-Roman World*, which does a remarkable job of synthesizing textual and material artifacts with methodological sophistication. Publication of writings in the field of archaeology have flourished in recent years. See especially Rachel Hachlili, ed., *Ancient Synagogues in Israel: Third-Seventh Century* C.E.*: Proceedings of Symposium, University of Haifa: May* 1987 (Oxford: B.A.R., 1989); Steven Fine, ed. *The Sacred Realm: the Emergence of the Synagogue in the Ancient World* (New York: Oxford University Press; Yeshiva University Museum, 1996); and Lee Levine, ed., *Ancient Synagogues Revealed* (Jerusalem/Detroit: The Israel Exploration Society/Wayne State University Press, 1982), among others. For background on the legal restrictions on Jews and their relative ineffectiveness, see Stemberger, *Jews and Christians in the Holy Land.* M. Avi-Yonah's *The Jews Under Roman and Byzantine Rule: A Political History from the Bar Kokhba War to the Arab Conquest* (New York: Schocken, 1984) likewise offers a comprehensive survey of this time period. For insight into the general complexity of the period, see E. Meyers, ed., *The Galilee Through the Centuries: A Confluence of Cultures* (Winona Lake: Eisenbrauns, 1999).

10 The fourth century appears to have been a watershed moment for relations between Jews and Christians and their own self-conceptions. See Gershon Cohen, "Esau as Symbol in Early Medieval Thought," in *Studies in the Variety of Rabbinic Cultures*, 243–69, for a presentation of this process via biblical exegesis. Levine's *The Ancient Synagogue* explores the issue from the perspective of that Jewish institution. Daniel Boyarin's *Dying for God: Martyrdom and the Making of Christianity and Judaism* (Stanford: Stanford University Press, 1999) focuses on the generative and complicated tensions between the two communities, while Shaye Cohen's *The Beginnings of Jewishness: Boundaries, Varieties, Uncertainties* (Berkeley: University of California Press, 1999) considers the issue from a more sociological-anthropological perspective. For insight into the Christian identity crisis, see Robert Wilken, *John Chrysostom and the Jews: Rhetoric and Reality in the Late Fourth Century* (Berkeley: University of California Press, 1983); Chrysostom's sermons on "Judaizing" offer a fascinating window into an inner-Christian dynamic in the century or so prior to Yannai. More generally, note the writings of Averil Cameron, including *Christianity and the Rhetoric of Empire* and *The Mediterranean in Late Antiquity.* See also the article by W. Kinzig, "'Non-Separation': Closeness and Co-operation between Jews and Christians in the Fourth Century," *Vigiliae Christianae* 45 (1991): 27–53; and Leonard V. Rutgers, "Archaeological Evidence for the Interaction of Jews and Non-Jews in Late Antiquity," *American Journal of Archaeology* 96 (1992): 101–18.

fresh and innovative perspectives. All material, including the piyyutim, is now being approached with new sophistication, thereby revealing fresh and enriching possibilities.

An intriguingly complicated picture of the societal and cultural milieu of sixth-century Palestine is gradually emerging now, and understanding the place of piyyut in this world—especially the works of Yannai, whose timing and style are pivotal and whose corpus is so intact—has become urgent. How do midrash, targum, and piyyut relate to one another? Are the poetic compositions related to mystical traditions, or are the apparent similarities misleading? Did these diverse liturgical and literary texts arise in the same setting, or do they reveal to us the existence of distinctive communities with diverse needs and ideas? What was the synagogue like in this, its first real golden age, and what was its place in society? In what ways was the liturgy standardized and the lectionary set, and by whom? And in terms of the larger culture, were the Jews influenced by the surrounding and increasingly dominant Christian culture, or was Judaism still shaping the younger faith? Alternatively, was the dynamic still fluid and reciprocal, despite increasingly articulated antagonism? In sum, with so much conflicting, incomplete, but tantalizing evidence, what can we say with any certainty?

This chapter seeks to draw limited but important inferences (if not conclusions) about Yannai's world from his own words and from other works of approximately this same period, not so much to settle these questions but to indicate directions future research may take. In general, piyyutim offer vital evidence about Jewish life in Late Antiquity. As an innovative, creative kind of writing, these poems offer insight into original developments within a dynamic culture, but their uses of tradition are as suggestive as their novelty. Yannai, in particular, was a critical participant in this renaissance; his works mark a watershed in the development not just of Jewish verse, but Jewish literature and culture. In his works we see exemplified the tensions, internal and external, that defined and energized Byzantine Judaism: continuity within diversity, originality within tradition, innovation within synthesis, "us" within "them." We will, thus, consider Yannai through an ever-widening lens: as a writer first within the rabbinic world, then within Jewish society more generally in Late Antiquity, and finally in light of Byzantine Christian hymnographic trends.

Piyyut as Rabbinic Text:

An Initial Example, the *Magen* for Genesis 12:1

Jewish culture in the Byzantine period—particularly the subset that would become known as rabbinic Judaism—was saturated in the Bible. Judaism in antiquity was an exegetical culture, a society in which contemporary events were refracted through the lens and language of biblical narrative, poetry, and prophecy. Scripture did not merely inform the narrative self-understanding of Jewish communities (for example, suggesting analogies between the exile of Jacob to Aram and their own dispossession); it provided the very words for articulating its self-expression—its idiom and in-group language. The act of interpreting the Bible helped shape an entire worldview as much as the worldview helped shape interpretations of text.

As discussed in the previous chapter, the most basic element of this complex social-exegetical relationship is a deep and pervasive intertextuality, exemplified by Yannai's rich and allusive reading of biblical texts. While the poet draws much of his vocabulary from the Jewish scriptures, his readings of biblical passages resonate strongly with aggadic traditions and methods, showing how thoroughly such approaches to Scripture permeated not only the methods by which the Bible was read but how more generally it was received. The key difference between piyyut and other forms of biblical interpretation from this period lies not so much in its themes, motifs, or contents (although Yannai innovates within each category), but most essentially in its rhetoric—how it shapes exegesis for liturgical performance and as poetry. Rather than laying out interpretations in a linear, narrative, explicatory manner, Yannai's compositions place much of the responsibility for generating interpretations on the audience. The community heard overtly biblical words and yet, at the same time, was expected to understand them in a way we might call "rabbinic." Thus, while Yannai's language may be thoroughly biblical, his use of these ancient words displays creativity and dramatic flair embedded in a rich tradition of interpretation. Exegesis becomes a shared endeavor.

Before delving into the intricacies of poetic exegesis and its relationship to other genres of writing and society in Late Antiquity, a single example will help demonstrate the range of issues involved in analyzing Yannai's dense and intricate works from this perspective. As a survey of the poems in this volume (and their annotations) indicates, Yannai's language is so pervasively textured with allusions to aggadah and implicit midrash that almost any poetic unit could illuminate some aspect of Yannai's exegetical richness. For the sake of simplicity, and to show how "thick" in meaning a single piece can be, we will here, for the moment, return to the *magen* (Poem One) for Gen 12:1, fruitfully used in Chapter Two as an example of Yannai's biblical intertextuality. Here it can highlight how still deeper layers of meaning can be drawn out of a single passage.[11]

The *magen* consists of twelve lines—three rhymed stanzas—followed by a series of six verses (one of which is missing in the MS) and a transition to the first blessing of the Amidah.[12] The biblical texts are, specifically, the first verse of the Torah portion (Gen 12:1)—i.e., the lemma—and a collection of four intertexts: Ps 45:11, Ps 45:12, Song 1:4, and Prov 3:6. In terms of exegesis, the first question concerns how Yannai uses these biblical quotations, but the issue of aggadah embedded in allusions, within the body of the poem, is important as well.

The physical structure of this poem immediately demonstrates several important facts about Yannai's context. First of all, it assumes the existence of both a lectionary and a liturgy. The first verse of the Torah portion is distinguished by the prefatory phrase "as it is written" (*ka-katuv*) while subsequent intertexts are introduced with a secondary rubric, "and it is said" (*ve-neʾemar*). The existence of the Amidah (*qua* Amidah), the central prayer of the Jewish liturgy, is immediately evident, but it appears in the form of an outline rather than the familiar fixed text of the later siddur (prayer book).[13] The transitional rubrics in the poem (the brief stanzas following the first three poems and the *silluq* that introduces the *qedushah*) indicate that the basic outlines of the *magen*, *gevurot*, and Qedushah (the first three blessings of the Amidah) were present and assumed by the poet and congregation. Likewise, the construction of the benedictions, with a transitional line smoothing the connection between the intertexts and the blessing, indicates that Yannai followed rabbinic norms—otherwise only attested in Babylonian sources—of prayer composition.[14] For instance,

---

11 The discussion in Chapter Two begins on p. 112. The text of Yannai's *qedushta* for Gen 12:1 can be found on p. 391.

12 See Appendix I for an outline of the typical *qedushta* structure and Appendix II for the text of the first three blessings of the Amidah.

13 By the Middle Ages, piyyutim adorned the fixed prayer texts of the Amidah and the Shema, rather than substituting for them. On the formation of the liturgy, in addition to the works of Elbogen, Heinemann, and Langer, see Reif, *Judaism and Hebrew Prayer*.

14 The form called a *shivʿata*—not studied in this volume but a common form in the Classical period and employed by Yannai—embellishes all seven blessings of the Sabbath or

Yannai consistently uses the root *n-g-n* ("to shield, protect") in the concluding stich of the transitional line in the *magen*, in anticipation of the key word "*magen*" ("shield," from the same root) in the benediction itself. It remains something of an open question whether the piyyutim are a rebellion against an already-fixed liturgy or evidence of the gradual crystallization of a still-fluid liturgy, but this much is clear: the basic liturgical outlines were firmly established by Yannai's time, but the wording of the blessings themselves (aside from the concluding formula and the overall scaffolding) remained or had become unfixed, at least on the Sabbath in Yannai's community.[15]

The collections of biblical texts that follow the *magen* offer a unique and important window into Yannai's cultural context. At first glance—as discussed in the previous chapter—the specific verses following the quotation from Gen 12:1 may seem peculiar, particularly Ps 45:11–12 and Song 1:4, which cast Abraham in the unlikely role of the ingénue/bride. Juxtaposed, these verses invite a kind of basic midrashic interpretation, where each sheds light on the other, all in the context of Abraham's call.[16] Read together with Gen 12:1, the psalm reads the patriarch as "my daughter" while the Song of Songs verse identifies Abraham with the female lover. Yannai, however, is not alone in linking these verses to Abraham; extant midrashic texts connect these very same verses explicitly to Abraham. Yannai's choice of these verses identifies him not as an innovator but as a participant in a

---

Festival Amidah. This genre indicates that the complete outline of that prayer, still in use today, was familiar in the Byzantine rite. In terms of halakhic norms, the issue here is Yannai's use of a literary transition to the benediction, as found in *b.Pesaḥ.* 104a; see Langer, *To Worship God Properly*, 26–27.

15 Piyyutim offer important data for reconstructing the history of the liturgy, but they have not settled the key dispute between Heinemann and his students, who argue for a fluid liturgy that gradually crystallized, and Fleischer and his students, who see piyyutim as a rebellion against an early-established fixity. For convenient English-language summaries of Heinemann and Fleischer, see Ruth Langer, "Revisiting Early Rabbinic Liturgy," *Prooftexts* 19 (1999): 179–204; Ezra Fleischer's response, "On the Origins of the Amidah," *Prooftexts* 20 (2000): 380–84; and Langer's response to Fleischer, "Consideration of Method: a Response to Ezra Fleischer," *Prooftexts* 20 (2000): 384–87. Yannai's poetry reflects a prayer tradition that is both fixed and fluid: the overall framework of the *qedushta* is quite standardized, not only in terms of poetic forms but the regular use of statutory liturgical phrases; yet the bodies of the different blessings—the *avot, gevurot,* and *qedushat ha-shem*—are not yet fixed, as those are the stations where the poetic compositions appear.

16 The importance of verse juxtaposition as the "essence" of midrash is articulated by Boyarin in *Intertextuality and the Reading of Midrash.* He provides the terminology of "intertext" (which he also calls "co-texts") as employed in the present study.

widespread exegetical tradition, an author who has taken familiar (and probably still fluid) interpretive conceits and shaped them to his own rhetorical ends. We see this because we know that Ps 45:11–12 are the *petiḥta* verses for the midrash in *GenR* 39:1, the teaching that opens the written collection of midrash on the Torah portion beginning with Gen 12:1. A *petiḥta* is a sophisticated and witty midrashic rhetorical structure in which the exegete opened (*pataḥ*) with "a verse from afar"—usually from the Writings section of the Hebrew Bible—and, through puns and other associations, connected the remote verse into the opening verse of the Torah portion. Because the content of the Torah portion was a given and the initial verse was readily anticipated by the congregation (as with the piyyut, which always has a known verse as its destination), the intellectual (and aesthetic) pleasure of the *petiḥta* form lies in anticipating how the exegete will arrive at his determined end-point from his opening salvo. The more unlikely the verse, then, the more intellectually satisfying the *petiḥta.*[17] In the case of Gen 12:1, the *Tanḥuma* traditions (both *Tanḥ Lekh Lekhah* 3 and *TanḥB Lekh Lekhah* 3), which like Yannai assume a Palestinian triennial lectionary, likewise connect these verses from Ps 45 to the Abraham story, albeit not in the *petiḥta* form.[18] Unlike these midrashic texts, however, Yannai's *qedushtaʾot* do not explicitly articulate the connections between *petiḥta* verse and lemma for his audience; the poet works entirely by allusion and juxtaposition. It is as if Yannai is playing by the same game as the prose exegete, but at a much faster pace and with the assumption that everyone already knows the rules.

What we cannot know, however, is whether Yannai could write so tersely and evocatively because his audience already in some sense knew the aggadic traditions—that is, they already knew how to understand the intertexts in light of the lemma—or because they were so steeped in the

---

17 Yannai's relationship to the *petiḥta* form is discussed further later in this chapter. My use of the *petiḥta*-piyyut analogy builds on the argument made by Shulamit Elizur that the structure of the *qedushta* as a whole recalls the structure of a *petiḥta.* See her article, "The Congregation at Prayer and the Early *Qedushta*" in *Knesset Ezra: Literature and Life in the Synagogue, Studies presented to Ezra Fleischer,* ed. Ezra Fleischer and Shulamit Elizur (Jerusalem: Yad Yitsḥak Ben-Zvi, 1994), 171–90 [Hebrew].

18 On the relationship of midrash to the triennial lectionary, see in particular Marc Bregman, "The Triennial Haftarot and the Perorations of the Midrashic Homilies," *Journal of Jewish Studies* 32 (1981): 74–84. Lieve Teugels, however, has attempted to complicate this association, at least in terms of midrash *aggadat bereshit,* in her article: "Aggadat Bereshit and the Triennial Lectionary Cycle," *Journal of Jewish Studies* 51 (2000): 117–32.

method of midrash that they could, in some sense, generate the aggadah themselves if given the raw materials.[19] Given that in many cases, as noted below, Yannai's intertexts are not paralleled in extant prose *midrashim*, it seems the *method* of generating midrash—of reading one verse in light of another—was the essential knowledge required of his listener, not familiarity with a vast body of aggadic lore in specific. Nevertheless, the close parallels between piyyut and midrash raise the question (for the moment vastly oversimplified) of whether Yannai is simply poeticizing established aggadah, or whether he and his community together were participating more actively in a still-fluid tradition. No matter the precise genetic relationship between the genres, the affinity of piyyut for midrash suggests how learned and intellectually engaged (and playful) at least some members of his audience were.[20]

The other intertexts within this unit suggest methodological resonances with midrash but leave open the possibility that the poet is engaging creatively with the tradition in terms of specific content. Song 1:4 is associated (almost incidentally) with Abraham in *GenR* 48:6 and 49:2, where the verse's final clause—"rightly do they love you"—is read in each midrash as "the righteous one [Abraham] loves you." The final extant intertext, Prov 3:6, is not explicitly linked to Abraham in the surviving rabbinic writings. However, a brief teaching in *b.Berakhot* 63a cites the verse in a way that might well apply to the patriarch: "Bar Kappara expounded: What short text is there upon which all the essential principles of the Torah depend? `In all your ways acknowledge Him and He will direct your paths.'" Bar Kappara doesn't mention Abraham, but in the context of the *qedushta*, the essential righteousness of Abraham lines up well with this brief statement: the future of Judaism—and therefore the future of the Torah—depends on the patriarch. Yannai may be particularizing the more general aggadic statement, linking the father of Israel with the single verse that Bar Kappara claims encapsulates the essence of Torah.

The complexity of this last example suggests the knottiness of the relationship between piyyut and midrash. Analysis that seeks primarily to connect piyyutim to rabbinic sources can, on the one hand, result in overwhelming lists of parallels but, on the other hand, overlook potentially

19 See Sarason, "Midrash in the Liturgy," especially pp. 484–92.

20 For an intriguing discussion of the *qedushta* as a work pitched at multiple intellectual levels, see Elizur, "The Congregation at Prayer and the Early *Qedushta*," cited above.

relevant but imperfect matches. At times, allusions may be indirect, and that slippage is, in and of itself, noteworthy. The close resemblance between Yannai's poem and the tradition recorded in *GenR* 39:1, both of which connect Abraham with the maiden-bride of Ps 45:11–12, indicates a profound and deep entwining of traditions—in this case, the poem and the midrash should be seen as two manifestations of the same basic (and, it should be noted, rather gender-bending) idea.[21] But it is not always the case that piyyut and midrash so closely resemble each other.

We see an example of the importance of less direct connections between them when we examine the juxtaposition of the Abraham story and the words of Song 1:4 and Prov 3:6. The connections here are weaker in the aggadah than in the piyyut but highlight the importance of *method* alongside *content.* Yannai's use of Song 1:4, not associated with Abraham in any major midrashic source, makes it clear that Yannai is not just poeticizing extant midrashic concepts. He shares traditions of interpretation with the *midrashim*, but he also apparently innovates, using similar methods but his own choice of intertexts. Song 1:4 eminently suits the romantic conceit of the *magen* itself, so Yannai felt free to adduce it, even if he was not relying on any external tradition for his inspiration. Indeed, the initial part of Song1:4, where the male lover beseeches his beloved to run away with him, resonates strongly with Abraham's response to "go forth" in the biblical narrative; reading the two passages together creates a biblically-based aggadic dialogue—all on the fly. Similarly, the language of "straight paths" and the reference to the Divine in Prov 3:6 accord well with the biblical story of Abraham's call as Yannai tells it, even if no other exegete connected it explicitly to Abraham. Yannai's use of Scripture recalls the midrashic process but not necessarily actual, extant *midrashim.*

Yannai, then, shares methods of exegesis and familiar interpretations with the Rabbis, but the differences between the piyyut and midrash reveal that Yannai was not merely repackaging prose writings for poetic use. Midrash and piyyut are, instead, different manifestations of the same broader phenomenon. The *payyetan* was creative as well as traditional, part of a larger cultural endeavor to discover and convey the deep meanings latent in sacred texts. Together with the abundant poetic remains of this period, the complex manuscript tradition behind the printed midrashic texts and the diversity of targumic materials from Palestine indicate just how fluid,

21 See Chapter Four for a discussion of Abraham as a feminized figure.

dynamic, and lively this exegetical culture was. Yannai was neither bound to nor limited by the printed texts we now have in hand (the convenience of printed versions, for modern scholars, can easily obscure the complicated manuscript traditions these printed works represent) or even, necessarily, by traditions of interpretation then in oral circulation. The poet worked within conventions but not necessarily according to any fixed script, and he wrote poetry that conveys a sense of textual saturation: the Bible and its exegesis permeate Yannai's poetry because they were, in a very fundamental way, his deep cultural vocabulary. Intertextuality was not only a technique but a worldview.

Yannai's engagement with aggadic tradition is not limited to specifically cited intertexts that follow the initial units of his *qedushtaʾot.* The exegetical verses are the most obvious biblical references in a *qedushta,* but echoes of midrash infuse almost every line of the poems. Scriptural allusions enrich stich upon stich, as noted in Chapter Two, and these bear with them their own insinuated histories of interpretation. Some allusions are quite simple. In the *magen* (Poem One) to Gen 12:1, the second line, "a creature You endowed, allowed to create" recalls the tradition in *GenR* 43:7 where God says, "I will regard you [Abraham] as though you were My partner with Me in the creation of the world." And the phrase, "You imbued him with a portion of Your power" in line 5 echoes teachings in *GenR* 39:11 and *GenR* 59:4, in which God dramatizes His empowerment of Abraham by stating that He will share His might with the patriarch. Likewise, the allusion to Song 8:8 ("we have a little sister") in the sixth line mirrors the use of that verse in several midrashim, including *GenR* 39:9 (in a *petiḥta*), *Tanḥ Lekh Lekhah* 2, *TanḥB Lekh Lekhah* 2, and *SongR* 8:10. Here Yannai draws on the tradition in which the Rabbis pun on "sister" (*ʾaḥot*) and "to stitch" (*ʾiḥah*), learning from the wordplay that Abraham "stitched together" (i.e., unified and united) all of creation through his realization of God's oneness and his dissemination of that insight. Similarly, the description of Abraham as "radiant" in the third line and "clear" in the seventh line brings to mind the tradition in *GenR* 2:3 where God identifies the primordial light with Abraham: "'And God said: Let there be light' (Gen 1:2)—This is Abraham." The intertext for this midrash is Isa 41:2, a passage that becomes an important subtext in the fourth poem of this *qedushta.* Finally, the provocative phrase "like sweet-talking a lass, You enticed him" in line 8 finds a parallel in a tradition quoted in *Midrash ha-Gadol Bereshit,* where God's call to Abraham is explicitly compared to courting a woman, and where the same root

פ-ת-ה ("to entice, seduce") appears.[22] Biblical words resonate deeply, creating layers and layers of resonant meaning. Hearing a piyyut involves detecting manifold echoes—and out of these echoes emerge something closely akin to midrash, and yet distinct. Where midrash is concrete and explicatory, piyyut evokes meaning through echoes, hints, and repetitions.

Even these examples reveal only the most obvious points of contact between this specific poem and the aggadic traditions of rabbinic literature. It is possible, for example, that the references to Abraham as "radiant" may also hint at the widespread tradition that Abraham was cast into Nimrod's furnace—a motif attested widely in the *midrashim* and also the *targumim* (both *TargN* and *TargPsJ* to Gen 21) as well as other sources. In this reading, Abraham was, quite literally, ablaze just prior to his call.

At this point it may be tempting to consider piyyut simply a poetic form of midrash. But, for all these similarities to midrashic works, it is also evident that Yannai uses the motifs in unique ways and to his own ends. His compositions are learned but not overtly didactic; his interpretations rely on juxtaposition and inference rather than explication. In terms of motifs, Yannai may well resemble more expansive aggadic narratives. In terms of both form and context, however, Yannai's piyyutim remain separate and distinctive. Furthermore, in terms of synagogue reality, the piyyutim are the most certain evidence we have of aggadic diffusion. The practical life-setting of targum and midrash are disputed— were they popular texts, or scholarly? Composed for use in the house of prayer or the house of study? Are the written texts we have in hand approximations of oral performance, or are they in fact later, scholastic works? Only the piyyutim are unambiguously "of the synagogue." And Yannai underscores for us the fact that the aggadic traditions that seem so tidy in their modern, written forms were still fluid—growing, developing, coalescing—in the Byzantine period. Yannai did not simply reap the fruits of aggadic creativity from centuries past; rather, he (and by extension his community) participated fully in the exegetical inventiveness of his age, just as much as the more famous Rabbis whose names have come down to us today.

Finally, we should notice how Yannai uses the brief, often unexplicated aggadic allusions to create meaning at deep levels, pulling together both

---

22 *Midrash ha-Gadol Bereshit,* p. 201, cited by Lieberman, "*Ḥazzanut Yannai,*" 237; *Midrash ha-Gadol* is a late work (12th century Yemenite), but the traditions it cites are probably much older—a dating supported by the appearance of a parallel in Yannai's work.

overt and implicit layers of interpretive understandings. The *magen* (Poem One) for Gen 12:1 is a love-song, drawing heavily on romantic language in the Bible as amplified and specified in post-biblical interpretation. Perhaps there is an implicit polemic here— a defense of Abraham (regarded as the first Jew) and an affirmation of God's enduring love for him in the face of Christian supersessionist claims. Are the references to "enemies"(line 1) and "darkness" (line 3) limited to Abraham's own context, in primitive, pagan Ur, or does the poet hint here at themes of chosenness, divine *eros*, and even martyrdom in his current milieu—ideas that are explicit in the prose aggadah? It is hard to know when to *stop* interpreting these works—this opening poem is not as explicit as some of the later units, and Yannai is fully capable of writing explicit polemic when he chooses.[23] In the end, we must remember that this poem is simply the opening unit of a much longer poetic work, which itself participates in a profound tradition of interpretation concerning the mystery of Abraham's call, the wonder of his response, and the place of his heirs in the larger—often hostile—world.

Comparison with extant prose aggadic texts sheds much light on the richness of Yannai's language in this poem, revealing both the depth of his relationship to attested methods and traditions and also the boldness of his creativity. Furthermore, the reliance on quotation and allusion clearly displays the responsibility that resides with the audience for recognizing and completing the implicit interpretations. For all that they reveal, however, these new insights raise deeper questions about the relationship of liturgical poetry to other forms of contemporary aggadic exegesis.

Having now delineated the complexity of the task through close scrutiny of a single example, a more systematic survey of the nature of common motifs, shared techniques, and broad cultural concerns will illustrate the connections between piyyut and aggadah (including midrash, targum, and mystical texts) and locate piyyut in the context of the synagogue edifice. Each new insight will, in turn, raise additional questions.

---

23 See his *qedushta* for Yom Kippur (Rabinovitz 2:221–22). The Aramaic piyyutim, particularly those for Purim, are even more gleefully polemical; see Sokoloff and Yahalom's edition of the Aramaic poems, *Jewish Palestinian Poetry from Late Antiquity*, and also the material in Chapter Four of this volume.

Aggadic and Liturgical Themes and Motifs

Yannai's writing relates to the biblical text and traditions of its interpretation in ways that are far from simple. Just as the underlying text of Scripture is itself multivalent—meaning many things simultaneously and, consequently, relying greatly on the skill of both the presenter (Yannai) and the interpreter (the congregation)—Yannai's use of this sacred text operates at multiple levels at once. His poems provide one kind of meaning on the surface level but, if considered more deeply, the meanings multiply and become significantly richer and more nuanced. Piyyut and midrash, both forms of exegesis flourishing in sixth-century Byzantine Galilee, share not only a common core text (the Bible) but common methods and traditions of interpretation, with both genres of writing exploring the overdetermined richness of the canonical text. At the same time, the liturgical context shapes the rhetoric, themes, and theologies of piyyutim in ways that make them inherently different from midrash and targum—texts that are not "prayed" in the same way as piyyut. To understand Yannai's piyyutim fully, this complex interrelationship between payyetanic and midrashic method and context must be considered.

The interconnections between piyyut and aggadah manifest most obviously at the levels of themes and motifs.[24] "Themes" refers to broad, sweeping arcs of interpretation, while "motifs" describe the small components that may or may not be essential to the interpretation as a whole. Both themes and motifs operate at a general, even superficial, level—the texts and traditions will not necessarily display the deeper bonds of the use of common exegetical verses, shared phrases, or embedded structures, although there may well be overlap. Thus, for example, the image of God "seducing" Abraham in the *magen* (Poem One) for Gen 12:1 echoes both themes and motifs attested in aggadic writings, at times drawing on shared exegetical traditions but still understandable in isolation. All these exegetical writings (piyyut, midrash, and targum) attempt to discern and understand, in one way or another, why Abraham received and followed the difficult demand to "go forth," the choice and command that sets an entire national drama—still ongoing—into motion. Both midrash and piyyut of-

---

24 The most exhaustive study to date of Yannai's relationship with other rabbinic sources is Rabinovitz, *Halakhah and Aggadah in the Liturgical Poems of Yannai.*

fer the same answer, albeit in different words and with different emphases: Abraham was called and went out of love.

In much of their exegesis, midrash and piyyut share an interest in "gap filling"—in finding the truths that lie between the lines of Scripture. When these gaps are filled by means of additional verses from the Bible, we call the interpretation "midrash"—the reader has sought (*darash*) and found answers in the text itself. One verse provides the key for unlocking the latent meaning in another. In other cases, the gap-filling may appear more fanciful, less rooted in texts. In such a case, we may call the teaching "aggadah," or simply narrative.[25]

As with the Gen 12:1 example, in some cases identifying the perceived gap in the biblical text is as important as understanding how the lacuna is filled; the exegetical inspirations can range from the obvious (why did God choose Abraham?) to the subtle (why did Abraham respond without a word?) to the inventive (what was God's tone of voice?). In many cases, the interpretive pretext for a piyyut lies within the initial words of the Torah portion.[26] For example, Gen 15:1 states, "After these things, the word of the Lord came to Abram in a vision, saying: `Fear not, Abram, I am a shield to you and your reward shall be very great.'" Upon reading this verse, one may well question the peculiar focus of God's revelation. Why does God open His declaration with, "Fear not"? Was Abram afraid? Of what? Inspired by the verse's opening phrase, "After these things," early interpreters connected Abram's fears in Gen 15:1 with the story of his battle against the Canaanite kings in the previous chapter. Yet, while multiple sources concur that

25 Yannai's interpretations display a particular affinity for a select corpus of rabbinic writings, particularly *Genesis Rabbah* (in the Genesis piyyutim), *Pirqe deRabbi Eliezer*, the *Tanḥumas*, *Pesiqta deRav Kehanah*, and the Palestinian Talmud. The overlap among these sources underscores Yannai's geographical location—he shows a strong preference for Palestinian Jewish sources and rarely alludes to traditions preserved only in Babylonian sources. In some cases, Yannai's use of a tradition predates the mainstream written versions of these materials, which may call into question the standard dates of such anthologies or the traditions they record. For a full study of Yannai's relationship to rabbinic sources, see Rabinovitz, *Halakhah and Aggadah in the Poetry of Yannai*. While Rabinovitz's work remains the standard in the field, further work remains to be done delineating the relationships between Yannai's piyyutim and specific midrashic corpora (particularly *Tanḥuma*); other early poets, particularly Qillir, would likewise make fruitful topics for such research.

26 Because many midrashim relate to the lectionary, as well, it is common to find overlap between the verses Yannai embellishes and verses that receive extensive midrashic embellishment. The relationship between Yannai's intertexts and midrashic prooftexts/*petiḥta* verses deserves serious inquiry.

Abram's fear must be explained, and many of these agree that the answer lies in Gen 14 , the exegetes offer a variety of interpretations to fill this gap.

According to *Tanḥ Lekh Lekha* 15 and *TanḥB Lekh Lekha* 15, Abram was anxious because he had killed sons of Shem, a righteous man, in the battle. This act, the patriarch fears, constitutes a terrible sin for which he should be punished. *GenR* 44:4, for its part, offers numerous reasons for Abram to be anxious. Perhaps he killed a righteous man among the wicked (foreshadowing Abraham's arguments on behalf of Sodom). Or, according to another Sage, the Canaanite kings may seek retribution. Or possibly, Abram's recent victory reflects a reward for merit spent in this world—and not, therefore, something to be reaped in the world to come. These various traditions, given in the name of different Sages in the *midrashim*, appear together (*sans* attribution, of course) in *TargN* and *TargPsJ* to Gen 15:1. And, finally a similar composite interpretation, likewise anonymous, appears in Yannai's *qedushta* for this Torah portion (Gen 15:1):

> The battle—as soon as it came to an end— / of a truth, trepidation in his heart was found
> For foes felled in Dan and Ḥovah / he trembled, lest it be thought a trespass [*ḥovah*] (Poem One, lines 4–7).

The specific reasons for Abraham's angst are not stated at this point—what, specifically, about his slain foes worries him? In the *magen* (Poem One), the poet emphasizes the fact that Abram's actions were in accord with God's commands. Nevertheless, Yannai grows more explicit in delineating the source of the patriarch's concern in Poem Five, when he writes:

> He was disturbed and distressed / over those he had killed // He hesitated to seek[27] / lest blood-justice be sought
> He trembled: Had there been a righteous man among them? // Or was a convert fated to arise from their midst? (Poem Five, lines 18–21)

These poetic motifs obviously resemble those found in prose midrashic and targumic traditions. It is clear that the poet is asking the same questions as the midrashic and targumic authors, and they are likewise in a general consensus that the battle in Gen 14 must be the source for the patriarch's anxiety. What distinguishes Yannai is his poetic form and the

---

27 I.e., Abram hesitated to petition God for his fair reward, a son, out of anxiety that God would instead punish him for bloodshed.

resultant rhetoric, which is elliptical and allusive in ways that the other sources are not, even if content suggests commonalities.

The similarities in content can be seen in many places. The notes and essays that accompany the translations of specific piyyutim frequently indicate these areas of common concern and point out congruities between the themes of piyyutim and discrete interpretations recorded in midrashic collections and *targumim*. Thus, for example, the theme of Yannai's *qedushta* for Gen 49:1—that God revealed the secrets of the end-time to Jacob but then concealed them when Jacob was going to teach this esoteric lore to his sons—finds parallels in both *TargN* and *TargPsJ* to Gen 49:1–2 as well as *GenR* 94. All of these traditions respond to a lacuna in the biblical text: Jacob tells his sons to assemble because he is going to tell them "what shall befall you in the end of days" (Gen 49:1), but the text that follows is a poem addressing the characteristics of the twelve tribes and not the esoteric knowledge implied by the phrase "end of days." The *payyetan, meturgeman*, and *darshan* all agree that between Gen 49:1 and Gen 49:2, God withdrew this special knowledge from Jacob, and they share an understanding of why as well.

One must bear in mind, however, that piyyutim—and likewise targumim—have their own unique histories. While the midrashic sources may contain the most articulate and developed versions of a tradition, this is largely a reflection of the distinctive editing and anthologizing process that midrashic collections underwent as well as the narrative nature of midrash itself. Genre conventions and context also play a part. The midrash seems intent on exploring why the prophecy was lost, while the piyyut focuses on recreating the experiential drama of the moment. One is intellectual, even edifying; the other is dramatic, even theatrical.[28] When looking back to Late Antiquity, we should consider that the traditions contained in these various texts were still fluid and diffuse, crystallizing in different fashions in different media, often at roughly the same time but sometimes separated by centuries. During the Byzantine period, each

28 The targumic versions of Gen 49:1–2 occupy something of a middle ground between midrash and piyyut—the medium of translation is conducive to verbose explication, but not multiplicities of opinion, and the focus within the *targumim* seems to be clarification and elucidation, perhaps with elements of theatricality, but not with performance and engagement as primary objectives. See L. Lieber, "O My Dove, in the Cranny of the Rocks, Let Me See Your Face," in *Paratext and Megatext in Jewish and Christian Traditions*, ed. A. den Hollander, U. Schmidt, and W.F. Smelik (Brill: Leiden, 2003), 109–35.

mode of interpretation (which may or may not have been committed to writing) was, in and of itself, in a fluid and productive state; the sense of creative motion and interplay is only intensified when we consider texts across genres. Exegetes—whether teaching, translating, or poeticizing—had access, it seems, to a common body of motifs, which each could employ creatively to suit his own needs.

Numerous similar examples could be cited in order to underscore the connections among these three genres, but some are more subtle than the shared themes used as examples above. For instance, in the *qedushta* for Gen 19:1, Yannai reflects the same understanding of angelic function attested in *GenR* 50:2, *TargN* 18:1, and *TargPsJ* to Gen 18:2—that each angel performs a distinct mission, and no angel may be sent on multiple missions. *Tanḥ Vayigash* 6, which also relates to the content of Gen 19, specifies that "dominion" and "fear" (in Job 25:2) are names for Michael and Gabriel, respectively, with Michael having been sent to announce Isaac's birth to Abraham and Gabriel appointed to overturn Sodom. While Yannai's understanding of how angels work clearly relates to these traditions (midrashic and targumic), the *qedushta* does not require specific knowledge of these aggadic and midrashic traditions for comprehension. Yannai's angelology may, in fact, be somewhat more vague than the parallels from prose sources; e.g., Yannai may be identifying the two angels of his piyyut with Gabriel and Raphael, with Raphael having been sent to rescue Lot and his family. Likewise, Yannai refers to angels as "dominion" and "fear" (Poem Six, line 1)—perhaps using these as angelic code names. But even if they are, they are not necessarily the same names as appear in the *Tanhuma* text. Yannai invokes the general idea—angels don't multitask, angels may be named for attributes—without displaying great concern with the specifics.

Indeed, angels are important figures in the *qedushtaʾot*, and the story of the *sidra* provides the poet with a pretext for augmenting the angelology latent within the liturgy.[29] The lack of specificity in the biblical story creates a pretext for gap-filling but does not necessarily dictate how the gap be filled. Yannai's embellishments of this motif reveal a certain amount of

29 See the discussion of angelology in Chapter Four of this volume for more detail specifically on Yannai and angels, and angels and the Qedushah; the issue here is that Yannai participates in a more general cultural milieu in which angels are a commonplace topic with which the poet can assume his audience had a certain familiarity.

consistency across genres but also indicate that the poet felt free to shape the general motif into the specifics he needed. In this example, the motif of angels resolves ambiguities in the lemma, a concern in all the genres. In Genesis, it is not clear precisely what the nature of the three messengers is, and whether one of them is, in fact, the deity and not an angel at all. The expansion of the role of angels is not merely determined by the content of the Torah portion, however. By amplifying the role of angels in this piyyut, Yannai may be appealing to his community's interests and practices (and the same may be true for the discussions of angels in other literary sources). We know that angels were a source of fascination in antiquity—for Jews, Christians, and pagans; at the popular level and among the elites; in the Land of Israel and in Babylonia. Both piyyut and midrash reflect a gap-filling compulsion and angelic fascination, but the details and functions such images, motifs, and concepts serve vary by genre and even individual example. When the midrashic writings elucidate the details of angels' functions, we should assume not that they are "inventing" an angelology but rather connecting existing beliefs about angels to specific textual contexts. But, because of the connections between the heavenly hosts and the recitation of the Qedushah, references to angels in a *qedushta* acquire added potency; during the Amidah—and thus in this piyyut—angels are more than theoretical; they are fundamentally present.

Payyetanic exegesis can also indicate the shared reality behind aggadic motifs, as well as a shared mythology. For instance, the *qedushta* for Gen 17:1 entertainingly describes the logical process by which Abraham learns precisely what "to circumcise" means and receives divine assistance in completing his own circumcision. The poet depicts a scene in which Abraham discerns what God has commanded him to do through logical inference: he makes an analogy from the pruning of trees to the "pruning" of his own member. This same teaching appears in *Tanḥ Lekh Lekhah* 18 (paralleled in *TanḥB Lekh Lekhah* 27), in which Abraham bases his reasoning on the word "and I will multiply" (*ve-arbeh*) and the agricultural practices in Lev 19:23. This conceit—God hints and Abraham reasons——is central to Yannai's depiction of the events of Gen 17. Certain details in Yannai's interpretation parallel midrashic and targumic traditions, indicating reliance on a common body of methods rather than direct dependence. For example, in line 6 of the *asiriyyah* (Poem Five), the poet describes Abraham's response to the commandment as "amazement" (not the laughter of Gen 17:17), a nuance in keeping with the renderings of that verse in both *TargN* and *TargPsJ*.[30] These aggadic embellishments and revisions, not rooted in the biblical text but in (we may imagine) the responses of later readers, supply a depth and richness to the events depicted in the poem, even though they are not actually necessary to understanding the events of the Torah portion—the "gap" being filled is one of nuance.

Poetic interpretations may also reflect living ritual practices. We see this possibility in the *rahit* for Gen 17:1, where Yannai refers to circumcision as "a fragrant formal rite" (line 12), which may refer to an actual practice of burning incense at the circumcision ceremony. Such a ritual is mentioned in *GenR* 47:7 and *SongR* 4:6 but is nowhere attested in the Bible. Read together, however, these sources suggest the existence of a "popular" ritual in Late Antiquity. Such details are important because they show us elements of Jewish practice taken for granted in Yannai's period, to the extent that these rituals were read back into Scripture. By making Scripture come alive for his congregation, Yannai unwittingly made his world a little more real to us.

Of course, most aggadic additions in Yannai's poems have primarily textual roots, in that an interpretive motif is usually adduced by means of an allusion to a biblical text, which, in turn, carries with it a well-known aggadic explication. For example, in the *qedushta* to Gen 8:15, the motif of celibacy aboard the Ark has its roots in the subtle difference in phrasing between Gen 6:18 ("Enter, you and your sons"—with wives mentioned later) and Gen 8:15 ("Go forth, you and your wife"—with sons mentioned later).[31] Yannai—like *GenR* 34:7, *Tanḥ. Noaḥ* 11, *TanḥB Noah* 17, *PRE* 29:20, and *j. Taʿan* 7:1—understands the first verse to imply sexual segregation aboard the Ark and the second to acknowledge a restoration of sexual union upon disembarking. This teaching, of course, depends entirely on an awareness of subtleties in the wording of Scripture—subtleties that Yannai articulates tersely but sufficiently. Similarly, the epithet "the hated one" for Leah (rooted in the language of Gen 29:31) evokes for Yannai a complete narrative subplot in the story. Leah, according to this tradition, was originally fated to marry Esau—the wicked one, who was also hated—

30 The Syriac poet Ephrem glosses the *Peshitta*'s faithful rendering of the Hebrew, which states that Abraham "laughed" at God (an act that might be construed as disrespectful), by explaining that Abraham "was astounded." See Sebastian Brock, "Jewish Traditions in Syriac Sources," *Journal of Jewish Studies* 30 (1979): 212–32.

31 This passage is discussed in more detail in Chapter Four.

a destiny she found so appalling that she cried herself blind, inspiring God's pity and resulting in her own loveless, but not hateful, marriage to Jacob. Being hated is Leah's sacrifice—a kind of martyrdom even. *GenR* 70:16 records this tradition as well, as does *b.Baba Batra* 123a, *Tanḥ Vayetze* 4, and *TargPsJ* to Gen 29:17. Yannai, in his *qedushta* for Gen 29:31, conjures and then amplifies the whole pathos-laden story of Leah's suffering (biblical and aggadic) through that single epithet—"hated"—which he poignantly juxtaposes with its antonym, "loved." Yannai's language is not merely a shorthand—simple metonymy—but rather a terse and allusive way of alluding to a broad range of traditions about why Leah (and by extension Israel) was hated and what good would emerge from her suffering. He has distilled the narrative to its emotional essence.

In some cases, the best parallels to certain aggadic motifs in Yannai appear not in midrashic texts but in other writings associated with the Rabbis or the synagogue. For instance, the drama of Judah's clash with Joseph (appearing as Pharaoh's vizier), described by Yannai in his *qedushta* for Gen 44:18, finds its closest parallel in a lengthy expansion in *TargN* to Gen 44:18–19—a rare instance where *TargN* preserves the most expansive version of a tradition, longer than any found in *GenR* or even *TargPsJ*. Similarly, the closest analogs to the praise of Abraham's old age found in Yannai's poem for Gen 24:1 lie not in aggadic midrash but more halakhic sources, including *m. Kidd.* 4:14, *j. Ḥag.* 9b, and *t. Kidd.* 5:14. An even more straightforwardly mishnaic teaching is alluded to in the description of the Land of Israel's holiness that opens Poem Six for Gen. 31:3, which practically quotes from *m. Kil.* 1:6. This range of commonalities suggests not only the array of traditions familiar to our poet and his community but the scope and fluidity of rabbinic interpretation as a whole during this period of creative ferment.

Indeed, most rabbinic sources—midrash aggadah, midrash halakhah, the Palestinian *Targumim*, the Mishnah, Tosefta, and the two Talmuds—contain traditions that resemble themes and motifs present in Yannai poems.[32] In some cases, a certain theme or motif may be widespread, occurring in diverse sources in approximately the same form; in other instances, a single, specific source provides the best parallel to one of Yannai's

32 Lieberman's "*Ḥazzanut Yannai*" began as an attempt to delineate some examples of Yannai's relationship to midrash and Talmud; Rabinovitz's *Halakhah and Aggadah in the Liturgical Poetry of Yannai* addresses this topic at length and lays the foundation for the work of compiling a critical edition.

teachings. It is significant that Yannai appears to be a thoroughly rabbinic writer, in terms not only of exegetical methods but of content as well. By the sixth century, these works suggest, rabbinic readings of Scripture and liturgical norms of halakhah were accepted, at least in Yannai's community.[33] There are, however, notable cases where Yannai's teachings are, in whole or in part, apparently original.

Of course, it is difficult to say that a motif is unique, or to ascertain when it is first attested. Given the vast size and the organic organization of traditional Jewish literature, something as small as a motif is easy to overlook or may yet be discovered. The problems in dating aggadic traditions (even more difficult than dating texts) raise further complications. A relatively late compositional date for a text does not necessitate a late date for the tradition itself. Since the discovery of the Cairo Genizah— which has so enriched the study of piyyut—the complex manuscript history of midrash has also become more evident, and the rich variety of texts suggests that midrashic traditions themselves were very fluid.

An example will perhaps elucidate the issues involved in the dating of texts. The *qedushta* for Gen 16:1 alludes to Gen 12:5 (particularly the phrase: "and the soul[s] they had made in Haran") when it states in Poem Five, "Abram and Sarai in confidence took refuge // because of all the souls that they made in Haran" (lines1–2). The idiom "to make souls" (*la`asot nefesh*) is understood by the Rabbis to mean "to create converts" (*GenR* 39:14, 84:4; *NumR* 14:10; *SongR* 1:22; *Tanḥ Lekh Lekha* 12; and others), an interpretation made explicit in the next line, where the poet states that "the reward of the souls / would be the gift of souls" (line 4). This specific "measure for measure" evaluation of Abram and Sarai's missionary efforts is paralleled only in one other source: *Pesiqta Rabbati* 43:6, a passage in which God rewards the ancestors' missionary efforts (i.e., the making of Jewish souls) with the birth of their own "soul," Isaac. *Pesiqta Rabbati* is generally dated to approximately the fifth to sixth century (the latter end overlaps with Yannai's approximate lifetime) and it is possible, if unlikely, that one source (the poet or the midrash) originated this interpretation, which subsequently spread and influenced the author of the other work. Alternatively, and more likely, Yannai and the author/ editor of *Pesiqta Rabbati* drew on a shared, but otherwise unpreserved, exegetical tradition

33 See the discussion below on the importance of seeing Yannai in his larger societal context.

about Gen 12:5, or each author independently arrived at this interpretation on his own. Similarly, when late sources, such as *Midrash ha-Gadol*, offer the best parallels for an earlier source, we cannot assume that the author (or editor) of the late work directly borrowed from the earlier source. It is possible, however, that the midrashic source reflects an older, albeit not well-attested, interpretation. In general, it is more fruitful to think of exegetes in Late Antiquity as living in an exegetical culture (or subculture)—a world richly infused with Scripture and its interpretation—rather than constructing an artificial scenario by which one author borrowed from another in a linear fashion.

Nevertheless, given Yannai's learning, creativity, and influence, when he innovates, it is possible that he is not merely transmitting an extant tradition but originating it. For example, Rabinovitz notes that the teaching in line 16 of the *asiriyyah* (Poem Five) for Gen 31:3 is, simply, unattested elsewhere. In this line, Yannai picks up on the fact that the lemma (Gen 31:3) says "turn back" (ש-ו-ב) and not "go back" (ח-ז-ר). To the poet, the choice of the root ש-ו-ב includes overtones of repentance (*teshuvah*, which is from the same root), and the biblical author's choice not to use the less theologically significant synonym must serve a purpose. Jacob had to repent as part of his process of physical return. As lovely as this teaching is, and as much in keeping with methods of rabbinic exegesis as it is, it appears at present to be unique to Yannai. Similarly, in the *silluq* (Poem Eight) for Gen 44:18 (line 5), there is no parallel elsewhere in surviving rabbinic writings or targum for the heavenly voice (*bat kol*) that cries out for battle—although the actual words uttered by the heavenly voice, "this is the time and the moment," are found in both the Palestinian Talmud and the liturgy.[34] As noted above and developed below, however, even when Yannai innovates, his exegetical methods strongly reflect those of rabbinic midrash. He is a poet of a high culture, not a counter- culture.

Indeed, there are places where Yannai blurs the line between *midrash*—in terms of exegetical method—and *melitzah* (sophisticated coinages, specifically the allusive, abbreviated invocation of phrases from the Bible as a narrative shorthand). Midrash itself is a profoundly complex

34 See Zulay, "Matters of Language in the Poetry of Yannai," 228, s.v. "עת ועונה." Zulay notes that while this idiom, "This is the time and this is the moment," is very ancient in Palestinian Hebrew, it is not included in dictionaries. Zulay cites multiple passages in the Palestinian Talmud that include it, including versions of the petitionary text *aneinu* ("answer us"), which is also found in the High Holiday liturgy and in the poetry by Qillir.

phenomenon, but as noted above, the most essential act of midrash is the application of one verse to clarify—often to specify—the meaning of another. The two verses exist simultaneously, the space between them collapsed and nullified by the interpreter. The new interpretation of Prov 3:6 in the *magen* for Gen 12:1, noted above, displays the exegetical power of juxtaposing a lemma with an intertext. Moreover, the generative power of intertextuality need not be limited to the first three poems of the *qedushta*, where lists of verses are juxtaposed with each other. It can be seen in the body of the *qedushta* as well. For example, a constant theme in Genesis is fraternal friction. The theme of familial conflict inspires Yannai in two different instances in his Genesis piyyutim to allude to Ps 133:1, "How good and pleasant it is when brothers dwell together." The first use of this allusion, an example of *melitzah* (intertextuality), occurs in Poem Six for the *qedushta* to Gen 32:4, in which the biblical reference adds a note of irony (or pathos) to the haste with which Jacob and Esau—temporarily at peace—separate from each other (line 39). The second allusion occurs in the opening stanza of the *meḥayyeh* (Poem Two) for the *qedushta* for Gen 37:1, where it again appears to be both ironic and, in this instance, pathos-laden, as the poet describes precisely how un-peaceful the life of Joseph and his brothers was, and how Joseph—naively and ineffectively—sought reconciliation with them, with the result that he was sold into slavery (line 1–2). Ps 133:1 is not connected elsewhere in rabbinic writings to either Jacob and Esau or Joseph and his brothers; this specific "midrash" seems to be unique to Yannai, although the content of the exegesis and his method (specifying concretely the general references in the Psalm verse) are wholly traditional. In Yannai's era, midrash was a vibrant and fluid genre, and it seems quite likely that our poet participated in its creation as well as its transmission.

In a *qedushta*, intertextuality is not limited to Scripture, however. Yannai's work integrates liturgical language and references as well.[35] As the above-cited example from the *silluq* (Poem Eight) for Gen 44:18 suggests, the relationship between Yannai and the liturgy is as complex as—although perhaps more taken for granted than—his relationship with aggadah. Obviously, the interweaving of liturgical texts is fundamental to the fixed structure of the *qedushta*, and it is somewhat analogous to the formal, pre-

35 Elements of the statutory liturgy can be seen as a genre of rabbinic literature; see J. Heineman, *Prayer in the Talmud.*

dictable pattern of the midrashic *petiḥta*—a double-*petiḥta*, in fact, because the *qedushta* possesses both scriptural and liturgical destinations.

The comparison of midrashic *petiḥta* and piyyut will be explored further in later sections, but here a summary will clarify the formal and rhetorical similarities. The *petiḥta*, as noted above, begins with one verse (one "from afar") and works its way towards its given conclusion (the lemma); it is a classic formal example of using Scripture to interpret Scripture, based on similarities of theme, action, or language. Similarly, in Yannai, each complete poetic cycle begins and ends with liturgical quotations: the first two blessings of the Amidah are integrated into the themes of the first two poetic units, while the *qedushah* poem works its way towards the Qedushah prayer (at least its key verses, Isa 6:3 and Ezek 3:12). Just as the *petiḥta* engages the audience by suggesting (but not immediately delineating) the connections between two verses, Yannai encourages the audience to anticipate how he will connect the fixed liturgical phrases to the themes and key verses of the Torah portion—all within the rhyme-scheme and other formal constraints, as well. Just as the *petiḥta* transitions at its conclusion into the first words of the Torah portion, the first poem of the *qedushta* works its way inexorably towards the first words of the first verse of the Torah portion—but the concluding stanza must accomplish an additional transition to the word *magen* ("shield"). Similarly, the second stanza concludes with references to dew—implicitly the dew of resurrection, emblematic of life renewed, which is the theme of the second benediction.[36] And throughout the *qedushta*, particularly beginning with Poem Three, the poet must introduce and integrate the element of holiness that he has found in the

36 One of the unusual elements of Yannai's *qedushtaʾot* is the mention of "dew" in almost every composition for which the second poem is extant and the absence of "rain" (*geshem*) in all but two, those for Gen 48:18 and Exod 12:29 (and those cases may reflect later scribal corrections). This despite the fact that his writings cover the complete Torah and were meant to be read during the course of roughly three and a half years. Zulay suggested that the Palestinian *payyetanim* (or at least some of them) were accustomed to pray for dew year-round ("*Meḥqrei Yannai,*" *Yediʿot ha-makhon le-ḥeqer ha-shirah ha-ivrit* 2 [1925]: 274–75. See also E. Fleischer, "*Iyyunim be-baʿayot tafqidam ha-liturgi shel sugei ha-piyyut ha-qodem,*" *Tarbiz* 40 (1970/71): 58n. Heinemann rather improbably suggests that *qedushtaʾot* were only recited during the long Sabbaths of summer ("The Machzor of the Triennial Cycle and the Annual Calendar," *Tarbiz* 33 [1964/65]: 368 [Hebrew]; an English version of the article appeared as: "The Triennial Lectionary Cycle," *Journal of Jewish Studies* 19 (1968): 41–48. Rabinovitz sidesteps the peculiarity by dissociating the dew of the poems and the dew mentioned in the seasonal prayer: the dew in the poems is not "dew" in any literal way but "the dew of resurrection." (*The Liturgical Poetry of Rabbi Yannai,* vol. 1, pp. 13–14).

Torah portion so that he can connect the biblical narrative to the third blessing of the Amidah. The language and themes of the blessings work like intertexts alongside the actual biblical verses cited, and as a result, the motifs of protection, resurrection, and holiness become part of the biblical story and its interpretation, and vice-versa.

Linking each Torah portion to the liturgical themes of the first two blessings of the Amidah—protection and resurrection—must have been a challenge for the poet, but in each case, the scope of the challenge was limited to individual units; the challenge could be met and quickly dispatched. The need to yoke the scriptural reading to the motif of holiness and the language of the Qedushah was more pervasive and began formally with the concluding phrase of the *meshallesh* (Poem Three), with its fixed quotation from Ps 22:4, "But You are Holy, enthroned on the praises of Israel." The concluding units of the *qedushta*—certainly the *qedushah* (Poem Nine) and often the prefatory *silluq* (Poem Eight)—make increasingly intense use of the word "holy" (*qadosh*) in anticipation of the threefold repetition of that word in Isa 6:3. Furthermore, due to the tripled repetition of "holy" in Isaiah, Yannai sought to distinguish not one but *three* connotations of holiness within his poetic theme in order to specify each repetition. Yannai's implicit rejection of any sense of redundancy in the repetition of "Holy, holy, holy" is consummately midrashic, as is the technique of breaking up phrases in interpreting them separately but in proximity. Yannai believes, like the Rabbis, that there are no superfluous words in Scripture, or, apparently, the liturgy—and how much the more so scriptural words *within* the liturgy. Thus we find, for example, in the *qedushta* for Gen 9:18, that the recitations of "holy" in Poem Nine describe the unique holiness of Noah's three sons: Shem, Yafet, and Ham. In the *qedushta* for Gen 28:10, "holy" is distributed over three kinds of angels who watched over Jacob: angels of mercy, angels of peace, and angels of hosts. And in the *qedushta* for Gen 48:10: the escaped of Judah, the captives of Jacob, and the remnant of Joseph are all contemporaries. In many *qedushta*ʾ*ot*, the poet goes beyond Isaiah 6:3 and also embellishes the word ממקומו ("from His place") from the second key verse of the Qedushah, Ezek 3:12. When Yannai does this, he likewise extends the threefold division of the "holy" section. As with the *petiḥta*, working its way towards the first verse of the Torah portion, the *qedushta* is working its way towards the explicit quotations of Isa 6:3 and Ezek 3:12—a pattern that is completely assumed, expected, and anticipated by the listeners.

In order to appreciate more fully the complex interrelationship between midrash and piyyut, as well as the role of the audience and liturgical context in shaping interpretation, piyyut's use of midrashic forms must be particularly scrutinized. After all, poetry is not merely a lexical assembly of resonant words; poems are constructed on the basis of specific rhetorical forms that themselves help shape their meanings. At times, aesthetics and poetics alone determine these forms.[37] In many cases, however, Yannai's rhetoric displays a deep affinity for midrash.

Piyyut and Midrash: Forms and Functions

In the previous section, we considered Yannai's poetry primarily from the per spective of its interpreted (if at times implicit) understandings of the biblical text. Comparison of piyyut with midrash and targum—the other major aggadic genres of biblical interpretation in Late Antiquity and into the Middle Ages—reveals numerous thematic parallels and common motifs.

As this section will show, piyyut and midrash share deep formal and structural affinities, as well. So strong is the resemblance between midrashic and payyetanic rhetoric that some scholars, notably Aharon Mirsky, have traced the origins of piyyut to prose midrashic forms.[38] For some poetic units—particularly the *rahit* (Poem Seven)—we agree that midrashic origins may, in fact, best account for the origin of the form. More generally, and cautiously speaking, however, the obvious parallels probably reflect somewhat more widespread aesthetic and intellectual trends influencing both midrash and poetry in the same period. The origins of piyyut, after all, lie in the same period when the classical midrashic traditions were coalescing and the Palestinian *Targumim* were being committed to writing. Yannai's exegesis shows a clear affinity for Palestinian traditions—especially those recorded in the major midrashic anthologies and the Palestinian Tal-

---

37 See Chapter Two.

38 The question of the origins of piyyut is addressed below. Mirsky is the strongest proponent of the theory that the roots of piyyut lie in rabbinic exegetical techniques. See, for example, his introduction to the poetry of Yose ben Yose (*Yose ben Yose: Poems*), 40–62, and the articles assembled in the anthology of his works, *The Piyyut* (Jerusalem: Magnes, 1990) [Hebrew]. Mirsky may overstate the case of payyetanic independence and downplay the possible influence of Christian (or other external) influences. However, when specific poems are examined, the resemblance to midrash is very strong, as the following analysis indicates. See also the discussion in Chapter Four.

mud.[39] As a result, perhaps we should not be surprised when these texts—especially midrash and piyyut, both of which are in Hebrew—share methods as well as content.

Intertexts

We have already examined the anthologies of verses that follow the first three poetic units in terms of how they create meaning (Chapter Two) and generate implicit midrash (earlier in this chapter). This juxtaposition of lemma and intertexts connects the first three piyyutim of the *qedushta*, in terms of both form and method, with midrashic prose.

At first glance, the catalogues of verses in the poems might suggest that Yannai has simply adapted and developed the way texts are used in the *seliḥot* compositions (assemblies of verses linked by shared words and themes, which may pre-date Yannai or be contemporary with him) and pre-Classical piyyutim of Yose ben Yose and other anonymous *payyetanim.*[40] The piyyutim of the century or so preceding Yannai typically employed lists of biblical quotations in some fashion.[41] In particular, the lists of verses in Yannai's piyyutim recall the structures found in poems originally composed for use in the context of the Rosh Hashanah Shofar service. The *malkhiyot*, *zikhronot*, and *shofarot* poems by the poet Yose ben Yose (roughly a century before Yannai) integrate lists of verses into their structure. The verses in these early poems for Rosh Hashanah resemble similar lists in the *seliḥot* prayers, also from the penitential season. The *seliḥot* are not actually poetry in most cases but rather thematically-linked litanies of verses recited in a liturgical context.[42] Yannai's inclusion of anthologies may be a continuation of these older liturgical forms.

The apparent similarities between these two kinds of writing may, how-

---

39 This preference for Palestinian Jewish sources—a critical factor in dating and placing our poet—are delineated most comprehensively in Rabinovitz, *Halakhah and Aggadah in the Liturgical Poetry of Yannai.* A brief synopsis can be found in the introduction to Rabinovitz's edition of Yannai's piyyutim (pp. 55–60) [Hebrew].

40 The precise date of the *seliḥot* compositions is difficult to fix; it seems likely that they are roughly contemporary with the rise of piyyut rather than predecessors to it. See Langer, "Biblical Texts in Jewish Prayers." For a more thorough exploration of the interrelationships of *seliḥot* texts and piyyut, see Lieber, "Penitential Themes in Early Synagogue Poetry."

41 Here the focus is on lists of biblical texts; the *avodah* poems quote Mishnah *Yoma* in much the same way. See Swartz and Yahalom, *Avodah.*

42 For a variety of perspectives on Jewish liturgical poetry and related texts, see the essays in Mark J. Boda, Daniel K. Falk, and Rodney Werline, eds., *Penitential Prayer: Origins, Development, and Impact*, vol. 3 (Atlanta: Society of Biblical Literature, 2008). The essays by

ever, be misleading. We know from *m. Rosh Hashanah* 4:5–6 and *m.Taʿan.* 2:2–4 that the recitation of specific biblical verses comprised the core of the Shofar service and penitential rites. They were not simply the prayer-leader's choice. These verses are central to, not ancillary embellishments of, the composition. The Shofar-service piyyutim provide an ornate framework for the recitation of the verses, but it is the verses themselves that possess the power.

To be sure, Yannai's inclusion of intertexts indicates a similar understanding of the liturgical role of Scripture, whereby the power of a verse is released by reciting it in a ritual, performative context. Specifically, the liturgical potency of Isa 6:3 and Ezek 3:12 in the Qedushah (and, thus, in poem nine of the *qedushta*) recalls the use of traditional, fixed, and liturgically-powerful quotations in the Shofar service and *seliḥot* ritual. These verses of angelic liturgy, brought to earth by the Prophets who overheard them from on high, are intrinsically potent, more important and powerful than the poetry in which they are embedded. In the opening units, the benediction and the lemma only, not the intertexts, are fixed; the poet had free rein to tailor other citations to his purposes. For Yannai, the poetry is primary, and the verses cited have primarily aesthetic and didactic functions. The verses quoted explicitly ("as it is written," and "as it is said") in a *qedushta* acquire power through their interpretation—that is, their potency is unleashed not through liturgical, talismanic recitation, but through juxtaposition with the lemma. The verses unlock one another; their potency does not derive from liturgical context alone but from exegesis. In this way, Yannai reveals himself to be a much more midrashic writer than the earlier *payyetanim*. Although Yose ben Yose and the other early *payyetanim* clearly knew rabbinic literature (particularly the Mishnah, which is quoted in the *avodah* piyyutim written for Yom Kippur), their compositions do not use texts to generate implicit midrash to the extent or with the depth that Yannai does.[43] Yose ben Yose alludes to rabbinic themes and motifs, while Yannai actively engages in their creation.[44] To put it another way, the earlier texts—the High Holiday poems and

---

Richard Sarason, Ruth Langer, and Laura Lieber are particularly pertinent to the present topic.

43 On the generation of midrash through the juxtaposition of texts—indeed , for a definition of midrash that relies on this method—see Boyarin, *Intertextuality and the Reading of Midrash.*

44 See Mirsky, *Formal Foundations of Piyyut,* discussed at length below.

seliḥot rituals, and the Qedushah as well—are writing *towards* Scripture with the recitation of verses as their objective. Yannai is writing *with* Scripture—using the powerful and evocative language of the interpreted Bible to create new and powerful works.[45]

Indeed, Yannai's poetry reveals deep and integral connections to the midrashic process. The opening example of this chapter—the *magen* (Poem One) for Gen 12:1—contains intertexts that were associated with the lemma (Gen 12:1) in midrashic works, such as Ps 45:11–12, which was a *petiḥta* verse in *GenR* and a key text in the *Tanḥumah* interpretations. The affinity between Yannai's intertexts and those that appear as key verses in midrashic *petiḥtot* is particularly intriguing, in that it seems hardly coincidental that one Rabbi's *petiḥta* verse should become one of Yannai's intertexts, the implication being that the two verses have a history of being connected.[46] The exegetical similarity is amplified by the fact that both the poem and the *petiḥta* derive a portion of their power from the element of delay involved in the resolution of the interpretation—i.e., the final synchronization of lemma, intertext, and (in Yannai's case especially) context. Rhetoric complements content and language.

Such overlap between piyyut and midrash happens frequently. In Yannai's *qedushta* for Gen 8:15, the second verse in the anthology following the *magen* is Prov 12:13, which opens the *petiḥta* in *GenR* 34:3 and also appears as an exegetical verse in *Tanḥ Noah* 10 and *TanḥB Noah* 16. Both the poet and the midrashic authors understand "the righteous one" to refer to Noah—"righteous" becomes an epithet for Noah throughout the poem—while "the wicked" are taken to be the generation of the flood. Similarly, Yannai includes Ps 142:8 as an intertext, a verse associated with Noah in *GenR* 34:1, *Tanḥ Noah* 11, and *TanḥB Noah* 17. These three midrashic sources, like the piyyut, understand Noah to be the speaker of the Psalms verse—an association indicated nowhere in the biblical text itself.

45 On the subject of "writing with Scripture," see the discussion in Chapter Two.

46 As noted above, the overlap between Yannai's intertext and the exegetical verses in classical rabbinic *petiḥtot* merits more extensive study than is possible here. The congruity is frequent enough to suggest that specific histories of interpretation were associated with the *petiḥta*-verses; at the same time, Yannai does not always cite *petiḥta*-verses among his intertexts, suggesting a more complex relationship than a poetic reliance on midrash. He displays freedom and creativity in his use of intertexts. Likewise, we should not dismiss the possibility that liturgical poetry helped shape the history of interpretation of some verses—i.e., verses first used as intertexts in piyyutim became important midrashic intertexts.

Even more intriguingly, *PRE* 23 (a text that may have been influenced by Yannai) states: "Through me—says Noah—all the righteous will crown You with a crown of sovereignty," a paraphrase of the poetic and midrashic interpretations of the second half of Ps 142:8. In Yannai's poetry, such interpretations are conveyed not by articulation but by juxtaposition—the simple act of placing a biblical verse in close proximity to a retold biblical story. The poet indicates the path, but the listener must finish the journey to meaning.

Many similar examples of shared intertextual traditions are easily adduced, and many (although far from all) are noted in the translations. For example, the *magen* (Poem One) for Gen 14:1 includes in its verse series Ps 37:4, which opens the proem in *GenR* 42:1 and appears in *Tanḥ Lekh Lekha* 7 and *TanḥB Lekh Lekha* 7. In the *magen* (Poem One) for Gen 16:1, Yannai cites: Ps 45:1, which *GenR* 45:1 applies to Sarai; Song 2:14, which likewise applies to Sarai in *GenR* 45:4, *SongR* 2:14, *Tanḥ Toledot* 9, and *b.Yev.* 64a; and Song 4:12, which appears also in *LevR* 32:5, *SongR* 4:12, and *PRK Veyehi Beshallaḥ* 7. These affinities between Yannai's intertexts and the exegetical verses in midrash strongly imply that both drew upon common exegetical traditions. One key difference remains, however: Yannai implicitly relies upon his audience to generate the interpretation that the midrashic texts explicitly teach.

Interestingly, in some cases, verses that Yannai selects as intertexts reappear later in a poem—a form of self-referential allusion. We see this, for example, in Yannai's use of the epithet "the righteous one" for Noah throughout the *qedushta* for Gen 8:15—a metonym rooted not only in Gen 6:9 but also, by extension, in Prov 12:13, cited as an intertext after the *magen* (Poem One). This is an example of a midrashic idea being assumed and internalized, and similar examples, such as the commonplace epithet "the pure one" (from Gen 25:27) for Jacob can be found throughout Yannai's writings. Other examples offer even stronger evidence of this phenomenon. For example, the *meḥayyeh* (Poem Two) for Gen 16:1 includes Prov 31:10 (the opening of "the woman of valor" passage) as its first intertext. The identification of Sarah with "the woman of valor" appears explicitly in *GenR* 45:1, *TanḥB Ḥayyei Sarah* 3, and *MidPs* 112:1. Nowhere in the *meḥayyeh* itself does the language of Prov 31:1 occur—nothing in the specific unit anticipates the quotation, although the exegesis of the verse is clear through context. Later in the *qedushta*, however—line 33 of Poem Six—the poet quotes Prov 31:26 ("she opens her mouth in wisdom"), as a way of describing Sarah's plan as "wise." This same association appears in *Tanḥ Ḥayyei Sarah* 4, which states: "`She opened her mouth in wisdom'—When? When she said to him [Abram], `Go, please, unto my handmaiden...'" The use of Prov 31:1 as an isolated intertext early in the *qedushta* prepares the listener for this deft allusion later in the poem. In effect, the poet teases members of the audience, alerting them to Sarah's identity as "the woman of valor" while waiting until later to make any use of the identification. Proverbs' "woman of valor," interpreted only through the active participation of the audience in its first appearance, becomes a building-block for the subsequent creation of meaning. The midrashic process not only edifies but engages.

These patterns of shared-verse traditions—the use of common exegetical verses harvested from throughout the Hebrew Bible in both piyyut and midrash—suggest deep affinities between the genres. The specific nature of the relationship, however, is unclear. We cannot know, for example, whether the poets were simply students of midrash, conveying in a public forum of the synagogue the type of exegesis prevalent in the academies; or whether the poets composed poems designed specifically to delight audiences already well-steeped in the exegesis of these verses. Perhaps *payyetan* and *darshan* simply shared a common approach to interpreting the Bible—the use of Scripture to interpret Scripture—and crafted this form of rhetoric in the ways best suited to their genres: pedagogical prose or prayerful poetry. Indeed, Yannai's poetry may suggest that the synagogues (*batei kenesset*) and academies (*batei midrash*) were not such separate institutions, at least not in Yannai's community (or time period), and the synagogue may, in the end, have to be reevaluated as a locus of midrashic creativity.[47] Too often it is tempting to oversimplify complicated cultural phenomena (particularly when some of the sources themselves present a simple, if not necessarily consistent, picture). The reality—or realities— probably involve a combination of the above hypotheses, and other factors as well.

For all that we cannot know, however, we can acknowledge that the poet's

47 The terms "house of study" or "academy" (*bet midrash*) and "house of assembly" or "synagogue" (*bet kenesset*) refer to complex social realities, and the precise relationship between the two—their overlap—is not a settled matter; the intensively aggadic content of piyyut may suggest a greater degree of overlap than has been commonly assumed in much recent literature. See Levine, *The Ancient Synagogue*, 381–411 and 476–78, and Catherine Hezser's summary of different views on these terms (particularly "house of study") and the possible realities reflected by them in *The Social Structure of the Rabbinic Movement in Roman Palestine*, 185–227.

reliance on implicit exegesis makes sophisticated demands of his audience. Yannai does not explicate the verses in any linear or explicit way. Rather, the full meaning of the texts must be drawn out by the audience using cues and contexts the poet has carefully presented prior to citing the verses. The exegesis in a Yannai *qedushta* is a kind of essentialized midrash. The responsibility placed on the audience may be one reason the poet includes verse anthologies only for the first three poetic units. We don't know the origins of these lists, but it is possible that, in theory, the poet could have fulfilled the most basic demands of the *qedushta* form by simply quoting the lemma—without including these series of additional verses. Maybe the anthologies served to engage the audience intellectually—like the *petiḥta.* In the case of the poem, the implicit task was not to identify the aggadic source or parallel (as is often the case in the way the poems are studied now, with the great search for parallels that shed light on what the poet may mean by his quotations and allusions) but to generate meaning. The cyclical, repetitive nature of many *qedushtaʾot* also suggests that key ideas were not meant to be grasped entirely at the first pass, but perhaps assembled and deepened over the course of the entire performance.

At the same time, we should not underestimate the biblical literacy of the ancient communities: while we cannot assume that the general populace would have mastered all of aggadic tradition, we can suppose that knowledge of the Hebrew Bible was relatively wide-spread—particularly the Torah, the *haftarot*, the *megillot*, and certain works such as Psalms—and that certain basic modes of reading text were also well known. Indeed, if the listeners knew any Hebrew, it would have been the Hebrew of the Bible.[48] Thus it may be that these anthologies of intertexts are not elitist but popular. They may constitute an opening volley, a challenge to engage and intrigue, which is followed—much as we find in the literary midrashic anthologies—by clearer, more expository teachings. Yannai's intertexts do not simply allude to midrash—that is an anachronistic scholarly assumption that renders the poet and audience more passive than they were. It also overestimates the fixity of midrashic teachings themselves. More likely, the piyyutim reflect the liveliness and fluidity of biblical exegesis in Late Antiquity. The verses Yannai cites are not just references awaiting footnotes; they are invitations to the audience to take what they know and create meanings of their own.

48 See discussion in Chapter Two.

Midrashic Tropes in Poetry

In his brief but seminal monograph, *The Formal Foundations of Piyyut*,[49] Aharon Mirsky delineates poetic structures common to early piyyut (including those of Yannai) that bear striking similarities to rabbinic exegesis preserved in the midrashic compendia and the two Talmuds. Mirsky endeavored in this study, as in many of his other works, to demonstrate that the roots of piyyut lie in aggadah—that is, for Mirsky, piyyut represents an organic development within Hebrew/ Rabbinic literature and was not a radical innovation borrowed from the Greco-Roman or Byzantine-Christian world. Leaving aside thorny questions of origin and directions of transmission (for the moment), we will focus on several ways in which Yannai's rhetoric and form clearly echo the rhetoric and form of attested aggadic traditions. The names given the categories are those found in Mirsky's study. Only a few representative examples—all from Yannai's *qedushta*ʾ*ot* for Genesis—are given for each trope, although noteworthy examples from elsewhere in Yannai's writings will be indicated upon occasion.

1. THE VERSE CLOSES THE *DRASH* (interpretation): This structure, which might be labeled "prooftexting," is defined by the use of a specific text to conclude a teaching (in piyyut, a phrase or word from a verse ends the stanza; in midrash, a complete verse may be cited). In *midrashim*, the verse that closes the *drash* is often prefaced by "as it is written" or another obvious marker (e.g., "thus" or "[Scripture] says"). As noted above, this formal device creates a superficial appearance of similarity between Yannai's *qedushta*ʾ*ot* and midrash, on the one hand, and the early piyyutim and the *seliḥot* rituals on the other. In the Shofar service, for example, the collocations of verses are prefaced by "as it is written in Your Torah" (for the citation from the Torah), "as it is written in Your holy words" (for the citations from Writings), and "as it is written by the hand of Your prophet" (for the verses from the Prophets). In Yannai, we have seen that the groupings after the first three poetic units use "as it is written" for the lectionary verses and "as it is said" for the subsequent intertexts, no matter what the source.[50] The subtle but significant difference in terminology reflects deeper differences in agenda. In the Shofar service, as already discussed,

49 Jerusalem: Magnes, 1985 [Hebrew].

50 See Chapter Two for a delineation of the form of the individual units that constitute a *qedushta* and Appendix I for an outline of the *qedushta* as a whole.

the series of verses is primary; in Yannai's poems—probably because the *qedushta* was an innovative form inserted in a developing liturgy rather than a literary genre developing around clusters of verses—the poetry itself and the embedded interpretations are central. Yannai and other authors of *qedushta'ot* appear to have had a freedom that Yose ben Yose and the other early *payyetanim* lacked because the *qedushta* itself had fewer predetermined features than the Shofar service and *seliḥot* rituals. In all cases, we can say that verses conclude the poems, but only with Yannai and the later poets is it truly appropriate to say that the poems themselves are "*drash.*"

At any rate, the anthologies of verses inserted in the first three poems are only one, and the most basic, way of understanding the device of "the verse closes the *drash.*" Mirsky cites examples by other poets in which a single verse is parsed out across multiple stanzas of a poem so that a single quotation concludes *multiple* stanzas, one phrase after each. This technique of breaking up a verse and interpreting the pieces in distinct but related ways clearly parallels midrashic techniques. It becomes particularly productive in poetry, however, where various forms of parallelism play important formal roles.[51] In Yannai, we see this pattern adapted to a distinctive and yet usually simple style: a *single* phrase from a single verse concludes *multiple* stanzas. Often units displaying this structure are prefaced by a somewhat longer quotation from the verse, which makes the biblical source of the language explicit (connecting this form to "the verse opens the *drash*" discussed below).[52] We see this phenomenon, for example, in the first *rahit* (Poem Seven[1]) for Gen 48:1. The first verse of the Torah portion states: "And it came to pass after these things, that he told Joseph, 'Lo, your father is ill'; and he took with him his two sons, Manasseh and Ephraim." The *rahit* is prefaced by the phrase, "And thus [it is written:] 'Manasseh and Ephraim'" (the final words of Gen 48:1). Each phrase of the *rahit* itself concludes with the names "Manasseh" and "Ephraim" in alternation. In reality, however, each pairing of Manasseh-Ephraim implies a

---

51 *Formal Foundations of Piyyut*, p. 101.

52 For example, Yannai's *qedushta* for the third Shabbat of Rebuke includes a unit that contrasts "the days of Moses" with "the days of Jeremiah" (Rabinovitz 2:309–10). The content closely parallels a passage in *PRK Divrei Yirmiyahu* 13. The midrash, however, explicates the series of prooftexts and is written from the perspective of Jeremiah, while Yannai's poem much more starkly juxtaposes scriptural quotations with poetic observations in the poet's own voice. The parallelism of the prose midrash is maintained but reduced to its most basic elements. (Other poems for this cycle, however, are in Jeremiah's voice.)

different intertext and thus a distinctive midrash; in each case, then, the abbreviated quotation from Gen 48:1 "closes" the *drash* implicit in the stanza. For example, the concluding stanza states:

> Years of hardship we have forgotten, as in the name *Manasseh*;
> We will bear fruit for goodness, as in the name *Ephraim*
> (Poem Seven[1], lines 21–22)

The language of this stanza depends on Gen 41:51–52, where the etymologies for the names of Joseph's sons are given. However, Yannai does not necessarily present just the simple meaning of these verses; instead, he understands them as a prophecy, foretelling events of his own day (hardship) and the future (reward). Thus, the verse becomes part of an implicit interpretation—a *drash*—in which the names of Joseph's sons acquire added prophetic significance: the "forgetting" of Manasseh's name extends forward into the future when Israel is redeemed; and the "fruitfulness" of Ephram—a pun on *peri* , "fruit"—likewise describes a time to come.

The exegesis of Gen 41:51–52 embedded in this stanza resembles a teaching in *ExodR* that does not explicate Gen 48:1 but that does explore the significance of the names of Joseph's sons:

> "And she [Zipporah] bore a son and he [Moses] called his name Gershom, for he said: I have been a stranger in a strange land" (Exod 2:22). It is the custom of the righteous to name their children based on some event that has occurred. What does it say in the case of Joseph? "And he called the name of the first-born *Manasseh*, for God has made me forget all my toil, and all my father's house" (Gen 41:51). "And the name of the second called he *Ephraim*; for God has made me fruitful in the land of my affliction" (Gen 41:52), so that he should always be mindful of the miracles God had done for him. So Moses called the name of his son Gershom on account of the miracle God had done unto him, for though he was a stranger in an alien country God caused him to prosper even there. (*ExodR* 1:33)

Both the midrashic exegete and the poet remind us of the deep significance of the names Ephraim and Manasseh, and both draw on Gen 41:51–52 in their interpretations. Formally, the primary difference is in verbosity: the midrash carefully explicates its interpretation, while the poet focuses on the terse requirements of his own form. The exegetical difference between the two texts, however, is that while the midrash emphasizes the "past tense" origin of the names, in keeping with the biblical text that lies behind them, Yannai reads them typologically. The names of the ancestors become paradigms for the sons. And, as Yannai constructs this *rahit*, this interpretation becomes embedded within the biblical phrase, "...and Manasseh and Ephraim," which—though broken up—closes each stich. These names are the final words of Gen 48:1, and by using the names to close each stanza, Yannai evokes a much lengthier midrashic tradition.

Other lines from this poem could provide additional parallels between aggadic sources and the pairings of Ephraim and Manasseh in this piyyut—although in no case does Yannai precisely echo any particular midrash in this specific poem. Instead, the lemma itself is broken in half and reinterpreted in twelve often novel ways. It is the exegetical *technique* more than the content that most recalls midrash here, and in each stich, the name contains a new revelation of meaning. To be sure, individual stanzas—as detailed in the notes to this poem—recall specific aggadic motifs. But the content here is essentially unique to Yannai; it is the *form* that engages with tradition. At the same time, it is possible that the sheer repetitiveness of this kind of rhetoric in the piyyut may have functioned not just exegetically but performatively as a kind of refrain, drawing in either the congregation or perhaps performed by a choir. Because this technique occurs so commonly in the *rahit*, when the poet is beginning his transition to the Qedushah, such a rhetorical-performative device would have served not only to convey a message to the listeners, but to rouse them for the drama of the liturgical experience to come.

2. The Verse Opens the *Drash* (interpretation): The structure of "the verse closes the *drash*," where the quotation comes at the end of a stich, line, or stanza, is very common in midrash and not rare in Yannai. For example, the *rahit* for Gen 35:9 concludes each line with "Israel," emphasizing the name change that occurs in the Torah portion (specifically, in Gen 35:10, which appears as an incipit before the unit: "and thus: `Israel will be your name'"), and implicitly the naming of the children of Israel, too; and the *rahit* for Gen 38:1 ends each line with "Judah" (from the first verse of the Torah portion, which again appears as an incipit: "And thus: `Then Judah went down from his brothers'"), which blurs the tense of the biblical narrative into the present and future. Yannai's preference, however, is for the related exegetical form, "the verse that opens the *drash*." Festival

piyyutim, such as the *qerova* and *shivʿata* for Passover—both poems embellish the entire Song of Songs, based on the opening words of each verse[53]—may employ extended text passages to structure an entire poetic cycle. In poems composed for the weekly service, simpler structures are typically used, with particular frequency in the *rahit.*

In essence, this pattern is quite similar to the previous structure except that the quotation from Scripture *precedes* each stanza rather than concludes it. In the *rahit* for Gen 28:10, a different verse opens up each stanza, with each verse edited so that the name "Jacob" concludes the quotation (and, in an impressive display of virtuosity, each verse contributes to an alphabetical acrostic, as well). The first extant stanza states:

> *For the Lord redeemed Jacob* (Jer 31:11)
> Redemption He will send again / just as He sent before
> Suddenly it will sprout up springing forth and coming swiftly
> (Poem Seven, lines 1–3)

In this stanza, the poet reads the quotation from Jeremiah as both an historical narration about the biblical patriarch Jacob and a prediction regarding the fate of Jacob's descendents, the Jews. The past tense of Jeremiah's prophecy speaks to both its historical content and, implicitly, of certain fulfillment in the time to come. Yannai's interpretation of the verse closely resembles the reading found in *GenR* 44:22:

> Rabbi Huna and Rabbi Dostai said in the name of Rabbi Samuel b. Naḥman: The mere speech of the Holy One, blessed be He, is equivalent to action… Rabbi Abin said: It is not written, "For the Lord *redeems* Jacob," but "For the Lord *redeemed* Jacob" (Jer 31:11).

This interpretation of Jer 31:11, like the piyyut, understands Jacob both as the patriarch and as the nation of Israel—a conflation necessary in many lines of this poem (and others as well). Exceptionally, each line of this *rahit* (Poem Seven) invokes a different biblical text; in some cases, the sense of the stanza depends upon the verse's simple meaning. In most instances, however, some more sophisticated form of exegesis is presumed.

53 The Passover poems are treated in Laura Lieber, *A Vocabulary of Desire: The Song of Songs in the Early Synagogue* (Leiden: Brill, forthcoming). In addition to the holiday piyyutim, it should also be noted that Yannai's *qedushta* for Lev 15:25 contains one extended passage, a *rahit* and *silluq*, which parses out Prov 31:10–31 ("the woman of valor"), one verse per stanza. Rabinovitz, vol. 1, pp. 437–41.

In the previous case, a single word ("Jacob") unifies numerous verses in an implicitly aggadic setting. More typically, however, a single verse (or a key word from a verse) is parsed out over multiple stanzas—much as was the case with "the verse closes the *drash*," only with the verse-element at the front of the stanza. Usually the chosen word or phrase comes from the first verse of the Torah portion, although occasionally Yannai may make use of the second verse instead. As with the previous trope, the verse almost invariably appears as an incipit or preface to the unit that articulates and emphasizes the connection between the verse and the *drash*. Yannai uses this structure with great frequency and skill, and Mirsky cites the second *rahit* for Gen 12:1, in which the single word "blessing" opens every stich, as an example of this form.[54] Likewise, both *r'hitim* for Gen 44:18 employ this structure. The first *rahit* begins every line with the opening words of the Torah portion, "Then he approached…" while the second *rahit* opens the first half of each line with "Please, my lord" and the second half with "do not" (both phrases from later within the lemma, as well). Unlike the example from "the verse closes the *drash*," in this instance the poet is not breaking up and explicating a word-pair but is rather using the formulaic phrasings within the lemma as structures for rewriting and extending the biblical scene itself. The verse opens Yannai's *drash*, as it were, but the *drash* itself is more aggadah than midrash.

The *r'hitim* for Gen 25:19 further develop our understanding of this verse-initial technique. Both units begin with the phrase, 'These are the generations of…', from the lemma, which (as expected) prefaces the section; the first *rahit* is relatively damaged and incomplete in the surviving manuscript, but the second reveals a complicated structure. Each line of the second *rahit* consists of two parts: an introductory dichotomy (the first trait is positive and applies to Jacob, the second is negative and applies to Esau) in the first half, and an explication of the dichotomy in the second half. For example:

> Descendents loved and loathed / loved, finding protection, and loathed, receiving rejection
> Descendents selected and rejected / selected as a treasure and rejected as something shunned

54 See Chapter Two for additional analysis of this *rahit*.

> Descendents of the kid and the leopard / a kid for favor and a leopard for a fight
> (Poem Seven², lines 1–6)

Keeping to this pattern, a later line states: "Generations of the birthright and the birthright lost / a birthright of sanctity and a birthright lost for a punishment" (Poem Seven², lines 9–10). The biblical subtext of this line comes from the conclusion of Gen 25, in which Esau sells his birthright to Jacob in exchange for a bowl of lentil stew. Implied in the *qedushta* is the tradition preserved in *GenR* 63:13, in which Esau's question in Gen 25:32, "What is this to me?" is interpreted as "What is This to me?"—a rejection of the God Jacob is eager to claim. ("This" being a rabbinic epithet for God; see Exod 15:2, "This is my God.") Between these two *r'hitim*, the simple opening phrase of the lemma—"These are the generations of…"—is broken open and forty-four new meanings are found. Yannai, as it were, reveals even more meaningful in the phrase than even the Rabbis found, but in a way that strongly recalls methods of rabbinic exegesis. He has intensified and multiplied the form as well as the content of midrashic interpretation, distilling it to its essence and transforming it to suit the needs of his poetry—and his performance.

3. An Item and Its Opposite: The second *rahit* from Gen 25:19, structured on antonymic pairs, anticipates the related form, "an item and its opposite." That is, Jacob is "an item" and Esau is "his opposite." Mirsky finds multiple examples of this rhetorical structure in the Talmud, such as the quotation from *b.Ḥag.* 15a, "For everything God created, He also created its opposite."[55] The technique of comparing opposites proves fruitful in both halakhic and aggadic contexts, and is particularly effective for articulating paradoxes. In the realm of halakhah, it plays up the paradoxical nature of certain commandments—for example, the prohibition against sleeping with your brother's wife but the commandment to fulfill levirate marriage. As *LevR* 22:10 explains, it is as if God has stated: "What I have forbidden you in one case, I have permitted in another." In aggadic contexts such as the interpretation of Gen 25 noted above, the dramatic difference between Jacob and Esau can be analyzed from a similar perspective. The very "twinness" of the two characters sharpens their differences. When

55 *Formal Foundations of Piyyut*, 68.

these terse rhetorical structures from prose writings are trimmed of intertexts and regularized in rhetoric—whittled down to their cores—they become strikingly similar to piyyutim that appear in the works of Yannai and Qillir. The highly patterned structure of this trope may well reflect the "oral" nature of some of these prose teachings—a kind of proto-poetic cadencing that would assist memorization. In the piyyutim, however, form has intrinsic importance, and we see this in the way the pithiness of this trope is distilled to its essence.

Mirsky's example of this phenomenon comes from the *rahit* for Gen 8:15, "Go forth from the ark." The opening phrases come from the lemma, quoted as a preface (thus again blending this structure with "a verse that opens a *drash*"): "Go forth from..."[56] The unit begins:

> *Go forth* from confinement to freedom // *Go forth* from trembling to tranquility
> *Go forth* from... // *Go forth* from oppression to exaltation
> *Go forth* from flux to firmness // *Go forth* from withdrawal to walking tall
> (Poem Seven[1], lines 1–6)

As this example shows, the poet takes a biblical phrase that does not seem, on the surface, to even have an antonym, and creates an element of opposition by making the second half of each line begin an element of direction, indicated by the repeated idea of "to," the opposite of "from." Thus the structure of the poem is built on antonyms: *from* one thing (confinement, darkness, trembling), *towards* its opposite (freedom, light, tranquility). The precise inspiration for this *rahit* is unknown—Mirsky suggests that it might lie in the pun on *teivah* ("ark") and *te'ievah* ("desire"), the final word-pair in the piyyut—but the formal structure shows that a generic exegetical trope could translate into poetry almost effortlessly. Poetry discovers the elegant, basic essence of this form. Again, this exegetical technique manifests primarily in the *r'hitim*, suggesting a contextual pressure behind the rhetorical form—its use as a refrain of some sort—beyond "simple" interpretation.

56 *Formal Foundations of Piyyut*, 77.

4. Measure for Measure: "A thing and its opposite" creates semantic and formal balance by juxtaposing antithetical pairs.[57] In the trope of "measure for measure," the opposite is true: an act of one kind attracts more of the *same*. In general, this category encompasses all structures that reflect "poetic justice" or what is called colloquially "irony," often created out of intensive word-play; in its purest form, the point is made by lining up identical episodes and drawing them into relation by virtue of their similarity. These structures can have an almost riddle-like quality—an ambiguity that the *midrashim* work to clarify but that the piyyutim exploit. This rhetorical structure is so intuitively pleasing and so common in Yannai's works (there is a reason we associate it with poets) that we can easily find examples outside the *rahit*. One poem that is particularly rich in "measure for measure" rhetoric is the *qedushta* for Gen 38:1, which treats the episode of Judah and Tamar. Multiple aggadic sources—*GenR* 84:19 and 85:11; *TanḥB Vayeshev* 17; and *TargN* and *TargPsJ* to Gen 38:25—connect Tamar's accusatory, "Examine this!" (Gen 38:25) with the identical phrase used by Judah in Gen 37:32, when he presented Joseph's torn and bloodied cloak to Jacob as evidence of Joseph's demise. *GenR* 85:11 states, for example,

> Rabbi Yoḥanan said: The Holy One, blessed be He, said to Judah: You said to your father, "Examine this"; by your life, Tamar shall say to you, "Examine this!"

Yannai pares this tradition down to its barest essentials: "An exchange: the one who said to his father, `Examine this!' // likewise hearkened unto `Examine this'"! (Poem Five, lines 15–16).[58]

Tamar is presented here as the vehicle for Judah's comeuppance, using the words with which he deceived Jacob as a means of revealing how he, himself, had been deceived. The specific referents are never clarified—such exposition would clutter up and dilute the power of the terse rhetoric. The brief allusions should (and must) suffice. Stripped down to these two essential words, the justice is delicious.

---

57 This section discusses the rhetorical elements of the "measure for measure" trope; the theological implications of this rhetorical structure are examined more closely in Chapter Four.

58 Interestingly, a significant number of lines in this *qedushta* employ "a thing and its opposite" as a trope, e.g., the descent of Joseph is really an ascent; Judah rises to be king of his brothers but falls from it after Joseph's sale, while Joseph is sold into slavery but rises to be vizier of Egypt; Judah becomes entangled with his son's wife Tamar, while Joseph flees from the clutches of Potiphar's wife.

5. In the Very Language. . .: This fifth rhetorical structure is a subset of "measure for measure"; in it, the specific language of the *sin* becomes the language of *justice*. While measure-for-measure can operate at the level of motifs and more general resemblance, "in the very language" requires parity of actual phrasing. The example given above from the story of Judah and Tamar could be considered an example: the phrase that encapsulates the totality of Judah's sin—"Examine this!"—becomes the language of his punishment: "Examine this!" Both the negative and the positive employ the same idiom. Mirsky associates a specific phrasing with this trope—a phrase that emphasizes the parity of language: "In the very language. . . ." (*bo be-lashon*).[59] Yannai's *qedushta* for Gen 11:1—a passage obsessed with language in any case—offers a perfect example of this rhetoric:

> As for the language (*be-lashon*) in which they spoke, with it (*bo*) were they answered // they said, "Come, let us go up!" and You said, "Come, let us go down!" (Poem Five, lines 11–12).

This teaching strongly recalls a passage preserved in *TanḥB Noaḥ* 25, which states:

> "Come, let us build ourselves a city" (Gen 11:4). The Holy One, blessed be He, said to them: You have said, "Come"'—by your lives, *in that very language* I will come down against you, as it is said, "Come, let Us go down and confound there their language" (Gen 11:7).

The poet, like the rabbinic exegete, delights in finding a wrong-doer's own words turned against the wrong-doer; the language of crime becomes the language of justice. As lovers of rhetoric, both Rabbis and poets delight in finding such wit encoded in Scripture itself. And sometimes, if the precisely perfect revenge-quotation is absent, the exegete may be inclined to invent it.

And these poems *are* inventive. While these examples may suggest that Yannai has simply stripped the prose midrash down to its essential elements of "tit-for-tat," the poet displays a noteworthy freedom with the text, even in comparison to midrash, which is hardly a "restrained" genre. For example, to increase the parity of crime and punishment in Gen 11, Yannai

59 *Formal Foundations of Piyyut*, 63–68.

"misquotes" the tower-builders, having them say, "Come, let us go up" (Poem Five, line 12) and not the accurate quotation, "Come, let us build," which we find in the *Tanḥuma.* This change has the effect of strengthening the antithesis; while "build" and "descend" are faithful to the text (and the word "Come" followed by a cohortative suffices for linking the two expressions in the midrashic source), "up" and "down" are an even better pair, and the poet is willing to depart from the letter of the text to sharpen his point. The goal of "in the selfsame language" is close congruity of language for the sake of terse, witty theological teachings: what goes around, comes around. Yannai, writing for a community at the bottom of that wheel, seems to particularly enjoy anticipating the enemies of the Jews—particularly Esau/Edom/Rome—getting their just desserts. This specific rhetorical trope is perhaps the most exquisite, razor-sharp articulation of this theology, which will be explored further in Chapter Four. What is most important to note here is the way the *payyetan*—like the *darshan*—picks up on the language of the biblical text itself, suitably altered when necessary.

Rhetoric of Terseness: the rahit

Midrashic rhetorical tropes seem to cluster with special intensity in the *rahit,* the seventh unit of a *qedushta.* The *rahit* in specific—but piyyut in general, as well—can be understood as an essentialization and distillation of midrashic modes of explication, as well as a transformation of them. This is not to say that Yannai consciously adapted the language of prose midrash into poetry, although that may well be the case at some deep level—Mirsky demonstrates the existence of profound parallels between piyyut and midrash beyond any doubt. It may be more accurate to understand Yannai as a poet writing within a deeply exegetical culture who, by nature or even instinct, employed aggadic forms within his works intuitively, drawing not specifically on the work we now know as "*Tanḥuma Buber,*" for example, but more generally on the exegetical-theological rhetoric of rabbinic exegesis itself. Understood this way, Yannai's interpretations may resemble midrash because he shares the same interpretive vocabulary. But he writes with that vocabulary in a fashion that suits the purposes, contexts, and aesthetics of liturgical poetry. The *rahit,* the most intricately abstract and artistic of the poetic style included in the *qedushta,* reveals the barest, most essential manifestation of this process, hinting, as well, at performative elements of piyyut that are unique to it as a genre.

Yannai's *qedushtaʾot* in general, and especially the *r'hitim*, are rich with terse, succinct allusions to rabbinic traditions. In a carefully crafted phrase, the poet presents profound and complicated ideas, which may take many lines to articulate in a prose medium, whether midrashic or targumic. In some cases, Yannai implicitly creates a new midrash by juxtaposing the lemma with a quotation from a remote biblical text—the essential act of midrash but without the explicit interpretive exposition. In other cases, the language of the poem is not allusive to any specific biblical text but offers instead a terse summary of a biblical or aggadic narrative. We can find examples of these various phenomena in the two *r'hitim* for Gen 15:1.

Both of these units follow the form of "the verse opens the *drash.*" The lemma itself states: "After these things, the word of the Lord came to Abram in a vision, saying: Do not fear, I am a shield to you, and your reward shall be very great" (Gen 15:1). The first *rahit* is built on two phrases from the lemma—"do not..." and "I am..."— while the second uses the latter part of the oracle as its skeleton: "your reward..." and "shall be very great..." Both *r'hitim* resemble what we might call "reverse *petiḥtot,*" in that they begin with the "near" verse—with the lemma itself—and allude to (but never quote) verses from afar. The "intertexts," however, may be either an actual biblical text or an allusion to an aggadic tradition. For example, the line, "*Do not* fear! *I am* your Hope // *Do not* cower! *I am* your Guardian" (Poem Seven[1], lines 1–2) uses the language of Gen 15:1 as part of its formal structure while simultaneously alluding to Isa 41:10, which closely parallels the structure of the lemma ("Do not fear; for I am with you; do not cower, for I am your God..."), Ps 39:8 ("my hope is in You"), and Ps 121, in which God is called "Your Guardian" three times (vv. 4, 5, and 7). We can imagine any of these verses being used as an exegetical verse with which to open a *petiḥta* leading into Gen 15:1, but in the present *rahit*, the lemma itself is quoted, emphatically, while the other texts are present only through implication.

Aggadic-midrashic motifs are likewise whittled down to their essentials in these poems. Continuing with the *rahit* from Gen 15:1, the simple line, "*Your reward* for the fire into which you went // *Shall be very great* for the converts you drew close" (Poem Seven[2], lines 1–2) carries with it the aggadic back-story of Abraham in Nimrod's ovens, rooted in the place name, Ur, as well as the familiar image of Abraham as master-proselytizer, based in part on the "souls he made" in Haran. These motifs, discussed above, appear in midrashic and targumic tradition and were apparently widespread and well known. The parallels to these allusions from both midrash and targum are rich in careful exegesis and expansive narration; they are, in essence, teaching the interpretation. In the piyyut, the same ideas are distilled to a phrase; the poet is not so much teaching as highlighting the artistry of scriptural exegesis and theology, as it were.

Alongside these midrashic allusions, we find concise references to biblical story arcs, in which whole episodes are summarized in a single phrase—e.g., "*Your reward* for the sinners you tried to spare" (Poem Seven^2, line 9) refers to Gen 18, in which Abraham pleads with God on behalf of Sodom and Gomorrah. The terse rhetoric of the *rahit* clarifies and essentializes God's promises to the patriarch; the brevity of the phrasing does not obscure the content but dramatizes it. In prose forms, attempts to convey such intensification may result in more drawn out, carefully articulated arguments bolstered by intertexts and analogies. In a *rahit*, the same effect is achieved using significantly fewer words. The emphasis in the *rahit* is as much on rhythm and sound as on content, reminding us that the performative element of piyyut should be considered in addition to the exegetical. These works were not studied but experienced.

A final example will highlight the complex interrelationship between biblical and aggadic language in Yannai's poetry. The opening lines of the *silluq* (Poem Eight) for Gen 48:1 state:

> Ephraim and Manasseh, the one to the other is joined / equal, one to the other
> Sometimes "Manasseh and Ephraim" / sometimes "Ephraim and Manasseh"
> The one is not greater than the other / the other not greater than the one.
> (Poem Eight, lines 1–6)

These lines follow immediately after the conclusion of the *rahit* discussed earlier, which is structured on the word-pair "Manasseh- Ephraim." The *silluq* appears, in part, to correct any potential misunderstanding arising from the rhetorical form of the previous piyyut. The *rahit* (Poem Seven) emphasized qualities that connected or differentiated the sons of Joseph; the *silluq* (Poem Eight) nullifies any misapprehension of *significant* difference. This interpretation somewhat contradicts aggadic interpretations preserved in other sources, in which Ephraim is favored. For example, *GenR* 97:5 asserts:

> "And he set Ephraim before Manasseh" (Gen 48:20). As he [Ephraim] preceded him [Manasseh] here, so did he in all cases... in generations... in genealogy... in inheritance... in standards...in princes...in judges... in kings... and in blessings...

Yannai, however, relies on biblical language to argue his case, alluding to the fact that sometimes Scripture mentions Manasseh first (four times, to be precise: Deut 34:4; Josh 17:17; 2 Chron 30:18 and 31:1) while other times Ephraim gets first mention (five times: Num 26:28; Josh 14:4, 16:4; and 2 Chron 34:6, 9). Yannai's reading strongly echoes a widespread theme found, for instance, in the prologue to the *Mekhilta deRabbi Ishmael*, which emphasizes the parity between Moses and Aaron based on the alternation of their names; and *TanḥB Shemot* 5, which applies the same exegesis-of-equality to the twelve tribes. Yannai reflects this same tradition of exegesis and the same thorough knowledge of Scripture along with its embedded meanings, but his specific exegesis is unparalleled. The language is, in part, biblical; the rhetorical form, identifiably midrashic; but the content is unique.

The shorter, more intricate, more constrained poems—particularly the *rahit*, but also the *silluq* (Poem Eight), and even the *asiriyyah* (Poem Five)—most overtly manifest the formal similarities between midrashic rhetoric and piyyut. Every unit of the *qedushta*, however, offers a potential locus for an allusion to an exegetical tradition, theme, or motif. These traditions of interpretation may be adduced by means of an explicit and completely quoted intertext, developed as a theme within the poem, embedded through a cryptic allusion to a biblical text—carrying with it familiar or innovative exegesis. Thus, the connections between piyyut and more traditional aggadic sources (midrash, targum, and Talmudic narrative) are obvious. Just as important, however, are those ways in which piyyut is a unique and distinctive mode of exegesis.

Viva la Difference: Midrash, Targum, and Piyyut

In terms of form, method, and content, strong and deep links connect the three major literary conduits of rabbinic exegetical tradition: midrash, targum, and piyyut. Midrash and piyyut—both primarily Hebrew genres—offer particularly compelling, and detectable, evidence of relationship, because shared language can easily be observed. Targum and piyyut, however, also merit comparison, for while the specific parallels can be harder to detect (due to the language difference), both genres—at least in theory—reflect literature of the ancient synagogue, a claim that is harder to sustain for midrash (at least in the form we now have it), a genre more closely associated with the rabbinic House of Study and, no matter its original *sitz im leben*, more altered over the centuries by the process of redaction and compilation. All three genres have specific associations with the Land of Israel, and as such, the Palestinian *targumim*, amoraic *midrashim*, and early piyyutim share clear affinities not common to works produced in Babylonia.[60]

Given the amount of overlap, it bears asking what each method of biblical interpretation offers that the others lack and what specific needs each genre met. That is, why do we have three such kinds of writing emerging and coalescing in the same period, different manifestations of the same general tradition, all in some fashion linked to the synagogue? My answers to these questions are speculative, based upon hypothetical reconstructions derived from an abundance of information that has not yet been satisfactorily analyzed. But certain basic observations can be made with (relative) confidence, and we will start with those.

The *targumim* (Aramaic versions of the Hebrew Bible) of the Land of Israel—*Targum Neophyti, Targum Pseudo-Jonathan* (also called *Targum Yerushalmi*), the Fragment *Targumim*, and other fragments of targumic texts from the Cairo Genizah[61]—are written in a dialect of Aramaic called "Jewish Palestinian Aramaic" or, in earlier scholarship, "Galilean Ara-

60 See Rabinovitz, *Halakhah and Aggadah in the Liturgical Poetry of Yannai* for the most thorough discussion of how Yannai relates to the Palestinian rabbinic traditions. The bibliography on targumic literature and its relationship to rabbinic writings is extensive; a good place to begin is D.R. J. Beattie and M. J. McNamara, eds., *The Aramaic Bible: Targums in their Historical Context* (Sheffield: JSOT Press, 1994); P.V. Flescher, ed., *Targum and Scripture: Studies in Aramaic Translation and Interpretation in Memory of Ernest G. Clarke* (Leiden: Brill, 2002); and K.J. Cathcart and M. Maher, eds., *Targumic and Cognate Studies: Essays in Honour of Martin McNamara* (Sheffield: Sheffield Academic Press, 1996).

61 The most accessible editions of these texts are: the series of Targum translations published by the Liturgical Press of Collegeville, MN, which includes editions of *Targum Onqelos, Neophyti*, and *Pseudo-Jonathan*, but these do not include the Aramaic text; Alejandro Diez-Macho, *Neophyti I: Targum Palestinense MS de la Biblioteca Vaticana*, 5 vols. (Madrid/Barcelone: Consejo Superior de Investigaciones Cientificas, 1968), which includes the Aramaic text and translations into Spanish, French, and English; and M. Klein, *The Fragment Targums of the Pentateuch: According to their Extant Sources* (Rome: Biblical Institute Press, 1980), which includes a wealth of textual sources as well as English translations.

maic."[62] For all the difference in their specific content, *targumim* are essentially expansive translations of biblical texts—that is, for every verse of Scripture, a *targum* will offer one rendering, which may be quite brief and faithful to the simple meaning of the text, or may be quite expansive, introducing large quantities of aggadah to its rendering or even inserting Aramaic poetry.[63] At least in theory, the *targumim* we now have reflect in some fashion the translations of the Bible that were presented in at least some early synagogues, in the period when Aramaic was the vernacular. They are, therefore, primarily didactic texts that aim to clarify what is unclear, flesh out what seems incomplete, correct what might be misunderstood, and—not to be overlooked—engage and entertain, as well. *Targumim* often harmonize apparent conflicts in Scripture and simplify what may appear to be confusingly complex. Based on the style in which the fragment *targumim* are written, as well as rabbinic descriptions of their use, it seems that the *targumim* were integrated into the Torah service.

According to the rabbinic conceptualization of the custom, translation in the early synagogue was an oral rather than a textual phenomenon, but for obvious reasons the surviving examples are written records.[64] We cannot know, therefore, whether the extant *targumim* we now possess were scholastic texts—written for study or perhaps memorization—or accurate reflections of the kinds of translations actually presented in any ancient synagogue.[65] What is clear, however, is that in the Land of Israel, written

---

62 For a clear delineation of some of the most idiosyncratic features of Jewish Palestinian Aramaic, see Kutscher, *Studies in Galilean Aramaic.*

63 The fact that Aramaic poems are inserted into the targumic manuscripts does not necessarily imply that they were recited as part of the targum's oral presentation. According to Sokoloff and Yahalom (*Jewish Palestinian Aramaic Poetry from Late Antiquity*), the Aramaic poems were not part of the synagogue rite but were popular works used to mark both joyous and sorrowful events—weddings, Purim celebrations, eulogies, etc. The targumic poems, however, do not date from any later than the seventh century and therefore reflect roughly the same cultural context as Yannai's poetry. See also Rand, "Observations on the Relationship Between JPA Poetry and the Hebrew Piyyut Tradition—The Case of the *Kinot.*"

64 For a full discussion of the importance of context and performance of translation in the synagogues of the Land of Israel in Late Antiquity, with thorough presentation of the relevant rabbinic sources, see Willem Smelik, "Code-switching: The Public Reading of the Bible in Hebrew, Aramaic and Greek," in *Was ist ein Text? Alttestamentliche, ägyptologische und altorientalistische Perspektiven*, ed. L. Morenz and S. Schorch (Berlin: Walter de Gruyter, 2007), 123–51.

65 See Willem Smelik, "Translation and Commentary in One: The Interplay of Pluses and Substitutions in the Targum to the Prophets," *Journal for the Study of Judaism in the Persian, Hellenistic and Roman Period* 29 (1998): 245–60; and "Orality, the Targums, and

targumim were occasionally used (a practice evidenced by its condemnation), and there was diversity in translational practices. In contrast, the more fixed and conservative traditions of Babylonia produced the relatively straightforward *Targum Onqelos*, which is quite minimal in terms of aggadic additions and was adopted as a communally-authorized translation. In the Land of Israel, creativity and diversity seem to have not only been the norm (piyyutim reflect this as much as *targumim*) but a value. We do not know who composed the *targumim*. In the rabbinic literature (Mishnah, Tosefta, and Talmud), the *meturgeman* (translator) was a lower-status functionary, but the reality may have been more complex, depending on local resources, the skill of the individual *meturgeman*, and the probability that individuals filled multiple roles. It is not clear whether the *targumim* were "rabbinic" (that is, written under rabbinic auspices) or independent. The frequent parallels between targum and midrash suggest common (and therefore possibly rabbinic) sources, but in several notable instances, the actual content of *targumim* differs from what rabbinic sources prescribe, suggesting that they may have arisen in slightly different but overlapping circles. Like the piyyutim, the Aramaic translations of Scripture (except, perhaps, the Fragmentary *Targumim*) indicate a relationship to the triennial Torah cycle of Palestine.[66]

Manuscript Reproduction." For a somewhat different perspective, see Avidgor Shinan, "Sermons, Targums, and the reading from Scriptures in the Ancient Synagogue," in *The Synagogue in Late Antiquity* (ed. Lee I. Levine; Philadelphia: Jewish Publication Society, 1987), 97–110; "The Aggadah of the Palestinian Targums of the Pentateuch and Rabbinic Aggadah: Some Methodological Considerations," in *The Aramaic Bible: Targums in their Historical Context* (*Journal for the Study of the Old Testament*, supp. 166; ed. D.R.G. Beattie and M.J. McNamara; Sheffield: JSOT Press, 1994), 203–17, and "The Aramaic Targum as a Mirror of Galilean Jewry," in *The Galilee in Late Antiquity* (ed. Lee Levine; New York: JTSA, 1992), 241–52. It is possible, of course, that this institution of translation goes back into the Second Temple period (e.g., Neh 8); see, for example, the discussion in L. Levine, "The Nature and Origin of the Palestinian Synagogue Reconsidered," *JBL* 115 (1996): 425–48.

66 See M. Klein, *Genizah Manuscripts of Palestinian Targum to the Pentateuch* (2 vols.; Cincinnati: HUC Press, 1986–1987), Klein notes that there is evidence of the triennial cycle in some of the manuscripts from the Genizah. In reference to the texts labeled by Klein as "the Fragment Targums" (passages of earlier *targums* specifically edited together by later redactors/editors), R.M. Campbell argues that they reflect the annual cycle and thus, in their present form, must be dated to the 10th century. See his essay "*Parashiyyot* and Their Implications for Dating the Fragment-Targums," in *Targums and Scripture : Studies in Aramaic Translation and Interpretation in Memory of Ernest G. Clarke* (ed. P.V. Flescher; Leiden: Brill, 2002), 105–14. Together, the evidence may best be understood as indicating both the diversity of manuscript traditions that survived in the Genizah and the fact that traditions themselves were in flux, particularly in the first millennium C.E.

Early *midrashim*, as we have them now, may be written in Hebrew (particularly the *Tannaitic midrashim*) or, especially in the Amoraic (200–500 C.E., approximately) compositions, in combinations of Hebrew and Jewish Palestinian Aramaic. These early *midrashim* appear to reflect the exegetical traditions of the Land of Israel from roughly the third to sixth centuries c.e.—the same period that saw the flourishing of the Palestinian targumic tradition and the first flowering of piyyut. The midrashic collections we have now are anthologies in which diverse interpretations, often associated with schools of teaching, have been edited together in the form of running, verse-centric commentaries. It is most likely that these various teachings arose in very disparate circumstances and circulated more loosely (perhaps orally), which is one reason we often have parallels and variations of a teaching in different anthologies (some of which are better texts than others). Certain details, such as the clustering of *petiḥtot* around specific verses, indicate the influence or assumption of a triennial Torah lectionary, as well.[67]

The patterns of overlap and difference among midrash, targum, and piyyut suggest that all three modes of interpretation shared common cultural and exegetical assumptions that crystallized in distinctive ways depending on the requirements of form, the demands of performance, and audience.[68] Each, in theory, had its roots in oral performance rather than written text, each related to the lectionary of the Palestinian synagogue in some fashion, and all reflected a kind of fluidity of interpretation, both within their genres and in comparison to each other.

Aramaic translations of Scripture, speaking broadly, approach the text linearly (verse-by-verse), usually simplifying the material as it goes. They smooth over textual "snags" and resolve potential misunderstandings of the text, while also embellishing the material in aggadic fashion. In terms of form, targum and piyyut seem quite different: targum is a prose Aramaic genre that values directness, while piyyut is a poetic genre, in Hebrew, that

67 See Bregman, "The Triennial Haftarot and the Perorations of the Midrashic Homilies." Recently, Teugels has expressed doubt about the usefulness of the Triennial cycle as an explanation for features of midrash; see her article "*Aggadat Bereshit* and the Triennial Lectionary Cycle." The relationship between some midrashic compendia and the Palestinian Torah cycle seems clear, however, and the resonances between Yannai's piyyutim and the *Tanḥuma* traditions are particularly intriguing.

68 For an early attempt to work out the precise relationships among these genres, see Lieber, "'O, My Dove in the Cranny of the Rocks, Let Me See Your Face!'"

delights in elliptical complexity. While it may seem, at first, unlikely that an audience that would require targum to understand the Torah portion would also be able to appreciate a *qedushta*, it is quite possible that genre and context, not audience sophistication, determined language. That is, the two kinds of writing (and their associated languages) served different functions, with Hebrew being particularly suited to statutory prayers (particularly the *qedushta*, which occupied a place of primary sanctity within the liturgy itself) and Aramaic to more streamlined explication in a non-liturgical setting.[69] Thus, while piyyutim and targum are very different as literature, they may conceivably have inhabited the same synagogues; certainly they reflect the same cultural orientation towards text and interpretation. For all the differences of form and language, targum and piyyut often share traditions of exegesis.

The general resemblance between midrash and piyyut is more obvious. *Midrashim* value creativity as well as clarity, and like piyyutim they embellish only some verses (although the midrashic anthologies contain explications of a majority of passages, edited into something resembling linear commentaries). Compared to targum, midrash is a "clever" genre of interpretation, interested in creating complexity where there may have been clarity, adding layers of meaning to the text, and discovering its manifold meaningfulness. Unlike piyyut, however, and to a lesser extent targum, the locus of the midrashic endeavor remains unresolved. It seems to have been, at least initially, the rabbinic academy rather than the synagogue—although the distinction between the two realms, as noted above, can be difficult to delineate and by Yannai's period the two social spheres may have collapsed into one, or at least begun their consolidation.[70]

In the end, midrash was presumably part of some kind of text study session, possibly in the synagogue in the context of the Torah service, but not necessarily (or exclusively). While midrashic texts are often didactic—intended to teach, sometimes at the popular register but other times at the equivalent of graduate student level—we cannot be certain

---

69 For a discussion of language-choice in rabbinic society, see especially S. Fraade, "Rabbinic Views on the Practice of *Targum* and Multilingualism in the Jewish Galilee of the Third–Sixth Centuries" in *The Galilee in Late Antiquity*, 253–86. The existence of Jewish Aramaic poetry—a very different kind of poetry from piyyut—supports the idea that context (the inclusion of a text in the statutory liturgy versus in an external context) played a large role in determining language selection. See discussion below.

70 In addition to the works discussed above, see L. Levine, "The Sages and the Synagogue in Late Antiquity" in *The Galilee in Late Antiquity*, 201–21.

exactly where or how, if ever, they were performed. That said, midrash is a definitive rabbinic genre. Sages are named in the text, and while the actual attribution of specific teachings to specific Sages may be regarded skeptically, the rabbinic imprimatur is unmistakable. The strong resemblance of Yannai's *qedushtaʾot* to midrash, both in terms of content and method, means that piyyutim offer insight into the locus of rabbinic teaching more generally. Whether or not *midrashim* were taught in the synagogue, midrash-like piyyutim were.

In a number of ways, piyyutim are quite similar to the *targumim*: both have their origins in public-liturgical (synagogal) practice, both have performative aspects, and both indicate a complicated relationship with rabbinic culture, although the piyyutim show something more of an affinity for rabbinic practices and rhetoric than targum. However, significant differences remain, even beyond language and the fact that targum is prose and piyyut poetry. For example, rather than explicating each verse singularly and in sequence, as the *targumim* do—one interpretation per verse—the demands of the *qedushta* form permit, even require, Yannai to take multiple passes at individual verses, continually refining and nuancing his interpretations.[71] Furthermore, the fact that *targumim* are, in some sense, translations minimizes their intertextuality—the Palestinian *targumim* contain aggadah, but rarely do they include midrash.[72] Piyyutim, however, are a profoundly intertextual genre. And finally, unlike the *targumim*, the piyyutim do not try to simplify or clarify the biblical verses; instead, they strive to engage and impress. Ultimately, the *targumim* are primarily didactic. While piyyutim may have served pedagogical functions and were no doubt valued for their aesthetics, they are noticeably more learned texts and were, ultimately, lived as part of a shared liturgical experience.

---

71 The presentation of multiple interpretations of a single verse is a phenomenon familiar from midrashic discourse, either as a result of an editor weaving together diverse interpretations (e.g., the familiar trope, *davar aḥer*, "another interpretation") or through the device of presenting exegesis as a conversational act. Midrashic interpretations, however, are typically associated with individual Sages—one Sage presents one reading, another Sage offers a different one—rather than a single Sage presenting multiple interpretations of a single passage.

72 Midrash in the strictest sense, using one verse to elucidate the meanings of another verse. This generalization is not to imply *targumim* are devoid of intertextuality; targum is in every way as rich a genre as piyyut and midrash, it simply reflects a different context and aesthetic. See, for example, Avidgor Shinan, *The Embroidered Targum: The Aggadah in Targum Pseudo-Jonathan of the Pentateuch* (Magnes: Jerusalem, 1992) [Hebrew].

These observations about piyyut *vis à vis* targum can be extended to the Aramaic poems embedded in the prose *targumim*. These poems did not likely originally appear as part of the Torah translation in the synagogue—they were presumably interpolated by later editors—but they offer a useful comparison to Hebrew piyyut.[73] The Aramaic poems are relatively simple in form and straightforward in contrast, compared with the Hebrew poems, which demand more and more intensive intellectual engagement from their audience (at least, they have that potential). We cannot know whether one kind of poetry was more popular than the other. The argument that the Aramaic poems were more popular because they are in a vernacular is countered by the significantly greater quantity of poetry in Hebrew that survived. In general, however, it seems likely these works either appealed to different audiences or, just as likely, reflect distinctive contexts. Indeed, evidence indicates that the Aramaic poems were not typically liturgical (in terms of playing a role in the statutory prayers) but were part of religious celebrations outside the synagogue rituals. Yannai's *qedushtaʾot*, by contrast, were recited in the context of the central prayer of the service.[74] Differences in language and form can just as easily be explained by context as by audience; if this line of thinking holds true, it may lead to a reevaluation of the sophistication of targum (appreciated by its scholars but not necessarily by outsiders to the field) as well as a broadening academic interest in the study of piyyut.

While the relationship between piyyut and targum is important, Yannai's *qedushtaʾot* have even more in common with midrash: they share a linguistic affinity (Hebrew); they have a fundamental, explicit intertextuality in common; and they often employ similar rhetorical strategies and exegetical techniques. In particular, beyond aggadic content, the two genres of writing revel in complexity, intertextuality, and multivocality; rather than seeing a single meaning in the text, midrashim and piyyutim delight in uncovering layers of meaning within Scripture's words. There remain, however, a number of important differences between the two genres. While certain prose rhetorical forms can be distilled into poetry, the fact remains that poetic expression operates as much by juxtaposition as explication,

73 The definitive edition of Aramaic poetry is M. Sokoloff and J. Yahalom. *Jewish Palestinian Aramaic Poetry from Late Antiquity* (Jerusalem: Ha-akademyah ha-le'umit ha-yisraelit le-madʿaim, 1999).

74 This point is made in the introduction to Sokoloff and Yahalom's *Jewish Palestinian Aramaic Poetry from Late Antiquity.*

relying on clues that set up expectations more than full articulations that clarify interpretations. Midrash *teaches*—shows the steps, connects the dots, and includes editorial asides—while piyyutim demand that the audience do much of that work themselves, particularly in the initial units (Poems One, Two, and Three).

This difference does not mean that piyyut is more "advanced" than midrash—of the two, piyyut is arguably the more "popular" literature, definitively composed for public recitation in the synagogue. More likely the differences reflect the demands of context: the conceit of midrash is of the teacher-pupil relationship (even if the classroom might have been the synagogue and the pupil every listener), in which cleverness is appreciated but clarity also important. Piyyut, as prayer and ritual, is participatory and performative, even theatrical—midrash is "story" where piyyut is "drama." While the poet guides the way, he is simultaneously part of the community at prayer; at the same time he must keep his community entertained and involved, active rather than passive. Thus while the midrashic anthologies juxtapose one teaching after another, Yannai's piyyutim typically revisit themes and motifs in an elliptical pattern, teasing and then confirming, but slowly moving through elements of the Torah portion so that multiple themes are gradually introduced and explored.

In sum, midrash is the classical "school house" text—the product of the academy (or the "academic" synagogue), an insider literature that, once its codes are decrypted, becomes a teaching tool in which modern readers join the teachers of antiquity in mining the text for new meanings. The *targumim,* meanwhile, are more straightforward and direct than the Hebrew poems, in a vernacular language, apparently interested in what the text *does* mean more than what it *could* mean, with a minimum of rhetorical flourishes. Translation and paraphrase smooth over ambiguity and provide the simple elegance of a single meaning for a given verse, in a single voice. Piyyut holds an intermediate position between these two genres: intellectual but popular; intricate yet ultimately clear; multivocal yet the work of a single hand; elevated but not rarefied. In the end, it seems as if the three genres are different facets of a single phenomenon, in which rhetoric, form, and language are shaped primarily by context. The similarities and differences among these genres of Jewish writing raise further questions. Given that the synagogue was the performative setting of Yannai's piyyutim, what role did the physical "stage" play in their interpretation? Furthermore, to frame the question of context even more broadly, where do

Yannai's *qedushta'ot* fit within the larger framework of Byzantine liturgical creativity? In short, is it possible to assemble these texts into a picture of the ancient synagogue and ancient Jewish life, the world in which piyyutim were lived?

The Bigger Picture: Piyyut in the Synagogue

The above discussion indicates the intertextual and exegetical richness of the piyyutim and the importance of contextualizing these poems among the other interpretive literatures of Judaism in the Byzantine period. While these aesthetics, techniques, and resonances possess intrinsic value, the public, performative, liturgical context of the piyyutim reveal much about the context as well as the content of their exegesis. Through their language, form, and content, Yannai's *qedushta'ot*, and the classical piyyutim in general, offer insights into certain realities of the synagogue in Late Antiquity—perhaps not all synagogues, but at least those in which these compositions were part of the service.

The *qedushta'ot* show us, for example, that in Yannai's congregation the Torah was read in a roughly three-and-a-half year (the so-called "triennial") cycle rather than the annual cycle that emerged in Babylonia, in which the complete Torah is read in one year.[75] The division of the Torah as indicated by the piyyutim of Yannai is in keeping with that of roughly

75 The relationship between the annual and triennial Torah reading cycles is disputed. E. Fleischer has argued that the triennial cycle supplanted a native Palestinian annual lectionary; see his articles "Inquiries Concerning the Triennial Cycle of Torah Reading in *Eretz Yisrael*," *HUCA* 62 (1991): 43–61 [Hebrew] and "The Annual and Triennial Torah Reading Cycles in the Early Synagogue," *Tarbiz* 61:1 (2003): 25–43 [Hebrew]. Fleischer's argument was provocative. Indeed, Fleischer and Shlomo Naeh engaged in a running dispute in the pages of *Tarbiz*; see S. Naeh, "The Torah Reading Cycle," *Tarbiz* 67:2 (2003): 167–87 [Hebrew] and "On the Septennial Cycle of the Torah Reading in Early Palestine," *Tarbiz* 74:1 (2005): 43–75 [Hebrew]. Naeh argues that the three-and-a-half year cycle was orchestrated so that every second cycle coordinated with the sabbatical year, with the Torah completed during Sukkot of the Sabbatical year. For an analysis and summary of the Fleischer-Naeh controversy in English, see Levine, *The Ancient Synagogue*, 537–38. In all likelihood, the lectionaries of individual communities varied and, while there may have been attempts to standardize or coordinate them, local differences were probably common.

The modern "triennial" cycle used in many modern (primarily Conservative) synagogues is quite different from the ancient "triennial" cycle. The modern triennial calendar follows the standard annual (Babylonian) schedule that has been the norm in Judaism since the Middle Ages but divides each reading into approximately three equal portions. Thus two-thirds of the Torah portion is skipped between weeks. The ancient triennial cycle read the Torah in linear order.

contemporary *midrashim* and *targumim*.[76] The composite evidence across all three genres indicates that there was no single, fixed lectionary unifying those communities that employed the triennial calendar. On the contrary, the specific divisions of Torah portions varied among different communities. The piyyutim have also shed much light on the role of the haftarah (the prophetic complement to the Torah portion) in the triennial cycle—indeed, the information embedded in piyyutim have enabled scholars to reconstruct complete, multiple haftarah lectionaries, a task previously involving a great deal of conjecture and uncertainty. As with the Torah portion, the emerging picture is one of diversity: haftarah selections varied, and there are traces of the existence of secondary haftarot as well, which implies that even within a single community there could be more than one haftarah.[77]

Piyyutim contain information on the liturgy as well as the lectionary. They show, for example, how the liturgy was fluid within certain established parameters. While the benedictions of the Amidah were formulaic by Yannai's day, as indicated by the cues for fixed liturgical rubrics within the poems themselves (as well as the cues indicated in the manuscripts), the material surrounding those fixed blessings varied, based on the Torah portion and the poet's skill. That is, the "text" of the Amidah (the "bodies" of the individual prayers preceding the benedictions) varied from week to week and community to community. Thus, the scaffolding of the Amidah—the themes of the prayers, the language of the benedictions and liturgical transitions, and possibly even the forms of the individual poetic units—was stable, while the actual content of the prayer-text within each section would have been distinctive.[78] Furthermore, the existence of the

76 In addition to the Bregman article noted above ("The Triennial Haftarot"), and the articles by Fleischer and Naeh just indicated, see Ben Zion Wacholder, Prolegomenon to *The Bible as Read and Preached in the Old Synagogue: a Study in the Cycles of the Readings from Torah and Prophets, as well as from Psalms, and in the Structure of the Midrashic Homilies*, by Jacob Mann (The Library of biblical Studies, vol.1; ed. Harry M. Orlinsky; New York: Ktav Publishing House, Inc., 1971), xi–xliii.

77 For the diversity of *haftarot* even within communities, with evidence drawn largely from Yannai's *qedushta'ot*, see Fried, "Alternative *Haftarot* in the Piyyutim of Yannai."

78 It seems that Yannai composed a single piyyut for most Torah portions—not, for example, a new poem for every Sabbath of his career but, by and large, a single poem for a single *sidra* (or, perhaps, his best composition for each portion was the one which was preserved). Thus, while the poeticized Amidah changed from week to week, the same poem would have eventually repeated when the same *sidra* was repeated after three or so years. Similarly, given the manuscript evidence of Yannai's work, it seems that his works were

qedushta as a genre indicates the centrality of reciting the Qedushah (that is, the recitation of Isa 6:3 and Ezek 3:12 in the third blessing of the Amidah) as part of the Sabbath service.[79] The momentous importance of the Qedushah—of joining the angels in prayer—is concretely conveyed by the fact that all but the first two units of the *qedushta* are oriented towards this third blessing of the Amidah.

Finally, as amply shown above, Yannai's *qedushtaʾot* suggest that rabbinic ways of reading Scripture—not just the content of the interpretations but the exegetical and rhetorical techniques that undergird them—were widespread and not restricted to a scholarly setting. To be sure, we cannot assume that the community for which Yannai wrote was representative of typical Late Ancient Judaism—it may have been unusually learned, or even closely connected to a specifically rabbinic circle. Nevertheless, Yannai's poems were written for public performance, and all evidence indicates that such works were enthusiastically, and broadly, received. Indeed, the material from the Genizah, both the abundance of piyyut texts and secondary references to poetry, shows that liturgical poetry was tremendously popular and not a rarefied field of interest. This clustering of evidence implies, as we will see, that what we might call "rabbinic culture" was taken for granted by the *payyetanim* and their listeners. The piyyutim do not support the idea of a priestly-rabbinic power struggle in the Byzantine synagogue, although they may well indicate the prominence of priestly families in the synagogue (and, perhaps, among the population of poets) and they encourage modern scholars to engage seriously with the idea that priestliness was an ongoing reality in Byzantine Judaism.[80] Even the term "*qerova*," indicating

---

popular, possibly in his lifetime and certainly afterwards, in which case there would have been some consistency across communities from week to week, both in terms of the Amidah and, presumably, the Torah reading cycle (*sidra* and haftarah) associated with the piyyutim.

79 The benediction "God's holiness" (*Qedushat ha-shem*) was recited daily; according to the Palestinian rite, that blessing stated simply: "You are holy and awesome is Your name; there is no God but You. Blessed are You, the holy God." It was the Qedushah—the charged recitation of Isa 6:3 and Ezek 3:12—that was reserved for the Sabbath. In Babylonia, the Qedushah was recited daily. See Elbogen, *Jewish Liturgy*, 210. On the attractiveness of the Qedushah, see also R. Langer, "Individual Recitation of the Kedushah," in *To Worship God Properly*, 188–244.

80 On the role of priests in the ancient synagogue, see Levine, *The Ancient Synagogue*, 519–29. Many early *payyetanim* appear to have been members of priestly families but, like Rabbis with similar epithets, their works can be considered "rabbinic" in the way that Yannai's is. Michael Swartz, in a thought-provoking comparison of the *avodah* poems with Mishnah *Yoma*, posits the liturgical poet as a third typology of leadership (along with priests

the genre of piyyut to which the *qedushta* belongs, with its echoes of the *qorban* offering, suggests that the poet functions as a kind of priest, offering up his poetry as part of the Amidah—the prayer which in rabbinic thought holds the place formerly filled by the Temple offerings. In sum, the liturgical poet overlaps in highly suggestive ways with rabbinic (exegetical-methodical) and priestly (ritual-performative) roles. This does not mean the piyyutim bespeak uniformity or homogeneity of Jewish culture in Late Antiquity, however—any more than the rabbinic textual sources do. Instead, the evidence from the piyyutim, combined with the diversity we find in the Palestinian *targumim* and *midrashim* and synagogue art and architecture, only confirms the impression of diversity and complexity in the ancient synagogue.

In the following sections, I consider two particular realms where the piyyutim may play an important role in reconstructing aspects of Jewish culture and society in Late Antiquity and the Byzantine period: the visual art of the early synagogue; and the relationship between Jewish and Christian hymnography in Late Antiquity.[81] These two areas—Jewish figurative art and Byzantine Christian poetry—are distinctive fields unto themselves, but ones where early piyyutim offer particularly important new insights. These two subjects suggest the potential richness of Yannai's work outside the confines in which he has traditionally been studied. The present treatment is not intended to be exhaustive, but rather introductory—a spur to

---

and Rabbis). See his essay "Sage, Priest and Poet" in *Jews, Christians, and Polytheists in the Ancient Synagogue*, ed. Steven Fine (New York: Routledge, 1999), 101–17. The *avodah* poems, as Swartz notes, closely resemble the mishnaic texts in many ways (even quoting lengthy passages from it), but where Mishnah *Yoma* reveals a strong anti-priestly inclination, the piyyutim are quite positive towards the priesthood.

81 The first major book-length study of piyyut that addresses the issue of these poems in their larger context from a contemporary scholarly perspective was written by Joseph Yahalom: *Poetry and Society in Jewish Galilee of Late Antiquity*. This slender but important monograph, which addresses the span of early poetry (from the period of Yose ben Yose and the anonymous *payyetanim*, to, briefly, post-Classical poets in Italy and Spain), examines piyyut from a variety of perspectives, with a particular focus on how piyyutim fit into both Jewish literary history and the literary context of Late Antiquity more generally. It addresses a range of topics—literary form, relationship of piyyut to targum and midrash, evidence of synagogue ritual, relationship to architecture, insight into history, inclusion of myth, priestliness, and rabbinicness, and other topics—that are of interest to the present study, as well. Yahalom's writings are of great significance for the modern study of piyyut; he is (along with Michael Swartz and Ophir Münz-Manor) one of the most original and creative thinkers on the topic in the present day. The translation and expansion of *Poetry and Society*, his most comprehensive work to date, would be welcome indeed.

further inquiry as the centrality and utility of these poems become increasingly clear.

Poetry and Synagogue Art

It is important to remember that Yannai's piyyutim were performed in a physical space, the synagogue. Synagogue building reached a peak—both numerically and artistically—in roughly the fourth to sixth centuries in the Galilee, the same period and place in which piyyutim first appeared and flourished.[82] The mosaics adorning these structures are often striking both for their beauty and their subjects, and the art becomes noticeably less figurative only in the wake of the Muslim conquest, the same period when the center of payyetanic creativity shifted from the Land of Israel to Italy and, in subsequent generations, the Rhineland.[83] Most likely, Yannai lived during or shortly after the apex of the period of synagogue building in Byzantine Palestine, enabling us to imagine his works being recited, performed, and heard in these structures. Taken together, the literary art of the *payyetanim* and the visual art of the physical synagogue space suggest just how vibrant and religiously rich the milieu of the early synagogue was. In order to explore this hypothetical cultural dynamic more fully, it may be useful, however tentatively, to consider poetry as a kind of verbal analog to synagogue art.

Judaism, particularly when compared to Christianity, was (and is) popularly considered to be iconoclastic, lacking any artist prior to Marc

---

82 J. Magness, along with Z. Ma'oz, Uzi Leibner, and others, has argued recently that archaeologists have consistently skewed the dating of the synagogue towards the early end of the spectrum (4th to early 5th century); see J. Magness, "Did Galilee Decline in the Fifth Century?" in *Religion, Ethnicity, and Identity in Ancient Galilee*, ed. Jürgen Zangenberg, Harold W. Attridge, Dale B. Martin (Tübingen: Mohr Siebeck, 2007), 259–74. For present purposes, the most important fact is the coincidence between the appearance of piyyut and the synagogue building boom, which is meaningful with either dating preference.

83 The subject of synagogue art has received serious renewed attention in recent years. The most impressive and important recent study is Steven Fine, *Art and Judaism in the Greco-Roman World*. In addition to subjecting Jewish art to a new and sophisticated reading, Fine reviews the complex history of the study of Jewish art. The various works of Rachel Hachlili are also of tremendous importance. On the ancient synagogue in general, see Levine, *The Ancient Synagogue* and Schwartz, *Imperialism and Jewish Society*. It is important to note that, throughout the centuries, many ritual items (Torah mantels, spice boxes, *ḥanukkiyot*, grave markers, liturgical manuscripts, and so forth) have been richly decorated, and that Jewish art was both influenced by and often in tension with the artistic norms of the surrounding majority culture. See K. Bland, *The Artless Jew: Medieval and Modern Affirmations and Denials of the Visual* (Princeton: Princeton University Press, 2000).

Chagall—a stereotype flatly contradicted by the rich artistic history of Jews.[84] From the Hellenistic period onwards, we have ample evidence of Jewish visual art—secular and religious, domestic and public, Palestinian and Diasporic. The simple existence of such a wealth of images, much of it figurative, from a period often envisioned as bleak and dispirited, has placed the field of art history at the center of controversies surrounding the nature of Byzantine Jewish culture. Some have read the art as indicating that these spaces were inhabited by "non-rabbinic" or "non-normative" Jewish communities. Others have seen the emphasis on Temple imagery as suggesting that the priests, not the Rabbis, determined synagogue ritual. In addition, there are contentious questions regarding the significance of the images themselves. Can Yannai's piyyutim, or piyyut more broadly, shed light on these matters?

Many of the images common in early synagogue art appear, on the surface, to be relatively non-controversial—that is, they depict objects and animals rather than the presumably more problematic human form. The prevalence of Temple imagery—incense shovels, the shofar, the lulav and etrog, the Torah shrine, and especially the seven-branched menorah—suggests that nostalgia for the Temple was strong, although it would be incorrect to limit the significance of these images to simple commemoration of the past.[85] Indeed, some of these items would have remained in use (such as the shofar, lulav, and etrog) and others, such as incense shovels, may have been modeled on contemporary, domestically-useful devices. Even further, the popularity of Temple items in the art may indicate that members of the priesthood, representing living continuity with the Temple traditions, remained in positions of synagogue leadership much longer than rabbinic sources indicate. Scholars inclined to pursue this model of synagogue leadership have seen the piyyutim—many of which were composed by poets of priestly lineage and deal with priestly concerns, such as the *mishmarot* (priestly watches)—as supporting the hypothesis that links Temple im-

84 See Bland, *The Artless Jew*, and the summary of the conventional wisdom in Fine, *Art and Judaism in the Greco-Roman World*.

85 On the persistence of Temple imagery and its relationship to the synagogue, see J. Magness, "Heaven on Earth: Helios and the Zodiac Cycle in Ancient Palestinian Synagogues," *Dumbarton Oaks Papers* 59 (2005): 1–52; and R. Elior, "From Earthly Temple to Heavenly Shrines: Prayer and Sacred Song in the Hekhalot Literature and Its Relation to Temple Traditions," *Jewish Studies Quarterly* 4 (1997): 217–67. The topic of Hekhalot mysticism is addressed further in Chapter Four.

agery in synagogue art to priestly leadership of the synagogue itself.[86] But this understanding, in many ways a strong and necessary corrective to earlier over-simplified understandings of rabbinic power, perhaps underestimates the fact that in a liturgical context, Temple imagery and priestly ritual naturally retain a place.

The Rabbis were, themselves, profoundly interested in matters of cultic ritual and its eventual reestablishment; and, similarly, priestly prominence in synagogue liturgy and ritual does not necessarily negate rabbinic presence.[87] If anything, the evidence of the piyyutim—deeply rabbinic works, even when in tension with specifics aspects of the rabbinic agenda or textual tradition—seems to take for granted a significant "rabbinic" presence, even if it is alongside "priestly" themes and concerns.

In the end, we do not have enough coherent documentation to be certain what groups constituted the leadership in the various synagogues or communities.[88] The presence of Temple items in synagogue art and expressions of nostalgia for the priesthood in some rituals does not contraindicate rabbinic influence any more than the pervasive use of rabbinic exegetical techniques, themes, and motifs removes piyyut from the realm of the priests. The poet, as prayer leader and thus priest, offers up his *qerova* (i.e., *qorban* offering?), but it is an offering richly textured by rabbinic ideas and content.[89] The data remain inconclusive, but the piyyutim suggest scholars should be wary of a hasty expulsion of the Rabbis from the Byzantine synagogue or a strong distinction between priests and Rabbis. To be sure, some

86 See the discussion in Irshai, "Confronting a Christian Empire," and J. Magness, "Heaven on Earth: Helios and the Zodiac Cycle in Ancient Palestinian Synagogues."

87 The prominence of the Priestly Blessing in modern synagogues and the granting of the first *aliyah* (summons to recite the benediction over the Torah reading) to members of the priestly families offer echoes of this role in modern synagogue ritual.

88 While the aggadic content of piyyutim suggests a strong rabbinic presence in at least some synagogues in the Byzantine Galilee, this does not mean that they necessarily support the traditional view of early rabbinic promulgation of the fixed liturgy—not just the framework, but the words. Piyyutim just as easily support the view of Joseph Heinemann, who regards the liturgy as slowly crystallizing over time—with first merely the framework of the Amidah established (for example) and only later the familiar wordings becoming fixed. Furthermore, the liturgy (like the piyyutim) displays a strong interest in "priestly" conceptions of worship. For a succinct presentation of the traditional view (championed, with some qualifications, by Ezra Fleischer) versus Heinemann's interpretation, see the exchange between Fleischer and Ruth Langer in *Prooftexts*, cited above (n. 15).

89 On the role of poet as priest, see M. Swartz, "Sage, Priest, and Prophet;" S. Fine, *This Holy Place: On the Sanctity of the Synagogue during the Greco- Roman Period* (Notre Dame, 1997), 552; and J. Yahalom, *Poetry and Society*, 64–92.

rabbinic sources indicate ambivalence about the House of Prayer, but many display a tremendous interest in the workings of the synagogue and the liturgy. The necessary scholarly correction to the popular picture may be one of recognizing the complexity of rabbinic culture rather than dividing Byzantine Judaism into ever more factions.

If the Temple images and nostalgia for the priesthood and its rites do not negate the possibility of rabbinic influence on the early synagogue, what of artistic representations that, with their boldly anthropomorphic depictions, might seem to be clear-cut violations of rabbinic law? These, too, turn out to be ambiguous, both in their own terms and even more so when the evidence of the piyyutim is introduced. Rabbinic sources display a nuanced ambivalence towards depictions of the human form, a compunction subject to renewed study and more careful articulation with the discovery of startlingly "pagan" images in the Byzantine synagogues.[90] The synagogue mosaics (including stunning depictions of Helios), have proven particularly intriguing, raising a host of questions about the communities that adorned their worship space with such images.

Rabbinic sources present a range of opinions on the subject, from the rigidly anti-iconic to the more delicately nuanced "anti-idolic."[91] Careful study of literary sources reveals changes in perspectives over time and depending on context. It suggests that Jewish attitudes towards art reflect a deeper struggle to craft self-identity and to create boundaries against imperialist majority cultures.[92] Rabbinic writings record stories about pietists who refused to look at coins bearing the Emperor's image (*j.Meg.* 15a: "Why was Naḥum [bar Simai] called `the holy of holies' man? Because he

90 R. Hachlili, "Synagogues in the Land of Israel: The Art and Architecture of the Late Antique Synagogues," in *The Sacred Realm: The Emergence of the Synagogue in the Ancient World,* ed. Steven Fine (Yeshiva University Museum/Oxford University Press: New York, 1996), 96–129, summarizes early modern understandings of Jewish "artlessness" (pp. 111–13). For a study of a specific synagogue in a particularly important Galilean location, see Z. Weiss and E. Netzer, *Promise and Redemption: The Synagogue Mosaic from Sepphoris* (Jerusalem: Israel Museum, 1996) and C. Meyers, E. Meyers, and E. Netzer, eds. *Sepphoris* (Winona Lake: Eisenbrauns, 1992). More recently, see Fine, *Art and Judaism in the Greco-Roman World,* which contains cogent critiques of many recent archaeological and art-historical publications.

91 See the discussion in Fine, *Art and Judaism in the Greco-Roman World,* 110–23. The term "anti-idolic" derives from his analysis.

92 Fine's monograph is a masterful delineation of the theoretical issues at stake here as well as specific changes over time; it is a sophisticated complement to Levine's magisterial volume, *The Ancient Synagogue.*

never in his life looked at the image imprinted on a coin"[93]). Nahum's extreme piety is, however, unusual—the explanation of the nickname in the Talmudic passage indicates the extraordinary character of his stringency. Rather than seeing the visual art of the synagogue as non-rabbinic, the physical artifacts of the synagogue can just as easily be understood as reflecting tensions and divisions *within* rabbinic Judaism.

The written sources of rabbinic Judaism do, in fact, preserve permissive statements regarding figurative art, often depending upon the kind of art and the specific contextual setting in which the art is encountered—although "toleration" should not be confused with "encouragement" nor "acquiescence" with "embrace." Most famously, *m. Avodah Zarah* 3:4 describes a scene in which a certain Proclus accosts Rabban Gamliel, who was bathing in the presence of a statue of Aphrodite. Gamliel explains that the statue is an adornment, not an object of worship, and furthermore the act of bathing in the image's presence debases and does not honor it. Of course, a bath is not a synagogue. What of other settings? We find the Palestinian Talmud stating, "In the days of Rabbi Yoḥanan, men began to paint pictures on the walls, and he [R. Yoḥanan] did not hinder them;" and: "In the days of Rabbi Abbun, men began to make designs of mosaics, and he did not hinder them" (both in *j.Avodah Zarah* 3:3, 48d).[94] These texts do not specify the location, which leaves open the possibility that the synagogue could have been a location for such embellishments. (The other likely location being the homes of wealthy Jews, which have also been discovered to be richly decorated.) Supporting this hypothesis, *TargPsJ* to Lev 26:1, in its rendering of the prohibition against idols, says: "…Nor shall you place a figured stone in your land to bow down towards it. But a pavement figured with images and likenesses you may make upon the floors of your synagogue[s], but do not bow down to it, for I am the Lord your God."[95] When taken together, these sources (notably all Palestinian in origin) appear to be attempting to nuance and refine complicated ideas (and reali-

93 For discussions of the figure of Naḥum, see Fine, *Art and Judaism in the Greco-Roman World*, 113–15; H.M.J. Loewe, *Render Unto Caesar: Religious and Political Loyalty in Palestine* (Cambridge: The University Press, 1940), 88–96; and P.C. Finney, "The Rabbi and the Coin Portrait (Mark 12:15b, 16): Rigorism Manqué," *JBL* 112.4 (Winter, 1993): 629–44.

94 On Gamliel and Proclus, see A. Wasserstein, "Rabban Gamliel and Proclus the Philosopher," *Zion* 45 (1980): 257–67.

95 This passages is discussed in Levine, *The Ancient Synagogue*, 618–23; and the article by M. Klein: "Palestinian Targum and Synagogue Mosaics," *Immanuel* 11 (1980): 33–45.

ties) about visual art—making allowance for location, use, subjects, and so forth. The biblical prohibitions may be read in strictly aniconic ways—but other understandings were not only possible during Late Antiquity but were apparently the norm.[96]

But stating that rabbinic attitudes towards images were nuanced and changed over time does not sufficiently account for the complexity that we see in specific archaeological remains. The zodiac, in particular, is a strikingly popular figure in Jewish art from the Byzantine period—clear evidence of "inculturation" and subsequent Judaizing of a non-Jewish iconography.[97] Even more perplexingly, scholars have noted that these visually stunning and enigmatic figures appear in the synagogue precisely during the period when such imagery was being *suppressed* (as pagan) in non-Jewish contexts by the Christian Church. How are we to understand this complex matrix of symbols—particularly the chariot-riding Helios figure at the center of an elaborate zodiac design—which appears in multiple ancient synagogues? The various examples resemble one another closely, and yet they are not replicas, nor are the synagogues even proximate to each other. What range of meanings could these works have signified, and why would Jews remain attached to these Judaized images for so long after the majority culture had rejected them?

Yannai's works (and early piyyutim more broadly) do not provide unambiguous answers to these questions. As Steven Fine notes, treating the

96 While our focus here is on visual art, we should also note the Rehov synagogue mosaic (6th century C.E.), a lengthy mosaic text that deals with agricultural regulations and practices in the region—arguably the oldest extant copy of a rabbinic source. It shows a strong affinity for rabbinic sources, including the Yerushalmi and the Tosefta; see the discussions in J. Sussman, "The Inscription at the Synagogue in Rehov," in *Ancient Synagogues Revealed*, 146–53 (pp. 152–53 offer a translation of the inscription). The fact that the quotation pertains to sabbatical laws, tithes, and priestly courses—all topics of priestly as well as rabbinic concern—only further supports the argument here that "priestly" topics do not negate "rabbinic" presence. The fact that the best parallels to this inscription are found in unambiguously rabbinic sources should not be overlooked. But note also the discussion in H. Sivan, *Palestine in Late Antiquity* (Oxford: Oxford University Press), 255–63.

97 See Fine, *Art and Judaism in the Greco-Roman World*, 196–205. Fine's views differ from those of Jodi Magness, who offers her own ideas on the zodiac and Helios, and like Fine, takes piyyut into account in her essay, "Helios and the Zodiac Cycle in Ancient Palestinian Synagogues," in *Symbiosis, Symbolism, and the Power of the Past. Canaan, Ancient Israel, and Their Neighbors from the Late Bronze Age through Roman Palaestina, Proceedings of the Centennial Symposium of the W.F. Albright Institute of Archaeological Research and American Schools of Oriental Research*, Jerusalem, May 29–31, 2000, ed. W.G. Dever and S. Gitin (Winona Lake, IN: Eisenbrauns, 2002), 363–89; and, more recently, "Heaven on Earth: Helios and the Zodiac Cycle in Ancient Palestinian Synagogues."

images of the ancient synagogue as "codes" to be "decoded" (i.e., the assumption that "image X means Y") leads to oversimplification or misunderstanding. But—as the commentaries on the piyyutim in this volume (especially those for Gen 1:1, Gen 8:15, and Gen 9:18) show in greater detail—Yannai's *qedushta'ot* may offer textual clues for readings of visual evidence.[98] Synagogue poetry, like synagogue art, displays a fascination with the zodiac and other strong visual images that intrigue and viscerally engage. Moreover, these images did exist in a context, and those who beheld them understood them within that context. Piyyutim—including the works of Yannai—reflect that same general cultural context. Indeed, the images help concretize and reify the imagery in the poems while the poems themselves suggest the potential significance of the images in thicker, deeper ways.

Images, even more than literary texts, are open to multiple interpretations. For example, something as simple as a mosaic depiction of a menorah raises questions: Does its presence attempt to create or invoke the ambience of the Temple, or does it have a deeper symbolic meaning, conjuring something of what the Temple's menorah itself sought to effect? Does it offer assurance of the divine presence, recall the cosmos (the seven lamps as the seven planets) and creation, give hope for restoration in the future, or act as a reminder of the glory of the past? Is its physical placement within the synagogue and in relation to other images simply aesthetic or is it symbolic and meaningful? And how could the meaning of these symbols have changed over time? By asking these questions, do we unintentionally burden the image with too much interpretation and fail to appreciate it as an object of beauty in its own right? We cannot know what the original artists "meant" by their art or why a work was commissioned. Would such knowledge even be helpful in reconstructing popular understandings?

Indeed, trying to reconstruct how ancient synagogue attendees would have received and themselves interpreted these images is an impossible

98 See J. Yahalom, "Piyyut as Poetry," in *The Synagogue in Late Antiquity*, ed. Lee Levine (Philadelphia: ASOR, 1987), 111–26. Piyyutim from outside of Genesis and by poets other than Yannai are important for this discussion, as well; Levine, Fine, and Schwartz all include piyyutim in their discussions of the art of the early synagogue. For example, Yannai's *qedushta* for Num 8:1 dwells at length on the image of the lamp, also an important visual element of synagogue decoration (see Fine, *Art and Judaism*, 158–63); and, as discussed below, anonymous laments composed for Tisha b'Av dwell at length on the zodiac.

task. We can, however, try to reconstruct how Yannai—a remarkably learned Jew in a position of some authority—might have understood images like those now uncovered by archaeologists. In most likelihood, these piyyutim somewhat post-date the most impressive synagogue mosaics, so we can imagine the poets' literary art being influenced by the visual art of the synagogue. And because of the poet's role as a public exegete and liturgist, his interpretations of images like those found in the synagogues may have shaped how those images were, in turn, understood—if not when they were first installed, then perhaps by generations that inherited them and sought to find them meaningful.

Hebrew piyyut and Aramaic poetry both are rich with poetic images that resonate with visual images popular in these early synagogues—and they suggest interpretations of the images that are strongly in keeping with what would become normative rabbinic traditions.[99] Thus, in the Torah portion that describes the menorah in the Tabernacle (Num 8:1–2), Yannai finds a pretext for exploring the menorah imagery that may have been familiar to his congregation. In his poetry, the menorah becomes a manifestly meaningful symbol of past glory and future hope, a concrete image of divine presence that connects the people to God. His poems lend specific shape to the general symbolism of the lamp.[100] We can imagine similar symbolic resonances in his poetic references to the lulav and etrog, the burning of incense, and the Torah itself.[101] The biblical origins of these items, images, and practices mean that the poet possesses not only pretext for but impetus to explore their significance in his works: simply put, they come up, both in the lectionary and in life.[102] These items are not restricted to any social

---

99 Fine (idem.) notes that "all of the issues that appear in the Sepphoris mosaic are dealt with by Yannai" (p. 188).

100 See Fine, idem., 158–63.

101 Aside from a partial *qedushta* for Shemini Atzeret (in Rabinovitz, *The Liturgical Poems of Rabbi Yannai* 2:227–35, which employs imagery of the sukkah and contains references to the Temple water-drawing ritual, as does his piyyut for Rosh Hashanah, in Rabinovitz, idem., 2:205), Yannai's piyyutim for Sukkot have not been recovered. Other early *payyetanim,* including Qillir, are known to have employed the imagery of the lulav and etrog, however, and this suggests that Yannai could have used similar imagery. See J. Rubenstein, "Cultic Themes in Sukkot Piyyutim," *Proceedings of the American Academy for Jewish Research* 59 (1993): 185–209.

102 Indeed, some objects, such as incense shovels, may have been used in daily life—for the perfuming of garments, for example—as well as in religious ritual. The design of incense shovels in visual arts likely reflects the appearance of such items in daily life, as familiar to the artists. See the discussion in D. A. Green, *The Aroma of Righteousness: Scent and Seduction in Rabbinic Literature* (University Park, PA: Penn State University Press, forthcoming).

circle—they are not the purview of the priests or under the authority of a specific group of Rabbis, but are, instead, the birthright of all Jews.

The same observations hold true for the representations of biblical narratives in the synagogue. There is possibly a significant congruity among the biblical characters—Noah, Abraham, and Daniel, especially—who routinely appear in both figurative art and in piyyut. Noah receives prominent treatment in Yannai's poetic corpus as a symbol of hope and renewal, transformed into an emblem of universal stability and particularist chosenness.[103] In this, Yannai builds on the prominence of Noah in the book of Isaiah, a story that became, in turn, a popular haftarah reading.[104] Abraham, meanwhile, would be important (at least in theory) to every Jew, not simply members of specific classes, because of his associations with covenant (both as the first Jew and, specifically, because of the centrality of circumcision) and possibly also in terms of martyrdom in a period when fascination with martyrdom in Judaism and Christianity was increasing. As with Noah, Abraham becomes a prominent figure within the Bible itself.[105] Finally, Daniel, who is associated with martyrdom and apocalypse, appears repeatedly in poetic works (the *qedushta* for Gen 32, for example) as well as in Jewish and Christian art.[106]

These biblical stories are part of the general patrimony of the Jewish community, and what we learn from the popularity of these figures gives

103 See the *qedushtaʾot* for Gen 8:1, 8:15, and 9:18 and the discussions in the commentaries.

104 The modern (annual, Babylonian) lectionary recognizes the importance of the Noah story in Isaiah as a powerful text, as well; Isa 54:1 appears as a haftarah not only for *parashat* Noaḥ but also *Ki Tetze* (one of the Sabbaths of Consolation). See Wacholder, "Prolegomenon," xxxii, where the author notes that two-thirds of the Palestinian *haftarot* are from Deutero-Isaiah (a full half are from Isaiah). Noah also appears in Ezek 14:14, 20, where he keeps company with Job and Dan(i)el (probably the Ugaritic wisdom-figure Dan'el rather than the biblical character Daniel, who may well be named for the ancient Canaanite figure). On the figure of Noah in piyyut, see L. Lieber, "Portraits of Righteousness: Noah in Early Christian and Jewish Hymnography," *Zeitschrift für Religions- und Geistesgeschichte* (forthcoming).

105 Abraham is particularly prominent in Deutero-Isaiah, notably: Isa 41:8, 51:2, and 63:16; also note Ezek 33:24, and Ps 105. On the importance of circumcision and Jewish identity, see S. Cohen, *Why aren't Jewish Women Circumcised? Gender and Covenant in Judaism* (Berkeley: University of California Press, 2005). On martyrdom, see Daniel Boyarin, *Dying for God.*

106 The bibliography on Daniel is extensive. On the subject of Daniel and piyyut, see the discussion in Yahalom, *Poetry and Society*, 102–6. More generally, see J. J. Collins, P. W. Flint, and Cameron VanEpps, eds., *The Book of Daniel: Composition and Reception* (Leiden: Brill, 2001); and L. DiTommaso, *The Book of Daniel and the Apocryphal Daniel Literature* (Leiden/Boston: Brill, 2005).

insight into distinctive communal concerns. The number of parallels between the images in the synagogue mosaics and the themes of classical piyyut are striking, and we can imagine the piyyutim existing in a kind of dialogue with the visual works, teaching a kind of interpretation of the extant visual context. Indeed, if we imagine that the art predates the poet, as seems probable, then the poetry functions as an *ex post facto* interpretation of the images—enabling the images to be invested (or reinvested) with meaning as times, interests, and understandings change.

The interpretive (even "koshering") function of piyyut, where poems offer interpretations for (re-)understanding potentially difficult or simply ambiguous visual representations, can be useful particularly when we consider somewhat surprising images, such as the dramatic Helios zodiacs, which seem quite "pagan" to modern eyes.[107] In context, these images resonate with important biblical and rabbinic concepts and would not have shocked the Jews of Yannai's time the way they startled the original excavators (although we may imagine that some Jews in antiquity would have disapproved). This zodiac imagery becomes so omnipresent that despite its roots in Greco-Roman iconography, the Judaized images of the heavenly dome eventually became typical of synagogue art—they became "Jewish."

Likewise, the zodiac is a popular motif in liturgical poetry from Late Antiquity. Why this sudden popularity? The most convincing arguments center on the significance of the calendar in Byzantine Judaism. Rabbinic sources display a keen interest in matters of intercalation, and (as the Qumran evidence makes clear) calendars are important means of communal self-definition. The liturgy, likewise, is fundamentally concerned with time: time of day and time of year are both essential to synagogue ritual. Calendars, art, and liturgy are all means of creating identity and delimiting boundaries, and those concerns intersect in the idea of the zodiac. The cosmic cycle and liturgical cycle come together in synagogue practice—and in synagogue art and liturgy.

Time is not the only significance Jews in antiquity might have found in the zodiac mosaics, however. If we understand the images as representing in some way the heavenly realm, as the menorah may have, the Helios and zodiac compositions could have reminded viewers of the ongoing presence of God and the heavenly hosts within the synagogue. This interpretation

---

107 See the discussion in Fine, "The Zodiac, Synagogue Mosaics, and Jewish Liturgy," in *Art and Judaism in the Greco-Roman World*, 196–205.

could certainly overlap with temporal concerns—God is both present and present-tense—but this latter conception underscores divine presence in the context of prayer. The image represents in some way the presence of the One who hearkens to prayer. The image, thus, grows thick with potential and latent meanings.

The piyyutim support this concept of there being an array of potential meanings; rather than limiting how we read images, they suggest multiple understandings that should be considered simultaneously. In the *silluq* for the *qedushta* for Gen 1:1, the signs of the zodiac appear as part of the Creation narrative. In a Qillir poem for Yom Kippur, Aries rejoices at the conclusion of the atonement rites, reflecting a kind of sympathy with the ram that has been offered up by the High Priest. And in an early anonymous lament for Tisha b'Av, the signs of the zodiac—the heavenly hosts—weep at the destruction of the Temple.[108] The motif of the zodiac is even more common in the Aramaic piyyutim. Read together, a cluster of interrelated themes emerges from these works: an idea of sanctified time; affirmation of the divine presence; the heavenly hosts as witness to history; and the suggestion that eternality is a form of consolation. Art and poetry enrich each other; the poet takes the images in his vicinity and invests them with particular meaning. The two art forms—visual and poetic—can be seen as reciprocally reinforcing one another.

For all this tantalizing potential interconnectedness, in the late sixth century—still the period of the Classical *payyetanim* and, in fact, the period when Qillir, the most prolific *payyetan*, probably lived—synagogue decoration began to move away from figurative art, favoring more abstract geometric and floral patterns and written inscriptions that strongly recall the artistic expression of the Second Temple period. In some cases (notably the Na'aran synagogue), all figurative depictions were removed and replaced with nonfigurative designs. It is probably not a coincidence that this same period reveals a Christian church beginning to embrace figurative art over abstract patterning. It appears that when the Christians adopted a practice, it became less appealing to the Jews. An inclination toward ab-

108 For a general discussion, particularly of the Qilliran and Anonymous works, see Yahalom, "Piyyut as Poetry." For the text of the anonymous lament, see Goldschmidt, *Order of Laments for Tisha b'Av* (Jerusalem: Mosad HaRav Kook, 1977), 29–30 [Hebrew]. A translation of the lament can be found in Schwartz, *Imperialism and Jewish Society*, 271. The *silluq* for Gen 1:1 ascribed by Rabinovitz to Yannai but now of disputed authorship (not discussed in Yahalom's article) appears in the present volume.

straction was further established in the Land of Israel with the arrival of Islam on the scene, bringing with it a new set of cultural norms with which the Jews would dynamically engage.

Beyond the Synagogue: The Christian Context of Piyyut

Context matters. It may be tempting to imagine that Jews' articulated antipathy for Christians and Christians' hostility towards Jews resulted in a radical separation between the church and the synagogue. The reality, however, appears to be significantly more complicated than superficial readings of the sources might suggest.[109] Indeed, certain figures—particularly Noah—appear commonly not only in Jewish worship spaces and piyyutim, as noted above, but in Christian settings and hymns as well—albeit with specific twists that help scholars understand the role that the biblical figure played for each community.[110] In terms of the visual arts, the same artisans appear to have worked in both Jewish and Christian buildings, perhaps from the same pattern books.[111] The similarities and differences in hymnography, however, suggest a deeper intellectual relationship between the two communities.[112] Through the arts, we can see evidence of each one attempting to draw clear boundaries for themselves against the other but we also see the places where they intersect. Liturgical texts—homilies, prayers, and poems—would have helped particularize the interpretations of a

109 For example, on the topic of Jewish and Christian biblical interpretation, see Marc Hirshman, *A Rivalry of Genius: Jewish and Christian Biblical Interpretation in Late Antiquity* (Albany: State University of New York Press, 1996).

110 See R. Hachlili, *Ancient Jewish Art and Archaeology in the Land of Israel* (Leiden: Brill, 1988), as well as Ancient Synagogues in Israel, which she edited.

111 Fine and Hachlili both note the apparent use of common pattern books. For a thorough and particularly pertinent "case study" of both the similarities between Jewish and Christian imagery and the notable differences, see R. Hachlili, "The Zodiac in Ancient Jewish Art: Representation and Significance," *Bulletin of the American Schools of Oriental Research* (1977): 61–77. It is worth noting that in some places, notably Zoar (near the Dead Sea, in modern Jordan), we have evidence of Jews and Christians sharing a common burial ground, which may well indicate extensive social mixing in life, too. On the Zoar tombstones, their social setting, and their resonance with rabbinic sources, see Y. Wilfand, "Aramaic Tombstones from Zoar and Jewish Conceptions of the Afterlife," *Journal for the Study of Judaism* (forthcoming).

112 A full comparative study of Jewish and Christian art exceeds the scope of this work. The notes above indicate some of the most important work being published in the field of synagogue studies; for parallel work in Christianity, see L. Safran, ed., *Heaven on Earth: Art and the Church in Byzantium* (University Park, PA: Penn State University Press, 2000). On Christian homiletics, see M. B. Cunningham and P. Allen, eds., *Preacher and Audience: Studies in Early Christian and Byzantine Homiletics* (Leiden: Brill, 1998).

seemingly common heritage of images and ideas while, simultaneously, suggesting unconscious mutual acculturation.[113] In sum, evidence both visual and literary indicates that Jews and Christians were not as isolated from each other as has previously been assumed—even if the differences remain telling.

Visual Arts: In the synagogue, artwork depicts the Temple and its implements (especially the menorah), which may have served a variety of functions (reminders of the Temple's importance and rites, hope for restoration, etc.); artwork presents biblical narratives that played key roles in self-understanding and national hopes (e.g., Abraham, who represents both the enduring covenant with Israel and the promise of salvation); and it reinforces of Jewish identity (e.g., via the complex nexus of meaning represented by the Torah and the Ark). Christian artwork, by contrast, emphasizes figures whose stories were read as foretelling individual (rather than national) salvation—Noah, Isaac, Moses, Jonah, and Daniel—depicted in ways that rendered these characters as typological foreshadowers of New Testament narratives and linchpins of Christian theology. As noted, some characters appear in both synagogue and church settings, a fact which reflects the common scriptural patrimony of the two communities. The episodes chosen for presentation and the physical contextualization of the images, however, indicate the confessional distinctions. For example, Jewish depictions of Noah focus on the renewal of creation as symbolized by the presence of animals; in Christian artwork, the images of Noah appear primarily in funerary contexts and emphasize parallels between the Ark and Jesus' tomb.[114] To be sure, Christian iconography is every bit as complicated and multivalent as Jewish art; what matters here is that the differences in contextualization and depiction suggest differences in understanding as well.

Strikingly, the image of the zodiac with Helios at the center is absent from Church iconography. Instead, Christian calendars—in keeping with Roman styles—personify the *months* (as kinds of labor), ignoring the zodiac entirely. These differences in artistic tastes suggest deeper differences

113 Hachlili, "Synagogues in the Land of Israel," 125.

114 For a discussion of Noah in late ancient Judaism and Christianity, see N. Koltun-Fromm, "Aphrahat and the Rabbis on Noah's Righteousness in Light of the Jewish-Christian Polemic," in *The Book of Genesis in Jewish and Oriental Christian Interpretation*, ed. E. Peter, J. Frishman, and L. van Rompay (Louvain: Peeters, 1997), 57–71. See also Lieber, "Portraits of Righteousness: Noah in Early Christian and Jewish Hymnography."

between Jews and Christians. Although Jews were apparently comfortable with an older (pagan) Roman style of iconography, it discomfited Christians. On the one hand, it may be that the zodiac was so "Judaized" by the fifth to sixth centuries that to include it in a church would have been considered a *judaization* of Christian space; or perhaps "pagan" imagery had become more threatening for the Church at this period (in the wake of Julian the Apostate's pro-pagan program in the fourth century) than it was for the Jews.

Non-Jewish Hymnography—An Overview: While Jewish and Christian visual art hints at the complex tensions between the two communities in the Galilee, the commonalities among Jewish, Samaritan, Syriac Christian, and Greek Christian poetry are even more directly suggestive. Discussions of the interrelations among these forms of poetry—whether on the level of forms or motifs—tend to focus on the thorny issue of origins. In brief, did Christians borrow their forms of religious poetry from the Jews, or did Jews borrow their poetry from the Christians? The first hypothesis, argued explicitly by Schirmann and Fleischer and implicitly by Mirsky, depends on an understanding of history in which Christianity derives its sacred literary traditions from its Jewish foundations because Judaism offers a unique kind of authenticity; the second hypothesis, put forth by Werner and endorsed implicitly by Levine, relies on a model in which the power of a majority culture (Christianity) leads to cultural influence on a subject minority (Judaism).[115] In more recent years, Joseph Yahalom has suggested

115 Schirmann, "Jewish Liturgical Poetry and Christian Hymnology," *JQR* New Series 44 (1953–54):123–61. Fleischer, *Hebrew Liturgical Poetry in the Middle Ages*, 63–97, focuses on piyyut as a wholly internal development within Judaism, but presents it controversially as a rebellion against the statutory liturgy, which he sees as having been fixed in wording at a very early date. Mirsky, *The Piyyut* (especially 11–29, 30–46, 57–76, 86–92, 146–65, and 202–8) focuses on rhetoric; see also Werner, *The Sacred Bridge*; and Levine, *The Ancient Synagogue*, (esp. 583–88). Most recently, see the work of Ophir Münz-Manor, who has spoken on the connections between Ephrem and Yannai; he sees the potential for mutual influence and dependency between Jewish and Christian poets. At the December 2007 meeting of the Association for Jewish Studies, he presented a paper entitled, "Many Voices, One Choir: Jewish, Christian and Samaritan Poets and the Rise of Neo-Semitic Poetry." His recent publication on Yannai's *qedushta'ot* for Gen 15:1 and 16:1 ("All About Sarah: Questions of Gender in Yannai's Poems on Sarah's (and Abraham's) Barrenness," *Prooftexts* 26:3 [Fall 2006]: 344–74), together with Susan Ashbrook Harvey's writings on women in the Syriac church and D. Krueger's writings about Romanos and other early Greek Christian poets, suggest how the study of poetry in Late Antiquity—Jewish and Christian—is developing in fascinating and highly sophisticated new directions.

a third source of influence on the Hebrew poetry: the Late Antique Roman literary aesthetic called "the jeweled style," in which ornamentation and lavish description replaced earlier models of classical proportion.[116] It is also possible that compositional styles were influenced by local poetic traditions—Ephrem's Syriac poetry in Edessa may have been shaped by a local Mesopotamian aesthetic totally alien to his Galilean contemporary, Yose ben Yose. At the same time, Yannai's poetry displays an awareness of Christian iconography and ritual, implying that he may have known Christian hymnography as well. If Ephrem's poetry presumably influenced Romanos' work, despite geographical distance, he could, perhaps, have also influenced Yannai. Conversely, perhaps early Jewish piyyutim shaped Christian hymnographic innovations.[117] If the visual arts show signs of contact, would the poetic arts be isolated?

Questions of origins may, in the end, prove more frustrating than illuminating. Just as midrash and piyyut appear to be entwined, differing reflections of common ways of reading, so, too, these earliest religious poems may partake of something shared—however unconsciously or unintentionally.[118] Different types of poems may have their origins in different settings (e.g., the *rahit* is very "rabbinic" but Poem Six in a *qedushta*, as we will see, resembles certain Christian styles of poetry). Furthermore, it is possible that the influences moved back and forth rather than in the linear direction that the word "origins" implies. Perhaps a form originated in a

116 See Michael Roberts, *The Jeweled Style: Poetry and Poetics in Late Antiquity* (Ithaca: Cornell University Press, 1989), and the descriptions of this style in Hebrew poetry that are found in Yahalom, *Poetry and Society.* In general, more research needs to be done contextualizing Late Antique hymnography—particularly piyyut—in the context of Greco-Roman poetics and rhetoric.

117 Yannai's knowledge of Christian ritual and belief appears in his polemical poems, such as his *qedushta* for Yom Kippur, mentioned above; he does not, however, indicate a nuanced awareness of the intense theological debates within Christianity (although he makes some references to Christians that seem to imply that they are a fragmented people, in contrast to Jewish unity; see his *qedushta* for Deut 6:4). Some Aramaic piyyutim display a similarly basic awareness of Christian doctrine. These Jewish works do not reveal a knowledge of the intricacy of Christian theological disputes in Late Antiquity, but rather imply a familiarity with basic doctrines and, perhaps, a sense of the general fractiousness of the Christian community, suggesting to modern readers the "trickle down" elements of public Christianity.

118 Yahalom states this idea of common and mutual patterns of influence succinctly: "...[T]here must have been common contemporary factors in the eastern prayer house and its rhetorical and cultural background that led to common—Jewish and Christian—developments in its poetry" ("Piyyut as Poetry," 124).

Jewish context, was developed in a Christian setting, and then re-imported, consciously or more diffusely, back into synagogue ritual. In the end, it may be most useful—and realistic—to understand the poets as public voices reflecting widespread and common cultural concerns and artistic developments of their days. Like the Jewish *payyetanim*, the Christian hymnists were participants in complex exegetical cultures—communities in which the world in general was read and understood through the lens of interpreted Scripture. Because much of this Scripture was shared with Jews and because these communities did come into significant and regular contact with each other, it should not be surprising that they came to use similar, though hardly identical, modes of expression in their poetry.

Poetry of the Samaritan rite and the hymns of the Eastern Church—i.e., the Syriac and Greek-language Byzantine congregations—display tantalizing parallels to early Jewish piyyutim. The works of the fourth-century Samaritan scholar-poet Marqa, his near-contemporary Syriac Church Father Ephrem the Syrian, and the sixth-century Greek-language poet (and contemporary of Yannai) Romanos the Melodist are highly reminiscent (to varying degrees) of the early Hebrew piyyutim in terms of both thematic content and poetic form. More work remains to be done in all these areas—Samaritan, Christian, and Jewish hymnography, both individually and comparatively— but what we do know is intriguing.[119] Striking similarities in structure, themes, and exegesis—even when couched in interreligious polemic— link these poems, despite their disparate communal contexts, religious concerns, and languages.

A full comparative study of Jewish, Samaritan, and Byzantine Christian hymnography far exceeds the scope of the present volume. What follows offers only a glimpse of the wealth latent in comparative ancient

---

119 For instance, it seems likely that these works were intoned in some fashion, either in whole or perhaps just sections—the Syriac and Greek hymns include cues indicating specific melodies, and the presence of vowel notations in the manuscripts of the piyyutim may suggest more than just basic pronunciation. While the earliest musical notation for a piyyut in Hebrew is that of a piyyut for Shavuot, notated by Obadiah the Proselyte (a Norman convert to Judaism in the twelfth century), we can assume that the piyyutim were performed in ways that resembled Christian traditions of liturgical performance in at least general ways. On the remarkable story of the earliest musical notation in Hebrew, see N. Golb, "Obadiah the Proselyte: Scribe of a Unique Twelfth-Century Hebrew Manuscript Containing Lombardic Neumes," *Journal of Religion* 45 (1965): 153–56. The article contains a reproduction of the MS.

hymnography while it also situates Yannai's poetry in its larger poetic context.

Samaritan Aramaic poetry: These works are arguably the least familiar of all these writings to modern readers—but they provide an intriguing parallel to Jewish hymnography. The Samaritan community, like the Jews of the Land of Israel, existed in tension with the Christian hegemonic empire. We might assume, then, that there would be a literary affinity between the communities as well as political sympathies, despite the historical tensions between the two groups.[120] Samaritan poetry is best reflected in the works of Marqa, who lived in the late fourth century C.E., roughly contemporaneous with the Christian poet Ephrem the Syrian (who wrote in a different dialect of Aramaic) as well as the early Jewish *payyetan* Yose ben Yose.[121] Most of Marqa's hymns are structured as simple alphabetic acrostics of 22 strophes (only one, MS Cowley 846, includes a signature—name—acrostic). While stanza length varies across hymns, within a single work they are consistent, from four to seven lines; there does not appear to be a fixed rhythm, as the lines have varying numbers of words and syllables. Formally, these Samaritan poems are simpler than either the Syriac or Hebrew poems of roughly the same period; they more closely resemble the Jewish Palestinian Aramaic poems (so-called "targumic" poems, which are likewise in Aramaic). In terms of content, Samaritan poems often employ images that strongly recall rabbinic traditions; for example, the hymn that

---

120 See Gray, "Palestine and Justinian's Legislation on Non-Christians," for a discussion of the relative status of Jews and Samaritans in 6th century Palestine and Lieber, "You Have Been Skirting this Hill Long Enough," for a discussion of Jewish and Samaritan relations during the reign of Justinian. For all the tension between the communities, it is known that Jews and Samaritans joined together in various anti-imperial rebellions in the 5th and 6th centuries.

121 See A. S. Rodrigues-Pereira, *Studies in Aramaic Poetry (c. 100 B.C.E–c. 600 C.E.): Selected Jewish, Christian, and Samaritan Hymns* (Assen: Van Gorcum, 1997). This work includes discussions and translations of works from the Qumranic community, the *Targumim*, Marqa, and Ephrem. On the Samaritan poetry specifically, see Ze'ev Ben-Ḥayyim, *The Literary and Oral Tradition of Hebrew and Aramaic Amongst the Samaritans* (5 vols; Jerusalem: The Academy of the Hebrew Language, 1957–77) [Hebrew]. For an introduction to the issues within the field of Christian hymnography, see S. Brock's monograph *From Ephrem to Romanos: Interactions between Syriac and Greek in Late Antiquity* (Aldershot; Brookfield, USA: Ashgate, 1999) and, from a more literary-critical perspective, Kreuger, *Writing and Holiness*, particularly his chapter on Romanos (159–88).

For Yose ben Yose, the definitive work is Mirsky, *Yose ben Yose: Poems*. For English translations of some of Yose's piyyutim, readers should consult Swartz and Yahalom, *Avodah*, which presents several of Yose's most important works with both Hebrew texts and translations.

describes the revelation of the Torah contains many parallels with rabbinic traditions about Sinai. Indeed, Marqa's hymns appear to be quite attuned to rabbinic theology as well as biblical Hebrew poetry (and not just the Samaritan translations of Scripture).

In general, the Samaritan liturgy and its poetic traditions have yet to be studied thoroughly, but the evidence that we do have suggests that this contact between Samaritans and Jews (and perhaps Christians) took place more on the level of ideas than on that of form and rhetoric—the formal similarities between Samaritan and Jewish Aramaic poetry being a notable and intriguing exception to this generalization. The existence of common themes and motifs should perhaps not be surprising, given not only the linguistic affinity of Samaritan Aramaic for Jewish Aramaic dialects (and Hebrew), but the relatively complicated relations between the Jewish and Samaritan communities during antiquity. Rabbinic sources attest to contacts (often fractious) between the two communities, while historical sources indicate that Jews participated in Samaritan uprisings against the Empire in the sixth century.[122] In terms of exegesis, parallels exist between Samaritan exegesis (e.g., the Samaritan aggadic anthology known as *Tebat Marqa*) and midrash.[123] Jewish poetry (Aramaic and Hebrew), both in form and content, may help scholars reconstruct a more detailed picture of how, ritually and intellectually, these two communities interacted in Late Antiquity.

Christian Hymnography:[124] The picture of hymnography in the Byzantine world becomes more complicated when we turn to Greek and Syriac poetic forms, which more closely resemble the intricate forms and functions of Hebrew piyyut, but display greater differences in terms of specific

122 See my article, "You Have Skirted This Hill Long Enough," *HUCA* 80 (forthcoming), on Yannai's *qedushta* for Deut 2:2, a text that addresses the sympathy Jews may have felt towards Samaritan uprisings and Yannai's disapproval of participation in such events.

123 The standard critical edition of *Tibat Marqa*, Marqa's major prose (midrashic) work, is Ze'ev Ben-Ḥayyim, ed. and trans., *Tibat Marqe: A Collection of Samaritan Midrashim* (Jerusalem: Jerusalem Israel Academy of Sciences and Humanities, 1988) [Hebrew]. For a more limited but nuanced study of how Samaritan exegetical traditions relate to rabbinic interpretations, see Kugel, *In Potiphar's House.*

124 For a succinct summary of Christian hymnography in Late Antiquity, see Michael Roberts, "Poetry and Hymnography (1): Christian Latin Poetry," in *The Oxford Handbook of Early Christian Studies*, ed. Susan Ashbrook Harvey and David G. Hunter (Oxford: Oxford University Press, 2008), 628–40; John McGuckin, "Poetry and Hymnography (2): The Greek World," idem., 641–56; and Sebastian Brock, "Poetry and Hymnography (3): Syriac," idem., 657–71.

interpretations and concerns. The task of delineating the history of Hebrew poetry in light of Christian poetic traditions has, as a result, been an intriguing, albeit at times more frustrating and uncertain, enterprise for many scholars of piyyut.

In the nineteenth and early twentieth century, scholars dated the early *payyetanim*, including Yannai, later (i.e., after the seventh century) than they are currently (i.e., in the sixth century). As a result, scholars (particularly Jewish scholars) generally hypothesized that the roots of Jewish piyyut lay in Christian liturgical poetry. Christian researchers in the field, meanwhile, for their own ideological reasons, were often more at pains to delineate continuity of transmission from synagogue poetry to the church.[125] However, given the antiquity of certain styles of Jewish poetry—particularly those forms that go back to the early centuries C.E.—the relationship is likely to be more complex than the more partisan schools would prefer.

In the end, the origins of Byzantine hymnography in general—Jewish and Christian—are uncertain. We can imagine that the Church—because of converts from Judaism who brought with them expectations and norms for worship, or because of a perception of Jews as in possession of liturgical authenticity, or simply because some Christian norms of worship were inherited from the synagogue—may have imported Jewish styles of liturgical poetry into Christian worship. At the same time, non-Jewish literary modes may well have entered the synagogue either via converts to Judaism or, more likely, via the simple power of a majority culture to set artistic norms and aesthetic tones. Ultimately, the reality is probably one of mutual, and not necessarily conscious, cross-pollination.[126]

Before we turn our attention to the complicated poetic forms of the Syriac and Greek traditions, a brief introduction to the cultural contexts of the major poet of each tradition, Ephrem of Edessa (Syriac) and Romanos the Melodist (Greek) may prove helpful.

Ephrem (CA. 306–373) was born into a Christian family in Nisibis, on

---

125 See, for example, Egon Wellesz, *A History of Byzantine Music and Hymnography* (Clarendon: Oxford, 1949), 11.

126 Note the apt statement by Stefan Reif that Judaism has an "excellent digestive system" (*Judaism and Hebrew Prayer*, 19). "Digestion," we should note, describes a process in which items are not only incorporated into a body but transformed radically. Likewise, the early Christian communities should be understood as borrowing and adapting from both Judaism and surrounding cultures.

the eastern border of Roman Syria and along the Silk Road that connected Rome to lands in the east. When Nisibis fell to the Persians in 363, Ephrem moved to Edessa. Although he spent most of his life caught up in the theological and political struggles of the fourth century (in the wake of the Council of Nicea), Ephrem was a prolific writer who frequently used his hymns to address contemporary topics—illustrating the potency of using hymns as pedagogical tools. In general Syriac Chistianity—in which the Aramaic language remained the liturgical language—retained closer connections to Judaism than to the more Hellenized and Greek-language Church of Constantinople. However, it was probably during Ephrem's lifetime, due to the power and influence of Constantine, that the Eastern Christian communities came into significant contact with the Western churches. Yannai's great predecessor, Yose ben Yose, lived at approximately the same time, or somewhat later. Ephrem displays a familiarity with some rabbinic-aggadic traditions and, though his writings about Jews are extremely polemical, we do know that there were Jews in Nisibis and Edessa during his lifetime and it is possible that he had some contact with them and perhaps their literature or liturgical traditions. Ephrem's works were popular in the Eastern Church, and evidence for their use is widespread, both in their original Syriac and in translation (a phenomenon *not* associated with Hebrew piyyut), well into Late Antiquity. Significantly, many manuscripts of his work survive from the sixth century—precisely Yannai's period.[127]

Ephrem, like the *payyetan* Yose ben Yose, was the first major poet of his tradition, and the origins of the forms in which he composed are just as mysterious as the origins of piyyut.[128] The parallels in dates and poetic

127 See C. Shephardson, *Anti-Judaism and Christian Orthodoxy: Ephrem's Hymns in Fourth Century Syria* (Washington, DC: Catholic University Press of America, 2008). The translation of Ephrem's hymns may reflect the general emphasis on translation in the early church, at the very same period when translation was falling out of favor in Judaism, with Hebrew becoming an increasingly symbolic "object" in its own right.

128 Ephrem has been the subject of more research, and translation, in English than Romanos; the works by Sebastian Brock offer a fine place to start a serious inquiry. An easily accessible volume of Ephrem's poetry in English is Ephrem the Syrian, *Hymns* (trans. K. McVey; New York: Paulist Press, 1989). More recently, and with a pronounced theoretical-philosophical bent, see Kees den Biesen, *Simple and Bold: Ephrem's Art of Symbolic Thought* (Piscataway, NJ: Gorgias, 2006). A study more directly pertinent to the subject at hand is T. Kronholm, *Motifs from Gen 1–11 in the Genuine Hymns of Ephrem the Syrian with Particular Reference to the Influence of Jewish Exegetical Tradition* (Lund : Liber Läromedel/ Gleerup, 1978). See also Shephardson, *Anti-Judaism and Christian Orthodoxy.*

developments between Ephrem and Yose suggest that perhaps both groups of poets—Jews and Christians—drew in the most general way on some common sources of inspiration, whether prose or poetic, Jewish or Christian. This is not to posit simple, linear transmission of either form or content; rather, it suggests that both communities were similarly influenced by larger factors or possibly by contact with one another, whether in positive or hostile settings, by means of converts or observation, or through the influence of a dominant culture. Given the span of multiple centuries under discussion here, and the complex social-commercial-political nexus of the Byzantine Empire, it seems possible that influences could have been reciprocal, particularly over time. Of course, it is also possible that each poet was shaped independently by local factors—Yose by the proto-poetic cadences of the *seliḥot* litanies and rabbinic midrash and Ephrem by local Mesopotamian works.[129] In any case, both Jewish and Christian poets were composing complex styles of poetry (more ornate than the Aramaic piyyutim or the poems of Marqa) by the late fourth century C.E. These poets certainly had influence within their own religious traditions, and just as we see Yannai as an heir to Yose ben Yose, we see Ephrem's influence in the works of the greatest Byzantine hymnist Romanos the Melodist.

One of the most famous of the Greek-language poets, Romanos is said to have been either a convert, or the child of converts, from Judaism. His Jewish origins are cited with (polemical) pride in a Christian hymn in his honor, in which he is compared to St. Paul—which suggests that his conversion may have taken place as an adult.[130] Romanos was born in the sec-

---

As Shephardson notes, Ephrem often condemns Jews (and "Arians") as "seekers"—implying that excessive probing of the biblical text is a trait that makes Christian heretics "Jewish." The resonance between this term of opprobrium and the term "midrash" (literally, "seeking") should not be glossed over.

129 The questions about the origins of Christian forms of hymnography are as manifold as those concerning the origins of piyyut. As Andrew Palmer, speaking of Ephrem, notes, "The earliest surviving Syriac poetry is so mature that it would seem to stand near the end of a development which stretches much further back in time" ("The Merchant of Nisibis: Saint Ephrem and His Faithful Quest for Union in Numbers," in *Early Christian Poetry*, ed. J. den Boeft and A. Hilhorst [Leiden: Brill, 1993], 167).

130 See P. Maas, Byzantinische Zeitschrift (1906), 20. The standard English translation of Romanos' oeuvre is *Kontakia of Romanos, Byzantine Melodist*, 2 vols., trans. M. Carpenter (Columbia: University of Missouri Press, 1970–1972). The standard critical edition of Romanos, with translations into French, is *Romanos le Mélode: Hymnes*, 5 vols. ed. and French trans. J. Grosdidier de Matons (Paris: Cerf, 1965–1981). For a more recent treatment of Romanos' putative Jewish origins, see J. Grosdidier de Matons, *Romanos le Mélode et les origins de la poésie religieuse à Byzance* (Paris: Beauchesne, 1977), 167–81.

ond half of the fifth century in Syrian Emesa and died in Constantinople sometime after 555 C.E. Given his Syrian birth, it seems possible that Romanos, the greatest Byzantine hymnist, likely knew the works of the most important Syriac church poet, Ephrem the Syrian, whose poetry had circulated as far as Constantinople in Greek translation.[131] Whether through Jewish or Syriac Christian channels, Romanos' poetry reveals a distinctive Semitic influence—e.g., correct scansion of Hebrew names in his poetry often require a Hebrew rather than Greek pronunciation to be assumed, and he often provides Hebrew words with Greek glosses within his poems.[132] Romanos' dates and Jewish origins take on added significance because Romanos' compositions bear striking resemblance to those of the classical *payyetanim* of the synagogue, despite significant differences.

This brief background sketch indicates that it is plausible to posit some form of contact between Jewish and Christian poetic traditions and tradents. For more specific insight into the complex intercultural phenomena in play here, however, we must look more closely at both poetic composition and content, both in Judaism and Christianity.

In matters of form, content, and reception, the parallels between Jewish and Christian hymnography are instructive, leading to similar questions if not simple answers. For example, the relatively sudden appearance of rhyme in the Syriac and, especially, in the Greek poems—by means of which rhyme probably entered the Latin rites, and from there the Western literary corpus—has puzzled scholars of Christian antiquity. It is not clear whether it developed organically or if it did, in fact, borrow from the more

---

131 See Brock, *From Ephrem to Romanos*, and also Krueger, *Writing and Holiness*, 162–63, for discussions of Emphrem's influence on Romanos. Also note M. Carpenter, "The Paper that Romanos Swallowed," *Speculum* 7 (1932): 3–22, which considers the question of the origin of the Kontakion.

132 The arguments for Romanos' bilingualism and connections to Ephrem have been well argued in recent years. See, in particular, William Petersen, "The Dependence of Romanos the Melodist upon the Syriac Ephrem: Its Importance for the Origin of the Kontakion," *Vigiliae Christianae* 39.2 (1985): 171–87; and the essays collected in Sebastian Brock, *From Ephrem to Romanos: Interactions between Syriac and Greek in Late Antiquity* (Aldershot ; Brookfield, USA : Ashgate, 1999). This said, while the connection between Ephrem and Romanos is well-established, Manolis Papoutsakis has recently called attention to the importance of Jacob of Sarug, in particular, as a writer who should be considered as influences upon Romanos, as well. Papoutsakis writes: "Peterson misleadingly confined the Melodist with Ephrem in the fourth century— undoubtedly Romanos belonged with his elder contemporary Jacob of Serugh with whom he shared the anxieties of the post-Chaledonian era" ("The Making of a Syriac Fable: From Ephrem to Romanos," *Le Muséon* 120 [2007]: 29–75).

thoroughly attested development of rhyme in synagogue poetry.[133] Rhyme does not appear in Greco-Latin poetry until after the emergence and spread of Christianity. Similarly, a Semitic model (entering Christianity from biblical or targumic models) explains Greek- and Latin-language Christian hymns that contain alphabetic acrostics ranging from *alpha–tau* and A-T rather than from *alpha-omega* or from A-Z.[134] (The ample presence of *biblical* models negates the hypothesis that the use of acrostics was

---

133 As noted in Chapter One, the origin of rhyme within piyyut is, itself, disputed, and one notable element of Yannai's poetry is his inconsistent use of rhyme, which may indicate the relative newness of the technique. Aharon Mirsky regards rhyme as an organic outgrowth of rabbinic prose stylizations, particularly the trope of "measure for measure," while Joseph Yahalom regards it as an amplification and development of biblical parallelism. See Mirsky, "Origins of Rhyme," 302–14; and Yahalom, *Poetry and Society*, 137–62, and "Piyyut as Poetry," 118–19. The present author sees the views of Mirsky and Yahalom as compatible, each delineating strong forces that acted within the world of Hebrew poetry. As Mirsky notes, key elements that contributed towards the development of rhyme in piyyut include the use of "theme words" in non-poetic ritual litanies and, by the time of Yose ben Yose, single-word refrains in liturgical poetry, such as the *shofarot* poem in which each line ends with the word *qol* ("voice, sound") or the *zikhronot* poem, in which each line ends with *zikkaron* ("memory"). This sort of proto-rhyme aesthetic can still be found in later poetry, including Yannai's works. *R'hitim*, in particular, which often use a single word or phrase as a kind of refrain (on top of Yannai's fully developed rhyme-schemes), resonate with this earlier style of writing. At the same time, Yannai's tendency to break up biblical parallels and construct new parallel material from those inherited constructions, as Yahalom so clearly delineates, not only contributes to the construction of rhyme but reflects a very "midrashic" approach to word-pairs (midrash is quite "tone deaf" to the aesthetics of biblical poetry but found the repetitions and redundancies rich in latent meaning); as in midrash, in piyyut an apparently simple phrase is broken open to reveal new layers of meaning. Unlike in prose midrashic texts, however, the force and wit of the new coinage is reinforced and amplified by rhyme.

134 See the discussion in J. Schirmann's seminal article "Hebrew Liturgical Poetry and Christian Hymnography." The ample presence of *biblical* models argues against Schirmann's hypothesis that the use of acrostics was borrowed from Jewish piyyut, however—the biblical models suffice to explain the significant increase in the popularity of acrostics in early Christian literature. The Septuagint does not replicate the actual acrostic structures of the underlying Hebrew when it translates acrostic texts; the Greek version of Lamentations (the first four chapters of which are alphabetic acrostics) and Ps 118/119 does include headings that indicate the Hebrew letter embedded in each stanza, but it is a question as to whether these headings are original or were added secondarily. See the summary and discussion in Albert Pietersma, "The Acrostic Poems of Lamentations in Greek Translation," in *Proceedings of the Eighth Congress of the International Organization for Septuagint and Cognate Studies, Paris* 1992, ed. Leonard Greenspoon and Olivier Munnich (Atlanta: Scholars Press: 1995), 183–201. As Kreuger notes, however, the Syriac version of Lamentations—which Romanos would have known, does replicate the acrostics; see *Writing and Holiness*, 170. It is important to note that acrostics are not unique to Semitic languages; Greek poets since the pre-classical period employed both name and alphabetic acrostics. See E. Courtney, "Greek and Latin Acrostichs," *Philologus* 134 (1990): 3–13.

borrowed from early Judaism.) Likewise, Byzantine Greek poetry largely abandoned the metrical schemes of classical Greek poetry, which raises questions concerning the origins of this innovative aesthetic: no matter the sources or directions of transmission, strongly resembles aspects of contemporary Jewish poetry. Additionally, certain Christian poetic forms blend biblical exegesis and liturgical function in the same way that Jewish piyyutim merge aggadah into the statutory prayers. Even the complaints against this new style of liturgical writing were similar although the geography was reversed: parallel to the resistance of the Babylonian Geonic authorities to piyyut, Christian authorities in the West resisted the inclusion of Eastern liturgical poems. Western Christian sources referred to popular religious poetry as *psalmi idiotici.*[135]

Christian Poetry: Ephrem and the Syriac Tradition

Syriac poetry, epitomized by Ephrem, is written in a dialect of Aramaic closely related to the Aramaic of the Babylonian Talmud. Syriac poetry employs many of the same forms as the pre-Classical and Classical piyyutim, including parallelism, acrostics (both in the biblical style, *alef-tav,* and—non-biblically—reverse acrostics from *tav-alef*), choral responses, and a strong rhythm. Given that Hebrew and Aramaic share many linguistic features, certain elements, such as the tendency to pun on related roots, are also common to both kinds of poetry. Furthermore, in content Ephrem's hymns (*madrashe* and *memre* being the two major genres) are often moralizing and draw on biblical texts with significant "aggadic" interpretation. Syriac hymns are formally more varied and more complex than the Samaritan or targumic Aramaic poems—the works with which they share the closest linguistic affinity. Thus in terms of structure, they are closer to Hebrew piyyut. For instance, the *soghitha,* related to the Syriac

135 *Psalmi idiodici* (lit. "private hymns"—works generally composed in the style of the Psalms) were popular lyrics that were banned by the Council of Laodicea in 320 and, though they persisted, were eventually supplanted in the Christian service by the recitation of biblical psalms. See R. E. Messenger, "Medieval Processional Hymns Before 1100," *Transactions and Proceedings of the American Philological Association* 80 (1949): 375–92; and, more recently, W. Evenepoel, "The Place of Poetry in Latin Christianity," *Early Christian Poetry,* ed. J. den Boeft and A. Hilhorst (Leiden: Brill, 1993), 35–60. Ruth Langer documents the controversy surrounding the inclusion of piyyut in the Babylonian and, later, medieval synagogues in *To Worship God Properly,* 110–87. It is intriguing to note the conflict in both Judaism and Christianity surrounding liturgical poetry; in the Christian tradition, however, we find poets self-consciously reflecting on the act of writing (beautifully delineated in D. Krueger, *Writing and Holiness*), which we do not find in the Classical piyyutim.

hymn form called a *madrasha* (a somewhat general term often translated as "hymn"), typically consists of a preface followed by a double acrostic, and it stands out for its extensive, structural use of dialogue. Another Syriac-Christian poetic form, the *enyana*, consists of literary mosaics blending poetry with scriptural quotations, rather like the opening stanzas of one of Yannai's *qedushta'ot* or the pre-Classical poetic styles of Yose ben Yose. The form referred to as a verse-homily (*memra*) recalls the more expansive units of the *qedushta*, such as Poem Six, although a *memra* is typically much longer than twenty-two lines and freer of form. Furthermore, Ephrem's pioneering use of signature acrostics and choral refrains recalls the use of similar devices in Yannai and his heirs.[136]

The exegesis embedded in Ephrem's poems also offers interesting parallels to Jewish aggadic traditions, including those found in the piyyutim. While on the surface many of Ephrem's poems reflect a profound antagonism towards Judaism, in both form and content the parallels to Hebrew poetry are suggestive. It seems highly unlikely that he would have directly borrowed Jewish models—if such models were available to be copied in his area. If Ephrem's use of "Jewish" forms was intentional, however, he may have been attempting to take on the Jews (or, perhaps, Christian "Judaizers") of his day on their own terms, and (almost literally) in their own language. Nevertheless, there are significant differences between Ephrem's poetry and Hebrew piyyut. Syriac poetry is generally based on a strictly regular syllable count—more fixed than the similar aesthetic of Hebrew poetry. Ephrem also famously employed a female choir—unlikely to have been employed in a synagogue—and, in general, he makes far more use of refrains than we see in early piyyut outside of some penitential Jewish hymns. And given that Hebrew poetry is so closely associated with the Land of Israel, the presence of influential Hebrew poetry at this early date in Syria seems unlikely. Furthermore, while Ephrem certainly includes anti-Jewish rhetoric in his poems, his polemics focus more on internal *Christian* heresies, including Marcionism, Arianism, and Manichaeism; indeed, Jews

136 On the question of Yannai's use of refrains, see Chapter One, n. 28. On Ephrem's use of choirs—notably female choirs—see Susan Ashbrook Harvey, "Spoken Words, Voiced Silence: Biblical Women in Syriac Tradition," *Journal of Early Christian Studies* 9 (2001): 105–31; and "Revisiting the Daughters of the Covenant: Women's Choirs and Sacred Song in Ancient Syriac Christianity," *Hugoye: Journal of Syriac Studies* 8.2 (July 2005), online [http://syrcom.cua.edu/Hugoye/Vol8No2/HV8N2Harvey.html]. When choirs are mentioned in Jewish sources (such as Nathan ha-Bavli's description of the choir present at the exilarch's installation), the choirs are apparently all male.

are more often a rhetorical foil for Ephrem in his struggle to articulate and define Christian orthodoxy, rather than a direct target.[137] Perhaps Jews were too disenfranchised, too weak, or too few in number to merit his concentrated attention.

Although it seems unlikely that Ephrem was directly influenced by contemporary Hebrew poetics (although it remains possible that he was familiar with "proto-payyetanic" synagogue writings, particularly through contact with the Jews in his area), the developments in Christian hymnography that Ephrem exemplifies may, in some fashion, have influenced the dramatic change in Hebrew poetry in the short period *between* Yose ben Yose and Yannai. That is, Yose and Ephrem offer us a start date within each tradition, and while it is difficult to establish a connection between these two founders, it becomes increasingly possible to posit connections among these writers' heirs. While we cannot assert contact with certainty, the diffusion of both piyyut and hymn throughout Byzantium suggests that some form of contact is not impossible.[138]

Christian Poetry: Romanos and the Greek Tradition

The complicated poetry of Romanos, the dominant poet of Byzantine Constantinople, must be studied more closely by those who wish to understand Yannai and his peers. Romanos, as noted above, was considered to have his roots in the synagogue of the fifth century (where he may have been familiar with the same piyyutim that inspired Yannai to his career). Though he moved at a young age from Syria to Constantinople, the cultural center of Byzantium, he lived in Syria, the homeland of Ephrem, for the first decades of his life (first in Emesa and then in Beirut). Based on semiticisms in his Greek, it seems likely that Syriac was, in fact, his first language. If the story of Jewish origins is true, he may well have had familiarity with Hebrew, as well. His hymns appear to be developed out of Syriac models.[139] He thus serves as a concrete link between Ephrem and Greek

137 See Shepherdson, *Anti-Jewish Polemic and Christian Orthodoxy*, for a substantial study of this complicated dynamic.

138 The poetry of Narsai (d. CA. 502) and Jacob of Serugh (d. 521), Syriac hymnists who lived closer to the period of Yannai, promises to yield especially intriguing results when much-needed comparative studies are finally done.

139 See Kreuger, *Writing and Holiness*, 166; and Brock, *From Ephrem to Romanos*, as well as note 130 above.

hymnography and, more hypothetically, a conduit between Christian and Jewish poetics.

Romanos was the first and earliest master of a form called the *kontakion.* Like the *qerova* in Hebrew piyyut, *kontakia* wed hymns to the lectionary, paraphrasing and interpreting the Bible in accord with communal traditions of interpretation and the liturgical setting.[140] Common to both the Hebrew and the Greek hymns are poetic prefaces, transitional stanzas, acrostics, dialogue, and rhyme. Often a short introductory stanza (called a *koukoulion* or *proimion*) announces the feast day, summarizes the theme of the hymn, and introduces the refrain (which may have been sung by a choir in a large cathedral or by the congregation in a smaller setting); the final strophe is a closing prayer explicitly addressing the contemporary audience. In some ways, these "bookends" recall the somewhat more complex but also highly organized structure of the *qedushta.* However, significant differences separate the *kontakion* from Yannai's style of writing. Its overall form is regular and uniform throughout, unlike the *qedushta,* which contains diverse component parts written in distinctive forms. Superficially, in this regularity, the *kontakion* has more in common with the pre-Classical Hebrew piyyut of Yose ben Yose or Aramaic hymns of the *targumim* and Marqa. Other elements are more complicated, however. *Kontakia,* like the Syriac hymns, display a much more formalized metrical system than piyyutim.[141] Additionally, the acrostics in the *kontakion* are significantly more complicated than the simple acrostics of the early piyyut. Romanos embeds lengthy signatures, such as "By the humble Romanos"[142]—a complexity of signature not seen in piyyut until several centuries after Yannai.[143] Early Hebrew piyyutim include only straightforward alphabetical acrostics (forward and reverse) and very basic name acrostics, such as the one first attested in Hebrew in the *qedushtaʾot* of Yannai.

An even more significant difference between piyyut and the *kontakion* form, noted by Schirmann, involves the relationship of the poetry to the

140 McGuckin states, "The kontakion bears the same role to the biblical text as midrash did in Jewish circles" ("Poetry and Hymnography (2): Greek," 649). The resemblance to piyyut—particularly the richly aggadic piyyutim of Yannai and his heirs—is even stronger.

141 Fixed, regular metrical patterns do not appear in Hebrew poetry until they are introduced by Dunash ibn Labrat in the tenth century, modeled on Arabic poetics.

142 See Kreuger, *Writing and Holiness,* 169–74.

143 See Fleischer, *Hebrew Liturgical Poetry in the Middle Ages,* where the subject of acrostics is discussed in various locations.

liturgy and the lectionary.[144] Piyyutim are always tied to a specific prayer and to the Torah portion of the week or holiday. The *kontakion* does not embellish a fixed liturgical text but rather the lectionary alone (i.e., the appropriate scriptural readings for a specific day).[145] We can, however, find Greek hymns that embellish the liturgy: the Byzantine poetic form called a *kanon*, which supplanted the *kontakion* in popularity after the seventh century. A *kanon* is built upon the prayer-text of the "nine odes" used for matins (eight hymns built on passages from the Old Testament and one from the Gospels). In a *kanon*, several stanzas embellish each ode and allude to its content prior to its citation, much as in a *qerova*—specifically, the subset of *qerova* called a *shivʿata*, which poetically adorns all seven blessings of the Sabbath Amidah. Both these genres—Hebrew *qerova* and Greek *kanon*—thus employ paraphrase of Scripture and interpolate exegesis into a liturgical station. In the end, it seems as if the twin functions of the *qerova*—embellishment of both liturgy and lectionary—have been split apart in the Greek tradition. But, these hymns all share a set of common impulses: the desire to renew the liturgy on a regular basis and to dramatize Scripture in a living, performative context. Poets from both traditions delight in diverse fixed forms—whether combined in one place, as in the *qedushta*, or restricted to specific forms and contexts.

Possibilities of Influence

Occasionally the language, imagery, or exegesis of two poems from separate traditions overlap so strongly that it is difficult to avoid discussing specific possibilities of influence—the depiction of Noah, noted above, offers an example of such a case. More often, however, alternative explanations can be offered. For example, the motif of "yearning for God" that both Ephrem and Yannai see behind the story of Gen 11 suggests the intrinsic power and appeal of that motif more than it does copying.[146] Or, to look more at rhet-

---

144 "Liturgical Poetry and Christian Hymnography," 160–61.

145 Syriac poetry contains a variety of topical hymns which are not pegged directly to decipherable calendrical events (e.g., Jacob of Serugh's "On Drunkenness"). The existence of these hymns in Syriac, and their absence from Hebrew piyyut, itself merits further inquiry.

146 It is regrettable that Yannai's poem for Gen 22 does not survive, as it would be fascinating to compare that work with Ephrem (or pseudo-Ephrem's) and Romanos' famous poetic treatments of the Binding of Isaac (also known by its Hebrew name, "the Akedah"). See S. Brock, "Two Syriac Verse Homilies on the Binding of Isaac," *Le Muséon* 99 (1986): 61–129; and M. Moskhos, "Romanos' Hymn on the Sacrifice of Abraham: A Discussion of

oric rather than theme, Romanos freely composes in the voice of biblical characters, collapsing the biblical story into the present tense—a technique common in Hebrew piyyut, but one which may reflect a common Greco-Roman background. Single, simple, potent conceptualizations and deft rhetorical techniques served the needs of all these authors. Other potential areas of commonality—notably matters of performance—are even more difficult to pin down definitively. Yet, accepting the importance of caution, the resonances are highly suggestive and much comparative work remains to be done.[147]

Indeed, for all their disagreement in matters of practice and theology, the liturgical poets were voices for their communities, and these communities did not live in isolation. As a result, the vast body of hymns from Late Antiquity may reveal issues that brought the Jewish and Christian worlds into conversation even if these specific poems (in terms of form) were not the vehicles by which the Jews and Christians communicated with one another. Rather, these poems indicate the internal discourse *within* the communities about issues of more general concern. For instance, when Yannai rejoices in the reunion of Noah and his wife—the cessation of the long period of celibacy in the Ark—he reflects the Jewish argument against a Christian interpretation of the story that appears in Ephrem's poem, which celebrates Noah as a celibate. For Jews, represented here by Yannai, the denial of marital intimacy was a temporary measure, necessitated by the situation; for a significant group within developing Christianity, as articulated by Ephrem, lifelong celibacy—presumably a "hard sell"—was promoted as an ideal. To be sure, these are voices on different sides of a broader cultural polemic. Christian prose sources passionately extol the virtues of abstinence while rabbinic sources openly mock the idea—even adducing stories that Noah's genitals were mauled by a lion, perhaps as a way of rebuffing the positive Christian interpretation of his lack of post-

the Sources and a Translation," *Byzantion* 44 (1974): 310–28. Also note the more general discussion in E. Kessler, *Bound by the Bible: Jews, Christians, and the Sacrifice of Isaac* (Cambridge, UK/New York: Cambridge University Press, 2004); this volume discusses, albeit briefly, Jewish and Christian liturgical poetry (from the Byzantine period) about the Akedah.

147 See Lieber, "Portraits of Righteousness," for a comparative study of Hebrew piyyut with Syriac and Greek Christian poetry through the lens of this polemic.

diluvium progeny.[148] Each side had some idea of what the other promoted, as evidenced by their response.

Yannai and Ephrem are, along with Romanos and Marqa, just two important and interesting voices among many, all engaged in a lively, ongoing cultural conversation, rooted in the meanings that texts acquire when read in living congregations of the faithful. Like their communities, these poets exist in tension with the other cultures—poetic exegetes linked by their common need to interpret a shared sacred text and meet the demands of a public-performative context. They are not the first voices on the subjects, and far from the last ones. And whether or not they were innovators of interpretation—the most potent or powerful voices—these poets were in the public realm. They were, within their communities, a public face of interpretation.

Conclusions

Jewish society in Late Antiquity and the Byzantine age produced works of stunning artistry and enduring importance. Although later sources would remember the Byzantine period as one exclusively of gloom and oppression for the Jews, the fourth to seventh centuries C.E. saw the flowering of a remarkable society. In defiance of imperial law, numerous synagogues were built, often decorated with some of the most beautiful Jewish art ever created. Diverse and inventive translations of Scripture were produced and, contrary to the wishes of some authorities, written down. In the rabbinic centers of the Galilee, major literary texts—most importantly the Amoraic midrashic collections but also the Palestinian Talmud—were edited and anthologized. And in the midst of this creative ferment, Jewish liturgical poetry, reflective of and in dynamic tension with all these other movements, likewise came into being. It was a period in which new interpretations, and new contexts for interpretation, flourished side by side with older traditions that were being consolidated and synthesized.

Yannai's remarkable creativity may, in part, have been a response to the tremendous tension of his period. For, while Jewish culture appears to have been thriving in the fifth century, the mid-sixth century and the reign of Justinian represents a kind of pivotal moment when life for Jews began to

148 Jewish polemics against Christianity will be discussed in the following chapter, which focuses on themes and motifs in the piyyutim.

take something of a turn for the worse. In this period, the Christian community was gaining in power, and the Jewish community often suffered as a result. That said, although the vice may have been tightening, the overall societal picture, its self-presentation, is not one of oppression and subjugation. The flowering of Jewish culture in this period—literary, artistic, and liturgical—suggests a society experiencing a renaissance, perhaps itself an act of defiance or a strategy of turning inward as a mode of cultural survival.[149] Indeed, the diversity and vigor of literary, artistic, and architectural creations from this era suggest that there were at least long moments (if not extended periods) of Jewish self-assertion in the face of real and perceived Christian imperialism. Anti-Christian polemics, for example, play a noticeable but not a dominant role in Yannai's piyyutim, especially when compared to the pointed opinions of the Jewish Aramaic poems from the same period.[150] Much greater than the subtext of oppression emerging from this literature is the sense of Jewish affirmation. Yannai knew enough about Christianity to attack it with some vigor, but by and large his preference seems to have been to focus his congregation inward, on themselves, rather than on their contemporary antagonists. Even the technique of couching his polemics in terms of "Rome/Edom" somewhat diminishes the sense of immediate threat, rendering the Byzantine Empire into the latest place-holder in the role of "enemy" in an ongoing Jewish narrative.[151]

Furthermore, the piyyutim help us create a portrait of Jewish leadership

---

149 P. T. R. Gray's characterization of the period is particularly appropriate: "We get a picture of local Jewish life in the villages of the Galilee turning in on itself to some extent in an era of increased hostility from Christians and the empire, but still vital, still devoted to its religious identity. The point is not just that the Judaism of the villages was a durable phenomenon—like the Samaritanism of a nearby area—unlikely to be susceptible to the kind of change Justinian's legislation aimed at producing. The point is also that such village-based Judaism could and did simply ignore the legislation." ("Palestine and Justinian's Legislation," 263).

150 The difference may be due to the contexts in which the poems were recited. That is, the Hebrew poems are set within the statutory liturgy, which, while not free of polemic, is focused on other concerns; additionally, it is possible that the Hebrew poems were more discreet because of the threat of Christian interference in the service. The Aramaic poems, recited outside of the statutory prayers, might have had greater freedom to speak in more aggressive language. This is not to downplay the polemic against Christianity in Yannai's poetry. Yannai's *qedushta* for Yom Kippur offers a particularly vituperative example of his anti-Christian polemic. (See Rabinovitz, *The Liturgical Poems of Rabbi Yannai*, 2:221–22.) But, also, note the cautions offered in W. Jac. van Bekkum, "Anti-Christian Polemics in Hebrew Liturgical Poetry (*Piyyut*) of the Sixth and Seventh Centuries."

151 See Chapter Four for a discussion of Yannai's treatment of Edom/Rome.

at a complicated and possibly pivotal moment in Jewish history. The piyyutim blend popular if otherworldly elements, such as the Qedushah and the zodiac, with levitical ("priestly") concerns, such as the priestly watches and Temple iconography, all in the context of a genre that seems to be overwhelmingly rabbinic in terms of motifs, methods, and liturgical structure. For all the subtle differences among the various genres of Jewish writing in this period, what emerges is most noteworthy for its complexity—a complexity that, perhaps paradoxically, reflects a broad cultural cohesion. The extant piyyutim do not simplify our picture of this world; they complicate it by suggesting a community composed of popular and elite, priestly and rabbinic, learned and playful all at once. It should not, however, come as a surprise that the roles, functions, and appeals of these literary genres overlap. Each kind of writing (at least as we have it now) probably reflects the needs and expectations of different audiences and contexts—the same basic "raw material" and methods crafted, shaped, and distilled or expanded to suit specific settings. The commonalities can be more misleading than the differences, whether the issue is shared midrashic and poetic tropes, common targumic and payyetanic motifs, or mutually engaged polemics across the Jewish-Christian divide. Yannai's piyyutim evoke an entire milieu—something much larger than just the ancient synagogue—in which textual interpretation formed worldviews. These works and their intertextual, even intercultural, thickness matter in part because they are a public manifestation of much broader realities.

Yannai and the other liturgical poets mediated or were permeated by multiple cultural influences—high and low, exoteric and esoteric, Jewish and Christian, fluid and fixed—and crafted from them works of meaningfulness and beautify, edification and entertainment, substance and sparkle.

The study above has presented the complexity of Yannai's work and his context, Jewish and more general, in necessarily broad strokes. In the following chapter, a similarly broad array of topics will be addressed, and as here, each could become a monograph in its own right. Specific elements will be explored in somewhat more detail, offering sketches of Yannai as both an active ancient Jewish theologian and a participant in an emotionally complex and politically charged Jewish community. These miniature studies will, in turn, suggest further ways in which Yannai's poems can be studied from a variety of interdisciplinary perspectives.

Chapter Four

"Threads of the Tapestry"

Selected Topics from Yannai's *Qedushta'ot* for Genesis

Poetry, Angels, and the Heavenly Hekhalot
The Concept of "Holiness"
The God of Yannai
The Covenant of the Land: Exile and Restoration
Esau and Apocalype: Jews, Christians, and "the Good Other"
Yannai's Women

The previous chapters have viewed Yannai and his works through an ever-widening lens: the relationship between form and function; the poet's use of language; and the complex Byzantine social and cultural contexts (Jewish and Christian) out of which the poems emerged and into which they were received. The following reflections explore Yannai's compositions on Genesis from the perspective of their thematic content. Divided into six essays-in-miniature, these explorations are not intended to be conclusive, exhaustive, or definitive. Instead, they should be regarded as starting points for further inquiry and analysis.

As a synagogue poet, Yannai not only reflected the theologies, politics, and social realities of his day; he also constructed and conveyed them. Rather than passively transmitting tradition, stitching together bits of Bible and aggadah into patchwork performance pieces, the poet actively used his medium to explore pressing issues: God's relationship to the Jewish people, the nature of prayer, the meaning of exile. There are meditations on values, morals, and even on the emotional experiences of life in his *qedushta'ot*. The poet was not trying to recover ancient societal norms in the way a modern biblical scholar would; instead, the situations, characters, and ideas of the past function as a lens through which he refracted his own time period. Furthermore, Yannai composed for a live audience, and whatever he taught must be understood as functioning within this public, performative, liturgical context. As the "popular" literature of the ancient synagogue, these piyyutim help us understand the life and times of the poet who composed them and the people who enjoyed them. The six essays highlight Yannai's creativity as a writer and tradent and revisit the importance of the liturgical context of the synagogue in understanding his work, particularly as it relates to (and differs from) other exegetical genres of writing from his time period. To be sure, this is a subjective enterprise. The working sample is, itself, limited to the poet's treatment of a single biblical book. Indeed, other readers may examine the same Genesis poems and find different emphases or interpretations.[1] They will certainly find other topics for further investigation.

Poetry, Angels, and the Heavenly Hekhalot

Angelology, liturgy, the early synagogue, Temple rituals, and the esoteric traditions clustered under the heading "Hekhalot mysticism" all achieved a new or transformed significance in Late Ancient Judaism.[2] This matrix of elements, in turn, overlaps significantly with the world of early piyyut. A full appreciation of this network of issues and piyyut's place within it requires a study of materials ranging from Qumranic prayer texts, such as the Songs of the Sabbath Sacrifice, to medieval Ashkenazic prayer rituals—works that are variously marginal, esoteric, and mainstream. The relationships among Qumranic liturgies, Temple and rabbinic prayer traditions, and early Jewish mysticism are particularly intriguing, and given the prominence of poetry in all three genres, the place of piyyutim amid these other writings has become an especially relevant issue.[3] Thus the question of

1 The discussions below relate to the texts presented in the second half of this volume, but in many cases, the essays that accompany piyyut translations expand the discussion of topics presented here.

2 The word "mysticism" defies easy definition. See E. Wolfson, "Mysticism and the Poetic-Liturgical Compositions from Qumran: a Response to Bilhah Nitzan, *Jewish Quarterly Review* 85 (1994): 185–202. Regarding the relationship of Hekhalot traditions to the liturgy, note the careful discussions in M. Swartz, *Mystical Prayer in Ancient Judaism: An Analysis of Maʿaseh Merkavah* (Tübingen: Mohr-Siebeck, 1992), and subsequently, in his monograph *Scholastic Magic: Ritual and Revelation in Early Jewish Mysticism* (Princeton: Princeton University Press, 1996). For the purposes of this study, "mysticism" is used as a shorthand for elements that stress the otherworldly or theologically-immediate elements of prayer—intense interest in angels and angelic praise of God as well as a sense of proximity to the divine, apprehension of and communication with the deity in a direct rather than abstract way. This is, admittedly, a "soft" mysticism—one that seeks neither *unia mystica* nor religious trance—but it allows sufficient flexibility to indicate further avenues of intellectual inquiry into these poems.

3 These issues, albeit with little direct treatment of early piyyut, have begun to receive

whether Yannai's poetry is in any way "mystical" deserves consideration. Mysticism is a difficult term to define, and for purposes of concision, only two elements often associated with early rabbinic mysticism will be considered here: Yannai's use and understanding of angelology and, more generally, the relationship of his works to the more thoroughly studied Hekhalot mystical texts and traditions.[4]

In Jewish sources, beginning with some of the pre-exilic Prophets, biblical sources display an increasing fascination with God's heavenly retinue. The later books of the Bible—Ezekiel, Zechariah, and Daniel, in particular—offer early evidence of that interest, which continues to develop throughout the Second Temple period (as evidenced in both apocryphal works such as Tobit and more esoteric writings such as Jubilees, the Dead Sea Scrolls, and Enoch).[5] Angels also play major roles in the Hekhalot

---

scholarly treatment. See, in addition to Wolfson's response to B. Nitzan, her original piece: B. Nitzan, "Harmonic and Mystical Characteristics in Poetic and Liturgical Writings from Qumran," *Jewish Quarterly Review* 85 (1994): 163–83. Also note R. Sarason, "The 'Intersections' of Rabbinic and Qumran Judaism," *Dead Sea Scrolls Discoveries* 8 (2001): 169–81; and M. Swartz, "The Dead Sea Scrolls and Later Jewish Magic and Mysticism," *Dead Sea Scrolls Discoveries* 8,2 (2001): 182–93.

4 As Wolfson notes in his response to Nitzan: "The Jewish sources, beginning with the apocalyptic and Qumran texts, may provide a different model [for understanding mysticism] based ... on the 'angelification' of the human being who crosses the boundary of space and time and becomes part of the heavenly realm, a motif that likely has its roots in ancient Near Eastern and Mesopotamian mythology" (186). To meet this contextual definition, Wolfson stipulates that there must be a "technique or praxis that facilitates the idealization of a human being into a divine or angelic being in the celestial abode" (187). This definition is stronger than the one employed here: I do not assert that the congregation at prayer made a spiritual ascent but rather participated, joined with, or harmonized with the angels at prayer in some not necessarily well-defined fashion. That said, the practice of reciting piyyutim (about which we know very few details in terms of ritual) may itself have constituted a kind of diffused or weakened translation of more ambitious mystical practices. To borrow the phrasing from Swartz's *Mystical Prayer in Ancient Judaism*, recitation of *qedushta'ot* may have promised "apprehension of and communication with the divine" (5).

5 For material evidence of popular interest in angelology, and the practical applications of angelogical knowledge, in both Palestine and Babylonia, see J. Naveh and S. Shaked, *Amulets and Magic Bowls: Aramaic Incantations from Late Antiquity* (Jerusalem: Magnes, 1998) and, by the same, *Magic Spells and Formulae: Aramaic Incantations from Late Antiquity* (Jerusalem: Magnes, 1993). The topic of magic has received renewed scholarly interest of late, although J. Trachtenberg's study *Jewish Magic and Superstition: a Study in Folk Religion* (New York: Berhmans, 1939; reissued: Philadelphia: University Penn Press, 2004) remains a classic. The following list offers a selection of recent works on the topic: M. Bar-Ilan, "Prayers of Jews to Angels and Other Intermediaries During the First Centuries C.E.," in *Saints and Role Models in Judaism and Christianity* (ed. M. Poorthuis and J. Schwartz; Leiden: Brill, 2004), 79–95; Swartz, *Scholastic Magic: Ritual and Revelation in Early Jewish Mys-*

sources, and although the dating of these traditions is difficult, they develop and amplify the biblical models and ideas from Late Antiquity. Yannai, for his part, reflects this apparently broad cultural interest in the heavenly hosts: angels often appear in his *qedushtaʾot* not only as characters in the biblical narratives our poet is embellishing but in their liturgical function as participants in the Qedushah. Yannai's development of this motif, especially his inclusion of angelic beings in poems lacking any biblical trigger for this element, suggest how keen his—or his community's—interest in this topic was. The question is: Was this motif in any way remarkable or was it merely a commonplace trope?

In general, angelic references in Yannai's piyyutim occur with particular frequency towards the end of the *qedushta*, in anticipation of the *Qedushat Ha-Shem* (the third blessing of the Amidah), into which the Qedushah is embedded.[6] The Qedushah focuses on Isa 6:3 and Ezek 3:12, understood from early on to be quotations from angelic liturgies overheard by the biblical Prophets—making these two verses particularly potent texts to quote in a ritual context.[7] Furthermore, according to traditions attested in Qumranic and early rabbinic sources, the human community reciting the Qedushah actually joined the angelic hosts in praise of God: when the Jews prayed these words, they prayed *with* the angels.[8] The moment of recitation

---

ticism; N. Janowitz, *Icons of Power: Ritual Practices in Late Antiquity* (University Park: Penn State University Press, 2002) and *Magic in the Roman World: Pagans, Jews and Christians* (London: Routledge, 2001); D. Sperber, *Magic and Folklore in Rabbinic Literature* (Ramat Gan: Bar Ilan University Press, 1994); and, most recently, G. Bohak, *Ancient Jewish Magic: A History* (Cambridge, UK/New York: Cambridge University Press, 2008). Popular and elite interests in angels and magic meet, sometimes harmoniously and sometimes with friction, in the context of the Qedushah prayer. See the discussion here and in Langer, *To Worship God Properly*, 188–244.

6 See the discussion of the *silluq* (Poem Eight) and *qedushah* (Poem Nine) in Chapter One.

7 Ruth Langer documents the controversy over individual recitation of the Qedushah (recitation in the absence of a *minyan* or quorum of ten adult males), which amply testifies to the prayer's popular appeal. See *To Worship God Properly*, 188–244.

8 See the convenient summary of the Qedushah in Late Antiquity with excellent notes in Levine, *The Ancient Synagogue*, 571–77; see also Arthur Green, *Keter: The Crown of God in Early Jewish Mysticism* (Princeton: Princeton University Press, 1997), especially pp. 12–19. Green's approach to the mystical traditions associated with the Qedushah prayer is worth noting: "Here I begin to betray my bias. Yes, there is a real religious phenomenon behind the [Hekhalot] texts... I do not believe that these are *only* literary/interpretive/imitative sources" (15n). That is, Green emphasizes the experiential reality of the texts—important to recall with piyyut, as well. Green's notes provide a good starting point for readers interested in gaining a more general background in Hekhalot mysticism in the liturgical context.

of this third blessing of the Amidah thus became a mystically-charged experience, an instant when earth and heaven joined not only in worship but in the very act of crowning the deity with their prayers.[9] As a result of the potency of this action and these specific words, the Qedushah was a popular and powerful liturgical moment, and resonant traditions have been found in the Dead Sea Scrolls, rabbinic literature, and the apocrypha and pseudepigrapha, all of which either predate Yannai or are roughly contemporary with his period.[10]

This is not to say that the connections among these works and their implied communities are simple, let alone linear. The differences (such as the striking absence of Isa 6:3 and Ezek 3:12 from the Qumranic Songs of the Sabbath Sacrifice) must be accounted for. Furthermore, shared texts do not indicate shared rituals or beliefs. The use of the Qedushah and the understanding of its efficacy and potency surely varied. As it is, the surviving texts—poetry and prose, exegesis and liturgy—leave us with a sense of broad cultural interest in certain esoteric matters, particularly the workings of heavenly creatures.[11] The phenomenon of the Qedushah must be studied contextually if we are to determine what the text "means."

It is not surprising that Yannai's poetry displays an intense interest in

9 In this, the ritual of the Qedushah (along with other rituals, particularly those of Rosh Hashanah) reflects a remarkable transformation and translation of ancient Near Eastern rituals of divine enthronement. On the continuity between ancient Near Eastern religion and rabbinic literature, see Fishbane, *Biblical Myth and Rabbinic Mythmaking.*

10 Levine notes that the origins of the Qedushah are pre-rabbinic. He locates its source among Qumranic sectarians, and considers the lack of discussion of the prayer in early rabbinic texts to indicate "the sages' lack of enthusiasm for this prayer, perhaps owing to its mystical, sectarian, or Christian associations" (*The Ancient Synagogue*, 575–76). While these specific conclusions are arguable, this quotation does bespeak the wide appeal of the prayer from an early date. The piyyutim provide among the most solid evidence for the centrality of the Qedushah in the Jewish liturgy of Late Antiquity.

11 As James Charlesworth notes in his introduction to the Songs of the Sabbath Sacrifice from Qumran: "The similarities in verbal style and in some forms of composition between the *Sabbath Songs* and the Hekhalot hymns are sufficient, when coupled with the basic similarities of the subject matter and association with the liturgical times for sacrifice and prayer, to establish a significant relationship between the *Sabbath Songs* and Hekalot literature. When taken together with the significant ways in which the *Sabbath Songs* differ from the Hekhalot material, one gains the impression of a complex literary tradition of description of angelic praise" (*The Dead Sea Scrolls: Hebrew, Aramaic, and Greek Texts with English Translations*, vol. 4b, *Angelic Liturgy: Songs of the Sabbath Sacrifice* [Mohr Siebeck/Westminster John Knox: Tubingen and Louisville, 1999], 11). The same could be stated of the relationship of piyyutim to both the Hekhalot and Qumranic materials, with the added awareness that the piyyutim are the most "exoteric" of all these genres.

angels, given that his poems have as an ultimate goal participation with the angels in praise—not seeking ascent to the heavens so much as a temporary erasure of any functional boundary between mortals and angels. What merits attention is the way Yannai employs and uses the motif in his individual works. He was not an academic theologian transmitting esoteric ideas to his disciples. His focus was on the world of the synagogue, where concepts such as "enthronement of God" and "angelology" possessed potent, real force. Through his words, Yannai enabled the community to experience the divine directly.

In their angelology, Yannai's Genesis *qedushtaʾot* recall well-established Jewish traditions about angels, usually grounded in imagery found in biblical passages. For example, in the *qedushah* (Poem Nine) for Gen 19:1, Yannai tells us that the angels sent to Abraham in Gen 19 were Michael (sent to announce Isaac's birth?); Gabriel (sent to overturn Sodom); and Raphael (sent to rescue Lot).[12] Each angel was charged with a specific task. This understanding of how angels fulfill missions resembles a tradition in *GenR* 50:2 that states:

> It was taught: One angel does not perform two missions, nor do two angels together perform one mission, yet you read that two [angels came to Sodom]? The fact is, however, that Michael announced his tidings [to Abraham] and departed, Gabriel was sent to overturn Sodom, and Rafael to rescue Lot.[13]

Yannai and the midrash share not only the basic idea about how angels work (one task per angel), but the identities of the angels intended for this specific episode. Both works are operating within the same tradition. Similarly, Yannai mentions in the same poem that each angel has his own host; this image resembles a teaching in *DeutR* 2:34 that states:

> Rabbi Isaac opened [his discourse] with the text "The Lord is my portion, says my soul; therefore will I hope in Him" (Lam 3:24). Rabbi Isaac said: This may be compared to a king who entered a province with his generals, rulers, and governors. Some of the citizens of the province chose a general as their Patron, others a ruler

12 The poem is fragmentary; it seems likely that the angels were identified earlier in the poem, as well. The commonalities between this passage and midrashic versions are discussed briefly in Chapter Three.

13 See also *b.Bava Metsia* 86b.

> and others a governor. One of them who was cleverer than the rest said, "I will choose the king." Why? All others are liable to be changed, but the king is never changed. Likewise, when God came down on Sinai, there also came down with Him many companies of angels: Michael and his company, Gabriel and his company. Some of the nations of the world chose for themselves [as their Patron] Michael, others Gabriel, but Israel chose for themselves God, exclaiming, "The Lord is my portion, says my soul"; this is the force of, "Hear, O Israel, the Lord is God, the Lord alone."

Again, by asserting that each named angel is the captain of an angelic host, Yannai does not innovate so much as tap into a wellspring of widespread beliefs about angels.

The angelology in other piyyutim by Yannai is in keeping with the mythology conveyed by conventional passages from various mainstream rabbinic writings describing angelic appearances and roles.[14] For instance, the *silluq* (Poem Eight) for Gen 12:1 (a passage with no associated tradition of angels) describes God's word as "enduringly bright among Your angels / who rush like lightning / and return like a bolt / fly like an arrow…" (lines 11–12).[15] Yannai's poeticized presentation of the angels would have engaged Yannai's audience more because of their lively, dynamic imagery than because of any hugely innovative content.

Indeed, Yannai's genre rather than his content distinguishes his uses of angelology from what we find in prose rabbinic sources. While the other sources of his day may describe the angels in terms similar to Yannai, Yannai presents them in a public-performative setting and as part of his own original composition. The angelology of the *qedushah* (Poems Eight and Nine) for Gen 19:1, noted above, is both "retold Bible" and performed midrash; that of the *qedushta* for Gen 12:1, a vivid verbal sensation ("you are there!") more than an explicit interpretation. As a result, while Yannai's

---

14 See, for example, *Mekhilta Beshallaḥ* 2, in which God arrays columns of angels before the Israelites at the Sea; *SongR* 3:24, which describes the angels in terms of fire and ice; and *GenR* 50:1, which uses Ezek 1:14 (alluded to in the passage cited above) to describe the appearance of angels. The opening chapters of Ezekiel provide particularly rich fodder for these elaborations, and Yannai's depiction in the *silluq* for Gen 12:1 participates in that tradition.

15 The dazzling appearance of heavenly beings is described in biblical works such as Ezekiel and is elaborated in both apocryphal works and in rabbinic midrash and Hekhalot texts. In addition to the passages discussed here, see also Yannai's *qedushta* for Exod 3:1 (Rabinovitz 1:263–274) which elaborates on the angelic creation from fire and ice.

angelology can be considered "traditional," his crafting of the imagery reflects his poetic imagination.

A quick survey of the *qedushta'ot* in this volume—particularly the *silluq* and the *qedushah* units, because of their proximity to the Qedushah prayer itself—reveals the quantity and nature of Yannai's angelology and his poetic interest in the workings of God's heavenly retinue. It remains a question, however, whether these poems are "mystical," at least in any esoteric sense; their commonalities with rabbinic aggadah suggest an exoteric quality that is at odds with the esotericism often associated with mysticism and mystical pursuits. Yannai may reflect a more popular understanding of the same traditions that are preserved in texts such as *Hekhalot rabbati, Sefer ha-razim*, and others. That is, his style of piyyut may be a "public face" of a *common* rabbinic mystical tradition. As noted, angels (and related motifs, such as the Zodiac, the heavenly court, the divine chariot/throne) were common elements of Jewish culture in the Byzantine world and mention of them apparently routine.

The popularity of the Qedushah, which has its origins in Temple ritual in some fashion, was probably rooted originally in the people's desire to recite these key biblical verses.[16] That desire appears from the earliest date to have been an integral part of this more general fascination: the wish to know more about, connect with, and, in magical context, manipulate or

---

16 The Qumranic evidence is particularly suggestive of the early influence of these biblical verses. See, in addition to the works noted above, M. Weinfeld, "The Traces of *Kedushat Yotzer* and the *Pesukey de-Zimra* in the Qumran Literature and Ben Sira," *Tarbiz* 45 (1976): 15–26 [Hebrew]; and J. Strugnell's classic, *The Angelic Liturgy at Qumran: 4Q Serek Shirot `Olat Ha-Shabbat* in *Vetus Testamentum*, Supp. 7 (Leiden; Brill, 1959–1960). Similarly, the Enochic material is important; see M. Mach, "Qedoshim Mal'akhim: Ha-'El ve-ha-Liturgiyah ha-Shamayemit," in *Massu'ot: Studies in Kabbalistic Literature and Jewish Philosophy in Memory of Prof. Ephraim Gottlieb* (ed. Ephraim Gottlieb, Michal Oron and Amos Goldreich; Jerusalem: Bialik, 1994), 298–310 [Hebrew]. The New Testament (Luke 2:14, Rev 4) likewise indicates the early popularity of the Qedushah or its forerunner. See Werner, *The Sacred Bridge*, vol. 2 , 112, as well—he posits an early date for the Qedushah but a Pharisaic/synagogal origin rather than the Temple, as he assumes a strong Sadducean influence at the Temple and accepts the idea that the Sadducees were anti-angelological in orientation. I. Gruenwald, conversely, argues convincingly for a Temple origin for the prayer; see his monograph, *Apocalyptic and Merkavah Mysticism* (Leiden: Brill, 1980); "Shirat ha-Mal'akhim, ha-Qedushah, u-Va'ayat Ḥibburah shel Sifrut Ha-Hekhalot," in *Peraqim be-Toledot Yerushalayim bi-Yemei Bayyit Sheni* (Jerusalem: Ben Zvi Institute, 1981), 459–81; and, most pertinent to the present topic, his article, "Piyyutei Yannai ve-Sifrut Yoredei Merkavah," *Tarbiz* 36 (1966–67): 257–77. More generally, see Levine, *The Ancient Synagogue*, 561–88.

benefit from the divine realm.[17] The popularity of the Qedushah, the centerpiece of the Shabbat morning liturgy in the Palestinian rite, is emblematic of this interest. So compelling were these potent, overheard words that individuals wished to recite them on their own, even in the absence of a *minyan*, and communities came to include the Qedushah on weekdays as well as Shabbat and holidays, in keeping with the Babylonian rite.[18]

The structure of the *qedushta*, emphasizing the Qedushah as it does (compared, for example, with the *shivaʿata*, which embellished a service lacking the recitation of the Qedushah), reveals that the piyyutim participated in this widespread cultural fascination. By including frequent reference to angels and the heavenly world, Yannai reflected the interests of his community as much as he was shaping them. Rather than seeing the piyyutim as separate from more esoteric mystical works, it may make more sense to see them as distinct manifestations of the very same impulses.[19]

In truth, Yannai's poetry displays some true affinities with the Hekhalot traditions of rabbinic mysticism, but not in the overt, obvious ways one might expect.[20] There are no strings of magical divine names or depictions of (or promises of) an ascent to heaven in these works. The mystical implications are, instead, more subtle, and the possible connections to more

---

17 Rabbinic mysticism should not, of course, be confused with medieval kabbalah. The goal of the rabbinic mystics in the Hekhalot ascent texts seems to have been to achieve an ecstatic experience and vision of the deity on His throne, surrounded by the divine retinue—to see and hear what Isaiah and Ezekiel saw, and what all the Israelites at Sinai witnessed. This vision was achieved by undergoing a spiritual journey through the seven heavens. According to some traditions, esoteric and secret wisdom could be brought back down to earth by the Sage; in other cases, simply beholding the Throne was the goal. The *Sar Torah* texts, which developed separately, present rituals that aimed to bring an angel down to earth, so that the mystic could acquire esoteric wisdom and skills. For a discussion of these beliefs and practices, see Swartz, *Mystical Prayer in Ancient Judaism* and *Scholastic Magic*.

18 See Langer, *To Worship God Properly*, 188–244. The Qedushah was recited daily in the Babylonian rite.

19 To be sure, based on the nature of the experience implied by the piyyutim, some readers may hesitate to refer to these works as "mystical"—based on the definitions one chooses, these works may fail to make the threshold. But, while Yannai's piyyutim do not indicate that they sought to generate an actual ascent to heaven, as we see in the Hekhalot ascent texts, the apparent collapsing of the boundaries between heaven and earth, even if in a vague and undefined fashion, suggests that some language relating to mysticism should be used to describe the experience.

20 Rabinovitz ("Introduction," 65–68), for example, downplays the mysticism of Yannai's *qedushtaʾot* because the piyyutim lack many formal features common in the Hekhalot texts, such as first person narration or strings of magical divine names. By Rabinovitz's standards, Yannai's works are not mystical but mainstream.

explicitly "mystical" writings and practices more complicated. Thus, while the connectedness of the two genres can be argued, another question remains. Are the mystical threads in Yannai's piyyutim weak popularizations of potent rabbinic mystical praxis or are they something more?

Resonances between the piyyutim and the Hekhalot traditions are evident most particularly at the levels of form and practice.[21] Some Hekhalot texts contain lists (called by Swartz "extended series"[22]) in which a single basic pattern becomes a paradigm for a more elaborate poem and doxological formulae. For example, in *Maʿaseh Merkavah* §594, we find two examples that resemble *r'hitim* in their verbal density and rhetorical structure, although they lack the formal features of the poetic texts, such as acrostics as structuring devices:

> *Example One*:
> Be blessed, praised
> Glorified, exalted, uplifted
> Magnified, acclaimed,
> Sanctified, adorned, beloved...

---

21 A complete bibliography of Hekhalot studies far exceeds the scope of the present essay. Some important works not already cited would include the following: Peter Schäfer, Margarete Schlüter, and Hans Georg von Mutius, *Synopse zur Hekhalot-Literatur* (Texte und Studien zum Antiken Judentum 2; Tübingen: JBC Mohr, 1981); David Halperin, *The Faces of the Chariot* (Tübingen: JBC Mohr, 1988); David J. Halperin, *The Merkabhah in Rabbinic Literature* (Leiden: Brill, 1980); R. Elior, "The Concept of God in Hekhalot Literature," in *Studies in Jewish Thought*, ed. J. Dan (New York: Praeger, 1989), 97–120. In terms of form, in addition to the above studies, readers should consult the pioneering work of Johann Maier, including his major book on this topic, *Vom Kultus zur Gnosis: Studien zur Vor- und Frühgeschichte der "jüdischen Gnosis"* (Salzburg: Otto Müller Verlag, 1964), as well as his essays, including, "Das *Gefährdungsmotiv* bei der Himmelsreise in der jüdischen Apokalyptik und 'Gnosis'," *Kairos* 5 (1963): 18–40; "Hekhalot Rabbati xxvi, 5," *Judaica* 21 (1965): 129–33; and "Hekhalot Rabbati xxvii, 2–5," *Judaica* 22 (1966): 209–17. Readers should also consult the early but important essay by A. Altmann, "Songs of the Qedushah in Early Heikhalot Literature," *Melilah* 2 (1945–1946): 1–24 [Hebrew]. Rachel Elior has developed Maier's connections between mysticism and the priestly rituals of the Temple in Jerusalem (and the trauma of the destruction of the Temple); of particular interest to the present discussion are R. Elior, "Mysticism, Magic, and Angelology: The Perception of Angels in Heikhalot Literature," *Jewish Studies Quarterly* 1 (1993–94): 3–53, also Elior, "From Earthly Temple to Heavenly Shrines." Elior articulates her ideas most fully in her recent monograph, *The Three Temples: Merkavah Tradition and the Beginnings of Early Jewish Mysticism* (trans. David Louvish; Oxford: Littman Library, 2003).

22 Swartz, *Mystical Prayer in Ancient Judaism*, 201–5. The opening phrases of the *Geʾulah* prayer following the Shemaʿ, and even the familiar language of the Kaddish, resembles such series as well. M. Smith argues that strings of epithets reflect a Hellenistic prayer mode; see M. Swartz, "On the *Yotzer* and Related Texts," in *The Synagogue in Late Antiquity* (ed. L.

Example Two:
Be blessed / by all the heavenly host;
Be beautified / by the Ofanim of beauty
Be sanctified / by the Cherubim of holiness
Be beautified / from the chambers of chambers
Be adorned / by the Troops of fire
Be glorified / by the Holy Creatures
Be praised / by Your throne of Glory[23]

These ecstatic runs strongly recall the formal structure of many of Yannai's *r'hitim*, while the doxologies echo the associative, semi-prose style of the *silluq* (not to mention the Kaddish). The angelic liturgies in the Hekhalot texts, meanwhile, draw on the language of the Qedushah itself.[24] Furthermore, prayer and poetry play important roles in the Hekhalot texts. As Rachel Elior summarizes:

> The worship of the angels in the heavenly palaces is the prototype of worship that the *yordey merkavah* [those who "descend" to the divine chariot] are imitating. The ceremony that the angels perform before the throne of glory, including immersion, the offerings of praises, the singing of hymns, recitations of prayers, binding of crowns, and mention of the Name, is conceived as the basic ritual structure that the *yordey merkavah* want to learn and imitate.[25]

To be sure, not all of these elements are present in Yannai's piyyutim. We do not know the specific ritual setting in which his poems were performed, but we have no indication that they were anything other than embellishments of the Sabbath and festival Amidah. It seems unlikely that

---

Levine; Philadelphia: JTSA and ASOR, 1987), 87–95.

23 These texts are from Swartz, *Mystical Prayer in Ancient Judaism*, 201–2; many similar examples can be found there, as well.

24 See Swartz, *Mystical Prayer in Ancient Judaism*, especially his translation of *Ma`aseh Merkavah* (pp. 224–51).

25 Elior, "Mysticism, Magic, and Angelology," 5. Related to this idea, Gruenwald, in *Apocalyptic and Merkavah Mysticism*, likewise notes: "On the whole, mystical ideas of prayer occupy in *Hekhalot Rabbati* a much more prominent place than has hitherto been noticed. A significant proportion of the description [of mystical experience] found in the book is in one way or another connected with the appearance of God on His throne. And as we have seen, God descends to the throne from His abode in the eighth heaven at the daily prayer-times of the people of Israel. If this idea is carried to its logical conclusion, it appears that a mystical descent to the Merkavah was carried out only during these official hours of prayer..." (155).

these works were associated with ritual immersion or theurgic recitation of the divine Name. But the rhetoric and form of the works suggest an affinity between Hekhalot works and Yannai's *qedushtaʾot* that should not be quickly dismissed.

Indeed, cautions noted, several of the distinctly mystical goals and practices of Hekhalot writings overlap with concerns of Yannai—particularly the singing of hymns and the recitation of prayers, and the language of those hymns and prayers. These similarities could imply that Yannai drew upon Hekhalot traditions in creating his poems—although in the process of "translating" them into the synagogue, he apparently tamed them, excluding *nomina barbara* and neutralizing the most overt incantational aspects of the mystical texts and transforming the goal from one of spiritual *ascent* to spiritual *participation*, so to speak. At the same time, depending on how one dates the Hekhalot texts (possibly not edited until Amoraic times, roughly third to sixth century C.E., or even later), it is quite possible that common liturgical practices—including the Qedushah prayer and norms of liturgical poetics—shaped Hekhalot traditions. The direction of influence could be the reverse of what is often suggested or assumed, meaning that the literature of the synagogue may have been taken and amplified by the mystics in their efforts to articulate their more daring and innovative beliefs. Likewise, the rituals of the synagogue and its hymns and prayers provided Yannai with a basis for imagining heavenly praise and worship. The visions of Isaiah and Ezekiel, filtered through the liturgy, were returned to the angelic realm of their origin. Alternatively, perhaps the two genres, Hekhalot poetry and piyyut, simply manifest the common Second Temple and post-Temple Jewish fascination with angels and their prayers in independently developed ways. It may well be that both kinds of poetry—the mostly esoteric Hekhalot hymns and the explicitly exoteric *qedushtaʾot*—drew on a common ecstatic-hymnic style already known from Tannaitic (pre-third-century C.E.) texts such as those found in *m.Pesaḥim* 10:5,with its cascading synonyms of praise prefacing the Hallel.

With so many dates and points of contact uncertain, attempting to determine rigid lines of direct influence can be not only frustrating but misleading. Rather than seeing the piyyutim as watered-down ecstatic mystical works, we should consider the possibility that the Hekhalot texts are piyyutim taken to a logical extreme. The liturgical ecstasy of the *rahit*, *silluq*, and *qedushah* may have inspired the even more mystically amplified rhetoric of the Hekhalot poems. Indeed, we may wonder how much human prayer attempts to replicate the praise of the angels, and how much the angelic liturgies transmitted by the mystics draw, in reality, on human prayer.

The similarities between Yannai's synagogue poems and the Hekhalot mystical texts remain instructive, even if the details continue to puzzle. For scholars of Yannai, the resonances suggest the depth of power with which these exoteric texts could be construed, indicating the poet's potential influence and creativity as a practical theologian. For those who study the Hekhalot texts, works such as Yannai's piyyutim provide the larger cultural context in which these obscure and often enigmatic mystical traditions should be understood. For example, both piyyut and Hekhalot writings were once classified as "non-rabbinic" traditions, in part because of their interest in Temple imagery and practices. And yet, both can be seen as fully rabbinic in origin—albeit products of a more complicated rabbinic society than was once envisioned. The literary evidence is, in turn, enriching the picture of the ancient synagogue—itself rich with nostalgia for Temple imagery but not, by Yannai's day, anything other than "rabbinic."

Boundaries drawn strongly and with confidence in previous decades seem much more permeable now. Additionally, Yannai's works suggest that the mystical content of some of the Hekhalot texts may not even be as esoteric as generally thought. Even such bold ideas as "the sage as mystical sacrifice"[26] have parallels in Yannai's *qedushtaʾot* for Genesis. The poet writes: "Take us whole, like whole offerings… Accept us, holy ones, like sacrifices" (*silluq* to Gen 33:18, lines 2 and 4). Is the poet invoking a mystical understanding of prayer as a "real," if existential, substitute for animal offerings?[27] Does he see an analogy between the angels, who are literally consumed in the act of prayer, and his congregation, willing (if unable) to join the angels even in that action?[28] Or is he simply taking the literary ideas

26 See A. B. Lieber, "Angels that Kill: Mediation and the Threat of Bodily Destruction in the *Hekhalot* Narratives," *Studies in Spirituality*, vol. 14 (2004): 17–35; and M. Swartz, "Sacrificial Themes in Jewish Magic," in *Ancient Magic and Ritual Power* (ed. Marvin Meyer and Paul Mirecki; Leiden: Brill, 1995), 303–17. Also, see R. Boustan, *From Martyr to Mystic: Rabbinic Martyrology and the Making of Merkavah Mysticism* (Texts and Studies in Ancient Judaism 112; Mohr Siebeck: Tübingen, 2005) and Elior, "From Earthly Temple to Heavenly Shrines."

27 See M. Fishbane, "'As If He Sacrificed a Soul': Forms of Ritual Simulation and Substitution," in *The Kiss of God: Spiritual and Mystical Death in Judaism* (University of Washington Press: Seattle/London, 1994), 87–124.

28 On the motif of angels being consumed in the act of prayer, see the hymns preserved in *Hekhalot Rabbati*; a convenient anthology of these texts in translation can be found in T.

of "wholeness" and "whole-offerings" to a striking but logical conclusion? Even more broadly, could the Temple imagery of the early piyyutim, often cited as evidence of their "priestliness," reflect ideas about the ritual life not of the terrestrial Temple, now razed, but of the Heavenly Hekhalot (lit., "palaces"), whose ritual functions have never been interrupted? And do these verbal images in fact shed light on the peculiar imagery in the early synagogue mosaics?

The rites and ritual items of the Temple suddenly have the potential to be "read" not only in the past and future tense—a physical domain destroyed but destined to be restored—but in the present, referring to the Temple that exists Above. And the fabulous mosaic depictions of the heavenly hosts—with the sun (Helios) on the chariot amid the constellations of the zodiac—read in light of the Hekhalot texts, appear to be representations not just of the calendar, but of the divine retinue so common in Yannai's piyyutim.[29] As the congregation prayed in time with the angels above, those angels may well have been standing "among" them, in the form of the synagogue mosaics.[30] The prayer experience was thus both hor-

---

Carmi, *The Penguin Book of Hebrew Verse* (New York: Penguin, 1981), 195–201.

29 Also see Chapter Three for a discussion of the zodiac mosaics in light of the piyyutim.

30 Lucille Roussin suggestively connects the zodiac mosaics to the actual "descent" practices of the *yoredei merkavah*, those who descend to the divine Chariot. While the idea that the rabbinic mystics crouched down to induce a head-rush has now been largely discredited (see D. Halperin, "Review: A New Edition of the Heikhalot Literature," *Journal of the American Oriental Society* 104 [1984]: 543–52, esp. pp. 549–51), it seems plausible that gazing downward in order to ascend (and hence the term, "descent" to the Chariot) may have been a part of Hekhalot mystical ritual. Inside the synagogue, "gazing down to see up" might have been a way in which the zodiac mosaics could have been employed in the prayer context (either by intention or as a form of secondary use). The use of Byzantine *ceiling* decorations on synagogue *floors* remains anomalous. Could they have functioned like figurative "shadowboxes" providing a safe way of "looking at the sun"—much like a pool of water could have been used in an outdoor setting? See Roussin's essay, "The Zodiac in Synagogue Decoration," in *Archaeology and the Galilee: Texts and Contexts in the Greco-Roman and Byzantine Periods* (ed. D. Edwards and C. McCollough; Atlanta: Scholars Press, 1997), 83–96.

Archaeologist Jodi Magness' analysis of the Helios mosaics in the synagogue supports Roussin's reading; see Magness, "Heaven on Earth." She writes: "I propose that Helios and the zodiac cycle should be understood within the context of several contemporary and related phenomena: the rise of Christianity; the emergence or strengthening of the Jewish priestly class in ate antique Palestine; and the magical-mystical beliefs and practices described in Hekhalot literature. Hekhalot literature is so called because it describes heavenly *hekhalot* (temples), where the heavens are a temple containing a varying number of shrines composed of firmaments, angels, chariots, legions, hosts, and other wondrous phenomena and beings. In my opinion, the figure of Helios was also intended to represent Metatron, the divine super-angel who has been compelled by an adept to appear and impart Torah

izontally integrated—linking people with each other and their physical surroundings—and vertically integrated—unifying the world below with the activities and images of the world above. The resonances between the piyyutim and the mystical texts suggest mystical readings of the synagogue structure, as well. The combination of piyyut and synagogue architecture reopens the question of how "esoteric" Hekhalot ideas really were.

The above discussion indicates possible directions for further study, both within Piyyut Studies and beyond. Given the wealth of sources, both literary and artistic, many reconstructions are possible, each supported by other texts and traditions and shaped by the inclinations of the modern reader as much as the ancient authors. The evocative, tantalizing imagery of Yannai's poems—the resonances that are not quotations, the echoes that are not allusions—intrigues modern readers as much by what it conceals as what it reveals. The angelic imagery and rapturous language of the piyyutim—particularly in proximity to the Qedushah prayer—convey to readers today the potency, majesty, and importance of the act and language of prayer experienced a millennium and a half ago. Hekhalot texts, if they drew on these poetic and liturgical traditions, intensified the already-potent prayer experience, taking it literally to a new level. And, in turn, the resonances may suggest a latent potency within the piyyutim themselves. The blurring of boundaries between esoteric and popular (as well as priestly and rabbinic, the Temple and the synagogue) reminds us that as much as division, boundaries, and distinctions may simplify life for those who come later, the reality of the ancient world resists such reductions. Yannai's angels and their heavenly realm may be, simultaneously, popular *and* mystical.[31] Ideas about heavenly liturgies may have influenced human rites of prayer—but equally plausibly, the direction of influence may have been the reverse: the terrestrial models of holy space and holy words may have shaped and colored how activities on high were envisioned. How else, we can imagine the listeners wondering, could one "pray"? At the very least, these images suggest how creative a theologian and liturgist Yannai

knowledge to the congregation" (6–7). Magness goes so far as to argue that Hekhalot rituals, including the use of secret divine names, were, in fact, part of synagogue ritual—an intriguing hypothesis that might well complicate our understanding of the role of the payyetan in this dynamic.

31 Magness notes that Byzantine art and literature in general reveled in ambiguity and multivalence; see "Heaven on Earth," 32–33. Fine, in *Art and Judaism in the Greco-Roman World*, emphasizes the mutlivocality of visual images in general and within the early synagogue in particular.

was; he did not merely receive and transmit ideas and images, but actively engaged with them, shaping them to suit his formal and interpretive needs, and quite possibly using the potent imagery associated with mysticism to draw in and engage his community. At this moment, many details, both those concerning this complex cultural matrix and Yannai's works in particular, remain uncertain. Nevertheless, if Yannai's works have complicated our picture, they also lend our understanding of this nexus of theology, ritual, and art both nuance and depth.

The Concept of "Holiness"

As Yannai's piyyut for Gen 14:1 states, "For You, holiness is the essence" (Poem Eight, line 5). In Late Antiquity, sanctity became an especially important idea, both in Christianity and in Judaism. The concept of "sacred space" was being redefined—churches, especially those built on sites of perceived historic significance, claimed a special sanctity, and the synagogue, in turn, became increasingly identified as a "holy place" (rather than a meeting place) within Judaism.[32] Archaeological remains offer tantalizing but unclear evidence of the gradual consecration of the synagogue, particularly through the increased incorporation of Temple iconography into its physical space. Both the significance and function of the synagogue were transformed when it became "holy." The presence of liturgy—and liturgical poetry—in these increasingly hallowed halls provides a literary corollary to the artistic representations that transformed the synagogue into the sanctuary it has become today. Beyond the creation of sacred space, however, Yannai's piyyutim offer a glimpse into the *experience* of the sacred. Through his emphasis on holiness, and his diverse ways of exploring this theme, Yannai created a powerful theology that was, in some fashion, received and enacted by his community.

In Yannai's works, a form or experience of sanctity emanates from the Qedushah—the same basic text that is so important in Qumranic liturgies,[33] in the Hekhalot texts, and in the developing Christian liturgy

---

32 See Levine, *The Ancient Synagogue*, 630–32; Fine, *This Holy Place* and *Judaism and Art in the Greco-Roman World*, 91; more generally, see also Eric Meyers and James Strange, *Archaeology, the Rabbis and Early Christianity: the Social and Historical Setting of Palestinian Judaism and Christianity* (Abingdon: Nashville, 1981).

33 The biblical angelic liturgies were important for the Qumran community but, as noted

(in the form of the Trisagion or Sanctus) as well.[34] This prayer has the concept of God's holiness quite literally at its center. As the *qedushta* progresses from unit to unit towards the inevitable recitation of Isa 6:3, the word "holy" becomes increasingly prominent in the poems, anticipating their ultimate liturgical destination. The foreshadowing begins early: the *meshallesh* concludes with a quotation from Ps 22:4 ("You are holy, enthroned on the praises of Israel"); Poem Four ends with the word "holy"; and sometimes the word "holy" forms the fourfold end-rhyme of stanzas in the sixth poetic unit.[35] It is perhaps significant that the word "holy" clusters at the end of these poems, which leave the strongest impression, aurally, before the transition to the *rahit*, a poem that, while not focused on the idea of holiness, formally resembles Hekhalot poetry most intensively. In the eighth and ninth poetic units, forms of the root ק-ד-ש ("holy") are commonplace, even definitive. What may be surprising, however, is the way the poet—writing as a theologian but one who shapes beliefs and practices in concrete rather than abstract terms—characterizes God's holiness, focusing as much on its immanent manifestations as on its transcendent qualities.

While mention of holiness occurs throughout many of the piyyutim, Yannai's audience anticipated the poet's extended meditations on holiness in a specific location: the *qedushah* (Poem Nine), which concludes the *qedushta* and which probably involved congregational participation in the

---

above, the actual Qedushah verses never appear in the Songs of the Sabbath Sacrifice—the so-called "angelic liturgies" of Qumran.

34 In Yannai's period, the Qedushah probably occurred twice in the Sabbath morning service: once as part of the *Yotzer* benediction before the Shema (on the theme of light), which may have been its original location; and again as the third blessing of the Amidah, which is where it occurs in Yannai's poetry. (Fleischer has documented early piyyutim embellishing the *Qedushah de-Yotzer*, but the *Yotzer* does not become a major genre of poetic composition until around the 8th–9th century C.E.) We do not know the origins of the third statutory Qedushah, the *Qedushah de-Sidra*, but it appears to have been added to the synagogue service sometime after Yannai's period; a "doxology after the Torah portion" (*aqdushah de-sidra*) is mentioned in *b. Sotah* 49a. In the Middle Ages, liturgical poets wrote extended poems for the *Qedushah de-Yotzer*, which were also full of angelic imagery. See E. Fleischer, *Ha-Yotzerot* (Jerusalem: Magnes, 1984) [Hebrew]. On the relationship between the Jewish Qedushah, the Greek Trisagion, and the Latin Sanctus, see: A. Gerhards, "Crossing Borders. The Kedusha and the Sanctus: a Case Study of the Convergence of Jewish and Christian Liturgy," in *Jewish and Christian Liturgy and Worship: New Insights into Its History and Interaction* (ed. A. Gerhards and C. Leonhard; Leiden: Brill, 2007), 21–41.

35 For examples, see the final stanza of Poem Six for Gen 12:1 and the next-to-last stanza of Poem Six for Gen 38:1 (the final stanza of this *Qedushta* has "the Lord" as the last word of each stich).

recitation of Isa 6:3 and Ezek 3:12. Elements of the final poem's form, as discussed in Chapter One, are fixed; especially important is the parsing out of the threefold "holy" from Isa 6:3, in which the poet associates each repetition of the theme word with a different nuance of holiness, somehow related to the themes of the Torah portion. For example, Yannai focuses on Noah's sons—Shem, Yafet, and Ham—in the *qedushah* for Gen 9:18, where they are a poetic focus throughout. By parsing out the repetitions of "holy" and linking them to the different sons, Yannai is able to highlight the ways that each character and his descendents embody a distinct facet of the concept: Shem possesses the most exalted holiness (especially knowledge of God's holy Name and the gift of the Torah); Yafet is gifted with a kind of literary holiness (the Greek language and the skill of translation); and Ham bequeaths a humble yet transformative holiness to his descendents, who are destined to become righteous converts. "Holiness" here is a quality shaped by the nature of those who possess it, as if it were a substance filtered and refracted by their inborn talents and proclivities. It reflects a hierarchy of divine knowledge and intimacy, anticipating the special holiness that will accrue to the heirs of Shem—i.e., the Jews. Each community acquires the specific version of holiness suited to it, however, and all have potential access to holiness. Sanctity is not just monolithic; it has nuance.

Similar organic, tripartite structures are easily found in other *qedushta'ot*, such as in the final poem for Gen 19:1. In that text, "holiness" describes three specific actions relating to the narrative events rather than three distinctive notions, and it is applied to angels rather than humans. In this *qedushta*, as noted above, the three angels (Michael, Gabriel, and Raphael) become the bearers of three kinds of holiness. The Holy One chose one angel for each of His three holy missions: one to announce Isaac's birth, a second to overturn Sodom, and a third to save Lot. Each task is considered a manifestation of divine and angelic holiness.

The story of Sodom and Gomorrah might seem devoid of sanctity to a modern reader, but Yannai not only finds holiness in the tale, he embellishes it, adding layers to the story he envisions. In addition to describing the three specific angels—characters in his story—Yannai broadens his focus to include the three major classes of angels (*Ḥayyot*, *Ofanim*, and *Cherubim*), as well as the specific angelic Hosts that follow each of the three named angels. Inspired by his liturgical context, Yannai takes a familiar midrashic trope—one angel, one task—and imbues it with a deeper significance, adding nuance to the angelic mission but also to the experience of hearing this tale recounted as part of prayer. Holiness is, again, specific but also widespread—and, through its presence in the participatory *qedushah* poem, it is embodied.

Other examples abound, indicating the poet's ability to construe holiness on a range of scales. One example indicates the loftiness of the concept as Yannai constructs it. The *qedushah* (Poem Nine) for Gen 1:1, building upon the cosmic scale of the Torah portion, describes the special sanctity of the heavens, land, and sea. In this case, rather than dividing specific traits among human communities, every aspect of nature is imbued with a distinct variety of sanctity, asserting, thereby, that all of creation partakes of "holiness." Every created entity (including the abstract Sabbath Day) responds to God with the repetition of the angelic "holy, holy, holy," and by doing so, all of creation reflects the divine image.

Other passages indicate, however, that Yannai could use this exact same structure and concept to more whimsical ends. The *qedushah* for Gen 24:1 (the only surviving fragment of the *qedushta*) offers such a case. The threefold repetition in that passage employs synonyms for graying hair and old age, as God's holiness is praised by the way it reflects in the dignity of elders: "the splendid glory that is the crown of old age," "the splendid grandeur that is the diadem of grey hair," and "the splendid treasure that is the glorious crest of hoary years." Going grey, according to this *qedushta*, is a manifestation not simply of the wisdom acquired with age, but of holiness.

In some cases, "holiness" manifests not just physically—in the heavenly spheres, throughout creation, or on the human body—but by means of ethical conduct. We see this, for example, in the *qedushah* (Poem Nine) for Gen 31:3, in which Jacob's purity and holiness result from his proper conduct and result in his restoration. Jacob walked a straight path, and therefore God made his pathways straight. Jacob's holiness manifests and enacts God's holiness. This reciprocity echoes a classical biblical injunction ("You shall be holy, for I, the Lord your God, am holy," Lev 19:2; see also Yannai's *qedushta* for this passage), but here it is modeled and enacted, not simply asserted—and there is no intertext, only a direct analogy. Likewise, in the *qedushah* for Gen 43:14, God's holiness is embodied in Joseph's compassion for his brothers. When Joseph has compassion upon those who had none, deals graciously with those who dealt gracelessly, and shows mercy to those who showed him none, he acts under the influence of God's holiness. God's holiness is not abstract but rather tangibly manifest in concrete behaviors—actions familiar from the biblical story, to be sure, but in a distinctive and elevated framework here. In keeping with biblical ideas, the ethical is sacred.

When Yannai describes God's holiness, he does not generally emphasize innate divine awesomeness but instead focuses on God's attentiveness to a character or the people or on some other action manifestly for the benefit of a lesser party (linking "holiness," in a way, with *ḥesed*, loyalty that defies a power differential). As wondrous as the angelic songs are, and as rapturous as the experience of joining the angels in prayer may be, the actual exertions of the Holy One emphasized in the Qedushah are generally actions on behalf of "the holy nation." Thus, for example, his *qedushah* for Gen 28:10, like that of Gen 19:1, focuses on the angels as manifestations of divine holiness and therefore divine attentiveness to human need. Three classes of angels accompany Jacob as he sets forth from Beer Sheba: angels of mercy, angels of peace, and angels of hosts. In this case, however, the angels have no intrinsic holiness but function as the retinue of the Holy One Himself. In this piyyut, it is God's holiness, which manifests as divine concern for Jacob. The retinue are symbolic and appropriate, but not definitive of sanctity or its direct bearers. It is God, in His capacity of "the Holy One," who accompanies Jacob, who guards him, and who appears to him in a dream. A second stanza of the *qedushah* for Gen 28:10 is also extant. In this passage, Yannai embellishes the phrase "from His place" (Ezek 3:12, repeated three times on the model of Isa 6:3) with thematically-appropriate biblical quotations, all of which emphasize divine providence. Again, the emphasis is as much on "doing holy" as on "being holy."

The association of providence with holiness is common. In the *qedushah* (Poem Nine) for Gen 32:4 Yannai emphasizes how the Holy One will, in the end, favor Jacob, who has true knowledge of God's holiness, over Esau, the profane pretender to holiness (as described in the *silluq*, Poem Eight).[36] This *qedushah* also has extant a secondary stanza juxtaposing "from His place" with biblical quotations that emphasize divine protection of Jacob and his descendents. Even the *qedushah* for Gen 30:22, a unit that overtly speaks of miracles on a grand scale—rainmaking, childbirth, and resurrection—reflects holiness in the terrestrial sphere. These three divine manifestations are not abstractions but refer to physical and existential

36 This poetic unit embeds an anti-Christian polemic, as well: Israel (the heir of Jacob) is holy; Christianity (the heir of Esau) emphatically is *not*.

"prisons" from which God can free Israel. Rain not only enables life but symbolizes redemption. Childbirth implies not only the creation of new life but the restoration of Zion. And resurrection hints not only at the undoing of death but redemption of a people that feels, metaphorically, dead. God's holiness here—the power for which He is so enthusiastically praised—does not simply dazzle the eyes of those who look upwards. It will, instead, take form as a tangible reality among the people. Holiness is an attribute of action.

On a human plane, Yannai's "holiness" is also not an abstract concept. It is real and pervasive, and it manifests in a variety of concrete ways, especially for God's holy people, the Jews. Holiness is expressed when people act ethically, when they acknowledge the holiness around them, and when they keep company—on the road or in prayer—with the holy angelic hosts. An attribute both awesome and intimate, holiness is a quality that connects the immanent and transcendent aspects of the divine. When divine holiness becomes manifest, it is often not for the purpose of simply impressing His worshippers above and below; instead, it is realized in ways that positively impact a community: all of creation, humanity in general, or Israel in particular. As a result of this diversity of expression, God's holiness itself becomes diverse and multifaceted.

People may, of course, respond to these manifestations of the sacred with ecstatic outbursts of praise, as the extant *silluq* (Poem Eight) for Gen 41:38 so clearly does:

> ...The Holy One in the splendor of holiness, in the holy language: holy, holy, holy! In the holy place to hallow You... the holy ones of the holy place, in a holy spirit, O my King, in holiness like the holy angels, as it is written: "And the one called..." ...[37]

God's holiness may manifest itself in humble, or hidden, ways, but the proper human response is clear: to rise up (or perhaps be lifted up, in a state approaching ecstasy) and to acknowledge the wonder and amazement of God's gifts, despite the inadequacy of any mortal response, and to do so with tremendous intensity. The rapturous repetitions of "holy, holy, holy!" throughout these *qedushta'ot* (strongly reminiscent of the ecstatic language of the Hekhalot mystics) reveal, through sheer

37 The ecstatic language of this *silluq* recalls the intense language of Hekhalot literature, discussed above.

exertion and the potency of repetition, a sense of joyful striving to enact the impossible and articulate the ineffable. Yannai takes traditional, even commonplace phrases and ideas—themes and motifs attested in midrashic parallels, for example, or rooted in familiar biblical language—and transforms them through his performative poetry. Indeed, it is important to recall that the congregation probably participated in reciting elements of these piyyutim, and the word "holy" would have been an easy one to anticipate.

Throughout his poetry, the poet quietly affirms that the distance between God and Israel is temporary, even illusory. The gap is closed every time the congregation below joins the angels above in praising Him. Yannai does not rely on explicit articulation of this created intimacy as he might in a more overtly and conveniently homiletical medium such as midrash or targum. He does not *say* in so many words that his is a message of consolation, hope, or affirmation. Instead, his truths emerge out of the juxtaposition of his poetry with the liturgical context and their setting in sacred space. The "holiness" of which he speaks only becomes real when it is enacted, but at the same time, performance ensures response.

The God of Yannai

Yannai, as a theologically invested biblical exegete, poet, and liturgist, displays a fascination with God—from exploring His more abstract qualities such as "holiness" to understanding the nature of His interactions with individuals and peoples, in the biblical past and in the present day. The prominence of God in liturgical-exegetical works such as these *qedushta'ot* is hardly surprising, but Yannai's specific treatment of this central figure should not be taken for granted. Working within a vast and fluid tradition, living at a pivotal moment in Jewish history, this poet creatively constructed his theologies to suit the themes of the Torah portion or his own particular ideas. The notes accompanying the translations in this volume often explore Yannai's implicit theology—his revealing portraits of God and His complex relationship with humanity, particularly Israel.

Because these poems were composed for public performance, Yannai wrote as a "constructive" theologian. His words, performed in the course of the synagogue service, were not so much studied as absorbed, and his ideas were reinforced or even transformed by the element of participation implicit in their liturgical setting. The theological themes and motifs in his works—weaving together biblical text, scriptural interpretation, and liturgy—should be approached neither as "mere" art nor as abstract philosophical musings. Instead, they are living engagements with a dynamic cultural nexus of exegesis (Jewish and Christian) and theology emerging from a variety of sources. Some elements of Yannai's theology are rooted in the Bible while others recall rabbinic modes of thought, but all must be approached with an awareness that he wrote not for the schoolhouse or private study and devotion, but for the synagogue. Synagogue poetry does not only reflect theology; it shapes it.[38]

Yannai's portrayals of God—the most complicated character in Jewish literature—are too diverse to be wholly or succinctly summarized here. But his philosophical diversity is itself significant. Unlike *midrashim*, which reflect a variety of theologies (due to a diversity of authorship and social and exegetical contexts and the discursive nature of much of the source material), or the *targumim*, which tend to simplify and streamline complicated passages, these *qedushtaʾot* are the work of a single individual. They do not seem concerned, however, with homogenizing God. For Yannai and thus his congregation, God was dynamic, even mercurial, yet steady and faithful; at times transparent and at other times mysterious. A complex deity emerges out of Yannai's intellectual and emotional engagement with his biblical sources, his involvement with rabbinic styles of exegesis, and the context of his works' performance. The examples below are neither exhaustive nor conclusive, but they do illustrate the diversity of theologies present in this collection of poems.

Payyetanic rhetoric, with its terse use of antithesis and parallelism for aural and aesthetic effect, lends itself particularly well to a theology called (appropriately) "poetic justice"—i.e., a system that understands God as doling out reward and punishment "measure for measure" (in Hebrew, *middah ke-neged middah*).[39] This particular theology finds its earliest and

38 Perhaps the most powerful examples of the formative power of synagogue poetry come not from Yannai's work but from those works that endured into modern prayer books. For instance, the early piyyut *Unetaneh Tokef*, with its famous litany of "who shall live and who shall die," has strongly influenced how many people even today understand what is at stake during the High Holy Days. The poetic imagery—and its poetic rhetoric—have shaped the very understanding of Rosh Hashanah and Yom Kippur. J. Spiegel has argued that *Unetaneh Tokef* not only dates to Yannai's period but should be considered the work of his hand; see his essay, "Clarification of the Words of the Piyyut," *Netuʿim* 8 (2001): 23–42 [Hebrew].

39 The rhetorical structures that undergird this theological mode were discussed in Chapter Three.

perhaps most eloquent expression in Deuteronomy and Deuteronomistic biblical sources, with their assertions that good will be rewarded and sin punished, and it is considered mainstream by the Rabbis. Poetry permits Yannai to present this theology with particular force.[40] This relatively simple but appealing construct is most evident, for example, in the theme of the *qedushta* for Gen 11:1, in which verbal transgression is punished by verbal confusion (see Poem Five, lines 11–12), or in that for Gen 38:1, in which Judah's transgression by means of "these" is repaid by his indictment by means of "these" (see Poem Five, lines 15–16). It depicts a fair, even arch, God dispensing people's just deserts.[41] People get what they deserve in an aesthetically pleasing fashion. This theology focuses on justice meted out by God (directly or indirectly) to whomever has earned it, whether the transgressor is an enemy, such as Esau, or the patriarch Jacob himself.

Yannai taps the latent force of the terse rhetoric of poetry in order to emphasize the quality of divine justice. The balance of poetic lines—the pleasing patterns repetition and parallelism—function to underscore and embody a theology in which God ultimately ensures a cosmic balance of justice, almost as if on the balances of scales. Yet, while "measure for measure" is probably the dominant theology in Yannai's poetry, it is not Yannai's only understanding of how God works in the world. His other theologies are not always easily categorized, nor are they systematic and fully developed. In many cases, our understanding of the poet's ideas about God emerges from a gestalt impression of a poem rather than through explicit "God talk." For example, the second *rahit* (Poem Seven) for Gen 30:22 consists of a simple acrostic litany of God's powers and His positive relationships with His followers; the alphabet, not theology, structures the list, which ranges from the esoteric ("revealing the concealed") to the intimate ("remembering the barren"), and which often adapts familiar biblical idioms and ideas to the specific language required by the *rahit*'s construction. The impression that emerges from this *rahit's* eclectic list is one of an attentive, involved, concerned, loving, and forgiving God, with an emphasis on God's vast knowledge and providential concern—clear but hardly simple. It is a theology of "attributes of action" rather than rigor-

40 For this theology in the Bible phrased with particular baldness, see, for example, Deut 28; for a synopsis of this construct in rabbinic works, see E. E. Urbach, *The Sages: Their Concepts and Beliefs* (trans. Israel Abrahams; Cambridge: Harvard University Press, 1979), 436–44.

41 See Chapter Three, "In the very language..." (p. 177)

ous, philosophical contemplation. Yannai's ideas about God are not systematic; instead, they are driven by the content of the weekly Torah portion and its traditions of interpretation, by diverse biblical assertions about God, and by the force of the performative, liturgical framework. The resulting poetry is theologically rich, philosophically diverse, and thoroughly non-systematic.

As a poet writing for a public venue, Yannai addresses his people's vulnerable circumstances: they have been displaced by Esau-Rome, denied a Temple, and dispersed into exile. They are, if not physically persecuted, existentially oppressed—acutely aware that the world is not as it should and will be. The Byzantine Empire, emerging from a period of turmoil and embattlement, experienced tremendous military, cultural, and religious expansion under the leadership of Justinian, and the Jewish communities in the Land of Israel, which earlier had flaunted imperial restrictions, may have felt increasing pressure to submit to imperial authority.[42] All evidence indicates that the sixth century was a period of intense messianism and turbulence.[43] Yannai's poetry often meets these homiletical demands and responds to the people's situation by emphasizing the theme of God's fidelity to keeping His promises—whether it is a comparatively small one made to a biblical character, such as His promise to give Abraham an heir, or a large one on the scale of national restoration. This theology discourages active attempts to force a redemption through armed rebellion—an option also attested in the historical sources, particularly through Jewish participation in the Samaritan revolts of the mid-sixth century.[44] Yannai's oblique acknowledgments of external realities indicate that the poet, aware

---

42 Averil Cameron, in her *Christianity and the Rhetoric of Empire*, offers a particularly vivid account of the Byzantine renaissance under Justinian, which is attested in both literary sources (Romanos' body of poetry and Procopius' histories, among others) and physical monuments.

43 See my forthcoming article, "You Have Skirted This Hill Long Enough."

44 On the Samaritan rebellions, see the entry, "Rebellions of the Samaritans in Palestine in the Romano-Byzantine Period," in *A Companion to Samaritan Studies*, eds. Alan D. Crown, Reinhard Pummer and Abraham Tal (Tübingen :Mohr-Siebeck), 1993), 199–203 for a concise summary of the events. For a political analysis of the events, see P. Mayerson, "Justinian's Novel 103 and the Reorganization of Palestine," *BASOR* 269 (1988): 65–71. For more detail, see: A. Scharf, *Jews and Other Minorities in Byzantium* (Ramat-Gan: Bar Ilan UP, 1995) [Hebrew] and, with a particular emphasis on the tension between Roman-Byzantine legal codes and social reality over time, A.M. Rabello, *The Jews in the Roman Empire: Legal Problems, from Herod to Justinian* (Aldershot; Burlington, VT. : Ashgate/Variorum, 2000).

of his surroundings, sought to direct his attention—and that of his listeners—inward.

As with the concept of "measure for measure," Yannai found the motifs of divine responsiveness, presence, and fidelity readily at hand in both biblical and rabbinic sources; through his choice of texts, intertexts, and poetic emphases, he selected this theological emphasis and brought it specifically to the fore with great clarity and consistency. The evidence of Yannai's piyyutim suggests that the assertion of God's fidelity to Israel was particularly compelling for Yannai and his community. Yannai stressed this message despite the fact that it may have seemed counterintuitive: his community (whether understood locally or on the ethnic-national scale) lived as a disempowered (if not physically persecuted) minority amid an increasingly empowered majority that regarded the Jews as rejected and dispossessed, superseded in this world and the next. Yannai responded to these messages and countered them, both directly and indirectly. In doing so, he articulated his own hopes: there is a strong messianic fervor in his works.[45] For example, in his *qedushta* for Gen 15:1, Yannai uses the first *rahit* to present a literal alphabet of such reassurance, a listing from *alef* to *tav* of assurances of God's fidelity in God's own voice. This unit opens:

> *Do not* fear! *I am* your Hope; *Do not* cower! *I am* your Guardian
> *Do not* tremble! *I am* your Shepherd; *Do not* cringe! *I am* your Creator
> *Do not* stumble! *I am* your Rock; *Do not* dread! *I am* your Ransomer
> (Poem Seven[1], lines 1–6)

While, in theory, the *rahit* presents God's affirmation of His word to the aged patriarch, the poet simultaneously offers these words as reassurance for his own congregation; grammatically and theologically, they are timeless. These phrases are not novel coinages—each has clear antecedents

---

45 On Jewish messianism in the 6th and early 7th centuries, see W. van Bekkum, "Jewish Messianic Expectations in the Age of Hereclius," in *The Reign of Heraclius (610–641): Crisis and Confrontation*, eds. G. J. Reinink, Bernard H. Stolte (Leuven: Peeters, 2002), 95–112;: P. J. Alexander, *The Byzantine Apocalyptic Tradition*, ed. Dorothy Abrahamse (Berkeley: University of CA Press, 1985); O. Irshai, "Dating the Eschaton: Jewish and Christian Apocalyptic Calculations in Late Antiquity," in *Apocalyptic Time*, ed. A. I. Baumgarten (Leiden: Brill, 2000), 113–53; D. M. Olster, "Byzantine Apocalypses," in *The Encyclopedia of Apocalypticism*, 3 vols. Ed. J. J. Collins, B. McGinn, and S. J. Stein (New York and London: Continuum, 1998), 2:48–73; and R. L. Wilken, "The Restoration of Israel in Biblical Prophecy: Christian and Jewish Responses in the Early Byzantine Period," in *"To See Ourselves as Others See Us": Christians, Jews, "Others" in Late Antiquity*, ed. J. Neusner and E. S. Fredrichs (Chico, CA.: Scholars Press, 1985), 443–71.

in the Bible—but their intense clustering here speaks both to the theme of the Torah portion and the more general appeal of the theology on a popular level. God is vividly, palpably immanent here. Furthermore, by culling and condensing these words into a single, intensely-patterned piece, the rhetorical force of the composition far exceeds the effect it would have as scattered phrases. The reiteration twenty-two times of the single idea—God's active, personal, reliable, and redemptive role in Israel's life, combined with the intensity of the direct and personal address— creates a vivid immediacy to the lines, as if the message from God is being heard *now*, in the present tense. God, through the poet, speaks directly to the congregation of individuals as much as to Abraham, and any temporal gulf between the two collapses. Explication, articulation, and etymology would clutter the experience of this work, not clarify it. This is poetic, performed theology.

This is not to imply that Yannai's deity is a simple personality playing a stereotypical role. God in Yannai's works has a range of moods and personalities, and the poet relates to Him and depicts His relationship with Israel in a variety of ways. At times, Yannai describes Him in quite tender terms. Often the *magen* poems conclude with images describing God as sheltering a vulnerable Israel in the palm of His hand or within His shadow (e.g., *qedushta'ot* to Gen 16:1, 31:3, 33:18, 44:18, 48:1).[46] God frequently behaves as a concerned and loving parent: protective of His creation and attentive to their needs and worries. At the same time, in keeping with the biblical and rabbinic traditions of bold, direct address of God, Yannai at times speaks to God in a forthright way, chastising Him for succumbing to inertia. But if God has become a little neglectful, prayer offers the chance to unsettle Him, to remind Him of His duty. So, for instance, we find in the *silluq* for Gen 33:18: "Bring us into a covenant, *in keeping with Your promise*/ Affirm us as of old, *in keeping with Your word*" (Poem Eight, lines 21–22; emphasis added). Behind such lines lies an assumption that God will be faithful, but the wording implies that He might lack urgency—that He needs a nudge. As a liturgist—one who addresses both God and

46 Unlike the *targumim*, Yannai displays no hesitancy in assigning God a physical body—or, at least, body parts—although much like with such passages in the biblical text, we should probably understand these references metaphorically. (On the Targumic phenomenon, see M. Klein, *The Translation of Anthropomorphisms and Anthropopathisms in the Targumim of the Pentateuch: With Parallel Citation from the Septuagint* [Jerusalem: Makor, 1982].)

congregation—Yannai steps into the potential breach between the two parties and reminds each to be faithful to the other.

God is not always gentle, however, nor passively remote from the world. Yannai's confidence in God's (perhaps imminent) salvation of Israel leads the poet to imagine God as violent and vengeful, particularly in those poems where the biblical focus is on Esau, ancestor of Rome. The *qedushta* for Gen 32:4 stands out for its recurring, gleeful depictions of divine violence. The conclusion of this poem's *magen* (Poem One), for example, is not tender, but brutal: "Your sword, O Ruddy One / will become drunk from the red one's blood" (*ḥatimah* to *magen*). Later, in a creative, disturbing, and vivid conflation of Song 5:10 and Isa 63:2, the poet exults in anticipation of retribution:

> A great slaughter in the land of *Edom* / A burning fire in the fields of *Edom*
> We yearn for You, O beloved, radiant and red (*edom*) / To appear in garments red with the blood of Edom" (Poem Seven[1], lines 9–12).

Implicit in the punning here we can see the conventional "measure for measure" theology, discussed above, jolted out of easy familiarity by the eroticization of brutality. This is a God of the sword, not the word. Indeed, much of the rest of this particular *qedushta* critiques Jacob for making conciliatory gestures towards Esau and juxtaposes the patriarch's fretful weakness with God's military might. Yannai was living in a period of great tension, with the Jews perhaps tempted both by rebellious and assimilationist impulses. It was a time when the empire was ever more confident in asserting its power over the Jews despite external pressures from the Persians. It is no wonder that the poet vividly imagined the restoration of his people and a day of judgment against Rome.

While Yannai confidently asserts God's eventual justice on Israel's behalf, and at times seems to project a sense of the imminence of the End, he concedes that the details of God's ways remain unknowable. In these moments, we sense him tempering his hopes and those of his listeners, and perhaps we hear echoes of disappointment in what has not yet come to pass. He acknowledges that the militant God, though faithful, is also enigmatic. Even the *qedushah* for Gen 32:4, which so vividly depicts Edom's downfall, opens: "Your counsel cannot be known / Your power cannot be diminished / Your Name cannot be changed" (Poem Nine, lines 1–3). In previous units, the poet described the eventual acts of divine justice with "you are there" vividness and delight, but he concedes, as he concludes, that aspects of God and His providence remain remote. The poet cannot predict when Esau's downfall will come—only what it will look like when it happens and his hope that it may come soon. These same enigmas, with less graphic violence but equal mysteriousness, color the deathbed scene of Jacob in the *qedushta* for Gen 49:1. For example: "A day You are bringing—who can calculate when it will come? // But like an oven shall it burn when you bring it" (Poem 3, lines 1 and 2); and, "In Your mind it was formed: / a day of vengeance! // But no creature standing upright / can fathom it" (Poem Four, lines 3 and 4). When he comes closest to the actual subject of his people's redemption, the poet's imagination is fired, but his God becomes remote.

Yannai's God does not entirely relish conflict, however. For example, the apocalyptic, aggressive characterization of God seen in the *qedushta* for Gen 32:4 can be contrasted with the reluctantly violent God of the *rahit* for Gen 14:1, in which the poet states, "You said: I am Peace, but they are war!" (quoting Ps 120:7; Poem Seven, line 3).[47] In this composition, God is fully present and active, but the violence occurs only with great reluctance: a necessary response, rather than a gleeful vendetta. God is, indeed, "a man of war," but warfare is a means, not an end. Similarly, in the following *qedushta* (Gen 15:1), God does not rejoice in Abraham's victory over the Canaanite kings, although He asserts the necessity of the battle. As God reassures the patriarch, "You wiped out wicked ones; your reward shall be very great" (Poem Five, line 23); this is not apocalyptic delight but a kind of "just war" theology.

Neither God nor patriarch rejoices in bloodshed, although violence holds an important place in the world. Indeed, the biblical Prophets, whose words saturate Yannai's writings, bequeathed to the poet this ambivalent perspective, with its yearnings for peace, practical advice towards quietism, and dire warnings of vivid apocalypse; rabbinic writings reflect these same mixed feelings; and in the end, even the individual poet Yannai cannot select one perspective. God's moods reflect his own. The most accurate generalization we can make, then, would be that Yannai understands divine violence to be contextually determined: in general, force may be necessary, but it is not enjoyed; against Esau-Edom-Rome, however,

47 As noted below (n. 72), the *rahit* of Yannai's *qedushta* for Deut 20:10 has, as its refrain, the word "peace" (*shalom*).

violence will not only prove essential, but intoxicating. God dislikes violence—with this one major exception.

Yannai's God of revenge and retribution dwells in the future, albeit one senses Yannai hopes it might be the very near future. When the poet writes of God in the present tense, he focuses on God's love, and His caring presence, even when He may seem to be remote. In piyyutim that strike this tone, the scale of the poetry feels more intimate, less grand, more comforting and consoling than energizing. The poet has at his fingertips an array of potential metaphors to describe this God-Israel relationship: parent and child, king and subjects, vintner and vine. However, the motif of divine *eros*—or, speaking more generally, the use of romantic metaphors to describe the relationship between God and His people— emerges as one of the most powerful and potent tones in Yannai's *qedushtaʾot*. In Yannai's writings, this motif appears most dramatically and pervasively in his Passover poems, built as they are on the Song of Songs.[48] Romance and *eros* also appear in his Genesis poems, however, most strikingly in the *qedushta* for Gen 12:1 (discussed in the previous two chapters), where God's call to Abraham to "go forth" is recast as a seduction and elopement. More poignantly, similar language of love—but primarily from the human perspective, directed *at* God rather than coming *from* Him—appears in the *qedushta* for Gen 29:31, which describes the lovelorn Leah's longings. God here is not so much the Lover as the object of (or the one worthy of) tremendous, heart-wrenching yearning. Leah's situation, like Israel's, is *eros* tinged with *pathos*.

At the same time, the motif of human love for the divine can strike a note of hope. In the same *silluq* quoted above, where Yannai reminds God of His promises, he uses the language of erotic love as well: "Entwine us, like lovers, in keeping with Your vow" (*qedushta* for Gen 33:18, Poem Eight, line 19). The overall tone of the poem is confident, so this line appears bold, perhaps even forward, but *not* pathetic. Both parties to the covenant not only express their love but have their worthiness to be loved affirmed. Leah's tragedy—and redemption—foreshadows that of her descendents.

Perhaps the most striking examples of divine-human intimacy can be

48 This theological-exegetical trend in early piyyut is considered more fully in Lieber, *A Vocabulary of Desire.*

seen in the very explicit parallels Yannai draws between God and Israel. For Yannai, some of the most important attributes of the deity are those that are bequeathed to His chosen people—the poet's version of *imitatio dei*.[49] We saw this parity with the concept of holiness, where God's holiness makes His people holy, and we see it in the first line of the *qedushta* for Gen 12:1, when the poet describes Abraham as a co-creator with God, stating: "A partner in Creation You considered him." This potent interpretation of Abraham has parallels in aggadah, notably *GenR* 43:7, which depicts God as rewarding Abraham's work as a proselytizer with the following words:

> Then the Holy One, blessed be He, said to [Abraham]: "My Name was not known among My creatures, but you have made it known among them: I will regard you as though you were associated with Me in the creation of the world."

Clearly, Yannai's words reflect this aggadic tradition, but compared to the midrash, the poetic phrasing is terser, and as a result stronger and sharper—and its presence at the opening of the *qedushta* lends it additional force. Later in the poem, the descriptions of Abraham make him so radiant he seems almost angelic, if not outright divine. Abraham's qualities and actions—creator, warrior, redeemer—reveal him to be a kind of analog to God.

Similarly, the poet casts Noah also as an analogue to the deity in the *qedushta* for Gen 8:15, where God asserts:

> The beast that had been by your hand / By your hand it stayed alive
> For like He who feeds all you created / In the same manner, you fed and kept alive
> (Poem Six, lines 9–12)

Here, Noah resembles God in His capacity as sustainer of life. In these poems, people are not simply reflections or echoes of the divine; the relationship Yannai describes is often truly reciprocal. We see this with great clarity in the *qedushta* for Gen 35:9, which describes the change of Jacob's name to Israel. In the third unit, Yannai asserts:

---

49 Yannai's *qedushta* for Exod 19:6 (Rabinovitz 1:318–21), not included in this volume, offers perhaps the boldest articulation of this parity. See my article, "The Exegesis of Love: Text and Context in the Poetry of the Early Synagogue," *Review of Rabbinic Judaism* 11 (2008): 73–99. See also the *qedushta* to Lev 19:1 (Rabinovitz 1: 444–48)

"Jacob" he was called / and You are "the God of Jacob"
"Israel" he is called / and You are "the God of Israel"
(Poem Three, lines 5–6)

Reversing the biblical understanding of events, the patriarch's name determines God's appellation. Even more boldly, in the *silluq* (Poem Eight), the poet states: "For Your blessing is in the name of Israel // and Your holiness is in the name of Jacob" (lines 1–2). While it is Israel's task to praise God with the angels, this praise involves Israel's own name. The two—God and people—are profoundly entwined. The nature of God—and the nature of Israel—render the tender intimacy between the two natural, even inevitable. Their fates are one.

To be sure, Yannai is neither the first nor the only Jewish writer to identify Israel so closely with God. A profound and mythic strain of aggadah articulates this bold theology, which often shifts from divine *eros* to *pathos* and participation in human suffering.[50] Yannai's poems tell us, however, that such bold theologies were not limited to elites with the training to understand them "properly." As with Hekhalot mysticism, discussed above, they were, at least to some extent, sufficiently common and widespread that they could be presented in the open forum of the synagogue. The appeal of such a theology seems obvious: to be so intimately bound to the deity surely means that, in the end, all will come out well. Or to phrase it even more strongly, it is as if Yannai says: We may appear lowly, but in reality, we are (practically) divine.

As the above analysis suggests, and the notes and commentaries on the individual poems bear out, little in the theology of Yannai stands out as inherently radical. The gleeful violence, bold eroticism, and daring divine-human parity—not to mention more obviously conventional themes such as "measure for measure justice" and "divine fidelity"—are firmly rooted in both the Bible and rabbinic traditions of interpretation. What makes this diversity noteworthy is its presence in the work of a single synagogue poet and the influence of his works as presented in a performative context. We are not dealing here with the expectedly varied theologies of different

---

50 On the topic of divine *pathos* more generally, see Fishbane's *Biblical Myth and Rabbinic Mythmaking*, 132–59; idem, *The Exegetical Imagination: on Jewish Thought and Theology* (Cambridge: Harvard University Press, 1998), 22–40; and Boyarin, *Intertextuality and the Reading of Midrash.*

authors, possibly from different times and places, as can be found in midrash or even the *targumim* (edited and supplemented, as most were, by later hands). If we think of Yannai as a "theological snapshot" of his moment, we see that his God is as varied, colorful, and perhaps unpredictable as the God of Scripture—in part because Yannai is poeticizing the God of Scripture but also because he is selectively shaping and emphasizing God's characteristics to suit the needs of his individual poems and his synagogue community.

The poet did not feel a need to tidy his presentations, either in terms of tone or imagery; God may be gentle in one *qedushta* and vindictive in another, reassuringly constant in one week's composition, distressingly remote in another. Yannai's God displays a complex personality. At the same time, as a communal poet, Yannai crafts the divine persona along specific lines of meaningfulness, wedding the biblical God's assertions and actions to the demands of the liturgy and the needs of the public. What may seem at first a hodge-podge, eclectic theology emerges instead as a contextually-astute collage.

To an extent, Yannai discovered and amplified theological elements within each week's Torah portion and the commentary developing alongside the biblical source. But his works were, we presume, compelling for his own audience and not merely of antiquarian interest. He wrote for his present, not the past. Nor is the God of these poems so fragmented that He seems to be many gods; He is, rather, the single most complex character of this cycle, at times mysterious and unknowable, at other times close and almost whimsical. Yannai feels no need to constrict or reduce this most complicated of personalities. The God of Yannai is neither simplistic nor disjointed but nuanced and alive, always responsive to the demands of the biblical narrative and the contemporary situation. In Yannai's works, we find the richness of a whole tradition reflected, unapologetically—a display of the competence and vigor of the poet and his community.

The Covenant of the Land: Exile and Restoration

The covenant between God and Israel—eternal, unbroken, and mutually affirmed—unites the multifaceted Jewish deity with His complex and cantankerous people. The creation of covenants can be considered a central theme of the Hebrew Bible: God makes a covenant with Noah that applies to all creation and defines human nature; with Abraham that signifies the special chosenness of a single human line; and with Israel, at Sinai, that ratifies the unique status of a single and singular nation.

Within the general concept, territory takes on special significance as the symbol of covenant fulfilled and maintained. When God makes his covenant with Noah, He seals the pact with a promise concerning "the land"—not any specific land, but simply the promise never again to destroy the earth itself by flood. When God makes a covenant with Abraham, and later with the people of Israel, He bequeaths upon them a very specific Land, the Land of Canaan, which becomes the Land of Israel. After Genesis 12 (itself a leave-taking transformed into a home-coming), the biblical narrative plays out as a series of exiles and restorations—a narrative trope that emerges as the overarching, cyclical narrative of Jewish history itself. The major stories of the Hebrew Bible revolve around the Land as the symbolic and physical turf of the Israelite national drama: inheritance of the territory, descent to Egypt, the Exodus, conquest, repossession, dispossession, exile, and eventually restoration. The Land becomes a physical manifestation of the covenant, to the point where pre-Exilic and Exilic biblical texts work through questions of whether loss of the Land meant that the covenant had been broken. Even territorial dispossession and the subsequent innovation of a text-based (Torah-centric) understanding of Judaism in the course of the Babylonian Exile—the creation of a "portable" religion able to exist without a Temple or territory—did not undercut the psychological centrality of the Land and the association of territorial restoration as one of the essential elements of restoration. Those Jews who chose to remain in the Diaspora after the Persian restoration in the sixth century B.C.E., voluntarily living outside the bounds of the Land of Israel (whether in Babylonia, Egypt, or elsewhere), still recognized the symbolic importance of possession and sovereignty of the homeland. The Land of Israel is central to the promise to the people of Israel—emblematic of the covenant even for those not actually living there.

Many of these fundamental Jewish themes—and the essential biblical plot of "promise, exile, restoration"—had renewed (although not universal) appeal in Late Antiquity and the Byzantine period, both in the flourishing Diaspora and in the Land of Israel itself. The exilic theme had particular potency for Jews in Palestine after the loss of sovereignty and the end of the Second Commonwealth in 63 B.C.E., when Pompey entered Jerusalem; after 70 C.E., when the Temple was destroyed; and after 135 C.E., when the Bar Kokhbah revolt was brutally suppressed. With the Christianization of the Roman Empire in the fourth century, the emotional experience of exile became particularly acute, as Jewish physical disempowerment was amplified by Christian assertions of Jews' religious and philosophical disinheritance. Exile became existential as well as territorial—it became alienation. Under Roman and Byzantine rule, the Jews were in exile within their own Land; even when physically on the Land, it was not theirs. Furthermore, the theological discourse emerging out of Christianity was one of supplantation: the covenant with the Jews was becoming "the old covenant," replaced by a "new covenant," that is, Christianity.[51] Competing with the traditional Jewish understanding of the eternal covenant between God and the Jews, Christianity developed a rival story that insisted God had put aside the old, stiff-necked people for a newer, better, more beloved one. Additionally, with the Christianization of the Roman Empire, "the Promised Land" actually became the property of "the New Israel"—that is, Christianity. The Jews—"old Israel," as it were—were wholly dispossessed, denied not only authority over their Land but even the right to claim it theoretically. According to this developing Christian narrative, Jewish loss of the Land—not only the Temple, but the very idea of sovereignty—symbolized Jewish loss of the covenant. Christian theology dispossessed the Jews not only physically but spiritually and existentially.[52]

Jews, of course, created a counter-narrative to the Christian story—one grounded in the traditional understanding of the covenant as eternal and that sees the present as part of an historical pattern of exile and restoration. This sense of a cyclical structure within history, culminating in a final redemption, permeates both Jewish biblical exegesis and the liturgy. The Land remained both a concrete geographic locale and an idealized symbol. It is an object of consistent, continual meditation and aspiration. Thus, while we might expect the Land to appear prominently in some piyyutim

---

51 While the bibliography on Christian anti-Jewish polemic and Jewish anti-Christian polemic is vast, readers are especially encouraged to consult Limor and Stroumsa, *Contra Iudaeos.*

52 The attitudes of Christianity towards the Land of Israel are far from simple; while the Byzantine Empire was politically motivated to retain control of the Land (and to subjugate the Jews), theologically, the universality of Christianity mitigated against claims that any specific location was more chosen than another. See W. D. Davies, *The Gospel and the Land: Early Christianity and Jewish Territorial Doctrine* (Berkeley: University of California Press, 1974); and P.W.L. Walker, *Holy City, Holy Places? Christian Attitudes to Jerusalem and the Holy Land in the Fourth Century* (Oxford: Clarendon; New York: Oxford University Press, 1990). More generally, see Ora Limor and Guy Stroumsa, eds., *Christians and Christianity in the Holy Land: From the Origins to the Latin Kingdom* (Turnhout : Brepols, 2006).

(those embellishing Torah portions where the Land is itself a major topic), we find that actually the Land plays a disproportionately significant role throughout Yannai's *oeuvre*—becoming a character in its own right in the poetic dramas, often introduced prominently in poems where it does not figure into the Torah portion at all. Implicitly, Yannai's affirmations of the promise of the Land confirm the covenant as a whole. The poet's praise of the Land—its fertility, beauty, life-giving qualities—constitutes a subtle polemic against any who would deny the Land or, by extension, the covenant to the Jews. The Land's intrinsic worth echoes and parallels the intrinsic worth of its rightful people and the God who has united the two.[53]

In some of Yannai's *qedushtaʾot*, the emphasis on the promise of the Land is subtle and part of an overall message assuring the community of the unbroken covenant. We see this, for example, in the *qedushta* for Gen 12:1.[54] Given that the subject of the Torah portion is God's promise of the Land to Abraham—"Go forth... to the land that I will show you" (Gen 12:1)—the audience may well have anticipated some discussion of the Land. And, indeed, we find intermixed with rapturous delineations of unending blessings concrete references to the specific importance of the Land for all of Abraham's heirs.[55] In the opening units, where Ps 45 and the Song of Songs set the tone, the Land becomes, implicitly, the bower where God and Abraham come together as lovers.

In the second *rahit*, meanwhile, Yannai describes the covenant abstractly as, "*A blessing*: true and enduring... *A blessing*: for him, and for his descendents" (Poem Seven², lines 6 and 12). The Land is not singled out, but God's promises to Abraham—all of them, including the bequest of territory—are affirmed as eternal and unceasing, never interrupted. In the first *rahit*, Yannai also seems to single out the Land explicitly, albeit cryptically: "You brought him into your 'Joy'" (Poem Seven¹, line 19). At first, this line appears strange—to what does "joy" refer? As it turns out, "joy" is an epi-

---

53 As this section delineates, the idea of the Land is essential to Yannai's poetic creativity, as is the idea of holiness, explored in the previous section. Intriguingly, however, his references to the Temple—to the restoration of the sacrificial cult and priestly elements of Jewish worship, arguably the locus of holiness and the capstone of restoration—are comparatively muted, particularly when compared to some other Byzantine *payyetanim* and the iconography of the early synagogue. This contrast merits further investigation.

54 Many of the themes discussed here have parallels in midrashic and targumic expositions of the biblical passages. The focus here is simply on Yannai's treatment of these ideas.

55 Writing before the Islamic conquest, Yannai does not dwell on the figure of Ishmael in his poems.

thet for Zion, based on Ps 48:3, which states: "The joy of all the earth is Mount Zion." While other readings of this stich are possible ("joy" could, for example, refer to the revelation of Torah, as in *NumR* 2:25), in the context of this *qedushta*, a territorial interpretation resonates with particular strength: God summoned Abraham to Canaan, after all, not Sinai.

These two examples from the *r'hitim* are somewhat indirect: the first speaks generally of the durability of blessings, not specifically of the Land, while the second implies the Land, but elusively and ambiguously. In the end, the Land is incidental to the piyyut, which dramatizes (and even eroticizes) the relationship between God and Abraham, emphasizing the loving and enduring nature of the relationship, not the bower. In Poem Six for this Torah potion, however, Yannai explicitly addresses the centrality of the Land. The next-to-last stanza has the word "earth/land" (*eretz*) as the conclusion to each stich:

> I called you from the ends of the *earth*
> I brought you near from the *earth's* far corners
> You are a faithful friend and you will dwell upon this piece of *earth*
> Trust in the One trusted to the ends of the *earth*
> (Poem Six, lines 37–40)

According to this stanza, God calls Abraham from the ends of the earth and admonishes him to remain faithful, in order to keep the gift of the Promised Land. The language echoes the prophetic promises of the ingathering, the drawing in of Israel's exiles from the four corners of the earth.[56] Abraham's call thus prefigures God's summoning of all of Israel. Yannai's use of plurals particularly draws attention to itself—the *ends* of the earth, the earth's far *corners*—as if Abraham were being called from multiple locations, the way his descendents will be gathered in the future. The placement of this stanza likewise hints at another level of meaning: the stanza describing "the Land" falls between a stanza on the theme of "righteousness" (in which *tzedeq* concludes each stich) and the final stanza, on the theme of divine holiness (*qodshi*, "My holiness" concludes each stich). Read contextually—as the stanza would have been experienced—the gift of the Land mediates Abraham's, and therefore Israel's, righteous behavior and God's own holiness. The Land is the reward for the former, but also the inevitable manifestation of God's own nature.

---

56 See Isa 41:9, 46:11.

In the *qedushta* for Gen 17:1, we again find Yannai musing about the Land in the midst of a larger meditation on the covenant—in this case, the covenant as expressed through circumcision. The surviving fragments of the poem focus primarily (and with some humor) on the patriarch's startled response to the divine command to circumcise himself and his intuition linking this "pruning" to the pruning of trees. Most of this poem should be read as a Jewish affirmation of circumcision in the face of Christian disregard for the practice.[57] Note, however, the confluence of topics in the surviving *rahit* (Poem Seven):

> *A covenant*: his purity You pressed into his flesh / his buffeted exiles You give root
> *A covenant*: at his loins You became one / Your hand keeping his hand steady
> *A covenant*: his glory, You cut / with his children, crowned, you wrote a contract
> *A covenant*: with him You joined[58] / and his descendents forever will You attend
> (Poem Seven, lines 17–24)

The imagery here is bold: Abraham and God are "joined," sharing a profoundly intimate moment; Abraham's children are crowned like brides and it is God who will forever attend Israel—the reverse of the typical power differential. Furthermore, by means of fulfilling and preserving the commandment of circumcision (an act associated with pruning elsewhere in the *qedushta*), the exiles "shall be given root." Does this imply territorial restoration? It seems so—and thus fidelity to the command to circumcise leads to territorial restoration.[59] Nowhere in this Torah portion does "the

---

57 For the complex cultural and historical significance of the practice of circumcision in Judaism, the Near East, and Christianity, see Cohen, *Why Aren't Women Circumcised*? and also his *The Beginnings of Jewishness.*

58 On the translation of the root *l-m-d* with the connotation of "cling, join," see Zulay, "Matters of Language in the Poetry of Yannai," s.v. למד (p. 206).

59 See *GenR* 46:9 for a midrash that draws a connection between maintenance of circumcision, specifically, and possession of/dispossession from the Land, stating: "'...If they [Abraham's descendents] accept circumcision, they accept My Divinity; if not, they do not accept My Divinity. If your children accept circumcision, they will enter the Promised Land; if not, they will not enter the Promised Land.' Rabbi Berekhiah and Rabbi Helbo in the name of Rabbi Abin b. Rabbi Yose said: It is written, 'And this is the reason (*davar*) why Joshua circumcised...' (Josh 5:4): Joshua spoke a word (*davar*) to them, and circumcised them. 'What are you thinking?' said he, upbraiding them, 'That you will enter the

Land" play a role, but when Yannai describes the benefits of circumcision for Abraham and his heirs, he also interweaves the gift of Land into the intimate covenant the Land represents. Circumcision becomes symbolic of the drama of exile and restoration.

A sense of exile (with its twin, anticipation of restoration, always latent in the background) permeates Yannai's poetry, both because of its prominence in the biblical narratives and because of its topicality in Yannai's own day. Not surprisingly, Jacob and Joseph—who leave home (the Promised Land) under duress—become figures of great interest to the poet. Likewise, these characters offer Yannai a generous canvas upon which to paint his picture of territory lost and regained. Abraham's peregrinations through the Land cannot equal the pathos of fraternal betrayal found in Jacob's flight from Esau or Joseph's sale into Egyptian slavery.

The Jacob cycle offers the greatest concentration of exile-restoration motifs, and, by reading it allegorically, Yannai mines from it a particularly powerful narrative. As retold by Yannai, the patriarch's biography mirrors the national history of Israel: he flees a threat to his life but answers a divine summons to return from exile, which constitutes a fulfillment of his birthright. This biblical plot line acquires potency because Jacob's primary antagonist at several junctures is Esau, his estranged twin brother, who by Yannai's day is thoroughly associated with Edom, and therefore with Rome, and therefore with Christianity, in the world of Jewish exegesis.[60] As he is understood by Yannai as well as other rabbinic exegetes, Jacob—renamed "Israel"—closely prefigures the lives of his children, who likewise engage in a struggle against a powerful, violent, seemingly favored "sibling": Christian Rome (i.e., Esau/Edom). While Israel's complicated relationship with Esau-Edom-Rome will be the focus of the following section, the role of the Land in two particular poems, the *qedushta'ot* for Gen 31:3 and 33:18, indicates how Yannai interpreted "the Land" in the context of the Jacob cycle.

Genesis 31:3 contains God's command to Jacob to return to his ancestral

---

Land uncircumcised!?'" The midrash is much clearer than Yannai's exposition, but much more verbose. Yannai's poem achieves a similar lesson but through juxtaposition and hint rather than elucidation.

60 See Gershon Cohen, "Esau as a Symbol in Early Medieval Thought," in *Studies in the Variety of Rabbinic Cultures* (Philadelphia/New York: JPS, 1991), 243–69, and also the discussion below.

Land—to go home at long last; Yannai consistently translates this message so that it speaks in the present tense, as well. The *qedushta* embellishing this passage contains multiple paeans to the Promised Land and descriptions of the end of exile, individual and national. The *magen* (Poem One) describes God "bringing near the far" (line 1) and fulfilling the decree that "a remnant would return" (line 10). These opening words clearly address Yannai's contemporary audience as much as they embellish the biblical story, given that Jacob returns with wives and children and flocks, hardly a "remnant" of his former self. Instead, "remnant" alludes to the biblical Prophets' visions of the restoration of the exiles. The *meḥayyeh* (Poem Two) describes Jacob telling his wives: "The end arrives, the return from exile" (line 7), despite the fact that for Rachel and Leah, this will be a journey parallel to Abraham's, a trek *away* from their father Laban's house in Aram. The *meshallesh* (Poem Three) describes the importance of piety in securing restoration: because Jacob was pious, "O Yah, You cared for him, restoring him to his burthplace, leading him to tranquility, granting him serenity and sending him home" (lines 7 and 8). The *asiriyyah* (Poem Five) emphasizes God's fidelity to His promise to restore Jacob to his homeland and concludes with a forthright petition by the poet to do the same for his congregation: "Yah, also restore us / and return us unto You // Let us live securely / and let us dwell in tranquility" (line 10). Poem Six, in particular, is a masterpiece: a twenty-two line Ode to Zion, an extended meditation on the beauty, majesty, and fecundity of the Land. Building on the opening phrase, "Return to the land of your ancestors," Yannai describes in every stanza the holiness, uniqueness, and chosenness of the Promised Land. It will sustain all who dwell upon her, her children will be Prophets, kings will seek her to pay tribute to her rulers, and her soil will grant eternal life. "Your claim upon her will not expire," the poet promises, "no strange land shall be your bower" (lines 35–36). The *rahit* (Poem Seven) continues in this vein, praising the Land and the people destined to inhabit her, while the *silluq* and *qedushah* (Poems Eight and Nine) assert that with God's favor and Israel's righteousness, restoration will surely come. For all that Yannai presumably lived, worked, and prayed in the Galilee—the most lush area of the Land of Israel—the place he describes in his piyyut seems almost dreamlike. He presents a vision not of the Land as it is, but of the Land restored. Just as restoration will renew the people in some existential way, it will likewise renew the Land; just as the people have experienced existential if not physical alienation from the Land, the Land itself has been dispossessed from its true potential. It, too, will be redeemed; it is the locus, the symbol, and the recipient of Israel's restoration.

The return commanded in Gen 31:3 reaches a first stage of completion in Gen 33:18. In this Torah portion, Jacob crosses the border into the Promised Land and purchases a territorial parcel in Shechem—the area of Shalem (identified midrashically as Jerusalem). Through this act, Jacob has secured his patrimony and acquired land he may bequeath to his heirs. Throughout this piyyut, Yannai builds on multiple valences of the word *shalem*: "whole, healthy" (and therefore a description of the patriarch's wellbeing), "fulfilled, completed" (and thus a reference to the promises of restoration), and "Jerusalem" (thereby providing the redemptive story with a concrete and meaningful location). Jacob and his children are *shalem*; God's word is *shalem*; and the scene of the story is *shalem*—i.e., the city of Jerusalem, but also a land that is healed through reunification of people, territory, and deity.[61] The *magen* (Poem One) for Gen 33:18 describes Jacob's homecoming, seeing in it a prefiguring of Israel's eventual national return. Israel, like Jacob, may be limping, but they will be healed, secure, and free. The *meḥayyeh* (Poem Two) asserts Jacob's unquestionable ownership of the Land of Shalem/Jerusalem. The *meshallesh* (Poem Three) anticipates the rebuke of Esau, the restoration of the Temple, and the complete restoration of the people—a restoration both physical and spiritual. Poem Four petitions the God who protected Jacob in his exile and upon his return to do the same for the children of Jacob—leading them in safety, like their ancestor, to the same lush and fertile Promised Land. The *asiriyyah* (Poem Five) concentrates on aspects of Jacob's piety—sacrifice, prayer, and Torah study—which prefigure the Temple that would someday stand (and will stand again) in Jerusalem. Poem Six describes a victorious Jacob's magnanimous entry to the Land; its final stichs are unambiguous:

> The full term of his exile completed // in Shalem he surrendered to peace and his vows he fulfilled (Poem Six, lines 43–44).

At long last, Jacob is able to fulfill the oaths he made in Gen 28, when he

61 Similar explorations of the word "*shalem*" occur in the midrash, but as noted before, the poetic medium allows Yannai to conflate, juxtapose, and play with the language in a way that prose exegetes cannot. While many of Yannai's individual interpretations resonate with readings found in *Genesis Rabbah* and other sources, indicating his participation in a rich interpretive tradition, poetry results in a different kind of composition and effect from prose.

fled the land to escape Esau's murderous wrath.. The complex *rahit* (Poem Seven) focuses on Jacob's piety and its rewards for his heirs, while the *silluq* and *qedushah* (Poems Eight and Nine) emphasize the eventual divine response on behalf of Jacob's descendents. Throughout the piyyut, Yannai paints a picture of absolute covenantal fidelity: God displays unwavering loyalty to Jacob and his descendents, while Jacob and his children possess unfailing piety. If it were possible for the poet to compel the redemption to come through sheer force of rhetoric, in this poem he would do so.

Of course, the story of the patriarchs of Genesis is one of displacement as much as possession; the necessity of exile as a precursor to restoration is an idea that the surviving fragments of the *qedushta* for Gen 37:1, the first major poem of the Joseph cycle, explore. When Joseph first appears as a character in Yannai's cycle of poetry, the audience hears the foreshadowing of his exile to come, and their own. Joseph's sojourn in Egypt—a long, dark period that ends generations later with the stunning story of the Exodus—becomes a template for Yannai's vision of his own day. Without exile, Yannai teaches, there can be no redemption. This *qedushta* indicates a transition in the poetic cycle, just as Gen 37 marks a shift in the Genesis narrative. The *magen* (Poem One) functions as a coda, summarizing Jacob's restoration to his ancestral Land—restoration that proves to be merely an interlude. The *meḥayyeh* (Poem Two), set in "the place in which brothers dwelled together" (line 1)—an image of peace echoing Ps 133—introduces the motifs of displacement and fracture. The brothers commit their sins, Joseph rats them out, and the narrator exclaims, "How they have fallen, these sons of the matriarchs!" (line 9). The *meshallesh* (Poem Three) maintains this despairing tone and sense of alienation:

> A restful dwelling place as yet we have not found // in all the lands to which we have gone forth…
> Oh, let them return and be restored / no longer blown here and there /
> in peaceful habitations may they dwell, securely settled…"
> (Poem Three, lines 1–2 and 7–8).

Exile is not a theme in the Torah portion itself, nor does the biblical text describe Joseph's sale into slavery in these nationalistic terms. At the same time, these wishes for peace and restoration are hardly unique to Yannai. What stands out is the poignancy of the poet's rhetoric, the delicacy with which he paints not only geographic but emotional portraits, drawing his congregants into a story that he presents as their own. In Yannai's realm, this poem works to create an especially ephemeral sensation: for only a few weeks, in liturgical time, did Jacob enjoy the Land! How quickly, in the end, it passed away, and not because of others, but because of the sins of Jacob's own sons.[62] And yet, the children of Jacob's children, the poet affirms, are destined for restoration. The story of Joseph is not remote; it is relived, in its whole range of emotions.

In the *qedushta* for Gen 39:1, Yannai tempers and moderates the gloominess of his piyyut for Gen 37:1, returning once again to the themes of divine plan and ultimate redemption. Just as Joseph did not despair when he was in Egypt, so Israel should not despair in its current exile. Indeed, by connecting Joseph's descent to Hos 11:4, "I drew them with human cords, with bonds of love, but I seemed to them like one who imposed a bit between their teeth, though I was offering them food," the poet tempers the experience of displacement and disempowerment by asserting that dispossession and alienation are not punishment, but part of a program of love.[63] If Joseph hadn't gone to Egypt, the other sons of Jacob would have starved. The one son suffered on behalf of many, so that, in the end, all would flourish. Mystery does not negate logic. By implication, there is some beneficent purpose behind Israel's present-day travails. Indeed, God never abandons Joseph, even in Egypt (and Egyptian prisons), and while the foes (whether Joseph's brothers or, by extension, contemporary Rome) believe they are determining history, they are wrong. In the third and final surviving poem, Yannai draws a clear analogy between Joseph, who was oppressed though innocent, and his own people. The children of Israel become, in this poem, the successors of Joseph—existential heirs to his legacy of betrayal and exile but also the promise of return.

When read closely, many—most, even—of Yannai's piyyutim for Genesis describe the Land and its significance and emphasize the promises of restoration. Indeed, the Genesis poems conclude with a *qedushta* that dwells on the set but unknown date of the restoration: Jacob's mystically-charged last words to his sons. Poems preceding the Jacob cycle likewise

62 The transience of Jacob's return may be a deeply embedded allusion to the "temporary" restoration of the Second Temple, which was ultimately destroyed, according to rabbinic lore, not by Rome but by the baseless hatred Jews bore for each other—just as Joseph and his brothers bring (temporary) ruin upon themselves in this sidra. See *b. Yoma* 9b.

63 *GenR* 86:1 and *TanhB Vayeshev* 18 read Hos 11:4 as an intertext for the Joseph story, as well. What stands out is not simply Yannai's familiarity with aggadic motifs and midrashic strands of interpretation, but the way he distills these traditions into his own medium.

engage with this central motif in a way that renders it enduring, and like much of midrash, outside of time. In the *qedushta* for Gen 16:1, the poet compares the matriarch Sarah to Zion personified, both childless, barren women who bear, in the end, children who will call them "mother" (Poem Three, line 10) and bring them joy. The Land is not always at the center of Yannai's poems, but it remains an emblem of Israel's national and existential story—a story whose end is known and written, for all that it has yet to transpire. The Promised Land—implying, as it does, the promise itself, the divine Promiser, and the Israelite promised—is not only the explicit setting for many of the stories, but a shorthand for describing restoration and its many positive results. "The Land" connotes safety, security, tranquility, and ease; it is a component of wholeness, its restoration, of cosmic rightness; and it represents divine immediacy and intimacy, something beyond the mere proximity of a God who is present with His exiled children. In some cases, particularly in his *qedushta* for Gen 31:3, the Land emerges as a character in its own right: it loves, yearns, awaits fulfillment. In other places, it seems more of an afterthought—something taken for granted, or simply assumed. Much as God and Israel can be depicted as separated lovers, Israel and its Land can be seen through the same lens. When the world is set right, all the lovers who populate this romance—the people of, the God of, and the Land of Israel—will be reunited. Images of the Land are tinged with almost erotic yearning.

For Yannai, even when his tone sounds despairing, the figure of "the Land" remains one of hope. He never directly confronts the Christian supersessionist interpretations he implicitly counters; such ideas do not seem to exist for him, except in his vigorous, implicit denial that such claims could even be made. The poet does not acknowledge that there are those who say the covenant is nullified, the Land lost. Instead, he asserts, over and over again, the actuality and inevitability of restoration and return, the fundamental impossibility of history having any other possible end. He does not deny the reality of exile—even in the Galilee, where Yannai lived, these poems teach us that the exilic sense was acute and the yearnings for restoration strong. But like the Rabbis, he teaches that dispossession is a burden that can be borne. The performative aspect of the poems only underscores and emphasizes the poet's teachings. Through Yannai's poetry, the community does not simply acknowledge this assertive optimism; they enact it and affirm it. The liturgical setting adds an experimental, non-intellectual component to the reality and worldview it helps create. In piyyut, as in other rabbinic writings, the acts of the fathers are a sign for the sons. Their merit is a lesson for their descendents, and so is their exile—and fated restoration. Yannai cannot teach Genesis in his day without reading it through the lens of his own situation. When Abraham, Jacob, and Joseph wander, it is his own loss he feels; and when Esau walks across the biblical stage, it is a very real anger that Yannai expresses.

Esau and Apocalypse: Jews, Christians, and "the Good Other"

The Promised Land is the poet's dreamscape: real, yet idealized; tangible, yet remote; possessed, but momentarily beyond his grasp. In Yannai's imagination, the Land becomes a maternal figure—life-giving, life-affirming, nurturing, nourishing, and protective—but also a damsel in distress, erotic and endangered. It is a destination of restoration but also itself in need of redemption.[64] The Land is a reward already promised, a future already tasted; it is what was and will be. It is, in short, Yannai's past and his future. In the present tense, however, Jewish life is more complicated: the Land is the locus of alienation and estrangement, and friction with the outside world readily felt. Indeed, between Yannai and his visions of peaceful, contented settlement on a land flowing with milk and honey lies one major, seemingly insurmountable, obstacle: the dominance of Rome.

Yet the assurances of biblical prophecies—from God's promises to the patriarchs in Genesis to the forecasts of the great Prophets in the later books and the insights of later Jewish exegetes—offer the conquered people of Israel hope of overcoming their powerful ancestral foe. Indeed, the geopolitical turmoil of the sixth century may have encouraged active messianic speculation and even insurrections among the Jewish population of Palestine.[65] At times, Yannai's vision of the downfall of Esau/Edom is leav-

64 On the maternal and erotic connotations of the Land, see the next section, on women.

65 On messianic speculation and even direct anti-imperial action on the part of Jews in 6th century Palestine, see my forthcoming article: "'You Have Been Skirting this Hill Long Enough,'" and also W. J. van Bekkum, "Messianic Expectations in the Age of Hereclius" and the sources cited above in n. 30. The funerary formulae from Jewish tombstones at Zoar further support the idea of intense messianic speculation among the Jewish population of the Land of Israel at this time. While Zoar is physically remote from the Galilee where Yannai presumably lived (Zoar is in modern Jordan, on the southeast shore of the Dead Sea), the tombstones overlap roughly in date with Yannai. They indicate among that community not only complicated beliefs about the afterlife but also messianic expectations, possibly imminent. These tombs and related epigraphic evidence from the 4th–6th centuries support the literary evidence of a widespread messianic expectation among Jews in

ened by poetic wit; in other instances, the poetry gives vent to apocalyptic yearnings; and at times, he verges upon despair.[66] Tracing the conflict between the Jews and Rome back to the days of the earliest ancestors, Yannai will regard his own day as a chapter in an ongoing story—but one to which he knows the eventual end.[67] At the same time, as we will also see, Yannai insists that not all gentiles are wicked, just as he will not say that all Israel is good.

The greatest concentration of anti-Esau/anti-Edom (i.e., anti-Byzantine Roman) polemic in the Genesis poems occurs, naturally, in poems where Esau is one of the primary characters in the Torah portion. If anti-

---

Byzantine Palestine. See Wilfand, "Aramaic Tombstones from Zoar and Jewish Conceptions of the Afterlife."

66 Yannai's most pessimistic poem about Edom does not occur in his Genesis piyyutim but in his *rahit* for Num 8:1, which begins: "The lamps of Edom are strengthened and increased / the lamps of Zion were swallowed up and destroyed // The lamps of Edom prevailed and glittered / the lamps of Zion were crushed and extinguished..." See the discussion of this poem (including its use of lamp imagery) in Fine, *Art and Judaism in the Greco-Roman World*, esp. 158–63. This piyyut is also discussed in van Bekkum, "Anti-Christian Polemic," 305.

67 Yahalom discusses Yannai's interest in Edom-Esau in his *Poetry and Society*, 183–93; see also W. van Bekkum, "The Hidden Reference: The Role of EDOM in Late Antique and Early Medieval Jewish Hymnography," in *Empsychoi Logoi: Religious Innovation in Antiquity, Studies in Honour of Pieter Willem van der Horst.* Edited by Alberdina Houtman, Albert de Jong, and Magda Misset-van de Weg (Leiden: Brill, 2008), 527–43. As vituperative as Yannai's poems can be towards Esau and all it symbolizes, they rarely reach the level of the Aramaic poems, which take particular glee in the denigration of non-Jews. By rooting his polemic in biblical language, imagery, and rhetoric and focusing his complaint on accusations of utmost seriousness and punishments that, violent though they are, reflect divine justice, Yannai never succumbs to precisely the kind of giddy mockery of "the other" that can sometimes be found in the Aramaic piyyutim. Yannai, for example, challenges Christian theology, asserting "You never fathered a son" (*qedushta* for Lev 12:1, opening line) and expresses disbelief with "the ones who cling to a dead man" (*qedushta* for Yom Kippur, poem 10).—"the dead one" being a common payyetanic epithet for Jesus. The Aramaic piyyutim for Purim, however, actively mock the Crucifixion, conflating it with the death of Haman in the context of Purim (see, for an example: Sokoloff and Yahalom, *Jewish Palestinian Aramaic Poetry from Late Antiquity*, 216, line 88).

It should be noted that even at its most vitriolic (works such as the non-liturgical text of *Toledot Yeshu*, a kind of Hebrew mock gospel narrative itself dated to the sixth century), Hebrew poetry does not reach the level of animosity and violence of Christian hymnography. While the anti-Jewish rhetoric of Late Antiquity—including the sermons of Chrysostom and the poems of Ephrem—are complicated (see Shepherdson, *Anti-Judaism and Orthodox Christianity*), in terms of Jewish literature the question arises over whether the relative lack of vitriol reflects imperial censorship (e.g., the law-codes and the idea that there was an official, watchful presence in the synagogue), Jewish self-censorship, or something else.

Roman sentiment was found exclusively in such locations, it would seem that Yannai's polemics were situational and their inclusion driven primarily by context. However, the figure of Edom/Rome appears both before and after the Jacob stories, particularly in Poem Three of the *qedushta* (the *meshallesh*), when the poet often addresses issues of contemporary concern.[68] Yannai seems to respond to a generic, structurally determined liturgical-poetical context (perhaps of his own devising) as much as he does to biblical pre-text.

The *qedushta* for Gen 11:1 provides a good example of how Esau-Rome may appear in a piyyut where the biblical character is in no way present (neither in the Torah portion nor in the haftarah). At the same time, this example highlights how Yannai uses familiar biblical texts to engage with traditions of exegesis in the construction of his creative theology. In the *meshallesh* (Poem Three) for this poem Yannai writes:

> You dwell in secret, laughing as all is revealed // for all secret laughter is revealed before You
> So pluck, now, from the earth (*adamah*) / the kingdom of deathly silence (*dumah*)
> (Poem Three, lines 1–3).

The line alludes to Isa 21:11 ("The burden of Dumah—One calls to me from Seir: Watchman, what of the night? Watchman, what of the night?"). This passage recalls the tradition recorded in the Palestinian Talmud that Rabbi Meir's codex connected "Dumah" with Rome ("'the burden of Dumah'—the burden of Rome"), based perhaps on the visual, orthographic similarities between "*dumah*" and "*adamah*" in Hebrew as well as the suitability of the prophecy.[69] Other traditions, notably those of the Babylonian Talmud, consider "Dumah" to be the name of the angel who presides over the dead. If Yannai also had this tradition in mind (or if members of his congregation knew it), Rome becomes some sort of horrific kingdom of death. The term "land" (*adamah*) in the first stich likewise puns on the name of the enemy, Edom, which comes from the

68 Esau becomes, for example, associated with the wicked Pharaoh of Exodus in the Exodus *qedushtaʾot*, and he is cited as a transgressor in the *qedushta* for Lev 14:33.

69 *j. Taʿan* 64a, 1:1. Compare with *b.San.* 94a, which leaves out the "the burden of Rome" from a similar passage. Jerome, in his commentary to Isa 21:11 mentions this tradition: "The burdens of Dumah, that some Jews read *Rumah* for *Dumah*, which means to say that they apply this prophecy to Rome."

same trilateral root, א-ד-ם. In this *meshallesh* (Poem Three), Yannai petitions God to restore the oneness lost at the Tower of Babel and to unify the nations of the world through common reverence for the deity—all the nations but Rome, that is. Yannai here *excludes* Rome, the archenemy, from his petition: "the nations" can participate in this utopian future; Rome he wants removed from the world entirely, plucked up and cast away.

In the passage above, and throughout this piyyut, Yannai depicts the Tower Builders (i.e., the Byzantine powers) as secretly mocking God. It may be that the hubris of the Empire manifests through their coerced unification of a polyglot Empire ("Their unity caused their division," Poem Two, line 3) as well as their "verbal" sins of anti-Jewish edicts and legislation. The Romans reenact the folly of the generation of the Tower-Builders, through both pride and abuse of power. Is this a subtle allusion to the conflicts and heresies that fragmented the Church in this period (despite its insistence on its unity), or perhaps a political statement against the Empire? Yannai leaves this poem open to interpretation—he may not have had a single reading in mind himself. He does, however, spell out his idea that the hubris of Babel evokes the arrogance of Rome. And Rome's downfall, Yannai hopes, will be just as spectacular.

Yannai's polemic, while pervasive, is often subtle, relying on contextual clues and the ability to perceive acid nuances of meaning embedded within witty constructions. The reference in Gen 11:1 requires engagement from the audience to decipher it. In isolation, it appears merely as a cryptic and passing remark. However, given that the reference occurs in the *meshallesh* (Poem Three, which introduces the haftarah), we can imagine that the congregation anticipated a political reference, and with such an assumption in mind, the anti-Roman rhetoric becomes easy to hear. This example is typical. Knowledge of the identity of "the enemy" often relies on complex exegesis—allusions not to Esau, Edom, or Rome explicitly, but to biblical verses (such as Isa 21:11) that carry with them interpretations that link them to this specific foe.

In other instances, however, simple but brief descriptors refer specifically (if still obliquely) to Rome. For example, in his *meshallesh* (Poem Three) for Gen 33:18, the poet pleads: "Burst forth against those who razed Shalem wholly!" (line 2). In context it is clear that "those who razed Shalem" means, "Those who destroyed the Temple" (or Jerusalem). This language is a potent allusion to Ps 137:7, which states: "Remember, O Lord, against the Edomites, the day of Jerusalem; they who said, `Raze it, raze it, to its foundation.'" Edom—the villain of the psalm, depicted as participating in the destruction of the First Temple—is a code-word for the Roman (and thus Byzantine) Empire, the power that destroyed the Second Temple. As a result, the enemies who destroyed Jerusalem in 586 B.C.E. seamlessly morph into the enemy that destroyed the Temple again in 70 C.E.—the imperial power that continues to antagonize Jews into Yannai's own day. In terse payyetanic rhetoric, the tragedy of Jerusalem, twice destroyed by Edom-Rome, can be invoked by a passing allusive phrase.

While references to Edom occur throughout Yannai's writings, Yannai reserves his most detailed, explicit, and developed polemics against Rome in those poems where Esau or Edom is an actual character. The cycle of weekly Torah readings, particularly in Genesis, provides the poet many weeks in which to explore the character of Esau, the father of Rome, as both a figure from Israel's past and future and an emblem of political oppression and religious usurpation in the present. This liturgical use of Scripture, much like midrashic readings of the text, transforms Esau- Rome from a simple historical character within the biblical narrative into a figure of contemporary urgency and import.

Liturgical poetry, even more than midrash, collapses the past into the present and works on the level of metaphor rather than simile. The terse vividness of his rhetoric lends his anti-Roman polemic extra force and sharpens his message with wit. For example, in the second *rahit* (Poem Seven^2) for Gen 25:19 (the portion in which the twins, Jacob and Esau, are born), Yannai uses clever puns to juxtapose the two as antithetical pairs. In doing so, he takes the rhetoric of antithesis present in Gen 25:27–28, where the biblical text contrasts the twins, and amplifies it. Jacob, for example, is "the ram," a kosher animal, fit for the altar of divine service. Esau is "the pig" (an animal associated with Rome, generally, and Christianity directly, because of their rejection of *kashrut*), destined for ruin (Poem Seven^2, lines 21–22).[70] Several lines later, we are told that Jacob is "the prince" while Esau is "the pretender"—one is a legitimate ruler (presumably of the Land of Israel), while the other is a usurper (lines 29–30), referring, we may assume, both to the political dominion of the Byzantine Empire over the Land of Israel and its theological claims of supersessionism.

70 The use of the word *ḥurban* ("ruin, destruction") here applied to Edom/Rome is a terse manifestation of "measure-for-measure" theology, in that just as Rome destroyed the Temple, Rome will be destroyed (in the selfsame language, even).

The differences are not merely in traits or tastes; they are existential. Forceful rhetoric underscores the essential truth of Yannai's message. The poem concludes that Jacob is "perfection" while Esau is "perversion." Jacob's perfection will lead to love, while Esau's perversion inspires loathing (lines 43–44). The traits associated with Jacob are all positive: he is lovable and worthy, choice and chosen, gentle and genteel, wise and pious, unique and unifying. Esau is his opposite: he inspires loathing and distaste, is vulgar and violent, a mocker and poseur, a liar and pervert. Jacob's touch heals while Esau's breaks. As the *silluq* (Poem Eight) summarizes, Esau "reddens people's faces" (line 3), shaming or bloodying them, while Jacob looks towards the face of God. And, as the poet enigmatically notes, "the one [Esau] is seen / while the other [Jacob] seems hidden" (line 4). That is, at the moment, Rome rules most of the known world. Everywhere in Yannai's world, Rome was a visible, domineering presence. Israel, by contrast, is small and barely visible.

Appearance, however, belies actual stature; in the eyes of God, Israel exceeds all others. The dramatic confrontation between these two opposites has been woven into the fabric of history, needing only the force of poetic rhetoric to make the contrast clear. In Scripture, the differences between Jacob and Esau are evident just verses after their birth. Yannai, like a *darshan*, took a biblical motif and ran with it; the poetic form distills the contrast between the two figures to its barest, most potent essence.

So pervasive is Esau's wickedness that Yannai, like many Jewish exegetes, detects his harmful, destructive influence even in stories where he is *not* explicitly mentioned. For example, in Yannai's *qedushta* for Gen 29:31, we learn that Leah's eyes are weak because when she realized that she was fated to marry the wicked, impious Esau, she literally cried herself almost blind in despair. God, moved by her prayer, altered her fate and decreed that she would instead marry Jacob (not necessarily a happier marriage but apparently a better one) and be granted impressive fertility. In this Torah portion, Esau isn't a factor at all, nor does the biblical text ever say that Leah was intended to marry anyone, let alone her brother-in-law.

Yannai's basic exegesis recalls a common midrashic understanding of how Leah's eyes became weak, but his use of the motif differs from that of the aggadah.[71] The poet does not directly articulate the cause of Leah's

71 *GenR* 70:16 describes how Leah's eyes were weakened when she learned that Rachel was destined to marry Jacob but she was doomed to marry Esau. So sincere were Leah's pleas

dimmed eyesight; instead, he assumes the broad outlines of the aggadah are known and uses his piyyut as a canvas for exploring Leah's emotional state and God's response. He is not interested in details but consequences. Yannai never articulates precisely what qualities made Esau such a horrible suitor. He is, simply, "the hated one"—the same epithet used for Leah in the opening verse of the Torah portion, a resonance that highlights the fact that hatred can be deserved or not. The congregation already knew Esau's nature and actions (both those narrated in the Bible and, presumably, in the aggadah) and could easily sympathize with Leah's horror. This background knowledge leaves the poet free to contemplate, along with Leah, relief at being spared an Esau-laden fate. The mood of this poem blends *pathos* with hope: *pathos* because Leah was hated, as Israel is hated, and hope because God recognized and rewarded Leah's piety and love, just as He will recognize and reward Israel's piety and love. For Israel, as for Leah, redemption involves being freed from a fate bound up with Esau. Esau, as Yannai sees it, has been a source and symbol of Jewish grief from the dawn of Israel's history; relief from Esau becomes synonymous with salvation. The poet identifies in this poem not with Jacob, but with Leah—not with the clever, assertive twin, but with the pious and vulnerable woman. Esau, in turn, is evidently a bully and a lout, but always off-stage; he need not even be present to make a girl cry herself almost blind at the idea of marrying him.

The *qedushta* for Gen 29:31 depicts a tender, empathetic, even romantic scenario: the tragedy of Leah's fate averted by gracious and timely divine intervention. Leah is the heroine, Esau the villain, and God the hero who saves her. More often, when Esau appears on the stage, the poet's mood becomes passionate to the point of apocalyptic. The *qedushta* for Gen 14:1 contains a fragmentary *rahit* in which God, "the man of war" (Exod 15:3), is convinced to put aside His preference for peace in order to enact justice upon Edom.[72] Yannai petitions:

---

that she not have to marry the wicked son, God altered the divine plan. "Rabbi Huna said: Great is prayer, that it annulled the decree, and she [Leah] even took precedence of her sister [Rachel]." Leah and Rachel are likewise compared in *GenR* 70:15 and *TanḥB Vayetze* 13. This motif appears in both *TargN* and *TargPsJ* to Gen 29:31, as well; the brevity of the targumic versions more closely recalls the rhetorical style of the piyyut, but the piyyut devotes much more extensive time to exploring Leah's inner state than any of the other sources.

72 The *qedushta* for Deut 20:1 (found in Rabinovitz 2:162–66), which has a *rahit* with the refrain "peace!" (*shalom*), forms a kind of bookend for this passage.

Exalting in Your ferocity on the day of *war*
Send us first one anointed for *war*
Let arise the one destined to arise for a time of *war*
He shall say: Up! Rise against her [Rome] for *war*
And then let us say: The Lord is valiant in *war*
(Poem Seven, lines 5–9)

As in the *meshallesh* (Poem Three) for Gen 11:1, the poet does not explicitly mention Rome, Esau, or Edom in these lines, but he nonetheless makes the object of his messianic/apocalyptic hope unambiguous. Yannai issues a stark call for battle, as the refrain makes clear (and we can imagine the congregation reciting the refrain in unison—a very potent experience). The world will not be made right simply by divine fiat, according to this vision; there will be battle. The apocalyptic visions of various later biblical books and traditions are adduced through allusion, with vengeful delight. The poet, we should note, does not encourage rebellion among his people—the *messianic leader* shall say, "Up! Rise against her for war," which implies clear divine authorization for militaristic action. Yannai eagerly anticipates both the battle and the justice of its results, but he does not encourage revolt. Rather, he assures that the time will come, and then, and only then, shall the battle commence.[73]

Yannai's most vivid apocalyptic visions in his Genesis *qedushtaʾot* appear in his poem for Gen 32:4. His coloring of the scene may be surprising, given that the Torah portion speaks of the peaceful, if awkward, reunion between the estranged twins. The fact that the haftarah for this Torah portion is the book of Obadiah, a single extended prophecy against Edom, either reflects Yannai's more confrontational mode of interpretation or helped shaped it. While Yannai continues to refrain from actively encouraging rebellion, he clearly takes delight in envisioning the various apocalypses of the Bible, all in the context of anti-Roman polemic. Nor is he at all cryptic here. The identity of the enemy is made explicit: the entire *qedushta* is an anthology of puns on the root א-ד-ם, Edom. The *magen* (Poem One), which is fragmentary, ends with the vivid prophecy: "Your sword, O Ruddy One / will become drunk from the red one's blood / You are our Shield, O Lord!"

73 Yannai never actually encourages his community to participate in rebellion against Rome, although the sources indicate that they would have had several opportunities to join the Samaritans in such a rebellion in the sixth century. War against Rome is God's responsibility. See Yahalom, *Poetry and Society*, 72–80, and my article, "You Have Skirted This Hill Long Enough."

The gory language of this *ḥatimah* relies on Isa 34:5, an unquoted intertext that states: "For My sword has drunk its fill in the heavens; behold, it shall come down upon Edom, and upon the people of My curse, to judgment." Yannai eagerly awaits this prophecy's fulfillment, when God, whom the poet describes as "radiant and ruddy" (Song 5:10) will deliver Israel from the enemy who is red and simply bloody.

In the *meḥayyeh* (Poem Two) for this piyyut, Yannai implicitly speaks to the present day: "He perceived that this world is his brother's world // so with begging and bribes he advances" (Poem Two, lines 9–10). On the one hand, this seems to describe Esau and Jacob in the *sidra*; Jacob does abase himself before his brother upon their reunion, and the poet (in keeping with aggadic tradition), chastises him for even appearing weak. That granted, the extreme power differential described applies much more accurately to Rome and Israel of Yannai's day; after all, the biblical text is quite clear that Jacob was, in fact, quite wealthy and powerful—that was the source of his fear of Esau, not his powerlessness. Unlike the biblical scenario, the world really did appear, in Late Antiquity, to belong to Rome.

The *meshallesh* (Poem Three) directly confronts the contemporary situation. In this poem, Yannai petitions God to liberate Israel from Edom's rule, and to judge and condemn Edom to famine, fire, and Hell—to fulfill, in essence, the words of Obadiah. In this unit, Yannai crafts a naked, desperate, and explicit polemic against Rome and a plea for a complete reversal of situation. For four brief lines, the poet reveals the agony of his condition—or at least one moment's experience. His patience runs thin.

After that third poem, Yannai's apocalyptic yearnings lie dormant until the first *rahit* (Poem Seven), which ends almost every stich with the word "Edom" or a related word, such as *adom* ("red"—in the sense of ruddy or bloody) or in one instance the rhyming "Sodom," the city whose cataclysmic fate prefigures the destiny of Rome. In this poem, Yannai anticipates:

> A great slaughter in the land of Edom / a burning fire in the fields of Edom…
> Spread Your net upon the land of Edom / You will hunt down the hunter, the father of Edom…
> Draw Your sword and sate it from Edom
> (Poem Seven[1], lines 9–10, 17–18, and 22)

This violent fate foreseen for Rome is fitting recompense for the vicious, bloody acts of murder and desecration committed by the Empire. There is possibly no more furious poem in all of Yannai's Genesis *qedushtaʾot.* The hot anger, yearning for justice and vengeance, and delight in the idea of retribution is palpable in this work, and we can imagine the communal anger arising as the congregation responds at the end of very stich with the refrain word: Edom! Edom! Edom! Rhetoric, politics, and performance combine for a fiery mix.

The next three units of the poem—the second and third *r'hitim* and the *silluq* (Poems Seven^2 and Seven^3, and Eight)—must be read together. They essentially retell the apocalyptic vision of Daniel 7; Yannai even composes these poems in Aramaic to evoke the biblical passage. The poet often quotes directly from the strange biblical story of Daniel's "Night Vision" of the Four Beasts, the fourth of which has ten horns.[74] For Yannai, Daniel's vision describes not Antiochus IV (the Seleucid ruler whose persecution of the Jews led to the Hasmonean revolt and whose brutality lies behind the story of Daniel), but Christian Rome. In the second *rahit*, Yannai includes what may be a subtle anti-Christian polemic: "The name of the last king is: `he changes'" (Poem Seven^2, line 21)—perhaps a jibe at Christian selective appropriation of the Torah or the Christian belief in a "Jewish" king who came and overturned the Torah.[75] The brief third *rahit*—an unusual feature in a form where one or two *r'hitim* are the norm—has almost a visionary quality, drawing on the imagery of Dan 7:9–11, in which the defeat of the beast is anticipated. The poet writes, "[D]ays come close and a day approaches // approaches the end, the killing of the beast" (Poem Seven^3, lines 1–2). While Yannai describes events that have not yet come to pass—i.e., the fall of Rome—the vivid and strange imagery creates a sensation of immediacy and proximity, as if in these three brief lines, the poet has *become* Daniel, or Daniel has become the poet. The *silluq* continues the Danielic imagery, focusing on the messianic figure predicted in Dan 7:13–14, the righteous king to whom God will grant eternal dominion and universal sovereignty—the "correct" version of a universal empire ruled by a proper king, an ideal perverted by the impostor Rome.

74 See Yahalom, *Poetry and Society,* 81–84, for a discussion of the payyetanic fascination with Dan 7.

75 The language of "change" returns in the first line of the *qedushah,* cited below, where God's immutability is asserted—continuing and developing the subtle polemic of the piece. Yannai's *qedushta* for Deut 6:4 contains a similar but more developed anti-Christian polemic based on the idea of a God or king who "changes."

The unusual *qedushah*, which concludes the poem, doubles each triad, using the poem as a way to continue highlighting the entwined, inverted fates of Jacob and Esau:

> Your counsel cannot be known / Your power cannot be diminished / Your name cannot be changed[76] / They respond, saying:
> *Holy, holy, holy is the Lord of Hosts; the whole world is filled with His glory!*
> "Holy" from the masters of counsel / "Holy" from the masters of power / "Holy" from the masters of name and deed
> "Holy"—He will confirm the counsel of Jacob / and overturn the counsel of Esau
> "Holy"—He will strengthen the weak power of Jacob / and uproot the power of Esau[77]
> "Holy"—He will favor the name of Jacob / over the deeds of Esau[78]
> (Poem Nine, lines 1–13)

The triads themselves refer to Israel (or perhaps an elite subset of the Jewish community) with somewhat mysterious overtones: they are "the masters of counsel," "the masters of power," and "masters of name and deed" (line 3). These esoteric epithets resonate well with the strange visions of Daniel 7 that preceded them. Continuing the unusual formal aspects of this poem, these epithets do not wholly structure the remainder of the *qedushah*; instead, the poet juxtaposes Jacob and Esau three times using one aspect of the opening triad. God will confirm the counsel of Jacob and overturn the counsel of Esau; strengthen the weak power of Jacob and uproot the power of Esau; and favor the name of Jacob over the deeds of Esau (lines 4–6).[79] The poet complicates the normally predictable *qedushah* structure in order to emphasize, one final time in the poem, the ultimate destiny of Esau.

Yannai does not envision a day of judgment only for his enemies, however; in his *qedushta* for Gen 44:18, he notes that Israel, too, may find itself

---

76 See Ps 71:19, Isa 49:4. This links back to the "false messiah" figure, named "He changes," mentioned above.

77 See Job 36:5, "Behold, God is mighty, and does not despise any; he is mighty in strength of wisdom."

78 The "deeds of Esau" refers to the irony implicit in Esau's name, which predicted righteous deeds but resulted in violence; the association of "name" with Jacob may refer to the importance of the name "Israel" which is given in this *sidra*.

79 The binary opposition recalls the parallel structures of the *rahit* for Gen 25:19.

judged. This poem describes not the sale of Joseph but the drama of his reunion with his brothers. Inspired by this biblical scene of confession and reconciliation, Yannai appends an additional poem to the end of the *qedushah*, which begins: "Woe to us for the Day of Judgment! Woe to us for the Day of Rebuke!" This exclamation—which appears almost verbatim in *GenR* 93:10,[80] but here functions as a refrain in a lengthy and intricate poetic composition—introduces a poem that speculates on the awesome terror that awaits *Israel* in the time to come. In most poems, the poet implicitly identifies with the "hero"—whether that be Noah, Abraham, Jacob, Leah, or Joseph. Here, however, he identifies with Joseph's brothers, the betrayers who sold their brother into slavery. Judah and the others anticipate the fate that awaits the Jews. Joseph, the judge, is the analog to the Judge. "Just as the brothers were not able to answer their brother // on the Day of Judgment, what will we say?" the poet asks in lines 5–6. Yannai laments: "The Living One, when He makes known the truth, how shall we stay standing?...The Lord—when He judges all flesh, our faces will fall" (lines 8 and 10[81]). The poet, typically so hopeful and consoling, here acknowledges that the yearned-for "Day of the Lord" may not be wholly joyful for Israel. By the concluding line, which expresses confidence in a second Ingathering and a restored Temple, anticipation of these events is tinged with rare self-criticism and anxiety.[82]

As a corollary to Yannai's treatment of Esau-Edom-Rome, we should

80 *GenR*, like Yannai, puts these words in the mouths of a later reader reflecting on the Joseph story. The midrash, however, presents the material as narrative, while in the *qedushta*, the congregation and poet *enact* the moment of regret and woe, consistently using the first-person plural form, "we," as opposed to the aggadic text's preference for a more impersonal third person. The *GenR* text states: "'And he wept aloud… and he said to his brothers: I am Joseph, is my father still alive? But his brothers could not answer him' (Gen 45:2). Simeon b. Eleazar quoted in the name of R. Eleazar b. `Azariah what he used to say in the name of Abba Kohen the son of Dalyeh: Woe to us for the day of judgment, woe to us for the day of rebuke! Balaam was the wisest of the heathens, yet he could not withstand his ass's rebuke… Joseph was the youngest of the tribal ancestors, yet his brethren could not withstand his rebuke… How much more then when the Holy One, blessed be He, comes and rebukes each man according to his deserts, as it says, `But I will reprove you, and set the cause before your eyes' (Ps 50:21)!" A shorter form of this tradition can be found in *GenR* 93:11.

81 Reading with MS against Rabinovitz's text. Rabinovitz's text is sustantially less intact than the Maʾagarim version.

82 Yannai's piyyutim for the Sabbaths of Rebuke preceding Tisha bʾAv, of course, depart from the generally positive pattern.

note that just as the Jews are not universally righteous, not all non-Jews are depicted as enemies. Indeed, Esau stands out for his consistent, pervasive villainy. In other cases, however, when Yannai depicts non-Jews, he crafts more complicated portraits. In some cases, this is simply in keeping with the tone of the biblical story—for example, the *qedushta* for Gen 38:1 valorizes the character of the Canaanite Tamar, amplifying her merits while remaining faithful to the biblical text in depicting her risky actions. Somewhat similar, although comparatively less rooted in Scripture, is Yannai's faint praise of the Pharaoh who rescues Joseph from the dungeon. We see this in the first *rahit* (Poem Seven[1]) for Gen 41:1, which seems to put recognition and praise of God in the mouth of Pharaoh. The final lines of the unit describe Pharaoh—if these are Pharaoh's words—as acknowledging God's sovereignty over Egypt and the Nile! If this reading is correct, a humbled Pharaoh assumes a place with Jethro and Rahab as a kind of *ger toshav* ("fellow traveler") or even a *ger tsedek* ("righteous convert").[83]

In the *qedushta* for Gen 9:18, Yannai offers his most intriguing discussion of non-Jews. In the ninth unit (the *qedushah*) Yannai presents all three of Noah's sons in highly favorable lights. Yannai's praise of Shem, the ancestor of the Jews, for his wisdom and learning seems natural; but his praise of Yafet and Ham comes as more of a surprise. Yafet, the ancestor of the Greeks, is praised as the one who translated the Torah "into a chosen tongue" and was "chose[n]... [to] utter honeyed words" (lines 12 and 17). This praise of the Greek language as "chosen" is particularly striking for a poet who composed in Hebrew in a culture where Greek was associated with the dominant culture and its Church. Despite this cultural baggage, Yannai depicts Yafet, in these brief lines, as the father of a beautiful literary tradition—beautiful because it resulted in the translation of the Bible into Greek![84] The cursed son Ham, meanwhile, experiences a redemption in

---

83 It is possible that these lines are merely narration, describing how Pharaoh was humbled. Given Yannai's use of dialogue, however, it is worth considering possibilities other than simple narration. See Cohen, *The Beginnings of Jewishness*, for an excellent and nuanced discussion of conversion in the Jewish tradition, particularly during the Greco-Roman period and Late Antiquity.

84 It may be that Yannai here alludes to the tradition that the Torah was translated into Greek by the proselyte Aquila. Nevertheless, in Yannai's period and place, the Greek translation (the Septuagint) would have been associated with Christianity and unlikely to be used in a synagogue. Translations in the Galilee would have been into Jewish Palestinian Aramaic, not Greek. See Saul Lieberman, *Greek in Jewish Palestine: Studies in the Life and Manners of Jewish Palestine in the II–IV Centuries* C.E. (New York: JTSA, 1942) and his *Hellenism in Jewish Palestine: Studies in the Literary Transmission, Beliefs and Manners of Palestine in*

this final poem, becoming the father of "enlightened ones who cling to the blessed [i.e., Israel]" (line 14), which Yannai clarifies as meaning, "righteous converts, meditating on His name" (line 18). In the biblical narrative, and indeed in the earlier parts of the piyyut, there are clearly two good sons—Shem and Yafet—and one flawed one, Ham. As the poem concludes, however, Yannai praises all three and depicts them as praising God, seeing the potential for good in the ancestor not only of the Jews, but those of the gentiles.

Much remains wholly unknown about Yannai's biography—even where or when precisely he lived—meaning that we can only speculate about his positive views of Greek culture and the Greek translation of the Bible, and about his praise of converts in this piyyut. What is the relationship of these comments to Yannai's cultural reality? Was he, in fact, living in a Greek-speaking or self-identified "Hellenistic" community? In terms of his time, place, body of work, and cultural context, it seems highly unlikely. Had he acquired a respect for the Greek Bible in some version, or at least in theory? It appears so, but we cannot determine what his familiarity with the text may have actually been, or with what text. Could the phrase "honeyed words" be, in reality, a subtle criticism—an implication that the Greeks (i.e., the Christians, who used the Greek Bible?) were superficial and lacked the substance of the sons of Shem, who "expound the fiery law" (line 16)? The question of converts is just as vexing. As early as the Byzantine law codes of the fourth century, we see restrictions on Christians converting to Judaism, which implies that these legal barriers were erected against a real, ongoing practice. Later law codes from Yannai's period (the sixth century) strengthen and specify these prohibitions. Likewise, the accusations of "Judaizing" that appear in the writings of the Church fathers (for example, John Chrysostom, although he addresses a Syrian, not a Galilean, population) suggest that Judaism did, in fact, continue to appeal to gentiles centuries after the rise of Christianity. Recall, however, that "judaizing" need not involve actual conversion (or, for that matter, actual Jews).[85]

---

the I Century B.C.E..–IV Century C.E. (New York: JTSA, 1950); J. T. Barrera, *The Jewish Bible and the Christian Bible: an Introduction to the History of the Bible* (Grand Rapids: Eerdmans, 1998); and Meyers, *The Galilee Through the Centuries.*

85 In addition to the lengthy discussion of "Judaizing" in Cohen's *The Beginnings of Jewishness*, see Kinzig, "'Non-Separation': Closeness and Cooperation between Jews and Christians in the Fourth Century." For the motif of conversion in other *qedushtaʾot*, see the poems of Gen 12:1 and15:1, as well.

Were converts to Judaism a reality in Yannai's community, or more of an abstraction, a rhetorical trope—an historically and textually grounded ideal? Again, we cannot know for certain, but this specific poem offers another piece of evidence from which a larger and more complex picture can be assembled.

What can we conclude from this brief survey of non-Jewish figures in Yannai's poems for Genesis? Yannai's polemic against Rome in his Genesis *qedushtaʾot*—particularly against its political dominion, although elsewhere against its Christianity—is unparalleled. Esau– Edom–Rome is *the* foe, and Yannai clearly relishes contemplating its demise, using every tool at his disposal—potent allusion, clever pun, intense rhetorical tropes, and divine ideals of justice—effectively to curse it. By emphasizing Rome's destined demise, Yannai consoles his community and shores up their endurance, reminding them that the present state of disempowerment and alienation will not last forever. We have seen that Yannai's complaint against Esau is pervasive. It appears before Esau does in the Genesis story and remains in the piyyutim long after he disappears from the biblical narrative. Yannai's crafting of Esau's character is colorful and vivid: Esau is a boar, a boor, a flame to be quenched, a bully, a suitor who makes his intended weep, a usurper to be deposed.

Fairly consistently, Jacob-Israel is presented as Esau's foil—as one falls, the other rises. When describing Rome's comeuppance, Yannai's glee takes on an apocalyptic vigor. His language and imagery may seem, to modern ears, inappropriately violent for the synagogue, but upon consideration they echo and amplify the visions of the biblical writers, particularly those who often provide the *haftarot* (Obadiah, Daniel, and Zechariah). Even when Yannai innovates, he offers us a window into the fantasies and hopes of his congregation. Importantly, however, he does not go so far as to encourage revolt. Responsibility for redemption, beginning with the toppling of the evil Empire, lies with God (and perhaps the Messiah, although Yannai does not dwell overmuch on messianism); Israel must wait it out. Yannai may dream of Rome burning, but he is not a firebrand. Furthermore, our poet does not conflate anti-Roman sentiment with anti-Gentile sentiment. Perhaps influenced by the possibilities for conversion to Judaism in his period, or perhaps simply influenced by the popularity of Deutero-Isaiah in his lectionary, he anticipates quite positively the day when “all will be one” (except Rome), and the nations (except Rome) will come to know the universal Jewish God. He does not anticipate a peaceful transition to such an age, but he expresses every confidence in its arrival—perhaps even thinking, or hoping, that the new era would be dawning soon.

In many cases, as the notes and commentaries to the individual poems indicate, Yannai's visions and interpretation resonate with established scriptural and aggadic tradition—little of what he hopes for falls outside of mainstream Jewish theology. And yet, his works differ from Second Temple apocalyptic writings and rabbinic fantasies of revenge against Rome, precisely because they are poetry and they are liturgical. As a synagogue poet, Yannai spoke not only for himself but for his community; these are fundamentally exoteric, public, popular texts, not sectarian or deeply cryptic. And while individual motifs and themes may echo aggadic writings from his period or earlier, poetic rhetoric presents them with a vividness, directness, and intensity more reminiscent of the biblical Prophets than of any prose text. The fate of Rome inspired intense anger and yearnings, and poetry provided Yannai a medium equal to the task of conveying rich and complex emotions. He was not simply a conduit of existing traditions, but one who actively shaped interpretations; in terms of form, content, and context, his works stand apart. One does not say "Amen" to midrash.

Yannai's Women[86]

Genesis is a populous book; major figures—Noah, Abraham, Jacob, Joseph, and others—accumulate almost too rapidly to count. We have seen how Yannai used two biblical actors—God and Esau—to address contemporary issues. Likewise, Yannai's depictions of two female figures—Zion and Leah—have been important in the discussion of other themes. In the *qedushta* for Gen 16:1, Yannai merged the characters of Zion and Sarah to represent barrenness redeemed, while Leah embodied the *pathos* and hope of the people Israel in the *qedushta* for Gen 29:31. Yannai's poetry, directly reflecting the wealth of female characters in the book of Genesis, offers a number of distinctive portrayals of women. To be sure, there are lacunae because of gaps in surviving manuscripts (e.g., we have no *qedushta* for Gen 2–3, where we might expect Eve to appear) or because Yannai simply

86 The following essay is a purely literary analysis; on the historical reality of women in the ancient synagogue, such as scholars have been able to reconstruct, see the convenient summary in Levine, *The Ancient Synagogue*, 499–518.

chose to focus on another character (e.g., the absence of Dinah from the *qedushta* for Gen 35, which deals explicitly with Jacob in Shechem). Yannai seems to have had little interest in the "wicked women" of Genesis.[87] Hagar plays a minimal role in the piyyut for Gen 16:1—less than her role in the biblical narrative, particularly when her role in Gen 21 is considered as well.[88] Potiphar's wife, meanwhile, makes only a cameo appearance in the poem for Gen 38:1, where she provides a foil for Tamar. In general, Yannai does not seek out pretexts for expanding the roles of minor female characters (such as Noah's wife) or for amplifying the roles of important women disproportionately (Sarah remains secondary to Abraham). Nevertheless, the strikingly feminine cast of the Genesis source material offers a chance to examine how Yannai drew upon and developed female imagery, both in the context of characters who are women and characters who—for reasons to be considered—take on feminine traits.

Many, if not most, female characters in the Bible play minor roles, and by and large they remain equally undeveloped in Yannai's works. For example, the wives of Noah and his sons are mentioned with equal brevity in Scripture and piyyut—in the context of the men's celibacy aboard the Ark in the *qedushta* for Gen 8:15.[89] The apparent passivity of the women in the poem reminds us that the commands for abstention from and resumption of conjugal relations, encoded in the Bible, are directed towards the men: "Enter, you and your sons" (Gen 6:8) and "Go forth, you and your wife" (Gen 8:15; both are cited in the second stanza of the *asiriyyah,* Poem Five).

---

87 This should not be extended too far; for example, see Yannai's treatment of Cozbi in his piyyut for Num 25:10 and the women of Midian in the poem for Num 25:1, as well as his treatment of the suspected adulteress in his poem for Num 5:11.

88 Hasty conclusions should be avoided, however. Hagar's apparent absence may be due to *lacunae* in the preserved material; we lack *qedushta'ot* for Gen 21 or Gen 22, where her character may have been more prominent.

89 *Midrashim* note the same textual issues as inspired Yannai, with the same biases. *GenR* 31:12 states, "Rabbi Judah son of Rabbi Simon and Rabbi Hanan in the name of Rabbi Samuel son of Rabbi Isaac said: As soon as Noah entered the Ark, cohabitation was interdicted to him… When he went out, He permitted it to him." Similarly, *PRE* 23 states: "Rabbi Levitas, a man of Yavneh, said: He separated the males from the females of all who came into the Ark when they came into the ark… Indeed, the males were on one side and the females on the other. When they went forth from the Ark, He caused the males to be joined with the females…. Indeed, a man would go forth with his wife. He blessed them that they might increase and multiply on the earth." On the topic of women in midrashic sources—a complicated subject made more so by the vast and intricate nature of the sources—see in particular J. Baskin, *Midrashic Women: Formations of the Feminine in Rabbinic Literature* (Hanover/London: University Press of New England, 2002).

Yannai neither develops the women's perspective on the command for abstinence nor praises them (as he praises Noah) for their participation in fulfilling it. Modern readers might find such topics worthy of "creative midrash," but Yannai did not take advantage of this particular opening. Similarly, in the *qedushta* for Gen 38:1, the character of Tamar is presented in a positive light, in keeping with her depiction in the Bible. However, the poet's focus is on Judah. Tamar's role is somewhat amplified, but not altered, and if anything, her role in the story (in the fragment of the *qedushta* that remains) is diminished somewhat, in order to make greater space for consideration of *Judah's* transformation.

Three of the four matriarchs, however—Sarah, Leah, and Rachel—do receive extensive treatment at Yannai's hand.[90] There is a *qedushta* devoted to each, reflecting her prominence in the biblical narratives and perhaps also in contemporary national consciousness. To be sure, the male characters get more attention, but Yannai's treatment of these three matriarchs remains noteworthy. In particular, while all of his poeticized accounts of the matriarchs resemble attested midrashic and aggadic expansions of their characters, in these piyyutim, the matriarchs are not fragmented, anthological, sporadically developed creations, but round and vivid characters with a distinct integrity all their own and character traits that reinforce important values for his community.

The *qedushta* for Gen 16:1, on Sarah, is the most complete of the matriarch poems (the first seven units have survived).[91] A particularly appealing aspect of Sarah's character, as developed by Yannai, is her active voice. While many of the individual motifs, tropes, and allusions in the poem

90 There are, unfortunately, gaps in Yannai's surviving corpus; of the poems where Rebecca might be expected to play a prominent role, only the very end (the *rahit*, *silluq*, and *qedushah*) to the *qedushta* for Gen 25:19 survives, and less than half of the poem for Gen 27:28. In the fragment of the *qedushta* for Gen 27:28, it is striking that Rebecca's role in the deception of Isaac is not mentioned except, perhaps, through the use of a passive verb in Poem Five, line 2. This could be because the passages where she is mentioned are lost, or because the poet chose to emphasize the patriarch's role and responsibility.

91 For a treatment of this poem—and Yannai's *qedushta* to Gen 15:1, too—from the perspective of gender theory and in the context of both rabbinic and Christian writings about women, see the gem of an article by Münz-Manor, "All About Sarah." This essay indicates the rich material latent within Yannai's piyyutim. Münz-Manor, building on the pioneering work of Susan Ashbrook Harvey, notes that the voice Yannai gives to Sarah resembles the prominence given to women's voices in Syriac hymnography (where women participated in the performance of liturgical poems—a practice unlikely to have in place in the synagogue). See Susan Ashbrook Harvey, "Spoken Words, Voiced Silence: Biblical Women in Syriac Tradition."

indicate Yannai's use of traditional interpretations, the composite that emerges is distinctive and full—rather than being a mosaic of interpretations as one would find in an anthology such as *Genesis Rabbah*, Yannai's Sarah is a round and complicated character by authorial design.[92] In the very first poem, we are told, "She cried out and knocked upon the latches of the lock" (line 7)—rebelling against her status as "a garden locked," an image from Song 4:12 applied to Sarah in line 5 of the *magen* (Poem One) that Yannai transforms into a metaphor for infertility rather than purity. She is not meek and passive, but forthright and forthcoming, and Yannai portrays these as very favorable characteristics.

Interestingly, Abraham's voice in the poem is subdued, while Sarah is given lines of great force, such was when she alludes to Eccl 3:2, stating: "'There is a time for bearing' // but I have been kept from bearing!" (Poem Two, lines 11–12).[93] But while with Abraham she is assertive and in charge, her internal voice is layered with despair, anger, and profound piety. As Yannai shapes her character, she is righteous and innocent but not excessively patient—a genuinely conflicted human personality. The *rahit* (Poem Seven), entirely in Sarah's voice, articulates a litany of woes—not conceived of on the national scale but presented as the tangible, believable complaint of a woman who cannot bear. Throughout the *qedushta*, Sarah pleads and petitions on her own behalf, often turning standard verse interpretations on their heads: "Like a bundle of myrrh He binds me" she exclaims (Poem Six, line 28), alluding to Song 1:13. This phrase may mean that Sarah has willingly suffered for the sake of God (as in *SongsR*, where this verse, tellingly, is applied to Abraham), but it could also describe the bitter irony Sarah experiences: she has been chosen by God, on the one hand, but "bound up" (rendered barren) by the very same God. Abraham's voice, by contrast, is remarkably muted, even more than in the biblical story, and Hagar is also sidelined. Sarah stands at center stage.

In general—whether one is looking at the Bible, midrash, or Yannai's piyyutim—Sarah is eclipsed by her spouse. In the poem for Gen 16:1, however, Yannai draws from both the biblical text and rabbinic modes of interpretation to emphasize elements of parity between them: both had faith, both wandered, both proselytized, both were tested, both had their

92 While the annotations in the translations cannot indicate every intertextual reference, biblical citation, or allusion to midrash, they indicate the major instances of overlap and suggest the complexity of the material.

93 This is a terrific example of "writing with Scripture." See Chapter Two.

names changed and their sins forgiven, and both were promised children. The poet acknowledges, however, that God did not treat them equally: God "yearned for their prayer" (Poem Five, line 11) but afflicted only Sarah; God promised them both offspring, but spoke only to Abraham—Sarah "had not been given word" (Poem Five, line 21). The divine logic will not win over modern readers, although midrashic parallels indicate that it was evidently popular with the Rabbis: in piyyut as in midrash, God kept Sarah barren and then denied her revelation in order to keep her from becoming haughty towards Abraham (alluding, perhaps, to Hagar's behavior, which is in keeping with this stereotype) or, as stated in a later poem, because He wished to hear her voice raised in prayer.[94] In the end, the birth of Isaac is presented as a gift to Sarah, compensation for "her abuse" (Poem Six, line 43). In context, "abuse" seems to refer to Hagar's mockery of Sarah—"`She heard her maid's taunt but kept silent // `Where is your righteous reward?'—thus her soul she [Hagar] oppressed" (Poem Six, line 21; the final stanza employs the root of the name Isaac, as foreshadowing). But seen as part of the poem as a whole, "her abuse" could refer to all of Sarah's suffering , which Sarah accepted and endured as part of her life with Abraham.[95]

In short, Yannai depicts Sarah as both strong and sympathetic. Rather than being undermined by any latent and explicit allegorical implications, her character imbues her allegorical extension with greater depth and pathos. When Yannai translates Sarah's barrenness into a metaphor for her heirs' dispossession and alienation (discussed below), he seems to have given a tremendous amount of thought to the individual, emotional cost of infertility as experienced by Sarah as a woman. Her character is some-

---

94 The *asiriyyah* (Poem Five), line 6 posits the anti-haughtiness interpretation; Poem Six, line 2 forwards the pleasing-voice hypothesis. These interpretations recall a variety of *midrashim*: see *SongR* 2:41, "Rabbi Azariah said in the name of Rabbi Hanina ben Papa: Why were the matriarchs so long childless? In order that they should not put on airs towards their husbands on account of their beauty." Also, *GenR* 45:4, "Why were the matriarchs so long childless?...Rabbi Azariah said in Rabbi Hanina's name: So that they might lean on their husbands in [spite of] their beauty." And finally, *SongR* 2:41, which states, "Rabbi Levi in the name of Rabbi Shila from Kfar Temarta and Rabbi Ḥelbo in the name of Rabbi Yoḥanan said: Why were the matriarchs so long barren? Because the Holy One, blessed be He, longed to hear their prayer. He said to them: `My dove, I will tell you why I have kept you childless; because I was longing to hear your prayer.' Hence it says, `For sweet is your voice, and your countenance is comely' (Song 2:14)." For this final interpretation, see also *GenR* 45:4.

95 In *SongR* 2:35, 8:18, *ExodR* 21:5 and elsewhere, the Rabbis present a reading in which God afflicts Israel in order to drive them to prayer—the same pattern displayed here with respect to Sarah.

what "improved" from the biblical version—the pettiness and insecurity that are evident in Sarah's dealings with Hagar are largely absent or even negated. Most of all, however, she is not simplified. Bold and determined, she is nevertheless able to surrender her fate to God. Yannai raises her up to be Abraham's equal; their marriage is one of mutual love, respect, and fidelity. Sarah is, in the end, as important to God's plan as any of the patriarchs, and Yannai depicts her as a worthy mother of Israel—an ancestor both realistic and idealized. Read with his depictions of Abraham, Yannai's listeners would come to understand that they inherited strength and integrity from both sides of the family tree.

The poems embellishing the lives of Leah and Rachel have not, unfortunately, survived in as intact a state as the *qedushta* for Gen 16. Hence we cannot ascertain as clearly how Yannai developed the characters of Jacob's wives. Nevertheless, despite the incomplete texts, interesting details and patterns emerge. Both sisters are depicted as active, like Sarah, and in a way, figures of both hope and pathos. Rachel's character may seem, at first, the most negative of the matriarchs—in spite of her generally positive depiction in Scripture as the beloved, beautiful wife of Jacob and mother of Joseph. For example, Rachel's assertion from Gen 30:1 "Give me children or else I am dead" becomes in Yannai's words the melodramatic, "Rachel was willing to die to provide her husband heirs" (*qedushta* to Gen 30:22, Poem Five, line 10).[96] It is true that in the rabbinic context Rachel's willingness to die so that her husband could have an heir could be (and was) read positively.[97] That said, Yannai does not gloss over the roughness of Rachel's character in the biblical text or downplay her jealousy: "Against her own sister, she felt harsh envy // indeed, envy is as harsh as Hell" (Poem Six, lines 3–4). His depiction is in keeping with Gen 30:1, which states simply that "Rachel envied her sister." The quotation from Song 8:6 ("envy is as harsh as Sheol [=hell]"), however, offers insight into the unpleasant emotional experience of such jealousy. Rachel lived the hell she wished upon her sister.

Yannai transforms potentially petty jealousy into deep sorrow and profound suffering, and he encourages his audience (whether all male or mixed) to identify with Rachel's wrenching grief.[98] As Yannai describes her,

---

96 This dramatic statement follows a catalogue of those who are dead while alive (the blind, the leper, the poor, and the childless). Rachel prefers physical to existential death.

97 See, for example, *GenR* 71:7.

98 Yannai's description is more sympathetic, and realistic, than the tradition preserved

she is brokenhearted and bereft, and the poetry richly and eloquently voices her range of feelings. Furthermore, when Rachel demands, "Give me sons!" (Poem Six, line 13, quoting Gen 30:1), Yannai does not include Jacob's angry reply but rather skips ahead, in the very next stanza, to the image of Rachel as a mother of not only a child, but of children: "She clutched to her bosom her sons" (Poem Six, line 15)—this despite the fact that in the biblical story Rachel dies embittered in the wake of Benjamin's birth. Yannai here focuses on her joy and reward (perhaps influenced by the allegorical reading of Rachel in Jer 31:14–15). Her petition is answered, but her dealings are not with Jacob but with God.

The *rahit* (Poem Seven) that follows this poem is an extended description of how God answered her plea—implying, perhaps, that her cry "Give me sons!" was not addressed to Jacob at all but to God, the source of her hope and new life. The remainder of the *rahit* focuses on God (the second *rahit* embellishes His attributes, while the *qedushah* (Poem Nine) focuses on His power over the natural world) rather than Rachel. But the quick sketches of her, preserved in the *asiriyyah* (Poem Five) and in Poem Six, reveal a Rachel enriched in terms of emotion and complexity but spared rebuke, both by the poet and by her spouse.

The figure of Rachel is never overpowered by explicit allegory. She remains distinctive and truly individual. And yet, implicitly, she becomes a representation of Yannai's contemporary community, and the matriarch's strength in the past bodes well for the redemption of her children in the future.

An even more *pathos*-laden figure than Rachel is her sister, Leah, whose character Yannai develops with particular sensitivity in his *qedushta* for Gen 29:31. Leah lacks the self-confident gumption of Sarah or the impatient anger of Rachel. Yannai never depicts her as asserting herself, either with her husband, who hated her, or with the other women, who slandered her. Leah seems to have been born on the cusp of defeat, and her only audiences are God and, as if eavesdropping, Yannai's liturgical community. In Leah, Yannai crafts a portrait of loneliness verging on despair. However, by granting her a profound rapport with the divine, the poet lets us see a powerful and complex dissonance between her external appearance—emotionally desolate, bereft of love if not sons—and her clear and blessed (if inadequately so) interior. Yannai's sensitivity to Leah's emotional world is touching. His presentation of her loneliness is stark, bare, and forceful. Even in the opening stanza he conjures up both her sense of isolation and the unlikely—and perhaps not wholly sensed—consolation of divine attention:

> Your might, O awesome One, is in the heavens // but You watch over all who set foot upon the streets
> Obvious to You is the love of the lovable // but the hated, the oppressed You seek out (Poem One, lines 1–4)

As the opening phrase tells us, God resides "far away," and for a brief moment, Yannai opens a gulf between the deity and humanity. One might think Him as remote, distant, and uncaring. But in this poem, the reverse is true: despite the distance, God pays attention to everyone, and rather than letting obvious things—like Jacob's love for Rachel—distract Him, He seeks out those who are easiest to overlook, the oppressed and unloved.

Fearful of a terrible fate (marriage to Esau who, unlike Leah, deserves to be hated), Leah cannot look to anyone other than God for help, and God—tender, caring, and attentive—to her joy, answers her prayers. His resolution to her problems may not seem perfect, but the poet must respect the boundaries of Scripture. Leah remains unloved by her husband (as Gen 29:30 tells us, "Jacob loved Rachel more than Leah"), but he honors her, and she bears him many sons, who bring them both respect. In the end, Yannai presents Leah's lifelong "romance" as being not with a human companion but with God. She sought a husband who would please *God*, she sought *God's* love, and rejoiced in the signs that *God* loved her. To others, she may have appeared to be hated (as the opening verse of the Torah portion states), but Leah (like the poet) knew better. For Leah—as for Israel—appearances of neglect can be misleading. There are deeper truths, and truer loves, at work in history. And subtly, but insistently, Yannai identifies the suffering of his own community—their appearance of being unloved and rejected—with that of Leah. When he reveals the deeper truths about her status as beloved by God, the more profound message is to his community: they are loved by God, despite all appearances and rumors to the contrary.

Looking beyond feminine characters, we should consider characters with feminine traits. As noted before, Abraham plays a "feminized" role in

---

in *GenR* 71:6, which states that Rachel envied Leah's good deeds. The midrash displays discomfort with Rachel's jealousy that Yannai apparently did not share.

the *qedushta* for Gen 12:1.[99] While the patriarch remains grammatically masculine throughout, much of the language used in the piyyut comes from the Song of Songs and Ps 45, where Abraham is cast as the female lover in the unfolding drama. Using this conceit, Yannai manipulates conventions of romance to create a specific tone for the story of Abraham's call (and response). By characterizing him as the ingénue, the relationship between God and patriarch acquires overtones of love, even *eros*—not simply command and obedience. God does not direct Abraham to go, as might appear from the biblical order, "Go forth" (Gen 12:1); He seduces him, woos him, courts him. God *desires* Abraham, and the poet's portrait of Abraham makes him eminently desirable: he is radiant, charming, and pure, as well as wise and bold. Yannai depicts him as he appears to God; we see him from the perspective of the smitten deity, and the promises we hear are those of a love-struck suitor who bestows gift after gift (blessing after blessing) upon the object of His desire.

In the *qedushta* for Gen 29:31, we gained insight into a person's love for God. Here we gain insight into God's love for a person. Both are profoundly intimate portraits, and the poet does not come out and say that this is what he is doing. He may not have consciously construed the relationship as he wrote. But this sense of intimacy with the divine—a mutual, reciprocal romance—is one of Yannai's gifts to his audience. He has overheard something wonderful, he implies, and he'll let his listeners in on it, too.[100]

A final type of feminine figure—perhaps the key figure in Yannai's writing—merits attention here: "the allegorical woman." Yannai's allegorical female characters have roots in the Bible, particularly in the figures of Wisdom and Folly (as in Prov 1–9) and Zion (in Hosea and Jeremiah, particularly). In Yannai's Genesis *qedushta*ʾ*ot*, Zion, representing both the Land and the people, is the most common allegorical woman—as, for

99 This section suggests but does not exhaust the complicated way Yannai constructs gender in his piyyutim. In his essay "All About Sarah: Questions of Gender in Yannai's Poems on Sarah's (and Abraham's) Barrenness," Ophir Münz-Manor explores the importance of construing Abraham as "barren"—a term usual reserved for female infertility—in Yannai's *qedushta* for Gen 15:1.

100 Again, many of the specific motifs and allusions in Yannai's text are—as noted in previous chapters—in keeping with midrashic readings of the patriarch. The rhetorical effect of presenting these ideas in performed poetry, rather than in the form of text-explication, should not be underestimated. The poetry creates a sense of immediacy and uses the language of *eros* and intimacy that is not softened by the process of exegesis.

example, in the *meshallesh* (Poem Three) for Gen 16:1, where Sarah's predicament offers an analog to that of Zion: barren, both are destined for motherhood.[101] Similarly, "the Land" in Poem Six for Gen 31:3 takes on maternal and spousal qualities, nourishing and sustaining her people Israel. She is fertile and luxuriant, beautiful and desirable, yielding and giving. There is an explicit eroticism to the poem—"Your claim upon her will not expire // no strange land shall be your bower" (Poem Six, lines 35–36)—and tones of jealousy, as well (others have laid claim to her love, but Israel knows she will be faithful). This language of sensual yearning tinges the more general desire for the Land, described above. It teaches in a vivid, almost non-intellectual way how and why the Land is important. Yannai uses the images of womanhood—often strong, sometimes anxious, but importantly *never victimized*—to convey complex emotions about a people and a place.

Once again, the piyyut focusing on Leah (the *qedushta* for 29:31) provides an instructive illustration of this phenomenon, as Yannai's sensitive depiction of the (seemingly) tragic matriarch grows out of his sensitivity to his people's own plight. In Poem Four, which opens "Our eyes are weak from our longing," it is clear that Leah *is* Israel, not in the realm of simile but as metaphor. The two identities collapse together and merge. Leah's condition—downtrodden, apparently unloved, alone in the world—becomes a mirror of Israel's own situation. Israel, like Leah, may seem to be lost, hated, and fated to suffer, but like Leah, Israel knows better. *Israel is loved.* God is paying attention and listening, and God will act. Like Leah, Israel wants to be loved by God, to do what God desires—and, in a way, create in God the same response that Abraham aroused in Him back in Gen 12. The pathos and hope ascribed to Leah provide a way of describing, in simple allegorical terms, the *pathos* and hope of being a Jew in the Byzantine world.

Yannai is hardly the first to characterize Israel (the Land and the people) as a woman, of course. We find both metaphors in Scripture itself and also—by means of a potent and formative allegory—in the Song of Songs.[102] Other writers, from the aggadic exegetes centuries before Yannai

101 As Münz-Manor points out in his article on Sarah's barrenness (cited above), the identification of Sarah with Zion is implicit in Isa 54:1, including the exact language used in the *meshallesh* for Yannai's *qedushta* to Gen 16:1.

102 Tikva Frymer-Kensky explores the idea that in the Bible, Israel identifies with feminine characters rather than masculine characters. See her seminal volume *In the Wake of*

to the poets and mystics of the centuries after him, found in the vocabulary of love a powerful shorthand for conveying the complex emotional and existential bond of the covenant. But Yannai, writing for the synagogue liturgy, makes particularly important and powerful use of this metaphor, and the social location of his poetry in the synagogue influences how we evaluate their importance. With a sensitivity and attentiveness that may surprise some readers, Yannai writes with tremendous feeling about biblical marriages. Abraham's love for Sarah and Jacob's love for Rachel embody the love and yearning, the mutual chosenness, that Yannai sees in Israel's relationship with God. In his piyyutim those feminine characters also embody a combination of vulnerability and strength, cleverness and motivation, a unique *pathos* but also singular charm.

Yannai was not writing to improve or change the lot of the women of his day, but his creation of feminine and feminized characters—nuanced and complex, appreciative of wisdom and aware of their humanity—displays both sensitivity and appreciation. Yannai neither sexualizes nor essentializes women in these poems, as is the common trend in Hellenistic Jewish writings and much of rabbinic literature. Given the public setting of his works, this difference deserves further study. If there were women in his congregation, he presented them not with role models so much as true characters. Even more strikingly, Yannai created female characters whom his presumably mostly (or even exclusively) *male* audience could both identify with and yearn for. In these figures of women (both human and allegorical), Yannai finds a vehicle for his story of hope and his message of consolation. Sarah, Leah, Rachel, Zion and Israel may all seem weak and disadvantaged, vulnerable and easily oppressed, but in these stories about women, Yannai finds meaning for everyone.

---

the Goddesses: Women, Culture, and the Biblical Transformation of Pagan Myth (New York: Fawcett Columbine, 1992). For a more general, theory-based discussion of this topic, see also Daniel Boyarin, *Unheroic Conduct: the Rise of Heterosexuality and the Invention of the Jewish Man* (Berkeley: University of California Press, 1997).

Conclusion

Directions Forward

Many brave men lived before Agamemnon;
but all are overwhelmed in eternal night, unwept, unknown,
because they lack a sacred poet.
Horace, *Odes*

The study of piyyut has, for too long, been a closed field. Barriers existed because of both language and content. Not only do the poems require mastery of a difficult idiom of Hebrew, but the scholarly literature has also been written primarily in Hebrew. Moreover, comprehensive study of piyyut requires engagement with a variety of disciplines, from literature and liturgy to archaeology and art. The reasons for undertaking such a complicated endeavor have not yet been thoroughly articulated. What, precisely, makes these obscure poems worth the massive efforts required to understand and appreciate them?

The essays and translations in this book attempt to answer this question by highlighting not only the richness of the texts themselves but the array of innovative ways they can be studied. In doing so many further questions emerge. What is the nature of the payyetanic idiom? Was its Hebrew a "Classical" language or a living dialect? Does payyetanic Hebrew have its own grammar or is it a variation of rabbinic Hebrew? What are the origins of the piyyut genre as a whole, and the *qedushta* in particular? Particularly in its pre-Classical and Classical form, what is piyyut's relationship to Qumranic poetry and other forms of Hebrew writing in Late Antiquity? How does piyyut intersect with the visual art of the synagogue? What are the possible connections between Byzantine Jewish poetic traditions and those of the early Church?

Based on the textual evidence alone, piyyutim appear *sui generis* in the third or fourth century. While they resemble the poetry of the nascent Church, the parallels are not decisive, and arguments in favor of origins within rabbinic modes of rhetoric cannot be dismissed. More specifically, Yannai is the earliest known poet to compose *qedushtaʾot.* Yet such a complex form hardly seems likely to have arisen spontaneously. Even the relationship between Yannai's *qedushtaʾot* and the earlier forms of piyyut, such as the *Avodah* poems, remain uncertain.

Within the Jewish cultural world, the knotty relationship of piyyut to the closely related genres of targum and midrash, while long the object of interest, is also just now coming into its own. The resonance between Yannai's intertexts and the *petiḥta* verses in *Genesis Rabbah* and the *Tanḥumah* traditions, for instance, are particularly suggestive of the complicated relationship between midrash and piyyut. Likewise, Yannai's resonances with specific rabbinic texts—*Genesis Rabbah, Tanḥuma, Pesiqta deRav Kehanah, Pirqe deRabbi Eliezer,* and the Palestinian Talmud, among others—indicate the fluidity and creativity of textual interpretation in the Land of Israel in Late Antiqutiy but raise questions about how the familiar prose texts came into existence and when this process took place.

At the same time, Yannai's creativity as an exegete exemplifies the innovative role of piyyut in the context of more familiar genres of writing. While his themes and motifs may strongly echo well-known prose texts, his works are not merely poeticized midrash. Even more intriguing are the possible connections between piyyut and the early rabbinic mystical traditions. While the piyyutim (particularly the early works) are rarely overtly "mystical," deep formal and thematic similarities between piyyut and some of the Hekhalot texts suggest common concerns, and possibly shared origins.

These questions in turn raise issues concerning the Jewish culture in Late Antiquity. In many of these texts, traces of literatures, rites, and Temple rituals can be detected, even as resonances with sectarian writings (particularly Qumran) complicate the picture. Tangled up in these historical issues are questions about the make-up of Jewish society and, more specifically, the synagogue in the Byzantine period—issues of priestly and rabbinic models of leadership, the relationship between the House of Study and the House of Prayer, the constituencies of the early synagogues, and the relationship between piyyut and other forms of synagogue expression—such as mosaic art and inscriptions. These questions about the place of piyyut in the world of the early synagogue inherently lead to questions about the place of the synagogue in Byzantine Roman society, and the potential contexts for understanding piyyutim widen further and further, until these poems become stones in the complex mosaic of Late Antique society as a whole.

At the same time, a study of piyyut can also focus inwards. The piyyut merit study not only because of their place in the culture and society of Late Antiquity, but as prayer and works of art. Throughout this study, Yannai's creativity as an artist, prayer leader, and exegete have been emphasized, even while connections to other forms of art and expression have been delineated. As a major genre of Hebrew writing, piyyutim would profit from being approached within the context of literary studies and comparative literature. They may be more obscure and difficult than the lyrics of Andalusia, but they are not lesser works, either in aesthetics or importance.

Finally, as this study demonstrates, ample opportunities for both synchronic and diachronic study of piyyut remain: studies of specific poets and specific types of piyyutim. To be sure, many such works have been written already—primarily in Hebrew. This volume, however, along with Swartz and Yahalom's edition of *Avodah* poetry, indicate the value of such works being undertaken in English and with translations. This study examined only a small selection of works; numerous other texts, poets, and genres of piyyut await similar attention. Genre studies, meanwhile, paint a more complex picture of change over time. In particular, piyyutim form a bridge between Jewish culture in Late Antiquity and that of medieval Ashkenaz, via Byzantine Italy. Studies of particular genres could illuminate details of this vast but obscure process of cultural transmission, continuity, and change.

This book, then, closes as it began: with an invitation. It is an invitation to scholars, whether already familiar with piyyutim or able to access them through the tools of related fields, to approach these beautiful and neglected texts using all the tools of their own disciplines. It is an encouragement to those in cognate areas of study (liturgical studies within Judaism and Christianity; rabbinic literature and targumic studies; the early synagogue and its art; Byzantine Christian culture and society; the history of biblical interpretation; comparative literature, and others) to engage with the piyyutim and bring them out into the larger conversation. The recovery of a vast "new" body of writing is a rare thing in the modern world—like the Dead Sea Scrolls, these treasures from the Cairo Genizah have energized the scholarly world with their intellectual equivalent of *terra incognita.* The piyyutim are poised to be rediscovered by those who knew them but did not really see them, and discovered for the first time by the majority who never knew they existed.

Yannai's works were composed for an audience; they come to life through engagement with a listener, or a reader. Their complicated rhetoric suggests that in the ancient synagogue, these works appealed to their audiences by working at a variety of registers, and the same is true today. Through these poems, we are offered access into a new world, or a new way of looking at a familiar one. Yannai's is a strong, singular voice speaking across the millennia, and his words invite all who hear them to listen.

Part Two

Yannai's *Qedushtaʾot* Embellishing Genesis

Qedushta to Genesis 1:1 בראשית א:א

"In the beginning God created..." בראשית ברא אלהים

This text is as damaged as it is tantalizing. The fragment of Poem Six retells in poetic form the story of creation which culminates with the creation of humanity in the image of the angels. The *rahit*, though badly damaged, draws parallels between the creation of the heavens and the earth. The lengthy *silluq* depicts the grandest elements of creation: the Zodiac, Leviathan, and Behemoth. These dramatic images form a backdrop to the drama of Adam's sin and redemption on the eve of the seventh day.[1] In the *qedushah*, all creation joins together with the angels in declaring God's holiness.

1 Poem Six and the *rahit* are present in the Maʾagarim text. Authorship of the *silluq* (Poem Eight), below, is uncertain. The Maʾagarim database identifies the *silluq* as part of an anonymous "*qedushta* for *Bereshit*." However, because this unit appears in the Rabinovitz volume, which remains the standard critical edition, and because of its zodiac imagery which is important in terms of the synagogue context of piyyut, I have chosen to include it (using the Maʾagarim text) here.

(6) …
"Let there be light"—just as You uttered
… water
to be a firmament amid the waters
…You built it with water[2]
And there was a firmament and the waters
…wisdom You spoke
and water to one side You moved
The beauty of the face of the earth You bared
and from it, green growth You made [sprout]
You complete lights and lamps
windows[3] of the heavens during the day making light
Night to be brightened
by the host of stars and planets[4]
Within the waters, swarming things You made swarm
many proud species You made[5]
Falcons[6] and raptors You gave wings to fly
from shallows You made water take flight
Speech – as You spoke it came to pass
and the earth writhed like an animal[7]
Dust to bring forth living beings
cattle and creeping things and all animals
You gathered (Your host): "Let Us make man"[8]
According to their likeness is the likeness of man[9]
They cried out: Why are You mindful of man[10]
when man does not abide with honor?[11]
You plucked[12] dust from the earth
with its body being of the earth
…to the angels on high You made it bear semblance
though she would sin and he resemble nothing[13]
In six days You completed all

---

2 See Ps 104:3.

3 A poetic term; see Jud 5:28 and Prov 7:6.

4 From Job 38:32, perhaps meaning "planets" (מזלות), as it is taken here, or referring to a specific constellation or cluster of constellations.

5 Job 28:8 mentions בני שחץ, perhaps referring to big game animals but here indicating the large sea animals (Gen 1:21).

6 Job 39:13

7 Ps 90:2

(ו)

...

וַיְהִי אוֹר כַּאֲשֶׁר בִּטֵיתָה

זע.. ... מַיִם

הֱיוֹת רָקִיעַ בְּתוֹךְ הַמַּיִם

... ..קֵירֵיתָה בַּמַּיִם

הָיָה רָקִיעַ בְּתוֹךְ הַמַּיִם

... ..חָוכְמָה הִיסַחְתָּה

וּמַיִם לְצַד אֶחָד הִיסַעְתָּה

יוֹפִי פְּנֵי גֵיא הִיחְסַפְתָּה

וּמֶנָּה צְמָחִים ה..בתה

כִּילַּלְתָּה אוֹר וּמְאוֹרוֹת

אֶשְׁנְבֵי שָׁמַיִם בַּיּוֹם מְאִירוֹת

לַיְלָה לִהְיוֹת מַזְהִירוֹת

צְבָא כּוֹכָבִים וּמַזָּרוֹת

מִמַּיִם שֶׁרֶץ הִשְׁרַצְתָּה

וְרוֹב מִינִים הִישְׁתַחְצְתָּה

נוֹצָה וְאֶבְרָה הֵיעֲפַפְתָּה

מֵרַקַק מַיִם הֵיעַפְתָּה

סִיחַ עַד לֹא סַחְתָּה הָיָה

וַתְּחוֹלֵל אֶרֶץ כְּמוֹ חַיָּה

עָפָר לְהוֹצִיא נֶפֶשׁ חַיָּה

בְּהֵימָה וָרֶמֶשׂ וְכָל חַיָּה

פִּיקַּדְתָּה נַעֲשֶׂה אָדָם

בִּדְמוּת פְּנֵיהֶם פְּנֵי אָדָם

צָעֲקוּ מַה תִּפְקוֹד אָדָם

וּבִיקָר לֹא יָלִין אָדָם

קָרַצְתָּה עָפָר מֵאֲדָמָה

וּגְלַמְתּוֹ הֱיוֹת עַל אֲדָמָה

ריש.. לְאֵילֵי מָרוֹם אוֹתוֹ דִימָּה

וְחָאטָא וּלְהֶבֶל דָּמָה

שֵׁשֶׁת יָמִים כֹּל כִּילַלְתָּה

---

8 The root פ-ק-ד in the *piel* occurs only in Isa 13:4, where it refers to mustering a military host; here the reference seems to be the aggadic motif in which God consults the angels (or other heavenly denizens) prior to the creation of humankind. See *GenR* 8:3–5.

9 That is, according to this piyyut, humanity is in the image of the angels.

10 An allusion to Ps 8:4.

11 Ps 49:13

12 See Job 33:6

13 Yannai here holds both Adam and Eve responsible for the transgression in the Garden.

and on the seventh You finished and were done
The completion You set forth as a sign to all generations
a day …You blessed

And thus, " …and the heavens and the earth"
(7) …the upper chambers of the heavens[14]
You formed the depths of the earth[15]
… the curtain of the heavens[16]
You knit tightly the dry land of the earth
…You established the heavens
And upon the wind You suspended the earth
With Your hand-span You measured the heavens
Strengthening a measure of the dust of the earth[17]
You laid out with Your right hand the heavens[18]
You founded with Your hand the earth
They recount Your glory[19] the heavens
for the sake of … [the earth]
You stretched out with wisdom the heavens[20]
planed … [the earth]
Your secrets are the clouds of the heavens
… [the earth]
You spread splendor [the heavens]
…
You fixed [the earth]

[The Fourth Day]
(8)[21] …
thirty days[22] and … day to day
and the Moon proclaims knowledge, night and day[23]
ascribing greatness to the One who dwells in secret on high.

---

14 Ps 104:3 15 Isa 44:23, Ps 63:10 16 Ps 104:2
17 This entire line reworks Isa 40:12, "Who has measured the waters in the hollow of his hand and marked off the heavens with a span, enclosed the dust of the earth in a measure and weighed the mountains in scales and the hills in a balance?"
18 Isa 48:13 19 Ps 19:2
20 See Isa 40:22
21 The first section of the *silluq* describes Day Four of creation (the creation of the heavenly hosts); the next describes Day Five of creation (sea and air creatures); the next describes Day Six (the creation of the land creatures, including humanity); the final lines

וּבַשְּׁבִיעִי כִּילִיתָה וְכָלַלְתָּה
תַּכְלִית אוֹת לְדוֹרוֹת עָרַכְתָּה
יוֹם ..ים בֵּירַכְתָּה

ובכן את השמים ואת הארץ
(ז) **א**..תה עֲלִיּוֹת שָׁמַיִם
בֵּירַרְתָּה תַחְתִּיּוֹת אָרֶץ
ג..ה יְרִיעוֹת שָׁמַיִם
דִּיבַּקְתָּה יַבָּשֶׁת אָרֶץ
... ... שָׁתָה שָׁמַיִם
וְעַל רוּחַ תָּלִיתָה אָרֶץ
זַרְתָךְ תִּיכְּנָה שָׁמַיִם
חִיזֵּק שָׁלִישׁ עֲפַר אָרֶץ
טִיפְּחָה יְמִינָךְ שָׁמַיִם
יָסְדָה יָדָךְ אָרֶץ
כְּבוֹדָךְ יְסַפְּרוּ שָׁמַיִם
לְמַעַן כ.. ...
מָתַחְתָּה בִּתְבוּנָה שָׁמַיִם
נָטִיתָה ...
סִיתָרָךְ עַנְנֵי שָׁמַיִם
... ...
פֵּירַסְתָּה הוֹד ...
... ...
קְבִיעַת מ.. ...

[יום רביעי]
(ח) ...
שְׁלוֹשִׁים יוֹם ו.. יוֹם לְיוֹם
וְסַהַר מְחַוֶּוה דַעַת לַיְלָה וָיוֹם
גְדֵולָּה לְיוֹשֵׁב בְּסֵתֶר עֶלְיוֹן

describe the creation of the Sabbath.

22 Presumably a reference to the length of a full month (**R**).

23 The poet here adapts Ps 19:3—"Day to day gives utterance, night to night proclaims knowledge"—to the story of Creation. **B1** connects this line to *GenR* 6:3 (paralleled in *SongR* 6:10); the relevant passage states: "Rabbi Nahman said: Esau counts by the sun, which is large: just as the sun rules by day but not by night, so does Esau enjoy this world, but has nothing in the World to Come. Jacob counts by the moon, which is small: just as the moon *rules by day and by night*, so, too, has Jacob a portion in this world and in the World to Come." The moon's "knowledge" may refer to astrology.

The stars cannot be counted
yet each one travels its appointed rounds,
going forward and returning back
seven (planets) going round ...without hesitation[24]
and twelve (constellations) ...shining (upon) every day;
six (of them) sparkling ...his companion's border he does not trespass
One sinks, the other rises ...[25]
[and Taurus'] eleven stars in the north proclaiming[26]
and four and a half (hours) between one (sign) and the other
keeping them apart[27] ... stationed in the South
and the eleven stars in the Scorpion do not blur together
... the Pleiades, not reckoned in their counting
are composed of seven fiery stars,
each leaning close to the next, their places crowded
and after forty-seven (days) of the third season,
    they begin to conceal themselves[28]
sinking and disappearing and not proclaiming;
and all of them by the name "Hyades" are called.[29]
To Aries they are a tail, while to Taurus they are a crown –
so they are reckoned
and between the realm of the Wagon and the Scorpion
dwell all the inhabitants of the world.[30]

---

24 **R** connects this imagery with material from *Sefer Yetzirah* of Judah ben Barzillai of Barcelona.

25 Based on what follows, the "sinking" constellation should be identified as Scorpio, the ascendant as Taurus/the Ox.

26 I have supplied "Taurus" based on the Genizah text cited by **R** in his note to this line.

27 The "four and a half hours" refers to the time it takes the Sun to pass between astrological signs; that is, the *time* refers to the *distance* that is the boundary between signs. For example, it takes the sun 30 days and 10.5 hours to travel from Aries to Taurus; 30 days and 6 hours are spent traveling within the space of the sign itself, but the remaining 4.5 hours are spent in the empty space between Aries and Taurus. This empty space is the boundary that is not trespassed. The clear demarcations of boundaries in the Zodiac mosaics may reflect this space.

28 The third season is that of Tishrei, which marks the autumnal equinox (the season beginning in the spring). The 47th day of the third season is the middle of Heshvan. Around this time, the Pleiades begin to rise at dawn, making them invisible during the day. **R** cites, among other related texts, *b.RH* 11b: "Rabbi Joshua said: That day [the day the Flood began] was the seventeenth day of Iyyar, when the constellation of Pleiades sets at daybreak and the fountains begin to dry up... Rabbi Eliezer said: That day was the seventeenth of Marheshvan, a day on which the constellation of Pleiades rises at daybreak, and [the season] when the fountains begin to fill."

אֵין מִסְפָּר לַכּוֹכָבִם
וְכָל אֶחָד בְּעִיתּוֹ לְפִי עִנְיָינוֹ
הוֹלְכִים וְשָׁבִים
שִׁבְעָה סוֹבְבִים ... וְלֹא מְעַכְּבִים
וּשְׁנֵים עָשָׂר ... שׂ בְּכָל יוֹם מַשְׁבִּיבִים
שִׁשָּׁה זוֹרְחִים ... לִגְבוּל חֲבֵירוֹ לֹא קוֹרְבִים
שׁוֹקֵיעַ אֶחָד וְעוֹלֶה אֶחָד דר..
... וְאַחַד עָשָׂר בְּצָפוֹן מְחַוִּוים
וְאַרְבַּע וָחֵיצִי בֵּין אֶחָד לְאֶחָד מַרְחִיבִים
... ... בְּתֵימָן נִיצָּבִים
וְאַחַד עָשָׂר בָּעַקְרָב לֹא מִתעָרְבִים
... כִּימָה אֵינָה נִימְנֵית בְּחִישּׁוּבִים
וּבָהּ שִׁבְעָה כּוֹכָבִים מַלְהִיבִים
וְכֻולָּם סְמוּכִים זֶה לָזֶה וּמְקוֹמָם מְעַבִּים
וּבְאַרְבָּעִים וְשִׁבְעָה לַתְּקוּפָה הַשְּׁלִישִׁית מִתְחַבִּים

שׁוֹקְעִים וּפוֹטְרִים וְלֹא מִתְחַוִּוים
וְכֻולָּם בְּשֵׁם כִּימָה נְקוּבִים
וְלַטָּלֶה זָנָב וְלַשּׁוֹר עֲטֶרֶת
הֵם מִתְחַשְּׁבִים
וּבֵין עֲגָלָה לְעַקְרָב כָּל בָּאֵי עוֹלָם יוֹשְׁבִים

Taurus [lit. "the ox"] is a sign associated with the Spring, particularly the months of Nisan and Iyyar, while Scorpio—the other sign highlighted in this piyyut—is autumnal, connected to the months of Tishrei and Heshvan. If the synagogue mosaics are used as models (imagine them as a wheel that turns, representing the movements of the constellations), when Scorpio sinks beneath the horizon, Taurus is on the ascent. Note that in standard rabbinic tradition, the world was created on Rosh Hashanah, the 1st of Tishrei. According to *PRE* 8, the season starting with Tishrei is also the season of sowing.

29 The name **כימה** is usually translated "Pleiades" (which is how **R** reads it, following Ibn Ezra to Amos 5:8), also called "the seven sisters," and such may indeed be the intention here, as above. However, the star cluster now called "Hyades" forms the forehead of Taurus (that is, its "crown"), the location where the two signs—Aries and Taurus—come closest together.

30 The word *ʿagalah*, here rendered as "Wagon," incorporates Rashi's understanding of the word ("these are stars that are formed like a wheel, and it is the constellation of Taurus"). *ʿAgalah*, literally "roller, wagon, basin" is sometimes understood as a cluster of stars ("Charles' Wain" or "Charles' Wagon") within Ursa Major, not Taurus. However, the consonants **עגלה**, vocalized as *ʿeglah*, can also be understood as "calf," a name for Taurus, an appealing alternative to suddenly introducing Ursa Major here. **R** cites *b.Pes.* 94a: "Come and hear: The Calf [Taurus] is in the north and the Scorpion [Scorpio] is in the south, the whole of the inhabited world lies between the Calf and Scorpio."

The rest of the stars can neither be counted nor reckoned,
yet all of them are called by name
by the One who dwells upon the Cherubim
and on the fourth day they prevailed because they are beloved
and the two lights went forth from a single window, like lovers
and within the curtain of the Third Heaven[31] they are set as attendants.[32]

[The Fifth Day]
… And on the fifth day …
"Let the waters swarm with all kinds of swarming things swarming"
… and swelling … all of them … bearing swarms of young
… Innumerable are those created to swarm
unending and limitless … dashing and s[mall] creatures among oppresors
all of them looking expectantly to You and darting about for food[33]
in seas and in rivers …
You give to them, they gather it up, they are glad
and all of them, groups upon groups, gather together
rushing, rejoicing …
And on the Fifth Day, too, You created the serpent with the twisted heart[34]
upon the waters of the Deep You make him ride all around
hard as stone his heart was cast
and like a seething cauldron[35] He makes (the sea), his length and breadth
firebrands and flames … from his mouth come his sparks
and from his nostrils smoke billows like an oven when he blazes
and like coals his breath burns from within him.
To him, any kind of iron is merely straw,
any kind of bronze merely worm-eaten wood.
Bow-shots and sling-stones do not move him from his place
and the brilliance of his raiment trailing after leaves his wake shining
with light.

---

31 Yannai uses the epithet *doq*, which is equated with *raqiʿa* based on Isa 40:22 ("He spreads forth the heavens (*shamayyim*) like a curtain [*ke-doq*]"). According to *GenR* 6:6, which **R** adduces, the Sun and Moon are fixed in this level: "Where are the spheres of the sun and the moon set? In the second heaven (*raqiʿa*), as it says, "And God set them in the firmament (*raqiʿa*) of the heaven.' (Gen 1:17)." Notice, however, that for Yannai, the stars are set in the third, not the second, heaven. Both Yannai's placement and naming of the third heaven (*doq/raqiʿa*) are in accord with the traditions found in *PRK* 23 and *DeutR* 2:32 (texts cited by **R**). Yannai, like other rabbinic sources, is not consistent in his naming of the seven heavens.

וְאֵין מִסְפָּר וְשִׁעוּר לִשְׁאָר הַכּוֹכָבִים
וּלְכֻולָּם בְּשֵׁם יִקְרָא שׁוֹכֵן כְּרוּבִים

וּבְיוֹם רְבִעִי גָּבְרוּ מִפְּנֵי שֶׁהֵם חֲבִיבִים
וּשְׁנֵי מְאוֹרוֹת יָצְאוּ מֵחַלּוֹן אֶחָד כְּאוֹהֲבִים
וּבְדוֹק שְׁלִישִׁי נִיתְּנוּ כְּקָאמִין וְיַיצִיבִין

[יום חמישי]
וּבַיּוֹם הַחֲמִישִׁי ... יִשְׁרְצוּ הַמַּיִם מִינֵי שְׁרָצִים
... וּמֵבִיצִים ... ... כּוּלָּם ... הֵם מַשְׁרִיצִים
וְאֵין מִסְפָּר לִמְשֻׁוקָּצִים
וְאֵין קִצְבָה וָסוֹף ... שְׁמִיצִים
וְחַיּוֹת קְטַנּוֹת ... בְּמֵצִים
כֻּולָּם אֵלֶיךָ יְסַבֵּרוּן וּלְאוֹכֶל רָצִים
בַּיַּמִּים וּבַנְּהָרוֹת ...
תִּתֵּן לָהֶם יִלְקוֹטוּן וְהֵם עֲלִיצִים
וְכֻולָּם כִּיתִּים כִּיתִּים נִקְבָּצִים
אָצִים גּוֹהֲצִים ...
וְעוֹד בַּחֲמִישִׁי יָצַרְתָּה נָחָשׁ בָּרִיחַ לְבָבוֹ
עַל מֵי תְּהוֹמוֹת הִרְכִּיבוֹ סְבִיבוֹ
וּכְמוֹ אֶבֶן יָצוּק לִבּוֹ
וְכַמֶּרְקָחָה יָשִׂים אָורְכּוֹ וְרָוחְבּוֹ
וְלַפִּידִים וְלֶהָבָה ... מִפִּי שְׁבִיבוֹ
וּמִנְחִירָיו עָשָׁן יוֹצֵא כְּכִבְשָׁן בְּהַשְׁבִּיבוֹ
וּכְגְחָלִים תְּלַהֵט נַפְשׁוֹ בְּקִרְבּוֹ
וְכָל מִין בַּרְזֶל לְתֶבֶן יְחַשְׁבוֹ
וְכָל מִין נְחוֹשֶׁת יַחֲשׁוֹב כְּעֵץ רִקָּבוֹן
וּמִקֶּשֶׁת וְאַבְנֵי קֶלַע לֹא יָזוּז מִמְּסִיבוֹ
וּמִזוֹהַר לְבוּשׁוֹ אַחֲרָיו יָאִיר נְתִיבוֹ

32 The heavenly luminaries, like the angels, stand ready to obey divine commands. The terms used here are Aramaic, and come from Dan 7:16.

33 **R** cites Ps 104:25–27, "So is this great and wide sea, where there are innumerable creeping things, living things, both small and great. There go the ships; and Leviathan, which You have made to play in it. These all look expectantly to You, that You may give them their food in due season." Cf. also Ps 145:15.

34 One of the "sea monsters" of Gen 1:21, traditionally identified as Leviathan. See Isa 27:1, which refers to Leviathan as "the twisted serpent." This passage draws heavily on Job 40–41.

35 Lit., "ointment pot"

In a place where he is, who may enter?
Yet when You desire, You frolic with him like a bird[36]
for this mighty Leviathan You created to sport with
and 800 [kinds of locusts] …You created on the fifth day
Nor can [the birds] be numbered …those who fly
spreaders of wing and pinion
… the firmament of heaven … all of them to their windows …[37]
[and they pour forth] their piercing, peeping prayer;[38]
of Your righteousness they chirp daily

[The Sixth Day]
On the Sixth Day You created all kinds of crawling things
[Upon the land, all] kinds of [creeping things] were placed[39]
from dust were they made
while upon the earth ... holes of dust ... were made
and within them, they were covered and hidden away.
And also species of cattle were …
…from a lump [of earth][40] they were made
Among them were the cud-chewers; and among them, the cloven-hoofed[41]
and among them … for beast and cattle that were made.
Ten (species) You made pure for `those who were carried'[42] to eat
and they rendered praise and tribute over all (God's) works
and from all the wondrous creations in this array.[43]
The sound of this one is never the same as the sound of that one[44]
… nor does the [appearance][45] … of this one resemble that one
nor does the mind[46] of this one resemble that one
nor does the hide[47] of this one resemble that one

---

36 See Ps 104:26, "… Leviathan, that You have formed to play with." The bird imagery comes from Job 40:29.

37 See Gen 7:11, Mal 3:10, 2 Kings 7:2, and Isa 24:18.

38 Reading with **B1**, who bases his reconstruction on Isa 26:16. This verse, however, is difficult to translate and probably has nothing to do with birds; "anguished whisper" is a better translation. The restored word "*tsaqon*" probably means "anguish" (taking it from the root צ-ו-ק) in the Isaian context. However, in the piyyut, the traditional, if not actual, meaning of "pouring forth" (from a homonymous root) seems more appropriate. **R** adduces Ps 104:12, which supplies a similar image (and which results in a slightly different reconstruction of the missing word).

39 Lacuna filled as in **B1**. 40 Completed according to **B1**.

41 Epithet for Israel, based on Isa 46:3. On the ten kosher species, **R** cites *LevR* 27:6: "Rabbi Judah son of Rabbi Simon observed: The Holy One, blessed be He, said: `I have given

וּבִמְקוֹם אֲשֶׁר הוּא שָׁם מִי יָבוֹא
וּבְעֵת אֲשֶׁר תַּחְפּוֹץ כְּצִפּוֹר תְּשַׂחֵק בּוֹ
לִיוְויָתָן זֶה יָצַרְתָּה לְשַׂחֵק בּוֹ
וּשְׁמוֹנֶה מֵאוֹת מִינֵי חֲגָבִים ... בָּרָאתָה בַּחֲמִישִׁי
וְאֵין מִסְפָּר לְעוֹפוֹת ... עָפִים
וּפוֹרְסֵי כְנָפַיִם וַאֲגַפִּים
... רְקִיעַ הַשָּׁמַיִם ... כּוּלָּם לַאֲרוּבּוֹתֵיהֶם ..פִים
וּבַצָּרָה לַחֲשָׁם צַהַל צִדְקָךְ מְצַפְצְפִים

[יום ששי]
וּבַיּוֹם הַשִּׁישִׁי בָּרָאתָה מִינֵי רְמָסִים.
... מִינֵי ... לְהָשִׂים
וּמִן הֶעָפָר הָיוּ נַעֲשִׂים
וְעַל הָאָרֶץ ... חוּרֵי עָפָר ... נַעֲשִׂים
וּבְתוֹכָם נִיכְסִים וְנִיכְמָסִים
וְעוֹד מִינֵי בְּהֵמָה ... שִׂים
וּמִגוּשׁ ... הֵם נַעֲשִׂים
מֵהֶם גּוֹדְרִים וּמֵהֶם מַפְרִיסִים
מֵהֶם ...
לְחַיָּיה וּבְהֵמָה הַנַעֲשִׂים
עֶשֶׂר טִיהַרְתָּה לְאוֹכֶל עֲמוּסִים
וְנָתְנוּ שֶׁבַח וְקִילוּס עַל כָּל מַעֲשִׂים
וּמִכָּל בְּרִיּוֹת הַכְּלוּלוֹת בְּעֵירֶךְ זֶה
אֵין קוֹל זֶה דוֹמֶה לָזֶה
וְלֹא ... דוֹמֶה לָזֶה
וְלֹא רֵעִי זֶה דוֹמֶה לָזֶה
וְלֹא לְבוּשׁ זֶה דוֹמֶה לָזֶה

---

you ten kinds of [kosher] beasts; three are in your domain and seven are not in your domain.'" The three in Israel's domain are the ox, sheep, and goat. These animals are to be used for offerings. The other seven are: the hart, the gazelle, the roebuck, the wild goat, the pygarg (perhaps a kind of antelope or gazelle), the antelope, and the mountain-sheep. This list of animals comes from Deut 14:4–5.

42 I.e., the kosher species

43 Or: "The array of This (i.e., God)." See n. 48.

44 Lit. "this one" (and this follows for the following lines).

45 Lacuna filled by **B1**.

46 See Ps 139:2 (רעי here is related to רעיון). Maʾagarim emends to ראי, "appearance." Both readings are feasible. With weakened gutterals, רעי and ראי are homonyms The text, as it is, seems to refer to the thought or mind of the beasts (*reʿi*). The best rabbinic parallel to this sequence is at *Seder Eliahu Rabbah* 2 (Friedmann, ed., p. 10), cited by **B1**.

47 Lit., "garment."

nor does the taste of this one resemble that one.
How great are Your works, O This[48], my God!
And furthermore You created Behemoth and You made him mighty[49];
his strength You put in his loins[50] ...his mouth ...
from pipes of bronze You made the stuff of his bones
and a thousand mountains grow grass for him, [for his pasture][51];
for, like any cow, tender grass is his food;
gardens and arbors fall under [his shadow][52]
... and the Jordan gushes forth towards his mouth.[53]

And also on the Sixth Day You created the human from the earth
and like one of the divine beings he seemed
but he sinned ... and to judgment he was brought in terror
and in the twelfth (hour), at the setting of the sun,
the Sabbath approached [and allieviated his guilt][54]
and his sentence was tempered: to work the land
and "a hymn: a song for the Sabbath day" (Ps. 92:1) – to sweetly sing
and also "to give thanks" (Ps 92:2)[55] to the Artist
whose works were thus perfected.[56]

48 "This" (*zeh*) is a common epithet for God in piyyutim. Specifically, the epithet paraphrases Exod 15:3, *zeh eli*. The intensive repetitions of "this" in the previous lines anticipate and strengthen the reference to God as "This" in this final stich.

49 In rabbinic Hebrew, the root י-פ-ה can have the connotation of "power" as well as beauty. This usage occurs in Yannai's *qedushta* for Gen 12:1 (Poem One, line 8; see notes 3 and 4), as well.

50 Maʾagarim here confirms **B1**'s hypothesized reading.

51 Lacuna filled as in **B1**.

52 Reading with **B1**.

53 See *LevR* 22:10 (**R**): "Rabbi Tanḥuma remarked: Great are the works of God! How strange are the works of the Holy One, blessed be He! Where does Behemoth drink from? Rabbi Yoḥanan and Rabbi Simeon son of Lakish give different answers. Rabbi Yoḥanan says: He makes a single draught of what the Jordan pours down in six months... Rabbi Simeon son of Lakish says: He makes a single draught of what the Jordan pours down in twelve months... and they contain but sufficient to moisten the beast's mouth. ...They do not [even] contain sufficient to moisten its mouth. Then where does it drink from? Rabbi Simeon bar Yoḥai learned: A river goes forth from Eden whose name is Yubal and from there it drinks." **R** also cites *PRK* 6 (p. 112) and *Tanḥ Pinhas* 12.

54 Lacuna filled as by **B1** [ופדתהו מאשמה]; lit., "bought him out of debt.". The motif of the Sabbath tempering God's wrath against Adam is stated most clearly in *MidPs* 92:3 (cited in part by **R**), where, as God is about to destroy both Adam and Eve for their transgression,

וְלֹא טַעַם זֶה דוֹמֶה לָזֶה
מַה גָּדְלוּ מַעֲשֶׂיךָ אֵלִי זֶה
וְעוֹד בָּרָאתָה בְּהֵימוֹת וַתְּיַיפֵּהוּ
כּוֹחוֹ תַּתָּה בְּמוֹתְנָיו ..פִּיהוּ
אֲפִיקֵי נְחוּשָׁה שַׁתָּה עֲצָמָיו לְעַצְמֵיהוּ
וְאֶלֶף הָרִים מְגַדְּלִים לוֹ עֵשֶׂב ...
כִּי חָצִיר כַּבָּקָר הוּא מַאֲכָלֵיהוּ
וְגַנּוֹת וְאִילָנוֹת מִיתְכַּסִּים
... וְיַרְדֵּן מֵיגִיחַ אֶל פִּיהוּ

וְעוֹד בַּשִּׁישִׁי יָצַרְתָּה אָדָם מִן הָאֲדָמָה
וּכְאֶחָד מִבְּנֵי אֵלִים נִדְמָה
וְחָטָא ... מַה וְלַדִּין הוּבָא בְּאֵימָה
וּבִשְׁתֵּים עֶשְׂרֵה עִם דִּימְדּוּמֵי חַמָּה
קֶדְמָה הַשַּׁבָּת ...
וְדִינוֹ נִגְמַר לַעֲבוֹד אֶת הָאֲדָמָה
וּמִזְמוֹר שִׁיר לְיוֹם הַשַּׁבָּת לְהַנְעִימָה
וְגַם לְהוֹדוֹת לַצַּיָּיר
אֲשֶׁר פְּעוּלָּתוֹ שְׁלֵימָה

---

the Sabbath intervenes, stating: "At that moment, the Sabbath arrived and became Adam's advocate, saying to the Holy One, blessed be He: `During the six days of Creation no one suffered punishment. And you will begin it with me? Is this my holiness? Is this my rest?' And thus Adam was saved by the Sabbath's pleas from destruction in Gehenna." See also *EcclR* 1:3, where it states: "Rabbi Berekhiah said: When Adam perceived the excellence of the Sabbath, that [for its unintentional desecration] one could bring an offering and gain atonement, he began to sing to the Holy One, blessed be He, praise and a psalm concerning it. That is what is written, `A Psalm, a Song for the Sabbath day' (Ps 92:1). R. Levi said: Adam composed that Psalm." This tradition also appears in *GenR* 22:13, *TanḥB Ber.* 25, *PRE* 18, and others.

55 This interpretation of the second verse of the psalm recalls another passage from *MidPs* on Ps 92:3, "When Adam saw the power of the Sabbath [to intercede on his behalf], he was about to sing a hymn in her honor. But the Sabbath said to him: `Are you going to sing to me? Rather, let us, you and I [together], sing a hymn to the Holy One, blessed be He.' Hence it is said: `It is a good thing to give thanks unto the Lord' (Ps 92:2)."

56 As **R** and **B1** both note, the poet here interprets Deut 32:4—"The Rock (*tsur*), whose works are perfect (*tamim*)" as "The Artist (*tsayyar*) whose works were complete." This is in accord with the interpretation of the biblical verse *in SifDeut Ha'azinu* 2. Also, **B1** suggests that the poet may be alluding to Ps 92:16, which refers to God as "my Rock, in whom there is no injustice." With redemption and praise introduced to creation, God's works are complete.

[The Seventh Day]
And the Seventh Day You blessed and hallowed
and on it You rested and were refreshed
And that day from all others—You separated it.
And as for its evening—You never let twilight set in.[55]
And as the first [of all holidays] You described it,[56]
for with light You enriched[57]
(a sum of) thirty-six hours ...You sanctified
twelve from the Sixth Day You fortified
and twenty-four ...You [sanctified] ...[58]
As an eternal sign You designated it
and from the very first Sabbath You have observed its rest
and [by] all Your works in holiness are You hallowed
As it is written: "And the one called ...Holy, Holy, Holy ..."

(9) Your works, Your formations, and Your creations
which You have made for Your glory, call out and say:
Holy, holy, holy is the Lord of Hosts! The whole earth is filled with His glory!
"*Holy*"—from[59] His work of the heavens
"*Holy*"—from His formation of the earth
"*Holy*"—from His creation of the seas
Holy, holy, holy is the Lord of Hosts! The whole earth is filled with His glory!
The Holy One worked into existence[60] the heavens and their hosts
The Holy One formed[61] the earth[62] and its creatures
The Holy One created the seas and all that are in them

---

55 As **R** notes, according to *MidPs* on *Ps* 92:1, first Sabbath was entirely of light (based on the absence of the word "evening" in Gen 1 in reference to the 7th day). See below.

56 Lacuna filled by **B1** (reiterated in **B2**). See Lev 23:3, where the importance of the Sabbath is stressed prior to the descriptions of the other holidays.

57 This alludes to the language of Prov 10:22, "The blessings of the Lord make rich." In *GenR* 11:1 (cited by both **R** and **B1**), this verse is applied to the Sabbath. **B1** suggests secondarily that this might also refer to the tradition recorded in *Maḥzor Vitry* according to which candles or lamps burn at greater length on the Shabbat, thus also enriching it with light.

58 Lacuna filled according to **B2**. Although the text of the piyyut is incomplete, the poet alludes here to a tradition preserved in multiple aggadic sources, including *GenR* 11:2 and 12:6, and *MidPs* 92:4. The *GenR* 11:2 version (cited by **R**) states: "Rabbi Levi said in the name of the son of Nezirah: That light [the light of the first Sabbath] functioned thirty-six hours: twelve on the eve of the Sabbath [i.e. Friday]; twelve during the night of the Sabbath; and

[יום שביעי]
וְיוֹם שְׁבִיעִי בֵּירַכְתָּה וְקִידַּשְׁתָּה
וּבוֹ נַחְתָּה וְנָפַשְׁתָּה
וְיוֹם מִיָּמִים אוֹתוֹ פֵּירַשְׁתָּה
וְעֶרֶב בּוֹ לֹא הֶאֱמַשְׁתָּה
וּבְרֹאשׁ ... פֵּירַשְׁתָּה
כִּי בְאוֹר אוֹתוֹ הֶעֱשַׁרְתָּה
שְׁלוֹשִׁים וָשֵׁשׁ שָׁעוֹת ... הִקְדַּשְׁתָּה
שְׁתֵּים עֶשְׂרֵה מִשִּׁשִּׁי יִישַּׁרְתָּה
וְעֶשְׂרִים וְאַרְבַּע מִשַּׁבָּת ...תָּה
וְאוֹת הִיא לְעוֹלָם אוֹתוֹ רָשַׁמְתָּה
וּמְנוּחָתוֹ מִשַּׁבָּת רִאשׁוֹנָה שִׁימַּרְתָּה
וְכָל מַעֲשֶׂיךָ בִּקְדוּשָּׁה נִתְקַדַּשְׁתָּה
ככתוב וקרא קדוש קדוש

(ט) מַעֲשֶׂיךָ וִיצוּרֶיךָ וּבְרִיוֹתֶיךָ
אֲשֶׁר לִכְבוֹדְךָ פָּעַלְתָּה יַעֲנוּ וְיֹאמְרוּ
קדוש קדוש קדוש יי צבאות מלא כל הארץ כבודו
קָדוֹשׁ מֵעֲשִׂיַּית שָׁמַיִם
קָדוֹשׁ מִיצִירַת אָרֶץ
קָדוֹשׁ מִבְּרִיַּית יַמִּים
קדוש קדוש קדוש יי צבאות מלא כל הארץ כבודו
קָדוֹשׁ עָשָׂה שָׁמַיִם וְצִבְאוֹתֵיהֶם
קָדוֹשׁ יָסַד אֲרָקִים וְצֶאֱצָאֵיהֶם
קָדוֹשׁ בָּרָא יַמִּים וְכָל אֲשֶׁר בָּהֶם

---

twelve on the Sabbath day." Thus Adam did not know "darkness" until after the end of the seventh day. The curses put upon Adam, which—according to *GenR* 12:6 included the diminution of the heavenly luminaries—did not take effect until after the end of the seventh day. When the first Sabbath ended, so did humanity's place in the Garden. The kindling of Sabbath lights and the rituals of havdalah are both traced to this primeval episode.

59 Or, "because of, on account of"

60 This translation attempts to replicate the repetition of the root ע-ש-ה ("to do, make") from the first line.

61 I have followed Mirsky's emendation here (accepted by **B1**), using the root י-צ-ר to maintain parallelism with the opening line of the poetic unit rather than the unparalleled י-ס-ד ("to found, establish") in the MS.

62 Yannai here uses an Aramaic word, ארק, found in Jer 10:11, for "earth," but with a Hebrew plural suffix.

Holy, holy, holy is the Lord of Hosts! The whole earth is filled with His glory!

"From His place"—He considered …

קדוש קדוש קדוש יי צבאות מלא כל הארץ כבודו

מִמְּקוֹמוֹ שָׁקַל ...

Commentary

It is regrettable for the history of Jewish biblical interpretation that this text is not better preserved. What survives tantalizes with its vivid imagery and dramatic narration. The *silluq*, in particular, provides a wealth of fascinating imagery–worth exploring even if its authorship is uncertain. The four days covered—the fourth, fifth, sixth, and the Sabbath—combine to create a powerful hymn to divine majesty. Each day also resonates with a variety of external sources, suggesting ways in which piyyutim can supplement and deepen our understanding of the culture of the early synagogue. At the same time, the surviving elements of Poem Six provide a lyrical retelling of the story of the creation, drawing heavily on Job and Isaiah, both of which imbue the narration with vivid images. And the *rahit* builds on this intertextual retelling of the story by emphasizing and creating parallels between heaven and earth–implicitly encompassing all of creation. Together, the various pieces of the piyyut, incomplete as they are, constitute a symphonic rapture at the wonder of the cosmos.

Of all the units presented here, the *silluq* is the most compelling. The stanzas embellishing Day Four provide a rich, if occasionally obscure, depiction of the heavenly bodies, with explicit reference to the Zodiac. One way of understanding this imagery is to see the cosmological depiction of the piyyut as a literary complement to the famous synagogue mosaics, several of which feature prominent depictions of the constellations. Archaeologists have uncovered visual depictions of the Zodia in floor mosaics in multiple synagogues in the Land of Israel (including those at Beit Alpha, Husifa, Ḥammat-Tiberias, Naʿaran, and Sepphoris, all with intriguing variations). The synagogue at Ein Gedi, meanwhile, preserves an eclectic inscription that lists the signs of the Zodiac and the ancestors as well. It may reflect a more conservative, iconoclastic tradition that incorporated the Zodiac into the synagogue without figurative depiction. Piyyutim featuring the Zodiac likewise appear to have been popular in Late Antiquity.[63] While it is difficult to know precisely how poetry about the Zodiac relates to images of the Zodiac in the synagogues, the two different styles of representation indicate, at the very least, the importance of the

63 See, for example, J. Yahalom, "Piyyut as Poetry," *The Synagogue in Late Antiquity*, ed. Lee Levine (JTSA/ASOR: Philadelphia, 1987), 111–26.

Zodiac in Late Ancient Judaism. The overlap may, however, suggest much more.[64]

It is worth considering how Yannai presents the motif in this particular *qedushta*. The overall emphasis of the astrological portion of the poem focuses on orderliness and scope: the dazzling expanse of the heavens and its barely-fathomable patterning are taken as ongoing evidence of the wonder of Creation. While this association is perhaps ironic in a poem for Gen 1—a text that strives to downplay any appearance of astral potency—in the context of the synagogues of Late Antiquity and the Byzantine era, the Zodiac should be seen as a conventional motif, beautifully executed not only in the visual world but in poetry as well.

This piyyut for Gen 1 is more than just an astrological treatise, however. The units describing the fifth and sixths days of creation add drama of a different kind to this work, particularly in their descriptions of Leviathan and Behemoth. Both of these fantastic beasts defy human scale and epitomize the majesty and power of God's work on Day Five (the sea creatures, of which Leviathan is the most terrible) and Day Six (the land creatures, of which Behemoth is the most awesome). According to commonplace rabbinic tradition, Leviathan and Behemoth will be the fish and meat courses in banquets to be served at the End of Time. In this poem, however (or at least the surviving fragments), there is no hint of the world's end; the poet focuses exclusively on creation.

As with the heavenly imagery that dominates Day Four, Yannai's focus in Days Five and Six is on the inherent majesty of these mythical beasts. He emphasizes the absolute wondrousness of their scale, making them beastly testimonials to the majesty of the heavens. In similar ways, the mundane, familiar animals of every day life are also praised: as individuals, they may not boggle the mind, but their wonderful diversity inspires our poet's awe. Recognition of the variety of life is articulated again and again as testimony to the greatest of wonders, Creation.

This *qedushta* for Gen 1 culminates in his presentation of the first Sabbath, which Yannai depicts as the "redeemer" of Adam. Connections between Adam and the Sabbath—two of the last creations—are commonplace in rabbinic literature, as evidenced in the notes

64 See Chapter Three for a discussion of the synagogue mosaics and Chapter Four, where the Zodiac is discussed in the context of Jewish mysticism.

accompanying the translation. Multiple textual sources credit Adam with the composition of Ps 92—the only psalm that bears a heading "for the Sabbath day." These sources link the Sabbath to the drama of Adam and Eve's expulsion from the Garden of Eden. Beyond the unique heading of this psalm, which led exegetes to connect it to the Sabbath, the psalm highlights divine attributes—love, faithfulness, power, subtlety, and unwavering justness—that can all bear upon the story of humanity's awkward first day. The drama of Adam and Eve is contextualized by these aggadic sources within creation itself, and the cycle of transgression and reprieve—with atonement enacted by the Sabbath—becomes part of the most basic human story.

Our poet participates in this general tradition of interpretation, but uses the vehicle of poetry to bring it vividly to life; it becomes more than exegesis or narration. As the poet recreates the scene, Adam's sin is an event with immediate cosmic effects, with the sun itself dramatically intervening on behalf of humanity. Human actions disrupt the natural symphony that opens this poem. When the Sabbath intercedes on Adam's behalf—securing his expulsion rather than his death—we realize that perhaps Mercy and Atonement are the final items created in this story. Only after Adam's punishment is tempered is God's work called "complete"; only with forgiveness and gratitude are God's works "perfected." Observance of the Sabbath, one of the central tenets of Judaism and one that during the biblical period became increasingly emphasized,[65] is here presented quite literally as the "salvation" of humanity, through its preservation of the first human being. This is a powerful lesson to teach to a community assembled in observance of the Sabbath—one that likely recited Ps 92 in honor of the Sabbath day. The primordial Sabbath becomes an eternal moment, one renewed and re-experienced every week.

65 Note, for example, Isa 58:13–14, "If you restrain your foot because of the Sabbath, from pursuing your business on My holy day; and call the Sabbath a delight, the holy day of the Lord honorable; and honor it, not following your own ways or pursuing your own business, or speaking of vain matters: then shall you delight yourself in the Lord; and I will cause you to ride upon the high places of the earth, and sustain you with the heritage of Jacob your father; for the mouth of the Lord has spoken it." The Sabbath is not always so strongly singled out in the Bible, but in Gen 1–2, it certainly can be seen as forming the capstone to creation.

Qedushta to Genesis 8:1 — בראשית ח:א

"Then God remembered Noah" — ויזכר אלהים את נח

While we have only fragments of a much longer poem before us, we can see from these few surviving lines that Yannai found an inspiration for bold theology in this Torah portion. The poet lauds Noah for specific virtues (both innate qualities and actions taken) that result in unprecedented divine favor. The righteousness of the father distinguishes his descendents, as well. Yannai does not preach simple reliance on ancestral merit, however. Divine favor derives from adherence to divine instruction. The commentary explores how the praise of Noah in this piyyut hints at his central place in Jewish art and literature in Late Antiquity.

(7)[1] Pure was he in his generations[2]
Peaceful in his words
Favored in the brightness of his speech
...
Modest in his ways[3]
doing...his...
Humble and upright in his deeds
Joyful in his portion, in his living creatures
Insightful in the shutting of his lips[4]
...
Learned ...
...his...
Knowing the needs of his beasts[5]
....
Pious in his good deeds
Pure and innocent in his...
Diligent in his works[6]
Thoughtful in (his) fidelity to decrees
Seeking His signs,
he decrees and God fulfills his utterance[7]
Blessed are the offspring of his generations
who have not strayed from his teachings[8]

(8) Uttering His praises
to the One crowned in the power of His holiness
in the circle of His holy ones
and by His host of holy beings
As it is written: "And the one called to..."

---

1 This unit is structured as a reverse (תשר"ק) acrostic in which each letter enumerates one of Noah's many virtues.

2 See Gen 6:9

3 From Mic 6:8.

4 Prov 17:28

5 The word rendered "needs" here is *nefesh*—i.e., life, breath, soul—and refers to all the requirements of keeping an animal healthy. As **R** notes, this language derives from Prov

(ז) **תָּ**מִים הָיָה בְדוֹרוֹתָיו
שָׁלֵים בְּמַאֲמָרוֹתָיו
רָצוּי בְדִבְרַת אוֹרוֹתָיו
קְנ.. ... ..עוֹתָיו
צָנוּעַ בְהֲלִיכוֹתָיו
פּוֹעֵל ... ..א..תָיו
עָנָיו וְיָשָׁר בְּמִפְעֲלוֹתָיו
שָׂמֵחַ בְּחֶלקוֹ בְנַפְשִׁיוֹתָיו
נָבוֹן בְּאֵיטֶם שְׂפָתוֹתָיו
...
לָמוּד ...
כ... ..אוֹתָיו
יוֹדֵיעַ מִנֶּפֶשׁ בַּהֲמוֹתָיו
...
חָסִיד בְּמַעֲשֶׂה טוֹבוֹתָיו
זַךְ וְנָקִי ב.. ...
וָתִיק בַּעֲבוֹדוֹתָיו
הוֹגֶה בְּאוֹמֶן עֵידוֹתָיו
דוֹרֵשׁ אֶת אוֹתוֹתָיו
גוֹזֵר וְאֵל מֵקִים אִימְרוֹתָיו
בָּרוּךְ בְּצֶאֱצָאֵי תוֹלְדוֹתָיו
אֲשֶׁר לֹא מָשׁ מִתּוֹרוֹתָיו

(ח) מַבִּיעַ תְּהִילוֹתָיו
לְנִכְתָּר בְּעֶרֶץ קְדוּשׁוֹתָיו
בְּסוֹד קְדוֹשִׁים
וּבִצְבָא קַדִּישִׁין
ככתוב וקרא זה אל

12:10, which opens: "A righteous man knows the needs of his beasts;" this verse is commonly associated with Noah in aggadic sources. Yannai identifies the "righteous man" with Noah, whose tasks aboard the ark included the most formidable challenges of animal husbandry ever undertaken.

6 Or, "worship" (עבודותיו)
7 Job 22:28 (**R**)
8 Or, "his Torahs" (תורותיו)

Commentary

The fact that this poem is so incomplete does not diminish our sense of its complexity. Yannai's use of language and allusion remains impressive, and the connections between the images evoked in these lines and other texts and traditions tantalize. Furthermore, the surviving portions of this piyyut offer an opportunity to understand the importance of the figure of Noah in Byzantine Judaism.

Before exploring the more general context and significance of the poem, we should pause to consider Yannai's rich use of intertextuality in these few lines.[9] In this briefest of fragments, the poem resonates with midrash and mishnah, with bold theological implications. The first extant stich echoes the language of Gen 6–9, itself; three lines later, Noah embodies the virtues of Mic 6:8; in line nine, his behavior is that of the wise man of Prov 17:28; and line thirteen draws upon a biblical text, Prov 12:10, which is applied to Noah in various *midrashim* (*Tanḥ Noaḥ* 7; *TanḥB Noaḥ* 10; *AggBer* 4; and others) as well; and the eighteenth line alludes to Job 22:28. Fragmentary as they are, these passages are enriched by the deftness of Yannai's use of biblical allusion.

It is also possible to detect an allusion to the Mishnah, which is uncommon in Yannai's piyyutim on Genesis (although more frequent in his more "halakhic" works, for *sedarim* later in the Torah). The language of the end of Poem Seven strongly evokes *m. Avot* 1:2, which states: "The world depends upon three things: upon the Torah, upon worship (*avodah*), and upon deeds of piety (*gemilut ḥasidim*)." Yannai's poetry echoes these ideas—using the very words *ḥesed*, *avodah* and *Torah* in the surviving *rahit*. Yannai in effect translates Noah's righteousness into an ideal of rabbinic practice. The parallels in language are too striking to dismiss as simple coincidence.

Intertextuality is not merely an aesthetic embellishment here. Yannai's characterization of Noah displays true innovation, and it relies on the power of biblical language. Lines 15–16 rework Ps 145:17: "The Lord is righteous in all His ways and pious in all His deeds." Through this allusion, Yannai has transferred divine attributes to the ancestor—a bold rhetorical move. Furthermore, not only does Noah possess attribute like God's, but God fulfills Noah's decrees. We see this same audacious theology in

9 Note that **R** and **B1** adduce more sources than those referenced here.

Tanḥ Va'era 19, where it is applied to Moses rather than Noah. In that midrash, the prooftext is Job 22:28—"You shall decree a thing and it shall be fulfilled for you"—the same verse upon which our poet draws when he writes, "He decrees and God fulfills his utterance." The application of this motif of divine-human parity to Noah appears to be unique to Yannai, according to whom God's covenant with humanity, symbolized by the rainbow, is Noah's idea.

What does this nexus of allusions, references, and images suggest? It appears that in the Byzantine synagogue, Noah was held in high esteem—higher than his overall ambivalent status in extent rabbinic literature alone might imply.[10] Exalting Noah is hardly a new trend in Hebrew literature, of course. Already in Ezek 14:14 and 20, Noah appears in a list alongside Daniel (probably the Ugaritic hero, Dan'el rather than the Hellenistic biblical character of the same name) and Job—three figures singled out by the Prophet because their merit as individuals saved the lives of others. In the final line of the first poetic unit above, Yannai echoes Ezekiel's assertion that individuals can save (or condemn) themselves. In the post-biblical period, apocryphal and pseudepigraphical works likewise provide intriguing complements to Yannai's depiction of Noah. For example, in a unit of the apocryphal Wisdom of Ben Sirah called "In Praise of Famous Men" (Sirah 44–50), Noah is the second of the ancestors listed, coming after Enoch and before Abraham, Isaac, Jacob, Moses, Aaron, and Phineas (Sirah 44:17–18). Much like Yannai, Sirah singles Noah out for both attributes and actions: his righteousness, his role in preserving life on earth, and the divine reward these qualities earn for him. The book of Jubilees (Jub 5–10), which is not included in any modern canon, expands Noah's role in more unusual ways; the flood story is dramatically shortened while other units, including one emphasizing the importance of the solar calendar, are added. Connecting Noah to the solar calendar,

10 Noah is also prominent in Christian iconography and texts in this period. See the discussion in the commentary for the next *qedushta*, as well, and also Naomi Koltun-Fromm, "Aphrahat and the Rabbis on Noah's Righteousness in Light of the Jewish-Christian Polemic," *The Book of Genesis in Jewish and Oriental Christian Interpretation*, eds. E. Peter, J. Frishman, and L. van Rompay (Louvain: Peeters, 1997), 57–71. Koltun-Fromm's article does not discuss piyyut, a lacuna filled by L. Lieber, "Portraits of Righteousness: Noah in Early Christian and Jewish Hymnography," *Zeitschrift für Religions- und Geistesgeschichte* 61 (2009): 332–55.

while most obvious in Jubilees, may have been widespread in antiquity. And it is to these connections that we now turn.

According to *PRE* 8, Noah is explicitly understood as having special knowledge of the heavens, of being an ancient astronomer, as it were:

> And Enoch delivered the principle of intercalation to Noah, and he was initiated into the principle of intercalation, and he intercalated the year, as it is said: "While the earth remains, seed time and harvest, and cold and heat, and summer and winter..." (Gen 8:22). "Seed time" refers to the season of Tishrei (fall), "harvest" refers to the season of Nisan (spring), "cold" refers to the season of Tevet (winter), and "heat" refers to the season of Tammuz (summer); "summer" in its season and "winter" in its season.

More subtly, *TargPsJ* renders Gen 8:22 in terms of the natural order linking the heavens and earth:

> During all the days of the earth, there shall be sowing at the season of Tishrei and harvest at the season of Nisan, cold at the season of Tevet and heat at the season of Tammuz, and summer and winter, and days and nights shall not cease.

Joining Noah—the father of all humanity—to the solar calendar (as Jubilees does) may reflect an awareness that the Jewish calendar was distinctive. Most of humanity—the children of Noah—rely upon the sun for their calendar; Jews employ a calendar that is lunar at base but corrected so that the seasons remain in synch with the solar calendar—the very topic of the passages just quoted from *PRE* and *TargPsJ*.[11]

The connection between the Noah story and continuity of the natural order can be seen in one additional variety of extra-canonical source: the visual arts. The story of Noah is depicted in two synagogue mosaics (at Gerasa and Mopsuestia) and on coins from Apamea Kibotos in Asia Minor (193 C.E.), as well.[12] Jewish visual depictions of Noah, like the literary sources discussed above, focus on the animals, most likely as symbolic of

---

11 For an articulation of the distinctiveness of the Jewish calendar, see *GenR* 6:3, which states: "R. Levi said in the name of R. Yose bar Lai: It is only natural that the great should count by the great, and the small by the small. Esau [Rome] counts [time] by the sun, which is large, and Jacob [the Jews] by the moon, which is small."

12 See Rachel Hachlili, *Ancient Jewish Art and Archaeology in the Land of Israel* (Leiden: Brill, 1988).

God's promise not to destroy the world with water again. This natural focus sets Jewish uses of Noah apart from Christian presentations of the same story, which emphasize a "death and resurrection" interpretation of the Flood narrative and are found primarily in funerary settings.

The covenant with Noah and its calendrical associations may shed light on a more common motif of synagogue art, as well. The remarkable depictions of the Zodiac on synagogue floors, often accompanied by figures denoting the seasons in the corners (or, in the case of the Ein Gedi synagogue, calendrical notations) may represent confidence in the eternal movement of the heavens. If this interpretation ever held sway (either at the time when the mosaics were laid, or simply in the eyes of later beholders), the mosaics implicitly invoke the unending cycle of seasons promised by God to Noah in Gen 8:21–22:

> ...And the Lord said in his heart, I will not again curse the ground any more for man's sake...nor will I again destroy every living thing, as I have done. While the earth remains, seed time and harvest, and cold and heat, and summer and winter, and day and night shall not cease.

The Jewish calendar, with its emphasis on the seasons (particularly the requirement that Passover always occur in the Spring), relies upon God's covenant with Noah.

His connections with the cycles of nature, the regularity of the calendar, and predictability of the seasons may be the greatest source of admiration of Noah in the Jewish world of Late Antiquity. In vivid form, both texts and images underscore the results of Noah's righteousness on behalf of the living world. Yannai's piyyut, small fragment that it is, sparkles like a stone in a newly revealed mosaic.

Qedushta for Genesis 8:15 — בראשית ח:טו

"Go Forth from the Ark" — צא מן התבה

Divine commandments offer the commanded both challenges and rewards. Some tests—notably the binding of Isaac—confront the tested (and the later reader) with stark existential and moral crises. This poem, however, describes a subtler trial: one of restraint rather than action, endurance rather than decisiveness. In Yannai's hands, the simple phrase, "Go forth, you and your wife" becomes a message of hope and restoration in both physical and metaphorical senses.

(1) Prisoners of Your hope[1], O Lord
…
…
The (others) were pacing in the presence of (Your) pure ones, quarrelling[2]

You concealed him until You destroyed them
And his ark, like a ship, You led
An angry torrent—and then it passed, and You released (him)
the sum of his suffering You had counted out.

His goodness and his purity You beheld
thus from the overflow You saved him
Just as You sheltered him with a command
so too You released him with a command[3]

As it is written: "Then God said to Noah: Go forth from the ark, you and your wife and yours sons, and your son's wives with you" (Gen 8:15–16)
And it is said: "In the sin of the lips is the trap of the wicked but the righteous one will go forth from dire straits" (Prov 12:13)[4]
And it is said: "When the wrath of a ruler flares up against you, do not leave your place, for calmness will put to rest great sins" (Eccl 10:4)[5]
And it is said: "Bring my life out from a prison, to praise Your name; through me, the righteous will make crowns, because You had compassion for me" (Ps 142:8)[6]
And it is said: "He brought me out to wide-open place; He drew me out because His desire was for me" (Ps 18:2)

---

1 Zech 9:12; Noah and his family are imprisoned within the ark yet hope that God will restore them to dry land.

2 As **R** notes, this stich appears to allude to the tradition found in *GenR* 30:7 and *TanḥB Noah* 10 that as Noah built the ark, the other inhabitants of the earth mocked and argued with him, calling him "contemptible old man" and offering other insults. Later, as they drowned, they sought to overturn the ark and drown Noah with them. Here, the poet includes Noah's sons in the scene.

3 See *Tanḥ Noaḥ* 8; just as Noah only entered the ark when God told him to do so, he would only leave the ark when he was commanded to do so. The imperative that opens this *sidra* ("go forth!") is the basis for this teaching.

4 See *GenR* 34:3 (*Pet*); *Tanḥ Noaḥ* 10; *TanḥB Noaḥ* 16 (**R**); these sources interpret the "wicked" of this verse as the generation of the Flood and the "righteous" as Noah. In the piyyut, "righteous" is a common epithet for Noah.

(א) אֲסִירֵי תִקְוָתְךָ אָדוֹן
ב.. ...
...
דּוֹרְכִים לְמוּל תְּמִימִים מָדוֹן

הַחְבֵיתם עַד אוֹתָם מָחִיתָ
וְתֵיבָתם כָּאֳנִיָּה נָחִיתָה
זַעַם עַד יַעֲבוֹר אָז פָּנִיתָה
חֶשְׁבּוֹן אִיסּוּרוֹ אֲשֶׁר מָנִיתָ

טוֹבָתוֹ וְתֻומָּתוֹ צָפִיתָה
יַעַן כִּי מִשֶּׁטֶף אֹתוֹ פָּצִיתָה
כְּמוֹ בִרְשׁוּת אוֹתוֹ הִצְפַּנְתָּה
לָכֵן בִּרְשׁוּת אוֹתוֹ הוֹצֵאתָ

ככתוב וידבר אלהים אל נח צא מן התבה אתה ואשתך ובניך ונשי בניך אתך

ונאמר בפשע שפתים מוקש רע ויצא מצרה צדיק

ונאמר אם רוח המושל תעלה עליך מקומך אל תנח כי מרפא יניח חטאים גדולים

ונאמר הוציאה ממסגר נפשי להודת את שמך בי יכתירו צדיקים כי תגמול עלי

ונאמר ויוציאני למרחב יחלצני כי חפץ בי

---

5 See *GenR* 34:4; *Tanḥ Noaḥ* 10 (**R**). The "place" one should not leave too early is understood specifically as the ark. The words for "leave" (תנח) and "put to rest" (יניח) are puns on the name Noah.

6 This verse occurs in reference to Noah in *GenR* 34:1, *Tanḥ Noaḥ* 11 (**R**); and also *TanḥB Noaḥ* 17. The imagery of the verse in the context of the *qedushta* evokes the tradition that the prayers of the Jews are woven into a divine crown by the angel Sandalfon, a mystically-charged tradition recorded in *b.Ḥag.*13b. The final line of this poem reinforces the connections between crowning and prayer. *PRE* 23 offers a parallel to this motif that specifically refers to Noah: "Through me," says Noah, "all the righteous will crown You with a crown of sovereignty." In all these sources, "crowning" is connected to prayer—in the Talmud and, implicitly, here, the context is one of routine prayer, while *PRE* may have the Rosh Hashanah shofar service (where God is "crowned" in the *malkhiyyot* section and Noah mentioned in the *zikhronot* sections) in mind.

And it is said: "God returns the solitary ones home, the imprisoned He brings forth to happiness; but the rebellious dwell in barrenness" (Ps 68:7)[7]

And it is said: "He does justice for the wronged, He gives bread to the hungry[8]; the Eternal sets prisoners free" (Ps 146:7)

Prisoners You set free
Indeed, for You we wait[9]
a shield, and we make crowns for You!
Blessed… Shield…

(2) The ones who were brought into the ark with Noah
they received good news—the Flood receded!
Yea, never will You reject
but unto the storm-tossed one You will give rest
You watched over the one whose reverence for You was pure[10]
one righteous in the law that makes pure
Rightness[11] for indeed, each is dependent on the righteous one in his purity[12]
… he is like the righteous in his purified law[13]
Keeping…
…
You hasten because Your time arrives
You will go forth…

As it is written: "Bring out with you every living thing of all flesh that is with you: birds, animals, and everything that creeps on earth; and let them swarm on the earth and be fertile and increase on earth" (Gen 8:17)

---

7 This verse is not connected to Noah in extant midrashic traditions, but it does occur in aggadic literature describing God as a matchmaker (e.g., *NumR* 3:6; **R** adduces *GenR* 68:4). The interpretation here derives its wit from the fact that "home" is a slang term or euphemism for "wife" in rabbinic Hebrew. In the present context, this verse comments on the restoration of marital satisfaction to the men and women of the ark who had abstained from sexual relations for the entire year of the Flood. The ones who had been "solitary" can go back "home" (note also that the word תיבה—"ark"—is an anagram for ביתה —"homeward"). The word *kosherot* ("happiness") can also mean "suitable women" (a meaning attested in other aggadic sources).

8 The line, not attached to the Noah story in the midrashic traditions, anticipates Noah's "god-like" role in providing for the people and animals of the ark later in the piyyut. The line may also suggest God's restoration of marital pleasures to the couples on board; "He

ונאמר אלהים מושיב יחידים ביתה מוציא אסירים בכושרות אך סוררים שכנו צחיחה

ונאמר עושה משפט לעשוקים נותן לחם לרעבים יי מתיר אסורים

אֲסוּרִים תַּתִּיר
כִּי לָךְ נַכְתִּיר
מָגֵן וְלָךְ נַעְתִּיר
ברוך... מגן...

(ב) **מ**וּבָאֵי לַתֵּיבָה עִם נֹחַ
נִתְבַּשְּׂרוּ כִּי מַבּוּל נִינּוֹחַ
סֶלָה לָעַד לֹא תַזְנִיחַ
עַד לַטָּרוּף תִּתֵּן מָנוֹחַ
פָּקַדְתָּה בְּיִרְאָתָךְ הַטְּהוֹרָה
צַדִּיק בְּדָת מְטוֹוהָרָה
קֹשֶׁט כִּי כָל טָפוּל לַצַּדִּיק בְּטָהֳרָה
רצ.. הוּא כַצַּדִּיק כְּדָת מְטוֹהָרָה
שׁוֹמֵר ...
...
תְּמַהֵר כִּי גָעָה עִתָּךְ
תֵּצֵא ...

ככתוב כל החיה אשר אתך מכל בשר בעוף ובבהמה ובכל הרמש הרמש על הארץ הוצא אתך ושרצו בארץ ופרו ורבו על הארץ

---

gives bread to the hungry" may allude to God permitting "bread" (wives; see Gen 39:6) to deprived husbands.

9 The reading in Maʾagarim is uncertain; here it is rendered in accord with Job 36:2. Alternatively, it could be translated as, "For You, we make a diadem" (in parallel with the third stich).

10 Ps 19:10, noted by **B1**.

11 *Qoshet* ("rightness, straightness, truth") may be a pun on a homonym, the biblical Hebrew loanword meaning "archer," thereby alluding to the rainbow (*qeshet*).

12 That is, everyone within the Ark depended on Noah (known as both "righteous" and "pure") to successfully navigate the Flood.

13 The text is somewhat uncertain; the second stich apparently refers to the new laws given to Noah after the Flood.

And as it is said: "A righteous man knows the life of his beast; but the heart of the wicked is cruel" (Prov. 12:10)
And as it is said….

…By Your righteousness lead us…
[*Blessed… Who resurrects…*]

(3) …
Their sinful ways You saw …
You plumbed …
… a dungeon You sustain …
each loyal one, and you pay heed…

As it is written: "To open blind eyes, bringing forth prisoners from confinement, those who dwell in darkness from the dungeon" (Isa 42:7)
And as it is said…
And You are Holy, enthroned on the prayers of Israel… *Please, God…*

(4) He frees the imprisoned[14] and fulfills every want;
He releases the bound and opens what is closed[15]
As for the man in the ark, You confined him; behind him You shut the door
but You let him lack for nothing and to him You brought glad news:
The rain has ended and the torrent ceased[16]
anger has abated and rage quieted down
the Flood has dried up the roaring deeps are quelled;
Go forth from the ark and fill the land of plenty[17]
Indeed, all who gaze out from in dire straits will someday see delight
Just as You promised, O Holy One!

(5) Then the hint was dropped and a word discretely spoken
upon his entry to the ark and upon his exit
Upon his entry, he was told, "Enter, you and your *sons*;"

---

14 Ps 68:7 (**B2**)

15 An unpopulated world "wants" (is in need of, lacks) people, a deficiency God appoints Noah to restore. Celibacy is again compared to imprisonment while reproduction fulfills both divine and human desires.

ונאמר יודעַ צדיק נפש בהמתו ורחמי רשעים אכזרי

ונאמר ...

... בְּצִדְקָתָךְ נְחֵינוּ
[ברוך... מחיה...]

(ג) ...
... הַעֲבִירָם תִּשְׁקוֹד
... ... אַתָּה חוֹקֵר ...
... ... בֵּית כֶּלֶא תְּקוֹמֵם ...
... כָּל חֶסֶר וְתַשְׁמִיעַ ...

ככתוב לפקוח עינים עורות להוציא ממסגר אסיר מבית הכלא ישבי חשך

ונאמר ...
ואתה קדוש יושב תהלות ישראל אל נא

(ד) מוֹצִיא אֲסִירִים וּמְמַלֵּא חֲסֵירִים
מַתִּיר אֲסוּרִים וּמְפַתֵּיחַ סְגוּרִים
לְאִישׁ בַּתֵּיבָה אֲסַרְתָּה וּבַעֲדוֹ סָגַרְתָּה
וְכֹל לֹא חִיסַּרְתָּה אוֹתוֹ בִּשַּׂרְתָּה
הַגֶּשֶׁם חָלַף וְהַשֶּׁטֶף הָלַךְ
זַעַם שָׁכַךְ וְזַעַף שָׁקַט
מַבּוּל יָבֵשׁ וּתְהוֹם כָּבֵישׁ
צֵא מִתֵּיבָה וּמַלֵּא גֵיְא תְּנוּבָה
כִּי כָל רוֹאֶה בְּצָרָה יִרְאֶה בִּרְוָחָה
כְּהִבְטַחְתָּה קָדוֹשׁ

(ה) אָז רָז נִרְמַז לוֹ וְדָבָר דִּבּוּר נִדְבַּר לוֹ
בְּבוֹאוֹ לַתֵּיבָה וּבְצֵאתוֹ מִתֵּיבָה
בְּבוֹאוֹ נֶאֱמַר לוֹ בּוֹא אַתָּה וּבָנֶיךָ

---

16 The language here echoes Song 2:11 (**R**).

17 As **R** notes, the Hebrew term here rendered "land" (גיא) means "valley" in biblical Hebrew; in later Hebrew it may be a pun on the Greek term "earth" (γη). The language of this verse echoes Isa 27:6 (**R** and **B1**).

But upon his exit, he was told, "Go forth, you and your *wife*"[18]
Indeed, upon his entry into captivity, she was forbidden to him
but upon his going forth to freedom, she was again permitted to him
Later generations would realize, deem wise, and affirm this:
do not increase at a time of decrease; do not be fruitful in a time of want
When trouble comes into the world, all suffer
and when joy comes to the world, all rejoice
And truly, a general rule can be learned from these laws:
how to act when wasted by want and hunger
His merit: he believed so he summoned and sustained;
Thus did he do well by every beast concealed in there with him[19]
A new mitzvah was made for him when he went forth from the ark
for the reward of a mitzvah is a mitzvah:[20] the reward of a life is a life
God granted him good sense gave him insight and made him wise
when He multiplied pure creatures but made the impure creatures few[21]
He went out among the pure and found an offering to offer
to the One who would renew a world out of the ruins
Please God…

"*Go forth from the ark*"
(6) I am He who shut the door behind you;
that this would last twelve months, I told you
By Myself did I adjure Myself
never again a flood to inflict
The earth revealed her face
ravaged by the arrogant, the hard of face;
Tread again My chamber, founded of old,
Your wife and all who are with you from before
The beast that had been by your hand
by your hand it stayed alive

---

18 The juxtaposition of these two phrases, from Gen 6:8 and Gen 8:15, is taken here, as in multiple aggadic passages (many noted by **R**), to indicate that the time spent in the ark was a time of celibacy for Noah and his family. They went in one-by-one, as it were, but upon disembarking, they came forth restored to marital pairs. See, among others, *GenR* 34:7; *TanḥB Noaḥ* 17; *Tanḥ Noaḥ* 11; *PRE* 29:20; and *j. Taʿan.* 7a.

19 This line teaches that Noah sustained each animal with appropriate food for the entire time on the ark. See, for example, *GenR* 34:14, "He brought branches for the elephants, brush for the deer…" (cited by **R**).

וּבְצֵאתוֹ נֶאֱמַר לוֹ צֵא אַתָּה וְאִשְׁתְּךָ
גַּם בְּבוֹאוֹ לְהֵיאָסֵר נֶאֶסְרָה לוֹ
וּבְצֵאתוֹ לְהִיוָּתֵר הֻותְּרָה לוֹ
דוֹרוֹת לְהַשְׂכִּיל וּלְהַסְכִּית וּלְהַסְכִּים
מִלְהַרְבּוֹת בְּעֵת מִיעוּט וּמִלְמַלְּאוֹת בְּעֵת חִיסּוּר
הַאִם בָּאַת צָרָה לָעוֹלָם לְהָצֵר בָּהּ
וְאִם בָּאַת שִׂמְחָה לָעוֹלָם לִשְׂמוֹחַ בָּהּ
וְאָמְנָם זֶה כְּלָל בְּחֻוקֵּי לִימּוּד
לִנְהוֹג בְּחֶסֶר וּבְכָפָן גַּלְמוּד
זְכוּת אֲשֶׁר הֶאֱמִין וְהִזְמִין וְהֵימִין
אֲשֶׁר עָשׂ שָׁם עִם כָּל מִין אֲשֶׁר אִיתּוֹ הִטְמִין
חֻודַּשׁ לוֹ מִצְוָוה בְּצֵאתוֹ מִתֵּיבָה
כִּי שְׂכַר מִצְוָוה מִצְוָוה וּשְׂכַר נְפָשׁוֹת נְפָשׁוֹת
טַעַם לוֹ הִתְכִּין וְהֵיבִין וְהֶחְכִּים
בְּעֵת כִּי רִיבָּה לוֹ בַּטְּהוֹרִים וּמִיעֵט לוֹ בַּטְּמֵאִים
יָצָא וַיִּמְצָא מִמֶּנָּה לְהַקְרִיב קָרְבָּן
לִמְחַדֵּשׁ לוֹ עוֹלָם מֵחָורְבָּן
אל נא

צא מן התבה
(ו) **אֲ**נִי הוּא אֲשֶׁר בַּעֲדָךְ סָגַרְתִּי
וְקֵץ שְׁנֵים־עָשָׂר חוֹדֶשׁ לָךְ מָסַרְתִּי
בִּשְׁבוּעָה עָלַיי אָסַרְתִּי
כִּי מַבּוּל לְעוֹלָם הֵיסַרְתִּי
גִּילָּת הָאָרֶץ פָּנִים
אֲשֶׁר בּוֹקְקָה וְעַזּוּ בָהּ פָּנִים
דְּרוֹךְ אֲגוּדָּה יְסוּדָה לְפָנִים
אִשָּׁה וְכָל אֲשֶׁר עִימָּךְ לִיפְנִים
הַחַיָּה אֲשֶׁר בְּיָדָךְ הָיְתָה
כְּמוֹ מִיָּדָךְ חָיְיתָה

20 Compare with *m. Avot* 4:2, "One mitzvah leads to [another] mitzvah;" the terseness of Yannai's language recalls the mishnaic phrasing. The meaning of this stich is: Because Noah faithfully obeyed God's command to build and go into the ark, upon his exit he was rewarded with the command that enabled him and his descendents to eat meat.

21 The understanding here—and again, it is rooted in the biblical story of Noah—is that the "pure" creatures are those who are *kasher*, consumable according to the Jewish dietary laws. The biblical text does not state this or even use the language of *kashrut*, but Noah intuits God's intent.

For like He who feeds all, you created[23]
In the same manner[24] you fed and kept alive
I remembered with kindness as enduring as the world
when I said, "Built up again shall be the world"[25]
I preserved you, to rebuild the foundations of the world
for the righteous are the pillar of the world
The droplets of the cloudy Curtain I stoppered
the [well-springs of] fountains of the Deep I sealed[26]
Those who go forth with you, wonders will they tell
for the eyes of all look to you with hope
All of My works I shall not again undo
The Curtain I shall not tatter nor the land again make melt
For My sake, for My own sake, shall I work
for My compassion falls upon every work
Never again shall there be waters to flood
but a downpour of My words instead
Their flow helps life to flourish
the soil sated, not saturated, shall be
So you asked the One who took the guise of the rainbow,[27]
(you) who survived the *Nephilim*,[28] with the vision of the rainbow
Because I see you do not trust in the war-bow
I will give you a sign in the clouds—the rainbow
Before your birth, I selected you for this covenant[29]
and I instructed you: "This is the sign of the covenant"[30]
I gave you light to shine morning and evening
to help you go forth and establish a remnant
A limit I set to the darkness—that it would end—
limits I imposed upon all, without exception
My compassion, however, I shall not restrain
never again will I work upon the world destruction
Those that came two-by-two: set them free, let them be;

23 God compares Noah's actions to His own—he creates (through his role in repopulating the world) and sustains. For God as "the one who feeds," see the Grace after Meals.

24 The poet uses the term "*middah*" ("measure, attribute") to describe Noah's action, suggesting that Noah shares these attributes (feeding others and keeping them alive) with the deity but also literally describing the act of apportioning food to animals in the ark.

25 A play on Ps 89:3.

26 Lacuna filled by **B1** on basis of Judg 5:4; the reading in the Ma'agarim database

וּכְזָן אֶת הַכֹּל בָּרָאתָ
בְּמִידָּה אֲשֶׁר זַנְתָּה וְחִיִּיתָה
זְכַרְתִּיךָ בְּחֶסֶד עוֹלָם
אֲשֶׁר בּוֹ אָמַרְתִּי יִיבָּנֶה עוֹלָם
חֲסַכְתִּיךָ לִבְנוֹת מוֹסְדֵי עוֹלָם
כִּי צַדִּיק הוּא יְסוֹד עוֹלָם
טִיפֵּי אֲרוּבּוֹת דּוֹק נִסְגָּרוּ
... מַעְיְינוֹת תְּהוֹם נִסְכָּרוּ
יוֹצְאֵי אִיתָּךְ פְּלָאוֹת יְסַפֵּירוּ
כִּי עֵינֵי כֹל אֵלֶיךָ יְשַׂבֵּרוּ
כָּלָה מַעֲשַׂיי לֹא אֶעֱשֶׂה
דּוֹק לֹא אֲמוֹטֵט וְגֵיא לֹא אַמְסֶה
לְמַעֲנִי לְמַעֲנִי אָז אֶעֱשֶׂה
כִּי רַחֲמַיי עַל כָּל מַעֲשֶׂה
מַיִם לְמַבּוּל עוֹד לֹא יִהְיֶה
כְּיְרִידָתוֹ דְּבָרִי יִהְיֶה
נוֹזֵל לְמִחְיָיה יִהְיֶה
נְשִׁיָּה לְהַשְׂבִּיעַ יִהְיֶה
סַחְתָּה לִמְדַמֶּה כְּמַרְאֶה קֶשֶׁת
לִמְלוֹט נְפִילִים בְּמַרְאֵה קָשֶׁת
עֲבוּר לָךְ רָאִיתִי לֹא בוֹטֵחַ בְּקָשֶׁת
אֶתֶּן לָךְ אוֹת בַּעֲנַן קֶשֶׁת
פְּקַדְתִּיךָ עַד לֹא נוֹלַדְתָּה בִּבְרִית
וְהִפְקַדְתִּי לָךְ זֹאת אוֹת הַבְּרִית
צִיהַרְתִּי לָךְ עַרְבִית וְשַׁחֲרִית
לָצֵאת וְלָשׁוּם לָךְ שְׁאֵירִית
קֵץ שָׂם לַחוֹשֶׁךְ הֵן כָּלָה
בְּקֵץ אֲשֶׁר תַּתִּי לְכָל תִּכְלָה
רַחֲמַיי מֵעַתָּה לֹא אֲכַלֶּה
מִלַּעֲשׂוֹת עוֹד בָּעוֹלָם כָּלָה
שְׁנַיִם שְׁנַיִם תִּפְטוֹר וְתִפְנֶה

supports **B1**'s conjecture.

27 God; cf. Ezek 1:28.

28 That is, Noah, who survived from the era of the *Nephilim* (lit., 'the fallen ones') (**B1**).

29 This may refer to *TanḥB Bereshit* 32, in which God shows "Noah and all the pure ones" to Adam in a prophetic dream. Alternatively, it could refer to *TanḥB Noaḥ* 6, which describes Noah as having been born circumcised. (**R** cites both possibilities.)

30 Quotations of Gen 9:12.

those that came seven-by-seven: Guard them well, keep accounts
Make offerings upon an altar—one you will build—
and thus recreate the world and in security dwell."

And so, "Go forth from the ark"
(7[1]) *Go forth from* confinement to freedom
Go forth from trembling to tranquility
Go forth from...
Go forth from oppression to exaltation
Go forth from flux to firmness
Go forth from withdrawal to walking tall
Go forth from darkness to light
Go forth from persecution to protection
Go forth from labor to leisure
Go forth from restriction to release
Go forth from mourning to merriment
Go forth from death to new life
Go forth from lamentation to celebration
Go forth from closed to opened
Go forth from effort to ease
Go forth from inside to out
Go forth from dire straits to delight
Go forth from curse to blessing
Go forth from fury to free-will
Go forth from conflict to calm
Go forth from the ark to a world of desire!

And thus, "With your sons and your wife, and your sons' wives ..."
(7[2]) With you, by merit of your kindness
a blessing upon the land is yours to give
A mighty "warrior," drawing your "sword"[31]
though your generation rejected such knowledge
So was it blotted out and I left only you

31 The first half of the line employs the language of Exod 15:9 in metaphorical terms, turning the military imagery into a euphemistic discussion of reproduction; the second half of the line suggests that the generation of the Flood refused to fulfill the command "be

שִׁבְעָה שִׁבְעָה תִּנְצוֹר וְתִמְנֶה
תֵּת בַּמִּזְבֵּחַ אֲשֶׁר תִּבְנֶה
וְעוֹלָם תִּקְנֶה וּבְבִטְחָתָה תַּחֲנֶה

ובכן צא מן התבה

(ז¹) צֵא מֵאֲסִירָה לְהַתָּרָה
צֵא מִבַּלָּהָה לְהֲנָחָה
צֵא מִגּ.. ...
צֵא מִדְּחִיקָה לְדִיצָה
צֵא מֵהוֹוָה לַהֲוָיָה
צֵא מִזְּעִימָה לִזְקִיפָה
צֵא מֵחֲשֵׁיכָה לְאוֹרָה
צֵא מִטַּלְטֵלָה לְהַבְטָחָה
צֵא מִיגִיעָה לִרְגִיעָה
צֵא מִכְּלִיאָה לִדְרָרָה
צֵא מִלְּחִיצָה לַעֲלִיצָה
צֵא מִמָּוְותָה לִתְחִיָּה
צֵא מִנְּהִיָּה לִנְהוֹרָה
צֵא מִסְּגִירָה לִפְתִיחָה
צֵא מֵעֲמִילָה לִנְפִישָׁה
צֵא מִפְּנִימָה לַחוּצָה
צֵא מִצָּרָה לִרְוָוחָה
צֵא מִקְּלָלָה לִבְרָכָה
צֵא מֵרְגִיזָה לִרְצִיָּה
צֵא מִשַּׁמָּה לְשַׁלְוָוה
צֵא מִתֵּיבָה לִתְאִיבָה

ובכן ובניך ואשתך ונשי בניך

(ז²) אִיתָּךְ בִּזְכוּת אֲמִיתָּךְ
בְּרָכָה לָאָרֶץ בְּתֵיתָךְ
גִּבּוֹר הָרֵק חֲנִיתָךְ
דּוֹרָךְ מָאַס בְּדַעְתָּךְ
הָומְחָה וְהִסְרַדְתִּי אוֹתָךְ

fruitful and multiply" given to Adam and Eve (see *Tanḥ Noaḥ* 12 and *PRE* 22) (**B1**). Noah and his family understood the importance of this commandment, but also understood the need to wait until the end of the Flood.

I hid you to revive you[32]
I remembered you to sustain you
I graced you with a graceful camp
I purified your impurity
I distinguished the lineage of your marital beds
I bedecked (you) with your love[33]
yours is the dew of childbearing
By you will the earth be filled
pleasing saplings are your blessing
Great indeed shall be those who come after you!
Your covenant will I sustain forever
A survivor [were you meant to be][34]
I only waited for your crowning prayer[35]
I brought your desire close
reclining [at rest, at last][36]
Peace and smooth-going shall be what you find
Let there be a [new] light upon your going forth[37]

(8) … light upon your path He shines light,
and He gives strength, and holiness… majestic in holiness
[As it is written: "And the one called to the other…"]

---

32 This refers specifically to reproduction (by Noah's sons), but also, metaphorically, to the role played by Noah and his family in preserving *all* life. The language evokes resurrection.

33 The language here suggests the ritual of crowning a bride; line nine refers to the reciprocal crowning of the groom.

34 Completed according to **B2**.

35 It seems that Noah's prayer induced God to release him from the ark. See Ps 142:8, quoted above: "Through me the righteous will make crowns" where the speaker is understood to be Noah.

36 Lacuna filled by **B2**. The imagery here functions at two levels: Noah and his family yearn for both physical rest—repose on dry land—but also intimacy with their spouses— reclining in bed, as it were. Thus "desire" and "reclining" should be heard as double entendres.

וְהֶחְבֵּיאתִיךָ לְהַחְיוֹתָךְ
זְכַרְתִּיךָ לְחַיּוֹתָךְ
חַנּוֹתִי לְחַנּוֹתָךְ
טִיהַרְתִּי טֻומְאָתָךְ
יִיחַסְתִּי מִיטָּתָךְ
כִּילַּלְתִּי אַהֲבָתָךְ
לָךְ טַל יַלְדוּתָךְ
מִמָּךְ אֲמַלֵּא אַדְמָתָךְ
נִטְעֵי נַעֲמָן בִּרְכָתָךְ
סַגִּיא מְאֹד תְּהִי אַחֲרִיתָךְ
עֲדֵי עַד קִיַּמְתִּי בְּרִיתָךְ
פלי.. ...
צִפִּיתִי לַעֲתִירָתָךְ
קֵירַבְ.. חִבָּתָךְ
ריבץ ...
שָׁלוֹם וּמִישׁוֹר מְצִיאָתָךְ
תְּהִי אוֹר חָ..שׁ לִיצִיאָתָךְ

(ח) ... אוֹר עַל דְּרָכָיו נָגַהּ אוֹר
וְנָתַן עוֹז וּקְדֻושָּׁה ... נֶאדָּר בַּקּוֹדֶשׁ
[ככתוב וקרא זה אל זה]

---

37 According to **B2**, this line recalls the teaching in *Tanḥ Ber.* 12 that understands the generation of the Flood as "rebels against the light" (citing Job 24:13) and Noah as their opposite—a polarity of "children of darkness and light." The idea of "new light" requires further comment, however. It could allude to a messianic light ("a new light shall shine upon Zion" from the *Yotzer Or*); or it may hint at the aggadah that the heavenly cycles of stars and planets (and, thereby, seasons and holidays) ceased during the great Flood and were in some way "renewed" upon its end.

See *GenR* 32:11, where it is written: "Rabbi Yohanan said: The planets did not function the whole twelve months [of the Flood]. Rabbi said Jonathan to him: They did function, but their effect was imperceptible. Rabbi Eliezer said: `They shall not cease' (Gen 8:22) implies that they never ceased. Rabbi Joshua deduced: `They shall not cease' — hence it follows that they had ceased!"

Commentary

This *qedushta* emphasizes the ways in which small-scale acts relate to cosmic reality. While on the ark, Noah fulfills a God-like role: just as God feeds and sustains the world, Noah feeds and sustains those living on the ark; just as God created the world, Noah and the animals embody the promise of re-creation; and just as God is, in some sense, fundamentally *alone*, Noah on the ark exists apart from his wife. The ark is, literally, a microcosm and Noah is its lord. This poem describes the restoration of the world to light and life (after a year of rain, death, and destruction) by focusing not on the cosmic scale, but on the restoration of a family. Noah's skill in animal husbandry earns him a reward of being restored as a husband.

Of all potential motifs available to Yannai in retelling the Flood story, that of temporary celibacy may strike modern readers as obscure, fanciful, or possibly even off-putting. And yet, not only does Yannai employ here a popular aggadic motif, but he selects one that emphasizes the deeper drama of the narrative. If we understand the Flood to be a drama about life and death, then celibacy becomes emblematic of destruction (denial of life and the future) while sexual intimacy represents the most essential kind of restoration (affirmation of life and creation of future). The motif of celibacy and its cessation is clearly articulated in *GenR* 31:12, which states:

> Rabbi Judah son of Rabbi Simon and Rabbi Hanan in the name of Rabbi Samuel son of Rabbi Isaac said: As soon as Noah entered the ark, cohabitation was interdicted to him...When he went out, He permitted it to him.

Similarly, *PRE* 23 notes:

> Rabbi Levitas, a man of Yavneh, said: He [God] separated the males from the females of all who came into the ark when they came into the ark...Indeed, the males were on one side and the females on the other. When they went forth from the ark, He caused the males to be joined with the females....Indeed, a male would go forth with his mate [lit. "wife"]. He blessed them that they might increase and multiply on the earth.

The interpersonal drama of abstinence, reunion, and fertility are thus linked with the cosmic scaled plot of destruction and restoration—a harmony of motifs the ancient exegetes discovered embedded in subtle clues within the biblical text. Why else the difference between "Enter, you and your sons" and "Go forth, you and your wife"? Why else the reiteration of the command to be fruitful and multiply?

Yannai articulates this motif delicately, echoing the understated nature of the biblical text itself. Initially, the poet is so subtle and allusive that the motif of the end of celibacy may be overlooked. In the first poem, the reader may wonder if celibacy is reckoned in "the sum of [Noah's] suffering" (line 8) or whether when God "released him" (line 12), if the release was from the bonds of abstinence. These readings become visible primarily in retrospect. At the same time, this sexualized reading lends clarity to the choice of texts that follow the first poem—notably Ps 18:2, Ps 68:7, and Ps 146:7. Psalm 18 uses the language of "desire" while Ps 146 may pun on the epithet "house" for wife; Psalm 68 provides the most suggestive intertext, however. While not elsewhere connected to the Noah story, this verse's history of interpretation is frequently connected to God's wisdom as a matchmaker and coordinator of connubial bliss. "Prison," such a common motif in this poem, is transformed from physical confinement into a euphemism for loneliness and isolation. Of course, the first poem makes sense on a simpler narrative level: it could describe actual release from the ark. But the wise may hear the word fitly spoken and anticipate from the opening lines the motif to follow.

In the opening of the *asiriyyah* (Poem Five), Yannai acknowledges the euphemistic nature of both the biblical text and the piyyut itself: "The hint was dropped and a word discretely spoken" (line 1). Following this acknowledgment, the poet more clearly articulates the theme of marital pleasure. In Poem Five, we find: "Upon his entry into captivity she [his wife] was forbidden to him // but upon his going forth to freedom, she was again permitted to him" (line 3–4). Similarly, in the second *rahit*, Yannai writes: "I distinguished the lineage of your marital beds / I bedecked your loves / yours is the dew of childbearing" (lines 10–12). Once the reader (or hearer) becomes conscious of these themes, they appear throughout the poem. For example, on several occasions the poet invokes the image of "narrow straits" (almost always contrasted with "delight"); "narrow straits" could simply mean generalized danger and suffering, but it may specifically suggest the self-restraint and emotional confinement of the ark-dwellers. "Delight," conversely, acknowledges the nature of the reward and the experience of release. Other word pairs, particularly in the first *rahit*, may allude to this dynamic, as well: restriction/release; mourning/

merriment; and—ultimately—death/life. The final line of the first *rahit* is especially tantalizing: "Go forth from the ark to a world of desire!" The ark—crowded in spatial terms, limited in food, void of intimacy—is the opposite of the post-diluvian world that awaits the ancestor and his fellow travelers.

The motif of Noah's celibacy invites comparison with non-Jewish hymnographic traditions. It was, perhaps not surprisingly, popular in early Christian hymns. The differences between the Christian interpretations and Yannai's suggest the cultural gap between the two communities in this period.[38] For Yannai (like the Rabbis), Noah's celibacy is a temporary, burdensome experience, necessitated by extreme circumstances and relieved immediately upon disembarkation; in Christian exegesis, Noah's celibacy becomes, and is praised as a proto-monastic permanent state.[39] Contrasting Noah's behavior with the licentiousness of his (doomed) generation, the Syriac poet Ephrem (fourth century C.E.) describes Noah as chaste even in marriage: "Because women had not defiled him, he consecrated / even the animals / all the couples who were in the ark: / the married man consecrated the marriage [into sexual abstinence]."[40] In Ephrem's corpus, Noah's righteousness is synonymous with his sexual abstinence, and the Flood that destroys creation consists of "waves of desire" to which Noah does not succumb.[41] Like Ephrem, Yannai repeatedly describes Noah as "pure," and this purity may have a specifically sexual component; for example, in the third stanza of the *magen* of this piyyut Yannai writes: "His goodness and his purity You beheld / thus from the overflow You saved him." Immediately after these lines, the first hint of abstinence is indicated. It is possible

38 See L. Lieber, "Portraits of Righteousness: Noah in Early Christian and Jewish Hymnography," *Zeitschrift für Religions- und Geistesgeschichte* 61 (2009): 332–55.

39 There is, in rabbinic literature, a tradition that Noah was castrated after the flood, either by a lion (*GenR* 36:4) or by his son Ham (*GenR* 36:7). These traditions exemplify the "negative Noah" strand of exegesis, in which Noah is far from heroic or idealized; his "celibacy" is a source of shame, not praise, and results from drunkenness. (It is not clear whether the castration traditions are engaging in anti-Christian polemic, but both traditions build on the fact that Noah did not father children after the Flood.) Yannai's depictions of Noah are wholly positive, however, and the castration motif is entirely absent.

40 *Carmen Nisibenum* I, 4:7–10; see T. Kronholm, *Motifs from Genesis 1–11 in the Genuine Hymns of Ephrem the Syrian* (CWK Gleerup Lund: Sweden, 1978), 180. According to Ephrem and other Syriac exegetes, Noah abstained from marital intercourse for the first 500 years of his life as well as the period after the Flood—not just while on the Ark—rendering him a model of monastic celibacy from the Old Testament period.

41 *Carmen Nisibenum* I, 4:3.

that the "purity" and "overflow" of the Hebrew verse pertain to sexuality, as in Ephrem's work. Similarly, Yannai indicts the generation of the Flood for their sexual immorality, as well—it is one facet of Noah's disagreement with his contemporaries. But this parallel holds only to a point. Ephrem criticizes the generation of the Flood for promiscuity; Yannai condemns that generation for its refusal to procreate (Poem 7^2, line 4). Furthermore, it is clear in the Jewish traditions that Noah's chastity was only to be temporary, an appropriate reaction to a time of extreme crisis, physical confinement, and lack of life-sustaining necessities. The post-diluvian world, in which husbands and wives are reunited, is a world of intimate pleasures as well as an imperative of reproduction. In the works of Ephrem (as in the earlier works of Origen) the motif of Noah's chastity is expanded to a general ideal, reflecting a distinctly different cultural context. Ephrem, with other church fathers, was engaged in the difficult task of promoting celibacy as an ideal; Yannai, however, in keeping with mainstream rabbinic tradition, affirmed the blessedness of a joyful marriage bed.

In our piyyut, the motifs of fertility and sexuality lend emotional immediacy and human realism to the larger themes of life and restoration that run throughout the poem. The composition as a whole affirms God's covenant and describes the renewal of life on the land. All of creation, from plants and animals to human beings, newly freed from the constraints of the ark, will be fruitful and flourish. Such renewal would not be possible had not Noah sustained the world-in-small (much as God promises to sustain the world itself) and it would not have lasted if creation had not been repopulated. The text acknowledges a balance, however: had the human and animal populations begun the process of reproducing while still aboard the ark, the results would have been disastrous. The virtue for which Noah is rewarded is not merely obedience, but insight: Noah excelled at "husbandry" in all of its possible meanings, shepherding his resources and managing the fertility of his flocks, and by fathering the founders of humanity. Noah's modest wisdom and practical efficiency merit the covenant of the rainbow and the privilege that Noah will bear to "recreate the world" (Poem Six, line 44). Humility and obedience are ultimately rewarded, however, not only with honor, but with delight.

Qedushta for Genesis 9:18 בראשית ט:יח

"The sons of Noah were" ויהיו בני נח

With the receding of the flood waters, it falls upon Noah and his family to reconstitute human society, establishing patterns that will persist thereafter. This poem employs the language of "fathers and sons" to describe both the events of the biblical passage it embellishes as well as the history of the communities who descend from these ancestors. The poet concludes this piyyut by emphasizing the spiritual and religious legacies of Noah's sons, Shem, Yafet, and Ham, rather than their geographical divisions and ethnic lines.

(1) You thought: "Let there be a sign of good"[1]
when You sat in judgment after the Flood[2]
And so, to their homes You restored the solitary,
those clans with love You settled

You permitted what they had foresworn –
You set the imprisoned ones free[3]
You remembered the restrained
You called to mind the confined

As for babes, they refrained from bearing
when settled on dry land, they bedded.
Those who were few, a mighty tribe they became
at the time when they, as families, went forth[4]

As it is written: "The sons of Noah who went forth from the ark were Shem and Ham, and Yafet; and Ham was the father of Canaan" (Gen 9:18)
And it is said: "He does justice for the oppressed; He gives food to the hungry—the Eternal sets prisoners free" (Ps 146:7)[5]
And it is said: "God returns the solitary ones home, the imprisoned He brings forth to happiness; but the rebellious dwell in barrenness" (Ps 68:7)
And it is said: "Saying to the imprisoned, `Go free,' and to those who are in darkness, `Show yourselves!' Upon the roads they shall pasture themselves, and upon every bare place shall be their pasture" (Isa 49:9)
And it is said: "God guards all of his faithful ones, but all of the wicked will He wipe out" (Ps 145:20)

May He wipe out His enemies
May He watch over His (sturdy) rocks
May He fell His foes
May He shield those He has sheltered[6]
Blessed are You… Shield…

---

1 "Sign for good" refers to the rainbow (**R**).

2 Ps 29:10, "The Lord was seated before the Flood." See *MidPs* to this verse, which understands this verse as depicting God seated in judgment over the wicked and listening to the prayers of the righteous in the ark (**R**).

3 This stanza refers back to one of the major motifs of the previous poem: that everyone on board the ark refrained from sexual intercourse and reproduction as a reaction to their confined living spaces. This chastity is here contrasted with God's command to them to "be fruitful and multiply" once they leave the ark.

(א) **א**וֹת לְטוֹבָה חָשַׁבְתָּה
בְּאַחַר לַמַּבּוּל יָשַׁבְתָּה
גַּם בַּיְתָה יְחִידִים הוֹשַׁבְתָּה
דְּגָלִים בְּחִיבָּה יִישַּׁבְתָּה

הִיתַּרְתָּה אֲסוּרִים
וְהוֹצֵאתָה אֲסִירִים
זָכַרְתָּה סְגוּרִים
חָשַׁבְתָּה סְגִרִים

טַפָּם בַּתֵּיבָה עֲבוּר הִצְנִיעוּ
יְשִׁיבָה עֲלֵי גֵיא הִיצִיעוּ
כִּי מְעַט הָיוּ וְהַרְבֵּה הוּצְבָּאוּ
לְעֵת לְמִשְׁפְּחוֹתָם יָצָאוּ

ככתוב ויהיו בני נח היצאים מן התבה שם וחם ויפת וחם הוא אבי כנען

ונאמר עושה משפט לעשוקים נתן לחם לרעבים יי מתיר אסורים

ונאמר אלים מושיב יחידים ביתה מוציא אסירים בכשרות אך סוררים שכנו צחיחה

ונאמר לאמר לאסורים צאו לאשר בחשך הגלו על דרכים ירעו ובכל שפיים מרעיתם

ונאמר שומר יי את כל אוהביו ואת כל הרשעים ישמיד

יַשְׁמִיד צָרָיו
יִשְׁמוֹר צוּרָיו
יְמַגֵּר צוֹרְרָיו
יְמַגֵּן נְצוּרָיו
ברוך... מגן...

---

4 Literally, "At a time when by their families they went forth." The unit juxtaposes the nature of the ark-dwellers as individuals on the ark and as members of families (procreating) upon their departure.

5 This verse (Ps 146:7) and the following text (Ps 68:7) are cited after the first unit of the previous *qedushta*, also. See Yannai on Gen 8:15 for additional notes on these passages.

6 The final words of each stich, though from different roots, constitute a potent rhyme: *tsarav* ("enemies") – *tsurav* ("His rocks") – *tsorerav* ("His foes") – *netsurav* ("He has sheltered").

(2) Forth from their loins the earth swarmed
Their shoots spread across the land
Their vines budded with blooms
Babes, like flowers, blossomed[7]
The precious few who belong the righteous [became abundantly many][8]
offshoots of the righteous man
Fi[xed firmly][9] is pillar of the world, the righteous one[10]
his virtue kept his tender saplings safe.
...And like *hallah* You separated them[11]
A world overflowing with good You gave them
...

(6)[12] ... These who were his kin
...
... They did
for upon their father's honor they had compassion
... every fruit which was planted
for Shem and for Yafet, with a word ...
... according to their days
and was not left behind...
... by their lives
... to their isles ...
...
... And they went out to the light
Nakedness ...[13]
...
Surviving the pelting rains of the Flood
When the primordial fountains were stoppered
and the waterworks sealed back in...
Hidden away until the wrathful outpouring should pass
They went forth, safely saved, from the Flow

---

7 *TanḥB Noaḥ* 20 describes the miraculous fecundity of Noah's garden. Here, the natural imagery describes the fertility of Noah's offspring.

8 Following **B2**'s reconstruction (פרצו לרוב טוב); see Gen 30:30. The epithet translated here as "precious few" (טוב מעט) comes from Ps 37:16, "The little (מעט) that belongs to the righteous man is better (טוב) than the riches of many wicked men" (**R**). "The righteous man" is here understood to be Noah, while the treasured possessions are his sons.

9 Gap filled according to **R**.

(ב) **מֵ**חַלְצֵיהֶם אֲדָמָה הִישְׁרִיצָה
נְטִיעָתָם בָּאָרֶץ הִפְרִיצָה
שָׂרִיגִים גַּפְנָם הֵינִיצָה
עוֹלָתָה כְּעָלְתָה נִיצָּה
פּ..וב טוֹב מְעַט לַצַּדִּיק
צִמְחֵי אִישׁ צַדִּיק
... יְסוֹד עוֹלָם הוּא הַצַּדִּיק
רַכָּיו עִימּוֹ הִיצְדִּיק
... וּכְחַלָּה הִפְרַשְׁתָּם
שֶׁפַע טוּב עוֹלָם הוֹרַשְׁתָּם
...

(ו) ... אֵלֶּה אֲשֶׁר נִיתְיַחֲסוּ
...
... עָשׂוּ
כִּי עַל כְּבוֹד אֲבִיהֶם חָסוּ
... כָּל פְּרִי הוּנְטָע
לְשֵׁם וּלְיֶפֶת בְּדְבַר.. ...
... ..ל
מ.. כִּימֵיהֶם
וְלֹא נוֹתַר ...
נ.. בְּחַיֵּיהֶם
... ..רוּ לְאֵייֶהֶם
סר.. ...
... וַיֵּצְאוּ לְאוֹר
עֶירְוַת ...
... ..תן בפ.. ...
פּלִיטִים מִסַּגְרִירֵי שֶׁטֶף
בְּהִסָּכֵר מַעְיָנוֹת וּבְהִסָּתֵם ...
צְפוּנִים עַד יַעֲבֹר זַעַם קֶצֶף
וַיֵּצְאוּ נִצוֹלִים מִשֶּׁצֶף קֶצֶף

---

10 **R** cites *GenR* 30:1, where it states: "'The righteous is an everlasting foundation' (Prov 10:25)—this refers to Noah.".

11 The poet here compares the sons of Noah with the portion of dough (*ḥallah*) offered by the priests.

12 First eight lines missing. This passage appears to deal with episode of Noah's drunkenness and subsequent shaming in Gen 9.

13 Either that of Noah (Gen 9:22), or the ravaged land (Gen 42:9, 12). Or עירות could mean towns; see n. 19, below.

[Called] by names in keeping with their actions[14]
Filial piety fulfilling good fates
The remote brother[15] was kept far from them
He was cursed – You made him unlike them[16]
The two were better than other one
For their deeds were much better
The loamy land from its desolation they resettled
one blessing leveled their field[17]

And thus, "And from these the whole world scattered forth"
(7[1]) *From these*, the edges of the earth were possessed
From these, houses of the covenant were built
From these, the borders or the land were [bounded][18]
From these generations of generations descended
From these, multitudes of multitudes were adorned
From these, remnants of communities were…
From these, the corners of this land were sown
From these, the furrows of the earth were plowed anew
From these, bannered towers were founded
From these, precious children appeared
From these, the foundation of all was made firm
From these, companies of learned were gathered
From these, settled encampments were filled
From these, ancestral pastures become possessions
From these, remnants of the fields …
From these, scholars in the Testimony arose[19]

---

14 Lacuna filled by **R**. In *GenR* 26:3, it is noted that Shem's name signified that God "set His name (*shemo*) upon him" as a special sign of favor, while the name Yafet, meaning "beautiful," speaks for itself. "Ham" probably derives from חמם, "heat," a reference to his association with the southern geographic regions. Based on Gen 10:6 and 10:20, "Ham" is used in the Bible as an epithet for Egypt (Ps 78:51; Ps 105:23, 27; Ps 106:22).

15 I.e., Ham.

16 This *qedushta* reflects a tension that can be detected in traditional interpretations of Gen 9. Is Ham a lesser son, or the equal to his brothers? The roots of the tension lie in the fact that in Gen 9:1, God blesses Noah and all three of his sons, while in v. 25, Noah curses Canaan, the son of Ham, in a place where the reader would expect Ham himself to be cursed. It may be that the previous blessing of Ham rendered him immune to the curse (see *GenR* 36:7, "There cannot be a curse where a blessing has been bestowed"). In numerous

ק.. שְׁמוּתָם כְּלוּלָה לָהֶם
וּמוֹרָא מוֹצִיאָם עֲלֵיהֶם
רֵוחַק אָח רָחוֹק א.. בָּהֶם
וְנֶאֱרַר תִּשְׁתַּנֶּה מֵהֶם
שְׁנַיִם מֵאֶחָד הוּטָבוּ
כִּי מַעֲשֵׂיהֶם הֵיטִיבוּ
תֵּבֵל וְחָרְבוֹתֶיהָ הוֹשִׁיבוּ
וּבִבְרָכָה זֶה לָזֶה הָשְׁווּ

ובכן ומאלה נפצה כל הארץ
(ז') מֵאֵלֶּה **אַ**פְסֵי **אֶ**רֶץ נֶאֱחָזוּ
מֵאֵלֶּה **בָּ**תֵּי **בְ**רִיּוֹת נִיבְנוּ
מֵאֵלֶּה **גְ**בוּלוֹת **גַּ**יְא ...
מֵאֵלֶּה **ד**וֹרוֹת **ד**וֹרוֹת נִדְרָכוּ
מֵאֵלֶּה **הֲ**מוֹנֵי **הֲ**מוֹנִים נֶהֱדָרוּ
מֵאֵלֶּה **וִ**יתּוּרֵי **וְ**וּעָדִים ...
מֵאֵלֶּה **זָ**וִיּוֹת **ז**ֹאת נִזְרָעוּ
מֵאֵלֶּה **חֲ**רוּשֵׁי **חֶ**לֶד נֶחֱלָפוּ
מֵאֵלֶּה **טֶ**כֶס **ט**ִירוֹת נִיטְבָּעוּ
מֵאֵלֶּה **יַ**קְרוּת **יְ**לָדִים נִירְאוּ
מֵאֵלֶּה **כַּ**נַּת **כֹּ**ל נִכְלָלוּ
מֵאֵלֶּה **לַ**הֲקוֹת **לְ**מוֹדִים נִלְקָחוּ
מֵאֵלֶּה **מַ**חֲנוֹת **מ**וֹשָׁבוֹת נִימְלָאוּ
מֵאֵלֶּה **נ**וֹוֹת **נְ**חָלוֹת נִינְחָלוּ
מֵאֵלֶּה **סְ**רִידֵי **שָׂ**דוֹת נס..
מֵאֵלֶּה **ע**וֹבְרֵי **עֲ**יָרוֹת נַעֲשׂוּ

midrashic sources, it is nonetheless Ham who is cursed, as he is here. In the final poetic unit, however, Ham is praised as a father of righteous converts from whom "a good reward" is derived. His curse, therefore, is temporary. It bears noting that Ephrem usually denigrates Ham, making him the antithesis of the righteous and the recipient of Noah's curse, but in one passage (*Sermones* III, 2:486) he describes the three sons of Noah as "the three holy vine-twigs," on par with each other.

17 A reworking of Eccl 4:9, "Two are better than one" (**R**). The biblical aphorism is here concretized and the referents specified. "The two" refers to Shem and Yafet while "the one" refers to Ham.

18 Lacunae in this stanza filled according to **B2**

19 Translating with **R**, who reads עובדי עדות; the Maʾagarim text translates as, "those who pass through the towns." For עירות as plural of עיר, see Jastrow, s.v. עיר (p. 1075).

From these, the heads of My handiwork[20] were set aside
From these, the districts of the dry land were [divided][21]
From these, the flocks of fellowship are summoned
From these, multitudinous myriads are multiplied
From these, roots of…are…
From these, the generations of the earth are…

And thus…
(7^2) *With* hope [*Which for their sake* You affirmed][22]
With … *Which for their sake* You…]
With [good will][23] *Which for their sake* You wished
With adornment *Which for their sake* You…
With … *Which for their sake* You…
With … *Which for their sake* You did
With a symbol *Which for their sake* You showed
With a signal *Which for their sake* You displayed
With kindness *Which for their sake* You kept
With resurrection *Which for their sake* You fated
With escorts *Which for their sake* You heartened
With anger *Which for their sake* You assuaged
With salvation *Which for their sake* You assured
With goodness *Which for their sake* You granted
With might *Which for their sake* You made mighty
With merit *Which for their sake* You minded
With distinction *Which for their sake* You designed
With wisdom *Which for their sake* You instructed
With speech *Which for their sake* You spoke[24]
With an oath *Which for their sake* You swore[25]
With a covenant *Which for their sake* You made clear
With a pledge *Which for their sake* You promised

(8) For You grandly turn back Your wrath

---

20 Epithet for the leaders of Israel; see Judg 20:2; 1 Sam 14:28; Isa 45:11 (**B1**).

21 Completed according to **B2**.

22 **B1**, whose completion is accepted here, notes the usage of the verb translated here as "affirmed" (תליתה) in an appropriate idiom in *b. Men.* 29b, which states: "If one puts his trust (תולה ב־) in the Holy One, blessed be He, behold, He becomes his refuge in this world and in the world to come."

מֵאֵלֶּה פִּינּוֹת פּוֹעַל נִפְרָדוּ
מֵאֵלֶּה צְדָדֵי צִיָּה נצ..
מֵאֵלֶּה קִינֵּי קְהָלִים נִקְרָאוּ
מֵאֵלֶּה רְבָבוֹת רַבִּים נִירְבָּבוּ
מֵאֵלֶּה שָׁרְשֵׁי שא.. ...
מֵאֵלֶּה תּוֹלְדוֹת תֵּבֵל נית..בו

ובכן

(ז[2]) בְּתִקְוָה ... ...
... ...
... אֲשֶׁר לָמוֹ רָצִיתָה
בְּקוֹשֶׁט אֲשֶׁר לָמוֹ ...
... ...
... אֲשֶׁר לָמוֹ פָּעַלְתָּה
בְּעֵידוּת אֲשֶׁר לָמוֹ עָרַכְתָּה
בְּסִימָן אֲשֶׁר לָמוֹ סָדַרְתָּה
בְּנוֹעַם אֲשֶׁר לָמוֹ נָצַרְתָּה
בְּמִחְיָיה אֲשֶׁר לָמוֹ מִינִּיתָה
בְּלִיווּי אֲשֶׁר לָמוֹ לִיבַּבְתָּה
בְּכַעַס אֲשֶׁר לָמוֹ כָּבַשְׁתָּה
בְּיֵשַׁע אֲשֶׁר לָמוֹ יִימַּנְתָּה
בְּטוֹב אֲשֶׁר לָמוֹ טִיעַמְתָּה
בְּחַיִל אֲשֶׁר לָמוֹ חִיזַּקְתָּה
בִּזְכוּת אֲשֶׁר לָמוֹ זָכַרְתָּה
בְּוָותִיקוּת אֲשֶׁר לָמוֹ וִיעַדְתָּה
בְּהַשְׂכֵּל אֲשֶׁר לָמוֹ הוֹרֵיתָה
בְּדָבָר אֲשֶׁר לָמוֹ דַּנְתָּה
בִּגְזֵרָה אֲשֶׁר לָמוֹ גָּזַרְתָּה
בִּבְרִית אֲשֶׁר לָמוֹ בֵּירַרְתָּה
בַּאֲמִירָה אֲשֶׁר לָמוֹ אִימַּנְתָּה

(ח) כִּי תַרְבֶּה לְהָשִׁיב אַפָּךְ

23 Gap filled by **R**.

24 The translation of this line emphasizes the parallelism with the lines to come; a more literal translation would state: "With a word (דבר) / Which for their sake You judged (דנתה)".

25 The final three lines of this poem refer to the symbol of the rainbow and the divine promise accompanying this sign. See Gen 9:11 and Isa 54:9.

and You magnanimously avert Your anger
and a finale You do not enact
because for Your own sake do You act
and Your mercy is over all Your actions
and Your compassion is upon all Your creatures
and generation to generation will praise
and generation to generation will recount
and this one will hear from that one
and this one will teach to that one
because not for nothing were they created
and for the sake of this one they were created
to bless Your name
to praise Your recollection
and to thank You
and to believe in You
and to sanctify You and to proclaim Your majesty
like those majestic ones on high, with the glory of holiness,
majestic in holiness,
majestic and holy one
As it is written…

(9) The descendants of those who went forth from enclosure,
those You brought out into space to breathe,[26]
let (them) say of the One who took them out:
Holy, holy, holy is the Lord of Hosts! The whole earth is filled with His glory!
"*Holy*"—from the masters of great name and deed[27]
"*Holy*"—from the masters of a choice tongue[28]
"*Holy*"—from the masters of a good reward[29]
Holy, holy, holy is the Lord of Hosts! The whole earth is filled with His glory!

---

26 "Space to breathe" renders the word רווחה (lit., "ease, respite"). The translation tries to capture the pun with the closely related word רווח ("wide, spacious")—by which the poet costructs a contrast to the physical and psychological experience of confinement of life on the ark.

27 That is, men both of great learning and action, i.e., the Jews. There is also a pun on the name Shem and its meaning (reputation, fame, renown). For the idiom "masters of name," see Gen 6:5 and Num 16:2 for the idiom "men of renown" (lit., "men of name"). It

וְתַשְׂגֶּה לְהַחֲזִיר זַעְפָּךְ
וְכָלָה לֹא תַעַשׂ
כִּי לְמַעֲנָךְ תַּעַשׂ
וְרַחֲמֶיךָ עַל כָּל מַעֲשֶׂיךָ
וְחֶמְלָתְךָ עַל כָּל בִּירְיוֹתֶיךָ
וְדוֹר לְדוֹר יְשַׁבֵּחַ
וְדוֹר לְדוֹר יְתַנֶּה
וְזֶה מִזֶּה יִשְׁמָעוּ
וְזֶה לָזֶה יְלַמֵּדוּ
כִּי לָרִיק לֹא נִיבְרָאוּ
וּבַעֲבוּר זֹאת נִבְרָאוּ
לְבָרֵךְ שְׁמָךְ
לְהַלֵּל זִיכְרָךְ
וּלְהוֹדוֹת לָךְ
וּלְהַאֲמִין בָּךְ
וּלְהַקְדִּישָׁךְ וּלְהַאְדִּירָךְ
כְּאַדִּירֵי מַעְלָה בְּאַדֶּרֶת קְדוּשָּׁה
נֶאְדָּר בַּקּוֹדֶשׁ
אַדִּיר וְקָדוֹשׁ
ככתוב

(ט) יוֹצְאֵי מִמַּסְגֵּר
אֲשֶׁר הוֹצֵאתָה לִרְוָוחָה
יְצוּאֵיהֶם יֹאמְרוּ
קדוש קדוש קדוש יי צבאות מלא כל הארץ כבודו
קָדוֹשׁ מִבַּעֲלֵי שֵׁם וּמַעֲשֶׂה
קָדוֹשׁ מִבַּעֲלֵי לָשׁוֹן מֻובְחָר
קָדוֹשׁ מִבַּעֲלֵי שָׂכָר טוֹב
קדוש קדוש קדוש יי צבאות מלא כל הארץ כבודו

---

could also be an allusion to the idea of the *baʿal shem*, "the master of the Holy Name," in which case it is suggestive of the theurgic potential latent within the Qedushah. On the pairing of the name "Shem" with God, see *GenR* 26:3. Yannai applies similar language to Jacob in the *qedushta* to Gen 32:4, Poem 9.

28 The poet praises Yafet, ancestor of the Greeks, by praising the sophisticated Greek language; see *GenR* 36:8.

29 Ham is, in this poem, lauded as the ancestor of righteous converts.

"*Holy*"—from Shem, He established those who wrap themselves in *tsitstit*,
(distinguished) in name and (great) in deed[30]
"*Holy*"—from Yafet, He established translations of the Torah
into a chosen tongue
"*Holy*"—from Ham, He established enlightened ones
who cling to the blessed[31]
The one towards the other…

"*From His place*"—He chose Shem:
that he would expound the fiery Torah[32]
"*From His place*"—He chose Yafet:
those who would utter honeyed words
"*From His place*"—He brought near from Ham:
righteous converts meditating on His name
Twice…

"*From His place*"—He brought out from the ark the children of [the
righteous one][33]
"*From His place*"—He built His world from the stock of the pure one
"*From His place*"—He bequeathed to them a world in fair parts divided[34]
Twice…

30 See *GenR* 36:6, where God gives Shem the *tallit* as a reward for covering his father's nakedness (**R**). (In that text, however, Yafet is granted a gift parallel to the *tsitstit*—the *pallium*-cloak—not the gift of translation as we have in this text.) **B1** notes that "those who wrap themselves in *tsitsit*" is an epithet for Israel. The idiom of "name and deed," rendered here as a combination of lineage and action, may also refer to commandment (the naming of the mitzvah of *tsitsit*) and fulfillment (the donning of *tsitsit*). There may also be a pun here on the phrase "*be-shem*:" The *tsitsit* will quite literally be "upon [the heirs of] Shem" when Jews don the *tallit.*

31 "The blessed" refers to Israel, and "those who cling" are the converts. **R** has a lengthy note indicating the parallels between this language and the aggadic traditions surrounding Abraham's servant Eliezer who, as a Canaanite, should have been cursed by and converted

קָדוֹשׁ מִשֵּׁם הֶעֱמִיד עוֹטֶה צִיצִית
בְּשֵׁם וּמַעֲשֶׂה
קָדוֹשׁ מִיֶּפֶת הֶעֱמִיד מַמְלִיצֵי דָת
בְּלָשׁוֹן מֻובְחָר
קָדוֹשׁ מֵחָם הֶעֱמִיד מַשְׂכִּילִים
דְּבֵיק בִּבְרוּכִים

לעומתם כל יא׳

מִמְּקוֹמוֹ בָּחַר בְּשֵׁם
כִּי דָרַשׁ אֵשׁ דָת
מִמְּקוֹמוֹ בָּחַר בְּיֶפֶת
הוֹגֵי נוֹפֶת צוּפִים
מִמְּקוֹמוֹ קֵירַב מֵחָם
גֵּירִים וְחוֹשְׁבֵי שְׁמוֹ

פעמים

מִמְּקוֹמוֹ הוֹצִיא מִתֵּיבָה יַלְדֵי ...

מִמְּקוֹמוֹ בָּנָה עוֹלָמוֹ מִגֶּיזַע תָּמִים
מִמְּקוֹמוֹ הוֹרִישׁ לָהֶם עוֹלָם לַחֲלָקִים

פעמים

---

by Abraham, received blessings instead. See *GenR* 59:9, 60:2, and 60:7. See discussion below.

32 "Fiery law" (the midrashic understanding of אשדת) is from Deut 33:2 (**R**). The virtue of the Jews (children of Shem) is described in relation to Scripture. The children of Yafet (here possibly meaning the "God-fearers" or even Christian gentiles) are attracted to the superficial content of scripture—the "honeyed words" of the Greek translation. The children of Ham are "righteous converts," who may lack the skill of the Jewish scholars to engage deeply in the law but who meditate on God's Name—perhaps an act of pious study somewhat deeper and more significant than just listening to honeyed words.

33 Lacuna filled by **B2**, who supplies צדיק.

34 For the image of the division of the land, see Josh 6:9 and 18:5 (**B1**).

Commentary

Where the *qedushta* for Gen 8:15 focused primarily on Noah, this piyyut explores the figures of Noah's sons and their signature roles in human history. Of the units that are preserved, the first focus on Shem, Yafet, and Ham generally, as progenitors of humanity in the post-diluvian world. Their individual characters are not developed until the final poem, where the poet implicitly divides the world into three classes of people: Shem is the forerunner of the Jews, Yafet of Greek-speakers, and Ham of righteous converts. Yannai is not describing universal human history here, as Genesis does, but rather the tripartite division of his own society, Byzantine Palestine. His depictions of Yafet and Ham are particularly intriguing. According to the biblical text, Shem is the ancestor of the Semites, understood here as the Jews; Yafet of the Mediterranean peoples; and Ham, the Africans. But Yannai regards these three sons of Noah as progenitors not of geographic populations but communities of belief and practice.

The aggadic association of Shem with Judaism—a more specific relationship than might be assumed given his genealogical distance from his descendent Abraham—can be detected in such midrashic commonplaces as "the academy of Shem and Eber," where Isaac studied and Rebecca sought an oracle, as well as a clear favoritism towards Shem in *midrashim* that denigrate Noah.[35] Yannai references this traditional association of Shem with Torah study when he describes Shem as "he who expounds (*darash*) fiery law"—an allusion to Deut 32:2 as well as to the axiomatic rabbinic enterprise of interpretation (*midrash*). Similarly, Shem is the first person to don *tsitsit* (ritual fringes), which are given as a reward for his clever use of a cloak (i.e., *tallit*) in covering his father's nakedness. Yannai's evocation of the image of Shem in traditional Jewish garments is in accord with the tradition preserved in *GenR* 36:6, *Tanḥ Noaḥ* 9, and *TanḥB Noaḥ* 21. Finally, only the Jews were given the gift of knowing God's proper name, and hence only the descendents of Shem could be *baʿalei shem*, "masters of the Name." Shem's praise is literally sung in this poem, and his merit manifests in terms of knowledge both deep and significant as well as in terms of deed.

Similarly, in Genesis Yafet is the progenitor of the Greeks and, by extension, all of Hellenistic culture. In the biblical text, Yafet—like Shem—re-

35 See the commentary to the *qedushtaʾot* for Gen 8:1 and 8:15.

ceives a blessing from Noah (Gen 9:26-27). To later exegetes, Yafet's blessing—that Yafet shall dwell in the tents of Shem (Gen 9:27)—would suggest a particular kind of cultural concord between Jews and Greeks. From an early date, this verse was understood to refer specifically to the incorporation of Greek language and literature into Judaism—an accommodation of Hellenism in a broad way—and the Greek translation of Scripture in particular. For example, in *GenR* 36:8, it is stated: "Bar Kappara explained it: Let the words of the Torah be uttered in the language of Yafet [i.e., in Greek] in the tents of Shem [i.e., the Jews]. R. Yudan said: From this [verse] we learn that a translation [of the Bible is permitted]." This association of Yafet with the Greek translation of Scripture—whether the Septuagint or another version—can also be found in *m. Meg.* 1:9; *j. Meg* 10a; and *b. Meg* 9b. While rabbinic texts express ambivalence about the influence of Greek thought upon Judaism, this piyyut appears to be quite favorable, twice referring to Greek as "a choice tongue" (*lashon muvḥar*). In praising Greek in Poem Nine, Yannai employs a rhetorical flourish of its own: to indicate "translation" in line 10, he uses the root מ-ל-ץ (literally, "to glide" or go between) found in Gen 42:23 (where it describes Joseph's use of a translator); to invoke Scripture in line 13, he evokes Ps 19:11 for the phrase "honeyed words," which rabbinic interpretations equate with Torah—here applied to a Greek translation of the same. Yannai appears, at least on the surface, to view "the Greeks" positively.

How are we to understand this apparent receptivity to Greek culture in Yannai's day? Could it be that when Yafet dwells in the tents of Shem, the implication is of conversion? We certainly see this in *Targ PsJ* to Gen 9:26, which states: "The Lord shall beautify the borders of Yafet, and his sons shall become converts and sit in the schools of Shem." Yannai's praise for Noah's second son could be rooted in a similar notion, but given the fact that Yannai emphasizes Ham, not Yafet, as the father of converts, other explanations seem more likely. In this poem Yafet is associated with text, specifically with both the translation and recitation of Scripture in Greek. These activities could be connected to two non-conversionary groups: "semi-proselytes" (perhaps comparable to the *seboumenoi*, or "God-Fearers" of the Second Temple period) who affiliate with Judaism; or gentiles who have converted to Christianity (but perhaps with Judaizing tendencies, as with the Ebionites). The number of "semi-proselytes" and Judaizing Christians (as well as actual converts to Judaism) in Yannai's era is difficult to determine, but their existence—as evidenced by the recurrent "Judaizing" heresies of the Byzantine era—seems clear, despite various imperial legal hurdles to such boundary-blurring and boundary-crossing behaviors and beliefs. Considering the second alternative—that Yafet here refers to Gentile Christians—there is evidence that in Late Antiquity, Jewish antagonism towards *gentiles* converting to Christianity was much less than their antagonism towards Jews who converted (e.g., the Nazoreans).[36] Either way, if we equate Yafet with these various "Judaizing" groups or "fellow travelers," it may be that Yannai's praise of Greek-speakers who utter honeyed words is, in fact, a sort of backhanded compliment. He is not overtly negative towards these well-meaning non-Jews, whether they are friendly to Judaism or converts to Christianity, but next to Shem—and even Ham—they appear deficient. When read in isolation, the lines describing Yafet seem like rich praise; but when juxtaposed with the other sons, it becomes clear that these children of Yafet are superficial: beautiful, but not profound; reading the text but not perceiving its deeper meanings; pleasant but slippery. No matter the birth order (which is debated in rabbinic and Christian tradition), Yafet is clearly a second son to Shem. This said, Yannai's praise of Greek-speakers stands out in an era when polemic is the expected tone.

The third son, Ham, whose son Canaan is (perplexingly) cursed in the biblical text, receives truly mixed blessings in this poem. As noted above, he cannot be denied the blessing that God bestows upon Noah and all his sons; at the same time, Ham's stature is diminished in comparison with his brothers when he lets Noah be shamed or, perhaps, actively participates in his father's humiliation. Furthermore, Ham is the ancestor of the Canaanites, those nations destined to be dispossessed by the Israelites. Ham, in short, is the father of a nation of future slaves whose fate, in some way, is determined by their ancestor's transgression. It is worth noting, however, than in the extant parts of this piyyut, Ham's son Canaan is never mentioned. Nor is Ham connected here with any geographic region in a meaningful way. The focus is purely on the relationship of Noah and his three

36 See R. Kimmelman, "*Birkat ha-minim* and the lack of evidence for an anti-Christian Jewish prayer in late antiquity," *Jewish and Christian Self-Definition*, vol. 2 (Fortress: Philadelphia, 1981), 226–24. See also the article by W. Kinzig, "'Non-Separation': Closeness and Co-operation between Jews and Christians in the Fourth Century," *Vigiliae Christianae* 45 (1991): 27–53. And, more generally, Leon V. Rutgers, "The Interaction of Jews and Non-Jews in Late Antiquity," *American Journal of Archaeology* 96 (1992): 101–18.

sons to the Torah and, thereby, to God and blessings. And according to this reading, Ham ends well.

In the final unit of this piyyut, Ham is presented not as a villain or failure but as a model proselyte. He gains a "good reward" (line 7); he fathers "enlightened ones who cling to the blessed" (line 11); and he is an ancestor of those "righteous converts" who meditate on God's name (line 13). The connection of Ham to converts recalls a tradition found in rabbinic literature; in *GenR* 60:7, we find the following:

> Rabbi Jose ben Rabbi Dosa said: Canaan was Eliezer [the servant of Abraham], yet because he faithfully served that righteous man, he passed from the category of the accursed into that of the blessed, as it says, "And [Laban] said: Come in, O blessed of the Lord" (Gen 24:31).

In this midrash, Abraham's faithful servant escapes the curse of Canaan (the son of Ham and bearer of this malediction) through his meritorious actions, which even the wicked Laban must recognize.[37] The language of this aggadah recalls the poet's choice of words; however, the redemption of Eliezer is a far cry from the potential redemption of all the Hamites. The closest parallel traditions to what we find in this piyyut occur in *Seder Olam Rabba* (23:8), a passage cited by Rashi in his commentary on Gen 19:18. This text depicts the Egyptians and Cushites—"sons of Ham"—converting to Judaism during the reign of Hezekiah, after the defeat of Sennacherib. But in general, Yannai's depiction of Ham as the ancestor of righteous converts is unusual; it completes his transformation of the biblical genealogy into a kind of spiritual lineage. Shem, Yafet, and Ham represent communities not of shared genes but shared texts and traditions.

It may be that Yannai is simply (but dramatically) amplifying the narrative of the *sidra*; perhaps he does not intend to convey any information about his contemporary context. Such a reading seems unlikely, however, because it leaves too many innovations unsatisfactorily unexplained. While our understanding of Yannai's historical setting remains deficient, this poem seems to suggest an unexpected cultural vibrancy and societal

---

37 According to *TargPsJ* to Gen14:14 and *PRE* 16, Eliezer is the son of Nimrod, and thus a great-grandson of Ham. Numerous midrashic sources teach that Eliezer was the only servant to accompany Abraham in his battle against the Canaanite kings. When these traditions are read together, Eliezer battled with his master against his Hamite kinsmen.

complexity. Combining the images of fertility and growth with which the poem opens and the language of universal Torah with which it closes, Yannai paints a picture of a thriving Judaism in which the Jews hew to their *mitzvot* and their neighbors—whether "semi-proselyte" sons of Yafet or righteously converted children of Ham—join them in their endeavors, to the best of their (admittedly limited) abilities. Given that this poem is followed by a piyyut about the destructive possibilities of hubristic unity (vividly brought to life by the Tower of Babel story), Yannai's *qedushta* for Gen 9:18 offers a positive picture of unity centered around Torah rather than ambition.

Qedushta for Genesis 11:1 — בראשית יא:א

"All the earth was" — ויהי כל הארץ

This *qedushta* stands out as one of Yannai's best. The themes of the Torah portion—the arrogant ambition of the builders of the Tower of Babel and the linguistic confusion that serves as their comeuppance—provide the poet with a remarkable opportunity to play with language. The result is a composition rich with wit and puns, which are used both to create aesthetic effects and to convey Yannai's theology of "measure for measure." The biblical story provides the perfect pretext for an exploration of poetic justice.

(1)[1] The land, which was mortally ill
twice afflicted with floods[2]
Even before her wounds were bound
her inhabitants pursued “disgrace.”

Most shameful folly their lips pronounced[3]
like fools, their lips brought ruin
The loathsome, though with a pestle beaten
were incapable of seeing in front of their faces.

Their heart's error exposed
the trap of their soul's own yearning
Their high tower—now swept away
when they lifted up their open lips so haughty.

As it is written: “And the earth was all of one language and unified of speech” (Gen 11:1)
And as it is said: “They neither know nor understand” (Isa 44:18)
And as it is said: “Even if you pound a fool with a pestle, in a mortar along with grain, his folly will not leave him” (Prov 27:22)
And as it is said: “Let lying lips be silenced, those that speak against the righteous, proudly with haughty contempt” (Ps 31:19)
And as it is said: “A lip of truth is established forever, a tongue of falsehood but a moment” (Prov 12:19)
And as it is said: “One who loves sin, loves strive; one who exalts his open (mouth) seeks destruction” (Prov 17:19)

Destruction, for us, bind up![4]
A crown, from us, put on!

---

1 An earlier translation of this poem, with extensive commentary, appeares in L. Lieber, “The Generation that Built the Tower: Yannai on Genesis 11,” *Review of Rabbinic Literature* (8, 2006): 161–88.

2 As **R** notes, according to rabbinic tradition, there were actually two great floods: one in the days of Noah, and a second in the days of Enosh. This idea may be based on the “floods” of Amos 5:8. See *GenR* 23:7, *j. Shek* 26a; *TanḥB Noaḥ* 24; *Mek. Yitro* 1. See also *TargPJ* to Gen 4:26. *Targum Onqelos* offers a different reading, asserting that in the days of Enosh “men desisted (or forbore) from praying in the name of the Lord.” *TargN* to Gen 4:26 lacks the motif of a flood, but includes idolatry: “In this manner the sons of man began to make themselves idols and to call them by the name of the Memra of the Lord.” The *masorah* to *TargN* is more expansive: “Lo, it was in this manner that they came to practice

(א)

אֶרֶץ אֲשֶׁר נֶאֱנָשָׁה
בִּשְׁנֵי מַבּוּלִים נֶעֱנָשָׁה
גַּם עַד לֹא נֶחְבָּשָׁה
דָּרֶיהָ בִּיקְשׁוּ בוּשָׁה

הוֹלֵילוֹת רָע שְׂפָתֵימוֹ בִּיטּוּ
וְכֶאֱוִיל שְׂפָתַיִים הִילְבִּיטוּ
זוֹלְלִים אֲשֶׁר בַּמַּכְתֵּשׁ נֶחְבָּטוּ
חֲסֵירֵי לֵב כִּי לֹא לְפָנִים בָּטוּ

טָעוּת לִבָּם נֶחֱסָפָה
יוֹקֶשׁ אֲשֶׁר נַפְשָׁם נִכְסָפָה
כַּנַּת גּוֹבְהָם נִסְחָפָה
לְעֵת כִּי הִיגְבִּיהוּ פִּתְחֵי שָׂפָה

ככתוב ויהי כל הארץ שפה אחת ודברים אחדים

ונאמר לא ידעו ולא יבינו
ונאמר אם תכתוש את האויל במכתש בתוך הריפות בעלי לא תסור מעליו אולתו

ונאמר תאלמנה שפתי שקר הדברות על צדיק עתק בגאוה ובוז

ונאמר שפת אמת תכון לעד ועד ארגיעה לשון שקר

ונאמר אוהב פשע אוהב מצה מגביה פתחו מבקש שבר

שֶׁבֶר מֶנּוּ תַּחְבּוֹשׁ
וְכֶתֶר מֶנּוּ תִּלְבּוֹשׁ

---

an alien cult and to call it by the name of the Memra of the Lord."

3 This language refers both to hubristic speech and idolatry. The language of this verse, which features unusual (archaic biblical Hebrew) pronominal suffixes, alludes to Ps 59:13 in theme as well as in morphology: "For the sin of their mouth (פימו), and the words of their lips (שפתימו), let them even be taken in their pride, and for cursing and lying which they speak." This verse is applied to the Tower-builders in *Tanḥ Noaḥ* 17 and *TanḥB Noaḥ* 23. Indeed, this verse from Psalms is implicit in the stanza, although it is not one of the prooftexts that follows it. Rather, it is subtly invoked through the unusual word choice and possibly through allusion to the midrashic reading of the verse.

4 Alludes to Isa 30:26, "On that day when the Lord binds up the wounds of His people" (**R**).

Exalt us as of old[5]
and seek for us a shield!
Blessed... Shield...

(2) From the ancients, they never learned[6]
Those perverts who rose up to do evil
When their speech was unified
they spoke blasphemously and feared nothing[7]
Their unity caused their division[8]
from their folly, their ruin
Their homes ejected them
their tranquility led them astray
They proclaimed aloud their slanderous speech
their utterance uprooted them from You
Their mighty arrogance, their own grandeur, they exalted
for along paths of ancient error they strayed

As it is written: "And it was when they strayed as of old[9], they came upon a valley in the land of Shinar and settled there." (Gen 11:2)
And as it is said: "At scoffers He scoffs, while with the lowly He deals graciously." (Prov 3:34)
And as it is said: "The inconstancy of the simple will destroy them, the complacency of fools is their doom." (Prov 1:32)
And as it is said: "Fear of the Lord is the hatred of evil; I hate arrogance and pride, and the evil path, and the duplicitous mouth." (Prov 8:13)
And as it is said: "Do not make much lofty, lofty speech; let arrogance depart from your mouths. For a knowing deity is the Eternal, and by Him are all deeds weighed." (1 Sam 2:3)

Deeds You weigh,
those of all You brought into being
"Our life," You are called;
to renew our lives with dew You have promised
Blessed... Who resurrects...

5 See Deut 26:18–19, a connection made in **B2**.
6 I.e., the generation of Enosh.
7 See *GenR* 38:5 (**B1**), *Tanḥ Noaḥ* 16, *TanḥB Noaḥ* 22, and others.
8 From the root פ-ל-ג; see below.

נַשְּׂאֵינוּ כְּבָרֹאשׁ
וּלְמָגִינֵינוּ תִּדְרוֹשׁ
ברוך... מגן...

(ב) **מ**ִקַּדְמוֹנִים לֹא לָמְדוּ
נַעֲוִוים אֲשֶׁר לְרָעָה עָמְדוּ
שִׂיחוֹתָם עֵת נֶאֱחָדוּ
עָתָק עָנוּ וְלֹא נִפְחָדוּ
פִּילְגָתַם הַשְּׁוָיִם
צִימְּתָתָם מְשׁוּבָתָם
קִילְעָתַם יְשִׁיבָתָם
רְדָפַתַם שַׁלְוָותָם
שֵׁימַע סָרָה הֵישִׂיחוּ
שִׁינּוּנָם מִמָּךְ הִיסִּיעוּ
תּוֹקֶף גֵּאָה וְגָאוֹן נָשָׂאוּ
תּוֹעִים כִּי מִקֶּדֶם נָסָעוּ

ככתוב ויהי בנסעם מקדם וימצאו בקעה בארץ שנער וישבו שם

ונאמר אם ללצים הוא יליץ ולענוים יתן חן

ונאמר כי משובת פתים תהרגם ושלות כסילים תאבדם

ונאמר יראת יי שנאת רע נאה וגאון ודרך רע ופי תהפוכות שנאתי

ונאמר אל תרבו תדברו גבהה גבהה יצא עתק מפיכם כי אל דעות יי ולא נתכנו עלילות

עֲלִילוֹת תִּיקַּנְתָּה
לְכָל אֲשֶׁר הִיתְקַנְתָּה
חַיֵּינוּ נִקְרֵאיתָה
לְהַחֲיֵינוּ בְּטַל הִקְרֵאתָה
ברוך... מחיה...

9 Reading the text according to the sense demanded by the piyyut (in keeping with, "from the ancients") rather than the contextual meaning of the verse in the Bible. The usual translation of Gen 11:2a is: "As they traveled from the East." For this second sense of the verse, see note 17, below.

(3) You dwell in secret, laughing as all is revealed
for all secret laughter is revealed before You[10]
Now pluck up from the earth the kingdom of deathly silence,[11]
and cast down fear upon every Nation
Yea, let them invoke Your name, all who have not invoked Your name
Let Your name be invoked upon all who invoke Your name.
Yah, just as Your unification is in Your nation
restore to all the nations a pure language to unify You

As it is written: "For then I will restore nations to a pure language, so that they all invoke the Eternal by name and serve Him with one accord." (Zeph 3:9)
And as it is said: "May the Eternal open my lips and my mouth to proclaim Your praise." (Ps 51:18)
Please, God...

(4) Who gives man mouth and lips?
Is it not You who creates the mouth's opening, and the phrase of the lips?
How could a people be so sharp of tongue and stammering of lip?
They open mouth and insult with lip.
Lofty, lofty speech nevertheless they spoke
But by the Loftiest of the Lofty they were humbled
Bricks into building blocks they baked
they knew nothing, comprehended nothing
As for the high tower they had erected:
a third is sunken a third is shattered and (only) a third still stands.[12]
But the word of He who lives and sustains forever is sustained
and unto each who is sustained, Your word is holy.

10 See *LamR pet.* 17 (**B1**).

11 "Kingdom of deathly silence (*dumah*)" attempts to translate several nuances of the word "*dumah*." "*Dumah*" (from דמם, to be silent) is, foremost, an epithet for the Roman Empire (first pagan and then Christian). **R** traces this appellation to *j. Taʿan.* 3a; in that passage, the "*Dumah* (silence) Pronouncement" of Isa 21:11 is explicitly understood as a prophecy against Rome. Isaiah's vision indicted "Dumah" (that is, Idumea, or Edom) and Seir, a mountain in Edomite territory. The name "Seir" is close to the word "hairy," which describes Esau in Gen 25:25 and 27:11. "Seir" thus stands in for Esau/Rome. "Edom" (meaning "red"—another attribute of the biblical Esau) likewise refers to Rome. Furthermore, in

(ג) **יָ**שַׁבְתָּה בַּסֵּתֶר שׁוֹחֵק עַל כָּל גָּלוּי
כִּי כָל שְׁחוֹק סֵיתֶר לְפָנֶיךָ גָּלוּי
נְתוֹשׁ נָא מֵאֲדָמָה מַלְכוּת דּוּמָה
וְתַפִּיל אֵימָה עַל כָּל אֻומָּה
יִקְרְאוּ בִשְׁמָךְ כֹּל לֹא קָרְאוּ בִשְׁמָךְ
יִיקָּרֵא שְׁמָךְ עַל קוֹרְאֵי שְׁמָךְ
יָהּ כְּמוֹ בְעַמָּךְ הוּא יִיחוּדָךְ
הֲפוֹךְ עַל כָּל עַמִּים שָׂפָה בְרוּרָה לְיַחֲדָךְ

ככתוב כי אז אהפוך אל עמים שפה ברורה לקרא כלם בשם יי לעבדו שכם אחד

ונאמר יי שפתי תפתח ופי יגיד תהלתך

ואתה קדוש יושב תהילות ישראל אל נא

(ד) מִי שָׂם לְאָדָם פֶּה וְשָׂפָה
הֲלוֹא אַתָּה בּוֹרֵא פֵּתַח פֶּה וְנִיב שָׂפָה
וְאֵיךְ עַם חַדֵּי פֶּה וּלְעוּגֵי שָׂפָה
פָּתְחוּ פֶּה וְהִפְטִיוּו שָׂפָה
גְּבוֹהָה גְּבוֹהָה עַל כִּי עָנוּ
מִגָּבוֹהַּ הַגָּבֹהָה נַעֲנוּ
לְבֵינִים לַאֲבָנִים לִיבְּנוּ
וְלֹא יָדְעוּ וְלֹא הֵיבִינוּ
כִּי מִגְדָּל הַגָּבוֹהַּ אֲשֶׁר בָּנוּ
שְׁלִישׁוֹ נִשְׁקַע וּשְׁלִישׁוֹ נִבְקַע וּשְׁלִישׁוֹ קַיָּם
כִּי דְבַר חַי וְקַיָּם לְעוֹלָם יִתְקַיָּם
וְעַל כֹּל מְקֻוּיָּם דְּבָרָךְ קָדוֹשׁ

Ps 115:17, "*dumah*" is symbolic of death or the realm of the dead, the underworld. Note that "*dumah*" also looks very much like "*romah*," the very name of Rome. The aural similarities between the words should also be considered; clearly *sound* plays a significant role in the pun as it is invoked here, in a performative piece.

12 As **R** notes, tripartite destruction of the Tower of Babel is described in the aggadah, although not precisely as in our poem. *GenR* 38:8 states that "a third sank, a third was burned, and a third remained standing;" *Tanḥ Noaḥ* 18 states that "a third was burned, a third was swallowed up, and a third remained standing;" *TanḥB Noaḥ* 25 and *b. San.* 109a state that "a third was swallowed up, a third fell down, and a third stands until today."

(5) Thus those of distorted speech had no wisdom in them[13]
indeed, those with an ugly stammer made no sense:
In the language of the world's creation
was their speech, but they corrupted it and to them it became unclear[14]
They feared lest floodwaters overwhelm them
when, according to the calendar, the month of Bul arrived[15]
This generation learned nothing from the generation of the Flood
that which they built up, by it they were confounded
Lo, Your statutes are not like those of man
and Your eyes perceive all of mankind
And as for the language in which they spoke, with it they were answered:
They said, "Come, let us go up" and You said, "Come, let Us go down"[16]
They schemed to build a city but became homeless in every city
they plotted to establish a name for themselves but by them no name was established
They thought from of old[17] to be one all together
but an East wind scattered them, and not one was with another
A heavenly palace You possess
You proclaimed the earth as mankind's dwelling
They plotted to establish their authority over both heaven and earth
but they did not reach heaven and they no longer dwell on earth
Please God… Forever…

"And all the land was…"
(6) United through their utterance of words
and sharp through their scorning of their curse

---

13 The decision to build the Tower revealed their lack of wisdom, which the confusion of languages serves to externalize and publicize.

14 The idea that the original language of humanity was Hebrew, the divine language of Creation, is attested in a number of sources, including: *GenR* 18:4; *Tanḥ Noaḥ* 19; *TanḥB Noaḥ* 28; *j. Meg* 10a. Also, it is found in *TargPJ* to Gen 11:1 (**R**).

15 The month of Bul was also known by the name "Mar (bitter) Heshvan," an identification adduced in this stich by the term "*ḥeshbon*" (calculation). The line alludes to the tradition that the builders of the Tower of Babel reckoned that another Flood was due (*TanḥB Noaḥ* 28; see also *Seder Olam Rabbah*–**R**). Because Noah's flood had occurred in Bul/Mar Heshvan, the Tower-builders assumed the next Flood would also occur at that time. According to this scenario, the tower was conceived of as a defense against drowning—but such preparation for divine punishment still indicates an assumption of guilt on the Tower Builders' part.

(ה) **אָ**ז לְעִמְקֵי שָׂפָה לֹא הָיָה בָם בִּינָה
כִּי אֶמֶת נִלְעַג לָשׁוֹן אֵין בִּינָה
בְּלָשׁוֹן אֲשֶׁר נִבְרָא בוֹ עוֹלָם
הָיָה שִׂיחָם וְנִיבְלוּהוּ וּמֵהֶם נֶעֱלָם
גָּרוּ פֶּן יְצִיפֵם שֶׁטֶף מַבּוּל
לְחֶשְׁבּוֹן שָׁנִים אֲשֶׁר בָּא בְּיֶרַח בּוּל
דּוֹר אֲשֶׁר לֹא לָמְדוּ מִדּוֹר מַבּוּל
אֲשֶׁר הוּקְמוּ גַּם הֵם לְנִיבּוּל
הֵן מִשְׁפָּטֶיךָ לֹא כְאָדָם
וְעֵינֶיךָ פְּקוּחוֹת עַל כָּל בְּנֵי אָדָם
וּבְלָשׁוֹן אֲשֶׁר עָנוּ בוֹ נַעֲנוּ
נָמוּ הָבָה נַעֲלֶה וְנַמְתָּה הָבָה נֵרְדָה
זָמְמוּ לִבְנוֹת עִיר וְנָדוּ מִדּוּר בְּכָל עִיר
עָצוּ לְהָקִים לָמוֹ שֵׁם וּמֵהֶם לֹא הוּקַם שֵׁם

חָשְׁבוּ מִקֶּדֶם לִהְיוֹת כּוּלָּם בְּצַד אֶחָד
וְרוּחַ הַקָּדִים הֱפִיצָם וְלֹא בְאֶחָד
טִירַת שָׁמַיִם לָךְ חִיסַּנְתָּה
וְדִירַת אֶרֶץ לִבְנֵי אָדָם יִיסַּדְתָּה
יָזְמוּ תֵּת רְשׁוּתָם בַּשָּׁמַיִם וּבָאָרֶץ
וְלֹא גָעוּ לַשָּׁמַיִם וְלֹא שָׁכְנוּ בָּאָרֶץ
אל נא ... לעולם

ויהי כל הארץ
(ו) **אֲ**חָדִים בְּשִׂיחַ מִילְלֵיהֶם
וְחַדִּים בְּבוּז קִלְלֵיהֶם

---

16 "Let us go up" does not occur in the biblical text, but "let Us go down" occurs in Gen 11:7. The poet's pseudo-quotation intensifies the parallelism of the stich, and the "measure for measure" theology. The language of "*bo' be-lashon*" is specifically associated with that rhetorical structure, and in *TanḥB Noaḥ* 25 (**R**), we find a strikingly similar language, where the Torah's use of "come, let us" (Gen 11:4, "Come, let us build a city") is juxtaposed with God's utterance of "Come, let Us go down." The similarities between the phrases permit the midrashic author to show how "in the language" (*be-lashon*) in which they sinned, "through it" (*bo'*) was their punishment. Poet and aggadist draw upon the same language and rhetorical structure exactly.

As for the plural "Us," it may allude to the aggadic teaching that seventy angels descended with God, each to teach a different language to the remnants of the Tower-building community. See *PRE* 24, *TargPsJ* to Gen 11:8, and Jub 10:22–23.

17 **R** has חשו ("they rushed [from the East]").

When the yowling of their yelling had risen to You
You weighed them according to their works
Once they lived securely in luxurious space
but now, how narrow is their place![18]
They imagined they could penetrate the highest place
Then they roamed, with no place to nest
A single multitude, of singular speech
they took counsel together: a single voice
Learning and teaching, one to the other
to make a "second" for the God who is One
Whatever they wished, it was theirs
but the fool's mouth speaks his ruin[19]
They plotted to work as one, lest their scheme be shattered
but they were dispersed like a shot.
They wanted to make themselves a name of renown
but were uprooted and made a desolation and waste[20]
Because against the One great in works
they plotted and stumbled in judgment[21]
Their minds turned heavy, like stone
while a brick became for them a stone
Therefore they were beaten like a stone
by God, whose words shatter[22] stone
They all muttered and mustered, speaking
mutiny against He who made all through speech
The potter exulted over the making of bricks
and bitumen was their mortar
Unified were they in caravan and camp
but they spoke in seventy tongues
Because of their sin, their outrage of lips
because of this, their lips withered
"Divided" is the name of their generation:[23]
they became divided in the tower of their dwelling
The Rock divided them and tore down their fence

---

18 Notice the puns in this line—the use of the terms *maqom* as both "place" and "the Omnipresent" and *tsar* as both "narrow" and "enemy."

19 See Prov 18:7 (**R**).

20 See Isa 24:12 (a prophecy against Tyre) for the idiom "desolation and waste" (*shamah u-sheʾiyah*) (**R**). This language puns quite splendidly with the poet's coinage of "name of

בַּעֲלוֹת לָךְ שְׁאוֹן יִילְלֵיהֶם
 דַּנְתָּם כְּפִי מַעַלְלֵיהֶם
גֵּירוּת בֶּטַח כְּרוֹחַב מָקוֹם
 וְאֵיךְ צַר לָהֶם הַמָּקוֹם
דִּימוּ לְקַנֵּן בְּרוּם מָקוֹם
 וְנָדְדוּ מִמְּצוֹא קֵן בְּכָל מָקוֹם
הָמוֹן אֶחָד וְדִיבּוּר אֶחָד
 וְנוֹסְדוּ יַחַד פֶּה אֶחָד
וְשָׁנוּ וְשִׁינְּנוּ אֶחָד לְאֶחָד
 לַעֲשׂוֹת שֵׁינִי לְאֵל אֶחָד
זֻומַּן לָהֶם אֵת אֲשֶׁר חָפָצוּ
 וּכְפִי כְסִיל מְחִיתָה פָּצוּ
חִשְּׁבוּ לְהִתְיַצֵּב פֶּן יְנֻופָּצוּ
 וּבְקִילּוּעַ קֶלַע נֻופָּצוּ
טָעֲמוּ עֲשׂוֹת לָמוֹ שֵׁם שְׁעִיָּה
 וְנֻותְּשׁוּ וְנַעֲשׂוּ שַׁמָּה וּשְׁאִיָּה
יַעַן כִּי לְרַב עֲלִילִיָּה
 זָדוּ וּפָקוּ פְּלִילִיָּה
כָּבַד לִבָּם כָּאָבֶן
 וּלְבֵינָה הָיָה לָהֶם לָאָבֶן
לָכֵן נִיפְּצָם כָּאָבֶן
 אֵל אֲשֶׁר דְּבָרוֹ מְפוֹצֵץ אָבֶן
מִילְּלוּ כֻּולָּם וְהִשְׁווּ אוֹמֶר
 לַחֲלוֹק עַל עוֹשֶׂה כֹּל בְּאוֹמֶר
נִיתְגַּדֵּל יוֹצֵר עַל חוֹמֶר
 וְחֵימָר הָיָה לָהֶם לַחוֹמֶר
סוֹד בַּחֲנִיָּיתָם וּבִנְסִיעָתָם
 לְשׁוֹן שִׁבְעִים הָיָה בְשִׂיחָתָם
עַל עֲנוֹתָם נְבָלָה בִּשְׂפָתָם
 בַּעֲבוּר כֵּן נָבְלָה שְׂפָתָם
פַּלָּגָה נִקְרָא דוֹרָם
 כִּי פָלְגוּ בְמִיגְדָּל דִּירָם
צוּר פִּילְּגָם וּפָרַץ גְּדֵירָם

renown" (*shem she'iyah*)—near homonyms with antonymic connotations.

21 This language comes from Isa 28:7 (**R**).

22 Jer 23:29.

23 The generation that built the Tower of Babel and was subsequently dispersed was referred to in rabbinic literature as "*dor ha-palagah.*"

and they were divided from one another in speech
The speaking of their lips was slick
as they spoke, so were they stricken[24]
They stormed and burned and kindled
by that which they sinned, they were smitten[25]
Equal and at ease with a single language
their dwelling had been one of comfort
But they desired loftiness, despised lowness
so in the end they were despised by the Lofty One
and torn away from below

And thus, "Unified of speech..."[26]

(7^{1}) Unified, united, one of speech, fools of the earth, they disparaged
They disparaged Him who tested their speech when they said, "Let us build a castle lofty"
Loftily, haughtily—they thought heroically—those valley-dwellers, arrogant blasphemers, they spoke
They spoke, they galloped, they soared, stomping, trampling, the trampling of Heaven
Heaven wrought their ruin; they were hung; He bent them, they were overturned and made fools
They were made fools, tongue-tied, unconscious, burnt, flooded, judged and this—
This because they plotted baseness: they were scorched, agitated, and scattered far afield
Far afield from their lovely dwelling, You showered arrows upon their army because they strutted
They strutted, they were fools, they erred and were devoured, exiled all together
Together they took counsel, plotted traps, stood firm, scheming thus
Thus all of them, as one, sinned, naming "power" to themselves[27]
To them You scorned to listen, mocking the mockers,[28] the makers of the tower

---

24 The Hebrew term *laqu'* ("afflicted") puns on the root ל-ק-ק ("to lap like a dog"), implying a devolution in their behavior beyond a loss of speech ability.

25 **R** reads באחד ("against the One") rather than באשר.

26 The second half of the first verse of the *sidra* provides the starting point for this unit.

וּפָלְגוּ זֶה עַל זֶה בְּדִיבּוּרָם
קְרִיאַת שִׂפְתוֹתָם אֲשֶׁר חָלָקוּ
כִּקְרִיאָתָם כֵּכֵן לָקוּ
רָגְשׁוּ וּבָעֲרוּ וְדָלָקוּ
וּבַאֲשֶׁר חָטְאוּ בָהּ לָקוּ
שִׁיווּי שִׁיפֵי שָׂפָה אֶחָת
וִישִׁיבָתָם יְשִׁיבַת נַחַת
תָּאֲבוּ רוּם וַיִּשְׂנְאוּ תָחַת
וְנִתְעֲבוּ מֵרוּם
וְנֻוּסְחוּ מִתָּחַת

ובכן ודברים אחדים

(ז׳) אֲחָדִים אֲחוּדִים אִימְרָה אַחַת אֱווִילֵי אֲדָמָה בִּיזּוּ
בִּיזּוּ בְּבוֹחֵן בִּיטּוּיָם בְּאָומְרָם בְּנוֹת בִּירָה גְבוֹהָה

גְּבוֹהָה גִּיבְּרוּ גָּרֵי גַּיְא גִּידּוּפֵי גַּאֲוָה דִּבֵּרוּ

דִּבֵּרוּ דָּהָרוּ דָּאוּ דְּרוּךְ דְּרוֹס דְּרִיסַת הַשָּׁמַיִם

הַשָּׁמַיִם הֵמָּה הִשְׁמִימוּם הוּתַל הִיטָּם הֲפַכְפַּךְ וְנוֹאָלוּ

וְנוֹאָלוּ וְנֶאֱלָמוּ וְנֶעֱלָמוּ וְנִשְׂרָפוּ וְנִשְׁטָפוּ וְנִשְׁפְּטוּ זֹאת

זֹאת זוֹלֵלוּת זוֹמָמוּ זוֹרָבוּ זוֹעָמוּ זוֹרוּ חוּץ

חוּץ חֲנִיַּית חֶמְדָתָם חֲצַצְתָּם חֵילָם חֵילֶף טָפוּ

טָפוּ טָפָשׁוּ טָעוּ טוֹרָפוּ טוּלְטְלוּ טַלְטֵלַת יָחַד

יַחַד יָעֲצוּ יָזְמוּ יוֹקֶשׁ יִתְיַצְּבוּ יִוָּוסְדוּ כֵּן
כֵּן כֻּולָּהֶם כְּאַחַת כָּפָרוּ כַּנּוֹת כֹּחַ לָמוֹ
לָמוֹ לַעֲגָתָה לְשָׁעָה לְהָלִיץ לַלֵּיצִים לְבוֹנֵה מִגְדָּל

---

27 The MS here is unclear; the translation follows **B2**. The implication is that the Tower Builders named the idol atop their tower "Power" in direct affront to God (to whom power truly belongs), thereby claiming power for themselves.

28 See above, the second proof-text for Poem Two (Prov 3:34).

The tower reaching the heights, the Fortress from whom they fled, fleeing
Fleeing, they dispersed, scattered, wandered, were shaken, seized by the storm
The storm raged against their windy words; their rebellious thoughts they spoke[29]
They spoke supposing that sneaking would be strategic for sinning successful sinning, thus disrupted was their deed
Their deed darkened their faces with shame; mouths still open, You dispersed them, O Rock!
O Rock, You wearied of their twittering, were put off by their protesting, and You shouted aloud
Aloud You called, O Indignant God, You shattered the wall, hurled from the nest their multitude
Their multitude pursued the wind of those who behold the Chariot of the Most High Almighty
O Almighty, You heard, You judged the folly of their noise, You despised
You despised those hoping to rise again; You desired those who hoped to repent.

And thus…

(7^2)

Your utterance	Cannot be altered;
Your covenant	Cannot be ended;
Your decree	Cannot be diminished;
Your word	Cannot be rejected;
Your splendor	Cannot be questioned;
Your superiority	Cannot be spoken;
Your call	Cannot be counterfeited;
Your residence	Cannot be revealed;
Your palace	Cannot be approached;
Your counsel	Cannot be known;
Your might	Cannot be exhausted;
Your dwelling	Cannot be demarked;
Your Self	Cannot be overthrown;[30]
Your timelessness	Cannot be tested;

29 On several occasions in this poem, the root ע-נ-ה (usually, "to answer") is understood as "to begin speaking." See M. Zulay, *Iyyunei Lashon be-Fiyutei Yannai*, p. 210.

מִגְדָּל מַגִּיעַ מָרוֹם מָעוֹז מְנוּסָם מֶנּוּ נוֹסָסוּ
נוֹסָסוּ נָזוֹרוּ נִתְפַּזָּרוּ נָעוּ נוֹעָרוּ נֹאחֱזוּ סָעַר

סָעַר סוּפַת סוֹעַ שִׂיחָם סֵיעֲפִים סָרָה עוֹנִים

עוֹנִים עֲשׂוֹת עָרְמָה עֶזְרָה עִינְיַין עִיוְעִים עֲוֹרְעֲרָה פְּעֻולָּתָם

פְּעֻולָּתָם פָּחָה פְּנֵיהֶם פֶּה פּוֹצְחִים פִּילַגְתָּם צוּר

צוּר צָפִיתָה צִיפְצוּפָם צָעִיתָה צִוְוחָתָם צָרַחְתָּה קוֹל

קוֹל קָרָאתָה קַנּוֹא קִיר קִירְקַרְתָּה קִינָּם קִילַּעְתָּה רֵובָּם

רֵובָּם רָדַף רוּחַ רוֹאִי רֶיכֶב רוּם שַׁדַּי

שַׁדַּי שָׁמַעְתָּה ש.. שָׁפַטְתָּה שְׁטוּת שְׁאוֹנָם תִּיעָבְתָּה
תִּיעַבְתָּה תּוֹלֵי תְקוּמָה תָּאַבְתָּה תְּלוּוֵיי תְשׁוּבָה

ובכן

(ז^{2}) אִימְרָתָךְ אֵין לְאַחֵר
בְּרִיתָךְ אֵין לְבַלּוֹת
גְּזֵירָתָךְ אֵין לִגְרוֹעַ
דִּבְרָתָךְ אֵין לִדְחוֹת
הַדְרָתָךְ אֵין לְהַרְהֵר
וִיתּוּרָךְ אֵין לאוֹמַר
זִכְרוֹנָךְ אֵין לְזַיֵּיף
חֲנִייָּתָךְ אֵין לַחֲקוֹר
טִירָתָךְ אֵין לִטְפּוֹף
יָעַצָךְ אֵין לֵידַע
כּוֹחָךְ אֵין לְכַלּוֹת
לִינָתָךְ אֵין לִלְחוֹץ
מִמָּךְ אֵין לִמְרוֹד
נִצְחָךְ אֵין לְנַסּוֹת

30 Literally, "Against You there can be no rebellion"; translation attempts to preserve the form of the unit.

Your secret	Cannot be fathomed;
Your [heights][31]	Cannot be scaled;
Your wonder	Cannot be divided;[32]
Your depiction	Cannot be drawn;
Your holiness	Cannot be approached;[33]
Your wind	Cannot be tamed;
Your authority	Cannot be limited;
Your lofty dwelling	Cannot be reached.

(8) From the heavens to the heavens of heavens / from the heavens of heavens to the Concealed Heavens / from the Concealed Heavens to the Lofty Abode / from Lofty Abode to the Hidden Lair / from Hidden Lair to the High Clouds / from the High Clouds to the Highest Heavens / from the Highest Heavens to the Exalted Throne / from the Exalted Throne to the Heavenly Chariot[34]:

Who could resemble You?[35] / Who might equal You? / Who saw? / Who reached? / Who dares lift his head? / Who would raise his eye? / Who tries with questions? / Who shall dare? / Who plots? / Who calculates in his heart? / Who boasts? / Who is proud? / Who shall evaluate?

And Your mount is a cherub / Your flight is on the wind / Your road is in the storm / Your path is in the gale / Your way is on the water / Your mission is through fire / Thousands upon thousands, myriads upon myriads / Become men / Become women / Become spirits / Become demons / Become every form / And perform every mission / With terror, with dread, with fear, with trembling, with quaking, with shaking, they open their mouths to mention Your holy Name:[36]

As it is written: "And the one called…"

---

31 Lacuna filled by **R**.

32 The term "divided" (לפלוג) here is from the same root as "Dispersed Generation" (פלג). See note above. The root can also mean "to dispute, debate."

33 God's holiness cannot be approached either physically or cognitively. In this attribute, He is wholly Other.

34 As **R** notes, the catalogue of the "seven heavens" can be found, with some variation in names and orders, in multiple rabbinic sources; see *LevR* 29:11; MisPsa 9:11; *SEZ* 9:3; *PRK Rosh Hashanah* 11; *b.* Ḥag 12b; ARN 37:9; and others, including mystical texts associated

סְפוּנָךְ   אֵין לִ**סְ**קוֹר

ע..   ... לַ**עֲ**לוֹת

פִּלְאָךְ   אֵין לִ**פְ**לוֹג

צוּרָתָךְ   אֵין לָ**צ**וּר

קְדוּשָּׁתָךְ   אֵין לִ**קְ**רַב

רוּחָךְ   אֵין לִ**רְ**כַּב

שִׁלְטוֹנָךְ   אֵין לְ**שַׁ**עֵר

תִּלּוּלָךְ   אֵין לִ**תְ**לוֹת

(ח) מִשָּׁמַיִם לִשְׁמֵי הַשָּׁמַיִם \ מִשְּׁמֵי שָׁמַיִם לַעֲרָפֶל \ מֵעֲרָפֶל לִזְבוּלָה \ מִזְּבוּלָה לִמְעוֹנָה \ מִמְּעוֹנָה לִשְׁחָקִים \ מִשְּׁחָקִים לַעֲרָבוֹת \ מֵעֲרָבוֹת לְרוּם כִּסֵּא \ וּמֵירוּם כִּסֵּא לְמֶרְכָּבָה

מִי יִדְמֶה לָּךְ \ מִי יִשְׁוֶוה לָּךְ \ מִי רָאָה \ מִי הִגִּיעַ \ מִי יִתְלֶה רֹאשׁ \ מִי יָרִים עַיִן \ מִי יַקְשֶׁה \ מִי יָעִיז \ מִי יָזִיד \ מִי יְחַשֵּׁב בַּלֵּב \ מִי יִגְאֶה \ מִי יִגַּס \ מִי יַעֲרוֹךְ

וּרְכוּבָךְ עַל כְּרוּב \ וְדִיאָתָךְ עַל רוּחַ \ וְאָורְחָךְ בְּסוּפָה \ וְדַרְכָּךְ בִּסְעָרָה \ וּשְׁבִילָךְ בְּמַיִם \ וּשְׁלִיחוּתָךְ בָּאֵשׁ \ אֶלֶף אֲלָפִים וְרִיבֵּי רְבָבוֹת \ נַעֲשִׂים אֲנָשִׁים \ נַעֲשִׂים נָשִׁים \ נַעֲשִׂים רוּחוֹת \ נַעֲשִׂים זִיקִים \ נַעֲשִׂים כָּל דְּמוּת \ וְעוֹשִׂים כָּל שְׁלִיחוּת \ בְּאֵימָה בְּיִרְאָה בְּפַחַד בְּרַעַד בְּרֶתֶת בְּזִיעַ \ יִפְתְּחוּ פֶּה לְהַזְכִּיר זֵיכֶר קָודְשָׁךְ ...

ככתוב וקרא זה אל זה

---

with *Hekhalot* traditions preserved in the modern anthologies *Otzar Ha-Midrashim* and *Batei Midrashot*. This list attests both to the widespread concept of "the seven heavens" and the diffuse nature of ideas associated with *Hekhalot* mysticism. The mystical texts and Yannai's piyyutim most likely represent different manifestations of a broader tradition; for a fuller discussion of this topic, see Chapter Three.

35 Compare to the prayer *Nishmat Kol Ḥai*.

36 **R** has שם קודשך; the Ma'agarim text recalls Ps 30:5 and Ps 97:12.

(9) In every lip and mouth and tongue,
with [clarity and] brightness and purity,
they declare and say:[37]
Holy, holy, holy is the Lord of Hosts! The whole earth is filled with His glory!
"*Holy*"—from those choice of tongue
"*Holy*"—from those clean of mouth
["*Holy*"—from those pure of] lip, true and steadfast
Holy, holy, holy is the Lord of Hosts! The whole earth is filled with His glory!
[The Holy One desired a tongue] learned in law[38]
The H[oly One desired a mouth …
[The Holy One desired a lip] … and holiness (etc.)

[*From His place*—… .like a gen]eration of one lip[39]
[*From His place*—…… He exam]ines a third like a generation [obscure] of tongue[40]
[*From His place*—……] like a generation sharp of mouth
[…*Twice*…]

37 Lacunae in this unit completed as in **R**.
38 See Isa 50:4.

(ט) בְּכָל שָׂפָה וּפֶה וְלָשׁוֹן
בִּיבְרִירוּת וּבִ[בְהִירוּת] וּבִינְקִיּוּת
יַעֲנוּ וְיֹאמְרוּ
קָדוֹשׁ קָדוֹשׁ קָדוֹשׁ [יי צבאות מלא כל הארץ כבודו]
קָדוֹשׁ מִבַּחוּרֵי לָשׁוֹן
קָדוֹשׁ מִנְקִיֵּי פֶה
[קָדוֹשׁ מִבְּרוּרֵי] שְׂפַת אֱמֶת הַנְּכוֹנָה
[קדוש קדוש קדוש יי צבאות מלא כל הארץ כבודו]
[קָדוֹשׁ חָשַׁק בִּלְשׁוֹן] לִימּוּדֵי דָת
קָדוֹשׁ חָשַׁק בְּפֶה ...
... וּקְדֻוּשָּׁה לְעוֹלָם

... כְּדוֹר שָׂפָה אַחַת
... ..חן שְׁלִישִׁי כְּדוֹר לָשׁוֹן ...

... כְּדוֹר חַדֵּי פֶה
...

39 I.e., language.
40 See Isa 28:11 and note in **B1**.

Commentary:

This piyyut ranks among Yannai's best by almost any measure. It is rich in allusions to aggadic and midrashic traditions, from the mundane to the near-mystical. It vividly brings the biblical story to life while also embedding within it contemporary political commentary. And in terms of richness and wittiness of language, it is exemplary. For a poet who delighted in language, the story of how God used language to punish the arrogant and idolatrous Tower Builders offered a remarkable opportunity to play with words.

Some of the most dazzling effects in this particular poem derive from its primary theme: the power of language. The theology emerging from this theme is "measure for measure": though seeking proximity to God through linguistic unity, the generation of the dispersion ended up alienated from both God and each other through disruption of language. Techniques such as puns, sound-play, and brilliantly complicated formalism acquire heightened significance in this theological-philosophical framework. Yannai's clever use of language ("the language of creation"—i.e., Hebrew—no less) implicitly distinguishes his community from the wayward Tower-Builders.

Yannai is not merely interested in the history of language; he is quite aware of its power in his own day. Indeed, as the poem develops, the poet juxtaposes the linguistic tragedy of the builders of Babel with the linguistic potency of his poem's liturgical setting: the heady, and constructive, act of praying the Qedushah. The builders of the Tower of Babel sought to be like the angels, among the hosts of heaven, but it is the community of Israel that holds that place instead; through transgression, every other nation has lost the linguistic (as well as cognitive) bond with Heaven. Myth and moment intersect in this composition. The experience of the *piyyutim* in the ancient synagogue was simultaneously intellectual and visceral: the recitation of Scripture, the performance of exegesis, and the act of prayer.

According to Gen 11, humanity sinned through abuse of language, and as a result it was punished through loss of language. The poet revels in the original story's irony: punishing hubristic speech by means of garbling all speech, and rewarding sedition with division. Yannai specifies that the "sins of the lips" were arrogance and hubris—and, perhaps unexpectedly for those not familiar with the aggadah on this portion, idolatry.[41] The building

41 Nowhere in the biblical text of Genesis 11 are we told that one of the sins of the

of the Tower is as much symbolic of these destructive behaviors as it is innately transgressive. Conversely, the poet teaches that appropriate speech and respectful assembly—implicitly including proper worship, for which his audience is gathered—may be expected to lead to continued effective divine attention and strengthened community. Motion up and down is particularly emphasized in the text. The Tower- builders sought to ascend upwards but were cast down; correct speech and ambition, however, may result in equally appropriate spiritual ascent and inspire the deity to act in the realms below.[42] In using both motifs—those of speech and motion—the poet depicts a God who is wholly and actively responsive. Between the theology of the poem and the liturgical context, it is natural that the poet frequently addresses God in the second person. The poem slips easily from narrative expansion into petition.

Emerging subtly from the repetitions of these fundamental motifs we can detect a single, coherent lesson on the nature of the world: human achievements, whether those of the Tower-builders of the ancient world or those of the poet's own day, are ultimately ephemeral. The most glorious accomplishments are fragile and beyond human power to preserve. The frustration of the dispersed generation is, in fact, ongoing: not merely in the communication challenge that emerged when one language became seventy, but the realization that any plan to reach God, when God does not want to be reached, is doomed and hubristic. In this poem, humans speak;

Tower-builders was idolatry. However, Yannai repeatedly includes this accusation in his description of that generation's transgressions: the terms "disgrace," "folly" and "error" in the first unit all allude to idolatry. Subsequently, the poet is more explicit: the Tower-builders sought "to make a `second' for the God who is One" (Poem 6, line 12); and—in what may be an anti-Christian, anti-trinitarian polemic—the poet asserts: "Your wonder: there is no dividing it" (second *rahit*, line 17). The interpretation (or interpolation) of idolatry into the story is not unique to the poet, however; *TargPsJ* to Gen 11:3 renders the biblical verse as: "Come, let us build ourselves a city and a tower, and the top of it shall come to the summit of the heavens; and let us make ourselves an idol for worship on the top of it, and put a sword in its hand so that it may draw up battle formations against Him, before we are scattered on the face of the earth." (*Targum Yerushalmi* has "house of worship" in place of "idol," suggesting an idolatrous temple.) *GenR* 38:6, *Mek Mishpatim* 20, and *b.San* 109a preserve similar traditions.

42 It is interesting to note a similar interpretation of the 4th century C.E. Christian poet, St. Ephrem the Syrian: "The symbol of the tower that the masses built looked for the One / for He was to descend and build on the earth the tower that leads up into heaven" (*De Nativitate* I, 44). The motifs of searching for God—inappropriately and too early—as well as the up/down motion are both present here. The complex relationships among piyyut, midrash, and early Christian hymnography are examined in Chapter Three.

God listens and reacts. Crumbling exemplifies mortality; enduring is divine. As the narrative line within the poem develops, the poet articulates God's remoteness (putatively from the builders of Babel) with increasing bittersweetness. The Tower-builders were fools to try to conquer the heavens, but speaking to a God who is so far away—higher than the highest heavens—might this not be an act just as foolish, or even futile? The act of praying carries a challenge to faith all its own. There is an occasional element of sympathy for the yearnings of the dispersed generation, and an urgency in the poet's own voice as he recites a soliloquy for two voices: his and God's. He asserts immanence while describing radical transcendence.

These multiple motifs—the potency of language, God's power and remoteness, the measure-for-measure justice that determined the Tower-builder's fate and that of other hubristic assemblies—occur in almost every unit of the poetic cycle. This elliptical style not only helps ensure understanding but also intensifies the potency of the message. Indeed, for all that the poem describes a remote, mythic past, contemporary concerns are easy to detect. First and foremost, text and context reassure the community that the act of prayer is far from futile. The community of Jews at prayer, the poet reassures his listeners, is fundamentally unlike that of the Tower-builders: their speech is humble, not hubristic. Their worship correct, not sinful. They act out of true knowledge of the divine, not in arrogant ignorance. And their petitions will be heard and received, not rejected and frustrated. Indeed, the entire poem moves towards the central prayer of the Amidah, the mystically charged Qedushah, which is based on the "angelic" liturgy of Isa 6:3 and Ezek 3:12. Israel, when she prays, joins the very heavenly hosts in the act of worship. Unlike the Tower-builders who "from the ancients never learned" (Poem 2, line 1), Israel possesses unique insights, which close the gap between earth and heaven. The biblical tale's tragic fable of destructive speech is linked, inexorably, with participation in mystical, powerful speech. The repetitions of the words "holy" and "proclaim" or "call out," so key in the Qedushah-prayer, subtly shift the audience's attention from the biblical story to their own moment in time.

The poet's contemporary world is explicitly adduced in the third poem of the cycle, the *meshallesh*, in which the poet has also embedded his name by means of an acrostic. Moving from the image of the futile plotting of the Tower-builders in the initial two stanzas, the poet turns his attention to the hubristic schemers of his own epoch: the Christianized Roman Empire, Byzantium. He envisions a day when that kingdom will be put to silence (through a pun on *dumah* [דומה], "silence" or an angel of death or even the underworld—a word that even physically resembles "Rome" [רומא] in Hebrew).[43] It may be that loss of speech is an even more extreme punishment than the disruption of dialect, but the evil of Rome merits dramatic affliction. *Edom* (the common epithet for Rome, which resonates with "*adamah*," or earth) will be cast down to the ground like the Tower-builders and not even granted language in the deadly aftermath. The poet, however, goes beyond drawing parallels between the biblical text and his own apocalyptic hopes. After the defeat of Rome, all humanity will, as one, invoke God and unify Him. Through this act of pious speech, the poet suggests, humanity itself may be reunified, a reality symbolized by a restored purity and unity of speech. That which was *overturned* will be *returned* to what it was—after the lesson has been learned. Poetic justice will result in restoration as well as destruction.

43 The association of Edom/Esau with Rome is a commonplace in rabbinic literature; see Chapter Four, as well as the later poems in this volume. This general identification was transferred to the christianized Empire and subsequently all of (Roman) Christianity in later antiquity.

Qedushta for Genesis 12:1 בראשית יב:א

ויאמר יי לאברם לך לך

"The Lord said to Abram, `Go forth'"

In this poem, Yannai explores God's selection of Abraham—and Abraham's response—in terms both dramatic and intimate. God rewards the trust Abraham showed in Him by following His call by bestowing eternal blessings and protections upon the patriarch and his descendents. These blessings are recalled in the poem itself, in the first benediction of the Amidah, where God is praised as "the shield of Abraham."

(1) A lover amidst Your enemies, You acquired
A creature You endowed, allowed to create[1]
One radiant among those dwelling in darkness You perceived
The ways of his heart You fathomed

Thus like an only daughter You led him
and like a little sister You drew him near[2]
Clear amidst the clouded when You saw him
like sweet-talking a lass, You enticed him[3]

They burdened without …
You imbued him with a portion of Your power[4]
Because You were so close…
Therefore, with a promise, You said to him, "Go forth!"

As it is written: "The Lord said to Abram, Go forth from your land and from your kindred and from your father's house to the land that I will show you" (Gen 12:1)
And it is said: "Pay heed, O daughter, and see; incline your ear, and forget your father's house" (Ps 45:11)[5]
And it is said: "And let the king be aroused by your charms, for he is your lord; bow down to him" (Ps 45:12)
And it is said: "Draw me after you and let us run! The king has brought me to his chambers; let us exult and rejoice in you! Let us extol your lovemaking beyond wine! Rightly do they love you." (Song 1:4)[6]

---

1 The phrase "endowed/allowed" captures the double nuance of the verb. As **B1** notes, the motif of Abraham becoming God's partner in creation appears frequently, both in this piyyut and in the midrash. See *GenR* 43:7, "Rabbi Isaac said: Abraham used to entertain wayfarers, and after they had eaten he would say to them, `Say a blessing.' `What shall we say?' they would ask. `Blessed be the God of the Universe of Whose bounty we have eaten,' he replied. Then the Holy One, blessed be He, said to him: `My Name was not known among My creatures, but you have made it known among them: I will regard you as though you were My partner with Me in the creation of the world.'" Compare with Noah in the Qedushta for Gen 8:15, and see also notes below.

2 Lit., "attached him." *GenR* 39:3 offers the same pun on *ʾaḥot* (sister) and *ʾiḥah* (to stitch), based on Song 8:8 ("We have a little sister"); see also *Tanḥ Lekh Lekha* 2 and *TanḥB Lekh Lekh*a 2 (**R**). This motif is discussed below.

3 The language is, in part, an adaptation of Prov 22:6, "Train (*ḥanakh*) a lad (*naʿar*) in the way he ought to go" (**B1**). Yannai has changed the gender of the object, however, from "lad" to the plural, "lasses" (or, possibly an abstract: youth). For the erotic connotations given here, however, see *Midrash ha-Gadol Bereshit* p. 216 (cited by **R**), where God's call to Abraham is compared to a man courting a woman, enticing her to leave her father's house

(א) **א**וֹהֵב מֵבִין שְׂנוּאִים קָנִיתָה
בְּרוּאִים אוֹתוֹ הִקְנֵיתָה
גִּיהַּ בֵּין חֲשׁוּכִים סָקַרְתָּה
דַּרְכֵי לִבּוֹ חָקַרְתָּה

הֵן כְּבַת יְחִידָה הִנְחֵיתוֹ
וּכְאָחוֹת קְטַנָּה אִחִיתוֹ
זַךְ בֵּין עֲכוּרִים כִּרְאִיתוֹ
חִינּוּךְ נַעֲרוֹת פִּתִּיתוֹ

טָעֲנוּ בְלֹא ...
יִיפִּיתוֹ בְּכֹחַ חֵילָךְ
כִּי אִיחָךְ ... לך
לָכֵן בְּהַבְטָחָה נַמְתָּה לוֹ לֶךְ־לְךָ

ככתוב ויאמר יי אל אברם לך לך מארצך וממולדתך ומית אביך אל הארץ אשר אראך

ונאמר שמעי בת וראי והטי אזנך ושכחי עמך ובית אביך

ונאמר ויתאיו המלך יפיך כי הוא אדניך והשתחוי לו

ונאמר משכני אחריך נרוצה הביאני המלך חדריו נגילה ונשמחה בך נזכירה דדיך מיין מישרים אהבוך

---

and come to his own. The midrash states: "Thus the Holy One, blessed be He, enticed our father Abraham to leave his land and his birthplace…" The root פ-ת-ה, which appears in the piyyut and the midrash, means "to flatter, persuade, seduce."

4 The translation ייפיתו of "imbued" attempts to capture the connotations of both "beautified, adorned" (as is the common meaning of the root יפה in biblical Hebrew) as well as "strengthened" (a valence of the root in rabbinic Hebrew). **B1** cites *GenR* 39:11, which states: "Rabbi Berekiah said: Seeing that it is already written, 'And I will bless you' (Gen 12:2), why is, 'And you will be a blessing' (ibid.) added? He [God] said to him [Abraham]: 'Previously, I had to bless My world; henceforth the blessings are entrusted to you: whom it pleases you to bless, bless!'" A similar comment is found in the midrash on Gen 24:1 ("And Abraham was old, advanced in years"): "Rabbi Samuel ben Isaac said: The Holy One, blessed be He, said to him: 'It is My function to dispense love; since you have embraced My function, come and don My raiment.'"

5 This verse and the following are the *petiḥta* verses in *GenR* 39:1 (**R**); they also appear as exegetical verses in *Tanḥ Lekh Lekha* 3 and *TanḥB Lekh Lekha* 3.

6 This verse occurs in *GenR* 49:2, where the final clause of the Song verse is understood as "the upright [i.e., the righteous, including Abraham] love You" (**R**).

And it is said: "In all your ways acknowledge Him and He will make your pathways straight" (Prov 3:6)

Our pathways may You set firm
and our hearts may You discern
and … may You shield!
Blessed… Shield…

(2) "Because you grasped the greatness of your Maker
I shall make you a great nation forever"
So You said…
thus he ran to seek the shelter of Your protection:
"Your steps will I guide in straightness
"Your every footfall will I reckon [fit]"[7]
"Your possessions[8] I will bless with abundance
"and when you hasten, you will fly on eagles' wings[9]
"Your name was `And he shall be'
"and thirty righteous…[10]
"You shall be blessed and by My blessing shall you live
"mightily blessed, a blessing shall you be!"

As it is written: "And I shall make you a great nation, and I shall bless you, and make your name great, and you shall be a blessing" (Gen 12:2)
And it is said: "A good name is preferable to great wealth; grace is better than silver or gold" (Prov 22:1)
And it is said: "A good name is better than good oil, and the day of one's death than the day of one's birth" (Eccl 7:1)[11]
And it is said: "The fragrance of your perfume is pleasing, oil poured forth is your name; therefore do the maidens love you" (Song 1:3)[12]

---

7 Gap filled by **B1**.

8 "Possessions" (קנינך) may refer to converts, the souls that Abraham "made" or acquired in Haran; see Gen 12:5. Alternatively, it could refer to Abraham's material belongings, cattle, and so forth (מקנה), as in Gen 13:2, the reading **R** favors.

9 **B1** refers to *MidPs* 110:3, and the similar tradition in *TanḥB Vayeshev* 8, where it says: "When Abraham pursued them [the Canaanite kings of Gen 14], the earth contracted before him." It appears there was a tradition that Abraham, like other *baʿalei shem*, could travel with supernatural speed (that is, by *kefitsat ha-derekh*, by means of a shortened road).

10 The numeric value of "*yihyeh*" is 30. See *GenR* 39:3, cited by **R**: "Rabbi Tanḥum said in the name of Rabbi Hus Elai in Rabbi Berekiah's name: He [God] informed him that the

ונאמר בכל דרכיך דעהו והוא יישר אורחותיך

אוֹרְחוֹתֵינוּ תְּכוֹנֵין
וְלִיבֵּינוּ תְּבוֹנֵין
... תְּגוֹנֵן
ברוך... מגן...

(ב) **מֵ**אֲשֶׁר דַּעְתָּה גּוֹדֶל עוֹשֶׁךָ
נֶצַח לְגוֹי גָּדוֹל אֶעֱשֶׂךָ
סַחְתָּה ....
עַל כֵּן רָץ לְצֵל מַחֲסֶךָ
פְּסִיעוֹתֶיךָ אַדְרִיךָ בְּיוֹשֶׁר
צְעָדֶיךָ אֶסְפּוֹר ...
קִנְיָנְךָ אֲבָרֵךְ בְּעוֹשֶׁר
רִיצָתְךָ אָעִיף כַּנֶּשֶׁר
שְׁמְךָ הָיָה וְיִהְיֶה
שְׁלֹשִׁים ... ה...
תְּבוֹרָךְ וּמִיבִּרְכָתִי תְּחְיֶיה
תּוֹקֶף בְּרָכָה בְּרוּכָה תִּהְיֶה

ככתוב ואעשך לגוי גדול ואברכך ואגדלה שמך והיה ברכה

ונאמר נבחר שם מעושר רב מכסף ומזהב חן טוב

ונאמר טוב שם משמן טוב ויום המות מיום הולדו

ונאמר לריח שמניך טובים שמן תורק שמך על כן עלמות אהבוך

---

world must never contain less than thirty righteous men like Abraham. Rabbi Judan and Rabbi Aḥa in Rabbi Alexandri's name deduced it from this verse: 'Seeing that Abraham shall surely be' (*hayo yihyeh*; Gen 18:18): *yod* is ten, *heh* five, *yod* ten, and *heh* five.'"

11 See *Tanḥ Vayaqhel* 1, where this verse is connected to Gen 12:2 (**R**).

12 **R** cites the *petiḥta* in *GenR* 39:2, which states: "Rabbi Berekiah opened: 'The fragrance of your perfume is pleasing' (Song 1:3). Said Rabbi Berekiah: What did Abraham resemble? A phial of myrrh sealed with a tight-fitting lid and lying in a corner, so that its fragrance was not disseminated; as soon as it was taken up, however, its fragrance was disseminated. Similarly, the Holy One, blessed be He, said to Abraham: 'Travel from place to place, and your name will become great in the world': hence, 'Go forth!...' (Gen 12:1)."

And it is said: "Those blessed by Him shall possess the land, but those He curses are cut off" (Ps 37:22)
And it is said: "Look back to Abraham your father, and to Sarah who brought you forth; for he was only one when I called him, but I blessed him and made him many" (Isa 51:2)

"And I will bless him," You uttered;
"And I make him great," You openly declared[13]
According to his blessing, let us be blessed!
With the dew of life renewed, give us strength!
Blessed... Who resurrects...

(3) A hand to the patriarch You extended[14]
And by his charms were You aroused
Before him did You walk upon the land to which You led him
He said, "If only I had the wings like a dove and like an eagle, to take flight!"
with a hopeful promise, You took him from the river's far shore
Because he followed in Your steps[15] and righteously proclaimed
therefore in his own steps' wake was righteousness proclaimed
The beauty of his blessing You multiplied for the many[16]
blessed seed from his seed[17] You made grow[18]

As it is written: "And I took your father, Abraham, from the river's shore, and I led him through all the land of Canaan, and I made his descendants a multitude, and I gave him Isaac" (Josh 24:3)
And it is said: "You are the Lord God, who chose Abram, who brought him out of Ur of the Chaldeans and changed his name to Abraham" (Neh 9:7)
And You are Holy, enthroned upon the praises of Israel...Please, O God...

(4) Within the eastern gates[19]

---

13 Following **B1**'s emendation (ואברכיהו נמתה / וארבה פצתה), which results in better parallelism.

14 The image is, as **B2** notes, as if God led Abraham by his hand to the Promised Land.

15 Or: "Because he submitted to Your instruction" (**R** cites Deut 33:3 for similar language). The translation here emphasizes the physicality of Abraham's journey from Ur.

16 **R** reads: "With the beauty of his blessings You blessed the many."

ונאמר כי מבורכיו ירשו ארץ ומקלליו יכרתו

ונאמר הביטו אל אברהם אביכם ואל שרה תחוללכם כי אחד קראתיו ואברכהו וארבהו

וַאֲבָרְכֵיהוּ וְאַרְבֵּהוּ נַמְתָּה
וַאֲבָרְכֵהוּ פַּצְתָּה
כְּבִרְכָתוֹ תְּבָרְכֵינוּ
בְּטַל לִתְחִיָּה תְּעוֹדְדֵינוּ
ברוך... מחיה...

(ג) **יָ**ד לָאָב נָתַתָּה
וּלְיָופְיוֹ נִתְאַוֵּיתָה
לְפָנָיו הִילַּכְתָּה בָּאָרֶץ אֲשֶׁר הוֹלַכְתָּה
נָם מִי יִתֵּן לִי כַּיּוֹנָה אֵבֶר וְכַנֶּשֶׁר הֶעֱלָה אֵבֶר
וּבְהַבְטָחַת סֵיבֶר לְקַחְתּוֹ מֵעֵיבֶר
יַעַן תֻּוכָּה לְרַגְלָךְ וּבְצֶדֶק קָרָא
עַל כֵּן לְרַגְלוֹ צֶדֶק הֻוקְרָא
יוֹפִי בִרְכָתוֹ לָרוֹב הִירְבִּיתָה
וְזֶרַע בְּרָכָה מִזַּרְעוֹ תַרְבִּיתָה

ככתוב ואקח את אביכם את אברהם מעבר הנהר ואוך אותו בכל ארץ כנען וארבה את זרעו ואתן לו את יצחק

ונאמר אתה הוא יי האלהים אשר בחרתה באברם והוצאתו מיאור־כשדים ושמת שמו אברהם

ואתה קדוש יושב תהלות ישראל אל נא

(ד) בְּשַׁעֲרֵי מִזְרָח

17 The words "seed" and "heirs" here translate the same word, *zera*^{c} ("seed"). The imagery of the stich is agricultural.

18 Reading הרביתה (an alternative cited in **R**'s annotations); the language of this verse may be influenced by Isa 61:9, "For they are a seed blessed by the Lord."

19 Presumably a reference to Abraham's origins in Ur. **R** has "From the eastern shore, " i.e., the horizon from which the sun appears.

arose one radiantly pure[20]
within the midst of darkness and gloom, he shone with a radiant light[21]
Indeed, the abominations[22] of Terah he rejected and cast aside
like a falcon, he burst forth and unto You he flew
His father's images he hammered to bits
and many lost souls he brought close to You
Though just a youth, he readied himself to fight for You
Trusting in the promises Your mouth uttered
…
He knew You a little, You made Yourself known to him well
He opened…
…close and holy
O, Awesome, Exalted, and Holy One

(5)[23] A mere boy of three was he, but brave
wonder and wisdom were set in his heart
Upon the heavens he gazed, upon their wonderful colored display
and he knew: "There is a Leader to all this host!"
So, too, like the words of the wise, which are heard in quiet[24]
he would entice whoever came to buy an idol from him
Knowledge he put in their hearts and their eyes, he opened
against the idols which at high cost You Yourself will take[25]
Thus from yesterday and the day before … renewed
and how the old would bow down to the new
But You are better than it, for You both hear and speak
… [not] hearing and not speaking[26]
Why on earth do you reject the God who made man

20 Heb. "*ezraḥ*," usually translated as "citizen," or "one born of the land"—an irony here, given that Abraham was born outside of the Promised Land. It probably means something like "one of pure descent." I have incorporated the nuances of radiance and purity in my translation. As **R** notes, *LevR* 9:1 and *PRK Parah* (p. 61) both transform this into one of Abraham's names by associating him with Ps 89:1, "A *maskil* of Eitan (`the brave one') the Ezrahite." For "the brave one," see poem 5, line 1.

21 Translation reflects **R**'s reading of נגה. The Ma'agarim version would be translated as "militant" or "vigilant."

22 **R** reads, "abominable lies." That is, idols (**B1**).

23 This unit, while not preserved fully intact, clearly refers to a cluster of aggadic traditions about Abraham's intuitive insightfulness and courage. The first two lines put forth the idea that Abraham logically discovered monotheism when he gazed upon the stars and

הֵיצִיץ אֶזְרָח
וּמֵאוֹפֶל וּמֵחוֹשֶׁךְ צָבָא וְזָרַח
כִּי בְתוֹעֲבוֹת תֶּרַח מָאַס וְטָרַח
וּכְעַיִיט פָּר וְעָדֶיךָ בָּרַח
צַלְמֵי אָבִיו כִּתֵּת וְשִׁיבֵּר
וְהַרְבֵּה תוֹעִים אֵלֶיךָ חִיבֵּר
נַעַר הָיָה וּכְגָבֵר עַצְמוֹ לָךְ גִּיבֵּר
בְּבִיטָּחוֹן אֲשֶׁר פִּיךָ לוֹ דִּיבֵּר
.....
יְדָעָךְ מְעַט נוֹדַעְתָּה לוֹ הַרְבֵּה
הוּא פָּתַח ...
.... קָרוֹב וְקָדוֹשׁ
נורא מרום וקדוש

(ה) **אָ**ז בֶּן שָׁלוֹשׁ שָׁנִים הָיָה אֵיתָן
וְיִרְאָה וְחָוכְמָה בְּלִיבּוֹ נִיתַּן
... הֵבִּיט וּבְמַרְאִית צִבְעָם
וְיָדַע כִּי יֵשׁ מַנְהִיג ...
גַּם כְּדִבְרֵי חֲכָמִים הַנִּישְׁמָעִים בְּנַחַת
הָיָה מְפַתֶּה לַבָּא צֶלֶם מֶנּוּ קַחַת
דַּעַת שִׂים לַלֵּב וְעֵינֶיךָ פְּקַח
בָּאֱלִיל אֲשֶׁר לָךְ בְּדָמִים תִּיקַּח
הֵן מֵאֶתְמוֹל וְשִׁלְשׁוֹם ... יְחוּדַּשׁ
וְאֵיךְ יִשְׁתַּחֲוֶוה יָשָׁן לְחָדָשׁ
וְאַתָּה טוֹב מֶנּוּ כִּי תִשְׁמַע וּתְדַבֵּר
... שׁוֹמֵעַ וְגַם לֹא מְדַבֵּר
זָנוֹחַ לָמָּה תִּזְנַח לְאֵל עוֹשֵׂה אָדָם

---

realized that they must have a maker (*TanḥB Lekh Lekha* 4, *EstR* 6:2, and *SongR* 5:16 all describe Abraham as being three years old when he recognizes his Creator; *GenR* 64:4 states that he was forty-eight). **R** cites the closest parallel, which comes from *AggBereshit* (p. 210), and notes a reasonably close parallel in *GenR* 39:1. The remaining lines seem to recount the famous legend that Abraham's father, Terah, was an idol-maker but Abraham, realizing that idols were powerless, rejected his father's practices and beliefs in order to follow his conscience. (See *GenR* 38:13; this tradition is so widespread that it appears in the *Qur'an* 6:74 and 21:51–71 as an organic part of the Abraham narrative). Moved by Abraham's recognition of His uniqueness, God called Abraham in Gen 12:1—choosing him because he was, intellectually and morally worthy of being chosen.

24 Eccl 9:17

25 דמים can mean "blood" or "money." 26 Ps 115:5–6

and bring offerings to one made by the hand of man?
...
... is known ... the One who knows the false
Your goodness with his reason ...
...
Unique was he[27], and Your unity he realized[28]
...

And thus: "Go forth from your land..."
(6) "You for whom I waited from the first
"Watching for you for ten generations
"Among all, I found your heart most true
"Thus into the fiery furnace I went with you"
He abhorred their abominations and deeds
for there was no point to cry out to their "protectors"
Their "caretakers" lack any sense
and just like them are those who made them!
"Incline your ear, forget your parents' house
"And become wise to all I will teach you!"
And he heard, and let himself be drawn after You[29]
so You brought him to Your mountains[30]
"Forsake your father, your family, and your land
"In My land, I will favor you as a father loves a son
"With might and power, I will make you awesome
"To a choice land, I will bring you swiftly as a stag
"This is the decree I declared to you:
"`My lover, arise, come away with Me!'
"`Let there come forth from you [a nation],[31] and let it hearken as you have
"My friend, My sister,[32] arise, come away!'
"You are called `the greatest man'[33]
"[Unto you I revealed] My great power[34]
"Therefore from you I will raise up a great nation

---

27 I.e., Abraham; see Ezek 33:24 (**B1**).
28 See *TanḥB Noaḥ* 24 (**B1**).
29 Song 1:4, cited as an intertext after the *magen*.
30 The hills of Judea; that is, the territory of Jerusalem (reading with **B1**).
31 Reading with **B1**.

וְתוֹבֵא לְעָשׂוּי בִּידֵי אָדָם
...
... יְדוּעַ ..וע הַיּוֹדֵעַ לָעוּת
טוּבְךָ בְּטָוֹעֲמוֹ ...
... ..נוּ
יָחִיד הָיָה וְיִיחוּדְךָ הִיכִּיר
...

ובכן לך לך מארצך

(ו) **אֲ**שֶׁר לָךְ מֵרֹאשׁ צִיפִּיתִי
וּבַעֲשָׂרָה דוֹר לָךְ צָפִיתִי
בְּכוּלָּם נֶאֱמָן לֵב לָךְ מָצָאתִי
לָכֵן בְּכִיבְשַׁן אֵשׁ לָךְ נִמְצֵאתִי
גָּעַל גִּילּוּלִים וּמַעֲשֵׂיהֶם
כִּי אֵין שׁוֹעַן לְמַחֲסֵיהֶם
דֵּיעָה חֲסֵירִים חוֹסֵיהֶם
כְּמוֹ הֵם יִהְיוּ עוֹשֵׂיהֶם
הַט אָזְנְךָ שְׁכַח בֵּית הוֹרֶיךָ
וְהַשְׂכֵּיל לְכָל אֲשֶׁר אוֹרֶיךָ
וְשָׁמַע וְנִימְשַׁךְ אַחֲרֶיךָ
וַתְּבִיאֵהוּ עַל חוֹרֶיךָ
זְנַח אָב וּמוֹלַדְתְּךָ וְאַרְצָךְ
וּבְאַרְצִי כְּאָב לְבֵן אֶרְצָךְ
חַיִיל וּגְבוּרָה אֶעֱרִיצָךְ
וּלְאֶרֶץ צְבִי כִּצְבִי אֲרִיצָךְ
טַעַם זֶה אֲשֶׁר נַמְתִּי לָךְ
אוֹהֲבִי עִימִּי קוּם לֵךְ לָךְ
יֵצֵא מִמְּךָ א.. וְתִישְׁמַע כְּמוֹ לָךְ
רַעֲיָיתִי אֲחוֹתִי קוּמִי לָךְ
כִּינּוּיָיךְ אָדָם גָּדוֹל
... כּוֹחִי הַגָּדוֹל
לָכֵן מִמְּךָ אָקִים לִי גּוֹי גָּדוֹל

32 Note the change from "my beautiful one" (*yafati*) in Song 2:10 to "my sister" (*ʾahoti*). This may, as above, be a reference to Abraham as God's "unifier," the one who was to spread monotheism.

33 See Jos 14:15

34 Lacuna filled as in **B1.**

"who bless themselves by your name[35]
"From Chaldean Ur I brought you forth
"For, a rose among thorns, I found you
"Roaming afar [as I commanded you][36]
"... just as I wished of you
"Indeed, I shall make all fear you, like a lion
"And with a promise, [you will lead them like a mother bear][37]
"With me, you shall fly like a falcon!
"And I will lead you like a ship at sail"
"I have opened to you the Gates of Righteousness
"And My right [hand], filled with righteousness, I extend to you"
"Your righteousness radiates, and all the mighty oaks of righteousness[38] exclaim:
"`Look how the Righteous one arises from the east!'[39]
"I called you from the ends of the earth[40]
"I brought you near from the earth's far corners
"Shepherd faithfully and dwell upon this piece of earth[41]
"Trust in the One trusted to the ends of the earth
"I summoned you with My word, so holy
"And to your name I added a letter from My own, so holy"
"I strengthened you with My arm, so holy
"To thereby sanctify, through you, [My people, so] holy!"[42]

And thus "I shall make..."
(7[1]) "A father to a multitude of nations I proclaim you[43]
"A new world from you shall I fashion"
"Your body from fire was saved:

---

35 **B1** notes that this is an allusion to the invocation of Abraham in the *avot*-prayer.

36 Lacuna filled as in **B2**.

37 For the restoration of this fragmentary line, see **B1**. He bases his reading on Job 38:32, "As a bear leads her cubs"—in context, this verse refers to the constellation of Ursa Major and the little stars ("cubs") that follow it. The *Targum*, however, understands the phrase from Job to mean, "As a hen leads her chicks." Cognates suggest that "lion" might also be an appropriate translation of *ʿayish.* I have chosen an interpretation ("mother bear") that emphasizes both the fierceness of the *ʿayish* as well as its maternal, protective qualities. Not to underestimate the qualities of a mother hen, but a bear seems more in keeping with the figures of the lion and the falcon. See discussion below.

38 Isa 61:3, where the term is an epithet for Israel, but here the nuance of איל is "prince" (see Exod 15:15, Ezek 17:13, 31:11, etc.) yielding the translation "righteous princes"—indicating universal recognition of Abraham—may be intended.

מְבָרְכִים בִּשְׁמָךְ שֵׁם גָּדוֹל
מֵאוּר־כַּשְׂדִּים הוֹצֵאתִיךְ
כִּי כְשׁוֹשַׁן בֵּין חוֹחִים מְצָאתִיךְ
נְדוֹד הַרְחֵיק כְּמ.. ..תִיךְ
... כְּמוֹ הִרְצֵיתִיךְ
שׂוֹם אָשִׂים עַל כֹּל אֵימָתָךְ כְּלָיִשׁ
וּבְבִיטְחָה ...
עִימָּדִי אֲעִיפָךְ כְּעָיִט
וְאַנְהִיגָךְ לִי כָאָונִי שָׁיִט
פָּתַחְתִּי לָךְ שַׁעֲרֵי צֶדֶק
וּפָשַׁטְתִּי ... יָמִין מְלֵיאָה צֶדֶק
צָמַח צִידְקָךְ וְנָמוּ אֵילֵי צֶדֶק

מִי הֵעִיר מִמִּזְרָח צֶדֶק
קְרָאתִיךְ מִקְצוֹת הָאָרֶץ
וְקֵירַבְתִּיךְ מִמֶּרְחַקֵּי אָרֶץ
רְעֵה אֱמוּנָה וּשְׁכוֹן אָרֶץ
בְּטַח בְּמִבְטַח כָּל קַצְוֵי אָרֶץ
שְׁימַּעְתִּיךְ דִּיבּוּר קָודְשִׁי
וְעַל שְׁמָךְ אוֹסִיף אוֹת מִשֵּׁם קָודְשִׁי
תִּיקַּפְתִּיךְ בִּזְרוֹעַ קָודְשִׁי
לְקַדֵּשׁ מִמָּךְ א.. קָודְשִׁי

ובכן ואעשך
(ז[1]) **אָ**ב לְכָל אֻומּוֹת אֲיַיחֲסָךְ
בִּירְיָיה חֲדָשָׁה אֶעֱשָׂךְ
גֵּיוְויָךְ אֲשֶׁר מֵאֵשׁ נֶחֱסַךְ

39 Isa 41:2.

40 Isa 41:9 (**R**).

41 The word *ʾeretz* (translated here consistently as "earth") concludes each stich of this stanza; the third stich could be translated, "Remain loyal and you will dwell upon this land," which is more felicitous English, but loses the force of the repeated word.

42 Lacuna filled as in **B1**.

43 The interpretation of this line involves a problem of universalism versus particularism. In *GenR* 39:10, it is stated that the genealogies of all nations are recorded only because of Abraham's merit; based on this, **R** understands the stich as teaching that all the nations of the earth owe their lineage to Abraham. **B2**, however, understands the stich in light of Gen 17:5, "father of a multitude of nations I will make you." The latter is the simpler, more compelling interpretation. As the stich stands, it could be interpreted as a reference to the dispersion of the Jews in exile, where they live among a multitude of nations.

"Know that I brought you through beneath My shield"
You spoke with love to one who sheltered with You
...
Rushing and running to Your refuge
Your merciful shelter ...
You purified him with ...
"Awe and wonder are your burden"
Just as You spoke to him, "I am your shelter"
...
"From violence, with My shield, I will protect you"
You comforted ...
He was chosen from among ...
Still more, I will bless (you), be your hope and protector"[44]
You opened Your mouth to express Your will
...
You brought him into Your "joy,"
You sated him with spiced wine[45]
...
You led him under the banner of Your blessing

And thus: "And he shall be a blessing"
(7^2) *A blessing:* To which there is no equal!
A blessing: With nothing lacking
A blessing: Revealed to every nation
A blessing: Until no more blessing is needed
A blessing: To be a father of a multitude
A blessing: True and lasting forever
A blessing: Recollected at all times[46]
A blessing: Graced with loving care
A blessing: Bearing great good
A blessing: Direct, without drawbacks
A blessing: Perfect for the blessing of all
A blessing: For him, and for his descendants
A blessing: Brimming to an overflow

---

44 Understanding *kisakh* as being from כ-ס-ה, to cover, protect, conceal.

45 "Joy" is an epithet for Zion, based upon Ps. 48:3, "The joy of all the earth is Mount Zion"; "spiced wine," from Song 8:2 is understood to be Torah (**B1**).

דַע כִּי הֶעֱבַרְתִּיךָ בְּסַךְ
הִגַּדְתָּה בְּאַהֲבָה לְחוֹסָךְ
...
זוֹרַז וְרָץ לִמְנוּסָךְ
חָס בְּצִילָךְ ... ..סָךְ
טִיהַרְתּוֹ בכי.. ...
יִירְאָה וּמוֹרָא עֲמָסָךְ
כְּנַמְתָּה לוֹ אָנֹכִי מַחֲסָךְ
... ..סָךְ
מִנֹּק בְּמָגִינֵי אֲכַסָּךְ
נִיחַמְתָּה בּוֹ ח.. ..סָךְ
סֻוגַּל מֶנּוּ מ.. ...
עוֹד אֲבָרֵךְ כִּיסְלָךְ וְכִיסָךְ
פִּצְתָּה לְרִיצָּךְ ...
...
קֵרַבְתּוֹ לִמְסוֹסָךְ
רִיוִּיתוֹ מֶרֶיקַח עֲסִיסָךְ
שׁרי ...
תִּירְגַּלְתּוֹ בְּבִרְכַּת טִיכּוּסָךְ

ובכן והיה ברכה

(ז[2]) בְּרָכָה **אֲ**שֶׁר כְּעֶרְכָּהּ **אֵ**ין
בְּרָכָה **בְּ**לִי חֶסְרוֹן **בָּ**הּ
בְּרָכָה **גְּ**לוּיָה לְכָל **גּ**וֹיִם
בְּרָכָה **דֵּ**י בְּלִי **דָ**יי
בְּרָכָה **הֱ**יוֹת לְאַב **הֲ**מוֹן
בְּרָכָה **וַ**ודַּיי עוֹד **וָ**עוֹד
בְּרָכָה **זְ**כוּרָה בְּכָל **זְ**מָן
בְּרָכָה **חֲ**נוּנָה אַהֲבַת **חָ**סֶד
בְּרָכָה **טְ**עוּנָה רוֹב **ט**וֹב
בְּרָכָה **יְ**שָׁרָה בְּאֵין **יָ**גָע
בְּרָכָה **כְּ**לוּלָה בְּבִרְכַּת **כֹּ**ל
בְּרָכָה **ל**וֹ וְגַם **לְ**זַרְעוֹ
בְּרָכָה **מ**וֹתֶרֶת וְיִתְרוֹן **מ**וֹסֶפֶת

46 Allusion to the fact that Abraham is mentioned in every prayer-service: weekday, Sabbath, festival (**B1**), as well as the Grace after Meals (*birkat ha-mazon*), the Passover Haggadah, and others.

A blessing: Firmly founded…
A blessing: Sustaining, fulfilling all wants[47]
A blessing: By grief never touched
A blessing: Opened…
A blessing: Poured out upon [your generations][48]
A blessing: …
A blessing: Abundant, sating with favor
A blessing: of all, of everything…[peace][49]
A blessing: Of healing, and of life renewed

(8) … and blessed / It stands forever;
It endures eternally; / It lasts for eternity
… / It does not cease nor does it diminish
It does not wither nor does it cause pain / …
Who can diminish? / Who can dilute?[50]
For You, O Lord, have blessed with Your own mouth / …
You have strengthened (him) with Your own right hand
You have brought (him) out by means of Your might
and You escorted (him) with Your Glory / and You called him with Your…
(Your word) stands firm in the heavens[51]
Enduringly bright among Your angels / who rush like lightning
And return like a bolt / [fly][52] like an arrow
and cry out in a tumult[53]
and respond, "Here we are!" until … not…the Name of the Holy One, the Hallowed, in Holiness …
As it is written "And the one called…"

---

47 Job 20:22 (**R**).
48 Lacuna filled as in **B2**.
49 Gen 24:1 (**B1**). The word "peace" (שלום) is present in **R** and Zulay.
50 As in the *silluq* for Gen 11:1, Yannai here employs a string of rhetorical questions.
51 Ps 119:89 (**R**); **B1**, in turn, cites *ExodR* 38:6, where this verse is connected explicitly to our lemma: "It is written: 'Forever, O Lord, Your word stands firm in the heavens' (Ps 119:89). Does then the word of God stand fast only in heaven, but not on earth? Rabbi Hezekiah ben Hiyya said: This is because God made a promise in heaven, which was fulfilled on earth for that righteous man [Abraham] after two hundred and ten years [when his descendents left Egypt]. How so? When the Holy One, blessed be He, said to Abraham:

בְּרָכָה **נְ**כוֹנָה מ.. ...
בְּרָכָה **סְ**מוּכָה מִלְּאוּי **שֶׁ**פֶק
בְּרָכָה **עֶ**צֶב אֵין **עִ**ימָּה
בְּרָכָה **פְּ**תוּחָה ב.. ...
בְּרָכָה **צֶ**קֶת עַל ...
בְּרָכָה ...
בְּרָכָה **רְ**צוּפָה שׂוֹבַע **רָ**צוֹן
בְּרָכָה **שְׁ**לֵימָה ...
בְּרָכָה **תְּ**רוּפָה וְגַם **תְּ**חִיָּיה

(ח)
... וּמְבוֹרָכָה \ עוֹמֶדֶת לָעַד
נִיצֶּבֶת עֲדֵי עַד \ וְקַיֶּמֶת לְעוֹלָם
... \ לֹא פוֹסֶקֶת וְלֹא חוֹסֶרֶת
לֹא בוֹצֶרֶת וְלֹא מַעֲצֶבֶת \ ...
מִי יַחֲסִיר \ מִי יַכְחִישׁ
וְאַתָּה יי בֵּירַכְתָּה בְּפִיךָ \ ...
אִמַּצְתָּה בִּימִינָךְ
וְהוֹצֵאתָה בְּכוֹחָךְ
וְלִוִּיתָה בִּכְבוֹדָךְ \ וְנִקְרֵאתָה ב..
נִיצָּב בַּשָּׁמַיִם
וּבָרוּר בְּמַלְאָכֶיךָ \ רָצִים כְּבָרָק
וְשָׁבִים כְּבָזָק \ ... כְּחֵץ
וְקוֹרְאִים הֲמוּלָּה
וְעוֹנִים הִינֵּינוּ עַד לא ..ת.. כר.. ... שֵׁם הַקּוֹדֶשׁ
הַנִּקְדָּשׁ בַּקּוֹדֶשׁ
ככתוב וקרא

`Go forth from your land... and I will make you a great nation' (Gen 12:1ff), the latter replied: `Lord of the Universe! What benefit do I derive from all these blessings since I am about to depart from this world childless?' Said God to him: `Are you sure you will never father a child?' The reply was: `Lord of the Universe! My planet [astrological sign] tells me that I will be childless.' `So you are afraid of the planet?' God responded; `As you live, it will be as impossible to number your offspring as it is to number the stars of heaven!'"

52 Lacuna filled by **B1**.

53 Allusion to Ezek 1:24, specifically "the sound of a tumult" but also the general depiction of the angelic hosts here. See also Job 38:35 for a depiction of the speed with which angels move, particularly as interpreted in *Mekh. Bo* 1.

(9) … Sons of the brave and constant one…
Holy, holy, holy is the Lord of Hosts! The whole earth is filled with His glory!
"*Holy*"—From those who know
Holy, holy, holy is the Lord of Hosts! The whole earth is filled with His glory!
"*Holy*"—You recognized him, and You said to him…
"*Holy*"—… Your might…
"*Holy*"—When You roused (him) to anger …

From His place—He walked with the father...
[From His place]—… from his birthplace
From His place—He…

(ט) ..הכר.. ... ..בְּנֵי אֵיתָן ...
קדוש קדוש קדוש יי צבאות מלא כל הארץ כבודו
קָדוֹשׁ מְמַכִּירֵי בי.. ...
קדוש קדוש קדוש יי צבאות מלא כל הארץ כבודו
קָדוֹשׁ הִיכַּרְתּוֹ וְנַמְתָּה לוֹ ...
... ..ש.. ..ע חֵילָךְ
קָדוֹשׁ כְּהַקְצַפְתָּה ...

מִמְּקוֹמוֹ לִיוָּוה לְאָב ...
... מִמּוֹלַדְתּוֹ
מִמְּקוֹמוֹ הוּא אֲשֶׁר ...

Commentary

In this poem, Yannai explores the relationship between God and Abraham by relying on metaphors from two discrete realms of experience: the world of nature, and the world of romance. The idea that God "seduces" Abraham (indeed, the casting of Abraham as the ingénue in the tale) has been discussed above, in Chapters Three and Four. Yannai's use of imagery from the world of nature, however—particularly his use of animals as symbolic of Abraham's various attributes—merits consideration, as well.

The first animals that Yannai associates with Abraham are raptors. Birds of prey, both the falcon (*ʿayit*) and the eagle (*nesher*), appear multiple times in this poem and play symbolic roles in Jewish literature. In the Bible, birds such as the eagle represent majesty and power: God compares Himself to an eagle who carries Israel out of exile as an eagle carries her chicks (Deut 32:11) while the arrogant kings of the nations are likened to eagles in Jer 48–49, Ezek 17, and Obadiah.[54] In rabbinic tradition, the eagle is the king of the birds (see *ExodR* 23:13; *SongR* 3:23) and one serves, in a mythic image, as a royal mount for King Solomon (*EcclR* 2:29). In this piyyut, Yannai transfers the vivid image of God carrying the Israelites to freedom "on eagles' wings" to the story of Abraham's individual exodus: Abraham's journey from Ur of the Chaldees anticipates the escape from Egypt in both action and metaphor, and thus becomes a paradigm for the redemption. In this poem, a personal-scale drama foreshadows what will happen eventually in national terms, down to the very imagery used to describe his flight.

The association of God with an eagle is a relatively common trope. Comparing Abraham with an eagle or other bird of prey, however, is relatively unusual. The most important parallel can be found in *GenR* 15:4, where Isa 46:11 ("I summoned a falcon from the East"—referring to Cyrus in context) is applied to Abraham. Based on this same verse, *AggBereshit* 56 lists "falcon" as one of Abraham's names. Yannai, for his part, uses bird of prey imagery four distinct times in this poem. In the *meḥayyeh* (Poem Two), God tells Abraham, "You will fly on eagles' wings" (line 8)—a more vivid and active formulation than "I will carry you." In the *meshallesh* (Poem

54 Obadiah's comparison of Edom to an eagle becomes particularly fruitful in later centuries when Edom is identified with Rome, which represented itself as an eagle, too.

Three), which opens with an allusion to Isa 46:11, Abraham wishes he were a dove or an eagle, so that "he could take flight" (line 4)—a wish that is fulfilled, as we see in the fourth poem, when Abraham bursts forth "like a falcon" (line 5). And in Poem Six, God reiterates this promise to Abraham, "You shall fly like a falcon" (line 31). The poet uses these images of raptors to connote speed, height, and power—an effortless mode of travel—as well as to perhaps create an association with the divine. By comparing Abraham to such regal birds, Abraham's stature is elevated and dignified, as is his act of leaving his ancestral land. The eagle imagery accords Abraham's prototypical journey a regal, majestic air, as if his exodus were self-empowered. No "flight" could be more dignified or powerful.

Yannai finds other animals with which to compare the patriarch, as well, beyond eagles and falcons. These other animals include the dove (Poem Three, line 4); the stag (Poem Six, line 16), and the lion and the bear (Poem Six, line 30). Abraham's wish—"If only I had the wings of a dove!"—is taken from Ps 55:7. The epithet "dove" is a common one for Israel, both in Psalms (see also Ps 68:14) and in Hosea (7:11 and 11:11—both times an epithet for Ephraim). According to traditional exegesis—including Yannai's piyyutim for Passover—references to the dove in Song 2:14, 5:2, and 6:9) likewise refer to Israel. "Dove" is not an epithet for Abraham, per se, but rather his descendents. Tellingly, Abraham asks for doves' wings, but is given the more majestic and powerful wings of eagles, heightening his resemblance to the divine. Abraham is no "silly dove" (Hos 7:11) but a regal, royal bird. Like the eagle, the stag is a majestic animal, untamed and swift, but also associated with piety (Ps 42:2). Growing out of the interpretation of the Song of Songs, the stag becomes a metaphor for God or the messiah (see Song 2:8–9, 17; 8:14 and the aggadic interpretations thereof, including Yannai's Passover poems), a symbol of redemption. By comparing Abraham to the stag, virtuous qualities—swiftness, vigilance, and devotion especially—are transferred to the patriarch, and divine, redemptive connotations are once again conjured. The lion, like the eagle and stag, is another regal animal, an image of might and power associated both with God and the nation. Beginning in Genesis 49, the lion represented Judah, and in Num 24:6, we see this identification broadened when Balaam compares the people Israel to a mighty lion. The lion symbolizes might in Judg 14, while prophets use lions to describe the awesome power of the nations God is sending against Israel (Isa 5; Jer 4). God Himself "roars" like a lion (Joel 4:16) and stalks His prey like one in Lamentations (3:10). When the poet describes a lion as "fearsome like a lion" in Poem Six, he is staying true to these connotations in their most positive aspect.

Yannai does not compare Abraham to any animal that is less than regal. The final animal from Yannai's bestiary is the *ʿayish*—which appears to mean "she-bear" or "lioness" in the context of Job 38:32, where the reference is to a constellation, probably Ursa Major (but which, we should note, the Targum translates as "hen"). Because Yannai uses the word in proximity to the word "lion" (*layyish*)—a powerful animal, as just noted—I have chosen "mother bear" as the best semantic parallel. Abraham will have the commanding presence of a male lion but the legendary protective instincts of a female bear. Mother-lions and mother-bears are powerful maternal images in the biblical corpus. A "bear robbed of her cubs" is an image of a person maddened by grief and anger in 2 Sam 17:8; in Ezek 19:2, Israel is told that her mother is a "lioness" who has nourished and raised healthy—but willful—whelps. In Joel 1:6, the lioness is noted primarily for her fangs. The targumic translation of "mother hen" cannot be simply rejected, however. Because of its familiarity to English-speakers, the image of "mother hen" effectively connotes the caring and nurturing that a patriarch would need to successfully lead his household through all their wanderings. The rendering "hen" would lend the scene a tranquility, humility, and domesticity that seems generally counter to the bold drama of the poem—a counterpoint rather than a complement.

All of these many animal metaphors contribute to the vivid imagery of the poem. They also perhaps should call to mind a proverbial reference to animals, found in *Pirke Avot*: "Be strong as a leopard, swift as an eagle, fleet as a stag, and valiant as a lion, to do the will of thy Father who is in heaven" (5:20). In this poem, Abraham is compared to three of these four animals—all regal analogs—as he seeks to do the will of God. Abraham, "the father of a multitude," encapsulates the drama of this proverb and serves as a model to all those who come after him, and who recall his name and his merit in their prayers.

Qedushta for Genesis 14:1 בראשית יד:א

ויהי בימי אמרפל

"And it came to pass in the days of Amraphel"

Only the first and final units of the piyyut are preserved, and even these are fragmentary. The beginning of the poem expands the biblical depiction of Abraham's battle against the four Canaanite kings. The piyyut then segues from this "historical" concern to a more philosophical and theologically-charged consideration of military engagement, particularly the image of God as "a man of war" (Exod 15:3) and Israel's messianic (even apocalyptic) expectations. The majority of the surviving poem focuses less on Abraham's epoch than on the poet's own historical context: the rescue of Lot from the Canaanites—and the Israelites from the Egyptians—becomes paradigmatic for the future redemption of the Jews.

(1) … You beat
… You drove out
… You put to flight
…

…with wickedness they drew their swords
… they spread
… evil, and upon the right-hand way they wander[1]
… they strayed

Cast upon them darkness
… a watchtower upon a hill
Deep gloom engulfed them[2]
their lot was cast with Amraphel

As it is written: "And it came to pass in the days of Amraphel, king of Shinar; Arioch, king of Elessar; Chedorlaomer, king of Elam; and Tidal, king of Goiim…" (Gen 14:1)

And it says: "The wicked draw their swords, bend their bows, to bring down the lowly and needy, to slaughter upright men" (Ps 37:14)[3]

And it says: "Though the wicked sprout like grass, though all workers of evil blossom, it is only in order to destroy them forever. But You are exalted, O Lord, for all time. For lo, Your enemies, O Lord, for lo, Your enemies shall perish, and all workers of evil shall be scattered" (Ps 92:8–10)[4]

And it says: "Nation was crushed by nation and city by city, for God threw them into panic with every kind of disaster" (2 Chron 15:6)

In all disaster and distress[5]
unto You I shall cry
with Your shield, vindicate us![6]
Blessed… Shield…

---

1 See Num 20:17; Deut 2:27. This language suggests the transgressive behavior of the Canaanite kings against whom Abraham battled. In context, in these verses, the Israelites promise to incline neither towards the right or left, in a gesture that indicates non-aggression. The Canaanite kings, however, behave with excessive aggressiveness, assaulting both sides without respite.

2 See *GenR* 42:4 (**R**).

3 This verse is the *petiḥta* verse in *GenR* 42:1; see also *TanḥB Lekh Lekha* 7 (**R**).

4 According to *MidPs* 92:10, this verse alludes to the coming of the Messiah. The midrash states: "When you see the wicked springing up like grass to cover the face of the earth then

(א)

... ..תתה
... כִּיתָּתָּה
... ..ש הִבְרַחְתָּה
... הִפְרַחְתָּה

... בְּרֶשַׁע חַרְבָּם פָּתְחוּ
... מָתְחוּ
... רַע וּבְדֶרֶךְ יָמִין תָּאוּ
... תָּעוּ

טַח עֲלֵיהֶם אוֹפֶל
... ..בַּחַן עוֹפֶל
כִּיסָּה עֲלֵימוֹ עֲרָפֶל
לְהַפִּילָם עִם אַמְרָפֶל

ככתוב ויהי בימי אמרפל מלך שנער אריוח מלך אלסר כדרלעמר מלך עילם ותדעל מלך גויים

ונאמר חרב פתחו רשעים ודרכו קשתם להפיל עני ואביון לטבוח ישרי דרך

ונאמר בפרח רשעים כמו עשב ויציצו כל פועלי און להשמדם עדי עד ואתה מרום לעולם יי כי הנה אויביך יי כי הנה איביך יאבדו יתפרדו כל פעלי און

ונאמר וכותתו גוי בגוי ועיר בעיר כי אלהים הממם בכל צרה

בְּכָל צָרָה וְצוּקָה
אֵלֶיךָ אֶצְעָקָה
בְּמָגִינָּךְ לָנוּ הַצְדִּיקָה
ברוך... מגן...

you may look forward to the days of the Messiah." Further in the passage, the appearance of the heir of David is described, based on vs. 13 of the Psalm: "Like the palm-tree, comely in its appearance, with all its fruits sweet and good, the son of David will be comely in his appearance and all of his works will be sweet and to the Holy One, blessed be He." While *MidPsa* does not connect this verse to Gen 14, Yannai articulates similar messianic themes in the final preserved poetic units.

5 Prov 1:27 (**B1**).

6 See *GenR* 42:2, where this passage is connected to the downfall of the Four Kingdoms, a prophecy first appearing in the biblical apocalypse of Daniel.

(2) From of old, You who "put and end to war"
You are called "A Man (who masters) War"[7]
[You set forth rules of engagement] in Your book of wars[8]
Answering one who cries out for warfare.
The edges[9] of Your sword are tongues of flame
the barbs of Your arrows are flashes of fire
[…]
he pursues them and does not despair.
[…]

(7) …
A time for peace and a time for *war*[10]—
You said: I am Peace, but they are *war*![11]
The enemies: haters of peace and lovers of *war*
Read in the book of wars and go forth to *war*!
Exalting in Your ferocity on the day of *war*[12]—
Send us first one anointed for *war*![13]
Let arise the one destined to arise for a time of *war*[14]—
He shall say: Up! Rise against her for *war*![15]
And then let us say: The Lord is valiant in *war*![16]

7 Citing Exod 15:3, "The Lord is a man of war" (**R**) as it is read in *GenR* 49:8 (**B1**): "Rabbi said: [Abraham pleaded:] A human being is mastered by his anger, but the Holy One, blessed be He, masters anger, as it says, `The Lord avenges and masters wrath (Nah 1:2).'" God is a "man of war" in the paradoxical sense that He is the One who can put an end to all war. God does not love or seek out war but rather works for its cessation. See Chapter Four.

8 That is, Deut 20:10–20 (**B1**); Bronznick (whose completion of the lacuna is accepted here) argues that this is not, as **R** suggests, a reference to the unknown historical chronicle, "The Wars of the Lord," referred to in Num 21:14. The motif of God's "book of wars" occurs again in Poem 7, line 5.

9 The translation follows **R**, who has פי חרבך (Gen 34:6, Exod 17:13, etc.); the Ma'agarim version would be rendered, "the snares of Your sword."

10 Eccl 3:8 (**R**)

11 Ps 120:7 (**R**)

12 Zech 14:3 (**R**)

13 This line and the ones following refer to messianic expectations (**R**). Line 6 possibly refers to the Messiah ben Joseph who is destined to come before the Messiah ben David. See *GenR* 75:8, "The Rabbis maintained: `Ox' is an allusion to the one anointed for battle

(ב)

מֵעוֹלָם מַשְׁבִּית מִלְחָמוֹת
נִקְרֵאתָה אִישׁ מִלְחָמוֹת
... לך סֵפֶר מִלְחָמוֹת
עֱנוֹת לְכָל קוֹרֵא לְמַהֲלוּמוֹת
פַּחֵי חַרְבְּךָ לַהֲטֵי אֵשׁ
צִינֵּי חִיצֶּיךָ בִּרְקֵי אֵשׁ
... לִפְנֵי ... אֵשׁ
רְדָפָם וְלֹא הִתְיָיאֵשׁ
[...]

(ז)

...

עֵת שָׁלוֹם וְעֵת	מִלְחָמָה
פַּצְתָּה אֲנִי שָׁלוֹם וְהֵמָּה	לַמִּלְחָמָה
צָרִים שׂוֹנְאֵי שָׁלוֹם וְאוֹהֲבֵי	מִלְחָמָה
קָרָא בְּסֵפֶר מִלְחָמוֹת וְצֵא	לַמִּלְחָמָה
רָם בְּהִילָּחֲמָךְ בְּיוֹם	מִלְחָמָה
שְׁלַח לָנוּ תְּחִילָּה מְשׁוּחַ	מִלְחָמָה
תַּצְמִיחַ צֶמַח צוֹמֵחַ בְּעוֹנַת	מִלְחָמָה
אוֹמֵר קוּמוּ וְנָקוּמָה עָלֶיהָ	לַמִּלְחָמָה
וְנֹאמַר יי גִּיבּוֹר	מִלְחָמָה

[the Messiah ben Joseph, who was destined to die], as it says, `His firstling bullock, majesty is his' (Deut 33:17; a verse describing the tribe of Joseph); `Ass' refers to the royal Messiah [the Messiah of the house of David], for it says of him, `Lowly, and riding upon an ass' (Zech 9:9)."

14 Literally, "Let sprout the branch destined to sprout up at a time of war." As **R** notes, the Messiah ben David is referred to as the "branch" in rabbinic literature, based on Zech 6:12. For the idea that the Messiah ben David will come at a time of war, see *GenR* 42:4, a midrashic explication of the base verse of this piyyut: "Another interpretation: `And it came to pass in the days of Amraphel, King of Shinar': this alludes to Babylon; `Arioch, King of Ellesar': that alludes to Greece; `Chedorlaomer, King of Elam': that is Media; `And Tidal, King of the Goyim' [lit. `nations']: this alludes to the wicked Power [i.e. Rome] which levies troops from all the nations of the world. Rabbi Eleazar b. Rabbi Abina said: When you see the Powers fighting each other, look for the coming [lit. `feet'] of the King Messiah. The proof is that in the days of Abraham, because these Powers fought against each other, greatness came to Abraham."

15 "Her" refers to Rome. **R** cites Obad 1:1, understood as an allusion to the messianic battle against Esau–Edom–Rome.

16 Ps 24:8 (**R**)

(8) For to You, O Lord, belongs greatness
and to You, O Lord, belongs might
and to You, the splendor of rule
and to You kingship is fitting
And for You holiness is the essence[17]:
the greatest of the great
the mightiest of the mighty
the ruler of all who rule
the king of kings
the holy of holies

As it is written, "And the one called…"

---

17 The root י-ס-ד ("to lay a foundation"). In the context of the Qedushah, this word resonates with "*sod*" ("circle of intimates, assembly"), in the sense of the angelic "circle" that joins Israel in reciting praise of God's holiness.

(ח) כִּי לְךָ יי הַגְּדוּלָּה
וְלָךְ הִיא הַגְּבוּרָה
וְלָךְ נָאֶה מֶמְשָׁלָה
וְלָךְ יָאֲתָה הַמְלוּכָה
וְלָךְ מְיֻוסֶּדֶת הַקְדוּשָּׁה
גְּדוֹל גְּדוֹלִים
גִּיבּוֹר גִּיבּוֹרִים
מוֹשֵׁל מוֹשְׁלִים
מֶלֶךְ מְלָכִים
קְדוֹשׁ קְדוֹשִׁים

ככתוב וקרא

Commentary

The extant portions of this poem transform Abraham's battle against the four Canaanite kings into a messianic, even apocalyptic, confrontation between God and the enemies of Israel. Paradoxically, however, the poem does not delight in war; it reflects the poet's ambivalence. Yannai walks a delicate line, inflaming and tempering passions simultaneously.

In the first poem, Yannai suggests violence by choosing verses that imply aggression and which, by interpretation, describe a destined day of reckoning. Through these intertexts, the biblical past speaks to the present and future. In the biblical text, Abraham, not God, appears responsible for victory, but Yannai's choice of verses imply that God effected the defeat of the Canaanite kings. The quotations of Ps 37:14 and 2 Chron 15:6 (the prophecy of Azariah ben Oded) speak generally of violence, just and unjust: the psalm speaks of how God vindicates the righteous who are under attack, while Azariah ben Oded affirms God's defense of Israel when they are faithful to Him. In the context of the *magen*, these two lines come to describe Abraham's battle against the Canaanite kings, but in the liturgical context, they are ripe to be understood as speaking in the present tense, as well. Just as the story of Abraham against the Canaanite kings anticipates the future fight of outnumbered, under-equipped Israel against Rome, the intertexts chosen by Yannai affirm God's ultimate vindication of the Jews against the nations. The remaining quotation—three verses from Ps 92, an unusually substantial citation from a single source—presents an even more obvious example of this dual temporal specificity. Read as part of the *magen*, the quoted selection seems to describe God's vindication of Abraham. But the psalm's history of interpretation rereads it as a future-looking text: *Midrash Tehillim* explicates the Psalm as a coded description of the battles the Messiah ben David will fight on behalf of Israel in the end of days. When these verses, with their language of promise, violence, and justice, are read together, they acquire additional militaristic qualities with resonances that go beyond the biblical story of Abraham and the Canaanite kings. As becomes clearer in the remaining fragments of the piyyut, Yannai uses the story of Abraham's victory to anticipate the future, dramatic redemption of Israel.[18]

---

18 *TanḥB Lekh* 12, like *GenR* 40:6, notes that whatever happens to Abraham will also befall his sons. Yannai likewise affirms this typological method of interpretation. The past contains the key to the future.

For all this aggressive language, Yannai simultaneously tempers the militarism in this piyyut, as becomes clear in the second poetic unit. Using the Bible's own phrases (e.g., Eccl 3:8 and Ps 120:7), he turns the familiar phrase, "God is a man of war" (Exod 15:3) on its head: as the master of warfare, God can (and will) put an end to war. Unlike humans, creatures vulnerable to overwhelming passions and vindictive urges, the divine prerogative is peace.[19] God fights not out of zeal but necessity, and He establishes laws of war in order to moderate the anarchy of human emotions. Thus, while God's arsenal is described in dynamic terms—His sword is flame, His arrows are fire—it is He who determines the rules of engagement. God only girds Himself for battle because others act in a way that demands a response (they "cry out for warfare" in line 4 of the *meḥayyeh*; they are "haters of peace" in line 3 of the *rahit*). He is a God of necessary warfare, not a lover of battle.

The *rahit*—with its refrain of "war!"—most clearly expresses the tensions embedded in this poem: war and peace each have a place in the world, and while God may be "peace" (line 3), the time for war appears to be coming. Noteworthy in this poem are the imperatives the poet uses: Read! Exalt! Send! Arise! Almost undermining the ambivalence of the earlier unit, the tone is enthusiastic, even intemperate. While God may temper His passions, the poet here indulges his. The conclusion of the *rahit* is a messianic call, urging the advent of the Messiah ben Joseph and the Messiah ben David and, ultimately, God Himself, to whom true might and victory belong. The tone is classically apocalyptic, and likely reflects a more general messianism among Jews in the mid-6th century.[20] However, as the poem transitions to the *silluq*, Yannai again tempers his militaristic enthusiasm; might and power are *facets* of God's holiness, not His essence. Battle is not the desired end but simply the means to recognition and acclaim of God's majesty. This shift in emphasis does not diminish or undercut the gleeful anticipation of apocalypse of the *rahit* but puts it firmly in a larger, non-militant context. To Yannai—and his congregation—God's march to victory, as anticipated by the Prophets of old, may seem the ultimate goal, but Yannai encourages his listeners to step back and regard

---

19 It is interesting to note that the *rahit* of Yannai's *qedushta* for Deut 20:19 in Rabinovitz 2:163–65) has the word "peace" (שלום) as its theme word.

20 On the topic of Jewish messianism, see Chapter Four, n. 42. On Yannai's cultural context in the mid-6th century, see my article, " 'You have skirted this hill long enough': the tension between rhetoric and history in a Byzantine piyyut," *HUCA* 79 (forthcoming).

the divine drama from a larger perspective in which the aftermath matters more than the battle, holiness more than destruction, the rightness of worship more than the relish of justice.

This key point—that power belongs to God, not humanity—is highlighted in a rabbinic interpretation of the verses upon which this poem is based. It is written in *GenR* 42:5 that the defeated Canaanite peoples wished Abraham to rule over them after he vanquished their kings, saying: "You are king over us! You are a god to us!" Abraham, of course, rejects this invitation to power, saying: "The world does not lack its king and the world does not lack its God." Yannai's piyyut is an appeal to this kingly deity, He who brought victory to Abraham in days of yore, that He may bring a much needed victory of the lowly over the mighty in the poet's day, as well; and it is a caution to his community that it is not their own sovereignty that they seek, but rather submission to the dominion of their God. In the end, the poet appeals not to his fellow Jews, but to God.

Qedushta for Genesis 15:1 בראשית טו:א

"After These Words: In a Vision" אחר הדברים האלה: במחזה

In the wake of his stunning victory over the combined forces of the four Canaanite kings in Gen 14, Abraham experiences a wave of anxious regret. Surveying the slaughter, the patriarch wonders if perhaps he went too far in his killing; and contemplating the miraculous victory, he worries that he has expended his accrued merit and reserves of divine favor rescuing his nephew, leaving God no reason to give him a son. God responds to Abraham's unspoken anxiety with firm, unwavering support. In the course of the conversation crafted by our poet, Abraham moves from a position of weakness and fear to one of empowerment and security. The divine attributes of Justice and Mercy are not at odds; both require that God repay His debt to His human counterpart, Abraham— repayment in the form of a child.

(1) The patriarch: You found his heart to be like Yours
To reward his heart's purity, his heart's desire You fulfilled[1]
You made sure his proud sword against his foe;
his fearful fretting You put to rest.[2]

The battle—as soon as it came to an end—
of a truth, trepidation in his heart was found
For foes felled in Dan and Ḥovah[3]
he trembled, lest it be thought a trespass

With an utterance, You answered him, granting him ease
"Beautiful and great is the reward I shall grant you!
"Indeed, their blood—you were told to let it flow!
"I am a shield to you; fear not!"

As it is written: "After these things, the word of the Lord came to Abram in a vision, saying: Fear not, Abram, I am a shield to you and your reward shall be very great" (Gen 15:1)

And it is said: "Then You spoke in a vision to Your faithful ones and said: I have conferred power upon a warrior; I have exalted one chosen out of the people" (Ps 89:20)[4]

And it is said: "You have ever drawn nigh when I called You; You have said: Fear not!" (Lam 3:57)

And it is said: "For the Lord God is sun and shield; the Lord bestows grace and glory; He does not withhold goodness from those who live in purity" (Ps 84:12)

---

1 **B2** cites Prov. 22:11, which *GenR* 41:8 applies to Abraham; **B1** refers to Job 34:11 for the language of this line.

2 The language of the third stich recalls Ps 21:9. The content of this opening stanza recalls aggadic traditions associated with Gen 15 (discussed below and adduced by **R** and **B1** throughout their commentaries). *GenR* 44:4 (**B1**) describes different sources of patriarchal anxiety: "Rabbi Levi said: Abraham was filled with misgiving, thinking to himself, `Maybe there was a righteous or God-fearing man among those troops which I slew'... Rabbi Levi made another comment: Abraham was fearful, saying, `Perhaps the sons of the kings that I slew will collect troops and come and wage war against me.'... The Rabbis explained it thus: Abraham was filled with misgivings, saying to himself, `I descended into the fiery furnace and was delivered; I went through famine and war and was delivered: perhaps then I have already received my reward in this world and have none left for the future world?' Therefore the Holy One, blessed be He, reassured him: `Fear not, Abram, I am a shield (*magen*) to you,' meaning, a gift of grace (*maggan*) to you. All that I have done for you in this world I did gratis; but in the future that is to come, `Your reward shall be exceedingly great',

(א)
אָב לִיבּוֹ כְּלִיבָּךְ מָצָאתָה
בְּטוֹהַר לִיבּוֹ כְּלִיבּוֹ לוֹ הִימְצֵאתָה
גַּאֲוַות חַרְבּוֹ בְּכָל צַר הִימְצֵאתָה
דִּבְרֵי חֲסִידוּתוֹ מִיצִּיתָה

הַמִּימִּלְחָמָה אַחַר הוּבָא
וַדַּיי הִירְהוּרִים בְּלִיבּוֹ חֻובָּא
זֵדִים אֲשֶׁר קִיטֵּל בְּדָן וּבְחוֹבָה
חָרַד פֶּן יֵיחָשֶׁב לוֹ חוֹבָה

טַעַם הֲשֵׁיבוֹתוֹ בַּעֲתִירָה
יוֹפִי רוֹב שָׂכָר לָךְ אוֹתִירָה
כִּי דָמַם תַּרְתִּי לָךְ לְהַתִּירָה
לָךְ אָנֹכִי מָגֵן אַל תִּירָא

ככתוב אחר הדברים האלה היה דבר יי אל אברם במחזה לאמר אל תירא אברם אנכי מגן לך שכרך הרבה מאד

ונאמר אז דיברתה בחזון לחסידיך ותאמר שויתי עזר על גבור הרימותי בחור מעם

ונאמר קרבתה ביום אקראך אמרת אל תירא

ונאמר כי שמש ומגן יי אלהים חן וכבוד יתן יי לא ימנע טוב להולכים בתמים

---

even as you read, `Oh how abundant is Your goodness, which You have laid up for them that fear You,' etc. (Ps 31:20).” The pun on “shield” and “gift” (near homonyms) is central to this initial piyyut. In *TanḥB Lekh* 19, Abraham fears that sons of Shem are among the dead.

3 The place names hint at the worries that will haunt Abraham: Will his slaying of the Canaanite kings in the areas of Dan and Ḥovah lead to a judgment (*din*) that he has committed trespass (*ḥovah*)?

4 **R** notes that this verse is applied to Abraham in *LevR* 1:4 where it is a *petiḥta* verse(see also *TanḥB Lekh* 18), “Rabbi Abin, in the name of Rabbi Berekiah the Elder, opened [his discourse with the verse], `Then You spoke in a vision to Your faithful ones' (Ps 89:20). This refers to Abraham, with whom He communicated by way of both word and vision. This is indicated by what is written, `After these things the *word* of the Lord came to Abraham in a *vision*, saying…(Gen 15:1).” “Word” and “vision” are the two of the highest forms of communication by which God speaks to humanity, and Abraham in this instance is rewarded with both. See Poem Three, below.

And it is said: "For I, the Lord, am your God, who grasped your right hand, who says to you: Fear not; I will be your help." (Isa 41:13)[5]

And it is said: "The Lord is at your right hand. He crushes kings in the day of His anger" (Ps 110:5)

And it is said: "The people I made for Myself, that they might recount My praise" (Isa 43:21)

And it is said: "The Lord is with me; I shall not fear. What can a man do to me?" (Ps 118:6)

For man in the image You formed[6]
in the likeness, You fashioned;
Shield[7] this people You created
Blessed... Shield...

(2) "But what is left for me?" The patriarch cried
"My soul grieves and my heart is in mourning
"Happiness in my heart? Over what should I rejoice?
"A withered tree am I, not verdant.
"My reward? What good is all my honor?
"Oh, for a shoot from my root[8]—but my branch is bare
"An accursed one[9] will inherit possession of my blessing
"If I depart[10] life still empty and bereft"
"The name `Justice' is mine[11]
"But the justice of a sapling I lack
"(In the past) I gave to you as You gave to me
"What can I give you, and what will You give me?

As it is written: "But Abram said: O Lord God, what will You give me, seeing that I shall die childless, and the one in charge of my household is Dammesek Eliezer!" (Gen 15:2)

---

5 **R** adduces *GenR* 44:3, where the entire pericope from Isaiah is applied to the biography of Abraham.

6 **B2** connects this to Gen 1:26; *GenR* 14:6 understands "the man" of Gen 1:26 as Abraham.

7 In light of the pun on shield/gift, this might be understood as "deal graciously with."

8 The Hebrew here is עקרי, literally "my essence" (but also a euphemism for the male member); the root also, however, recalls the word *ʿaqarah* ("barren"). While barrenness is usually considered a feminine condition, in Deut.7:14, we find the term applied to males, as well. On this topic, see the insightful article by Ophir Münz-Manor, "All about Sarah: Questions of Gender in Yannai's Poems on Sarah's (and Abraham's) Barrenness," *Prooftexts*

ונאמר כי אני יי אליך מחזיק ימינך האמר לך אל תירא אני עזרתיך

ונאמר יי על ימינך מחץ ביום אפו מלכים

ונאמר עם זו יצרתי לי תהלתי יספרו

ונאמר יי לי לא אירא מה יעשה לי אדם

אָדָם בִּדְמוּת צַרְתָּה
וּבְצֶלֶם צִיַּינְתָּה
מַגֵּן עַם זוּ יָצַרְתָּה
ברוך... מגן...

(ב) **מַ**ה יִתְרוֹן לִי אָב נִיתְחַנָּן
נַפְשִׁי עֲגוּמָה וְלִיבִּי מִתְאוֹנֵן
שִׂמְחָה בְלִיבִּי מַה יְרוֹנָּן
עֵץ סְרַק אָנוֹכִי וְלֹא רַעֲנָן
פָּוּעֳלִי מַה בְּכָל יְקָרִי
צִיץ עִיָּרִי עֲקָרִי בִּמְקוֹרִי
קִינְיַין בִּרְכָתִי יִירַשׁ אֲרוּרִי
רֵיק אִם אֶפְנֶה וַעֲרִירִי
שֵׁם צֶדֶק יֵשׁ לִי
שֶׁתֶּל צֶדֶק אֵין לִי
תַּתִּי לָךְ וְנָתַתָּה לִי
מָה אֶתֵּן לָךְ וּמַה תִּיתֵּן לִי

ככתוב ויאמר אברם אדני אלהים מה תתן לי ואנכי הולך ערירי ובן משק ביתי הוא דמשק
אליעזר

---

26 (2006): 344–74.

9 **R** notes that according to Genesis, and the midrashic expansions thereof, "the accursed one" is Damascene Eliezer, Abraham's servant (a descendant of the cursed Ham; see *qedushtah* to Gen 9). However, Yannai could also be hinting at Lot in this line, based on a pun: the name "Lot" (לוט) closely resembles a word meaning "cursed" (ליטא). Neither Eliezer nor Lot is an acceptable heir in the eyes of Abraham.

10 "Depart" translates the sense of "go" (הלך), from the biblical verse.

11 Lit. *tsedek*; the translation given here (and used throughout the poem) anticipates the poet's use of the term as the complement to "mercy" in Poem Six.

And it says: "There is hope for a tree: if it is cut down it will renew itself; its shoots will not cease" (Job 14:7)
And it says: "May He grant you as your heart desires, and fulfill your every plan" (Ps 20:5)
And it says: "If you are righteous, what do you give Him? What does He receive from your hand?" (Job 35:7)
And it says: "You will listen to the entreaty of the lowly, O Lord; You will make their hearts firm; You will incline Your ear" (Ps 10:17)

Your ear is inclined
to (hear) our every aspiration
O You who make dew, renew life with the blowing winds![12]
Blessed... Who resurrects...

(3) Oh Yah! Ten kinds of utterances You have hewn[13]
and with ten kinds of language You proclaim prophecy
Prophecy, vision, command, speech, saying,
discourse, [par]able, metaphor, burden, riddle[14]
The glory to the brave one was then made known
For through three of these ten glorious types You made Yourself known
To wit: speech, saying, and vision
to speak, to say, to hear and give ear

As it is written: "The vision of Isaiah, son of Amoz, which he beheld concerning Judah and Jerusalem in the days of Uzziah, Yotam, Ahaz, and Hezekiah, Kings of Judah" (Isa 1:1)
And it says: "In accordance with all these words and this entire vision thus did Nathan speak to David" (1 Sam 7:17)[15]

And You are Holy, enthroned on the praises of Israel...Please, God...

---

12 The language of this concluding line suggests the winter-time Amidah insertion, "...who causes the winds to blow and the rain to fall," rather than the usual blessing for dew alone.

13 According to **B1**, this image seems to come from Hos 6:5, "Therefore have I hewn them by the prophets." It may also resonate with *Sefer Yetsira* 2:2, "Twenty two letters He engraved and hewed forth." This phrase recollected the idea that the world was created by ten utterances and the Torah was given by means of ten utterances; likewise God communicates with His prophets by means of ten utterances—ten *kinds* of utterance.

14 A parallel to this motif of "ten kinds of divine speech" is found in *GenR* 44:6:

ונאמר כי יש לעץ תקוה אם יכרת ועוד יחליף וינקתו לא תחדל

ונאמר יתן לך כלבבך וכל עצתך ימלא

ונאמר אם צדקתה מה תתן לי או מה מידך יקח

ונאמר תאוות ענוים שמעת יי תכין לבם תקשיב אזנך

אָזְנֶיךָ קַשּׁוּבוֹת
לְכָל מַחֲשָׁבוֹת
מַטְלִיל תְּחִי בְּרוּחוֹת נִישָּׁבוֹת
ברוך... מחיה...

(ג) יָהּ מַאֲמָרוֹת עֲשָׂרָה חָתַכְתָּה
וּבִילְשׁוֹנוֹת עֲשָׂרָה נְבוּאָה קָרָאתָה
נְבוּאָה חָזוֹן צִיוּוּי דִּיבֵּר אֲמִירָה
הַטָּפָה מָשָׁל מְלִיצָה מַשָּׂא חָדָה
יְקָר לְאֵיתָן אָז הוֹדַעְתָּה
כִּי בִשְׁלֹשֶׁת הַיְקָרִים שֶׁבָּהֶם לוֹ נוֹדַעְתָּה
יִידּוּעַ דִּיבֵּר וְאוֹמֶר וְחָזוֹן
לְדַבֵּר וְלֹאוֹמַר לִשְׁמוֹעַ וְלֶאֱזוֹן

ככתוב חזון ישעיהו בן אמוץ אשר חזה על יהודה וירושלם בימי עזיהו יותם אחז יחזקיהו מלכי יהודה

ונאמר ככל הדברים האלה וככל החזיון הזה כן דבר נתן אל דוד

ואתה קדוש יושב תהלות ישראל אל נא

"[Prophecy] is called by ten names: prophecy, vision, discourse [lit. `flow'], speech, saying, command, burden, parable, metaphor, and riddle. And which is the severest form? Rabbi Leazar said: Vision, as it says, `A grievous vision is declared unto me' (Isa 21:2). Rabbi Yoḥanan said: Speech (*dibbur*), as it says, `The man, the lord of the land, spoke (*dibber*) roughly with us,' etc. (Gen 42:30). The Rabbis said: Burden, as it says, `As a heavy burden' (Ps 38:5). Great then was the power of Abraham that [divine] converse was held with him in both vision and in speech."

15 See *LevR* 1:4, where this verse is quoted as part of an extensive *petiḥta* (it is the *petiḥta* verse) on forms of divine speech with favored individuals (**R**).

(4) To the patriarch—before he yet beheld a vision
or had insight into any deed —
You appeared (to him) in a vision
and You became for him a shelter
And that over which he fretted in his heart
and upon which his mind mused
You let him know—O You who probe the heart
and examine the mind—
Because he had become afraid
You said to him: Fear not![16]
And because it was a word that had him rattled,
with a word he was reassured
And because it was thought that had him thinking—
with thought he was put at ease:
"I am your shield; who can harm you?
"I have grasped your hand;[17]
"Who dares strike you?
"I will give you your reward
"Who would diminish it?"
—You gained his trust, O Holy One

(5) O [Lord] God[18], Your brave one entreats you
he whom in mercy and justice You had graced with all Your gifts
And thus he argued: "If I am to have none,[19]
for mercy's sake, still give me!
And he said: If there will be one for me
for the sake of justice, let him be given me!"
He moaned: "What can You give me?
"I have much yet I have nothing:
"I have the means to father children
"But as yet I lack a son!
"Plenty of good reward, `in all things'[20] You have given me

16 Yannai refers here to Abraham's fears that his actions against the Canaanite kings will lead him to harm, whether through retributive violence, loss of merit, or failure to father a son. The rhetoric of this passage is classic "measure for measure"—a variant of `in the self-same language' structure discussed in Chapter Three. The translation is somewhat loose to reflect the rhetoric.

(ד) לְאָב עַד לֹא חָז מַחֲזֶה
וְהֵיבִין בְּכָל מַעֲשֶׂה
נִירְאֵיתָה בַּמַּחֲזֶה
וְנִהְיֵיתָה לוֹ מַחֲסֶה
וַאֲשֶׁר הִירהֵר בַּלֵּב
וְחִישֵּׁב בַּכְּלָיוֹת
יִידַּעְתּוֹ חוֹקֵר לֵב
וּבוֹחֵן כְּלָיוֹת
מֵאֲשֶׁר נִיתְיָירָא
נַמְתָּה לוֹ אַל תִּירָא
וּבְדָבָר אֲשֶׁר נֵוהַם
בּוֹ בְדָבָר נֵוחַם
וּבְאוֹמֶר כִּי נִיתְחַשֵּׁב
בּוֹ בְאוֹמֶר נִיתְיַישָּׁב
אָנֹכִי מָגִינָךְ מִי יַמְגִּינָךְ
אָנֹכִי מַחֲזִיקָךְ
מִי יַזִיקָךְ
אָנֹכִי מַשְׂכִּירָךְ
וּמִי יַחֲסִירָךְ
הִבְטַחְתּוֹ קָדוֹשׁ

(ה) [יי] **אֱ**לֹהִים חִינְנָךְ אֵיתָנָךְ
כִּי בְּרַחֲמִים וּבְדִין חֲנַנְתּוֹ בְּכָל מַתָּנָךְ
בְּכֵן פָּץ אִם אֵין לִי
בְּרַחֲמִים תֵּן לִי
וְנָם אִם יֵשׁ לִי
בְּדִין יִינָּתֵן לִי
גָּעָה מַה תִּיתֵּן לִי
וְיֵשׁ לִי וְאֵין לִי
מוֹלִיד יֵשׁ לִי
וְיֶלֶד אֵין לִי
דֵּי שָׂכָר טוֹב בַּכֹּל נָתַתָּה לִי

---

17 Lit., "I have strengthed/seized you."**B1** connects to Isa 41:3; see *GenR* 44:3

18 "Lord" (which appears in **R** and Zulay) is the divine name associated with mercy; "God"' is the term associated with justice (see *GenR* 14:1).

19 That is, no sons.

20 An allusion to Gen 24:1 (**R**) and its aggadic interpretations.

"But the reward of fruit from my loins—that You have not given me!
"Is it not said, `What profit have I for all of my labor?'[21]—
"if the son of my brother or the son of my house
"Shall inherit all from me?"
So You said to him: "Fear not—neither one nor the other
Neither one nor the other shall inherit."
He was disturbed and distressed over those he had killed
He hesitated to seek[22] lest blood-justice be sought
He trembled: Had there been a righteous man among them?
Or was a convert destined to arise from their midst?
You gave him sound advice:[23] "Don't overdo righteousness![24]
"You wiped out wicked ones; your reward shall be great
"You fret—like a sage who frets though shunning evil
"But for each fearsome fate you fret over,
"Glad tidings shall come forth from your mouth"

Forever…

"In a Vision…"
(6) A thousand shields You hung about the patriarch[25]
and over those who shield the earth[26] You exalted him
By the shield[27] with which You blessed him—
By "the shield of Abraham"[28] You are blessed.
[A splendid] sun[29] and shield You were for him
and the shield of Your salvation You gave him
Like a banner then You appeared over him
O God, Our Shield, You saw (him)
You showed him his reward
for one shall not keep the wages of a hired worker with him[30]

---

21 Adapted from Eccl 1:3 (**R**).

22 Presumably Yannai means that Abraham hesitated to petition God for his fair reward, a son, out of anxiety that God would instead punish him for bloodshed, recognizing that a gift of life is an incongruous reward for the taking of life.

23 Prov 26:16 (**B1**).

24 *EcclR* 7:25, addressed to Saul (**B1**); this passage recalls God's mild rebuke of Abraham in *GenR* 44:2, "`Be not wise in your own eyes; fear the Lord' (Prov 3:7). Do not accept as wise that which you see with your own eyes [i.e., astrology may appear convincing but its scientific appearance misleads]; can you say that I will cause you to beget or that I will not cause you to beget?' `Fear the Lord' [the verse says—implying `do not fear anything else']:

וְשָׂכָר פְּרִי הַבֶּטֶן לֹא נָתַתָּה לִי
הֲלֹא מַה יִתְרוֹן לִי בְּכָל עֲמָלִי
אִם בֶּן אָחִי אוֹ בֶן בֵּיתִי
יוֹרֵשׁ אוֹתִי
וְנַמְתָּה לוֹ אַל תִּירָא לֹא מִזֶּה וְלֹא מִזֶּה
לֹא יִירָשְׁךָ לֹא זֶה וְלֹא זֶה
זָחַל וְעָרַג עַל אֲשֶׁר הָרַג
וְהִרְהֵר לִדְרוֹשׁ פֶּן דָּמָם תִּדְרוֹשׁ
חָרַד פֶּן יִהְיֶה צַדִּיק בֵּינֵיהֶם
אוֹ גֵר עָתִיד לַעֲמוֹד מִבְּנֵיהֶם
טַעַם הֱשִׁיבוֹתוֹ אַל תְּהִי צַדִּיק הַרְבֵּה
רְשָׁעִים הִכְחַדְתָּה שְׂכָרְךָ הַרְבֵּה
יְרֵאֲךָ כְּחָכָם יָרֵא וְסָר מֵרָע
וּבְכָל רָע אֲשֶׁר יָרָא
טוֹב מְפִיךְ בּוֹשֵׂר

לעולם

במחזה

(ו) אֶלֶף הַמָּגֵן לְאָב תָּלִיתָה
וְעַל מָגִינֵּי אֶרֶץ עִילִּיתָה
בְּמָגֵן אֲשֶׁר אוֹתוֹ בֵּירַכְתָּה
בְּמָגֵן אַבְרָהָם נִיתְבָּרַכְתָּה
ג.. שֶׁמֶשׁ וּמָגֵן לוֹ הָיִיתָה
וּמָגֵן יִשְׁעֲךָ לוֹ נָתַתָּה
דָּגוּל בְּעֵת אֵלָיו נִירְאֵיתָה
מָגִינֵּינוּ אֱלֹהִים רָאִיתָה
הֵירְאֵיתָה לוֹ שְׂכָרוֹ אִתּוֹ
כִּי לֹא הֵילִין שְׂכַר שָׂכִיר אִיתּוֹ

thus it is written, `Fear not, Abraham! I am a shield to you' (Gen 15:1). See also *b. Shab.* 156a, in which Abraham sees in a horoscope that he is destined to die childless.

25 Allusion to Song 4:4 (**R**).

26 See Ps 47:10, "The great of the peoples are gathered together, the retinue of Abraham's God; for the ones who shield the earth (מגני ארץ) belong to God; He is greatly exalted." The implication here may be that Abraham is exalted above the angels.

27 Again, possibly punning on the near-homonym *maggan*, "gift."

28 **R** notes that this is apparently a shorthand reference to the Amidah.

29 **B1** fills this lacuna according to Judg 5:31; Ps 84:12

30 Lev 19:13 (**R**); applied to Abraham in *GenR* 42:1

And you brought him glad tidings: what was closed would open[31]
paying him his due reward
Your [merit][32] went before him
To teach that childless he should not go
The [might of][33] his justice would go before him
the same justice that goes before Him[34]
Aggrieved over his lack of an heir
lest to a stranger his portion should fall
You informed him from the first
that in the end a son of his own would inherit
Your glory You revealed to him
the dullness of his perception You lifted
The wormwood, bitter in his mouth, You sweetened
with the goodness that Your own mouth spoke
From the rocky peaks You hewed Your rock;[35]
From the summit of faith You established the faithful one
From his lofty dwelling You led him outside
and to the starry hosts of heavens You led his gaze
You said to him: Thus shall be your offspring
thirty, equal to you, from your line[36]
Forever and ever shall your flame burn undimmed[37]
that which you have kindled with your insight
Wonders did You work for Your right-hand man[38]
You accounted him righteous for his belief in You[39]
Splendor for the just, [the foundation of] Your works[40]
Your partner in creating creatures for You[41]
You called out to the one who summoned strays to You
You brought close [he who brought others close] to You[42]

---

31 That is, his childlessness would be at an end because Sarah's closed womb would be opened.

32 Lacuna filled as by **R**.

33 Reading חוזק צדקו, with **B1**.

34 **R** cites Ps 85:14, "Justice goes before Him and He makes for His footsteps a way." This stanza is difficult, both in terms of translation (each line ends with a form of ה-ל-ך, but with nuances including "precede, die, march") and meaning. It seems to be drawing an equivalence between Abraham's reputation (which "goes before him") and God's.

35 That is, Abraham.

36 **R** notes that this is an allusion to the thirty righteous descendents of Abraham who

וּבִישַּׂרְתּוֹ לְפֶתַח מַסְגֵּורְתּוֹ
וּלְשַׁלֶּם לוֹ מַשְׂכֻּורְתּוֹ
זִי..ךְ לְפָנָיו הֵילֵךְ
לְהוֹדִיעוֹ כִּי עֲרִירִי לֹא הוֹלֵךְ
חָז צִידְקוֹ לְפָנָיו מְהַלֵּךְ
בְּצֶדֶק אֲשֶׁר לְפָנָיו יְהַלֵּךְ
טָרוּחַ עֲלֵי יְרֻושָּׁתוֹ
פֶּן לְזָר תִּיהְיֶה מוֹרַשְׁתּוֹ
יִידַּעְתּוֹ מֵרֵאשִׁיתוֹ
כִּי בְאַחֲרִיתוֹ בְּנוֹ יִירַשׁ אוֹתוֹ
כְּבוֹדָךְ עָלָיו גִּילִּיתָה
וְכוֹבֶד אָוזְנוֹ גָּלִיתָה
לַעֲנוֹת אֲשֶׁר הָג פִּיו הִמְגָּדְתָּה
בְּטוֹבוֹת אֲשֶׁר בְּפִיךְ לוֹ הִיגָּדְתָּה
מֵרֹאשׁ צוּרִים צוּר חֲצַבְתּוֹ
וּמֵרֹאשׁ אֲמָנָה מַאֲמִין הִיצַּבְתּוֹ
נְוֵה מְרוֹמִים חוּצָה הוֹצֵאתוֹ
וּצְבָא כוֹכָבִים הִצְפֵּיתוֹ
סַחְתָּה לּוֹ כֹּה יִהְיֶה זַרְעָךְ
שְׁלוֹשִׁים כְּעֶרְכָּךְ מִגִּיזְעָךְ
עֲדֵי עַד נֵירָךְ לֹא יִדְעָךְ
אֲשֶׁר הֵיאַרְתָּה בְּמַדָּעָךְ
פְּלָאוֹת הִפְלֵאתָה לְמַיְימִינָךְ
וְחָשַׁבְתָּה צְדָקָה לְמַאֲמִינָךְ
צְבִי לַצַּדִּיק ... בִּנְיָינָךְ
אֲשֶׁר הִיקְנֵיתָה קִינְיָינָךְ
קָרָאתָה לְמַקְרִיא תוֹעִים לָךְ
וְקֵירַבְתָּה ... ..ים לָךְ

will inhabit the world at any given time; see *qedushta* to Gen 12, Poem Two, line 10 and *GenR* 49:3, which is cited in my commentary there.

37 Abraham is associated with the image of light; **B1** cites *GenR* 2:3 for this stich.

38 Ps 110:1, as interpreted in *TanḥB Lekh* 17 (**B1**).

39 Gen 15:6 (**R**).

40 An allusion to Prov 10:25, "The just man is the foundation of the earth, an everlasting foundation" (**B2**, who uses this language to complete the lacuna).

41 The reference here seems to be to Abraham's "missionary" activities, commonly attested in the midrash; see also the *qedushta* to Gen 12:1.

42 Line completed according to text of **B1**.

Mercies of your own I will give you
Justice, like your name, I shall proclaim for you[43]
Good tidings of fatherhood You shall let him hear
And from tidings of ill You shall guard him
Gifts of three from him You took with favor[44]
and from chariots-of-three You saved him.

And thus: "Fear not; I am your shield"

(7^1) *Do not* fear! *I am your* Hope
Do not cower! *I am your* Guardian
Do not tremble! *I am your* Shepherd
Do not cringe! *I am your* Creator
Do not stumble! *I am your* Rock
Do not dread! *I am your* Ransomer
Do not blanch! *I am with* you;
Do not shudder! *I am your* Support
Do not stray! *I am your* place of ease
Do not reel! *I am your* Foundation
Do not tarry! *I am your* escort
Do not sorrow! *I am your* Cup
Do not quail! *I am your* Savior
Do not feel hunted! *I am your* rocky Shelter
Do not weaken! *I am your* Might
Do not quake in terror! *I am your* strong Arm
Do not act the fool! *I am your* Source of praise
Do not worry! *I am your* lofty Banner
Do not lose hope! *I am your* Redeemer
Do not shrink away! *I am your* Maker
Do not dwell in darkness! *I am your* Light!

And thus: "Your reward shall be very great!"

(7^2) *Your reward* for the fire into which you went
Shall be very great for the converts you drew close
Your reward for the paths upon which you led others

43 See above, Poem Two, line 9, where "Justice" is given as a name of Abraham. The poet here alludes to the fact that Abraham merited blessings from both of God's attributes: Justice

רַחֲמִים מִשֶּׁלָּךְ אֶתֵּן לָךְ
  וְצֶדֶק בִּשְׁמָךְ אֶקְרָא לָךְ
שְׁמוּעָה טוֹבָה לְאָב שִׁימַּעְתָּה
  וּמִשְּׁמוּעָה רָעָה אוֹתוֹ שִׁימַּרְתָּה
תְּשׁוּרַת שִׁלּוּשִׁים מֶנּוּ שַׁעְתָּה
  וּמִשָּׁלִישִׁים אוֹתוֹ הוֹשַׁעְתָּה

ובכן אל תירא אנכי מגן לך

(ז[1]) אַל תִּירָא אָנֹכִי תּוֹחַלְתָּךְ
אַל תִּשְׁתָּע אָנֹכִי שׁוֹמְרָךְ
אַל תִּרְעַד אָנֹכִי רוֹעָךְ
אַל תְּקַנֵּא אָנֹכִי קוֹנָךְ
אַל תֵּצַר אָנֹכִי צוּרָךְ
אַל תִּפְחַד אָנֹכִי פּוֹדָךְ
אַל תַּעֲרוֹץ אָנֹכִי עִימָּךְ
אַל תִּסְמַר אָנֹכִי סוֹמְכָךְ
אַל תָּנוּד אָנֹכִי נוּחָךְ
אַל תִּמּוֹג אָנֹכִי מָגִינָּךְ
אַל תִּלְאֶה אָנֹכִי לִיוּוּיָךְ
אַל תִּכְעַס אָנֹכִי כּוּסָךְ
אַל תֵּיחַת אָנֹכִי יִשְׁעָךְ
אַל תְּטוֹרָף אָנֹכִי טוּרָךְ
אַל תֶּחֱלֶה אָנֹכִי חֵילָךְ
אַל תִּזְחַל אָנֹכִי זְרוֹעָךְ
אַל תְּהוֹלָל אָנֹכִי הִילּוּלָךְ
אַל תִּדְאַג אָנֹכִי דִּיגְלָךְ
אַל תָּגֹר אָנֹכִי גּוֹאֲלָךְ
אַל תְּבוֹהָל אָנֹכִי בּוֹרְאָךְ
אַל תֵּאָפֵל אָנֹכִי אוֹרָךְ

ובכן שכרך הרבה מאד

(ז[2]) שְׂכָרָךְ בָּאֵשׁ אֲשֶׁר בָּאתָה
  הַרְבֵּה מְאֹד בְּגֵירִים אֲשֶׁר דִּיבַּקְתָּה
שְׂכָרָךְ בַּהֲלִיכוֹת אֲשֶׁר וִיעַדְתָּה

---

and Mercy.

44 Gen 15:9 (**R**).

Shall be very great for merit which to you was reckoned[45]
Your reward for wanderings that spread the word
Shall be very great for the strength with which you gave heart
Your reward for the kings whom you defeated
Shall be very great for the utterance of your response
Your reward for the sinners you tried to spare
Shall be very great for the truth by which you made (Me) great[46]
Your reward for the oath that you heard
Shall be very great for the promises you claimed

(8) *Your reward*—is given justly
Shall be very great—in its mercy
for God is just
and the Lord is merciful
Through him, You sanctify Your name [in justice]
and by him, You are sanctified through mercy
like the sanctification on high
As it is written: "And the one called out to the other..."

45 Gen 15:6 (**B1**).

הַרְבֵּה מְאֹד בִּ**זְ**כוּת אֲשֶׁר **חִ**ישַּׁבְתָּה
שְׂכָרְךָ בְּ**ט**וֹעִים אֲשֶׁר **יִ**ידַּעְתָּה
הַרְבֵּה מְאֹד בְּ**כ**וֹחַ אֲשֶׁר **לִ**יבַּבְתָּה
שְׂכָרְךָ בִּ**מְ**לָכִים אֲשֶׁר **נָ**צַחְתָּה
הַרְבֵּה מְאֹד בְּ**שִׂ**יחַ אֲשֶׁר **עָ**נִיתָה
שְׂכָרְךָ בְּ**פ**וֹשְׁעִים אֲשֶׁר **צִ**ידַּקְתָּה
הַרְבֵּה מְאֹד בְּ**קֹ**וֶט אֲשֶׁר **רִ**יבִּיתָה
שְׂכָרְךָ בִּ**שְׁ**בוּעָה אֲשֶׁר **שָׁ**מַעְתָּה
הַרְבֵּה מְאֹד בִּ**תְּ**נָיִים אֲשֶׁר **תָּ**בַעְתָּה

(ח) שְׂכָרְךָ בְּדִין
הַרְבֵּה מְאֹד בְּרַחֲמִים
כִּי אֱלֹהִים דִּין
וַיי רַחֲמִים
בּוֹ קִידַּשְׁתָּה שְׁמָךְ ...
וּבוֹ נִיתְקַדַּשְׁתָּה בְּרַחֲמִים
כִּקְדֻושַּׁת עֶלְיוֹנִים
ככתוב וקרא זה אל זה

46 See *GenR* 55:1 (**B1**).

Comments

In this piyyut, Yannai focuses on two specific themes that emerge from the biblical text: the anxiety-provoking connection Abraham makes between his triumph over the Canaanite kings and his childlessness; and God's reassurance that Abraham acted well and that he will soon become a father. Yannai roots these dual emotions, anxiety and affirmation, in the language of Gen 15:1, which states, "*After these things* [דברים], the word of the Lord came to Abram in a vision, saying: *Fear not*, Abram; I am a shield to you and your reward shall be very great" (italics added). The poet, along with other ancient exegetes, looks to the story of what happened before this verse to understand the opening of the *sidra*: the "things" that precede divine consolation are understood as "words" (and thus become Abraham's internal monologue) while God's reassurance—"Fear not!"—now responds directly to the patriarch's understood but unstated concerns.

These two threads—human anxiety and divine reassurance—run throughout the poem, from the first stanza to the final surviving lines. The alternation of these two ideas throughout the composition results in an unusually conversational piyyut. The dialogue created within the poem expands the dialogue already present within the biblical pericope; the poet's voice merges into that of the biblical narrator. In Poem One, Yannai lets us hear God's voice, as He responds to the patriarch's inward, unarticulated fear. In Poem Two, Abraham responds forcefully to God's speech, accepting God's assertion of his innocence and using his vindication to plead vigorously on his own behalf. The petition for offspring segues neatly into the prayer for renewed life. Poem Three is entirely in the narrator's voice, while Poem Four contains primarily narration, but recalls Poem One in that God responds to the patriarch's inward thoughts. Poem Five contains both sides of the dialogue, and in Poem Six, the poet mediates the divine-human interchange, as if turning from one party to the other. The *r'hitim* are in God's voice, with God speaking to Abraham, while the *silluq* is again in the narrator's voice, this time turned towards his own congregation. The *qedushta*, complex as it is, constitutes a single overheard conversation.

Although the twin tones of anxiety and reassurance are voiced repeatedly, the extended dialogue (emerging out of the first verse of the *sidra*) results in repeated affirmations of Abraham's merit and multiple reiterations of God's promises to the patriarch and—explicitly as well as implicitly—his offspring, who constitute the community for which this piyyut was composed. Particularly noteworthy is the boldness of Abraham's language. As pathos-laden as the intimations of guilt may be, the assertiveness of Abraham's plea for offspring—already strong in the biblical passage—stands out. Abraham reminds God (and Yannai reminds his audience) that Abraham was virile, stating, for example: "I have the means to father children / but as yet I lack a child!" (Poem Five, line 9–10); the problem is not physical. In Abraham's petition, fatherhood becomes a matter of, if not justice, then mercy. The patriarch appeals to both of God's attributes by employing both of His names ("Lord" as well as "God" in the opening of Poem Five). God assents to Abraham's demand for a child on both grounds: Abraham shall have an heir not only because he wants one but because it is his due. Abraham is not criticized for his boldness, but praised. The final line of the second *rahit* commends the patriarch for his assertiveness: "[*Your reward*] *shall be very great*: for the promises you [Abraham] claimed [from God]" (line 12). To paraphrase the poem, Abraham is a worker who has earned his wage. He believed in God and God counted his faith to his merit (Gen 15:6); Abraham fought wars and followed divine commands; Abraham brought gentiles under the wings of the Shekhinah and made God's reputation great in the world. Now, when Abraham said that God stands in his debt, God agrees.

Embedded in the story of Abraham's childlessness is the idea that Abraham is the father of converts. Yannai first hints at this motif in the conclusion of the *magen* (Poem One). While he describes God as creator of humanity, Yannai subtly joins humanity in general (אדם) with the specific nation of Israel ("this people"—עם זו). The tension between the universal and the particular can be resolved by conversion, and the sensitive listener may connect Abraham with Adam (as in the aggadah) and thus with conversion. Abraham acknowledges his connection to conversion explicitly when he worries that he may have killed a future righteous convert in his battle against the Canaanite kings (Poem Five, lines 18–21). In Poem Six (line 36) and in the second *rahit* (lines 2 and 5), Yannai describes Abraham as a co-creator with God—that is, the patriarch "creates" through his missionary activities. Indeed, leading another to conversion can be seen as a kind of parenthood—an idea implicit in the fact that a convert takes the name "son/daughter of Abraham."[47] In this composition, however, Yannai

47 See the *qedushta* to Gen 12 for more on this theme.

suggests that fathering spiritual offspring is *not* equal to fathering biological offspring; converts cannot compensate for barrenness, at least not in Abraham's eyes. Converts reflect Abraham's power and goodness but they satisfy God's yearning for progeny, not Abraham's. Abraham's success as a missionary increases God's indebtedness to him, intensifying rather than ameliorating Abraham's right to a biological child. The motif of "creation" thus provides a conversational counterpoint to Abraham's demands. The patriarch is—as Yannai audaciously and repeatedly asserts—God's counterpart on earth, but where God has many children—children granted to Him by Abraham!—Abraham has none.

Yannai starts with the complexity of Abraham's character in the biblical corpus and its aggadic interpretation and then amplifies it by distilling it to a conversational essence. The poet sketches Abraham's righteousness and courage as well as his humility and frailty in bold strokes. It is not hard to imagine the appeal of Abraham's character to Yannai's audience: modest and fragile yet boldly asserting his claim upon God—he is, in every way, a model for a community that wishes to balance piety with a sense of due justice. The poet crafts a poem which affirms Abraham and, by extension, validates and consoles his own community. In the poetic conversation, the poet shifts the burden of explanation and justification from Abraham to God. Offspring are granted to Abraham as a result of God's mercy and out of a divine sense of justice. The poet almost says as much in the final line of the second *rahit*: God owes Abraham. And as Abraham asks in Gen 18:25, "Shall not the Judge of all the earth do justice?" From deep within his fear, Abraham finds the courage to ask for fairness—and his voice, ultimately, is not his own but rather that of the poet Yannai, speaking for himself and his community.

Qedushta for Genesis 16:1 בראשית טז:א

"Now Sarai, the wife of Abram" ושרי אשת אברם

In *Targum Neophyti* to Gen 16:5, we find the following account: "And Sarai said to Abram: My judgment and my humiliation, my insult and the beginning of my affliction are given into your hand. I forsook my country, and the house of my birth, and the house of my father, and I came with you faithfully. I went with you before the kings of the earth: before Pharaoh, king of Egypt; and before Abimelech, king of Gerar; and I said, `He is my brother,' so that they would not kill you. And when I saw that I did not bear (children), I took Hagar the Egyptian, my handmaid, and I gave her to you as wife." As in the targumic expansion, in this piyyut the figure of Sarai becomes complex and compelling, and she speaks with a strong, distinctive voice. In the matriarch, Yannai creates a character who defies simplistic interpretation or maginalization, and the poem he composes around her nuances Sarai's character and gives her a powerful, poignant presence.

(1) A matriarch, like a dove in the cranny of a stone
Her belly having been blocked as by a stone
... and stone
the doors of her womb to open with a supplication

She was like a garden locked
and she was sealed like fountain locked[1]
She cried out and knocked upon the latches of the lock
O Gracious One to grant her from her husband, a child.[2]

Pure and sacred, she suited him[3]
and for ten years she tried to fulfill him[4]
The wisest of women, she acted on his behalf
to do right by him, having not borne to him[5]

As it is written: "Now Sarai, the wife of Abram, had not borne to him, but she had an Egyptian handmaid by the name of Hagar" (Gen 16:1)
And it is said: "The wisest of women builds her house, but the foolish one tears it down with her own hands" (Prov 14:1)
And it is said: "Royal princesses are your favorites; the consort stands at your right hand, decked in gold of Ophir" (Ps 45:1)
And it is said: "O my dove, in the cranny of the stone, hidden by the cliff, let me see your face, let me hear your voice; for your voice is sweet and your face is comely" (Song 2:14)
And it is said: "A garden locked is my sister, my bride, a fountain locked, a spring sealed" (Song 4:12)

Sealed upon the heart
Not forgotten from the heart
in order to shield the children of the pure of heart.[6]
Blessed... Shield...

---

1 Line completed according to Song 4:12, cited as an intertext, and in keeping with the suggestions of Zulay (cited by **R**) and **B1**.

2 This line alludes to Song 5:2 and 5:5, as well.

3 **R** and **B1** connect this phrase with Exod 30:35, where "pure and sacred" describes the "sweet spices" to be compounded for use in the sanctuary. The translation, "she suited him," is an attempt to capture the nuance of *mulḥah* (lit., "salted"). It refers to Sarah's compatibility with Abraham.

4 According to *m. Yev.* 7:6, a man is permitted (some later authorities would argue

(א) **אֵ**ם כְּיוֹנָה בְּחַגְוֵי סֶלַע
בִּיטְנָהּ בִּהְיוֹת חָסוּם כְּסֶלַע
... ..ודה וְסֶלַע
דַּלְתֵי רַחְמָהּ לִפְתּוֹחַ בְּסֶלַח

הָיְתָה כְּמוֹ גַּן נָעוּל
וַחֲתוּמָה כְּמוֹ גַל נָעוּל
זָעֲקָה וְדָפְקָה כַּפּוֹת הַמַּנְעוּל
חַנּוּן לְחָונְנָהּ מִבַּעֲלָהּ עוּל.

טוֹהַר וְקוֹדֶשׁ מֻולְּחָה לוֹ
יְמוֹת שְׁנוֹת עֶשֶׂר מִילְּאָה לוֹ
כְּחַכְמוֹת נָשִׁים פָּעֲלָה לוֹ
לְהַצְדִּיק כִּי לֹא יָלְדָה לוֹ

ככתוב ושרי אשת אברם לא ילדה לו ולה שפחה מצרית ושמה הגר

ונאמר חכמות נשים בנתה ביתה ואולת בידיה תהרסנו

ונאמר בנות מלכים ביקרותיך נצבה שגל לימינך בכתם אופיר

ונאמר יונתי בחגוי הסלע בסתר המדרגה הראיני את מראיך השמיעיני את קולך ערב ומראך נאוה

ונאמר גן נעול אחותי כלה גל נעול מעין חתום

חָתוּם עַל לֵב
לֹא תִישָּׁכַח מִלֵּב
לְמַגֵּן בְּנֵי בָרֵי לֵב
ברוך... מגן...

---

required) to divorce his wife if, after ten years, she has not borne him children. *GenR* 45:3 applies this halakhah specifically to the events of this *sidra* but argues that Abraham's years outside the Land of Israel are not counted towards the ten (**R**). See also *b. Yev.* 64a-b, which connects this mishnah to the story of the patriarchs and matriarchs.

5 That is, she took it up on herself to help Abraham acquire the merit of a child, even if such merit was to be denied her personally. See *Tanḥ Ḥayyei Sarah* 4.

6 "Pure of heart" is an epithet for Israel, based on Ps 73:1, "A psalm of Asaph: Truly God is good to Israel, to those who are pure of heart" (**B2**).

(2) "My own family? I have failed to build it[7]
So please, from my maid, build me up."
So mused "she who discerned"[8] to "the father" aloud
"Yet I, too, may be built up into a camp
"A visitation[9] of peace and pleasure?
"The righteous one[10] shall find no pleasure with me—[11]
"Until my distress he puts to rest
"Until the promise of my deed he fulfills"[12]
The father listened to she-who-would-bear[13]
Perhaps to find hope
She replied to him: "There is a time for bearing
"But I have been kept from bearing"

As it is written: "Then Sarai said to Abram: `You must see that the Lord has kept me from bearing. Come now, please, unto my maid--perhaps I will be built up from her.' And Abram hearkened to the voice of Sarai" (Gen 16:2)

And it is said: "A woman of valor: who can find her? Her worth is more than rubies" (Prov 31:10)

And it is said: "Whatever He tears down cannot be rebuilt; whatever He shuts against a man cannot be opened" (Job 12:14)

And it is said: "The stone that the builders rejected has become the chief cornerstone" (Ps 118:22)

A cornerstone exalted
Set us as high as heaven!
And we will live again, through dew that flows from on high!
Blessed… Who resurrects…

(3) O Yah: You compared Zion to the wife of the brave one[14]

---

7 Literally, "From my family, I have no builder"—i.e., a son. (See the reverse of the same pun in the famous passage of *b. Ber.* 64a, "Do not read `your sons' [*banayikh*] but rather `your builders' [*bonayikh*]".) This stanza puns extensively on the words build/son. There may also be an implicit criticism of Abram, who has failed to "build" a house with Sarai.

8 The implication seems to be that Sarah foresaw that she would also someday be a mother (either biologically or through her handmaid Hagar); the appellation "father" alludes to Abraham's paternal destiny. **B1** cites *b. Meg.* 14a: "Sarah [is one of seven prophetesses], as it is written: `The father of Milkah and the father of Yiskah' (Gen 11:29). Rabbi Isaac said [on this]. Yiskah is Sarah; and why was she called Yiskah? Because she discerned [*sakethah*] by means of the holy spirit… Another explanation is: Because all gazed [*sakin*] at her beauty."

(ב) **מ**ִמִּשְׁפַּחְתִּי אֵין לִי בּוֹנֶה
נָא מִשִּׁיפְחָתִי אוּלַי אִיבָּנֶה
סָחָה יִסְכָּה לְאָב בְּמַעֲנֶה
עַד גַּם אֲנִי אִיבָּן בַּמַּחֲנֶה
פְּקֻודַּת שָׁלוֹם וְשָׁלֵיו
צַדִּיק עִימִּי לֹא יִשְׁלָיו
קֵץ קִינְאָתִי עַד יַשְׁלֵם
רְצוֹן פּוֹעֲלִי עַד יְשַׁלֵּם
שָׁמַע אָב לְתְחוֹלֶלֶת
שֶׁמָּה לִמְצוֹא תוֹחֶלֶת
תַּנוּתָהּ לוֹ עֵת לָלֶדֶת
תַּחַת כִּי נֶעֱצַרְתִּי מִלֶּדֶת

ככתוב ותאמר שרי אל אברם הנה נא עצרני יי מלדת בא נא אל שפחתי אולי אבנה ממנה ויאמע אברם לקול שרה

ונאמר אשת חיל מי ימצא ורחוק מפנינים מכרה

ונאמר הן יהרוס ולא יבנה יסגור על איש ולא יפתח

ונאמר אבן מאסו הבונים היתה לראש פנה

פִּינָּה מְעוּלֶּה
תְּשִׂימֵינוּ עַד לְמָעְלָה
וְנִיחְיֶיה בְּטַל זִילַת מָעְלָה
ברוך... מחיה...

(ג) **יָ**הּ לְאֵשֶׁת אֵיתָן צִיּוֹן הִישְׁוֵיתָה

---

9 The term "visitation" (*pekudah*) is here used in the sense of marital intimacy (**B1**). See Job 5:24, "You will know that all is well in your tent; When you visit (פ-ק-ד) your wife you will never fail," as well as *b. Yev.* 62b; *LevR* 18:1. According to this interpretation, Sarah realized that a son (biological or surrogate) was necessary for restoration of a full marital relationship with Abraham.

10 Abraham

11 Reading לאי שליו as לא ישליו/ישלו, with Zulay (cited by **R**). See Ps 122:6 and Job 12:6.

12 The subject of the verbs "puts to rest" and "fulfils," is here taken to be Abraham but could also be God.

13 The names here foreshadow the happy events to come.

14 Abraham; see *qedushta* for Gen 12:1.

equal tests and trials upon each You set[15]
It is said about Sarah, the princess, that she could not bear
and it was said about Zion, My principality, that she would never bear again[16]
The one who sat childless at home
was then seated at the center of the House
So shall You settle within the house[17]
she who was uprooted from her own house[18]
Fair-crested, the precious one
by Your own mouth called "Mother"
Rejoice, O barren one
Unto your children He will call!

As it is written: "Rejoice, O barren one, you who bore no child! Shout aloud for joy, you who did not bear! For the children of the wife forlorn shall outnumber those of the espoused -- said the Lord" (Isa 54:1)
And it is said: "He sets the childless woman among her household as a happy mother of children. Hallelujah!" (Ps 113:9)
And You are Holy, enthroned upon the prayers of Israel… Please, God…

(4) "O You who unbinds the bound, unbind my bindings
"And heal my afflictions," Sarai cried out[19]
"Alas, was I created unable to bear future fruit?
"If only I could fathom why I am barren!
"Is my fault that I cannot bear
"Or is it my husband—that he cannot beget?"
"Let him come unto my handmaid; then I will know if he can father!"
At the appointed time he came, and at once with her he became a father[20]
She trusted in her prayer she did not whitewash her plea:[21]
"You who set limits for all,[22]
"Do not withhold Your mercy from me!"
O Holy One…

---

15 Lit., "Upon her."

16 This line picks up on the language of Lam 1:1, where שרתי (*sarati*, "my princess") is an epithet for Zion. The term obviously recalls the name of Sarah.

17 The language here recalls Ps 128:3 (**R**); the word "house" here most probably refers to the Temple.

18 This line hints at the multiple meanings of *bayit* in rabbinic Hebrew, where it can be used to refer to a literal "house" but also used as shorthand for "wife" and "Temple." See also the third stanza of Poem Six.

19 This line contains a powerful wordplay on the roots א-ס-ר (`to bind'); י-ס-ר (`to suffer');

בְּנִיסּוּי וּמַסָּה אֲשֶׁר עָלֶיהָ שִׁיוִּיתָה
נֶאֱמַר עַל שָׂרָה לֹא יָלָדָה
וְנֶאֱמַר עַל שָׂרָתִי לֹא יָלָדָה
יוֹשֶׁבֶת עֲקֶרֶת הַבָּיִית
יָשְׁבָה בְּעִיקָּר בָּיִת
כֵּן תּוֹשִׁיב בְּיַירְכְּתֵי בָיִית
נֶעֱקֶרֶת מִבָּיִית
יְפֵה נוֹף הַיִּיקָרָא
אֲשֶׁר פִּיךָ אֵם קָרָא
רָונִּי עֲקָרָה
עַל בָּנַיִךְ יִקְרָא

ככתוב רוני עקרה לא ילדה פצחי רנה וצהלי לא חלה כי רבים בני שוממה מבני בעולה אמר יי

ונאמר מושיבי עקרת הבית אם הבנים שמחה הללויה

ואתה קדוש יושב תהלות ישראל אל נא

(ד) מַתִּיר אֲסוּרִים הַתֵּר אֲסוּרָיי
וְרַפֵּא יִיסּוּרָיי צָעֲקָה שָׂרָיי
לוּ לֹא נוֹצַרְתִּי כִּי נֶעֱצָרְתִּי
מַה נֶּחֱקַרְתִּי כִּי נֶעֱקָרְתִּי
אִם מִמֶּנִּי הִיא כִּי לֹא אוֹלִיד
וְאִם מֵאִיִּי הִיא כִּי לֹא מוֹלִיד
יָבוֹא נָא אֶל אֲמָתִי וְאֵידַע מִי מוֹלִיד
וְעֵת בָּא מִיַּד מִמֶּנָּה הוֹלִיד
בָּטְחָה בִּתְפִילָּה וְלֹא טָחָה תִיפְלָה
שָׂם קֵץ לְכָל תִּכְלָה
רַחֲמֶיךָ לֹא תִכְלָא מִמֶּנִּי
קָדוֹשׁ

---

and *sarah* (Sarai's name). It alludes to Ps 146:7, which refers to God as "He who releases (*mattir*) the bound (*ʾasurim*)"—here understood to refer to infertility. Bitterness, hopefulness, praise, and complaint are all packed into these few words.

20 Alludes to the aggadic tradition that Abram only had intercourse with Hagar once, sparing Sarai the humiliation of an extended affair and himself from charges of profligacy. See *GenR* 45:4 (**R**).

21 See Ezek 13:10 and Job 1:25 (**R**).

22 Ps 119:96, "I have seen that all things have their limit, but Your commandment is broad beyond measure" (**B1**).

(5) Abram and Sarai in confidence took refuge
because of all the souls that they made in Haran[23]
In the Creator of All[24] they rejoiced when from their land they wandered[25]
for the reward of the souls would be a gift of souls[26]
By great things were they tested but the Almighty[27] they did not test[28]
at the time when they tarried though parenthood came not quickly
Their course was examined and checked;
their deeds were refined and tested:
would their faith stay firm until their elder days?
Such were their deeds; in their works He rejoiced;
He yearned for their prayer and the entreaty of their words
Lest towards her husband she act haughty
He reckoned it best she be barren;
and lest she be too pampered from giving suck was she delayed.[29]
Thus while Sarah was yet "Sarai" and Abraham merely "Abram;"
Fate was a hindrance until the exalted God willed change[30]
Then He transformed their names and renewed their souls,
forgave their sins and rebuilt their ruins[31]
A decree: "Thus shall it be!" It was promised: "Indeed, it shall surely be!"[32]
In his heart he kept the secret his sorrow was restrained
Because as yet Sarai had not been given word
"He has closed me up!" she said yet for salvation she still hoped[33]
Forever…

---

23 Gen 12:5; the language of "acquiring souls" is understood in Rabbinic tradition as creating converts to the worship of God.

24 Jer 10:16.

25 This refers to Abraham and Sarah's voluntary departure from their ancestral land and family (Gen 12) to the land of Israel. See *GenR* 39:8 (**B1**).

26 See *qedushta* to Gen 8:15, Poem Five, above.

27 Literally, "*gevurot*," the divine attribute of power.

28 I.e., Abraham and Sarah did not "test" God by pestering him with petitions for offspring. **R** cites *PesR* 43.

29 See *SongR* 2:41, "Rabbi Azariah said in the name of Rabbi Ḥanina ben Papa: Why were the matriarchs so long childless? In order that they should not put on airs towards their husbands on account of their beauty." **R** cites a variant of this tradition, *GenR* 45:4, which states: "Why were the matriarchs so long childless?. . .Rabbi Azariah said in Rabbi Ḥanina's name: So that they might lean on their husbands in [spite of] their beauty." The explanation seems to be that the matriarchs were so beautiful and otherwise blessed with riches and

(ה) אַבְרָם וְשָׂרַי בְּהַבְטָחָה חָסוּ
בְּכָל נֶפֶשׁ אֲשֶׁר בְּחָרָן עָשׂוּ
בְּיוֹצֵר כֹּל גָּלוּ וּמֵאַרְצָם גָּלוּ
כִּי שְׂכַר נוּפָשׁוֹת אֶתְנַן נְפָשׁוֹת
גְּדוֹלוֹת נִסּוּ וּגְבוּרוֹת לֹא נִיסּוּ
בְּעֵת אֲשֶׁר אִיחֲרוּ וּלְהוֹלִיד לֹא מִיהֲרוּ
דַּרְכָּם לִבְחוֹן וְלִבְדּוֹק
וּפָעֳלָם לִצְרוֹף וּלְנַסּוֹת
אִם עָמְדוּ בְּמֵימֵיהֶם עַד זִיקְנַת יְמֵיהֶם
הָיָה פּוֹעֳלָם שָׂמֵיחַ בְּמִפְעָלָם
מִיתְאַוֶּוה לְפִילְלָם וּלְתַחֲנוּנֵי מִילְלָם
וּפֶן עַל בַּעֲלָהּ תִּיתְרַפֵּק
נֶחְשַׁב כִּי לֹא תִיתְאַפֵּק
וּפֶן תִּיתְפַּנֵּק עֲוֹכְבָה מִיוֹנֵק
זֹאת הָיְתָה שָׂרָה שָׂרַיי וְאַבְרָהָם אַבְרָם
וּמַזָּל הָיָה מְעַכְּבָם עַד חָפֵץ אֵל רָם
חִילֵּף שְׁמוֹתָם וְחִידֵּשׁ נִישְׁמוֹתָם
וְכִיפֵּר אַשְׁמוֹתָם לִבְנוֹת שׁוֹמְמוֹתָם
טַעַם כֹּה יִהְיֶה הָובְטַח הָיוֹ יִהְיֶה
בְּלִיבּוֹ כָּבַשׁ וְעוֹצְבּוֹ חֲבָשׁ
יַעַן כִּי שָׂרַי לֹא נִיתְבַּשְּׂרָה
עֲצָרַנִי סִיפְּרָה וּלְיֵשַׁע סִיבְּרָה

לעולם

confidence that had they also had children early in their lives, they would have been entirely too self-sufficient and content with themselves.

30 This recalls *GenR* 45:10, which states: "Rabbi Samuel b. Isaac commented: [Abraham said:] My planetary fate (*mazzal*) oppresses me and declares, 'Abram cannot beget a child.' Said the Holy One, blessed be He, to him: 'Let it be even as your words: Abram and Sarai cannot beget but Abraham and Sarah can beget'" (**R**). A change of name results in a change of destiny. See also *TanḥB Ḥayyeh Sarah* 6.

31 When God changes Abram to Abraham and Sarai to Sarah, it is as if He has returned humanity to the very beginning: a fresh start, full of promise, free of any history of transgression. **B1** cites *GenR* 39:11, "'I will make you a great nation'—after I have created you as a new creation, you will be fruitful and multiply." See also *TanḥB Ḥayyei Sarah* 6 (**B1**).

32 The two quotations in this line come from Gen 15:5 and 18:18, respectively (**R**).

33 The last two lines of the *asiriyyah* imply that Abram did not confide God's promise to Sarai but waited, instead, until God Himself would reveal the truth to her, as happens in Gen 18.

And Sarai…

(6) Whose womb had been compared to a heap of wheat:[34]
her womb was dry and her breasts were withered[35]
While she was pure, her womb unswollen[36]
she was granted a reward: fruit of the womb
The lot was cast: she was meant for Abram
while they were yet in their mothers' wombs[37]
Their quantity of sighs was not for naught
though "youth and black hair are fleeting"[38]
She was the patriarch's portion, along with wealth and home;[39]
with a fair sapling, a wife, taking root within the home
And she was the essence of the home
she who dwelled childless in the home[40]
Despondent, she despaired of having children
shattered like a mother bereft—without sons[41]
But, at last, she had milk to suckle children
for the heritage of the Lord is children
The goodness of her work[42] shone for her husband;
she sowed righteousness just as he sowed
For she had kept herself pure from the seed of strangers;[43]
she was righteous and innocent, and, for the right seed, fertile
Honored she was, and treasured
carried high upon the heights of the city
For the sake of her entreaty her womb was rendered bare[44]

---

34 Song 7:3 (**R**).

35 Hos 9:14, "Give them, O Lord; what will you give? Give them a miscarrying womb and withered breasts" (**B1**). See also Num 11:6 (**B2**).

36 "Unswollen" could contrast simply to the round belly of the pregnant woman—Hagar, in particular. More likely, however, it alludes to the ritual of the suspected adulteress ('Sotah'); see Num 5:25–28 (**R**). This understanding of "unswollen" indicates that during her captivities with Pharaoh and Abimelech, Sarah maintained her purity and fidelity to Abraham. She was granted a son as a reward.

37 According to *PRE* 30, Abraham and Sarah were fated for each other from before birth (**R**). The text states: "Rabbi Yehudah said: In that night [when Sarah asked Abraham to send Hagar away; see Gen 20:10] the Holy One, blessed be He, was revealed to him [Abraham]. He said to him: 'Abraham! Do you not know that Sarah was appointed to you for a wife from her mother's womb? She is your companion and the wife of your covenant…Nor is Hagar called your wife, but your handmaid." **R** also mentions *PRK* 23:8, and *LevR* 29:8.

38 Eccl 11:10 (**R**).

39 Based on Prov 19:14, "House and wealth are inherited from fathers; but a prudent wife

ושרי

(ו) **אֲ**שֶׁר נִימְשְׁלָה בַּעֲרֵימַת בֶּטֶן
וְיָבְשָׁה בְּבֶטֶן וְצָמְקָה בְעֶטֶן
בְּעֵת טָהֲרָה מִילַּצְבּוֹת בֶּטֶן
נֶחְנְנָה שָׂכָר פְּרִי הַבָּטֶן
גּוֹרָל עָלְתָה לְאַבְרָם חֶבֶל
עוֹדָם בִּמְעֵי אִימָּם הֶבֶל
דֵּי יְגִיעָם לֹא הָיָה לְהֵיבֶל
כִּי הַיַּלְדוּת וְהַשַּׁחְרוּת הָבֶל
הָיְתָה נַחֲלַת אָבוֹת בְּהוֹן וָבָיִת
וּשְׁתוּלָה בְּיַרְכְּתֵי הַבָּיִת
וְהִיא הָיְתָה עִיקָּר הַבָּיִת
וְיוֹשֶׁבֶת עֲקֶרֶת הַבָּיִת
זְנוּחָה מְיוֹאָשָׁה הָיְתָה מִבָּנִים
רְטוּוָּה כְּאֵם עַל בָּנִים בְּלִי בָנִים
חָלָב בְּסוֹף הֵינִיקָה בָנִים
כִּי נַחֲלַת יְיָ בָּנִים
טוֹב פָּוּעֳלָהּ כְּבַעֲלָהּ זָרַח
וְזָרְעָה לִצְדָקָה כְּמוֹ זָרַע
יַעַן טָהֲרָה מִזָּרוּת זֶרַע
צָדְקָה וְנִיקְּתָה וְנִיזְרְעָה זָרַע
כְּבוּדָה הָיְתָה וּמְיֻקֶּרֶת
טְעוּנָה עַל גַּפֵּי מְרוֹמֵי קָרֶת
לְמַעַן לְחַנֵּין הָיְתָה מְעֻוקֶּבֶת

---

is from the Lord" (**R** and **B1**).

40 See above in the *meḥayyeh.*

41 Hos 10:14 (**R**). This line compares Sarai's grief over her childlessness with that of a mother bereft of her children.

42 Sarah's "good work" may refer to her willingness to follow Abraham's demands of her in Gen 20:13 or her generosity in creating the arrangement between Abraham and Hagar.

43 That is, she guarded her chastity while in the courts of Pharaoh and Abimelech. Her fidelity to Abraham in those situations earned her the reward of a son later. See Gen 12 and 20, and *SifN* 19 (**B1**).

44 According to aggadic tradition, God rendered the matriarchs barren because the sound of their prayer was so sweet. See *SongsR* 2:41, "Rabbi Levi in the name of Rabbi Shila from Kfar Temarta and Rabbi Helbo in the name of Rabbi Yohanan said: Why were the matriarchs so long barren? Because the Holy One, blessed be He, longed to hear their prayer. He said to them: 'My dove, I will tell you why I have kept you childless; because I was longing to hear your prayer.' Hence it says, 'For sweet is your voice, and your countenance is comely' (Song 2:14)." See also *GenR* 45:4.

but to bring forth babes she was "pierced" with her husband's "hammer."[45]
"From birthing," she said, "Lo, I am prevented!
"If only with a womb for bearing I were created![46]
"Alas, from my youth, my afflictions have been many
"But like a bundle of myrrh He binds me"[47]
A princess she was, over all the realm
no ill-fame did she bear over intimate matters
She who was barren became fruitful and multiplied
until she blossomed like a verdant vine
She opened her mouth in wisdom[47]
for the building up of her house was her longing
She suppressed her wrath and restrained her anger
she cast no evil eye upon her maid
Her jealousy consumed her heart, in her sorrow
though she would have a reward for her labor[48]
Her spirit ached in her anguish
until at ninety she was granted relief
She heard her maid's taunt but kept silent
"Where is your righteous reward?"—thus her soul she oppressed[49]
You gave her a gift, compensated her abuse
and in the end her wish was granted.

---

45 The language of this line depends on Isa 51:1 (**B1**), and implicitly on vs. 2, as well: "Listen to me, you who follow after righteousness, you who seek the Lord; look to the rock from which you have been hewn, and to the hole of the pit from which you were dug. Look to Abraham your father, and to Sarah who gave birth to you; for he was only one when I called him, and blessed him, and increased him." The Isaiah verse is here understood as euphemistic for the sexual intercourse necessary for Abraham and Sarah to increase in numbers.

46 *b. Yev.* 64b records a tradition that Sarai was born without a womb, making her eventual motherhood that much more miraculous.

47 As **B1** notes, this seems to apply to Sarai a tradition regarding Abraham preserved in *SongR* 1:49 (interpreting Song 1:13): "Just as when anyone gathers myrrh (*mor*) his hands

אֲבָל לְהוֹלִיד נֻוקְרָה בְמַקֶּבֶת
מִלֶּדֶת נָמָה הִנֵּא נָא עֲצָרָנִי
לוּ לֹא בִמְעֵי יוֹלֶדֶת יְצָרָנִי
נָא מִנְּעוּרַיי רַבַּת צְרָרוּנִי
כִּצְרוֹר הַמּוֹר צְרָרָנִי
שָׂרַת הָיְתָה עַל כָּל בִּירְיָה
וְלֹא סָרַת בְּכָל דְּבַר עֶרְיָיה
עֲצוּרָה הָיְתָה בְּפִירְיָיה וְרִיבְיָיה
עַד פָּרְחָה כְּגֶפֶן פּוֹרִיָּיה
פִּיהָ פָּתְחָה בְּחָוכְמָתָהּ
אֲשֶׁר לְבִינְיַין בֵּיתָהּ הָיְתָה כְּמִיהָתָהּ
צָדָה אֵימָתָה וְכָבְשָׁה חֲמָתָהּ
וְלֹא רָעָה עֵינָהּ בַּאֲמָתָהּ
קִינְאָה אָכְלָה לִיבָּהּ מֵעוֹצֶב
וְהָיָה לָהּ מוֹתָר בְּכָל עֶיצֶב
רוּחָהּ קָפְדָה מִקּוֹצֶר
עַד לְתִשְׁעִים נִיתַּן לָהּ קָצֶב
שָׁמְעָה הוֹנָיוֹת וְשָׁתָקָה
אֵיפֹה צִדְקָהּ וְנַפְשָׁהּ שָׁחָקָה
תַּתָּה לָהּ אֶיתְנָן עַל אֲשֶׁר נֶעֶשָׁקָה
וּבְאָחֲרִית וְתִיקְוָוה נֶחֱשָׁקָה

---

smart, so Abraham afflicted (*memarer*) himself and castigated himself." This passage could refer to some form of extreme ascetic practice, but might also indicate a willingness to suffer on account of the demands God made of the couple, and the opposition their teachings may have aroused.

48 Prov 31:26.

49 **R** connects to Prov 14:23; the implication here is that while giving Hagar to Abraham caused Sarah tremendous pain, she would ultimately reap rewards for the sacrifice.

50 See *GenR* 45:4, which states, "Hagar would tell [the local women]: `My mistress Sarai is not inwardly what she is outwardly: she appears to be a righteous woman, but she is not. For had she been a righteous woman, she would not have passed so many years without conceiving, while I conceived in one night!" (**R**).

And thus, "*Lo*[51], I am prevented from bearing"
(7) *Lo*, I am mute for want of one to raise[52]
Lo, I am too old for a son
Lo, I am cut down to a barren stump[53]
Lo, I am cast off from my tribe
Lo, I am drained of splendor[54]
Lo, I am in ruins for lack of offspring
Lo, I am scattered, my seed unsown
Lo, I am lacking one to swaddle[55]
Lo, I am torn for want of a tot
Lo, I am desperate, in need of a nursling
Lo, I cut off from my foundation
Lo, I am wrinkled and withered[56] …

---

51 It is important to consider the opening phrase, *hinneh na'*, here rendered simply as "lo," in an attempt to be as vague and inclusive of nuance as possible. In biblical Hebrew, this phrase connotes immediacy and request, along the lines of, "Hey, now, look here!" In Yannai, however, the particle נא can mean something along the lines of "truly" or "thus." It may even be an epithet for God, meaning, therefore, "Take note, O God!". For an extended discussion, see M. Zulay, *ʿIyyunei Lashon BeFiyyutei Yannai* (Schocken: Jerusalem, 1945), pp. 207–9. For a description of this idiom (הנה נא) in biblical Hebrew, see Joüon-Muraoka, *A Grammar of Biblical Hebrew*, §105 c, d.

52 The word rendered "to raise" (אומן) has connotations of fostering or surrogacy. In biblical Hebrew, a nurse is אומנת and Mordecai is called Esther's אמן ("foster father"; Est 2:7—

ובכן הנה נא עצרני

(ז) הִנֵּה נָא נֶ**אֱ**לַמְתִּי מֵ**א**וֹמֶן

הִנֵּה נָא נִ**בְ**לֵיתִי מִ**בֵּ**ן

הִנֵּה נָא נִ**גְ**רַעְתִּי מִ**גֶּ**יזַע

הִנֵּה נָא נִ**דְ**חֵיתִי מִ**דֶּ**גֶל

הִנֵּה נָא נֶ**הֱ**מַמְתִּי מֵ**ה**וֹד

הִנֵּה נָא נֱ**וֹ**תַצְתִּי מִ**וָּ**ולֶד

הִנֵּה נָא נִ**זְ**רֵיתִי מִ**זֶּ**רַע

הִנֵּה נָא נֶ**חְ**דַּלְתִּי מֵ**ח**וֹתֶל

הִנֵּה נָא נִ**טְ**רַפְתִּי מִ**טָּ**ף

הִנֵּה נָא נִיתְיָיאַשְׁתִּי מִיּוֹנֵק

הִנֵּה נָא נִי**כְ**רַתִּי מִ**כָּ**אן

הִנֵּה נָא נִ**לְ**חַצְתִּי מִי**לֶּ**חַ

R cites this verse). The term is used here for the sake of the acrostic and refers to Sarai's desire for biological offspring.

53 This language inverts the image of a stump that experiences renewed life in Isa 11:1 (cited by **R**).

54 Jer 51:34 (**R**).

55 Ezek 16:4 (**R**).

56 Literally, "I have been oppressed by salt/dryness." The implication is that Sarah regards herself as not only barren but unattractive. **B2** connects this with *b. BM* 87a, "Rabbi Ḥisda said: After [Sarah's] flesh was worn and the wrinkles multiplied, [her] flesh was rejuvenated, the wrinkles were smoothed out, and beauty returned to its place."

Commentary

The most compelling aspect of this poem is the figure of Sarai, both the personality Yannai constructs for her and the way he constructs it. She is simultaneously weak and strong: "weak" in the sense of being full of doubt, anxiety, grief, even bitterness; and "strong" in the sense of being bold, assertive, and proactive. She is tested and tests; she despairs and hopes. By depicting Sarai as such a complex character, Yannai amplifies the personality already present in the biblical narrative. At the same time, the matriarch here is more than merely an expanded version of her biblical counterpart. In the liturgical and exegetical context of the *qedushta*, Sarai becomes a voice for her long hoped-for offspring, the community of Israel. Many of Yannai's embellishments of Sarai's personality are paralleled in rabbinic aggadah, but what is most striking in this piyyut is the narrative and emotional arc of the poem as a whole. Complaint gives way to silence, and hope succumbs to despair, but not forever. Sarai's character is not static; during the course of the poem, she articulates a range of often conflicting human emotions.[57]

The first poem, as expected, sets the stage, delineating the two key elements of the story: Sarai's barrenness and her decision to employ Hagar, her Egyptian handmaid, as a remedy for her plight. Throughout the *magen*—and, in fact, repeatedly throughout the poem—Yannai evokes and inverts the language of the Song of Songs. The language of chastity from the biblical poem ("a garden locked…a spring sealed," quoted from Song 4:12) appears here as a wry descriptor of Sarai's infertile womb. A maiden's virtue becomes a wife's despair. Sarai does not suffer in silence, however. Her reaction—"she cried out and knocked upon the latches of the lock" (line 7)—echoes Song 5:2 ("Hark, my beloved knocks: `Open to me, my sister, my love, my dove, my perfect one...'"), but with a gender reversal: she knocks upon His door. Finally, the quotation from Song 2:14 in the list of verses following the *magen* suggests that Sarai's angry, despairing plea is precisely what God wishes to hear—an idea developed throughout the piyyut. From this first poem, the loving, reassuring tone of the intertexts

57 For a thorough and sophisticated study of this piyyut (and also Yannai's *qedushta* for Gen 15:1), particularly from the perspective of gender theory, see the essay by Ophir Münz-Manor, "All About Sarah: Questions of Gender in Yannai's Poems on Sarah's (And Abraham's) Barrenness," *Prooftexts* 26:3 (Fall 2006): 344–74.

provide a counterpoint to Sarai's anxiety. The congregation—Sarai's descendents—experience Sarai's desperation while consoled by an awareness she lacked; in fact, the first word of the piyyut gives away the game and calls her "mother." The transition to the benediction, with its reference to sons, likewise hints at the happy ending that awaits the future matriarch.

The *magen* (Poem One) narrates Sarai's predicament; in the *meḥayyeh* (Poem Two), we hear her voice directly, as she explains her planned resolution to Abram. In this unit, Sarai is forthright, even courageous—despair is not the same as despondency—but there is also a bleakness implicit in her resolve. As in the biblical text, her plan arises out of desperation; in the poem, Yannai hints at the disruption of the couple's married life. In describing Abram's reaction, Yannai uses the language of optimism: "The father listened to she-who-would-bear // Perhaps to find hope" (lines 9–10), but in her response—"There is a time for bearing // but I have been kept from bearing" (lines 11–12), we hear flintiness. The intertexts are, in this poem, more enigmatic than in the first. Sarai is praised as a women of valor (Prov 31:10), and the quotation from Psalms cautions against superficial negative judgments; but the quotation from Job—"whatever He shuts against a man cannot be opened" (12:14)— dampens the mood. Sarai has knocked upon the door but, this verse implies, it may not be *her* door that He opens. The matriarch has made a bold but difficult choice, choosing the path of righteousness but not necessarily joy.

Any concession to despair vanishes in the *meshallesh* (Poem Three), where Yannai transforms Sarai's trial into a national allegory. Stepping out of the biblical narrative, the poet directly compares the matriarch to the Land of Israel. When he shifts from Sarai's desperate resolution in the past to Zion's dire straits in the present, Yannai's mood becomes wholly confident. The previous two poems hinted at hope, conveying a fundamental optimism that rings true because the drama's conclusion is well known. In the third unit, Yannai translates this confidence into the future tense: just as Sarai, unable to perceive her happy destiny, experienced moments of anguish, so, too, Zion may appear doomed and bereft; and just as Sarai's end was happy, so will Zion's be. The conclusion of the present moment is, in fact, also known; it just has yet to be experienced.

The joyful "Hallelujah" of Ps 113:9, which concludes the *meshallesh*, tempers what might otherwise be the most heartbreaking passage in the poem: Sarai's lament in Poem Four. In this poem, Sarai's outcry (mentioned in the first poem, suppressed in the second) is articulated. When speaking to

Abram in the *meḥayyeh*, Sarai is curt and to the point; addressing God in Poem Four, she pours out her heart, voicing her fears and anxieties, articulating the deeper plan behind the Hagar scheme (to test Abram's fertility), and affirming, for all her protest, her piety. Now that she knows Abram can father a child, Sarai beseeches God for a child of her own. God wished to hear her voice—or so the quotation from Song 2:14 suggests—and now she speaks. Her voice, while aggrieved, can be heard clearly and strongly.

Yannai articulates the dynamic between Sarai and God more explicitly in the *asiriyyah* (Poem Five), explicating motives previously only hinted at by context and intertext. Childlessness for both Abram and Sarai is presented as a test, and the correct response is prayer: recalling Song 2:14, "[God] yearned for their prayer and the entreaty of their words" (line 10). God's dealings with Sarai—He confirms that Abram will become a father but does not yet tell Sarai that she will become a mother, and this behavior is explained in terms of keeping Sarai from becoming haughty—may seem cruel and off-putting to modern readers, but Sarai's persistence in her faith and good works *despite* God's silence (and Abram's) underscores her merit. As Yannai crafts the story in this poem, Sarai—in all other ways Abram's equal—accrues additional merit through additional tests. This poem, which most fully articulates the divine perspective, indicates that Sarai's complaints in the previous poems are valid: God has, in fact, closed her womb, for His sake, and for hers. Thus she acts with piety despite a lack of explanation.

In Poem Six, Yannai knits together a welter of themes. The opening stanza summarizes the problem and its resolution: evoking the woman from the Song of Songs once again, Sarai is paradoxically beautiful and barren: "a heap of wheat" is transformed in the first stich from an image of ripe roundness to withered desiccation. The second line, however, anticipates the end: as a reward for her virtues, she is granted a child. The rest of the poem continues this alternation, veering between recollections of her youth (even before her birth: "she was meant for Abram // while they were yet in their mothers' wombs," lines 5–6) and anticipation of her future as a mother ("and in the end, her wish was granted," line 44). Throughout the poem, Yannai juxtaposes Sarai's physical and moral virtues (her beauty, her righteousness, her propriety as a wife) with acknowledgment of her well- deserved happy ending. Counterbalancing both motifs, however, the poet gives clear voice to both her yearning and her suffering: she is wise but jealous and her insightfulness increases her anguish. It is not that she lacks negative feelings, but that she overcomes them. The motif of Sarai's suffering increases in the final three stanzas of the poem: Hagar is a "rival" (line 36) to whom Sarai submits; Sarai is consumed by jealousy and questions her lack of a reward (lines 37–38); her spirit "aches" (line 39); and in the face of her handmaid's taunt, Sarai—previously so articulate—falls silent (line 41). Even in the midst of these dark lines, however, the poet reaffirms her happy destiny: "at ninety she was granted relief" (line 20); "and in the end, her wish was granted" (line 44). The seesawing emotions of this unit recreate the uneven, ambivalent experience of the matriarch. She is certain of her righteousness and unclear on why she suffers, but her fate is confronted with fortitude, and in the end, she receives her reward. She triumphs over herself—a struggle the poet conveys by vacillating among her diverse experiences as he builds towards her eventual reward.

The language of Poem Six connects back to the vocabulary of the *magen*. The vocabulary of biblical wisdom literature textures the poem, and once again, the Song of Songs is inverted, its rhetoric of yearning employed to give voice to Sarai's despair. The phrase "like a bundle of myrrh He binds me" (line 14) alludes to Song 1:13 but transforms the intimacy of the biblical text into one of constraint and restriction. What should be a bond of love has become, instead, bondage to infertility. The potent allusions add depth to the drama of the poem, and help weave the piece into a single whole.

The final preserved poem is fragmentary—the first half of a *rahit*. With this poem, Yannai has shifted back once again to a tone of lamentation. Each stich articulates Sarai's hopelessness in a new way. We can imagine that the next poem—presumably a second *rahit*—would contain a divine response to her fears, and that the poem would end on a hopefully, reassuring note, anticipating the birth of Isaac and the future of the Jewish people. And yet, it is somehow fitting that this poem breaks off where it does. As often as Yannai acknowledges Sarai's eventual happiness, he does not shy away from letting her voice her fears, her jealousy, and her complaints. She is not a stoic, a patient martyr to her fate. She has opinions, yearnings, and sufficient insight (and courage) to understand and assert that her barrenness cannot be punishment.[58] God loves to hear her voice, even when it may seem less than sweet. This synthesis of two ideas—the righteous complaint as a yearned for voice—combine powerfully in the

58 Sarai's bold voice is a fitting counterpart to Abraham's insistence on both compassion and justice in the *qedushta* for Gen 15:1.

context of prayer. Like Sarai, Yannai's congregants may wonder at their current state. Do they deserve exile? Will their hopes for restoration be fufilled? Must they bear the taunts of lesser people who, for mysterious reasons, seem favored with power? Has their hope withered? In this poem, the community is told that they need not keep silent. God is שומע תפילה, He who hears prayer. Through Sarai, we hear the voice of the people, raised in hope against despair, lifted sweetly, if plaintively, to God.

But only through Yannai do we hear any divine response. Although Yannai recalls God's words to Abram (Poem Five, line 19), and God speaks to the community through the intertexts, He never speaks directly to Sarai, either in the biblical text or in the piyyut. Her merit comes, in part, from her ultimately pious resolve in the face of divine silence. And this divine silence (at least in the surviving poem), combined with the poem's abrupt conclusion, leaves the reader with a lingering lack of resolution. Amid the welter of Sarai's emotions—her highs and lows, her hopes and fears—lingers a question: Why does God not answer her? Where, in the present tense, is the voice of God?

Qedushta for Genesis 17:1 בראשית יז:א

"When Abram was 90 years old" ויהי אברם בן תשעים

In this poem, Yannai exalts the commandment of circumcision, both dramatizing the commandment's origin and exploring its enduring significance. As Yannai presents it, circumcision is not merely a test of Abraham's devotion to God; it is, literally, the embodiment of the covenant. Indeed, for many people (from biblical times to the present day), circumcision is the identifier of Jewish males *par excellence*. A complex ritual made more complicated by its symbolism, the act of *berit milah* provides Yannai with a pretext for meditating at length on the covenant between God and Israel: its challenges and its pain, but also its joy and rewards.

(5)[1] Happy are they who despise the foreskin and choose circumcision;
for despised is the foreskin and chosen is circumcision
Despite all the commandments the ancestor fulfilled while still with his foreskin
he was not considered perfect until he circumcised his foreskin[2]
So, too, when commanded that he should cut?
He stood, amazed:[3] from what limb to cut[4]
You granted him insight to understand based on the trees of the field:
A man, himself, is like the tree of the field
A tree is pruned from the place where it brings forth fruit
so too a man is pruned from the place where he brings forth fruit[5]
So he steeled himself and prevailed over himself
and the foreskin of his flesh he excised from his flesh
He sacrificed his inclination to his Maker
and like with his neck…on account of his suffering
The ornamental seal, forever upon him, was cut
as an eternal [law][6], an eternal covenant with him was cut
Before he was circumcised, when the Rock would speak
he[7] would fall upon his face, out of fear of the Speaker
(But on) the day he was circumcised, he arose at the heavenly voice's word to him
and was speaking with Him as a man speaks with his friend

---

1 The final five lines of the *asiriyyah* are absent from **R** but included both in the *Ma'agarim* version and in Shalom Spiegel, *Fathers of Piyyut*, 53–55.

2 This is an anti-Christian polemic which rejects the Christian view that Abraham was "saved" without circumcision, based on his faith alone (see Paul's interpretation of Gen 15:6 in Rom 4). Rabbinic tradition considers Abraham imperfect until his circumsion. Consider the tradition preserved in *TargPsJ* to Gen 17:1: "Worship Me *and be perfect in your flesh*." The poet builds on the juxtaposition of the command to circumcise with the second half of the verse, "And [the Lord] said to him, `I am the Almighty God; walk before me, and be perfect.'"

3 *TargPsJ* to Gen 17:17 and the Christian poet Ephrem (commenting on the Peshitta's literal translation of the verse) likewise describe Abraham as "amazed" rather than as "laughing" (as in the biblical text). See S. Brock, "Jewish Traditions in Syriac Sources," *Journal of Jewish Studies* 30 (1979): 212–32.

4 The word rendered here as "cut" is from the root ג-ז-ר, which can also acquire the meaning of "circumcise" and "decree' (*rahit*, lines 5–6) in this context. I have translated the phrase usually rendered "to make a covenant" in its literal sense of "to cut a covenant" in

(ה) **אַ**שְׁרֵי מוֹאֲסֵי עָרְלָה וּבוֹחֲרֵי מִילָה
כִּי מְאוּסָה עָרְלָה וּבְחוּרָה מִילָה
בְּכָל מִצְוֹת אֲשֶׁר עָשׂ אָב וְהוּא בְעָרְלָתוֹ

לֹא נִמְצָא שָׁלֵם עַד שֶׁמָּל עָרְלָתוֹ
גַּם בְּעֵת נִגְזַר עָלָיו כִּי יִגְזוֹר
צָג תָּמֵיהַּ מֵאֵיזֶה אֵבֶר לִגְזוֹר
דֵּעָה הִשְׂכַּלְתּוֹ לְהָבִין מֵעֵץ הַשָּׂדֶה
כִּי הָאָדָם עֵץ הַשָּׂדֶה
הָעָרְלַת הָעֵץ מִמְּקוֹם פֵּירוֹתָיו
וְעָרְלַת אָדָם מִמְּקוֹם פֵּירְיוֹתָיו
וְהִגְבִּיר עַצְמוֹ וְגָבַר בְּעַצְמוֹ
וְעָרְלַת בְּשָׂרוֹ חָתַךְ מִבְּשָׂרוֹ
זָבַח יִצְרוֹ לִפְנֵי יוֹצְרוֹ
וּכְמוֹ בְצַוָּארוֹ ש..טר בְּצַעֲרוֹ
חוֹתָם נוֹיי עֲדֵי עַד בְּעַדוֹ נִכְרַת
... עוֹלָם בְּרִית עוֹלָם עִמּוֹ נִכְרַת
טֶרֶם אֲשֶׁר מָל הָיָה צוֹר מְדַבֵּר
וְנוֹפֵל עַל פָּנָיו מֵאֵימַת הַדָּבָר
יוֹם אֲשֶׁר מָל קָם בְּבַת קוֹל דְּבָרוֹ

וְהָיָה מְדַבֵּר בּוֹ כְּאָדָם לַחֲבֵירוֹ

---

this piyyut to highlight the connections between the national-legal-spiritual covenant and its physical manifestation in *berit milah*.

5 According to *TanḥB Lekh Lekha* 27, Abraham didn't know which part of his body was implicated in the command to circumcise, so God hinted to him through the use of the term "I will multiply you" (*arbeh*) in Gen 17:2; following that lead, Abraham make an analogy to the laws concerning fruit trees in Lev 19:23. **R** cites multiple other sources, including *GenR* 46:4, *LevR* 25:6, *Tanḥ Lekh Lekha* 18, and others. *GenR* 46:4 nicely highlights the parallels between this piyyut and midrashic rhetoric: "R. Huna said in Bar Kappara's name: Abraham pondered [God's command] and drew an inference: *ʿorlah* (foreskin) is said here (Gen 17:11), and *ʿorlah* occurs in reference to a tree (Lev 19:23): just as *ʿorlah* in the case of trees refers to the place where it yields fruit, so *ʿorlah* employed in reference to man means the member which produces offspring [fruit]." By implication, circumcision will result in fatherhood. Yannai's line distills this basic analogical reasoning down to its essence, stripped of prooftexts and discursive reasoning.

6 Lacuna filled by Spiegel (p. 55) as "לחוק עולם".

7 Abraham

(6) …

And thus: "And I will establish My covenant[8] *between Me and you"*

(7) *A covenant:* with him You confirmed
You bound him, You taught (him)[9]
A covenant: by it You made him pure
through it You made him strong
A covenant: You circumcised his member
cuttings of proud waters (in return) You decreed[10]
A covenant: of words (of) his (covenant) You spoke
the freedom offspring You secured[11]
A covenant: his splendor You adorned
it was his path, and You laid it straight[12]
A covenant: for his testimony You made enduring
the fragrant formal rite[13] You fixed
A covenant: You linked its merit to him
to his descendents You gave this gift
A covenant: his wound You bound
a seal of life[14] You engraved in his flesh
A covenant: his purity You pressed (into his flesh)
his buffeted exiles You give root
A covenant: at his loins You became one
Your hand keeping his hand steady[15]
A covenant: for his glory You cut
with his children crowned You also wrote (a contract)
A covenant: with him You joined[16]

---

8 Fundamental to this unit is the use of "covenant" (*berit*) as shorthand for "covenant of circumcision" (*berit milah*).

9 Taking אילפתה from the Aramaic root for "educated" (א-ל-ף as in *ulpan*).

10 As a reward for Abraham's merit in fulfilling the command to circumcise himself, God parted the waters of the Red Sea for his descendents. On the image of "proud waters," see Job 38:11 and Ps 89:10 (**B1**). According to *Mekhilta Beshallaḥ* 4 (cited by **R**), God cut the sea into twelve parts (hence the plural, "cuttings"). The word rendered "circumcised" is *gazarta*; the word rendered "cuttings" is *gezarim*; and the word rendered "decreed" is *gizarta*all from the root ג-ז-ר.

11 **R** notes Fleischer's citation of *m. Avot* 6:2, "No one is free (בן חורין) except he who engages in Torah and *mitzvot*."

12 The language of this stich depends in part on Isa 28:25 (**B1**).

13 This appears to allude to the custom of burning incense as part of the circumcision ceremony; see also *GenR* 47:7 and *SongR* 4:6 (**B1**).

(ו) ...

ובכן ואתנה בריתי ביני ובינך

(ז) בְּרִית **אִ**תּוֹ **אִ**ימַּנְתָּה

אִיזַּרְתָּה **אוֹ**תוֹ **אִ**ילַּפְתָּה

בְּרִית **בִּ**בְשָׂרוֹ **בֵּ**ירַרְתָּה

בָּהּ **בּ**וֹ **בָּ**חַרְתָּא

בְּרִית **גִּ**יוְיוֹ **גָּ**זַרְתָּה

גָּאון **גְּ**זָרִים **גִּ**יזַּרְתָּה

בְּרִית **דּ**וֹבְרוֹ **דִּ**יבַּרְתָּה

דְּרוֹר **דָּ**לִיּוֹתָיו **דִּ**יבַּקְתָּה

בְּרִית **ה**וֹדוֹ **הִ**ידַּרְתָּ

הִיא **הִ**ילּוּכוֹ **הִ**שְׁוֵיתָה

בְּרִית **וִ**יעוּדוֹ **וִ**יתַּקְתָּה

וֶסֶת **וְ**רָדָיו **וִ**יעַדְתָּה

בְּרִית **זְ**כוּתוֹ **זִ**ימַּנְתָּה

זַרְעוֹ **ז**ֹאת **זָ**בַדְתָּ

בְּרִית **חָ**לְיוֹ **חִ**יתַּלְתָּ

חוֹתַם **חַ**יִּים **חָ**קַקְתָּ

בְּרִית **טָ**הֳרוֹ **טָ**בַעְתָּ

טֵירוּף **טִ**לְטוּלוֹ **טָ**עַתָּה

בְּרִית **יְ**רֵכָיו **יִ**יחַדְתָּה

יְדַךְ **יָ**דוֹ **יָ**שַׁרְתָּ

בְּרִית **כְּ**בוֹדוֹ **כָּ**רַתָּה

כְּלוּלָיו **כֵּ**ן **כָּ**תַבְתָּ

בְּרִית **ל**וֹ **לִ**ימַּדְתָּ

14 See the interpretations of Ezek 16:6"In your blood, live!"in *Mekh. Pisḥah* 5; *ExodR* 19:5 (**B1**).

15 See *SongR* 4:15, "Rabbi Abin said in Rabbi Simeon's name: God assisted Abraham with His right hand to circumcise him, as it says, `You made a covenant [i.e., circumcision] with [i.e. assisting] him' (Neh 9:8)." The Nehemiah verse refers to "cutting a covenant" in its context, but here it is read in more literal terms. This interpretation is rooted in the use of the *nifal* in Gen 17:11, which could be rendered as a reflexive ("you shall circumcise yourselves") but more commonly understood as a passive ("you shall be circumcised")if Abraham was, passively, circumcised, someone else must have actually done the rite. God's participation in Abraham's *bris* is derived from the principle that only one who is circumcised/pure may circumcise another. Since Abraham was the first to circumcise, God had to assist him in the operation. It was also probably an indication of moral support.

16 On the translation of ל-מ-ד with the connotation of `cling, join,' see Zulay, *`Iyyunei lashon*, s.v. למד (p. 206).

and his offspring forever will You attend
A covenant: from him You pruned,
the blemish from his body You cut back
A covenant: everlasting You established[17] with him
forever with awesome wonders You will keep (his descendents) safe
A covenant: his sign You set
a mystery everlasting You laid out[18]
A covenant: with him You made
forever and ever You linked Yourself to him
A covenant: its wonders You worked
a command for his `yielding of fruit' You pronounced[19]
A covenant: for his distinction You fashioned
the splendor of righteousness You stored away[20]
A covenant: his statute You established
before "a Voice" You had yet proclaimed[21]
A covenant: by this sign You exalted
the pleasure of his scent You sent wide[22]
A covenant: his welfare You looked after
his praiseworthy (new) name You praised
A covenant: his perfection You established
in the path of life eternal You led his children's steps

(8) His right hand You grasped his foreskin You clipped[23]

---

17 **R** cites Gen 17:7, "And I will establish my covenant between me and you and your seed after you in their generations for an everlasting covenant, to be a God to you, and to your seed after you."

18 That is, God revealed the mystery of circumcision to Abraham and his descendents. See *Tanḥ Lekh Lekha* 19, which uses Ps 25:14 to interpret the lemma (**R**).

19 This stich can be understood in two ways. The first interpretation, given by **R**, understands it as God giving a command to Abraham that is incumbent upon his children ("fruit") as well. The other meaning, offered by **B1**, understands the line as alluding to the specific procedures of circumcision (*peri`ah*, punning on *peri*, "fruit"), which includes uncovering the *glans*, the "source of fruitfulness," tearing the membrane, and then pulling it down. Bronznick's interpretation suggests that Yannai's understanding of this story is different from those aggadot that assert that "Abraham was not commanded to tear..." (*DeutR* 6).

20 For the first stich, **R** cites *SongR* 1:64, which specifies the distinction of circumcision ("Just as the dove is distinguished [by its coloring], so Israel is distinguished through [abstention from] shaving, through circumcision, through fringes"). The splendor (and honor) of circumcision was "stored away" until it was time to bestow it upon Abraham. **B1**

לְנִינָיו לָעַד לִוִּיתָה
בְּרִית מֶנּוּ מָלְתָּה
מוּם מִגּוּפוֹ מָנַעְתָּה
בְּרִית נִצְחוֹ נָתַתָּה
נֶצַח נוֹרָאוֹת נוֹסַסְתָּה
בְּרִית סִימָנוֹ שַׂמְתָּה
סוֹד סֶלָה סָדַרְתָּ
בְּרִית עִמּוֹ עָשִׂיתָ
עַד עוֹלָמִים עֲרַסְתָּה
בְּרִית פִּלְאוֹ פָּעַלְתָּ
פֶּקֶד פְּרִי פָּתַחְתָּה
בְּרִית צִיּוּנוֹ צָרְתָּה
צְבִי צְדָקָה צָפַנְתָּה
בְּרִית קִיּוּמוֹ קוֹמַמְתָּ
קֶדֶם קוֹל קָרָאתָה
בְּרִית רִישׁוּמוֹ רִיבִּיתָה
רִיצּוּי רֵיחוֹ רָוִיתָה
בְּרִית שְׁלֹמוֹ שָׁעִתָּה
שְׁבַח שְׁמוֹ שִׁיבַּחְתָּה
בְּרִית תֻּומּוֹ תַּתָּה
תֶּחִי תוֹלְדוֹתָיו תִּרְגַּלְתָּה

(ח) בִּימִינוֹ תָּמַכְתָּה וְעָרְלָתוֹ חָתַכְתָּה

adds citations for *TanḥB Lekh Lekha* 25; *GenR* 46:3. "Righteous" is also an epithet for Abraham, as we have seen in previous piyyutim. So circumcision is a sign of righteousness in its own right—a commandment that carries its own reward—but it is also a sign of being of the lineage of Abraham, the righteous one.

21 The poet here alludes to the fact that circumcision is a commandment that predates the giving of the Torah (a fact alluded to by the phrase, "a Voice [i.e., Torah, revelation] that You proclaimed," which is rooted in Deut 4:12 [cited by **B1**], "And the Lord spoke to you out of the midst of the fire; you heard the sound of the words, but saw no form; you only heard *a voice*").

22 **R** connects this with *GenR* 47:7, "Rabbi Aibu said: When Abraham circumcised those that were born in his house, he set up a hillock of foreskins; the sun shone upon them and they putrefied, and their odor ascended to the Lord like sweet incense. God then said: `When My children lapse into sinful ways, I will remember that odor to their favor and be filled with compassion for them.'"

23 Yannai here employs the language and imagery from halakhah of the father circumcising his son. Just as Abraham will circumcise Ishmael and Isaac, God (his "Father"in the same way that Abraham becomes the father of all subsequent converts) circumcises him.

his covenant You cut and his circumcision You did twofold[24]
His blood You cleansed[25] and like a father You took delight[26]
his weakness You strengthened and his suffering You made weak[27]
and with him You covenanted and a statute You engraved upon him
You taught and You entrusted and You decided[28] and You swore:
"From now on, My lover are you!" For on that day You circumcised him
Happiness was before You[29] and joy in the place of Your camp;
delight dwells among the angels and they say, this one to that,
"Sing to God and rejoice before Him mightily"[30]—
"Those who exult in joy"[31] continually and who celebrate together in joy
and who open their mouths in purity and respond, the one to the other,
in holiness" *As it is written: "And one called to the other…"*

(9) With trust, with faith, and with obedience the father was drawn to You
and his sons answer and say:
Holy, holy, holy is the Lord of Hosts! The whole earth is filled with His glory!
"*Holy*"—are they who trust in You
"*Holy*"—are those who believe in You
"*Holy*"—are those who hearken to You
Holy, holy, holy is the Lord of Hosts! The whole earth is filled with His glory!
"*Holy*"—when at the age of forty-eight he trusted in you
and went off into exile[32]
"*Holy*"—when at the age of seventy-five he believed in You
and walked in Your ways
"*Holy*"—when at the age of ninety-nine he hearkened You
and circumcised himself
Holy, holy, holy is the Lord of Hosts! The whole earth is filled with His glory!
"*Holy*"—from the *Ḥayyot*;
"*Holy*"—from the *Ofanim*;
"*Holy*"—from the *Cherubim* *… The one towards the other…*

---

24 See *j. Shabb.* 87b (which contradicts *b. Yev.* 71b), cited by **R**. The Palestinian tradition teaches (based on the infinitive absolute construction in Gen 17:13) that Abraham was given the two-fold circumcision procedure in which the corona of the penis is revealed at circumcision. The Babylonian tradition states that this method was not given to the Israelites until the time of Joshua. See note above.

25 See Isa 4:4 (**B2**).

26 Isa 63:12; Jer 31:19 (**B1**).

27 **B1** notes the appealing parallelism of these two phrases: Weakness God makes strong, while strong affliction He makes weak.

וּבְרִיתוֹ כָּרַתָּה וּמִילָתוֹ פָּרַעְתָּה
וְדָמָיו הִידַּחְתָּה וּכְאָב אוֹתוֹ שִׁעֲשַׁעְתָּה
וְרִפְיוֹנוֹ חִיזַּקְתָּה וְצַעֲרוֹ רִפֵּאתָה
וְעִמּוֹ קִיַּמְתָּ וְחוֹק לוֹ חָקַקְתָּה
וְהִתְנֵיתָה וְהִבְטַחְתָּה וְגָזַרְתָּה וְנִשְׁבַּעְתָּה
מֵעַתָּה אֹהֲבִי אָתָּה כִּי בַּיּוֹם אֲשֶׁר אוֹתוֹ מַלְתָּה
שִׂמְחָה הָיְתָה לְפָנֶיךָ וְחֶדְוָה בִּמְקוֹם מַחֲנֶיךָ
וְגִילָה בֵּין מַלְאָכֶיךָ וְנָמוּ זֶה לָזֶה
סוֹלּוּ לָאֵל וְעִלְזוּ לְפָנָיו בְּחֵיל
הַמְסַלְּדִים תָּמִיד בְּחִילָה וּמְסַלְסְלִים יַחַד בְּגִילָה
וּפוֹתְחִים פִּיהֶם בְּטָהֳרָה וְעוֹנִים לָז לְלָז בִּקְדֻשָּׁה
ככתוב וקרא זה אל זה

(ט) בְּבִטָּחוֹן וּבְאוֹמֶן וּבְשֶׁמַע נִגְרַר לָךְ אָב
וּבָנָיו יַעֲנוּ וְיֹאמְרוּ
קדוש קדוש קדוש יי צבאות מלא כל הארץ כבודו
קָדוֹשׁ מִבּוֹטְחֵי בָךְ
קָדוֹשׁ מִמַּאֲמִינֵי בָךְ
קָדוֹשׁ מִשּׁוֹמְעֵי לָךְ
קדוש קדוש קדוש יי צבאות מלא כל הארץ כבודו
קָדוֹשׁ בֶּן אַרְבָּעִים שָׁנָה וּשְׁמֹנָה בָּטַח בָּךְ
וְגָלָה
קָדוֹשׁ בֶּן שִׁבְעִים וַחֲמִשָּׁה הֶאֱמִין בָּךְ
וְהָלַךְ
קָדוֹשׁ בֶּן תִּשְׁעִים וָתֵשַׁע שָׁמַע לָךְ
וָמָל
קדוש קדוש קדוש מלא כל הארץ כבודו
קָדוֹשׁ מחיה
קָדוֹשׁ מאופן
קָדוֹשׁ מכרוב לעומתן

---

28 "Decided" attempts to reflect the pun on ג-ז-ר, both "to cut" (as in "decisive") and "decree."

29 Yannai refers here to the religious duty to celebrate at the time of circumcision (**B1**). See *Tanḥ Ḥayyei Sarah* 7 and others.

30 Ps 68:5 (**R**).

31 Or, "in strength." From Job 6:10 (**R**); this is generally construed as "those who exalt in anguish," but **R** notes that elsewhere it means "joy" as translated here. In this instance, it functions as a descriptor of Israel.

32 The idea that Abraham was forty eight at the time when he "recognized his Creator"

Commentary

This is not, strictly speaking, an example of a "circumcision poem"; circumcision poems are a medieval genre of poetry, and unlike the present text, they were composed for recitation at the actual ceremony of the *berit milah*.[33] That said, this composition resembles what will come to be called "circumcision poems," and it is tempting to connect it to Jewish ritual practices in Late Antiquity. In particular, rabbinic sources roughly contemporary with Yannai mention that poems were recited at the circumcision of Elisha ben Abuyah. According to one tradition, Elisha is reported to have said: "My father, Abuyah, was one of the notable men of his generation, and at my circumcision he invited all the notables of Jerusalem, including Rabbi Eliezer and Rabbi Joshua. After they had eaten and drunk, they sang: some [singing] ordinary songs and others alphabetical acrostics" (*RuthR* 6:2). Although it is a life-cycle event on par with weddings and funerals, the ceremony of circumcision may not strike modern readers as a poetic ritual. Yet for many centuries it was one of the most important events in both communal and familial Jewish life. The composition and recitation of poetry reflected the centrality of this uniquely Jewish rite.[34]

The present poem embellishes the theme of circumcision (*berit milah*, literally "covenant of circumcision") not because of a life-cycle event of the poet's day, but because the Torah portion for the week introduces the rite of circumcision into the Jewish tradition. As such, it is perhaps fitting that this poem be understood as a kind of archetype of the liturgical poetry that celebrates the ritual itself. Understood as a prototypical circumcision poem, this work signifies both the creation and the continuity of Israel's covenant with God, simultaneously profoundly personal and public.

---

also occurs in *GenR* 30:9. Alternatively, some MSS lack the number "eight," which accords with the tradition in GenR 39:9 that Abraham was forty when God called him to "go forth" in Gen 12:1.

33 However, Shalom Spiegel notes that a fragment of this piyyut was preserved in a South African circumcision poem (*Fathers of Piyyut*, 56). The most famous circumcision poems were composed a millennium after Yannai by the 17th century Yemenite poet, Shalem Shabazi.

34 Circumcision itself is not, of course, unique to Jews; but infant circumcision is definitively associated with Judaism. For a cross-cultural anthropological study of Jewish circumcision, see H. Goldberg, *Jewish Passages: Cycles of Jewish Life* (Berkeley: University of California Press, 2003), 28–76.

The essence of this poem can be found in the range of meanings associated with the Hebrew root ג-ז-ר: to cut, decree, decide, and (although it is not the standard verb for the act in Hebrew) circumcise.[35] For example, in the opening lines of the first extant poem, we find its connotations of "command" and "cut/circumcise" juxtaposed: "So, too, when commanded (*nigzar*) that he should cut/circumcise (*yigzor*) // he stood amazed at the limb he was to cut/circumcise (*ligzor*)." As these translations imply, the root ג-ז-ר offers a semantic parallel to the root כ-ר-ת, "to cut," as in the idiom, "to cut a covenant" (see *rahit*, line 21). Circumcision quite literally embodies the covenant, by means of a cut; it is evidence of connection between God and Israel "sealed into the flesh" (to paraphrase the Grace After Meals). In Abraham's case, God directly participates in the cutting of the covenant by assisting in the circumcision, the way a father assists a son. Through various puns and repetitions, Yannai links key events—Abraham's call, the parting of the Red Sea, and Israel's ultimate redemption—to the covenant and its most personal manifestation. With deft humor, startling vividness, and profound gravity, Yannai places both the philosophical ideal and the physical reality at the center of Israel's existence.

While we lack the *meshallesh* of this *qedushta*—the one most likely to overtly refer to the poet's own historical context—the explicit and emphatic praise of circumcision, its status as *the* marker (*par excellence*) of God's covenant with Israel and male Jewish identity, and the reinforcement of its statutory, mandatory status should probably all be understood in the context of vigorous Christian repudiation (and denigration) of the practice from the time of Paul.[36] This opposition became more entrenched and virulent in subsequent centuries.[37] Judaism, however, retained and even

35 The standard Hebrew root for circumcision is מ-ל-ל, as in *milah*.

36 See Acts 15; Gal 5; and, noted above, Rom. 4. We have ample evidence that Jews and non-Jews alike considered circumcision one of the key identity markers of Judaism, despite the fact that it was not an exclusively Jewish practice. See Shaye Cohen, *The Beginnings of Jewishness* (Berkeley: U of California P, 1999) as well as his *Why Aren't Jewish Women Circumcised* (Berkeley: U of California P, 2005); and Louis Feldman, *Jew and Gentile in the Ancient World* (Princeton: Princeton UP, 1993).

37 For example, consider the words of Justin Martyr in his "Dialogue with Trypho" (2nd century C.E.): "The custom of circumcising the flesh, handed down from Abraham, was given to you [Jews] as a distinguishing mark, to set you off from other nations and from us Christians. The purpose of this was that you and only you might suffer the afflictions that are now justly yours; that only your land be desolated, and your cities ruined by fire, that the fruits of your land be eaten by strangers before your very eyes; that not one of you be permitted to enter your city of Jerusalem. Your circumcision of the flesh is the only mark by which you can certainly be distinguished from other men…"

emphasized the equation of "circumcision" with "covenant," as evident through the fact that a singular term is used for both: *berit*. The word "*berit*" (in Ashkenazic pronunciation, *bris*, the colloquial shorthand for the ritual of circumcision) is the theme-word of the *rahit*. The poem is a vigorous defense of a distinctive and definitive practice.

Another important, and related, motif in this poem is the paradoxical function of "cutting" as an act of "joining"(the English word "cleave" replicates the ambiguity). Circumcision may seem like an intensely personal act, but it is one primarily of communal significance. Thus cutting a piece of flesh joins the individual to his community. This implicit significance of *milah*, however, is not emphasized in the poem; instead, the poet dramatizes the intimate bond that circumcision creates with God. This motif finds its most powerful expression in the *rahit*, particularly in lines 19–20: "*A covenant*: at his loins You became one (ייחדתה) / Your hand keeping his hand steady." Similarly, several lines later, Yannai writes: "*A covenant*: ...forever and ever You linked Yourself to him" (line 32). The act of circumcision becomes not a test but a moment of profound, almost conjugal, intimacy between patriarch and deity. Abraham's physical act seals the act of "leaving and cleaving" that began in Genesis 12. The first test was enacted on a large scale: Abraham's radical and complete departure, family in tow, from "his father's house." Now, five chapters and decades later, the chosen test is intimate, requiring tremendous trust on Abraham's part and creating a bond between and individual and his God. The deity Himself participates in this intimate rite, and the sign of circumcision is the seal of the covenant that all Abraham's descendents will bear. The covenant of circumcision departs from (metaphorical) ways in which others bind themselves to God; it is not simply a vow or a sacrifice of another creature, but a potent ritual and sacrifice of the self. The act of cutting becomes an act of cleaving, a joining of God to both an individual and a community composed of similarly marked individuals. The rite of circumcision, the *berit milah*, so praised by Yannai, retains this paradoxical power and potent symbolism to the present day. The very difficulty, even strangeness, of the ritual—which still compels an echo of Abraham's amazement in many modern witnesses—has helped create its enduring significance.

Qedushta to Genesis 18:1 בראשית יח:א

"Then the Lord appeared to him" וירא אליו יי

The surviving fragments of this piyyut suggestively juxtapose themes and images, many of which resonate with the aggadic interpretations of Gen 18:1–2. In the first fragment, from the *asiriyyah*, we have an earthy depiction of Abraham confiding in his three visitors about the command of circumcision (the topic of the previous *qedushta*); the fragment of the *rahit* appears to describe the angelic visitation and Abraham's hospitality; and the surviving lines of the *silluq* depict the appearance and experience of the heavenly hosts as they assemble for prayer, with no explicit connection to the themes of the *sidra* beyond the prominence of angels in both.

(5) When You disclosed to him the command of circumcision,
(Abraham) disclosed to his companions his bafflement at circumcision[1]
He never rebelled[2] against any utterance of Your mouth
though now he took counsel with Eshkol, Aner, and Mamre
With utmost arrogance did Eshkol and Aner answer him
and concerning the snipping of skin they discouraged him
But `*avec le conseil sage et le bon sens'* did Mamre respond[3]
and at the grove of Mamre You appeared to him, while he was sitting
...

(7) ...
... fluttering wings ...
...
... I found...
And faithful of heart ...
... I was found
He uttered and entreated, "Please, fetch a little water"[4]
... to bathe in water ...[5]
... then I bathed you in water...[6]
He proclaimed, "Rest yourselves under the tree"[7]
... Each tree became verdant and ...
And glad tidings were brought and ... the tree had ...
And for the sake of sons in the wilderness He brought forth bread
... and You give bread
... offerings of bread ...

1 Lit., "the secret of his circumcision." The idea that Abraham conferred with his friends at this moment is absent from the biblical text. As **R** notes, the opening lines recall an aggadic tradition preserved in multiple midrashic sources, including *GenR* 42:8, *Tanḥ Vayera* 3; and *AggB* 19:3. The *GenR* version states: "`Now (Abraham) was dwelling in the groves of Mamre' (Gen 14:13)...And why was he called Mamre? Rabbi Azariah said in the name of Rabbi Judah: Because he scolded (*himrah*) Abraham. When the Holy One, blessed be He, commanded Abraham to circumcise himself, he went and took counsel with his three friends (Mamre, Eshkol, and Aner). Aner said to him: `You are already a hundred years old, yet you would inflict this pain upon yourself?' Eshkol said to him: `Why should you go and make yourself distinguishable to your enemies?' But Mamre said to him: `When did He not stand by you—in the fiery furnace, in famine, and in your war with the kings? Will you not obey Him, then, in this matter!' Said the Holy One, blessed be He, to him (Mamre): `You gave him good advice, to circumcise himself. By your life! I will reveal Myself

(ה) **אָ**ז בְּגַלּוֹתָךְ לוֹ חוֹק מִילָתוֹ
גִּילָה לְאֲהֲבָיו סוֹד מִילָתוֹ
בְּכָל אִמְרֵי פִּיךָ לֹא הָיָה מַמְרֶה
וְנִמְלַךְ בְּאֶשְׁכּוֹל עָנֵר וּמַמְרֵא
גְּבוֹהָה גְבוֹהָה אֶשְׁכֹּל וְעָנֵר עָנוּהוּ
וְעַל חֲתִיכַת בְּשָׂרוֹ הוֹנוּהוּ
דַּעַת עֵטָה וּטְעֵם מַמְרֵא לוֹ הֵשִׁיב
וּבְאֵלוֹנֵי מַמְרֵא נִרְאָה לוֹ וְהוּא יוֹשֵׁב
...

(ז) ... רוק רש..
... מְעוֹפְפִים בִּכְנָפַיִם
... ..עה כי ני..
... מָצָאתִי
וְנֶאֱמָן לֵב ל..
נִמְצֵאתִי ....
פֶּץ וְחִינֵּן יֻוקַּח נָא מְעַט מַיִם
... לְהַרְחִיץ בַּמַּיִם
ו.. ..א וְאֶרְחָצְךָ בַּמַּיִם
קָרָא וְהִשָּׁעֲנוּ תַּחַת הָעֵץ
... כָּל עֵץ רַעֲנָן וְיֵשׁ ... ..עֵץ
ובושר כ.. ..ו יֵשׁ לָעֵץ.
וּלְבָנָיו בַּמִּדְבָּר הוֹצִיא לֶחֶם
... אַתָּה נוֹתֵן לֶחֶם
... מי.. קוֹרְבָּנוֹת לֶחֶם ...

to him (Abraham) only in your (Mamre's) palace.' Hence it is written, And the Lord appeared unto him in the groves of Mamre (Gen 18:1)."

2 The word "rebelled" is *mamreh*

3 French used to represent the Aramaic, which would be rendered as, "with wise counsel and good sense." **B1** notes that the poet quotes Dan 2:14, perhaps to emphasize Mamre's identity as an Amorite (on the assumption that Amorites would have spoken Aramaic). See comment below.

4 Gen 18:4

5 Perhaps a reference to the merit Abraham acquired when he fetched waters for the divine messengers in Gen 18:3; see *GenR* 48:10, where it is stated that this bringing of water will result in Israel being blessed in terms of water (**R**).

6 Ezek 16:9

7 Gen 18:4

(8) And He appeared …
And He appeared:[8] in their wings, wind with …
And He appeared …
And He appeared …
And He appeared: the splendor of their eyes is like flashes of flames
And He appeared: their bodies, like the gleam of …[9]
And He appeared …
And He appeared: the music[10] of their voices … like the multitude ..
And He appeared: flying … sixty[11]
And He appeared …
And He appeared: with the appearance of lightning
And He appeared …
And He appeared: from mighty ones..
And He appeared: awesome ones and frightful ones and harsh ones
And He appeared: holy ones
And He appeared: completing their missions and not desisting
And thus …
And He appeared: … and wonders crowding …
And He appeared: a great host whispering
And He appeared: a still, small voice …[12]
And He appeared: running and returning and not resting
And He appeared: … to the ones who are made holy
And He appeared: … who crown and who hallow
… The One whose holiness is proclaimed …
… "*And the one called out …*"

8 The Maʾagarim text for this unit is superior to **R**. It is now clear that it contains both an acrostic and a refrain. It may be necessary to reclassify this unit as a *rahit*, which it strongly resembles.

9 The language describing the angels' appearance draws primarily upon the imagery of Ezek 1. If the word קדם appears in the stich (the MS is very faint), the phrase may also draw on Ps 119:148, "My eyes anticipate the watches of the night (קדמו עיני אשמורות), that I may meditate on your utterance;" the presence of that word would yield a translation something

(ח)

וַיֵּרָא [**א**] ... ..שים

וַיֵּרָא **בְ**כַנְפֵיהֶם רוּחַ בד.. ....

[וַיֵּרָא **ג**]

[וַיֵּרָא **ד**]

וַיֵּרָא **ה**וֹד עֵינֵיהֶם כְּלַפִּידֵי אִישִׁים

... **וּ**גְוִיָּתָם כְּעֵין ....

[וַיֵּרָא **ז**] ... ..שים

וַיֵּרָא **חַ**לֵּל קוֹלָם כַּהֲמוֹן ..שים

[וַיֵּרָא **ט**] ... ראשים

[וַיֵּרָא **י**]

וַיֵּרָא **כְּ**מַרְאֵה בָּזָק מְאֻוּשָּׁשִׁים

[וַיֵּרָא **ל**] ... ..שים

וַיֵּרָא **מִ**גְבוּרֹת.. ... ..שים

וַיֵּרָא **נוֹ**רָאִים וְאֵימִים וְקָשִׁים

[וַיֵּרָא **ס**] ... קְדֹשִׁים

וַיֵּרָא **עוֹ**שִׂים שְׁלִיחוּתָם וְלֹא מָשִׁים

וּבְכֵן...

וַיֵּרָא [**פ**]..אים וְנִיפְלָאוֹת רוֹחֲשִׁים

וַיֵּרָא **צְ**בָא גְדוֹלוֹת לוֹחֲשִׁים

וַיֵּרָא **קוֹ**ל דְּמָמָה דַקָּה ..שים

וַיֵּרָא **רָ**צִים וְשָׁבִים וְלֹא נוֹפְשִׁים

וַיֵּרָא [**ש**]... ..ים אֶל מְקוּדָּשִׁים

וַיֵּרָא [**ת**] ..ידים וּמַכְתִּירִים וּמַקְדִּישִׁים

... ... הַנִּיזְכָּר קָדוֹשׁ

... וקרא

---

like, "as the eye greets..." and refer to the act of beholding the angels rather than their specific visual appearance of the heavenly beings.

10 Taking חלל in the sense of playing a flute or other musical instrument; see 1 Kgs 1:40, והעם מחללים בחללים.

11 Reading this stich with **R**, who has "...וטסים...ששים" The Maʾagarim text would be rendered, "And He appeared: ... heads..."

12 1 Kgs 19:12, which describes a theophany to Elijah.

Commentary

As fragmentary as this poem is, the surviving lines are tantalizing. The complete *qedushta* must have been remarkable.

One simple, beautiful, but nigh-untranslatable moment in this poem is Yannai's playful use of Aramaic in line 7 of the *asiriyyah*.[13] The translation of that phrase relies on French in an attempt to create the same sense of *difference*. As noted by Bronznick, Yannai's decision to refer to Mamre's counsel in Aramaic (while the rest of the poem is in Yannai's typically artful Hebrew) may reflect a belief that Mamre, who is an Amorite according to the biblical text, spoke Aramaic. The poet may have indulged in this little bilingual flourish because the phrase appears in the biblical text of Daniel (a rich source of language and imagery for him in his *qedushta* to Gen 32:4) or because Aramaic (albeit a different dialect—Jewish Palestinian Aramaic) was the community's own vernacular. The phrase (*daʿat ʿiṭah u-ṭeʿim*) appears to have been chosen for its meaning and idiom; it does not contribute significantly to the sound-play of the line or poem overall. While it is possible that the missing parts of the poem contain more word-plays of this type, at present, the slip into Aramaic seems to be almost purely a glimmer of poetic wit, a brief and fleeting "insider's joke" rooted in language, Scripture, and exegesis.

Yannai's depiction of the angelic beings, while conveyed only fitfully by the fragmented text, engages with an even more intriguing topic. The *sidra* itself invites this focus—the enigmatic angelic (divine?) visitors are prominent characters in the story, and aggadic treatments of the passage show great interest in exploring its implicit angelology. Indeed, Yannai rarely overlooks an opportunity to explore the world of angels and to describe the heavenly realm; his fascination with angels—probably reflecting a more general interest in such matters—may well be another facet of the same cultural force that led to the creation of the *qedushta* itself. The *qedushta*, after all, builds up to the mystically-charged experience of joining the angels in prayer, as heaven and earth together recite the Qedushah.

Yannai's imagery in the *silluq* fragment is radiant and bold, drawing

13 Yannai rarely employs Aramaic in his poetry; the *r'hitim* in his *qedushta* for Gen 32:4 are a rare exception, but the Aramaic employed there is adapted directly from the biblical Aramaic of Daniel, as is this. See M. Sokoloff and J. Yahalom, "Aramaic Piyyutim from the Byzantine Period," *JQR* 75 (1985): 310. For more on Aramaic poetry, see the discussion in Chapter Three.

heavily on Ezek 1 as it describes how God manifests amid the angelic hosts. For all the luminosity of its language, it does not approach the mystical incantatory rapture of the *Hekhalot* or *Merkavah* texts, but neither is it precisely "tame." The poet instead creates the sensation of being in the presence of these beings: he opens with a description of beating wings and brilliant eyes, moves to their voices and overwhelming masses; and then describes them in terms of their dazzling and terrifying radiance. The composite experience of this piyyut is one of overwhelming numbers, noise, and light, all restless and rushing to and fro. The sound-picture Yannai creates is dynamic: he conveys the sensation of a tremendous hum generated by myriads of angels engaging in voiceless, obedient activity. The vivid language, appealing to multiple senses (visual, auditory, even tactile), draws the congregation almost physically into the experience of heavenly prayer.

The poet also introduces another kind of voice, one mentioned in the context of God's advent in 1 Kings 19:12: literally "a sound of thinnest whisper," more familiarly rendered as "a still, small voice." Here as in the biblical source, the paradoxical "sound of silence" seems to be the voice of God. As Yannai presents it, this voice arises from God's ceaseless response to those who call Him holy: angels and Israel. The hosts and Israel together proclaim God's holiness, crowning Him with prayers, and His voice answers, holiness for holiness. Those who hallow become holy.

Or so it seems. The poem is fragmentary, and its incomplete language tempting; much of the reconstruction is conjecture with optimism for mortar. Those cautions noted, the idea of the ceaseless, silent divine voice, however, has particular appeal in this poem. God revealed Himself to Abraham in multiple ways: in speech, in saying, and in vision. In the poet's time, and down to the present day, however, the divine is much harder to perceive. There is comfort and consolation in the idea that God's voice continues ceaselessly but silently, responsive and responding in a register that angels if not humans can hear. The act of prayer—ever an act of hope—is transformed from a monologue into a conversation, as angels, Jews, and God call out to each other.

Qedushta for Genesis 19:1 | בראשית יט:א

"Then came two angels" | ויבאו שני המלאכים

This piyyut explores the nature and function of the angelic beings central to the events of Genesis 18 and 19—a motif that attracted Yannai's attention in the *qedushta* for Gen 18, as well. In the surviving fragments of this poem, the poet describes the nature of angelic agency, both in general and in relation to the specific missions of each messenger. His depictions of the angels, while "conventional" within rabbinic angelology, remain dramatic and vivid, and Yannai's expansion of the biblical scene intensifies the sense of cosmic drama implicit beneath the surface of the story's events.

(1) Your ʾ*Erelim*, when he escorted …
… when You sent them, they buckled their gear
Mighty ones who, like lightning …
the appearance of the messengers…

The two (of them) going …
… Your word they do not alter
… You send and they hasten
… they seek…and they tarry

… when they did not see
noble ones[1] who appeared like men[2]
… yet like angels they appeared and they did not dissemble
[to do] their duty, they went to Sodom

As it is written: "Then came the two angels towards Sodom in the evening" (Gen 19:1)
And it is said: "He makes the winds His messengers, the fiery flames His servants" (Ps 104:4)
And it is said: "Praise Him, all His angels! Praise Him, all His hosts!" (Ps 148:2)
And it is said: "He sends forth His word to the earth; swiftly yet His utterance runs" (Ps 147:15)
…

(3) … Princes of Sodom
… Indeed You will restore us from our captivity[3]
…
… You will bring upon her terror at [even-]tide[4]

Please, God…

(4) … Angels of mercy, angels of … They hesitated for You, Lord …
… You will argue with those who honor haughtiness[5]

---

1 That is, angels.

2 *TargPsJ* and *TargN* to Gen 18:2 both render the Hebrew "three men" as "three angels in the form of men." See also *GenR* 50:2 (cited by **R**): "Here you call them angels, but earlier they were termed men? Earlier, when the Shekhinah was above them, they were men; but as soon as the Shekhinah departed from them they assumed the form of angels. Rabbi Levi said: To Abraham, whose [moral] strength was great, they looked like men; but to Lot they

(א) אֶרְאֶלֶיךָ כְּלִיוָּוה ...
... לשא.. כִּשְׁלַחְתָּם הֵם חָגְרוּ ...
גִּיבּוֹרִים אֲשֶׁר כַּבָּזָק ...
דְּמוּת הַשְּׁלוּחִים לש.. ...

הַשֵּׁינִי מְהַלֵּךְ ...
... דְּבָרְךָ לֹא יָמִירוּ
ז.. ... תִּשְׁלַח וִימַהֵרוּ
חמ.. ... בִּיקְשׁוּ וַיְאַחֵרוּ

... כְּלֹא רָאוּ
יְקָרִים ... כַּאֲנָשִׁים נִרְאוּ
כְּמַלְאָכִים נִרְאוּ וְלֹא נֶחְבָּאוּ
... מַלְאֲכוּתָם סְדוֹמָה בָּאוּ

ככתוב ויבאו שני המלאכים סדומה בערב

ונאמר עושה מלאכיו רוחות משרתיו אש לוהט

ונאמר הללוהו כל מלאכיו הללוהו כל צבאיו

ונאמר השולח אמרתו ארץ עד מהרה ירוץ דברו

...

(ג) ... קַצִינֵי סְדוֹם
... כִּי תָשִׁיב שְׁבוּתֵינוּ
... ..ים כ..
תָּבִיא לָהּ בַּלָּהָה לְעֵת ...

אל נא

(ד) מַלְאֲכֵי רַחֲמִים מַלְאֲכֵי ... ..ם חִיכּוּ לְךָ אָדוֹן
ל..תא תִּידוֹן בְּמַכְבִּידֵי זָדוֹן

---

appeared as angels, because his strength was feeble."

3 See Jer 32:44; 32:7, 11; Ezek 39:25; Joel 4:1; Lam 2:14.

4 Isa 17:14.

5 "Haughtiness" (*zadon*; lit. "intentional, premeditated sin") may refer to idolatry. See *GenR* 47:1, where idolatry is listed as one of Sodom's four sins (inhospitality, bloodshed, and adultery are the other three).

... According to their measure ...
Whether... or whether with mercy, in accord with their cruel ways ...
Angels... and instantaneously...
... he goes forth
but no righteous person could be found[6]
Angels of peace ...
they became angels of wrath, wreaking ruin[7]

(5) ... You confirmed
and their word goes throughout the world, as You directed
... ...
... in their going forth and returning[8]
An eternal decree does not go forth ...
... and drop ... living ...
The matter of the mission was singular; it would not be doubled
and two missions [fall not upon one][9]
Does not each his mission do,
whether for good or ill, whether of favor or anger?
Good as done as soon as heard,[10] they rush to their mission
... but in Sodom, they delayed their commission:
The father of a multitude had sought their merit
Indeed, he was standing and pleading for them
They hesitated, for You taught, "Upon the wicked I will have mercy"
and as for the cruel—according to Your word—"I will relent"[11]
In a single flight, the whole world they could cover

---

6 See *GenR* 49:9, where God says to Abraham, who has just asked whether God will sweep away the innocent along with the guilty: "'You desire that judgment of the wicked should be suspended for the sake of the righteous; but are they righteous? Surely they are but counterfeit righteous!' For Rabbi Yoḥanan said: Wherever *zaddikim* (righteous ones) occurs in connection with Sodom, it is spelled defectively."

7 See *Tanḥ Tazri*ʿ*a* 9, which states: "Only angels of peace stand before the Holy Blessed One, while angels of wrath are far from Him." The destructive element of the angelic mission could only take place out of proximity to God.

8 The phrase "goings forth and returning" (*ratzo va-shov*) comes from Ezek 1:14, "And the living creatures [the *ḥayyot* of the divine chariot] went forth and returned like the appearance of a flash of lightning." This verse is applied to the angelic mission to Sodom in *GenR* 50:1, quoted below.

9 Lacuna filled by **R**. See *TargN* to Gen 18:1, which states, "The three [angels] were sent for three things, because it is impossible for any angel from on high to be sent for more than one thing." **R** cites *GenR* 50:2, "It was taught: One angel does not perform two missions,

... כְּמִידָתָם
אִם ... אִם כְּרַחֲמִים כְּאַכְזָרִיּוּתָם דַּרְכָּם
מַלְאֲכֵי שׁ.. ... וּכְהֶרֶף עַיִן
... יֵצֵא
וְצַדִּיק לֹא נִימְצָא
מַלְאֲכֵי שָׁלוֹם ...
נַעֲשׂוּ מַלְאֲכֵי חֵימָה לַעֲשׂוֹת רָע ...

(ה) ... תַּאֲמִין
וְקִוּוּם בְּכָל הָעוֹלָם תְּיַימֵּין
ב.. ...
... בְּרָצוֹא וָשׁוֹב
גְזֵירָה עַד לֹא תֵּצֵא ...
..ב ...
דְּבַר שְׁלִיחוּת אַחַת בִּשְׁנַיִים לֹא תֵּיעָשֶׂה
וּשְׁתֵּי שְׁלִיחוּיוֹת ...
הֲלֹא כָּל אֶחָד שְׁלִיחוּתוֹ יַעַשׂ
אִם לְטוֹב אִם לְרָע אִם לְרָצוֹן אִם לְכַעַס
וּמַעֲשֶׂה לְמִשְׁמָע מַקְדִּימִים בְּמִשְׁלַחְתָּם
וּבִסְדוֹם נִיתְמַהְמְהוּ בִּשְׁלִיחוּתָם
זְכוּת הָיָה חוֹפֵשׂ אַב הֲמוֹן לָהֶם
כִּי הָיָה עוֹמֵד וּמִתְחַנֵּן עֲלֵיהֶם
חִיכּוּ כִּי כְלִימוּדָךְ עַל הָרָעָה תְּנָחֵם
עַל אַכְזָרִיים כְּדוֹבְרָךְ תְּרַחֵם
טִיסָה אַחַת כָּל הָעוֹלָם יַעֲשׂוּ

---

nor do two angels together perform one mission, yet you read that two [angels came to Sodom, and three had come to Abraham]? The fact is, however, that Michael told [Abraham] his tidings and departed; Gabriel was sent to overturn Sodom, and Raphael to rescue Lot."

10 **B1** notes that the language echoes Ps 103:20; the use of this verse in *b. Shabb.* 88a is particularly telling: "Rabbi Eleazar said: When the Israelites gave precedence to `we will do' over `we will hearken' [Exod 24:7] a Heavenly Voice went forth and exclaimed to them, `Who revealed to My children this secret, which is employed by the Ministering Angels, as it is written: "Bless the Lord, O angels of His, O mighty in strength, that fulfill His word, who hearken unto the voice of his word"—first they fulfill and then they hearken!'"

11 **B1** connects this language in both these stichs with Jer 18:7–8, "If at any time I shall speak concerning a nation, and concerning a kingdom, that I will pluck it up, and that I will pull it down, and that I will destroy it; but if that nation, against whom I have pronounced, turns from its evil, I will repent of the evil that I intended to do to them." See also *GenR* 50:1, cited below, which describes the angels' hesitation (even dawdling) on account of the fact that Abraham might yet justify mercy upon the Sodomites.

but from the [righteous] one's dwelling their trip took a day[12]
Because the judgment against the wicked comes in the evening
therefore they entered at even[tide][13]

Forever…

"*And then came…*"
(6) Angels fear and ruin[14] …
roaming at the end of a single wind
Lightening … those who were sent …
every single one with a single mission
Mighty ones: their bodies are like *tarshish*[15]
which were turned …
In hot pursuit towards Sodom …
those who burn …
The one to save [Lot from the cities][16]
… and the one to lay bare the cities
When the hand is stretched against the flinty hills[17]
[to overturn][18] the root of the hills
They hurried … afternoon
because his righteousness was like the shining sun of noon
… two evenings
indeed …

---

12 Lacuna filled by **R**. The meaning is that it took the angels one day to travel from Abraham's home to Sodom—faster than humans could travel, but not instantaneously as angels might be expected to go. *GenR* 50:1 sheds light on the larger concerns of this passage: "'And the two angels came to Sodom in the evening' (Gen 19:1). It is written, 'And the living creature ran (*ratzo*) and returned as the appearance of a flash of lightning (Ezek 1:14). Rabbi Aibu said: Not *ratzot* (running) is written but *ratzo*: they are eager (*ratzin*) to perform their mission. 'Like the appearance of a flash of lightning (*bazak*).' Rabbi Judah b. Rabbi Simon said in the name of Rabbi Levi b. Parta: [Like the flames breaking forth] when one scatters (*bozek*) olive refuse in a stove. R. Ḥiyya b. Abba said: It was like wind driving sparks (*zika*). The Rabbis said: Like a lightning-flash to the eye. So [how is it that such fast beings] they took their leave of Abraham at noon, and didn't arrive in Sodom in the evening!? The fact is, however, that they were angels of mercy, and they delayed, thinking that perhaps Abraham might find something in their favor; but when he found nothing in their favor, 'The two angels came to Sodom in the evening.'" (**R** and **B1** both adduce this midrash at various points.)

13 Lacuna filled by **R**. See *TanḥB Vayera* 15.

14 Isa 24:17.

15 See Dan 10:6. This line connects the angels with the "mighty men of renown" in Gen 6:4.

וּמִינְוֵוה ... מַהֲלַךְ יוֹם אֶחָד עָשׂוּ
יַעַן מִשְׁפַּט רְשָׁעִים בָּעֶרֶב
עַל כֵּן נִכְנְסוּ ל.. ... עֶרֶב

לעולם

ויבאו ...
(ו) אֵילֵי פַּחַד וָפַחַת
מְשׁוֹטְטִים בִּקְצֵה רוּחַ אַחַת
בְּרָקִים הַנִּישְׁלָחִים ...
כָּל אֶחָד וְאֶחָד שְׁלִיחוּת אַחַת
גִּיבּוֹרִים גְּוִיָּתָם כְּתַרְשִׁשׁ
אֲשֶׁר נִיפְנוּ ...
דְּלִיקָה לִסְדוֹמָה ל..ש
הַדּוֹלְקִים ואח.. ... ..ש
הָאֶחָד לְמַלֵּט ...
וְאֶחָד לְעַרְעֵר הֶעָרִים
וּבְחַלְמִי יַד הָרִים
... ..שׁוֹרֶשׁ הָרִים
זוּרְזוּ ... צָהֳרָיִם
כִּי הָיָה צִידְקוּ כְצָהוֹרַיִים
... ..רי ... ..עַרְבַּיִים
כִּי ...

GenR 26:7 describes the tremendous stature of these ancient, otherwordly beings. "*Tarshish*" appears to be construed here as a term for size as well as brilliance. Multiple rabbinic sources identity Tarshish with "the great sea" (i.e., the Mediterranean)—see, for example, *b. Ḥull.* 91b, which states: "And of an angel it is written: `His body was like the Tarshish' (Dan 10:6), and we have a tradition that the Tarshish [Great Sea] is two thousand parasangs long." The angels are thus as tall as the ocean is wide. For the image of *tarshish* as a radiant gemstone (beryl or yellow jaspser) which the "bodies" of divine or angelic beings resemble, see again Dan 10:6 (the language of which forms the basis for this stich, as Bronznick reads it): "His body also was like *tarshish*, and his face like the appearance of lightning, and his eyes like lamps of fire, and his arms and his feet in color like polished bronze, and the sound of his words like the voice of a multitude." Also note Ezek 1:16, "As for the appearance and structure of the wheels (*ofanim*), they gleamed like *tarshish*."

16 Accepting **R**'s completion here.

17 See Job 28:9 as interpreted in *GenR* 51:4 (**B1**): "Rabbi Levi said in the name of Rabbi Samuel b. Naḥman: These five cities [of the plain—see Gen 19:25] were built on one rock, so the angel stretched out his hand and overturned them, as it is written, `He puts forth his hand against the flinty rock; he overturns the mountains by the roots' (Job 28:9)."

18 Lacuna as filled by **B1**.

For "And there appeared to him"

(9) Messengers upon Your missions, the kingship of the king of kings,
they enthrone and say:[19]
Holy, holy, holy is the Lord of Hosts! The whole earth is filled with His glory!
"*Holy*"—from the multitudes of Michael
"*Holy*"—from the legions of Gabriel
"*Holy*"—from the bands of Raphael[20]
Holy, holy, holy is the Lord of Hosts! The whole earth is filled with His glory!
"*Holy*"—to bear news to the old ones that they would bear a son—
He sent for Michael
"*Holy*"—to overturn Sodom and her suburbs—
He sent for Gabriel
"*Holy*"—to spare Lot from being swallowed in the enveloping shroud[21]—
He sent for Raphael
Holy, holy, holy is the Lord of Hosts! The whole earth is filled with His glory!
"*Holy*"—from the *Ḥayyot*;
"*Holy*"—from the *Ofanim*;
"*Holy*"—from the *Cherubim*
Towards each other …

19 This line ties back to Ps 148:2, cited after the *magen*. That verse describes how angels are compelled to praise God, and here they do.

20 In reference to the angels possessing their own hosts, and not merely being part of God's Host, **B1** cites *DeutR* 2:34, "…When God came down on Sinai, there also came down with Him many companies of angels, Michael and his company, Gabriel and his company. Some of the nations of the world chose for themselves [as their patron] Michael, others Gabriel, but Israel chose for themselves God." See also *SongR* 2:4, 2:15, 6:10. In this case, the

לוירא אליו

(ט) מַלְאָכִים בְּמַלְאֲכוֹתֶיךָ מַלְכוּת מֶלֶךְ מְלָכִים
מַמְלִיכִים וְאוֹמְרִים
קדוש קדוש קדוש יי צבאות מלא כל הארץ כבודו
קָדוֹשׁ מֵרִיבְבוֹת מִיכָאֵל
קָדוֹשׁ מֵאַלְפֵי גַבְרִיאֵל
קָדוֹשׁ מִגְּדוּדֵי רְפָאֵל
קדוש קדוש קדוש יי צבאות מלא כל הארץ כבודו
קָדוֹשׁ לְבַשֵּׂר זְקֵינִים כִּי יֵלֵדוּ
שִׁילַּח לְמִיכָאֵל
קָדוֹשׁ לַהֲפוֹךְ סְדֹם וּבְנוֹתֶיהָ
שִׁילַּח לְגַבְרִיאֵל
קדוש לְמַלֵּט לוֹט מִבִּילוּעַ הַלּוֹט הַלּוֹט
שִׁילַּח לִרְפָאֵל
קדוש קדוש קדוש יי צבאות מלא כל הארץ כבודו
קדוש מחיה
קדוש מאופן
קדוש מכרוב

לעומתם

poet describes three troops because there are three angels (a convenient detail when it comes to parsing out the threefold repetition of "holy" in the Qedushah). Michael receives the largest host ("multitudes"—10,000 troops each), perhaps because (as Bronznick notes) he is the angel associated with Israel in Dan 10:21 and 12:1. For more on angels in Yannai, see Chapter Four.

21 The language of this line comes from Isa 25:7 (**R**) and puns on the name "Lot": *hallot hallot* (`the enveloping shroud'; i.e., impending doom).

Commentary

The focus of this poem is upon angels and angelic missions. Neither the Bible nor rabbinic textual traditions present the modern reader with a systematic angelology; however, as the individual notes make clear, what Yannai presents here is consistent with strands of Jewish belief about God's celestial host as they developed in the Hellenistic and Late Ancient worlds. Several ideas stand out: the belief that angels appear human and yet are somehow visibly distinct; the understanding that each angel has a singular mission, meaning that no angel can have more than one task nor can two angels be assigned to a single mission; and the notion that angels are beings of almost complete and instantaneous obedience to the divine will. In this piyyut, however, we are given other information, as well: angels can also hesitate, because of their knowledge of Torah. The angels delay their mission to destroy Sodom because they know that God's will may change, should Abraham convince him that He should have mercy on Sodom. By means of this simple, fleeting expression of uncertainty, the angels (as depicted here) acknowledge both the mutability of divine will and the power of human intercession. Abraham, for all his mortal limitations (and his limited appearance in this piyyut), has more power than the mighty angels Michael, Gabriel, and Raphael. In the liturgical context, the privileging and empowering of the human voice has particular significance.

While rabbinic traditions associate the angels with the morning liturgy (see *b. Ḥul.* 91b), this poem does not emphasize the ritual functions of angels except through its citation of Ps 148:2 and the stereotypical inclusion of angelic with human praise in the opening line of Poem Nine. While rabbinic writings often suggest that angels are opponents of humanity (e.g., *GenR* 8:4 in which God creates Adam against the wishes of the angels), and the biblical source itself teaches of their superiority (Ps 8:6, "For you have made [man] a little lower than the angels, and have crowned him with glory and honor"), in Yannai's works Israel is consistently superior to but in overall harmony with the heavenly hosts. He depicts no tension between angels and humans here; if anything, humanity (or, rather, Abraham) appears to be more powerful than the heavenly beings. We see this power inversion through the apparent hesitancy the angels show in executing their missions in Sodom lest Abraham change God's mind. For all their might, swiftness, and splendor, the angels could or would act as boldly as Abraham, despite their superior abilities and powers. In terms of moral influence, Abraham is the mightier being.

The three angels specified by Yannai—Michael, Gabriel, and Raphael—are among the most important in Jewish tradition, a trend already evident in Second Temple period writings. Michael appears in the biblical book of Daniel as well as the apocryphal books of Judith and 1 Esdras and the New Testament book of Revelations; Gabriel likewise appears in Daniel, as well as in the New Testament gospel of Luke; and Raphael is a major character in the apocryphal book of Tobit. The same angels appear (often together) in rabbinic literature, as well; Michael and Gabriel are especially frequently paired. For example, in *GenR* 8:13, they are Adam's groomsmen; in *ExodR* 18:5, they smite Israel's enemies and rescue Israelites from danger; and *EcclR* 9:13 describes them as "kings of angels" (but nonetheless afraid of Moses). It is also worth noting that the Rabbis understood Michael and Gabriel to have had an enduring relationship with Abraham. Based on the biblical story of the angel who saves Daniel's friends in Dan 3, the Rabbis read an angelic role into Abraham's test in the furnaces of Chaldean Ur (see *GenR* 44:13; *ExodR* 8:5; and *b. Pes.* 118a). These angels, however, are not unconditionally beneficent to Israel; they manifest God's will, and at times God wishes to harm His people. Note, for instance, the tradition preserved in *Yalqut* to Lam 1:2, which describes Michael and Gabriel as destroying the Temple as punishment for saying it was dearer to them than the people of Israel. This tradition appears to underlie a teaching recorded in *LamR* 1:27, in which "All her friends have dealt treacherously with her, all her friends become enemies" (Lam 1:2) which Rabbi Jacob of *Kefar Ḥanan* explains as, "This alludes to Michael and Gabriel." As in this poem, angels are instruments of divine agency; when justice requires punishment, angels of mercy become angels of wrath.

Evidence of interest in angels and their connection with Abraham is not limited to literary sources. Depictions of the angels' visitation to Abraham prior to their mission to Sodom, while common in ancient churches (where it is understood to prefigure Gabriel's annunciation to Mary in the New Testament)—is largely unattested in synagogue art. In fact, this motif appears only once in any current excavated ancient synagogue, in the floor mosaic of the synagogue in Sepphoris in the Galilee (ca. 6th century C.E.). In this mosaic, the angels appears alongside a two-paneled depiction of the Binding of Isaac. The panel depicting Abraham, Sarah, and the angelic visitors on the floor of the Sepphoris synagogue is badly damaged, but the existence of this depiction remains suggestive. At least for this one community—and Sepphoris was a major Jewish center in the Roman and Byzantine periods—the story of the angels visiting Abraham was important enough to inspire the effort and expense required to represent it in a synagogue mosaic. While visual images are particularly open to interpretation, in the context of the Akedah, the implied narrative seems to be one of promise and fulfillment. In the scene of the angelic visitation, God promises Abraham and Sarah a son together, a promise that is fulfilled. In the scene of the binding of Isaac, Abraham demonstrates his faithfulness to God through his willingness to sacrifice that son, and God responds with a blessing upon all of Abraham's descendents. Although other readings are certainly possible (and could easily coexist with the one just proposed), in a liturgical context, the story of God's promises to Abraham are particularly appealing.

In our poem, the juxtaposition of these same angels with the motif of divine justice and mercy (rather than divine test and promise) creates an optimistic interpretation of a story that can be as troubling as the Akedah on its own: on the one hand, the presence of angels (who are angels of peace and mercy by default) exist to protect Israel and bring good tidings; on the other hand, their presence—and the fate of Sodom—indicates that in the end justice will be served. For a poet writing in the Roman-dominated, Christianized Galilee of the Late Antiquity, such motifs are as significant in literary form as in visual representation.

While it might be stretching the limits of fancy to imagine the mosaic and poem being "read" together, the common elements of these roughly contemporary works of art (mosaic and literary)—along with other textual sources—indicate just how potent and attractive the angelic motifs were in Late Antiquity. Angels were central to both popular and esoteric forms of speculation. The origins of this fascination lie in the early Second Temple period, if not earlier (Ezekiel, Zechariah, Daniel come to mind as the earliest Jewish sources), but their enduring appeal is clear. The angelology here, which affirms heavenly might and responsiveness, also asserts human integrity and influence—and it creates a sense that the Jews of the 6th century in the Galilee are living in the midst of an almost-invisible cosmic drama just as much as Abraham was. For Yannai's listeners, this deeply embedded, even latent, conception of their own historical epoch may have been particularly compelling.

Qedushta for Genesis 24:1 בראשית כד:א

"Now, Abraham was old" ואברהם זקן

While only the final unit of the piyyut survives in an intelligible form, the text we have presents a rich and charming depiction of the patriarch's grand and dignified later years.[1]

1 The Maʾagarim database includes fragments of what appear to be earlier units of this *qedushta*, perhaps Poem Six and a *rahit*. As those passages are very badly damaged, they were not included here.

(9) From the insight of the elders:[2] to the One who makes all grow old but He does not grow old, all say:
Holy, holy, holy is the Lord of hosts! The whole world is filled with His glory!
"*Holy*"—from the possessors of old age;
"*Holy*"—from the possessors of gray hair;
"*Holy*"—from the possessors of hoary years
Holy, holy, holy is the Lord of hosts! The whole world is filled with His glory!
"*Holy*"—from the splendid glory that is the crown of old age[3]
"*Holy*"—from the splendid grandeur that is the diadem of gray hair[4]
"*Holy*"—rom the splendid treasure that is the glorious crest of hoary years[5]
Holy, holy, holy is the Lord of hosts! The whole world is filled with His glory!
"*Holy*"—from the *Ḥayyot*
"*Holy*"—from the *Ofanim*
"*Holy*"—from the *Cherubim*
Towards each other, they all say: "*Blessed is His Glory from His place*"

"*From His place*"—a blessing with which He blessed the patriarch
in his childhood *And He is in His place*
"*From His place*"—He favored him
in his black-haired days[6] *And He is in His place*
"*From His place*"—He doubled for him (his reward)
when he became a gray-beard[7] *And He is in His place*

From His place, let Him turn to the people, the ones who unify (His name) twice every day and who say twice with love...[8]

---

2 Job 12:20, "He deprives trusty men of speech, and takes away the discernment of elders" (**R**). In other instances, this verse is applied negatively to Isaac and Jacob, who sought to reveal divine secrets inappropriately (see *Tanḥ Vayeḥi* 8, *GenR* 99:5, and Yannai's *qedushta* to Gen 49). Here, however, Yannai alludes only to the b-part of the verse, using it implicitly to praise Abraham's age-earned wisdom.

3 See Prov 17:6 (**B1**).

4 Prov 16:31 (**B1**), interpreted as applying to Abraham in *GenR* 59:1.

5 1 Kgs 7:9 (**B1**).

6 Eccl 11:9 and 12:1 (**R**).

7 **R** connects this line with *m. Kidd.* 4:14, "And thus you find about our father Abraham

(ט) מִטַּעַם זְקֵנִים לְמַזְקִין כֹּל
וְהוּא לֹא יַזְקִין הַכֹּל אוֹמְרִים
קדוש קדוש קדוש יי צבאות מלא כל הארץ כבודו
קָדוֹשׁ מִבַּעֲלֵי זִקְנָה
קָדוֹשׁ מִבַּעֲלֵי שֵׂיבָה
קָדוֹשׁ מִבַּעֲלֵי יְשִׁישׁוּת
קדוש קדוש קדוש יי צבאות מלא כל הארץ כבודו
קָדוֹשׁ מִזִּיו הוֹדוֹ הִיא עֲטֶרֶת זִקְנָה
קָדוֹשׁ מִזִּיו הֲדָרוֹ הִיא תִּפְאֶרֶת שֵׂיבָה
קָדוֹשׁ מִזִּיו יְקָרוֹ הִיא כְּבוּדַּת יְשִׁישׁוּת
קדוש קדוש קדוש יי צבאות מלא כל הארץ כבודו
קדוש מחיה
קדוש מאופן
קדוש מכרוב
לעומתם כל יאמרו ברוך כבוד ממקומו

מִמְּקוֹמוֹ בְּרָכָה אֲשֶׁר בֵּירַךְ
לְאָב בְּנַעֲרוּתוֹ — והוא במקומו
מִמְּקוֹמוֹ הֶעְדִּיפָה לוֹ
בְּבַחְירוּתוֹ — והוא במקומו
מִמְּקוֹמוֹ הִכְפִּילָה לוֹ
לְעֵת זְקוּנָתוֹ — והוא במקומו

מִמְּקוֹמוֹ יִיפֶן בְּעַם הַמְיַחֲדִים בְּכָל יוֹם
פַּעֲמַיִם וְאוֹמְרִים פַּעֲמַיִם בְּאַהֲבָה...

(peace be upon him) that the Omnipresent blessed him in his childhood and in his old age." Our poem addresses the three ages of man: childhood, youthful vigor, and old age. For the language of `doubling' (of wealth and blessing) in old age, **B1** cites *j. Ḥag.* 9b, which explicates Job 42:12. Yannai applies that passage's interpretation to Abraham rather than to Job. **R** and **B1** also refer to *t. Kidd.* 5:14, which states that God blessed Abraham even more in his old age than in his youth; blessing is then defined in terms of wealth. See also *TanḥB Emor* 6. *GenR* 59:7 may have a similar, if non-monetary, idea of reward in mind when it says God's final "blessing" upon Abraham was an absence of any further trials.

8 "To unify God's name" is a reference to the Shema (particularly its opening verse, Deut 6:4).

Commentary

In this poem, the last of Yannai's Abraham cycle, the poet lauds the aged patriarch whose physical bearing embodies and reflects his wisdom and dignity. The poet lauds the patriarch both for his receipt of divine favor and for the gray hair and beard that symbolize this achievement. Indeed, the biblical notice of Abraham's age inspires an anonymous voice in the Talmud to assert, "Until Abraham, there was no old age" (*b.Bava Metzia* 87a). According to this passage, physical appearance as an elder was one manifestation of Abraham's virtue. *GenR* 65:9, likewise commenting on Gen 24:1, contains an expanded version of the same tradition:

> Judah b. Simon said: Abraham requested [the appearance of] old age, pleading before Him: "Sovereign of the Universe! When a man and his son enter a town, none know whom to honor! But if You would crown him [the father] with [the appearance of] old age, everyone will know whom to honor." Said the Holy One, blessed be He, to him: "By your life! You have asked well, and so it [old age] will commence with you." Thus from the beginning of the book [Genesis] until here `old age' is not mentioned, but when Abraham arose [the appearance of] old age was granted to him: "And Abraham was old, well stricken in age" (Gen 24:1).[9]

Similarly, *Pirqe de-Rabbi Eliezer* lists Abraham's advanced age as one of the "seven wonders of the world":

> The third wonder: From the day that the heavens and earth were created, grey hair did not appear among humanity until Abraham our father, upon whom grey hair did appear, as it is said, "And Abraham was old, advanced in age" (Gen 24:1). Rabbi Levitas, a man of Yavneh, said: Just as a crown makes the head of the king splendid, so, too, grey hair is splendid and an honor to the elderly, as it is said: "The glory of youths is their strength; the splendor of old men is their grey hair" (Prov 20:29).

According to this body of tradition, in which Yannai participates, all the

9 This tradition is paralleled in *Tanḥ Noaḥ* 16 and *Toledot* 6; *TanḥB Noaḥ* 20 and *Toledot* 7; in reality, in the biblical text, the word "old" (זקן) does, in fact, occur prior to Gen 24:1, but its earliest use (Gen 18:11) does occur in the context of the Abraham story.

signs of old age—particularly gray hair—constitute a unique blessing to humanity, one bestowed at Abraham's request.

Age alone inspires admiration, but Abraham stands out not only for the age he achieved, but the dignity he possessed until the very end of his life. This motif, also present in the piyyut, aligns closely with a tradition found in *GenR* 59:6, which states:

> Rabbi Aha said: Some have [the dignity of] old age without actual length of days, while others have years without the dignity of age; but here [in the case of Abraham] the dignity of age corresponded to long life, and long life to the dignity of age, as it says, "He [Abraham] was old, advanced in days" (Gen 24:1)."

The doubled clause that opens the *sidra* (the use of both "old" and "advanced in days") is taken by prose exegetes and poet alike as indicative of a doubling of qualities: not only life-span but quality of life. The extant poem praises Abraham at every stage of life—childhood, youth, and old age—but singles out his senectitude as laudable in its own right: Abraham is a model of aging well and of old age as a blessing. At each stage of his life, he inspires emulation. The final image of this rapturous *qedushah* is one of a geriatric choir praising the One who, while He does not age, is nonetheless sometimes called the "Ancient One of Days" (Dan 7:9).

Qedushta for Genesis 25:19 בראשית כה:יט

"And these are the descendents" ואלה תולדות

This is the first Torah portion in which Jacob and Esau appear. These twins, entangled with and struggling against each other from before birth, foreshadow the conflict that will plague their descendents: Israel and Rome. Fraternal twins, Jacob and Esau are portrayed here as opposites, mirror images of each other. Yannai thus transforms the biblical story from a domestic clash to a national struggle, using allegory to emphasize the entangled nature of the relationship between the two. The triumph of the younger (Jacob) over the elder (Esau) predicted in Rebecca's oracle (Gen 25:23) foretells the eventual triumph of the weaker nation (Israel) over the stronger (Byzantine Rome).

[And thus, "And these are the descendents...]"

(7[1]) The descendents of the steadfast believers[1] of him whom his father loved[2]
[The descendents of] ...
The descendents of the stump of the raiding band of Gad[3] ...
The descendents of the one who knocked on the doors of interpreted wisdom[4]
The descendents of the crown ... and he ...
The descendents of ... My everlasting assembly
The descendents of the pure seed scattered ...
The descendents of desire ... delighting in devotion
The descendents of ... good, clear sense
The descendents of the bearing of ... a beloved one going forth
The descendents of the stock of the vineyard[5] ... all of it ...
The descendents of the bands[6] of the hearty, to father forever
The descendents of the planting of the quarry[7], the blessed source[8]
[The descendents of ...] the faithful one whose lineage was listed[9]
The descendents of the branch, the choice vine, cherished and chosen[10]
The descendents of an eternal people ...
The descendents of fruitfulness, of she who bore the fruit of divine visitation[11]
The descendents of the blossoming sprout, the most refined righteous[12]
[The descendents of ...] the line of the proclamation of truth[13]
The descendents of the gentle one made many, of fragrance favored[14]
The descendents of a transplanted shoot sent forth ...
The descendents of praising the powerful One, exalted by splendor!

---

1 Isa 25:1

2 The language of this phrase comes from Gen 44:20, where it refers to Jacob's love of Benjamin. Here, however, it describes Abraham's love for Isaac, as in Gen 22:2, or God's love for Israel.

3 See Gen 49:19.

4 **R** notes that this is an allusion to the common aggadic tradition that Jacob, "he who sits in tents" (Gen 25:27), was a Torah scholar, even from before his birth. See *TanḥB Toledot* 13; *GenR* 63:6.

5 See Ps 80:16.

6 The term "bands" appears only in 1 Sam 19:20 and, possibly, Prov 30:17.

7 The "quarry" refers to the womb of the matriarch Rebecca, the mother of Israel.

8 Abraham's fathering of Isaac is probably meant here, or possibly Isaac's fathering of Jacob; see Isa 51:1–2 (**R**).

[ולכן ואלה תולדות]

(ז׳) תּוֹלְדוֹת אֱמוּנֵי אוֹמֶן אֲהֵיבוֹ אָבִיו
[תּוֹלְדוֹת ב..] ... בר..
תּוֹלְדוֹת גֶּזַע גּוּר גַּד גְּדוּד
תּוֹלְדוֹת דּוֹפֵק דַּלְתוֹת דְּרִישַׁת דָּתוֹת

תּוֹלְדוֹת הַנֵּזֶר ה..צה הוּא ...
תּוֹלְדוֹת ו.. ... וְעוּדֵי וָעֶד
תּוֹלְדוֹת ז..ע זַךְ זֵירוּזֵי ז..
תּוֹלְדוֹת חָמַד ח..ק חָפֵץ חָסֶד
תּוֹלְדוֹת ... טוּב טַעַם טָהוֹר
תּוֹלְדוֹת יְלִידַת יו.. יוֹצֵא יָדִיד
תּוֹלְדוֹת כַּנַּת כֶּרֶם ... כּוּלוֹ כ..
תּוֹלְדוֹת לַהֲקֵי לִיבּוּב לְהוֹלִיד לָעַד
תּוֹלְדוֹת מַטַּע מַקֶּבֶת מָקוֹר מְבוֹרָךְ
[תּוֹלְדוֹת נ..] ... נֶאֱמָן נִמְנָה נִתְיַחֵס
תּוֹלְדוֹת סָרִיג סוֹרֵק סִלְסוּל סֶגֶל
תּוֹלְדוֹת עַם עוֹלָם ...
תּוֹלְדוֹת פְּרִי פּוֹרִיָּה פְּקוּדַת פֶּלֶא

תּוֹלְדוֹת צִיץ צֶמַח צְרִיפוּת צֶדֶק
[תּוֹלְדוֹת ק..ת] קַו קְרִיאַת קוֹשֶׁט
תּוֹלְדוֹת רִיבּוּי רַךְ רִיצּוּי רֵיחַ
תּוֹלְדוֹת שֶׁלַח שֶׁתֶל ש.. ש..
תּוֹלְדוֹת תְּהִלַּת תּוֹקֶף תִּילֵל תִּפְאָרָה

9 Isaac is the referent here; see Gen 25:20, the second verse of the *sidra*, where his genealogy is listed.

10 The imagery here is of Abraham, Isaac, and Jacob as the roots of the chosen people.

11 The phrase "divine visitation" (from the root פ-ק-ד) may refer back to Gen 21:1, when God remembered (*paqad*) Sarah's plight of infertility. Or the phrase may anticipate Rebecca's conception, which was—miraculously—not complicated by difficulties but rather occurred as soon as Isaac prayed on her behalf (Gen 25:21).

12 This line echoes Jer 23:5.

13 The word "truth" (קושט) is an Aramaicism, employed because it fits the acrostic. The stich is otherwise a paraphrase of Prov 22:21.

14 This line alludes to Ezek 20:41, "I will favor your sweet fragrance, when I bring you out from the peoples, and gather you from the countries where you have been scattered; and I will be sanctified in you before the nations" (**B2**).

(7²)[15] Descendents loved and loathed[16]
loved, and finding compassion,[17] and loathed, receiving rejection
Descendents selected and rejected
selected as a treasure[18] and rejected as something shunned[19]
Descendents of the kid and the leopard[20]
a kid for favor and a leopard for a fight
Descendents sought and snubbed
sought for seeing and snubbed in disgust[21]
Descendents of the birthright and the birthright lost
a birthright of sanctity and a birthright lost for a sin[22]
Descendents of experience and inexperience
experience in the tent[23] and inexperience with trembling[24]
Descendents of pure and polluted[25]
pure in innocence and polluted by sin
Descendents of the pious and the apostate
the pious getting loyalty and the apostate getting lack[26]
Descendents of the lamb and the wolf[27]
the lamb dwelling in safety and a wolf hurled outside

15 The similarities between this *rahit* and the previous one suggests the way that Yannai plays with and develops his own formal conventions. Formally, this poem is simple, but it is more complicated than the preceding one, which it closely resembles. The first *rahit* begins with the word "generations" from the *sidra* and expands it with four words sharing an acrostic letter (e.g., *toledot* a-a-a-a, *toledot* b-b-b-b, *toledot* c-c-c-c). The second *rahit* is also an alphabetic acrostic, built upon the same word: *toledot* ("[these are the] descendents..."). Here, however, the acrostic is complemented by antithesis. That is, through clever puns, Jacob and Esau are juxtaposed as antithetical pairs; first the pairing alone is stated (Jacob is always first, and the acrostic follows his attributes), and then—in the second stich—the comparison is fleshed out (without an acrostic element). The terseness of the rhetoric and its reliance on puns and rhymes render this unit particularly difficult to translate.

16 Mal 1:3 (**R**). "Loved" refers to Jacob; "loathed" refers to Esau.

17 Understanding this as from the root חוס. Alternatively, this could be read as "lineage, genealogy."

18 Understanding *segel* as "treasure." See Exod 19:5, in which God refers to Israel as His *segulah* (treasure); and Deut 7:2, which refers to Israel as *ʿam segulah*, "a treasured people."

19 **B1** cites Num 12:14, where Miriam is stricken with *tsaraʿat* and excluded from the camp as a result of her slandering of Moses. "Excluded" is from the same root and stem (ס-ג-ר), translated here as "shunned."

20 See Isa 11:6, "The wolf also shall live with the lamb, and the leopard shall lie down with the kid; and the calf and the young lion and the fatling together; and a little child shall lead them" (**B1**). The kid is not only a kosher animal, fit for use in ritual, but also a symbol of purity, docility, and innocence—a fitting analog to the "pure" and gentle Jacob. (**B2** notes that Israel is symbolized by a kid in the Passover song, *Ḥad Gadya*.) That which comes from the kid—and, by analogy, that which comes from the children of Israel (e.g., prayer), is fit

(ז[2])

תּוֹלְדוֹת **אָ**הוּב וְשָׂנאוּי
אָהוּב לְיַיחֵס וְשָׂנאוּי לְמַאֵס
תּוֹלְדוֹת **בָּ**חוּר וּבָזוּי
בָּחוּר לְסֶגֶל וּבָזוּי לְסֶגֶר
תּוֹלְדוֹת **גְּ**דִי וְנָמֵר
גְּדִי לְרִצּוּי וְנָמֵר לְנִיצּוּי
תּוֹלְדוֹת **דָּ**רוּשׁ וְדָחוּף
דָּרוּשׁ לְרֵיאָיוֹן וְדָחוּף לְדֵירָאוֹן
תּוֹלְדוֹת **הַ**בְּכוֹר וְהַמְבַכֵּר
הַבְּכוֹר לְקוֹדֶשׁ וְהַמְבַכֵּר לְעוֹנֶשׁ
תּוֹלְדוֹת **וָ**תִיק וַעֲוִיל
וָתִיק לְאֹהֶל וַעֲוִיל לְבוֹהֶל
תּוֹלְדוֹת **זַ**ךְ וְזֵד
זַךְ לִזְכוּת וְזֵד לְחוֹבָה
תּוֹלְדוֹת **חָ**סִיד וְחָנֵף
חָסִיד לְחֶסֶד וְחָנֵף לְחֶסֶר
תּוֹלְדוֹת **טָ**לֶה וּזְאֵב
טָלֶה לְטִילּוּל וּזְאֵב לְטִלְטוּל

---

and acceptable to God. The leopard, conversely, is a wild animal, non-kosher and ritually unfit, and furthermore representative of wildness, intractability, and violence. In *SongR* 4:8, the leopard is a symbol of Esau/Rome.

21 The implication here is that Jacob and his line merited intimacy with the divine—most manifestly in the image of Jacob on the divine throne (see *GenR* 82:2), which God beholds. Esau, meanwhile, was repugnant and unworthy of such divine favor.

22 The allusion here is the episode in which Esau sells his birthright for a bowl of red lentil stew in Gen 25. Clearly Esau's disparagement of his birthright is to be criticized. Furthermore, according to *GenR* 63:13, Esau's question, "What is `this' (*zeh*)" is read as a rejection not simply of the birthright but of God (who is called "This"—see n. 46, below). Esau thus denied God, while Jacob claims Him.

23 The tent of Torah or as a House of Study, that is. This is rooted in interpretations of Gen 25:27 (cited by **R**; see *GenR* 63:9 and others). The appellation "experienced scholar (*talmid vatiq*)" is attested in rabbinic literature as a term of high praise.

24 The referent here is not clear. **B1** links it to fearlessness in the hunt (which seems positive for a hunter, if not a good hobby for the budding scholar), while **R** links it to Exod 15:15, which implies Esau never knew the (positive) trembling of standing at Sinai.

25 The pair "pure and polluted" comes from Prov 21:8 (**B1**).

26 "Lack" in the sense of famine and loss of physical sustenance, the "reward" of rejecting God who provides for human needs. **R** cites Job 30:3, "Through want and famine they are solitary; they flee into the wilderness, into a gloomy waste and desolation."

27 Isa 65:25, "The wolf and the lamb shall feed together, and the lion shall eat straw like the ox; and dust shall be the serpent's food. They shall not hurt nor destroy in all my holy mountain, says the Lord" (cited by **B1**). This is Deutero-Isaiah's interpretation of Isa 11:6, quoted above.

Descendents of the unique and the arrogant
    the unique to unify and the arrogant breaking to shards[28]
Descendents of ram and pig[29]
    ram for the altar and the pig for the ruin[30]
Descendents of mastery and mockery
    mastery for the student and the mocker expelled[31]
Descendents of the singer and the shamed
    the singer for sweet sanctuary[32] and the shamed doomed to roam
Descendents of fitness and folly
    fitness for holy service and folly fit for filth[33]
Descendents of the prince and the pretender
    the prince to rule and the pretender to roam[34]
Descendents of the strong and the strident
    the strong for strength[35] and the strident for wild Azazel[36]
Descendents of the bold and the barbaric
    the bold blossoming forth and the barbaric bursting asunder[37]

---

28 "Unify" is a reference to the Shema, in which Israel proclaims God's "oneness." Precisely what "unification" means can vary but the central importance of the act remains constant and is central to Judaism's own unified identity. The image of fragmentation associated with Esau could refer to the debates within Christianity on trinitarianism or the nature of Jesus in Byzantine Christianity, which took place during the 5th–7th centuries, precisely the period when Yannai lived. It could also refer to political disunity in the late Empire or Rome's role in the creation of the Diaspora. Contrast this with the teaching in *b. Ber.* 6a: "The Holy One, blessed be He, said to Israel: `You have made me a unique entity in the world, and I shall make you a unique entity in the world.' `You have made me a unique entity in the world', as it is said: `Hear, O Israel, the Lord our God, the Lord is one' (Deut 6:4). `And I shall make you a unique entity in the world', as it is said: `And who is like Your people Israel, a nation one in the earth' (1 Chron 18:21)."

29 As above, the kosher animal represents Israel, while the pig stands for paganism, Rome, and Christianity (i.e., those who eat pork). Ps 80:14, "The boar of the forest ravages," was a favorite prooftext in this tradition of exegesis well into the Middle Ages. **R** cites *GenR* 65:1, which states: "It is written, `The boar of the forest ravages, that which moves in the field feeds on it (Ps 80:14). Rabbi Phinehas and Rabbi Ḥelkiah in Rabbi Simon's name said: Of all the prophets, only two, Moses and Asaph, exposed it [the treacherousness of Rome]. Asaph [wrote]: `The boar of the forest ravages'; while Moses said: `And the swine, because his hoof is cloven…' (Deut 14:8). Why does he compare it [the Roman State] to a swine? For this reason: when the swine is lying down, it puts out its hoofs, as if to say, `I am clean'; so does this wicked State rob and oppress, yet pretend to be executing justice. So for forty years Esau used to ensnare married women and violate them, yet when he attained forty years he compared himself to his father, saying, `As my father was forty years old when he married, so I will marry at the age of forty.' — This passage reveals how the image of the pig, Rome, and Esau were all thoroughly intertwined in the rabbinic textual tradition.

תּוֹלְדוֹת **יָ**חִיד וְיָהִיר
יָחִיד לְיַחֵד וְיָהִיר לְיַחֵת
תּוֹלְדוֹת **כֶּ**בֶשׂ וְחֲזִיר
כֶּבֶשׂ לְקָרְבָּן וְחֲזִיר לְחָרְבָּן
תּוֹלְדוֹת **לִ**מּוּד וְלֵץ
לִמּוּד לְחַנֵּיךְ וְלֵץ לְגָרֵשׁ
תּוֹלְדוֹת **מְ**זַמֵּר וּמְחָרֵף
מְזַמֵּר לְנוֹעַם וּמְחָרֵף לְנוֹעַ
תּוֹלְדוֹת **נָ**קִי וּמְנֻוּבָל
נָקִי לְשֵׁירוּת וּמְנֻבָּל לְשִׁיחוּת
תּוֹלְדוֹת **שַׂ**ר וְסוֹרֵר
שַׂר לְשָׂרֵר וְסוֹרֵר לְשָׁרֵךְ
תּוֹלְדוֹת **ע**וֹז וְעֵז
עוֹז לֶעֱזוּז וְעֵז לַעֲזָאזֵל
תּוֹלְדוֹת **פּ**וֹרֵץ וּפָרִיץ
פּוֹרֵץ לִגְדּוֹר וּפָרִיץ לִפְרוֹץ

30 The term חורבן alludes to the destruction of the Temple (both by Edom, as in Ps 137:7; and by the Romans). Yannai's language here suggests that just as Rome destroyed the Temple, Rome will in turn be destroyed, and the Temple ("altar") rebuilt.

31 See note above on Esau's denial of God.

32 **B1** cites *GenR* 68:11, which teaches that the entire time that Jacob lived with his uncle Laban, he did not sleep but rather stayed up all night reciting the psalms of David, the "sweet singer of Israel" (2 Sam 23:1). The epithet "sweet singer of Israel" includes overtones beyond simply the songs: the idea of restoration of the Temple and its rites—in short, all the connotations of permanence, restoration, and tranquility associated with the reestablishment of the Temple.

33 The language here draws upon Job 9:31, which refers to a pit filled with filth (**B1**). "Folly" refers to Esau's numerous sins, including the shedding of blood and immoral sexual practices. See *GenR* 63:10 and 63:12.

34 See Jer 2:23

35 "Strength" (עוז) is an epithet for Torah derived from Ps 29:11. See *LevR* 31:5, *SongsR* 1:23 and 2:12; and *MidPs* 7:3, 8:4, 21:2, and 29:2.

36 The translation "wild Azazel" attempts to reproduce the double connotations of "Azazel" as both a place of desolation and a kind of demonic presence. See *b. Yoma* 67b; *Sifra* to Lev 16:8; and others. Here Azazel, located at the farthest imaginable point from "holiness" (see Lev 16), is antithetical to the power and sanctity of Torah.

37 This entire line puns on a single root: פ-ר-ץ, which can have positive and negative connotations. In each case, Jacob reflects the positive, domestic, fruitful connotations of the root while Esau encapsulates the overwhelming, destructive, wild, and negative qualities of the same. Furthermore, the biblical figure Peretz (see Gen 38:29 and Ruth 4:12, 18), descended from Jacob, is an ancestor of—and shorthand for—the messiah. I read נפרץ with **B1** (a reference to 1 Sam 3:1) against the Maʾagarim's uncertain לגדוד ("to band together").

Descendents of the righteous and the wicked
the righteous for life and the wicked for death[38]
Descendents of truth and falsehood
truth of God and falsehood of idols[39]
Descendents of the soft-spoken and the brusque
the soft-spoken to bring together and the brusque to break apart
Descendents of wholeness and fragmentation
wholeness for peace and fragmentation for fearful trembling
Descendents of perfection and perversion
perfection leading to love and perversion leading to loathing

(8) Esau and Jacob, Edom and Israel[40]
Esau, named for deeds and Jacob, called a "heel"[41]
Edom, making red people's faces[42] while Israel looks towards God
the one is seen while the other seems hidden[43]
The one sunken down while the other sprouts up
the one fallen while the other will be exalted
the one extinguished while the other will shine[44]
For Edom, this world but for Israel, the world to come and this world as well.
And by his name each is called the one and the other[45]

---

38 In *GenR* 63:11 and 14, Esau denies the concept of resurrection of the dead, understood as the birthright he has scorned (and which Jacob has acquired). By rejecting the afterlife, he condemns himself to death, while Jacob will inherit eternal life.

39 The second half of this line blends Gen 31:29 with Job 24:25.

40 The explicit identification of Esau as Rome and Jacob as Israel is unusually reminiscent of the directness of midrashic rhetoric.

41 The poet here puns on the names Esau and Jacob. Esau can be understood as related to the word "deeds" (from the root ע-ש-ה) implying that he should have been destined for a life of exemplary behavior—or perhaps alluding to the aggadic teaching that Esau was born "done," complete with hair, beard, and molars (see *Targ PsJ* to Gen 25:25; **R** cites *GenR* 71:3 and *TanḥB Shelah* 10). Jacob, meanwhile, is presented in Gen 26:26 as a grasping, greedy younger son. Their actual life stories prove how incorrect these names were: Esau's deeds were wicked, while Jacob was the righteous twin.

42 The idiom "to redden the face" generally refers to shaming, but **B2** understands it as describing Edom's violent habits.

43 At first, it might seem like the poet has switched Esau and Jacob in the pairing of "seen" and "hidden." However, because the order is otherwise fixed in this poem, this couplet probably refers to superficial appearance in this world and not reality: Esau/Rome is a

תּוֹלְדוֹת **צַ**דִּיק וְרָשָׁע

צַדִּיק לְחַיִּים וְרָשָׁע לְמָוֶת

תּוֹלְדוֹת **קוֹ**שֶׁט וָשֶׁקֶר

קוֹשֶׁט לָאֵל וְשֶׁקֶר לֶאֱלִיל

תּוֹלְדוֹת **רַךְ** וָרָב

רַךְ לְאַסֵּף וְרַב לְהָסֵיף

תּוֹלְדוֹת **שָׁ**לֵם וּמְעֻוָּת

שָׁלֵם לְשָׁלוֹם וּמְעֻוָּת לְרוֹגֶז

תּוֹלְדוֹת **תָּם** וְתָע

תָּם לְתַאֵב וְתָע לְתַעֵב

(ח) עֵשָׂו וְיַעֲקֹב אֱדוֹם וְיִשְׂרָאֵל

עֵשָׂו לְפִי מַעֲשָׂיו וְיַעֲקֹב בְּשֵׁם נָקוּב

אֱדוֹם מַאְדִּים פָּנִים וְיִשְׂרָאֵל יָשׁוֹר לָאֵל

נִרְאֶה זֶה נִטְמַן זֶה

נִשְׁקַע זֶה הֵצִיץ זֶה

נָפַל זֶה יָרוּם זֶה

כָּבָה זֶה יָאִיר זֶה

לֶאֱדוֹם עוֹלָם זֶה וּלְיִשְׂרָאֵל עוֹלָם בָּא ועוֹלָם זֶה

וּבִשְׁמוֹ קָראוּי זֶה זֶה אֶל זֶה

---

highly visible presence, while Jacob/Israel barely registers. This outward manifestation belies the deeper truth of Israel's "visibility" (in the divine eye) and ultimate triumphal destiny. See next note.

44 **R** cites *GenR* 6:3, "Rabbi Naḥman said: As long as the light of the greater luminary functions, the light of the smaller one is not noticeable, but when the light of the greater one sets, the light of the smaller one becomes noticeable; even so, as long as the light of Esau prevails, the light of Jacob cannot be distinguished; but when the light of Esau sets, that of Jacob shall be distinguished…" In this stanza, the messianism of this piyyut becomes more explicit.

45 Here and in the following stich, "the one and the other" renders (lit.), "this and this." The blurring of identities is significant, and the names "Jacob" and "Israel" here apply to the patriarch, the angelic hosts, and the congregation. It may also have geographic significance, with the first assembly of angels("the host of Jacob") being those who escorted Jacob from Aram to the border of Canaan, and the second ("the host of Israel") being the host of angels that watched over him within the Land. Thus Israel and its national angelic hosts, both in the Land and in exile, join together in praising God and reciting the Qedushah. See also the *qedushta* for Gen 35:9, particularly the *silluq* (**B1** draws a parallel between this passage and the *silluq* for the *qedushta* for Gen 28:10).

are crowning This One,[46] like the one and like the other
with the one and with the other from the one and from the other
As it is written, "And the one called out ..."

Ofan

(9)[47] None can compare to You,[48]
the One who called the epochs and generations after Your name,[49] saying:
Holy, holy, holy is the Lord of Hosts! The whole earth is filled with His glory!
"Holy"—from the earliest epochs
"Holy"—until the last descendents
"Holy"—from fathers and sons
Holy, holy, holy is the Lord of Hosts! The whole earth is filled with His glory!
"Holy"—both father and son, He foresaw all from the earliest epoch[50]
"Holy"—on account of their descendents, upon later descendents
He will have mercy[51]
"Holy"—because of their name He said that both fathers and sons
will henceforth be called[52]
Holy, holy, holy is the Lord of Hosts! The whole earth is filled with His glory!
Towards each other ...

---

46 "This" is a name for God in payyetanic and rabbinic literature, based on sources such as Exod 15:2, "*This* is my God." (**B1** notes this and includes other sources in his discussion. Also see above, where Esau's rejection of "this" (birthright) is understood as a rejection of "This" (God).

47 This poem is built upon the triad of the patriarchs—Abraham, Isaac, and Jacob/Israel—reflecting the theme of the portion's opening words, "descendents." Each benefited the future generations in his own way, and is therefore recalled to Israel's benefit in the present. This poetic unit hearkens back to the first benediction of the Amidah, the *avot*, in which the merit of these ancestors is specifically invoked. By "the earliest epochs" and "the last descendents" Yannai includes his own community, which falls between the two

48 Ps 40:6, "Many, O Lord my God, are Your wonderful works that you have done, and Your thoughts, which are toward us; none can compare to You; if I would declare and tell of them, they would be more than can be numbered."

49 **R** cites Isa 41:4, "Who has wrought and achieved this? He who announced the generations from the start—I, the Lord, who was first and will be with the last ; I am He." God has foreseen all (and revealed one aspect of this to Rebecca through the oracle in Gen 25:23, in this *sidra*); the downfall of Esau/Edom/Rome and the ascent of Jacob/Israel are thus certainties.

50 **B1** contains a lengthy discussion of this line. "Father and son" probably refers to

מַכְתִּירִים לְזֶה כָּזֶה וְכָזֶה
בָּזֶה וּבָזֶה מִזֶּה וּמִזֶּה
ככתוב וקרא

אופן
(ט) אֵין לַעֲרוֹךְ אֵלֶיךָ
קוֹרֵא הַדּוֹרוֹת וְתוֹלְדוֹת לְשִׁמְךָ אוֹמְרִים
קדוש קדוש קדוש יי צבאות מלא כל הארץ כבודו
קָדוֹשׁ מִדּוֹרוֹת רִאשׁוֹנִים
קָדוֹשׁ מִתּוֹלְדוֹת אַחֲרוֹנִים
קָדוֹשׁ מֵאָבוֹת וּבָנִים
קדוש קדוש קדוש יי צבאות מלא כל הארץ כבודו
קָדוֹשׁ לְאָב וּבֵן צָפָה מִכָּל דּוֹרוֹת רִאשֹׁנִים
קָדוֹשׁ עַל תּוֹלְדוֹתָם יִיחֵס תּוֹלְדוֹת אַחֲרֹנִים

קָדוֹשׁ עַל שְׁמָם נָם יִקָּרְאוּ אָבוֹת וּבָנִים

קדוש קדוש קדוש יי צבאות מלא כל הארץ כבודו
לעומתם

Abraham and Isaac—the first and second generations of Israel—possibly in the specific context of the binding of Isaac (Gen 22), where they are most frequently described as "father" and "son." "Foreseen from the earliest epoch" refers to the aggadic conception that Abraham was destined to emerge as a uniquely righteous individual from the beginning of time. He stands at the apex of twenty flawed generations, with ten generations from Adam to Noah and another ten from Noah to Abraham. God has, therefore, been waiting for Abraham, Isaac, and Jacob for many generations. See *m. Avot* 5:2, *GenR* 39:4, etc.

51 As **R** notes, this verse seems to refer back to the binding of Isaac, an act in which Isaac was (according to rabbinic aggadah) an active participant. Isaac's merit benefits all his descendents ever since. (Yannai's *qedushta* for Gen 22 remains unrecovered.)

52 There are two different interpretive possibilities here, both arising out of the awkwardness of the phrase "their name." The first reading (given by **R**, citing *GenR* 63:3) emphasizes the idea of "name" and understands the poem as referring to the name "Israel," in which case Jacob receives the greatest honor, bestowing his name upon both the nation (the children of Israel) and God. Alternatively, as argued by **B1**, the suffix "their" is of primary importance, in which case the phrase refers to the three patriarchs all together; this reading bases itself in part on Jer 33:29 ("the seed of Abraham, Isaac, and Jacob"), which serves as a prooftext in *b. Ber.* 16b. Given the importance of Jacob in this poem, I am inclined to read against Bronznick's interpretation, although it has its merits.

Commentary

Only the final four units of this *qedushta* are preserved, and the surviving passages are damaged; nonetheless, a clear line of interpretation emerges. In particular, in the two interior units Yannai contrasts the eponymous ancestor of Israel, Jacob, with his twin brother, Esau, the ancestor of Rome. The simple juxtaposition of these two brothers is hardly innovative; the *sidra* upon which this poem is built invites the comparison from the birth of the brothers, and rabbinic exegesis freely developed and amplified their differences The poem's creativity and nuance lie in the way the poet constructs his comparison. Yannai begins with the biblical distinctions—hairy versus smooth-skinned, for example—and expands them into radical, ontological polarities. Most noteworthy among these are those that emphasize unity/multiplicity, and inclusion/exclusion.

The first kind of contrast, prominent at the conclusion of the second *rahit,* focuses on the actions of the individual characters: Jacob is consistently associated with language of unity and harmony, particularly as expressed through his assertions of God's oneness. Esau, by contrast, is depicted as Jacob's opposite: Esau shatters, creates discord, and denies the unity of God. In line 20, Jacob is characterized as "the unique one to unify," while Esau is "the boastful one" who "breaks to shards." In line 34, Jacob "blossoms forth"—a productive, positive image—while Esau "bursts asunder," causing damage to the world around. Jacob's heirs will stand in the breach, healing it, while Esau's descendents will create it. Similarly, in line 40, Jacob "will bring together" with his gentle speech, while Esau will "break [things] apart" with his arrogant approach to his world. In the next to last stanza, Jacob is associated with "wholeness" (which leads to peace) and Esau with "fragmentation" (the line is unclear, but "discord" would be a likely term to fill the lacuna). In sum, Jacob's actions are generative and result in positive consequences for his heirs, while Esau is the essence of destructiveness and such is his legacy. Yannai's emphasis on the creation and destruction of unity stands out because it is both vivid (kinetic and concrete) and evocative. What precisely does Yannai mean by this imagery? Perhaps the poet implies a critique of trinitarianism, of Christianity's "breaking" of the divine unity. Alternatively, he could be hinting at a political situation—depicting Jewish unity despite the fragmenting effects of the Diaspora (which were amplified by imperial policies), in contrast to the imperial and religious schisms within the Byzantine empire in the sixth century C.E. Or perhaps he does not intend any "contemporary" referent at all, revealing instead a facet of a deep philosophical idealism that values wholeness and dislikes destruction, as one understanding excludes the others.

The second category, inclusion and exclusion, introduces God into the twins' interpersonal dynamic. The divine response to Jacob and Esau can be summarized generally as "favor and disfavor," and the poet amplifies this overall reaction through the use of descriptors with unambiguous valences ("pure, righteous, pious"; associations with kosher or *treyf* animals; access or lack of access to the divine). Much of the specific language used to describe God's relation to each ancestor relies on the language of physical proximity and possession. Jacob is "a keepsake"—implicitly treasured and kept close—while Esau is "kept out" (7^2, line 4); Jacob is "sought" while Esau is "snubbed" (line 8). Jacob "dwells in safety" while Esau is "hurled outside" (line 18). Human actions affect proximity to God, but not in an abstract way. The words chosen are both emotional and strong, with vigorous, active connotations. It is a subtle touch but hardly accidental that "loving" and "loathing"—terms that describe God's feelings—are the polarity that open and close the second *rahit*.

The importance of physical space is underscored in the *silluq* where the imagery conveys inversion as reality is contrasted with appearance. At the present moment, Esau/Rome seems to have the advantage in the physical realm: he is exalted and brilliant, visible to all. His presence intrudes everywhere, inescapable and unavoidable. Jacob is lowly, even invisible. In the end, however, the existential reality of Israel's spiritual prominence will align with its physical space, and Esau will fall into darkness. The present world is, in a way, a mirror of the world-to-come. Just as the twins are opposites of each other, reverses of each other, so, too, will they exchange fate and status. Jacob, however, is the true image—the real figure—while Esau is the illusion in the glass.

Through the juxtaposition of vivid word-pairs, the poet dramatizes the choreography of the dynamic relationships among the three characters: Jacob, Esau, and God. The contrast between unity and multiplicity emphasizes the human actions, while the duality of inclusion and exclusion summarizes the divine response. By creating the category of inclusion/exclusion, the interactions take on concrete and tangible qualities. Despite possibly contrary outward appearances, Jacob (because of his actions and innate qualities) is "in," while Esau (for the same reasons) is "out." The reward for Jacob's righteousness is intimacy with the divine; being cut-off is Esau's punishment. At the same time, language of intense familiarity—of embracing, kissing or seeing God face-to-face—is not used. It is purely a "geographical" favoritism. All that is sought, all that is withheld, is proximity.

Qedushta for Genesis 27:28 בראשית כז:כח

"So may God give you" ויתן לך האלהים

The subject of this poem is Isaac's blessing of Jacob, a blessing the poet sees as both stolen and freely granted. Yannai explicates the content of the blessings (Gen 27:28-29) with a particular emphasis on two motifs. The first is "resurrection"—not only because "dew" is mentioned in the *sidra* but perhaps also because Isaac, who bequeaths the blessing, was so closely associated with that motif, both in the aggadah and in the liturgy. The second is the ongoing durability of these ancient blessings given to Israel's eponymous ancestor by Isaac—but confirmed and bestowed by God.

(4) …
(You) upon whom the pure one relied
forever affirm for him (a blessing):
Your shadow shall not leave him
goodness shall not diminish from its rightful owner.
The blessing of the fathers will bless the sons
and fathers and sons will bless Your holy name

(5) The pure man put on the most delightful garb[1]
and with the skins of kids he was bedecked
In cunning[2] he came[3] yet he did not—such a sin!—con him;[4]
but as for the con-man, who came with his "game"
  "The con-man shall not enjoy his game."[5]
Kids he cooked into tasty dishes for his father
with the scent of Eden spiced, they were savory to his palate[6]
You planned to bless him long before his father blessed him;[7]

---

1 A reference to the garments of Esau, which, according to legend, belonged to Adam and Nimrod the mighty hunter of Gen 10. See *GenR* 63:13 (which describes Esau's acquisition of the garments) and *GenR* 63:16 (which identifies the garment worn by Jacob in this *sidra* as Nimrod's). This motif is also present in *TargPsJ* Gen 27:15, *TanḥB Toledot* 12; and *NumR* 4:8.

2 This line is replete with difficult puns and double entendres. The phrase "*be-mirmah,*" usually translated as "with guile" or "deceitfully," here may be understood in accord with the targumic rendering, "with wisdom." See *GenR* 68:4, where Rabbi Yohanan states, "[Jacob] came with the wisdom of his Torah." The present translation attempts to reproduce this ambiguity, necessary for capturing the repetitions of the same root in the subsequent stichs. Similarly, the word צידו is translated as "game" (rather than, say, "prey") in order to capture the doubled meaning of the Hebrew, which is read in *GenR* 63:1 and *Tanḥ Toledot* 8 as teaching that Esau, the hunter, "ensnared" people with his words.

3 The verb "*huvah*" appears passive, indicating that Rebecca brought Jacob in; our lack of the earlier units of the poem prevents us from knowing how Yannai characterized the role of Jacob's mother in this story, but a reading of the verb as passive somewhat excuses Jacob and gives Rebecca the active role. However, in rabbinic and payyetanic Hebrew, the *hofal* can sometimes have the meaning of an active verb, indicating Jacob came on his own. **B1** notes *TanḥB Metzorah* 8 for the *hofal* of "to come" as a simple active verb, and cites Yahalom, *Sefat ha-shir* p. 62 for a more general discussion of this kind of slippage. It is possible that in this specific instance, the audience might have heard "he came" (הוא בא, with the verb in the *qal*). In the end, Hebraic ambiguity enables exegetical ambivalence.

4 This stich is difficult. The printed text says, "He did not deceive him—a sin." **R** follows Zulay, who emends the Hebrew רימיתו (deceive him) to דימיתו (seem to him), with the result that "It did not seem to him a sin." The Maʾagarim database's annotations suggest reading this in terms of Jacob's quick preparation, in contrast to Esau's delay described in *GenR* 67:2, cited in the following note (and mentioned by **R**).

5 Prov 12:27, translated to suit this context (cited by **R**). This Proverbs verse occurs as a

(ד) ...
... אֲשֶׁר נִסְמַךְ תָּם עָלָיו
לָנֶצַח כּוֹנְנָה עָלָיו
צִלְּךָ לֹא יָסוּר מֵעָלָיו
וְאַל יִמְנַע טוֹב מִבַּעֲלָו
בִּרְכַּת אָבוֹת יְבוֹרְכוּ בָנִים
וְאָבוֹת וּבָנִים יְבָרְכוּ שִׁמְךָ קָדוֹשׁ

(ה) **א**ִשׁ תָּם לָבַשׁ חֲמוּדוֹת עֲדָיִים
וַיִּתְלַבֵּשׁ בְּעוֹרוֹת גְּדָיִים
בְּמִרְמָה הוּבָא וְלֹא רִימִתוֹ חוּבָה
עַד אִישׁ מִרְמָה בָּא בְּצֵידוֹ
וְלֹא יַחֲרוֹךְ רְמִיָּה צֵידוֹ
גְּדָיִים אֲשֶׁר עָשׂ מַטְעַמִּים לְאָבִיו
מֵרִיחַ עֵדֶן עֲוּדְנוּ וְנִטְעֲמוּ לְפִיו
דָּרַשְׁתָּה לְבָרְכוֹ טֶרֶם אָב בֵּירְכוֹ

---

prooftext in *GenR* 67:2, where "the deceptive man" is identified as Esau. "Rabbi Leazar ben Rabbi Simeon said: O you snarer, how you have been ensnared! O you breaker of gates, how are your gates broken and destroyed!' Thus it is written, "The deceitful man shall not roast his game' (Prov 12:27). The Rabbis interpreted it: The Holy One, blessed be He, will not permit the trickster long to enjoy (*ya'arikh*) his game, nor delay (*ye'akher*) [in requiting him]. Rabbi Liezer, the son of Rabbi Yose ha-Galilee, interpreted it: Shall not the Holy One, blessed be He, delay and postpone the trickster's prey? For Rabbi Joshua ben Levi said: Esau spent the whole of that day catching deer and trussing them, but an angel came and freed them; also birds, which he tied together, an angel came and liberated them. And why was this? Because, as it is written, "But the substance of the man of glory is determined" (ibid.), i.e. so that Jacob who was the glory of the world might come and receive the blessings that had been determined as his from the very beginning of the world." See also *Tanḥ Toledot* 11 and *TanḥB Toledot* 17 (**R**).

6 This aggadic allusion is obscure. While offerings typically emit "a soothing odor" in the Bible, in this story it is usually Jacob's garments that smell of Eden, not the meat, as seems to be the case here. It may be that the pleasant scent was general, imbuing Jacob, his clothes, and his food with the odor of Eden; **R** cites *GenR* 65:22 (and parallels), which states: "The fact, however, is that when Jacob went in to his father the Garden of Eden entered with him." It could also be that the kid possessed the Edenic scent associated with the Passover offering. According to *TargPsJ* to Gen 27:9, the two kids Jacob fetched for Rebecca were for the Passover and Festival offerings.

7 Jacob was destined from the beginning of creation to receive the blessings conveyed in this chapter. **B1** adduces *GenR* 67:2, which states: "Jacob who was the glory of the world might come and receive the blessings that had been determined as his from the very beginning of the world." In this same passage, the Rabbis explain that Isaac weeps in this passage out of relief that he was not coerced by birth order into blessing the unworthy son, Esau, who—as a wicked person—had no right to God's blessing.

for You bless the righteous, and he is blessed
His blessing began with the beneficence of dew[8]
therefore You said: "I will be for Israel like dew."[9]
Those who curse him will be cursed like the one closed-of-eye[10]
but those who bless him shall be blessed like he who was never dull of eye[11]
The merit of the pure one went first and strode before him[12]
lest he be exposed[13] to his father and be ashamed[14]
You strengthened his right hand and You brought one unto the other
perfect blessings to place upon him
Dew does good for both living and dead
for within it lies both life and good[15]
Splendid in summer and lovely in winter,
in this world and the world to come

(6) [For His faithfulness[16]] you shall not want
from you and from your seed it shall not be turned aside[17]
Trusted shall you be and gladdened by good tidings
for mixed wine shall never be wanting[18]

---

8 Gen 27:28, the actual patriarchal blessing, opens with a reference to the dew. Here this is understood to be the dew of resurrection, which was among Isaac's gifts to Jacob. *TarPsJ* to Gen 27:6 states, "And Rebecca said to her son Jacob, saying, `Behold, tonight the heavenly beings praise the Lord of the world and the storehouses of dews are opened.'" See also *PRE* 32.

9 Hos 14:6 (**R**).

10 **R** connects this with Num 23:3, 15 (a reference to Balaam, who was blind to God's will). See Judith Baskin, "Origen on Balaam: The Dilemma of the Unworthy Prophet," *Vigiliae Christianae* 37 (1983): 22–35.

11 That is, Moses (see, as **R** notes, Deut 34:7). See both *Targ N* and *TargPJ* to Gen 27:29 for this same juxtaposition of cursed-as-Balaam and blessed-as-Moses, also in connection with this *sidra*. See also *TanḥB Toledot* 16 and *GenR* 66:4.

12 Jacob's merit, here personified, preceded him and protect him from being revealed as an imposter; a similar idea is expressed in *GenR* 65:19 (**R**), which describes two angels supporting Jacob at the moment when the stress of deceiving his father threatened to make him faint.

13 Reading יתגלה in place of יתגלע with **R**. The weakening of the guttural (interchanging ע and ה) is well-attested in Jewish-Palestinian dialects. See E.Y. Kutscher, *Studies in Galilean Aramaic*, trans. M. Sokoloff (Bar Ilan University Press: Ramat Gan, 1976), 70–78. Alternatively, this could be construed in accord with Prov 18:1 and 20:3, in which the word יתגלע is usually translated as "he who isolates, ensnares himself" but which may, **B2** argues, be regarded as synonymous with יתגלה, "he who reveals himself, is exposed."

14 Literally, "and his face grow pale." The idiom comes from Isa 29:22, which concludes,

כִּי אַתָּה תְּבָרֵךְ צַדִּיק וְיִתְבָּרֵךְ
הַתְחָלַת בִּרְכָתוֹ הָיְתָה בְּטוּב טָל
לָכֵן נַמְתָּה אֶהְיֶה לְיִשְׂרָאֵל כַּטָּל
וְאוֹרְרָיו אֲרוּרִים כִּשְׁתוּם הָעָיִן
וּמְבוֹרְכָיו בְּרוּכִים כְּלֹא נִכְהָא בָּעָיִן
זְכוּת תָּם קִידְּמָה וְהָלְכָה לְפָנָיו
פֶּן יִתְגַּלַּע לָאָב וְיֶחֱוְרוּ פָּנָיו
חִיזַּקְתָּה יְמִינוֹ וַתְּבִיאוֹ אֵלָיו
בְּרָכוֹת גְּמוּרוֹת לְהַשִּׂיא עָלָיו
טַל אֲשֶׁר לַחַיִּים וְלַמֵּתִים הוּא טוֹב
וּבוֹ נִכְלְלוּ הַחַיִּים וְהַטּוֹב
יָפֶה בְּחוֹרֶב וְנָעִים בְּחוֹרֶף
בָּעוֹלָם הַזֶּה וְלָעוֹלָם הַבָּא

(ו) ... לֹא תֶחְסַר
מִמָּךְ וּמִזַּרְעָךְ לֹא תוּסַר
בָּטוּחַ תְּהִי וּמְבֻוּשָּׂר
כִּי הַמֶּזֶג לֹא יֶחְסָר

---

appropriately enough for our context: "No more shall Jacob be shamed, no longer his face grow pale."

15 **R** cites *TanḥB Toledot* 19, which states: "Dew is symbolic of resurrection of the dead, and thus Isaiah said: `Your dead men shall live, together with my dead body shall they arise. Awake and sing, you who dwell in dust; for your dew is as the dew of herbs, and the earth shall cast out the shades of the dead' (Isa 26:19). **R** also mentions *PRK Va-Tomer Zion* 8, where the superiority of dew over rain is explicated, based on Hos 14:6, cited above. It is possible that the dew that is good for the living ("in this world") is Torah; see *Sifre Deut Ha'azinu* 1. These meanings carry over into the following line.

16 God's love/truth as symbolized by Torah. The restoration may be "his love" (אהבתו), as supplied by **R**, or "truth" (אמונתו), as preferred by **B1** (based on Mic 7:20, "You will show truth to Jacob, and loyalty to Abraham, as you have sworn to our fathers from the days of old."). This translation accommodates nuances of both possibilities.

17 See *TargPsJ* to Gen 27:13, in which Rebecca states: "If he blesses you with blessings, let them come upon you and upon your children." In this piyyut, however, the source of the blessing is God; the patriarch is simply the vehicle. "It" refers to the blessing.

18 Based on Song 7:3 (**R**). See *SongR* 7:6, where "mixed wine" (מזג) is understood as the "needs (*nizga*) of the world," which God (the "Butler"—*mazga*) provides (see also *GenR* 66:3). There may also be an allusion to the tradition preserved in *TargPJ* to Gen 27:24, which tells that when Jacob brought the cooked dishes to his father, in order to secure the blessing, "he had no wine, but an angel mixed it for him, from the wine that had been kept in its grapes from the days of the beginning of the world; and he gave it into Jacob's hand, and Jacob brought it to his father, and he drank."

The power of bountiful dripping dew,[19]
when the dew upon you drops,
The grain—young men—shall He renew
and new wine shall He pour forth for the maidens[20]
. . .[21]
The paternal possession and the mother's domain:[22]
dominion over the father's brother
and authority over the mother's brother[23]
He hastens to hearken to his father and his mother,[24]
to taste the fruit of honoring father and mother[25]
What is yours and not yours is given you
all that is yours shall be given you;[26]
Those below and those above are with you;[27]
they sanctify the Name of Him who chose you[28]

(7[1]) Stones not whole will become one whole stone[29]
he had faith: indeed, his bed would be whole[30]

---

19 Yannai here alludes to the interpretation of Ps 68:10 that is preserved in *LevR* 28:3: "Rabbi Berekhiah expounded: I, [says God], am your Cook, so will you not let me taste of your broth, so that I may know what you require, whether dew or rain? This is what David meant when he said, 'Rain, a free gift, pour down, O God' (Ps 68:10). David said to the Holy One, blessed be He: 'Sovereign of the Universe! If the land requires rain, give it as "a free gift" and if it requires dew, 'Pour down, O God'" (**B1**). The blessing for dew is inserted in the prayer known as "[God's] Power (*gevurah*)," which also mentions the resurrection of the dead. Dew is commonly associated with resurrection and renewed life. See *m. Ta'an.* 1:1 (**R**).

20 **R** connects with Zech 9:17, a difficult verse: "How lovely, how beautiful they shall be, producing young men like new grain, young women like new wine!" He also cites *GenR* 66:3 for an interpretation of this verse in the context of the *sidra*. The image is one of God reviving the young men and women of Israel—resurrection restoring all people to their youthful vigor.

21 Gap of fourteen lines.

22 **B1** notes here that the phrase "mother's domain" (*naḥalat ha-em*) may refer to the fact that according to *b. Git.* 77a, women could not purchase property but could inherit it.

23 That is, the descendents of Ishmael and Laban; this is in accord with Gen 27:29 (**R**). It may be that Yannai regards Laban as the progenitor of more recent oppressors, including the Hellenistic empires (the Seleucid rulers, most notably Antiochus IV, who desecrated the Temple in the 2nd century B.C.E., leading to the Maccabean revolt) and Rome (an association perhaps based on an anagram: *Arami/Romai*). Or, more generally, Laban may represent any power that seeks to destroy Jacob/Israel—similar to Pharaoh and Amalek, but worse for being a member of the family.

24 According to *GenR* 68:8 (cited by **B2**), Jacob possessed the power of "shortening the way" (קפיצת הדרך), reaching Padan Aram in a single day, out of obedience to his parents' wishes that he go there.

גְבוּרַת הַטַל הַמְנוּפֵף
וְכַטַל עָלֶיךָ יְחוּפֵף
דָּגָן בַּחוּרִים יְשׁוֹבֵב
וְתִירוֹשׁ לִבְתוּלוֹת יְנוֹבֵב
...
קִנְיַן אָב וְנַחֲלַת הָאֵם
שִׁלְטוֹן אֲחִי אָב
וְהַמְשֵׁל אֲחִי אֵם
רָץ שְׁמוֹעַ אֶל אָב וְאֶל אֵם
אָכוֹל מִפְּרִי כִּיבּוּד אָב וָאֵם
שֶׁלָּךְ וְשֶׁלֹּא לָךְ יֻיתַּן לָךְ
וּמִשֶּׁלָּךְ יִנָּתֶן לָךְ
תַּחְתּוֹנִים וְעֶלְיוֹנִים בָּךְ
יַקְדִּישׁוּ שֵׁם בּוֹחֵר בָּךְ

(ז[1]) **אֲ**בָנִים לֹא שְׁלֵימוֹת כְּנַעֲשׂוּ אֶבֶן שְׁלֵימָה
הֶאֱמִין כִּי מִטָּתוֹ לִהְיוֹת שְׁלֵימָה

25 See *m. Pe'ah* 1:1, where honoring one's parents is listed as among the actions for which a person "enjoys the fruits" (lives off the "interest") in this world while even more merit (the "principle") remains in the world to come (**R**).

26 **R** connects with *GenR* 66:3, "`So may God give you' (Gen 27:28, the opening verse of the *sidra*). May He give you again and again. May He give you blessings and give you the means for holding them. May He give you what is yours, and give you of your father's; may He give you yours and give you of your brother's. Rabbi Aḥa said: `May He give you of His own divine strength. When? When you need it.'"

27 The pronoun in the first stich refers to Jacob. "Those below" probably refers to Jacob's family, while "those above" refers to the angels who guard Jacob on his flight from Esau and throughout his exile.

28 Ps 135:4, "For the Lord has chosen Jacob for Himself." In *GenR* 76:1, Jacob is identified as "the chosen one of the patriarchs," who received divine assurance and yet remained afraid. Ps 135:4 is the proof text for Jacob's distinct chosenness. **B2** cites Isa 41:8 in *Sifre Deut* 27.

29 Perhaps a description of the twelve tribes descended from Jacob who will become one nation; see *GenR* 68:11.

30 "Bed" is here understood as a euphemism for progeny (i.e., the offspring of the marital bed)—Jacob's flight is not only from Esau but towards marriage and fatherhood. "Whole" may refer to the moral qualities of his sons, as in the next line; to their unity, as in the previous stich; or to the broader health, welfare, and prosperity of his descendents. *LevR* 36:5 is particularly appropriate to note here, both for its very similar language and its exegetical contours. It states: "Why is the expression `*af*' used in connection with Abraham and Isaac but not in connection with Jacob? Because the latter's `bed' was perfect before Him. From Abraham sprang Ishmael and all the sons of Keturah; from Isaac sprang Esau and all the chiefs of Edom; but Jacob's bed was perfect, all his sons being righteous." This idea is continued in the following line.

Without begetting, like his fathers, both righteous and wicked
one righteous and one wicked[31]
He approached the place "He will see,"[32] and he saw (in) a dream
And God appeared like the awesome angels appear
The image of the ladder unfurled from the Footstool to the Throne[33]
to compare (him) with the image engraved on the Throne …
…

(7²) Then, when he went forth, he resembled a gazelle
and glory to the righteous will resound through the land[34]
In order to find for him comfort
before its time, the sun sank[35]
Heaped and loaded with the blessings of plenty[36]
Fleeing from the one who abhorred the seven
Tears dripped as he wept[37]
as he went forth empty handed from Beer Sheba[38]
…

---

31 That is, Jacob's children would all be righteous; see note above.

32 Perhaps associating Beth El with Mt. Moriah, renamed "The Lord will see" in Gen 22:14.

33 That is, from the earth to heaven; see Isa 66:1.

34 The phrase "glory to the righteous" comes from Isa 24:16, which colors the imagery in the second stich, as well. The line puns on "gazelle" and "glory" (both of which are צבי).

35 *GenR* 68:10 states: "The Rabbis said: The Holy One, blessed be He, caused the sun to

בְּלִי לְהוֹלִיד כְּהוֹרָיו בְּצֶדֶק וּבְרֶשַׁע
אֶחָד צַדִּיק וְאֶחָד רָשָׁע
גָּשׁ לְמָקוֹם יֵרָאֶה וַחֲלוֹם רָאָה
וְאֵל אֵלָיו נִרְאֶה כְּמַלְאֲכֵי מוֹרָא מַרְאֵה
דְּמוּת סוּלָם זָקוּף מֵהֲדוֹם לְכִסֵּא
לִדְמוּת דְּמוּת אֲשֶׁר חֲקוּקָה בְּכִסֵּא
...

(ז[2]) **אָ**ז בְּצֵאתוֹ לִצְבִי דָמָה
וּצְבִי לְצַדִּיק צִלְצְלָה אֲדָמָה
בַּעֲבוּר לְהַמְצִיא לוֹ נֶחָמָה
לְלֹא עִתָּהּ שָׁקְעָה חַמָּה
גָּדוּשׁ וּטָעוּן בְּרָכוֹת שָׁבֵעַ
בּוֹרֵחַ מִמְּתוּעָב שֶׁבַע
דְּמָעוֹת הֵטִיף שָׁוֵעַ
בְּצֵאתוֹ רֵיקָם מִבְּאֵר־שֶׁבַע
...

set prematurely, in order to speak in privacy with our father Jacob."

36 That is, the blessings Isaac gave Jacob in Gen 27:28–29. It may also pun on "seven," as in the "Seven Blessings" of the wedding service, indicating Jacob's forthcoming marriage (and perhaps anticipating the burdens that will come with his two wives and their family).

37 Jacob's tears are here implicitly contrasted with those of Esau in Gen 27:34.

38 See Gen 28:10. According to *GenR* 68:3, Isaac sent Jacob away from Beer Sheba empty handed.

Commentary

In the extant fragments of the *qedushta*, Yannai confronts a question that troubles many readers of the Jacob story: Did Jacob steal the blessing of the first-born from Isaac—tricking a blind man, his own father, no less? Or did he gain it legitimately, with Isaac playing along with the ruse? Was Jacob's conscience at ease, or was he troubled? Yannai hedges. He does not aggressively read the biblical text against the contextual meaning, in order to fully clear Jacob's character (despite precedent in rabbinic tradition for such "strong" interpretations) but neither does he condemn the patriarch's actions. Jacob here is "cunning" (Poem Five, line 3) and he feels anxiety "lest he be exposed" to Isaac and suffer shame for his actions (Poem Five, line 14). At the same time, the poet makes clear that God—not just Rebecca (who is absent from the surviving passages of the poem, except perhaps through the presence of a passive verb)—was actively behind the conspiracy. In Poem Five, line 4, it is stated that God had already determined that Jacob should receive this blessing, while in line 15, God steadies Jacob's trembling hand. Indeed, Jacob's hypostasized merit escorts him into the room (line 13) This divine involvement affirms that Jacob is, in fact, "pure" (Poem Four, line 1) of any deception and suggests his reluctance to trick his blind father. The only character labeled "deceptive" in this poem is Esau (Poem Five, line 4), although the allusion to Laban (Poem Six, line 10) may hint at the trickster who lies in Jacob's future. The overall motion within the fragment is from insecurity to confidence, as Jacob assumes ownership of a blessing that has in truth been his all along. Confidence in the future mitigates the fragility of the present.

The blessings Isaac bestows upon Jacob focus upon two things: resurrection, including life in the world to come; and triumph of Israel over less worthy relations (primarily Esau, but also Ishmael and Laban). The motif of resurrection in the piyyut is rooted in the prominence of "dew" in Gen 27:28, and dew's association with resurrection, both in general (see *m. Taʿanit* 1:1; *PRE* 33 and 34; and many others) and specifically in the second blessing of the Amidah, *gevurah* ("God's Might") where control over life and death symbolizes the scope of divine power—the seasonal prayer for dew occurs in the context of the second prayer of the Amidah, and Yannai mentions dew at the end of almost every *meḥayyeh* unit. Furthermore, the belief that Isaac was actually sacrificed and then resurrected underlies an association of Isaac with the second benediction of the Amidah, and this colors the association of Isaac with life-giving dew.[41] The second motif, which emphasizes Jacob's triumph over his foes and his temporary dire straits, continues the nationalized allegory of the Jacob-Esau story begun in the *qedushta* for Gen 25. Even when Yannai appears to be recalling and expanding the biblical story, he simultaneously develops a contemporary lesson for his congregation. He collapses the sense of time that separates Jacob from his descendents, and his children from "the children of Israel," leading his listeners to understand the ancient tale as their own story.

Prophecies of restoration, vindication, and justice implicit in the Jacob-Esau allegory remain unfulfilled, but this poem provides true consolation. The intense and intimate involvement of God in every moment of Israel's history—in planning Jacob's blessing from the beginning of time, guiding the plot that secured the blessing, maintaining the blessing through the generations after Jacob, and promising that all conditions of the blessing will, in the end, be fulfilled—can be imagined as instilling hope at a moment when the Byzantine empire was tilting towards ever more constrictive practices in its relations with non-Christians subjects. In the brief fragment of the poem that remains to us, affirmation of the continuity of divine providence occurs with great frequency. This message can be read as a continued development of Yannai's general program of "disengagement": affirming confidence in divine justice and salvation in order to forestall more direct confrontation with the imperial powers.

These important contextual elements aside, it is particularly delightful that this common theological trope of God blessing Israel is embedded in the context of Israel sanctifying God. The relationships become mutually reinforcing: God blesses fathers, fathers bless sons, sons bless God. The poet's construction thus creates a sense of rapturous reciprocity as the sacred act of reciting the Qedushah approaches. While the poet acknowledges, obliquely, elements of his present-day context, his attention is fixed on God.

41 The classic study of Isaac's near (or actual) sacrifice and subsequent resurrection in Jewish tradition is Shalom Spiegel, *The Last Trial,* trans. Judah Goldin (New York: Behrman House, 1979). For a more recent treatment of the motif, see Jon Levenson, *The Death and Resurrection of the Beloved Son* (New Haven: Yale University Press, 1993).

Qedushta for Genesis 28:10 — בראשית כח:י

"Then Jacob went forth" — ויצא יעקב

The biblical story of Jacob's dream at Beth El during his flight from Esau is both vivid and enigmatic. In particular, Jacob's vision of the ladder to heaven and the angels ascending and descending upon it invites speculation on the nature and function of angels. Yannai accepts the invitation, presenting a relatively extensive angelology that illuminates the nature of Jacob-Israel as well. Yannai constructs a poetic scaffolding for these thematic concerns with the result that, despite the fragmentary nature of the surviving poem, this composition offers insight into both his poetic creativity and the exegetical richness of piyyut.

(7) [*For the Lord redeemed Jacob* (Jer 31:11)[1]]
Redemption He will send again,[2] just as He sent before
Suddenly it will sprout up,[3] springing forth and coming swiftly

Command salvation for Jacob! (Ps 44:5)
Righteous and saved in righteousness he rejoices
For Your salvation we cry: out Save us, and we shall be saved!

The voice is the voice of Jacob (Gen 27:22)
A voice pleasant in majesty and also very sweet[4]
Purer than milk, sweeter than honey

Shout for joy in Jacob (Jer 31:7)
Celebrate with fitting songs, with proper melodies[5]
Men and women making music[6] upon every melodic instrument[7]

Hearken to me, O Jacob (Isa 48:12)
You summoned with an utterance[8]: "Hearken!" [And they replied: "Hear"][9]
You heard the reply: "We will do as we have heard"[10]

You gave Truth to Jacob (Mic. 7:20)
Strong in faith and to testimony, faithful[11]
Held in faith shall it be to those who keep the faith

---

1 Completion supplied by **R**. This verse is explicated in relation to the patriarch Jacob in *GenR* 44:22, and it also recalls the conclusion of the blessing that follows the Shema, the *geʾulah.*

2 Ps 111.9 (**B2**).

3 Mal 3:1 (**B2**).

4 The first stich alludes to Isa 30:30 (**B1**), "And the Eternal shall make His majestic voice heard," but here describes Jacob's voice. The idea that Jacob's voice (identified with Israel's voice) is especially powerful may also derive from its ability to silence even the angelic hosts when it is raised in prayer; see *GenR* 65:21, which states: "`The voice is the voice of Jacob': This is the voice that silences heavenly and earthly beings…When Israel says, `Hear O Israel', the angels are silent and then drop their wings; and what do they [later] proclaim? `Blessed be the name of His glorious kingdom for all eternity.'" The source of Jacob's power, however, is Torah. According to *GenR* 65:20 (cited by **B1**), Jacob's voice is "sweet" when he and his descendents study Torah, which is like milk and honey under the tongue (see *DeutR* 7:3; *SongR* 1:19, 2:14).

5 כישרות (from ישר), but perhaps read כּוֹשָׁרוֹת. **B1**suggests that this line draws on Ps 68:7, which is a challenging text. In *Mekh. Pisḥah* 16, this verse is used to describe the joy of the Israelites during the Exodus (an event commemorated in the Song at the Sea, Exod 15). While the language is difficult, the imagery is clear: the future redemption, like the first, will be a celebration.

(ז)

...

פְּדוּת עוֹד יִשְׁלַח אֲשֶׁר כְּבָר שָׁלַח
וּפִתְאוֹם תִּצְמַח וְתָבוֹא וְתִצְלַח

צַוֵּה יְשׁוּעוֹת יַעֲקֹב
צַדִּיק וְנוֹשָׁע בְּצֶדֶק נְשָׁוְעָשַׁע
וּלְיֶשְׁעֲךָ נְשַׁוֵּעַ הוֹשִׁיעֵנוּ וְנִוָּשֵׁעַ

קוֹל קוֹל יַעֲקֹב
קוֹל נָעִים בְּהוֹד וְגַם עָרֵב מְאֹד
נָקִי מֵחָלָב וּמָתוֹק מִדְּבָשׁ

רָנּוּ לְיַעֲקֹב שִׂמְחָה
רְנָנוֹת מֻוכְשָׁרוֹת בְּנִיגּוּן כִּישָׁרוֹת
שָׁרִים וְשָׁרוֹת בְּכָל כְּלֵי שִׁירוֹת

שְׁמַע אֵלַי יַעֲקֹב
שִׁמַּעְתָּה שׁוֹמֵעַ שִׁימְעוּ
וְשָׁמַעְתָּה שֵׁימַע נַעֲשֶׂה וְנִשְׁמָע

תִּתֵּן אֱמֶת לְיַעֲקֹב
תּוֹקֶף אֱמוּנָה וְעֵדוּת נֶאֱמָנָה
וַתְּהִי מוּאֳמָנָה לְבַעֲלֵי אֲמָנָה

---

6 **B1** connects with 2 Sam 19:36, describing the luxuries of David's court (see also Eccl 2:8, also describing courtly opulence).

7 Amos 6:5, cited by **B1**, where musical entertainment symbolizes the decadent pleasures of Ephraim's wealthy class. Yannai uses the imagery in a positive way: music as emblem of happiness.

8 For the root שמע in the Piel, see 1 Sam 15:4 and 23:8. Reading שימע with **B1**.

9 Lacuna filled according to **B1**, who inserts: ועני שמע. This line may refer to the tradition of exegesis surrounding Gen 49:1–2 (see *qedushta* for Gen 49, as well as the *qedushta* for Deut 6:4), when Jacob summons his sons to his deathbed with the imperative, "Hearken!" When Jacob tells his sons that he is worried they will succumb to sin and transgress against God's unity after his death, the sons reply with the Shema: "Hear, O Israel, the Lord is our God, the Lord is One" (Deut 6:4). This verse from Deuteronomy is thus reread: "Israel" is the patriarch, not the nation, and the general affirmation of monotheism is specified. See *GenR* 98:3; *DeutR* 2:35, and the *targumim* (*N* and *PsJ*) to Gen 49:1–2 and Deut. 6:4.

10 The ultimate ratification of Jacob's sons' fidelity to their father's admonishment is the acceptance of the Torah and the yoke of the commandments at Sinai, signified here by the quotation of Exod 24:7 (cited by **R**).

11 The language of this line alludes to Ps 19:8–10; according to *j. RH* 18a, *PRK* 2:4, and others, "Truth" (אמת)is an appelation for Torah (**B1**). Yannai thus reads the base-text for this stanza, Mic 7:20, in light of this intertext, as referring to God's gift of the Torah to Israel.

(8) For Your trust is in Jacob and Your testimony is in Israel
for (You) see the image of Jacob[12]
They sanctify You, O Holy One of Israel and they recall the Name of Jacob
and they stand in awe of the God of Israel[13]
You are called "the God of Jacob" and also "the God of Israel;"
and at the manifestation[14] of Your camps of angels:
One proclaims the name "Jacob" and another proclaims the name "Israel,"[15]
and the first one says, "Holy is He!"
And the second one says, "Blessed is He!" and this one calls out to the other
and this one listens well to the other[16]
and this one agrees with the other and this one is aligned with the other;
and the one inquires of the other[17]
and the other teaches the one[18]; one brings glad tidings to a thousand
and a thousand to a multitude
and a multitude to multitudes a thousand thousands open up
and a multitude of multitudes respond
and the rest, whose words were unrecorded, in thinnest silence whisper;[19]
and they draw The Chariot
and in their mustering, they sway and with their wings, they fly
and at the time when they assemble[20],
They take flight and they seem to be above Him
but nothing is above Him
the stature of each one of them is like the span of the Great Sea
and they stoop their stature down for Him[21]
and they shroud the front of the throne and the sound
of its wheels go forth

12 Referring to the image of Jacob engraved on the divine chariot; see *GenR* 68:12 (**R**); *b.Hul.* 91b; *Tanḥ Bamidbar* 19; *TanḥB Bamidbar* 22; *PRE* 35; *TargN* to Gen 28:12; and others.

13 See Isa 29:23 (**R**).

14 This translation follows Maʾagarim, which suggests that the root of the word דגם is the rabbinic loanword from Greek, as is the Hebrew term, דוגמא.

15 The language here is from Isa 44:5; the application of this verse to the angels occurs in *Mek. Mishpatim* 18. **R** notes that this passage assumes that there are two camps of angels, and cites *GenR* 68:12; there, the "ascending" angels of Jacob's dream are identified as the angels who escorted Jacob from his father's house to the borders of the Land of Israel (and are now returning to heaven), while the "descending" angels are those who escorted him once he left the Land—thus the first cohort are "exilic" angels and the second "domestic," These two camps of angels participate antiphonally in the divine worship. (See also *Tanḥ Vayishlaḥ.* 3 and *TanḥB Vayishlaḥ.* 3.) It would seem, by extension, that the divine names "Holy One" and "Blessed One" reflect ways of describing God in exile and in the Land of Israel.

(ח) כִּי אֱמוּנָתְךָ בְּיַעֲקֹב וְעֵדוּת הִיא בְּיִשְׂרָאֵל
כִּי רוֹאֶה דְמוּת יַעֲקֹב
יַקְדִּישׁוּךָ קְדוֹשׁ יִשְׂרָאֵל וּמַזְכִּירֵי שֵׁם יַעֲקֹב
יַעֲרִיצוּךָ אֱלֹהֵי יִשְׂרָאֵל
נִקְרֵאתָה אֱלֹהֵי יַעֲקֹב וְגַם אֱלֹהֵי יִשְׂרָאֵל
וּדְגַם מַחֲנוֹת מַלְאָכֶיךָ
זֶה יִקְרָא בְּשֵׁם יַעֲקֹב וְזֶה יְכַנֶּה בְּשֵׁם יִשְׂרָאֵל
זֶה יֹאמַר קָדוֹשׁ הוּא
וְזֶה יֹאמַר בָּרוּךְ הוּא וְזֶה אֶל זֶה יִקְרָאוּ
וְזֶה מִזֶּה יְקַבֵּלוּ
וְזֶה עִם זֶה יִשְׁווּ וְזֵה בָּזֶה יִפְגָּשׁוּ
וְזֶה אֶת זֶה יִשְׁאָלוּ
וְזֶה לָזֶה יְלַמֵּדוּ אֶחָד יְבַשֵּׂר לְאֶלֶף
וְאֶלֶף לִרְבָבָה
וּרְבָבָה לִרְבָבוֹת אֶלֶף אֲלָפִים יִפְתָּחוּ
וְרִיבּוֹ רְבָבוֹת יַעֲנוּ
וְהַשְׁאָר אֲשֶׁר לֹא כָתוּב דְּמָמָה דַקָּה יֶחֱשׁוּ
וְהַמֶּרְכָּבָה יַעֲגִילוּ
וּבַאֲגַפֵּיהֶם יְנוֹפֵפוּ וּבְכַנְפֵיהֶם יְעוֹפֵפוּ
וְעֵת אֲשֶׁר יְטַפְסְרוּ
וְיָטוּסוּ יֵירָאוּ מִמַּעַל לוֹ
אֲבָל אֵין מִמַּעַל לוֹ
וְקוֹמַת כָּל אֶחָד מֵהֶם כְּאוֹרֶךְ הַיָּם הַגָּדוֹל
וְיַגְהִינוּ לוֹ קוֹמָתָם
וִיאַחֲזוּ פְּנֵי כִסֵּא
וְיֵלֵךְ קוֹל גַּלְגַּלָּיו

16 Or: "This one is parallel to/matches that one." See the *Targum* of Isa 6:3 (**R**).

17 One cohort of angels asks, "Where is the place of His glory?" (a question embedded in the *musaf* Qedushah, as discussed by both **R** and **B1**). The other angels teach the reply: "Blessed is the glory of the Eternal from His place!" (Ezek 3:12).

18 This may be a reference to the tradition that angels are created anew each morning; as a result, they must teach themselves the response, "Blessed is the Lord from His place," in response to their own question, "Where is the place of His glory?" (**B1**). As with the story surrounding Jacob's son's reciting the Shema, cited above, a liturgical text is recast as having origins in a kind of narrative.

19 A play on the theopanic images in 1 Kgs 19:17.

20 The verb here is יטפשרו, which occurs only as a nominal form in the Hebrew Bible, with the sense of "scribe, marshal." See Nah 3:17 (**R**), Jer 51:27. The nuance of the root suggests rigorous orderliness.

21 Reading ויגחינו with **R**.

And those that are listed as being upon the throne[22]
give glory to the One who sits upon the throne:[23]
The lion roars and the ox bellows
the eagle shrieks and the human[24] cries aloud
from here and from there from this one and from the other
These are of fire and these are of snow;[25]
these are of Jacob and these are of Israel:
a singular delight, all of them as one,
as it is written, "And one called out..."

(9) Their delight is in Jacob
They sanctify you, O Holy One of Jacob
and they sing out and say:
Holy, holy, holy is the Lord of Hosts! The whole earth is filled with His glory!
"*Holy*"—from the angels of mercy
"*Holy*"—from the angels of peace
"*Holy*"—from the angels of the hosts
Holy, holy, holy is the Lord of Hosts! The whole earth is filled with His glory!
"*Holy*"—With the angels of mercy
He accompanies Jacob in his going forth[26]
"*Holy*"—With the angels of peace
He guards him in the place of his sleeping
"*Holy*"—With the angels of the hosts
He revealed Himself to him in his dream
Holy, holy, holy is the Lord of Hosts! The whole earth is filled with His glory!
... Towards each other...

---

22 See Ezek 1:10, which lists the four creatures whose faces appear on the four sides of the divine throne (**R**).

23 Ps 16:9.

24 According to *PRE* 35 (among others), the human face of the chariot-drawing creatures looks like Jacob (**R**).

25 On "the river of fire" from which the angels come, see Dan 7:10. "Angels of snow" and "angels of fire" are a common duality in rabbinic angelology; see *NumR* 12:8; *DeutR* 5:12; *SongR* 3:24. For comparisons of angels and Israel using this imagery, see *ExodR* 15:7, "The angels renew themselves each day, praise the Lord, and then return to the river of fire from

וְהָרְשׁוּמִים בַּכִּסֵּא
יְפָאֲרוּ לְיוֹשֵׁב עַל כִּסֵּא
אַרְיֵה יִשְׁאַג וְשׁוֹר יִגְעֶה
נֶשֶׁר יְצַפְצֵף וְאָדָם יִצְוָוח
מִפֹּה וּמִפֹּה מִזֶּה וּמִזֶּה
אֵילוּ מֵאֵשׁ וְאֵילוּ מִשֶּׁלֶג
אֵילוּ בְּיַעֲקֹב וְאֵילוּ בְּיִשְׂרָאֵל
נְעִימָה אַחַת כּוּלָּם כְּאֶחָת
ככתוב וקרא

(ט) נְעִימָתָם לְיַעֲקֹב
מַקְדִּישֶׁךָ קְדוֹשׁ יַעֲקֹב
עוֹנִים וְאוֹמְרִים
קדוש קדוש קדוש יי צבאות מלא כל הארץ כבודו
קָדוֹשׁ מִמַּלְאֲכֵי רַחֲמִים
קָדוֹשׁ מִמַּלְאֲכֵי שָׁלוֹם
קָדוֹשׁ מִמַּלְאֲכֵי צְבָאוֹת
קדוש קדוש קדוש יי צבאות מלא כל הארץ כבודו
קָדוֹשׁ בְּמַלְאֲכֵי רַחֲמִים
לִיוָּוה לְיַעֲקֹב בְּצֵאתוֹ
קָדוֹשׁ בְּמַלְאֲכֵי שָׁלוֹם
שִׁימְּרוּ בִּמְקוֹם יָשְׁנוֹ
קָדוֹשׁ בְּמַלְאֲכֵי צְבָאוֹת
נִיגְלָה לוֹ בִּמְקוֹמוֹ
...

לעומתן

which they emerged, and the Lord renews them and restores them to their former condition; for it says: 'They are new every morning' (Lam 3:23). So also Israel is sunk in iniquity on account of the evil impulse that is within them, but they do penitence, and God each year pardons their iniquities and renews their heart to fear Him; for it says: 'A new heart also will I give you' (Ezek. 36:26)." See also *LamR* 3:8 for a more extensive version of this aggadah. See, too, Yannai's *qedushta* for Exod 3:1 (**R**, I:263–274).

26 See *GenR* 68:11 (**R**). The use of the preposition -ב ("with") here in place of the more common -מן ("from," used in the initial lines of this unit) or the absence of a proposition is unusual.

"From His place"

He went down, and brought down His hosts
to see the image of Jacob[27]

"From His place"

He spoke to him, "'Here I am with you'[28]—
just as your image is with Me"

"From His place"

He spoke to him, "Though you sleep,
your Guardian does not slumber"[29]

. . . Twice. . .

---

27 See note above on the image of Jacob on the divine throne in *GenR* 68:12 *et al.*

מִמְּקוֹמוֹ

יָרַד וְהוֹרִיד צְבָאָיו

רְאוֹת דְּמוּת יַעֲקֹב

מִמְּקוֹמוֹ

נָם לוֹ הִנְנִי עִמָּךְ

כִּי דְמוּתָךְ עִימִּי

מִמְּקוֹמוֹ

נָם לוֹ אִם תִּישָׁן

שׁוֹמְרָךְ לֹא יִישָׁן

פעמים

28 Gen 28:15 (**R**). 29 Ps 121:4 (**R**).

Commentary

Formally, and ultimately exegetically, the *rahit* for this poem—fragmentary though it is—differs from all the other *qedushta'ot* presented in this volume. These incipits both share and construct the formal elements that define the unit: each quotation begins with a word that builds an alphabetical acrostic (the fragment opens with the letter "*peh*") and concludes with the name "Jacob." The naming of Jacob in each incipit provides the refrain-like repetition that typifies the strongly rhythmic poetic unit, but the diversity of texts is otherwise a unique structuring device in this body of work, although Yannai uses somewhat similar patterns elsewhere.[30] Despite the fact that only the final six stanzas of an original twenty-two remain, Yannai draws on all three sections of the *Tanakh* in his incipits for the surviving lines of the *rahit*: Torah (Gen 27:22, from the previous week's *sidra*); Prophets (Isa 48:12; Jer 31:7, 11; Mic 7:20); and Writings (Ps 44:5). In most cases, these verses are construed midrashically, acquiring meaning through implied interpretation or on multiple levels at once: "Jacob" may refer to the nation in Isa 48:12, but in the *piyyut* it is initially understood as the patriarch himself; conversely, Gen 27:22 is spoken by Isaac to his son, Jacob, but the poet interprets it broadly as both the people and its eponymous ancestor. Epithets for Torah, rooted in aggadic traditions, are also prominent in this poem. As a result of the apocopated, terse nature of the *rahit*, form becomes essential to the generation of meaning: by juxtaposing quotation with poem, without intervening explication, the poet creates a composition of particularly dense exegetical possibilities. The surviving fragment indicates a kind of narrative progression and conversation: the annunciation of redemption, an articulation of yearning for Israel's sweet voice, the sweet voice responding in celebratory song, a divine reiteration of covenant, and affirmation of Torah. Rather than stating this directly, however, Yannai relies on the subtle interplay of biblical language, rabbinic exegesis, and the insightful listener to construct a meaning from this richly textured text.

There are elements of this poem's rhetoric that might seem, at first, confusing, precisely because Yannai relies heavily on ambiguity. However,

30 The use of distinct verses from different locations in Scripture seems to be unique to this poem, within Yannai's *oeuvre*. See, however, the *qedushta* for Lev 15:25, which quite intriguingly, uses the text of Prov 31 ("the woman of valor") as a base text; also noteworthy are Yannai's *shivʿata* and *qedushta* for Passover, in which the entire Song of Songs—not just the opening verses—are embellished poetically.

rather than being a flaw in his poetry, the uncertainly Yannai creates appears to be both intentional and fruitful. Just as the exegesis implicit in the *rahit* intentionally blurs the identity of Jacob/Israel as both an individual and a nation, the *silluq* and *qedushah* build upon interpretive traditions that obscure the distinctions among the patriarch, the nation, and the angelic hosts devoted to their protection. This overlapping of names begins in the first lines of the *silluq*, where one camp of angels calls out the name "Jacob" (addressing the angels who are outside the Land, or the human community?) and the other calls out, in response, the name "Israel" (addressing those within the borders of the Land, or also naming the human congregation?). The identities of the parties named here are merged and synthetized.[31] These two heavenly hosts not only guard the doubly named patriarch and his descendents, and by implication they guard the children of Israel both in the Land and wherever they wander, but they also seem to be known by the names of their charges. Further complicating the overlap is the physical resemblance between the mortal Jacob and the human face on God's chariot. "Jacob" blurs into the name of an individual, a nation, and an angelic host—beings terrestrial, heavenly, and traveling in between. To quote the *silluq*, these various identities coalesce and become "a singular delight / all of them as one" (lines 33–34).

Although rabbinic literature provides parallels to many of Yannai's interpretations, it is worth considering what the poet gains by playing with the identity confusion enabled by aggadic traditions and so easily exploited in the terse, elliptical language of poetry. On a basic level, just as poetic rhetoric collapses the past into the present, as the patriarch is identified with his heirs, so, too, he merges the terrestrial into the heavenly, as people join the angels in prayer. That is, through this device of ambiguity, the children of Jacob—the community assembled to hear the piyyut and participate in its liturgy—find themselves intimately, almost interchangeably, linked to the divine retinue. So closely bound are the guardian angels to their mortal charges that they have become existentially "one." If humankind is "little less than the angels" (to paraphrase Ps 8:6), then Israel is the closest to God to them of all. Furthermore, humans and angels come together when they recite the Qedushah, further blurring their boundaries: their voices become one. The relative superiority of the angels to humanity is completely

31 This passage is discussed at length in my article, "The Experience of Piyyut: Liturgical Poetry as Performance," *Journal of Religion*, forthcoming.

undermined by the end of the piyyut. In the final poem, both God and His host delight in Jacob (Poem Nine, line 1); both God and His host protect him at every stage of his journey; and both God and the angels focus on Jacob and his image, gazing upon him with fascination and devotion. Indeed, while the angels exist to praise God, God—in the final lines of this poem—seems to exist to dote on Jacob. Coming so close to being among the angels, it is as if Jacob and his descendents have, in fact, surpassed them.

Qedushta for Genesis 29:31 בראשית כט:לא

וירא יי כי שנואה

"Then the Lord saw that she was hated"

This piyyut focuses on the matriarch Leah, whose story of trial and triumph foreshadows the fate of her children's nation. Built primarily around the antonymic pair "loved-hated," Yannai reflects on the idea that those who appear most despised may be, in fact, the most beloved. Just as Leah's virtue—despite tragic circumstances—earned her a magnificent reward, so, too, will Israel's perseverance—despite its overtly sorry situation—result in the fulfillment of a splendid destiny.

(1) Your might, O Awesome One, is in the heavens[1]
but You watch over all who set foot upon the streets[2]
Obvious to You is the love of the lovable
but the hated, the oppressed, You seek out[3]

The hated woman, with her weakened eyes,
was in prayer to You with uplifted eyes[4]
By her merit, she preceded her with whom she shared the womb;[5]
You graced her first with fruit of the womb.

You granted satisfaction in place of sorrow
her shame You transformed to honor
The confinement of her captivity You released,[6]
in place of hatred You opened up love[7]

As it is written: "Then the Lord saw that Leah was hated, so He opened her womb; but Rachel was barren" (Gen 29:31)
And it is said: "The eyes of the Lord are in all places, observing bad and the good" (Prov 15:3)
And it is said: "Hatred rouses strife, but love covers over all sins" (Prov 10:12)
And it is said: "Better is reproof revealed than love concealed" (Prov 27:5)
And it is said: "Set me as a seal upon your heart, as a seal upon your arm, for love is stronger than death, jealousy harder than Sheol, its darts are darts of fire, of divine flame" (Song 8:6)[8]
And it is said: "For the Lord listens to the needy, and His fettered ones He does not spurn" (Ps 69:34)
And it is said: "He sets the childless woman among her household as a happy mother of children. Hallelujah" (Ps 113:9)

---

1 The language here blends Prov 8:28 (**R**) with Ps 68:35 and 89:8 (**B1**).

2 That is, all people, including the most humble and lowly.

3 The word translated as "obvious" means, literally, "apparent, self-evident, revealed." See *TanḥB Vayetze* 10 (**R**).

4 **B1** highlights the importance of comparison with the Palestinian *targumim* to this passage. The language of *TargN* to Gen 29:17 is particularly apt; it states: "And the eyes of Leah were raised in prayer, begging that she be married to the just Jacob." *TargPsJ* to the verse contains a variant of the same: "Leah's eyes were running because she used to weep and pray before the Lord that He would not destine her for Esau the wicked."

5 That is, Rachel. She and Leah were daughters of the same mother, and hence they shared a womb; it may even be hinted here that they were twins, just like Jacob and Esau (see *Tanḥ Vayetze* 4 , cited by **R** and **B1**; and *TanḥB Vayetze* 12, cited by **R**). **R** quotes *GenR* 70:16 which describes how Leah's eyes were weakened when she learned that Rachel was destined to

(א) אָמְצָךְ אָיוֹם בַּשְּׁחָקִים
בּוֹטֶה בְּכָל צוֹדְדֵי שְׁוָוקִים
גָּלוּי לָךְ אַהֲבַת חֲשׁוּקִים
דָּרוּשׁ לָךְ גַּם שִׂנְאַת עֲשׁוּקִים

הַנִּשְׂנֵאת בְּרוֹךְ עֵינַיִם
וּבְפֶלֶל לָךְ נָשְׂאָה עֵינַיִם
זְכוּתָהּ קִדַּמְתָּה לַאֲחוֹת מֵיעַיִים
חֲנַנְתָּה תְּחִילָּה פְּרִי מֵיעַיִם

טוֹבָה לְרָעָתָהּ נָתַתָּה
יְקָר לְבִיזּוּיָהּ חִילַּפְתָּה
כְּלִיאַת אֲסִירָתָהּ פִּיתַּחְתָּה
לְשִׂנְאָתָהּ אַהֲבָה פָּתַחְתָּה

ככתוב וירא יי כִּי שנואה לאה ויפתח את רחמה ורחל עקרה

ונאמר בכל מקום עיני יי צופות רעים וטובים

ונאמר שנאה תעורר מדנים ועל כל פשעים תכסה אהבה
ונאמר טובה תוכחת מגלה מאהבה מסותרת
ונאמר שימני כחותם על לבך כחותם על זרועך כי עזה כמות אהבה קשה כשאול קנאה רשפיה רשפי אש שלהבתיה

ונאמר כִּי שמע אל אביונים יי ואת אסיריו לא בזה

ונאמר מושיבי עקרת הבית אם הבנים שמחה הללויה

---

marry Jacob but she was doomed to marry Esau. So sincere were Leah's pleas that she not have to marry the wicked son, God altered the divine plan. "Rabbi Huna said: Great is prayer, that it annulled the decree, and she [Leah] even took precedence over her sister [Rachel]." Leah and Rachel are likewise paralleled in *GenR* 70:15 and *TanḥB Vayetze* 13. See also the *Targums* noted above.

6 "Captivity" refers here to infertility, which the Rabbis likened to a prison sentence; see notes below and the *qedushta* to Gen 30:22. (**R** cites *GenR* 71:1.)

7 God opens Leah's womb and also shows her love. "Love" in this stich—*ahavah*—puns implicitly on רחם in the first verse of the *sidra*. "*Reḥem*" suggests both "compassion" and "womb." Through the act of opening up Leah's womb, love enters Leah's life. Yannai's reading of the lemma is, therefore, perhaps along the lines of: "The Lord saw that Leah was hated, so He opened her up with love."

8 See also *qedushta* to Gen 48, Poem 2, where this verse is also a prooftext.

"Hallelujah," let us say
To the One who fulfills for us (His) words
To the One who shields us let it be said:
Blessed... Shield...

(2) The hated one who was troubled[9]
bore heirs to the pure one and acquired acclaim[10]
Her reward: her womb bore fruit first[11]
and then by her neighbors she was no longer distressed[12]
Mouths reckoned her...
...

[And it is written: "And Leah conceived, and bore a son, and she called his name Reuben; for she said, Surely the Lord has seen my affliction; now, therefore, my husband will love me" (Gen 29:32).]

"Then the Lord saw that Leah was hated..."
(3) O Yah, love those who love You
and hate those who hate You;
Watch over Your lovers
Watch out for Your haters
Glorify...she who was hated for her voice
Call to her, because of her voice[13]
and love her, she who is pleasant of voice
She sits upon the stones[14]
like a woman bereft of children;
but You are the Father of children
and she is a mother of children[15]

9 Reading the root א-ק-ר in place of ע-ק-ר, based on the weakening of the gutturals; see Kutscher, *Studies in Galilean Aramaic*, p. 81. For the language of this verse, see Prov 15:6 (**B1**).

10 Lit. "bore the portion of the pure one"—that is, she bore sons to Jacob. "*Naḥalah*" (ancestral portion) refers to the patrimony inherited by sons. While bearing sons to Jacob did not earn Leah love, it did gain her respect.

11 I.e., Reuben, whose birth is recorded in the second verse of the *sidra*. This translation avoids the more literal rendering, "Fruit of the Womb"!

12 See *GenR* 71:2, cited below. The neighbor women gossiped that Leah's infertility was punishment for her cooperation in Jacob's deception earlier in Gen 29; compare Hagar's slander of Sarah, noted in the *qedushta* for Gen 16:1. As a result of this tale-bearing, Leah

הַלְלוּיָהּ נֹאמַר
לְמֵיקִים לָנוּ מַאֲמַר
לְמָגִינֵּינוּ יֵאָמַר
ברוך... מגן...

(ב) **מְ**ושְׂנֵאת אֲשֶׁר אִיכְּרָה
נַחֲלַת תָּם וְנִיתְיַקָּרָא
שָׂכָר פְּרִי הַבֶּטֶן עֵת בִּיכָּרָה
עוֹד מִשְׁכֵנִים לֹא נֶעְכָּרָה
פִּיוֹת מוֹנֶיהָ רָחֲשׁוּ
...

וירא יי כי שנואה לאה
(ג) **יָ**הּ אֱהוֹב אוֹהֲבֶיךָ
וּשְׂנָא שׂוֹנְאֶיךָ
נְצוֹר לִמְאַהֲבֶיךָ
נְטוֹר לִמְשַׂנְאֶיךָ
נַוֵוה ... אֲשֶׁר נִשְׂנְאָה בְּקוֹלָהּ
קְרָא לָהּ בְּקוֹלָהּ
וֶאֱהוֹב נוֹעַם קוֹלָהּ
יָשְׁבָה עַל אֲבָנִים
כַּעֲקָרָה מִבָּנִים
וְאַתָּה אַב בָּנִים
וְהִיא אֵם הַבָּנִים

---

was an outcast both at home and among her people; Reuben's birth, however, improved her domestic and social situation.

13 That is, her voice raised in prayer and pleasant to hear when she offers praise.

14 To dwell or sit upon rocks or rubble is a biblical image for homelessness (see Jer 48:28), a literal marginality. Israel, metaphorically barren and outcast, is thus implicitly contrasted with the happy mother of children who dwells at the center of the house (Ps 113:9; 128:3—**B1** cites both, **R** only the first). The second stich teaches that Israel's destiny is to be precisely at the *center* of the house, a happy mother of many children—an image of complete restoration. See the following notes for more on the inside/outside distinction associated with childlessness.

15 In this line, the figure of the people of Israel blurs, it seems, into the figure of Zion.

Let her be called "espoused," transform her rejection![16]
She shall be "she who is loved" instead of being "she who is hated"!

[As it is written: "Whereas you have been forsaken, rejected, with none passing through, I will make you a pride everlasting, A joy for generation after generation" (Isa 60:15)]

(4) Our eyes are weak with longing love for You, O Lover;
we are hated by a hateful foe
O please, see our suffering at home (within)
and heed how we are hated outside (without)[17]
As with Leah, whose suffering You saw
You heeded how she was harassed by hate
At home (within), her haters were against her[18]
and outside (without), they were making her hated more[19]
Not all the lovable are loved
and not all worthy of hatred are hated
There are some who are hated below but beloved on high
Your haters are hated and those who love You are loved
We are hated because we love You, O Holy One.[20]

---

16 See Jer 33:16 and Isa 62:4—the language again blurring together the images of the people of Israel and Zion.

17 "Within" refers to within the territory of Israel; "without" refers to the Diaspora. Both communities are, existentially if not literally, in exile; local enemies inflict one kind of suffering while the Roman Empire, from its imperial seat, inflicts another.

18 Those who hated Leah "within" are Jacob and Rachel. **R** cites *GenR* 71:2, which explicated the first verse of this *sidra.* It states: "Rabbi Judah b. Rabbi Simon and Rabbi Ḥanan said in the name of Rabbi Samuel b. Rabbi Isaac: When the Patriarch Jacob saw how Leah deceived him by pretending to be her sister, he determined to divorce her. But as soon as the Holy One, blessed be He, visited her with children, he exclaimed, `Shall I divorce the mother of these children?' Eventually he gave thanks for her, as it says, `And Israel bowed down [in thanksgiving] at the bed's head' (Gen 47:31). Who was `the head' (i.e., first) of our father Jacob's bed? Surely Leah!" Thus, before she became a mother, Jacob hated her, and until she herself became a mother, Rachel hated her.

In allegorical terms, this line refers to "those who hate Israel" both at home and abroad—possibly referring to the impact of the Christianization of the Empire and increasing restrictions on and denigrations of Judaism in the public sphere.

19 Being hated "outside" the house probably refers to the unfavorable gossip and rumor mongering to which Leah was subjected—much like Sarah (see *qedushta* for Gen 16:1). **B1** cites *GenR* 71:2, "All hated [i.e. abused] her [Leah]: sea-travelers abused her, land-travelers

יִקְרָא לָהּ בְּעוּלָה תְּמוּר עֲזוּבָה
וְתִהְיֶה אֲהוּבָה תַּחַת הָיְתָה שְׂנוּאָה

(ד) כָּלוּ עֵינֵינוּ לְאַהֲבָתְךָ אוֹהֵב
נִישְׂנָאִים מִשִּׂינְאַת אוֹיֵב
רְאֵה נָא בְעָנְיֵנוּ מִבַּיִת
וְשׁוּר שִׂנְאָתֵינוּ מִבַּחוּץ
כְּלֵאָה אֲשֶׁר רָאִיתָה בְּעָנְיָהּ
וְשַׁרְתָּה בְּשִׂנְאַת עִינּוּיָהּ
מִבַּיִת הָיוּ לָהּ שׂוֹנְאִים
וּבַחוּץ הָיוּ לָהּ מַשְׂנִיאִים
וְלֹא כָּל אָהוּב אָהוּב
וְלֹא כָּל שָׂנאוּי שָׂנאוּי
יֵשׁ שְׂנוּאִים בְּמַטָּה וַאֲהוּבִים בְּמָעְלָה
שְׂנוּאֶיךָ שְׂנוּאִים וַאֲהוּבֶיךָ אֲהוּבִים
שִׂינְאָתֵינוּ כִּי אֲהַבְנוּךָ קָדוֹשׁ

---

abused her, and even the women behind the vine-press abused her, saying: `This Leah leads a double life! She pretends to be righteous, yet is not so, for if she were righteous, would she have deceived her sister?'" Again, her sorrow derives from the same source as her joy: her wedding night, where she tricked Jacob but avoided marrying Esau.

In terms of the inside/outside dichotomy, *GenR* 71:1 sheds some light on the imagery of this line. This midrash interprets Ps 69:34 (cited as a text after Poem 1) as referring to Israel ("the needy") and barren women ("His fettered ones"). Because conception lies in the hands of God, barren women are uniquely "imprisoned" by God. It also appears that shame at childlessness might have kept a woman physically shut up within the house. Similarly, *GenR* 71:2 states, "`The Lord lifts all that fall' (Ps 144:14)—that is, childless women who fall [i.e. are disgraced] in their own homes; `And He raises up all those that are bowed down' (ibid.)—as soon as God remembers them with children, they [barren women] are raised up. The proof is that Leah was hated in her house, yet when the Holy One, blessed be He, visited her, she was raised up."

By analogy, Israel is the "barren woman" whose restoration and health likewise lie in the hands of God.

20 This phrase strongly recalls the teaching in *SongR* 2:16, which states: "Another explanation of, `For I am sick with love' (Song 2:5): the Community of Israel said before the Holy One, blessed be He: `Sovereign of the Universe, the reason for all the sufferings that the nations inflict upon me is because I love You'" (**B2**).

(5) Once, to the name of the hated one was Leah called
thus "the hated one" she also was called[21]
When she saw that the deeds of the pure one were good,[22]
She prayed to You, the One who sees everything, bad and good
Her soul wished and wanted for You to show her love,
and You loved her who loved You, and by You she was beloved
You saw her despair; You then saw her bear;
and as she was seen to be seemly, she saw sons
Indeed, because she was loved, she was first hated[23]
and because she was hated, she was first to bear[24]
Her love and her hatred exalted her[25]
her beloved sister she never wished ill[26]
She tended her garden, his first fruit was hers;[27]
she was given six sons, like the six days of creation
Engraved and imprinted were the symbols of their names
each upon one of the stones (of the breastplate) were their six names[28]
Their names a reward for the deeds of their mother,
great ones for whom God worked great wonders.[29]
Because her eyes were weak (with weeping)
she would become the wellspring[30] of those whose eyes are pools[31]
...

---

21 In this unit, we return to the theme of Leah as averting her original destiny—marriage to Esau, "the hated one"—through prayer. She paid a price for her role in the deception of Jacob, but her actions were rewarded in the end.

22 That is, Jacob.

23 The reading suggested by **B1** is also possible: הן באבתה להינשא ("because of her love she was the first to wed").

24 See *Tanḥ Vayetze* 4.

25 Love for Jacob, hatred for Esau.

26 Lit. "Her eye never afflicted [Rachel] because of the love of her sister;" that is, Leah never wished her sister ill despite the fact that Jacob loved Rachel and not her (**B1**). The idiom of "an eye afflicting" refers to giving someone the evil eye.

27 According to *GenR* 99:6, cited by **B1**, the phrase "first of my strength" in Gen 49:3 ("Reuben, you are my firstborn, my might, and the first of my strength, the excellency of dignity, and the excellency of power") should be understood as saying that Reuben was

(ה) **אָ**ז לְשֵׁם שָׂנאוּי הָיְתָה מְקוֹרָאָה לֵאָה
לָכֵן שְׂנ וּאָה הָיְתָה נִקְרָאָה
בִּרְאוֹתָהּ מַעֲשֵׂה תָם הַטּוֹבִים
פִּילְלָה לָךְ רוֹאֶה רָעִים וְטוֹבִים
גָּהֲצָה וְחָפְצָה נַפְשָׁהּ לְאוֹהֲבָךְ
וַתֶּאֱהַב אֶת אוֹהֲבָךְ וַאֲהוּבָךְ
דּוֹנֶיהָ רָאִיתָה רוֹאֵה נוֹלָדִים
וְכִרְאוּיָה מֵרָאוּי רָאֲתָה יְלָדִים
הֵן בְּאַהֲבָתָהּ לְהִשָּׂנֵא קָדְמָה
וּבְשִׂנְאָתָהּ לְהוֹלִיד קִדְּמָה
וְאַהֲבָתָהּ וְשִׂנְאָתָהּ הוֹעִילוּ אוֹתָהּ
כִּי לֹא צָרָה עֵינָהּ בְּאַהֲבַת אֲחוֹתָהּ
זֵירוּעֶיהָ הִצְמִיחָה מִתְּבוּאַת רֵאשִׁית
וְנִתַּן לָהּ שִׁשָּׁה כְּשֵׁשֶׁת יְמֵי בְרֵאשִׁית
חֲרוּתִים חֲרוּטִים כִּינּוּי שְׁמוֹתָם
בְּאַחַת מֵאֲבָנִים שִׁשָּׁה מִשְּׁמוֹתָם
טַעֲמֵי שְׁמוֹתָם לְשֵׁם מַעֲשֵׂה אִמָּם
גְּדוֹלִים אֲשֶׁר הִגְדִּיל אֵל עִמָּם
יַעַן כִּי הָיְתָה עֵינֶיהָ רַכּוֹת
הֶעֱמִידָה כַּנַּת עֵינֶיהָ בְּרֵיכוֹת
...

---

conceived the very first time Jacob and Leah had intercourse. The second verse of this *sidra* describes the birth of Reuben.

28 See Exod 39, where it is described how the High Priest's breastplate bears the names of the twelve tribes. Six of the twelve tribes trace their ancestry back to Jacob's less-favored wife.

29 See 1 Sam 12:24 (**B1**). The sense here is that Leah gave her sons names that destined them for greatness—destinies which God fulfilled. This is an instance of "*zekhut imahot*," merit accrued to one's female ancestors for the benefit of later generations.

30 More literally, "foundation," but rendered in keeping with the water imagery.

31 The final extant line returns to the theme of Leah's righteousness, as expressed in her intense opposition to a marriage with Esau. This righteousness justifies her status as the mother of six of the twelve tribes. The scholars descended from her are said to have "eyes like pools" (from Song 7:5, as interpreted in *SongR* 7:10; **R**). Her virtue, resulting in weakened eyes, leads to generations of virtue among those who study Torah with clear-sighted eyes.

Commentary

Several intriguing themes are woven into Yannai's emotionally rich, profoundly touching portrait of the tragic matriarch, Leah. The only matriarch *not* afflicted with barrenness—not for even a single day, according to rabbinic tradition, was she ever infertile—Leah's prayers are nonetheless among the most heartfelt written by Yannai. Finding a creative space between the first two verses of the *sidra*—the first focusing on how Leah was hated, the second on the birth of her first son—the poet paints an intimate, emotional portrait of this mother of Israel. Where the nationalized allegory of the twins Jacob and Esau is a story of right versus wrong, the story of the matriarchal sisters, Leah and Rachel, is a tale of much greater complexity. In the end, Leah is loved despite her flaws and in spite of appearing hated, and the poet asserts that the same holds true for Israel.

And, like the husband for whose love she yearns, Yannai's Leah is flawed. In keeping with one line of rabbinic interpretation, the poet sees Leah as culpable for the deception of Jacob on his wedding night. The first poem alludes to this story in subtle ways, primarily through intertexts that assert God's omniscience and forgiveness: Yannai observes that God sees both "the bad and the good" (Prov 15:3), associating Leah with something negative as well as positive; he reminds us that "love covers all sins" (Prov 10:12), suggesting that God's love of Leah, compensates for her transgressions (although it may also indicate that Leah's love of Jacob ameliorates his own sins); and he notes that "Jealousy is harder than Sheol," for Leah was, indeed, jealous of Rachel. Yannai hints at the reasons for Leah's poor reputation in Poem Two (line 2) and Poem Four (line 7): she did, in fact, betray Jacob's trust when she complied with Laban's scheme to deny Jacob his chosen bride. Neither Leah's purposes nor her actions are simple; she is an ambiguous, complicated figure. This moral complexity is part of her legacy to her children, the nation Israel. The phrase, "she was hated for her voice" (Poem Three, line 2) alludes to Jer 12:8, in which God spurns Israel, saying: "My own possession [people] acted toward Me like a lion in the forest; she raised her voice against Me—therefore I have rejected her!" Leah sinned through silence and complicity; Israel through vocal brazenness. Each has, in some measure, earned the reputations that cause their intimates (spouse or deity) and neighbors (the locals or the nations) to assume the worst about them and to speak against them. Assumptions about guilt and culpability are not entirely misplaced. But, the poet teaches, the story does not end there; the story ends with love. Leah and Israel are loved *despite* being, at times, unlovable.

For all Leah's faults, Yannai finds her worthy of tremendous love—both for her positive actions and ambitions, and because of her profound loneliness. Numerous times, the poet asserts that God loved Leah, precisely because she was unloved. Her isolation and suffering, justified or not, produced in her a character of humility and piety. For Leah, suffering atones, and her prayers change God's decree. Learning that she is fated to be married to the elder brother—to the wicked Esau—Leah's heart breaks. Her frantic, even self-damaging, rejection of this destiny earns her God's love, even as it leads to her deception of Jacob on their wedding night. Her sacrifice—as well as his—is rewarded. Similarly, in Poem Three, Israel's voice can be as self-redeeming as it was self-condemning. The emphasis on the redemptive power of prayer, in particular, is both common and potent in the context of the piyyut. Implicitly, the poet suggests the redemptive power of his own poem.

In the biblical narrative, and in many post-biblical traditions as well, Rachel is far and away the more lovable and loved of the two sisters. It is Rachel whom Jacob wished to marry; Rachel whose beauty wins hearts while she tends her father's flock; Rachel who dies tragically in childbirth; and Rachel who, like Zion personified, weeps for her exiled children and receives God's comfort in Jeremiah 31. As a love story, the tale of Jacob and Rachel leaves no room for a third party. Leah, excluded and despised, occasionally petty and manipulative, comes across as pathetic more than tragic, a bitter Peninah to Rachel's Hannah. But by focusing on the intrinsic value of Leah's longing and her choice of degradation (through marriage to Jacob) rather than evil (through marriage to Esau), Yannai transforms her story into an emotionally potent allegory. The people of Israel are not always lovable; their motives can be mixed and less than wholly pure; their choices can seem poor, even wrong. Israel's lowly place in the world—exiled and disempowered—may seem to indicate divine rejection, to confirm the suspicion that God hates Israel (see Amos 5:1) the way Jacob hated Leah. And yet, with Israel as with Leah, appearances prove misleading. God loves Israel, despite her flaws, and Israel is ultimately worthy of His love. The future holds the promise of honor and status, but even the present tense is not empty of reward. Love is reciprocated, in the end, even if its manifestation is subtle rather than overt. Both Leah and Israel suffer for their love of God, and God can only love them both the more for it.

Qedushta for Genesis 30:22 בראשית ל:כב

“Then God remembered Rachel” ויזכור אלהים את רחל

Although the surviving poem is fragmentary, in the surviving passages Yannai weaves together a complex matrix of motifs. In general, he transforms the small-scale drama of Rachel's barrenness and eventual motherhood by using it to foreshadow the parallel national-scale drama of Israel's exile and restoration. Despite this allegorical reading of the *sidra*, however, Yannai focuses almost exclusively on the character of Rachel and her interactions with God in this piyyut. The tone of the poem is thus almost relentlessly personal, even when the scale is implicitly epic.

(5)[1] …
The blind, in darkness, eyes shut to the light of the world
truly these shut-ins are dead to the world[2]
A man with eruptions, whose flesh rots away:[3]
he is dead while alive, his soul trapped in his flesh.
One poor and oppressed for want of wealth and one weak for want of power:
like one dead is he considered for his speech goes unheeded[4]
The childless who will not father a child in the world
Better he were dead rather than alive in the world[5]
And thus Rachel was willing to die to provide her husband heirs
because children are the heirs[6] of the Lord
…

[*And He remembered Rachel…*]
(6) "Sister"—thus Rachel had been called
until, by her broken heart, she was torn[7]
Against her own sister she felt harsh envy
indeed, envy is as harsh as hell[8]

And He remembered Rachel (etc.)[9]

A lady, loved by the breeder of the flock[10]
who, when he came, spied her coming with her flock
He sought to establish with her the young of his own flock
who are destined to overwhelm the scorner's folk[11]

And He remembered Rachel (etc.)

---

1 According to *GenR* 71:6, cited by **R**, there are four categories of living people who are regarded as dead: the blind, the leper, the impoverished, and the childless. This aggadic tradition undergirds this unit and something along the lines of this understanding probably opened the poem. (*TanḥB Vayetze* 22 lists only childlessness.)

2 According to *GenR* 65:10, the blind stayed at home: "The Holy One, blessed be He, said: `Shall Isaac go out into the market place and people say: Here is the father of that scoundrel (Esau)! Rather, I will make his eyes dim, so that he shall stay at home'" (**B1**). See also *GenR* 65:4.

3 That is, the leper. **R** cites Zulay, *Iyyunei lashon*, s.v. "רטפש".

4 Eccl 9:16 (**R**); powerlessness, equated with poverty, is here likened to death. **B1** connects with *m. Avot* 5:21.

5 See *m. Ḥag.* 2:1 (**R**).

6 Lit. "portion," related to the word "heir," because heirs inherit their parents' portions. For "children are the portion of the Lord," see Ps 127:3 (**R**).

7 This line exploits the pun between the word for "sister" (אחות) and "to stitch together" (איחה) also appearing in the *qedushta* for Gen 12:1. The first stich describes Rachel's unity with Leah—as sisters, they were "stitched together." The second stich describes how Rachel's

(ה)

...

בְּמַחְשָׁךְ לֹא רָאוּ אוֹר עוֹלָם
אָמְנָם כְּלוּיִים הֵם כְּמֵיתֵי עוֹלָם
גֶּבֶר אֲשֶׁר בְּצֵירוּעַ רֻוטֲפַשׁ בְּשָׂרוֹ
מֵת הוּא בְּחַיָּיו וְנַפְשׁוֹ אֲנוּסָה בִּבְשָׂרוֹ
דַּל וְדַךְ בְּהוֹנוֹ וְרָעֵב בְּאוֹנוֹ
כְּמוֹ מֵת חָשׁוּב כִּי אֵן שִׂיחוֹ קָשׁוּב
הָעֲרִירִי אֲשֶׁר לֹא הוֹלִיד בֵּן בָּעוֹלָם
רָתוּי לוֹ כְּמוֹ מֵת בָּא לָעוֹלָם
וְעַל כֵּן מֵתָה רָחֵל בַּעֲבוּר לִנְחוֹל בָּנִים
כִּי נַחֲלַת יי בָּנִים

...

...

(ו)

אָחוֹת אֲשֶׁר רָחֵל נִקְרָאָה
אֲשֶׁר בְּשִׁבְרוֹן לֵבָב נִקְרָעָה
בַּאֲחוֹתָהּ בְּקוֹשִׁי קִנְּאָה
כִּי קָשָׁה כִּשְׁאוֹל קִנְאָה

ויזכר את רחל וג׳

גְּבֶרֶת אֲשֶׁר אָהַב מְיַיחֵם צֹאן
אֲשֶׁר בְּבוֹאוֹ שָׂר בָּאָה עִם הַצֹּאן
דָּרַשׁ לְהַצִּיב מֶנָּה צְעִירֵי הַצֹּאן
הָעֲתִידִים לִסְחוֹף עַם לָצוֹן

ויזכר את רחל וג׳

---

experience with barrenness, in the face of Leah's fertility, rent the bond between them. For more on this pun, see the *qedushta* for Gen 12:1.

8 Lit. "Sheol," but "hell" connotes the unpleasantness of the emotional state and strengthens the alliteration. This stich alludes to Song 8:6, "Love is as strong as death, envy as harsh as Sheol." (**R** notes the verse.)

9 The Maʾagarim text, unlike **R**, indicates the use of the incipit as a refrain which concludes each stanza.

10 I.e., Jacob.

11 According to *GenR* 73:7, *TanḥB Vayetze* 15, and *PRK* 3:13, discussed by **R**, Esau will be defeated by the sons of Rachel. Thus Joseph's descendants ("flock") are fated to overcome the sons of Esau ("the scorner's folk"). The *GenR* version, explaining why Jacob wished to leave Laban as soon as Joseph was born, states: "For Rabbi Phinehas said in the name of Rabbi Samuel b. Naḥman: It is a tradition that Esau will fall at the hands of none other than Rachel's descendants." Jacob was apparently anxious to begin the final confrontation. Similarly, in *Targ PsJ* to Gen 30:25, Jacob states: "Those of the house of Joseph are destined to be like a flame that will destroy those of the house of Esau…From now on, I will not be afraid of Esau and his legions."

Most praised and beautiful of women
the seed of mankind would be given to her
She built up her house with a woman's wisdom[12]
women and men rejoiced for her[13]

And He remembered Rachel (etc.)

She cried out, "Give me sons!
Lest I be scorned like a cast-down stone"[14]
She clutched to her bosom her sons[15]
and fathers and sons were joyful for her

And He remembered Rachel (etc.)

...

(7[1]) ...
Then He created creation anew in her womb
Then He unlocked the shutters deep within her body[16]
Then He knocked open the dripping lock of her door
Then He murmured, listening, to her whispered prayer
Then He shone, to give her life-giving power at the brink of death[17]
Then He remembered her silence, to her merit[18]
Then He renewed her weakened power, her potency
Then He planted a sapling, seedling of her purity
Then He created a companion, joining her uniqueness[19]
Then He firmed the fertile path of her belly

---

12 This stich weaves together the language of Gen 30:3, in which Rachel seeks to be "built up" by means of Bilhah's children, and Prov 14:1 (**R**), in which "The wisdom of women builds her house."

13 Where Leah suffered from ill-repute, Rachel suffered despite having the love of her husband and the praise of her neighbors.

14 "To be cast about like a stone" is an idiom expressing contempt in rabbinic Hebrew. **B1** mentions *LevR* 4:5, which states: "Likewise [as in the preceding parable] God will say to the body: `Why have you sinned before Me?' and the body will reply: `O Master of the Universe, I have not sinned! Rather, it is the soul that has sinned. Why, since it left me, *I am cast about like a stone thrown upon the ground.* Have I then sinned before You?' What will the Holy One, blessed be He, do to them? He will bring the soul and force it into the body, and judge both as one." See also *PRE* 24 (**B1**).

15 The plural here, required by the rhyme scheme, is nonetheless a problem. Yannai could be describing here Dan and Naftali, Rachel's sons by Bilhah, in addition to Joseph, or the plural could simply be an idiom. (Benjamin does not suit timeline, or tone, here, since Rachel died upon his birth.)

16 The architectural references in this stanza recall *LevR* 14:4 (cited by **R**), which describes

הֲדוּרָה הַיָּפָה בְּנָשִׁים
וְנִיתַּן לָהּ זֶרַע אֲנָשִׁים
וּבָנְתָה בֵיתָהּ כְּחַכְמוֹת נָשִׁים
וְשָׂמְחוּ לָהּ נָשִׁים וַאֲנָשִׁים

ויזכר את רחל וג׳

זוֹעֶקֶת הָבָה לִי בָנִים
פֶּן אִימָּאֵס כַּאֲבָנִים
חִיבְּקָה בְתוֹךְ חֵיקָהּ בָּנִים
וְשָׂשׂוּ לָהּ אָבוֹת וּבָנִים

ויזכר את רחל וג׳

...

(ז[1])

...
וַיִּבְרָא בְּרִיָּיה חֲדָשָׁה בְּבִטְנָהּ
וַיְגַל סְגִירַת קֶרֶב גִּיוְיָהּ
וַיִּדְפּוֹק מַנְעוּל טוֹרֵד דַּלְתָּהּ
וַיֶּהֱמֶה לְהַאֲזִין לְחִישַׁת הֲגִיגָהּ
וַיּוֹפִיעַ לְהַחֲיוֹת מִיתָתָהּ וְכוֹחָהּ
וַיִּזְכּוֹר שְׁתִיקַת זְכוּתָהּ
וַיְחַדֵּשׁ תַּשּׁוּת כּוֹחַ חֵילָהּ
וַיִּטַּע שֶׁתֶל זֵרוּעַ טָהֳרָהּ
וַיִּיצֶר תֹּאַם דִּיבּוּק יִיחוּדָהּ
וַיְכוֹנֵן אוֹרַח רִיבּוּעַ כְּרֵיסָהּ

---

the woman's body as having doors, locks, and hinges: "Rabbi Eliezer and Rabbi Joshua and Rabbi Akiba gave explanations (for Job 38:3: 'Who shut up the sea with doors, when it broke forth, and issued out of the womb?'). Rabbi Eliezer said: Just as a house has doors, so a woman, too, has doors, as it is written, 'Because it shut not up the doors of my [mother's] womb' (Job 3:10). Rabbi Joshua said: Just as for a house there are keys (*maftehot*), so, likewise, for a woman, as it is written, 'And God hearkened to her, and opened (*pathah*) her womb' (Gen 33:22)." Rabbi Akiba said: Just as a house has hinges (*zirim*), even so has a woman birthpangs (*zirim*), as it is written, 'She knelt and gave birth, for her pangs (*zirim*) came suddenly upon her (1 Sam 4:19)."

17 Rachel, who saw herself as nearly dead, was instead granted the power of creating new life.

18 GenR 73:4, "What did He remember in her [Rachel's] favor? Her silence on her sister's behalf. When Leah was being given to [Jacob], she [Rachel] knew it and yet was silent" (**R**). See also *LamR Pet.* 24.

19 The word תאם connotes symmetry. This may refer to the fact that Joseph was, like Rachel, "beautiful of appearance" (Gen 29:16; Gen 39:6), the only man so described. Others so described are Abigail (1 Sam 25:3) and Esther (Est 2:7).

Then He heartened her heart with her heart's desire
Then He fulfilled the lack of eggs in her inward parts[20]
Then He made shine the darkness of her soul like a candle
Then He enlarged the small gift of her clustered seed[21]
Then He answered abundantly the plea of her prayers
Then He opened the shut place, a reward for her works
Then He created a babe midst the pangs of her birthing[22]
Then He thickened the seed of `the nation-founder' within her[23]
Then He had mercy upon her womb in accord with His great mercy[24]
Then He heard her whisper and He heeded her cry for help
Then He gave her pregnancy and progeny

And thus, "For You are..."

(7) Sustaining offspring
Beholding births[25]
Foreseeing the future
Answering petitions
Giving power
Clothing the righteous
Knowing (Your) creation
Perceiving secrets
Strengthening the weak
Seeking the lost
Testing the hearts

Hearkening to prayers
Summoning generations
Remembering the barren
Forgiving sins
Recounting deeds
Crowning the beloved
Good to all (Your) creatures
Straightening the bent
Planning the good
Revealing the concealed
Loving the pure

(8) And on account of all His deeds, let Him be magnified
and on account of all His works, let Him be sanctified
In purity and holiness in the mouths of all the holy divinities,
as it is written: "And the one called out..."

---

20 See Isa 48:19 for the language of this line (**B1**). The word here rendered "eggs" is literally "pebbles" or "grains."

21 The imagery here is of a cluster of grapes, but they describe human fertility.

22 The language here draws on 1 Sam 4:19 (see *LevR* 14:4, cited above) (**R**).

23 The nation-founder is Jacob/Israel, according to **R** who reads "*ʾum*" in light of Gen 25:23; alternatively, the line could be translated according to Bronznick as, "He gelled the seed of the womb within her." **B1** understands "*ʾum*" as meaning "womb" (a possible meaning in rabbinic Hebrew).

24 This line puns on the word "*reḥem*" (womb, but with the connotation of mercy in its

וַיְלַבֵּב לֵב תְּשׁוּקַת לִבָּהּ
וַיְמַלֵּא חֶסְרוֹן מְעֻוַת מֵ..הּ
וַיְנַהֵר מַחְשַׁבֵי נִשְׁמַת נֵירָהּ
וַיְסַגֶּה מִיעוּט חֲנִינַת סִיגוּלָהּ
וַיַּעַן עֶתֶר סִיחַ עֲטִיפָתָהּ
וַיִּפְתַּח מַסְגּוֹרֶת מַסְכּוֹרֶת פְּעֻולָּתָהּ
וַיָּצֶר וָולָד בַּחֲלָל צִירֶיהָ
וַיַּקְפִּיא זֶרַע אוֹם קְרָבֶיהָ
וַיְרַחֵם כְּרוֹב רַחֲמָיו אֶת רַחְמָהּ
וַיִּשְׁמַע לַחֲשָׁהּ וַיִּשַׁע שַׁוְעָתָהּ
וַיִּתֵּן לָהּ הֵירָיוֹן תּוֹלָדוֹת

ובכן כי אתה

(ז[2]) תּוֹמֵךְ תּוֹלָדוֹת — שׁוֹמֵעַ תְּפִילוֹת
רוֹאֶה נוֹלָדוֹת — קוֹרֵא דוֹרוֹת
צוֹפֶה עֲתִידוֹת — פּוֹקֵד עֲקָרוֹת
עוֹנֶה עֲתִירוֹת — סוֹלֵחַ עֲוֹנוֹת
נוֹתֵן תַּעֲצוּמוֹת — מוֹנֶה סְפוֹרוֹת
לוֹבֵשׁ צְדָקוֹת — כּוֹלֵל אֲהָבוֹת
יוֹדֵעַ יְצִירוֹת — טוֹב לְכָל פְּעֻולוֹת
חוֹקֵר נִיסְתָּרוֹת — זוֹקֵף כְּפוּפוֹת
וּמַחֲזִיק רָפוֹת — הוֹגֶה טוֹבוֹת
דּוֹרֵשׁ נִשְׁכָּחוֹת — גּוֹלֶה עֲמוּקוֹת
בּוֹחֵן לְבָבוֹת. — אוֹהֵב טְהוֹרוֹת

(ח) וְעַל כָּל מַעֲשָׂיו יִתְגַּדֵּל
וְעַל כָּל מִפְעָלָיו יִתְקַדֵּשׁ
בְּטָהֳרָה וּבִקְדֻשָּׁה בְּפִי אֵילֵי קוֹדֶשׁ
ככתוב וקרא

---

derived forms). This line may hint at the aggadic tradition found in *TanḥB Vayetze* 20, in which Rachel fears that her infertility will cause Jacob to divorce her, which could result in her being married off to Esau. See also Rashi to Gen 30:22.

25 The idiom rendered here as “beholding births” (*roʾeh noladot*) could be translated, perhaps more idiomatically, in accord with *m. Avot* 2:9, as “discerning what will come to be”; however, my more literal and less idiomatic translation emphasizes the way this language resonates with the themes of this *sidra*. **R** cites *Tanḥ Ber.* 30, which links the two idioms of the line, “beholding births” and “summoning generations” (Isa 41:4) and which understands the phrase `beholding births' in a literal sense.

(9)[26] You shake the highest heavens[27]
You pay heed to the barren
You open the graves
For the people who say of Your name:
"*Holy, holy, holy! The whole world is filled with His glory!*"
"*Holy*"—from the heavens from which He will answer them[28]
"*Holy*"—from the barren ones whom He recalls
"*Holy*"—from the graves which He will open

"*Holy*"—from those who come forth from the womb,
for upon them You bestow life and loyalty
"*Holy*"—from those who come forth from the grave,
for You renew life and resurrect them in great loyalty
"*Holy*"—from those who mention You in the prison of exile,[29]
for You will call to them and they will go forth,
at a word from the One who delights in mercy[30]
All towards one another…

"*From His place*"—He heard Rachel's prayer and He remembered her
"*From His place*"—He hearkened to the moans of her entreaties
and He recollected her
"*From His place*"—He saw her despair lest she be forgotten
from bearing a son and He kept her in mind[31]
Twice…

---

26 The *qedushah* focuses upon three elements: exile, childlessness, and death, all of which are kinds of imprisonment from which God can and will free Israel. This selection of motifs resembles a common rabbinic motif, that God possesses keys to rain, sustenance, resurrection, and childbirth. All four keys are listed in *TargN* to Gen 30:22. The base verse of this piyyut. *b.Ta*ʿ*an.* 2b (**R**) initially lists only three keys: rain, death, and childbirth, but it notes that "in Palestine they said: Also the Key of Sustenance, for it is said, `You open Your hand…" (Ps 145:16). Why does Rabbi Yohanan not include also this [key]? – Because in his view sustenance is [included in] Rain." See also *TanḥB Vayetze* 16 (**R**), which associates each of the four keys with a different biblical character: Elijah holds the key to rain; Noah holds the key to sustenance; Ezekiel holds the key to graves; and Elisha holds the key to the womb. Yannai, however, does not here use the imagery of keys, and he connects national redemption to this cluster of motifs.

27 At first, this appears to refer simply to the Key of Rain, which God can unlock and thereby regulate a prosperous and sustaining harvest. Based on the rest of the poem, however, "highest heavens" (*aravot*) seems to stand for more than the natural phenomenon of rain. According to *b. Ḥag.* 12b, cited by **B1** in a lengthy note, *aravot* ("clouds") is the highest (describable) level of heaven. The description of *aravot* states: "*Aravot* is that [heaven] in which there are Right and Judgment and Righteousness, the treasures of life and the treasures

(ט)

עֲרָבוֹת תִּשְׁקוֹד
עֲקָרוֹת תִּפְקוֹד
קְבָרוֹת תִּפְתַּח
בְּעַם אוֹמְרִים לִשְׁמָךְ
קדוש קדוש קדוש יי צבאות מלוא כל הארץ כבודו
קָדוֹשׁ מֵעֲרָבוֹת כִּי יֵוֹנְעָם
קָדוֹשׁ מֵעֲקָרוֹת כִּי יִפְקְדֵם
קָדוֹשׁ מִקְּבָרוֹת כִּי יִפְתָּחֵם

קָדוֹשׁ מִיּוֹצְאֵי רֶחֶם
כִּי עִימָּם יַעַשׂ חַיִּים וָחֶסֶד
קָדוֹשׁ מִיּוֹצְאֵי קֶבֶר
כִּי תְחַיֵּים וְתַעֲמִידֵם בְּרוֹב חֶסֶד
קָדוֹשׁ מִמַּזְכִּירֶיךָ בְּמַסְגֵּר
קְרוֹא לָמוֹ וְיֵצְאוּ
בִּדְבַר חָפֵץ חֶסֶד
לעומתם כל

מִמְּקוֹמוֹ שָׁמַע תְּפִילַּת רָחֵל וַיִּזְכְּרֶהָ
מִמְּקוֹמוֹ הִקְשִׁיב נַאֲקַת תַּחֲנוּנָהּ
וַיִּפְקְדֶהָ
מִמְּקוֹמוֹ רָאָה שַׁחְקָהּ כִּי נִשְׁכָּחָה
מִבֵּן וַיִּפְקְדֶהָ

פעמים

---

of peace, and the treasures of blessing, the souls of the righteous and the spirits and the souls that are yet to be born, and dew wherewith the Holy One, blessed be He, will hereafter revive the dead." This passage links the themes of childbirth (souls) and resurrection (the dew), and also the motif of redemption, because when God shakes the heavens, these things—blessings, righteousness, peace, and judgment—will rain down upon the world. Rain is symbolic of the granting of these three kinds of "freedom."

28 The translation follows the emendation suggested by **R** (citing Zulay), which reads the verb here (יונעם, which is a passive verbal form) as ינעם (from the root ענה, "to answer," with a pronominal suffix), in parallel with the other verbal forms (all imperfects with pronominal suffixes). According to this reconstruction, it draws on Hos 2:23.

29 See *ExodR* 15:11, 18:10, 19:8, 36:1; *DeutR* 4:9; and others for descriptions of "exile" as "prison" and redemption from exile as being freed from prison.

30 God is called "He who delights in mercy" in Mic 7:18, in the context of the redemptive vision that concludes the book.

31 In a departure from his usual practice, Yannai repeats a single root in the same exact form at the conclusion of the final two lines (the root he repeats is פ-ק-ד). Perhaps he had two different nuances in mind: the first being the simple idea of memory, the second that of *acting* upon that memory.

Commentary

Yannai—in true midrashic fashion—delights in discovering meaningful relationships among seemingly disparate entities. In this piyyut, he compares categories of people in both negative and positive situations, and then highlights the connections they share. The opening fragment juxtaposes the blind, the leper, the poor, and the barren as classes of people who are all "the living dead." Despite the fact that all four of these kinds of people are, physically, alive, in a critical social sense they don't exist, at least not in the world of Jewish Late Antiquity (and, in more subtle ways, many would argue, even today). Similarly, in the final poem, childlessness, death, and exile (symbolized by drought) are described as metaphorical prisons from which God will set the imprisoned free. Through this comparative rhetoric, the poet subtly moves from the narrative of the *sidra*—Rachel's childlessness as a kind of individual death sentence from which she is rescued—to a more nationalistic drama of exile and restoration. Just as Rachel was released from her prison and granted new life (as she created new life—Joseph, her son), so, too, will Israel be released from its national confinement—and even her dead will live again. And yet, for all that the themes of the piyyut easily translate into national allegory, the poet's presentation of this material remains almost exclusively non-allegorical. This poem concentrates not on the nation, but on the singular, compelling figure of Rachel. Instead of moving from the specific (stories of individuals) to the general (national, allegorical), as he often does, in this poem Yannai consistently moves from the general to the specific: from major analytical categories to the individual story of Rachel. The allegorizing of Rachel occurs implicitly, through the listeners' identification with the matriarch. Her story, fundamentally, becomes theirs.

Yannai also departs from his customary form in the final poem. While this might be simply chalked up to compositional fatigue—with the pressure of generating these new works week after week, might the poet not simply have an "off" moment or choose to experiment for a change?—his failure to maintain strict patterns may reveal a struggle to articulate something particularly complex or to create a specific emphasis. For example, the first two categories in the *qedushah* are presented in strictly parallel terms: "those who go forth from..." (Poem Nine, lines 9–10). The exiles, however, break the parallelism; they "mention" God while "still in the prison of exile" (line 11). The other groups are, in some fashion, already free—children can be born at any time, and all the dead await resurrection. These are ultimately individual concerns, and the responses will be individual as well, even if (as with resurrection) the experience will also be communal. Exile, however, is presented as a collective phenomenon; the concern is not with the individual in Diaspora, but the people as a whole—with, in particular, Yannai's audience and community. The poet also departs from his own conventions in other ways in this *qedushah*, such as his repetitions of specific words and roots: ח-ס-ד ("loyalty") concludes lines 9–10, while the root פ-ק-ד ("to keep in mind"— often with connotations of redemption or granting fertility) concludes the final two lines of the poem. Finally, in the last three lines of the *qedushah*, rather than keeping his focus broad and general, as in the earlier lines of this final unit, Yannai returns his focus to the individual character of Rachel, and her particular experience of God's redemption. Thus the poem concludes by articulating not the national perspective (although Rachel's story has national consequences), but with a personal tone.

Throughout the surviving elements of this *qedushta*, the poet dwells on God's relationship with this specific matriarch. He emphasizes the realistic emotional turmoil and psychological price Rachel. the beloved wife, paid for her privileged status (dwelling, in particular, on her troubled relationship with Leah in Poem Six), but he balances those with clear (if not very impressive) reiterations of God's providential care for her. The first unit depicts God's responsiveness to Rachel's pleas, while the second subtly enlarges the frame of the story, presenting God's concern for Rachel as typifying His divine character—and, by implication, suggesting providential concern for the wellbeing of Israel on both the national and individual scales. Like Leah, Rachel can easily be read as a symbol for the nation as a whole. However, while Leah's story affirms the emotional bond between God and Israel, Rachel symbolizes the mysterious process of redemption that flows naturally from the divine-human love. In this *qedushta*, the birth of a child embodies redemption on a small, but still miraculous, scale. The implicit message of consolation is clear: Yannai leaves the image of national rebirth and resurrection—against all odds and appearances—in the mind of his audience without having to come out and say it. Israel may feel itself to be in a kind of living death—exile—but just as Rachel's redemption came and just as she was never actually forgotten, so will the nation's time arrive. All these doors—personal and national—God will unlock, and rescue those who are imprisoned. By speaking so tenderly of

Rachel, Yannai addresses his community not simply as a collective but also as an assembly of individuals. The singular can be even more powerful, and meaningful, than the plural.

Qedushta for Genesis 31:3 בראשית לא:ג

"Return to the Land of your fathers" שוב אל ארץ אבותיך

In this poem, the life of the father becomes a sign to the sons—that is, Jacob's biography anticipates Israel's national history. The mood of the poem is intensely optimistic, in keeping with the heady events of the *sidra*: restoration to the Land from which the patriarch-nation has long been exiled. By implication, the poet creates a sense that the end of suffering is at hand, restoration is imminent, and the bountiful Land awaits. The most striking theme of the poem, however, is its presentation of the Land as a character in its own right.

(1) Your ways bring near those who are far
Those driven to wander so far a-field
Exiles, far flung among those who reject You
Their path keeps them far from evil
Indeed, just like the man of purity, who had been near but had gone afar[1]
Fleeing the man of rejection[2]
This is the Land bequeathed to him
"Return to it"—with a word, He spoke and compelled him
Your decree: he would not return empty;[3]
You declared: a remnant would return[4]
Though the storm of the hairy one, like a dragon, approached[5]
To the smooth one You said, "Return to your portion!"

As it is written: "Then the Eternal said to Jacob: `Return to the Land of your ancestors and to your birthplace, and I will be with you'" (Gen 31:3)
And it is said: "A remnant shall return, a remnant of Jacob, to a mighty God" (Isa 10:21)
And it is said: "I cry out to You, O Eternal; (I say), `You are my refuge, my portion in the (living) land'" (Ps 142:6)[6]
And it is said: "Say, `To you will I give the land of Canaan, your allotted portion'" (Ps 105:11)
And it is said: "And He confirmed as a decree for Jacob, for Israel as an eternal covenant" (Ps 105:10)

The world You founded[7]
You built it with Your steadfast love

---

1 This refers to Jacob, who had to flee the land of Canaan in order to avoid his brother Esau's murderous wrath (Gen 27).

2 That is, Esau, the consummate apostate who rejects (keeps far from) all the positive attributes embodied by Jacob.

3 `Empty' could have several possible meanings. In keeping with the end of Gen 31:3 (cited by **B1**), it could mean that Jacob will not return alone, but rather that God would be with him. It could also describe Jacob's return as a prosperous family man, although he left home alone and as a penniless fugitive. This meaning emerges from Gen 31:42, in which Jacob tells Laban: "Had not the God of my father, the God of Abraham, and the fear of Isaac, been with me, surely you would have sent me away now empty. God has seen my affliction and the labor of my hands and rebuked you last night." Finally, it could refer to the fact that God's promises are not empty words, but are destined to be fulfilled; **R** cites Isa 55:11, "So shall my word be that goes out of my mouth; it shall not return to me empty, but it shall

(א) **א**וֹמָנָךְ מִקָּרֵב רְחוֹקִים
בְּדוּדֵי נְדוּדֵי מֶרְחַקִּים
גוֹלִים וּמִמֶּרְחֲקוֹתֶיךָ רוֹחֲקִים
דַּרְכָּם מֵעֲלֵיהֶם מַרְחִיקִם
הֵן כְּאִישׁ תָּם הַקָּרוֹב אֲשֶׁר רָחַק
וּבָרַח מֵאִישׁ הַמְרֻוחָק
זאֹת הָאָרֶץ אֲשֶׁר לוֹ הוּחַק
חֲזוֹר לָהּ דִּיבֵּר אֵלָיו דָּחַק
טַעֲמָךְ אֲשֶׁר רֵיק לֹא יָשׁוּב
יִידַּעְתָּה אֶת שְׁאָר יָשׁוּב
כְּבָה סַעַר שָׂעִיר כְּעַכְשׁוּב
לְחָלְק נַמְתָּה לְחֶלְקָךְ שׁוּב

ככתוב ויאמר יי אל יעקב שוב אל ארץ אבותיך ולמולדתך ואהיה עמך

ונאמר שאר ישוב שאר יעקב אל אל גבור

ונאמר זעקתי אליך יי אמרתי אתה מחסי חלקי בארץ החיים

ונאמר לאמר לך אתן את ארץ כנען חבל נחלתכם

ונאמר ויעמידה ליעקב לחק לישראל ברית עולם

עוֹלָם יְסוֹדָךְ
בָּנִיתָה בְחַסְדָּךְ

---

accomplish that which I please, and it shall prosper in the thing for which I sent it."

4 In addition to the prooftext from Isa 10:21 (**R**), see Isa 7:3, where one of Isaiah's sons is named, prophetically, "A remnant shall return" (*sheʾar yashuv*). Here the national prophecy is applied to the patriarch; God's promise will not go unfulfilled.

5 Reading כבא with **R** and Zulay. The "hairy one" (*seir*) being a code-name for Esau, who is contrasted with the smooth-skinned Jacob. The poet seems to have in mind the aggadic tradition that Esau was coming towards Jacob with the intent to wage war against him, but God's promise to be with him (Gen 31:3) gives him the courage to move forward. See *ExodR* 27:1. The image of Esau's militant approach contradicts Yannai's retelling of these events in the *qedushta* for Gen 32:4, in which Esau is going on his own way and Jacob deliberately intercepts him.

6 Cited in *TanḥB Vayetze* 23.

7 "World" (*ʿolam*) here picks up an "eternal" (*ʿolam*) at the end of Ps 105:10.

O Shield of the children of Your faithful one[8]
Blessed… Shield…

(2) The queens[9] among his treasures
the wives of the pure one, his favorites[10]
His stalwarts, sturdy sheltering walls:
the very structure of his dwelling, they stand by
Mindful of what had been revealed
he joined them, and to them he revealed:
"The end arrives, the return from exile"
Desiring that rebuke be revealed[11]
He perceived that the matter was urgent;
he sent for them while he waited outside
Pure women, and wise, free of disdain
the pure one in his wisdom called them to council

As it is written: "Then Jacob sent and called Rachel and Leah to the field, to his flock" (Gen 31:4)
And it is said: "Daughters of queens are among your treasures; your consort stands at your right hand, decked in the fine gold of Ophir" (Ps 45:10)
And it is said: "He has told you, O mortal, what is good, and what the Eternal seeks from you: nothing except doing justice, keeping loyalty, and walking in wisdom[12] with your God" (Mic 6:8)
And it is said: "The Eternal is for me, I fear nothing; what can a man do to me?" (Ps 118:6)

Man and beast You save[13]
O God who saves
Life-giving dew You pour over us!
Blessed… Who resurrects…

---

8 The language of this line recalls Ps 89:3, which states, "For I have said, 'The world is built by steadfast love (*ḥesed*); as for the heavens, you shall establish your faithfulness (*emunah*) among them.'" Although the referent here is God, the psalm is attributed to "Etan the Ezrahite," construed midrashically as a name for Abraham. By "rewriting" a psalm attributed to Abraham and using it as a transition to the *ḥatimah*, Yannai creates a close but very subtle connection between the patriarch, the congregation, and the blessing.

9 That is, Rachel and Leah, the two high-status wives. The concubines, Zilpah and Bilhah, may be implicit in the following line: four wives representing the four walls of a house. Note, also, that "house" is a rabbinic euphemism meaning 'wife.' See *ExodR* 28:2, *LevR* 20:9, *EcclR* 9:8, *b. Shabb.* 118b, *b. Yoma* 2a.

מְמַגֵּן בְּנֵי חֲסִידָךְ
ברוך... מגן...

(ב) **מְ**לָכוֹת בִּיקְרוֹתָיו
נְשׂוּאוֹת תָּם יְקָרוֹתָיו
סוֹכְנוֹתָיו צֵל קוֹרוֹתָיו
עוֹמְדוֹת תַּבְנִית קִירוֹתָיו
פִּקּוּד אֲשֶׁר אֵלָיו נִגְלָה
צִימְּדָם וְלָהֶם גִּילָה
קֵץ גַּע לָשׁוּב מִגּוֹלָה
רְצוּיָה תּוֹכַחַת מְגוּלָּה
שָׂר הַדָּבָר כִּי נָחוּץ
שִׁילַּח אַחֲרֵיהֶם וְהוּא בַחוּץ
תְּמִימוֹת וּצְנוּעוֹת מִנִּיאוּץ
תָּם בְּהַצְנֵיעַ קְרָאָם לְיִעוּץ

ככתוב וישלח יעקב ויקרא לרחל וללאה השדה אל צאנו

ונאמר בנות מלכים ביקרותיך נצבה שגל לימינך בכתם אופיר

ונאמר הגיד לך אדם מה טוב ומה יי דורש ממך כי אם עשות משפט ואהבת חסד והצנע לכת עם אלהיך

ונאמר יי לי לא אירא מה יעשה לי אדם

אָדָם וּבְהֵמָה תּוֹשִׁיעַ
אֵל הַמּוֹשִׁיעַ
תְּחִיַּית טַל לָנוּ תַּשְׁפִּיעַ
ברוך... מחיה...

---

10 Ps 45:10; see also *GenR* 45:1 (**R**).

11 This alludes to Prov 27:5, "Revealed [open] rebuke is better than concealed love" (**R**). The intended meaning seems to be that Jacob wished to reveal to Leah and Rachel their father's duplicity, which had been disguised as love.

12 The poet uses the root צ-נ-ע according to its Aramaic meaning, "discretion, cleverness, wit," rather than the more common Hebrew meaning, "modesty." The somewhat awkward translation of Micah reflects the implicit interpretation.

13 Ps 36:7 (**R**), interpreted in *GenR* 33:1 as: "Man You preserve for the sake of the beasts," contrary to the reverse interpretation, which might seem more intuitive. This line may also hint that Jacob's sustenance of his flocks is parallel to God's sustenance of His "flock."

(3) Fear and awe are nothing to those who fear You
For in their fear of You, all who oppose You become nothing
You said to the man who felt fear: "Of what are you afraid?
How can a God-fearing man[14] fear one who doesn't know fear?"[15]
He[16] feared You in his own land and outside his land as well;
You fulfilled his desire and You kept his counsel
O Yah, You cared for him, restoring him to his birthplace
leading him to tranquility, granting him serenity, and sending him home.

As it is written: "As for you: have no fear, my servant Jacob, says the Eternal; be not dismayed, O Israel, for here I am! I am delivering you from afar, and your descendants as well, from the land of captivity. And Jacob shall again have serenity and peacefulness, and nothing shall make him tremble" (Jer 30:10).

And it is said: "Station yourselves towards Zion,[17] set up signposts; set your hearts upon the highway, the path you walk. Return, O maiden Israel! Return to these towns of yours!" (Jer 31:20)

You are Holy, enthroned on the praises of Israel... *Please, God...*

(4) The Aramean would have destroyed my father[18] while he dwelt with him
had You not been his guard and protector
He deceived and tricked, but You were faithful;[19]
he was false and fibbed, but You kept faith
He gave him mottled ones, but You watched over them
speckled and spotted ones, and You made them conceive
During the day, he showed him the younger one
but at night he brought him the elder[20]

---

14 A version of the epithet, "the Fear (*paḥad*) of Isaac" (see Gen 31:42 for the use of that divine name in this *sidra*); Yannai uses the root י-ר-א instead of פ-ח-ד, however, to suit the formal needs of this poem.

15 Jacob is a pious man, a God-fearing person; Esau, foolishly proud, does not fear anyone, not even God (see the interpretation of Deut 25:18 in *ExodR* 27:1, cited in **B1**).

16 The identification of the character meant here is open to interpretation. According to one reading, adopted in this translation, "he" refers to Jacob/Israel, whose piety remained true both in the Land and in the Diaspora/exile. Alternatively (and with **R**), this line could be understood as describing not Jacob, but *Esau.* In this reading, Esau feared Jacob, as in Deut 2:4, "And charge the people as follows: You will be passing through the territory of your kinsmen, the descendants of Esau, who live in Seir. Though they will be afraid of you, be very careful." Yannai would then mean that at the time of the Redemption, Rome

(ג) יִרְאָה וּמוֹרָה לִירֵאֶיךָ אָיִין
כִּי בְּיִרְאָתְךָ כֹּל נֶגְדְּךָ כְּאַיִן
נַמְתָּה לְאִישׁ מִיתְיָירֵא מַה תִּיתְיָרֵא
אֵיךְ גֶּבֶר יָרֵא יִירָא מִלֹּא יָרֵא
יִירָאֲךָ בְּאַרְצוֹ וְגַם חוּץ לְאַרְצוֹ
מְלֶאכְתָּה חֶפְצוֹ וְהִשְׁלַמְתָּה יְעָצוֹ
יָהּ תִּרְגַּלְתּוֹ לְמוֹלַדְתּוֹ לַהֲשִׁיבוֹ
לְשַׁאֲנְנוֹ לְהַשְׁלִיווֹ וּלְהַשְׁקִיטוֹ וּלְיַישְׁבוֹ

ככתוב ואתה אל תירא עבדי יעקב נאם יי ואל תחת ישראל כי הנני מושיעך מרחוק ואת
זרעך מארץ שבים ושב יעקב ושקט ושאנן ואין מחריד

ונאמר הציבי לך צינים שמי לך תמרורים שתי לבך למסלה דרך הלכתי שובי בתולת
ישראל שבי אל עריך אלה

ואתה קדוש יושב תהלות ישראל אל נא

(ד) אֲרַמִּי אוֹבֵד אָבִי בְּעֵת הָיָה אֶצְלוֹ
לוּלֵי כִּי הָיִתָה שׁוֹמְרוֹ וְצִילּוֹ
הִיתֵּל וְרִימָּה וְאַתָּה אוֹמָּן
כִּיזֵּב וְשִׁקֵּר וְאַתָּה נֶאֱמָן
נָתַן לוֹ בְּרֻודִּים וּפִקַּדְתָּם
עֲקֻודִּים נְקֻודִּים וְיִיחַמְתָּם
הֶרְאָה לוֹ בַּיּוֹם לַצְּעִירָה
וְהֵבִיא לוֹ בַּלַּיְלָה לַבְּכִירָה

(=Esau) will fear Israel throughout the Empire, and not simply in Palestine. If read this way, the first half of the line continues God's direct speech to the patriarch.

17 The phrase is usually translated "erect markers for yourselves"; however, the noun ציונים contains in it a pun on the word "Zion," which may, by turn, be an epithet for those who will dwell in Zion, the children of Jacob.

18 **R** cites Deut 26:5, "A wandering (*ʾoved*) Aramean was my father," but as interpreted in rabbinic tradition by means of a repunctuation (*ʾibbed*), most famously in the Passover Haggadah and, as **B1** notes, in the *targumim*. The Aramean is, in this case, Laban, although in other contexts it refers to "Rome."

19 **R** and **B1** both adduce *GenR* 74:3, which reads "He (God) has been with me (*ʿimadi*)" (Gen 31:5,a verse of the *sidra*) as "God has been my pillar/support (*ʿamudi*)."

20 That is, Laban promised Rachel to Jacob but delivered Leah on the wedding night.

But he, because he worked in earnest, his works were his own, in earnest;
though the Aramean was a swindler, advising him with deceit
And You, Guardian of Israel, are called "Holy!"

(5) He reversed and reneged, twisted and tricked
he distorted and deceived, perverted and warped
You knew how Laban treated the pure one, whom You made pure[21]
The perverse, You treat perversely but with the pure, Your acts are pure
His body ravaged by frost and his form scorched by fire
near his end, because of the heat and nigh finished, because of the cold[22]
He sought to consume his strength and his labors[23]
his wares and his wages and, in the end, his life[24]
He starved him countless times and he aged him early, without end
but You have seen that every affliction meets a foretold fate
The time appointed for his return had arrived it approached
    and You said to him, "Return!"
As he trusted in You back when he said, "I will return"[25]
    You promised him, "I will return you!"[26]
A stranger and foreigner he was considered[27]
in a foreign land, one wholly strange, he dwelled.
"Go back" is not what was said to him
    "Turn back" is what was said to him;
when he was brought back to take shelter and repentance to do[28]
We have strayed among foreigners and scattered among strangers are we
we are mixed up among the multitudes and mixed in with the nations
Yah, again return to us, and turn us unto You![29]
Let us live securely and settle us in serenity!
… *Forever*…

---

21 This may allude to the tradition that Jacob was born circumcised; see *Tanḥ Noaḥ* 5 (**B1**).

22 Yannai alludes to Jacob's suffering at Laban's hands. In Gen 31:4, Jacob says to Laban: "Thus I was; in the day the drought consumed me, and the frost by night; and my sleep departed from my eyes" (**R**).

23 I.e., Laban sought to acquire Jacob's hard-earned property.

24 See first line of Poem Four.

25 Gen 28:21 (**R**).

26 Gen 28:15 (**R**).

27 This could refer to the fact that Jacob was not yet "Israel" (a "stranger" being a "non-Israelite") or that his status as one who lived outside the promised land made him functionally "other."

הוּא כְּפוֹעֵל אֱמֶת פְּעָלוֹ בֶּאֱמֶת
וַאֲרַמִּי כְּאִישׁ מִרְמוֹת עָץ עָלָיו לְרַמּוֹת
וְשׁוֹמֵר יִשְׂרָאֵל נִקְרֵאתָה קָדוֹשׁ

(ה) **א**ִיחוּר וַהֲפַכְפַּךְ עִיקּוּשׁ וּפְתַלְתּוֹל
מִרְמוֹת וָתוֹךְ הָותֶל וַעֲקַלְקוֹל
בַּנְתָּה כִּי עָשׂ לָבָן לְתָם אֲשֶׁר הִתְמָמְתָּה
וְעִם עִיקֵּשׁ נִתְעַקַּשְׁתָּה וְעִם תָּמִים נִיתַּתְמָמְתָּה
גִּיוְיוֹ שָׁחַף קֶרַח וְגוּפוֹ שָׁזַף קֶדַח
קָץ מִפְּנֵי חוֹרֶב וְקָט מִפְּנֵי חוֹרֶף
דִּימָּה לֶאֱכוֹל חֵילוֹ וִיגִיעוֹ
סַחְרוֹ וּשְׂכָרוֹ וּבַסּוֹף נַפְשׁוֹ
הִקְטִינוּ לְלֹא עֵת וְהִזְקִינוּ לְלֹא קֵץ
וּלְכָל תִּיכְלָה רָאִיתָ קֵץ
וְקֵץ שִׁיבְתּוֹ לָשׁוּב קָרַב
וְנַמְתָּה לוֹ שׁוּב
כְּבָטַח בָּךְ וְנָם וְשַׁבְתִּי
וְהִבְטַחְתּוֹ וַהֲשִׁיבוֹתִיךָ
זָר וְגַם נָוכְרִי יֵיחָשֵׁב
בְּאֶרֶץ נָוכְרִיָּיה וְזָרָה כָּל בָּהּ יוֹשֵׁב
חֲזוֹר לֹא נֶאֱמַר לוֹ
וְשׁוּב נֶאֱמַר לוֹ
בְּמַחֲזִירוֹ לַחֲסוֹת וּתְשׁוּבָה לַעֲסוֹת
טָעִינוּ בֵּין נָוכְרִים וְנִיזְרִינוּ בֵּין זָרִים
עוֹרַבְנוּ בַּגּוֹיִם נִיבְלַלְנוּ בָּעַמִּים
יָהּ עוֹד שׁוּבֵינוּ וְאֵלֶיךָ שׁוֹבְבֵינוּ
בֶּטַח הוֹשִׁיבֵנוּ וְשֶׁקֶט יַשְׁבֵּינוּ
לעולם

---

28 The pun here is on the root ש-ו-ב, which can mean "return" but also "repent." As **R** notes, the poet here states that the biblical author *could* have used the synonym ח-ז-ר for "return," but that would lack the penitential connotation. God is returning Jacob to his homeland both so that he can take shelter (under the wings of the divine presence) and also do repentance for his years of living away from the Promised Land. Yannai asks for both kinds of restoration for his own community: a restoration to divine shelter, and a restoration to communal integrity (people of Israel in the Land of Israel) so that they can finally do repentance that is otherwise denied them.

29 Reading השיבינו with **R** and Zulay. This line also employs the root ש-ו-ב in its dual sense of "restore" and "repent." See Lam 5:21, "Turn us to you, O Eternal One, and we shall be turned; renew our days as of old" (**R**). This verse concludes the modern Torah service liturgy (the Ark closing).

"Return to the land of your ancestors…"

(6) The land of Israel is hallowed[30]
and made more holy than any other land
Among the ten most holy, it is holiest[31]
and the holy ones who are within her, she hallows[32]
The boundaries of the territory of the seven nations
for which I raised My hand in an oath[33]
"Banners" born of she who hewed her seven;[34]
they divided their apportioned portion into seven once again[35]
I gave a promise to the grandfather: "I will surely return"
and to father and son with, "We will bow down and then return"[36]
And lo, also to you it was said, "Return!"
for [I will restore you from your] captive dwellings[37]
Flowing with honey and milk is she
and unlike all other lands is she
Your destined portion, the pride of Jacob is she[38]
the Land of Israel—named for you is she
Fine and wide and fertile
abundant in her fruit
Her dwellings unlike any other
free from all pestilence and plague[39]
As when your mouth brought forth your beautiful voice
as when you went forth from your father's house, staff in hand,[40]

---

30 **R** reads: "Land of holiness, hallowed" (אדמת קודש המקודשת).

31 See *m. Kil.* 1:6 (**R**).

32 See *Mekh. Kaspa* 2 (**B1**); Yannai's reasoning here is as follows: because a number of *mitzvot*—particularly agricultural commandments—can only be fulfilled within in the Land of Israel, living in Israel and fulfilling those *mitzvot* increases one's sanctity.

33 This is the land that God swore to give to Abraham and his descendents, "the Promised Land."

34 This line is opaque; based on the allusions to Prov 9:1 ("Wisdom has hewn her seven pillars," cited by **R**) and Prov 14:1 ("The wisdom of women builds her house," added by **B1**), and the use of 'banners" as a byword for "sons, descendents," the line seems to refer to the Israelites as the sons of "wisdom" (i.e., Torah) or, more likely, "wise women": Rachel, Leah, Bilhah, and Zilpah who collectively built Jacob's house. See note above, where "house" is a euphemism for "wife." The seven pillars of wisdom are juxtaposed here against the seven Canaanite nations.

35 This refers to the division of the Land into seven parts in the time of Joshua. See Josh 18:6, "When you have written down the description of the land in seven parts, bring it here to me. Then I will cast lots for you here before the Eternal One our God" (**R**).

36 "Grandfather" and "father" both refer to Abraham, while "son" refers to Isaac; the

שוב אל ארץ

(ו) **א**ַדְמַת יִשְׂרָאֵל הַמְקוּדֶּשֶׁת
מִכָּל אֲרָצוֹת מוּקְדֶּשֶׁת
בְּעֶשֶׂר קְדוּשׁוֹת נִקְדֶּשֶׁת
וּקְדוֹשִׁים אֲשֶׁר בָּהּ מְקַדֶּשֶׁת
גְּבוּל נַחֲלַת עֲמָמִים שִׁבְעָה
אֲשֶׁר נָשָׂאתִי יָדִי בִּשְׁבוּעָה
דִּגְלֵי חֲצוּבֵי חָצְבָה שִׁבְעָה
יְחַלְּקוּהָ מְחַלְּקֵי חֵלֶק לְשִׁבְעָה
הִבְטַחְתִּי לַשָּׁב בְּשׁוּב אָשׁוּב
וְלָאָב וְלַבֵּן בְּנִשְׁתַּחֲוֶה וְנָשׁוּב
וְהִנֵּה גַם לָךְ נֶאֱמַר שׁוּב
כִּי שְׁבוּת ... ..שׁוּב.
זָבַת חָלָב וּדְבַשׁ הִיא
וְלֹא כִשְׁאָר כָּל אֲרָצוֹת הִיא
חֶבֶל נַחֲלָתְךָ גְּאוֹן יַעֲקֹב הִיא
אֶרֶץ־יִשְׂרָאֵל לְשִׁמְךָ הִיא
טוֹבָה וּרְחָבָה וּשְׁמֵינָה
וּבְפֵירוֹתֶיהָ מְשׁוּמָּנָה
יְשִׁיבָתָהּ מִכֹּל מְשׁוּנָּה
וּמִימַּזִּיק וּמִימַּחֲרִיד מְשׁוּאֲנָנָה
כְּהוֹצִיא פִיךָ בְּנוֹי קוֹלָךְ
כְּצֵאתְךָ מִבֵּית אָבִיךָ בְּמַקְלָךְ

---

first quotation comes from Gen 18:10, while the second is from Gen 22:5 (**R**). Zulay and **R** lack the word לבן ("to the son"), which would suggest "father" refers to Isaac, not Abraham.

37 From Jer 30:18 (**B1**). Zulay's reading (כי שבות אהליך אשוב) is accepted here.

38 The language of this line draws on Ps 105:11 ("your destined portion") and Ps 47:5 ("He chooses our portion for us, the pride of Jacob whom he loves. Selah") (**B2**). The word rendered here as "portion" (*naḥalah*) has connotations of inheritance, birthright. The referent may be the entire Land or Zion in particular.

39 Lev 26:5–6 (**B1**) states: "And your threshing shall last to the time of vintage, and the vintage shall last to the sowing time; and you shall eat your bread to the full and dwell in your land safely. And I will give peace in the land, and you shall lie down, and none shall make you afraid; and I will remove evil beasts from the Land, nor shall the sword go through your Land" (**B1**). The terms "pestilence" and "harm" may refer not only to various diseases and blights but the demons (*maziqin*, the plural of the word translated as "pestilence" here) associated with such plagues in rabbinic literature. See also *Sifra* to the cited verse (**R** and **B1**).

40 The first stich seems to refer to Jacob's oath in Gen 28:21 (cited by **R**), "So that I will come back to my father's house in peace; then shall the Eternal One be my God." The second draws upon the imagery of Gen 32:11 (**R**).

Tremble not; return with your great cohort[41]
for your birthplace will receive you for good
Your bearer and begetter are seeking you[42]
praying for your protection from the proud one's prideful party[43]
Your descendents, all of them, look to you
radiant[44], refined, and regal are they
The choicest dwelling, desired by kings[45]—
who are destined to lick your dust[46]
With you upon the way shall there be walking
camps of hosts of angels
Her fruits and her yields she grants;
to you and to your offspring it is granted
Your claim upon her will not expire
no strange land shall be your bower
Her stones are streaked with iron pure
and from her hills is copper hewn[47]
Hurry, scale her walls upon which My ladder leans;
just as I said, as I stood by you[48]
For her name is "the land of life"
because her dead will be the first to return to life
Those who brought you forth are still among the living[49]
and years of life await you

And thus, "I will be with you…"
(7[1]) My angels and I are with you
I will not abandon you
Your brother's glory will fade before you
I will instruct you in ways of peace
Neither wealth nor health will you lack

---

41 That is, with your wives and sons.

42 "Bearer" refers to Rebecca, who was still alive when Jacob set out on his return journey; "begetter" refers to Isaac. See *GenR* 74:1, discussed below.

43 That is, Esau and his cohort.

44 From Isa 6:6, where the term describes glowing coals.

45 This alludes to the fact that so many kings attempted to conquer the Land of Israel; they sought to possess it, but they were merely sojourners there. See *SifD Eqev* 1 (**B1**).

46 Isa 49:23 provides this vivid image (**R**).

47 See Deut 8:9, "A land where you may eat without stint, where you will lack nothing; a

לֹא תִשְׁתָּע שׁוּב בְּרוֹב קְהָלָךְ
כִּי מוֹלַדְתָּךְ בְּטוֹב תְּקַבְּלָךְ
מוֹלַדְתָּךְ וּמוֹלִידָךְ לָךְ מְצַפִּים
מְחַנֲנִים כִּי תֻוצַּל מֵחֲצוּפִים
נִינֶיךְ כֻּולָּם לָךְ צוֹפִים
רְצוּפִים צְרוּפִים וּצְנוּפִים
סְגֻולַּת מוֹשַׁב הַמְּלָכִים
הָעֲתִידִים הֱיוֹת עֲפָרָךְ מְלַחֲכִים
עִימָּךְ בַּדֶּרֶךְ יִהְיוּ מְהַלְּכִים
מַחֲנוֹת כִּיתֵּי מַלְאָכִים
פִּירְיָהּ וִיבוּלָהּ נוֹתֶנֶת
לָךְ וּלְזַרְעָךְ נִיתֶּנֶת
צִדְקָתָךְ בָּהּ לֹא מִתְמַתֶּנֶת
וְזָרָה בָּךְ לֹא מִתְחַתֶּנֶת
קִיבּוּעַ אֲבָנֶיהָ בַּרְזֶל נִיקְצָב
וְהֲרָרֶיהָ נְחוֹשֶׁת נֶחְצָב
רוּץ וְדַלֵּג שׁוּר וּבָהּ תּוּצָּב
כְּסַחְתִּי לָךְ וַאֲנִי עָלֶיךְ נִיצָּב
שֶׁשְּׁמָהּ אֶרֶץ הַחַיִּים
כִּי מֵיתֶיהָ תְחִילָּה חָיִים
תְּחוֹלְלֹתֶיךְ עַד הֵם בַּחַיִּים
וְיוֹסִיפוּ לָךְ שְׁנוֹת חַיִּים

ובכן ואהיה עמך
(ז[1]) **א**ֲנִי וּמַלְאָכַי עִימָּךְ
בַּל אֶעָתֵק מֵעִימָּךְ
גְּאוֹן אָח לְפָנֶיךָ יִימָךְ
דֶּרֶךְ שָׁלוֹם אַחְכִּימָךְ
הוֹן וָנֶפֶשׁ לֹא יֶיחְסַר מִמָּךְ

land whose rocks are iron and from whose hills you can mine copper" (**R**).

48 This line refers to the story of Jacob's vision of the ladder at Beth El; see Gen 28:13 (**R**).

49 By the time Jacob returns home, Rebecca, his mother, is dead; however, it appears that when Jacob left for home, she was still alive. See *GenR* 74:1, which interprets the opening verse of this *sidra* as follows: "'Return to the land of your fathers, and to your kindred, and I will be with you' (Gen 31:3): ["Your fathers" means:] Your father waits for you [there], [`your kindred' means:] your mother waits for you, ["I will be with you" means:] and I Myself wait for you." Because Rebecca has not yet died, God's words to Jacob are not false as might first seem to be the case here. See above, Poem 6, lines 25–26.

You will brighten your mother's and father's faces[50]
Shining and sheltered from harm are you
Graced, just as in your vision dreamed
Stepping swiftly in your purity
Your right hand in Mine, supporting you
On My throne of glory I have engraved you
Never shall I decree your doom[51]
How lovely are the tents of your dwellings[52]
Forever among them shall I sustain you
Your utterance—like honey drip your words
So sweet in lovely voice are your declarations
I watch over you in mercy, full of mercy for you
I have commanded your rescue, to exalt you
You are holy, and I will not reckon your sin
I keep you from your pursuer's grasp
My name I have joined to yours,[53]
And you will return to your birthplace in peace

And thus…

(7^2) You will bring us back from all foreign gates
When gates sunk low are lifted[54]
Lifted shall be the stooped of stature
With stature and status, distinguish us![55]
Distinguish us, the chief cornerstone
A cornerstone, a precious gem, on high
On high, over all, set us
Set us, and over every head exalt us
Exalt us, and lift us up to the heights[56]
Upon the heights, exalted of old, You shall dwell![57]

---

50 See previous note.

51 On Israel's permanence, see 2 Kgs 14:27 (cited by **B1**), "And the Eternal One did not say that he would blot out the name of Israel from under heaven."

52 Num 24:5 (**R**), well-known for its inclusion in the morning liturgy in "*Mah tovu.*"

53 Yannai refers to the incorporation of the theophoric element "El" into the name Israel.

54 The gates here are those of Jerusalem or the Temple itself (see Lam 2:9, which opens: "Her gates are sunk into the ground"—**R**)—symbolic of both political autonomy and a restored cult. See also Isa 3:26, 26:2, 60:11; Ps 24:7, 9 (**B1**); and others. As part of Israel's redemption, God will lift (i.e., rebuild) these gates.

וּתְחַלֶּה פְּנֵי אָבִיךָ וְאִמָּךְ
זָךְ וּמוּצַּל מִילוֹחֲמָךְ
חַנּוּן כְּמוֹ מַרְאֵה חֲלוֹמָךְ
טוּסָה וְהִתְהַלֵּךְ בְּתֻוּמָּךְ
יְמִינָךְ בִּימִינִי תֻּוּתְמָךְ
כִּיסֵּא כְּבוֹדִי בּוֹ אֶחְתְּמָךְ
לָעַד לֹא אַתִּימָּךְ
מַה טוֹבוּ אוֹהָלֵי מְקוֹמָךְ
נֶצַח בָּהֶם אֲקִימָךְ
סִיחַ הִיטִיף נָוְאֲמָךְ
עָרֵב בְּקוֹל נוֹיִי טַעֲמָךְ
פְּקַדְתִּיךָ בְּרַחֲמִים לְרַחֲמָךְ
צִיוִּיתִי יִשְׁעָךְ לְרוֹמְמָךְ
קָדוֹשׁ אַתָּה וְלֹא אַאֲשִׁימָךְ
רוֹדְפָךְ בְּיָדוֹ לֹא אַשְׁלִימָךְ
שְׁמִי עֵרַבְתִּי בִּשְׁמָךְ
תָּשׁוּב לְמוֹלַדְתָּךְ בִּשְׁלוֹמָךְ

ובכן

(ז[2]) תְּשִׁיבֵנוּ מִכָּל שְׁעָרִים
שְׁעָרִים טָבְעוּ רוֹמֵם
רוֹמֵס כְּפוּפֵי קוֹמָה
קוֹמָה וְקוֹמְמִיּוּת צַיְּינֵנוּ
צַיְּינֵנוּ לְרֹאשׁ פִּינָּה
פִּינָּה וְיִקְרַת עֶלְיוֹן
עֶלְיוֹן עַל כֹּל שִׂימֵינוּ
שִׂימֵינוּ וּלְכָל רֹאשׁ נַשְּׂאֵינוּ
נַשְּׂאֵינוּ נַטְּלֵינוּ מָרוֹם
מָרוֹם מֵרִאשׁוֹן לִינָה

55 **R** cites Lev 26:13, "I am the Eternal One your God, who brought you out of the land of Egypt, that you should not be their slaves; and I have broken the bars of your yoke and made you go upright."

56 **B1** cites Deut 28:1, "And it shall come to pass, if you shall give heed diligently to the voice of the Eternal One your God, to observe and to do all his commandments which I command you this day, that the Eternal One your God will set you on the heights above all nations of the earth."

57 As part of the restoration, the Temple will be rebuilt, and God will again dwell in His house. The poet uses the imperative in this line.

Dwell with us amidst the scattered[58]
Scattered, then ransomed, shall be the precious ones
Precious ones, honored though we have strayed!
We strayed, though in the land of our desire[59]
Desired and delightful—a land flowing
Flowing with milk and honey
Honey clear and unpolluted[60]
Unpolluted, she shall not expel her dwellers
Her dwellers who are her keepers[61]
Her keepers keep her covenant
Her covenant was made with her in truth[62]
Truth within her bounds flourishes

(8) May You cause us to flourish and prosper us;
may You come and bring us along;
may You return and restore us;
may You approach and be brought near;
may You arise and raise us up,
we who return to You!
we are your witnesses[63]
and the children of Your servants;
we serve You with awe,
"Your holy branch"[64]
"those who sanctify You,"
As it is written: "And one called..."

---

58 This stanza, lines 11–12 of the unit, contains difficult puns on the root כ-פ-ר, which can mean "henna blossoms" (Song 7:12} "atonement" (as in Yom Kippur), "ransom" (Isa 43:3), and "scattered villages" (see *SongR* to the just cited verse; see also the common village prefix, "Kfar..."), among other nuances of this root, whose essential meaning is "to cover over" (**R** and **B1** both discuss the allusions in this passage). The sense of the line conveys a plea for God to be present in exile, among the henna spray and scattered villages, and while among the exiles for Him to bring about their rescue and ransom, motivated both by divine mercy and Israel's atonement.

59 A reference to the sin of the spies who brought back evil report about the Land in Num 13–14, using the language of Ps 106:24, which describes the episode. *j. Taʿan.* 23b explicitly connects the sin of the spies with the destruction of the Temple. (**B2**).

60 This translation reflects the enchainment technique (anadiplosis) of the Hebrew original. This line and the following, more literally, draw a parallel between honey, which does

לִינָה עִימָּנוּ בְּתוֹךְ כְּפָרִים
כְּפָרִים מְכַפְּרִים בְּעַד יְקָרִים
יְקָרִים נִכְבָּדִים טָעִינוּ
טָעִינוּ בְּאֶרֶץ חֶמְדָּה
חֶמְדָּה וְתַאֲוַת זָבַת
זָבַת חָלָב וּדְבָשׁ
וּדְבָשׁ בְּלִי בוֹ הֲקָאָה
הֲקָאָה וּבַל תָּקִיא דָּרֶיהָ
דָּרֶיהָ אֲשֶׁר הֵם גְּדֵירֶיהָ
גְּדֵירֶיהָ וּמוֹסְדֵי בְּרִיתָהּ
בְּרִיתָהּ כְּרוּתָה לָהּ אֱמֶת
אֱמֶת מִתּוֹכָהּ תִּצְמָח

(ח)

תִּצְמַח וְתַצְלִיחַ
תָּבוֹא וְתָבִיא
תָּשׁוּב וְתָשִׁיב
תִּקְרַב וּתְקָרֵב
תָּקוּם וְתָקִים
שָׁבֵי עָדֶיךְ
אֲשֶׁר הֵם עֵידֶיךְ
וּבְנֵי עֲבָדֶיךְ
בְּיִרְאָה עוֹבְדֶיךְ
כַּנַּת קְדוֹשֶׁיךְ
כִּינּוּי מַקְדִּישֶׁיךְ
ככתוב וקרא

---

not cause vomiting, and the Land, which will not vomit out its inhabitants. For the language underlying these lines, see Prov 25:16 and Lev 20:22 (**R**).

61 The poet here puns on the fact that the Land is "kept" by means of keeping the commandments. A fence around the Torah amounts to a fence around the Land, and the result is an interdependence of protection.

62 **B2** connects this with *Sifra Beḥukotai* 8:9 (to Lev 26:42), which asserts that God made a covenant with the Land itself. At the same time, the language ties in with Ps 105:9–11, which teaches that the covenant binding Abraham, Isaac, Jacob, and their heirs to the Land is eternal and unbreakable. The covenant is thus both *with* the Land and *of* the Land.

63 Following Isa 43:10 (**R**).

64 **R** adduces Psa. 80:15–16, "Return, we beseech you, O God of hosts; look down from heaven, and behold, and have regard for this vine; and the vineyard which your right hand has planted, and the branch that you made strong for yourself."

(9) By the pure ones You are purified and by the holy ones you are hallowed,
for continually they are saying:
Holy, holy, holy is the Lord of Hosts! The whole earth is filled with His glory!
"*Holy*"—from those who are pure of path
"*Holy*"—from those who are straight of course
"*Holy*"—from those who are smoothed of way
[Holy, holy, holy is the Lord of Hosts! The whole earth is filled with His glory!]
[“*Holy*"—He made pure] the pure path for the pure one,
in accord with his purity[65]
"*Holy*"—He made straight the straight course for him,
in accord with his straightness
"*Holy*"—[He made smooth for him a smooth] way,
in accord with his smoothness[66]
The one towards the other... together...

"*From His place*"—He said to the smooth one:
"Return, I am restoring your fortune"[67]
"*From His place*"—He will restore to Himself the penitent
of whom He said, "I will return"[68]
"*From His place*"—He brings his restoration, his return,
as He spoke: "And I will return you."[69]

Twice...

65 Here, "Holy" should probably be understood as "The Holy One"—i.e., God. The translation emphasizes the common form.

66 A pun on Jacob's smooth skin (Gen 27:11) and cleverness. See below.

(ט) בִּתְמִימִים תְּוּתְמָם וּבִקְדוֹשִׁים תְּוּקְדָּשׁ
בְּמַתְמִידִים וְאוֹמְרִים
קדוש קדוש קדוש יי צבאות מלא כל הארץ כבודו
קָדוֹשׁ מִתְּמִימֵי דֶרֶךְ
קָדוֹשׁ מִמְּיַישְּׁרֵי הֵילֶךְ
קָדוֹשׁ מִשְּׁפוּיֵי הֵיפֶךְ
...
... לְתָם תּוֹם דֶּרֶךְ
לְפִי תֻּומָּתוֹ
קָדוֹשׁ יִישֵּׁר לוֹ יוֹשֶׁר הֵילֶךְ
לְפִי יַשְּׁרוּתוֹ
קָדוֹשׁ ... הֵילֶךְ
לְפִי שְׁפִיוּתוֹ
לעומתם ... כל

...
מִמְּקוֹמוֹ נָם לְחָלָק
שׁוּב שַׁבְתִּי שְׁבוּתָךְ
מִמְּקוֹמוֹ הֵשִׁיב לוֹ תְּשׁוּבַת
אֲשֶׁר נָם וְשַׁבְתִּי
מִמְּקוֹמוֹ הֱשִׁיבוֹ וְשׁוֹבְבוֹ
כְּנָם וַהֲשִׁיבוֹתִיךְ

פעמים

67 Jer 30:3 (**R**).
68 Perhaps an allusion to Amos 9:14.
69 Isa 49:5 (**R**).

Commentary

This piyyut features a dramatic cast of characters: Jacob and God are the leads, with Rachel and Leah in supporting roles; Esau and Laban, meanwhile, make villainous return appearances. The most striking "character" in this poem, however, is the Land of Israel itself. In Poem Six, in particular, Yannai presents an extended paean to the "Holy Land"—a title that can be understood in a variety of ways.

Land of the holy ones: This understanding of "Holy Land" highlights the intense, organic bond between the Land and the nation of Israel, called in Deut 26:19 "a Holy People." The identification of Land and people as "holy" renders their shared destiny both natural and necessary. The Land's chosenness manifests through its remarkable fertility and productivity, which Yannai describes as a nearly Edenic state of effortless agriculture. She grants her yield to her tenants, and her veins run rich with resources. A land of milk and honey, "unlike all other lands is she" (line 14). Her holiness protects her inhabitants from pestilence and plague, and she gives freely to the people of all that she possesses. Jacob and his descendents are organically part of this Land, even sharing a name: "the Land and children of Israel." The Land is so attractive that others have always had designs on her—she is "desired by kings" (line 29) and temporarily possessed by the seven Canaanite nations—but only the chosen people, Israel, merit her and her bounty. Indeed, because God has been with Israel throughout the experience of exile and landlessness, "redemption" here is defined in terms of return to the Land, not in a specifically nationalist way (through the restoration of the monarchy, for example) but in naturalistic language. The people and Land are described as lovers who have been apart; the end of exile will be the restoration of a natural, almost cosmic, balance.

Land of the Holy One: The Land of Israel is not holy simply because of innate superior qualities; it is holy because the Holy One has chosen it. Of all the holy places, it is the most holy, to paraphrase *m. Kil.* 1:6—a text to which the opening stanza of Poem Six alludes. God Himself has sworn an oath concerning it, and it is God who controls when and how Israel the nation will return to Israel the Land. Israel may dwell on the Land, but the people cannot own it. The Land is as much a destiny as a destination. Reunion with the Land will mean restoration of a three-part fragmentation: the Land, the nation, and the God of Israel once again all together. They share the name "Israel" but in the exilic status quo, the ideal reality is fractured. Holiness, however, is whole.

Land that makes holy: The junction of people and territory, both blessed by God, creates a special kind of holiness: reciprocal, cyclical, and reinforcing. The holiness of the Land is not static; the Land itself creates opportunities for the generation of sanctity. How so? By having specific *mitzvot* (commandments) attached to it—every obligation in the Torah that begins, "When you are in the Land…" In exile, these *mitzvot* lie fallow, unfulfilled; when Israel is restored, they will be revived. In return, the inhabitants of the Land will be the first people to be revived at the time of the resurrection. The Land gives life, the people cultivate life, and the Land renews life.

Land of Holy Union: The longing that the poet expresses for the Land verges upon the erotic; like the ideal mother-wife, the Land of Israel nurtures, sustains, and protects. At moments, the identity of "she who bore you" is ambiguous, most likely referring to Rebecca, Jacob's birth mother and a matriarch of the nation, but also possibly describing the Land as a kind of "mother" who "bears" children in a metaphorical way, a real "birthplace." Similarly, referring to Jacob's wives, individually, as "she who hewed her seven" juxtaposes Rachel and Leah (and Bilhah and Zilpah) with the physical territory of Canaan, hewed into seven parts among the seven nations. The Land is described as eager and fecund, "fine, wide, and fertile" (line 17). She is relentlessly, lovingly personified. Never barren, never demanding, chosen and blessed, the Land becomes an idealized woman; she is the unmentioned matriarch. Each patriarch wed a woman who became a mother of the nation; the people as a whole entered into "*qiddushin*," as it were—a holy bond—with the Land of Israel. Separated from each other, in exile, they yearn for each other and trust that God, their creator-matchmaker, will restore them once again.

Yannai's ode to Zion, his paean to the beauty of the Land of Israel, expresses a national, collective yearning. The vision of the Land that emerges is idealized and dreamlike, tinged with both loss and hope. Yannai writes this poem despite living, technically, within the borders of the Promised Land, in the Galilee. Yet, his yearning tells us that so long as Esau and Laban, the enemies of the Jews, hold power over the Land, Israel is in exile, even in the Land of Israel. God has not yet uttered the command: "Return!" But when He does, Yannai's ears, and those of his listeners, are primed to hear, and yearning to obey.

Qedushta for Genesis 32:4 — בראשית לב:ד

"Then Jacob sent" — וישלח יעקב

This poem interweaves a number of related themes. The national allegory developed in the previous *qedushta* continues, only now the fraught encounter between Jacob and Esau—Israel and Rome—takes on apocalyptic overtones. At the same time, Yannai develops the character of Jacob in this poem, making him a more complex, perhaps less sympathetic, figure. While the patriarch successfully navigates this dangerous encounter with his potentially murderous twin, he does so at a cost that will be borne by his descendents. The motif of "real" versus "superficial" occurs several times in the context of Jacob's deception of his brother, as the trickster continues his tricks—with mixed results.

(1) … Terrifying and awesome is Your fearsomeness
thus: "Who shall not fear you?"[1]
… will see you …
… yet of *him* you are afraid?

… was so very filled with fear
yet always he was afraid …
… against him united
…

[The pure one, fearful,][2] honored him
The one puffed with pride[3] when he heard; lo, they were before him
… to you, to bend knee before him
… emissaries went before him

As it is written: "Then Jacob sent messengers before him to Esau his brother, to the land of Seir, the fields of Edom" (Gen 34:2)
And it is said: "A soft answer turns away wrath, a thoughtful word lifts anger" (Prov 15:1)
And it is said: "The oracle concerning Dumah: A call comes to me from Seir, `Watchman, what of the night? Watchman, what of the night?'" (Isa 21:11)[4]
And it is said :…
And it is said :…
And it is said: "Happy is the man who is anxious always, but he who hardens his heart will fall into misfortune" (Prov 28:14)
And it is said: "The poor man speaks beseechingly but the rich man's answer is harsh" (Prov 18:23)
And it is said: …

Your sword, O Ruddy One
will become drunk from the red one's blood
You are our Shield, O Lord[5]
[Blessed are You… Shield…]

---

1 These opening stanzas are damaged; the first line most likely describes God's awesomeness, while the second and third may indicate that Jacob fears Esau instead of God—showing honor to the wrong party.

2 Lacuna filled according to **B2**.

3 "One puffed with pride" is used here as an epithet for Esau; the phrase derives from Prov 21:24, "The proud, insolent man, scoffer is his name, acts in a frenzy of insolence."

4 "Dumah" is understood to refer to Edom/Rome.

(א) אָיוֹם וְנוֹרָא מוֹרָאָךְ
בְּכֵן מִי לֹא יִירָאָךְ
... ..א יִרְאָךְ
ד.. ... מֶנּוּ יְרֵיאָךְ

... מְאוֹד מִתְפַּחֵד
וְתָמִיד הָיָה מְפַחֵד
ז..ן עָלָיו יִתְיַחֵד
ח.. ...

... נָשָׂא פָּנָיו
יָהִיר בְּשָׁומְעוֹ הֵן לְפָנָיו
... לָךְ לְהַכְרִיעוֹ מִלְּפָנָיו
... שְׁלוּחִים לְפָנָיו

ככתוב וישלח יעקב מלאכים לפניו אל עשיו אחיו ארצה שעיר שדה אדום

ונאמר מעינה [רך ישיב חמה ודבר עצב יעלה אף]

ונאמר משא דומה אלי קרא משעיר שמר מה מלילה שמר מה מליל

ונאמר ...
ונאמר ... ..
ונאמר אשרי אדם מפקד תמיד ומקשה לבו יפול ברעה

ונאמר תחנונים ידבר רש ועשיר יענה עזות

ונאמר יי ...

חַרְבְּךָ אֱדוֹם
תְּרַוֶּוה מֵאֱדוֹם
וּתְמַגְּנֵינוּ אָדוֹן
...

5 For the imagery, see Isa 34:5 ("For My sword has drunk its fill in the heavens; behold, it shall come down upon Edom, and upon the people of my curse, to judgment") and its interpretation in *GenR* 75:1, quoted in the commentary below (**R**). The rhyme for this stanza consists of *adom-edom-adon*—an imperfect but effective rhyme. In particular, the divine epithet "Ruddy One" (as **B1** notes, from Song 5:10, "My beloved is radiant and ruddy" is juxtaposed effectively with "red one," or Edom, a name of Esau as well as the name of the nations descended from him, including Rome. See also *GenR* 75:4 (**B1**).

(2) An answer mild turns anger aside
So with "please" the smooth one answered the hairy[6]
Lest stormy wrath should be his reply,
lest the harsh one answer him harshly
The murmurs of the mild mouth
soft spoken, bowing low to the ground
Hearing his words, the harsh one wept
"Great was our suffering!" He said, holding on to his hope in You[7]
He perceived that this world is his brother's world
so with begging and bribes he advanced
Wise emissaries that he sent forward
his woes he commanded they recount

As it is written: "Then he commanded them, saying: `Thus you shall say to my lord Esau'" (Gen 32:5)

And it is said: "What will you say when he shall punish you, for you have taught them to be your captains, your chiefs over you; shall not pangs seize you like a woman in labor?" (Jer 13:21)[8]

And it is said: "Though the misfortunes of the righteous are many, the Lord will save him from them all" (Ps 34:20)[9]

And it is said: "If you faint on the day of adversity, your strength is small" (Prov 24:10)[10]

And it is said: "Since my youth so often they afflicted me!—let Israel now declare—since my youth so often they afflicted me, but they have never overcome me" (Ps 129:1–2)

And it is said, "No more shall a villain be called `prince' nor shall `nobleman' be said of a knave" (Isa 32:5)

O Noble One, You delighted in us[11]
Let no evil befall us
and with the dew of life redeem us
Blessed are you… Who resurrects…

---

6 Gen 33:14 (**R**).

7 The subject of this line is Jacob. See below, where the idea that this world belongs to Rome/Esau but the World-to-Come belongs to Israel.

8 This verse is a *petiḥta* verse in *GenR* 75:3 (**R**).

9 This verse is cited in *GenR* 79:2 (**R**).

(ב) **מִ**ילּוּל מַדְּ אַף מֵישִׁיב
נָא חֲלָק לְשָׂעִיר הֵישִׁיב
סַעַר עָלָיו פֶּן יָשִׁיב
עָז עֲזוּת לְבַל יַקְשִׁיב
פֶּיצַח לָשׁוֹן רַכָּה
צִיפְצֵף וְשָׁפַל עַד דַּכָּה
קָושְׁבוֹ דְבָרָיו בִּיכָּה
רַבַּת צְרָרוּנִי פָּץ וְלָךְ חִיכָּה
שָׂר וְזֶה עוֹלָם שֶׁלּוֹ
שֶׁיוַע וְשׁוֹחַד לִימֵּד לוֹ
תַּחְכְּמוֹנִים אֲשֶׁר שִׁילַּח לוֹ
תְּלָאוֹתָיו צִיוָּה לְתַנּוֹת לוֹ

ככתוב ויצו אתם לאמר כה תאמרון לאדני לעשו

ונאמר מה תאמרי כי יפקוד עליך ואת לימדת אותם עליך אלפים לראש הלוא חבלים יאחזוך כמו אשת לידה

ונאמר רבות רעות צדיק ומכלם יצילנו יי

ונאמר התרפיתה ביום צרה צר כחכה

ונאמר רבת צררוני מנעורי יאמר נא ישראל רבות צררוני מנעורי גם לא יכלו לי

ונאמר לא יקרא עוד לנבל נדיב ולכילי לא יאמר שוע

שׁוֹעַ תְּשַׁעַשְׁעֵינוּ
וְאַל תַּרְשִׁיעֵינוּ
וּכְטַל לְתֶחִי הוֹשִׁיעֵינוּ
ברוך... מחיה...

10 This verse is cited in *TanḥB Vayishlaḥ* 6 (**R**).

11 Language from Isa 66:12 (**R**), where it has connotations of "dandling a baby on the knee," "cuddling," "doting on playfully"—a range of intimate, warm, protective, endearing associations. The poet here evokes a complex association of puns between the roots שעע ("to delight"), שוע ("to cry out" but also "noble"), and ישע ("to save, redeem").

(3)[12] Oh Yah, do not be silent—even if our mouths are struck dumb—
let us be freed from Edom and Edom a possession become[13]
His endless enmity and his insolent impudence
You will cause to pass away, O Lord; You will contend and judge
Let them descend to hell and let them know the Judge;
Stretch forth your spear against Tyre and Sidon[14]
Famine shall be their fate and fire fills their future
but You will hear our outcry as You showed Obadiah the seer

As it is written: "The vision of Obadiah: Thus says the Lord to Edom…" (Obad 1:1)
And it says: "And saviors shall ascend Mount Zion to judge the Mount of Esau; and the kingdom shall be the Lord's" (Obad 1:21)[15]
And You are Holy… Please, God…

(4) Twin multitudes of heavenly hosts
You deployed when the pure man went forth[16]
His paths to keep straight, his ways to make smooth
his presence to proclaim in the face of "doom"[17]
Lest a host encamp against him
and then he see and feel afraid of "he who feels no fear"[18]
These same angels were with him
when he went forth from his parents' house
They were there upon the ladder in his dream
they supported him in his in-law's house[19]
They were with him when he went forth

---

12 Wout J. van Bekkum discusses this unit in his article, "Anti-Christian Polemics in Hebrew Liturgical Poetry (*Piyyut*) of the Sixth and Seventh Centuries," *Early Christian Poetry* (Leiden: Brill, 1993), 297–308.

13 See Num 24:18, "Edom shall become a possession, and Seir a possession of its enemies; but Israel shall be triumphant" (**R**).

14 "Tyre" is an attested epithet for Rome, and Sidon is the greatest city in Tyre. **B1** cites *GenR* 61:7, which states: "Rabbi Eleazar said: Whenever *Ẓur* [Tyre] is written full in Scripture, it means the province of Tyre; where it is defective [thus spelling, "he who afflicts; an enemy"], Scripture alludes to Rome."

15 The entire text of Obadiah, a single, extended prophecy against Edom, is the haftarah for this *sidra*, as indicated by the quotation here of the first and last lines of the book. (See Mann, *The Synagogue as Read and Preached in the Old Synagogue*, 260).

16 The idea of two camps of angels comes from the name of the place where Jacob encamped, *Maḥanayim*, which means "two camps." See *GenR* 75:10 (**R**).

(ג) יָהּ לֹא תִדּוֹם אִם פִּינוּ יִדּוֹם
לְהִיפָּרַע מֵאֱדוֹם וִירֵשָׁה תִהְיֶה אֱדוֹם
נֶצַח מָדוֹן וּמֵצַח זָדוֹן
תַּעֲבִיר אָדוֹן וְתָרִיב וְתָדוֹן
יֵרְדוּ לָאֲבַדּוֹן וְיֵדְעוּ שַׁדּוּן
וְתִנְטֶה כִידוֹן עַל צוֹר וְצִידוֹן
יְשׁוּלַּח בָּם רָזוֹן וְיִהְיוּ לְאֵשׁ מָזוֹן
וְצַעֲקָתֵינוּ תֶאֱזוֹן כְּהוֹדַעְתָּה לְעוֹבַדְיָה חָזוֹן

ככתוב חזון עובדיה כה אמר יי לאדום

ונאמר ועלו מושיעים בהר ציון לשפט את הר עשו והיתה ליי המלוכה

ואתה קדוש אל נא

(ד) רִיבּוֹתַיִים מַלְאֲכֵי צְבָאוֹת
צִיוִּיתָה לְאִישׁ תָּם בְּתוֹצָאוֹת
דְּרָכָיו לְלַוּוֹת אָורְחוֹתָיו לְנַוּוֹת
וְאוֹתוֹ לְחַוּוֹת אֶת פֶּה הַוּוֹת
פֶּן תַּחֲנֶה עָלָיו מַחֲנֶה
וְיִרָא וְיִיתְיָרֵא מִלֹּא יָרֵא
הֵם הַמַּלְאָכִים אֲשֶׁר הָיוּ עִימּוֹ
בְּצֵאתוֹ מִבֵּית אָבִיו וְאִמּוֹ
וְהֵם רָאָה בְּסֻולָּם בַּחֲלוֹמוֹ
וְהֵם סִיעֲדוּהוּ בְּבֵית חוֹתְנוֹ
וְהֵם הָיוּ בְּצֵאתוֹ

---

17 That is, Esau and his host; see *ExodR* 27:1, where it describes how Esau came out to kill Jacob when he heard that Jacob had left Aram. The heavenly hosts accompany Jacob as he approaches this confrontation and announce Jacob's powerful presence to the oncoming enemy.

18 "He who feels no fear" refers to Esau, an idea occurring in the *qedushta* for Gen 25:19 (Poem 7[2], line 6). See, also, *ExodR* 27:1, where Deut 25:18 ("he did not fear God," speaking of Amalek) is applied to Esau.

19 According to rabbinic tradition, angels guarded Jacob at every step of his journey; his vision at Bethel (Gen 28) was merely one of the changing of the guard; see the piyyut on that *sidra.* The angels who escorted him to Aram now protect him on his return trip. **B1** cites ExodR 32:9, "And what did Jacob say to his children? `The angel who redeemed me from all evil…" (Gen 48:16). He redeemed me from the hand of Esau and from Laban, and he it was who fed and sustained me during the years of famine.'" This same angel will guard all of Jacob's children.

and they were with him as he returned
they are the ones who wrestled him[20]
and they went forth to do his bidding To a brother
and upon them stumbled the brother—the camp of Your angels,
the assembly of Your kingdom,[21] O Holy One![22]

(5) The man who resembled a flickering flame
He understood: it was time to make sport of the one likened to stubble[23]
His household he divided lest the spoils be divided[24]
the smooth-skinned man: his estate he parceled out[25]
The one[26] was on his own path, to meet the other he was not intending
but with propriety the pure one performed
    and on the honor of his Maker he did not impose[27]
Words of conquest, the softest of speech
he sent to him, in the region of evil
You made him rich, You made him strong,
but words of weakness he sent to him
He[28] heard him, but remembered the day of his birthright's sale;
he came to greet him with his weapon drawn[29]
"This One," the Lord of the worlds, said to him, "Your Lord am I!"[30]
but his faith faltered and he ordered, "Thus shall you say to my lord"[31]
Thus exchanged, other lords will rule his sons

---

20 Although the verb here is plural, to maintain parallelism, the stich alludes to the wound Jacob received as he wrestled the angel in Gen 32. **B1** cites *Tanḥ Vayishlaḥ* 3.

21 Zech 7:2.

22 The image here is of an "accidental" encounter between Jacob's angelic emissaries and Esau's retinue, a theme developed in the next poem.

23 The comparisons here—Jacob/Israel to a flame, Esau/Edom to stubble—come from Obad 18, in the haftarah.

24 **B1** connects with Zech 14:1, "Behold, the day of the Lord comes, and the plunder taken from you shall be divided in your midst."

25 Referring to the procedure described in Gen 32:17, in which Jacob parcels out his vast estate in advance of meeting Esau, *GenR* 76:8 (**B1**) notes: "Why did he not bring them [all his flocks] to him all mixed together? In order to dazzle him by his gift. And why did he not bring them to him all at once? In order to satiate the eyes of that wicked man." This strategy is wise, but as we will see, Jacob's craftiness goes too far and results in generations of slavery for his children.

26 Here, Esau. "The other" is Jacob.

27 The language of this line strongly recalls a teaching in *GenR* 75:1, which states: "Rabbi Joshua of Siknin interpreted in Rabbi Levi's name: [Jacob said, paraphrasing Ps.17:13:] Deliver my soul from that wicked one who will fall one day by Your sword, as it says, `For My

וְהֵם הָיוּ בְּבוֹאוֹ
וְהֵם פָּגְעוּ בוֹ
וְהֵם שֻׁולְּחוּ בִשְׁלִיחוּתוֹ אֶל אָח
וּבָם פָּגַשׁ אָח מַחַן מַלְאֲכוֹתֶיךָ
וְרֶגֶם מַלְכוּתָךְ. קָדוֹשׁ

(ה) **א**ִישׁ אֲשֶׁר נִימְשַׁל בְּאֵשׁ מַשָּׂקֶת
בָּן וְהִנֵּה הָעֵת לִמְשׁוֹל קַשׁ שׁוֹחָקֶת
בָּתָיו חִילָּק פֶּן שָׁלָל יְחוּלָּק
אִישׁ הֶחָלָק כָּבוֹד לוֹ נֶחֱלַק
גַּם לְדַרְכּוֹ הָיָה וְלִקְרָאתוֹ לֹה הָיָה
וְדֶרֶךְ אֶרֶץ תָּם עָשׂ
וְעַל כְּבוֹד קוֹנוֹ חָס
דִּבְרֵי כִיבּוּשִׁים וְרִיכּוּכֵי שִׁיעָה
שִׁילַּח אֵלָיו לִגְבוּל רִישְׁעָה
הֶעֱשַׁרְתּוֹ וְהֶחֱזַקְתּוֹ וְדִבְרֵי עֲנִיּוּת שִׁילַּח אֵלָיו
וּבְדִבְרֵי רַכּוּת שִׁילַּח אֵלָיו
וְשָׁמַע וְנִזְכַּר יוֹם מְכִירָתוֹ
וּבָא לִקְרָאתוֹ אֲחוּז מְכֵרָתוֹ
זֶה אֲדוֹן עוֹלָמִים נָם לוֹ אֲדוֹנָךְ אֲנִי
וְלֹא הֶאֱמִין וְנָם כֹּה תֹאמְרוּן לַאֲדֹנִי
חֵלֶף כֵּן לְבָנָיו בְּעָלוּם אֲדוֹנִים

sword has drunk its fill in heaven; behold, it shall come down upon Edom' (Isa 34:5). Said the Holy One, blessed be He, to him [Jacob]: 'He [Esau] was going his own way, but you send to him, saying, 'Thus says your servant, Jacob…'!" The implication is that Esau was not hunting Jacob down; rather, he was going on his own way and Jacob actively brought about the confrontation by sending messengers to intercept his brother. In contrast to the teaching of *GenR* 75:1, however, Jacob does not impose on God, demanding that God intervene on his behalf to save him (**B2** offers *b. Taʿan.* 24a as an example of "imposing on God"). Instead, Jacob defeats his brother on his own, by exploiting his egotism—a method that our poet, in keeping with other traditions of interpretation, does not find free of flaws. See also *TanḥB Vayishlaḥ* 2.

28 Esau.

29 As noted, Esau was also "going on his own way," not seeking out Jacob in order to exact his revenge; however, upon hearing of Jacob's approach, his first emotion was anger and the danger to Jacob the same as if his twin had been planning revenge all along. Jacob's "soft words" did not, at first, achieve their intended effect.

30 A quotation of Isa 41:10 (**R**) and Isa 44:21 (**B2**).

31 Gen 32:5; Yannai's interpretation accords with that of *GenR* 75:11 (**R**), in which Israel is condemned to serve eight different kingdoms because Jacob doubted God and called Esau "my lord" eight times in this *sidra*. See also *TanḥB Vayishlaḥ* 5 (**R**).

other than You, the Lord of the lord of lords[31]
The Good One said to him,[32] "I created you to be My servant;
"My servant are you," but he said (to Esau), "Thus said *your* servant"[33]
For this, then, slaves have enslaved us;
upon You [hang] our eyes like those of slaves[34]
Forever …

(6) Mighty ones, strong ones, ones who have dominion …[35]
…
Despising … those who heed
for flattery finds favor with the wicked

…
In their hands, a gift of honor[36]
Words of peace to those who have no honor
but it is not seemly to honor the fool[37]

… in his hand, to the Edomite
What profit can be won from my blood?"[38]
He sheltered him at once
… the Aramean…

They trembled when…he advised
the tyrant became weak with terror[39]
[The pious one prepared] a prayer at a fateful time

---

31 See Isa 26:13 ("O Lord our God, other masters beside you have had dominion over us") and Deut 10:17 ("For the Lord your God is God of gods, and Lord of lords") (**B1**).

32 That is, God said to Jacob.

33 In these lines, Isa 41:8–11 (**R**), in which God describes Israel as His servant, is juxtaposed with Gen 33:5, in which Jacob refers to himself as Esau's servant.

34 Lacuna filled as in **B1** (תלויות).

35 The opening of this poem is damaged; this first line may quote Jacob's flattery of Esau and his host; or, it may describe the angels who accompanied Jacob on his journeys and whom he sent forth on a mission to Esau. See line 13.

36 The word "gift" (תשורה) appears only in 1 Sam 9:7 in the biblical text.

37 Prov 26:1.

38 The question quotes from Ps 30:10. In the *qedushta* for Gen 38 (Poem Five) it is associated with the sale of Joseph by his brothers. Although the line is fragmentary, it seems that Esau has come at Jacob aggressively; Jacob deflects his brother's aggression by appealing to

זוּלַת אֲדוֹן אֲדוֹנֵי הָאֲדֹנִים
טוֹב סָח לוֹ יְצַרְתִּיךָ לְעֶבֶד לִי
עַבְדִּי אַתָּה וְסָח כֹּה אָמַר עַבְדְּךָ
יַעַן כִּי עֲבָדִים בָּנוּ מַעֲבִידִים
אֵילֶיךָ ... עֵינֵינוּ כַּעֲבָדִים
לעולם

(ו) **א**ֱיָילִים חַיָּילִים וּמוֹשִׁיעִים
... ..שעים
בָּזוּי לכ.. ..מַשְׁעִים
כִּי מַחֲנִיפִים לִרְשָׁעִים

...
בְּיָדָם תְּשׁוּרַת כָּבוֹד
דִּבְרֵי שָׁלוֹם לְאֵין בָּם כָּבוֹד
וְלֹא נָאֶה כְּסִיל כָּבוֹד

... בְּיָדוֹ לֶאֱדוֹמִי
... ..מַה בֶּצַע בְּדָמִי
וְהִיצִּילוּ מִיַּד ...
... ..אֲרַמִּי

זְרִיזִים באמ.. יוֹעֲצוֹ
לֶעָרִיץ לְהַרְפּוֹתוֹ מֵעָורְצוֹ
... תְּפִילָּה לְעֵת מְצוֹא

---

his greed—hence the comparison with Laban, "the Aramean," best known for his avarice.

39 By sending angels as his messengers, Jacob underscores his possession of divine favor. **B1** cites *GenR* 75:10, "Four thousand ministering angels disguised themselves for Jacob's sake, and they all looked like king's troops; some were clad in armor, others were horsemen, others again were charioteers. When [Esau] met those clad in armor, he asked them, `To whom do you belong?' and they answered, `To Jacob.' Then he met the cavalry and asked them, `To whom do you belong?' and they answered, `To Jacob.' Then he met the charioteers and asked them, 'To whom do you belong?' and they too answered, `To Jacob'...This conduct of Jacob is similar to that of the man who invited his neighbor to dine with him, and, perceiving that he desired to murder him, remarked, `This dish tastes like that which I ate in the royal palace.' `The king then is acquainted with him!' the other exclaimed, and he was filled with fear and did not kill him. Similarly, when Jacob said to Esau, `Seeing your face is like seeing the face of God' (Gen 33:10), Esau exclaimed, `Seeing that the Holy One, blessed be He, has promoted him to such honor, I can no longer prevail against him.'"

when, perhaps, favor can be found[40]

Gentle were the claims he made upon the one compared to straw;
he (spoke of) peace and they of war
He undertook to undo his brother's fear
for a soft reply turns back anger[41]

He[42] (recounted) all the woes his eye had seen
in his in-law's house, his evil eye upon him
Lest he come into his camp and smite him to smithereens
for (Esau's) eye would have no pity upon him

Heavenly hosts He showed to him,[43]
God Himself revealed them to him
He had grown wiser than he who felt no fear
for fear is the beginning of wisdom[44]

Speaking entreatingly to a man hard to appease
lest his spring be muddied by his own hand[45]
The strong one who tramples on all
tramples himself for the sake of a silvery bribe

Having persuaded him who pities neither fathers nor sons
lest a mother be dashed to death with her babes[46]
He cried out to You, who feel a father's compassion for his sons
lest his nest be raided of both mothers and babes[47]

---

40 **B1** connects this to Ps 32:6 (which he uses to fill the lacuna earlier this stanza), "Therefore shall every one who is pious pray to You in a fateful time (lit: `a time of finding'); then surely the floods of great waters shall not come near him." According to *GenR* 92:2, "a fateful time (`*et matzo*')" is a time of danger. For Jacob, likewise, this is a time when God's favor—or lack thereof—will be revealed, through the results of his encounter with Esau.

41 A paraphrase of Prov 15:1 (**R**), altered to suit the form of this line; the biblical verse is quoted after the *magen.*

42 Jacob

43 That is, God showed Esau the divine nature of Jacob's escort—so **R** understands it. Alternatively, this could refer to Jacob revealing his divine escort to Esau and describing God's previous revelations in the course of telling his brother his story. The Hebrew is ambiguous in a way that English (because of the convention of capitalizing the divine pronoun) cannot be.

44 As **R** and **B1** both note, the second stich paraphrases Ps 111:10, "Fear of the Lord is the beginning of wisdom." Esau lacks this fear of God, as noted above.

חֵן בְּעֵינָיו אוּלַי לִמְצוֹא

טַעֲנוֹת רַכּוֹת לְקַשׁ בִּמְדוּמֶּה
הוּא שָׁלוֹם וְהֵם לַמִּלְחָמָה
יָזַם לְהַכְחִישׁ בּוֹ אֵימָה
כִּי מַעֲנֶה רַךְ יָשִׁיב חֵימָה

כָּל צָרוֹת אֲשֶׁר רָאֲתָה עֵינוֹ
בְּבֵית חוֹתְנוֹ אֲשֶׁר בּוֹ צָרָה עֵינוֹ
לָבַל יָבוֹא בְמַחֲנוֹ וְיַךְ וְאֵינוֹ
לֹא עָלָיו תָּחוּס עֵינוֹ

מַלְאָכִים מִמַּחֲנוֹת אֲשֶׁר לוֹ הֶרְאָה
אֶל אֲשֶׁר אֵלָיו נִירְאָה
נִיתְחַכַּם עַל אִישׁ אֵין בּוֹ יִרְאָה
וְרֵאשִׁית חָוכְמָה הִיא יִרְאָה

סִיחַ רָצוֹן לְאִישׁ קָשֶׁה לְרַפֵּס
מְקוֹרוֹ בְּיָדוֹ פֶּן יֵרָפֵס
עָז אֲשֶׁר הוּא הַכֹּל מְרַפֵּס
וּבְרַצֵּי כֶסֶף הוּא מִתְרַפֵּס

פִּיתּוּיִים לְאֵין לוֹ חִיסָה עַל אָבוֹת וּבָנִים
פֶּן יְרֻוטָּשׁ אֵם עַל בָּנִים
צָעַק לָךְ מְרַחֵם כְּאָב עַל בָּנִים
פֶּן תִּילָּקַח קִינּוֹ אֵם וּבָנִים

---

45 See *GenR* 75:2, cited by **R**: "Rabbi Judah b. Rabbi Simon opened his discourse: `Just as a troubled fountain, and a corrupted spring, so is a righteous man who gives way before the wicked' (Prov 25:26). As a fountain cannot be [permanently] troubled [i.e., muddied] nor a spring [permanently] corrupted, so is it impossible for the righteous to sink [permanently] before the wicked; and just as a troubled fountain and a corrupted spring, so is a righteous man who abases himself before the wicked. Said the Holy One, blessed be He, to him [Jacob]: `He [Esau] was going his own way, nevertheless you sent [messengers] to him, saying, `Thus says your servant Jacob'!" Jacob is in no lasting danger from Esau, but he brought this danger on his own head nonetheless.

46 For all of Jacob's culpability in generating the encounter, Esau's character is not redeemed; Jacob's fears, expressed in a prayer in Gen 32:12, are reinforced here: "Save me, I beseech you, from the hand of my brother, from the hand of Esau; for I fear him, lest he will come and strike me, and the mother with the children."

47 In *GenR* 76:6, Esau is accused of violating the commandments against killing both mothers and children (**R**); see Lev 22:8 and Deut 22:6.

Advancing a gift and all their goods[48]
towards the wicked man who calls what is wicked "good"
He hastened to separate himself from "how good and pleasant it is"[49]
and from "he who is wise about a matter will find good"[50]

Messengers sent to set straight the crooked
to catch the crooked with crafty words[51]
So he said: "Thus says your servant Jacob"
though it was said to him: "Do not fear, My servant Jacob"[52]

And thus, "Towards the land of Seir..."[53]
(7^1) The ruddy one, the man of Edom
despised his birthright for the red food of Edom
The land of his possession, the realm of red Edom
his allies were reddened with bloodiness of Edom
He loved red blood so his name was Edom[54]
He is Esau and he is ruddy Edom
Remember, O Lord, the sons of Edom
the destruction wrought by the daughters of Edom
A great slaughter in the land of Edom
A burning fire in the fields of Edom
We yearn for You, O Beloved, radiant and red (*adom*)[55]
To appear in garments red with the blood of Edom[56]
From the Heavens will be cast down the Prince of Edom[57]
Your sandal You will cast against Edom[58]
Set Your vengeance against Edom
You will yet wipe out wisdom from Edom[59]
Spread Your net upon the land of Edom

---

48 A pun on "goods" in the sense of "wares" (i.e., Jacob's material wealth) and also "goodness" (i.e., all the intangible goodness that traveled with Jacob, the good people, good beliefs), and even the "Good God." Perhaps read מחנה ("camps") in place of מנחה ("gift").

49 The poet ironically quotes Ps 133:1 ("How good and pleasant it is when brothers dwell together"—**R** indicates the quotation) to describe the haste with which Jacob and Esau parted company.

50 Quotation of Prov 16:20.

51 This line is difficult, and my interpretation follows **B1**'s reading. The overall sense of the passage is that Jacob got himself into a dangerous situation by seeking out Esau; in order to get himself and his family out of danger, he will have to cater to Esau's ego. However, through this indulgent course of action, Jacob will accrue a punishment for later generations.

52 This final line of the unit returns to the theme of Poem Five, Jacob's culpability for

קִידּוּם מִנְחָה וְכָל טוּב
לְאִישׁ רָע הָאוֹמֵר לָרָע טוּב
רָץ לְהַפְרִידוֹ מֵהִנֵּה מַה טּוֹב
וּמַשְׂכִּיל עַל דָּבָר יִמְצָא טוֹב

שְׁלוּחִים לְיַשֵּׁר אֶת עָקוֹב
פְּנֵי עָקוֹב עֲקוּבוֹת לִנְקוֹב
תִּינָּה כֹּה אָמַר עַבְדְּךָ יַעֲקֹב
וְנֶאֱמַר לוֹ אַל תִּירָא עַבְדִּי יַעֲקֹב

ובכן ארצה שעיר

(ז[1]) **אַ**דְמוֹנִי אִישׁ   הָאָדוֹם
בָּז בְּכוֹרָה בְּמַאֲכָל   אָדוֹם
גֵּיא יְרֵושָּׁתוֹ גְּבוּל   אֱדוֹם
דְּבוּקָיו מְאֻודָּמִים כְּדָם   אָדוֹם
הוּא אָהַב דָּם לָכֵן שְׁמוֹ   אֱדוֹם
וְהוּא עֵשָׂו וְהוּא   אֱדוֹם
זְכוֹר יי לִבְנֵי   אֱדוֹם
חֻורְבַּן אֲשֶׁר עָשְׂתָה בַּת   אֱדוֹם
טֶבַח גָּדוֹל בְּאֶרֶץ   אֱדוֹם
יְקֵידַת אֵשׁ בִּשְׂדֵה   אֱדוֹם
כְּמַהְנוּ לָךְ דּוֹד צַח   וְאָדוֹם
לְהֵירָאוֹת בִּלְבוּשׁ   אָדוֹם
מִמָּרוֹם תַּפִּיל שַׂר   אֱדוֹם
נַעֲלָךְ תַּשְׁלִיךְ עַל   אֱדוֹם
שִׂימָה נִקְמָתָךְ   בֶּאֱדוֹם
עוֹד תְּאַבֵּד חֲכָמִים   מֵאֱדוֹם
פְּרוֹס מְצוּדָה בִּבְאֶרֶץ   אֱדוֹם

---

debasing himself before Esau. The first stich quotes Jacob's instructions to his messengers in Gen 32:5; the second stich quotes God's assurances to Israel in Isa 44:2 and Jer 30:10 (**R**).

53 This *rahit* depends on various connotations of the root א-ד-ם, as in "Edom" and "red" (*adom*). The translation attempts to preserve this feature by ending almost every stich with "Edom."

54 Blood (*dam*), anticipating the name Edom in both sound and implied coloration.

55 Song 5:10 (**R**).

56 Isa 63:2 (**R**), which describes God as coming from Bozrah—a major Edomite city—in bloody garments.

57 That is, Edom's guardian angel.

58 Ps 60:10 (**R**).

59 Obad 1:8 (**R**).

You will hunt down the hunter, the father of Edom[60]
Cut off the ten horns from Edom!
Upturn and overthrow the throne and footstool (of Edom)[61]
Set it upside down like Sodom
Draw Your sword and sate it from Edom
You will shine, and we will say: "Who is this who comes from Edom?"[62]
Kingship will restored to You from Edom

And thus...[63]

(7^2) Edom who...fearsome
a beast unknown by any name[64]
Its body like that of a mighty boar
of all its cohort, it gave the most frightening sight
Did it not roar like the river Euphrates?
And did it not dwarf the others by right of its might?
It is the smallest but the arrogant fear it;[65]
It is the Fourth Beast and great is its power
Its bronze claw slashed

---

60 "Hunter" is an epithet for Esau (based on Gen 25:27, cited by **R**), the progenitor of the Edomites/Romans. The language of the first stich is based on two verses from Ezekiel, however (**B1**): Ezek 17:20 ("And I will spread my net upon him, and he shall be taken in my snare...") and 32:3 ("Thus says the Lord God: I will therefore spread out my net over you with a company of many people; and they shall bring you up in my net"). Both these verses depict the use of the hunting net.

61 This is based on Dan 7 (**R**), detailed below. Here it is translated into a prayer for the dissolution of the Byzantine Roman Empire. For the specific language, **B1** adduces Hag 2:22, "And I will overthrow the throne of kingdoms, and I will destroy the strength of the kingdoms of the nations; and I will overthrow the chariots, and those who ride in them; and the horses and their riders shall come down, everyone by the sword of his brother." "The sword of his brother" may have been understood as "the sword of Jacob." The imagery of "the throne and footstool of Edom" recalls the language applied to God's relation to the heavens and earth in Isa 66:1 (**R**), indicating perhaps the grandiosity and hubris of Rome.

62 Quotation of Isa 63:1 (**R**).

63 A highly patterned acrostic poem, this *rahit* is built upon the eschatological imagery of Daniel 7, which also forms the basis for the aggadic tradition of Esau's downfall recorded in *GenR* 76:6. The key verses of Daniel state: "After this [the visions of the first three beasts], I saw in the night visions, and behold a fourth beast, dreadful and terrible, and exceedingly strong; and it had great iron teeth; it devoured and broke in pieces, and stamped the residue with its feet; and it was different from all the beasts that were before it; and it had ten horns. I considered the horns, and, behold, there came up among them another little horn, before which three of the first horns were plucked up by the roots; and, behold, in this horn were

צוֹד תָּצוּד לְאִישׁ צַיִּיד אֱבִי אֱדוֹם
קְרָנוֹת עֶשֶׂר גַּדֵּע מֵאֱדוֹם
רָם הֲפוֹךְ עָלֶיהָ כֵּס וַהֲדוֹם
שִׁיתָהּ מַהְפֵּכָה כִּסְדוֹם
שְׁלִיפַת חַרְבָּךְ תְּרַוֶּה מֵאֱדוֹם
תּוֹפִיעַ וְנֹאמַר מִי זֶה בָּא מֵאֱדוֹם
תִּיסוֹב לָךְ מְלוּכָה מֵאֱדוֹם

ובכן

(ז[2]) אֱדוֹם אֲשֶׁר ... אֵימְתָּנִי
בְּחֵיוָתָא לָא הִתְפַּרְשַׁת בְּשֵׁם
גּוּשְׁמָה מְתִיל בַּחֲזִיר גִּיבַּר
דְּחִילָה בְּחֶבְרָתָהּ חָזוּת דִּמְיוֹנָהּ
הֲלֹא כִנְהַר פְּרָת הָמְיָיה
וּמְהַשַּׁנְיָיא מִן כָּולְהֵין וְתַקִּיפָא
זְעֵרָא הִיא וְרַבְרְבָן הֵם זְוָעֲתָהּ
חֵיוָה רְבִיעָאָה וְיַתִּירָה חַיִּיל
טִיפְרָה דִי נְחַשׁ טִיבָה

eyes like the eyes of man, and a mouth speaking great things" (Dan 7:7–8). As M. Sokoloff and J. Yahalom note, the use of Aramaic in Yannai's piyyutim (separate from the influence of Aramaic on his Hebrew) is unusual; Yannai's Aramaic typically derives from Daniel, as is the case here. See M. Sokoloff and J. Yahalom, "Aramaic Piyyutim from the Byzantine Period," *Jewish Quarterly Review* 75 (1985): 310.

64 Dan 7 describes four fearsome beasts (a lion, a bear, a leopard, and a fourth beast, which is unnamed—all of which have eagles' wings). Each animal represents a kingdom that will gain and then lose dominion over Israel. The fourth, most terrible beast, is associated with Edom/Esau/Rome, as the association with the boar in the following line underscores (**R** cites *LevR* 13:5 and others). See also J. Yahalom, *Poetry and Society*, 81–84.

65 While the motif of the "small horn" appears in the Daniel verses, the poet has not yet reached his description of the horns. Therefore, this stich most probably alludes to Obad 2 (**B1**), from the haftarah: "Behold, I will make you small among the nations…" (the same phrase occurs in Jer 49:15, in the context of Jeremiah's prophecy against Edom). See the interpretation of this verse in *GenR* 65:11, offered by **B1**: "Rabbi Leazar b. Rabbi Simon said: `This ([Isaac] called Esau his great/elder son' in Gen 27:1) may be compared to a country that was levying a bodyguard for the king. Now a certain woman there had a son, a dwarf, whom she used to call `Tallswift.' Said she: `My son is tall and swift; why then do you not appoint him?' `If in your eyes he is tall and swift,' they retorted, `in ours he is but a dwarf.' In like manner, his [Esau's] father called him great, that is, `He called Esau his great son'; his mother too called him great: `And Rebecca took the choicest garments of Esau her great son (Gen 27:15). Said the Holy One, blessed be He, to them: `Though in your eyes he is great, in Mine he is small,' as it says, `Behold, I make you small among the nations' (Obad 2)."

its iron teeth finished off
Thus all the land is devoured
it was given to it in a vision in the night
It stomped and devoured what remained
goring, it was crowned with ten horns
Then appeared the form of one small horn sprouting
with eyes like human eyes upon it
Its mouth, uttering insolence, is open
its royal crown is Bozrah besieged[66]
It waged war against the holy ones[67]
Its authority over the ten kings is written[68]
The name of the last king is "he changes"[69]
He suspends matters out of mighty scorn

(7^3)[70] Mighty One and Ancient of Days
days close in and a day approaches
Approaches the end, the killing of the beast
the beast: abolished is its body
Its body consigned to flames of fire
fire consuming fire

(8) And from the house of Jacob there will be fire, a Man will sprout[71]
and among the clouds of heaven he will fly
and up to the Ancient One of Days he will ascend
and dominion over the world will be given unto him
and glory and kingship he will possess
and his dominion will not pass away
and His glory will not cease

---

66 The end of this line is unclear and the reading a conjecture. Bozrah was an important city in Edom, a "crown jewel" of the territory. The Fourth Beast (Edom), in its arrogance, seeks to assail the very heavens but here, as in Daniel 7, God nullifies its ambitions.

67 This may refer to Israel or the angels, or both.

68 See Dan 7:23, "And the ten horns are ten kings that shall arise out of this kingdom, and another shall rise after them; and he shall be different from the former ones, and he shall subdue three kings." This passage was understood by Yannai and the Rabbis as a prophecy foretelling Rome's long imperial history—and ultimate doom.

69 The name "he changes (*shanei*)" comes from Dan 7:24–25, in that this beast differs from his predecessors and he will think to change the law. In its original context, this verse describes Antiochus IV, the Seleucid ruler whose politically-rooted antagonism towards

יע.. זְשִׁינַהּ דִי פַרְזֶל יָכִיל
כָּל אַרְעָה אָכְלָה כִּדְנָה
לַהּ הִתְיְהֵב חֶזְוֵי לֵילְיָא
מַדְּקָה וְאָכְלָה שְׁאָר מֵאכָלַהּ
נִיגּוּחַ עֲשַׂר קַרְנִין נִיכְתְּרָה
סוּם קֶרֶן זְעֵירָה סִילְקָת
עֵינִין כְּעַיְנֵי אֶנָשָׁה עֲלוֹהִי
פּוּמָהּ מְמַלֵּל רַבְרְבָן פְּתִיחַ
צְנִיף מַלְכוּתָהּ בצירה צירה
קְרָב עָבְדָא עִם קַדִּישִׁין
רִישְׁיוֹנָהּ עַשְׂרָה מַלְכִין רְשִׁים
שֵׁם מֶלֶךְ אָחֳרָן שָׁנֵי
תָּלֵי מִלִּין לְצַד תַּקִּיפָה

(ז[3])
תַּקִּיפָה וְעַתִּק יוֹמַיָּה
יוֹמַיָּה יִקְרְבוּן וְיוֹם יֶאֱתֶה
יֶאֱתֶה קֵץ קְטִילַת חֵיוָותָה
חֵיוָותָה וְהוּבַד גּוּשְׁמָהּ
גּוּשְׁמָהּ לִיקֵידַת אֶשָּׁא
אֶשָּׁא אָכְלָה אֶשָּׁא

(ח)
וּמִן בֵּית יַעֲקֹב אִשׁ יִצְמַח אֱנָשׁ
וְעִם עֲנָנֵי שְׁמַיָּה יְטוּס
וְעַד עַתִּיק יוֹמַיָּיה יִמְטֵי
וְיִתְיְהֵב לֵיהּ שָׁולְטָן עָלַם
וִיקָר וּמַלְכוּ יִתְאַחֲסַן
שָׁולְטָנֵהּ דִי לָא יֶעְדֵּי
וִיקָרֵהּ דִי לָא יִפְסֵק

Judaism instigated the Hasmonean revolt. In this poem, however, it may refer to Jesus ("king of the Jews") and the antinomian stance of Christianity (according to which the laws "are changed") and Christianity's fracturing (or "doubling," שנה) of God's being. **B1** cites *GenR* 76:6, where this beast is termed "*ben natsar*, "the son of Natsar." While the Soncino translation of *Midrash Rabbah*, following Graetz, identifies "*Natsar*" as "a robber chief who became the founder of a dynasty, *viz.* Odenathus of Palmyra," the likelihood of this referring to, or punning on like, "*ben Notsri*," the Nazarene—i.e., Jesus—seems hard to ignore.

70 This poem, an unusual third *rahit* (employing anadiplosis), is based on Dan 7:9–11.

71 The imagery here is messianic; the messiah is often depicted as "sprouting" or as a "shoot" of the house of David. **B1** cites Jer 23:5, Zech 6:12, as well as *SongR* 3:5. For the image of the messianic figure rising up to the Ancient One of Days (God), see Dan 7:13–14.

and His kingdom will not be destroyed
and the peoples Will submit to Him
and the nations will serve Him
and their tongues will worship Him
And the kingdom and dominion and grandeur will be given
to the nation of the holy ones[72]
the ones who hallow the Name of the Holy One
As it is written, "And the one called out..."

(9) Your counsel cannot be known
Your power cannot be diminished
Your name cannot be changed[73]
They respond, saying:
Holy, holy, holy is the Lord of Hosts! The whole earth is filled with His glory!
"Holy"—from the masters of counsel
"Holy"—from the masters of power
"Holy"—from the masters of name and deed
"Holy"— He will confirm the counsel of Jacob
  and overturn the counsel of Esau[74]
"Holy"— He will strengthen the weak power of Jacob
  and uproot the power of Esau[75]
"Holy"— He will favor the name of Jacob
  over the deeds of Esau[76]
Each calls out towards the other...

"From His place"—He said to the pure one:
  "When you see your brother, do not fear"[77]
"From His place"—He said to him:
  "When you pass through water, you will not be overwhelmed"[78]
"From His place"—He said to him:
  "When you walk in fire, you will not be consumed"[79]
Etc... Twice...

---

72 "The nation of the holy ones" (*ʿam qaddishin*) occurs in Dan 7:21, where it refers to the angels. Here, however, it seems to refer to Israel. Blurring of the identity of Israel and the heavenly hosts is particularly likely in such proximity to the Qedushah.

73 See Ps 71:19, Isa 49:4. This links back to the "false messiah" figure, "He changes," above.

74 This line juxtaposes Isa 44:26 with Ps 33:10 (**B1**). "Holy" here refers to "the Holy One."

75 **B1** connects with Job 36:5, "Behold, God is mighty, and does not despise any; he is mighty in strength of wisdom."

76 The "deeds of Esau" refers to irony of Esau's name, which predicted righteous deeds

וּמַלְכוּתֵיהּ דִי לָא תִתְחַבַּל
וְעַמְמַיָּה לֵיהּ יַשְׁלְמוּן
וְאוּמַיָּה לֵיהּ יִשְׁתַּעְבְּדוּן
וְלִישָׁנַיָּה לֵיהּ יִפְלְחוּן
וּמַלְכוּתָה וְשָׁולְטָנָה וּרְבוּתָה תִּתְיְהֵב
לְעַם קַדִּישִׁין
הַמַּקְדִישִׁים שֵׁם הַקּוֹדֶשׁ
ככתוב וקרא

(ט) עֲצָתְךָ אֵין לֵידַע
כּוֹחֲךָ אֵין לְבַלּוֹת
שְׁמָךְ אֵין לְהַחֲלִיף
יַעֲנוּ וְיֹאמְרוּ
קדוש קדוש קדוש יי צבאות מלא כל הארץ כבודו
קָדוֹשׁ מִבַּעֲלֵי עֵיצָה
קָדוֹשׁ מִבַּעֲלֵי כוֹחַ
קָדוֹשׁ מִבַּעֲלֵי שֵׁם וּמַעֲשֶׂה
קָדוֹשׁ הִשְׁלִים אֶת עֲצַת יַעֲקֹב
וְהֵפֵר אֶת עֲצַת עֵשָׂו
קָדוֹשׁ הִכְבִּיד תַּשׁוּת כּוֹחַ יַעֲקֹב
וְהִתִּישׁ כּוֹחַ עֵשָׂו
קָדוֹשׁ הֵיטִיב שֵׁם יַעֲקֹב
מִמַּעֲשֵׂה עֵשָׂו
לעומתם כל

מִמְּקוֹמוֹ נָם לְתָם
אִם תִּרְאֶה לְאָח לֹא תִיתְיָרֵא
מִמְּקוֹמוֹ נָם לוֹ
אִם תַּעֲבוֹר בַּמַּיִם לֹא תִשָּׁטֵף
מִמְּקוֹמוֹ נָם לוֹ
אִם תֵּלֵךְ בְּמוֹ אֵשׁ לֹא תִיכָּוֶה
וגו'. פעמים

but resulted in violence; the association of "name" with Jacob may refer to the importance of the name "Israel," which is given in this *sidra*.

77 Quotation from Isa 43:1 (**R**), possibly a secondary haftarah for this *sidra* (suggested by the inclusion of Isa 43:2 in the next line).

78 From Isa 43:2 (**R**).

79 From Isa 43:2, also; this verse ties in nicely with Obad 18, in which "the house of Jacob" is compared to a fire—imagery that has occurred repeatedly in this poem. Israel, like the burning bush, will burn but not be consumed.

Commentary

In *GenR* 75:1, we find several interpretations of Ps 17:13, a verse that states: "Arise, O Lord, confront him, cast him down; save my soul from the wicked, by your sword." The rather lengthy *petiḥta* concludes:

> Deliver my soul from that wicked one [Esau-Edom] who advances [against me] by virtue of that sword about which (Scripture) says, "By your sword you shall live" (Gen 27:40, Jacob blessing Esau).
>
> Another interpretation of "Your sword": He [Esau] is Your sword, for with him do You chastise the world.
>
> [Another interpretation:] Deliver my soul from that wicked one who will fall one day by Your sword, as it says, "For My sword has drunk its fill in heaven; behold, it shall come down upon Edom" (Isa 44:5).
>
> Said the Holy One, blessed be He, to him [Jacob]: `He [Esau] was going his own way, but you sent to him, saying, `Thus says your servant Jacob' (Gen 32:4)!

This compact series of interpretations shares a variety of motifs and scriptural allusions with this piyyut. Most obviously (and commonly) both texts understand Esau as referring to Rome, a violent empire that dominates the world in fulfillment of divine command but which is ultimately destined for destruction. Esau, however, is not the only figure criticized in both midrash and poem. If Esau inflicts suffering in this world, he is merely an instrument of God; and if Israel suffers, it is—at least in part—because he calls Esau's attention to himself. Esau may be violent, but—according to the interpretations of this *sidra*'s opening words—Jacob provokes. By extension, the Jews are not wholly innocent victims, even if they will ultimately be redeemed.

Tensions between redemption and reprimand permeate this piyyut. As fragmentary as the opening poem is, we nonetheless find in it a tone of rebuke ("Yet of him you are afraid?" line 4) and reassurance (God's sword "will become drunk from the red one's blood…" line 22, the transition to the benediction). Isa 44:5, quoted in the midrash above, is the text to which the final line of the *magen* alludes. These paired tones color the rest of the piyyut even more strongly. The second poem focuses on Jacob's clever manipulation of Esau, describing how Jacob humbled himself in order to achieve the upper hand, and used bribes to stave off potential robbery.

Cleverness is one of Jacob's dominant personality traits, but here (as in the biblical stories), an excess of cleverness can lead to trouble. Poems Three and Four are largely positive, emphasizing the ultimate redemption of Israel, with Poem Four acting as a prologue to the encounter between the estranged twins. But in Poems Five and Six, the element of rebuke returns. Poem Five opens with Jacob's decision to make sport of Esau but ends with a note of tragedy: "Therefore slaves have enslaved us" (line 19). Both Poems Five and Six conclude with a rebuke of Jacob for flattering Esau by calling him "lord" and deprecating himself as his brother's "servant"—relationships and loyalties owed not to any human power but to God alone. Jacob's flattery of his estranged brother, while effective, comes at the expense of his special relationship with the deity. According to the midrash above, as well as Yannai, Jacob cannot serve two masters, not even as a pretence or out of expediency.[80] By extension, Rome does not bear singular responsibility for the current situation; Israel's servitude to Rome is fulfillment of Jacob's own foolish words.

Yannai is not content merely to alternate between rebuke and consolation, however. The final units strike notes of increasing apocalypticism. The message gains momentum, exploiting the overwhelmingly "chronological" structure of the *qedushta* as a whole. The doom of Edom dominates the unusual triple *rahit*. The first *rahit* cleverly puns on connotations of the root א-ד-ם, hammering out the fate of Edom like a drum-beat; the second links Esau's fate to the mystical visions of the terrible and strange beasts of Daniel 7; the third, for all its brevity, continues the Daniel apocalypse, graphically depicting the death of "the beast" at the hands of the Ancient One of Days. The *silluq* (Poem Eight), which follows Daniel's vision to its conclusion, describes the arrival of the Messiah and the establishment of God's eternal dominion over all false gods and usurper kings, including Rome and its Church. The final poem, the *qedushah*, focuses on the redemption of Jacob, who will be made strong, wise, and safe, while Esau will be weakened, mocked, and vanquished. This future is assured;

80 This is in contrast to the lesson derived by the same scenario in *PRE* 37, which states: "'Thus says your servant Jacob' (Gen 32:4). The Holy Blessed One said to him: Jacob! That which was holy [i.e., our relationship] you have made profane [by transferring terms to Esau]! He replied to Him: Lord of the world! I flatter the wicked so that he will not slay me. Hence the Sages say we may flatter the wicked in this world for the sake of peace." Eventually, however, Jacob's flattery of Esau goes too far; God tells him, "By your life! It shall be according to your own words. He shall rule over you in this world and you shall rule over him in the world to come." Yannai keeps his focus on *this* world.

Esau will be weakened, mocked, and vanquished. This future is assured; Jacob's transgression only served to delay the inevitable. In both poem and midrash, one can sense divine exasperation at moments in the poem, but God's love for Israel will triumph—not only over Esau's wickedness but over Israel's failings.

The general themes of this poem—the certainty of Israel's redemption and Edom's downfall, the mild rebuke of Jacob and the villainization of Edom—are common and well-attested both in rabbinic writings and within Yannai's own corpus. Collectively, they may suggest immanent messianic expectations within Yannai's community.[81] Nonetheless, Yannai uses the extended piyyut format to develop his characters in detail and with nuance, while also constructing a clear theology. The poet's vehemence in the concluding poems, particularly the unusual triple *rahit*, is tangible. Edom is a bloody, monstrous foe, and his end will, in return, be bloody. Edom is arrogant but gullible, and his thoughtless hubris will be his downfall. He is mighty, but not as mighty as the enemy he acquired by challenging God Himself. The ecstatic messianism of the *silluq* giddily anticipates a day when a true king will reign with real dominion, guided by the deity. All this enthusiasm does not temper the poet's critique of Jacob—and, by extension, Yannai's Jewish contemporaries. Jacob is arrogant as well, trusting in his own cleverness; as in the biblical text, he is duplicitous, seeking to trick his brother into kindness not yet earned. While Yannai hints that Jacob sought out his brother with reconciliation in mind ("He undertook to undo his brother's fear // for a soft reply turns back anger"; Poem Six, line 10), there are also hints that he enjoyed the sport of tricking his twin. While Jacob's course of action should have avoided requiring divine intervention ("on the honor of his Maker he did not impose;" Poem Five, line 3), in the end Jacob made much more work for God, when he took his trick too far and flattered Esau by calling him "lord." The tone of rebuke is unmistakable, as are the consequences of Jacob's choice. "Thus exchanged, other lords will rule his [Jacob's] sons," Yannai writes in Poem Five (line 8). This is not a theology of blame, but of responsibility.

Esau-Edom-Rome is a dangerous master for Jacob to serve; Yannai does not downplay the bloodthirstiness of Esau's realization that Jacob is nearby ("he came to greet him / with his weapon drawn;" Poem Five, line 6). Furthermore, Esau remains thoughtless and gullible. He is taken in by Jacob's

81 See the discussion of Jewish messianism in the 6th century in Chapter Four.

crafty scheme and permits himself to be manipulated, revealing a true weakness at the sight of his brother's feigned defenselessness. But for all of Esau's wickedness and possible vulnerability (a combination that echoes the biblical character's complexity), the poet's message is ultimately one of passivity: do not follow in the ancestor's footsteps. Jacob sought out Esau, with mixed if generally good intentions; his behavior, however, was reckless. Jacob aggressively brought himself into danger by seeking out his enemy. It would have been better had each brother gone his separate way rather than Jacob willingly expose himself and his family to such peril. Jacob's decision to confront his brother resulted in excessive, inappropriate self-humiliation. The oppression of Yannai's audience, real or existential, under the yoke of Esau still, is presented as a direct result of Jacob's action. Perhaps Yannai dwells on Jacob's decision to seek out Esau in order to condemn those who sought out imperial favor or cooperated beyond bare necessity with the Byzantine authorities. Seeking confrontation with Esau could, however, also be understood as condemning attempts to force the coming of the Messiah. To paraphrase the phrase in Song of Songs, Jacob tried to rouse love either in the wrong party or at the wrong time. Yannai advises separation and diffidence: do not antagonize Esau, nor fawn over him. Just wait, for his time will come. Yannai here, as elsewhere, attempts to turn his community inward, to disengage from Esau entirely, both in terms of positive contact and confrontation.

The lesson of this poem? Jacob sinned against God's will and his descendants by calling Esau's attention to himself. The apocalypse will come, but on God's schedule, not Israel's. Esau will be the cause of his own downfall; he does not need Jacob's help. The Jews, according to the interpretation embedded in this week's poem, should not encourage attention from Rome: they should avoid conflict (perhaps an allusion to social unrest in the mid-6th century in the Land of Israel) but also flattery, and they must resist the impulse to play the humble servant when Rome is not their true master.[82] The Jews have their own Lord, and it will be on His timetable, at His initiative, that the prophecies of Obadiah and Daniel will come to fruition. The Jews should not trust in their own cleverness, or even their guardian angels, but in God. Scheming, no matter how clever, can only prolong the sentence. Our poet turns his community away from the temptation to force God's hand. He turns their eyes upwards, instead, to God.

82 On both the militaristic and accomodationist impulses among the Jews in Yannai's period, see my article, "You have skirted this hill long enough" *HUCA* 79, forthcoming.

Qedushta for Genesis 33:18 בראשית לג:יח

"Then Jacob came to Shalem" ויבא יעקב שלם

In this *sidra*, Jacob returns from his exile in Aram to the land of Canaan, to the town of Shalem, a city of Shechem, destined to be the burial place of Joseph and the future site of Jerusalem. There Jacob purchases property upon which to build an altar and thus he acquires a toe-hold in the Promised Land much as his grandfather Abraham did with his purchase of the cave of Makhpelah. In this piyyut, Yannai explores the many valences of the word "*shalem*": peace, wholeness, health, restoration, retribution, perfection, fulfillment, and others. The use of this word in Gen 33:18 offers Yannai the opportunity to construct a nuanced, complex interpretation of the history of Jacob and his heirs—poetry exploiting lexical ambiguity rather than resolving it. Seen through this lens of multiple possibilities, the place Shalem becomes a frame of mind, a site of hope, and a state of grace.

(1) The paths of the pure one You made straight
his coming and his going You protected
His splendid strength You made strong[1]
the banner-bearers of his camp You enobled[2]

He who sowed in tears of shame[3]
thus reaped in joy the fruits of his loyalty
A stronghold of salvation was set aside for him
much desired blessings he has in his store

A Prince (of heaven) pursued him but he prevailed[4]
he was afflicted with a limp, by the sinew now forbidden[5]
He was healed because he did not reject discipline[6]
thus to Shalem he came home whole and undiminished.

As it is written: "Then Jacob came to Shalem, a city of Shechem, which was in the land of Canaan, when he came from Padan-Aram, and he camped facing towards the city" (Gen 33:18)[7]
And it is said: "You will know that there is peace in your tent; when you visit your dwelling, you shall not fail" (Job 5:24)
And it is said: "The Lord will guard your going forth and your coming in, from now and forever" (Ps 121:8)[8]
And it is said: "Those who sow in tears shall reap in joy" (Ps 126:5)[9]
And it is said: "Though he walks and weeps while carrying a sack of seed, he shall surely come back in joy, bearing his sheaves" (Ps 126:6)
And it is said: "Great shall be the peace of those who love Your Torah; they shall encounter no stumbling block" (Ps 119:165)

There shall be no stumbling block before us
when we go forth and when we come in;
in Your shadow, O our Shield, let us take shelter
Blessed are You... Shield...

---

1 For the language of this stich, see Ezek 24:21 (**B1**); as **B1** notes, "splendid strength" there refers to the Temple, but here it alludes to Torah, for which "strength" (*ʿoz*) is a common epithet.

2 "Banner-bearers," or simply "banners," here refer to Jacob's twelve sons, the tribes of Israel.

3 The translation of חסד here as "shame" follows its use in Lev 20:17 and Prov 25:10, as discussed by **B1**. See *GenR* 65:15, which describes how Jacob wept while he deceived his father at his mother's command—an act constituting both "shame" and "loyalty." As the next stich makes clear, however, all worked out for the best. See also *GenR* 74:4.

4 That is, the guardian angel of Esau, with whom Jacob wrestled at the river crossing in

(א) **אָ**ורְחוֹת תָּם יִישַּׁרְתָּה
בּוֹאוֹ וְצֵאתוֹ שִׁימַּרְתָּה
גְּאוֹן עֻזּוֹ אִישַּׁרְתָּה
דִּיגְלֵי מַחֲנוֹתָיו הִיכְשַׁרְתָּה

הוּא זָרַע בְּדִמְעַת חֶסֶד
וּבְרִינָּה קָצַר לְפִי חֶסֶד
זֻוּמְּנוּ לוֹ יְשׁוּעוֹת חוֹסֶן
חֶמְדַת בִּרְכוֹת אוֹסֶם

טָס עָלָיו שָׂר וַיָּשַׂר
יֻוּסַּר בְּהַצְלָעַת גִּיד אֲשֶׁר יוּסָּר
כָּעֵת נִרְפָּא וְלֹא קָץ בְּמוּסָּר
לְשָׁלֵם בָּא שָׁלֵם וְלֹא מְחֻוסָּר

ככתוב ויבא יעקב שלם עיר שכם בארץ כנען מפדן ארם ויחן את פני העיר

ונאמר וידעת כי שלום אהלך ופקדת נוך ולא תחטא

ונאמר יי ישמר צאתך ובואך מעתה ועד עולם

ונאמר הזורעים בדמעה ברנה יקצרו
ונאמר הלוך ילך ובכה נשא משך הזרע בא יבא ברנה נשא אלמתיו

ונאמר שלום רב לאהבי תורתך ואין למו מכשול

מִכְשׁוֹל לֹא יָבוֹא לָנוּ
בְּצֵאתֵינוּ וּבוֹאֵינוּ
בְּצֵל מָגִינָּךְ הַחְבִּאֵינוּ
ברוך... מגן...

Gen 32 (**R**).

5 See Gen 32:33.

6 Prov 3:11

7 Note that, in addition to the midrashic sources cited by **R**, **B1**, and **B2** (and throughout this essay), *TargPsJ* translates the opening of this verse as: "Jacob arrived *safely with all that he had* in the city of Shechem…" *TargN* renders it: "And Jacob came, *perfect in good work*, to the fortress of Shechem…" The italics highlight interpretations that resonate with this piyyut's interpretation.

8 Cited in *GenR* 74:2, *TanḥB Vayishlaḥ* 10 (**R**).

9 The *petiḥta* verse in *GenR* 74:4 (**R**, although R does not indicated *petiḥta* verses).

(2) The place of the portion to be possessed
Truly, the smooth one possessed it
Forever he would bequeath it to his descendents
the city of [Shechem had by him][10] been acquired
He surveyed and settled, for there he came to see
that `Tsafnat' would find final rest there[11]
A hundred *kesitahs* [he gave to get it][12]
(the place) where, like a field, his fame wafts throughout[13]
Peace presided in his citadel
calm serenity among his mighty host
[The boundary of Shechem was][14] his estate
he settled in and pitched his tent firmly.

As it is written: "Then he purchased the parcel of land where he had pitched his tent from the hand of the children of Hamor, the father of Shechem, for a hundred *kesitahs*" (Gen 33:19)

And as it is said: "God said, by His holiness, that I would rejoice and divide up Shechem, and the valley of Sukkot I would measure" (Ps 60:8)

And as it is said:....

And as it is said: "I will give possessions to those who love me, and their storehouses will I fill" (Prov 8:21)

And as it is said: "He chose for us our portion, the pride of Jacob whom he loved forever" (Ps 47:5)

Forever[15] is the blessing of Your name
...
through the dew of life may Your name be blessed
Blessed are You... who resurrects...

(3) Yah, from Shalem[16] pay back Your foes completely[17]

---

10 Lacuna filled according to **B2**.

11 "Tsafnat" was the name/title given to Joseph in Egypt in Gen 41:45; its root, according to the Hebrew folk etymology, is related to צפה, "to see, to be a seer." In Josh 24:33, cited by **B1**, we find an allusion to this *sidra* as well as a description of the burial of Joseph's bones: "And the bones of Joseph, which the people of Israel brought out of Egypt, buried them in Shechem, in a parcel of ground that Jacob bought from the sons of Hamor the father of Shechem for a hundred pieces of silver; and it became the inheritance of the sons of Joseph." According to Yannai, Jacob's purchase of the burial plot indicates that he was also a seer.

12 Lacuna filled as by **B1**.

13 The letter *resh* is apparently absent from the acrostic. The translation takes liberties in order to convey both the sense of the line and its allusiveness. It alludes to the good repu-

(ב) **מְ**קוֹם נַחֲלַת מִקְנָה
נָא חָלָק בָּהּ קָנָה
סֶלָה לְנִינָיו הִיקְנָה
עִיר ... נִיתְקַנָּה
פָּנָה וְנָח בָּהּ כִּי בָן בָּהּ
צָפְנַת כִּי יָנוּחַ בָּהּ
קְסִיטוֹת מֵאָה ...
אֲשֶׁר כְּשָׂדֶה הֵיפִיחַ בָּהּ
שָׁלוֹם שָׂר בְּחֵילוֹ
שָׁלָו וְשָׁקַט בַּחָיָילוֹ
... ... בְּנָוחֲלוֹ
תִּיכֵּן וְנָטָה שָׁם אָהֳלוֹ

ככתוב ויקן את חלקת השדה אשר נטה שם אהלו
מיד בני חמור אבי שכם במאה קשיטה

ונאמר אלהים דבר בקדשו אעלזה אחלקה שכם ועמק סכות אמדד

ונאמר ...
ונאמר להנחיל אוהבי יש ואצרתיהם אמלא

ונאמר יבחר לנו את נחלתינו את גאון יעקב אשר אהב סלה

סֶלָה בִּבְכַּת שְׁמָךְ
...
בְּטַל תְּחִי יְבוֹרָךְ שְׁמָךְ
ברוך... מחיה...

(ג) יָהּ מְשַׁלֵּם גְּמוּלוֹת מְשַׁלֵּם

tation of Joseph (a "branch" of Jacob's tree) who is compared to a "fruitful bough" (hence fragrant) in Gen 49:22; also drawn upon is Gen 27:27 (**B1**), "The scent of my son [Jacob] is like the scent of the field;" this imagery is combined with Eccl 7:1, "A good name (reputation) is better than fragrant oil" (**B1**) and Song 4:16, "Blow upon my garden that its scent may spread" (**R**). The implication is that Jacob's good reputation spread throughout the land.

14 **B2**'s restoration of the text.

15 The Hebrew rendered as "forever" here and in line 2 of this poem is the liturgical lexeme, "*selah*."

16 "Shalem" is here understood as short for "Jerusalem." See Gen 14:18 and Gen 33:18. See the Commentary for more on this key word.

17 The language here alludes to Isa 66:6 (**B1**).

burst forth [wholly] against those who razed it wholly[18]
Let us behold your Tabernacle in Shalem a building once again whole
and just as the pure one came back whole
[to You] we give [thanks] wholeheartedly[19]
May they receive complete repayment
for an evil people, payment-in-full!
and let this be called a "year of payment fulfilled"
They worship You with whole-offerings a people wholly devoted to You
and they shall be restored in whole numerous again and whole

As it is written: "Thus says the Lord: Even as they are whole and many, they will be cut off and pass away; as surely as I afflicted you, I will afflict you no more" (Nah 1:12)
And as it is said: "Lord, may You appoint peace for us, for indeed, all that we have done, You have done for us" (Isa 26:12)
And You are Holy… Please, God…

(4) O Guardian of Israel [his stronghold, his rock][20]
Indeed from all evil protecting him
"God of Israel" is His name[21]
He affirmed for him[22] His promise
and He confirmed for [him His favor][23]
He brought the blameless one to a blameless end[24]
and dealt blamelessly with him
for he walked in purity
When he went forth and when he entered and when he was brought back
His guardian and his protection [at his right hand][25]
Bring him back whole and let him dwell in peace
restore him to tranquility and let him draw forth blessings
…

18 That is, the Edomites/Rome. Edom participated in the destruction of the First Temple while Rome destroyed the Second.

19 The language here puns on the conceptual response of `fullness of gratitude', which those returning from exile would feel, and the concrete act of sacrificing the whole-offering, which those who are restored from exile (Jacob and those in the present) would make as thanksgiving. The restoration draws on Ps 56:13, adduced by **B1**.

20 The restoration, suggested by **B1**, draws on Ps 31:3.

21 In *GenR* 82:3, God notes that Jacob is the last of the patriarchs, the last with whom He will "unite" His name (as in "God of Abraham, of Isaac, and of Jacob" in Exod 3:16) (**R**).

פְּרַע ... לְמַחֲרִיבֵי שָׁלֵם
נַחַז סֻוכָּךְ בְּשָׁלֵם בְּבִינְיָן שָׁלֵם
וּכְתָם הַבָּא שָׁלֵם
... נְשַׁלֵּם
יְשׁוּלָּמוּ תַּשְׁלוּמִים
לְגוֹי רָע מְשַׁלְּמִים
וְתִיקָּרֵא שְׁנַת שִׁילּוּמִים
יַחְלוּף בִּשְׁלָמִים עִם לָךְ מוּשְׁלָמִים
וְיִהְיוּ מְשׁוּלָּמִים רַבִּים וְכֵן שְׁלֵמִים

ככתוב כה אמר יי אם שלימים וכן רבים וכן נגוזו
ועבר וענתיך לא אענך עוד

ונאמר יה תשפות שלום לנו כי גם כל מעשינו פעלת לנו

ואתה קדוש אל נא

(ד) שׁוֹמֵר יִשְׂרָאֵל ...
כִּי מִכָּל רָע שְׁמָרוֹ
אֱלֹהֵי יִשְׂרָאֵל שְׁמוֹ
הֵיקִים לָנוּ נוּאֲמוֹ
וְכוֹנֵן עָלָיו ...
תֹּם הֲתִימוֹ
הִתְמִימוֹ
כִּי הֵילֵךְ בְּתֻומּוֹ
בְּצֵאתוֹ וּבוֹאוֹ וּמוּבָאוֹ
שׁוֹמְרוֹ וְצִילּוֹ ...
שָׁלֵם הֱשִׁיבוֹ וְשָׁלוֹם הוֹשִׁיבוֹ
שָׁלֵיו יֵישְׁבוּ וּבְרָכוֹת הִשְׁאִיבוֹ
... ...

Abraham and Jacob, in particular, have elements of divine names incorporated into new names given to them by God (the "h" from Yah in Abraham; the element "El" in Israel).

22 **R** reads the word "for us" (לנו) here.

23 Lacuna filled by **B1**, based on Ps 90:17. This refers to God's promises to bring Jacob back healthily, wealthily, and peacefully in Gen 28:15, "And, behold, I am with you, and will keep you in all places where you go, and will bring you back to this land; for I will not leave you, until I have done that about which I have spoken to you" (**R**).

24 See 2 Sam 20:18.

25 The language **B1** uses to restore this line draws upon Ps 121:4–7.

Give him wide land and luxury, let him not know thirst
like a well-watered garden let him flourish
and in all things let him prosper
O Holy One!

(5)[26] The man, pure upon his return, was whole and in peace
in the company of angels of peace, he reached a resting place of peace
Before the day of rest was made known to the meek[27]
the one who sat in his tent[28] taught it to his sons[29]
As the sun set, he set the boundary for the Sabbath
and those who went forth from his loins, he commanded concerning going forth on the Sabbath[30]
The confines of his camp he squared, two thousand cubits in each direction
he resided and rested there, in ease of spirit[31]
Appeasement he made for the important people of his town;
gifts he gave to the sons of his neighbors[32]
He fixed the pillars of his dwelling facing the town of Shechem;[33]
to worship, he pitched tent in Shechem
and God caused His presence to dwell there[34]
The pure one dressed in his best[35] within the tent he had pitched;
God inclined His ear towards the Name which he would utter[36]

---

26 This unit works through the themes of the first three verses of the *sidra*, cited at the beginning of the Commentary.

27 That is, before the Sabbath was revealed to Moses. Moses is called "meek" (or "humble") in Exod 12:3 (**B2**).

28 That is, Jacob; see Gen 25:27 (**R**).

29 This appears to reflect a tradition in which Jacob did not merely observe the Sabbath himself but taught the command to his children and required its observance by them. For the idea that Jacob kept the Sabbath (and not Abraham) and therefore received a greater reward than his grandfather, see *GenR* 11:7 (cited by **B2**).

30 That is, he taught them the acceptable limits within one can travel on the Sabbath without violating the Sabbath (two thousand cubits in any direction). See *GenR* 11:7 (**B2**), and also Yannai's *qedushta* for Exod 16:28 (**R**).

31 The words rendered "direction" and "spirit" here both reflect the same underlying Hebrew word, "*ruaḥ*." The meaning here is that he delineated the boundaries of Sabbath travel, two thousand cubits in each direction from the center of the settlement, creating a "square" if that distance is traveled in each of the cardinal directions from a center point (**R** cites *m. Erub.* 4:8). These boundaries determined, Jacob is able to rest and enjoy his Sabbath.

הִרְחִיבוֹ וְלֹא הִצְמִיאוֹ
כְּגַן רָוֶה הִצְמִיחוֹ
וּבַכֹּל הִצְלִיחוֹ
קדוש

(ה) **א**ִישׁ תָּם בְּחָוזְרוֹ שָׁלֵם וְשָׁלוֹם
בְּלִיוּוּי מַלְאֲכֵי שָׁלוֹם הִישִּׂיג מְנוּחַת שָׁלוֹם
בְּטֶרֶם יוֹם מְנוּחָה נוֹדַע לֶעָנָיו
יוֹשֵׁב אוֹהָלִים יִידְעוּ לְבָנָיו
גִּשְׁתּוֹ בְדִמְדּוּם חַמָּה קָבַע גְּבוּל שַׁבָּת
וּלְיוֹצְאֵי חֲלָצָיו צִיוָּה יְצִיאוֹת שַׁבָּת

דֶּיגֶל מַחֲנוֹ רִיבֵּעַ אַלְפַּיִם לְכָל רוּחַ

וַיִּיחַן וַיָּנַח שָׁם בְּנָחַת רוּחַ
הֲנָחָה עָשָׂה פְּנֵי מִשְׁכְּנוֹתָיו
וּמַשְּׂאֹת נָתַן לִבְנֵי שְׁכִינוֹתָיו
וְקָבַע יְתֵידוֹת שָׁכֵן פְּנֵי הָעִיר שְׁכֶם
וְלַעֲבוֹדָה הִיטָּה שֶׁכֶם
וְאֵל כְּבוֹדוֹ שִׁיכֵּן
זָךְ חֲמוּדוֹת עָטָה בְּאוֹהֶל אֲשֶׁר נָטָה
וְאֵל אוֹזֶן הִיטָּה לַשֵּׁם אֲשֶׁר בִּיטָּה

---

32 **R** cites *GenR* 74:6, "He showed his regard (*ḥanan*) for the important men (*panim*) of the city by sending them gifts."

33 Picking up on the interpretation of the previous line, the imagery here may be metaphorical: just as in English, the term "pillar of the community" can refer to an important person (see *GenR* 43:8, where the three patriarchs are called "pillars"), so, too, here, Jacob may be "grounding" and supporting his family within the community. And as in the midrash cited above, *panim* (here rendered as "facing") can mean "important people." Thus Jacob set himself up on par with the local inhabitants, not as a subservient sojourner. Building an altar, as he does in the next stich, is a further sign of his independence and self-possession as well as piety.

34 With Jacob's return from exile, God returns to the Land as well.

35 **R** adduces *GenR* 79:3 (among other texts), in which Job 8:6, "If you are pure and upright," is applied to Jacob at the time of his return. "Dressed in his best" translates a phrase literally, "he wrapped [in] choice garments," using the same term that was used for Esau's best clothes in Gen 27, about which there were, in turn, many aggadic traditions (see also the previous *qedushta*). The image here, however, is of priestly vestments, not "secular" garb.

36 That is, Jacob in the act of prayer.

Mighty is the name he called it[37] and by the same he was also called;[38]
by it was the source sustained, kingship and priesthood[39]
He assembled his altar and gave his offering
and he offered unto the lawful Lord[40] thanksgiving for his portion
"Israel" and "his God" He called his name[41]
In time His name would be proclaimed upon those who proclaim
His name...
Forever...

"Then Jacob came..."
(6) When he went out, the sun went down[42]
for God's lovers are like the sun rising[43]
Upon his return, the sun shone upon him
for God is a sun a shield to those who seek His shelter
Whole in goodness and fulfilled[44]
(He is) over all, honored by all
The Presence of his Escort at all times he sought[45]
as he walked upright, he was uplifted

---

37 That is, the altar.

38 In Gen 33:20, it is written: "And he erected there an altar, and called it `*El-Elohe-Israel* [El, the God of Israel]'" (**B1**). In *GenR* 79:8 (**R**), this verse is interpreted: "He [Jacob] declared to Him: `You are God in the celestial spheres and I am God in the terrestrial sphere.'" According to Ibn Ezra's interpretation of the verse, "El" means "mighty;" in any case, it is a powerful name for the altar. The second stich recalls the interpretation of the verse in *b.* Meg. 18a (**R**), "Rabbi Aḥa also said in the name of Rabbi Eleazar: How do we know that the Holy One, blessed be He, called Jacob El [God]? Because it says, `And the God of Israel called him [Jacob] El.' For should you suppose that [what the text means is that] Jacob called the altar El, then it should be written, `And Jacob called it.' But [as it is not written so], we must translate, `He called Jacob El.' And who called him so? The God of Israel." See also *GenR* 98:3, in which Gen 49:2 is rendered as "Your father Israel is as a god: as God creates worlds, so does your father create worlds; as God distributes worlds, so does your father distribute worlds." **R** also suggests that this plays on the epithet "mighty" (*gevurah*, transformed here to *ḥayil* to suit the acrostic) as a divine name.

39 See Ps 80:16. Jacob, as the father of all Israel (a nation called by his name), is the father of both Levi (the priests) and Judah (the monarchy), the two institutions that signify the core of Israelite society. **B1** connects this with Exod 19:6, "And you shall be to me a kingdom of priests, and a holy nation." Finally, unlike Abraham (father of Ishmael) and Isaac (father of Esau), Jacob fathered no wicked children.

40 That is, the God who is faithful to his promises, who keeps His covenants and grants laws by which Israel can display fidelity. **B1** cites Ps 105:10, "He confirmed the same [covenant] to Jacob for a law, and to Israel for an everlasting covenant."

41 Yannai again adduces the epithet "God of Israel" as a name for Jacob; see note above.

חֵיל שֵׁם אֲשֶׁר כִּינָּה בּוֹ נִתְכַּנָּה
וּבוֹ נִתְכּוֹנְנָה כַּנָּה מַלְכוּת וּכְהֻונָּה
טִיכֵּס מִזְבְּחוֹ וְנָתַן זִיבְחוֹ
וְשָׁם לְבַעַל חֵוּקוֹ הוֹדָיָה עַל חֶלְקוֹ
יִשְׂרָאֵל וֵאלֹהָיו קָרָא אֶת שְׁמוֹ
עֵת יִיקָּרֵא שְׁמוֹ עַל קוֹרְאֵי שְׁמוֹ

לעולם

ויבא יעקב

(ו) אָז בְּצֵאתוֹ בָּא לוֹ שֶׁמֶשׁ
כִּי אוֹהֲבֵי אֵל כְּצֵאת הַשֶּׁמֶשׁ
בְּבוֹאוֹ זָרַח לוֹ הַשֶּׁמֶשׁ
כִּי אֵל לְחוֹסָיו מָגֵן וְשֶׁמֶשׁ
גָּמֵור בַּטּוֹב וּמְמֻולָּא
וְעַל הַכֹּל בַּכּוֹל מְעֻולָּא
דְּמוּת מְלַוּוֹ בְּכָל עֵת מְחַלֶּה
בְּהֵילָךְ קוֹמְמִיּוּת מְתֻולֶּא

42 The phrase translated here as "the sun went down (*ba ha-shemesh*)," could be interpreted several ways, and *GenR* 68:10 (cited by **R**) offers several clues: "The Rabbis said: This teaches that the Holy One, blessed be He, caused the sun to set prematurely, in order to speak in privacy with our father Jacob…Rabbi Phinehas said in the name of Rabbi Ḥanin: He [Jacob] heard the voices of the angels saying, 'The sun comes (*ba ha-shemesh*)! The sun comes!'…When did the Holy One, blessed be He, restore to him those two hours by which He had caused [the sun prematurely] to set on his account on his departure from his father's house? When he was returning to his father's house…" The first interpretation understands the sun's departure as creating a moment of intimacy between God and Jacob; the second teaches that "sun" was an epithet for Jacob; the final interpretation associates sunset with exile, sunrise with restoration. In the piyyut, Jacob—"the sun"—went "down" into exile in Laban's house, but this departure set the stage for divine intimacy.

43 From Judg 5:31, which opens: "So may all Your enemies perish, O Lord! But may His friends be as the sun rising in might!..." (**R**). Jacob's departure has the effect of a sunset—he leaves and takes light with him, and those who remain are left in darkness.

44 The word translated as "goodness" for reasons of alliteration is actually *tov* (good), and is probably an epithet for Torah; see *GenR* 98:12 (**B1**). The language of the verse depends upon Prov 28:10, "Whoever causes the righteous to go astray in an evil way, he shall fall himself into his own pit; but the pure shall inherit goodness" (**B1**) The word rendered as "fulfilled" (*memulla'*) recalls *GenR* 79:5, cited by **B1**, which describes how Jacob returned to his ancestral home with all his wealth intact.

45 Ps 45:13 and 105:4, cited by **B1**, provide some of the imagery of this stich. The image here is not one of constant prayer but rather a more general seeking of divine favor and presence.

The ones to come were rooted in him,
they who were worthy of his mother[46]
He merited that they should be from him
for the portion of the Lord is his people
Sown like light, shining like a luminary
his splendor and radiance go forth and shine
Cleared of every ugly accusation[47]
in peace he crossed the river Jabbok
His tender babes with him followed close
the path he chose for them was both gentle and straight
Children pure and proper
like the apple of his eye, well-guarded
Crowned with splendor and his good name
wherever he went, his name went forth
Upon his approach, men of renown would speak:
"Blessed be he who comes in His name, who is called by His name!"
He who rejoices in joy, like a bearer of sheaves
gladdened by the goodness of dreams[48]
He was kept from all harm
heir of the goodness of both worlds
The whole of his "property" he kept near his heart[49]
just as the righteous rejoices in his "portion."
He was protected from the "flame of fire" that seized him[50]
and from the ruddy one[51] who clung to him—
    who embraced him by the throat, to strangle him![52]
Among the mighty of the city of Shechem he settled
a portion of Shechem's own stones he acquired[53]
A distinguished altar of stone[54] there he built
to give thanks to Him who brings near the far

---

46 **R** cites *GenR* 63:3, "It was taught in Rabbi Nehemiah's name: Rebecca merited that the twelve tribes should spring directly from her."

47 That is, innocent of Laban's accusations (Gen 31).(Text spells כעור as כאור).

48 This line draws on Ps 126:5 and Gen 28:12 (**R**).

49 "His property (*segulato*)" here refers to both his material wealth and his Torah-learning, reflecting the same ambiguity as "good (*tov*)" above. **B1** connects the following stich to *m. Avot* 4:1, "Who is happy? He who rejoices in his portion (*ḥelko*)." "Portion" here, likewise, can have a double meaning of "Torah" or "possessions."

50 That is, the angel of fire with whom Jacob wrestled on the night before his crossing. **R** cites *GenR* 77:2, "Rabbi Huna said: Eventually he [the angel] said to himself: Shall I not

הַבָּאִים אֲשֶׁר הִשְׁרִישׁ עִמּוֹ
אֲשֶׁר הָיוּ רְאוּיִים לְאִימּוֹ
וְצָדָק כִּי יִהְיוּ מִימּוֹ
כִּי חֵלֶק יי עַמּוֹ
זָרוּעַ כָּאוֹר זָרוּחַ כְּמָאוֹר
וְזִיו זָוהֲרוֹ הוֹלֵךְ וָאוֹר
חָסוּךְ מִכָּל דָּבָר כָּאוּר
בְּשָׁלוֹם עָבַר יַבּוּק יְאוֹר
טַפָּיו אִיתּוֹ מְקוּשָּׁרִים
וּמַסְלוּלָיו בְּנַחַת מְיוּשָּׁרִים
יְלָדִים תְּמִימִים וּמְוּכְשָׁרִים
כְּבָבַת עַיִן מְשֻׁומָּרִים
כָּלוּל בְּהָדָר וּבְטוּב שֵׁם
בְּכָל סְבִיבָיו יָצָא לוֹ שֵׁם
לְבוֹאוֹ סָחוּ אַנְשֵׁי שֵׁם
בָּרוּךְ הַבָּא בְּשֵׁם קוֹרְאוֹ בַּשֵּׁם
מְרַנֵּין בְּגִיל כְּנוֹשֵׂא אֲלוּמּוֹת
מְבוּשָּׂר טוֹבוֹת בַּחֲלוֹמוֹת
נָצוּר מִכָּל מַהֲלוּמוֹת
נָחוּל טוֹבַת שְׁנֵי עוֹלָמוֹת
סְגוּלָּתוֹ שְׁלֵימָה בְּחֵיקוֹ
כְּצַדִּיק שָׂמֵיחַ בְּחֶלְקוֹ
עָזוּר מִלַּהַב אֵשׁ אֲשֶׁר אֲבָקוֹ
וּמֵאַדְמוֹנִי אֲשֶׁר דִּיבְּקוֹ
וְחִיבְּקוֹ בַּעֲנָקוֹ לְחָונְקוֹ
פְּנֵי הָעִיר שְׁכֶם אָז חָנָה
וְחֶלְקָה מֵאַבְנֵי שְׁכֶם קָנָה
צִיּוּן מִזְבֵּחַ שָׁם בָּנָה
וְתוֹדָה לִמְקָרֵב רְחוֹקִים עָנָה

---

inform him with whom he is engaged? What did he do? He put his finger on the earth, whereupon the earth began spurting fire. Said Jacob to him: `Would you terrify me with that? Why, I am altogether of that stuff!' Thus it is written, `And the house of Jacob shall be a fire,' etc. (Obad 18)."

51 Esau

52 This line is unusually long, containing an entire extra stich.

53 That is, the stones with which he built the altar. The first stich, "among the mighty," would literally be "at the face, towards the face," but the translation maintains the interpretation found in the previous unit, which these lines recall.

54 See Jer 31:21, Ezek 39:15 for the use of ציון with the sense of a stone monument.

He gave gifts and made appeasement
when the time of rest and repose arrived
The spirit of all (people) found pleasure in him
just as the spirit of God rested upon him[55]
Whole in all ways and preferred over all
into the hand of his hater he was not handed over
The full term of his exile completed
in Shalem he surrendered to peace, his vows he fulfilled[56]

And thus, "Then Jacob came to Shalem..."[57]

(7) Perfect in his faith   Perfected in his tent
    To fulfill his trust, a sign was spoken
Perfect in his entry   Perfected in his offspring[58]
    To fulfill his vision, a clearly-worded vow
Perfect in his body   Perfected in his soul[59]
    To fulfill his promise, upholding his pledge
Perfect in his ways   Perfected in his words
    To fulfill his speech's exalted reward
Perfect in his form   Perfected in his following
    To fulfill the honor of his meditative knowledge
...[60]
    ...
Perfect in his visage   Perfected in his sons
    To fulfill the merit of his amazing memory[61]
Perfect in his holdings   Perfected in his freedom
    To fulfill his promise, given from grace
Perfect in his good[62]   Perfected in his babes
    To fulfill his utterance uttered before he fled[63]

---

55 *m. Avot* 3:10 indicates that "spirit of all" refers to people, not the deity (**B2**).

56 That is, the vows Jacob swore at Beth El (to build an altar and tithe), when he fled Esau's wrath (Gen. 28) (**B1**).

57 As **R** notes, this *rahit* contains a second *rahit* embedded within, in the third stich of each line. Formally, the entire poem is structured on the pattern *shalem b- – meshullam b- – leshallem*, rendered here as "perfect in...perfected in...to fulfill..." The first two stichs each consist of a single word (with a third masculine singular suffice, "his"), following an alphabetical acrostic; the third stich continues the same alphabetic acrostic, but contains three words, each starting with the letter required by the acrostic. The full structure, then, is: *shalem b-(A)...meshullam b-(A)...leshallem (A-A-A)*, where "A" represents a word beginning with the acrostically-required letter. In terms of content, the first stich describe Jacob's physical return, the second generally describes his offspring and familial situation

קָבַע מַשְׂאֵת וְעָשׂ הֲנָחָה
  כְּהִישִׂיג מַרְגֵּיעָה וּמְנוּחָה
רוּחַ הַכֹּל מִמֶּנּוּ נוֹחָה
  כִּי רוּחַ אֵל עָלָיו נָחָה
שָׁלֵם בַּכֹּל וּמְשׁוּלָּם
  כִּי בְּיַד שׂוֹנְאוֹ לֹא הֻושְׁלָם
תֶּכֶל קֵץ גָּלוּתוֹ שָׁלָם
  וּבְשָׁלֵם הֻושְׁלָם וְנִידְרוֹ שִׁילֵם

ובכן ויבא יעקב שלם

(ז) שָׁלֵם בְּאָומְנוֹ   מְשׁוּלָּם בְּאָוהֳלוֹ
  לְשַׁלֵּם אוֹמֶן אוֹת אָמְרוֹ
שָׁלֵם בְּבוֹאוֹ   מְשׁוּלָּם בְּבָנָיו
  לְשַׁלֵּם בִּיאוּר בֵּירוּר בִּיטּוּיוֹ
שָׁלֵם בְּגוּפוֹ   מְשׁוּלָּם בְּגִיוְיוֹ
  לְשַׁלֵּם גְּמוּל גְּזֵירַת גּוֹמְרוֹ
שָׁלֵם בִּדְרָכָיו   מְשׁוּלָּם בִּדְבָרָיו
  לְשַׁלֵּם דֶּבֶב דִּיגּוּל דְּבָרוֹ
שָׁלֵם בְּהוֹנוֹ   מְשׁוּלָּם בַּהֲמוֹנוֹ
  לְשַׁלֵּם הִידּוּר הוֹרָיַית הֶגְיוֹנוֹ
…   …
…
שָׁלֵם בְּזִיווֹ   מְשׁוּלָּם בִּזְרוֹעוֹ
  לְשַׁלֵּם זְכוּת זוֹהַר זִיכְרוֹנוֹ
שָׁלֵם בְּחֵילוֹ   מְשׁוּלָּם בְּחָופְשׁוֹ
  לְשַׁלֵּם חוֹק חִינּוּן חִיבּוּיוֹ
שָׁלֵם בְּטוּבוֹ   מְשׁוּלָּם בְּטַפָּיו
  לְשַׁלֵּם טַעַם טָעַן טֶרֶם טָס

(the ripple-effect of his perfection), and the third (the internal *rahit*) elaborates upon the purpose of his and his family's return: the fulfillment of the oath made at Beth El in Gen 28.

58 In *GenR* 79:1, Jacob's return "*shalem*" is understood to mean "Jacob did not depart from the world until he saw thirty myriads of his descendents." The multiple references to Jacob's offspring reflect, in part, this line of interpretation.

59 Lit., "self" or perhaps the male organ (i.e., offspring).

60 The MS lacks a line for the letter *vav*.

61 **B2** cites *GenR* 79:5, which describes Jacob as "whole in his learning," in contrast to Joseph "who forgot his."

62 That is, Torah, as used above.

63 The oath sworn before he fled to Haran.

Perfect in his thighs[64] Perfected in his children
To fulfill his Maker's precious unity
Perfect in his might Perfected in all[65]
To fulfill honor of the covenant he had cut
Perfect in his [learning][66] Perfected in his companions[67]
To fulfill the lesson of his learned tongue
Perfect in his property Perfected in his camp
To fulfill his mitzvah's murmured response
Perfect in his beauty Perfected in his portion
To fulfill the pleasure of his vocalized vow
Perfect in his shelter Perfected in his hope
To fulfill the whispered wishes of his lips
Perfect in his fertility[68] Perfected in his `flocks'
To fulfill the pledge of orderly offerings
Perfect in his prayer Perfected in his vigilance
To fulfill his clearly worded words of mouth
Perfect in his herds Perfected in his provision
To fulfill the just joy of his Maker
Perfect in his promise Perfected in his possession
To fulfill the sacred sacrifices to his Creator
Perfect in his fellowship Perfected in his followers
To fulfill the fragrant offering for his Friend
Perfect in his return Perfected in his tribes
To fulfill the sacrifice of whole-burnt lambs
Perfect in his purity Perfected in his generations
To fulfill the essence of thankful offerings

And thus…
(8)[69] Make us mighty like the twins[70]

---

64 This stich contains a double entendre: on the one hand, it implies that Jacob was healed of the wound he received to his thigh when he wrestled with the angel by the river Jabbok (see *GenR* 79:5); on the other, it implies the purity of Jacob's offspring, the subject of the following stich.

65 Based on midrashic interpretations of "all (*kol*)," **B2** suggests that this most likely means a son (*kol* and *ben* have the same value according to gematria); it might also mean wealth or old age. Jacob, of course, possessed all of these in abundance.

66 Reading with **B1**.

67 That is, given the structure of this poem, his children.

68 This probably refers to his ability to effortlessly breed his sheep or raise his crops; it could also refer to his remarkable number of children. "Flocks" in the following stich

שָׁלֵם בִּירֵיכָיו מְשׁוּלָּם בִּילָדָיו
לְשַׁלֵּם יְקַר יִיחוּד יוֹצְרוֹ
שָׁלֵם בְּכוֹחוֹ מְשׁוּלָּם בַּכֹּל
לְשַׁלֵּם כִּיבּוּד כְּמוֹ כָּרַת
שָׁלֵם בְּלִינָתוֹ מְשׁוּלָּם בְּלִיוּוּיוֹ
לְשַׁלֵּם לֶיקַח לִימּוּד לְשׁוֹנוֹ
שָׁלֵם בְּמָמוֹנוֹ מְשׁוּלָּם בְּמַחֲנוֹ
לְשַׁלֵּם מִצְוַת מוֹצָא מַעֲנוֹ
שָׁלֵם בְּנוֹאִיו מְשׁוּלָּם בְּנָוֹחֲלוֹ
לְשַׁלֵּם נוֹעַם נוֹאַם נִידְרוֹ
שָׁלֵם בְּסֵוּכוֹ מְשׁוּלָּם בְּסִיבְרוֹ
לְשַׁלֵּם סִיחַ סֵידֶר שְׂפָתָיו
שָׁלֵם בְּעִיבּוּרוֹ מְשׁוּלָּם בַּעֲדָרָיו
לְשַׁלֵּם עִינְיַין עֲבוֹדַת עֶרְכּוֹ
שָׁלֵם בְּפִילּוּלוֹ מְשׁוּלָּם בְּפָוּקְדוֹ
לְשַׁלֵּם פֶּיצַח פֵּירוּשׁ פִּיו
שָׁלֵם בְּצֹאנוֹ מְשׁוּלָּם בְּצֵידוֹ
לְשַׁלֵּם צֶדֶק צַהַל צוּרוֹ
שָׁלֵם בְּקִינּוֹ מְשׁוּלָּם בְּקִינְיָינוֹ
לְשַׁלֵּם קָורְבָּן קִידּוּשׁ קוֹנוֹ
שָׁלֵם בְּרִיגְשׁוֹ מְשׁוּלָּם בְּרִיבּוּיוֹ
לְשַׁלֵּם רִיצּוּי רֵיחַ רֵיעוֹ
שָׁלֵם בְּשֵׁובוֹ מְשׁוּלָּם בְּשְׁבָטָיו
לְשַׁלֵּם שְׁחִיטַת שֵׂיֵי שְׁלָמָיו
שָׁלֵם בְּתֻומּוֹ מְשׁוּלָּם בְּתוֹלְדוֹתָיו
לְשַׁלֵּם תּוֹכֶן תְּרוּמוֹת תּוֹדוֹתָיו

ובכן

(ח) תְּתְנֵינוּ תַּקִּיפִים כִּתְאוֹמִים

---

probably refers to his children.

69 This *silluq* is unusually poetic (it is composed as an acrostic, with each letter tripled in its stich, and the third word of each stich beginning with the prefix -כּ); indeed, it is ornate even by the standards of a *rahit*, an it might be more appropriate to regard it a second *rahit* rather than a *silluq*.

70 This reference is tantalizing; as **B1** suggests, it probably refers to Peretz and Zerah, the twin sons of Judah and Tamar (see *GenR* 85:13, where it states: "Here [Gen 38:27] `twins' is written fully, indicating that both [Perez and Zerah] were righteous; whereas in the earlier case [of Jacob and Esau] `twins' is written defectively, because one was righteous and the other wicked."). It might, however, contain an allusion to the famous twins of the Zodiac (Castor and Pollux).

Take us whole like whole offerings
Raise us high, like the exalted *re᾿em*[71]
Accept us, holy ones, like sacrifices
Station us, stately like the Hosts[72]
Recall, to our favor, the fragrant blossoming vine[73]
Crown us on high among clouds[74]
Set us, supreme, as speakers wise
Sustain us as befits princes
Fill us with perfection, like angels
Accompany us forever as You accompanied us before
Found us firmly, like Your glory
Unify us as one, like Your splendor
Build us well, like Your ramparts walled
Shield us strongly with Your strength
Make us shine, radiant like Your splendor
Assemble us together, like when You gave revelation
Adorn us with the glory, like Your procession
Entwine us, like lovers, in keeping with Your vow[75]
Redeem us, O Great One, in accord with Your greatness
Bring us into a covenant, in keeping with Your promise
Affirm us as of old, in keeping with Your word
Let us declare with those who say "Holy"
Hallowed, in the beauty of the Holy One
As it is written: "And the one called…"

(9) Whole in every way
for them, You perfect every thing
for those who fulfill (vows) and say:
Holy, holy, holy [is the Lord of Hosts! The whole earth is filled with His glory!

---

71 "Unicorn" or "wild ox" (*re'em*), a mythical animal of enormous height, based on its name (lit. "height"). It is mentioned in the Bible in Isa 34:7 and Ps 29:6. In *MidPs.* 22:28, King David mistakes the *re᾿em* for a mountain, while in *MidPs* 92:11, we learn that "the *re᾿em* has high horns and gores in all directions."

72 Most obviously, this refers to the heavenly hosts who join Israel in reciting the Qedushah; however, it may also include the patriarchs or martyrs, as **R** notes (based on *SongR* 2:18).

73 That is, Joseph son of Jacob; see above, where Joseph brought into the piyyut because he was buried in Shechem. The language of scent has to do with the contagious pervasiveness of the good reputation of, if not the current generation, the ancestors whose merit

תְּשִׁיתֵינוּ **שְׁ**לֵימִים כִּשְׁלָמִים
תְּרוֹמְמֵינוּ **רָ**מִים כִּרְאֵימִים
תְּקַבְּלֵינוּ **קְ**דוֹשִׁים כְּקָורְבָּנוֹת
תַּצִּיבֵינוּ **צַ**דִּיקִים כִּצְבָאוֹת
תִּפְקְדֵינוּ **פְ**רוּחִים כְּפֵירוֹת
תְּעַטְּרֵינוּ **עֶ**לְיוֹנִים כַּעֲנָנִים
תְּשִׂימֵינוּ **סַ**גִּיאִים כְּסִיחִים
תְּנַהֲגֵינוּ **נְ**חוּלִים כַּנְּדִיבִים
תְּמַלְּאֵינוּ **מִ**כְּלָל כְּמַלְאָכִים
תְּלַוֵּינוּ **לָ**עַד כִּלְוּוּיָךְ
תְּכוֹנְנֵינוּ **כֵּ**נָּה כִּכְבוֹדָךְ
תְּיַחֲדֵינוּ **יַ**חַד כִּיקָרָךְ
תְּטָעֵינוּ **טוֹ**בִים כְּטִיכּוּסָךְ
תְּחַסְּנֵינוּ **חֲ**זָקָה כְּחֵילָךְ
תַּזְרִיחֵינוּ **זוֹ**הַר כְּזִיוָךְ
תְּוַעֲדֵינוּ **וַ**עַד כִּוִידוּיָךְ
תְּהַדְּרֵינוּ **הוֹ**ד כְּהִילּוּכָךְ
תַּדְבִּיקֵינוּ **דוֹ**דִים כְּדִיבּוּרָךְ
תִּגְאָלֵינוּ **גָּ**דוֹל כְּגָודְלָךְ
תְּבִיאֵינוּ **בִּ**בְרִית כְּבִיטְחוֹנָךְ
תַּאֲמִירֵינוּ **כְּאָ**ז כְּאָומְרָךְ
וְנַאֲמִירָךְ כְּאוֹמְרֵי קָדוֹשׁ
בִּקְדֻשָּׁה בְּהַדְרַת קוֹדֶשׁ
ככתוב וקרא

(ט) שְׁלֵימִים בְּכָל דָּבָר
עִימָּם תְּשַׁלֵּם כָּל דָּבָר
מְשַׁלְּמִים וְאוֹמְרִים
קדוש קדוש קדוש יי צבאות מלא כל הארץ כבודו

stands in their favor. See Deborah A. Green, *The Aroma of Righteousness* (University Park: Penn State University; forthcoming) for an in-depth study of the nexus of scent, merit, and memory in rabbinic literature.

74 **R** connects with the messianic imagery of Dan 7:13: "I saw in the night visions, and, behold, one like a son of man came with the clouds of heaven, and came to the ancient of days, and they brought him near before him."

75 **B1** connects with Jer 13:11, "For as the belt fits tightly to the loins of a man, so have I caused the whole house of Israel and the whole house of Judah to hold tightly to Me, says the Lord; that they might be to me for a people, and for a name, and for a praise, and for a glory; but they would not hear."

"*Holy*"—from those who are wholly Yours
"*Holy*"—from those who perfect Your [will]
"*Holy*"—from those who fulfill [vows] to You[76]
O Holy One,[77] You fulfilled the what the pure one lacked
because he was wholeheartedly Yours[78]
O Holy One, You perfectly punished his enemies before him
because he perfected himself before You
O Holy One, You protected him (with) peace all the way to Shalem
because he fulfilled his vows to You
Each to the other…

"*From His place*"—He kept the pure one when he went out and came in
because he kept His laws
"*From His place*"—He blessed him with all that was his and not his
because he blessed His name
"*From His place*"—He saved him from fire and water[79]
because he saved himself for His sake[80]

Twice

---

76 This poem, like the *rahit,* plays with the root ש-ל-ם in three stems: the *qal* (rendered here as a form of "whole"); the *piel* (translated as a form of "to fulfill"); and the *hiphil* (rendered here as a form of "perfect"). The choice of stem is not consistent within each category.

77 Unusually, this *qedushah* uses "Holy One" (קדוש alone) rather than the more usual "Holy from…" (קדוש מ־) construction.

קָדוֹשׁ מְשַׁלְּמֵי לָךְ
קָדוֹשׁ מְמַשְׁלִימֵי לָךְ
קָדוֹשׁ מְמַשַׁלְּמֵי לָךְ
קָדוֹשׁ שִׁילַּמְתָּה חֵיסְרוֹנֵי תָם
כִּי הָיָה שָׁלֵם לָךְ
קָדוֹשׁ גַּם אוֹיְבָיו הִישְׁלַמְתָּה לוֹ
כִּי עַצְמוֹ הִשְׁלִים לָךְ
קָדוֹשׁ שָׁלוֹם עַד שָׁלֵם שִׁימַּרְתּוֹ
כִּי נְדָרָיו שִׁילֵּם לָךְ
לעומתם כולם

מִמְּקוֹמוֹ שִׁימֵּר לְתָם בְּצֵאתוֹ ובוֹאוֹ
כִּי שָׁמַר חֻוקּוֹ
מִמְּקוֹמוֹ בֵּירְכוֹ בְּשֶׁלּוֹ וְלֹא לוֹ
כִּי בֵּירַךְ שְׁמוֹ
מִמְּקוֹמוֹ הוֹשִׁיעוֹ מֵאֵשׁ וּמִמַּיִם
כִּי נוֹשַׁע בּוֹ

פעמים

78 Jacob "lacked" that which he gave as gifts to Esau but God remedied any deficiency; see *GenR* 79:5 (**B2**).

79 "Fire" refers to the angel Jacob wrestled by the river, while "water" refers to Esau directly; for the language of this line, see Ps 66:12 (**R**), Isa 17:12 and Ps 32:6 (**B1**).

80 The implication of this line is that God saves those who wish to be saved for His sake—in this case, Jacob's desperate wish to fulfill the oath he had sworn at Beth El.

Commentary

> *And Jacob came* shalem, *a city of Shechem, which is in the land of Canaan, when he came from Padan-Aram; and pitched his tent before the city. And he bought a parcel of a field, where he had spread his tent, at the hand of the children of Hamor, Shechem's father, for a hundred kesitahs of money. And he erected there an altar, and called it* El-Elohei-Israel. *(*Gen 33:18–20*)*

The base-verse of this piyyut, the first verse of the *sidra*, contains a phrase that lends itself to two variant understandings: did Jacob return to a place called "Shalem" (perhaps to be identified with Jerusalem?), or did he return in a state of *shelemut* ("wholeness")? Most modern translations (the New JPS, the New Revised Standard, and others), along with the three major *targumim* (Onqelos, Neophyti, Pseudo-Jonathan), Rashi and Ibn Ezra, include the latter, adverbial meaning of the phrase, while the Septuagint, Rashbam, and the King James Version treat Shalem as the proper name of a place.

Yannai, having both the generous canvas of the *qedushta* form and the openness of poetic rhetoric at his disposal, does not have to choose one meaning over the other; indeed, this entire piyyut is a study in the range of possible meanings of the word *shalem*. Throughout this poem, he employs every available nuance of the root ש-ל-ם: verbal, adverbial, adjectival, and nominal. In truth, the present translation often obscures the aural richness of the poem because it must rely on multiple words to render the common root. No single English lexeme shares anything like the breadth of meaning of the Hebrew term. The semantic range of שָׁלֵם includes: totality, peace, health, perfection, completion, fulfillment, repayment, restitution, and retribution. It can refer to a kind of offering (one that was wholly burnt, which may have effected "wholeness" in the divine-human relationship, if breeched) or a psycho-social state of being. In all cases, there is an element of "restoring to wholeness," whether the lack results from ill health, poverty, war, debt, or—most centrally here— exile. The city of "Shalem" (familiar from the English name, Salem, which reflects the Greek transcription and pronunciation) first appears in the Abraham story (Gen 14:18) and was (and is) possibly to be identified with Jerusalem, itself contains these lexical nuances. According to folk etymology, Jerusalem is "the city of peace," the city that reflects a unique potential and aspiration for wholeness in the Jewish worldview. Jerusalem is the city where the world can be made *shalem*—the city to which exiles will return, make their whole offerings, and achieve peace, health, and fulfillment.

Thus, for Yannai, when Jacob returns *shalem*, he returns to an absolute and complete wholeness: his health is restored, his safety assured, promises of peace fulfilled, wealth regained, his family complete, and he is fully vindicated in the face of heaven (the angelic host), neighbors (the Shechemites), and foes (Esau and Laban). And all this takes place in the city of Shalem—the city of wholeness—Jerusalem. Every valence of "wholeness" possible—almost every interpretation of the verse found in the body of *midrashim* on this passage—finds its way into this piyyut.

Jacob as depicted here is not the complex, flawed figure of the previous poem. He is, instead, a picture of piety: perfect in the eyes of people and God. His actions are just, his Torah complete, and his very being right with God. He is wounded but healed, accused but unjustly, attacked but ultimately vindicated. The rich rewards Jacob receives—which manifest both materially and existentially, in the present tense and the future—are completely deserved, with Jacob's return to Canaan cast not simply as the end of an exile, but a pilgrimage made to fulfill a decades old vow. Why these differences from Yannai's other depictions of the patriarch? Why the absence of criticism when the previous poem did not shy away from more than gentle rebuke? It may well be the theme of pervasive restoration that permeates the entire poem. As Poem Six concludes, "The full term of his exile completed (*shalam*) // in Shalem he surrendered to peace (*be-shalem hushlam*) / and his vows he fulfilled (*shillem*)." From the first poem, where Ps 126 is quoted (two verses, in fact), to the very end of the *qedushah*, a motif of a dreamlike restoration is presented. A world awry is set aright. Harmony and peace are renewed and reestablished. Foes are met with justice and the hierarchy of truth rather than appearances is recreated. God and Jacob work in tandem, with Jacob earning the rewards God gladly bestows upon him. "*Shalem*" stands for this restored Edenic state. Critique of the central figure would fracture this whole.

Read this way, the opening verses of the *sidra* take on forward-looking, even messianic importance. They allude to the ultimate restoration to wholeness of all of Jacob's descendents; explicitly, in Poem Three, justice and retribution—aspects of ש-ל-ם—are sought. Restitution anticipates restoration: of the Temple, of worship, of the people who are the heirs of Jacob. The emphasis on keeping the Sabbath in Poem Five becomes part of the messianic program; Jacob is depicted as teaching his sons the same value being practiced by the community that constitutes the audience. By implication, the Sabbath becomes a kind of "homecoming" irrespective of geographic location. It is a day perfected through sheer human willpower, and in accord with divine will. By extension, the motif of worship in general (growing out of the peculiar altar-name in Gen 33:20) likewise stands out. Thanksgiving rituals at the present moment are incomplete for lack of the Temple but destined for restored perfection, as soon as the present exile is over. Eventually—(God willing)—the children of Israel will be restored—that is, made whole again—just as their father was: in body, in soul, in learning, in progeny, in all ways imaginable. The initiative clearly lies with God—as always, Yannai is not a hawk—but the yearning, the pleading, and dreaming are evident. Unquoted, but apt, is the first verse of Ps 126: "When the Lord restores the captives of Zion, we will have become like dreamers." In this *qedushta*, Yannai permits himself a rapturous vision, though he ascribes the experience to Jacob (a figure himself known for his dreams, and the father of Joseph, the dream-interpreter). It is a vision so real, so fully anticipated that he can already see it: fulfilled, perfectly, in whole.

Qedushta for Genesis 35:9 בראשית לה:ט

"Then God appeared to Jacob" וירא אלהים אל יעקב

This piyyut develops the motif of Jacob's grief—first over Rebecca's nurse, then for his parents, and then over Rebecca herself—and God's tender, humble consolation of the mourning patriarch. The confirmation of Jacob/Israel's change of name is presented as an element of divine comfort. God's act of consoling the bereaved exemplifies a cardinal virtue and serves as a model for Jacob and his descendents, but it also reflects the intimate bond connecting God, Jacob, and Jacob's descendents. The patriarch cannot shield his children from suffering, but he can arm them against it with a durable, heartfelt hope. While the themes of loss and consolation in this piyyut resemble similar motifs from other *qedushta'ot*, the tone here is personal rather than overtly national-allegorical throughout.

(1) Great is Your perfect faithfulness;
Faith in You leads to greatness
Even more, Your great humility grants great honor to others[1]
Those who seek You, You make grand and great.[2]

You gave greatly to the pure one while he sat in mourning,
grieving and seeking comfort
The grandeur of Your presence You shone forth to comfort him
when he was in need of comfort and consolation[3]

Goodness for the sake of the good one You showed
while he sat sighing, You saw his need
The glory of Your works You showed to him
to show him Your face, You appeared

As it is written: "Then God appeared to Jacob yet again while he was coming from Paddan Aram, and He blessed him" (Gen 35:9)
And as it is said: "Let Your works be seen by Your servants, and Your ways by their sons" (Ps 90:16)
And as it is said: "Blessed are you when you come, and blessed are you when you go forth" (Deut 28:6)[4]
And as it is said: "You decree and it will be fulfilled, and light will shine upon Your ways" (Job 22:28)
And as it is said: "And lo, in this way will the man who fears the Lord be blessed" (Ps 128:4)

O Lord, our God
With Your strong staff, lead us
and show to us Your shield
Blessed are you… Shield…

---

1 The line alludes to Ps 18:36, which is the exegetical verse for a *petiḥta* in *GenR* 48:1 (**B1**). The motifs and interpretations implied here are developed and expanded in Poem 5. According to *GenR* 8:13, and other sources, God humbled Himself by taking on very human roles: rejoicing with the bride and groom (Adam and Eve), visiting the ill (Abraham), consoling the bereaved (Jacob), and burying the dead (Moses). Each of these cases models virtuous behavior for humankind; when people behave in accord with God's example, their humility makes them great in His eyes. (For these ideals as human obligations see *m. Peah* 1:1 and *b. Shabb* 127a, now in the morning liturgy.)In this poem, God's humility

(א) אוֹמֶן אֱמוּנָתְךָ רַבָּה
בְּנֶאֱמָנֶיךָ מִתְרַבָּה
גַּם עִינְוָותְךָ מְאֹד מְרֻבָּה
דּוֹרְשֶׁיךָ מַרְבָּה וּמְרַבָּה

הִרְבֵּיתָה לְתָם בְּשִׁבְתּוֹ אוֹנֵן
וּמִתְאוֹנֵן וּמִתְחַנֵּן
זִיו יְקָרְךָ הוֹפַעְתָּה חוֹנֵן
חֲנוּנָיו לָחוֹן וּלְחוֹנֵן

טוֹב לְהֵיטִיב הִירְאֵיתָה
יְשִׁיבָתוֹ בְּאֶנַח עֵת רָאִיתָה
כְּבוֹד פּוֹעָלְךָ עָלָיו הֶרְאֵיתָה
לְהַרְאוֹת לוֹ פָּנִים נִרְאֵיתָה

ככתוב וירא אלהים אל יעקב בבואו מפדן ארם ויברך אתו

ונאמר יראה על עבדיך והדרך על בניהם

ונאמר ברוך אתה בבאך וברוך אתה בצאתך

ונאמר ותגזר אומר ויקם לך ועל דרכיך נגה אור

ונאמר הנה כי כן יבורך גבר ירא יי

יי אֱלֹהֵינוּ
בְּעוֹז שִׁיבְטָךְ נְחֵינוּ
וּמָגִינָּךְ הַרְאֵינוּ
ברוך... מגן...

honors Jacob. For the motif of God's appearance as an act of consolation, see *GenR* 81:5 and 82:1; *TanḥB Vayishlaḥ* 23 and 26 (**R** cites the last of these); *TargN* to Gen 35:9; and others.

2 The opening stanza depends heavily on repetitions of the root רבה in various stems.

3 This stanza repeats forms of the root חנן/חון, here translated as "comfort" rather than the more usual "grace."

4 The use of a Torah text in the litany of verses following the first verse of the *sidra* is highly unusual. The language is evoked again in the first line of Poem Four.

(2) A fortress for the pure one You became
leading him [like a shepherd with his flock][5]
...
...
... from his mother's womb
You commanded Your salvation...[6]
...
...
Your name with his You entwined[7]
His remnant You guaranteed for good
...
...

[As it is written: "Then God said to him: Your name is Jacob, but no longer shall your name be called `Jacob' but rather `Israel' shall be your name. Thus He called his name `Israel.'" (Gen 35:10)]

(3) Your name will be known[8] and Your people will know Your name[9]
and all who are called by Your name [will make known][10] Your name
"The prince"[11] You created for Your glory
and You fashioned his likeness upon Your Throne of Glory[12]
"Jacob" he was called, and You are "the God of Jacob;"
"Israel" he is called, and You are "the God of Israel"[13]

---

5 Ps 80:2 provides the language for **B1**'s restoration.

6 The first stich may allude to traditions such as those preserved in *GenR* 63:6 that describe Jacob's struggles *in utero* with Esau, as well as Rebecca's merit. The language of the second stich comes from Ps 44:5 (**B2**) but here the phrasing suggests the midrashic motif that God participates in Israel's suffering and, like Israel, needs redemption. On the motif of divine pathos, see Michael Fishbane, *Biblical Myth and Rabbinic Mythmaking* (Oxford: Oxford University Press, 2003), 132–59.

7 That is, Jacob had the theophoric element "El" incorporated into his new name: Isra-*El*. (This is similar to the abbreviated element "Yah" added to change Abram's name to Abraham and Sarai to Sarah.) The very name "Israel" serves as a reminder to the nation of its national history, status, and destiny.

8 Isa 64:1 (**B2**).

9 Isa 52:6 (**R**); **B2** also cites *MidPs* 91:8, which teaches that Israel's prayers are not answered in this world because Israel does not know God's proper name (השם המפורש) any more, but in the future, God will restore this knowledge to them, at which moment all their prayers will be answered.

(ב) **מ**ִשְׂגָּב לְתָם נִהְיֵיתָה
נוֹהֵג ...
...
...
... מִמְּעֵי אִימּוֹ
צִיוִּיתָה יִשְׁעָךְ ...
...
...
שְׁמָךְ בִּשְׁמוֹ עֵירַבְתָּה
שְׁאֵירִיתוֹ לְטוֹב עָרַבְתָּה
...
...

(ג) **י**ִוָּודַע שְׁמָךְ וְיֵידַע עַמָּךְ שְׁמָךְ
וְכֹל הַנִּקְרָא בִשְׁמָךְ ... שְׁמָךְ
נִין אֲשֶׁר יָצַרְתָּה לִכְבוֹדָךְ
וְצַרְתָּה דְמוּתוֹ בְּכִסֵּא כְבוֹדָךְ
יַעֲקֹב נִיקְרָא וְאַתָּה אֱלֹהֵי יַעֲקֹב
יִשְׂרָאֵל נִיקְרָא וְאַתָּה אֱלֹהֵי יִשְׂרָאֵל

10 Gap filled as by **R**.

11 I.e., Jacob. For בין as "prince" rather than "son," see **B1**.

12 The motif of Jacob's visage appearing on the divine throne is cited in connection with this *sidra* in *GenR* 82:2, which states: "If I bless him who builds an altar in My name, how much the more should I appear to Jacob, whose features are engraved on My Throne, and bless him…If I appear to him who offered a ram in My name and bless him, how much the more should I appear to Jacob whose features are engraved on My throne, and bless him." There may also be a hint of the etymology of "Israel" that understands it as a contraction of *ish-raʾah-el*, "the man who has seen God." See *GenR* 78:3.

13 See *GenR* 78:3, where we are told: "It was not intended that the name of Jacob should disappear, but that `Israel' should be his principal name and `Jacob' a secondary one." *GenR* 46:8, however, notes an alternate tradition to the reverse effect, using the second verse of this *sidra* as a prooftext: "Rabbi Zebida interpreted in Rabbi Aḥa's name: At all events, `Your name is Jacob, save that, but Israel [too] shall be your name' (Gen 35:10, translated in accord with the exegetical sense): `Jacob' will be the principal name, while `Israel' will be an additional one."

Oh Yah, fulfill for him what You proclaimed to him
and make come true all that You said to him:

As it is written: "And now, thus says the Lord who formed you, O Jacob, who formed you, O Israel: Fear not, for I will redeem you; I called you by your name. You are mine." (Isa 43:1)
And as it is said: "Each who is called by My name, and whom I formed for My glory, I created him, indeed, I made him" (Isa 43:7)
And You are holy, enthroned on the praises of Israel ... Please, God...

(4) When he went forth and when he came back, Jacob was blessed[14]
he who by his name You are blessed, O God of Jacob
Mentioning his name and blessing Your name
for You recalled his name in the mention of Your name
In the dwelling of splendor he appeared yet again
and You gave him a great blessing that there be no adding to his pain[15]
For You will bless and the righteous will be blessed[16]
blessed are You, O Lord, God of Israel
For by the name of Israel You will be blessed, blessed and holy

(5) God of the world, from the first days of the world
You taught humility to those born into the world[17]
The blessing of the bridegroom You taught
through the created one and his helpmeet[18]
and visiting the sick through the father of circumcision[19] when he was cut
Likewise, consoling the bereaved You revealed through the pure one[20]
when, while he was on the road from Paddan, You revealed Yourself to him
"The path of all"—for such is fate—was the nurse-maid's way
The news of Rebecca came, that she had set forth on her journey[21]
Not yet at ease from the pain in the soles of his feet[22]—

14The language of this unit, which emphasizes the root ב-ר-ך, initiates a resonance of liturgical phraseology, which permeate this *qedushta*. The first line evokes Deut 28:6, an intertext from Poem One.

15 "Blessing" is here used with a double sense. On the one hand, God "blessed" Jacob with sons, wealth, wives, and a safe return to his homeland. He is also graced with status as a patriarch, a divine change of name, his visage on the divine throne, and here a personal revelation. Additionally, however, in the context of this *sidra*, God "blesses" Jacob by teaching him the mourner's blessings and gracing him with His presence. Part of the blessing of consolation is to wish the bereaved an end of suffering, as implied in the final stich of the line.

יָהּ הָקֵם לוֹ אֶת אֲשֶׁר קָרָאתָה
וְכוֹנֵן עָלָיו כָּל אֲשֶׁר אָמַרְתָּה

ככתוב ועתה כה אמר יי בוראך יעקב ויצרך ישראל אל תירא כי גאלתיך קראתי בשמך לי אתה

ונאמר כל הנקרא בשמי ולכבודי בראתיו יצרתיו אף עשיתיו

ואתה קדוש יושב תהלות ישראל אל נא

(ד) בְּצֵאתוֹ וּבְבוֹאוֹ בּוֹרַךְ יַעֲקֹב
אֲשֶׁר בִּשְׁמוֹ תְבוֹרַךְ אֱלֹהֵי יַעֲקֹב
מַזְכִּירִים שְׁמוֹ וּמְבָרְכִים שְׁמָךְ
כִּי הִזְכַּרְתָּה שְׁמוֹ בְּזִיכְרוֹן שְׁמָךְ
בִּשְׁכִינַת הוֹד נִירְאֵיתָה עוֹד
וּבֵירַכְתּוֹ לִמְאוֹד בְּלִי לִמְעוֹד
כִּי אַתָּה תְבָרֵךְ וְצַדִּיק יִתְבָּרֵךְ
בָּרוּךְ יי אֱלֹהֵי יִשְׂרָאֵל
כִּי בְשֵׁם יִשְׂרָאֵל תִּתְבָּרֵךְ בָּרוּךְ וְקָדוֹשׁ

(ה) אֱלֹהֵי עוֹלָם מִימוֹת עוֹלָם
לִימַּדְתָּה עֲנָוָוה לְבָאֵי עוֹלָם
בְּרְכַּת חֲתָנִים לִימַּדְתָּה
מִיצִיר וְעֶזְרוֹ
וּבִיקּוּר חוֹלִים מֵאַב מִילָה בְּגָוזְרוֹ
גַּם נִיחוּם אֲבֵילִים מֵאִישׁ תָּם הוֹדָעְתָּה
בְּעֵת בְּדֶרֶךְ פַּדָּן עָלָיו נוֹדַעְתָּה
דֶּרֶךְ כֹּל כְּהוּקְרָא בַדֶּרֶךְ לַמֵּינִיקָה
בְּשׂוֹרַת רִבְקָה בָּאָה כִּי נֶעְתָּקָה
הוּא לֹא שָׁלֵיו מִכְאֵיב כַּף יָרֵךְ

16 See Ps 5:13 (**R**), which is construed as applying to Jacob.

17 This poem expands on the traditions mentioned in note 1. God's actions in these stories—rejoicing with bride and groom, visiting the sick, consoling the bereaved—all speak of tremendous divine humility as a counterpoint to His honoring of His creatures.

18 I.e., Adam and Eve.

19 Abraham

20 Jacob

21 For the language of the final stich, see Gen 12:8 and Job 14:18 (**B1**). The language of traveling a path (lit. dislodged or moved') is here used for the ultimate journey: death.

22 That is, Jacob was still in the midst of his long, difficult trek home.

before he had quiet from [Deborah's] death upon the road
the nursemaid of "she who writhed in childbirth"[23]—
He began to tremble hearing of the death of she who gave him birth[24]
He cried out and was grieved, weeping [doubly much][25]
therefore that selfsame place was called "Another Weeping"[26]
To the living You appeared, to console him
and with the blessing for mourners You blessed him, on account of
his mother[27]
By the coinage of a new name You called him
he was called by the name You gave him and the name he earned[28]
"By `Jacob' you shall no longer be known
"though Jacob shall not be supplanted[29]
"You rule over the princes of God,[30] `Israel' shall you be called"[31]

Forever...

"Then God appeared..."[32]
(6) To the mourning father, wounded with grief[33]
at the time when he sat, sitting shiva
To let him know that He was watched over
[For His name is] "The Holy One of Israel," his savior[34]
To the one engraved upon the throne of Glory

---

23 Lacuna filled according to **B1**. "She who writhed in childbirth" refers to Rebecca.

24 While Jacob was mourning his mother's nursemaid, news of his own mother's death reached him. **R** footnotes but does not discuss *GenR* 81:5, "And Deborah, Rebecca's nurse, died, and she was buried beneath Beth-El under an oak; and the name of it was called *ʾAllon-Bachut* [a terebinth of weeping]" (Gen 35:8). Rabbi Samuel ben Naḥman said: This is Greek, in which *allon* means `another,' indicating that while he was mourning for Deborah, tidings reached him that his mother had died. Hence it is written, `And God appeared to Jacob again...and blessed him.' With what blessing did He bless him? Said Rabbi Aḥa in Rabbi Jonathan's name: With the mourners' blessing." Yannai assumes this meaning of the name in the next line. How did Rebecca's nurse end up in Jacob's company? **B1** cites *Midrash ha-Gadol* and Rashi (citing Moses ha-Darshan) on Gen 35:8, texts that teach that Rebecca had dispatched her nurse to summon Jacob home, but Deborah died on the return journey.

25 Lacuna filled according to **B1**, who bases his reconstruction on *GenR* 81:5.

26 Lit., "a grave of weeping," but see discussion below.

27 **B1** connects this line with *m. Ber.* 2:7 (and its *gemarra, b. Ber.* 16b). These texts discuss the procedures for mourning household slaves (such as Deborah would be considered), indicating that Jacob would recite the mourner's blessing for his mother, not for Deborah. (This is implicit in *GenR* 81:5, above, as well—God only teaches Jacob this blessing when he is mourning his mother, not Deborah.)

28 That is, Jacob retained two names: both Jacob (a name understood to be given by God)

וְטֶרֶם שָׁקַט מִמֵּיתָה עָלָיו בַּדֶּרֶךְ
ו.. ... מֵינֶקֶת הַמְּחוֹלֶלֶת
בָּא רוֹגֶז עַל מִיתַת תְּחוֹלֶלֶת
זָעַק וְנֶאֱבַל מש.. לִבְכּוֹת
לָכֵן לְאוֹתוֹ מָקוֹם נִיקְרָא אַלּוֹן בָּכוּת
חַי בְּכֵן נִרְאֵיתָה לוֹ לְנַחֲמוֹ
וּבִרְכַּת אֲבֵילִים בֵּרַכְתּוֹ עַל אִימּוֹ

טִיכּוּס שֵׁם חָדָשׁ אוֹתוֹ בְּקוֹרְאָךְ
נִקְרָא קְרוּאָךְ וּמְקוֹרָאָךְ
יַעֲקֹב לֹא ... תָּוּנְקֵב
וְגַם לֹא תְּוּעֲקַב
יָשַׂרְתָּה לְשָׂרֵי אֵל תִּיקָּרֵא יִשְׂרָאֵל

לעולם

וירא אלהים
(ו) אֶל אָב אָבֵיל עַל פִּישְׁעוֹ
בְּעֵת יָשַׁב לִשְׁמוֹר שְׁבוּעוֹ
בַּעֲבוּר לְיַדְּעוֹ כִּי הוּא מַשְׁעוֹ
... קְדוֹשׁ יִשְׂרָאֵל מוֹשִׁיעוֹ
אֶל גָּלוּם בְּכִסֵּא כָבוֹד

---

and Israel (a second divinely-given name Jacob earned for himself when he wrestled the angel). See *Tanḥ Shemot* 4. As **B2** notes, this renaming is also a sign of tremendous honor, and the word translated here as "called by" could also be more loosely rendered as `honored with.'

29 A pun on the name "Jacob," which indicates both the permanence of the original name as well as his unchanged chosen status.

30 This stich and the following pun on the etymology of "Israel" through a variety of roots: שרה, ישר, and שור. The language of the line as a whole recalls Hos 12:4–5 (cited by **R**). A less-bold but equally legitimate translation could be, "you prevailed over the princes of God" (i.e., the angels). Either way, the poet emphasizes Jacob's superiority to the angels.

31 See the note above on Jacob's dual name, which is considered distinct against Abraham and Sarah, who are truly renamed (see *GenR* 46:8).

32 This poem is unusual in that every stanza opens with the word אל ("to") in addition to the standard alphabetical acrostic. This addition supports the hypothesis that the incipit from the biblical text functioned as a refrain repeated at the head of every stanza.

33 Jacob, earlier "wounded" from wrestling with the angel of God, is here "wounded" by the news of his mother's death.

34 See Isa 43:3 (**R**) and 47:4 (**B1**), which provide the basis for the reconstruction. The meaning of the line is that "the Holy One of Israel" pays special attention to the feelings of Israel; when Israel/Jacob grieved, God came to comfort him.

in a place where there was no glory[35]
He sought [for God, that He grant][36] him some glory
and the glory of the glorious God He revealed
To the one who bred his flock by his staff[37]—
the Shepherd of Israel led him like a lamb
And He protected him from the people of scorn
and crowned him with the shield of good fortune
To the one who recalled the forgotten vow
for which his little lamb would be punished[38]—
His terrible trials He made him forget
while He let him know he wasn't forgotten
To the pure one, whose ways were straight[39]
who bore the burdens of his wanderings
His descendents, when they appear, are blessed[40]
the hosts of angels bless themselves by them[41]
To the one who stored up birthright and blessing
and was called "first-born son" and "father of blessing"[42]
When he went forth, he was blessed in full;
when he returned, his blessing was doubled[43]
To the one who was brought from Aram quadrupled;
his camps, he divided into four[44]
Wives and concubines numbering four
....

35 This probably refers to Laban's house, whose idols would have rendered it unfit for revelation (see *Tanḥ Vayetze* 10 [**B1**]). While in Laban's house, Jacob felt more cut off from God than while on the road home or in his homeland.

36 Lacuna filled according to **B1**.

37 See Gen 30, as well as *LevR* 31:4 (**B2**), which interprets Jacob's rod in light of the divine oath: "This signifies hat the Holy One, blessed be He, bound Himself (*asar*) by an oath that He wpuld cause His Presence to dwell under the rafters (*rehitin*) of Jacob...Rabbi Levi said: It is by reason of the merit of Jacob, of whom it is written, 'And he set the rods which he had peeled over against the flocks in the gutters (*barehatim*)' (Gen 30:38)."

38 The stich puns on the name Rachel (which means "lamb"). According to the Rabbis, Jacob was culpable for delaying fulfillment of the vow he made in Gen 28:20–22; the punishment for such delinquency is, according to *Tanḥ Vayishlaḥ* 8, the death of one's wife; see also *GenR* 81:1 (**R**). The trouble that comes upon Jacob in this *sidra* is the consequence of his own inactions. In Gen 35:19, Rachel dies in childbirth. Jacob, who builds the altar in vs. 14, is too late to escape punishment entirely, although his consolation comes from God Himself.

39 Ps 119:1 (**B1**).

בִּמְקוֹם אֲשֶׁר אֵין שָׁם כָּבוֹד
דָּרַשׁ ... לַחֲלוֹק לוֹ כָּבוֹד
וְנִגְלָה לוֹ כְּבוֹד אֵל הַכָּבוֹד
אֶל **הַ**מְּיַיחֵם בְּמַקְלוֹ צֹאן
רוֹעֵה יִשְׂרָאֵל נִיהֲגוֹ כַּצֹּאן
וּמִילְּטוֹ מֵאַנְשֵׁי לָצוֹן
וְעִיטְּרוֹ כַּצִּינָּה רָצוֹן
אֶל **זָ**כוּר נִדְרוֹ אֲשֶׁר נָשָׁה
וְכִיבְשָׁתוֹ לָכֵן נֶעֱנָשָׁה
חֶרְדַּת עֲמָלוֹ אִתּוֹ נִישָּׂא
וְהוֹדִיעוֹ כִּי לֹא נֻושָּׂא
אֶל **טָ**הוֹר וּתְמִים דְּרָכִים
אֲשֶׁר טָעַן טַרְחוּת דְּרָכִים
יְלָדָיו בְּהֵירָאוֹת בְּרוּכִים
מַלְאֲכֵי צְבָאוֹת בָּם מְבָרְכִים
אֶל **כּ**וֹמֵס בְּכוֹרָה וּבְרָכָה
וְנִקְרָא בֵּן בְּכוֹר וְאַב בְּרָכָה
לְעֵת יָצָא נִיכְלְלָה לוֹ בְּרָכָה
וְעֵת בָּא נִיכְפְּלָה לוֹ בְּרָכָה
אֶל **מ**וּבָא מֵאֲרַם מְרוּבָּע
וּבְמַחֲנוֹתָיו נִתְרַבַּע
נָשִׁים וּפִילַגְשִׁים אַרְבַּע

...

---

40 See Gen 35:11, in which God tells Jacob to "be fruitful and multiply." The stich could mean "appear" in the literal sense—when they are born—but more likely means "appear before God in worship (sacrifice or prayer)." In the act of blessing God, they are themselves blessed.

41 This line is difficult, but it seems to reference the idea that the angels bless God with the epithet "God of Israel" (i.e., the sons of Israel/Jacob). Thus Jacob/Israel (both in the sense of the patriarch and the community of Yannai's day) is the vehicle for the prayers and praises of the heavenly hosts.

42 For these epithets, see Exod 4:22 and Gen 28:14, as well as *Tanḥ Mikketz* 3. The term "father of blessings" is intended to convey Jacob's "archetypal" nature, with "father" used in the same sense as in "*binyan ʾav*" (a major halakhic category) or "*ʾav melakhah*" (major category of labor).

43 See Gen 28:13–14 and 35:11–12 as well as *GenR* 82:2 (**B1**).

44 Jacob returned from Laban's house with great material wealth—more than fourfold what he fled with—and also with a large family, due to his two wives and two concubines. In Gen 32, he divides his camp into four cohorts before meeting Esau, an attempt to conceal his wealth which also emphasizes it.

[To] ...
    ... He built up his house from her[45]
    Upon him He established [a world like stone[46]]
    his foot never hurt by stone[47]
To the one who was freed, who in purity walked[48]
    and whose wrenched hip He bound with perfect healing[49]
    The righteousness of his blessing to seal
    that not forever would his offspring be orphans
To the one who was called by the name "Jacob"
    but who would no longer be called "Jacob"
    ... in uprightness he was clever
    and by a name like His name he was called
To him who was whole in each and every way
    [with a multitude of][50] blessings completed
    [The power of] His name[51] mixed with his, faultless[52]
    and his name gone forth, famous[53]

And thus, "And ['Israel'] shall be your name..."[54]

(7) You are the God of   Israel
In You rejoices Jacob and delights   Israel
Great is Your name in   Israel
Your word is wholly good[55] about   Israel
You shall be as a father for   Israel
And the foundation stone of   Israel[56]
This one shall be called   Israel
Engraved are the tablets of   Israel
Before [You gave] the law to   Israel[57]

---

45 The language here recalls Gen 35:9–16 as well as Ruth 4:11. See *GenR* 71:2, which interprets Rachel's description as "barren (*ʿaqarah*) in the house" as "principle (*ʿiqarah*) of the house" (**B2**).

46 I.e., eternal. The lacuna is filled on the basis of *GenR* 75:11, in which David quotes Prov 10:25 to describe Jacob as a pillar and foundation of the world (**B2**).

47 Ps 91:12 (**R**).

48 Prov 10:9 and Ps 144:7 (**B1**); I read אל פצוי with **B1** in place of אל פונה, ("to one who turns"), the reading favored by **R**. The epithet "one who was freed" refers to Jacob's flight from Laban's oppressive household.

49 For the motif of Jacob's healing, see *GenR* 78:5 and 79:5 (**B2**).

50 Lacuna completed by **R**.

51 That is, the theophoric element "El" in Isra-*el*.

...

בֵּיתוֹ מִמֶּנָּה יִיבֶן
עָלָיו כּוֹנֵן ...
רַגְלוֹ לֹא נֶוֹגְפָה בָאָבֶן
אֶל פּוֹנֶה וְהוֹלֵךְ בַּתּוֹם
וְלִקְהִיַּתוֹ חָבַשׁ מְתוֹם
צִדְקַת בִּרְכָתוֹ לַחְתּוֹם
כִּי לָעַד לֹא פִּרְיוֹ יִתּוֹם
אֶל קָרוּאִי הָיָה בְּשֵׁם יַעֲקֹב
לְבַל יִיקָּרֵא עוֹד יַעֲקֹב
... ..ותו בְּמִישׁוֹר עָקוֹב
וְשֵׁם כִּשְׁמוֹ אִתּוֹ לִנְקוֹב
אֶל שָׁלֵם בַּכֹּל וּמְכוּלָּל
... בְּרָכוֹת נִיתְכַּלָּל
ת.. שְׁמוֹ נִיבְלַל וְנִיכְלַל
וּשְׁמוֹ יָצָא וְנִיתְמַלָּל

ובכן ... יהיה שמך

(ז) אַתָּה אֱלֹהֵי יִשְׂרָאֵל
בָּךְ יָגֵל יַעֲקֹב וְיִשְׂמַח יִשְׂרָאֵל
גָּדוֹל הוּא שְׁמָךְ בְּיִשְׂרָאֵל
דְּבָרָךְ אַךְ טוֹב עַל יִשְׂרָאֵל
הֱיוֹתָךְ לְאָב לְיִשְׂרָאֵל
וּמִשְׁתִיַּת אֶבֶן יִשְׂרָאֵל
זֶה יִקְרָא בְשֵׁם יִשְׂרָאֵל
חֲקוּקָה עֵידוּת לְיִשְׂרָאֵל
טֶרֶם ... חוֹק לְיִשְׂרָאֵל

52 "El" here is understood as a name of power (akin to its association with the divine harsh/strong Attribute of Justice). In *GenR* 82:3, God remarks that Jacob is the last person with whom He will join His name, thus making Jacob the last of the patriarchs. This recalls the language of the first blessing of the Amidah, in which God is invoked as the "God of Abraham, God of Isaac, God of Jacob." The lacuna in this line is filled in accordance with **B1**.

53 That is, the name "Israel" will become famous.

54 The name "Israel" constitutes a refrain.

55 Ps 23:6

56 Gen 49:24 (**R**).

57 Lacuna filled by **R**. **B1** cites Ps 105:10 in support; the implication of this stanza is that God intended to be known as "the God of Israel" even before Jacob's name change.

You are known as the God of Israel
For You are God in Israel
Therefore let us say, O Israel
Your kingship is as king of Israel[58]
Standing, though enthroned on the praise of Israel[59]
The saying, "Behold your gods, O Israel"[60]
Shall no longer be recalled in Israel
Record the number of the sons of Israel[61]
The hosts of the mortals of Israel[62]
Unswerving is your happiness, O Israel
First-fruit of the Holy One is Israel
Praise of Your majesty is upon Israel
O bless the house of Israel!

(8) For your blessing is in the name of Israel
and Your holiness is in the name of Jacob
And the Hosts above and below—
This one calls out the name of Jacob
And that one confirms the name of Israel;
and this one says, "Blessed is He"
And that one says, "Holy is He"
And He is blessed by them and sanctified by them,
as it is written: "And the one called..."

58 Isa 44:6 (**B1**).

59 When Israel prays, their prayers form a throne for God, but God—rather than being seated upon it—manifests in their midst. See *GenR* 48:7, in which it states: "Rabbi Samuel b. Rabbi Hiyya and R. Yudan in Rabbi Hanina's name said: Every time that Israel praises the Holy One, blessed be He, He causes His Shekhinah to rest upon them. What is the proof? 'Yet You are holy, O You who are enthroned upon the praises of Israel' (Ps 22:4). A fuller version

יִידַּעְתָּה אֱלֹהֵי יִשְׂרָאֵל
כִּי אַתָּה אֱלֹהִים בְּיִשְׂרָאֵל
לָכֵן יֹאמַר נָא יִשְׂרָאֵל
מַלְכוּתְךָ מֶלֶךְ יִשְׂרָאֵל
נִיצָּב יוֹשֵׁב תְּהִילּוֹת יִשְׂרָאֵל
סִיחַ אֵלֶּה אֱלֹהֶיךָ יִשְׂרָאֵל
עוֹד לֹא יִיזָּכֵר בְּיִשְׂרָאֵל
פְּקוֹד מִסְפַּר בְּנֵי יִשְׂרָאֵל
צְבָאוֹת מְתֵי יִשְׂרָאֵל
קוֹשֵׁט אַשְׁרֶיךָ יִשְׂרָאֵל
רֵאשִׁית קוֹדֶשׁ יִשְׂרָאֵל
שְׁבַח גַּאֲוָתְךָ עַל יִשְׂרָאֵל
תְּבָרֵךְ אֶת בֵּית יִשְׂרָאֵל

(ח) כִּי בִּרְכָתְךָ בְּשֵׁם יִשְׂרָאֵל
וּקְדוּשָּׁתְךָ בְּשֵׁם יַעֲקֹב
וְצִבְאוֹת מַעְלָה וּמַטָּה
זֶה יִקְרָא בְּשֵׁם יַעֲקֹב
וְזֶה יְכַנֶּה בְּשֵׁם יִשְׂרָאֵל
זֶה יֹאמַר בָּרוּךְ הוּא
וְזֶה יֹאמַר קָדוֹשׁ הוּא
וְהוּא מְבוֹרָךְ בָּם וְנִקְדָּשׁ בָּם
ככתוב וקרא זה אל זה וג׳

of this tradition is preserved in *SongR* 2:24 (**B1**). The verse that is the prooftext here is cited at the conclusion of Poem 3 of the *qedushta*, as part of the form's conventional structure.

60 The idolatrous phrase uttered in reference to the Golden Calf in Exod 32:4 (**R**), and again by Jeraboam in 1 Kgs 12:28.

61 Num 3:40 (**R**) and Hos 2:1 (**B2**).

62 Isa 41:14 (**B2**).

Commentary

With its themes of grief and consolation, humility and greatness, this piyyut strikes some of the same chords as the most famous mourner's prayer, the "orphan's" or "mourner's" kaddish (*kaddish yatom*, or, for many, simply "The Kaddish"), not only in terms of its mournful context and associations but also its redemptive and optimistic conclusions.

Key words in the opening units of this piyyut—"great" (*rabbah*), "blessed" (*mevorakh*), "name" (*shem*), and others—are particularly suggestive of a kaddish connection. Chronologically, textual evidence suggests that the mourner's kaddish, as it is known and used today, emerged at approximately Yannai's period or somewhat after, in the Palestinian Jewish context. Recitation of kaddish is associated with mourners in *PRE* 17, in the post-Talmudic tractates *Soferim* 19:2 (dated to perhaps 600 C.E.—roughly contemporary with Yannai) and *Semaḥot* 8, and in *Tana deVey Eliyahu Rabba* 120:20 and *Tana deVey Eliyahu Zuta* 23:17.[63] To be sure, the present poem does not actually allude to the mourner's kaddish; it may, however, reflect the gradual association of such language with mourning, or simply echo a more general understanding of themes associated with consoling the bereaved, both individually and collectively. Just as the mourner's kaddish contains no overt references to death but rather focuses on God's majesty and ultimate triumph, so too the consolation of Jacob focuses not on death, but on confidence deriving from God's presence, providence, and promise of redemption.

The resemblance between this piyyut and the kaddish prayer is strongest in the poem's opening unit, which emphasizes God's greatness. The "blessings" referenced throughout the piyyut refer more to the patriarch (who benefits from them) than to God (for whom they are merely praise), although the relationship between mortal and divine is ultimately reciprocal. Furthermore, the poem emphasizes God's humility, which paradoxically augments His majesty, while the kaddish offers mourners an undiluted doxology. However, even if the echoes are ultimately only contextual—the liturgical language of praise and intertwined with lamentation—the poem remains a stately evocation of the ultimate and

63 The kaddish itself, in some basic form, may date back to Tannaitic times or earlier; its development into different forms for use in different contexts, however, extended over a period of centuries. See J. Heinemann, *Prayer in the Talmud*, esp. 256–57 and 266–68; and I. Elbogen, *The Jewish Liturgy*, esp. 80–84.

essential human experiences of mourning and comforting, cast here in the divine image.

In Genesis 35, Jacob *needs* consolation. In this one biblical chapter, the patriarch suffers losses of increasing intensity: Deborah (a beloved servant), Rebecca (his mother), Isaac (his father), and Rachel (his favored wife) all die. Jacob's triumphal return transforms into a mournful procession led by the patriarch, now orphaned and widowed. How can he be comforted? Wealth did not protect him; cleverness could not shield him; not even God's favor could deflect this fate. The path of mortality is one all will walk, and the poet does not offer any pat, easy answers or cheap condolences. The individuality of grief stands at the center of the poem. Jacob's experience is that of an individual; Yannai relates to him not primarily as a symbol or an archetype, but as a person. In this piyyut, even God acts in very human ways, His behavior exemplifying what others should do.

Jacob may have felt alone, but he was not. In his grief, he was surrounded by children and comforted by God. Both divine assurance and the promise of new generations give Jacob, despite his grief, a respite of hope and reasons to continue his trek back to a now empty home. God, in particular, is emphatically "present" throughout the poem: active and intimately involved.

While the relationship between God and Jacob is unique even among the patriarchs, Jacob is also a highly representative figure, the eponymous ancestor of a people well acquainted with sorrow and loss. Thus when God comforts the singular individual Israel, He implicitly consoles all the children of Israel. We sense this, for example, when the poet writes: "Not forever would his offspring be orphans" (Poem Six, line 36). At the time when this line is spoken, Jacob is the orphan, not his sons; yet by the end of Gen 35, Joseph and Benjamin will also have lost their mother, and the grief of the orphan is something most children will eventually know. None of these characters will mourn alone, however; the consolation given to Jacob extends to all his heirs; grief in the Jewish tradition is never a solitary experience. The poet does not minimize the pain of bereavement—if anything, he intensifies and personalizes it, particularly in Poem Five. But he does not dwell exclusively on grief; like Jacob consoled by God, the poet turns his audience's attention to the future. Jacob may be tempted to look to the past, but God teaches him how to see what lies ahead. The poet does the same for his audience: he does not negate grief, but he dilutes it with hope. These are not framed as nationalistic losses and expectations, however, but deeply human, profoundly emotional experiences of grief mingled with optimism.

And how does Jacob emerge from these experiences? Changed. He is still "Jacob," our text texts us, but he is now *also* "Israel." He has struggled with God, and he has seen God. Struggle and belief, fatigue and faith become in this poem components of grief and recovery. The present may seem unbearable, but the future offers encouragement—both to the patriarch and the nation he fathers. This ending, then, echoes that of the Mourner's Kaddish: the One who makes peace in the heavens will cause peace to descend upon (all) Israel.

Qedushta for Genesis 37:1 בראשית לז:א

"Then Jacob settled" וישב יעקב

In this piyyut, we are introduced to the complex figure of Joseph, whose experiences echo his father's tale of exile, while they also anticipate the drama of Israel's history of loss and redemption. The *sidra* begins with Gen 37:1, a biblical coda that summarizes how, at long last, Jacob has returned to the land of Canaan. The *magen* emphasizes the permanence of this territorial gift—a reassuring prelude, perhaps, to the tale of displacement that follows; the *meḥayyeh* introduces the central motif of brotherly strife; the *meshallesh*—the most poignant unit—connects Joseph's sale into slavery with the exilic conditions of Yannai's own day. Throughout the surviving fragments of the piyyut, themes of generational continuity and conflict recur alongside images of loss of and restoration to the Promised Land. The flawed but evocative figure of Joseph and the tragic consequences of his sale into slavery at the hands of his own brothers becomes the dramatic lens through which we see the past, present, and future.

(1) You speak and it happens
Your word, once uttered, becomes deed[1]
The man who trusted in You,
he had faith in Your word, and it was fulfilled[2]

You entrusted [the land to the one saved] from fire[3]
You promised it to the one bound on an altar over fire[4]
You appointed it [to the one who wrestled with an angel of fire][5]
He encamped there, he and his whole house, all likened to fire[6]

The good one[7] You drenched with blessings;
The hairy one of hubris [will inherit Mt. Seir][8]
In due time, You restored him peacefully;
safely, untroubled, You settled him in.

As it is written: "Then Jacob settled in the land of his father's sojourning, the land of Canaan" (Gen 37:1)
And it says: "Saying, `To you I will give the land of Canaan as your allotted heritage. You were then few in number, a a handful, merely sojourning in it" (1 Chron 16:18–19)

In it[9] may You root us
and from it do not weed us out
[within it, may You shield][10] our shoots!
Blessed are You… Shield…

---

1 This *magen* focuses on God's reiterated promises of the Land to the patriarchs—a promise that remains effective even in exile. For the idea of divine word being automatically fact, **B1** cites *GenR* 44:22, where it states: "Rabbi Huna and Rabbi Dostai said in the name of Rabbi Samuel b. Naḥman: The mere speech of the Holy One, blessed be He, is equivalent to action, for it says, `Unto your seed I have given' (Gen 15:18)—not `I will give' but rather `have given'." God's promise to give something in the future is phrased in the past tense, indicating that it has, in essence, already come to pass.

2 See *GenR* 84:1, where Isaiah 57:13 ("But he who puts his trust in Me shall possess the land and shall inherit My holy mountain") is applied to Jacob.

3 That is, Abraham, who was saved from the ovens of Ur and who received the first promise of the land in Gen 12. Lacuna filled by **R**.

4 This refers to Isaac in Gen 22. Note that God said to Isaac: "Do not go down to Egypt… Sojourn in this land, and I will be with you, and will bless you; for to you, and to your seed, I will give all this territory…" (Gen 26:2–3). The key here is the promise of the land to Isaac's descendents, and also the language of *not* going down to Egypt (which Joseph will do involuntarily, and Jacob and his other sons will do voluntarily).

(א) אַתָּה אוֹמֵר וְעוֹשֶׂה
בֵּיאוּר מַאֲמָרָךְ מַעֲשֶׂה
גֶּבֶר אֲשֶׁר בָּךְ יֶחֱסֶה
דְּבָרָךְ בּוֹ יָקוּם וְיֵעָשֶׂה

הִבְטַחְתָּה ... אֵשׁ
וְהֶחֱסִיתָהּ לְנֶעֱקַד בְּמִזְבַּח אֵשׁ
זִימַנְתָּה ...
חָנָה בָּהּ הוּא וּבֵיתוֹ הַמָּשׁוּל בָּאֵשׁ

טוֹב בְּרָכוֹת הִשְׁאַבְתּוֹ
יָהִיר ...
כָּעֵת אֲשֶׁר בְּשָׁלוֹם הֵישַׁבְתּוֹ
לָבֶטַח בָּדָד הוֹשַׁבְתּוֹ

ככתוב וישב יעקב בארץ מגורי אביו בארץ כנען

ונאמר לאמר לך אתן ארץ כנען חבל נחלתכם בהיותכם מתי מספר כמעט וגרים בה

בָּהּ תִּיטָעֵינוּ
וּמֶנָּה בַּל תַּטְעֵינוּ
... נְטָעֵינוּ
ברוך... מגן...

---

5 A reference to Jacob's struggle with the angel by the Jabbok river (Gen. 32). Lacuna filled by **R**.

6 This entire line refers to Jacob; as **R** notes, the final stich alludes to Obad 18, "And the house of Jacob shall be fire, and the house of Joseph flame, and the house of Esau stubble, and they shall burn them and consume them; and none shall remain of the house of Esau; for the Lord has spoken it." Jacob, like his father and grandfather before him, received an unconditional promise of the Land.

7 That is, Jacob.

8 This stich refers to Esau. The completion is based on **B1**'s reconstruction, which relies on Gen 36:8 ("Thus lived Esau in Mount Seir; Esau is Edom") and Jos 24:4 ("I gave to Isaac Jacob and Esau; and I gave to Esau Mount Seir, to possess it. But Jacob and his children went down to Egypt"). Yannai puns here on the words "arrogant" (*yahir*), "mountain" (*har*), and "*Seir,*" which can also mean "hairy;" he thus evokes Esau's personality, territory, and dominent physical attributes.

9 I.e., the Land.

10 Lacuna filled according to **B1**.

(2) In the place in which brothers dwelled together[11]
there arose a quarrel among the brothers[12]
The good and pleasant one [sought their peace][13]
hoping [that this would] appease his brothers[14]
Their doing of such wicked deeds[15]
involving their own flock while they were the shepherds—
Too truthful, to his father he spun his tale,
the mild one skilled at seeming pleasing.[16]
How they have fallen, these sons of the matriarchs!
How they are humbled, these sons of handmaidens![17]
Rewarded with embraces from the handmaidens' sons[18]
He became mighty, and the birthright he bore.

As it is written: "These are the generations of Jacob: Joseph was seventeen years old, shepherding with his brothers the flock, and he was a lad with the sons of Bilhah and the sons of Zilpah, his father's wives, and Joseph brought report of their bad conduct to their father" (Gen 37:2)

---

11 This refers to the Land of Israel; the "brothers" are both Jacob and Esau as well as Joseph and his brothers. The quarrel between Joseph and his brothers reiterates, and amplifies, the quarrels of Jacob and Esau, and even Isaac and Ishmael.

12 These lines recall the general theme of sibling rivalry and strife that permeate Genesis. The poet may have a specific incident in mind or he may be alluding to a series of general incidents—**B1** adduces Reuben's inappropriate relations with Jacob's concubine in Gen 35, which *Tanḥ Vayeshev* 1 says lead to Reuben's disinheritance in favor of Joseph (see 1 Chron 5:1); Joseph's snitching on his brothers in Gen 37; or Joseph's hubristic dreams in the same chapter. Over the course of Gen 35–37, relations between Joseph and his brothers deteriorates until finally they sell Joseph into slavery. The sale of Joseph is the ultimate act of sibling violence among the patriarchal families; it exceeds any actual violence Esau did to Jacob (despite Esau's threat of fratricide).

13 "Good and pleasant one" refers to Joseph, based on the language of Prov 20:11 (**R**). "Seeking their peace (*shelomam*)" alludes to both their health and welfare, as well as actual peacefulness, and also reflects the norms of simple civility. See Gen 37:4, where we are told that the brothers could not say "*shalom*" to Joseph. Yannai's depiction here introduces an implied comparison—Joseph did say "*shalom*" to his brothers (as he is instructed to in Gen 37:14, cited by **B1**). See also Gen 43:27, where Joseph (now as Pharaoh's vizier) inquires after his family's welfare (*shalom*). Lacuna filled according to **B1**.

14 Joseph is depicted here as attempting to restore relations among his brothers; see *TanḥB Vayeshev* 7 and *MidGadol ad loc* (**B1**), which cite Ps 133:1 (alluded to in the first stich of this poem) as a prooftext. Lacuna filled according to **B1**.

15 Apparently Joseph's attempts to set things right fails, and his brothers continue to transgress. Yannai alludes first to the rumor reported by Joseph to Jacob that the other brothers ate limbs torn from living animals (also in *PsJ* to Gen 37:2 and *TanḥB Vayeshev* 6); in the next line, the report that the sons of Leah mocked the sons of Bilhah (Dan and Naftali) and Zilpah (Gad and Asher) as "sons of slaves" is intended. **B1** cites *GenR* 84:7,

(ב) **מָ**קוֹם אֲשֶׁר יָשְׁבוּ אַחִים
נִתַּן קְטָטָה בֵּין אַחִים
ס.. ... טוֹב וְנָעִים
עֲבוּר ... אֶחָיו נָחִים
פְּעוּלַּת מַעַלְלֵיהֶם הָרָעִים
צֹאן בְּעֵת הָיוּ רוֹעִים
קוֹשֶׁט לִפְנֵי אָב הִנְעִים
רַךְ הַנִּיכָּר בְּמַעֲלָלָיו כִּי נָעִים
שָׁפְלוּ בְּנֵי אִימָּהוֹת
שַׁחוּ בְּנֵי אֲמָהוֹת
תְּמוּר כִּי מָצוּי קֵן לְיַלְדוּת
תָּקַף וְנִיתְיַיחֵס רֹאשׁ לְתוֹלָדוֹת

ככתוב אלה תולדות יעקב יוסף בן שבע עשרה שנה היה רעה את אחיו בצאן והוא נער
את בני בלהה ואת בני זלפה נשי אביו ויבא יוסף את דבתם רעה אל אביהם

"Rabbi Meir said: [Joseph told Jacob]: Your children are to be suspected of [eating] limbs torn from the living animals. Rabbi Judah said: They insult the sons of the bondmaids [Bilhah and Zilpah] and call them slaves. Rabbi Simeon said: They cast their eyes on the daughters of the country." According to Rabbi Judah b. Simeon, we should note, these accusations were false.

16 The word קושט has multiple valences. It may mean "truth" but it can also have the meaning of "gossip" (or, more accurately, "snitching"; see *GenR* 98:18—cited by **B1**). Joseph may be truthful, but his actions are nonetheless inappropriate. The language draws on Prov 20:11 (**R**), cited as a prooftext in this unit.

17 The theology here is "measure for measure" but complicated by the issues of social status; the apostrophe is an unusual insertion of the poet-narrator's voice into the scene. For this specific language and interpretation, see **B1**, who cites Isa 2:9 and who notes that according to Rashi, "a person (*adam*) is humbled" refers to a regular person—in this case, the sons of the handmaidens—while "a man (*ish*) is brought low" refers to a man of importance, here the sons of Leah and, through his own sins, Joseph as well. See also *Tanḥ Ki Tissa* 4.

18 This translation follows the emendation supplied by **B1** (מנשקן לילדות). The letters are clear but rejected by **R**, Zulay, and **B1** as garbled. He relies on a tradition preserved in *MidGadol Bereshit* ad. loc., which understands the phrase "[Joseph] was a lad with the sons of Bilhah and the sons of Zilpah" as, "the sons of the handmaidens were kissing Joseph and hugging him." It appears that this affectionate association between Joseph and the sons of the handmaids (who suffered at the hands of the sons of Leah) was considered praiseworthy and was one reason that Joseph became "head of his generations"—translated here in the image of "bearing the birthright." See 1 Chron 5:1, which states: "Now the sons of Reuben the firstborn of Israel (for he was the firstborn; but, since he defiled his father's bed, his birthright was given to the sons of Joseph the son of Israel, so that the genealogy is not to be considered after the birthright)." See also *Tanḥ Vayeshev* 1 and its interpretation of Gen 37:2.

And it says: "You sit and speak against your brother, [you slander] your own mother's son" (Ps 50:20)
And it says: "Put crookedness of speech away from you, and keep deviousness of utterance far from you" (Prov 4:24)
And it says: "A child may be dissembling in his behavior even though his actions are blameless and proper" (Prov 20:11)
And it says: "Come and behold the deeds of the Lord, how He has wrought desolation on the earth" (Ps 46:9)
And it says: "O Shepherd of Israel, give ear! O Leader of the flock of Joseph, You who are enthroned on the cherubim, shine forth!" (Ps 80:2)

Shine forth from the heights
over us, in mercy
and let fall the dew for waking the deep sleepers!
Blessed are You… Who resurrects…

(3) A restful dwelling place as yet we have not found
in all the lands to which we have since gone forth[19]
We resemble the pure one who dwelled in many dwellings[20]
the enemies' eye peers cruelly upon our once-beautiful dwellings[21]
The tribes of the offspring of the righteous shall never settle down
until they undo the payment of silver for which they sold the righteous[22]

---

19 See *ExodR* 26:1, where the interpretation of the Four Kingdoms motif recalls the language here (**B2**).

20 The peripatetic patriarch, Jacob, whom his descendents resemble. From the day of Joseph's supposed death, Jacob knew no peace, and the act of selling Joseph doomed the descendents of Jacob to generations of slavery, either the generations of servitude in Egypt, or the exile that continues to the present day. As **B2** notes, Yannai may also have in mind here the tradition preserved in *GenR* 84:3, in which Jacob—because he was not content with his life in this world nor with what was stored up for him in the World-to-Come—was continually afflicted (by Esau, Laban, Dinah, and finally Joseph).

21 Jerusalem and the Temple Mount. The line contains an implied pun: "the prisons of our (current) dwellings"

22 The "righteous" in the first stich refers to Jacob; in the second, Joseph. The language and imagery here depend upon Deut 24:7 ("If a person is found to have kidnapped a fellow Israelite, enslaving him or selling him, that kidnapper shall die") and Amos 2:6 ("they sold for silver he whose cause was just"). The motif of the ongoing punishment earned by the sons of Jacob on account of Joseph's sale was popular in antiquity and the Middle Ages—a tradition placing it on a par with the the sin of the Golden Calf. Indeed, greed is equated with idolatry, incest, and murder in *j. Yoma* 4b and is there blamed for the destruction of the Temple. According to Jubilees 34:18, Joseph was sold into slavery on Yom Kippur, and

ונאמר תשב באחיך תדבר בבן אמך תתן דפי

ונאמר הסר ממך עקשות פה ולזות שפתים הרחק ממך

ונאמר גם במעלליו יתנכר נער אם זך ואם ישר פעלו

ונאמר לכו חזו מפעלות יי אשר שם שמות בארץ

ונאמר רעה ישראל האזינה נהג כצאן יוסף יושב הכרובים הופיעה

הוֹפִיעָה מִמְּרוֹמִים
עָלֵינוּ בְּרַחֲמִים
וְהַטְלִיל תְּחִיַּית רְדוּמִים
ברוך... מחיה...

(ג) יְשִׁיבַת מָנוֹחַ אָז לֹא מָצָאנוּ
בְּכָל הָאֲרָצוֹת אֲשֶׁר יָצָאנוּ
נִידְמִינוּ לְאִישׁ תָּם אֲשֶׁר יָשַׁב בְּמוֹשְׁבוֹתָיו
וַתְּעוֹלֵל עַיִן בְּנוֹאֵי יְשִׁיבוֹתֵינוּ
יְשִׁיבָה אֵין לְשִׁבְטֵי זֶרַע צַדִּיק
עַד יִפְרְעוּ כֶּסֶף אֲשֶׁר מָכְרוּ צַדִּיק

---

hence that became and remains the Day of Atonement. The ten days of repentance may be linked to the ten brothers who sinned. Also, the fact that it was ten brothers may account for the fact that it was ten Sages who were martyred in Jewish legends linking the Hadrianic persecutions to the story of Joseph's sale. In *Midrash Eleh Ezkarah* (dated to the Geonic period, with several versions published in Jellinek's *Batei Midrashot*), we find a lengthy discourse based on the Joseph story. This midrash depicts the Roman emperor as filling his palace with shoes, then asking the ten great Sages to judge the case of a kidnapper who has sold his brother for a pair of sandals. They condemn the hypothetical perpetrator, and in doing so, condemn themselves, for they must bear the punishment their ancestors escaped. Contrary to the Talmudic versions of this martyrology (*b. AZ* 17b-18a), in which all ten Sages are executed in accord with a single decree, here all ten Sages are executed in the same hour. This theme proved fruitful for several *payyetanim*; in addition to the poetic version of *Eleh Ezkarah* recited on Yom Kippur mornings (written by a poet probably roughly contemporary with Yannai), attention should be drawn to the piyyutim of Pinḥas ha-Kohen (7th century, Tiberias), who wrote, "*Aḥ be-naʿalayin mekhartem* (You sold a brother for the price of shoes)" and Meir bar Yeḥiel (13th century, Rhineland), author of "*Arzei Levanon* (The Cedars of Lebanon)." Additional sources pertinent to this motif include: *TargPsJ* to Gen 37:28; *Tanḥ Noaḥ* 5 and *Vayeshev* 2; *PRE* 38; and the *Testament of Zebulun* 3:2, and others.

Oh, let them return and be restored no longer blown here and there
in peaceful habitations may they dwell, securely settled.

As it is written: "Then My people shall dwell in peaceful habitations, in secure dwellings, in untroubled places of rest" (Isa 32:18)
And it says: "And they shall dwell upon their land" (Ezek 28:25)
And You are holy, enthroned upon the prayers of Israel… Please, God…

יָבוֹאוּ וְיָשׁוּבוּ וְעוֹד לֹא יֻונְשָׁבוּ
כִּי בִנְוֵה שָׁלוֹם יֵשְׁבוּ וְיִתְיַשָּׁבוּ

ככתוב וישב עמי בנוה שלום ובמשכנות מבטחים ובמנוחת שאננות

ונאמר וישבו על אדמתם
ואתה קדוש יושב תהלות ישראל אל נא

Commentary

As in a number of the *qedushta'ot* earlier in the Genesis cycle, Yannai's focus here is upon land: its acquisition, its loss, and its eventual restoration.[23] From the opening lines of the piyyut, Yannai sets up a tension between the divine promise of the Land and the flawed, complex human actions that will result in its loss. The extant fragment of the poem offers a clear historical narrative: the Land is won, the Land is lost, the Land awaits Israel's redemption. The opening of the poem expresses confidence in God's promises to and the righteousness of the patriarchs. God has pledged the Land to Abraham, Isaac, and Jacob, each of whom endured a trial of fire and faith to merit this reward. In this unit, the ancestors are idealized and recipients of bounty; even Esau, briefly mentioned, receives his patrimony of Mount Seir.[24] For a brief moment, there is a territory for every party, and each party dwells safely upon its portion. This idyll is interrupted by the fractious quarrelling of Jacob's eleven sons: the sons of Leah mock the sons of the handmaids, Reuben loses his birthright through sexual impropriety, and Joseph shows himself a tattletale, earning the enmity of them all. In retribution—or just comeuppance—the brothers sell Joseph into slavery, and unwittingly also sell off their rights to the Land. God gave, but God has taken away, and while the promises remain, the poet's own state of exile is here blamed not on the wickedness of Esau, but on the violence perpetrated by many brothers upon one. The Land, settled and secure at the beginning of the poem, reverts to being merely an unfulfilled divine promise by the conclusion of the fragment.

At the heart of this ongoing tragedy lies the conflict among brothers. There are echoes of the previous generation's quarrel between Jacob and Esau, but Yannai's focus—reflecting the content of the *sidra*—is on the characters of Joseph and Jacob's other sons. Yannai draws Joseph, much like his father Jacob, as a thoroughly ambiguous character. Joseph attempts to make peace among his quarrelling brothers, and defends the sons of the handmaids from the snobbish pretensions of Leah's sons—both positive actions. At the same time, he brings a negative, if truthful, report of his brother's actions to their father, thus sowing the seeds of his own dramatic

23 See discussion of this theme in Chapter Four.

24 See Yannai's *qedushta* for Deut 2:2 (which appears in translation in my article, "You have skirted this hill") for more on God's fidelity to Esau's territorial gift.

downfall and, ultimately, the exile of all their descendents. Joseph's actions beget a cycle of violence and no one is wholly innocent or completely blameworthy: Jacob is passive and obtuse, the brothers are jealous and vindictive, Joseph vain and spoiled. Nevertheless, Joseph is still called "good," "pleasant," "mild," and "righteous," and by the end of the second poem, he has made peace with the sons of Bilhah and Zilpah, and acquired the birthright as well. The life of Joseph, like that of his father, becomes a metaphor for the experience of the Jewish people: he is blessed but prone to error; he acquires a birthright but must endure servitude.

The final surviving stanza of the poem, the *meshallesh*, focuses on the aftermath of the events of Genesis 37, as the poet shifts to the present tense and a communal voice. He yearns for an end of the cycle of violence and exile begun in the time of Joseph and laments the heritage of loss and injustice that Jacob's sons left to their heirs. Tapping into a potent and peculiar aggadic motif, the landlessness that has plagued the Jews on multiple occasions is here blamed on a familial tragedy: the sale of Joseph for silver, his exchange for a pair of shoes. The sentence is still being served and the children of these ancestral figures continue to suffer. At the same time, the promise that opened the piyyut remains intact: God has promised the Land to the children of Jacob, and God's word is true. In the future, Yannai assures, the tranquility and ease with which the poem opened will be restored, but this time, for good.

Qedushta for Genesis 38:1 בראשית לח:א

ויהי בעת ההיא וירד יהודה
"And it came to pass at that time that Judah went down"

In this poem, Yannai develops and expands the character of Judah. Judah, as Yannai depicts him, is, much like his father Jacob: a complex, even ambiguous, character. On the one hand, Judah bears responsibility for the sale of Joseph into slavery and the life-threatening predicament of Tamar. On the other hand, Judah recognizes Tamar's merit (at the risk of self-humiliation), and his decision to recognize her righteousness ultimately earns him the reward of founding the Davidic line, making him the ancestor of the messianic Redeemer. In this piyyut, we see Judah mature. He displays a willingness to sacrifice himself for the sake of justice—a value we will see him display again when, as leader of his brothers, he confronts Pharaoh's vizier (the disguised Joseph) in Egypt (Gen 44). In the course of this poem, Judah acquires, loses, and regains status and leadership among his brothers, and Yannai transforms the story of his individual self-redemption into an allegory for Judah's descendents, the Jews.

(5) The man, Judah, would begin a *mitzvah* but not complete it
He was one who spoke then turned and changed[1]
When his brothers sought to murder and spill blood (he asked:)
"How do we profit from his blood? Let us sell him for money"[2]
Likewise, the prince of Judah began to make his descent
before the descent Joseph was forced to make
Diminished was "the worthy one of Jacob"[3] at that moment
and it was heard in his house…
… the one who sells[4] and the one who was sold[5]
the descent of the sold one was in fact his ascent
The one was king but [from kingship he fell][6]
[While the other was] into captivity brought down but he ascended the throne[7]
The one was snarled in the snare of his own son's wife
while the other fled from his master's wife's clutches[8]
An exchange: the one who said to his father, "Examine this!"
likewise hearkened unto "Examine this!"[9]
[The Good One's hand] is open to each who repents[10]
He accepted his repentance at the time when he sat in judgment
Because he said she was right,[11] right he also was[12]

---

1 The restorations supplied by the Maʾagarim Historical Dictionary also appear in Shalom Spiegel's *Fathers of Piyyut* (60), which includes additional text used to fill lacunae here. The opening lines praise Judah for his role in saving Joseph's life, as he argued that Joseph should be sold rather than murdered. But they also criticize him for his failure to save Joseph from slavery. See *GenR* 85:3 and *TanḥB Vayeshev* 8, which point out that Judah did only half of a good deed. Realizing that there was no benefit in Joseph's death, he should have led him back to their father's house rather than selling him into slavery in search of a profit. The theology of this opening unit is "measure for measure." The series of verbs appear to be epithets characterizing Judah in general (at least initially) rather than for his specific actions.

2 The first half of Judah's question is meritorious; the second half costs him the merit he just gained. Judah's question comes from Ps 30:10 and is used by Jacob to dissuade Esau from attacking him in the *qedushta* for Gen 32:4 (Poem Six, line 10).

3 The phrase, from Isa 17:4, refers specifically to Judah, whose status and stature have been diminished by his role in the sale of Joseph (**B1**); by extension, however, Judah's actions diminished the honor of Jacob's entire household, as well. All later generations, according to one line of midrashic tradition, continue to pay the price for the sin which Judah did not prevent (see *qedushta* for Gen 37).

4 Judah

5 Joseph

(ה) **א**ִישׁ יְהוּדָה הֵחֵיל בַּמִּצְוָה וְלֹא גְמָרָהּ
אֲמָרָהּ וְחָזַר וְהֵמִירָהּ
בְּבַקְּשָׁם אַחִים לַהֲרֹג אָח וְלִשְׁפּוֹךְ דָּמִים
מַה בֶּצַע בְּדָמוֹ נִימְכְּרֶנּוּ בְדָמִים
גַּם לְנִין יְהוּדָה רֵידָה אֲשֶׁר יָרַד
קָדְמָה לַיְּרִידָה אֲשֶׁר יוֹסֵף הוּרַד
דַּל כְּבוֹד יַעֲקֹב בָּעֵת הַהִיא
וְנִשְׁמַע בְּבֵיתוֹ ב.. ...
... מוֹכֵר וּמָכוּר
עֲלִיָּיא הָיְתָה יְרִידַת מָכוּר
וְזֶה הָיָה מֶלֶךְ ו.. ...
... ..שָׁבוּי וְהוּרַד וְעָלָה לִמְלוּכָה

זֶה נוֹקֵשׁ בִּמְצוּדַת אֵשֶׁת נִינַיו
וְזֶה בָּרַח ... אֲדֹנָיו
חֵילֶף אֲשֶׁר פָּץ לָאָב הַכֶּר נָא
גַּם הוּא הִקְשִׁיב מִזֶּה הַכֶּר נָא
... פְּתוּחָה לְכָל שָׁב
שָׁעָה תְשׁוּבָתוֹ עֵת בַּדִּין יָשָׁב
יַעַן פָּץ צְדָקָה צָדַק גַּם הוּא

6 That is, Judah, who is contrasted with Joseph in the following stich. See *TanḥB Vayeshev* 12 (**R**). According to this midrashic tradition, Judah had been made king over the brothers, but Jacob's refusal to be comforted over the loss of Joseph led to Judah's removal from leadership—hence his descent from authority and kingship. Judah's sovereignty over his brothers is also mentioned in *GenR* 85:2 (**R**).

7 Completion in this stanza according to **R**.

8 The (successful) entrapment of Judah by Tamar is contrasted with the (mostly unsuccessful) entrapment of Joseph by Potiphar's wife.

9 The identical phrase, "Examine this (*hakker na*)!" is used both in Gen 37:32, when Joseph's bloodied garment is shown to Jacob, and in Gen 38:25, when Judah is presented with his seal, cord, and staff—evidence of his paternity of Tamar's unborn child. See *GenR* 84:19 (**R**) and 85:11, as well as *TargN* and *TargPsJ* to Gen 38:25.

10 Ps 25:8; the imagery is of turning in repentance (**B1**, who filled this lacunae); the image of God's open hand comes from Ps 145:16.

11 Alluding to Judah's declaration of Tamar's innocence in Gen 38:26.

12 The root translated here as "right" (צדק) also has the connotation of "innocent" in the juridical context. This may imply that Judah's union with Tamar "atoned" for his previous marriage to a Canaanite woman (see *GenR* 85:1); his children by Tamar are of purer stock than his first three sons—indeed, Judah merits becoming the ancestor of the Messiah through her.

upright,[13] not ashamed to give praise, his brothers will praise him[14]
Please God... Forever...

"*And it came to pass at that time...*"
(6) The man who sold "the fruitful bough" to the Midianites[15]
came into his brothers' hands for judgment[16]
Judah was a traitor with the traders[17]
and he went down and intermarried with the Canaanites
A lord (among his brothers), until he saw what he had brought about[18]
(when,) "My way is hidden!" his father cried out[19]
He fretted and feared his (father's) fierce grieving
so he turned and strayed, towards Hirah's house[20]
When the lion then lifted up his legs[21]
a woman of valor there he married[22]
And chief justice of the court he there acted
and in judgment there he was exalted[23]

---

13 "*Temor,*" a pun on the name Tamar (who, though her actions may have seemed questionable, behaved valorously—she was also upright). A *temorah* is also an "exchange," which may hint at Judah's actions in Gen 44:33, when Judah offers to remain in Egypt as a slave in place of Benjamin, finally atoning for the sale of Joseph.

14 At issue here is the interpretation of Judah's admission of guilt in Gen 38:26, in which he risks shaming himself in order to spare Tamar the penalty for harlotry (dramatically depicted in *TargN* and *TargPsJ*). See *TanḥB Vayeshev* 11, which cites Prov 28:13 and discusses the power of confession. Note also the wording of *TargN* of Gen 38:25: "A voice came forth from heaven and said: They are both meritorious; from before the Lord the situation has come about." Also note *ExodR* 30:19, quoted in n. 22, below. Judah's brothers praise him in Gen 49:8; this may also allude to the messianic lineage created by the union of Judah and Tamar. See also *GenR* 85:1 (**B1**).

15 Yannai may have in mind the interpretation of "fruitful bough" (*porat yosef*; Gen 49:22) found in *GenR* 98:18, in which the phrase is interpreted, "A son who broke faith with his brothers [by bringing unfavorable reports] and a son whose brothers broke faith with him [by selling him into slavery]" (**B2**).

16 This line alludes to the aggadic tradition that Judah's brothers held him responsible for the sale of Joseph and their father's resultant grief; and as a result, they excommunicated him. The midrash depends on understanding the term "to descend" (which opens the *sidra*) as "to be excommunicated." See *Tanḥ Ki Tissa* 22, *ExodR* 42:3, and others (**B1**). This line also anticipates the motif of the trial, which is so central to the story of Judah and Tamar.

17 The term "Canaanite" in biblical Hebrew can refer either to the ethnic, non-Israelite population of the Land of Israel or the practice of trading so associated with them that "Canaanite" came to mean anyone who engaged in trade. The first reference uses the term in the context of "trading," when Judah sold Joseph to the caravaners in Gen 37:28 (this verse identifies the traders first as Midianites and then as Ishmaelites), while the second understands the term in its ethnic sense. According to *GenR* 85:4, Judah's wife was the daughter of a prominent and important Canaanite (**R**). His intermarriage is here treated

תְּמוּר לֹא בוֹשׁ לְהוֹדוֹת אֶחָיו יוֹדוּהוּ

אל נא לעולם

ויהי בעת ההיא

(ו) אִישׁ אֲשֶׁר מָכַר פּוֹרָת לְמִידְיָנִים

וְנוֹתַן בְּיַד אַחִים מְדָנִים

בָּגַד יְהוּדָה בְּכִינְעָנִים

וְרַד וְנִתְחַתֵּן לִכְנַעֲנִים

גְּבִיר בִּירְאוֹתוֹ מַה הָקְרָה

וְנִסְתְּרָה דַּרְכֵּי אָב קָרָא

דָּאַג וּמִגַּחַלְתּוֹ יָרָא

וַיֵּט וַיֵּשְׁטְ עַד חִירָה

הָאַרְיֵיה רַגְלָיו אָז נָשָׂא

וְאֵשֶׁת חַיִל שָׁם נָשָׂא

וְאַב בֵּית דִּין שָׁם נַעֲשָׂה

וּבַדִּין שָׁם הוּא נִיתְנַשָּׂא

---

with ambivalence: it is a sign of his moral descent, but as with the sale of Joseph, it could have been much worse.

18 That is, he saw the sorrow that the loss of Joseph caused Jacob.

19 According to *GenR* 91:10, this is the only "idle" phrase ever uttered by Jacob (**R**). According to *TanḥB Vayeshev* 8, however, Jacob refused to be comforted by his sons because he knew Joseph was alive and was, therefore, both unwilling to be comforted as a mourner (he was not in mourning) and aware of his other sons' treachery. This midrashic passage also introduces the motif that Jacob's grief led to Judah's dethronement.

20 The language of this stich recalls Prov 7:25, "Let not your heart turn aside to her [the adulteress'] ways, do not stray into her paths" (**B1**).

21 A fanciful image for a journey.

22 Although Judah's urge to intermarry was a sinful impulse, the Canaanite woman he wed is here depicted positively and is regarded by the aggadah as the daughter of a righteous man (see *GenR* 85:4 which calls her father Shua "a light of that place"). Similarly, while Tamar is not an Israelite, she merits becoming the mother of the messianic line (and acquires, in the aggadah, a Shemite lineage).

23 This seems to imply that Judah routinely sat as chief of the court, not only at Tamar's trial. The aggadah in *ExodR* 30:19, cited in **B1**, illustrates this point: "Why did God give the crown to Judah? Surely, he was not the only brave one of all his brothers; were not Simeon and Levi and the others valiant too? Rather, it was because he dealt justly with Tamar that he became the judge of the world [i.e., the king, who sits in judgment, and ancestor of the Messiah who will judge the world as its king]. It is like a judge who tried an orphan girl and found means to declare her innocent, so when the case of Tamar came before Judah, under sentence to be burnt, he acquitted her, finding a plea on her behalf. What happened there? Isaac and Jacob and all his brothers sat there trying to shield him [by arguing that though the cord and seal were Judah's, he might simply have lost them] but Judah recognized the circumstances and said, 'The thing is correct; she is more righteous than I' (Gen 38:26). For this, God made him a prince."

His "fruitful branch"[24] produced three boughs
but two of them were wastrels
They sinned and turned their backs
breaching all that had been fenced in[25]
He claimed for Er, his first-born, a bride
her name was Tamar and she was like "my sister, my bride"[26]
Yah saw his wickedness,[27] how completely it was done
and for the evil that he did, he was completely done in[28]
He waited for Onan because he was her levir[29]
and he was compelled to come to her as her levir[30]
He did not desire for her seed or fertility
he destroyed his seed to prevent her fertility[31]
From on high God beheld his wickedness[32]
and like "the smitten ones"[33] was his destruction
Well-known was his wickedness
so as He killed his brother, He killed him
Judah, a man of certainty,[34] spoke up
to his daughter-in-law…certainty:
"The Mighty One saw fit to kill two portions[35]
"Go back, and live in widowhood"
The lion understood [that this] was a sign
so he pitied his third son, the only remnant left
"Wait[36] until he grows, for he is just a lad,"[37]

---

24 As **B1** notes, this is a euphemism for Judah's genitals, the means of male fruitfulness (see, as a parallel, *GenR* 46:4 as well as the *qedushta* to Gen 17). The "boughs" are Judah's sons: Er, Onan, and Shelah.

25 Judah's two elder sons sinned through sexual deviance; according to Gen 38:9, Onan's sin was "spilling his seed" (an act called, after him, *onanism*); for this sin, God killed him. The Bible does not specify the nature of Er's sin, simply saying that he was "displeasing to the Lord," so God killed him. According to *GenR* 85:4, he "plowed on roofs," meaning that he engaged in anal rather than vaginal intercourse, which was the reason that Tamar never conceived from him.

26 The quotation is from Song 7:8 (**R**). According to *GenR* 85:10 and *TanḥB Vayeshev* 17, Tamar is the daughter of the Shem, the son of Noah, head of the first Torah academy and a priest. This explains why Judah called for her to be burned when she was accused of harlotry (see Lev 21:9).

27 That is, God saw Er's wickedness; see Gen 38:7.

28 The two stichs pun on the root כלה, "to be finished, done, complete."

29 "Levir," a term coming from Latin, refers to the custom of a childless widow marrying a brother of her husband or another close kinsman of her husband. (See Deut 25:5–10.)

זמוֹרָתוֹ נָתְנָה שְׁלוֹשָׁה סָרִיגִים
שְׁנַיִם מֵהֶם נַעֲשׂוּ סִיגִים
חַטָּאִים וְאָחוֹר נְסוֹגִים
פְּרוּצִים בְּכָל אֲשֶׁר נִיסּוֹגִים
טָעַן לְעֵר בְּכוֹרוֹ כַּלָּה
שְׁמָהּ תָּמָר בַּאֲחוֹתִי כַלָּה
יָהּ שָׂר רָעָתוֹ מְכַלָּה
וּבְרָעָה עָשׂ בּוֹ כָּלָה
כִּיתֵּר לְאוֹנָן עֲבוּר לְיַבְּמָהּ
וְנֶאֱנַס לָבוֹא וּלְיַבְּמָהּ
לֹא אָבָה לְזָורְעָהּ וּלְרַחֲמָהּ
וְהִשְׁחִית זַרְעוֹ מִלְּרַחֲמָהּ
מִמָּרוֹם הִשְׁקִיף אֵל בְּרִישְׁעָתוֹ
וְכִמְחוּיִים הָיְתָה הַשְׁחִיתוֹ
נוֹדְעָה כִּי רַבָּה רָעָתוֹ
וּכְמִיתַת אָח הֵימִית גַּם אוֹתוֹ
סָח יְהוּדָה אִישׁ אֱמוּנוֹת
לְכַלָּתוֹ במש.. ..אֲמָנוֹת
עוֹז עָשׂ לְאַבֵּד שְׁתֵּי מָנוֹת
שׁוּבִי וּשְׁבִי כְאַלְמָנוּת
פָּתַר לָבִיא כִּי סִימָן הוּא
וְחָס עַל שְׁלִישִׁי כִּי פָלִיט הוּא
צְרִי עַד יִגְדַּל כִּי נַעַר הוּא

---

30 A baraita in *b.Yev.* 54a (cited by **B2**) notes that even "unnatural" intercourse can consummate a levirate union.

31 Reading here with **B1**, who emends the root רחם (womb) to יחם (fertile); the Maʾagarim text, like **R**, would be translated: "He did not desire her to have seed in her womb // he destroyed his seed before it got to her womb" [or: his offspring rather than love her].

32 The language of this stich draws on Ps 102:20 (**B2**).

33 That is, the generation destroyed in the Flood; according to *PRE* 22 (**B1**), that generation also engaged in immoral sexual practices, including onanism.

34 The word rendered "certainty" is literally "truth, surety" (אמת). **B1** cites *GenR* 93:8 for the characterization of Judah as a man who spoke only of matters about which he was certain.

35 The two portions are Tamar's two husbands (and Judah's two sons); the phrase "Mighty One" (from Ps 59:10—**B1**) could also be rendered "Divine wrath" here. Maʾagarim corrects the word עוז ("strength") to עוון ("misdeed, sin"), which would result in a line translated as, "A sin did he commit, to destroy two portions." Presumably Judah, a man of truth, here speaks of his son's sin and not in accusation of God, although such a reading is possible.

36 From the root נ-צ-ר, "keep watch, protect.".

37 That is, the youngest son, Shelah.

for he thought, "Lest he also die!"
Tamar hallowed the Holy Name
for she hoped for holy seed
She harlequinned and played the holy harlot
and her holy path He prospered
She preserved her widowhood before the Lord
the Lord did not return her empty[38]
She longed to grow the garden of the Lord
for they are the seed the Lord has blessed

And thus: "Then Judah went down [from his brothers]..."
(7) His brothers were called "Jews" after the name of Judah
And thus: More powerful than his brothers was Judah[39]
Great is His name, which was made known in Judah
You said: "My scepter is Judah"[40]
You made Your sanctuary in Judah
Your regal crowds are the princes of Judah[41]
You have bequeathed kingship to Judah
Defeat and destroy the enemies of Judah
Remove and repair the sins of Judah
Let all be blessed in Judah
Just as Tamar bore children to Judah
Forever may you dwell, O Judah
Those who come forth from the "spring" of Judah[42]
Let them fill again the cities of Judah
Surely shall You restore kingship to Judah
Indeed, only to a lion can he be compared, O[43] Judah

---

38 See *GenR* 85:7 (cited by **R**), in which Tamar prays, "May it be Your will that I not leave this place [*Petaḥ Enayim*—"opening the eyes"—the site of her seduction of Judah] empty." In aggadic tradition, God often takes responsibility for the tawdry events of Gen 38; see *GenR* 85:12, *TanḥB Vayeshev* 17, *TargN* and *TargPsJ* to Gen 38:25.

39 On Judah's merit relative to his brothers, due to his willingness to risk public shame on behalf of Tamar, note *b. Sota* 10b, which states: "`And Judah acknowledged them, and said: She is more righteous than I' (Gen 38: 26). That is what Rabbi Ḥanin b. Bizna said in the name of Rabbi Simeon the Pious: Joseph who sanctified the heavenly Name in private (by showing restraint during the episode with Potiphar's wife) merited that one letter should be added to him from the Name of the Holy One, blessed be He, as it is written: `He appointed it in Joseph for a testimony' (Ps 81:6, in which Joseph is spelled with the addition

כִּי אָמַר פֶּן יָמוּת גַּם הוּא
קִידְּשָׁה שֵׁם תָּמָר הַקְּדוֹשָׁה
אֲשֶׁר כָּמְהָא לְזֶרַע קְדֻושָּׁה
רִימַּת וְעָשְׂתָה קִידֵּשָׁה
וְהִצְלִיחַ דַּרְכָּהּ קְדוֹשָׁהּ
שִׁימְּרָה אַלְמְנוּתָהּ פְּנֵי יְיָ
וְרֵיקָם לֹא הֱשִׁיבָהּ יְיָ
תַּאֲוָוה לְהַגְזִיעַ בְּעַם יְיָ
כִּי הֵם זֶרַע בֵּירַךְ יְיָ

ובכן וירד יהודה

(ז) **א**ֶחָיו נִקְרְאוּ יְהוּדִים לְשֵׁם — יְהוּדָה
בְּכֵן בְּאֶחָיו גָּבַר — יְהוּדָה
גּוֹדֶל שִׁמְךָ נוֹדַע — בִּיהוּדָה
דִּיבַּרְתָּה מְחוֹקְקִי — יְהוּדָה
הָיְיתָה לְקָדְשָׁךְ — יְהוּדָה
וְרִיגְמָתָךְ שָׂרֵי — יְהוּדָה
זָבַדְתָּה מְלוּכָה — לִיהוּדָה
חָלוֹשׁ וְקַטֵּל צָרֵי — יְהוּדָה
טְמוֹן וּמְחֵא חַטַּאת — יְהוּדָה
יְבוֹרְכוּ הַכֹּל — בִּיהוּדָה
כְּמוֹ יָלְדָה תָּמָר — לִיהוּדָה
לְעוֹלָם תֵּשֵׁב — יְהוּדָה
מוּצָאֵי מִמְּתֵי — יְהוּדָה
נָא יְמַלְּאוּ עָרֵי — יְהוּדָה
סוֹב תִּסּוֹב מְלוּכָה — לִיהוּדָה
עֲבוּר כִּי כְּאַרְיֵה נִמְשַׁל — יְהוּדָה

---

of the letter *heh*). Judah, however, who sanctified the heavenly Name in public (at Tamar's trial) merited that the whole of his name should be called after the Name of the Holy One, blessed be He." – The importance of this passage applies to the previous *qedushta*, as well, in that it helps explain why the King Messiah comes from Judah's line, and only the secondary messiah comes from Joseph's lineage.

40 **R** adduces Ps 60:9; God's kingship is enacted through the line of Judah (the Messianic line).

41 Ps 68:28; רגמה has regal valences of action ("command") or dress (royal purple).

42 **B1** connects with Isa 48:1; "spring" is a euphemism for Judah's male organ. By extension, it refers to all of Judah's offspring—i.e., the Jews.

43 Just as the lion is the king of beasts, the heir of Judah will be the King Messiah.

Keep watch, and they will rejoice in You, these sons of Judah
He commanded…like Judah
Judah
It is hinted: " And he went up first"[44]—meaning Judah
Set… [Judah]
… house of Judah

(8) For, under the name of "Judah" you became united[45]
… your memory, and bowing in thanks
As it is written: "The one called out…"

44 Judg 1:1–2 (**R**); see the interpretation of these verses in *Tanḥ Bemidar* 14 (**B1**), in which it is taught that just as Judah was first to go up in battle at the time of the conquest, Judah will also be the first to receive messianic tidings.

45 The descendents of all the tribes are called "Jews" in honor of Judah, who unified God's name. **B1** cites *GenR* 98:6 ("a man does not say `I am a Reubenite' or `I am a

פְּקוֹד וְיִשְׂמְחוּ בָךְ בְּנֵי	יְהוּדָה
צַוֵּה צ..	כִיהוּדָה
...	יְהוּדָה
רְמוֹז וְיַעַל בַּתְּחִילָּה	יְהוּדָה
שִׁיתָה כתח..	...
... בֵּית	יְהוּדָה

(ח) כִּי בְשֵׁם יְהוּדָה נִיתְיַיחַדְתָּה ...
..חד אֶת זִיכְרָךְ וּמוֹדִים בְּהוֹדוֹת ...
ככתוב וקרא

Simeonite' but 'I am a *Yehudi* [Judahite, i.e., Jew]'"), and also *EstR* 6:2 and *TanḥB Yitro* 5. This teaching is based on a subtle pun between the letters *heh* (as in the name Judah) and *ḥet* (as in the word "unify"). Judah—and by extension, Jews—unify God's name when they assert God's oneness (as in the Shema, which may have been included in the recitation of the Qedushah in Yannai's time).

Commentary

Just as Jacob became Israel—a single ancestor giving his name to a nation—so, too, is Judah (*Yehudah*) the father of the Jews (*Yehudim*). When characters have such dual identities and eponymous roles, it is particularly important to consider how the poet depicts them because they are of historical and contemporary importance. As we have seen, Yannai skillfully uses poetic rhetoric to collapse the identities of biblical characters into their latter day heirs. Skimming the biblical stories about these figures may lead the casual reader to focus on the "problems" of Jacob and Judah, particularly their deceitfulness and apparent callousness towards members of their own families. Conversely, if one were to mine the aggadah selectively, one could easily construct entirely valorized character sketches of them. And, indeed, we might suppose that such positive interpretations would be the ones taught in the ancient synagogue, both because of the "positive" nature of the Sabbath and the importance of ancestral merit (*zekhut ʾavot*). Yannai, however, was apparently not particularly interested in protecting the reputations of the ancestors. Instead, he acknowledged and explored their moral complexities. Like their descendants, these are characters that seriously sin before they redeem themselves.

In a midrashic text, different interpretations of a character can (and, to an extent, must) be understood as part of the editorial process that led to the texts' composition. The *midrashim* preserved for us are written texts, the works of an editor who wove together multiple traditions of exegesis. The complexity of the *midrashim* is often the result of discrete traditions being juxtaposed in the process of compiling a larger text. Ambiguity in the characterization of Judah in the *midrashim* often reflects the boldness or openness of the editor, not necessarily of the individual exegetes. In the piyyutim, however, we have the work of a single author. Any ambivalence towards Judah, then, is in some fashion Yannai's own and not the result of later re-contextualization or anthologization.

It is impossible, of course, to know Yannai's reasons for depicting Jacob and Judah (among others) in complex rather than simple fashions. Genre itself offers a clue: poetry is not a form that enables the intricate exegesis often needed for highly valorized readings of these figures but is, instead, a form that thrives on ambiguity and resonance. The rhetoric of poetry, with its emphasis on pun and juxtaposition, encourages multivalent readings and paradox. However, because of the clear similarities between midrash and piyyut, it would still seem feasible for the poet to dwell on the positive. Why might Yannai have nonetheless chosen to complicate things for his audience?

The tension between good storytelling and pastoral homiletics may provide a partial explanation. Fragmentary though the poem is, it moves from the narrative of the biblical story in Poems Five and Six to a national allegory in the *rahit*, and along the way it changes from critique to praise. Judah, as an individual, sins and suffers; he has positive instincts but consistently muddles them with incomplete or inept actions. He is shamed, he sulks, he is excommunicated, his sons are louts, and his treatment of Tamar, while sympathetic, remains questionable. Yet, confronted with his own embarrassing behavior, he could have acted the coward. At the key moment at Tamar's trial, however, he behaves publicly with courage, accepting the blame both for Tamar's lack of a husband and her awkward pregnancy. For this act, he is rewarded, regaining both his pride and his place of kingship. Yannai finds in Judah's story a tale of atonement—one that continues to be developed further when Judah reunites with Joseph. Judah is not whitewashed. On the contrary, he undergoes a very Jewish—and very human—process of transgression and restoration.

This process, in which sin is recognized, confronted, and if possible atoned for, has meaning at the national-allegorical level, as well. But when the poet turns his attention to his community, he softens his critique, emphasizing redemption rather than critique. In Poem Seven (the *rahit*), Yannai shifts from understanding Judah as a character to seeing him as a symbol of the Jews. In some lines, Yannai clearly has the individual character in mind. In others, he blurs Judah's identity into the corporate identity of his descendents. On one level, the imagery in this final extant poem of this *qedushta* is messianic, as the poet draws upon the fact that Judah and Tamar are the ancestors of the Davidic Messiah. The very name "Judah" moves from past tense to future, as the restoration of the royal house of Judah is anticipated. As the poem moves from story to allegory, the poet becomes increasingly positive. He does not draw parallels between Judah's sinfulness and that of his contemporaries, nor does he call for his community to engage in similar acts of repentance. Instead, Yannai tempers his critique of the ancestor with consolation and encouragement of his own community.

What do we learn from these nuances of presentation? Perhaps due to the structure and liturgical context of his poetry, Yannai becomes more positive as he approaches the conclusion. Excessive critique amplifies the biblical narrative but, in the allegory, would impugn his audience, which Yannai does not seem eager to do, unless the liturgy itself demands it (e.g., the Sabbaths of Rebuke prior to Tisha b'Av—but note the conclusion of the *qedushta* for Gen 48:1 where Judah's story again prompts serious, self-critical reflection). In terms of communal address, Yannai is a poet of gentle rebuke and insistent consolation. Judah's story is sordid, albeit redemptive, and retold with entertaining flair; the *qedushah*, however, is heavenly and pure, and in the radical present tense: to be participated in rather than merely observed or recounted. The poet ends with hope—he spins a tale that engages but also teaches. The poet *may* chastise, but he *must* inspire. Out of this delicate balance, Judah and the other biblical characters emerge as round characters. They are not necessarily figures Yannai's audience could (or would want to) "relate to," but their examples are nonetheless instructive: Who in Yannai's community sinned as seriously as Judah, and who has experienced such redemption? At the same time, certain characteristics—in Judah's case, bravery, exemplified by the frequent comparisons to a lion—are emphasized, and this emphasis could well be pedagogical. Yannai does not exaggerate the lesson of Judah's life, but he does not conceal it. He presents it with drama, memorably.

Embedded in the drama of Judah's life are his misadventures with women. Contrary to the expectations one may have, the two women in this story—Judah's wife (Bat Shua) and Tamar—are positive figures, for all that they are gentiles. Judah's marriage was contracted with the intent to sin, or at least a disinterest in behaving correctly; nevertheless, perhaps through providence, the marriage works out well, and marks a transition to a more successful period in Judah's life. Bat Shua is a "woman of valor" (Poem Six, line 10), and Judah—like the husband in Prov 31—is able to sit at the city gates (the place where courts were held) because of her merits. Similarly, Tamar plays the harlot, but not for her own gratification. She acts out of her desire to become a mother of Jews (Poem Six, lines 43–44). She resorts to tricking a trickster, but for the sake of Heaven. These events, experienced by these characters, underscore the sense of a divine plan being at work. God's will *will* be done.

A divine plan does not mean predestination, however. For all that Yannai promises his audiences a happy ending, the stories of Judah and the other characters also affirm the theology of "measure for measure." Judah was the "king" of his brothers before they sold Joseph into slavery; the drama in Judah's life derives from his difficult path towards regaining his regal status (a status that the Messiah, emerging from Judah's line, will restore and exceed). A theology of "poetic justice" is not only aesthetically pleasing but psychologically potent, especially to a disempowered population with memories of past glory and prophecies of future restoration. From the earliest surviving lines of this piyyut, we find the motif of reversals: he who is high will be brought low, and the lowly will become exalted. In the previous *qedushta*, we saw that Joseph did, in fact, sin against his brothers, and as a result he was punished. Judah, likewise, sins against his family, and he must also suffer. But these reversals—favorite son to slave, dominant sibling to outcast—are themselves fated to be reversed. In this way, these figures become beacons of hope to the Jews of Yannai's time. The very lowness of Jewish status in the present tense strengthens their hopes for a coming redemption.

Qedushta for Genesis 39:1 בראשית לט:א

ויוסף הורד מצרימה

"But Joseph was brought down to Egypt"

Fragmentary as it is, in this poem Yannai draws evocative parallels between Joseph's servitude in Egypt and his own experience of exile. In the end, both slavery and exile are presented as part of a divine plan. A related motif, the frustration of Joseph's brothers, anticipates the disempowerment that Rome-Byzantium, the empire "enslaving" the Jews in Yannai's day, will someday experience. Appearances of human victimhood are as illusory as a pretence of power; all, in the end, yield to the will of God and participate in His mysterious plan.

(1) … from the young ox[1]
with grace and loyalty adorned
Your decree, O God, not to be undone
… Potiphar

In bonds drawn down to a foreign land
to be a slave to slaves[2] he was sold
The innocent one, through his works renown[3]
[through His favor] he gained fame[4] all who saw him could see it[5]

Just as, pure of heart when he was cast down[6]
his heart stayed whole and against You he did not rebel
So, too, he was when deprived of all he had,
brought down to a land not his own[7]

And it is written: "But Joseph was brought down to Egypt and Potiphar, an officer of Pharaoh, captain of the guard, an Egyptian man, bought him from the Ishmaelites who brought him down there" (Gen 39:1)
And it is said: "He sent a man before them as a servant, the sold-one, Joseph" (Ps 105:17)
And it is said: "I drew them with human cords, with bonds of love, but I seemed to them like one who imposed a bit between their teeth, though I was offering them food" (Hos 11:4)[8]
And it is said: "Though your beginning was small, by your end you will greatly increase" (Job 8:7)
And it is said: "He imposed it as a decree upon Joseph, when he went forth to the land of Egypt; I listened to a language I had never heard" (Ps 81:6)

I will listen for good news[9]
for the Lord has spoken of good
to shield the sons of "he took one tender and good"[10]
Blessed are You… Shield…

---

1 The specific phrase here adapts language from Judg 6:25; the image of Joseph as an ox (or bull—also associated with the sign Taurus) comes from Deut 33:17, "Like firstling bull in his majesty, he has horns like the horns of the wild-ox" (**R**).

2 That is, the Egyptians. See Lam 5:8.

3 Prov 20:11 (**R**).

4 Lit. "His grace was recalled"—meaning that God's favoring of Joseph gained the attention of those around him. The lacuna is filled according to **B1**'s reading.

5 This line elaborates on Gen 39:3, "When his master saw that the Lord was with him and that the Lord lent success to everything he undertook…" Based on the interpretation of

(א) **א**.. ... מִשּׁוֹר פָּר
בְּחֵן וְחֶסֶד מְשׁוּפָּר
גְּיזֵרָתְךָ אֵל בַּל תּוּפָּר
... **ל**.. פּוֹטִיפָר

הַבַּעֲבוֹעוֹת נִמְשַׁךְ לְגֵיא נֵיכָר
וְלַעֲבָדִים לְעֶבֶד הוּא נִמְכָּר
זַךְ אֲשֶׁר בְּמַעֲלָלָיו נִיכָּר
ח.. נִיזְכָּר וּבְרוֹאָיו נִיכָּר

טוֹהַר לֵב אֲשֶׁר גַּם בַּמּוֹרָד
יִיחַד יִיצְרוֹ וּבָךְ לֹא מָרָד
כְּמוֹ כֵן מִשֶּׁלּוֹ הָפְרָד
לְאֶרֶץ לֹא לוֹ הוּרָד

ככתוב ויוסף הורד מצרימה ויקנהו פוטיפר סריס פרעה שר הטבחים איש מצרי מיד הישמעאלים אשר הורדהו שמה

ונאמר שלח לפניהם איש לעבד נמכר יוסף

ונאמר בחבלי אדם אמשכם בעבתות אהבה ואהיה להם כמרימי על על לחיהם ואט אליו אוכיל

ונאמר והיה מראשיתך מצער ואחריתך תשגה מאד

ונאמר עדות ביהוסף שמו בצאתו על ארץ מצרים שפת לא שמעתי אשמע

אֶשְׁמַע שֵׁימַע טוֹב
כִּי יְיָ דִּיבֵּר טוֹב
לְמַגֵּן בְּנֵי קַח רַךְ וָטוֹב
ברוך... מגן...

GenR 86:5, in which Potiphar beholds the Divine Presence hovering over Joseph, the final stich of this line might be translated "all who saw him could see Him."

6 **B1** connects this to Gen 37:24, referring to the well into which his brothers threw him; the next line draws a parallel between that experience and his exile to Egypt.

7 This alludes to the phrase in Gen 15:13, where God tells Abram that his children will be exiled to "a land not theirs" (**B2**).

8 Exegetical verse in *GenR* 86:1 and *TanḥB Vayeshev* 18.

9 The use of the first person in this transitional phrase is unusual although not unique.

10 I.e., Abraham, with the epithet taken from Gen 18:7 (**R**).

(2) Drawn down and bound by human cords
You led (him) like a man leads a lamb[11]
Lest his foes believe their power prevailed,[12]
as a slave[13] they sold the one who loved them
Every work of his hands prospered
the beauty of his righteousness flourished there[14]
Clinging close to God with pious whispers[15]
he ruled over their land until He could bring the others near[16]
O Almighty! You were zealous for his zeal
the power of his purchaser You gave him[17]
His nearly-lost life You revived
Always, in all straits,[18] You were with him

As it is written: "And it was that the Lord was with him, and he was a prosperous man, and he was in the house of his Egyptian master" (Gen 39:2)

And as it is said: "In the presence of all their captors, He dealt with them mercifully" (Ps 106:46)

And as it is said: "May Your loyalty, O Lord, be upon us, for we have put our hope in You" (Ps 33:22)

And as it is said: "O Shepherd of Israel, give ear, You who leads Joseph like a flock! You who shine forth, enthroned on cherubim!" (Ps 80:2)

Shine forth from on high,
O One full of mercy[19]
and the dew of reviving life drip down!
Blessed are You… Who resurrects…

---

11 The image of Joseph as a "lamb" is perhaps a play on his usual association with the ox. The final phrase, lit. "flock of man" (צאן אדם) derives from Ezek 36:37, 38.

12 "His foes" refers to Joseph's brothers; the language derives from Deut 32:27 (**B1**).

13 Reading עבד in place of עבור ("because").

14 This stich draws on Isa 4:2 (**R**), but may also serve to remind the audience of Joseph's famous beauty—both physical and (as implied here) moral.

15 This recalls Gen 39:3 as interpreted in *GenR* 86:5, which states: "Rabbi Huna interpreted in Rabbi Aḥa's name: He [Joseph] whispered [God's name] whenever he came in and whenever he went out." A fuller version of this interpretation is preserved in *Tanḥ Vayeshev* 8 (**B1**).

16 The verb rendered "bring…near" in the second stich recalls the language of Judg 1:14, where the same root (צ-נ-ח) is used to mean "descend" (**B1**). The negative connotations of "descent" are not present here, however, as they are (for example) in the previous *qedushta*.

(ב) מָשׁוּךְ בְּחַבְלֵי אָדָם
נִיהַגְתָּה כְּצֹאן אָדָם
שׂוֹנְאָיו פֶּן תֵּירוֹם יָדָם
עֲבוּר כִּי מָכְרוּ יְדִידָם
פּוֹעַל יָדָיו בַּכֹּל הִצְלִיחַ
צְבִי צִדְקוֹ שָׁם הִצְמִיחַ
קִירְבַת אֱלֹהִים הִיצְנִיעַ
רְדוֹת בְּאַרְצָם עַד הִצְנִיחַ
שַׁדַּי קִינְאָתוֹ קִינֵּאתָה
שִׁלְטוֹן קוֹנָיו אוֹתוֹ הִיקְנֵיתָה
תְּמוּתַת נַפְשׁוֹ חִיֵּיתָה
תָּמִיד בְּכָל צַר אִתּוֹ הָיִיתָה

ככתוב ויהי יי את יוסף ויהי איש מצליח ויהי בבית אדניו המצרי

ונאמר ויתן אותם לרחמים לפני כל שוביהם

ונאמר יהי חסדך יי עלינו כאשר יחלנו לך

ונאמר רועה ישראל האזינה נוהג כצאן יוסף ישב הכרובים הופיעה

הוֹפִיעָה מִמְּרוֹמִים
מָלֵא רַחֲמִים
מַטְלִיל לְהַחֲיוֹת רְדוּמִים
ברוך... מחיה...

See Gen 47:21; Joseph ruled first over Potiphar's house and then over all of Egypt, all as part of a divine plan in which God would bring the rest of Jacob's family down to Egypt. See *GenR* 86:1, *Tanḥ Vayeshev* 4, and *TanḥB Vayeshev* 16 (**B1** offers these citations).

17 That is, Joseph's brother's sold him to be a slave, but he rose to a position of authority, first in the house of his purchaser (Potiphar), and eventually in Pharaoh's court. The language reflects the same phrasing as the opening words of *GenR* 86:3 (**R**), and puns on קנא (jealousy/zeal) and קני (acquisition). Joseph's brothers were jealous, which inspired God's zeal, and led to Potiphar's purchase, and Joseph's acquisition of power.

18 The translation here reflects the unclear text oh the MS, which may be read either as צר ("affliction, trouble") or צד (with the connotation of "place"). The language of the phrase when read with the first possibility recalls Isa 63:9, as the Masoretic text reads it.

19 As **B1** notes, this language recalls that of the penitential *Taḥanun* prayers, particularly as they appear in the Ashkenazi rite.

(3) Yah, remember Your beloved ones who are oppressed for no cause
who seek You in the streets[20] though You are in the heavens
Gather the dispersed and undo affliction
Continue to grace to the traces of Joseph
Hand and Help[21] shall You be, as for Joseph, freely
for, like slaves, their eyes follow You[22]
[Yah, You promised them they would][23] be redeemed for free
just as we were sold off, for free

As it is written: "For thus says the Lord: You were sold for free, and thus you shall be redeemed without money" (Isa 52:3)
And as it is said: "For thus said the Lord God: Of old, My people went down to Egypt, to sojourn there; but Assyria oppressed them for no cause" (Isa 52:4)
And as it is said:

Please God ...

20 See Song 3:2 and Ps 10:1 (**B1**).
21 Lit. "staff," which echoes the shepherd imagery above.

(ג) יָהּ זְכוֹר חֲשׁוּקִים אֲשֶׁר בְּאֶפֶס עֲשׁוּקִים
מְבַקְשֶׁיךָ בַּשְּׁוָוקִים וְאַתָּה בַשְּׁחָקִים
נְדוּדִים אַסֵּף וְצָרוֹת הָסֵף
וְלָחוֹן הוֹסֵף עַל שְׁאֵירִית יוֹסֵף
יָד וּמַשְׁעֵינָה תִּהְיֶה כְּיוֹסֵף חִינָּם
כִּי כַּעֲבָדִים לָךְ עֵינָם
י.. לְהִגָּאֵל חִינָּם
כְּמוֹ נִמְכְּרוּ חִינָּם

ככתוב כה אמר יי חינם נמכרתם ולא בכסף תגאלו

ונאמר כִּי כה אמר יי מצרים ירד עמי בראשונה לגור שם ואשור באפס עשקו

ונאמר ...

אל נא

22 Ps 123:2 (**R**).
23 Lacuna filled by **B1**, based on the language of Isa 52:3, in the following line.

Commentary

Only the first three units of this *qedushta* are extant, but within this fragment, Yannai develops a clear and simple (although hardly simplistic) theme: the continuity of divine providence even through the bleakest of times. Joseph's sufferings—and by extension, the real and perceived oppression of the Jews of the poet's own day—constitute discrete elements within a larger divine plan. Yannai roots his emphasis on providence in the biblical text itself: the passive verb in the opening verse of the *sidra* raises the question of agency: by whom was Joseph brought down to Egypt? In Genesis 50:20, Joseph answers this question when he reassures his brothers, "Besides, although you intended me harm, God intended it for good, so as to bring about the present result—the survival of many people." While the narrator of Genesis is cryptic, Joseph interprets the text of his experience: the divine hand guides human actions and shapes individual destinies.

Yannai, however, does not draw upon Gen 50:20 directly—at least in the preserved lines of this piyyut. Instead, Hos 11:4, cited after the first poem, forms the key to his reading of this week's passage. The verse from Hosea, which introduces both the divine perspective on providence and the human perception of enslavement, captures well the paradoxes Yannai keeps in a careful tension—paradoxes which, on the surface, apply to Joseph, but which akso spoke clearly and meaningfully to Yannai's own community.

Both of the first two poems, focusing on the Joseph story itself, employ the language of Hosea to describe how Joseph came to be in Egypt: "in bonds drawn down to a foreign land" (Poem One, line 5) and "drawn down and bound by human cords" (Poem Two, line 1). Despite a situation that might have led to mutual rejection (Joseph rebuffing the God who appears to have rejected him—a corollary to the potential appeal of apostasy by Jews, on the one hand, and the Christian supersessionist perspective, on the other), God and Joseph remain true to each other. Though Joseph suffered, "his heart stayed whole" (Poem One, line 10), and God responds in kind to Joseph's faith, protecting him and allowing him to prosper through his period of exile. Yannai unequivocally diminishes the role of the brothers in determining Joseph's fate: God has carefully and over a long period of time created a scenario that will force the brothers to recognize that it was not their own power that permitted these indignities to be visited upon Joseph but rather divine design. Presumption of power is illusory.

Poem Three, which is explicitly attached to verses from Isaiah (the first verse of the haftarah), highlights the themes of the second half of the Hosea verse. The Isaiah passage acknowledges directly that God's plans can seem like unwelcome discipline, for all that they lead to good ends. Yannai casts his contemporaries, collectively, in Joseph's role, using his rhetoric to help them identify with their ancestor, but he speaks his words entirely to God: the people, Yannai asserts, endure exile because they remain confident in God's goodness and full of yearning for His nearer presence. Israel's appearance as "enslaved" is misleading, for they are, in truth, slaves only to God, not to those who appear to be their mortal masters. In this context, the words of Isaiah, which recall the sale of Joseph and the period of Egyptian slavery in paradigmatic terms, reassure the community that their term of servitude will likewise come to an end and justice will be served, all within the scope of God's providential plan. The biblical story, in reality, describes the present.

Throughout this poem, two opposing motions predominate: the motion of the eyes downwards, servant-like; counterbalanced by the motion of the eyes upwards, towards the heavens. The movement downward connotes defeat, subservience, and despair, but the upward gaze indicates defiance, hope, and longing. The juxtaposition of the two creates a tension between exterior appearance and internal experience. Outwardly, the Jews—like Joseph—may appear downtrodden and defeated. They act, and look, like the vanquished. But inwardly, these "losers" retain a defiant, rebellious hope revealed, if at all, only by a furtive upwards glance. Joseph's experiences become a model for a deep, quiet form of resistance. Yannai never advocates active rebellion against the powers of his day—indeed, he actively discourages it[24]—but this poem promotes a different kind of resistance: the refusal to look only down in despair.

24 See discussion in Chapter Four.

Qedushta for Genesis 41:1 בראשית מא:א

"And it came to pass at the end of" ויהי מקץ

This poem focuses on Pharaoh's mysterious dreams and Joseph's interpretations of them. Royal dreams are here associated with divine prophecy, which leads Yannai to explore the sources of power—real and perceived—at play in this story. Along the way, the poet increasingly attends to questions of truth and knowledge, particularly the tension between the truth that ultimate redemption will come and the knowledge that the details of the divine plan must (for God's own reasons) remain hidden. Justice delayed, according to this poem, is nonetheless still justice.

(4) To this master of dreams[1]
You revealed a secret: true-vision dreams
Because of dreams he was sent forth and because of dreams he was found[2]
from one pit he was drawn up but in another he was confined[3]
Hated for a dream for which he needed explanation;
loved for a dream that only he could explain
He was sold [as a slave][4] but over his brothers will rule
when fulfilled is the interpretation of "will you truly rule?"[5]
Indeed, one who emerges from the prison house can be a king[6]
Forever, [O Lord],[7] does Your word endure
And he will stand and he will arise and he will be and he will succeed
... by means of dreams
And wondrous signs he will one day do[8]
O awesome, exalted, and holy One!

(5) A man who, for good reason, went down to that beautiful land[9]
an end-point was set for his sentence in the darkness down there
In the pit and on the path and in his master's place, he was not forsaken[10]
but why to the prison-house was he cast away?[11]
...

(6) He fretted...
he saw, and they swallowed up the good ones
Strength...those who bear messages[12]
for the visions that appeared terrified him[13]

---

1 That is, Joseph (see Gen 37:19).

2 See *TanḥB Miqqetz* 3, where it states that Pharaoh had this dream only for the sake of rescuing Joseph from prison.

3 The first pit refers to the well in which Joseph's brothers kept him while they decided his fate; the second pit refers to his prison in Egypt, in which he languished for twelve years.

4 Lacuna filled by **B1**.

5 In Gen 37:8, the brothers, interpreting Joseph's dream, ask him, "Would you rule over us?" By the end of Genesis, Joseph has fulfilled this utterance of his jealous brothers. It may also have overtones of the messianic figure of the Messiah ben Joseph, possibly alluded to in the next lines.

6 Eccl 4:14

7 Lacuna filled by **R.**

8 The word read here as "signs" (אותות) by **R** could alternatively be reconstructed as "destiny" (אותיות, from אתה, as in Isa 44:7, 45:11; **B1** points out these verses.).

9 That is, Egypt, as in Jer 46:20. The language is ambiguous regarding the reasons for Joseph's exile to Egypt: Was it merely part of God's plan, or did Joseph bear some respon-

(ד) לְבַעַל חֲלוֹמוֹת הַלָּזֶה
גִּלִּיתָה סוֹד חֲלוֹמוֹת מַחֲזֶה
מֵחֲלוֹמוֹת יָצָא וַחֲלֹמוֹת מָצָא
מִבּוֹר הֻודְלָה וּבַבּוֹר הֻוכְלָא
נִשְׂנָא בַּחֲלוֹם אֲשֶׁר לוֹ נִפְתָּר
וְנֶאֱהַב בַּחֲלוֹם אֲשֶׁר הוּא פָּתָר
נִמְכַּר ... וְעַל אֶחָיו יִמְלֹךְ
וְקָם פִּתְרוֹן חֲלוֹם הֶמָּלֶךְ תִּמְלֹךְ
כִּי לְמִבֵּית הֲסוּרִים יָצָא לִמְלֹךְ
לְעוֹלָם ... דְּבָרְךָ נִצָּב
וַיַּעֲמֹד וְיָקוּם וְיִהְיֶה וְיַצְלִיחַ
... עַל יְדֵי חֲלוֹמוֹת
וְסִימָנֵי אוֹתוֹת יַעֲשֶׂה
נוֹרָא מָרוֹם וְקָדוֹשׁ

(ה) **א**ִישׁ אֲשֶׁר בַּעֲלִילָה רָד לִיפֵיפִיָּה
קֵץ נִיתַּן עַד אַיִן יִהְיֶה בְּמַאְפֵּלְיָה
בַּבּוֹר וּבַדֶּרֶךְ וּבְבֵית אֲדֹנָיו לֹא נֻוטָשׁ
בְּבֵית הָאֲסוּרִים לָמָּה רֻוטָשׁ
...

(ו) **ז**ָחַל מ..הר ...
אֲשֶׁר שָׂר וְהֵם לַטּוֹבֹת בּוֹלְעוֹת
חַיִּיל ... סוֹבְלֵי קוֹרְאוֹת
וּבִיעֲתוּהוּ מַרְאוֹת נִירְאוֹת

---

sibility for his fate? **B1** cites *Tanḥ Vayeshev* 4; see also *TargPsJ* 41:8 and *GenR* 89:6.

10 For an expansion on the nature of "the pit," see *GenR* 84:16 and *Tanḥ Vayeshev* 2, both of which interpret Gen 37:23; for God's providence to Joseph on "the path," see *Mekh Beshallaḥ* 5, which offers a midrash on Gen 37:25 (**B1**). The idiom "his master's house" comes from Gen 39:2-6 (**B1**).

11 The word translated as "cast away" here is from the root ר-ט-ש, which generally means "dashed to pieces" in biblical Hebrew but has the valence of "abandoned, renounced, forsaken, banished" in Aramaic. The Aramaic meaning is more likely here, but the English translation attempts to capture the nuance of the Hebrew as well.

12 The word rendered "messages" is the feminine plural participle, קוראות (lit., "proclamations, summonses"), which suggests that the cows of the dream bear a prophetic message for the king.

13 This could also mean that those of awful appearance (that is, the scrawny, ugly cows of his dream) afflicted Pharaoh. The *vision* (dream) of their *appearance* (both *mar'ot* in Hebrew) distressed the Egyptian king. The word ניראות (translated as "appeared") puns on "to see" (from its actual root, ראה) and "awful/awesome" (from the root ירא)

He was torn and troubled but slept once more[14]
when the image within his dream changed yet again!
He planned…to stand in counsel[15]
but among the council of the Lord, who may stand?
Each vision was beheld in one night
seven in the midst of a single stalk[16]
A refuge from…he saw sheaves joined together
and the two dreams were really one
Filled with grain were they, and piles of it[17]
and like the wheat of Minnit[18] heaped up
Up sprouted another seven, abhorrent to see:[19]
blighted dry grain, scorched and charred
His [skin] crawled[20] within his chambers …
such visions he suffered at that time!
Because stalks consumed the other stalks
just as the cows had done!
As for Pharaoh, when he started up startled from his dream
in terror trembling from his dream
He cried out, in search of an interpretation of his dreams,
for his foolish "wise men" and sorcerers
Then arose the cup-bearer, who had forgotten to mention
the one who mentioned to him to mention him
    at a propitious time for mentioning[21]
He who was wanted by the king said: "If I may now make mention—
"My sin do I now recall"[22]
The cupbearer informed the king what had happened:
"For the baker: death; but for me: life"
"You will make great …
"Just as he interpreted for us, so it happened."

---

14 See Gen 41:8 (**B1**).

15 Jer 23:22; both "in counsel" and "among the council" in this line render the Hebrew בסוד

16 The text is unfortunately damaged and difficult to reconstruct, but the language here suggests that Yannai is connecting Joseph's dream of the sheaves in Gen 37 with Pharaoh's dream of sheaves in Gen 41.

17 The word translated as "grain" (בר) is used several times in Gen 41.

18 "Wheat of Minit" occurs in Ezek 27:17; in *LamR* 3:6 and *EcclR* 1:23, the grain is praised as the source for innumerable (*ke-minyan minit*) recipes or, based on the numerical value of Minit, at least 500 recipes. The term indicates profound abundance. Reading the preposi-

טוֹרָף וְנִתְפָּעַם וַיִּישַׁן עוֹד
וְנִשְׁנָה לוֹ מַרְאֵה חֲלוֹם עוֹד
יָזַם ע..ר בְּסוֹד לַעֲמוֹד
וּבְסוֹד יְיָ מִי יַעֲמוֹד
כָּל מַחֲזֶה הָיָה בְּלַיְלָה אֶחָד
שֶׁבַע בְּתוֹךְ קָנֶה אֶחָד
לִינַת ... חָז שִׁבֳּולִים עוֹד נִתְיַיחֵד
וּשְׁנֵי חֲלוֹמוֹת הָיוּ חֲלוֹם אֶחָד
מְלֵיאוֹת בָּר הָיוּ וּדְגוּנוֹת
בְּחִיטֵּי מִינִּית מְדֻוּגָּנוֹת
נִצְמַח עוֹד שֶׁבַע מְגֻוּנוֹת
צְנוּמוֹת דַּקּוֹת שְׁדוּפוֹת וּגְחוּנוֹת
סָמַר קִירוֹת ... ..יסו
חֶזְיוֹנוֹת לוֹ בְּעֵת נִיסּוּ
עֲבוּר שִׁבֳּולִים בְּשִׁיבֳּולִים עִיסּוּ
כְּמוֹ פָּרוֹת לְפָרוֹת עָשׂוּ
פַּרְעֹה כְּהֵיקִיץ מֵחֲלוֹמוֹ
מִבְּעִיתוּת תּוֹעַ חֲלוֹמוֹ
צִוַּח לְבַקֵּשׁ פִּיתְרוֹן מֵחֲכָמָיו
וְנוֹאֲלוּ חֲכָמָיו וְחַרְטֻמָּיו
קָם מַשְׁקֶה אֲשֶׁר שָׁכַח לְהַזְכִּיר
לְמַזְכִּירוֹ לְהַזְכִּירוֹ
בְּעֵת הִזְכִּיר
רֵוּצָה לְמַלְכּוֹ נָא אִם אַזְכִּיר
אֶת חֲטָאַיי אֲנִי מַזְכִּיר
שִׁימַּע מַשְׁקֶה לַמֶּלֶךְ מֶה הָיָה
לְאוֹפֶה מִתָּה וְלִי חַיָּיה
תֶּרֶב .. ...
בַּאֲשֶׁר פָּתַר לָנוּ כֵּן הָיָה

---

tion כ־ in place of the preposition ב־.

19 The word מגונות is from the root גני, which has the connotation of “deserving to be covered up, indecent, ugly” in rabbinic Hebrew.

20 Ps 119:120 supplies the missing word (**B2**), or could read with Job 4:15.

21 This line is rich with puns on the root ז-כ-ר. The language draws on Gen 40:14, 23; the biblical phrase, “when it shall be well with you” (vs. 14) is here interpreted as a propitious moment for Joseph. See also *GenR* 88:7 (**B1**).

22 **B1** has נם (“said”) in the first stich rather than נא (“please”). I take “said” as implied. The implication is that the cupbearer risks self-incrimination to (at last) do right by Joseph. The language suggests hesitation.

And thus, "And it came to pass at the end of two years"

(7¹) Then "the reeds by the river, upon the shore of the river"—
in a dream You showed the dragon of the river[23]
Great is Your counsel, O regal and radiant One[24]
courses You established for the light and the luminary[25]
And thus: "And it came to pass at the end of two years"[26]

You who turn wise men to fools,[27]
if You bless, who can curse?
You are clear and pure of eyes;[28]
such are visions of Your visage, radiant and splendid[29]
And thus: "And it came to pass at the end of two years"

The pure from amid the impure You rushed to choose[30]
a hand You sent forth through the keyhole[31]
Like a lion, You roar and crouch[32]
cowing the violent beasts[33]
And thus: "And it came to pass at the end of two years"

You lack nothing and nothing hinders You
Our lives You keep in Your hand
The trust of Your creatures You keep
unto the thousands (of generations) You stay loyal
And thus: "And it came to pass at the end of two years"

The fate of Your faithful ones[34] You guard;
as for Your enemies, their pride You shatter
You have set a sentence for blackest darkness;[35]

---

23 That is, God revealed to Pharaoh the fate of Egypt and its leaders. The river here is the Nile, and the dragon who swims within it is Pharaoh; as **R** notes, the language recalls Isa 19:7 ("The reeds by the river, by the mouth of the river, and every thing sown by the river, shall wither, be driven away, and be no more"), here shown as a prophecy to Pharaoh; and Ezek 29:3 ("Speak, and say, Thus says the Lord God: Behold, I am against you, Pharaoh king of Egypt, the great crocodile that lies in the midst of his streams, which has said, My river is my own, and I have made it for myself").

24 Ps 76:5 (**B1**).

25 Job 38:19 (**R**); the imagery hints at the journey Joseph has made from the darkness of the prison to the light of freedom and power.

26 Maʾagarim includes this phrase—the opening words of the Torah portion—as a refrain.

27 See Isa 44:25 (**R**); for more on this motif in the context of Joseph before Pharaoh, see *GenR* 89:6 (**B1**).

ובכן ויהי מקץ שנתים ימים וג׳

(ז[1]) **אָ**ז עָרוֹת עַל יְאוֹר עַל פִּי יְאוֹר
בַּחֲלוֹם הֶרְאֵיתָה לְתַנִּין יְאוֹר
גְּדוֹל עֵצָה אַדִּיר וְנָאוֹר
דְּרָכִים שַׂמְתָּה לְאוֹר וּמָאוֹר

ובכן ויהי מקץ וג׳

הַמֵּשִׁיב חֲכָמִים אָחוֹר
וְאַתָּה תְּבָרֵךְ וּמִי יָאוֹר
זַךְ וּבְעֵינַיִם טָהוֹר
חֲזוּת מַרְאָךְ צַח וְצָהוֹר

ובכן ויהי מקץ וג׳

טָהוֹר מִטָּמֵא כְּאַצְתָּה לִבְחוֹר
יָד שָׁלַחְתָּה מִן הַחוֹר
כְּאַרְיֵה תִּשְׁאַג וְתִגְהוֹר
לִפְרִיצֵי חַיּוֹת תִּגְעוֹר

ובכן ויהי מקץ וג׳

מַחְסוֹר אֵין לָךְ וְלֹא מַעְצוֹר
נַפְשֵׁינוּ בְּיָדְךָ תֶּאֱצוֹר
סְמִיכַת יֵצֶר תִּצּוֹר
עַד אֲלָפִים חֶסֶד תִּנְצוֹר

ובכן ויהי מקץ וג׳

פְּקֻודָּה לְפוֹקְדֶיךָ תִּשְׁמוֹר
צוֹרְרֶיךָ גְּאוֹנָם תִּשְׁבּוֹר
קֵץ שַׂמְתָּה לְמַחְשַׁךְ שְׁחוֹר

28 See Hab 1:13 (**R**). 29 A play on Song 5:10.

30 The language here is from Job 14:4 (**R**). The interpretation recalls the description of the Exodus in *SongR* 2:8. "The pure" refers to Israel; "the impure" the nations among whom Israel is exiled—in this case, Egypt.

31 This alludes to Song 5:4 (cited by **R**); Yannai, drawing on the history of exegesis of this verse, also applies this language to the Exodus in his *qerova* on the Song of Songs for Passover, line 89 (Rabinovitz, II, 281). The "hand" refers to Moses.

32 See Hos 11:10 (**B2**).

33 That is, God's obvious power and might intimidates those who pretend to power—as displayed through acts of violence.

34 Isa 26:16 (**B2**).

35 The period of slavery and exile, both Joseph's and contemporary. **B1** cites *Tanḥ Miqqetz* 1.

O Exalted One, You reign over Nof and the black river[36]
Your allies You lead in straight ways[37]
the twisted thread of dreams You unknot[38]
And thus: "And it came to pass at the end of two years"

And thus:
(7²) The One who says what will come to pass
The One who creates what will…
The One who reveals what is coming
The One who speaks what is unsaid
The One who utters what is murmured
The One who … what will be
The One who devises what shall be devised
The One who delves deeply into thoughts
The One who pierces the veil of the hidden
The One who knows what will …
The One who completes what is promised
The One who…
The One who declares what shall be from the start
The One who…
The One who hides what must be hidden
The One who…
The One who explains what defies explanation
The One who…
The One who proclaims what shall come to be…

(8) … Who keeps precious things deep[39] …
…
the One who reveals deep things and who magnifies salvation[40]
…
In the circle of those on high and those below,[41]
as it is written: "And the one called…"

---

36 "Nof" is a name for the Egyptian city Memphis; "the black river" refers to the Nile. Pharaoh may believe himself ruler—even creator—of his realm, but he is mistaken on both counts. See Ezek 29 for a description of this mythic self-image on the part of Pharaoh.

37 This draws on Ps 27:11 and 143:10; see also *Tanḥ Beshallaḥ* 3.

38 Literally, "explain." Yannai draws on the language of Dan 5:12 (**R**), a scene which itself draws on this *sidra*, in which Daniel is called upon to interpret Belshazzar's dream.

39 See Zech 14:6 (**R**). The biblical text should probably yield a translation of "who makes

רָם מָשַׁלְתָּה נוֹף בְּשִׁיחוֹר
שְׁלוּמֶיךָ תַּנְחֶה בְּמִישׁוֹר
תּוֹכֶן עִיקּוּם חֲלוֹמוֹת תִּפְשׁוֹר

ובכן ויהי מקץ וג׳

ובכן

(ז²) הָאוֹמֵר מַה יֶּאֱתֶא
הַבּוֹרֵא מַה יִב..
הַגּוֹלֶה מַה יִּגַּשׁ
הַדּוֹבֵר מַה יִּדּוֹם
הַהוֹגֶה מַה יְּהַרְהֵר
..בִין מַה יִּהְיֶה
הַזּוֹמֵם מַה יְּזוֹמֵם
הַחוֹקֵר מַה יְּחוֹשֵׁב
הַטּוֹעֵן מַה יְּטוּמָּן
הַיּוֹדֵעַ מַה י..
הַכּוֹלֵל מַה יִּכּוֹן
... מַה ...
הַמַּגִּיד מַה מֵּרֹאשׁ
...
הַסּוֹתֵר מַה יִּסָּתֵר
...
הַפּוֹתֵר מַה יַּפְלִיא
...
הַקּוֹרֵא ...

(ח) ... הַמַּקְפִּיא יְקָרוֹת
המ.. ...
הַמְּגַלֶּה עֲמוּקוֹת הַמַּגְדִּיל יְשׁוּעוֹת
ה.. ...
בְּסוֹד עֶלְיוֹנִים וְתַחְתּוֹנִים
ככתוב וקרא

---

the frost sparkle" in this context, but I have tried to translate it in accord with the aggadic readings found in *b. Pes.* 50a, *Tanḥ Ḥukkat* 8, *TanḥB Ḥukkat* 24, *PRK Parah* 18, and *NumR* 19:6 (also on the Red Heifer), all of which understand the text as hinting at revelations in the World-to-Come of important secrets that are concealed in this world.

40 The language draws on Job 12:22 and Ps 18:51 (**B1**); the psalm verse (familiar to many from the Grace after Meals), in particular, has strong messianic overtones.

41 See Poem Six, line 7–8, where Pharaoh is implicitly denied a place in this group.

Commentary

This poem develops, in a thorough yet understated way, the motif of reversals, which typifies many of the poems of the Genesis cycle: Pharaoh, the dragon of the Nile, is rendered powerless by nightmares of cattle and grain, while Joseph, an imprisoned slave, is empowered by his ability to interpret mysterious signs. The wise become fools, the cupbearer becomes a hero, and a Pharaoh becomes dependent on his Israelite vizier.

The true power behind the throne here is of course God. God is the only character who is never in the dark, never at a loss, never subject to cyclical ascents and descents. Scripture privileges its human readers by offering insight into the divine mind, which results in a heightened awareness of irony: Joseph is in slavery because of his dreams—and his brothers' interpretations; but Joseph gets out of slavery because of Pharaoh's dreams—and Joseph's interpretations. Power and efficacy do not reside in the dream itself (or, by implication, the prophecy) but in the ability to explicate its meaning. Visions and their decipherment are two halves of a puzzle, both of which come from God. The mistake made by the ignorant—including, in the *sidra*, both Pharaoh and the cupbearer—is to confuse the human conveyor of interpretation with its actual (divine) source. Joseph, and by extension, his latter-day kinsmen, the Jews, do not fall into this error but rather recognize and credit the Source of mysteries (as the second *rahit* and the *silluq* expansively indicate). Indeed, as the poem concludes, the poet focuses his attention on the vast scope of God's incomparable knowledge and power, a common motif throughout the poems of the Joseph cycle. Human power—whether presumed by Judah or Pharaoh or, implicitly, Rome—is a pathetic illusion.

What is the appeal of this recurring motif of reversal? The theme of visions and their fulfillment in the *sidra* reflects the poet's own concern with prophecy and its realization: Israel's restoration is assured by divine prophecy and promise, yet God operates on a timetable that is deeply and frustratingly mysterious. Just as Joseph's redemption from slavery and imprisonment must be understood as occurring within the context of an elaborate, enigmatic, but in the end elegant and transparent divine plan, so, likewise, must Yannai and his compatriots understand their own situation as existing in a state of uncertain certainty. The poet consistently draws parallels between Joseph's release, the Exodus from Egypt, and the redemption yet to come: all are simply variants of the same reliable pattern of which a struggle against impatience is an integral part.

The primary significance of the Joseph story, then, emerges out of its paradigmatic power. Even more than Jacob, who at least fled from Esau under his own agency, Joseph is both a victim and a victor. In Poem Five, the poet acknowledges the anxiety and confusion humans can feel, caught up in the moment: "But why to the prison-house was he cast away?" (line 4). The question is phrased bluntly, and it connotes anger at the long years Joseph spent languishing in his cell—years that foreshadow the centuries the Jews spent in exile and under Esau's rule. Yannai does not answer his own heartfelt question, beyond the satisfaction of Joseph's eventual triumph, when he bests Pharaoh's wise men and earns his freedom—the lowest of the low becomes the most exalted. As the poem progresses, however, Yannai emphatically affirms that salvation is a certainty, even if the specifics of its timing are unknown. Yannai, while perhaps at times impatient, struggles to emulate Joseph's confidence in dreams.

Qedushta to Genesis 41:38 בראשית מא:לח

"Can we find one such as this?" הנמצא כזה

This fragmentary piyyut picks up with the final lines of a first *rahit* in which Egyptians praise Joseph and his incomparable wisdom. The surviving portion of the second *rahit* describes God's unique majesty and fidelity, and the rewards Israel realized from those divine qualities. The final unit—a fragment of the *silluq*—verges on *hekhalot*-like intensity, with its rapturous repetitions of the root ק-ד-ש, "holy."

(7¹)[1] [Can we find one such as this]: fit[2] to foresee a famine?
Can we find one such as this: principled, princely, peaceful, praised?[3]
[Can we find one such as this]: pure and pious?

(7²) ... the depths
Who is diligent for deep counsels
...
Those called by You from the most remote realms
...statutes
Safeguarding from stumbling those who are sure in You[4]
...
Your lips pour forth wisdom
... radiant
rare, refined, and renowned
... poured forth
complete, righteous, forged strong
... and shouts
goodness You hear, and righteousness You do[5]
... land for You to lay waste
remembrances in Your records to reward
... in order to declare clean
multitudes of Your hosts to muster
Your words becomes deed without flattery[6]
Your utterances never return unfulfilled[7]
... [whose wings] kiss[8]
with us is truth entwined[9]

---

1 This unit was constructed as an alphabetic acrostic; letters *resh*, *shin*, and *tav* have been preserved.

2 Lacunae in this unit filled as by **R**.

3 The language here suggests that of Gen 14:17, which refers to the Valley of Shaveh (rendered here "principled," in an attempt to capture the two valences of "straight" and "prosperous"), the Valley of the King (implied by the poet's use of *shalit*, "prince," which suits the acrostic, in place of the lemma's more familiar *melekh*).

4 The rare word here translated as "stumbling" comes from 1 Sam 25:31 (**R**). The word rendered "sure" for the sake of alliteration in English more literally means "hope."

5 "Goodness" may be generic but more likely refers to obedience to God's will and law

(ז¹) ... רָאוּי רָעָב רוֹאֶה
הֲנִמְצָה כָּזֶה שָׁוֶוה שַׁלִּיט שָׁלֵם שֶׁבַח
... ... תְּמִים תְּהִילָּה

(ז²) ... עֲמוּקוֹת
שׁוֹקֵד עֵיצוֹת מַעֲמַקּוֹת
... ..ות
קְרוּאֵי לְךָ קִיצֵי חֲוּקוֹת
... ..חֲוּקוֹת
פּוֹדֶה קוֹוֶיךָ מִיפּוּקוֹת
... ..קות
שִׂיפְתוֹתֶיךָ חָכְמוֹת מְפִיקוֹת
... מַבְהִיקוֹת
מְבוּחָנוֹת צְרוּפוֹת וּבְדוּקוֹת
... מוּצָקוֹת
כּוֹלְלוֹת צְדָקוֹת וּמְצוּקוֹת
... וּצְעָקוֹת
טוֹב תַּקְשִׁיב וְתַעַשׂ צְדָקוֹת
... תֵּבֵל לָךְ לְבַקּוֹת
זִכְרוֹנוֹת בְּסִיפְרָךְ לְחַקּוֹת
... ..נך לְמַעַן לְנַקּוֹת
הֲמוֹנֵי צִיבְאוֹת לְהָקוֹת
דְּבָרֶיךָ יַעֲשׂוּ בְּלִי חֲלָקוֹת
גְּזֵירוֹתֶיךָ לֹא יָשׁוּבוּ רֵיקוֹת
... ..יך בְּמַשִּׁיקוֹת
אִיתָּנוּ אֱמֶת מְחוּשָּׁקוֹת

(e.g. 1 Kgs 12:7—**B2**); in response to human fidelity, God responds with righteousness.

6 The line alludes to Ps 73:18, "You surround them with flattery, You make them fall through blandishments" (**B1**), where flattery is a base motive for action through which God misleads the wicked; for the righteous, no such inducement is necessary. The verb in the stich is here read as active *Qal*, but could also be pointed as passive *Nifal* (as **B1** prefers). The translation treats the phrase as an impersonal construction.

7 Isa. 55:11.

8 That is, brush against each other; this is a reference to the angels (see Ezek 3:13).

9 The word rendered "entwined" (from the root ח-ש-ק) has connotations of both attachment and desire.

(8) …The Holy One
in the splendor of holiness
in the holy language:
Holy, holy, holy!
In the holy place to hallow You …
The holy ones of the holy place, in a holy spirit,
O my King, in holiness, like the holy angels,
as it is written: "And the one called…"

(ח) ... הַקּוֹדֶשׁ
בְּהַדְרַת קוֹדֶשׁ
בְּלָשׁוֹן קוֹדֶשׁ
קוֹדֶשׁ קוֹדֶשׁ קוֹדֶשׁ
בְּקוֹדֶשׁ לְהַקְדִּישָׁךְ ... ..ש
קוֹדְשֵׁי קוֹדֶשׁ בְּרוּחַ קוֹדֶשׁ
מַלְכִּי בַּקּוֹדֶשׁ כְּמַלְאֲכֵי קוֹדֶשׁ
ככתוב וקרא

Commentary

In this poem, the majesty of Joseph in the eyes of Pharaoh and the Egyptians reflects the splendor of God in the eyes of His worshippers, human and angelic. Pharaoh's exclamations of wonder—which recall the teaching in *GenR* 90:1, "'Pharaoh said unto his servants: Can we find such a one as this [in whom the spirit of God dwells] (Gen 41:38)?' If we go to the end of the world, shall we actually find such a person!?"—convey uncertainty, hesitancy, and disbelief commingled with awe. The communal language, however, articulates the intimacy and immediacy of God's presence among the worshippers, and conveys a rapturous sense of divine immanence. The poet thus contrasts the authentic sense of wonder his listeners feel as they achieve proximity to the divine with Pharaoh's incomplete experience of the same. Joseph provides Pharaoh and his court with a brief glimpse of this reality. They have no access on their own; without an intermediary, they are cut off. The experience leaves them gropingly aware of the experience of God to which Yannai and his community have fuller access and deeper understanding. Despite His majesty, God relates to Israel with directness and profound, even stunning, immediacy. Pharaoh can commune only with God's servant, while the poet and his congregation are able to approach Him directly. Yet within their limits—and Pharaoh's limits are greater than those of the humble slave, Joseph—each receives a kind of revelation. The only possible response to this awesome awareness of proximity is amazement.

Qedushta for Genesis 43:14 בראשית מג:יד

ואל שדי יתן לכם רחמים

"And may God Almighty grant you mercy"

Only the final units of this poem survive.[1] The opening verse of the *sidra* speaks of Jacob's hopes that the vizier of Egypt—the unrecognized Joseph—will be moved by God to have mercy on his sons. In the extant piyyut, however, it seems that "the man" may also be God.[2] This recognition leads the poet to meditate on the divine personality, which leads, in turn, to reflections on prayer.

Let us praise you, O Our God!
(7[1])[3] You are God, to You belongs mercy
And thus You will have mercy upon …
… to You …
those attached to You and beloved by You[4]
Are You not exalted in the heights?
So too they are exalted, and You they extol
You graced them as with the strength of the *re᾿emim*
And You distinguished them as with the dignity of the *re᾿emim*[5]
Good are Your people, making themselves pure
You know the lifespan of the pure[6]
Gathering the waters of the sea as in a bottle[7]
Arrayed before You are all their days
Confounding the conspiracies of the crafty
Being pleasant and clothing the naked;[8]
Sate us with prosperous and pleasant days
The power of everlasting triumph[9]
Opening the mouths of the mute
Your commandments are not obscure
Singing sweetly of Your holiness
A multitude that is sweet to You[10]
Tribes of the pure one[11] from the people who are consumed[12]
May You soothe their suffering![13]

---

1 Rabinovitz, working off less extensive textual sources, categorizes the opening four units presented here—the triple *rahit* and the *silluq*—as a single, extended silluq. Based, however, on the formal intricacy of these works, I have chosen to understand the formal structure as it appears here: a triple *rahit* (embedding three complete acrostics, one per unit) and a very terse *silluq*.

2 **R** connects this piyyut with *GenR* 92:3, in which R. Joshua b. Levi interprets this verse according to the understanding that "the man" refers to God. Rather ironically, the prooftext for this association is the phrase "God is a man of war" in Exod 15:3. God may be a man of war, when the situation requires it, but He is also a man of mercy.

3 This unit embeds a complete alphabetical acrostic from *alef* to *tav* (one letter per stich).

4 For the root ר-ח-ם in this sense, see Ps 18:2 (**B2**).

5 *Re᾿em* refers to a wild ox or unicorn; see Num 23:22 (**B2**) and Deut 33:17, both of which use this image to describe the power and majesty of the tribes of Israel. On the translation "unicorn" see the note to the *qedushta* to Gen 33:18, poem 8, line 3. The final stich of this line could, thus, alternatively be rendered, "You made them one like the horn of the unicorn" based on a similar use of the verb in *b. Ber.* 6a (**R**).

ונעריצך אלהינו

(ז'[1]) אַתָּה הוּא אֱלֹהִים לְךָ הָרַחֲמִים
בְּכֵן תְּרַחֵם אֵל ל.. ..מִים
גד.. ... לך ...
דְּבוּקִים בָּךְ וּלְךָ מְרֻוחָמִים
הֲלֹא אַתָּה רָם בִּמְרוֹמִים
וְהֵם רָמִים וְלָךְ מְרוֹמְמִים
זִימַּנְתָּם כְּתוֹעֲפוֹת רְאֵמִים
חֲטִיבָתָם כְּקַרְנֵי רְאֵמִים
טוֹב עַמָּךְ מַתְמִימִים
יוֹדֵעַ יְמֵי תְמִימִים
כּוֹנֵס כְּנוּדוֹת מֵי יַמִּים
לְפָנֶיךָ סְדוּרִים כָּל יָמִים
מֵפֵר מַחְשְׁבוֹת עֲרוּמִים
נָעִים וּמַלְבִּישׁ עֲרֻומִים
שַׂבְּעֵינוּ טוֹבִים וּנְעִימִים
עוֹז תְּשׁוּעַת עוֹלָמִים
פּוֹתֵחַ פִּיּוֹת נֶאֱלָמִים
צִיוּוּיָךְ לֹא נֶעֱלָמִים
קְדֻושָּׁתָךְ מַנְעִימִים
רְבָבָה אֲשֶׁר לָךְ מֻונְעָמִים
שִׁבְטֵי תָם מֵעַמִּים לְחוּמִים
תִּתֵּן לְעָצְבָּם נִיחוּמִים

6 Perhaps an allusion to the idea articulated in *GenR* 92:2, "'At a propitious time (*le'et matzo*; in Ps 33:2, the *petiḥta* verse) means at the moment of exacting (*mizuy*) justice; also, when the soul is being pressed out (*mizuy*) from the body [that is, at the time of death, when one is in agony]; and lastly, when the final account is rendered [that is, when your suffering outweighs your sins, you should pray for your suffering to cease]. Thus when Jacob saw that his account was complete, he poured out his supplications: 'And may God Almighty grant you mercy…'"

7 Ps 33:7

8 According to Ps 135:3 (cited and discussed in **B2**), 'Pleasant' is a divine name. See *Tanḥ Vayigash* 10, which notes in connection with Gen 3 that the Torah begins with an act of loving kindness, God's decision to clothe the exiled Adam and Eve.

9 Isa 45:17 (**B1**).

10 The multitude refers to Israel; reading with **B1** who connects this line with Ezek 16:7.

11 That is, Jacob/Israel

12 The poet here blends the language of Deut 32:24 and Ps 14:4 (**B1**).

13 This echoes Gen 5:29, cited in **B2**, in which Noah is named.

(7^{2})[14] And let us always know Your strength
And let us sing Your praises
And let us rejoice in Your acceptance[15]
And let us proclaim Your holiness[16]
And let us make a diadem of Your righteousness[17]
And let us declaim Your wonders
And let us exult in Your exaltation
And let us jump for Your joy[18]
And let us delight in Your victory
And let us taste Your sweet words[19]
And let us be bound upon Your heart
And let us make a crown of Your glory
And let us unify Your oneness
And let us make Your rulings flow
And let us be strong in Your strength
And let us mention Your memory
And let us make known Your assembly
And let us make splendid Your splendor
And let us speak Your word
And let us declare Your greatness
And let us utter Your blessings
And let us be strengthened by Your strength

(7^{3})[20] He who is glorious in holiness[21]
whose image is hidden
who is glorified forever
who remembers loyalty
whose goodness is unique[22]
whose honor is eternal
The everlasting King
whose is arrayed[23] strength

---

14 This section contains a reverse acrostic (תשר"ק).
15 **R** reads, "Your joy-giving" (רינונך).
16 Foreshadowing the recitation of the Qedushah.
17 See Isa 62:3 (**B1**), where God speaks similar words (our poet's source) as a promise to Israel. Here, Israel reciprocates.
18 See Job 6:10

(ז^{2})

וְנַתְמִיד תָּקְפָּךְ
וְנָשִׁיר שְׁבָחָךְ
וּנְרַנֵּן רִיצּוּיָךְ
וְנִקְרָא קִידּוּשָׁךְ
וְנַצְנִיף צִדְקָךְ
וְנַפְלִיא פִּלְאָךְ
וְנַעֲלֶה עִילּוּזָךְ
וּנְסַלֵּד סִילּוּדָךְ
וְנַנְעִים נִצְחָךְ
וְנַמְתִּיק מִילּוּלָךְ
וּנְלַבֵּב לִיבּוּבָךְ
וְנַכְתִּיר כִּתְרָךְ
וּנְיַחֵד יִחוּדָךְ
וְנַטִּיף טַעֲמָךְ
וּנְחַסֵּן חֵילָךְ
וּנְזַמֵּר זִכְרָךְ
וּנְוָועֵד וִועוּדָךְ
וּנְהַדֵּר הוֹדָךְ
וּנְדַבֵּר דְּבָרָךְ
וְנַגִּיד גָּדְלָךְ
וְנַבִּיעַ בִּרְכָתָךְ
וּנְאַמֵּץ אָמְצָךְ

(ז^{3})

הָאַדִּיר בַּקּוֹדֶשׁ
הֶגָּנוּז דְּמוּת
הֶהָדוּר וָעַד
הַזּוֹכֵר חֶסֶד
הַטּוֹב יַחְדָּיו
הַכָּבוּד לָעַד
הַמֶּלֶךְ נֶצַח
הַסָּדוּר עוֹז

---

19 These lines recall, indirectly, the interpretation of Song 8:13 found in *SongR* 8:17, discussed below.

20 This unit embeds a complete alphabetic acrostic (*alef* to *tav*), with one letter per word.

21 Exod 15:11.

22 Perhaps יחדיו should be taken as from the root ח-ד-ה, "to rejoice." See Jer 31:13.

23 Lit., "ordered, regulated."

who works hidden wonders
sanctified with songs
the Almighty so strong!

(8) He who is endowed with loyalty we will sanctify because of Your beneficent mercies
and Your loyalty … to You …
threefold …for the sake of Your glory
As it is written: "And the one called to the other…"

Ofan

(9) Compassionate One, Gracious One, Merciful One,
the pure one prayed for his descendents;
and also now may You lead those who say:
Holy, holy, holy is the Lord of Hosts! The whole earth is filled with His glory!
"*Holy*"—from the masters of compassion
"*Holy*"—from the masters of grace
"*Holy*"—from the masters of mercy
Holy, holy, holy is the Lord of Hosts! The whole earth is filled with His glory!
The Holy One put compassion within the brother[24]
for his brothers who felt no compassion for him
The Holy One gave him to be gracious towards those
who showed him no grace
The Holy One filled him with mercy towards those
who granted him no mercy
"*Holy*"—from the *Hayyot*;
"*Holy*"—from the *Ofanim*;
"*Holy*"—from the *Cherubim*,
the one towards the other (etc.)…
Twice (etc.) …

---

24 Joseph

הַמַּ**פְ**לִיא **צ**וֹפֶן
הַקָּדוֹשׁ **רְ**נוֹת
הַשַּׁדַּי **תּ**וֹקֶף

(ח) חָסוּד וְנַקְדִּישֶׁיךָ עַל טוּב רַחֲמֶיךָ

וְחַסָדֶיךָ ... לָךְ ...
שְׁלֹשָׁה לְשֵׁם כְּבוֹדָךְ
ככתוב וקרא זה אל זה וג׳

אופן

(ט) חוֹמֵל וְחוֹנֵן וּמְרַחֵם
פִּילֵל תָּם לְנִינָיו
וְגַם עַתָּה תַּנְהִיג לְאוֹמְרִים
קדוש קדוש קדוש יי צבאות מלא כל הארץ כבודו
קָדוֹשׁ מִבַּעֲלֵי חֶמְלָה
קָדוֹשׁ מִבַּעֲלֵי חֲנִינָה
קָדוֹשׁ מִבַּעֲלֵי רַחֲמִים
קדוש קדוש קדוש יי צבאות מלא כל הארץ כבודו
קָדוֹשׁ שָׂם חֶמְלָה בְּאָח
עַל אַחִים אֲשֶׁר לֹא חֲמָלוּהוּ
קָדוֹשׁ נָתַן בּוֹ חֲנִינָה עֲלֵיהֶם
כִּי לֹא חֲנָנוּהוּ
קָדוֹשׁ מִילְאוֹ רַחֲמִים עֲלֵיהֶם
כִּי לֹא רִיחֲמוּהוּ
קדוש מחיה
קדוש מאופן
קדוש מכרוב
לעומתן וג׳ ...
פעמים וג׳

Commentary

This poem balances petition and praise, each in heightened form. On the one hand, as is typical of the final poems of a Yannai *qedushta*, the focus is increasingly on God's majesty and awesomeness. The sense of the divine presence elicits a response of wonder and exclamation of "Holy!" from mortals and angels alike. At the same time, the plea for mercy expressed in the first verse of the *sidra* creates an opening for the poet to meditate on the fundamental divine attribute of compassion and responsiveness. The density of language in the poems (particularly the triple *rahit*) intensifies both elements of the text, with the poet shifting almost breathlessly from praise to petition and back again, often blurring the two concepts as he petitions God for the ability to more fully and freely praise Him.

The liturgy as we now have it offers many reasons why God should spare His people's suffering, even if punishment is deserved: the potency of ancestral merit; the power of repentance and prayer; the need to protect the divine reputation; and fidelity to ancient oaths, among others. In this poem, however, the poet appeals to God's own nature. God will have mercy because He is a merciful God. For Joseph, disguised and empowered by his role as Pharaoh's vizier, to spare the brothers who sold him into slavery may have been unexpected: it is not human nature to deal so graciously with the graceless, to feel pity for the pitiless, to have mercy on the merciless. Indeed, according to Poem Nine, God had to create these generous feelings in Joseph's heart—the implication being that without God, Joseph might not have dealt so gently with his brothers.

Mercy, in this piyyut, becomes a defining divine characteristic. As a result, Yannai does not here plead his people's case (at least not in the surviving fragment). He does not justify or defend their actions, boast of their virtues, or dramatize their repentance. The poet does not emphasize Joseph's righteousness, innocence, faith, or wisdom as a kind of ancestral merit, nor does he dramatize the brothers' repentance, atonement, or change of heart. Yannai doesn't even offer reminders of prophetic promises of reward as reminders of God's yet-unfulfilled obligations to His people. Instead, the simple fact of God's merciful nature and His tremendous power—the will and the way—are affirmed. Upon hearing this poem, who can doubt that God will someday act with compassion towards His suffering people? How can He *not* act, when He is a God of mercy?

At the same time, this divine reality is acknowledged in the context of ecstatic prayer by a community that, for all its mention of needing divine aid and the articulation of a sense of "existential exile" in many of the *qedushta'ot,* here seems strong and privileged, confident and sure. This poem rejoices exuberantly over a topic normally associated with petition. Here a rabbinic midrash may provide an interesting parallel. The basis for this midrash is Song 8:13, "O you who dwell in the gardens, the companions listen for your voice; let me hear it."

> Rabbi Nathan said in the name of Rabbi Aḥa: [God here is compared] to a king who was angry with his servants and threw them into prison. He then took all his officers and servants and went to listen to the song of praise that they were chanting. He heard them saying: "Our lord the king, he is the object of our praise, he is our life; we will never fail our lord the king." He said to them: "My children, raise your voices, so that the companions who are nearby you may hear." So although Israelites are occupied with their work for the six days of the week, on the Sabbath they rise early and go to the synagogue and recite the Shema and pass in front of the ark and read the Torah and a passage from the Prophets, and the Holy One, blessed be He, says: "My children, raise your voices so that the companions standing by may hear"—the word "companions" denoting the ministering angels—"and take good heed that you do not hate one another nor be jealous of one another, nor wrangle with one another, nor shame one another, in order that the ministering angels may not say before Me: `Sovereign of the Universe, the Torah that You gave to Israel is not practiced by them, and lo, there is enmity, jealousy, hatred and quarrelling among them,' but you in fact are fulfilling it in peace." Bar Kappara said: Why are the ministering angels called "companions"? Because there exists among them neither enmity nor jealousy nor hatred nor quarrelling nor strife nor altercation.

It is impossible to know if Song 8:13 was an intertext earlier in this piyyut, nor is this midrash an exact parallel to our poem, but the themes common to this midrash and the extant piyyut fragment are intriguing. In the parable, there is no reason given why the servants were thrown into prison— recalling the poet's bafflement in the *qedushta* for Gen 41:1, where the poet wondered why Joseph had to be put in the Egyptian jail (Poem 5, line 2). Implicitly, the midrash suggests bafflement at the current situation of the Jews. The response to this possibly unfair treatment, however, is not criticism or complaint, but praise and assertion of fidelity to the king. This recalls the poem's praise for God, with almost no mention of individual or communal suffering. At the same time, the midrash carefully articulates the complex scenario and exegesis that underlie the aggadic tradition, while Yannai asserts and embodies it. The two genres share themes and theology, but presentation differs dramatically. The midrash inspires thought, while the piyyut creates an experience. Yannai does not deny the problematic situation of the Jews; he transcends it.

The midrashic interpretation of Song 8:13 resonates with themes and motifs from our poem and more generally with the payyetanic endeavor. Implicitly in the midrash, the "prison" is the workaday world of Jews living in exile—the same world in which Yannai and his community lived, and which the poet addresses in his "present tense." In the midrash, God yearns to hear words of praise, prayer, and Torah study in the synagogue on the Sabbath—the very context for which this piyyut was composed. In the midrash, God asks specifically to hear words of Torah and the Prophets (i.e., the words of the Torah service), the very texts that Yannai "teaches" through his compositions. Finally, the midrash introduces the perception of humanity through the eyes of the angels, with an implicit note of critique; as God notes in the midrash, human nature is inclined towards strife, and people must work to master this disposition through Torah study. Yannai does not introduce these motifs—people here are humble, not arrogant, in need of rescue rather than critique, and they work (and pray) in concert with the angels, not in opposition. Nonetheless, the tranquility of the heavens—where the God of mercy rules over the angels of peace—suggests the ideal world to which Yannai aspires and where he leads his congregation in prayer. In this poem, as in the midrash, rather than the past being the paradigm, the heavenly is. And through his poetry, Yannai is able to fulfill God's wish, by raising his voice in praise and song so that God—and His angelic host—may hear it.

Qedushta for Genesis 44:18

בראשית מד:יח

"Then he approached him"

ויגש אליו

In this lengthy and formally unusual *qedushta,* Yannai dramatizes the conflict between the estranged brothers, Joseph and Judah, over the fate of the Jacob's youngest son, Benjamin. The poet articulates rapidly shifting emotions from a multiplicity of perspectives. He pays substantial and sympathetic attention to the feelings and experiences of the brothers collectively. As the poem progresses, the narrative also develops, culminating with Joseph's dramatic disclosure of his identity to his brothers. Yannai creates an extended analogy between this moment of self-revelation and self-discovery and the eventual Day of Judgment that will be faced by all.

(1) Trembling seized hold of the pure one's tribes[1]
as soon as the man ordered them back
While he had searched all they had for a goblet,
they worried as they listened and looked on

He started, he finished, and he found[2]
and the lad was destined for slavery
With what followed, he who had pledged[3] was pained:
he begged and beseeched before the officer

The lion[4] kept leashed his anger:
"Please, let your servant speak!"—wisdom whet his words
Like a young lion he roared against him
but the young ox[5] did not react rashly

As it is written: "Then Judah approached him, saying, "Please, my lord, let your servant speak a word in the ear of my lord, and let not your face grow hot against your servant, for you are just like Pharaoh" (Gen 44:18)

And it is said: "My son, if you may a pledge to a friend, if you have given your hand for a stranger" (Prov 6:1)[6]

And it is said: "Do this, then, my son, to redeem yourself, for you have come into the power of your fellow: go grovel, and badger your fellow" (Prov 6:3)[7]

And it is said: "One approaches the other, and a breath cannot pass between them" (Job 41:8)[8]

And it is said: "Thus the kings joined forces; they advanced together" (Ps 48:5)

And it is said: "The lion is mightiest among the beasts and recoils before the presence of none" (Prov 30:30).

---

1 The language of "trembling seizing" comes from Isa 33:14 (**B2**). It is intriguing that the sons of Jacob began to tremble even before the planted evidence (the goblet) is found. Their body language betrays a deeper guilt.

2 Gen 44:12 (**R**), which describes Joseph's "discovery" of the planted goblet among Benjamin's possessions.

3 That is, Judah; see Gen 43:9.

4 "Lion" and its variants ("young lion," "lion's whelp," etc.) are common epithets for Judah, rooted in Gen 49:9. The imagery is frequently adduced in aggadic and targumic

(א) **אֲ**חֲזָה רְעָדָה לְשִׁבְטֵי תָם
בְּעֵת הֵשִׁיב הָאִישׁ אֹתָם
גָּבִיעַ בְּהִידָּרֵשׁ מֵאִתָּם
דָּאֲגוּ בְּשׁוּמְעָם וּבִרְאוֹתָם

הֵחֵל וְכִילָּה וּמָצָא
וְנַעַר לְעֶבֶד נִימְצָא
זֹאת עָשׂ עוֹרְבוֹ נֶעֱצָב
חִינֵּן וְנִתְרַפֵּס פְּנֵי נִיצָּב

טָעַן אַרְיֵה אֶת חֲמָתוֹ
יְדַבֵּר נָא פִּי שִׂיחַ שָׂח בְּחָכְמָתוֹ
כִּכְפִיר שָׁאַג לְעוּמָּתוֹ
לֹא נֶחְפַּז שׁוֹר מִנַּהֲמָתוֹ

ככתוב ויגש אליו יהודה ויאמר בי אדני ידבר נא עבדך דבר באזני אדני ואל יחר אפך בעבדך כי כמוך כפרעה

ונאמר בני אם ערבת לרעיך תקעת לזר כפיך

ונאמר עשה זאת אפוא בני והנצל כי באת בכף רעך לך התרפס ורהב רעיך

ונאמר אחד באחד יגשו ורוח לא יבוא ביניהם

ונאמר כי הנה המלכים נועדו עברו יחדיו

ונאמר ליש גיבור בבהמה ולא ישוב מפני כל

versions of this episode (e.g., *TargN* Gen 4:18 states, "He roared *like a lion* and said…"; the italicized words are added in the Aramaic rendition).

5 The ox (or "bull"—also the sign Taurus) represents Joseph (see Deut 33:17, cited by **R**).

6 Cited in *TanḥB Vayiggash* 4.

7 Cited in *TanḥB Vayiggash* 3, which also includes the figures of the ox and lion in a parable describing their confrontation. This text notes that while each of these men is destined to have a messiah spring from his line, the messiah of Judah's line will be primary.

8 Interpreted in relation to this portion in GenR 93:2, as is the next verse (**R**).

All is the work of Your hands
And all is held in Your hands
Shield us in the shelter of Your hands—
Blessed are You… Shield…

(2) Deep coursed the devisings of that one's heart[9]
but when the wise one[10] saw him, he saw his brokenness of heart
The brothers spoke to him with all their heart
on behalf of a brother they poured out heart and soul[11]
"The children of one man are we all
and One Rock is our King
"Once, against one brother, we sinned
 but our wickedness is now repaid in full
"Once we were whole but now we are lacking
Such you sought to know of us, and we shield no secrets
You demanded, and the truth we made known to you
Please, my lord, do not judge against us."

As it is written: "My lord asked his servants, saying: Do you have a father or a brother?" (Gen 44:19)
And it is said: "Have you not all one father? Has not one God created us? Why do we deal treacherously, one man against his brother, profaning the covenant of our fathers?" (Mal 2:10)
And it is said: "Deep waters are the counsels of a man's heart but a man of insight draws them forth" (Prov 20:5)[12]
And it is said: "Apples of gold in silver filigree is a word fitly spoken" (Prov 25:11)[13]
And it is said: "By long forbearing is a prince persuaded, and a soft tongue breaks the bone" (Prov 25:15)
And it is said: "The living, the living shall praise You, as I do this day; the father to his children shall make known Your truth" (Isa 38:19)

Your truth is forever

---

9 That is, Joseph.
10 That is, Judah. The language of this stich derives from Prov 20:5, cited among the prooftexts that follow.
11 Although in the Torah portion only Judah speaks, here the poet employs the plural and

כֹּל מַעֲשֶׂה יָדֶיךָ
וְהַכֹּל בְּיָדֶיךָ
מַגְּנֵינוּ בְּצֵל יָדֶיךָ
ברוך... מגן...

(ב) **מַ**יִם עֲמוּקִים עֲצַת לֵב
נָבוֹן בְּשׁוּרוֹ שִׁבְרוֹן לֵב
סָחוּ לוֹ אַחִים בְּכָל לֵב
עַל אָח נִשְׁפּוֹךְ נֶפֶשׁ וָלֵב
פְּרִי אִישׁ אֶחָד כֻּלָּנוּ
צוּר אֶחָד הוּא מַלְכֵּינוּ
קֶדֶם בְּאָח אֶחָד אָשַׁמְנוּ
רִשְׁעֵנוּ לָכֵן עַתָּה שִׁוּלָּמְנוּ
שְׁלֵמִים הָיִינוּ וְחָסַרְנוּ
שְׁאַלְתָּנוּ וּמִמְּךָ לֹא הִסְתַּרְנוּ
תָּבַעְתָּה וֶאֱמֶת לְךָ הוֹדֵינוּ
בִּי אֲדוֹנִי אַל נָא תְּנִידֵנוּ

ככתוב אדוני שאל את עבדיו לאמר היש לכם אב או אח

ונאמר הלא אב אחד לכלנו הלא אל אחד בראנו מדוע ניבגד איש באחיו לחלל ברית אבותינו

ונאמר מים עמוקים עצה בלב איש ואיש תבונה ידלנה

ונאמר תפוחי זהב במשכיות כסף דבר דבור על אפניו

ונאמר בארך אפים יפתה קצין ולשון רכה תשבר גרם

ונאמר חי חי הוא יודך כמוני היום אב לבנים יודיע אל אמתך

אֲמִתְּךָ מֵעוֹלָם

---

depicts all the brothers as speaking.

12 As **R** notes, both *GenR* 93:4 and *TanḥB Vayiggash* 2 associate this verse with Judah's confrontation of Joseph.

13 *GenR* 93:3 (**R**).

Your loyalty is forever and ever[14]
and You resurrect us with Your rain, O Eternal God![15]

Your truth comforts us
Your light leads us[16]
and with rain You resurrect us from Sheol
Blessed are You… Who resurrects…

(3) Together they draw close
as one they come together;[17]
the one who plows against the one who reaps: they rush;
the one who treads against the one who gathers: they hurry[18]
He approached for close battle, You brought him to the point of battle[19]
indeed, in every approaching of battle unto us You draw near![20]
Yah roared like a lion at the building of the Ariel[21]
You will appear in the image of a lion as appeared … the lion cub
The enemies of Judah went down[22] in a storm like …
the sons of Judah were victorious as with the approach … Gilgal …:

As it is written: "The sons of Judah approached Joshua and Caleb the son of Jephunneh the Kenizzite said to him at Gilgal: You know what instructions the Lord spoke to Moses, the man of God, concerning me and you, at Kadesh-Barnea" (Josh 14:6)
And it is said: "Lo, days are coming, says the Lord, when the plowman shall meet the reaper and the treader of grapes he who sows the seed; when

---

14 The language of the first two stichs derives from Ps 103:17 (**B1**). The double conclusion here suggests the preservation of two distinctive conclusions to the unit. Personally, one or the other would have been recited.

15 These lines are our first indication of unusual forms and constructions in this poem. First, the doubled conclusion (present in both **R** and Zulay, also) should perhaps be understood as alternates. That said, quite surprisingly, both variants clearly refer to rain rather than dew, as would be expected—but to the "rain of resurrection" and not simply the weather phenomenon. Something like "abundant dew of resurrection" may be intended. See *Mekh. Baḥodesh* 9 (H-R, 236), which connects "abundant rain" (גשם נדבות; Ps 68:10) with the resurrection of Israel after its shock at the revelation at Sinai; this passage closely parallels the aggadic traditions incorporated here, in which Judah and his brothers "die" when their souls fly out of them at the shock of Joseph's self-revelation.

16 The language of the first two stichs blends Ps 117:2 with Ps 43:3 (**B1**).

17 Aggadic descriptions of Judah's confrontation with Joseph are rich and found frequently in Jewish writings from Late Antiquity. There is a lengthy version of this episode in

חַסְדְּךָ מֵעוֹלָם וְעַד עוֹלָם
הַחֲיֵינוּ בְּגִשְׁמָךְ אֱלֹהֵי עוֹלָם

אֲמִיתָּיךְ תְּנַחֲמֵינוּ
וְאוֹרָךְ יַנְחֵינוּ
בְּגֶשֶׁם מִשְׁאוֹל יְחַיֵּינוּ
ברוך... מחיה...

(ג) יַחְדָּו יִגָּשׁוּ
כְּאַחַת יִפְגָּשׁוּ
חוֹרֵשׁ בַּקּוֹצֵר יָחוּשׁוּ
דּוֹרֵךְ בַּבּוֹצֵר יָעוּשׁוּ
נִיגַּשׁ לִקְרָב קֵרַבְתּוֹ לִקְרָב
כִּי בְּכָל גִּישַׁת קְרָב אֵלֵינוּ תִיקְרָב
יָהּ שָׁאַג כְּאַרְיֵה בְּבִינְיַן אֲרִיאֵל
וְתוֹפִיעַ דְּמוּת אַרְיֵה כְּהוֹפִיעַ גּוּר אַרְיֵה
יָרְדוּ צָרֵי יְהוּדָה בְּסַעַר כגל.. ...
נִצְּחוּ בְּנֵי יְהוּדָה כְּגִישַׁת ... ..גִּלְגָּל

ככתוב ויגשו בני יהודה אל יהושע בגלגל ויאמר אליו כלב בן יפנה הקניזי אתה ידעת את הדבר אשר דבר יי אל משה איש האלהים על אדותי ועל אדותיך בקדש-ברנע

ונאמר הנה ימים באים נאם יי ונגש חורש בקוצר ודורך ענבים במושך הזרע והטיפו ההרים עסיס וכל הגבעות תתמוגגנה

TargN to Gen 44:18 and also in many Fragmentary *Targumim* and multiple *toseftas* (see Klein 1:132–43), and a briefer version in *TargPsJ* to the same; in the *midrashim*, the same basic traditions are scattered throughout *GenR* and the *Tanḥuma* collections. Citations in this translation will indicate some, but not all, parallels.

18 The imagery and language of this verse come from Amos 9:13, cited as an intertext; see note, below.

19 For this grammatical construction, see Ezek 36:8.

20 This line, which puns on nuances of ק-ר-ב ("to come close, draw near" but, as a noun, with aggressive intentions), transitions the poem from narrative expansion of the biblical story to almost apocalyptic contemplation of Israel's future. Yet Yannai turns aside from Judah's militarism—it is God here who acts and achieves victory and he does so without bloodshed.

21 I.e., the Temple; see Isa 29:1–2.

22 The first lines convey irony: the foes will physically descend upon Jerusalem, but this will lead to a decline in their power, as well.

the mountains shall drip sweet wine and all the hills shall melt" (Amos 9:13)[23]

And You are holy, enthroned on the praises of Israel... Please, God...

(4) Angels on high looked at the young ox [and lion][24]
...
... the flesh of the donkeys[25] is softened like kneaded dough[26]
... Judah sent...
Then the hairs of his chest burst out through his clothing[27] ...
The lion roars; who shall not fear?[28]
A lion's whelp is Judah, lord over every beast
Master over every animal
You made him strong; You made him mighty
O awesome, most high, and holy One

ʿAssiriyah

(5)[29] One against the other, like iron sharpening iron[30]
truly, brother against brother they drew close and came together[31]
An approach of entreaty was his first approach[32]
and after that he drew close opposite him, ready for war[33]
The lion drew close, opposite the ox, and said:
"If I but say the word all Zoan[34] will be done for!

---

23 *GenR* 93:5 (**B1**); according to this midrash, the scene described by Amos is not a confrontation between Joseph and Judah but the Messiah ben Joseph who prepares the way for the Messiah ben David. Although the use of the Amos verse for this scenario is not attested elsewhere, *TanḥB Vayiggash.* 3 (also cited by **B1**) alludes to a similar scene.

24 Lacuna filled by **B2**. I.e., they saw Joseph (the ox) and Judah (the lion); **R** cites *Tanḥ Vayiggash.* 4, which describes how, when Judah and Joseph confronted each other, the angels said, "Come, led us descend to down below and see the ox and the lion shoving, the one at the other!" Maʾagarim, however, suggests the translation "the angels on high looked down to see," reading לשור as the infinitive of שור.

25 That is, Egypt (an epithet derived from Ezek 23:20, cited by **R**).

26 Perhaps Judah here remarks on the weak, defenseless state of the Egyptians (the "donkeys"—a derogatory term whether compared to an ox or a lion). Note *TargN* to Gen 44:18, which states (in part): "By an oath, if I draw my sword from the scabbard I will not return it within it until I have killed all the Egyptians! I will begin with you and finish with Pharaoh, your master..." See also *GenR* 93:8 and *TanḥB Vayiggash* 6 and 7.

27 For this image, see *GenR* 93:6 (**R**), *Tanḥ Vayiggash* 3 (**R**), and *TargN* and *TargPsJ* to Gen 44:19.

28 Amos 3:8

ואתה קדוש יושב תהלות ישראל. אל נא

(ד) מַלְאֲכֵי מָרוֹם הִבִּיטוּ לָשׁוֹר ...
...
... בְּשַׂר חֲמוֹרִים נִימַּק כְּלָיִישׁ
... יְהוּדָה שָׁלַח ...
וַיֵּצְאוּ חוּץ לְבוּשׁוֹ שַׂעֲרוֹת לִבּוֹ
אַרְיֵה יִשְׁאַג מִי לֹא יִירָא
גּוּר אַרְיֵה יְהוּדָה רֹאשׁ עַל כָּל בְּהֵמָה
גִּיבּוֹר עַל כָּל חַיָּיה
אֱיָילְתּוֹ וְחִיַּילְתּוֹ
נוֹרָא מָרוֹם וְקָדוֹשׁ

עשיריה

(ה) **אֶ**חָד בְּאֶחָד כְּבַרְזֶל בְּבַרְזֶל
אָמְנָם אָח בְּאָח גָּשׁוּ וְנִפְגָּשׁוּ
בְּגִישַׁת תְּחִינָּה נִגַּשׁ תְּחִלָּה
וְאַחֲרֵיכֵן נִגַּשׁ אֶצְלוֹ לַמִּלְחָמָה
גָּשׁ אַרְיֵה לְמוּל שׁוֹר וְאָמַר
אִם אוֹצִיא מַאֲמָר כָּל צוֹעַן תְּוּגְמָר

---

29 Shalom Spiegel, *Fathers of Piyyut*, ed. M. Schmelzer (New York/Jerusalem: JTSA, 1996), 61–65, includes additional annotation and discussion of the *ʿasiriyyah* and the first two stanzas of Poem Six (absent from **R**'s text), with some discussion of the piyyut as a whole.

30 Job 41:8 and Prov 27:17; see *TanḥB Vayiggash* 6 (**R**).

31 The confrontation is depicted here in simultaneously positive and negative terms; while conflict is not the ideal state, the brothers "sharpen" each other, which can be understood as beneficial. See *TanḥB Vayiggash* 6 (**R**), in which the fraternal confrontation is praised and Prov 27:17 ("As iron sharpens iron, so one man sharpens his friend") is cited, offering a positive reading of the scene.

32 **R** cites *GenR* 93:6, one aggadic location in which the idiom "to approach towards" is explained as having three possible meanings: for purposes of battle, petition, or prayer. Judah is ready for all three.

33 The tension between aggression and appeasement here is suggested also in *TargN* to Gen 44:18, which opens, "And Judah approached him (Joseph), *raging in words and contrite in tongue*..." (italics indicate the aggadic expansion in the targum).

34 Egypt (see Num 13:11); No-Ammon refers to Thebes/Alexandria (Nah 3:8). "No[-Ammon]" is adduced in the context of this scene through a pun on the particle of entreaty, *na'*, as in *TanḥB Vayiggash*. 6.

"As for justice—for how long, sir, will you pervert it against us?[35]
If I but speak the word, sir a plague against Nof I will bring, sir!
So spoke he of the sparkling eye to the vine fruitful before eye:[36]
"Where have you `set your eye'?[37] You promised us regarding the one
    pleasant of eye![38]
"If a slave you need to serve you, here I am! I am your slave![39]
"Better me than he let it be upon me and not him[40]
"This is the law of God—if you fear God:
"Twofold recompense let the thief repay[41]
    [If it is in his hand, twice what was stolen shall he repay][42]
"And one who snatched, slaughtered, and sold[43]
    fourfold and fivefold he repays.
"For his thievery, he is sold if he cannot repay
"Take for yourself our great wealth but to this lad show mercy;
"We give to you all that we have so that we shall not be shamed."
Joseph, upon hearing his words his compassion was kindled
his guts were in knots and he revealed himself to his brothers!

(6) A lion powerful and unrestrained[44]
like the approach of the plowman towards the reaper:[45]

---

35 **R** cites *GenR* 93:5 6 , which puns on Judah's use of *bi* (in the idiom, "please [*bi*], my lord") and the Greek word *bia* ("injustice"). At issue is the fact that Benjamin is being punished for a crime he did not commit—whether that crime is the theft of a goblet (for which he could pay restitution; see Exod 22:2ff cited in *GenR* 93:5 and below) or the sale of Joseph (for which Judah and the other brothers, but not Benjamin, do deserve to die). See also *Tanḥ Vayiggash* 5, cited by **B1**.

36 That is, Judah (Gen 49:12) and Joseph (Gen 49:22) (**R**). The phrase rendered here as "before the eye" is usually translated as "by springs of water" or, midrashically, as "before the eye" (*GenR* 88:10, which describes how Joseph obstructed Esau's gaze from tainting his mother in Gen 33:7). The present translation follows the midrashic reading, in order to preserve the parallelism.

37 The idiom "to set one's eye upon another" has a connotation of "to look after, to take care of"; see Jer 39:12, 40:4. Judah criticizes Joseph for promising to care for Benjamin (he is quoted using this idiom, in Gen 44:21) and instead threatening to enslave him. *TargPsJ* to Gen 44:21 clarifies the nuance in the original by adding the phrase "for good" to the original lemma.

38 The one "pleasant of eye" is Benjamin (**R** cites *GenR* 93:6), and the implication may be that Benjamin was as handsome as Joseph and their mother Rachel or, in keeping with the idiom in Prov 22:5 that he was generous. *GenR* 93:8 brings forward the interpretation that the brother's accuse Joseph of bringing them in under false pretenses.

דִין עַד אָנָה בָּנוּ תַּעֲבוֹר נָא
דָּבָר אִם אֲדַבֶּר נָא דֶּבֶר בְּנוֹף אָשִׂימָה נָא
הֵשִׁיב חַכְלִיל עַיִן לְבֶן פּוֹרָת עֲלֵי עָיִן
אַיֵּה הֲשָׂמַת עַיִן שֶׁהִבְטַחְתָּנוּ בְּטוֹבַת עָיִן

וְאִם עֶבֶד לְעַבְדָּךְ הֵן אֲנִי עַבְדָּךְ
מוּטָב לִי וְלֹא לוֹ בִּי אֲדוֹנִי וְלֹא בוֹ
זֹאת הִיא דַּת אֱלֹהִים אִם אַתָּה יְרֵא אֱלֹהִים
תַּשְׁלוּמֵי כֶּפֶל גַּנָּב מְשַׁלֵּם
[אִם בְּיָדוֹ הַגְּנֵבָה שְׁנַיִם יְשַׁלֵּם]
חָטַף וְטָבַח וּמָכַר
רִיבּוּעַ וָחוֹמֶשׁ יְשַׁלֵּם
וְנִמְכָּר בִּגְנֵיבָתוֹ אִם אֵין לוֹ לְשַׁלֵּם
טוֹל לָךְ רַב הוֹן וְעַל הַנַּעַר חוֹן
לָתֵת לָךְ רַב יֵשׁ שֶׁלֹּא נִתְבַּיֵּשׁ
יוֹסֵף כְּשֵׁמַע אֲמָרָיו נִכְמְרוּ רַחֲמָיו
וְהָמוּ מֵעָיו לְהִתְוַדַּע לְאֶחָיו

(ו) **א**ֲרִי בְכוֹחַ בְּלִי לְהֵעָצֵר
כְּגִישַׁת חוֹרֵשׁ בַּקּוֹצֵר

39 See again *GenR* 93:6 (**R**), where Judah, the "king" of Jacob's sons, offers to be Joseph's hewer of wood and drawer of water (the lowest occupations in biblical society).

40 Yannai here rereads the biblical phrase, "Please, my lord" (בי אדוני) midrashically as "[let the burden be] upon/against me (בי), my lord—and not upon/against him (בו)"—see *GenR* 93:6.

41 A resonant teaching is found in *TanḥB Vayiggash.* 5, cited by **R**, where Judah accuses Joseph of violating both royal and divine legal standards; *TargN* and *TargPsJ* to Gen 4:18 assert, somewhat more weakly, that Joseph's judgments have turned from being those of the Lord to "those of Pharaoh, your master" and suggests that where Joseph once feared the Lord, "now you say, `Of Pharaoh I am afraid.'" See Exod 22:6, where the thief, if he cannot repay double what he stole, is sold into indentured servitude. Judah here describes himself as the one who "stole" his brother(s).

42 The final stich is in Spiegel, *Fathers of Piyyut*, 63. The entire line draws on Exod 22:3, אם המצא תמצא בידו הגנבה... שנים ישלם.

43 See Exod 21:37 (**R**). The verse refers to an ox or sheep, here an allusion to Joseph (the ox) and the deception of Jacob. See *GenR* 93:6 and *TargPsJ* to Gen 44:18.

44 The initial stichs of the first four lines of Poem Six are absent from **R** but appear in Spiegel, *Fathers of Piyyut*, 63 64 , as well as the Maʾagarim database. Where there are differences, Spiegel's text is favored.

44 This revisits the language of Amos 9:13, used in Poem 3.

"Please, my lord, by me was he spared[45]
"A brother from his brothers shall not be hidden away"

A powerful warrior, he was called a young lion[46]
and he said to the provider, the interpreter, the comely one:[47]
"The matter of `in the pit' and a vow do not nullify[48]
Lest our faces before the face of our father be shamed"[49]

...
indeed the rent in the father's garment remains unmended still[50]
...
until now, the father has not ceased (yearning) for their brother

This he responded ...
"Do not open a breach ...
...
Indeed, their borders ...

The slaughterer said, "I will contain you in your borders
I will ... your servants, and to smite your great ones
"Our hand held still until the time you fell upon us[51]
Now, indeed, in my bloody garment I will fall upon you"

Most mighty warrior of the brothers in his wrath
He drew close for battle and for war
The lion is the most mighty of beasts[52]
He made the ox [recoil in fear] from him[53]

He made No-Ammon tremble when he roared like a lion[54]

---

45 See Gen 37:26 27 . This stich suggests that Judah began his confrontation with Joseph defensively, a defensiveness which he moderates with an admission of guilt in line 4.

46 The word rendered "young lion" is *kefir* (Judg 14:5, Ezek 32:2) and describes Judah, based on Gen 49:9 ("Judah is a lion's whelp [*gur ariyeh*]"). Ezek 32:2, coincidentally, applies the term to the king of Egypt.

47 Epithets for Joseph based on his provisioning of Egypt (Gen 42:6, cited by **R**), his wisdom in dream interpretation (Gen 44:21), and his beauty (Gen 39:6, cited by **B1**).

48 The language of the first phrase seems to allude to Gen 37:29, where Reuben discovers that Joseph is missing from the pit—a cryptic reference to the sale of Joseph, and an admission of guilt on Judah's part; the second phrase, "a vow do not nullify" may entreat the vizier not to force the brothers to go back to Jacob without Benjamin, the son they swore to protect. Spiegel, however, suggests that "the vow" refers to Joseph's complicity in hiding the truth—that he was alive—from his father, in fidelity to an oath his brothers swore at the pit when they sold him, and in which God was complicit, as well (64). See *PRE* 38.

בִּי אֲדוֹנִי מֶנִּי הִנָּצֵר
אָח מֵאַחִים לֹא יִבָּצֵר

גִּבּוֹר בָּעוֹז הַנִּקְרָא כְּפִיר
וְשָׂח לַמַּשְׁבִּיר וּמַסְבִּיר וּמַשְׁפִּיר
דָּבָר בַּבּוֹר וְנֶדֶר אַל תָּפֵיר
פֶּן פָּנֵינוּ בִּפְנֵי אָב תַּחְפִּיר

...

כִּי קֶירַע אָב עַד אָנָה לֹא נִיתְאָח

...

עַד עַתָּה אָב לֹא נָח מֵאָח

זֹאת הֵשִׁיב לשׁ.. ...
... אַל נָא תִּפְרוֹץ פֶּרֶץ

...

כִּי בִגְבוּלָם יה.. ...

טֶבַח סָח אָשִׁית בִּגְבוּלְךָ
ואח.. ... ..מְשָׁרְתֶיךָ לְהַכּוֹת בְּגָדְלְךָ
יָד הֶרֶף עַד מָתַי הִיתְגּוֹלְלָךְ
כִּי בְשִׂמְלָתִי בְדָמָיו אֲגוֹלְלָךְ

כַּבִּיר גְּבִיר אַחִים בְּחֵימָה
וּקְרָב לִקְרָב וְלַמִּלְחָמָה
לַיִשׁ גִּיבּוֹר בַּבְּהֵמָה
וְשׁוֹר מֶנּוּ הִיתִישׁ חֵימָה

מַרְעִישׁ נוֹא בְּשַׁאֲגוֹ כְּלָבִיא

49 See Gen 44:26 (**B1**).

50 A reference to Jacob's rites of mourning in Gen 37:34 (**B1**).

51 See Gen 43:18 (**R**); literally, "in order to roll against us"—i.e., to assail us.

52 Prov 30:30 (**B1**).

53 The manuscript is difficult; the translation here follows **B1** (who reads יירתע in place of היתיש). The *Ma'agarim* text yields "the ox purged his anger from him," but that seems to fit the narrative flow less well.

54 See *GenR* 93:6 (and the variant in *TargN* to Gen 44:19), where, in response to Judah's threats, Joseph becomes agitated and signals his son, Manasseh, with a stamp of his foot [or, in some version, Manasseh stamps his foot], causing the whole palace to tremble with a might that can only come from the line of Jacob. According to the Neophyti version, Jacob is agitated not by Judah's threat of violence against himself, Pharaoh, and all Egypt, but by compassion and the realization that Judah's haughtiness is gone, replaced by a desire to protect Benjamin and their father.

towards Pithom [he cried out] like a prophet[55]
"I pledged myself for this boy to my father
"Give him back, and the wrath of my heart will be appeased."

He said to him: "Against me should your hand be, sir
"I will be his substitute, like a servant shall I serve you
"Why against us did you plot such a secret
"And not act in complete good faith?"[56]

A powerful outburst, making himself known[57]
the fruitful vine, when he stood to save him,
Zaphenat-Paneah[58] thus they beheld
"I am he who was completely torn asunder," they heard[59]

His voice! – When they heard it they fainted
their spirits .... from them flew out[60]
Seeing them, "the horns of the *re'em*"[61] ...
for the one decrees made his thanksgiving and rejoiced[62]

The roar reached as far as Tahpenes [and Hanes][63]
...
"Know that, indeed, I am Joseph!"[64]
... [and you shall] dwell[65] with me ...

[Then Judah approached...]

(7[1]) ...
Then he approached: the one who plows,
    the hot wrath of ... sharp his sword
Then he approached: he who tears prey[66],

---

55 The rhyme here depends on "lion" (*labi'*) and "prophet" (*nabi'*); according to *GenR* 93:7, all Egypt trembled at the power of Judah's voice. Lacuna filled as by **B1**.

56 Gen 44:21 (**B1**).

57 See above, where Manasseh's foot stomp gives their lineage away; according to *TargN* to Gen 44:19, "And Joseph beckoned to his son Manasseh; he stamped with his foot on the palace and all the palace was shaken." This powerful stomp reveals that the official before whom the brothers stand can only be Joseph. The following lines describe their response to this revelation. **B1** connects the language to Judg 5:7, 11.

58 A name for Joseph in Gen 41:45.

59 Joseph here quotes what the brothers told Jacob in Gen 37:33.

60 **B1** cites *Tanḥ Vayiggash.* 5; the shock of seeing Joseph alive causes the brothers' souls to fly out of them, but angels restore the souls and thus resurrect the brothers. See below.

61 That is, Joseph, according to Deut 33:17 (**R**)

לְעוּמַּת פּוֹתֵר ... כְּמוֹ נָבִיא
נַעַר עָרַבְתִּי מֵאָבִי
תְּנָה וְהָשֵׁךְ שַׂעֲרַת לְבָבִי

שָׂח לוֹ. בִּי תְּהִי נָא יָדְךָ
אֲנִי תְּמוּרוֹ כְּעֶבֶד אֶעֱבָדְךָ
עָלֵינוּ לָמָּה הֶעֱרַמְתָּה סוֹדְךָ
וְלֹא שִׁילַּמְתָּה פְּעוּלַּת חַסְדָּךְ

פִּירְזוֹן גְּבוּרָה בְּהוֹדִיעוֹ
פּוֹרַת כְּעָמַד לְהוֹשִׁיעוֹ
צָפְנַת פַּעְנֵיחַ בְּכֵן שָׁעוֹ
אֲנִי טָרוֹף טוֹרַף הִשְׁמִיעוֹ

קוֹלוֹ בְּקָוֹשְׁבָם נִתְעַלָּפוּ
רוּחִי.. מֵהֶם הוּעָפוּ
רְאוֹתָם קַרְנֵי רְאֵם ...
לְגוֹזֵר וְעָשׂ הוֹדוּ וְתוֹפִיפוּ

שְׁאוֹן תַּחְפַּנְחֵס הֶאָסֵף
...
תֵּדְעוּ כִּי אֲנִי הוּא יוֹסֵף
... ..שבתם אִתִּי ...

[...]

... (ז')
וַיִּגַּשׁ **ח**וֹרֵשׁ **ח**ֵימַת **ח**ָרוֹן
..ל **ח**וּד **ח**ַרְבּוֹ
וַיִּגַּשׁ **ט**וֹרֵף **ט**ֶיבַח

62 The final verb is from תפף, literally, "to sound the timbrel."

63 The Ma'agarim text would be translated, "A crowd was gathered in Tahpenes," but the reading offered in **B1** seems preferable. Tahpenes and Hanes are cities in Egypt; see Isa 30:4 and Jer 43:7, and this indicates both the power of Judah's voice and the drama of the conflict between the brothers.

64 Gen 45:3 (**B1**). According to *GenR* 93:8 and 10 (**B1** cites the latter), the brothers do not believe Joseph is their long-lost brother until he shows them the sign of his circumcision— hence the translation here, "*See*, I am Joseph…" (indicating that he offered visual proof of his identity). Joseph's self-revelation to his brothers is described in detail later in this piyyut.

65 Only the letters שבתם אתי are visible in the MS. Presumably the verb is either from ישב ("to dwell"), as rendered here, or from שוב ("to return").

66 That is, the lion (**B2** cites Ps 7:3, 22:4, and others.)—meaning Judah.

casting off good sense of his purity[67]
Then he approached: Judah descended
together … fear of his pride[68]
Then he approached: a lion whelp,
the stored up … the profit of his honor
Then he approached: a lion, learned
to sustain[69] … his flesh[70]
Then he approached: king facing the king
of … the gift of his insight[71]
Then he approached: roaring
raising the banner of … the crown of his triumph
Then he approached: a straight-spined prince,
stormy in … his suffering[72]
Then he approached: one who pledged an eternal pledge:[73]
his freedom[74]
Then he approached: an officer
… his reason
Then he approached: a messenger
… crying out his victory
Then he approached: proclaiming a vow
in a voice … his inmost self
Then he approached: … a net,
shaking with the strength of his wrath
Then he approached: roaring, panting,
audibly, a weapon in his grip[75]
Then he approached: seeking to give comfort,
in strength of praise is his honor[76]

---

67 "Purity" in the sense of mercy or kindness. For "good sense," see Ps 119:66.

68 This line and the following recall the themes of the *qedushta* to Gen 38, in which Judah's new-found humility (there when he admitted to his guilt in the affair with Tamar, here when he expresses remorse for the fate of Joseph) results in an increase in his honor. Judah's maturation is one reason why the most important messianic figure—that of the Davidic line—will spring from Judah's lineage rather than that of another brother (e.g., Joseph) who might seem, superficially, more worthy.

69 Isa 50:4

70 Zeph 1:7; alternatively, it could be understood as "his food" or, perhaps, "his battle."

71 **B2** cites Eccl 7:7. See *GenR* 93:3, *TanḥB Vayiggash*. 6, and *TargN* and *TargPsJ* to Gen 44:18.

טוֹרֵד בְּטוּב טַעַם טָוהֳרוֹ
וַיִּגַּשׁ יְהוּדָה יָרַד
יַחַד ... יִרְאַת יְקָרוֹ
וַיִּגַּשׁ כְּפִיר כָּמוּס
כ.. ... כִּישְׁרוֹן כְּבוֹדוֹ
וַיִּגַּשׁ לָבִיא לָמוּד
לָעוּת ... לְחוֹמוֹ
וַיִּגַּשׁ מֶלֶךְ מוּל מֶלֶךְ
... מַתְּנַת מַדָּעוֹ
וַיִּגַּשׁ נוֹהֵם נֹשֵׂא נֵס
... נֵיזֶר נִיצְחוֹ
וַיִּגַּשׁ שַׂר סָעוּד
סַעַר ב.. ..ל סִיחָתוֹ
וַיִּגַּשׁ עוֹרֵב עֲרוּבַת עוֹלָם
ב.. ... עַצְמוֹ
וַיִּגַּשׁ פָּקִיד פ..
... ב.. ... פֵּירוּשׁוֹ
וַיִּגַּשׁ צִיר ...
..קה בצ.. צַעֲקַת צוֹלְחוֹ
וַיִּגַּשׁ קוֹרֵא ... קִיוּם
בְּקוֹל ק.. קִירְבּוֹ
וַיִּגַּשׁ ר.. ... רֶשֶׁת
בְּרַעַשׁ רֶגֶשׁ רָוגְזוֹ
וַיִּגַּשׁ ... שָׁאַג שׁוֹאֵף
בְּשֶׁימַע שֶׁלַח שׁוֹעֲלוֹ
וַיִּגַּשׁ תּוֹבֵעַ תֵּת תַּעֲנוּג
בְּתוֹקֶף תְּהִילוֹת תִּיפְאַרְתּוֹ

72 The word rendered "suffering" here (סיחתו) in the sense that it has in 1 Sam 1:16, where it is in parallel with "distress" (pointed out in **B2**). A more common translation would be simply "speech."

73 The language here draws on Prov 17:18 (**B2**).

74 Lit., "himself" (עצמו). That is, Judah offered himself as a slave in Benjamin's stead (Gen 44:32); see also *Tanḥ Vayiggash* 2 (**B2**).

75 See 2 Chron 23:10, 32:5 for שלח as "weapon;" the word rendered "grip" is, literally, "handful."

76 This final line seems to suggest that Judah's moral qualities, not his physique, are the source of his power. All the physical vigor and energizing anger of the earlier lines seems to evaporate here, as Judah turns from confrontation to appeasement.

And thus, "He said, `Please ..."[77]

(7²) *Please, my lord,* a father *do not* cast away;
Please, my lord, a son *do not* seek![78]
Please, my lord, a kid *do not* steal;
Please, my lord, justice *do not* thrust aside![79]
Please, my lord, a promise *do not* overturn;
Please, my lord, as for you: *do not* tarry!
Please, my lord, "this"[80] *do not* remember;
Please, my lord, a sin *do not* recollect!
Please, my lord, a slaughter *do not* cause;
Please, my lord, a boy *do not* break!
Please, my lord, an honest man *do not* make crooked
Please, my lord, against us *do not* make war!
Please, my lord, a word *do not* warp;
Please, my lord, testimony *do not* transgress!
Please, my lord, hatred *do not* feel;
Please, my lord, a wicked deed *do not* do!
Please, my lord, our faces *do not* cast into darkness;
Please, my lord, our radiance *do not* dim![81]
Please, my lord, a relative *do not* rob;
Please, my lord, a quarrel *do not* create!
Please, my lord, a tribe[82] *do not* wipe out;
Please, my lord, Tahpenes *do not* destroy!

Silluqah

(8) The ox was not terrified nor did the lion flee
this one speaks and the other responds
this one says and the other replies,[83]
The seller and the sold;
and a heavenly voice from above answers:
"This is the time and the moment!
"Here is battle And here is war!"

---

77 This entire unit is based on the bilingual pun between *bi* (Hebrew for "please" in Gen 44:18) and *bia* (Greek for "injustice") noted above.

78 The first two lines recall the language of Eccl 3:6, "A time to seek, and a time to lose; a time to keep, and a time to cast away" (**B1**).

79 The MS contains the word תחדוף, an error; Maʾagarim and **B2** emend to תדחוף, accepted here. **B2** contains a discussion.

ובכן ויאמר בי

(ז[2]) בִּי אֲדֹנִי אָב   אַל תְּאַבֵּד
בִּי אֲדֹנִי בֵּן   אַל תְּבַקֵּשׁ
בִּי אֲדֹנִי גְּדִי   אַל תִּגְזוֹל
בִּי אֲדֹנִי דִּין   אַל תִּדְחוֹף
בִּי אֲדֹנִי הַבְטָחָה   אַל תַּהֲפוֹךְ
בִּי אֲדֹנִי וְאַתָּה   אַל תּוֹחִיל
בִּי אֲדֹנִי זֹאת   אַל תִּזְכּוֹר
בִּי אֲדֹנִי חֵטְא   אַל תַּחְשׁוֹב
בִּי אֲדֹנִי טֶבַח   אַל תָּטִיל
בִּי אֲדֹנִי יֶלֶד   אַל תְּיַיחֵת
בִּי אֲדֹנִי כֵּן   אַל תַּכְרִיעַ
בִּי אֲדֹנִי לָנוּ   אַל תִּלָּחֵם
בִּי אֲדֹנִי מִלָּה   אַל תָּמִיר
בִּי אֲדֹנִי נוֹכְחֵינוּ   אַל תִּנְאַץ
בִּי אֲדֹנִי שִׂנְאָה   אַל תִּשְׂנָא
בִּי אֲדֹנִי עֲלִילָה   אַל תַּעַשׂ
בִּי אֲדֹנִי פָּנֵינוּ   אַל תַּפִּיל
בִּי אֲדֹנִי צָוהֳרֵינוּ   אַל תְּצַאֲנֵן
בִּי אֲדֹנִי קָרֹב   אַל תִּקְבַּע
בִּי אֲדֹנִי רִיב   אַל תָּרִיב
בִּי אֲדֹנִי שֵׁבֶט   אַל תַּשְׁבִּית
בִּי אֲדֹנִי תַּחְפַּנְחֵס   אַל תַּתִּים

סילוקה

(ח) וְלֹא נִבְהַל שׁוֹר וְלֹא נֶחְפַּז אֲרִי
זֶה מְדַבֵּר וְזֶה מֵשִׁיב
זֶה אוֹמֵר וְזֶה מְקַבֵּל
מוֹכֵר וּמָכוּר
וּבַת קוֹל מִמָּרוֹם עוֹנָה
הִנֵּה הָעֵת וְהָעוֹנָה
הִנֵּה קְרָב וְהִנֵּה מִלְחָמָה

---

80 The sale of Joseph (from which serious and abiding guilt were incurred), or more contextually, the "crime" of Benjamin's supposed theft of the goblet (for which the party is innocent anyway).

81 This stanza draws on the language of Job 29:24. (**B1**)

82 That is, Benjamin.

83 The language here suggests confrontation.

Though the Lord is a man of war
He says: "A time of peace is this!"
As for the vizier,[84] his stomach is in knots:
should he reveal himself to his brothers?
And when it was that he was revealed to them
his most private parts he uncovered to them[85]
They fell on their faces and trembling seized them
throes like a birthing woman enveloped them
and the walls of their hearts trembled[86]
Their spirits grew faint and their souls grew weak
but angels accompanied him
and a heavenly voice called out to them from on high[87]
Behold, his sheaf stood[88]
and his dreams came true[89]
and they opened their mouths and gave praise
to the One who fulfills His word and who sustains His counsel
For with this He is sanctified
And the one called…

(9) And angels on high … protecting His treasure …
… praising and sanctifying…the Helper of the tribes …
… when they stand, replying [and reciting]:
Holy, holy, holy is the Lord of Hosts! The whole earth is filled with His glory!
"*Holy*"—from the remnant of Judah
"*Holy*"—from the remainder of Joseph
"*Holy*"—from those left of Benjamin[90]
Holy, holy, holy is the Lord of Hosts! The whole earth is filled with His glory!
"*Holy*"—the deed that was done when Judah drew near to Joseph
"*Holy*"—the deed that was done when Joseph answered Judah
"*Holy*"—was the peace made between them on account of Benjamin[91]
Holy, holy, holy is the Lord of Hosts! The whole earth is filled with His glory!

---

84 Yannai here uses the same term of office that appears in Gen 42:6 (**B2**).

85 That is, Joseph proved his identity by revealing his circumcision to his brothers. See *GenR* 93:8, 10. On the translation of פניו ("his face") as a euphemism for genitalia, see Hos 2:4, *b. Nid.* 14b, and *b. Shab.* 41a (**B1**).

86 An image of faintness and fear. For the language, see Job 37:1 (**B2**)

87 This alludes to the angels who restored the brothers' souls (and lives) to them; see

וְיָיָ אִישׁ מִלְחָמָה
אוֹמֵר עֵת שָׁלוֹם הִיא
וְהַשַּׁלִּיט מֵעָיו הוֹמִים
לְהִתְוַדַּע אֶל אֶחָיו
וְעֵת אֲשֶׁר נִגְלָה לָהֶם
וּפָנָיו גִּילָּה לָהֶם
נָפְלוּ עַל פְּנֵיהֶם וּרְעָדָה אֲחָזָתָם
חִיל כַּיּוֹלֵדָה אֲפָפָם
וַיִּתֵּר קִיר לִבָּם
וַתִּתְעַלֵּף רוּחָם וַתִּתְעַטֵּף נַפְשָׁם
וּמַלְאָכִים אֲשֶׁר לִיווּהוּ
וּבַת קוֹל מִמָּרוֹם קָרְאוּ לָהֶם
הִנֵּה קָמָה אֲלֻומָּתוֹ
וְנִצְּבוּ חֲלוֹמוֹתָיו
וּפָתְחוּ פִּיהֶם וְנָתְנוּ שֶׁבַח
לִמְקַיֵּים דְּבָרוֹ וּמַעֲמִיד עֲצָתוֹ
כִּי בְכֵן יוּקְדַּשׁ
וקרא זה

(ט) וּמַלְאֲכֵי מָרוֹם מ.. ... מַחְסֵנֵי יִקְרָתוֹ
מ.. ... מַעֲרִיצִים וּמַקְדִּישִׁים ... עֶזְרַת הַשְּׁבָטִים
ב.. ... מַעֲמָדָם עוֹנִים ...
קדוש קדוש קדוש יי צבאות מלא כל הארץ כבודו
קָדוֹשׁ מִפְּלֵיטַת יְהוּדָה
קָדוֹשׁ מִשְּׁאֵרִית יוֹסֵף
קָדוֹשׁ מִתּוֹתֶרֶת בִּנְיָמִין
קדוש קדוש קדוש יי צבאות מלא כל הארץ כבודו
קָדוֹשׁ עֲלִילָה עָשָׂה גִּישַׁת יְהוּדָה אֶל יוֹסֵף
קָדוֹשׁ עֲלִילָה עָשָׂה עֲנִיוּת יוֹסֵף לִיהוּדָה
קָדוֹשׁ שָׁלוֹם עָשׂ בֵּינֵיהֶם עֲדֵי בִּנְיָמִין
קדוש קדוש קדוש יי צבאות מלא כל הארץ כבודו

Tanḥ Vayiggash 4 (**R**).

88 Here the poet explicitly alludes to Joseph's dream in Gen 37.

89 Lit., "stood."

90 These epithets come from Isa 37:31 (Judah), Amos 5:15 (Joseph) (cited in **B1**).

91 This seems to be a play on Gen 49:27, but taking עדי as a preposition rather than the noun meaning "spoils, booty."

"Holy"—from the *Ḥayyot*
"Holy"—from the *Ofanim*
"Holy"—from the *Cherubim*
Towards each other, all say, "Blessed is the glory of the Lord from this place"

"From His place"—He praised Joseph when he said, "I am Joseph"[92]
and He is in His place
"From His place"—He restored the souls of the brothers of Joseph,
and He is in His place
"From His place"—He will return and He will be gracious to the
remnant of Joseph [*and He is in His place*]
Twice

Woe to us for the Day of Judgment! Woe[93] *to us for the Day of Rebuke!*[94]

The most loved of the brothers[95] when he revealed himself to his brothers
against his rebuke they could not stand
Woe to us for the Day of Judgment!...

Even more so, how shall we stand on the Day of Rebuke
when the Judge says "Come, let us reason together"[96]
Woe to us for the Day of Judgment!...

Just as the brothers were not able to answer their brother
on the Day of Judgment what will we say?
Woe to us for the Day of Judgment!...

'This one,' when he made himself known, no one could stay standing[97]
The Living One, when He rebukes him, how does he stand?
Woe to us for the Day of Judgment!...

His voice—when they heard it, they fell on (their) faces
The Lord—when He judges, (our) faces will fall[98]
Woe to us for the Day of Judgment!...

---

92 **B1** cites Gen 45:4, "And Joseph said to his brothers, Come near me, I beg you. And they came near. And he said, I am Joseph your brother, whom you sold into Egypt..." Joseph's comments indicate that he was privy to the divine mind and plan.

93 For this form of "woe" (אי, perhaps a contraction of אוי), see Eccl 10:16.

94 This opening line functions as a refrain; the section is structured as a complete alphabetical acrostic. **R** compares this passage to *GenR* 93:10, which states: "Woe to us for the day of judgment, woe to us for the day of rebuke!... Joseph was the youngest of the tribal ancestors, yet his brethren could not withstand his rebuke, as it says, 'And his brothers could

קָדוֹשׁ מחיה
קָדוֹשׁ מאופן
קדוש מכרוב
לעומתם כל יאמרו ברוך כבוד יי ממקומו

מִמְּקוֹמוֹ שִׁיבַּח לְיוֹסֵף כְּנָם אֲנִי יוֹסֵף
והוא במקומו
מִמְּקוֹמוֹ הֵשִׁיב אֶת נֶפֶשׁ אֲחֵי יוֹסֵף
והוא במקומו
מִמְּקוֹמוֹ יָשׁוּב וְיָחוֹן
אֶת שְׁאֵירִית יוֹסֵף

פעמים

אִי לָנוּ מִיּוֹם דִּין אִי לָנוּ מִיּוֹם תּוֹכֵיחָה

אָהוּב אַחִים בְּהִתְוַדְּעוֹ לְאַחִים
בְּתוֹכַחְתּוֹ לֹא קָמוּ אַחִים

אי לנו מיום דין וג׳

גַּם מַה נַּעֲשֶׂה לְיוֹם תּוֹכֵיחָה
דַּיָּן בְּאָמְרוֹ לְכוּ נָא וְנִוָּוכְחָה

אי לנו מיום דין וג׳

הֵן אַחִים לְאַח לֹא יָכְלוּ עֲנוֹת
וּבְיוֹם דִּין מַה יֵּשׁ לַעֲנוֹת

אי לנו מיום דין

זֶה בְּהִתְוַדְּעוֹ אִישׁ לֹא עָמַד
חַי בְּהוֹכִיחוֹ אֵיךְ יֵשׁ מַעֲמָד

אי לנו

טַעֲמוּ בְקָושְׁבָם נָפְלוּ עַל פָּנִים
יָהּ בְּשָׁפְטוֹ אֵיךְ יֵשׁ תָּלוּי פָּנִים

אי לנו

---

not answer him' (Gen45:2)—how much more then when the Holy One, blessed be He, comes and rebukes each man according to his deserts!..."

95 Gen 37:3 (**B1**).

96 Isa 1:18

97 Joseph's dream of Gen 37, in which the sheaves and stars bow before him, comes to pass.

98 Reading יפלו with **B1**; see also Gen 4:5 and Jer 25:31 for this language. Ma'agarim's תלוי would be translated as "suspended, hung," perhaps also with a connotation of "to lay low" or paralysis.

As one they knelt and bent their stature
In the future, God will rebuke; how will anyone stand?
Woe to us for the Day of Judgment!...

Before his face, they trembled, when he said, "I am your brother!"
"A lad you sold for your pairs of sandals"[99]
Woe to us for the Day of Judgment!...

His speech—when they heard it, they fretted with fear
They offered no answer and for them, and wisdom was hidden from them
Woe to us for the Day of Judgment!...

Fear and trembling seized them there
Their tears poured forth, and their sweat
Woe to us for the Day of Judgment!...

Near, like a destroyer, he will come from Shaddai
Far and near, they will say, "How shall we come?"
Woe to us for the Day of Judgment!...

We heard and were astonished at the trembling of Joseph[100]
Astonishment and trembling will there be at the time when You gather
Your right hand will gather a second time
You will make heard to a people whom You will gather to Your Abode
"To be to you as a God ..."[101]

99 The final words of this line are visible in the MS and cited by **B1**. See the *qedushta* for Gen 37:1 for more on this motif.

100 Note that it is Joseph who trembles, not Judah. Will God—the Judge—tremble at the

כְּאַחַת כָּרְעוּ וְכָפְפוּ קוֹמָה
לְעֵת יוֹכִיחַ אֵל אֵיךְ יֵשׁ תְּקוּמָה

אי לנו

מִפָּנָיו נִבְהֲלוּ כְּסָח אֲנִי אֲחִיכֶם
נַעַר מְכַרְתֶּם בְּנַעֲלֵיכֶם

אי לנו

סִיחָתוֹ בְשָׁמְעָם דָּאֲגוּ מֵאֵימָה
עֲנִייָה לֹא עָנוּ וּמֵהֶם נֶעְלְמָה חָכְמָה

אי לנו

פְּחָדָה וּרְעָדָה שָׁם אֲחָזָתַם
צָקֶה דִּימְעָתָם וְזֵיעָתָם

אי לנו

קָרוֹב כְּשׁוֹד מִשַּׁדַּי יָבוֹא
רְחוֹקִים וּקְרוֹבִים יֹאמְרוּ אֵיךְ נָבוֹא

אי לנו

שָׁמַעְנוּ וְנִתְמָהַנוּ לְחֵרֶדֶת יוֹסֵף
תִּימָּהוֹן וַחֲרָדָה עֵת תֵּאָסֵף
יַד יְמִינְךָ שֵׁנִית תּוֹסֵף
וְתַשְׁמִיעַ לְעָם אֲשֶׁר לְנָוְוךָ תֵּאָסֵף
להיות לכם לאלהים וג׳

---

repentance of Israel?

101 Lev 22:33, 25:38; and Num 15:41; in each verse God's declaration is made in connection with the Exodus from Egypt.

Commentary

Formally, this piyyut is unusual in several respects: Poem Two (the *meḥayyeh*) is followed by a doubled conclusion which mentions rain rather than dew in both variations; Poem Five (the *ʿasiriyyah*) reaches a level of linguistic complexity normally associated with the *rahit*; and Poem Nine (the *qedushah*) is both atypically long and includes an exceptional appendix. This appendix builds on the central episode of the *sidra*, the moment of confrontation and reconciliation between the brothers. However, Yannai reads that episode as an encoded warning about the ultimate day of judgment, which traditional Judaism teaches all are destined to face.

Indeed, while the messianism found here has parallels in other works by Yannai, the motif of redemption usually inspires a tone of confidence and optimism, resolution and hope. In contrast, here the tenor is anxious and introspective. Not only does Yannai use the story of Genesis 44 as a warning for his community—"Woe for us!" for we will stand before one much more powerful than Pharaoh's "vizier," and in need of so much more forgiveness—but some of the darker elements of rabbinic lore are found here, such as the passing reference to the doomed messiah of the house of Joseph. Through the rhetoric of this poem, Yannai encourages his listeners to identify with Joseph's brothers, who momentarily die of shock and must be revived by angels when Joseph reveals himself. Their mortifying astonishment comes not from the judgment God passes on them for their crimes, but the judgment they pass on themselves in that moment of radical and traumatic self-awareness. Even the messianic scenario envisioned by Amos, that the land will be so fertile that the sower will meet the reaper, takes on grim, confrontational overtones.

Overall, throughout the piyyut, the poet affirms God's magnanimous nature and the coming redemption. In the third poem, which stresses the imagery of the great battle against Edom at the end of days, the poet assures his audience of Judah's inevitable victory. Nowhere in the piyyut, however, does the poet downplay guilt, communal or individual. The sale of Joseph was a crime in its own right, an offense not only against Joseph but the entire family of Jacob; all consequent suffering was self-inflicted. Down to the present day and into the future, there remains the potential for renewed violence: Joseph considers revenge while Judah vows to prevent a second tragedy. Each party bears a legitimate grudge, and justice is not easy to determine.

It is not clear who the "hero" of this poem is: both Judah and Joseph have their merits and embody the agony of their individual predicaments, but each also moves precipitously towards violent conflict. The poet conveys a range of complex emotions by focusing on the welter of feelings that course through the minds and hearts of Joseph, Judah, and the other brothers. Rather than emphasizing any single tone or action—anger, petition, magnanimity—Yannai here creates a complicated composition in which moods and feelings welter and shift, rise and fall, from moment to moment. The unstable emotional ambiance generates a vivid impression of immediacy and realism. Everyone in this poem is haunted and conflicted, manifesting in the world of action deeply felt internal agonies. At the level of allegory, this poem may well encapsulate Yannai's own anxiety regarding the seductive lure of apocalypse and active messianism (which he himself voices in the *meshallesh*)—hopes vividly alive in Yannai's own day but which he ultimately rejects, over and over again.[101]

The potential for violence on a scale that is both familial and national is a powerful recurring motif throughout this piyyut. The battle between the lion and the ox—one the natural prey of the other—recalls the mythic battle between Leviathan and Behemoth in the final chapters of the Book of Job. The poet's distressed depiction of this struggle reflects anxiety over the possibility of fratricide. The conflict at the heart of this Torah portion is not one the poet can anticipate with glee; calamity lurks close to the surface as brother faces off with brother. Unlike Jacob and Esau, whose kinship is rarely emphasized despite the fact that they are twins, the sons of Jacob are all one people. In his allegory, Yannai does not call Rome to account, but the Jews. As such, for all the tension that he generates, the poet—amplifying the structure of the *sidra*—keeps the violence from materializing. The pain is all moral and self-inflicted; it comes not from external agents but from judgments individuals pass on themselves.

The presence of angels and the heavenly hosts add an otherworldly element to this poem and broaden its scale from the familial and national to the cosmic. In Poems Six and Eight, angels are positive and work on behalf of humans. In Poem Nine, they join the humans, singing hymns to God. But in Poem Eight, a darker note is introduced. Picking up on the binary structure of Eccl 3, the poet introduces a heavenly voice that cries

---

102 See Chapter Four.

out that this is a moment for war, apparently encouraging the confrontation between Joseph and Judah, egging on their darker, more violent impulses. Physical conflict is only averted when God intervenes. Despite being a "man of war," God declares that the encounter between Judah and Joseph is a time for making peace. No other voice in the poem seems capable of diffusing the hostility that seems ready to erupt between the two protagonists.

Ultimately, in this poem, humans act while God reacts. Even when the combatants are ambivalent and conflicted, they possess the ability to inflict serious harm on themselves and others. On a national level, Yannai reflects the Jewish struggle with the militarism implicit in messianism, which he believes the children of Judah must overcome just as Judah did. On a familial level, in the arena of mythic history, Joseph, Judah, and even the heavenly host are ready to wage war against one another, a microcosm of civil war. Here Yannai perhaps obliquely addresses a fragmented Jewish community, divided against itself as it seeks survival strategies against an increasingly powerful and confident Byzantine Empire.

On an individual level, every person is destined for a personal confrontation with his own lifetime tally of actions, the consequences of personal choices and individual restraint. Inspired by this solemn idea and the dramatic narrative of his biblical canvas, the poet creates vivid dramatic tensions. He juxtaposes Judah's newfound maturity and wisdom with his enduring instincts for violence and Joseph's deep emotional response to his brothers' transformations with his sense of justice and self-preservation. Along the way, we also witness the brothers' transformative experience of self-recognition—Joseph reveals himself, but all the brothers learn about themselves. Their history is not what they thought it was; they do not know their own life stories. The world is suddenly, totally different. Rather than filling the poet with hope, however, these imagined encounters seem to fill Yannai with doubt and dread; looking inward rather than outward, the poet keenly acknowledges the failings of creation. The poem opens with trembling and concludes with the Day of Judgment—albeit one which concludes with a faint hint of redemption; the struggle that fills the lines in between are a plea to God to make things other than the way they seem doomed to be.

Qedushta for Genesis 48:1 בראשית מח:א

ויאמר ליוסף הנה אביך חלה

"Then he said to Joseph, `Lo, your father is ill'"

This piyyut focuses less on the narrative content of the *sidra* and more on philosophical concepts that the Torah portion suggests: in this case, what purposes do illness and suffering serve? Jacob is the first character in the biblical story said to fall ill; in keeping with midrashic methods of reading, his illness teaches us something about the nature of sickness and suffering. According to this poem, sickness came into the world to inspire people to put their affairs in order, both as individuals (through repentance) and as members of a family (by creating blessings, wills, and testaments). In this context, Yannai presents a tender portrait of an intimate family scene while also depicting the dignity of old age. Blessings, meanwhile, link the generations one to another.

(1) …

And it is written: "And it came to pass after these things, that he told Joseph, `Lo, your father is ill;' and he took with him his two sons, Manasseh and Ephraim" (Gen 48:1)
And it is said: "A man's spirit will sustain him through illness; but [low spirits]—who can bear them?" (Prov 18:14)
And it is said: "Listen to your father who begot you; do not disdain your mother when she is old" (Prov 23:22)
And it is said: "The sons of one's sons are a crown of old age, and the glory of children is their parents" (Prov 17:6)[1]
And it is said: "Yea, you shall see your children's children and peace will be upon Israel" (Ps 128:6)[2]

Israel is [the work of Your hand][3]
and they are the flock of Your hand[4]
Shield them in the shelter of Your hand
Blessed are You… Shield…

(2) … flame
beauty, pleasure he loved
The pure one placed …
a love strong as death was his love[5]
His turning towards death …
…
He called and paid him honor[6]
trembling, to seek …
… that ached
upon his hearing, the one who saw You yearned to see him
[He hastened and] was strengthened and was seated[7]
Bolstered, he sat upon the bed.

As it is written: "When Jacob was told, `Here, your son Joseph has come to see you,' Israel gathered his strength and sat up in bed" (Gen 48:2)

---

1 In this context, this verse refers to Ephraim and Manasseh, Joseph's sons, who are "like Reuben and Simeon" (**R**).

2 This puns on the ambiguity of "Israel" – in its original context, the verse refers to the nation, but here, in the aggadic-midrashic setting, it refers specifically to the patriarch Jacob.

3 Completed according to **B2**, based on Isa 45:11 and 60:21.

4 Ps 95:7 (**B2**).

(א) ....

ונאמר איש יכלכל מחלהו ורוח נכאה מי ישאנה

ונאמר שמע לאביך זה ילדך ואל תבוז כי זקנה אמך

ונאמר עטרת זקינים בני בנים ותפארת בנים אבותם

ונאמר וראה בנים לבניך שלום על ישראל

יִשְׂרָאֵל ... ..דך
וְהֵם צֹאן יָדָךְ
גּוֹנְנֵם בְּצֵל יָדָךְ
ברוך... מגן...

(ב) ... ..אד לַהַב
נוֹאי נוֹעַם אָהָב
שָׂם תָּם ...
עַזָּה כַּמָּוֶות אַהֲבָה אֲשֶׁר אָהָב
פְּנוֹתוֹ לְמִיתָה ...
... ..וד
קָרָא וְחָלַק לוֹ כָבוֹד
רָעַד לְבַקֵּשׁ ...
... אֲשֶׁר כָּאָב
שָׁמְעוֹ הֵן שׁוֹרָךְ לְשׁוּרֵנוּ תָּאָב
... נִתְחַזֵּק וְנִיתְיַישָּׁב
תָּמַךְ וְעַל מִיטָּה יָשָׁב

ככתוב ויגד ליעקב ויאמר הנה בנך יוסף בא אליך ויתחזק ישראל וישב על המטה

---

5 The second stich reworks Song 8:6, cited below.

6 See *GenR* 97 (**R**), which states: "'And Israel strengthened himself and sat up upon the bed' (Gen 48:2)—in order to pay honor to royalty." The image is that Jacob accords Joseph the honor due to his Egyptian status, thus fulfilling the dream in Gen 37. Joseph's power and station, however, cannot shield Jacob from mortality or the son from grief.

7 Lacuna filled as by **B1**. The language of this stich recalls that of the second *rahit*.

And as it is said: "Many seek audience with a ruler, but man's justice is from the Lord" (Prov 29:26)
And as it is said: "Set me like a seal upon your heart, like the seal upon your arm, for as strong as death is love, passion as hard as Sheol; its darts are darts of fire, a heavenly flame" (Song 8:6)[8]
And as it is said: "For this let every pious man pray to You at the time of finding, that the rushing mighty waters not draw near overwhelming him" (Ps 32:6)[9]

The time draws near[10]
to renew the old,
to revive the sleepers with the dew.[11]
Blessed are You… Who resurrects…

(3) You decreed that each will die
but [You made each thing] beautiful in its season[12]
a cup is mixed for each[13]
for each will end like the other[14]
They worried over the illness [but rejoiced on the day of death][15]
because the day of death will atone for their lives[16]
Princely power is nothing on the day of death
for who does not fear death until he is swallowed by death?
The first sickness was a warning; the second sickness You granted as well

8 This verse also occurs as a prooftext in the *qedushta* on Gen 29:31; there, Yannai emphasizes Leah as unloved by Jacob but loved by God, while here he focuses on Jacob, whose love for God was strong even at the time of his death. The language of "heavenly fire (*shalhevet Yah*)" may be suggestive of his deathbed suffering, which was fierce but sent by God.

9 See *GenR* 92:2 (**R**).

10 This stich, which concerns the messianic era, builds on the language of Ps 32:6 ("drawing near" with the connotation of overwhelming or drowning) and Eccl 12:1, which states: "Remember now your Creator in the days of your youth, before the evil days come, and the years draw near, when you shall say, I have no pleasure in them." In the Psalms verse, being touched (by water) is a threatening image of being washed away; the Ecclesiastes verse, however, refers to the day of reckoning faced by each individual on the day of death. The poet draws these verses together, but transforms them from pleas and warnings to reminders of what awaits the people after illness and death: new life in the world renewed.

11 For this language, see Isa 26:19 and Dan 12:2 (**B2**). Lacuna filled by **R**.

ונאמר רבים מבקשים פני מושל ומיי משפט איש

ונאמר שימיני כחותם על לבך כחותם על זרועך כי עזה כמות אהבה קשה כשאול קנאה רשפיה רשפי אש שלהבתיה

ונאמר על זאת יתפלל כל חסיד אליך לעת מצוא רק לשטף מים רבים אליו לא יגיעו

יַגִּיעוּ שָׁנִים
לְחַדֵּשׁ יְשָׁנִים
... בְּטַל יְשֵׁינִים
ברוך... מחיה...

(ג) יָזַמְתָּה מִיתָה לַכֹּל
וְיָפֶה בְּעִתּוֹ ... כֹּל
כּוֹס מָסוּךְ לַכֹּל
וְהַכֹּל כַּאֲשֶׁר לַכֹּל
נֶעֱצָבִים בְּחוֹלִי ... ..תה
בַּעֲבוּר כִּי עַל חַיֵּיהֶם יְכַפֵּר יוֹם מִיתָה
יַד שִׁילְטוֹן אֵין בְּיוֹם הַמָּוֶת
וּמִי לֹא יִרְאֶה הַמָּוֶת עַד יְבוּלַּע מָוֶת
יְקוֹשׁ חוֹלִי רִאשׁוֹן וְחוֹלִי שֵׁינִי הֶחֱלֵיתָה

---

12 Lacuna filled by **R**.

13 Lacuna filled by **B1**. See *b. Ket.* 8b (**R**), which discusses the language of the mourner's blessing. In particular, the following is appropriate: "He [Resh Lakish] then said to him [Judah ben Naḥmani]: Rise [and] say something with regard to the mourners. He spoke and said: `Our brethren, who are worn out, who are crushed by this bereavement, set your heart to consider this: This it is [that] stands for ever, it is a path from the six days of creation. Many have drunk, many will drink [from the cup of sorrow], as the drinking of the first ones, so will be that of the last ones. Our brethren, the Lord of consolation comfort you. Blessed be He who comforts the mourners...."

14 Eccl 9:2.

15 Completion according to **B1**, based on Prov 31:25 as interpreted in *GenR* 62:2 (which describes the death of Abraham) as teaching that God shows the righteous their destined reward immediately before they die, bringing them joy.

16 See *GenR* 62:2, which interprets Prov 31:25 (**B1**); also note *Mekh. de Rabbi Ishmael Yitro* 7 (**R**).

At the request of the prophets of righteousness, all this You began[17]

And it is written: "Elisha was sick with the sickness of which he would die, and Joash, the king of Israel, came down to him, and he wept over his face and cried, `Father! Father! Israel's chariots and horsemen!'" (2 Kings 13:14)

And it is said: "What man can live and not see death, can save himself from the clutches of Sheol?" (Ps 89:49)

And it is said: "The death of His faithful ones is precious in the sight of the Lord" (Ps 116:15)

And it is said: "No man has power over the lifebreath—to hold back the lifebreath; there is no power over the day of death. There is no mustering out from that war; wickedness is powerless to save its owner" (Eccl 8:8)

And You are holy, enthroned on the praises of Israel… Please, God…

(4) The days of the pure ones You know[18]
but the day of death You do not let them know
So that whether they will grow sick or grow old,
their property they will ready and their heirs they will prepare[19]
Like "the father" and "his only one," when they saw
that they had reached their old age:[20]
They worried when the day of death would be
and they commanded their households what should be[21]
So, too, the pure one, when he fell ill he called to his son, to Joseph
before he was gathered up[22]
Upon him to add additional blessings:[23]

---

17 The "prophets of righteousness" are Jacob, Hezekiah, and Elisha; see *GenR* 97:1 and *b. BMʿa* 87a (**R** cites *GenR* 65:9). According to the traditions cited in these passages, Abraham requested God to create old age, Isaac requested suffering, and Jacob illness; then Hezekiah requested repeated illness. Before Elisha, however, no one recovered from illness; the fact that this verse specifies that this was the illness of which the Prophet would die teaches that before, a person (such as Jacob) simply died as soon as he became ill. Assuming that the haftarah extended to vs. 21 ("And it came to pass, as they were burying a man, that, behold, they spied a band of men; and they cast the man into the sepulcher of Elisha; and when the man was let down, and touched the bones of Elisha, he revived, and stood up on his feet"), the motif of resurrection—the ultimate healing of the ultimate malady, death—is introduced here, as well.

18 In the sense of lifespan.

לִנְבִיאֵי צֶדֶק וּמֵהֶם הַחִילוֹתָה

ככתוב ואלישע חלה את חליו אשר ימות בו וירד אליו יואש מלך ישראל ויבך על פניו ויאמר אבי אבי רכב ישראל ופרשיו

ונאמר מי גבר יחיה ולא יראה מות ימלט נפשו מיד שאול סלה

ונאמר יקר בעיני יי המותה לחסידיו

ונאמר אין אדם שליט ברוח לכלוא את הרוח ואין שלטון ביום המות ואין משלחת במלחמה ולא ימלט רשע את בעליו

ואתה קדוש יושב תהלות ישראל אל נא

(ד) יְמֵי תְמִימִים אַתָּה יוֹדֵיעַ
וְיוֹם מִיתָה לָהֶם לֹא מוֹדִיעַ
לְמַעַן אִם יֶחֱלוּ וְאִם יַזְקִינוּ
מְלַאכְתָּם יַתְקִינוּ וְיוֹרְשֵׁמוֹ יַתְקִינוּ
כְּאָב וִיחִידוֹ אֲשֶׁר בָּטוּ
כִּי לִימוֹת זִיקְנָה נָטוּ
וְדָאֲגוּ פֶּן יוֹם מִיתָה יִהְיֶה
וְצִיווּ עַל בָּתֵּיהֶם מַה יִּהְיֶה
וְתָם בְּעֵת חָלָה קָרָא לִבְנוֹ לְיוֹסֵף
עַד לֹא יֵאָסֵיף
עָלָיו לְהוֹסִיף תּוֹסֶפֶת בְּרָכוֹת

19 The final stich could also be translated: "they will set their affairs in order." The implication is that before death one should arrange one's affairs, in both material (i.e., property distribution) but also—as this last stich indicates—in spiritual and interpersonal terms.

20 That is, Abraham ("the father") and Isaac ("his only one"), both of whom set their affairs in order (in terms of property and blessing) before their deaths; see *TanḥB Vayeḥi* 5 (**R**) and *GenR* 59:11 (**B1**). Jacob (the pure one) follows this familial example.

21 For Abraham, see Gen 18:19; for Isaac, see Gen 28:1–4 (**B2**).

22 That is, Jacob has summoned Joseph so that he could arrange his affairs with him (including designating Ephraim and Manassah as heirs on par with Reuben and Simon, Jacob's first two sons) before he died of this final illness.

23 This line puns on the name Joseph, which is implied through the double repetition of the root for "add/additional" (יסף), in the first stich *le-hoseph*, and in the second *tosephet.*

"Ephraim will be like Reuben, Manasseh will be like Simon"[24]
and then the Holy One confirmed it

(5) So "the father,"[25] when he came into lengthy days, introduced old age
to make known that old age is the end of one's days[26]
Mortal man, when he arrives in his elder days
always fears the day of his death
Likewise "his only one"[27] invented suffering
for sufferings surrender a man to his death
Fretful, for every man frets, fearing such suffering,
lest his breath be cut short and he be surrendered to death unprepared[28]
Thus after "the pure one[29] was sickness introduced
for if a man becomes sick, he will tremble and writhe
Then he will repent in his illness, for he will fear death[30]
just as a sickness summons death.
The pure one called to the one spared defiling of the loins:[31]
"Swear to me by the seal[32] upon your loins!
"God forbid you that you should bury a lamb in the land of asses[33]
"but rather in the place we acquired from the Amorites"[34]
"Abrekh"[35] brought close to him his babes
Then he blessed them and said: "By you may he be blessed![36]
"May Ephraim grow greatly and Manasseh multiply
"Eternally is Ephraim Mine and forever will Manassah belong to Me"[37]

God… Forever You are Exalted…

---

24 That is, Ephraim will be the firstborn of Joseph's sons, as Reuben was for his generation; see the first *rahit*, line 4.

25 Abraham (a pun on his name, as in Gen 17:4–5).

26 The idea that Abraham "invented" old age is attested in aggadic literature (see above), but this specific rationale for his request appears to be unique to Yannai.

27 Isaac (an epithet from Gen 22:2).

28 The language here draws on Num 21:4 ("breath be cut short") and Ps 118:18 ("but He has not surrendered me to death") (**B2**). For the content of this line, see *GenR* 65:9 (**B1**), noted above and discussed in the commentary.

29 Jacob (Gen 25:27).

30 The stich seems to allude to the tradition that Hezekiah asked God to institute *multiple* illnesses prior to death in order to inspire full repentance (*GenR* 65:9). According to this same midrash, the reason Jacob gives for instituting illness in the first place is so that it will inspire

אֶפְרַיִם כִּרְאוּבֵן מְנַשֶּׁה כְּשִׁמְעוֹן
וְאָז הִסְכַּמְתָּה קָדוֹשׁ

(ה) **אָ**ז בְּזִיקְנָה הִתְחִיל אָב בָּא בַיָּמִים
לְהוֹדִיעַ כִּי זִיקְנָה הוּא סוֹף יָמִים
בֵּן אָדָם בְּהַגִּיעוֹ לְזִקְנַת יְמוֹתָיו
יְפַחֵד תָּמִיד מִפְּנֵי יוֹם מוֹתָיו
גַּם יְחִידוֹ הֵחֵל בְּיִסּוּרִים
כִּי הֵם לְאָדָם לְמִיתָה מוֹסְרִים
דָּאוֹג עֲבוּר יֵודְאַג כָּל אִישׁ אִם יְוַסֵּר
פֶּן תִּקְצַר נַפְשׁוֹ וְלַמָּוְותָה יִמָּסֵר
הֵן מֵאִישׁ תָּם הַחוֹלִי הִיתְחִיל
כִּי אִם יֶחֱלֶה אָדָם יֵיחַת וְיָחִיל
וְיָשׁוּב בְּחָלְיוֹ כִּי יִירָא מִמָּוֶת
כִּי הַחוֹלִי קֹרֵא לַמָּוֶות
זָעַק תָּם לְנֶחֱסַךְ מִלְּטַמֵּא יָרֵךְ
הִישָּׁבְעָה לִי בְּחוֹתַם יָרֵךְ
חָלִילָה לָּךְ מִלִּקְבּוֹר שֶׂה בְּצַד חֲמוֹרִים
כִּי אִם בַּאֲשֶׁר קָנִינוּ מֵאֱמוֹרִים
טִיפּוּחָיו הִיגִּישׁ לוֹ אֲבָרֵךְ
וַיְבָרְכֵם וַיֹּאמֶר בְּךָ יְבָרֵךְ
יַרְבִּיב אֶפְרַיִם וַיַּאֲלִיף מְנַשֶּׁה
לְעוֹלָם לִי אֶפְרַיִם וָלָעַד לִי מְנַשֶּׁה

אל לעולם תוערץ

---

a man to think about dividing his property among his heirs, in Jacob's case, Joseph's sons.

31 The epithet used here, "the one spared defiling his loins" alludes to Joseph's refusal to sin with Potiphar's wife.

32 That is, his circumcision; as **R** notes, the language alludes to Gen 47:29, just prior to this *sidra*; **B1** connects with *GenR* 59:5. The language of the line also evokes Song 8:6.

33 The "lamb" is Jacob; "the land of asses" is Egypt; see *Tanḥ Vayeḥi* 5 .

34 That is, the cave of Makhpelah (**R**).

35 I.e., Joseph; see Gen 41:43.

36 See Prov 17:6; the pronouns here are ambiguous—God, Joseph, Ephraim and Manassah all recirocally bless each other.

37 The language of this line draws on Deut 32:17 and Gen 48:20 (**R**), and Ps 60:9 (**B1**). Note also *SifN Behaʿalotekha* 34, where, as **B1** notes, divine assertions of "Mine" always means "forever."

["Then he said to Joseph, `Lo…'"]
(6) "The father whom your soul loves
"He is sick …
"Because of (his) love for you which is like a flame,
"He was drawn down by the bonds of love[38]
"He is deteriorating and declining, near death
"He desires you and says, `This time I will die'"[39]
"The Judge, who releases the children of death[40]
"Precious in his eyes is the death of the righteous
"Your parent, yea, he is gathered unto his people
"And good is the blessing that shall be added to his people."
He took his two sons with him
so that he could bless them with prophecy and prosperity.[41]
Hot fever flushed the face of the father
and weakness seized hold of his hands
But the sick one, when he heard, "Here he is!" gathered strength
seeking renewed strength in his blessings
"He who bore you and dandled you on his knees
"Is burdened by illness and now bent in his knees."
Joseph, when he heard this, lent his strength to his knees[42]
to help him bestow the blessing to those born on his knees
"The one who bore you yearns to behold you
"His soul is faint and weak"
Therefore he did not dawdle when he went up
and his sons he brought up with him
"He who loved you most of all his sons
"He is sick and calls to you, of all of sons"
He bequeathed to his sons[43] a blessing like the greatest of his sons
for the sons of ones sons are like sons
"Your parent approaches the end of his days

---

38 For the language of this line, see Song 8:6 (**B1**) and Hos 11:4 (**R**); the interpretation recalls *GenR* 86:1 (**B1**), discussed in the notes of the *qedushta* for Gen 39. Earlier, the langage described how God led Joseph to Egypt. Here Jacob's love for his son leads him into exile.

39 "Drawn to"—to Egypt. The language of the final stich draws on Prov 6:11 and, even more closely, Eccl 12:5 (citations in **B1**); the implication is that now, after this final illness, Jacob is ready to die.

40 I.e., mortals. See Ps 79:11 (**R**).

41 Based on the use of קח (which appears to be an imperative) as a perfect in Ezek 17:5, I

[ויאמר ליוסף הנה

(ו) **אָ**ב אֲשֶׁר נַפְשׁוֹ לָךְ אֲהֵבָה
חָלָה וג.. ..
בַּעֲבוּר אַהֲבָתָךְ אֲשֶׁר כְּלֶהָבָה
נִמְשַׁךְ בַּעֲבֹתוֹת אַהֲבָה
גוֹוֵעַ וְנָטָה לְמִיתָה
אִוָּה לָךְ וְנָם הַפַּעַם אָמוּתָה
דַּיָּין הַמּוֹתִיר בְּנֵי תְמוּתָה
יָקָר בְּעֵינָיו לַחֲסִידָיו הַמָּוְתָה
הוֹרָךְ הֵן נֶאֱסָף אֶל עַמּוֹ
וְטוֹב בְּרָכָה נֶאֱסֶפֶת עִימּוֹ
וְקָח אֶת שְׁנֵי בָנָיו עִמּוֹ
כִּי יְבָרְכֵם בְּנָאֳמוֹ וְנָעֳמוֹ
זַעַם חוֹלִי עַל אָב חֲוזַק
וְרִפְיוֹן יָדַיִם חִיזַּק
חוֹלְלוֹ בְּשָׁמְעוֹ הִינּוֹ נִיתְחַזֵּק
בִּבְרְכוֹתָיו אֹתוֹ לְחַזֵּק
טוֹעֲנָךְ וְנוֹשְׂאָךְ עַל בִּרְכָּיו
טָעַן חוֹלִי וְכָרַע עַל בִּרְכָּיו
יוֹסֵף בְּקָשְׁבוֹ אִימֵּץ בִּרְכָּיו
לְהַטְעִין בְּרָכָה לְנוֹלְדוּ עַל בִּרְכָּיו
כָּמָּה מְחוֹלְלָךְ לָךְ לְחַלּוֹת
נַפְשׁוֹ בְּהִתְעַטֵּף וּבְהֵחָלוֹת
לָכֵן לֹא הִתְמַהְמַהּ לַעֲלוֹת
וְאֶת בָּנָיו עִמּוֹ לְהַעֲלוֹת
מַאֲהִיבָךְ בֵּן הַבָּנִים
חָלָה וְלָךְ קָרָא מִכָּל בָּנִים
נִיחֵל בָּנָיו בְּרָכָה בִּגְדוֹלֵי בָנִים
כִּי בְּנֵי בָנִים כְּבָנִים
סָמַךְ הוֹרָךְ לְסוֹף יְמוֹתָיו

have followed **B2** (a revision of his opinion in **B1**), which construes this line as the beginning of the poet's narration. Alternatively, it could be construed as continuing the speech of the anonymous messenger: "Take his two `sons' in with him / so that he may bless them…" The reference to Ephraim and Manasseh as Jacob's "sons" rather than grandsons would suggest that Jacob was understood as adopting his grandsons.

42 Joseph supported his weakened father as he struggled to sit up and bless Ephraim and Manasseh.

43 Joseph's sons, Ephraim and Manasseh.

"And he is soon to dwell with his fathers"[44]
He went up, and those who came forth from his loins
to establish upon them inclusion in his blessing
"God had a fate—He who sets fates for all—
"For your father, who shares the fate of all"
"The Rock of all[45] all things are like all others[46]
"What is fair, in due time, He does for all
"The one who called you here has been called;
"his summons to die has come[47]
"And who is so strong, that he can live and never die?"[48]
He hurried to behold him with a hopeful face
as if he were finding the face of God's own Presence[49]
He who kept the commandment for which the reward is the breath of life:
honoring the father who loved you with all the love of his every breath[50]
He leaned close to receive his last breath[51]
and to give praise to the Lord of every breath[52]

And thus, "Manasseh and Ephraim..."

(7[1])	Truth you declared to	Manasseh
	With strength is crowned the head of	Ephraim[53]
	The dignity of the firstborn's belonged to	Manasseh
	But You said: My first born is	Ephraim

---

44 The language of this stich draws on Jer 14:8 and Ps 25:13. The combination creates a sense of transience and yet also ease.

45 This epithet for God (צור הכל) appears to be unique, although "Rock" is common; as **B2** notes, one aspect of the name "Rock" is "creator" (taking it from the root י-צ-ר; see *j. Ḥag.* 10a; *SifD* 307). If this is the case, the epithet means "Creator of All," a more commonplace attribution, albeit still an unusual coinage.

46 Eccl 9:2 (**R**).

47 That is, the one who has summoned you is being summoned by death; it could also have the connotation of "named," but Rachel named Joseph, not Jacob. The word מקרא (called) may also pun on the word מקרה ("fate"), as in Eccl 3:19: the one who has summoned you is fated to die.

48 See Ps 89:49 (**B1**).

49 See *b. Ned.* 40a, "Rabin also said in Rab's name: From where do we know that the Divine Presence rests above an invalid's bed? From the verse, 'The Lord sets Himself upon the bed of languishing' (Ps 41:4)." The translation here follows the MS, which has the word זה (lit. "as if he were finding this, the presence of the visage"). Zulay (cited by both **R** and **B1**) emends the text to read זיו ("the splendor of the presence of the visage"—i.e., the splendor / appearance of the Divine Presence). "This" is a widely attested payyetanic and

וְנָטָה לָלוּן עִם אֲבוֹתָיו
עָלָה הוּא וְיוֹצְאֵי יְרֵיכוֹתָיו
לְכוֹנֵן עֲלֵיהֶם כְּלַל בִּרְכוֹתָיו
פָּקַד הָאֵל פּוֹקֵד כֹּל
לְאָבִיךָ פְּקֻדַּת הַכֹּל
צוּר הַכֹּל כֹּל כַּאֲשֶׁר לַכֹּל
יָפֶה בְעִתּוֹ עָשָׂה כֹּל
קוֹרְאֲךָ קָרָא
מִקְרָאוֹ לָמוּת
וּמִי גֶבֶר יִחְיֶה וְלֹא יָמוּת
רָץ לְחַלּוֹתוֹ בְּסֵיבֶר דְּמוּת
כִּמְחַלֶּה זֶה שְׁכִינַת דְּמוּת
שׁוֹמֵר מִצְוָה שְׂכָרָהּ חַיֵּי נֶפֶשׁ
לְכִיבּוּד אָב אֲהֵיבָךְ אַהֲבַת נֶפֶשׁ
תָּכַף לְקַבֵּל מֵינוּ נֶפֶשׁ
וְלָתֵת תְּהִלָּה לַאֲדוֹן כָּל נֶפֶשׁ

ובכן את מנשה ואת אפרים

(ז[1])
אֱמֶת הֶאֱמַרְתָּה	לִמְנַשֶּׁה
בְּמָעוֹז רֹאשׁ נִיכְתַּר	אֶפְרָיִם
גִּידוּל בְּכוֹר הָיָה	מְנַשֶּׁה
דִּיבַּרְתָּה בְּכוֹרִי הוּא	אֶפְרָיִם

---

aggadic epithet for God (based on Exod 15:2).

50 Apparently these two lines are an extended epithetical description of Joseph. The line is intriguing but unclear. **B1** notes that the language recalls Prov 19:16 ("He who keeps the commandment keeps his own soul [life-breath]; but he who despises his ways shall die"), which implies that honoring one's parents leads to longer life in this world. It is also possible, however, to understand the verse as does Zulay in *`Iyyunei Lashon* (cited by **R**), as implying that honoring parents receives a reward of life in the world-to-come. These two readings are not mutually exclusive.

51 This probably means to close the eyes of the deceased, in accord with m. *Shab.* 23:5; see also the description of events in *GenR* 96, which interprets Gen 46:4, where Jacob says, "Joseph will put his hands upon my eyes" (**B1**). Closing the eyes of the deceased is described in the midrash as a great act of love: "A man sometimes honors his father through fear or shame, but this [act of] love after death is a true love." More existentially, Joseph may also have leaned in so as to receive Jacob's "soul blessing" (*birkat nefesh*), as in Gen 27:25 (**R**).

52 That is, to recite the blessing one recites upon learning of a death (or other bad news), "Blessed are You…the True Judge (*dayyan emet*)" (**B1**).

53 The agent here is Jacob. **R** cites Gen 48:19, in which Jacob prophesies that while Manasseh will be a great tribe, Ephraim—the younger son—will be the greater.

Everyone blesses by Manasseh
And all bless themselves by the name of Ephraim[54]
Designated like Simon shall be Manasseh
Beloved like Reuben shall be Ephraim
Before he was even born—that is, Manasseh
Foreseen was the descendants of Ephraim[55]
The glory of circumcision accrued to Manasseh
Accompanying the Sabbath [is the heritage of] Ephraim[56]
A city of refuge is within the borders of Manasseh
And one likewise found in the hill country of Ephraim
A hand crossed over upon the head of Manasseh
Right hand crowned upon the head of Ephraim
Wonders You worked for the children of Manasseh[57]
Righteousness You raised up for the tribe of Ephraim[58]
You summoned the myriads of Manasseh
You multiplied the multitudes of Ephraim
Years of hardship we have forgotten, as in the name Manasseh
We will bear fruit for goodness, as in the name Ephraim

(8) Ephraim and Manasseh, the one to the other is joined
Equal, one with the other
Sometimes "Manasseh and Ephraim"
Sometimes "Ephraim and Manasseh"[59]
The one not greater than the other
the other not greater than the one
By one You are praised, by the other You are sanctified
In the circle of Your hosts You are called
And they answer, one to the other, *as it is written: "And one called..."*

---

54 This line is open to two possible interpretations, both offered in **B1**. According to the first, it may refer to a singular blessing invoking the names of both Ephraim and Manasseh. Alternatively, it may refer to two different blessings, one in the name of each son, as in the final lines of this poem: Manasseh is invoked when one wishes to expunge the memory of sorrowful events, while Ephraim is recalled when positive blessings are recited. (See the first *rahit*, lines 21–22).

55 That is, the Messiah of Joseph's line, who will descend from Ephraim; see *GenR* 1:4, 2:4; and *Tanḥ Naso* 11 (**B1**).

56 Completed according to **R**. See *GenR* 11:8, where the Sabbath is called Israel's partner (**B2**). The implication is that Israel (here represented by Ephraim) has a special bond with the Sabbath. **R** connects this stich to the special offerings made by the leader of Ephraim

הכל מברכים מנשה
ומתברכים בשם אפרים
זומן כשמעון מנשה
חושק כראובן אפרים
טרם נולד מנשה
יודעה תולדות אפרים
כבוד מילה עלה למנשה
ליווי שבת ... אפרים
מקום מקלט בגבול מנשה
ניתן כן בהר אפרים
שוכלה יד על ראש מנשה
עוטרה ימין בראש אפרים
פלאים היפלאיתה לבני מנשה
צדק היצמחתה למטה אפרים
קיהלתה אלפי מנשה
ריבבתה ריבבות אפרים
שנות רע נשינו כשם מנשה
תפרינו לטוב כשם אפרים

(ח) אפרים ומנשה זה וזה צמודים
שקולים זה בזה
פעמים מנשה ואפרים
פעמים אפרים ומנשה
לא זה גדול מזה
ולא זה גדול מזה
מזה תוערץ ומזה תוקדש
בסוד צבאותיך הקוראים
ועונים זה אל זה ככתוב וקרא

(Num 7:48); see *TanḥB Naso* 31; *NumR* 14:1, and others. "The seventh day" in Num 7:48 ("On the seventh day, it was the chieftain of the Ephraimites, Elishama son of Ammihud") is understood in the interpretations to be the Sabbath.

57 Possibly an allusion to Gideon (see *Tanḥ Vayeḥi* 10) (**R**, **B1**).

58 As **R** notes (**B1** concurs), another allusion to the Messiah ben Joseph; **B1** cites Isa 45:8, 61:10; and Ps 98:2 for the language.

59 As **B1** notes, five times in the Bible (Num 26:28; Josh 14:4, 16:4; 2 Chron 34:6, 9), Ephraim precedes Manasseh, and four times the reverse is true (Deut 34:4; Josh 17:17; 2 Chron. 30:18, 31:1). This alternation indicates their parity (**R** cites TanḥB *Shemot* 5). See the prologue to the *Mekhilta* for a similar interpretation of the alternation of Moses and Aaron. **R** notes the alternative interpretation of *GenR* 97:5.

"And thus: `So Israel gathered (his) strength and sat up upon the bed'"[60]
(7^2) "So he gathered strength" with faith, with courage, to show his fellowship[61]
"And he sat" in discernment, with perceptiveness, to bless his sons
"So he gathered strength" with light … to … his lads
"And he sat" in knowledge, in joy, to make his troop sleek[62]
"So he gathered strength" [in] splendor, in grandeur, to save his horde
"And he sat" in introspection, in readiness, to appoint his assembly
"So he gathered strength" with memory, with might, to acquit his minders[63]
"And he sat" in a vision, with happiness, to favor his favored ones
"So he gathered strength" with ceremony, with decree, to protect his lambs
"And he sat" in awe, in beauty, in honor, to honor his children
"So he gathered strength" with power, with potency, to confirm his crowns[64]
"And he sat" in concentration, in dignity, to hearten his offshoots
"So he gathered strength" with awe, with fairness, to address to his remnant
"And he sat" in splendor, in prophecy, to console his heirs
"So he gathered strength" with hope, with mystery, to strengthen his shoots
"And he sat" in cleverness, in humility, to help[65] his flock
"So he gathered strength" with freedom, with care, to glorify his blooms
"And he sat" in splendor, in joy, to justify his host
"So he gathered strength" in truth, with bowing, to lift his community
"And he sat" in trembling, in joy, to have mercy on his offspring
"So he gathered strength" in silence, in serenity, to adorn his saplings
"And he sat" in desire, in exaltation,[66] to sustain his pure ones

---

60 The pattern of this poem consists of splitting the biblical verse into two parts, completing each half with two adverbial phrases followed by a verb of blessing (or some other positive connotations) that has the sons of Jacob (implied through an epithet: "force," "flock," "shoots," etc.) as its recipient. Each adverb, verb, and epithet begins with the appropriate letter of the alphabetical acrostic. The *Ma'agarim* database ascribes this unit to Shimon bar Megas, a poet who lived a generation after Yannai but also of the Classical period; it is attributed to Yannai, however, by **R** and Zulay and is included here.

61 Lit. "band," "union."

62 Lit., "fat" meaning prosperous.

ובכן ויתחזק ישראל וישב על המטה

(ז[2]) וַיִּתְחַזֵּק בְּאוֹמֶן בְּאוֹמֶץ לְאַשֵּׁר אֲגוּדָיו
וַיֵּשֶׁב בְּבֶדֶק בְּבִינָה לְבָרֵךְ בָּנָיו
וַיִּתְחַזֵּק בְּגִיהַ לג.. בְּגוּרָיו
וַיֵּשֶׁב בְּדֵיעָה בְּדִיץ לְדַשֵּׁן דְּגָלָיו
וַיִּתְחַזֵּק הָדוּר בְּהוֹד לְהוֹשִׁיעַ הֲמוֹנָיו
וַיֵּשֶׁב בְּוִידּוּי בְּוִכּוּחַ לְוַכֵּחַ וְעוּדָיו
וַיִּתְחַזֵּק בְּזִכָּרוֹן בִּזְרוֹעַ לְזַכּוֹת זְכָרָיו
וַיֵּשֶׁב בְּחִזָּיוֹן בְּחִדוֹת לְחַנֵּךְ חֲנִינָיו
וַיִּתְחַזֵּק בְּטֶכֶס בְּטַעַם לְטַלֵּל טְלָאָיו
וַיֵּשֶׁב בְּיִרְאָה בְּיוֹפִי בִּיקָר לְיַקֵּר יְלָדָיו
וַיִּתְחַזֵּק בְּכוֹחַ בְּכִישׁוֹר לְכוֹנֵן כֹּתָרָיו
וַיֵּשֶׁב בְּלַהַג בְּלַהַק לְלַבֵּב לְלָבָיו
וַיִּתְחַזֵּק בְּמוֹרָא בְּמִישׁוֹר לְמַלֵּל לְמְלִיטָיו
וַיֵּשֶׁב בְּנוֹי בִּנְבוּאָה לְנַחֵם נְחָלָיו
וַיִּתְחַזֵּק בְּסִבְרוֹן בְּסוֹד לְשַׂגֵּב סָרִיגָיו
וַיֵּשֶׁב בְּעָרְמָה בַּעֲנָוָה לְעוֹדֵד עֲדָרָיו
וַיִּתְחַזֵּק בְּפִרְזוֹן בִּפְקִידָה לְפָאֵר פְּרָחָיו
וַיֵּשֶׁב בְּצֹהַר בְּצַהַל לְצַדֵּק צְבָאָיו
וַיִּתְחַזֵּק בְּקֹשְׁטְ בְּקִידָּה לְקַמֵּם קְהָלָיו
וַיֵּשֶׁב בְּרֶגֶשׁ בְּרוֹן לְרַחֵם רְבִיעָיו
וַיִּתְחַזֵּק בְּשֶׁקֶט בְּשָׁלוֹם לְשַׁפֵּר שְׁתוּלָיו
וַיֵּשֶׁב בְּתַאֲוָוה בְּתִילּוּל לִתְמֹךְ תְּמִימָיו

63 The adverbs and verb here have connotations of both power and virtue (rather than simply brute force).

64 That is, his grandsons, Ephraim and Manasseh (see Prov 17:6, cited as a prooftext for the *magen* and mentioned by **B2**).

65 See 1 Chron 12:34

66 **B1** cites Gen 49:26, "The blessings of your father surpass the blessings of my ancestors, to the utmost bounds of the eternal hills. May they rest on the head of Joseph, on the brow of the elect of his brothers."

Commentary

Jacob, on his deathbed, is frail but stubborn, and firmly in control of his faculties and his family. According to a tradition recorded in *GenR* 65:9, even Jacob's illness came at his initiative—indeed, he invented sickness:

> Jacob demanded illness, saying to Him: "Sovereign of the Universe! A man dies without previous illness and does not settle his affairs with his children; but if he were ill two or three days, he would settle his affairs with his children." Said the Holy One, blessed be He, to him: "By your life, you have asked well, and it will commence with you." Hence, "And he said to Joseph: Behold, your father is ill" (Gen 48:1).

Like the author of this midrash, Yannai understands that Gen 48:1 is rich in latent meaning. In the quiet bedside scene of Jacob, Joseph, Ephraim and Manasseh, the poet finds a pretext for exploring the individual and familial dynamics of death.

This poem addresses two interrelated issues: on the personal level, we have a very human picture of an individual striving to maintain his dignity and set his affairs in order as he endures a final illness. However, because one of Jacob's final tasks is blessing Joseph's two sons, in the last unit of the poem national and messianic concerns are introduced. This broadens the scope of the poem's themes through the interpretive technique of allegory. The children blessed by Jacob are transformed into representatives of Yannai's own contemporary community and their shared blessing constitutes national destiny.

Jacob, only rarely a figure of dignity in the biblical story and hardly a model father, is here depicted in touching, parental terms. Through the verses accompanying the first three poems, Yannai introduces elements of filial piety, fatherly pride, deep love, and resolute optimism. Parents, children, and God are all bound together in a web of mutual responsibility to honor and care for one another. The reality of death is addressed unflinchingly—Who can escape it? Who does not fear it?—as is the potential for depression, as the quotation from Prov 18:14 acknowledges. Yannai, however, is philosophical rather than pessimistic. Alluding to Ecclesiastes, he recognizes that everything, even mortality, is beautiful in its season. At the same time, death is the final mystery: like every day of judgment, we cannot know when it will happen, only that it will. Nevertheless, illness and death serve purposes. Most immediately, knowledge of mortality encourages atonement for sins (Poem Three, line 6) and inspires repentance. More important, it paves the way for acquiring eternal life. Illness, for its part, presents children and parents, here exemplified by Joseph and Jacob, with an opportunity to demonstrate a very concrete form of filial piety and parental love. These motifs are most poignantly explored in Poem Six. In this unit, the anonymous voice of the opening verse of the *sidra* becomes the narrator of the scene, instructing the uncertain Joseph on how to approach his failing father and describing for Joseph (and the listeners) the love and anxiety inherent in Jacob's request to see his children. The tender scene of their meeting seems to end with Jacob's death (although Jacob does not die at this moment in the Genesis narrative). Joseph, a loving son, runs to greet his father with a "hopeful face" (line 39) perhaps believing that Jacob's illness will only be temporary. Jacob, however, is presented as a realist, ready, even anxious, to set his affairs in order.

On his deathbed, Jacob does not become mired in thoughts of his own mortality. Instead, he turns his attention—and ours—to the future as he bestows his blessings upon Joseph's sons, Ephraim and Manasseh. Yannai expands upon the themes, language, and content of those biblical blessings, and while he does at times extend the idea of the "children" of Israel into its broad, national semantic range, he generally keeps the focus on the biblical characters themselves, resisting the potential to turn the story wholly into allegory. For example, in the first *rahit*, the poet moves gradually from the biblical episode's setting to motifs such as the cities of refuge (mentioned in Deuteronomy and Joshua), concluding with the poet's own day, when he speaks in the present tense and communal sense of "we have forgotten" and "we will bear." Along the way, Yannai hints at the eschatological future, dropping veiled references to the messiah of Joseph's line.

Nevertheless, the poet's scale remains small and his tone is hardly apocalyptic. He focuses on past and present—often blurring the line between the two, as in Poem Eight (the *silluq*). He concentrates on embellishing the family dynamics, emphasizing interpretations that have an affirming, even healing bent, such as the motif that Ephraim and Manasseh are, in the end, equals.

From the days of Isaac and Ishmael, Jacob and Esau, Joseph and his brothers, the biblical narrative dwells on contests for superiority, pitting younger and elder sons against one another. Jacob seems to continue this tradition, favoring the younger Ephraim over his elder brother Manasseh.

Yannai, however, indicates that this deeply embedded cycle has come to an end. Joseph, the child most victimized by sibling rivalry, will not see that sad dynamic passed on as an inheritance to his sons.

In the final extant poem of this cycle, Yannai yokes all these varied images and themes together: through the repetition of the opening phrases (taken from Gen 48:2), the poet emphasizes the strength, acuity, and dignity of the elderly Jacob. The very repetition of the two verbs ("he gathered (his) strength…he sat up…") adds a sense of exertion to the actions: in every stanza, as it were, Jacob draws on inner reserves of energy and pride. The strength here is emotional rather than physical—he does not "gather his power" to smite an Esau, wrestle an angel, or argue with God. Jacob now is a frail mortal, one for whom his final illness has made something as simple as sitting up in bed an heroic act. We can easily imagine the scene: an elderly relative mustering his inner will and physical strength during his final days to put on such a display for beloved relatives.

Jacob's mortality humanizes him. Following each refrain-like phrase, Yannai presents the different emotions and attitudes he imagines the patriarch to be experiencing: faith, happiness, readiness, dignity, humility, and concentration. No single description suffices; instead, the poet offers multiple perspectives on the complex experiences of aging, illness, leave-taking, and death. And just as the blessing of one's heirs leads to thoughts of the future, Yannai uses this scenario to extend the biblical scene into his present day. The blessings Jacob bestows upon his grandsons extend seamlessly from one generation to the next. Just as the grandsons are regarded as "sons," so, too, is every subsequent child born a "child of Jacob/Israel." Jacob's final acts, according to this poem, are tender and protective, healing and strengthening. In his last moments, it is Jacob who consoles his children, and his blessings and consolations overflow into the present tense.

Yannai has here crafted a dignified elegy for the patriarch Jacob while simultaneously speaking to all of Jacob's heirs. It is as if the poet has gathered not only Joseph, Ephraim and Manasseh, but all of Jacob's descendants—all of Israel's children—around Jacob's bed to receive the patriarch's enduring wisdom and ongoing blessings.

Qedushta for Genesis 49:1 — בראשית מט:א

"Then Jacob summoned his sons" — ויקרא יעקב אל בניו

Picking up on a narrative embellishment popular in both *midrashim* and *targumim*, Yannai has here composed an evocative poem about the limits of human knowledge and the boundaries of prophetic insight. The information specifically hoped for—and denied—concerns the date of the end of days: when will redemption come? Expanding on the tantalizing language of Jacob's enigmatic death-bed scene (nuances all intensified by the fragmentary nature of the surviving poetic text), the poet tells us that the patriarch possessed this secret knowledge, but when he sought to pass it on to his sons, it became lost to him.

(1) Signs of the Day-to-Come,
in Your heart sealed up and hidden,[1]
Yet, out of the might of great love,
visions You revealed to each prophetic ancestor[2]

The man, the pure one, reaching out from near death,
the spirit of insight enveloping him[3]
He summoned around his bed his tribes:
a revelation of things to come to tell to them[4]

The meanings of matters
O Yah, You hid from his eyes
For the mystery which was shared between You and he[5]
in order to reveal it, he summoned his sons[6]

As it is written: "Then Jacob summoned his sons, saying, `Let them gather together that I may tell them that which will befall them at the End of Days'" (Gen 49:1).

And as it is said: "Who like Me can announce, can foretell it—and match Me thereby? Even as I told the future to an ancient people, so let him foretell coming events to them" (Isa 44:7).

And as it is said: "See, the things once predicted have come to pass, and now I foretell new things, announcing to you before they sprout up" (Isa 42:9).

And as it is said: "He told His commands to Jacob, His statutes and rules to Israel" (Ps 147:19).

And as it is said: "I call upon God Most High, upon the deity who has shown me the End" (Ps 57:3).[7]

---

1 The timing of the redemption is among God's most closely guarded secrets. He hasn't even revealed it fully to Himself or His retinue. See *b. San.* 99a, where it states: "Rabbi Yoḥanan said [that God said]: `To My heart I have revealed it [the date of the end-time], but not to My limbs.' Rabbi Shimon ben Lakish said: `To My heart I have revealed it, but not to My ministering angels.'" See also *MidPs* to Ps 9:2 (cited by **R** in reference to line 43).

2 According to aggadic tradition, God granted each of the patriarchs visions of both the suffering and the redemption of future generations, but this knowledge was not to be shared (when Isaac wished to share his information with Esau, he went blind; when Jacob tries to do the same in this *sidra*, his insight is taken away). See *GenR* 44:15, *LevR* 29:2, and *Tanḥ Vayeḥi* 8, in particular (referenced by **B1**). According to this poem, the prophetic knowledge granted to each patriarch was in the form of visions rather than explicit, direct speech.

3 This language draws upon Judg 6:34 (**B1**). The imagery here suggests that as Jacob's physical strength waned, his spiritual strength increased.

(א) אוֹתוֹתֵי יוֹם הַבָּא
בְּלִיבָּךְ סָתוּם וְנֶחְבָּא
גַּם מֵעוֹצֶם רוֹב חִיבָּה
דִּמְיוֹנוֹת גִּלִּיתָה לְכָל אָב הַנִּיבָּא

הָאִישׁ תָּם לְמִיתָה בִּנְטוֹת
וְרוּחַ שֶׂכֶל בַּעֲטוֹת
זִיעֵק סְבִיב מִיטָּתוֹ מַטּוֹת
חוֹקֶר אוֹתִיוֹת לָמוֹ לְבַטּוֹת

טַעְמֵי עִינְיָנָיו
יָהּ עִילַּמְתָּה מֵעֵינָיו
כִּי סוֹד אֲשֶׁר הָיָה בֵּינָךְ לבניו
לְגַלּוֹתוֹ קָרָא לְבָנָיו

ככתוב ויקרא יעקב אל בניו ויאמר האספו ואגידה לכם את אשר יקרא אתכם באחרית הימים

ונאמר ומי כמוני יקרא ויגידה ויערכה לי משומי עם עולם ואתיות ואשר תבאנה יגידו למו

ונאמר הראשונות הנה באו וחדשות אני מגיד בטרם תצמחנה אשמיע אתכם

ונאמר מגיד דבריו ליעקב חקיו ומשפטיו לישראל

ונאמר אקרא לאלהים עליון לאל גמר עלי

---

4 The language here alludes to Prov 25:2, cited below.

5 Understanding לבניו as from בין ("between") rather than as "his sons" or "for his understanding," although those are alternatives. See Josh 3:4 and 8:11 (**B1**), for ביניו where one would expect בינו (in both cases a *ketiv*). **R** leaves unpointed.

6 For parallels to this tradition, see *TargN*, *TargPsJ*, and the *FragTargs* to Gen 49:1–2, which contain expansive renderings of the text that often recall the interpretation present here, as well as *GenR* 94, 96, and 98:2–3, *b.* Pes. 56a, and *Tanḥ Vayeḥi* 8 (**R**, **B1**, and **B2** all reference these traditions). The overall depiction of the scene in Gen 49 recalls works such as the Testament of the Twelve Patriarchs and Qumranic texts on the patriarchal blessings. The language of the *targumim*, like the piyyut, suggests the influence of apocalyptic texts such as Dan 2. The motif of God revealing then concealing knowledge of the redemption is discussed in the commentary.

7 **R** notes that this verse and the following are cited in *GenR* 94 (new version, Albeck p. 1203).

And as it is said: "It is the glory of God to conceal a matter, and the glory of kings to reveal a matter" (Prov 25:2).
And as it is said: "Many are the thoughts in the heart of man, but it is the plan of the Eternal that is established" (Prov 19:21).
And as it is said: "You have had a vision of all, one like the words of a sealed document. If it is handed to one who can read and he is asked to read it, he will say, `I can't, because it is sealed'" (Isa 29:11).
And as it is said: "And if the document is given to one who does not know how to read, saying, `Please read this,' then he will say, `I am unable to read'" (Isa 29:12)
And as it is said: "A voice says, `Proclaim!' and it says, `What shall I proclaim?' `All flesh is grass, and all its righteousness like the flower of the field'" (Isa 40:6).
And as it is said: "For a day of vengeance is in My mind, the year of My redemption approaches" (Isa 63:4).[8]

The time approaches,
the season comes:
O our Shield, let us be gathered together by You!
Blessed are You… Shield…

(2) Near death was the one called "pure" at birth[9]
and his offspring, in keeping with their purity, he summoned:
"Gather round, so that to you I may proclaim
"the Time[10] which has not been revealed to any man
"… you will stray
"the Rock, with one accord, shall you serve"[11]
…
…
Hearken, and your souls shall live[12]
Peaceful shall be your rest"[13]
…

8 Cited in *GenR* 65:12 and *EcclR* 11:5 (**R**). The *GenR* version states: "It was taught: Seven things are concealed from man: the day of death, the day of comfort [when Jerusalem will be rebuilt], and the absolute truth of judgment. Again, no man knows through what he will profit, no man knows what is in his neighbor's heart, no man knows what a woman is bearing [the child's sex or fate], and when the wicked State [Rome] will fall." The Isaiah verse quoted here is the prooftext for the unknowability of the date of Rome's destined fall.

9 Jacob was called "pure" from birth because he was born circumcised. See *qedushta* to Gen 31 and *Tanh Noah* 5.

ונאמר כבוד אלהים הסתר דבר וכבוד מלכים חקר דבר

ונאמר רבות מחשבות בלב איש ועצת יי היא תקום

ונאמר ותהי לכם חזות הכל כדברי הספר החתום אשר יתנו אותו אל יודע הספר לאמר קרא נא זה ואמר לא אוכל כי חתום הוא

ונאמר ונתן הספר על אשר לא ידע ספר לאמר קרא נא זה ואמר לא ידעתי ספר

ונאמר קול אומר קרא ואמר מה אקרא כל הבשר חציר וכל חסדו כציץ השדה

ונאמר כי יום נקם בלבי שנת גאולי באה

בָּאָה הָעֵת
הִגִּיעַ מוֹעֵד
מָגִנֵּינוּ לָךְ נִוָּועֵד
ברוך... מגן...

(ב) **מְ**וּתְמָם אֲשֶׁר תָּם נִיקְרָא
נִינָיו לְפִי תֻּוּמָן קָרָא
סוֹבּוּ וַאֲלֵיכֶם אֶקְרָא
עֵת אֲשֶׁר לָאָדָם לֹא חָקְרָה
פ..ר ... תֹּאבֵדוּ
צוּר שְׁכֶם אֶחָד תַּעֲבוֹדוּ
...
...
שִׁמְעוּ וּתְחִי נַפְשְׁכֶם
שַׁאֲנָן יְהִי נוּפְשְׁכֶם
...

10 That is, the End-Time, the details of the messianic era.

11 Zeph 3:9

12 A reference to resurrection.

13 Reading נופשכם, with **B2**; lit. "your rest, refreshment." See Jer 30:10, "Therefore do not fear, O my servant Jacob, says the Lord; nor be dismayed, O Israel; for, behold, I will save you from afar, and your seed from the land of their captivity; and Jacob shall return, and shall be quiet and at ease, and none shall make him afraid." Here it seems Jacob speaks of his sons' future comfort, although he, soon to die, will more literally be "at rest."

[if you listen][14] to Israel, your father"

As it is written: "Gather together and hear, O sons of Jacob, that which will happen to you in the End of Days" (Gen 49:2).
And as it says: "Hear, O sons, the insight of a father, and listen closely, in order to gain wisdom" (Prov 4:1).
And as it says: "Incline your ear and come to Me; hear, and your soul shall be revived. And I will make with you an eternal covenant, the enduring loyalty promised to David" (Isa 55:3).
And as it says: "Hear insight and become wise; do not spurn it" (Prov 8:33).
And as it says: "The spirit of the Eternal speaks through me and His word is on my tongue" (2 Sam 23:2).
And as it says: "In the assemblies, bless God, the Eternal from the (off-)spring of Israel" (Ps 68:27).
And as it says: "Then you will rejoice on account of the Eternal, and I will set you astride the heights of the land, and I will let you eat from the portion of Jacob, your father, for the mouth of the Eternal has spoken" (Isa 58:14).

He said to us, "He will arise"[15]
and You said: "Now I will arise;"
Let the dew drip; let life renew; let Him establish (this) for all.
Blessed are you… Who resurrects…

(3)[16] A day You are bringing—who can calculate when it will come?
But like an oven shall it burn when You bring it
Concealed in Your treasury[17] hidden in Your heart[18]
And by Your own accord, from of old, Your mind is not revealed
"You strive against Me," You said to the pure one,
"Making known the End which from you is hidden
"Your dear ones you brought close
on the day when (your end) you approached;
"Them you held close but Me you did not call!"[19]

---

14 Lacuna filled as by **B2** (תשמעו).

15 A reference to resurrection or perhaps to the Messiah. In the next line God Himself will come.

16 Shalom Spiegel discusses this passage and Poem Four in *Fathers of Piyyut*, ed. M. Schmelzer (New York/Jerusalem: JTSA, 1996), 359.

17 Deut 32:34 (**R**).

... לְיִשְׂרָאֵל אֲבִיכֶם

ככתוב הקבצו ושמעו בני יעקב את אשר יקרא אתכם באחרית הימים

ונאמר שמעו בנים מוסר אב והקשיבו לדעת בינה

ונאמר הטו אזנכם ולכו אלי שמעו ותחי נפשכם ואכרות לכם חסדי דוד הנאמנים

ונאמר שמעו מוסר וחכמו ואל תפרעו
ונאמר רוח יי דבר בי ומלתו על לשוני

ונאמר במקהלות ברכו אלהים אדני ממקור ישראל

ונאמר אז תתענג על יי והרכבתיך על במתי ארץ והאכלתיך נחלת יעקב אביך כי פי יי דבר

דִּיבֵּר לָנוּ יָקוּם
וְתֹאמַר עַתָּה אָקוּם
וְתַטְלִיל תְּחִי לְכָל יְקוּם
ברוך... מחיה...

(ג) יוֹם מוֹבָאֲךָ מִי יְכַלְכֵּל בּוֹאוֹ
כִּי כְּתַנּוּר בּוֹעֵר הוּא מוֹבָאוֹ
נִיכְמַס בְּאוֹצָרָךְ וְנִיגְנַז בְּלִיבָּךְ
וּלְפִיךָ מֵאָז לֹא גִילָּה לִבָּךְ
יָגַעְתָּ בִּי נַמְוֹתָה לְאִישׁ תָּם
לְהוֹדִיעַ אַחֲרִית אֲשֶׁר מִימָּךְ נֶחְתָּם
יְדִידָךְ קֵירַבְתָּה
בְּיוֹם אֲשֶׁר קָרַבְתָּה
אוֹתָם הוֹקַרְתָּה וְאוֹתִי לֹא קָרָאתָה

18 See note, above.

19 When Jacob's death drew near, he called his sons close and said he would tell them "what would happen at the End of Days" (Gen 49:1–2), not words of blessing in the name of God and not words that God had revealed to him—either of which would have constituted a mention of God's name. Jacob should have mentioned God's name when he called his sons close, either as the source of revelation or of blessing.

As it is written: "But Me you have not mentioned, O Jacob; rather, you strive against Me, O Israel" (Isa 43:22).
And as it says: "Listen to Me, O Jacob, O Israel whom I have called; the First is Mine as is the Last" (Isa 48:12).
And You are holy, enthroned upon the praises of Israel… Please, God…

(4) Suppressed and concealed, hidden and sealed
secreted and covered, closeted and veiled:
In Your mind it was formed: a day of vengeance!
But no creature standing upright can fathom it
Your mind did not reveal to Your mouth[20]
and as for its End, how could it be revealed to the world?
just a few of them did You reveal to Jacob[21]
The One who told His words to Jacob,[22]
He said: "Gather together and listen, O sons of Jacob
"And let the crooked heart become straight[23]
"And I will make known to you from the beginning
"What will be in the End"
For You are the One who foretold the End from the beginning
the First and the Last, the Holy One

(5) The man whom You gathered in[24]
and who is called by the name You gave him:
"I will add unto those he has gathered[25]
and I will call unto those who bear his name"
Coming … how long will You tarry?
and You cheered him and exalted him with another word

---

20 Here "heart" is rendered "mind," as suits the context. The stich has two possible interpretations. If "mouth" is understood as a reference to the Prophets (as in **B1**), then God did not reveal this secret to His Prophets (including Jacob), and when Jacob opened his mouth to utter it, it evaporated. In short, no human knows the date of redemption and can articulate it. Alternatively, or simultaneously, Yannai references here the idea found in *b. San.* 99a (and *MidPs* 9:2), in which God states that the date of the day of vengeance is within His heart/mind but even His mouth does not know it to reveal it—that is, God has concealed this mystery even from the divine self, so one should certainly not give credence to any person who claims to possess this knowledge.

21 That is, God did not share the full picture or complete information with Jacob. Even this incomplete revelation, however, was too much to share.

ככתוב ולא אותי קראת יעקב כי יגעת בי ישראל

ונאמר שמע אלי יעקב וישראל מקראי אני הוא ראשון אף אני אחרון

ואתה קדוש יושב תהלות ישראל אל נא

(ד)
כָּמוּס וְסָתוּם. גָּנוּז וְחָתוּם
טָמוּן וְסָפוּן. עָמוּם וְצָפוּן
בְּלִיבָּךְ רֻוקַם כִּי יוֹם נָקָם
וְכָל יְצוּר הֻוקַם וְעָלָיו לֹא קָם
לִיבָּךְ לְפִיךְ לֹא גִילָּה
וְקִיצוֹ אֵיךְ לִבְרִיָּיא נִגְלָה
מִקְצָת מֶינּוּ גִּלִּיתָה לְיַעֲקֹב
הַמַּגִּיד דְּבָרָיו לְיַעֲקֹב
וְנָם הִקָּבְצוּ וְשִׁמְעוּ בְּנֵי יַעֲקֹב
וְיַשְּׁרוּ לֵב עָקוֹב
וְאוֹדִיעֲכֶם מֵרֵאשִׁית
מַה יִּהְיֶה בְּאַחֲרִית
וְאַתָּה הוּא הַמַּגִּיד אַחֲרִית מֵרֵאשִׁית
רִאשׁוֹן וְאַחֲרוֹן קָדוֹשׁ

(ה)
אִישׁ אֲשֶׁר אֱסוּפָךְ
וּקְרוּאָךְ נִיקְרָא
אֲסוּפָיו אוֹסִיף
וּקְרוּאָיו קָרָא
בָּא ... ... עַד כַּמָּה יְאַחֵר
וְהִבְלַגְתּוֹ וְהִסֵּיאַתוֹ לְדָבָר אַחֵר

22 Ps 147:19 (**R**).

23 See *GenR* 98:2, which depicts Jacob as being on the verge of revealing the forbidden knowledge to his sons but, upon seeing the Divine Presence hovering above him, he offers them ethical advice, instead.

24 This line puns on various connotations of the roots יסף and אסף ("to add, gather, assemble"). The language of this specific phrase derives from Mic 2:12 ("I will surely gather Jacob, all of you…" – **R**), which alludes to the ingathering of the exiles. In this poem, the assembly of Jacob's sons at Jacob's bed foreshadows the ingathering of their descendants at the time of the redemption.

25 See Isa 56:8, "Thus declares the Lord God…: `I will gather still more to those already gathered'" (**B1**). Also note Eccl 12:11; later exegetes understood בעלי אסופות to be the Sages.

Commentary

The tension between the known and the unknowable lies at the heart of this *qedushta*. The End of Days, when the exile will end and the people of Israel will be restored to its former glory, is woven into the very fabric of creation. At the same time, the specifics of when the End will come are shrouded in mystery—apparently even God does not know them. As precious and urgently desired as this insight is, even those few who possess such knowledge lose it when they attempt to articulate it. Redemption is thus both wholly known and completely unknowable.

This tension verges close to paradox: knowledge exists yet is unknowable; God hasn't even revealed these secrets fully to Himself. Try to communicate this knowledge, as Jacob does, and the knowledge vanishes. It is as if the insight is present only in the corner of the viewer's eye; attempt to see it directly, and it is as if it was never there.

These roots of this paradox—this sense of found-then-lost, effervescent and evaporating knowledge—lie within the verses that open this *sidra*: on the one hand, Jacob tells his sons that he is going to reveal to them what will befall them "in the End of Days" (Gen 49:1, repeated in 49:2). The content of the verses that follow these tantalizing pronouncements, however, are neither apocalyptic nor messianic. Instead, they catalogue the dominant personality traits (and, to an extent, fates) of the individual tribes.[26] Early interpreters of this biblical passage noticed the gap between what the patriarch promised and what he actually articulated; midrashim, targumim, and poetry all concur that *something happened* between Gen. 49:2 and 49:3: either the patriarch changed his mind and decided, at the last minute, not to reveal what he knew, or he lost the knowledge itself. Yannai seems to suggest both possibilities: God "had hidden it from his eyes" (Poem One, line 10), but God also never revealed the full truth to him at all (Poem Four, line 7).

For a community such as Yannai's, intensely interested in the topic of the

26 The language "end of days" (also translated, "days to come") does not, in the Hebrew rhetoric of the book of Genesis, connote a messianic end-time but simply the future; only in prophetic literature does the same idiom come to refer to an "end time" (*eschaton*), a culmination of history. Later readers, including Yannai, read the later meaning into the Genesis verses and detected the paradox at the heart of this poem. (The repetition of the phrase is due to the fact that Gen 49:1 is the prose introduction to the poem that begins in vs. 2.)

end of their own exile, anticipating the defeat of the Byzantine empire (read through the lens of biblical prophecies), energized by messianic expectations, and yearning for the restoration of Israel, the tensions within the opening verses of the *sidra* must have been electrifying; it encourages speculation even as it denies it. The promised End is absolutely certain to come and to bring with it justice long delayed: "Like an oven shall it burn" (Poem Three, line 2); in God's mind, it already exists as "a day of vengeance" (Poem Four, line 3). But Yannai, inspiring apocalyptic fantasies at one moment, discourages speculation in another. In a dazzling rhetorical display, the poet conjures eight synonyms for `hidden' in the opening line of Poem Four. The rest of that unit underscores the mystery: God knows the day, but He has never revealed it even to his prophets or even Himself—meaning that one may scour the sacred scriptures yet find no concrete information on this most tantalizing subject.

Navigating the tensions within this poem, it seems that the poet has, perhaps unwittingly, articulated his internal conflict with messianic expectations and his ambivalence about the yearning for such information in his community. With some force of will, he pulls back from this tempting speculation and—following the lead of the rest of the *sidra*—turns to ethical matters. Rather than worrying about the End of Days, he suggests, worry about making one's ways straight and not crooked; and rather than probing the depths of the End Time, ponder the majesty of the One who decreed it, instead (Poem Four, lines 13–14)—wholly exoteric, non-mystical teachings, suitable for all ages and populations. At the same time, almost undermining this safe approach to the topic, these lines suggest that perhaps, with enough ethical discipline, more may somehow gain insight into the End. It is as if the poet can't help but stare at something from which he knows he should avert his gaze.

Shortly after this point, the poem breaks off, but at a tantalizing junction. For while in Poem Four, the poet seems to accept the unknowability of the date of the Redemption, he cannot resist in the opening lines of the very next poem asking, "...How long will You tarry?..." (Poem Five, line 5). Like the prophets of old, the poet stands in the breech between his community and God, impatient with the deity despite his deference, and he is sympathetic to his listeners' pain, anxiety, and hope. Yannai shows himself able to counsel patience but unable to practice it. He advises acceptance but not resignation. Yannai advocates for both sides. A hint of his hope-against-hope may be evident even in the unusual number of intertexts that follow the first poem. These verses highlight the tension between revealing and concealing that is at the heart of the poet's interpretation. God *has* shared wisdom with Jacob, revealed secrets to Israel, hinted at mysteries to the prophets; despite what Yannai says in Poem Four, suggesting that no prophet ever received the date, Yannai adduces texts that suggest the opposite. He draws a parallel between the End of Time and the sealed document of Isa 29—begging the question of whether the Torah in whole or part is the sealed document which, if opened correctly (by means of interpretation) could reveal all the secrets of the Kingdom. The sheer density of Deutero-Isaiah among these citations lends the text fragment a kind of messianic fervor. Most telling, the final intertext of the first poem says that "the year of My redemption approaches" (Isa 63:4). Does Yannai, for all his protestations of ignorance, believe—or just want to believe—the End is near?

These verses, and the poem itself, suggest a final tension in the composition—or perhaps within the poet. His sense of existential exile and his messianic hopes are keen, which make his ignorance frustrating, but in the end, the sense of mystery offers protection. It is not the End that fails to come; rather, it is the human mind that fails to fathom the secrets of the divine. It is not God who has disappointed, the poet seems to warn himself here; the questions themselves were, perhaps, too much to ask. So he continues to wonder, "How long?" and he continues to answer himself: in God's time. Just as Yannai collapses the past into the present, he himself blurs into Jacob. Like Jacob, Yannai has a sense, a tingling awareness even, of things to come, but like Jacob, he finds the wisest counsel is restraint—or perhaps, like Jacob, words simply fail him. Perhaps speaking the words aloud breaks the spell.

Searching for the end of exile, yearning to understand God's mysterious responses to human yearnings for redemption: the themes of this poem form a fitting prelude to the redemptive, paradigmatic story of the book of Exodus. The poet, standing in the breech, speaks to God and his people. As he does so, he shapes the stories and the language of the past—the mythic, ancestral past—into meaningful strategies for living in the present. And possibly, just possibly, he finds clues to the future along the way.

Appendix I

Amidah for the Morning Service (Blessings 1-3)

(Nusach Ashkenaz, Adapted)

This appendix presents the typical language of the first three blessings of the Sabbath Amidah as they appear in contemporary "traditional" prayerbooks. Language which appears in Yannai's *qedushta'ot* in full or part appears here in boldface.

1. אבות (מגן)

ברוך אתה יי אלהינו ואלהי אבותינו, אלהי אברהם, אלהי יצחק, ואלהי יעקב, האל הגדול הגבור והנורא, אל עליון, גומל חסדים טובים, וקנה הכל, וזוכר חסדי אבות, ומביא גואל לבני בניהם, למען שמו באהבה. מלך עוזר ומושיע ומגן.**ברוך אתה יי מגן אברהם.**

"God of the Ancestors" (magen)

Blessed are You, O Lord our God and God of our ancestors, God of Abraham, God of Isaac, and God of Jacob, the great, the mighty, and the awesome God, God almighty, who bestows lovingkindness, and creates all, who remembers the faithfulness of the ancestors, and who brings a redeemer to their children's children, for the sake of His name, with love. O King, helper, savior, and shield! **Blessed are You, O Lord, shield of Abraham.**

2. גבורות (מחיה)

אתה גבור לעולם אדני, מחיה מתים אתה, רב להושיע.
(בקיץ: מוריד הטל. בחורף: משיב הרוח ומוריד הגשם.)
מכלכל חיים בחסד, מחיה מתים ברחמים רבים, סומך נופלים, ורופא חולים, ומתיר אסורים, ומקים אמונתו לישני עפר, מי כמוך בעל גבורות ומי דומה לך, מלך ממית ומחיה ומצמיח ישועה. ונאמן אתה להחיות מתים.**ברוך אתה יי מחיה המתים.**

"God's Might" (meḥayyeh)

You are eternally mighty, my Lord; You resurrect the dead, You are mighty to save. (*In summer, according to the Sefardic rite:* You cause the dew to fall. *In winter*: You cause the wind to blow and the rain to fall.) You sustain the living with kindness, You resurrect the dead with great mercy, You support the fallen, and heal the sick, and free the captive, and keep faith with those who sleep in the dust. Who is like You, possessor of might? And who resembles You, O King who causes death and gives life and causes salvation to spring forth? And you are faithful, resurrecting the dead. **Blessed are You, O Lord, who resurrects the dead.**

3. קדושת השם (קדושה)
נקדש את שמך בעולם, כשם שמקדישים אותו בשמי מרום, ככתוב על יד נביאך, **וקרא זה אל זה ואמר:**

קדוש, קדוש, קדוש, יי צבאות, מלא כל הארץ כבודו

אז בקול רעש גדול אדיר וחזק, משמיעים קול, מתנשאים לעמת שרפים, לעמתם ברוך יאמרו:
ברוך כבוד יי ממקומו

ממקומך מלכנו תופיע, ותמלך עלינו, כי מחכים אנחנו לך. מתי תמלך בציון, בקרוב בימינו, לעולם ועד תשכון. תתגדל ותתקדש בתוך ירושלים עירך, לדור ודור ולנצח נצחים. ועינינו תראינה מלכותך, כדבר האמור בשירי עזך, על ידי דוד משיח צדקך: ימלך יי לעולם, אלהיך ציון, לדר ודר, הללויה. לדור ודור נגיד גדלך, ולנצח נצחים קדשתך נקדיש, ושבחך, אלהינו, מפינו לא ימוש לעולם ועד, כי אל מלך גדול וקדוש אתה. **ברוך אתה יי האל הקדוש**

"God's Holiness" (Qedushah)
Let us sanctify Your name in the world, just as they (the angels) sanctify it in the highest heavens, as it is written by the hand of Your prophet: **"And this one called to that one and said:**

Holy, holy, holy is the Lord of hosts! His glory fills all the earth!

Then in sound of tumult, great and might and strong, they make their voices heard, and lifting themselves up towards the Seraphim, towards them they will say, "Blessed!"

Blessed is the Glory of the Lord from His place!

From Your place You will shine forth, You will rule over us, for we wait for you. When will you rule over Zion? Soon, in our days, forever and ever may You dwell there. May You be magnified and sanctified within Jerusalem, Your city, from generation to generation, forever and ever. Let our eyes see Your kingdom, according to the word that was spoken in the songs of Your might by the hand of David, Your righteous anointed: "The Lord will reign forever, your God, O Zion, from generation to generation, Hallelujah!" From generation to generation, we will proclaim Your greatness, forever and ever wee will hallow Your holiness, and Your praises, God, will never cease from our mouths, not for eternity, because, O God, You are a great and holy King. **Blessed are You, the holy God.**

Appendix II

Outline of the Generic Qedushta Form

(This outline is typical, but among the works presented here there are often variations)

1. *magen*:
    Six lines embedding an acrostic from *alef* to *lamed*
    Quotation of first verse of Torah portion
    List of intertexts
    Transition to blessing
    First blessing of Amidah: “Blessed are You… shield of Abraham”

2. *meḥayyeh*:
    Six lines embedding an acrostic from *mem* to *tav*
    Quotation of second verse of Torah portion
    List of intertexts
    Transition to blessing
    Second blessing of Amidah: “Blessed are You…who resurrects …”

3. *meshallesh*:
    Four lines embedding the signature acrostic, י-נ-י-י
    Quotation of first verse of Haftarah
    List of intertexts
    Quotation of Ps 22:4 and “God, we beseech” (*el naʾ*)

4. Poem Four:
    No fixed form, concludes with “holy” (*qadosh*)

5. *asiriyyah*:
    Ten lines embedding an acrostic from *alef* to *yod*
    Concludes with some variation of “O God, may You be revered forever” (*el naʾ le/0ʿolam tuʿaratz*)

6. Poem Six:
    Twenty two lines embedding a complete alphabetical acrostic, *alef* to *tav*
    Incipit—usually from the first or second verse of the *seder*—may have functioned as refrain

7. *rahit*:
    The most intricate unit
    Typically embeds at least one acrostic, possibly multiple acrostics
    Often includes a refrain
    Qedushtaʾot often have two or more *r'hitim*

8. *silluq*:

No fixed form; typically rhythmic prose
Often makes concentrated use of the root *q-d-sh* ("holy")
Concludes with: "As it is written: `The one called…'" from Isa 6:3

9. *qedushah*:

Prose-like preface to quotation of Isa 6:3
Quotation of Isa 6:3
The threefold repetition of *qadosh* ("holy") is parsed out to reflect three elements from the Torah portion:

"Holy from…."
"Holy from…"
"Holy from…"

May also parse out Ezek 3:12, "From His place"

Bibliography

Aaron, D. "The Doctrine of Hebrew Language Usage." In *The Blackwell Companion to Judaism*. Edited by J. Neusner and A. J. Avery-Peck. Oxford/Malden, MA: Blackwell, 2003, 268–87.

Altmann, A. "Songs of the Qedushah in Early Heikhalot Literature." *Melilah* 2 (1945–46): 1–24. [Hebrew].

Ashbrook Harvey, Susan. "Spoken Words, Voiced Silence: Biblical Women in Syriac Tradition." *Journal of Early Christian Studies* 9 (2001): 105–31.

——. "Revisiting the Daughters of the Covenant: Women's Choirs and Sacred Song in Ancient Syriac Christianity." *Hugoye: Journal of Syriac Studies* 8,2 (July 2005), [online http://syrcom.cua.edu/Hugoye/Vol8No2/HV8N2Harvey.html].

Avi-Yonah, Michael. *The Jews Under Roman and Byzantine Rule: A Political History from the Bar Kokhba War to the Arab Conquest*. New York: Schocken, 1984.

——. *The Jews of Palestine*. New York: Schocken, 1976.

Bakhos, Carol, editor. *Current Trends in the Study of Midrash*. Leiden: Brill, 2006. Jerusalem: Jerusalem Israel Academy of Sciences and Humanities, 1988 [Hebrew].

Bar-Ilan, M. "Prayers of Jews to Angels and Other Intermediaries During the First Centuries C.E.." In *Saints and Role Models in Judaism and Christianity*. Edited by M. Poorthuis and J. Schwartz; Leiden: Brill, 2004, 79–95.

Barrera, J. T. *The Jewish Bible and the Christian Bible: An Introduction to the History of the Bible*. Grand Rapids: Eerdmans, 1998.

Baskin, J. *Midrashic Women: Formations of the Feminine in Rabbinic Literature*. Hanover/Lebanon, NH: University Press of New England, 2002.

Beattie, D. R. J. and M. J. McNamara, editors. *The Aramaic Bible: Targums in their Historical Context*. Sheffield: JSOT Press, 1994.

Ben-Hayyim, Ze'ev. *The Literary and Oral Tradition of Hebrew and Aramaic Amongst the Samaritans*. 5 vols. Jerusalem: The Academy of the Hebrew Language, 1957–77 [Hebrew].

Ben-Hayyim, Ze'ev, editor and translator. *Tibat Marqe: A Collection of Samaritan Midrashim*. Jerusalem: Israel Academy of Sciences and Humanities, 1988 [Hebrew].

Biesen, Kees den. *Simple and Bold: Ephrem's Art of Symbolic Thought*. Piscataway, NJ: Gorgias, 2006.

Bland, K. *The Artless Jew: Medieval and Modern Affirmations and Denials of the Visual*. Princeton: Princeton University Press, 2000.

Boda, Mark J., Daniel K. Falk, and Rodney Werline, editors. *Penitential Prayer: Origins, Development, and Impact*. Vol. 3. Atlanta: Society of Biblical Literature, 2008.

Bohak, G. *Ancient Jewish Magic: A History*. Cambridge and New York: Cambridge University Press, 2008.

Boustan, R. *From Martyr to Mystic: Rabbinic Martyrology and the Making of Merkavah Mysticism*. Texts and Studies in Ancient Judaism 112. Tübingen: Mohr Siebeck, 2005.

Boyarin, Daniel. *Intertextuality and the Reading of Midrash*. Bloomington: University of Indiana Press, 1990.

——. *Dying for God: Martyrdom and the Making of Christianity and Judaism*. Stanford: Stanford University Press, 1999.

——. *Unheroic Conduct: the Rise of Heterosexuality and the Invention of the Jewish Man*. Berkeley: University of California Press, 1997.

Bregman, Marc. "The Triennial Haftarot and the Perorations of the Midrashic Homilies." *Journal of Jewish Studies* 32 (1981): 74–84.

——. "Past and Present in Midrashic Literature," *Hebrew Annual Review* 2 (1978): 45–59.

Brock, Sebastian. "Jewish Traditions in Syriac Sources." *Journal of Jewish Studies* 30 (1979): 212–32.

——. *From Ephrem to Romanos: Interactions between Syriac and Greek in Late Antiquity.* Farnham: Ashgate Publishing, 1999.

——. "Two Syriac Verse Homilies on the Binding of Isaac." *Le Muséon* 99 (1986): 61–129.

Bronznick, Nachum M. *The Liturgical Poetry of Yannai.* 2 vols. Jerusalem: Rubin Mass, 2000. Supplement 2005.

Cameron, Averil. *Christianity and the Rhetoric of Empire: The Development of Christian Discourse.* Berkeley: University of California Press, 1991.

——. *The Mediterranean World in Late Antiquity, A.D. 395–600.* London: Routledge, 1993.

Campbell, R. M. "*Parashiyyot* and Their Implications for Dating the Fragment-Targums." In *Targums and Scripture: Studies in Aramaic Translation and Interpretation in Memory of Ernest G. Clarke.* Edited by P.V. Flescher; Leiden: Brill, 2002, 105–14.

Carmi, T. *The Penguin Book of Hebrew Verse.* New York: Penguin, 1981.

Carpenter, M. "The Paper that Romanos Swallowed," *Speculum* 7 (1932): 3–22.

Cathcart, K. J., and M. Maher, editors. *Targumic and Cognate Studies: Essays in Honour of Martin McNamara.* Sheffield: Sheffield Academic Press, 1996.

Charlesworth, J., editor. *The Old Testament Pseudepigrapha.* 2 vols. Garden City, NY: Doubleday, 1983–85.

——. *The Dead Sea Scrolls: Hebrew, Aramaic, and Greek Texts with English Translation.*, Vol. 4b, *Angelic Liturgy: Songs of the Sabbath Sacrifice.* Tubingen: Mohr Siebeck / Louisville: Westminster John Knox, 1999.

Chazon, E., R. Clements and A. Pinnick, editors. *Liturgical Perspectives: Prayer and Poetry in Light of the Dead Sea Scrolls*: Proceedings of the Fifth International Symposium of the Orion Center for the Study of the Dead Sea Scrolls and Associated Literature, 19–23 January, 2000. Leiden: Brill, 2003.

Cohen, Gershon. *Studies in the Variety of Rabbinic Cultures.* Philadelphia: Jewish Publication Society, 1991.

——. "Esau as a Symbol in Early Medieval Thought." In *Studies in the Variety of Rabbinic Cultures.* Philadelphia/New York: Jewish Publication Society, 1991, 243–69.

Cohen, Shaye. *The Beginnings of Jewishness: Boundaries, Varieties, Uncertainties.* Berkeley: University of California Press, 1999.

------. *Why aren't Jewish Women Circumcised?: Gender and Covenant in Judaism.* Berkeley: University of California Press, 2005.

Cole, Peter. *The Dream of the Poem: Hebrew Poetry from Muslim and Christian Spain, 950–1492.* Princeton: Princeton University Press, 2007.

Collins, J. J., P. W. Flint, and Cameron Van Epps, editors. *The Book of Daniel: Composition and Reception.* Leiden: Brill, 2001.

Courtney, E. "Greek and Latin Acrostichs." *Philologus* 134 (1990): 3–13.

Culler, Jonathan D. *Structuralist Poetics: Structuralism, Linguistics, and the Study of Literature.* Ithaca: Cornell University Press, 1975.

Cunningham, M. B., and P. Allen, eds. *Preacher and Audience: Studies in Early Christian and Byzantine Homiletics.* Leiden: Brill, 1998.

Davidson, Israel. *Machzor Yannai: A Liturgical Work of the Seventh Century.* New York: Jewish Theological Seminary of America, 1919.

Davies, W. D. *The Gospel and the Land: Early Christianity and Jewish Territorial Doctrine.* Berkeley: University of California Press, 1974.

Delitzsch, Franz . *Zur Geschichte der jüdischen Poesie seit dem Abschluss der Schriften des Alten Bundes.* Leipzig: Karl Tauchnitz, 1836.

Diez-Macho, Alejandro. *Neophyti I: Targum Palestinense MS de la Biblioteca Vaticana.* 5 vols. Madrid/Barcelona: Consejo Superior de Investigaciones Cientificas, 1968.

DiTommaso, L. *The Book of Daniel and the Apocryphal Daniel Literature.* Leiden/Boston: Brill, 2005.

Elbogen, I. *Jewish Liturgy: a Comprehensive History.* Translated by R. Scheindlin. Philadelphia: Jewish Publication Society; New York: Jewish Theological Seminary of America, 1993.

Elior, R. "From Earthly Temple to Heavenly Shrines: Prayer and Sacred Song in the Hekhalot Literature and Its Relation to Temple Traditions." *Jewish Studies Quarterly* 4 (1997): 217–67.

____. "The Concept of God in Heikhalot Literature." In *Studies in Jewish Thought,* edited by. J. Dan. New York: Praeger, 1989. 97–120.

____. "Mysticism, Magic, and Angelology: The Perception of Angels in Heikhalot Literature." *Jewish Studies Quarterly* 1 (1993–94): 3–53.

____. *The Three Temples: Merkavah Tradition and the Beginnings of Early Jewish Mysticism.* Translated by David Louvish. Portland, OR/Oxford: Littman Library, 2003.

Elizur, Shulamit. "From Piyyut to Midrash." In *The Mordecai Bauer Festschrift.* Vol. 2. Edited by Moshe Bar-Asher. Jerusalem: Akademon, 1992: 283–97 [Hebrew].

____. "The Congregation at Prayer and the Early *Qedushta.*" In *Knesset Ezra: Literature and Life in the Synagogue, Studies presented to Ezra Fleischer.* Edited by E. Fleischer and Shulamit Elizur. Jerusalem: Yad Yitsḥak Ben-Zvi, 1994: 171–90 [Hebrew].

____. "The Use of Biblical Verses in Hebrew Liturgical Poetry." In *Praying by the Book: Scripturalization of Prayer in Second Temple Judaism.* Edited by Judith Newman. Atlanta: Scholars Press, 1999, 83–100.

Ephrem the Syrian. *Hymns.* Translated by K. McVey. New York: Paulist Press, 1989.

Fine, Steven. *Art and Judaism in the Greco-Roman World: Towards a New Jewish Archaeology.* Cambridge/New York: Cambridge University Press, 2005.

Fine, Steven, editor. *The Sacred Realm: the Emergence of the Synagogue in the Ancient World.* New York: Oxford University Press; Yeshiva University Museum, 1996.

Finney, P. C. "The Rabbi and the Coin Portrait (Mark 12:15b, 16): Rigorism Manqué," *Journal of Biblical Literature* 112 (Winter, 1993): 629–44.

Fishbane, Michael. *Biblical Myth and Rabbinic Mythmaking.* New York: Oxford University Press, 2003.

____. "'As If He Sacrificed a Soul': Forms of Ritual Simulation and Substitution." In *The Kiss of God: Spiritual and Mystical Death in Judaism.* Seattle: University of Washington Press: 1994, 87–124.

____. *The Exegetical Imagination: On Jewish Thought and Theology.* Cambridge: Harvard University Press, 1998.

Fleischer, E. *Hebrew Liturgical Poetry in the Middle Ages.* Jerusalem: Keter, 1975 [Hebrew].

____. "Iyyunim be-baʿayot tafqidam ha-liturgi shel sugei ha-piyyut ha-qodem." *Tarbiẓ* 40 (1970/71): 41–63 [Hebrew].

____. "On the Antiquity of the Qedushta." *Ha-Sifrut* 2 (1971): 390–414 [Hebrew].

____. "Inquiries in the Structure of the Classical *Qedushta.*" In *Proceedings of the Fifth World Congress of Jewish Studies,* vol.3. Jerusalem: World Union of Jewish Studies, 1969, 291–95 [Hebrew].

———. *The Refrains of Anonymous.* Jerusalem: Ha-Akademyah ha-le᾿umit ha-yisra᾿elit le-mada῾im, 1974.
———. *The Poems of Shelomo Ha-Bavli: Critical Edition with Introduction and Commentary.* Jerusalem: Ha-Akademyah ha-le᾿umit ha-yisra᾿elit le-mada῾im, 1973.
———. "Towards a Solution of Some Fundamental Problems in the Structure of the Classical `*Qedushta.*'" In Henoch Yalon Memorial Volume, ed. E. Y. Kutscher, S. Lieberman, and M. Z. Kaddari, Jerusalem: Kiryat Sefer, 1974: 444–70.
———. "Inquiries Concerning the Triennial Cycle of Torah Reading in *Eretz Yisrael.*" *HebrewUnion College Annual* 62 (1991): 43–61 [Hebrew].
———. "The Annual and Triennial Torah Reading Cycles in the Early Synagogue." *Tarbiẓ* 61:1 (2003): 25–43 [Hebrew].
———. "On the Origins of the Amidah." *Prooftexts* 20 (2000): 380–84.
———. *Ha-Yotzerot.* Jerusalem: Magnes, 1984 [Hebrew].
Flescher, P. V., editor. *Targum and Scripture: Studies in Aramaic Translation and Interpretation in Memory of Ernest G. Clarke.* Leiden: Brill, 2002.
Fraade, S. "Rabbinic Views on the Practice of *Targum*, and Multilingualism in the Jewish Galilee of the Third-Sixth Centuries." In *The Galilee in Late Antiquity.* Edited by Lee Levine. New York: Jewish Theological Seminary of America, 1992, 253–86.
Fried, Natan. "Alternative Haftarot in the Piyyutim of Yannai and the Other Early Payyetanim." *Sinai* 61 (1966–67): 268–90 [Hebrew].
Frymer-Kensky, Tikva. *In the Wake of the Goddesses: Women, Culture, and the Biblical Transformation of Pagan Myth.* New York: Fawcett Columbine, 1992.
Gerhardsson, Birger and Eric J. Sharpe. *Memory and Manuscript: Oral Tradition and Written Transmission in Rabbinic Judaism and Early Christianity; with Tradition and Transmission in Early Christianity.* Grand Rapids: Eerdmans, 1998.
Gerhards, A. "Crossing Borders. The *Kedusha* and the *Sanctus*: a Case Study of the Convergence of Jewish and Christian Liturgy." In *Jewish and Christian Liturgy and Worship: New Insights into Its History and Interaction.* Edited by A. Gerhards and C. Leonhard; Leiden: Brill, 2007, 21–41.
Gershom Me᾿or Ha-Golah. *Teshuvot Rabbenu Gershom Me᾿Or HaGolah.* Edited by S. Eidelberg. New York: Yeshiva University, 1955 (EBRW)
Ginsberg, Louis, editor. *Ginzei Schechter.* Vol 2. New York: Jewish Theological Seminary of America, 1928–29 [Hebrew].
Goitein, S. D. *Jewish Education in Muslim Countries Based on Records from the Cairo Genizah.* Jerusalem: Yad Yitzchak Ben-Zvi, 1962 [Hebrew].
Golb, N. "Obadiah the Proselyte: Scribe of a Unique Twelfth-Century Hebrew Manuscript Containing Lombardic Neumes." *Journal of Religion* 45 (1965): 153–56.
Goldschmidt. *Order of Laments for Tisha b᾿Av.* Jerusalem: Mosad HaRav Kook, 1977 [Hebrew].
Gray, P. T. R. "Palestine and Justinian's Legislation on Non-Christian Religions." In *Law, Politics and Society in the Ancient Mediterranean World.* Edited by Baruch Halpern and Deborah W. Hobson. Sheffield: Sheffield Academic Press, 1993, 241–70.
Green, Arthur. *Keter: The Crown of God in Early Jewish Mysticism.* Princeton: Princeton University Press, 1997.
Green, D. A. *The Aroma of Righteousness: Scent and Seduction in Rabbinic Literature.* University Park, PA: Penn State University Press, forthcoming.
Green, William Scott, and Jacob Neusner. *Writing with Scripture: The Authority and Uses of the Hebrew Bible in the Torah of Formative Judaism.* Minneapolis: Fortress Press, 1989.
Grosdidier de Matons, J. *Romanos le Mélode et les origins de la poésie religieuse a` Byzance.* Paris: Beauchesne, 1977.

Gruenwald, I. *Apocalyptic and Merkavah Mysticism.* Leiden: Brill, 1980.

____. "Shirat ha-malʾakhim, ha-qedushah, u-vaʿayat ḥibburah shel sifrut ha-heikhalot." In *Peraqim be-toledot yerushalayim bi-yemei bayyit sheni.* Jerusalem: Ben Zvi Institute, 1981, 459–81.

____. "Piyyutei yannai ve-sifrut yoredei merkavah." *Tarbiẓ* 36 (1966–67): 257–77.

Hachlili, Rachel, ed. *Ancient Synagogues in Israel: Third–Seventh Centuries C.E.: Proceedings of Symposium, University of Haifa: May 1987.* Oxford: B.A.R., 1989.

Hachlili, Rachel. "Synagogues in the Land of Israel: The Art and Architecture of the Late Antique Synagogues." In *The Sacred Realm: The Emergence of the Synagogue in the Ancient World.* Edited by Steven Fine. Yeshiva University Museum/Oxford University Press: New York, 1996, 96–129.

____. *Ancient Jewish Art and Archaeology in the Land of Israel.* Leiden: Brill, 1988.

____. "The Zodiac in Ancient Jewish Art: Representation and Significance." *Bulletin of the American Schools of Oriental Research* (1977): 61–77.

Halperin, David J. *The Merkavah in Rabbinic Literature.* New Haven: American Oriental Society, 1980.

____. "Review: A New Edition of the Heikhalot Literature." *Journal of the American Oriental Society* 104 (1984! 543–52.

Hasan-Rokem, Galit., and David Shulman, editors. *Untying the Knot: Riddles and Other Enigmatic Modes.* New York: Oxford University Press, 1996.

Heinemann, J. *Prayer in the Talmud.* Translated by R. Sarason. Berlin; New York: De Gruyter, 1977.

____. "The Triennial Lectionary Cycle," *Journal of Jewish Studies* 19 (1968): 41–48.

____. "The Machzor of the Triennial Cycle and the Annual Calendar." *Tarbiẓ* 33 [1964/65]: 362–68 [Hebrew].

Heszer, Catherine. *The Social Structure of the Rabbinic Movement in Roman Palestine.* Tübingen: Mohr-Siebeck, 1997.

____. *Jewish Literacy in Roman Palestine.* Tübingen: Mohr Siebeck, 2001.

Hirshman, Marc. *A Rivalry of Genius: Jewish and Christian Biblical Interpretation in Late Antiquity.* Albany: State University of New York Press, 1996.

Hoffman, L. *The Canonization of the Synagogue Service.* Notre Dame: University of Notre Dame Press, 1979.

Hrushovski, B. "Note on the Systems of Hebrew Versification." In *The Penguin Book of Hebrew Verse.* Edited and translated by T. Carmi. New York: Penguin Books, 1981, 57–72.

Idelsohn, A. Z. *Jewish Liturgy and Its Development.* New York: Henry Holt and Co., 1932.

Irshai, O. "Confronting a Christian Empire: Jewish Culture in the World of Byzantium." In *Cultures of the Jews: a New History.* Edited by D. Biale; New York: Schocken, 2002, 180–221.

____. "Dating the Eschaton: Jewish and Christian Apocalyptic Calculations in Late Antiquity." In *Apocalyptic Time,* edited by A. I. Baumgarten. Leiden: Brill, 2000, 113–53.

Jacobs, Andrew S. "Visible Ghosts and Invisible Demons: The Place of Jews in Early Christian Terra Sancta." In Eric Meyers, editor. *The Galilee Through the Centuries: A Confluence of Cultures.* Winona Lake: Eisenbrauns, 1999, 359–76.

Jaffee, M. *Torah in the Mouth: Writing and Oral Tradition in Palestinian Judaism, 200 B.C.E.–400 C.E.* Oxford; New York: Oxford University Press, 2001.

Janowitz, N. *Icons of Power: Ritual Practices in Late Antiquity.* University Park: Penn State University Press, 2002.

____. *Magic in the Roman World: Pagans, Jews and Christians.* London: Routledge, 2001.

Jeffrey, P. "Werner's *The Sacred Bridge*, Volume 2: A Review Essay," *Jewish Quarterly Review*, 77 (1987): 203–29.
Kahle, Paul. E. *The Cairo Geniza.* London: The British Academy, 1947.
——. *The Cairo Genizah.* 2nd ed. Oxford: Blackwell, 1959.
——."Kerobas aus dem Mahzor des Jannai." In *Masoreten des Westens.* vol.1, Hildesheim: Georg Olms Verlagsbuchhandlung, 1967, 87–89.
Kalimi, Isaac, and Peter J. Haas, eds. *Biblical Interpretation in Judaism and Christianity.* New York: T&T Clark, 2006.
Kessler, E. *Bound by the Bible: Jews, Christians, and the Sacrifice of Isaac.* New York: Cambridge University Press, 2004.
Kinzig, W. "'Non-Separation': Closeness and Co-operation between Jews and Christians in the Fourth Century." *Vigiliae Christianae* 45 (1991): 27–53.
Klar, B. *The Chronicle of Aḥimaatz.* Jerusalem: Tarshish, 1974.
Klein, M. *The Fragment Targums of the Pentateuch According to their Extant Sources.* 2 vols. Rome: Pontifical Institute, 1980.
——. *Genizah Manuscripts of Palestinian Targum to the Pentateuch.* 2 vols. Cincinnati: Hebrew Union College Press, 1986–87.
——. *The Translation of Anthropomorphisms and Anthropopathisms in the Targumim of the Pentateuch: With Parallel Citation from the Septuagint.* Jerusalem: Makor, 1982.
——. "Palestinian Targum and Synagogue Mosaics." *Immanuel* 11 (1980): 33–45.
Koltun-Fromm, N. "Aphrahat and the Rabbis on Noah's Righteousness in Light of the Jewish–Christian Polemic." In *The Book of Genesis in Jewish and Oriental Christian Interpretation.* Edited by E. Peter, J. Frishman, and L. van Rompay. Louvain: Peeters, 1997, 57–71.
Kronholm, T. *Motifs from Genesis 1–11 in the Genuine Hymns of Ephrem the Syrian with Particular Reference to the Influence of Jewish Exegetical Tradition.* Lund : LiberLaromedel/ Gleerup, 1978.
Krueger, Derek. *Writing and Holiness: The Practice of Authorship in the Early Christian East.* Philadelphia: University of Pennsylvania Press, 2004.
Kugel, J. *The Idea of Biblical Poetry: Parallelism and Its History.* New Haven: Yale University Press, 1981.
——. *In Potiphar's House: The Interpretive Life of Biblical Texts.* San Francisco: Harper and Row, 1990.
——., ed.. *Prayers that Cite Scripture.* Cambridge, Mass.: Harvard University Center for Jewish Studies, 2006.
Kutscher, E.Y. *Studies in Galilean Aramaic.* Translated by M. Sokoloff. Jerusalem: Ahvah Press, 1976.
Landshuth, Eliezer. *Amudei ha-avodah: Reshimat rashe ha-paytanim u-meat mi-toldotehem al sedar alfa beta ʿim mispar piyutehem ha-nimtsaʾim be-sifre tefilot.* Berlin: Bernstein, 1857–62 [Hebrew].
Langer, Ruth. *To Worship God Properly: Tensions between Liturgical Custom and Halakhah in Judaism.* Cincinnati: Hebrew Union College Press, 1998.
——. "Liturgy and Sensory Experience." In *Christianity in Jewish Terms.* Edited by Tikva Frymer-Kensky, David Novak, Peter Ochs, David Fox Sandmel, and Michael A. Signer. Boulder, Colo.: Westview Press, 2000, 189–95, 386–87
——. "From Study of Scripture to a Reenactment of Sinai." *Worship* 72 (1998): 43–67. = *Journal of Synagogue Music* 31 (2006): 104–25.

_____. "Biblical Texts in Jewish Prayers: Their History and Function." In *Jewish and Christian Liturgy and Worship: New Insights into its History and Interaction*. Jewish and Christian Perspectives. Edited by Albert Gerhards and Clemens Leonhard. Leiden: Brill, 2007, 63–90.

_____. "Revisiting Early Rabbinic Liturgy," *Prooftexts* 19 (1999): 179–204.

_____. "Consideration of Method: a Response to Ezra Fleischer," *Prooftexts* 20 (2000): 384–87.

Levine, Lee. *The Ancient Synagogue: the First Thousand Years*. 2nd ed. New Haven: Yale University Press, 2000.

_____. "The Nature and Origin of the Palestinian Synagogue Reconsidered." *Journal of Biblical Literature* 115 (1996): 425–48.

_____. "The Sages and the Synagogue in Late Antiquity." In *The Galilee in Late Antiquity*. Edited by Lee Levine; New York: Jewish Theological Seminary of America, 1992, 201–21.

_____. ed. *Ancient Synagogues Revealed*. Jerusalem/Detroit: The Israel Exploration Society/Wayne State University Press, 1982.

Lieber, A.B. "Angels that Kill: Mediation and the Threat of Bodily Destruction in the *Hekhalot* Narratives." *Studies in Spirituality* 14 (2004): 17–35.

Lieber, L. "O My Dove, Let Me See Your Face: Targum, Piyyut, and the Literary Life of the Ancient Synagogue." In *Paratext and Megatext as Channels of Jewish and Christian Traditions*. Edited by A. den Hollander, U. Schmid, and W. Smelik. Leiden: Brill, 2003, 109–35.

_____. "Piyyut." In *The Encyclopedia of Judaism*. Edited by Jacob Neusner, Alan J. Avery-Peck and William Scott Green. Leiden: Brill, 2005, vol.3, 2000–2019.

_____. "Confessing from A to Z: Penitential Themes in Early Synagogue Poetry." In *Penitential Prayer: Origins, Development, and Impact*. Edited by Mark J. Boda, Daniel K. Falk, and Rodney Werline. Atlanta: Society of Biblical Literature, 2008, vol. 3, 99–125.

_____. "'You Have Skirted This Hill Long Enough': The Tension Between Rhetoric and History in a Byzantine Piyyut" *Hebrew Union College Annual* 79 (forthcoming).

_____. "Portraits of Righteousness: Noah in Early Christian and Jewish Hymnography," *Zeitschrift für Religions- und Geistesgeschichte* 61 (2009): 332–355.

_____. "The Exegesis of Love: Text and Context in the Poetry of the Early Synagogue." *Review of Rabbinic Judaism* 11 (2008): 73–99.

Lieberman, Saul. "*Ḥazzanut Yannai*." *Sinai* 4 (1938): 221–50. Reprinted in *Studies in Palestinian Talmudic Literature*. Jerusalem: Magnes, 1991, 123–52 [Hebrew].

_____. *Greek in Jewish Palestine: Studies in the Life and Manners of Jewish Palestine in the II–IV Centuries* C.E. New York: Jewish Theological Seminary of America, 1942.

_____. *Hellenism in Jewish Palestine: Studies in the Literary Transmission, Beliefs and Manners of Palestine in the I Century* B.C.E.*–IV Century* C.E. New York: Jewish Theological Seminary of America, 1950.

Limor, Ora, and Guy G. Stroumsa, eds. *Contra Iudaeos: Ancient and Medieval Polemics between Christians and Jews*. Tübingen: Mohr Siebeck, 1996.

_____. *Christians and Christianity in the Holy Land: From the Origins to the Latin Kingdom*. Turnhout : Brepols, 2006.

Loewe, H.M.J. *Render Unto Caesar: Religious and Political Loyalty in Palestine*. Cambridge: The University Press, 1940.

Mach, M. "Qedoshim malʾakhim: Ha-ʾEl ve-ha-liturgiyah ha-shamayemit." In *Massuʾot: Studies in Kabbalistic Literature and Jewish Philosophy in Memory of Prof. Ephraim Gottlieb*. Edited by Ephraim Gottlieb, Michal Oron and Amos Goldreich. Jerusalem: Bialik, 1994: 298–310 [Hebrew].

Magness, J. “Did Galilee Decline in the Fifth Century?” In *Religion, Ethnicity, and Identity in Ancient Galilee.* Edited by Jürgen Zangenberg, Harold W. Attridge, Dale B. Martin. Tübingen: Mohr Siebeck, 2007, 259–74.

——. “Helios and the Zodiac Cycle in Ancient Palestinian Synagogues.” In *Symbiosis, Symbolism, and the Power of the Past. Canaan, Ancient Israel, and Their Neighbors from the Late Bronze Age through Roman Palaestina, Proceedings of the Centennial Symposium of the W.F. Albright Institute of Archaeological Research and American Schools of Oriental Research, Jerusalem, May 29–31, 2000.* Edited by W. G. Dever and S. Gitin. Winona Lake, Eisenbrauns, 2002, 363–89.

——. “Heaven on Earth: Helios and the Zodiac Cycle in Ancient Palestinian Synagogues.” *Dumbarton Oaks Papers* 59 (2005): 1–52.

Maier, Johann. *Vom Kultus zur Gnosis: Studien zur Vor- und Fruhgeschichte der “jüdischen Gnosis.”* Salzburg: Otto Müller Verlag, 1964.

——. “Das *Gefährdungsmotiv* bei der Himmelsreise in der jüdischen Apokalyptik und 'Gnosis'.” *Kairos* 5 (1963): 18–40.

——. “Hekhalot Rabbati xxvi, 5.” *Judaica* 21 (1965): 129–33.

——. “Hekhalot Rabbati xxvii, 2–5.” *Judaica* 22 (1966): 209–17.

Marcus, J. “Studies in the Chronicle of Aḥimaaz,” *Proceedings of the American Academy for Jewish Research* 5 (1933–34): 85–93.

Messenger, R. E. “Medieval Processional Hymns Before 1100.” *Transactions and Proceedings of the American Philological Association* 80 (1949): 375–392.

Meyers, Eric, ed. *The Galilee Through the Centuries: A Confluence of Cultures.* Winona Lake: Eisenbrauns, 1999.

Meyers, Eric, and James Strange. *Archaeology, the Rabbis and Early Christianity: the Social and Historical Setting of Palestinian Judaism and Christianity.* Abingdon: Nashville, 1981.

Meyers, C., E. Meyers, and E. Netzer, eds. *Sepphoris.* Winona Lake: Eisenbrauns, 1992.

Mirsky, A. *Formal Foundations of Piyyut.* Jerusalem: Magnes, 1985 [Hebrew].

——. *The Piyyut.* Jerusalem: Magnes, 1990 [Hebrew]

——. *Yose ben Yose: Poems.* 2nd ed. Jerusalem: Mosad Bialik, 1991 [Hebrew].

Moskhos, M. “Romanos' Hymn on the Sacrifice of Abraham: A Discussion of the Sources and a Translation,” *Byzantion* 44 (1974): 310–28.

Münz-Manor, Ophir. “All About Sarah: Questions of Gender in Yannai's Poems on Sarah's (and Abraham's) Barrenness.” *Prooftexts* 26 (2006): 344–74.

Murtonen A. (with G. J. Ormann). *Materials for a Non-Masoretic Hebrew Grammar.* 2 vols. Helsinki, 1958.

Naeh, S. “The Torah Reading Cycle.” *Tarbiẓ* 67:2 (2003): 167–87 [Hebrew].

——. “On the Septennial Cycle of the Torah Reading in Early Palestine.” *Tarbiẓ* 74:1 (2005): 43–75 [Hebrew].

Naiman, H. *Seconding Sinai: The Development of Mosaic Discourse in Second Temple Judaism.* Leiden: Brill, 2003.

Naveh, J., and S. Shaked. *Amulets and Magic Bowls: Aramaic Incantations from Late Antiquity.* Jerusalem: Magnes, 1998.

——. *Magic Spells and Formulae: Aramaic Incantations from Late Antiquity.* Jerusalem: Magnes, 1993

——. *On Stone and Mosaic: The Aramaic and Hebrew Inscriptions from Ancient Synagogues.* Jerusalem: Maariv, 1978 [Hebrew].

Nelson, D. “Orality and Mnemonics in Aggadic Literature.” In *Midrash and Context: Proceedings of the SBL Consultation on Midrash, 2004–2005.* Piscataway, NJ: Gorgias Press, 2007, 123–38.

Newman, Judith. *Praying By the Book: Scripturalization of Prayer in Second Temple Judaism.* Atlanta: Scholars Press, 1999.

Nickelsburg, G. *Ancient Judaism and Christian Origins: Diversity, Continuity, and Transformation.* Minneapolis: Fortress, 2003.

Nitzan, B. "Harmonic and Mystical Characteristics in Poetic and Liturgical Writings from Qumran." *Jewish Quarterly Review* 85 (1994): 163–83.

The Oxford Handbook of Early Christian Studies. Edited by Susan Ashbrook Harvey and David G. Hunter. Oxford: Oxford University Press, 2008.

Palmer, Andrew. "The Merchant of Nisibis: Saint Ephrem and His Faithful Quest for Union in Numbers." In *Early Christian Poetry,* ed. J. den Boeft and A. Hilhorst. Leiden: Brill, 1993, 167–233.

Papoutsakis, Manolis. "The Making of a Syriac Fable: From Ephrem to Romanos." *Le Muséon* 120 (2007): 29–75.

Petuchowski, Jakob Josef. *Prayerbook Reform in Europe: The Liturgy of European Liberal and Reform Judaism.* New York: World Union for Progressive Judaism, 1968.

____. *Theology and Poetry: Studies in the Medieval Piyyut.* London; Boston: Routledge and Kegan Paul, 1978.

Pietersma, Albert. "The Acrostic Poems of Lamentations in Greek Translation." In *Proceedings of the Eighth Congress of the International Organization for Septuagint and Cognate Studies, Paris 1992* Edited by Leonard Greenspoon and Olivier Munnich. Atlanta: Scholars Press: 1995, 183–201.

Plaut, Gunther, ed. *The Rise of Reform Judaism.* New York: World Union for Progressive Judaism, 1963.

Rabinovitz, Zvi Meir. *Halakhah and Aggadah in the Liturgical Poetry of Yannai.* Tel Aviv: Alexander Kohut, 1965 [Hebrew].

____. *The Liturgical Poems of Rabbi Yannai According to the Triennial Cycle of the Pentanteuch and the Holidays.* 2 vols. Jerusalem: Mosad Bialik, 1985–87 [Hebrew].

Rand, Michael. "The *Seder Beriyot* in Byzantine-Era Piyyut." *Jewish Quarterly Review* 95 (2005): 667–83.

____. *Introduction to the Grammar of Hebrew Poetry in Byzantine Palestine.* Piscataway, NJ: Gorgias Press, 2006.

____. "Observations on the Relationship Between JPA Poetry and the Hebrew Piyyut Tradition – The Case of the *Kinot.*" In *Jewish and Christian Liturgy and Worship: New Insights into its History and Interaction.* Jewish and Christian Perspectives Edited by Albert Gerhards and Clemens Leonhard. Leiden: Brill, 2007, 127–44.

Romanos. *Kontakia of Romanos, Byzantine Melodist.* 2 vols. Translated by M. Carpenter. Columbia: University of Missouri Press, 1970–72.

____. *Romanos le Mélode: Hymnes.* 5 vols. Edited and translated to French J. Grosdidier de Matons. Paris: Cerf, 1965–81.

Reif, S. *Judaism and Hebrew Prayer: New Perspectives on Jewish Liturgical History.* New York: Cambridge University Press, 1993.

Roberts, Michael. *The Jeweled Style: Poetry and Poetics in Late Antiquity.* Ithaca: Cornell University Press, 1989.

Rodrigues-Pereira, A.S. *Studies in Aramaic Poetry (c. 100 B.C.E. – c. 600 C.E.): Selected Jewish, Christian, and Samaritan Hymns.* Assen: Van Gorcum, 1997.

Roussin, Lucille. "The Zodiac in Synagogue Decoration." In *Archaeology and the Galilee: Texts and Contexts in the Greco-Roman and Byzantine Periods.* Edited by D. Edwards and C. McCollough. Atlanta: Scholars Press, 1997, 83–96.

Rubenstein, J. "Cultic Themes in Sukkot Piyyutim." *Proceedings of the American Academy for Jewish Research* 59 (1993): 185–209.

Saadia ben Joseph (Saadia Gaon). *Sefer ha-Egron.* Edited by N. Allony. Jerusalem: Ha-Akademyah ha-le'umit ha-yisra'elit le-mada'im, 1969 [Hebrew].

Safran, L., editor. *Heaven on Earth: Art and the Church in Byzantium.* University Park, PA: Penn State University Press, 2000.

Sarason, R. "Midrash in Liturgy." In *Encyclopedia of Midrash: Biblical Interpretation in Formative Judaism.* Edited by Jacob Neusner and Alan J. Avery-Peck. 2 vols. Leiden: E.J. Brill, 2004, 463–92.

———. "The `Intersections' of Rabbinic and Qumran Judaism." *Dead Sea Scrolls Discoveries* 8 (2001): 169–81.

Schafer, Peter, Margarete Schluter, and Hans Georg von Mutius. *Synopse zur Heikhalot-Literatur,.* Texte und Studien zum Antiken Judentum 2. Tubingen: JBC Mohr, 1981.

Scheindlin, Raymond. *The Gazelle: Medieval Hebrew Poems on God, Israel and the Soul.* Philadelphia: Jewish Publication Society, 1991.

Schirmann. "Jewish Liturgical Poetry and Christian Hymnology." *Jewish Quarterly Review* New Series 44 (1953):123–61.

Schmelzer, M. "The Contribution of the Genizah to the Study of Liturgy and Poetry." *Proceedings for the American Academy for Jewish Research* 63 (1997–2001): 163–79.

Schwartz, Seth. *Imperialism and Jewish Society, 200 B.C.E.. to 640 C.E.* Princeton: Princeton University Press, 2001.

Shephardson, Christine. *Anti-Judaism and Christian Orthodoxy: Ephrem's Hymns in Fourth Century Syria.* Washington, DC: Catholic University Press of America, 2008.

Shinan, Avigdor. "Sermons, Targums, and the Reading from Scriptures in the Ancient Synagogue." In *The Synagogue in Late Antiquity.* Edited by Lee I. Levine. Philadelphia: Jewish Publication Society, 1987, 97–110.

———. "The Aggadah of the Palestinian Targums of the Pentateuch and Rabbinic Aggadah: Some Methodological Considerations." In *The Aramaic Bible: Targums in their Historical Context. Journal for the Study of the Old Testament,* supp. 166. Edited by. D. R. G. Beattie and M. J. McNamara. Sheffield: JSOT Press, 1994, 203–17.

———. "The Aramaic Targum as a Mirror of Galilean Jewry." In *The Galilee in Late Antiquity.* Edited by Lee Levine; New York: JTSA, 1992, 241–52.

———. *The Embroidered Targum: The Aggadah in Targum Pseudo-Jonathan of the Pentateuch.* Magnes: Jerusalem, 1992 [Hebrew].

Sivan, H. *Palestine in Late Antiquity.* Oxford: Oxford University Press, 2008.

Smelik, Willem F. "Orality, the Targums, and Manuscript Reproduction." In *Paratext and Megatext in Jewish and Christian* Traditions*: The Textual Markers of Contextualization.* Edited by. A. den Hollander, U. Schmidt and W.F. Smelik. Leiden: Brill, 2003, 49–81.

———. "Translation and Commentary in One: The Interplay of Pluses and Substitutions in the Targum to the Prophets." *Journal for the Study of Judaism in the Persian, Hellenistic and Roman Period* 29 (1998): 245–60.

———. "Code-switching: The Public Reading of the Bible in Hebrew, Aramaic and Greek," in *Was ist ein Text? Alttestamentliche, ägyptologische und altorientalistische Perspektiven,* ed. L. Morenz and S. Schorch (Berlin: Walter de Gruyter, 2007), 123–51.

Sokoloff, M., and J. Yahalom. *Jewish Palestinian Aramaic Poetry from Late Antiquity.* Jerusalem: Ha-Akademyah ha-le'umit ha-yisra'elit le-mada'im, 1999.

Sperber, D. *Magic and Folklore in Rabbinic Literature.* Ramat Gan: Bar Ilan University Press, 1994.

Spiegel, Jacob. "Clarification of the Words of the Piyyut, `But Repentance, Prayer, and Charity Avert the Evil Decree,' and the Payyetanic Commitment to Halakhah." *Netuʿim* 8 (2001): 23–42 [Hebrew].
Spiegel, Shalom. "On the Language of the Payyetanim." *Ha-Doʾar* 43:23 (1962–63): 397–400 [Hebrew].
____. *Fathers of Piyyut: Texts and Studies toward a History of the Piyyut in Eretz Yisrael.* Edited by M. Schmelzer. Jerusalem; New York: Jewish Theological Seminary of America, 1996 [Hebrew].
Stemberger, Günter. *Jews and Christians in the Holy Land: Palestine in the Fourth Century.* Translated by R. Tushling. Edinburgh: T&T Clark, 2000.
Strugnell J. *The Angelic Liturgy at Qumran: 4Q Serek Shirot ʿOlat Ha-Shabbat;* in *Vetus Testamentum,* Supp. 7. Leiden; Brill, 1959–60.
Swartz, Michael D., and Joseph Yahalom, editors and translators. *Avodah: An Anthology of Ancient Poetry for Yom Kippur.* University Park, PA.: Penn State University Press, 2005.
Swartz, M. *Mystical Prayer in Ancient Judaism: an Analysis of Maʿaseh Merkavah.* Tübingen: Mohr-Siebeck, 1992.
____. *Scholastic Magic: Ritual and Revelation in Early Jewish Mysticism.* Princeton: Princeton University Press, 1996.
____. "The Dead Sea Scrolls and Later Jewish Magic and Mysticism," *Dead Sea Scrolls Discoveries* 8 (2001): 182–93.
____. "On the Yotzer and Related Texts." In *The Synagogue in Late Antiquity.* Edited by L. Levine. Philadelphia: Jewish Theological Seminary of America and American Schools of Oriental Research, 1987, 87–95.
____. "Sacrificial Themes in Jewish Magic." In *Ancient Magic and Ritual Power.* Edited by Marvin Meyer and Paul Mirecki. Leiden: Brill, 1995, 303–17.
____. "Sage, Priest and Poet." In *Jews, Christians, and Polytheists in the Ancient Synagogue.* Edited by Steven Fine. New York: Routledge, 1999, 101–17.
Teugels, L. "Aggadat Bereshit and the Triennial Lectionary Cycle," *Journal of Jewish Studies* 51 (2000): 117–32.
Trachtenberg, J. *Jewish Magic and Superstition: A Study in Folk Religion.* New York: Berhmans, 1939. Reissued: Philadelphia: University of Pennsylvania Press, 2004.
Urbach, E. E. *The Sages: Their Concepts and Beliefs.* Translated by Israel Abrahams. Cambridge: Harvard University Press, 1979.
Van Bekkum, W. J. "Anti-Christian Polemics in Hebrew Liturgical Poetry (Piyyut) in the Sixth and Seventh Centuries." In *Early Christian Poetry: A Collection of Essays.* Edited by J. den Boeft and A. Hilhorst; Leiden: Brill, 1993, 297–308.
____. *Hebrew Poetry from Late Antiquity: Liturgical Poems of Yehudah.* Leiden: Brill, 1998.
____. "Hearing and Understanding Piyyut in the Liturgy of the Synagogue." *Zutot* 1 (2001): 58–63.
____. "Messianic Expectations in the Age of Hereclius." In *The Reign of Heraclius (610–641): Crisis and Confrontation.* Edited by G. J. Reinink, Bernard H. Stolte. Leuven: Peeters, 2002, 95–112.
____. "The Hidden Reference: The Role of EDOM in Late Antique and Early Medieval Jewish Hymnography." In *Empsychoi Logoi: Religious Innovation in Antiquity, Studies in Honour of Pieter Willem van der Horst.* Edited by Alberdina Houtman, Albert de Jong, and Magda Misset-van de Weg. Leiden: Brill, 2008, 527–43.
Wacholder, Ben Zion. *Prolegomenon to The Bible as Read and Preached in the Old Synagogue: A Study in the Cycles of the Readings from Torah and Prophets, as well as from Psalms, and in the Structure of the Midrashic Homilies,* by Jacob Mann. The Library of Biblical Studies. Vol.1. Edited by Harry M. Orlinsky. New York: Ktav, 1971.

Walker, P.W.L. *Holy City, Holy Places? Christian Attitudes to Jerusalem and the Holy Land in the Fourth Century.* Oxford: Clarendon; New York: Oxford University Press, 1990.

Wasserstein, A. "Rabban Gamliel and Proclus the Philosopher." *Zion* 45 (1980): 257–67.

Weinberger, L. *Jewish Hymnography: A Literary History.* London; Portland, OR: Littman Library, 1998.

Weinfeld, M. "The Traces of *Kedushat Yotzer* and the *Pesukey de-Zimra* in the Qumran Literature and Ben Sira." *Tarbiẓ* 45 (1976): 15–26 [Hebrew].

Weiss, Z., and E. Netzer. *Promise and Redemption: The Synagogue Mosaic from Sepphoris.* Jerusalem: Israel Museum, 1996.

Wellesz, Egon. *A History of Byzantine Music and Hymnography.* Clarendon: Oxford, 1949.

Werner, Eric. *The Sacred Bridge: The Interdependence of Church and Synagogue During the First Millennium.* Vol. 1 New York: Columbia University Press, 1959. Vol. 2. New York: Ktav, 1984.

Wilfand, Yael "Aramaic Tombstones from Zoar and Jewish Conceptions of the Afterlife." *Journal for the Study of Judaism* 40 (2009): 510–539.

Wilken, Robert Louis. *John Chrysostom and the Jews: Rhetoric and Reality in the Late Fourth Century.* Berkeley: University of California Press, 1983.

———. "The Restoration of Israel in Biblical Prophecy: Christian and Jewish Responses in the Early Byzantine Period." Pages 443–471 In *"To See Ourselves as Others See Us": Christians, Jews, "Others" in Late Antiquity.* Edited by J. Neusner and E. S. Fredrichs. Chico, CA.: Scholars Press, 1985, 443–71.

Wolfson, E. "Mysticism and the Poetic-Liturgical Compositions from Qumran: a Response to Bilhah Nitzan." *Jewish Quarterly Review* 85 (1994): 185–202.

Yahalom, Joseph. *Poetry and Society in Jewish Galilee of Late Antiquity.* Tel-Aviv: Hakibbutz Hameuchad; Jerusalem: Yad Yitshak Ben-Zvi, 1999 [Hebrew].

———. *Sefat ha-shir: shel ha-piyut ha-erets-yisa'eli ha-kadum.* Jerusalem: Magnes, 1985 [Hebrew].

———. "Piyyut as Poetry." In *The Synagogue in Late Antiquity.* Edited by Lee Levine. Philadelphia: American Schools of Oriental Research, 1987, 111–26.

Zulay, Menachem. *The Liturgical Poems of Yannai: Collected from Geniza-Manuscripts and Other Sources.* Berlin: Shocken, 1938.

———. *Eretz Yisrael and Its Poetry.* Edited by E. Hazan. Jerusalem: Magnes, 1995 [Hebrew].

———. "Matters of Language in the Poetry of Yannai." In *Studies of the Research Institute for Hebrew Poetry in Jerusalem.* Vol. 6. Schocken: Jerusalem, 1945: 165–247 [Hebrew].

———. "Meḥqrei Yannai," *Yediʿot ha-makhon le-ḥeqer ha-shirah ha-ʿivrit* 2 (1925): 213–391.

Zunz, Leopold. *Literaturgeschichte der synagogalen Poesie.* Berlin: L. Gerschel Verlagsbuchhandlung, 1865.

———. *Der Ritus des synagogalen Gottesdienstes.* Berlin: J. Springer, 1859.

———. *Die synagogale Poesie des Mittelalters* . 1st ed. Frankfurt am Main: J. Kaufmann, 1920.

Index

About the Author

Laura Lieber received her rabbinical ordination from the Hebrew Union College–Jewish Institute of Religion and her Ph.D. in the History of Judaism from the University of Chicago. She taught in the departments of Classics and Religion at Middlebury College in Vermont for five years, and is now assistant professor of Late Ancient Judaism at Duke University. Dr. Lieber co-edited *A Scriptural Exegesis: The Shapes of Culture and Religious Imagination, a Festschrift in Honour of Michael Fishbane* (2009) and has authored A *Reader's Guide to the JPS Haftarah Commentary* (2002), *The Vocabulary of Desire: The Song of Songs in the Early Synagogue* (forthcoming), and several articles and chapters in books.

Monographs of the Hebrew Union College

1. Lewis M. Barth, *An Analysis of Vatican 30*
2. Samson H. Levey, *The Messiah: An Aramaic Interpretation*
3. Ben Zion Wacholder, *Eupolemus: A Study of Judaeo-Greek Literature*
4. Richard Victor Bergren, *The Prophets and the Law*
5. Benny Kraut, *From Reform Judaism to Ethical Culture: The Religious Evolution of Felix Adler*
6. David B. Ruderman, *The World of a Renaissance Jew: The Life and Thought of Abraham ben Mordecai Farrisol*
7. Alan Mendelson, *Secular Education in Philo of Alexandria*
8. Ben Zion Wacholder, *The Dawn of Qumran: The Sectarian Torah and the Teacher of Righteousness*
9. Stephen M. Passamaneck, *The Traditional Jewish Law of Sale: Shulḥan Arukh, Ḥoshen Mishpat, Chapters 189–240*
10. Yael S. Feldman, *Modernism and Cultural Transfer: Gabriel Preil and the Tradition of Jewish Literary Bilingualism*
11. Raphael Jospe, *Torah and Sophia: The Life and Thought of Shem Tov ibn Falaquera*
12. Richard Kalmin, *The Redaction of the Babylonian Talmud: Amoraic or Saboraic?*
13. Shuly Rubin Schwartz, *The Emergence of Jewish Scholarship in America: The Publication of the Jewish Encyclopedia*
14. John C. Reeves, *Jewish Lore in Manichaean Cosmogony: Studies in the Book of Giants Traditions*
15. Robert Kirschner, *Baraita De Melekhet Ha-Mishkan: A Critical Edition with Introduction and Translation*
16. Philip E. Miller, *Karaite Separatism in Nineteenth-Century Russia: Joseph Solomon Lutski's Epistle of Israel's Deliverance*
17. Warran Bargad, *"To Write the Lips of Sleepers": The Poetry of Amir Gilboa*
18. Marc Saperstein, *"Your Voice Like a Ram's Horn": Themes and Texts in Traditional Jewish Preaching*
19. Emanuel Melzer, *No Way Out: The Politics of Polish Jewry, 1935–1939*
20. Eric L. Friedland, *"Were Our Mouths Filled With Song": Studies in Liberal Jewish Liturgy*
21. Edward Fram, *Ideals Face Reality: Jewish Law and Life in Poland, 1550–1655*
22. Ruth Langer, *To Worship God Properly: Tensions Between Liturgical Custom and Halakhah in Judaism*

23. Nili Sacher Fox, *In the Service of the King: Officialdom in Ancient Israel and Judah*
24. Carole B. Balin, *To Reveal Our Hearts: Jewish Women Writers in Tsarist Russia*
25. Shaul Bar, *A Letter That Has Not Been Read: Dreams in the Hebrew Bible*
26. Eric Caplan, *From Ideology to Liturgy: Reconstructionist Worship and American Liberal Judaism*
27. Rina Lapidus, *Between Snow and Desert Heat: Russian Influences on Hebrew Literature, 1870–1970*
28. Howard L. Apothaker, *Sifra, Dibbura de Sinai: Rhetorical Formulae, Literary Structures, and Legal Traditions*
29. Hava Tirosh-Samuelson, *Happiness in Premodern Judaism: Virtue, Knowledge, and Well-Being*
30. Zafrira Lidovsky Cohen, *"Loosen the Fetters of Thy tongue, Woman": The Poetry and Poetics of Yona Wallach*
31. Louis Feldman, *"Remember Amalek": Vengeance, Zealotry, and Group Destruction*
32. Marc Saperstein, *Exile in Amsterdam: Saul Levi Morteira's Sermons to a Congregation of New Christians*
33. Edward Fram, *"My Dear Daughter": Rabbi Benjamin Slonik and the Education of Jewish Women in Sixteenth-Century Poland*
34. Elizabeth Loentz*: Let Me Continue to Speak the Truth: Bertha Pappenheim as Author and Activist*
35. Michael Chernick*: A Great Voice that Did Not Cease: The Growth of the Rabbinic Canon and Its Interpretation*
36. Laura S. Lieber*: Yannai on Genesis: An Invitation to Piyyut*